LITERATURE

READING ◊ REACTING ◊ WRITING

PORTABLE EDITION

 *is*

A Harcourt Higher Learning Company

Now you will find Harcourt Brace's distinguished innovation, leadership, and support under a different name . . . a new brand that continues our unsurpassed quality, service, and commitment to education.

We are combining the strengths of our college imprints into one worldwide brand: Harcourt

Our mission is to make learning accessible to anyone, anywhere, anytime—reinforcing our commitment to lifelong learning.

We are now Harcourt College Publishers. Ask for us by name.

One Company
"Where Learning Comes to Life."

www.harcourtcollege.com
www.harcourt.com

LITERATURE

READING ◆ REACTING ◆ WRITING

PORTABLE EDITION

LAURIE G. KIRSZNER
University of the Sciences in Philadelphia

STEPHEN R. MANDELL
Drexel University

HARCOURT COLLEGE PUBLISHERS

Fort Worth Philadelphia San Diego New York Orlando Austin San Antonio
Toronto Montreal London Sydney Tokyo

Publisher	Earl McPeek
Acquisitions Editor	Bill Hoffman
Market Strategist	John Meyers
Developmental Editor	Camille Adkins
Project Editor	Jon Davies
Art Director	David Day
Production Manager	Cindy Young

ISBN: 0-15-506902-0
Library of Congress Catalog Card Number: 00-102634

Copyright © 2001 by Harcourt, Inc.

All rights reserved. No part of this publication may be reproduced or transmitted in any form or by any means, electronic or mechanical, including photocopy, recording, or any information storage and retrieval system, without permission in writing from the publisher.

Requests for permission to make copies of any part of the work should be mailed to the following address: Permissions Department, Harcourt, Inc., 6277 Sea Harbor Drive, Orlando, FL 32887–6777.

Copyrights and Acknowledgments appear on page 991, which constitutes a continuation of the copyright page.

Address for Domestic Orders
Harcourt College Publishers, 6277 Sea Harbor Drive, Orlando, FL
32887–6777
800-782-4479

Address for International Orders
International Customer Service
Harcourt, Inc., 6277 Sea Harbor Drive, Orlando, FL 32887–6777
407-345-3800
(fax) 407-345-4060
(e-mail) hbintl@harcourt.com

Address for Editorial Correspondence
Harcourt College Publishers, 301 Commerce Street, Suite 3700, Fort Worth, TX 76102

Web Site Address
http://www.harcourtcollege.com

Harcourt College Publishers will provide complimentary supplements or supplement packages to those adopters qualified under our adoption policy. Please contact your sales representative to learn how you qualify. If as an adopter or potential user you receive supplements you do not need, please return them to your sales representative or send them to: Attn: Returns Department, Troy Warehouse, 465 South Lincoln Drive, Troy, MO 63379.

Printed in the United States of America

0 1 2 3 4 5 6 7 8 9   039   9 8 7 6 5 4 3 2 1

Harcourt College Publishers

❖ ❖ ❖
Preface

We wrote *Literature: Reading, Reacting, Writing,* Portable Edition (the portable companion volume to the full-length and compact versions of *Literature: Reading, Reacting, Writing*), in response to the many instructors who told us they wanted a book that was truly a realistic size for a one-semester or a one-quarter course. The portable edition of *Literature* is that book: extensive enough to provide a variety of interesting selections, yet compact enough for students to bring to class. It contains just the essentials: brief introductions to literary genres and works, the works themselves, and study questions. Thus, students are not forced to pay for selections they will not read or for features they will never use. To keep the portable edition of *Literature* short, we do not include the extensive apparatus that characterizes the other two versions of our text. For example, we have eliminated all discussion of literary research. (Instructors who have not developed their own materials for teaching literary research can refer students to the *MLA Handbook for Writers of Research Papers* or to one of the many Web sites that summarize this documentation style.)

Despite the relatively small size of the portable edition of *Literature,* its purpose is the same as that of our other two literature books: to expand students' appreciation of literature and to suggest to them the many possibilities for self-discovery that literature offers. Central to our approach is the idea that writing is a vital part of understanding literature. For this reason, we include writing instruction not as an afterthought, tucked away in an appendix, but in the book's first chapter. In Chapter 1, "Reading and Writing about Literature," we discuss reading, interpreting, and evaluating literature, as well as the process of gathering and arranging ideas, drafting, and revising, and we explain how these concepts apply specifically to writing about literature. At the end of this chapter, we include three model student papers, one on a short story, Alberto Alvaro Ríos's "The Secret Lion" (p. 281); one comparing two poems, Robert Hayden's "Those Winter Sundays" (p. 311) and Seamus Heaney's "Digging" (p. 312); and one analyzing a play, Susan Glaspell's *Trifles* (p. 586). We believe this chapter will prepare students to approach the literary works in this anthology with confidence and creativity and to write about them intelligently and creatively.

Other features enhance and strengthen the text's emphasis on reading and writing about literature. Each section of the book begins with a chapter that orients readers to a particular genre—fiction, poetry, or drama—and each chapter in the book includes a Writing Checklist. In the chapters that focus on the various elements of fiction (plot, setting, point of view, and so on), we include a wide variety of short stories. Some, such as "The Lottery" and "A Rose for Emily," are perennial favorites; others are less familiar but equally compelling—for example, "Once upon a Time" and "Doe Season." Throughout the poetry section, we maintain a balance between old and new with works by classic poets such as Robert Frost and Emily Dickinson placed alongside works by more contemporary poets such as Sylvia Plath and Michael Ondaatje. The drama section also juxtaposes the classic and contemporary, with selections ranging from Shakespeare's *Hamlet* to Milcha Sanchez-Scott's *The Cuban Swimmer* and Alice Childress's *Florence*.

Throughout the portable edition of *Literature,* Reading and Reacting questions (including suggestions for journal entries) follow many selections. These questions ask students to interpret and evaluate what they have read, with many of the journal entries encouraging students to make connections—between two works, between two genres, between two themes, or between a literary work and their own experiences. After each set of Reading and Reacting questions is a Related Works feature that enables students to make connections among works and among genres—connections they can explore in class discussions as well as in their writing. Writing Suggestions appear at the end of each chapter.

To assist users of *Literature: Reading, Reacting, Writing,* Portable Edition, the following ancillary materials are available from Harcourt:

Internet Writing Activities—online activities for each chapter, many of them linked to other online resources. Students may use these activities to develop their writing and critical-thinking skills. To access these activities, students should go to the Harcourt Web site (www.harcourtcollege.com).

Instructor's Resource Guide—discussion and activities for every story, poem, and play in the anthology; thematic table of contents; semester and quarter syllabi.

The Harcourt Brace Casebook Series in Literature—ten complete casebooks, each providing in one convenient location all the materials a college student needs to complete a literary research paper.

FICTION

"A Rose for Emily" by William Faulkner
"The Yellow Wall-Paper" by Charlotte Perkins Gilman
"A Good Man Is Hard to Fine" by Flannery O'Connor
"A&P" by John Updike
"A Worn Path" by Eudora Welty

POETRY

A Collection of Poems by Emily Dickinson
A Collection of Poems by Langston Hughes
A Collection of Poems by Walt Whitman

DRAMA

"Master Harold" . . . *and the Boys* by Athol Fugard
Hamlet by William Shakespeare

The Harcourt Brace Original Film Series in Literature—film adaptations of Eudora Welty's "A Worn Path" and John Updike's "A&P." Each film lasts thirty minutes or less and includes an interview with the author.

Additional Videos—14 videos, including adaptations of plays in the portable edition.

ACKNOWLEDGMENTS
◊ ◊ ◊

From start to finish, this text has been a true collaboration for us, not only with each other, but also with our students and colleagues. We have worked hard on the book, and many people at Harcourt have worked along with us. As always, the credit for the endless day-to-day coordination of people and pages goes to our smart, funny, and incredibly patient developmental editor, Camille Adkins. Claire Brantley, acquisitions editor, worked hard to make good things happen, and Jon Davies, project editor, guided the manuscript through production with patience and skill. David Day oversaw the creation of yet another beautiful design, and Cindy Young managed the book's production with professionalism and ease. We also thank Laura Mandell Zaidman of the University of South Carolina and Sandy Richardson of Central Carolina Technical College for writing the Instructor's Resource Guide.

We are grateful to the following reviewers of the full-length and compact fourth editions on which the portable edition is based: Crystal V. Bacon, Glouchester County College; Gwen Barklay-Toy, North Carolina State University; Eric Birdsall, University of Akron; John Doyle, Quinnipiac College; David Fear, Valencia Community College; Elizabeth Keats Flores, College of Lake Country; Linda Gruber, Kishwaukee College; Lynn Hildenbrand, Chesapeake College; Teresa Kennedy, Mary Washington College; Michael Kraus, Marian College of Fond du Lac; Teri Maddox, Jackson State Community College; Judith P. Moray, Moraine Valley Community College; Mary Beth Namm, North Carolina State University; Rodney D. Newton, Central Texas College; Monte Prater, Tulsa Community College—Northeast; Gail Rung, Black Hawk College; Robert M. Temple, Manatee Community College; Maria W. Warren, University of West Florida; Donnie Yeilding, Central Texas College; and Laura Mandell Zaidman, University of South Carolina—Sumter.

We would also like to thank all the reviewers who made valuable contributions to the third edition: Ben Accardi, University of Kansas; Thomas Bailey, Western Michigan University; John Bails, University of Sioux Falls; Leigh Boyd, Temple Junior College; Cathy Cowan, Cabrillo College; Pat Cowart, Frostburg State University; Kitty Dean, Nassau Community College; Jo Devine, University of Alaska—Southeast; Jack Doyle, University of South Carolina—Sumter; Lynn Fauth, Oxnard College; David Fear, Valencia Community College; Mary Fleming, Jackson

State Community College; Ann Fogg, University of Maine; Wayne Gilbert, Community College of Aurora; Shain Graham, Orange Coast College; Linda Gruber, Kishwaukee College; Chris Hacskaylo, University of Alaska—Ketchikan; Richard Hascal, Contra Costa College; Gwen Hauk, Temple Junior College; Michael Herzog, Gonzaga University; Andrew Kelly, Jackson State Community College; Benna Kime, Jackson State Community College; Amy Sparks Kolker, University of Kansas; Michael Kraus, Marian College of Fond du Lac; Heidi Ledett, Ulster County Community College; Teri Maddox, Jackson State Community College; Jeanne Mauzy, Valencia Community College; Fred Milley, Anderson University; Robert Milliken, University of Southern Maine; Andrew Moody, University of Kansas; Paul Perry, Palo Alto Community College; Angela Rapkin, Manatee Community College; Jean Reynolds, Polk Community College; Ellen Robbins, Ulster County Community College; Paul Rogalus, Plymouth State College; Neil Sebacher, Valencia Community College; Larry Severeid, College of Eastern Utah; Sharon Small, Des Moines Area Community College; Virginia Streamer, Dundalk Community College; Robert Temple, Manatee Community College; Margie Whelan, Mt. San Antonio College; Mike White, Odessa College; Rebecca Yancey, Jackson State Community College; Donnie Yielding, Central Texas College; and Martha Zamorano, Miami Dade—Kendall Campus.

Reviewers of the second edition were Deborah Barberbousse, Horry-Georgetown Technical College; Bob Mayberry, University of Nevada—Las Vegas; Shireen Carroll, University of Miami; Stephen Wright, Seminole Community College; Robert Dees, Orange Coast College; Larry Gray, Southeastern Louisiana University; Nancy Rayl, Cypress College; James Clemmer, Austin Peay State University; Roberta Kramer, Nassau Community College.

Reviewers of the first edition included Anne Agee, Anne Arundel Community College; Lucien Agosta, California State University—Sacramento; Diana Austin, University of New Brunswick; Judith Bechtel, Northern Kentucky University; Laureen Belmont, North Idaho College; Vivian Brown, Laredo Junior College; Rebecca Butler, Dalton Junior College; Susan Coffey, Central Virginia Community College; Douglas Crowell, Texas Tech University; Shirley Ann Curtis, Polk Community College; Kitty Dean, Nassau Community College; Robert Dees, Orange Coast College; Joyce Dempsey, Arkansas Tech University; Mindy Doyle, Orange County Community College; James Egan, University of Akron; Susan Fenyves, University of North Carolina—Charlotte; Marvin Garrett, University of Cincinnati; Ann Gebhard, State University of New York—Cortland; Emma Givaltney, Arkansas Tech University; Corrinne Hales, California State University—Fresno; Gary Hall, North Harris County College; Iris Hart, Santa Fe Community College; James Helvey, Davidson County Community College; Chris Henson, California State University—Fresno; Gloria Hochstein, University of Wisconsin—Eau Claire; Angela Ingram, Southwest Texas State University; John Iorio, University of South Florida; George Ives, North Idaho College; Lavinia Jennings, University of North Carolina—Chapel Hill; Judy Kidd, North Carolina State University; Leonard Leff, Oklahoma State University; Michael Matthews, Tarrant County Junior College—Northeast; Craig McLuckie, Okanagan College; Candy Meier, Des Moines Area Community College; Judith Michna, DeKalb College—North; Christopher O'Hearn, Los Angeles Harbor College; James O'Neil, Edison Community College; Melissa Pennell, University of Lowell; Sam Phillips, Gaston College; Robbie Pinter, Belmont College; Joseph Sternberg, Harper College; Kathleen Tickner, Brevard Community College; Betty Wells, Central Virginia Community College; Susan Yaeger, Monroe Business Institute.

We would also like to thank our families—Mark, Adam, and Rebecca Kirszner and Demi, David, and Sarah Mandell—for being there when we needed them. And finally, we each thank the person on the other side of the ampersand for making our collaboration work one more time.

Brief Contents

Preface v
1 Reading and Writing about Literature 1

◆ FICTION

2 Understanding Fiction 34
3 Plot 39
4 Character 61
5 Setting 85
6 Point of View 117
7 Style, Tone, and Language 159
8 Symbol and Allegory 192
9 Theme 225
FICTION FOR FURTHER READING 265

◆ POETRY

10 Understanding Poetry 296
11 Voice 328
12 Word Choice, Word Order 362
13 Imagery 387
14 Figures of Speech 402
15 Sound 427
16 Form 452
17 Symbol, Allegory, Allusion, Myth 478
POETRY FOR FURTHER READING 503

◆ DRAMA

18 Understanding Drama 564
19 Plot 581
20 Character 656
21 Staging 859
22 Theme 921
Acknowledgments 991
Index of Authors, Titles, and First Lines of Poetry 1001

Contents

Preface v

◆ **CHAPTER 1   READING AND WRITING ABOUT LITERATURE   1**

READING LITERATURE 1
Previewing 1
Highlighting 3
CHECKLIST: Using Highlighting Symbols 3
   MAYA ANGELOU, "My Arkansas" 4
Annotating 5

WRITING ABOUT LITERATURE 6
Planning an Essay 6
Drafting an Essay 13
Revising and Editing an Essay 14
✓ *EDITING CHECKLIST:* Conventions of Writing about Literature 19

THREE MODEL STUDENT PAPERS 20
"'The Secret Lion': Everything Changes" 21
"Digging for Memories" 24
"Desperate Measures: Acts of Defiance in *Trifles*" 28

FICTION

◆ **CHAPTER 2   UNDERSTANDING FICTION   34**

THE SHORT STORY 36

READING FICTION 37

◆ **CHAPTER 3   PLOT   39**

CONFLICT 39

STAGES OF PLOT 40

ORDER AND SEQUENCE 41

A FINAL NOTE 42
✓ *CHECKLIST:* Writing about Plot 42
   KATE CHOPIN, "The Story of an Hour" 43

xiii

NADINE GORDIMER, "Once upon a Time"   46
WILLIAM FAULKNER, "A Rose for Emily"   51

Writing Suggestions: Plot   60

◆ CHAPTER 4 CHARACTER   61

ROUND AND FLAT CHARACTERS   61

DYNAMIC AND STATIC CHARACTERS   62

MOTIVATION   63

✓ *CHECKLIST:* Writing about Character   63
JOHN UPDIKE, "A&P"   64
KATHERINE MANSFIELD, "Miss Brill"   70
ANN PETRY, "Like a Winding Sheet"   75

Writing Suggestions: Character   84

◆ CHAPTER 5 SETTING   85

HISTORICAL SETTING   86

GEOGRAPHICAL SETTING   86

PHYSICAL SETTING   87

✓ *CHECKLIST:* Writing about Setting   88
KATE CHOPIN, "The Storm"   89
TILLIE OLSEN, "I Stand Here Ironing"   94
CHARLOTTE PERKINS GILMAN, "The Yellow Wall-Paper"   102

Writing Suggestions: Setting   116

◆ CHAPTER 6 POINT OF VIEW   117

FIRST-PERSON NARRATOR   117
Unreliable Narrators   118

THIRD-PERSON NARRATOR   120
Omniscient   120
Limited Omniscient   121
Objective   122
SELECTING AN APPROPRIATE POINT OF VIEW: Review   122
✓ *CHECKLIST:* Writing about Point of View   123

RICHARD WRIGHT, "Big Black Good Man"   124
EDGAR ALLAN POE, "The Cask of Amontillado"   135
WILLIAM FAULKNER, "Barn Burning"   142

Writing Suggestions: Point of View   157

◆ CHAPTER 7   STYLE, TONE, AND LANGUAGE   159

LEVEL OF DICTION   161
Formal Diction   161
Informal Diction   162

IMAGERY AND FIGURATIVE LANGUAGE   163
Imagery   163
Figurative Language   164

A FINAL NOTE   165
✓ CHECKLIST: Writing about Style, Tone, and Language   165
JAMES JOYCE, "Araby"   166
ERNEST HEMINGWAY, "A Clean, Well-Lighted Place"   172
FLANNERY O'CONNOR, "A Good Man Is Hard to Find"   177

Writing Suggestions: Style, Tone, and Language   190

◆ CHAPTER 8   SYMBOL AND ALLEGORY   192

LITERARY SYMBOLS   193
Recognizing Symbols   194
The Purpose of Symbols   194

ALLEGORY   194
✓ CHECKLIST: Writing about Symbol and Allegory   197
NATHANIEL HAWTHORNE, "Young Goodman Brown"   197
SHIRLEY JACKSON, "The Lottery"   209
ALICE WALKER, "Everyday Use"   216

Writing Suggestions: Symbol and Allegory   224

◆ CHAPTER 9   THEME   225

UNDERSTANDING THEME   226

IDENTIFYING THEMES   227

✓ CHECKLIST: Writing about Theme 229
    DAVID MICHAEL KAPLAN, "Doe Season" 230
    D. H. LAWRENCE, "The Rocking-Horse Winner" 242
    EUDORA WELTY, "A Worn Path" 256

Writing Suggestions: Theme 263

FICTION FOR FURTHER READING 265

    RAYMOND CARVER, "Popular Mechanics" 265
    JAMAICA KINCAID, "Girl" 266
    JOYCE CAROL OATES, "Where are You Going, Where Have You Been?" 268
    ALBERTO ALVARO RÍOS, "The Secret Lion" 281
    AMY TAN, "Two Kinds" 285

POETRY

◆ CHAPTER 10 UNDERSTANDING POETRY 296

    NIKKI GIOVANNI, "Poetry" 296
    ARCHIBALD MACLEISH, "Ars Poetica" 297
    MARIANNE MOORE, "Poetry" 298

DEFINING POETRY 299
    WILLIAM SHAKESPEARE, "That Time of Year Thou Mayst in Me Behold" 300
    LOUIS ZUKOFSKY, "I Walk in the Old Street" 301
    E. E. CUMMINGS, "l(a" 302

READING POETRY 303

RECOGNIZING KINDS OF POETRY 304
Narrative Poetry 304
Lyric Poetry 305

DISCOVERING THEMES IN POETRY 305
    ADRIENNE RICH, "A Woman Mourned by Daughters" 306
    RAYMOND CARVER, "Photograph of My Father in His Twenty-Second Year" 307
    JUDITH ORTIZ COFER, "My Father in the Navy: A Childhood Memory" 308

POEMS FOR FURTHER READING: POEMS ABOUT PARENTS 309
THEODORE ROETHKE, "My Papa's Waltz" 309
DYLAN THOMAS, "Do Not Go Gentle into That Good Night" 310
LUCILLE CLIFTON, "My Mama Moved among the Days" 311
ROBERT HAYDEN, "Those Winter Sundays" 311
SEAMUS HEANEY, "Digging" 312
Reading and Reacting: Poems about Parents 313

POEMS FOR FURTHER READING: POEMS ABOUT LOVE 313
CHRISTOPHER MARLOWE, "The Passionate Shepherd to His Love" 313
SIR WALTER RALEIGH, "The Nymph's Reply to the Shepherd" 314
THOMAS CAMPION, "There Is a Garden in Her Face" 315
WILLIAM SHAKESPEARE, "My Mistress' Eyes Are Nothing like the Sun" 315
ROBERT BROWNING, "Meeting at Night" 316
ROBERT BROWNING, "Parting at Morning" 316
ELIZABETH BARRETT BROWNING, "How Do I Love Thee?" 317
DOROTHY PARKER, "General Review of the Sex Situation" 317
SYLVIA PLATH, "Wreath for a Bridal" 318
TED HUGHES, "A Pink Wool Knitted Dress" 318
Reading and Reacting: Poems about Love 320

POEMS FOR FURTHER READING: POEMS ABOUT WAR 320
RUPERT BROOKE, "The Soldier" 320
WILFRED OWEN, "Anthem for Doomed Youth" 321
WILLIAM BUTLER YEATS, "An Irish Airman Foresees His Death" 322
ROBERT LOWELL, "For the Union Dead" 322
DENISE LEVERTOV, "What Were They Like?" 324
BORIS SLUTSKY, "How Did They Kill My Grandmother?" 325
YUSEF KOMUNYAKAA, "Facing It" 326
Reading and Reacting: Poems about War 327

◆ CHAPTER 11   VOICE   328

    EMILY DICKINSON, "I'm Nobody! Who Are You?"   328

    THE SPEAKER IN THE POEM   328
        LOUISE GLÜCK, "Gretel in Darkness"   330
        LEONARD ADAMÉ, "My Grandmother Would Rock Quietly and Hum"   331
        LANGSTON HUGHES, "Negro"   333
        ROBERT BROWNING, "My Last Duchess"   334
    POEMS FOR FURTHER READING: THE SPEAKER IN THE POEM   337
        LESLIE MARMON SILKO, "Where Mountain Lion Lay Down with Deer"   337
        JANICE MIRIKITANI, "Suicide Note"   338

    THE TONE OF THE POEM   340
        ROBERT FROST, "Fire and Ice"   340
        THOMAS HARDY, "The Man He Killed"   341
        AMY LOWELL, "Patterns"   342
    POEMS FOR FURTHER READING: THE TONE OF THE POEM   345
        WILLIAM WORDSWORTH, "The World Is Too Much with Us"   345
        SYLVIA PLATH, "Morning Song"   346
        ROBERT HERRICK, "To the Virgins, to Make Much of Time"   347

    IRONY   348
        ROBERT BROWNING, "Porphyria's Lover"   349
        PERCY BYSSHE SHELLEY, "Ozymandias"   351
        ARIEL DORFMAN, "Hope"   352
    POEMS FOR FURTHER READING: IRONY   354
        W. H. AUDEN, "The Unknown Citizen"   354
        ANNE SEXTON, "Cinderella"   355
        DUDLEY RANDALL, "Ballad of Birmingham"   358
✓ CHECKLIST: Writing about Voice   360

Writing Suggestions: Voice   360

◆ CHAPTER 12   WORD CHOICE, WORD ORDER   362

    SIPHO SEPAMLA, "Words, Words, Words"   362

    WORD CHOICE   363
        WALT WHITMAN, "When I Heard the Learn'd Astronomer"   364
        WILLIAM STAFFORD, "For the Grave of Daniel Boone"   366

POEMS FOR FURTHER READING: WORD CHOICE 368
    JAMES WRIGHT, "Autumn Begins in Martins Ferry, Ohio" 368
    E. E. CUMMINGS, "in Just-" 369
    THEODORE ROETHKE, "I Knew a Woman" 370

LEVELS OF DICTION 371
Formal Diction 371
    MARGARET ATWOOD, "The City Planners" 372
Informal Diction 373
    JIM SAGEL, "Baca Grande" 373
POEMS FOR FURTHER READING: LEVELS OF DICTION 375
    BARBARA L. GREENBERG, "The Faithful Wife" 375
    RICHARD WILBUR, "For the Student Strikers" 376
    CHARLES BUKOWSKI, "Dog Fight" 377

WORD ORDER 379
    EDMUND SPENSER, "One Day I Wrote Her Name upon the Strand" 379
    E. E. CUMMINGS, "anyone lived in a pretty how town" 381
POEMS FOR FURTHER READING: WORD ORDER 382
    A. E. HOUSMAN, "To an Athlete Dying Young" 382
    EMILY DICKINSON, "My Life Had Stood—A Loaded Gun" 383
✓ CHECKLIST: Writing about Word Choice and Word Order 385

Writing Suggestions: Word Choice, Word Order 386

◆ CHAPTER 13   IMAGERY   387

    JANE FLANDERS, "Cloud Painter" 387
    WILLIAM CARLOS WILLIAMS, "Red Wheelbarrow" 390
    EZRA POUND, "In a Station of the Metro" 391
    GARY SNYDER, "Some Good Things to Be Said for the Iron Age" 391
    SUZANNE E. BERGER, "The Meal" 392
    WILLIAM CARLOS WILLIAMS, "The Great Figure" 393
POEMS FOR FURTHER READING: IMAGERY 395
    MATSUO BASHO, "Four Haiku" 395
    CAROLYN KIZER, "After Basho" 396
    RICHARD WILBUR, "Sleepless at Crown Point" 397
    ROBERT FROST, "Nothing Gold Can Stay" 397

JEAN TOOMER, "Reapers" 398
WILFRED OWEN, "Dulce et Decorum Est" 399
✓ CHECKLIST: Writing about Imagery 400

Writing Suggestions: Imagery 400

◆ CHAPTER 14 FIGURES OF SPEECH 402

WILLIAM SHAKESPEARE, "Shall I Compare Thee to a Summer's Day?" 402

SIMILE, METAPHOR, AND PERSONIFICATION 403
LANGSTON HUGHES, "Harlem" 404
LAWRENCE FERLINGHETTI, "Constantly Risking Absurdity" 405
AUDRE LORDE, "Rooming Houses Are Old Women" 406

POEMS FOR FURTHER READING: SIMILE, METAPHOR, AND PERSONIFICATION 407
ROBERT BURNS, "Oh, My Love Is like a Red, Red, Rose" 407
JOHN UPDIKE, "Ex-Basketball Player" 408
RANDALL JARRELL, "The Death of the Ball Turret Gunner" 410
MARGE PIERCY, "The Secretary Chant" 410
JOHN DONNE, "A Valediction: Forbidding Mourning" 411

HYPERBOLE AND UNDERSTATEMENT 413
SYLVIA PLATH, "Daddy" 413
DAVID HUDDLE, "Holes Commence Falling" 416

POEMS FOR FURTHER READING: HYPERBOLE AND UNDERSTATEMENT 418
ANNE BRADSTREET, "To My Dear and Loving Husband" 418
ANDREW MARVELL, "To His Coy Mistress" 419
ROBERT FROST, "'Out, Out—'" 420
DONALD HALL, "My Son, My Executioner" 422
MARGARET ATWOOD, "You Fit into Me" 423

METONYMY AND SYNECDOCHE 423
RICHARD LOVELACE, "To Lucasta Going to the Wars" 424

APOSTROPHE 424
SONIA SANCHEZ, "On Passing thru Morgantown, Pa." 425
✓ CHECKLIST: Writing about Figures of Speech 425

Writing Suggestions: Figures of Speech 426

◆ Chapter 15   Sound   427

Walt Whitman, "Had I the Choice"   427

Rhythm   427
    Gwendolyn Brooks, "Sadie and Maud"   428

Meter   430
    Emily Dickinson, "I Like to See It Lap the Miles"   433

<u>Poems for Further Reading: Rhythm and Meter   436</u>
    Adrienne Rich, "Aunt Jennifer's Tigers"   436
    Etheridge Knight, "For Malcolm, a Year After"   437

Alliteration and Assonance   438
    Alfred, Lord Tennyson, "The Eagle"   439
    N. Scott Momaday, "Comparatives"   439
    Robert Herrick, "Delight in Disorder"   441

Rhyme   441
    Ogden Nash, "The Lama"   443
    Richard Wilbur, "A Sketch"   443

<u>Poems for Further Reading: Alliteration, Assonance, and Rhyme   446</u>
    Gerard Manley Hopkins, "Pied Beauty"   446
    W. H. Auden, "As I Walked Out One Evening"   447
    Lewis Carroll, "Jabberwocky"   449

✓ **Checklist:** Writing about Sound   450

Writing Suggestions: Sound   450

◆ Chapter 16   Form   452

John Keats, "On the Sonnet"   452

Closed Form   454
Blank Verse   454
Stanza   455
The Sonnet   456
    William Shakespeare, "When, in Disgrace with Fortune and Men's Eyes"   457

<u>Poems for Further Reading: The Sonnet   458</u>
    Claude McKay, "The White City"   458
    John Keats, "On First Looking into Chapman's Homer"   459
    Gwendolyn Brooks, "First Fight. Then Fiddle"   460

Haiku   460
 RICHARD BRAUTIGAN, "Widow's Lament"   461
POEMS FOR FURTHER READING: HAIKU   462
 RICHARD WRIGHT, "Hokku Poems"   462

OPEN FORM   463
 CARL SANDBURG, "Chicago"   464
 LOUISE GLÜCK, "Life Is a Nice Place"   465
 E. E. CUMMINGS, "the sky was can dy"   467
POEMS FOR FURTHER READING: OPEN FORM   468
 WALT WHITMAN, from "Out of the Cradle Endlessly Rocking"   468
 DIANE WAKOSKI, "Sleep"   469
 ROBERT HAYDEN, "Monet's 'Waterlilies'"   470
 WILLIAM CARLOS WILLIAMS, "Spring and All"   471
 CAROLYN FORCHÉ, "The Colonel"   472

CONCRETE POETRY   473
 MAY SWENSON, "Women"   474
POEM FOR FURTHER READING: CONCRETE POETRY   475
 GEORGE HERBERT, "Easter Wings"   475
✓ CHECKLIST: Writing about Form   476

Writing Suggestions: Form   476

◆ CHAPTER 17 SYMBOL, ALLEGORY, ALLUSION, MYTH   478

 WILLIAM BLAKE, "The Sick Rose"   478

SYMBOL   478
 ROBERT FROST, "For Once, Then, Something"   479
 JIM SIMMERMAN, "Child's Grave, Hale County, Alabama"   480
 EMILY DICKINSON, "Volcanoes Be in Sicily"   482
POEMS FOR FURTHER READING: SYMBOL   483
 LANGSTON HUGHES, "Island"   483
 THEODORE ROETHKE, "Night Crow"   484

ALLEGORY   484
 CHRISTINA ROSSETTI, "Uphill"   485
POEM FOR FURTHER READING: ALLEGORY   486
 ADRIENNE RICH, "Diving into the Wreck"   486

ALLUSION   488
   WOLE SOYINKA, "Future Plans"   489
   WILLIAM MEREDITH, "Dreams of Suicide"   491
  POEM FOR FURTHER READING: ALLUSION   492
   DELMORE SCHWARTZ, "The True-Blue American"   492

MYTH   493
   COUNTEE CULLEN, "Yet Do I Marvel"   494
  POEMS FOR FURTHER READING: MYTH   495
   LOUISE ERDRICH, "Windigo"   495
   WILLIAM BUTLER YEATS, "Leda and the Swan"   497
   DEREK WALCOTT, "Sea Grapes"   498
   W. H. AUDEN, "Musée des Beaux Arts"   499
✓ CHECKLIST: Writing about Symbol, Allegory, Allusion, Myth   500

Writing Suggestions: Symbol, Allegory, Allusion, Myth   501

POETRY FOR FURTHER READING   503

  MATTHEW ARNOLD, "Dover Beach"   503
  WILLIAM BLAKE, "The Chimney Sweeper"   504
  WILLIAM BLAKE, "The Lamb"   505
  WILLIAM BLAKE, "London"   506
  WILLIAM BLAKE, "The Tyger"   506
  GWENDOLYN BROOKS, "The *Chicago Defender* Sends a Man to Little Rock"   507
  GWENDOLYN BROOKS, "Medgar Evers"   509
  GWENDOLYN BROOKS, "We Real Cool"   509
  GEORGE GORDON, LORD BYRON, "She Walks in Beauty"   510
  SAMUEL TAYLOR COLERIDGE, "Kubla Khan"   510
  E. E. CUMMINGS, "Buffalo Bill's"   512
  E. E. CUMMINGS, "next to of course god america i"   513
  EMILY DICKINSON, "After Great Pain, a Formal Feeling Comes"   513
  EMILY DICKINSON, "Because I Could Not Stop for Death"   514
  EMILY DICKINSON, "I Heard a Fly Buzz—When I Died"   514
  EMILY DICKINSON, "The Soul Selects Her Own Society"   515
  EMILY DICKINSON, "Wild Nights—Wild Nights!"   515
  JOHN DONNE, "Death Be Not Proud"   516

Rita Dove, "The Satisfaction Coal Company" 516
Paul Laurence Dunbar, "We Wear the Mask" 518
T. S. Eliot, "The Love Song of J. Alfred Prufrock" 519
James A. Emanuel, "Emmett Till" 523
Robert Frost, "Acquainted with the Night" 523
Robert Frost, "Birches" 524
Robert Frost, "Mending Wall" 525
Robert Frost, "The Road Not Taken" 526
Robert Frost, "Stopping by Woods on a Snowy Evening" 527
Thomas Hardy, "The Convergence of the Twain" 528
Gerard Manley Hopkins, "The Windhover" 529
Langston Hughes, "The Negro Speaks of Rivers" 530
John Keats, "La Belle Dame sans Merci: A Ballad" 531
John Keats, "Bright Star! Would I Were as Steadfast as Thou Art" 533
John Keats, "Ode on a Grecian Urn" 533
John Keats, "When I Have Fears" 535
Claude McKay, "If We Must Die" 536
John Milton, "When I Consider How My Light Is Spent" 536
Pablo Neruda, "The United Fruit Co." 537
Sharon Olds, "Rite of Passage" 538
Michael Ondaatje, "Dates" 539
Linda Pastan, "Ethics" 540
Marge Piercy, "Barbie Doll" 541
Sylvia Plath, "Metaphors" 541
Ezra Pound, "The River-Merchant's Wife: A Letter" 542
Edwin Arlington Robinson, "Miniver Cheevy" 543
Edwin Arlington Robinson, "Richard Cory" 544
Carl Sandburg, "Fog" 545
William Shakespeare, "Let Me Not to the Marriage of True Minds" 545
William Shakespeare, "Not Marble, nor the Gilded Monuments" 546
Percy Bysshe Shelley, "Ode to the West Wind" 546
Stevie Smith, "Not Waving but Drowning" 549
Gary Soto, "Black Hair" 549
William Stafford, "Traveling through the Dark" 550
Wallace Stevens, "Anecdote of the Jar" 551
Wallace Stevens, "The Emperor of Ice-Cream" 551
Alfred, Lord Tennyson, "Ulysses" 552
Margaret Walker, "Lineage" 554
Edmund Waller, "Go, Lovely Rose" 554

Phillis Wheatley, "On Being Brought from Africa to America"   555
Walt Whitman, "A Noiseless Patient Spider"   555
Walt Whitman, from "Song of Myself"   556
William Wordsworth, "Composed upon Westminster Bridge, September 3, 1802"   557
William Wordsworth, "She Dwelt among the Untrodden Ways"   558
James Wright, "A Blessing"   558
William Butler Yeats, "The Lake Isle of Innisfree"   559
William Butler Yeats, "Sailing to Byzantium"   559
William Butler Yeats, "The Second Coming"   560

DRAMA

◆ Chapter 18   Understanding Drama   564

Dramatic Literature   564

The Origins of the Modern Theater   565
The Ancient Greek Theater   565
The Elizabethan Theater   567
The Modern Theater   570

Kinds of Drama   573
Tragedy   573
Comedy   576

Reading Drama   579

◆ Chapter 19   Plot   581

Plot Structure   581
Plot and Subplot   582

Plot Development   583
Flashbacks   584
Foreshadowing   584
✓ *Checklist:* Writing about Plot   585
   Susan Glaspell, *Trifles*   585
   Henrik Ibsen, *A Doll House*   598

Writing Suggestions: Plot   655

◆ CHAPTER 20 CHARACTER 656

CHARACTERS' WORDS 657
Formal and Informal Language 659
Plain and Elaborate Style 659
Tone 661
Irony 662

CHARACTERS' ACTIONS 663

STAGE DIRECTIONS 663

ACTORS' INTERPRETATIONS 665

✓ CHECKLIST: Writing about Character 667
  ANTON CHEKHOV, *The Brute* 668
  WILLIAM SHAKESPEARE, *Hamlet* 681
  ARTHUR MILLER, *Death of a Salesman* 782

Writing Suggestions: Character 857

◆ CHAPTER 21 STAGING 859

STAGE DIRECTIONS 859

THE USES OF STAGING 861
Costumes 861
Props 861
Scenery and Lighting 862
Music and Sound Effects 863

A FINAL NOTE 864

✓ CHECKLIST: Writing about Staging 864
  MILCHA SANCHEZ-SCOTT, *The Cuban Swimmer* 865
  SOPHOCLES, *Oedipus the King* 878

Writing Suggestions: Staging 920

◆ CHAPTER 22 THEME 921

TITLES 921

CONFLICTS 921

DIALOGUE 923

CHARACTERS 923

STAGING 924

A FINAL NOTE 925
✓ *CHECKLIST:* Writing about Theme   925
    ALICE CHILDRESS, *Florence*   926
    TENNESSEE WILLIAMS, *The Glass Menagerie*   938

Writing Suggestions: Theme   989

◊ ACKNOWLEDGMENTS   991

◊ INDEX OF AUTHORS, TITLES, AND FIRST LINES OF POETRY   1001

CHAPTER 1

Reading and Writing about Literature

READING LITERATURE

❖ ❖ ❖

The process of writing about literature starts the moment you begin to read, when you begin interacting with a work and start to discover ideas about it. This process of **active reading** helps you to interpret what you read and, eventually, to develop your ideas into a clear and logical paper.

Most readers are passive; that is, they expect the text to give them everything they need, and they don't expect to contribute much to the reading process. Active readers, however, participate in the reading process—thinking about what they read, asking questions, and challenging ideas. Active reading is excellent preparation for the discussion and writing you will do in college literature classes. And, because it helps you understand and appreciate the works you read, active reading will continue to be of value to you long after your formal classroom study of literature has ended.

Three strategies in particular—*previewing, highlighting,* and *annotating*—will help you to become a more effective reader. Remember, though, that reading and responding to what you read is not an orderly process—or even a sequential one. You will most likely find yourself doing more than one thing at a time—annotating at the same time you highlight, for example. For the sake of clarity, however, we discuss each active reading strategy separately in the pages that follow.

PREVIEWING

You begin the active reading process by **previewing** a work to get a general idea of what to look for later, when you read it more carefully.

Start with the work's most obvious physical characteristics. For example, how long is a short story? How many acts and scenes does a play have? Is a poem divided into stanzas? The answers to these and similar questions will help you begin to notice more subtle aspects of the work's form. For example, previewing may reveal that a contemporary short story is presented entirely in a question-and-answer format, that it is organized as diary entries, or that it is divided into sections by headings. Previewing may identify poems that seem to lack formal structure, such as E. E. Cummings's unconventional "l(a" (p. 302); those written in traditional forms (such as sonnets) or in experimental forms, such as the numbered list of questions and answers in Denise Levertov's "What Were They Like?" (p. 324); or concrete poems such as George Herbert's "Easter Wings" (p. 475). Your awareness of these and other distinctive features at this point may help you gain insight into a work later on.

Perhaps the most physically distinctive element of a work is its title. Not only can the title give you a general idea of what the work is about, as straightforward titles like "Miss Brill" and "The Cask of Amontillado" do, but it can also isolate (and thus call attention to) a word or phrase that emphasizes an important idea. For example, the title of Amy Tan's short story "Two Kinds" (p. 285) refers to two kinds of daughters—Chinese and American—suggesting the two perspectives that create the story's conflict. A title can also be an allusion to another work. Thus, *The Sound and the Fury,* the title of a novel by William Faulkner, alludes to a speech from Shakespeare's *Macbeth* that reinforces the major theme of the novel. Finally, a title can introduce a symbol that will gain meaning in the course of a work—as the image of a shroud does in Ann Petry's story "Like a Winding Sheet" (p. 76).

Other physical elements—such as paragraphing, capitalization, italics, and punctuation—can also provide clues about how to read a work. In William Faulkner's short story "Barn Burning" (p. 142), for instance, previewing would help you to notice passages in italic type, indicating the protagonist's thoughts, which occasionally interrupt the narrator's story.

Finally, previewing can enable you to see some of the more obvious stylistic and structural features of a work—the point of view used in a story, how many characters a play has and where it is set, or the repetition of certain words or lines in a poem, for example. Such features may or may not be important; at this stage, your goal is to observe, not to analyze or evaluate.

Previewing is a useful strategy not because it provides answers but because it suggests questions to ask later, as you read more closely. For instance, *why* does Faulkner use italics in "Barn Burning," and *why* does Herbert shape his poem on the page as he does? Elements such as those described may be noticeable as you preview, but they will gain significance as you read more carefully and review your notes.

HIGHLIGHTING

When you go on to read a work closely, you will notice additional, sometimes more subtle, elements that you may want to examine further. At this point, you should begin **highlighting**—physically marking the text to identify key details and to note relationships among ideas.

What should you highlight? As you read, ask yourself whether repeated words or phrases form a pattern, as they do in Ernest Hemingway's short story "A Clean, Well-Lighted Place" (p. 173), in which the Spanish word *nada* ("nothing") appears again and again. Because this word appears so frequently, and because it appears at key points in the story, it helps to reinforce the story's pessimistic theme—that all human experience amounts to *nada*, or nothingness. Repeated words and phrases are particularly important in poetry. In Dylan Thomas's "Do Not Go Gentle into That Good Night" (p. 310), for example, the repetition of two of the poem's nineteen lines four times each enhances the poem's rhythmic, almost monotonous, cadence. As you read, highlight your text to identify such repeated words and phrases. Later on, you can consider *why* they are repeated.

During the highlighting stage, also pay particular attention to images that occur repeatedly in a work, keeping in mind that such repeated images may form patterns that can help you to interpret the work. When you reread the work, you can begin to determine what pattern the images form and perhaps decide how this pattern enhances the work's ideas. When highlighting Robert Frost's "Stopping by Woods on a Snowy Evening" (p. 527), for instance, you might identify the related images of silence, cold, and darkness. Later, you can consider their significance.

The following poem by Maya Angelou has been highlighted by a student preparing to write about it. Notice how the student uses highlighting symbols to help him identify stylistic features, key points, and patterns of repetition that he may want to examine later.

✱ Checklist: Using Highlighting Symbols

- ✓ Underline important ideas that you should read again.
- ✓ Box or circle repeated words, phrases, or images.
- ✓ Put question marks beside confusing passages, unfamiliar references, or words that need to be defined.
- ✓ Draw lines or arrows to connect related ideas or images.
- ✓ Number incidents that occur in sequence.
- ✓ Set off a long portion of the text with a vertical line in the margin.
- ✓ Place stars beside particularly important ideas.

MAYA ANGELOU
(1928–)

My Arkansas
(1978)

There is a **deep brooding**
in Arkansas.
Old crimes like moss **pend**
from poplar trees.
5 The sullen earth
is much too
red for comfort.

Sunrise seems to hesitate
and in that second
10 lose its
incandescent aim, and
dusk no more shadows
than the noon.
The past is brighter yet.

15 Old hates and
ante-bellum lace are **rent**
but not discarded.
Today is yet to come
in Arkansas.
20 It writhes. It writhes in awful
waves of **brooding.**

This student identifies repeated words and phases ("brooding"; "it writhes") and places question marks beside the two words ("pend" and "rent") that he plans to look up in a dictionary. He also boxes two phrases—"old crimes" and "ante-bellum lace"—that he needs to think more about. Finally, he stars what he tentatively identifies as the poem's key ideas. When he rereads the poem, his highlighting will make it easier for him to react to and interpret the writer's ideas.

Annotating

At the same time you highlight a text, you also **annotate** it, recording your reactions as marginal notes. In these notes you may define new words, identify allusions, identify patterns of language or imagery, summarize plot relationships, list a work's possible themes, suggest a character's motivation, examine the possible significance of particular images or symbols, or record questions that occur to you as you read. Ideally, your annotations will help you find ideas to write about.

The following paragraph from John Updike's 1961 short story "A&P" (p. 65) was highlighted and annotated by a student in an introduction to literature course who was writing an essay in response to the question "Why does Sammy quit his job?":

> Lengel sighs and begins to look very patient and old and gray. He's been a friend of my parents for years. "Sammy, you don't want to do this to your Mom and Dad," he tells me. It's true, I don't. But it seems to me that once you begin a gesture it's fatal not to go through with it. I fold the apron, "Sammy" stitched in red on the pocket, and put it on the counter, and drop the bow tie on top of it. The bow tie is theirs, if you've ever wondered. "You'll feel this for the rest of your life," Lengel says, and I know that's true, too, but remembering how he made the pretty girl blush makes me so scrunchy inside I punch the No Sale tab and the machine whirs "pee-pul" and the drawer splats out. One advantage to this scene taking place in summer, I can follow this up with a clean exit, there's no fumbling around getting your coat and galoshes, I just saunter into the electric eye in my white shirt that my mother ironed the night before, and the door heaves itself open, and outside the sunshine is skating around on the asphalt.

Annotations (margin notes):
- Action doesn't seem to be the result of thought.
- Sammy reacts to the girl's embarrassment.
- ✱ Need for a clean exit — reinforces immature romantic ideas.
- Romantic cowboy, but his mother irons his shirt. Irony.

Because the instructor had discussed the story in class and given the class a specific assignment, the student's annotations are quite focused. In addition to highlighting important information, she notes her reactions to the story and tries to interpret Sammy's actions. Sometimes, however, you annotate a work before you have decided on a topic—in fact, the process of reading and responding to your text can help you to focus on a topic. In the absence of a topic, your annotations are likely to be less focused, so you will probably need to repeat the process when your paper's direction is clearer.

WRITING ABOUT LITERATURE

Writing about literature—or about anything else, for that matter—is an idiosyncratic process during which many activities occur at once: as you write, you think of ideas; as you think of ideas, you clarify the focus of your essay; and as you clarify your focus, you reshape your paragraphs and sentences and refine your word choice. Even though this process sounds chaotic, it has three stages: *planning, drafting,* and *revising and editing.*

PLANNING AN ESSAY

Considering Your Audience

Sometimes—for example, in a journal entry—you write primarily for yourself. At other times, however, you write for others. As you write an essay, you should consider the special requirements of that **audience**. Is your audience your classmates or your instructor? Can you assume your readers are familiar with your paper's topic and with any technical terms you will use, or will they need brief plot summaries or definitions of key terms? If your audience is your instructor, remember that he or she is a representative of a larger academic audience and therefore expects accurate information; standard English; correct grammar, mechanics, and spelling; logical arguments; and a certain degree of stylistic fluency. In addition, your instructor expects you to support your statements with specific information, to express yourself clearly and explicitly, and to document your sources. In short, your instructor wants to see how clearly you think and whether you are able to arrange your ideas into a well-organized, coherent essay.

In addition to being a member of a general academic audience, your instructor is also a member of a particular community of scholars—in this case, those who study literature. By writing about literature, you engage in a dialogue with this community. For this reason, you should adhere to the specific **conventions**—procedures that by habitual use have become accepted practice—its members follow. Many of the conventions that apply specifically to writing about literature—matters of style, format, and the like—will be discussed in this book. (The Editing Checklist on page 19 addresses some of these conventions.)

Understanding Your Purpose

Sometimes you write with a single **purpose** in mind; at other times, a writing assignment may suggest more than one purpose. In general terms, you may write for any of the following reasons:

Writing to Respond   When you write to *respond,* your goal is to discover and express your reactions to a work. To record your responses you engage in relatively informal activities, such as brainstorming, listing, and journal writing (see pp. 9–11). As you write, you explore your own ideas, forming and reforming your impressions of the work.

Writing to Interpret   When you write to *interpret,* your aim is to explain a work's possible meanings. To do so, you may summarize, give examples, or compare and contrast the work to other works or to your own experiences. Then, you may go on to analyze the work, studying each of its elements in turn, putting complex statements in your own words, defining difficult concepts, or placing ideas in context.

Writing to Evaluate   When you write to *evaluate,* your purpose is to assess a work's literary merits. You may consider not only its aesthetic appeal, but also its ability to retain that appeal over time and across national or cultural boundaries. As you write, you use your own critical sense and the opinions of experts in the field to help you make judgments about the work.

Choosing a Topic

When you write an essay about literature, you develop and support an idea about a literary work or works. Before you begin your writing, you should make certain that you understand your assignment. Do you know how much time you have to complete your essay? Are you expected to rely on your own ideas, or are you able to consult outside sources? Is your essay to focus on a specific work or on a particular element of literature? Do you have to write on an assigned topic, or are you free to choose a topic? About how long should your essay be? Do you understand exactly what the assignment is asking you to do?

Sometimes your assignment limits your options by telling you what you should discuss:

- ◇ Write an essay in which you analyze Thomas Hardy's use of irony in his poem "The Man He Killed."
- ◇ Discuss Hawthorne's use of allegory in his short story "Young Goodman Brown."
- ◇ Write a short essay in which you explain Nora's actions at the end of Ibsen's *A Doll House.*

At other times, however, your instructor will give you few guidelines other than a paper's length and format. In such situations, where you must choose a topic on your own, you can often find a topic by brainstorming or by writing journal entries. As you engage in these activities, however, keep in mind that you have many options for writing papers about literature:

- ◇ You can compare two works of literature. ("Related Works" listed at the end of each set of "Reading and Reacting" questions in the text suggest possible connections.)

- You can compare two characters or discuss some trait those characters share.
- You can trace a common theme—jealousy, revenge, power, coming of age—in several works.
- You can consider how a common subject—war, love, nature—is treated in several works.
- You can examine a single element in one or more works—for instance, plot, point of view, or character development.
- You can focus on a single aspect of that element, such as the use of flashbacks, the effect of a shifting narrative perspective, or the role of a minor character.
- You can apply a critical theory to a work of literature—for instance, apply a feminist perspective to Tillie Olsen's "I Stand Here Ironing."
- You can examine connections between an issue treated in a work of literature—for instance, spousal abuse in Ann Petry's "Like a Winding Sheet"—and that same issue as it is treated in sociological or psychological journals or in the popular press.
- You can examine some aspect of history or biography and consider its impact on a literary work—for instance, the influence of World War I on Wilfred Owen's poems.
- You can explore a problem within a work and propose a possible solution—for example, consider Montresor's actual reason for killing Fortunato in Edgar Allan Poe's "The Cask of Amontillado."

Any of the preceding options may lead you to an interesting topic. Remember, however, that you will still have to narrow the scope of your topic so that it fits within the limits of your assignment.

Finding Something to Say

Once you have a topic, you have to find something to say about it. The information you collected when you highlighted and annotated will help you formulate the statement that will be the central idea of your essay and find ideas that can support that statement.

You can use a variety of different strategies to find supporting material:

- You can discuss ideas with others—friends, classmates, instructors, or parents, for example.
- You can ask questions.
- You can do research, either in the library or on the Internet.
- You can *freewrite*—that is, keep writing on your topic for a given period of time without pausing to consider style, structure, or content.

Three additional strategies—*brainstorming, keeping a journal,* and *listing*—are especially helpful.

Brainstorming   When you **brainstorm,** you record ideas—single words, phrases, or sentences; statements or questions; quotations, paraphrases, summaries, or your own ideas—as they occur to you, moving as quickly as possible. Your starting point may be a general assignment, a particular work (or works) of literature, a specific topic, or even a thesis statement; in fact, you can brainstorm at any stage of the writing process (alone or in a group), and you can repeat this activity as often as you like.

The brainstorming notes that follow were made by a student preparing to write a paper on the relationships between children and parents in four poems. She began by brainstorming about each poem and went on to consider thematic relationships among the poems. These notes are her preliminary reactions to one of the four poems she planned to study, Adrienne Rich's "A Woman Mourned by Daughters" (p. 306):

```
(Memory:) then and now
        Then: leaf, straw, dead insect ( = light);
              ignored
        Now: swollen, puffed up, weight ( = heavy);
              focus of attention. controls their
              movements.
*Kitchen = a "universe"
        (Teaspoons, goblets, etc.) = concrete
              representations of mother;
              also = obligations, responsibilities
              (like plants and father)
        →(weigh on them, keep
         them under her spell)
    Milestones of past: weddings, being fed as children
    "You breathe upon us now"
              PARADOX? (Dead, she breathes, has weight,
    fills house and sky. Alive, she was a dead insect,
    no one paid attention to her.)
```

Keeping a Journal A journal can be a notebook, a small notepad, or a computer file. You can use a journal to find ideas—and, later, to help you to find a topic or a thesis. In a **journal** you expand your marginal annotations, recording your responses to works you have read, noting questions, exploring emerging ideas, experimenting with possible paper topics, trying to paraphrase or summarize difficult concepts, or speculating about a work's ambiguities. A journal is the place to take chances, to try out ideas that may initially seem frivolous or irrelevant; here you can think on paper (or on a computer screen) until connections become clear or ideas crystallize. You can also use your journal as a convenient place to collect your brainstorming notes and, later, your lists of related ideas.

As he prepared to write a paper analyzing the role of Jim, the "gentleman caller" in Tennessee Williams's play *The Glass Menagerie* (p. 938), a student explored ideas in the following journal entry:

> When he tells Laura that being disappointed is not the same as being discouraged, and that he's disappointed but not discouraged, Jim reveals his role as a symbol of the power of newness and change--a "bulldozer" that will clear out whatever is in its path, even delicate people like Laura. But the fact that he is disappointed shows Jim's human side. He has run into problems since high school, and these problems have blocked his progress toward a successful future. Working at the warehouse, Jim needs Tom's friendship to remind him of what he used to be (and what he still can be?), and this shows his insecurity. He isn't as sure of himself as he seems to be.

This journal entry, which represents the student's preliminary explorations, can help him to decide on a specific direction for his essay.

Seeing Connections

Listing After you have actively read a work, you should have a good many underlinings and marginal notes. Some of this material will be useful, and some will be irrelevant. **Listing** is the process of reviewing your notes, deciding which ideas are most interesting, and arranging related ideas into lists. Listing enables you to discover patterns: to see repeated images, similar characters, recurring words and phrases, and interrelated themes or ideas. Identifying these patterns can help you to decide which points to make in your paper and what information you will use to support these points. A student preparing a paper about D. H.

Lawrence's short story "The Rocking-Horse Winner" (p. 243) made the following list of related details:

> Secrets
> > Mother can't feel love
> > Paul gambles
> > Paul gives mother money
> > Family lives beyond means
> > Paul gets information from horse
>
> Religion
> > Gambling becomes like a religion
> > They all worship money
> > Specific references: "serious as a church"; "It's as if he had it from heaven"; "secret, religious voice"
>
> Luck
> > Father is unlucky
> > Mother is desperate for luck
> > Paul is lucky (ironic)

This kind of listing can be a very helpful preliminary organizing strategy, but remember that the lists you make now do not necessarily reflect the order or emphasis of ideas in your paper. As your thoughts become more focused, you will add, delete, and rearrange material.

Deciding on a Thesis

Whenever you are ready, you should try to express the main idea of your emerging essay in a tentative **thesis statement**—an idea, often expressed in a single sentence, that the rest of your essay supports. This idea should emerge logically out of your highlighting, annotating, brainstorming notes, journal entries, and lists. Eventually, you will write a **thesis-and-support** paper: stating your thesis in your introduction, supporting the thesis in the body paragraphs of your essay, and reinforcing the thesis or summarizing your points in your conclusion.

An effective thesis statement tells readers what your essay will discuss and how you will approach your material. Consequently, it should be precisely worded, making its point clear to your readers, and it should contain no vague words or inexact diction that will make it difficult for readers to follow your discussion. Although the statement "The use of sound in Tennyson's poem 'The Eagle' is interesting" is accurate, it does not convey a precise idea to your readers because the words *sound* and *interesting* are not specific. A more effective thesis statement would be "Unity in 'The Eagle' is achieved by Tennyson's use of alliteration, assonance, and rhyme throughout the poem." In addition to being specific, your thesis statement should give your readers an accurate sense of the scope and direction of your essay. It should not make promises that you do not intend to fulfill or contain extraneous details that might confuse your readers. If, for example, you are going to write a paper about the dominant image in a poem, your thesis should not imply that you will focus on the poem's setting or tone.

Remember that as you organize your ideas and as you write, you will probably modify and sharpen your tentative thesis. Sometimes you will even begin planning your essay with one thesis in mind and end it with an entirely different idea. If this happens, be sure to revise your support paragraphs so that they are consistent with your changes and so that the points you include support your new thesis. If you find that your thoughts about your topic are changing, don't be concerned; remember that this is how the writing process works.

Preparing an Outline

Once you have decided on a tentative thesis and have some idea of how you will support it, you can begin to plan your essay's structure. Quite often, an outline can help you to shape your essay. Not all writers outline, but many do because it helps them to clarify their ideas and the relationship of these ideas to one another. Realizing, however, that they will discover many new ideas as they write, these writers seldom take the time to prepare a detailed formal outline, preferring instead to make a scratch outline that lists just the major points they plan to discuss.

A **scratch outline** is perhaps the most useful kind of outline for a short paper. An informal list of the main points you will discuss in your essay, a scratch outline is more focused than a simple list of related points because it presents ideas in the order in which they will be introduced. As its name implies, however, a scratch outline lacks the detail and the degree of organization of a more formal outline. The main purpose of a scratch outline is to give you a sense of the shape and order of your paper and thus enable you to begin writing. A student writing a short essay on Edwin Arlington Robinson's use of irony in his poem "Miniver Cheevy" (p. 543) used the following scratch outline as a guide:

<u>Speaker's Attitude</u>
    Ironic
    Cynical
    Critical
<u>Use of Diction</u>
    Formal
    Detached
<u>Use of Allusions</u>
    Thebes
    Camelot

```
            Priam
            Medici
Use of Repetition
            "Miniver"
            "thought"
            regular rhyme scheme
```

Once this outline was complete, the student was ready to write a first draft.

Drafting an Essay

Your first draft is a preliminary version of your paper, something to react to and revise. Still, before you actually begin drafting your paper, you should review the material you have collected to support your thesis.

First, make sure you have collected enough information to support your thesis. The points you make are only as convincing as the evidence you present to support them. As you read and took notes, you collected examples from the work or works about which you are writing—summaries, paraphrases, or quoted lines of narrative, verse, or dialogue—to back up your statements. Just how many of these examples you need to use in your draft depends on the breadth of your thesis and how skeptical you believe your audience to be. In general, the more inclusive your thesis, the more material you need to support it. For example, if you were supporting the rather narrow thesis that the speech of a certain character in the second scene of a play was wooden or awkward, only a few examples would be needed. However, if you wanted to support the inclusive thesis that Nora and Torvald Helmer in Henrik Ibsen's 1879 play *A Doll House* (p. 599) are trapped in their roles, you would need to present a wide range of examples.

Second, see if the work includes any details that contradict your thesis. Before you begin writing, you should test the validity of your thesis by looking for details that contradict it. For example, if you plan to support the thesis that in *A Doll House* Ibsen makes a strong case for the rights of women, you should look for counterexamples. Can you find subtle hints in the play that suggest women should remain locked in their traditional roles and continue to defer to their fathers and husbands? If so, you will want to modify your thesis accordingly.

Finally, consider whether you need to use literary criticism to help you support your thesis. You could, for example, strengthen the thesis that *A Doll House* challenged contemporary attitudes about marriage by including the information that when the play first opened, Ibsen was convinced by an apprehensive theater manager to write another ending. In the new ending, Ibsen had Nora decide, after she stopped briefly to look in at her sleeping children, that she could not leave her family. Sometimes information from another source can even lead you to change your thesis. For example, after reading *A Doll House,* you might have decided that Ibsen's purpose was to make a strong case for the rights of women. In class, however, you might learn that Ibsen repeatedly said that his play was about the rights of all human beings, not just of women. This information could lead you to a thesis that suggests Torvald is just as trapped in his role as Nora is in hers. Naturally, Ibsen's interpretation of his work does not invalidate your first judgment, but it does suggest another conclusion that is worth investigating.

After you have carefully evaluated the completeness, relevance, and validity of your supporting material, you can begin drafting your essay, using your scratch outline as your guide. Your goal is to get your ideas down on paper, so you should write quickly. Once you have a draft, you will be able to examine the connections among ideas and to evaluate preliminary versions of your paragraphs and sentences. Your focus in this draft should be on the body of your essay; this is not the time to worry about constructing the "perfect" introduction and conclusion. In fact, many writers, knowing that their ideas will change as they write, postpone writing these paragraphs until a later draft, preferring instead to begin with just their tentative thesis. As you write, remember that your first draft is naturally going to be rough and will probably not be as clear as you would like it to be; still, it will enable you to see the ideas you have outlined begin to take shape.

REVISING AND EDITING AN ESSAY

As soon as you begin to draft your essay, you begin the process of revision. When you **revise,** you literally "re-see" your draft and, in many cases, you go on to reorder and rewrite substantial portions of your essay. Before you are satisfied with your essay, you will probably write several drafts, each more closely focused and more coherent than the previous one.

Strategies for Revision

Two strategies can help you to revise your drafts: *peer review* and a *dialogue with your instructor.*

Peer review is a process in which students assess each other's work-in-progress. This activity may be carried out in informal sessions, during which one student comments on another's draft, or it may be a formal process in which a student responds to specific questions on a form supplied by the instructor. In either case, one student's reactions can help another student revise.

A **dialogue with your instructor**—in conference or by e-mail—can give you a sense of how to proceed with your revision. Establishing such an oral or written dialogue can help you learn how to respond critically to your own writing, and your reactions to your instructor's comments on any draft can help you to clarify your essay's goals. (If your instructor is not available, try to schedule a conference with a writing center tutor, if your school offers this service.) Using your own responses as well as those of your classmates and your instructor, you can write drafts that are increasingly more consistent with these goals.

The Revision Process

As you move through successive drafts, the task of revising your essay will be easier if you follow a systematic process. As you read and react to your essay, begin by assessing the effectiveness of the larger elements—thesis and support, for instance—and proceed to examine increasingly smaller elements.

Thesis Statement First, reconsider your **thesis statement.** Is it carefully and precisely worded? Does it provide a realistic idea of what your essay will cover? Does it make a point that is worth supporting? It is not enough, for instance, to base an essay about literature on a vague thesis.

> **Vague:** Many important reasons exist to explain why Margot Macomber's shooting of her husband was probably intentional.
>
> **Vague:** Dickens's characters are a lot like those of Addison and Steele.

To give focus and direction to your essay, a thesis statement must be more pointed and more specific:

> **Revised:** Although Hemingway's text states that Margot Macomber "shot at the buffalo," a careful analysis of her relationship with her husband suggests that in fact she intended to kill him.
>
> **Revised:** With their extremely familiar, almost caricature-like physical and moral traits, many of Charles Dickens's minor characters reveal that he owes a debt to the "characters" created by the seventeenth-century essayists Joseph Addison and Richard Steele for the newspaper <u>The Spectator</u>.

Support Next, assess the appropriateness of your **supporting ideas** and consider whether you present enough support for your thesis and whether all the details you include are relevant to that thesis. Make sure you have supported all points with specific, concrete examples from the work or works you are discussing, briefly summarizing key events, quoting dialogue or description, describing characters or settings, or paraphrasing important ideas. Make certain, however, that your own ideas control the essay and that you have not substituted plot summary for analysis and interpretation. Your goal is to draw a conclusion about one or more works and to support that conclusion with pertinent details. If a plot detail supports a point you wish to make, include a *brief* summary of the event or series of events, showing its relevance by explicitly connecting the summary to the point you are making. In the following excerpt from a paper on a short story by James Joyce, the first sentence summarizes a key event and the second sentence explains its significance:

> At the end of "Counterparts," when Farrington returns home after a day of frustration and abuse at work, his reaction is to strike out at his son Tom. This act shows that although he and his son are similarly victimized, Farrington is also the counterpart of his tyrannical boss.

Topic Sentences Now, turn your attention to the **topic sentences** that present the main idea of each body paragraph, making sure that they are clearly worded and that they communicate the direction of your ideas and the precise relationships of ideas to one another.

Be especially careful to avoid abstractions and vague generalities in topic sentences:

> **Vague:** One similarity revolves around the dominance of the men by women. *(What exactly is the similarity?)*
>
> **Revised:** In both stories, a man is dominated by a woman.
>
> **Vague:** There is one reason for the fact that Jay Gatsby remains a mystery. *(What is the reason?)*
>
> **Revised:** Because <u>The Great Gatsby</u> is narrated by the outsider Nick Carraway, Jay Gatsby himself remains a mystery.

When revising topic sentences that are intended to move readers from one point (or section of your paper) to another, be sure the relationship between the ideas they link is clear:

> **Relationship between ideas unclear:** Now the poem's imagery will be discussed.
>
> **Revised:** Another reason for the poem's effectiveness is its unusual imagery.
>
> **Relationship between ideas unclear:** The sheriff's wife is another interesting character.
>
> **Revised:** Like her friend Mrs. Hale, the sheriff's wife has mixed feelings about what Mrs. Wright has done.

Introductions and Conclusions   When you are satisfied with the body of your essay, you can go on to examine your paper's *introduction* and *conclusion*.

The **introduction** of an essay about literature should identify the works to be discussed and indicate the emphasis of the discussion to follow. Depending on your purpose and on your paper's topic, you may want to provide some historical background or biographical information or to briefly discuss the work in relation to other, similar works. Like all introductions, the one you write for an essay about literature should create interest in your topic and include a clear thesis statement.

The following introduction, although adequate for a first draft, is in need of revision:

> Revenge, which is defined as "the chance to retaliate, get satisfaction, take vengeance, or inflict damage or injury in return for an injury, insult, etc.," is a major component in many of the stories we have read. The stories that will be discussed here deal with a variety of ways to seek revenge. In my essay, I will show some of these differences.

Although the student clearly identifies her paper's topic, she does not identify the works she will discuss or the particular point she will make about revenge. Her tired opening strategy, a dictionary definition, is not likely to create interest in her topic, and her announcement of her intention in the last sentence is awkward and unnecessary. The following revision is much more effective:

> In Edgar Allan Poe's "The Cask of Amontillado" Montresor vows revenge on Fortunato for an unspecified "insult"; in Ring Lardner's "Haircut"

Paul, a young retarded man, gets even with a cruel practical joker who has taunted him for years. Both of these stories present characters who seek revenge, and both stories end in murder. However, the murderers' motivations are presented very differently. In "Haircut" the unreliable narrator is unaware of the significance of many events, and his ignorance helps to create sympathy for the murderer. In "The Cask of Amontillado," where the untrustworthy narrator is the murderer himself, Montresor's inability to offer a convincing motive turns the reader against him.

In your **conclusion** you restate your thesis or sum up your essay's main points; then, you make a graceful exit.

The concluding paragraph that follows is acceptable for a first draft, but it communicates little information:

Although the characters of Montresor and Paul were created by different authors at different times, they do have similar motives and goals. However, they are portrayed very differently.

The following revision reinforces the essay's main point, effectively incorporating a brief quotation from "The Cask of Amontillado" (p. 136):

In fact, then, what is significant is not whether or not each murderer's act is justified, but rather how each murderer, and each victim, is portrayed by the narrator. Montresor--driven by a thirst to avenge "a thousand injuries" as well as a final insult--is shown to be sadistic and unrepentant; in "Haircut" it is Jim, the victim, whose sadism and lack of remorse are revealed to the reader.

Sentences and Words Now, focus on the individual sentences and words of your essay. Begin by evaluating your **transitions**, the words and phrases that link sentences and paragraphs. Be sure that every necessary transitional element has been supplied and that each word or phrase you have selected accurately conveys the exact relationship (sequence, contradiction, and so on) between ideas. When you are satisfied with the clarity and appropriateness of your paper's transitions, consider sentence variety and word choice.

First, be sure you have varied your sentence structure. You will bore your readers if all your sentences begin the same way ("The story . . . "; "The story . . . "), or if they are all about the same length. In addition, make sure that all the words you select accurately communicate your ideas and that you have not used vague, inexact diction. For example, saying that a character is *bad* is a lot less effective than characterizing him or her as *ruthless, conniving,* or *malicious*. Finally, eliminate subjective expressions, such as *I think, in my opinion, I believe, it seems to me,* and *I feel*. These phrases weaken your essay by suggesting that its ideas are "only" opinions and have no objective validity.

Editing

Once you have finished revising, you **edit**—that is, you make certain that your paper's grammar, punctuation, spelling, and mechanics are correct. Always run a spell check—but remember that you still have to proofread carefully for errors that the spell checker will not identify. These include homophones (*brake* incorrectly used instead of *break*), typos that create correctly spelled words (*work* instead of *word*), and proper nouns that may not be in your computer's dictionary. If you use a grammar checker, remember that grammar programs may identify potential problems—long sentences, for example—but may not be able to determine whether or not a particular long sentence is grammatically correct (let alone stylistically pleasing). Always keep a style handbook as well as a dictionary nearby so that you can double check any problems a spell checker or grammar checker highlights in your writing.

As you edit, pay particular attention to the mechanical conventions of literary essays, some of which are addressed in the Editing Checklist that follows. When your editing is complete, give your essay a descriptive title; before you retype or reprint it, be sure that its format conforms to your instructor's requirements.

✸ Editing Checklist: Conventions of Writing about Literature

✓ Use present-tense verbs when discussing works of literature: "The character of Mrs. Mallard's husband *is* not developed. . . . "

✓ Use past-tense verbs only when discussing historical events ("Owen's poem conveys the destructiveness of World War I, which at the time the poem *was* written *was* considered to be . . ."), when presenting historical or biographical data ("Her first novel which *was* published in 1811 when Austen *was* thirty-six, . . ."), or when identifying events that occurred prior to the time of the story's main action ("Miss Emily is a recluse; since her father *died* she has lived alone except for a servant").

✓ Support all points with specific, concrete examples from the work you are discussing, briefly summarizing key events, quoting dialogue or description, describing characters or setting, or paraphrasing ideas.

✓ Avoid unnecessary plot summary. Your goal is to draw a conclusion about one or more works and to support that conclusion with pertinent details. If a plot detail supports a point you wish to make, a *brief* summary is acceptable. But plot summary is no substitute for analysis.

✓ Use *literary terms* accurately. For example, be careful not to confuse *narrator* or *speaker* with *author;* feelings or opinions expressed by a narrator or character do not necessarily represent those of the author. You should not say, "In the poem's last stanza, *Frost* expresses his indecision" when you mean that the poem's *speaker* is indecisive.

✓ Underline titles of novels and plays; place titles of short stories and poems within quotation marks.

✓ Refer to authors of literary works by their full names *(Edgar Allan Poe)* in your first reference to them and by their last names *(Poe)* in subsequent references. Never refer to authors by their first names, and never use titles that indicate marital status *(Flannery O'Connor* or *O'Connor,* never *Flannery* or *Miss O'Connor).*

Three Model Student Papers

✦ ✦ ✦

The three papers in this section were written by students in an introduction to literature course. The first, by John Frei, analyzes the short story "The Secret Lion" (p. 281); the second, by Catherine Whittaker, compares the poems "Those Winter Sundays" (p. 311) and "Digging" (p. 312); the third, by Kimberly Allison, discusses the play <u>Trifles</u> (p. 586). As they planned, drafted, and revised these papers, the students followed the writing process described in this chapter.

John Frei
Professor Nyysola
English 102
14 April 2000

"The Secret Lion": Everything Changes

The first paragraph of Alberto Alvaro Ríos's "The Secret Lion" presents a twelve-year-old's view of growing up: everything changes. When the magician pulls a tablecloth out from under a pile of dishes, the child is amazed at the "staying-the-same part" (281); adults focus on the tablecloth. As adults, we have the benefit of experience; we know the trick will work as long as the technique is correct. We gain confidence, but we lose our innocence, and we lose our sense of wonder. The price we pay for knowledge is a permanent sense of loss, and this tradeoff is central to "The Secret Lion," a story whose key symbols reinforce its central theme: that change is inevitable and that change is always accompanied by loss.

The golf course is one symbol that helps to convey this theme. When the boys first see the golf course, it is "heaven" (284). Lush and green and carefully tended, it is the antithesis of the dry, brown Arizona landscape and the polluted arroyo. In fact, to the boys it is another world, as exotic as Oz and ultimately as unreal. Before long, the Emerald City becomes black and white again. They learn that there is no such thing as a "Coke-holder," that their "acting 'rich'" is just an act, and that their heaven is only a golf course (285). As the narrator acknowledges, "Something got taken away from us that moment. Heaven" (285).

The arroyo, a dry gulch that can fill up with water, is another symbol that reflects the idea of the inevitability of change and of the loss that accompanies change. It is a special, Edenlike place for the boys--a place where they can rebel by shouting forbidden words and by swimming in forbidden waters. Although it is a retreat from the disillusionment of the golf course, it is still their "personal Mississippi" (281), full of possibilities. Eventually, though, the arroyo too disappoints the boys, and they stop going there. As the narrator says, "Nature seemed to keep pushing us around one way or another, teaching us the same thing every place we ended up" (283). The lesson they keep learning is that nothing is permanent.

The grinding ball, round and perfect, suggests permanence and stability. But when the boys find it, they realize at once that they cannot keep it forever, just as they cannot remain balanced forever between childhood and adulthood. Like a child's life, the ball is perfect--but temporary. Burying it is their desperate attempt to stop time, to preserve perfection in an imperfect world, innocence in an adult world. But the boys are already twelve years old, and they have learned nature's lesson well enough to know that this action will not work. Even if they had been able to find the ball, the perfection and the innocence it suggests to them would still be unattainable. Perhaps that is why they do not try very hard to find it.

Like the story's other symbols, the secret lion itself suggests the most profound kind of change: the movement from innocence to experience, from childhood to adulthood, from expectation to disappointment to resignation. The narrator explains that when he was twelve, "something happened that we didn't have a name for, but it was there nonetheless like a lion, and roaring, roaring that way the biggest things do. Everything changed" (281). School was different, girls were different, language was different. Despite its loud roar, the lion remained paradoxically "secret," unnoticed until it passed. Like adolescence, the secret lion is a roaring disturbance that unsettles everything for a brief time and then passes, leaving everything changed.

In an attempt to make things stay the same, to make time stand still, the boys bury the grinding ball "because it was perfect.[. . .] It was the lion" (285). The grinding ball is "like that place, that whole arroyo" (282): secret and perfect. The ball and the arroyo and the lion are all perfect, but all, ironically, are temporary. The first paragraph of "The Secret Lion" tells us "Everything changed" (281); by the last paragraph we learn what this change means: "Things get taken away" (285). In other words, change implies loss. Heaven turns out to be just a golf course; the round, perfect object only "a cannonball thing used in mining" (282); the arroyo just a polluted stream; and childhood just a phase. "Things get taken away," and this knowledge that things do not last is the lion, secret yet roaring.

Catherine Whittaker
Professor Jackson
English 102
6 March 2000

Digging for Memories

  Robert Hayden's "Those Winter Sundays" and Seamus Heaney's "Digging" are two literary pieces that are tributes to the speakers' fathers. Although the depiction of the families and the tones of the two poems are different, the common thread of love between fathers and children extends through the two poems, and each speaker is inspired by his father's example.

  Many other poets have written about children and their fathers. Simon J. Ortiz in "My Father's Song" writes a touching tribute to a father who taught the speaker to respect and care for the lives of animals and to appreciate earthly wonders. In other poems, such as Theodore Roethke's "My Papa's Waltz" and Colleen J. McElroy's "My Father's Wars," fathers are depicted as imperfect, vulnerable people who try to cope with life as well as possible.

  As all these poems reveal, reflections on childhood can bring complex memories to light, as they do for Hayden's and Heaney's speakers. Now adults, they reminisce about their childhoods with a mature sense of enlightenment not found in childhood. Both speakers describe their fathers' hard work and dedication to their families. Hayden's speaker remembers that even after working hard all week, his father would get up early on Sunday to warm the house in preparation for his sleeping children. The speaker vividly portrays his father's hands, describing "cracked hands that ached from labor in the weekday weather" (3-4). And yet, these

Whittaker 2

same hands not only built the fires that drove out the cold, but also polished his children's good shoes. In a similar way, Heaney's speaker reminisces about his father's and grandfather's digging of soil and sod, pointing out their skill and their dedication to their tasks.

    The fathers in these poems appear to be hard workers, laborers who struggled to support their families. Not only were they dedicated to their work, but they also loved their children. Looking back, Hayden's speaker realizes that, although his childhood may not have been perfect and his family life was not entirely without problems, his father loved him. Heaney's description of the potato picking makes us imagine a loving family led by a father and grandfather who worked together and included the children in both work and celebration. Heaney's speaker grows into a man who has nothing but respect for his father and grandfather, wishing to be like them and to somehow fill their shoes.

    Although some similarities exist between the sons and fathers in the poems, the family life the two poems depict is very different. Perhaps it is the tone of the poems that best reveals the family atmosphere. The tone of "Digging" is wholesome, earthy, natural, and happy, emphasizing the healthy and caring nature of the speaker's childhood. Heaney's speaker seems to have no bad memories of his father or family. In contrast, the tone of Hayden's poem is very much like the coldness of the Sunday mornings. Even though the father warmed the house, the "chronic angers of that house" (9) did not leave with the cold. The speaker, as a child, seems to have resented his father, no doubt blaming him for the family's problems. The reader senses

Whittaker 3

that the warm relationship between the father and the son in Heaney's poem is absent in Hayden's.

In spite of these differences, the reader cannot go away from either poem without the impression that both speakers learned important lessons from their fathers. Both fathers had a great amount of inner strength and dedication to their families. As the years pass, Hayden's speaker has come to realize the depth of his father's devotion to his family. He uses the image of the "blueblack cold" (2) that was splintered and broken by the fires lovingly prepared by his father to suggest the father's efforts to keep his family free from harm. The cold suggests the tensions of the family that the father is determined to force out of the house through his "austere and lonely offices" (14).

In Heaney's poem, the father and grandfather also had a profound impact on the young speaker. As the memories come pouring back, the speaker's admiration for the men who came before him forces him to reflect on his own life and work. He realizes that he will never have the ability (or the desire) to do the physical labor of his relatives: "I've no spade to follow men like them" (28). However, just as the spade was the tool of his father and grandfather, the pen will be the tool with which the speaker will work. The shovel suggests the hard work, effort, and determination of the men who came before him, and the pen is the literary equivalent of the shovel. Heaney's speaker has been inspired by his father and grandfather and hopes to accomplish with a pen in the world of literature what they accomplished with a shovel on the land.

"Digging" and "Those Winter Sundays" are poems written from the perspective of sons, admiring and appreciating their fathers. Childhood memories not only act as images of the past but also evoke the speakers' self-realization and enlightenment. Even after childhood, the fathers' influence over their sons is evident; only now, however, do the speakers appreciate its true importance.

Allison 1

Kimberly Allison
English 1013
Professor Johnson
1 March 2000

Desperate Measures: Acts of
Defiance in *Trifles*

Susan Glaspell wrote her best-known play, *Trifles*, in 1916, at a time when women were beginning to challenge their socially defined roles, realizing that their identities as wives and domestics kept them in a subordinate position in society. Because women were demanding more autonomy, traditional institutions such as marriage, which confined women to the home and made them mere extensions of their husbands, were beginning to be reexamined.

As a married woman, Glaspell was evidently touched by these concerns, perhaps because when she wrote *Trifles* she was at the mercy of her husband's wishes and encountered barriers in pursuing her career as a writer because she was a woman. But for whatever reason, Glaspell chose as the play's protagonist a married woman, Minnie Foster (Mrs. Wright), who has challenged society's expectations in a very extreme way: by murdering her husband. Minnie's defiant act has occurred before the action begins, and as the play unfolds two women, Mrs. Peters and Mrs. Hale, who accompany their husbands on an investigation of the murder scene, piece together the details of the situation surrounding the murder. As the events unfold, however, it becomes clear that the focus of *Trifles* is not on who killed John Wright, but on the themes of the subordinate role of women, the confinement of the wife in the home, and the experiences all women share; through these themes,

Glaspell shows her audience the desperate measures women had to take to achieve autonomy.

The subordinate role of women, particularly Minnie's role in her marriage, becomes evident in the first few minutes of the play when Mr. Hale observes that the victim, John Wright, had little concern for his wife's opinions: "I didn't know as what his wife wanted made much difference to John" (587). Here Mr. Hale suggests that Minnie was powerless against the wishes of her husband. Indeed, as these characters imply, Minnie's every act and thought were controlled by her husband, who tried to break her spirit by forcing her to perform repetitive domestic chores alone in the home. Minnie's only power in the household remained her kitchen work, a situation that Mrs. Peters and Mrs. Hale understand because each of these women's behavior is determined by her husband. Therefore, when Sheriff Peters makes fun of Minnie's concern about her preserves, saying, "Well, can you beat the woman! Held for murder and worrying about her preserves" (589), he is, in a sense, criticizing all three of the women for worrying about domestic matters rather than about the murder that has been committed. Indeed, the sheriff's comment suggests that he assumes women's lives are trivial, an assumption that influences the thoughts and speech of all three men.

Mrs. Peters and Mrs. Hale are similar to Minnie in another way as well: throughout the play, they are confined to the kitchen of the Wrights' house. As a result, the kitchen becomes the focal point of the play. The women find that the kitchen holds the clues to Mrs. Wright's loneliness and to the details of the murder. Mrs. Peters and

Allison 3

Mrs. Hale remain confined to the kitchen while their husbands enter and exit the house at will. This scenario mirrors Minnie's daily life, as she remained in the home while her husband went to work and into town. The two women discuss Minnie's isolation in being housebound: "Not having children makes less work--but it makes a quiet house, and Wright out to work all day, and no company when he did come in" (594). Beginning to identify with Minnie's loneliness, Mrs. Peters and Mrs. Hale recognize that, busy in their own homes, they have, in fact, participated in isolating and confining Minnie. Mrs. Hale declares, "I <u>wish</u> I'd come over here once in a while! That was a crime! That was a crime! Who's going to punish that? [. . .] I might have known she needed help!" (596).

Soon the two women discover that Minnie's only connection to the outside world was her bird, the symbol of her confinement; Minnie was a caged bird who was kept from singing and communicating with others because of her restrictive husband. And piecing together the evidence--the disorderly kitchen, the misstitched quilt pieces, and the dead canary--the women come to believe that John Wright broke the bird's neck just as he had broken Minnie's spirit. At this point, Mrs. Peters and Mrs. Hale figure out the connection between the dead canary and Minnie's situation. The stage directions describe the moment when the women become aware of the truth behind the murder: "<u>Their eyes meet</u>," and the women share "<u>A look of growing comprehension, of horror</u>" (594).

Through their observations and discussions in Mrs. Wright's kitchen, Mrs. Hale and Mrs. Peters come to understand the commonality of women's

Allison 4

experiences. Mrs. Hale speaks for both of them when she says, "I know how things can be--for women. [. . .] We all go through the same things--it's all just a different kind of the same thing" (961). And, once the two women realize the experiences they share, they begin to recognize that they must join together in order to challenge a male-oriented society; although their experiences may seem trivial to the men, the "trifles" of their lives are significant to them. They realize that Minnie's independence and identity were crushed by her husband and that their own husbands have asserted that women's lives are trivial and unimportant as well. This realization leads them to commit an act as defiant as the one that has gotten Minnie into trouble: they conceal their discovery from their husbands and from the law.

Significantly, Mrs. Peters does acknowledge that "the law is the law," yet she understands that because Mr. Wright treated his wife badly, Minnie is justified in killing him. They also realize, however, that for men the law is black and white and that an all-male jury will not take into account the extenuating circumstances that prompted Minnie to kill her husband. And even if Minnie were allowed to communicate to the all-male court the psychological abuse she has suffered, the law would undoubtedly view her experience as trivial because a woman who complained about how her husband treated her would be seen as ungrateful.

Nevertheless, because Mrs. Hale and Mrs. Peters empathize with Minnie's condition, they suppress the evidence they find, enduring their husbands' condescension rather than standing up to them. And, through this desperate action, the women break through the boundaries of their social role, just

Allison 5

as Minnie has done. Although Minnie is imprisoned for her crime, she has freed herself; and, although Mrs. Peters and Mrs. Hale conceal their knowledge, fearing the men will laugh at them, these women are really challenging society and freeing themselves as well.

In <u>Trifles</u>, Susan Glaspell addresses many of the problems shared by early twentieth-century women, including their subordinate status and their confinement in the home. In order to emphasize the pervasiveness of these problems and the desperate measures women had to take to break out of restrictive social roles, Glaspell does more than focus on the plight of a woman who has ended her isolation and loneliness by committing a heinous crime against society. By presenting three male and two female characters who demonstrate the vast differences between male and female experience, she illustrates how men define the roles of women and how women can challenge these roles in search of their own significance in society and their eventual independence.

Fiction

CHAPTER 2

Understanding Fiction

A **narrative** tells a story by presenting events in some logical or orderly way. Works of narrative fiction originate in the imagination of the author, not in history or fact. Certainly some fiction—historical or autobiographical fiction, for example—focuses on real people and actual events, but the way the characters interact and how the plot unfolds are the author's invention.

Even before they know how to read, most people have learned how narratives are structured. Once children can tell a story, they also know how to exaggerate, how to add or delete details, how to rearrange events, and how to bend facts—in other words, how to fictionalize a narrative to achieve a desired effect. This kind of informal, personal narrative is similar in many ways to the more structured literary narratives included in this anthology.

Our earliest examples of narrative fiction are stories and songs that came out of a prehistoric oral tradition. These stories, embellished with each telling, were often quite long, embodying the history, the central myths, and the religious beliefs of the cultures in which they originated. Eventually transcribed, these extended narratives became **epics**—long narrative poems about heroic figures whose actions determine the fate of a nation or an entire race. Homer's *Iliad* and *Odyssey*, the ancient Babylonian *Epic of Gilgamesh*, the Hindu *Bhagavad Gita*, and the Anglo-Saxon *Beowulf* are examples. Many of the tales of the Old Testament also came out of this tradition. The setting of an epic is vast—sometimes worldwide or cosmic, including heaven and hell—and the action commonly involves a battle or a perilous journey. Quite often divine beings participate in the action and influence the outcome of events, as they do in the Trojan War in the *Iliad* and in the founding of Rome in Vergil's *Aeneid*.

Folktales and **fairy tales** also come out of an oral tradition. These tales, which developed along with other narrative forms, have influenced works as diverse as Chaucer's *The Canterbury Tales* and D. H. Lawrence's "The Rocking-Horse Winner" (p. 243). The folktales and fairy tales that survive (such as "Cinderella" and Aesop's *Fables*) are contemporary versions of old, even ancient, tales that can be traced back centuries through many different cultures. Folktales and fairy tales share several characteristics. First, they feature simple characters who illustrate a quality or trait that can be summed up in a few words. Much of the appeal of "Cinderella," for example, depends on the contrast between the selfish, sadistic stepsisters and poor, gentle, victimized Cinderella. In addition, the folktale or fairy tale has an obvious theme or moral—good triumphing over evil, for instance. The stories move directly to their conclusions, never interrupted by ingenious or unexpected twists of plot. (Love is temporarily thwarted, but the prince eventually finds Cinderella and marries her.) Finally, these tales are anchored not in specific times or places but in "Once upon a time" settings, green worlds of prehistory filled with royalty, talking animals, and magic.

During the Middle Ages, the **romance** supplanted the epic. Written initially in verse but later in prose, the romance replaced the epic's gods, goddesses, and central heroic figures with knights, kings, and damsels in distress. Events were controlled by enchantments rather than by the will of divine beings. *Sir Gawain and the Green Knight* and other tales of King Arthur and the Knights of the Round Table are examples of romances. Eventually the romance gave way to other types of narratives. Short prose tales, such as those collected in Giovanni Boccaccio's *The Decameron*, originated in fourteenth-century Italy, and the **picaresque,** an episodic, often satirical work about a rogue or rascal, such as Miguel de Cervantes's *Don Quixote*, emerged in seventeenth-century Spain. The **pastoral romance,** a prose tale set in an idealized rural world, and the **character,** a brief satirical sketch illustrating a type of personality, both became popular in Renaissance England.

From these diverse sources emerged the **novel.** The English writer Daniel Defoe is commonly given credit for writing the first novel in 1719. His *Robinson Crusoe* is an episodic narrative similar to a picaresque but unified by a single setting as well as by a central character. By the nineteenth century, the novel reached a high point in its development, replacing other kinds of extended narratives. Because of its ability to present a wide range of characters in realistic settings and to develop them in depth, the novel appealed to members of the rising middle class, who seemed to have an insatiable desire to see themselves portrayed. Writers such as George Eliot, Charles Dickens, William Thackeray, and Charlotte and Emily Brontë appealed to this desire by creating large fictional worlds populated by many different characters who reflected the complexity—and at times the melodrama—of Victorian society. From these roots, the novel as a literary form continued to develop throughout the twentieth century.

The Short Story

✧ ✧ ✧

Like the novel, the short story evolved from the various forms of narrative discussed earlier. Because the short story comes from so many different sources from all over the world, it is difficult to determine where it originated. We can say with certainty, however, that in the United States during the nineteenth century a group of writers—in particular Nathaniel Hawthorne and Edgar Allan Poe—took it seriously and exploited its fictional possibilities. Because the short story was embraced so readily and developed so quickly in the United States, it is commonly, although not quite accurately, thought of as an American literary form.

Whereas the novel is an extended piece of narrative fiction, the **short story** is limited in length and scope. These limitations account for the characteristics that distinguish the short story from longer prose forms. Unlike the novelist, the short story writer cannot devote a great deal of space to developing a highly complex plot or a large number of characters. As a result, the short story begins close to or at the height of action and develops only one character in depth. Usually concentrating on a single incident, the writer develops a character by showing his or her responses to events. (This attention to character development, as well as its detailed description of setting, is what distinguishes the short story from earlier short narrative forms, such as folktales and fairy tales.) In many contemporary stories, a character experiences an **epiphany,** a moment of illumination in which something hidden or not understood becomes immediately clear. Examples of epiphany are found in this anthology in James Joyce's "Araby," John Updike's "A&P," and David Michael Kaplan's "Doe Season."

Today the term *short story* is applied to a wide variety of prose narratives: stories like most of those in this text; **short short stories,** which are under five pages in length; and long stories, which may more accurately be called short novels or **novellas.**

As the selections in this anthology show, the possibilities of the short story are infinite. A short story may be comic or tragic; its subject may be growing up, marriage, crime and punishment, war, sexual awakening, death, or any number of other human concerns. The setting can be an imaginary world, the old West, rural America, the jungles of Uruguay, nineteenth-century Russia, pre-communist China, or modern Egypt. The story may have a conventional form, with a definite beginning, middle, and end, or it may be structured as a letter, as a diary entry, or even as a collection of random notes. The narrator of a story may be trustworthy or unreliable, involved in the action or a disinterested observer, sympathetic or deserving of scorn, extremely ignorant or highly insightful, limited in vision or able to see inside the minds of all the characters.

Reading Fiction

⋄ ⋄ ⋄

The following guidelines, designed to help you explore works of fiction, focus on issues that will be examined in depth in chapters to come.

◇ Look at the **plot** of the story. How do the events in the story relate to one another, and how do they relate to the story as a whole? What conflicts occur in the story, and how are these conflicts developed or resolved? Does the story include any noteworthy plot devices, such as flashbacks or foreshadowing? (See Chapter 3.)

◇ Analyze the **characters** of the story. What are their most striking traits? How do these individuals interact with one another? What motivates them? Are the characters fully developed, or are they stereotypes whose sole purpose is to express a single trait (good, evil, generosity) or to move the plot along? (See Chapter 4.)

◇ Identify the **setting** of the story. At what time period and in what geographic location does the action of the story occur? How does the setting affect the characters of the story? How does it determine the relationships among the characters? How does the setting affect the plot? Does the setting create a mood for the story? In what way does the setting reinforce the central ideas that the story examines? (See Chapter 5.)

◇ Examine the narrative **point of view** of the story. What person or persons are telling the story? Is the story told in the first person (*I* or *we*) or in the third person (*he, she,* or *they*)? Does the narrator see from various perspectives, or is the story restricted to the perspective of one person—a major character, a minor character, or just an observer? How much does the narrator know about the events in the story? Does the narrator present an accurate or inaccurate picture of events? Does the narrator understand the full significance of the story he or she is telling? (See Chapter 6.)

◇ Analyze the **style, tone,** and **language** of the story. Does the writer make any unusual use of diction or syntax? Does the writer use imaginative figures of speech? Patterns of imagery? What styles or levels of speech are associated with particular characters? What words or phrases are repeated throughout the work? Is the story's style plain or elaborate? Does the narrator's tone reveal his or her attitude toward characters or events? Are there any discrepancies between the narrator's attitude and the attitude of the author? Is the tone of the story playful, humorous, ironic, satirical, serious, somber, solemn, bitter,

condescending, formal, informal—or does the tone suggest some other attitude? (See Chapter 7.)
- ◊ Focus on **symbolism** and **allegory**. Does the author use any objects or ideas symbolically? What characters or objects in the story are part of an *allegorical framework?* How does an object establish its symbolic or allegorical significance in the story? Does the same object have different meanings at different places in the story? Are the symbols or *allegorical figures* conventional or unusual? At what points in the story do symbols or allegorical figures appear? (See Chapter 8.)
- ◊ Identify the **themes** of the story. What is the central theme? How is this idea or concept expressed in the work? What elements of the story develop the central theme? How do character, plot, setting, point of view, and symbols reinforce the central theme? How does the title of the story contribute to readers' understanding of the central theme? What other themes are explored? (See Chapter 9.)

Chapter 3

Plot

Alfred Hitchcock's 1951 film *Strangers on a Train*, based on a suspense novel by Patricia Highsmith, offers an intriguing premise: two men, strangers, each can murder someone the other wishes dead; because they have no apparent connection to their victims, both can escape suspicion. Many people would describe this ingenious scheme as the film's "plot," but in fact it is simply the gimmick around which the complex plot revolves. Certainly a clever twist can be an important ingredient of a story's plot, but plot is more than "what happens"; it is how what happens is presented. **Plot** is the way in which a story's events are arranged; it is shaped by causal connections—historical, social, and personal—by the interaction between characters, and by the juxtaposition of events. In *Strangers on a Train*, as in many well-developed works of fiction, the plot that unfolds is complex, with one character directing the events and determining their order while the other character is drawn into the action against his will. The same elements that enrich the plot of the film—unexpected events, conflict, suspense, flashbacks, foreshadowing—can also enrich the plot of a work of short fiction.

CONFLICT

❖ ❖ ❖

Readers' interest and involvement are heightened by a story's **conflict,** the struggle between opposing forces that emerges as the action develops. This conflict is a clash between the **protagonist,** a story's principal character, and an **antagonist,** someone or something presented in opposition to the protagonist. Sometimes the antagonist is a villain; more often, he or she simply represents a conflicting point of view or advocates a course of action different from the one the protagonist follows. Sometimes the antagonist is not a character at all but a situation (for instance, war or poverty) or an event (a natural disaster, such as a flood or a storm, for example) that challenges the protagonist. In other stories, the protagonist may struggle against a supernatural force, or the conflict may occur within a character's mind. It may, for example, be a struggle between two moral choices, such as whether to stay at home and care for an aging parent or to leave and make a new life.

Stages of Plot

◊ ◊ ◊

A work's plot explores one or more conflicts, moving from *exposition* through a series of *complications* to a *climax* and, finally, to a *resolution*.

In a story's **exposition** the writer presents the basic information readers need to understand the events that follow. Typically, the exposition sets the story in motion: it establishes the scene, introduces the major characters, and perhaps suggests the major events or conflicts to come. Sometimes a single sentence can present exposition clearly and economically, giving readers information vital to their understanding of the plot that will unfold. For example, the opening sentence of Amy Tan's "Two Kinds" (p. 285)—"My mother believed you could be anything you wanted to be in America"—establishes an important fact about a central character. Similarly, the opening sentence of Shirley Jackson's "The Lottery" (p. 209)—"The morning of June 27th was clear and sunny, with the fresh warmth of a full-summer day; the flowers were blossoming profusely and the grass was richly green"—introduces the picture-perfect setting that is essential to the story's irony. At other times, as in John Updike's "A&P" (p. 65), a more fully developed exposition section establishes the story's setting, introduces the main characters, and suggests possible conflicts. In some experimental stories a distinct exposition component may even be absent.

As the plot progresses, the story's conflict unfolds through a series of complications that will eventually lead readers to the story's climax. The action may include several crises. A **crisis** is a peak in the story's action, a moment of considerable tension or importance; the **climax** is the point of greatest tension or importance, the scene that presents a story's decisive action or event.

The final stage of plot, the **resolution,** or **denouement** (French for "untying of the knot"), draws the action to a close and accounts for all remaining loose ends. Sometimes this resolution is achieved with the help of a **deus ex machina** (Latin for "a god from a machine"), an intervention of some force or agent previously extraneous to the story—for example, the appearance of a long-lost relative or a fortuitous inheritance, the discovery of a character's true identity, a last-minute rescue by a character not previously introduced. Usually, however, the resolution is more plausible: all the events lead logically and convincingly (although not necessarily predictably) to the resolution. Sometimes the ending of a story is indefinite—that is, readers are not quite sure what the protagonist will do, or what will happen next.

This kind of resolution, although it may leave some readers feeling cheated, has its advantages: it mirrors the complexity of life, where closure rarely occurs, and it can draw readers into the action as they try to understand the significance of the story's ending or to decide how conflicts should have been resolved.

ORDER AND SEQUENCE
◊ ◊ ◊

A writer may present a story's events in strict chronological order, with each event presented in the sequence in which it actually took place. More often, however, especially in relatively modern fiction, writers do not present events chronologically. Instead, they present incidents out of expected order, or in no apparent order. For example, a writer may choose to begin **in medias res** (Latin for "in the midst of things"), starting with a key event and later going back in time to explain events that preceded it, as Tillie Olsen does in "I Stand Here Ironing" (p. 94). Or, a writer can decide to begin a work of fiction at the end and then move back to reconstruct events that led up to the final outcome, as William Faulkner does in "A Rose for Emily" (p. 52). Many sequences are possible as the writer manipulates events to create interest, suspense, confusion, wonder, or some other effect.

Writers who wish to depart from strict chronological order use *flashbacks* and *foreshadowing*. A **flashback** moves out of sequence to examine an event or situation that occurred before the time in which the story's action takes place. A character can remember an earlier event, or a story's narrator can re-create an earlier situation. For example, in Alberto Alvaro Ríos's "The Secret Lion" (p. 281), the adult narrator looks back at events that occurred when he was twelve years old—and then moves further back in time to consider related events that occurred when he was five. In Edgar Allan Poe's "The Cask of Amontillado" (p. 136), the entire story is told as a flashback. Flashbacks are valuable because they can substitute for or supplement formal exposition by presenting background vital to the readers' understanding of a story's events. One disadvantage of flashbacks is that, because they interrupt the natural flow of events, they may be intrusive or distracting. Such distractions, however, can be an advantage if the writer wishes to reveal events gradually and subtly or to obscure causal links.

Foreshadowing is the introduction early in a story of situations, events, characters, or objects that hint at things to come. A chance remark, a natural occurrence, or a seemingly trivial event is eventually revealed to have great significance. For example, a dark cloud passing across the sky can foreshadow future problems. In this way, foreshadowing allows a writer to hint provocatively at what is to come, so that readers only gradually become aware of a particular detail's role in a story. Thus, foreshadowing helps readers sense what will occur and grow increasingly involved as they see the likelihood (or even the inevitability) of a particular outcome.

In addition to employing conventional techniques like flashbacks and foreshadowing, writers may experiment with sequence by substantially tampering with—or even dispensing with—chronological order. An example is the scrambled chronology of "A Rose for Emily." In such instances the experimental form enhances interest and encourages readers to become involved with the story as they work to untangle or reorder the events and determine their logical and causal connections.

A Final Note

◊ ◊ ◊

In popular fiction, plot is likely to dominate the story, as it does, for example, in mystery or adventure stories, which tend to lack fully developed characters, complex themes, and elaborately described settings. In richer, more complicated works of fiction, however, plot is often more complex and less obvious.

 ## Checklist: Writing about Plot

- ✓ What happens in the story?
- ✓ Where does the story's formal exposition section end? What do readers learn about characters in this section? What do readers learn about setting? What possible conflicts are suggested here?
- ✓ What is the story's central conflict? What other conflicts are presented? Who is the protagonist? Who (or what) serves as the antagonist?
- ✓ Identify the story's crisis or crises.
- ✓ Identify the story's climax.
- ✓ How is the story's central conflict resolved? Is this resolution plausible? Satisfying?
- ✓ Which portion of the story constitutes the resolution? Do any problems remain unresolved? Does any uncertainty remain? If so, does this uncertainty strengthen or weaken the story? Would another ending be more effective?
- ✓ How are the story's events arranged? Are they presented in chronological order? What events are presented out of logical sequence? Does the story use foreshadowing? Flashbacks? Are the causal connections between events clear? Logical? If not, can you explain why?

◆ **KATE CHOPIN** (1851–1904) must, in a sense, be considered a contemporary writer. Her honest, sexually frank stories were rediscovered in the 1960s and 1970s, influencing a new generation. A popular contributor of stories and sketches to the magazines of her day, Chopin scandalized many critics with her outspoken novel *The Awakening* (1899), in which a woman seeks sexual and emotional fulfillment with a man who is not her husband.

Chopin was born Katherine O'Flaherty, the daughter of a wealthy St. Louis merchant and his Creole wife. She married Oscar Chopin, a Louisiana cotton broker, who took her to live on a plantation in central Louisiana. Chopin's representations of the Cane River region and its people are the foundation of her reputation as a local colorist.

◆ ◆ ◆

KATE CHOPIN

The Story of an Hour
(1894)

Knowing that Mrs. Mallard was afflicted with a heart trouble, great care was taken to break to her as gently as possible the news of her husband's death.

It was her sister Josephine who told her, in broken sentences, veiled hints that revealed in half concealing. Her husband's friend Richards was there, too, near her. It was he who had been in the newspaper office when intelligence of the railroad disaster was received, with Brently Mallard's name leading the list of "killed." He had only taken the time to assure himself of its truth by a second telegram, and had hastened to forestall any less careful, less tender friend in bearing the sad message.

She did not hear the story as many women have heard the same, with a paralyzed inability to accept its significance. She wept at once, with sudden, wild abandonment, in her sister's arms. When the storm of grief had spent itself she went away to her room alone. She would have no one follow her.

There stood, facing the open window, a comfortable, roomy armchair. Into this she sank, pressed down by a physical exhaustion that haunted her body and seemed to reach into her soul.

5   She could see in the open square before her house the tops of trees that were all aquiver with the new spring life. The delicious breath of rain was in the air. In the street below a peddler was crying his wares. The notes of a distant song which some one was singing reached her faintly, and countless sparrows were twittering in the eaves.

There were patches of blue sky showing here and there through the clouds that had met and piled one above the other in the west facing her window.

She sat with her head thrown back upon the cushion of the chair, quite motionless, except when a sob came up into her throat and shook her, as a child who has cried itself to sleep continues to sob in its dreams.

She was young, with a fair, calm face, whose lines bespoke repression and even a certain strength. But now there was a dull stare in her eyes, whose gaze was fixed away off yonder on one of those patches of blue sky. It was not a glance of reflection, but rather indicated a suspension of intelligent thought.

There was something coming to her and she was waiting for it, fearfully. What was it? She did not know; it was too subtle and elusive to name. But she felt it, creeping out of the sky, reaching toward her through the sounds, the scents, the color that filled the air.

Now her bosom rose and fell tumultuously. She was beginning to recognize this thing that was approaching to possess her, and she was striving to beat it back with her will—as powerless as her two white slender hands would have been.

When she abandoned herself a little whispered word escaped her slightly parted lips. She said it over and over under her breath: "Free, free, free!" The vacant stare and the look of terror that had followed it went from her eyes. They stayed keen and bright. Her pulses beat fast, and the coursing blood warmed and relaxed every inch of her body.

She did not stop to ask if it were not a monstrous joy that held her. A clear and exalted perception enabled her to dismiss the suggestion as trivial.

She knew that she would weep again when she saw the kind, tender hands folded in death; the face that had never looked save with love upon her, fixed and gray and dead. But she saw beyond that bitter moment a long procession of years to come that would belong to her absolutely. And she opened and spread her arms out to them in welcome.

There would be no one to live for during those coming years; she would live for herself. There would be no powerful will bending her in that blind persistence with which men and women believe they have a right to impose a private will upon a fellow creature. A kind intention or a cruel intention made the act seem no less a crime as she looked upon it in that brief moment of illumination.

And yet she had loved him—sometimes. Often she had not. What did it matter! What could love, the unsolved mystery, count for in face of this possession of self-assertion which she suddenly recognized as the strongest impulse of her being.

"Free! Body and soul free!" she kept whispering.

Josephine was kneeling before the closed door with her lips to the keyhole, imploring for admission. "Louise, open the door! I beg; open the door—you will make yourself ill. What are you doing, Louise? For heaven's sake open the door."

"Go away. I am not making myself ill." No; she was drinking in a very elixir of life through that open window.

Her fancy was running riot along those days ahead of her. Spring days, and summer days, and all sorts of days that would be her own. She breathed a quick prayer that life might be long. It was only yesterday she had thought with a shudder that life might be long.

20   She arose at length and opened the door to her sister's importunities. There as a feverish triumph in her eyes, and she carried herself unwittingly like a goddess of Victory. She clasped her sister's waist, and together they descended the stairs. Richards stood waiting for them at the bottom.

Some one was opening the front door with a latchkey. It was Brently Mallard who entered, a little travel-stained, composedly carrying his gripsack and umbrella. He had been far from the scene of the accident, and did not even know there had been one. He stood amazed at Josephine's piercing cry; at Richards' quick motion to screen him from the view of his wife.

But Richards was too late.

When the doctors came they said she had died of heart disease—of joy that kills.

READING AND REACTING

1. The story's basic exposition is presented in its first two paragraphs. What additional information about character or setting would you like to know? Why do you suppose the writer does not supply this information?
2. "The Story of an Hour" is a very economical story, with little action or dialogue. Is this a strength or a weakness? Explain.
3. When "The Story of an Hour" was first published in *Vogue* magazine in 1894, the magazine's editors titled it "The Dream of an Hour." A film version, echoing the last words of the story, is called *The Joy That Kills*. Which of the three titles do you believe most accurately represents what happens in the story?
4. Did Brently Mallard abuse his wife? Did he love her? Did she love him? Exactly why was she so relieved to be rid of him? Can you answer any of these questions with certainty?
5. What is the nature of the conflict in this story? Who, or what, do you see as Mrs. Mallard's antagonist?
6. What emotions does Mrs. Mallard experience during the hour she spends alone in her room? What events do you imagine take place during this same period outside her room? Outside her house?
7. Do you find the story's ending satisfying? Believable? Contrived?
8. Was the story's ending unexpected, or were you prepared for it? What elements foreshadowed this ending?

9. **Journal Entry** Rewrite the story's ending, substituting a few paragraphs of your own for the last three paragraphs of the story.

Related Works: "The Storm" (p. 89), "The Yellow Wall-Paper" (p. 102), "Women" (p. 474), *A Doll House* (p. 599)

◊ **NADINE GORDIMER** (1923–   ), winner of the 1991 Nobel Prize in literature, has been publishing short stories, essays, and novels about South Africa, her native country, since she was fifteen, but her work was often banned in her own country because of its condemnation of apartheid. *New York Times* book critic Michiko Kakutani suggests that in the attempt to illustrate that apartheid debases the lives of both blacks and whites, "she has mapped out the social, political and emotional geography of that troubled land with extraordinary passion and precision."

◊ ◊ ◊

NADINE GORDIMER

Once upon a Time
(1991)

Someone has written to ask me to contribute to an anthology of stories for children. I reply that I don't write children's stories; and he writes back that at a recent congress/book fair/seminar a certain novelist said every writer ought to write at least one story for children. I think of sending a postcard saying I don't accept that I 'ought' to write anything.

And then last night I woke up—or rather was wakened without knowing what had roused me.

A voice in the echo-chamber of the subconscious?

A sound.

A creaking of the kind made by the weight carried by one foot after another along a wooden floor. I listened. I felt the apertures of my ears distend with concentration. Again: the creaking. I was waiting for it; waiting to hear if it indicated that feet were moving from room to room, coming up the passage—to my door. I have no burglar bars, no gun under the pillow, but I have the same fears as people who do take these precautions, and my windowpanes are thin as rime, could shatter like a wineglass. A woman was murdered (how do they put it) in broad daylight in a house two blocks away, last year, and the fierce dogs who guarded an old widower and his collection of antique clocks were strangled before he was knifed by a casual labourer he had dismissed without pay.

I was staring at the door, making it out in my mind rather than seeing it, in the dark. I lay quite still—a victim already—but the arrhythmia of my heart was fleeing, knocking this way and that against its body-cage. How finely tuned the senses are, just out of rest, sleep! I could never listen intently as that in the distractions of the day; I was reading every faintest sound, identifying and classifying its possible threat.

But I learned that I was to be neither threatened nor spared. There was no human weight pressing on the boards, the creaking was a buckling, an epicentre of stress. I was in it. The house that surrounds me while I sleep is built on undermined ground; far beneath my bed, the floor, the house's foundations, the stopes and passages of gold mines have hollowed the rock, and when some face trembles, detaches and falls, three thousand feet below, the whole house shifts slightly, bringing uneasy strain to the balance and counterbalance of brick, cement, wood and glass that hold it as a structure around me. The misbeats of my heart tailed off like the last muffled flourishes on one of the wooden xylophones made by the Chopi and Tsonga migrant miners who might have been down there, under me in the earth at that moment. The stope where the fall was could have been disused, dripping water from its ruptured veins; or men might now be interred there in the most profound of tombs.

I couldn't find a position in which my mind would let go of my body—release me to sleep again. So I began to tell myself a story; a bedtime story.

In a house, in a suburb, in a city, there were a man and his wife who loved each other very much and were living happily ever after. They had a little boy, and they loved him very much. They had a cat and a dog that the little boy loved very much. They had a car and a caravan trailer for holidays, and a swimming-pool which was fenced so that the little boy and his playmates would not fall in and drown. They had a housemaid who was absolutely trustworthy and an itinerant gardener who was highly recommended by the neighbours. For when they began to live happily ever after they were warned, by that wise old witch, the husband's mother, not to take on anyone off the street. They were inscribed in a medical benefit society, their pet dog was licensed, they were insured against fire, flood damage and theft, and subscribed to the local Neighbourhood Watch, which supplied them with a plaque for their gates lettered YOU HAVE BEEN WARNED over the silhouette of a would-be intruder. He was masked; it could not be said if he was black or white, and therefore proved the property owner was no racist.

10   It was not possible to insure the house, the swimming pool or the car against riot damage. There were riots, but these were outside the city,

where people of another colour were quartered. These people were not allowed into the suburb except as reliable housemaids and gardeners, so there was nothing to fear, the husband told the wife. Yet she was afraid that some day such people might come up the street and tear off the plaque YOU HAVE BEEN WARNED and open the gates and stream in . . . Nonsense, my dear, said the husband, there are police and soldiers and tear-gas and guns to keep them away. But to please her—for he loved her very much and buses were being burned, cars stoned, and schoolchildren shot by the police in those quarters out of sight and hearing of the suburb—he had electronically-controlled gates fitted. Anyone who pulled off the sign YOU HAVE BEEN WARNED and tried to open the gates would have to announce his intentions by pressing a button and speaking into a receiver relayed to the house. The little boy was fascinated by the device and used it as a walkie-talkie in cops and robbers play with his small friends.

The riots were suppressed, but there were many burglaries in the suburb and somebody's trusted housemaid was tied up and shut in a cupboard by thieves while she was in charge of her employers' house. The trusted housemaid of the man and wife and little boy was so upset by this misfortune befalling a friend left, as she herself often was, with responsibility for the possessions of the man and his wife and the little boy that she implored her employers to have burglar bars attached to the doors and windows of the house, and an alarm system installed. The wife said, She is right, let us take heed to her advice. So from every window and door in the house where they were living happily ever after they now saw the trees and sky through bars, and when the little boy's pet cat tried to climb in by the fanlight to keep him company in his little bed at night, as it customarily had done, it set off the alarm keening through the house.

The alarm was often answered—it seemed—by other burglar alarms, in other houses, that had been triggered by pet cats or nibbling mice. The alarms called to one another across the gardens in shrills and bleats and wails that everyone soon became accustomed to, so that the din roused the inhabitants of the suburb no more than the croak of frogs and musical grating of cicadas' legs. Under cover of the electronic harpies' discourse intruders sawed the iron bars and broke into homes, taking away hi-fi equipment, television sets, cassette players, cameras and radios, jewellery and clothing, and sometimes were hungry enough to devour everything in the refrigerator or paused audaciously to drink the whisky in the cabinets or patio bars. Insurance companies paid no compensation for single malt, a loss made keener by the property owner's knowledge that the thieves wouldn't even have been able to appreciate what it was they were drinking.

Then the time came when many of the people who were not trusted housemaids and gardeners hung about the suburb because they were unemployed. Some importuned for a job: weeding or painting a roof; anything, *baas*, madam. But the man and his wife remembered the warning about taking on anyone off the street. Some drank liquor and fouled the street with discarded bottles. Some begged, waiting for the man or his wife to drive the car out of the electronically-operated gates. They sat about with their feet in the gutters, under the jacaranda trees that made a green tunnel of the street—for it was a beautiful suburb, spoilt only by their presence—and sometimes they fell asleep lying right before the gates in the midday sun. The wife could never see anyone go hungry. She sent the trusted housemaid out with bread and tea, but the trusted housemaid said these were loafers and *tsotsis*,[1] who would come and tie her up and shut her in a cupboard. The husband said, She's right. Take heed of her advice. You only encourage them with your bread and tea. They are looking for their chance . . . And he brought the little boy's tricycle from the garden into the house every night, because if the house was surely secure, once locked and with the alarm set, someone might still be able to climb over the wall or the electronically-closed gates into the garden.

You are right, said the wife, then the wall should be higher. And the wise old witch, the husband's mother, paid for the extra bricks as her Christmas present to her son and his wife—the little boy got a Space Man outfit and a book of fairy tales.

But every week there were more reports of intrusion: in broad daylight and the dead of night, in the early hours of the morning, and even in the lovely summer twilight—a certain family was at dinner while the bedrooms were being ransacked upstairs. The man and his wife, talking of the latest armed robbery in the suburb, were distracted by the sight of the little boy's pet cat effortlessly arriving over the seven-foot wall, descending first with a rapid bracing of extended forepaws down on the sheer vertical surface, and then a graceful launch, landing with swishing tail within the property. The whitewashed wall was marked with the cat's comings and goings; and on the street side of the wall there were larger red-earth smudges that could have been made by the kind of broken running shoes, seen on the feet of unemployed loiterers, that had no innocent destination.

When the man and wife and little boy took the pet dog for its walk round the neighbourhood streets they no longer paused to admire this show of roses or that perfect lawn; these were hidden behind an array of different varieties of security fences, walls and devices. The man, wife, little boy and dog passed a remarkable choice: there was the low-cost option of pieces of broken glass embedded in cement along the top of walls, there were iron grilles ending in lance-points, there were attempts at reconciling the aesthetics of prison architecture with the Spanish Villa style (spikes painted pink) and with the plaster urns of neoclassical façades (twelve-inch pikes finned like zigzags of lightning and painted pure white). Some walls had a small board affixed, giving the name and telephone number of the firm responsible for the installation of the devices. While the little boy and the pet dog raced ahead, the husband

---

[1] Criminals.

and wife found themselves comparing the possible effectiveness of each style against its appearance; and after several weeks when they paused before this barricade or that without needing to speak, both came out with the conclusion that only one was worth considering. It was the ugliest but the most honest in its suggestion of the pure concentration-camp style, no frills, all evident efficacy. Placed the length of walls, it consisted of a continuous coil of stiff and shining metal serrated into jagged blades, so that there would be no way of climbing over it and no way through its tunnel without getting entangled in its fangs. There would be no way out, only a struggle getting bloodier and bloodier, a deeper and sharper hooking and tearing of flesh. The wife shuddered to look at it. You're right, said the husband, anyone would think twice . . . And they took heed of the advice on a small board fixed to the wall: Consult DRAGON'S TEETH The People for Total Security.

Next day a gang of workmen came and stretched the razor-bladed coils all round the walls of the house where the husband and wife and little boy and pet dog and cat were living happily ever after. The sunlight flashed and slashed, off the serrations, the cornice of razor thorns encircled the home, shining. The husband said, Never mind. It will weather. The wife said, You're wrong. They guarantee it's rust-proof. And she waited until the little boy had run off to play before she said, I hope the cat will take heed . . . The husband said, Don't worry, my dear, cats always look before they leap. And it was true that from that day on the cat slept in the little boy's bed and kept to the garden, never risking a try at breaching security.

One evening, the mother read the little boy to sleep with a fairy story from the book the wise old witch had given him at Christmas. Next day he pretended to be the Prince who braves the terrible thicket of thorns to enter the palace and kiss the Sleeping Beauty back to life: he dragged a ladder to the wall, the shining coiled tunnel was just wide enough for his little body to creep in, and with the first fixing of its razor-teeth in his knees and hands and head he screamed and struggled deeper into its tangle. The trusted housemaid and the itinerant gardener, whose 'day' it was, came running, the first to see and to scream with him, and the itinerant gardener tore his hands trying to get at the little boy. Then the man and his wife burst wildly into the garden and for some reason (the cat, probably) the alarm set up wailing against the screams while the bleeding mass of the little boy was hacked out of the security coil with saws, wire-cutters, choppers, and they carried it— the man, the wife, the hysterical trusted housemaid and the weeping gardener—into the house.

READING AND REACTING

1. How is the introduction—paragraphs 1 through 8—related thematically to the fairy tale the narrator tells? What specific plot elements do they share?

2. In what respects is the story that begins with paragraph 9 of "Once upon a Time" similar to a fairy tale? In what respects is it different? Would the story be more or less effective without the narrator's introduction?
3. In paragraph 8, the narrator characterizes the paragraphs that follow as a "bedtime story." How does her tale differ from your idea of a bedtime story?
4. The story's events are presented in strict chronological order. Give some examples of words and phrases that move readers from one time period to another. Why is chronological order so important?
5. Imagine Gordimer's fairy tale dramatized, perhaps as a television documentary. Where would you interrupt the story to provide commercial breaks or station identification? How would you present the introduction? Explain your decisions.
6. Throughout the fairy tale, various objects and events (and even specific warnings) foreshadow the grim ending. Give several examples of such hints, and explain how each anticipates the ending.
7. Which characters are in conflict in the fairy tale? Does the story have a hero? A villain? What larger forces are in conflict? Are the conflicts between these forces resolved at the end? Explain.
8. What tendencies in her society do you think the author of "Once upon a Time" means to criticize? Do you agree that these tendencies are dangerous?
9. **JOURNAL ENTRY** "Once upon a Time" is set in South Africa. Could it have been set in the United States?

Related Works: "The Rocking-Horse Winner" (p. 243), "Gretel in Darkness" (p. 330), "Cinderella" (p. 355), "The Chimney Sweeper" (p. 504)

◆ **WILLIAM FAULKNER** (1897–1962), winner of the 1949 Nobel Prize in literature and the 1955 and 1963 Pulitzer prizes for fiction, was an unabashedly "Southern" writer whose work continues to transcend the regional label. His nineteen novels explore a wide range of human experience—from high comedy to tragedy—as seen in the life of one community, the fictional "Yoknapatawpha County" (modeled on the area around Faulkner's own hometown of Oxford, Mississippi).

Local legends and gossip frequently served as the spark for Faulkner's stories. As John B. Cullen notes, "A Rose for Emily" was based on Oxford's aristocratic "Miss Mary" Neilson, who married the charming Yankee foreman of a street-paving crew, over her family's shocked protests. He didn't meet the fate of Emily's lover, but Faulkner created his story "out of fears and rumors"—the dire predictions about what *might* happen if Mary Neilson married her Yankee.

◊ ◊ ◊

WILLIAM FAULKNER

A Rose for Emily
(1930)

I

When Miss Emily Grierson died, our whole town went to her funeral: the men through a sort of respectful affection for a fallen monument, the women mostly out of curiosity to see the inside of her house, which no one save an old manservant—a combined gardener and cook—had seen in at least ten years.

It was a big, squarish frame house that had once been white, decorated with cupolas and spires and scrolled balconies in the heavily lightsome style of the seventies, set on what had once been our most select street. But garages and cotton gins had encroached and obliterated even the august names of that neighborhood; only Miss Emily's house was left, lifting its stubborn and coquettish decay above the cotton wagons and the gasoline pumps—an eyesore among eyesores. And now Miss Emily had gone to join the representatives of those august names where they lay in the cedar-bemused cemetery among the ranked and anonymous graves of Union and Confederate soldiers who fell at the battle of Jefferson.

Alive, Miss Emily had been a tradition, a duty, and a care; a sort of hereditary obligation upon the town, dating from that day in 1894 when Colonel Sartoris, the mayor—he who fathered the edict that no Negro woman should appear on the streets without an apron—remitted her taxes, the dispensation dating from the death of her father on into perpetuity. Not that Miss Emily would have accepted charity. Colonel Sartoris invented an involved tale to the effect that Miss Emily's father had loaned money to the town, which the town, as a matter of business, preferred this way of repaying. Only a man of Colonel Sartoris' generation and thought could have invented it, and only a woman could have believed it.

When the next generation, with its more modern ideas, became mayors and aldermen, this arrangement created some little dissatisfaction. On the first of the year they mailed her a tax notice. February came, and there was no reply. They wrote her a formal letter, asking her to call at the sheriff's office at her convenience. A week later the mayor wrote her himself, offering to call or to send his car for her, and received in reply a note on paper of an archaic shape, in a thin, flowing calligraphy in faded ink, to the effect that she no longer went out at all. The tax notice was also enclosed, without comment.

They called a special meeting of the Board of Aldermen. A deputation waited upon her, knocked at the door through which no visitor had passed since she ceased giving china-painting lessons eight or ten years earlier. They were admitted by the old Negro into a dim hall from which a stairway mounted into still more shadow. It smelled of dust and disuse—a close, dank smell. The Negro led them into the parlor. It was furnished in heavy, leather-covered furniture. When the Negro opened the blinds of one window, they could see that the leather was cracked; and when they sat down, a faint dust rose sluggishly about their thighs, spinning with slow motes in the single sun-ray. On a tarnished gilt easel before the fireplace stood a crayon portrait of Miss Emily's father.

They rose when she entered—a small, fat woman in black, with a thin gold chain descending to her waist and vanishing into her belt, leaning on an ebony cane with a tarnished gold head. Her skeleton was small and spare; perhaps that was why what would have been merely plumpness in another was obesity in her. She looked bloated, like a body long submerged in motionless water, and of that pallid hue. Her eyes, lost in the fatty ridges of her face, looked like two small pieces of coal pressed into a lump of dough as they moved from one face to another while the visitors stated their errand.

She did not ask them to sit. She just stood in the door and listened quietly until the spokesman came to a stumbling halt. Then they could hear the invisible watch ticking at the end of the gold chain.

Her voice was dry and cold. "I have no taxes in Jefferson. Colonel Sartoris explained it to me. Perhaps one of you can gain access to the city records and satisfy yourselves."

"But we have. We are the city authorities, Miss Emily. Didn't you get a notice from the sheriff, signed by him?"

"I received a paper, yes," Miss Emily said. "Perhaps he considers himself the sheriff . . . I have no taxes in Jefferson."

"But there is nothing on the books to show that, you see. We must go by the—"

"See Colonel Sartoris. I have no taxes in Jefferson."

"But, Miss Emily—"

"See Colonel Sartoris." (Colonel Sartoris had been dead almost ten years.) "I have no taxes in Jefferson. Tobe!" The Negro appeared. "Show these gentlemen out."

II

So she vanquished them, horse and foot, just as she had vanquished their fathers thirty years before about the smell. That was two years after her father's death and a short time after her sweetheart—the one we believed would marry her—had deserted her. After her father's death she went out very little; after her sweetheart went away, people hardly saw her at all. A few of the ladies had the temerity to call, but were not received, and the only sign of life about the place was the Negro man—a young man then—going in and out with a market basket.

"Just as if a man—any man—could keep a kitchen properly," the ladies said; so they were not surprised when the smell developed. It was another link between the gross, teeming world and the high and mighty Griersons.

A neighbor, a woman, complained to the mayor, Judge Stevens, eighty years old.

"But what will you have me do about it, madam?" he said.

"Why, send her word to stop it," the woman said. "Isn't there a law?"

"I'm sure that won't be necessary," Judge Stevens said. "It's probably just a snake or a rat that nigger of hers killed in the yard. I'll speak to him about it."

The next day he received two more complaints, one from a man who came in diffident deprecation. "We really must do something about it, Judge. I'd be the last one in the world to bother Miss Emily, but we've got to do something." That night the Board of Aldermen met—three graybeards and one younger man, a member of the rising generation.

"It's simple enough," he said. "Send her word to have her place cleaned up. Give her a certain time to do it in, and if she don't . . ."

"Dammit, sir," Judge Stevens said, "will you accuse a lady to her face of smelling bad?"

So the next night, after midnight, four men crossed Miss Emily's lawn and slunk about the house like burglars, sniffing along the base of the brickwork and at the cellar openings while one of them performed a regular sowing motion with his hand out of a sack slung from his shoulder. They broke open the cellar door and sprinkled lime there, and in all the outbuildings. As they recrossed the lawn, a window that had been dark was lighted and Miss Emily sat in it, the light behind her, and her upright torso motionless as that of an idol. They crept quietly across the lawn and into the shadow of the locusts that lined the street. After a week or two the smell went away.

That was when people had begun to feel really sorry for her. People in our town, remembering how old lady Wyatt, her great-aunt, had gone completely crazy at last, believed that the Griersons held themselves a little too high for what they really were. None of the young men were quite good enough for Miss Emily and such. We had long thought of them as a tableau, Miss Emily a slender figure in white in the background, her father a spraddled silhouette in the foreground, his back to her and clutching a horsewhip, the two of them framed by the back-flung front door. So when she got to be thirty and was still single, we were not pleased exactly, but vindicated; even with insanity in the family she wouldn't have turned down all of her chances if they had really materialized.

When her father died, it got about that the house was all that was left to her; and in a way, people were glad. At last they could pity Miss

Emily. Being left alone, and a pauper, she had become humanized. Now she too would know the old thrill and the old despair of a penny more or less.

The day after his death all the ladies prepared to call at the house and offer condolence and aid, as is our custom. Miss Emily met them at the door, dressed as usual and with no trace of grief on her face. She told them that her father was not dead. She did that for three days, with the ministers calling on her, and the doctors, trying to persuade her to let them dispose of the body. Just as they were about to resort to law and force, she broke down, and they buried her father quickly.

We did not say she was crazy then. We believed she had to do that. We remembered all the young men her father had driven away, and we knew that with nothing left, she would have to cling to that which had robbed her, as people will.

III

She was sick for a long time. When we saw her again, her hair was cut short, making her look like a girl, with a vague resemblance to those angels in colored church windows—sort of tragic and serene.

The town had just let the contracts for paving the sidewalks, and in the summer after her father's death they began the work. The construction company came with niggers and mules and machinery, and a foreman named Homer Barron, a Yankee—a big, dark, ready man, with a big voice and eyes lighter than his face. The little boys would follow in groups to hear him cuss the niggers, and the niggers singing in time to the rise and fall of picks. Pretty soon he knew everybody in town. Whenever you heard a lot of laughing anywhere about the square, Homer Barron would be in the center of the group. Presently we began to see him and Miss Emily on Sunday afternoons driving in the yellow-wheeled buggy and the matched team of bays from the livery stable.

At first we were glad that Miss Emily would have an interest, because the ladies all said, "Of course a Grierson would not think seriously of a Northerner, a day laborer." But there were still others, older people, who said that even grief could not cause a real lady to forget *noblesse oblige*[1]—without calling it *noblesse oblige*. They just said, "Poor Emily. Her kinsfolk should come to her." She had some kin in Alabama; but years ago her father had fallen out with them over the estate of old lady Wyatt, the crazy woman, and there was no communication between the two families. They had not even been represented at the funeral.

And as soon as the old people said, "Poor Emily," the whispering began. "Do you suppose it's really so?" they said to one another. "Of course it is. What else could . . ." This behind their hands; rustling of craned silk and satin behind jalousies closed upon the sun of Sunday

---

[1] The obligation of those of high birth or rank to behave in an honorable fashion.

afternoon as the thin, swift clop-clop-clop of the matched team passed: "Poor Emily."

She carried her head high enough—even when we believed that she was fallen. It was as if she demanded more than ever the recognition of her dignity as the last Grierson; as if it had wanted that touch of earthiness to reaffirm her imperviousness. Like when she bought the rat poison, the arsenic. That was over a year after they had begun to say "Poor Emily," and while the two female cousins were visiting her.

"I want some poison," she said to the druggist. She was over thirty then, still a slight woman, though thinner than usual, with cold, haughty black eyes in a face the flesh of which was strained across the temples and about the eye-sockets as you imagine a lighthouse-keeper's face ought to look. "I want some poison," she said.

"Yes, Miss Emily. What kind? For rats and such? I'd recom—"

"I want the best you have. I don't care what kind."

The druggist named several. "They'll kill anything up to an elephant. But what you want is—"

"Arsenic," Miss Emily said. "Is that a good one?"

"Is . . . arsenic? Yes, ma'am. But what you want—"

"I want arsenic."

The druggist looked down at her. She looked back at him, erect, her face like a strained flag. "Why, of course," the druggist said. "If that's what you want. But the law requires you to tell what you are going to use it for."

Miss Emily just stared at him, her head tilted back in order to look him eye for eye, until he looked away and went and got the arsenic and wrapped it up. The Negro delivery boy brought her the package; the druggist didn't come back. When she opened the package at home there was written on the box, under the skull and bones: "For rats."

IV

So the next day we all said, "She will kill herself"; and we said it would be the best thing. When she had first begun to be seen with Homer Barron, we had said, "She will marry him." Then we said, "She will persuade him yet," because Homer himself had remarked—he liked men, and it was known that he drank with the younger men in the Elks' Club—that he was not a marrying man. Later we said, "Poor Emily" behind the jalousies as they passed on Sunday afternoon in the glittering buggy, Miss Emily with her head high and Homer Barron with his hat cocked and a cigar in his teeth, reins and whip in a yellow glove.

Then some of the ladies began to say that it was a disgrace to the town and a bad example to the young people. The men did not want to interfere, but at last the ladies forced the Baptist minister—Miss Emily's people were Episcopal—to call upon her. He would never divulge what happened during that interview, but he refused to go back again. The next Sunday they again drove about the streets, and the following day the minister's wife wrote to Miss Emily's relations in Alabama.

So she had blood-kin under her roof again and we sat back to watch developments. At first nothing happened. Then we were sure that they were to be married. We learned that Miss Emily had been to the jeweler's and ordered a man's toilet set in silver, with the letters H. B. on each piece. Two days later we learned that she had bought a complete outfit of men's clothing, including a nightshirt, and we said, "They are married." We were really glad. We were glad because the two female cousins were even more Grierson than Miss Emily had ever been.

So we were not surprised when Homer Barron—the streets had been finished some time since—was gone. We were a little disappointed that there was not a public blowing-off, but we believed that he had gone on to prepare for Miss Emily's coming, or to give her a chance to get rid of the cousins. (By that time it was a cabal, and we were all Miss Emily's allies to help circumvent the cousins.) Sure enough, after another week they departed. And, as we had expected all along, within three days Homer Barron was back in town. A neighbor saw the Negro man admit him at the kitchen door at dusk one evening.

And that was the last we saw of Homer Barron. And of Miss Emily for some time. The Negro man went in and out with the market basket, but the front door remained closed. Now and then we would see her at a window for a moment, as the men did that night when they sprinkled the lime, but for almost six months she did not appear on the streets. Then we knew that this was to be expected too; as if that quality of her father which had thwarted her woman's life so many times had been too virulent and too furious to die.

When we next saw Miss Emily, she had grown fat and her hair was turning gray. During the next few years it grew grayer and grayer until it attained an even pepper-and-salt iron-gray, when it ceased turning. Up to the day of her death at seventy-four it was still that vigorous iron-gray, like the hair of an active man.

From that time on her front door remained closed, save for a period of six or seven years, when she was about forty, during which she gave lessons in china-painting. She fitted up a studio in one of the downstairs rooms, where the daughters and granddaughters of Colonel Sartoris' contemporaries were sent to her with the same regularity and in the same spirit that they were sent to church on Sundays with a twenty-five-cent piece for the collection plate. Meanwhile her taxes had been remitted.

Then the newer generation became the backbone and the spirit of the town, and the painting pupils grew up and fell away and did not send their children to her with boxes of color and tedious brushes and pictures cut from the ladies' magazines. The front door closed upon the last one and remained closed for good. When the town got free postal delivery, Miss Emily alone refused to let them fasten the metal numbers above her door and attach a mailbox to it. She would not listen to them.

Daily, monthly, yearly we watched the Negro grow grayer and more stooped, going in and out with the market basket. Each December we sent her a tax notice, which would be returned by the post office a week later, unclaimed. Now and then we would see her in one of the downstairs windows—she had evidently shut up the top floor of the house—like the carven torso of an idol in a niche, looking or not looking at us, we could never tell which. Thus she passed from generation to generation—dear, inescapable, impervious, tranquil, and perverse.

And so she died. Fell ill in the house filled with dust and shadows, with only a doddering Negro man to wait on her. We did not even know she was sick; we had long since given up trying to get any information from the Negro. He talked to no one, probably not even to her, for his voice had grown harsh and rusty, as if from disuse.

She died in one of the downstairs rooms, in a heavy walnut bed with a curtain, her gray head propped on a pillow yellow and moldy with age and lack of sunlight.

V

The Negro met the first of the ladies at the front door and let them in, with their hushed, sibilant voices and their quick, curious glances, and then he disappeared. He walked right through the house and out the back and was not seen again.

The two female cousins came at once. They held the funeral on the second day, with the town coming to look at Miss Emily beneath a mass of bought flowers, with the crayon face of her father musing profoundly above the bier and the ladies sibilant and macabre; and the very old men—some in their brushed Confederate uniforms—on the porch and the lawn, talking of Miss Emily as if she had been a contemporary of theirs, believing that they had danced with her and courted her perhaps, confusing time with its mathematical progression, as the old do, to whom all the past is not a diminishing road but, instead, a huge meadow which no winter ever quite touches, divided from them now by the narrow bottle-neck of the most recent decade of years.

Already we knew that there was one room in that region above stairs which no one had seen in forty years, and which would have to be forced. They waited until Miss Emily was decently in the ground before they opened it.

The violence of breaking down the door seemed to fill this room with pervading dust. A thin, acrid pall as of the tomb seemed to lie everywhere upon this room decked and furnished as for a bridal: upon the valance curtains of faded rose color, upon the rose-shaded lights, upon the dressing table, upon the delicate array of crystal and the man's toilet things backed with tarnished silver, silver so tarnished that the monogram was obscured. Among them lay collar and tie, as if they had just been removed, which, lifted, left upon the surface a pale crescent in the dust. Upon a chair hung the suit, carefully folded; beneath it the two mute shoes and the discarded socks.

The man himself lay in the bed.

For a long while we just stood there, looking down at the profound and fleshless grin. The body had apparently once lain in the attitude of an embrace, but now the long sleep that outlasts love, that conquers even the grimace of love, had cuckolded him. What was left of him, rotted beneath what was left of the nightshirt, had become inextricable from the bed in which he lay; and upon him and upon the pillow beside him lay that even coating of the patient and biding dust.

Then we noticed that in the second pillow was the indentation of a head. One of us lifted something from it, and leaning forward, that faint and invisible dust dry and acrid in the nostrils, we saw a long strand of iron-gray hair.

READING AND REACTING

1. Arrange these events in the sequence in which they actually occur: Homer's arrival in town, the aldermen's visit, Emily's purchase of poison, Colonel Sartoris's decision to remit Emily's taxes, the development of the odor around Emily's house, Emily's father's death, the arrival of Emily's relatives, Homer's disappearance. Then, list the events in the sequence in which they are presented in the story. Why do you suppose Faulkner presents these events out of their actual chronological order?
2. Despite the story's confusing sequence, many events are foreshadowed. Give some examples of this technique. How does foreshadowing enrich the story?
3. Where does the exposition end and the movement toward the story's climax begin? Where does the resolution stage begin?
4. Emily is clearly the story's protagonist. In the sense that he opposes her wishes, Homer is the antagonist. What other characters—or what larger forces—are in conflict with Emily?
5. Explain how each of these phrases moves the story's plot along: "So she vanquished them, horse and foot [. . .]" (15); "After a week or two the smell went away" (24); "And that was the last we saw of Homer Barron" (47); "And so she died" (52); "The man himself lay in the bed" (58).
6. The narrator of the story is an observer, not a participant. Who might this narrator be? How do you suppose the narrator might know so much about Emily? Why do you think the narrator uses *we* instead of *I?*
7. The original version of "A Rose for Emily" included a two-page deathbed scene in which Emily tells a servant that Homer's body lies upstairs. Why do you think Faulkner deleted this scene? Do you think he made the right decision?
8. Some critics have suggested that Miss Emily Grierson is a kind of symbol of the Old South, the last defender of its outdated ideas of chivalry, formal manners, and tradition. Do you think this interpretation is justified? Would you characterize Miss

Emily as a champion or a victim of the values her town tries to preserve?

9. **Journal Entry** When asked at a seminar at the University of Virginia about the meaning of the title "A Rose for Emily," Faulkner replied, "Oh, it's simply the poor woman had no life at all. Her father had kept her more or less locked up and then she had a lover who was about to quit her, she had to murder him. It was just 'A Rose for Emily'—that's all." In another interview, asked the same question, he replied, "I pitied her and this was a salute, just as if you were to make a gesture, a salute, to anyone; to a woman you would hand a rose, as you would lift a cup of *sake* to a man." What do you make of Faulkner's responses? Can you offer other possible interpretations of the title's significance?

Related Works: "Miss Brill" (p. 71), "Porphyria's Lover" (p. 349), *Trifles* (p. 586)

◆ Writing Suggestions: Plot

1. Write a sequel to "The Story of an Hour," telling the story in the voice of Brently Mallard. Use flashbacks to provide information about his view of the Mallards' marriage.
2. Locate a newspaper story you find disturbing. Then, write a "once upon a time" story like Gordimer's in which you retell the story's events in a detached tone without adding analysis or commentary.
3. "The Story of an Hour" includes a *deus ex machina,* an outside force or agent that suddenly appears to change the course of events. Consider the possible effects of a *deus ex machina* on the other two stories in this chapter. What might this outside force be in each story? How might it change the story's action? How plausible would such a dramatic turn of events be in each case?
4. Like Emily in "A Rose for Emily," the narrator of "The Yellow Wall-Paper" (Chapter 5) is a privileged, protected woman driven to the edge of madness by events she cannot control. Despite similarities in the two women's situations, however, their tragic stories are resolved in very different ways. What factors account for the two stories' different outcomes?
5. Like "Once upon a Time," D. H. Lawrence's "The Rocking-Horse Winner" (Chapter 9) focuses on a young boy whose life comes to a tragic end as a result of social forces beyond his control. Compare and contrast these two stories. (If you like, you may consider how each story resembles a tradtional fairy tale.)

CHAPTER 4

Character

A **character** is a fictional representation of a person—usually (but not necessarily) a psychologically realistic depiction. **Characterization** is the way writers develop characters and reveal those characters' traits to readers. Writers may portray characters through their actions, through their reactions to situations or to other characters, through their physical appearance, through their speech and gestures and expressions, and even through their names.

Generally speaking, characters are developed in two ways. First, readers can be *told* about characters. Third-person narrators can give us information about what characters are doing and thinking, what experiences they have had, what they look like, how they are dressed, and so on. Sometimes they also offer analysis of and judgments about a character's behavior. Similarly, first-person narrators can tell us about themselves or about other characters. Thus, Sammy in John Updike's "A&P" (p. 65) tells us that he lives with his parents and that he disapproves of the supermarket's customers. He also tells us what various characters are wearing and describes their actions, attitudes, and gestures. (For more information about first-person narrators, see Chapter 6, "Point of View.")

Alternatively, a character's personality traits and motivation may be *revealed* through actions, dialogue, or thoughts. For instance, Sammy's vivid fantasies and his disapproval of his customers' lives suggest to readers that he is something of a nonconformist; however, Sammy himself does not actually tell us this information.

ROUND AND FLAT CHARACTERS

⋄ ⋄ ⋄

In his influential 1927 work *Aspects of the Novel,* English novelist E. M. Forster classifies characters as **round** (well developed, closely involved in and responsive to the action) or **flat** (barely developed or stereotypical). In an effective story, the major characters will usually be complex and fully developed; if they are not, readers will not care what happens to them. In much fiction, readers are encouraged to become involved with the characters, even to identify with them. This empathy is possible only when we know something about the characters—their strengths and weaknesses, for example, or their likes and dislikes. We must know at least enough to understand why characters act the way they do. In some cases, of course, a story can be effective even when its central characters are not well developed. Sometimes, in fact, a story's effectiveness is enhanced by an *absence* of character development, as in Shirley Jackson's "The Lottery" (p. 209).

Readers often expect characters to behave as "real people" in their situation might behave. Real people are not perfect, and realistic characters cannot be perfect either. The flaws that are revealed as round characters are developed—greed, gullibility, naïveté, shyness, a quick temper, or a lack of insight or judgment or tolerance or even intelligence—make them believable. In modern fiction, the protagonist is seldom if ever the noble "hero"; more often, he or she is at least partly a victim, someone to whom some unpleasant things happen, and someone who is sometimes ill-equipped to cope with events.

Unlike major characters, minor characters are frequently not well developed. Often they are flat, perhaps acting as *foils* for the protagonist. A **foil** is a supporting character whose role in the story is to highlight a major character by presenting a contrast with him or her. For instance, in "A&P," Stokesie, another young checkout clerk, is a foil for Sammy. Because he is a little older than Sammy and shows none of Sammy's imagination, restlessness, or nonconformity, Stokesie suggests what Sammy might become if he were to continue to work at the A&P. Some flat characters are **stock characters,** easily identifiable types who behave so consistently that readers can readily recognize them. The kindly old priest, the tough young bully, the ruthless business executive, and the reckless adventurer are all stock characters. Some flat characters can even be **caricatures,** characterized by a single dominant trait, such as miserliness, or even by one physical trait, such as nearsightedness.

DYNAMIC AND STATIC CHARACTERS
◊ ◊ ◊

Characters may also be classified as either *dynamic* or *static*. **Dynamic** characters grow and change in the course of a story, developing as they react to events and to other characters. In "A&P," for instance, Sammy's decision to speak out in defense of the girls—as well as the events that lead him to do so—changes him. His view of the world has changed at the end of the story, and as a result his position in the world will change too. A **static** character may face the same challenges a dynamic character might face but will remain essentially unchanged: a static character who was selfish and arrogant will remain selfish and arrogant, regardless of the nature of the story's conflict. In the fairy tale "Cinderella," for example, the title character is as sweet and good-natured at the end of the story—despite her mistreatment by her family—as she is at the beginning. Her situation may have changed, but her character has not.

Whereas round characters tend to be dynamic, flat characters tend to be static. But even a very complex, well-developed major character may be static; sometimes, in fact, the point of a story may hinge on a character's inability to change. A familiar example is the title character in William Faulkner's "A Rose for Emily" (p. 52), who lives a wasted, empty life, at least in part because she is unwilling or unable to accept that the world around her and the people in it have changed.

A story's minor characters are often static; their growth is not usually relevant to the story's development. Moreover, we usually do not learn enough about a minor character's traits, thoughts, actions, or motivation to determine whether or not the character changes significantly.

Motivation

Because round characters are complex, they are not always easy to understand. They may act differently in similar situations, just as real people do. They wrestle with decisions, resist or succumb to temptation, make mistakes, ask questions, search for answers, hope and dream, rejoice and despair. What is important is not whether we approve of a character's actions but whether those actions are *plausible*—whether the actions make sense in light of what we know about the character. We need to see a character's **motivation**—the reasons behind his or her behavior—or we will not believe or accept that behavior. For instance, given Sammy's age, his dissatisfaction with his job, and his desire to impress the young woman he calls Queenie, the decision he makes at the end of the story is perfectly plausible. Without having established his motivation, Updike could not have expected readers to accept Sammy's actions.

Even when readers get to know a character, they still are not able to predict how a complex, round character will behave in a given situation; only a flat character is predictable. The tension that develops as readers wait to see how a character will act or react, and thus how a story's conflict will be resolved, is what holds readers' interest and keeps them involved as a story's action unfolds.

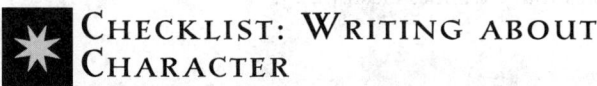
Checklist: Writing about Character

✓ Who is the story's protagonist? Who is the antagonist? Who are the other major characters?

- ✓ Who are the minor characters? What roles do they play in the story? How would the story be different without them?
- ✓ What do the major characters look like? Is their physical appearance important?
- ✓ What are the major characters' most noticeable traits?
- ✓ What are the major characters' likes and dislikes? Their strengths and weaknesses?
- ✓ What are we told about the major characters' backgrounds and prior experiences? What can we infer?
- ✓ Are characters developed for the most part through the narrator's comments and descriptions or through the characters' actions and dialogue?
- ✓ Are the characters round or flat?
- ✓ Are the characters dynamic or static?
- ✓ Does the story include any stock characters? Any caricatures? Does any character serve as a foil?
- ✓ Do the characters act in a way that is consistent with how readers expect them to act?
- ✓ With which characters are readers likely to be most (and least) sympathetic?

◆ **JOHN UPDIKE** (1932–) is a prolific writer of novels, short stories, essays, poems, plays, and children's tales. In early stories such as "A&P," Updike draws on memories of his childhood and teenage years for the sort of "small" scenes and stories for which he quickly became famous. "There is a great deal to be said about almost anything," Updike comments in an interview in *Contemporary Authors*. "All people can be equally interesting. [. . .] Now either nobody is a hero or everybody is. I vote for everybody. My subject is the American Protestant small-town middle class. I like middles. It is in middles that extremes clash [. . .]."

JOHN UPDIKE

A&P
(1961)

In walks these three girls in nothing but bathing suits. I'm in the third check-out slot, with my back to the door, so I don't see them until they're over by the bread. The one that caught my eye first was the one in the plaid green two-piece. She was a chunky kid, with a good tan and a sweet broad soft-looking can with those two crescents of white just under it, where the sun never seems to hit, at the top of the backs of her legs. I stood there with my hand on a box of HiHo crackers trying to remember if I rang it up or not. I ring it up again and the customer starts giving me hell. She's one of these cash-register-watchers, a witch about fifty with rouge on her cheekbones and no eyebrows, and I know it made her day to trip me up. She'd been watching cash registers for fifty years and probably never seen a mistake before.

By the time I got her feathers smoothed and her goodies into a bag—she gives me a little snort in passing, if she'd been born at the right time they would have burned her over in Salem—by the time I get her on her way the girls had circled around the bread and were coming back, without a push-cart, back my way along the counters, in the aisle between the check-outs and the Special bins. They didn't even have shoes on. There was this chunky one, with the two-piece—it was bright green and the seams on the bra were still sharp and her belly was still pretty pale so I guessed she just got it (the suit)—there was this one, with one of those chubby berry-faces, the lips all bunched together under her nose, this one, and a tall one, with black hair that hadn't quite frizzed right, and one of these sunburns right across under the eyes, and a chin that was too long—you know, the kind of girl other girls think is very "striking" and "attractive" but never quite makes it, as they very well know, which is why they like her so much—and then the third one, that wasn't quite so tall. She was the queen. She kind of led them, the other two peeking around and making their shoulders round. She didn't look around, not this queen, she just walked straight on slowly, on these long white prima-donna legs. She came down a little hard on her heels, as if she didn't walk in her bare feet that much, putting down her heels and then letting the weight move along to her toes as if she was testing the floor with every step, putting a little deliberate extra action into it. You never know for sure how girls' minds work (do you really think it's a mind in there or just a little buzz like a bee in a glass jar?) but you got the idea she had talked the other two into coming in here with her, and now she was showing them how to do it, walk slow and hold yourself straight.

She had on a kind of dirty-pink—beige maybe, I don't know—bathing suit with a little nubble all over it and, what got me, the straps were down. They were off her shoulders looped loose around the cool tops of her arms, and I guess as a result the suit had slipped a little on her, so all around the top of the cloth there was this shining rim. If it hadn't been there you wouldn't have known there could have been anything whiter than those shoulders. With the straps pushed off, there was nothing between the top of the suit and the top of her head except just *her*, this clean bare plane of the top of her chest down from the shoulder bones like a dented sheet of metal tilted in the light. I mean, it was more than pretty.

She had sort of oaky hair that the sun and salt had bleached, done up in a bun that was unravelling, and a kind of prim face. Walking into the A&P with your straps down, I suppose it's the only kind of face you *can* have. She held her head so high her neck, coming up out of those white shoulders, looked kind of stretched, but I didn't mind. The longer her neck was, the more of her there was.

5   She must have felt in the corner of her eye me and over my shoulder Stokesie in the second slot watching, but she didn't tip. Not this queen. She kept her eyes moving across the racks, and stopped, and turned so slow it made my stomach rub the inside of my apron, and buzzed to the other two, who kind of huddled against her for relief, and they all three of them went up the cat-and-dog-food-breakfast-cereal-macaroni-rice-raisins-seasonings-spreads-spaghetti-soft-drinks-crackers-and-cookies aisle. From the third slot I look straight up this aisle to the meat counter, and I watched them all the way. The fat one with the tan sort of fumbled with the cookies, but on second thought she put the packages back. The sheep pushing their carts down the aisle—the girls were walking against the usual traffic (not that we have one-way signs or anything)—were pretty hilarious. You could see them, when Queenie's white shoulders dawned on them, kind of jerk, or hop, or hiccup, but their eyes snapped back to their own baskets and on they pushed. I bet you could set off dynamite in an A&P and the people would by and large keep reaching and checking oatmeal off their lists and muttering "Let me see, there was a third thing, began with A, asparagus, no, ah, yes, applesauce!" or whatever it is they do mutter. But there was no doubt, this jiggled them. A few houseslaves in pin curlers even looked around after pushing their carts past to make sure what they had seen was correct.

You know, it's one thing to have a girl in a bathing suit down on the beach, where what with the glare nobody can look at each other much anyway, and another thing in the cool of the A&P, under the fluorescent lights, against all those stacked packages, with her feet paddling along naked over our checkerboard green-and-cream rubber-tile floor.

"Oh Daddy," Stokesie said beside me. "I feel so faint."

"Darling," I said. "Hold me tight." Stokesie's married, with two babies chalked up on his fuselage already, but as far as I can tell that's the only difference. He's twenty-two, and I was nineteen this April.

"Is it done?" he asks, the responsible married man finding his voice. I forgot to say he thinks he's going to be manager some sunny day, maybe in 1990 when it's called the Great Alexandrov and Petrooshki Tea Company or something.

What he meant was, our town is five miles from a beach, with a big summer colony out on the Point, but we're right in the middle of town, and the women generally put on a shirt or shorts or something before they get out of the car into the street. And anyway these are usually women with six children and varicose veins mapping their legs and nobody, including them, could care less. As I say, we're right in the middle of town, and if you stand at our front doors you can see two banks and the Congregational church and the newspaper store and three real-estate offices and about twenty-seven old freeloaders tearing up Central Street because the sewer broke again. It's not as if we're on the Cape; we're north of Boston and there's people in this town haven't seen the ocean for twenty years.

The girls had reached the meat counter and were asking McMahon something. He pointed, they pointed, and they shuffled out of sight behind a pyramid of Diet Delight peaches. All that was left for us to see was old McMahon patting his mouth and looking after them sizing up their joints. Poor kids, I began to feel sorry for them, they couldn't help it.

Now here comes the sad part of the story, at least my family says it's sad but I don't think it's sad myself. The store's pretty empty, it being Thursday afternoon, so there was nothing much to do except lean on the register and wait for the girls to show up again. The whole store was like a pinball machine and I didn't know which tunnel they'd come out of. After a while they come around out of the far aisle, around the light bulbs, records at discount of the Caribbean Six or Tony Martin Sings or some such gunk you wonder they waste the wax on, sixpacks of candy bars, and plastic toys done up in cellophane that fall apart when a kid looks at them anyway. Around they come, Queenie still leading the way, and holding a little gray jar in her hand. Slots Three through Seven are unmanned and I could see her wondering between Stokes and me, but Stokesie with his usual luck draws an old party in baggy gray pants who stumbles up with four giant cans of pineapple juice (what do these bums *do* with all that pineapple juice? I've often asked myself) so the girls come to me. Queenie puts down the jar and I take it into my fingers icy cold. Kingfish Fancy Herring Snacks in Pure Sour Cream: 49. Now her hands are empty, not a ring or a bracelet, bare as God made them, and I wonder where the money's coming from. Still with that prim look she lifts a folded dollar bill out of the hollow at the center of her nubbled pink top. The jar went heavy in my hand. Really, I thought that was so cute.

Then everybody's luck begins to run out. Lengel comes in from haggling with a truck full of cabbages on the lot and is about to scuttle into that door marked MANAGER behind which he hides all day when the girls touch his eye. Lengel's pretty dreary, teaches Sunday school and the rest, but he doesn't miss that much. He comes over and says, "Girls, this isn't the beach."

Queenie blushes, though maybe it's just a brush of sunburn I was noticing for the first time, now that she was so close. "My mother asked me to pick up a jar of herring snacks." Her voice kind of startled me, the way voices do when you see the people first, coming out so flat and dumb yet kind of tony, too, the way it ticked over "pick up" and "snacks." All of a sudden I slid right down her voice into her living room. Her father and the other men were standing around in ice-cream coats and bow ties and the women were in sandals picking up herring snacks on toothpicks off a big plate and they were all holding drinks the color of water with olives and sprigs of mint in them. When my parents have somebody over they get lemonade and if it's a real racy affair Schlitz in tall glasses with "They'll Do It Every Time" cartoons stenciled on.

15 "That's all right," Lengel said. "But this isn't the beach." His repeating this struck me as funny, as if it had just occurred to him, and he had been thinking all these years the A&P was a great big dune and he was the head lifeguard. He didn't like my smiling—as I say he doesn't miss much—but he concentrates on giving the girls that sad Sunday-school-superintendent stare.

Queenie's blush is no sunburn now, and the plump one in plaid, that I liked better from the back—a really sweet can—pipes up, "We weren't doing any shopping. We just came in for the one thing."

"That makes no difference," Lengel tells her, and I could see from the way his eyes went that he hadn't noticed she was wearing a two-piece before. "We want you decently dressed when you come in here."

"We *are* decent," Queenie says suddenly, her lower lip pushing, getting sore now that she remembers her place, a place from which the crowd that runs the A&P must look pretty crummy. Fancy Herring Snacks flashed in her very blue eyes.

"Girls, I don't want to argue with you. After this come in here with your shoulders covered. It's our policy." He turns his back. That's policy for you. Policy is what the kingpins want. What the others want is juvenile delinquency.

20 All this while, the customers had been showing up with their carts but, you know, sheep, seeing a scene, they had all bunched up on Stokesie, who shook open a paper bag as gently as peeling a peach, not wanting to miss a word. I could feel in the silence everybody getting nervous, most of all Lengel, who asks me, "Sammy, have you rung up this purchase?"

I thought and said "No" but it wasn't about that I was thinking. I go through the punches, 4, 9, GROC, TOT—it's more complicated than you think, and after you do it often enough, it begins to make a little song, that you hear words to, in my case "Hello *(bing)* there, you *(gung)* hap-py pee-pul *(splat)*!"—the *splat* being the drawer flying out. I uncrease the bill, tenderly as you may imagine, it just having come from between the two smoothest scoops of vanilla I had ever known were there, and pass a half and a penny into her narrow pink palm, and nestle the herrings in a bag and twist its neck and hand it over, all the time thinking.

The girls, and who'd blame them, are in a hurry to get out, so I say "I quit" to Lengel quick enough for them to hear, hoping they'll stop and watch me, their unsuspected hero. They keep right on going, into the electric eye; the door flies open and they flicker across the lot to their car, Queenie and Plaid and Big Tall Goony-Goony (not that as raw material she was so bad), leaving me with Lengel and a kink in his eyebrow.

"Did you say something, Sammy?"

"I said I quit."

"I thought you did."

"You didn't have to embarrass them."

"It was they who were embarrassing us."

I started to say something that came out "Fiddle-de-doo." It's a saying of my grandmother's, and I know she would have been pleased.

"I don't think you know what you're saying," Lengel said.

"I know you don't," I said. "But I do." I pull the bow at the back of my apron and start shrugging it off my shoulders. A couple customers that had been heading for my slot begin to knock against each other, like scared pigs in a chute.

Lengel sighs and begins to look very patient and old and gray. He's been a friend of my parents for years. "Sammy, you don't want to do this to your Mom and Dad," he tells me. It's true, I don't. But it seems to me that once you begin a gesture it's fatal not to go through with it. I fold the apron, "Sammy" stitched in red on the pocket, and put it on the counter, and drop the bow tie on top of it. The bow tie is theirs, if you've ever wondered. "You'll feel this for the rest of your life," Lengel says, and I know that's true, too, but remembering how he made that pretty girl blush makes me so scrunchy inside I punch the No Sale tab and the machine whirs "pee-pul" and the drawer splats out. One advantage to this scene taking place in summer, I can follow this up with a clean exit, there's no fumbling around getting your coat and galoshes, I just saunter into the electric eye in my white shirt that my mother ironed the night before, and the door heaves itself open, and outside the sunshine is skating around the asphalt.

I look around for my girls, but they're gone, of course. There wasn't anybody but some young married screaming with her children about some candy they didn't get by the door of a powder-blue Falcon station wagon. Looking back in the big windows, over the bags of peat moss and aluminum lawn furniture stacked on the pavement, I could see Lengel in my place in the slot, checking the sheep through. His face was dark gray and his back stiff, as if he'd just had an injection of iron, and my stomach kind of fell as I felt how hard the world was going to be to me hereafter.

Reading and Reacting

1. Summarize the information Sammy gives readers about his tastes and background. Why is this exposition vital to the story's development?
2. List some of the most obvious physical characteristics of the A&P's customers. How do these characteristics make them foils for Queenie and her friends?
3. What is it about Queenie and her friends that appeals to Sammy?
4. Is Queenie a stock character? Explain.
5. What rules and conventions are customers expected to follow in a supermarket? How does the behavior of Queenie and her friends violate these conventions?
6. Is the supermarket setting vital to the story? Could the story have been set in a car wash? In a fast-food restaurant?
7. How accurate are Sammy's judgments about the other characters? How might the characters be portrayed if the story were told by Lengel?
8. Given what you learn about Sammy during the course of the story, what do you see as his *primary* motivation for quitting his job? What other factors motivate him?
9. **JOURNAL ENTRY** Where do you think Sammy will find himself in ten years? Why?

Related Works: "Araby" (p. 167), "Ex-Basketball Player" (p. 408), "The Road Not Taken" (p.526)

◆ **KATHERINE MANSFIELD** (1888–1923), one of the pioneers of the modern short story, was born in New Zealand and educated in England. At the age of nineteen, she began publishing stories and reviews in many of the most influential literary magazines of the day.

A writer of great versatility, Mansfield produced sparkling social comedies as well as more intellectually and technically complex works. According to one critic, her best works "[w]ith delicate plainness [. . .] present elusive moments of decision, defeat, and small triumph." One notable theme in Mansfield's work is the *dame seule,* the "woman alone," a character spotlighted in the poignant "Miss Brill."

KATHERINE MANSFIELD

Miss Brill
(1922)

Although it was so brilliantly fine—the blue sky powdered with gold and great spots of light like white wine splashed over the Jardins Publiques[1]—Miss Brill was glad that she had decided on her fur. The air was motionless, but when you opened your mouth there was just a faint chill, like a chill from a glass of iced water before you sip, and now and again a leaf came drifting—from nowhere, from the sky. Miss Brill put up her hand and touched her fur. Dear little thing! It was nice to feel it again. She had taken it out of its box that afternoon, shaken out the moth-powder, given it a good brush, and rubbed the life back into the dim little eyes. "What has been happening to me?" said the sad little eyes. Oh, how sweet it was to see them snap at her again from the red eiderdown! . . . But the nose, which was of some black composition, wasn't at all firm. It must have had a knock, somehow. Never mind—a little dab of black sealing-wax when the time came—when it was absolutely necessary. . . . Little rogue! Yes, she really felt like that about it. Little rogue biting its tail just by her left ear. She could have taken it off and laid in on her lap and stroked it. She felt a tingling in her hands and arms, but that came from walking, she supposed. And when she breathed, something light and sad—no, not sad, exactly—something gentle seemed to move in her bosom.

There were a number of people out this afternoon, far more than last Sunday. And the band sounded louder and gayer. That was because the Season had begun. For although the band played all year round on Sundays, out of season it was never the same. It was like some one playing with only the family to listen; it didn't care how it played if there weren't any strangers present. Wasn't the conductor wearing a new coat, too? She was sure it was new. He scraped with his foot and flapped his arms like a rooster about to crow, and the bandsmen sitting in the green rotunda blew out their cheeks and glared at the music. Now there came a little "flutey" bit—very pretty!—a little chain of bright drops. She was sure it would be repeated. It was; she lifted her head and smiled.

Only two people shared her "special" seat: a fine old man in a velvet coat, his hands clasped over a huge carved walking-stick, and a big old woman, sitting upright, with a roll of knitting on her embroidered apron. They did not speak. This was disappointing, for Miss Brill always looked forward to the conversation. She had become really quite expert, she thought, at listening as though she didn't listen, at sitting in other people's lives just for a minute while they talked round her.

---

[1] Public Gardens (French).

She glanced, sideways, at the old couple. Perhaps they would go soon. Last Sunday, too, hadn't been as interesting as usual. An Englishman and his wife, he wearing a dreadful Panama hat and she button boots. And she'd gone on the whole time about how she ought to wear spectacles; she knew she needed them; but that it was no good getting any; they'd be sure to break and they'd never keep on. And he'd been so patient. He'd suggested everything—gold rims, the kind that curved round your ears, little pads inside the bridge. No, nothing would please her. "They'll always be sliding down my nose!" Miss Brill wanted to shake her.

5   The old people sat on the bench, still as statues. Never mind, there was always the crowd to watch. To and fro, in front of the flower-beds and the band rotunda, the couples and groups paraded, stopped to talk, to greet, to buy a handful of flowers from the old beggar who had his tray fixed to the railings. Little children ran among them, swooping and laughing; little boys with big white silk bows under their chins, little girls, little French dolls, dressed up in velvet and lace. And sometimes a tiny staggerer came suddenly rocking into the open from under the trees, stopped, stared, as suddenly sat down "flop," until its small high-stepping mother, like a young hen, rushed scolding to its rescue. Other people sat on the benches and green chairs, but they were nearly always the same, Sunday after Sunday, and—Miss Brill had often noticed—there was something funny about nearly all of them. They were odd, silent, nearly all old, and from the way they stared they looked as though they'd just come from dark little rooms or even—even cupboards!

Behind the rotunda the slender trees with yellow leaves down drooping, and through them just a line of sea, and beyond the blue sky with gold-veined clouds.

Tum-tum-tum tiddle-um! tiddle-um! tum tiddley-um tum ta! blew the band.

Two young girls in red came by and two young soldiers in blue met them, and they laughed and paired and went off arm-in-arm. Two peasant women with funny straw hats passed, gravely, leading beautiful smoke-colored donkeys. A cold, pale nun hurried by. A beautiful woman came along and dropped her bunch of violets, and a little boy ran after to hand them to her, and she took them and threw them away as if they'd been poisoned. Dear me! Miss Brill didn't know whether to admire that or not! And now an ermine toque[2] and a gentleman in grey met just in front of her. He was tall, stiff, dignified, and she was wearing the ermine toque she'd bought when her hair was yellow. Now everything, her hair, her face, even her eyes, was the same color as the shabby ermine, and her hand, in its cleaned glove, lifted to dab her lips, was a tiny yellowish paw. Oh, she was so pleased to see him—delighted! She rather thought they were going to meet that afternoon. She described

---

[2] Small, close-fitting woman's hat.

where she'd been—everywhere, here, there, along by the sea. The day was so charming—didn't he agree? And wouldn't he, perhaps? . . . But he shook his head, lighted a cigarette, slowly breathed a great deep puff into her face, and, even while she was still talking and laughing, flicked the match away and walked on. The ermine toque was alone; she smiled more brightly than ever. But even the band seemed to know what she was feeling and played more softly, played tenderly, and the drum beat, "The Brute! The Brute!" over and over. What would she do? What was going to happen now? But as Miss Brill wondered, the ermine toque turned, raised her hand as though she'd seen some one else, much nicer, just over there, and pattered away. And the band changed again and played more quickly, more gaily than ever, and the old couple on Miss Brill's seat got up and marched away, and such a funny old man with long whiskers hobbled along in time to the music and was nearly knocked over by four girls walking abreast.

Oh, how fascinating it was! How she enjoyed it! How she loved sitting here, watching it all! It was like a play. It was exactly like a play. Who could believe the sky at the back wasn't painted? But it wasn't till a little brown dog trotted on solemn and then slowly trotted off, like a little "theatre" dog, a little dog that had been drugged, that Miss Brill discovered what it was that made it so exciting. They were all on the stage. They weren't only the audience, not only looking on; they were acting. Even she had a part and came every Sunday. No doubt somebody would have noticed if she hadn't been there; she was part of the performance after all. How strange she'd never thought of it like that before! And yet it explained why she made such a point of starting from home at just the same time each week—so as not to be late for the performance—and it also explained why she had quite a queer, shy feeling at telling her English pupils how she spent her Sunday afternoons. No wonder! Miss Brill nearly laughed out loud. She was on the stage. She thought of the old invalid gentleman to whom she read the newspaper four afternoons a week while he slept in the garden. She had got quite used to the frail head on the cotton pillow, the hollowed eyes, the open mouth and the high pinched nose. If he'd been dead she mightn't have noticed for weeks; she wouldn't have minded. But suddenly he knew he was having the paper read to him by an actress! "An actress!" The old head lifted; two points of light quivered in the old eyes. "An actress—are ye?" And Miss Brill smoothed the newspaper as though it were the manuscript of her part and said gently: "Yes, I have been an actress for a long time."

10   The band had been having a rest. Now they started again. And what they played was warm, sunny, yet there was just a faint chill—a something, what was it?—not sadness—no, not sadness—a something that made you want to sing. The tune lifted, lifted, the light shone; and it seemed to Miss Brill that in another moment all of them, all the whole company, would begin singing. The young ones, the laughing ones who were moving together, they would begin, and the men's voices, very

resolute and brave, would join them. And then she too, she too, and the others on the benches—they would come in with a kind of accompaniment—something low, that scarcely rose or fell, something so beautiful—moving. . . . And Miss Brill's eyes filled with tears and she looked smiling at all the other members of the company. Yes, we understand, we understand, she thought—though what they understood she didn't know.

Just at that moment a boy and a girl came and sat down where the old couple had been. They were beautifully dressed; they were in love. The hero and heroine, of course, just arrived from his father's yacht. And still soundlessly singing, still with that trembling smile, Miss Brill prepared to listen.

"No, not now," said the girl. "Not here, I can't."

"But why? Because of that stupid old thing at the end there?" asked the boy. "Why does she come here at all—who wants her? Why doesn't she keep her silly old mug at home?"

"It's her fu-fur which is so funny," giggled the girl. "It's exactly like a fried whiting."[3]

"Ah, be off with you!" said the boy in an angry whisper. Then: "Tell me, my petite chérie—"[4]

"No, not here," said the girl. "Not *yet*."

On her way home she usually bought a slice of honeycake at the baker's. It was her Sunday treat. Sometimes there was an almond in her slice, sometimes not. It made a great difference. If there was an almond it was like carrying home a tiny present—a surprise—something that might very well not have been there. She hurried on the almond Sundays and struck the match for the kettle in quite a dashing way.

But to-day she passed the baker's boy, climbed the stairs, went into the little dark room—her room like a cupboard—and sat down on the red eiderdown. She sat there for a long time. The box that the fur came out of was on the bed. She unclasped the necklet quickly; quickly, without looking, laid it inside. But when she put the lid on she thought she heard something crying.

READING AND REACTING

1. What specific details can you infer about Miss Brill's character (and, perhaps, about her life) from this statement: "She had become really quite expert, she thought, at listening as though she didn't listen, at sitting in other people's lives just for a minute while they talked round her" (3)?

---

[3] Food fish related to the cod.
[4] Little darling (French).

2. How do Miss Brill's observations of the people around her give us insight into her own character? Why do you suppose she doesn't interact with any of the people she observes?
3. In paragraph 9, Miss Brill realizes that the scene she observes is "exactly like a play" and that "even she had a part and came every Sunday." What part does Miss Brill play? Is she a stock character in this play, or is she a three-dimensional character? Does she play a lead role or a supporting role?
4. What do you think Miss Brill means when she says, "I have been an actress for a long time" (9)? What does this comment reveal about how Miss Brill sees herself? Is her view of herself similar to or different from the view the other characters have of her?
5. What role does Miss Brill's fur piece play in the story? In what sense, if any, does it function as a character?
6. What happens in paragraphs 11–16 to break Miss Brill's mood? Why is the scene she observes so upsetting to her?
7. At the end of the story, has Miss Brill changed as a result of what she has overheard, or is she the same person she was at the beginning? Do you think she will return to the park the following Sunday?
8. The story's last paragraph describes Miss Brill's room as being "like a cupboard." Where else has this image appeared in the story? What does its repetition in the conclusion tell us?
9. **JOURNAL ENTRY** Write a character sketch of Miss Brill, inventing a plausible family and personal history that might help to explain the character you see in the story.

Related Works: "A Clean, Well-Lighted Place" (p. 173), "Rooming Houses Are Old Women" (p. 406), "After Great Pain, a Formal Feeling Comes" (p. 513), "Acquainted with the Night" (p. 523)

◆ **ANN PETRY** (1908–1997) was born in Old Saybrook, Connecticut. She studied pharmacy and between 1931 and 1938 worked as a pharmacist in her hometown. In 1938, she moved to New York City to pursue a writing career. Her novel *The Street* (1946) was the first novel by an African-American woman to focus on poor urban blacks and was also the first best-seller by an African-American woman. Petry published just two other novels in addition to a number of books aimed at young people.

"Like a Winding Sheet" is a grim reminder of how the insult of injustice can fester into anger and blind violence.

ANN PETRY

Like a Winding Sheet
(1945)

He had planned to get up before Mae did and surprise her by fixing breakfast. Instead he went back to sleep and she got out of bed so quietly he didn't know she wasn't there beside him until he woke up and heard the queer soft gurgle of water running out of the sink in the bathroom.

He knew he ought to get up but instead he put his arms across his forehead to shut the afternoon sunlight out of his eyes, pulled his legs up close to his body, testing them to see if the ache was still in them.

Mae had finished in the bathroom. He could tell because she never closed the door when she was in there and now the sweet smell of talcum powder was drifting down the hall and into the bedroom. Then he heard her coming down the hall.

"Hi, babe," she said affectionately.

"Hum," he grunted, and moved his arms away from his head, opened one eye.

"It's a nice morning."

"Yeah." He rolled over and the sheet twisted around him, outlining his thighs, his chest. "You mean afternoon, don't ya?"

Mae looked at the twisted sheet and giggled. "Looks like a winding sheet," she said. "A shroud—"[1] Laughter tangled with her words and she had to pause for a moment before she could continue. "You look like a huckleberry—in a winding sheet—"

"That's no way to talk. Early in the day like this," he protested.

He looked at his arms silhouetted against the white of the sheets. They were inky black by contrast and he had to smile in spite of himself and he lay there smiling and savoring the sweet sound of Mae's giggling.

"Early?" She pointed a finger at the alarm clock on the table near the bed and giggled again. "It's almost four o'clock. And if you don't spring up out of there, you're going to be late again."

"What do you mean 'again'?"

"Twice last week. Three times the week before. And once the week before and—"

"I can't get used to sleeping in the daytime," he said fretfully. He pushed his legs out from under the covers experimentally. Some of the ache had gone out of them but they weren't really rested yet. "It's too light for good sleeping. And all that standing beats the hell out of my legs."

"After two years you oughta be used to it," Mae said.

---

[1] Cloth wrapped around a corpse; a winding sheet.

He watched her as she fixed her hair, powdered her face, slipped into a pair of blue denim overalls. She moved quickly and yet she didn't seem to hurry.

"You look like you'd had plenty of sleep," he said lazily. He had to get up but he kept putting the moment off, not wanting to move, yet he didn't dare let his legs go completely limp because if he did he'd go back to sleep. It was getting later and later but the thought of putting his weight on his legs kept him lying there.

When he finally got up he had to hurry, and he gulped his breakfast so fast that he wondered if his stomach could possibly use food thrown at it at such a rate of speed. He was still wondering about it as he and Mae were putting their coats on in the hall.

Mae paused to look at the calendar. "It's the thirteenth," she said. Then a faint excitement in her voice. "Why, it's Friday the thirteenth." She had one arm in her coat sleeve and she held it there while she stared at the calendar. "I oughta stay home," she said. "I shouldn't go outa the house."

"Aw, don't be a fool," he said. "Today's payday. And payday is a good luck day everywhere, any way you look at it." And as she stood hesitating he said, "Aw, come on."

And he was late for work again because they spent fifteen minutes arguing before he could convince her she ought to go to work just the same. He had to talk persuasively, urging her gently, and it took time. But he couldn't bring himself to talk to her roughly or threaten to strike her like a lot of men might have done. He wasn't made that way.

So when he reached the plant he was late and he had to wait to punch the time clock because the day-shift workers were streaming out in long lines, in groups and bunches that impeded his progress.

Even now just starting his workday his legs ached. He had to force himself to struggle past the outgoing workers, punch the time clock, and get the little cart he pushed around all night, because he kept toying with the idea of going home and getting back in bed.

He pushed the cart out on the concrete floor, thinking that if this was his plant he'd make a lot of changes in it. There were too many standing-up jobs for one thing. He'd figure out some way most of 'em could be done sitting down and he'd put a lot more benches around. And this job he had—this job that forced him to walk ten hours a night, pushing this little cart, well, he'd turn it into a sitting-down job. One of those little trucks they used around railroad stations would be good for a job like this. Guys sat on a seat and the thing moved easily, taking up little room and turning in hardly any space at all like on a dime.

He pushed the car near the foreman. He never could remember to refer to her as the forelady even in his mind. It was funny to have a white woman for a boss in a plant like this one.

She was sore about something. He could tell by the way her face was red and her eyes were half-shut until they were slits. Probably been out late and didn't get enough sleep. He avoided looking at her and hurried a little, head down, as he passed her though he couldn't resist stealing a glance at her out of the corner of his eye. He saw the edge of the light-colored slacks she wore and the tip end of a big tan shoe.

"Hey, Johnson!" the woman said.

The machines had started full blast. The whirr and the grinding made the building shake, made it impossible to hear conversations. The men and women at the machines talked to each other but looking at them from just a little distance away, they appeared to be simply moving their lips because you couldn't hear what they were saying. Yet the woman's voice cut across the machine sounds—harsh, angry.

He turned his head slowly. "Good evenin', Mrs. Scott," he said, and waited.

30 "You're late again."

"That's right. My legs were bothering me."

The woman's face grew redder, angrier looking. "Half this shift comes in late," she said. "And you're the worst one of all. You're always late. Whatsa matter with ya?"

"It's my legs," he said. "Somehow they don't ever get rested. I don't seem to get used to sleeping days. And I just can't get started."

"Excuses. You guys always got excuses," her anger grew and spread. "Every guy comes in here late always has an excuse. His wife's sick or his grandmother died or somebody in the family had to go to the hospital," she paused, drew a deep breath. "And the niggers is the worse. I don't care what's wrong with your legs. You get in here on time. I'm sick of you niggers—"

35 "You got the right to get mad," he interrupted softly. "You got the right to cuss me four ways to Sunday but I ain't letting nobody call me a nigger."

He stepped closer to her. His fists were doubled. His lips were drawn back in a thin narrow line. A vein in his forehead stood out swollen, thick.

And the woman backed away from him, not hurriedly but slowly—two, three steps back.

"Aw, forget it," she said. "I didn't mean nothing by it. It slipped out. It was an accident." The red of her face deepened until the small blood vessels in her cheeks were purple. "Go on and get to work," she urged. And she took three more slow backward steps.

He stood motionless for a moment and then turned away from the sight of the red lipstick on her mouth that made him remember that the foreman was a woman. And he couldn't bring himself to hit a woman. He felt a curious tingling in his fingers and he looked down at his hands. They were clenched tight, hard, ready to smash some of those small purple veins in her face.

40 He pushed the cart ahead of him, walking slowly. When he turned his head, she was staring in his direction, mopping her forehead with a dark blue handkerchief. Their eyes met and then they both looked away.

He didn't glance in her direction again but moved past the long work benches, carefully collecting the finished parts, going slowly and steadily up and down, and back and forth the length of the building, and as he walked he forced himself to swallow his anger, get rid of it.

And he succeeded so that he was able to think about what had happened without getting upset about it. An hour went by but the tension stayed in his hands. They were clenched and knotted on the handles of the cart as though ready to aim a blow.

And he thought he should have hit her anyway, smacked her hard in the face, felt the soft flesh of her face give under the hardness of his hands. He tried to make his hands relax by offering them a description of what it would have been like to strike her because he had the queer feeling that his hands were not exactly a part of him anymore—they had developed a separate life of their own over which he had no control. So he dwelt on the pleasure his hands would have felt—both of them cracking at her, first one and then the other. If he had done that his hands would have felt good now—relaxed, rested.

And he decided that even if he'd lost his job for it, he should have let her have it and it would have been a long time, maybe the rest of her life, before she called anybody else a nigger.

The only trouble was he couldn't hit a woman. A woman couldn't hit back the same way a man did. But it would have been a deeply satisfying thing to have cracked her narrow lips wide open with just one blow, beautifully timed and with all his weight in back of it. That way he would have gotten rid of all the energy and tension his anger had created in him. He kept remembering how his heart had started pumping blood so fast he had felt it tingle even in the tips of his fingers.

With the approach of night, fatigue nibbled at him. The corners of his mouth drooped, the frown between his eyes deepened, his shoulders sagged; but his hands stayed tight and tense. As the hours dragged by he noticed that the women workers had started to snap and snarl at each other. He couldn't hear what they said because of the sound of machines but he could see the quick lip movements that sent words tumbling from the sides of their mouths. They gestured irritably with their hands and scowled as their mouths moved.

Their violent jerky motions told him that it was getting close on to quitting time but somehow he felt that the night still stretched ahead of him, composed of endless hours of steady walking on his aching legs. When the whistle finally blew he went on pushing the cart, unable to believe that it had sounded. The whirring of the machines died away to a murmur and he knew then that he'd really heard the whistle. He stood still for a moment, filled with a relief that made him sigh.

Then he moved briskly, putting the cart in the storeroom, hurrying to take his place in the line forming before the paymaster. That was another thing he'd change, he thought. He'd have the pay envelopes handed to the people right at their benches so there wouldn't be ten or fifteen minutes lost waiting for the pay. He always got home about fifteen minutes late on payday. They did it better in the plant where Mae worked, brought the money right to them at their benches.

He stuck his pay envelope in his pants' pocket and followed the line of workers heading for the subway in a slow-moving stream. He glanced up at the sky. It was a nice night, the sky looked packed full to running over with stars. And he thought if he and Mae would go right to bed when they got home from work they'd catch a few hours of darkness for sleeping. But they never did. They fooled around—cooking and eating and listening to the radio and he always stayed in a big chair in the living room and went almost but not quite to sleep and when they finally got to bed it was five or six in the morning and daylight was already seeping around the edges of the sky.

He walked slowly, putting off the moment when he would have to plunge into the crowd hurrying toward the subway. It was a long ride to Harlem and tonight the thought of it appalled him. He paused outside an all-night restaurant to kill time, so that some of the first rush of workers would be gone when he reached the subway.

The lights in the restaurant were brilliant, enticing. There was life and motion inside. And as he looked through the window he thought that everything within range of his eyes gleamed—the long imitation marble counter, the tall stools, the white porcelain-topped tables and especially the big metal coffee urn right near the window. Steam issued from its top and a gas flame flickered under it—a lively, dancing, blue flame.

A lot of the workers from his shift—men and women—were lining up near the coffee urn. He watched them walk to the porcelain-topped tables carrying steaming cups of coffee and he saw that just the smell of the coffee lessened the fatigue lines in their faces. After the first sip their faces softened, they smiled, they began to talk and laugh.

On a sudden impulse he shoved the door open and joined the line in front of the coffee urn. The line moved slowly. And as he stood there the smell of the coffee, the sound of the laughter and the voices, helped dull the sharp ache in his legs.

He didn't pay any attention to the white girl who was serving the coffee at the urn. He kept looking at the cups in the hands of the men who had been ahead of him. Each time a man stepped out of the line with one of the thick white cups the fragrant steam got in his nostrils. He saw that they walked carefully so as not to spill a single drop. There was a froth of bubbles at the top of each cup and he thought about how he would let the bubbles break against his lips before he actually took a big deep swallow.

Then it was his turn. "A cup of coffee," he said, just as he had heard the others say.

The white girl looked past him, put her hands up to her head and gently lifted her hair away from the back of her neck, tossing her head back a little. "No more coffee for a while," she said.

He wasn't certain he'd heard her correctly and he said "What?" blankly.

"No more coffee for a while," she repeated.

There was silence behind him and then uneasy movement. He thought someone would say something, ask why or protest, but there was only silence and then a faint shuffling sound as though the men standing behind him had simultaneously shifted their weight from one foot to the other.

He looked at the girl without saying anything. He felt his hands begin to tingle and the tingling went all the way down to his finger tips so that he glanced down at them. They were clenched tight, hard, into fists. Then he looked at the girl again. What he wanted to do was hit her so hard that the scarlet lipstick on her mouth would smear and spread over her nose, her chin, out toward her cheeks, so hard that she would never toss her head again and refuse a man a cup of coffee because he was black.

He estimated the distance across the counter and reached forward, balancing his weight on the balls of his feet, ready to let the blow go. And then his hands fell back down to his sides because he forced himself to lower them, to unclench them and make them dangle loose. The effort took his breath away because his hands fought against him. But he couldn't hit her. He couldn't even now bring himself to hit a woman, not even this one, who had refused him a cup of coffee with a toss of her head. He kept seeing the gesture with which she had lifted the length of her blond hair from the back of her neck as expressive of her contempt for him.

When he went out the door he didn't look back. If he had he would have seen the flickering blue flame under the shiny coffee urn being extinguished. The line of men who had stood behind him lingered a moment to watch the people drinking coffee at the tables and then they left just as he had without having had the coffee they wanted so badly. The girl behind the counter poured water in the urn and swabbed it out and as she waited for the water to run out, she lifted her hair gently from the back of her neck and tossed her head before she began making a fresh pot of coffee.

But he had walked away without a backward look, his head down, his hands in his pockets, raging at himself and whatever it was inside of him that had forced him to stand quiet and still when he wanted to strike out.

The subway was crowded and he had to stand. He tried grasping an overhead strap and his hands were too tense to grip it. So he moved near the train door and stood there swaying back and forth with the rocking of the train. The roar of the train beat inside his head, making it ache and throb, and the pain in his legs clawed up into his groin so that he seemed to be bursting with pain and he told himself that it was due to all that anger-born energy that had piled up in him and not been used and so it had spread through him like a poison—from his feet and legs all the way up to his head.

Mae was in the house before he was. He knew she was home before he put the key in the door of the apartment. The radio was going. She had it turned up loud and she was singing along with it.

"Hello, babe," she called out, as soon as he opened the door.

He tried to say "hello" and it came out half grunt and half sigh.

"You sure sound cheerful," she said.

She was in the bedroom and he went and leaned against the doorjamb. The denim overalls she wore to work were carefully draped over the back of a chair by the bed. She was standing in front of the dresser, tying the sash of a yellow housecoat around her waist and chewing gum vigorously as she admired her reflection in the mirror over the dresser.

"Whatsa matter?" she said. "You get bawled out by the boss or somep'n?"

"Just tired," he said slowly. "For God's sake, do you have to crack that gum like that?"

"You don't have to lissen to me," she said complacently. She patted a curl in place near the side of her head and then lifted her hair away from the back of her neck, ducking her head forward and then back.

He winced away from the gesture. "What you got to be always fooling with your hair for?" he protested.

"Say, what's the matter with you anyway?" She turned away from the mirror to face him, put her hands on her hips. "You ain't been in the house two minutes and you're picking on me."

He didn't answer her because her eyes were angry and he didn't want to quarrel with her. They'd been married too long and got along too well and so he walked all the way into the room and sat down in the chair by the bed and stretched his legs out in front of him, putting his weight on the heels of his shoes, leaning way back in the chair, not saying anything.

"Lissen," she said sharply. "I've got to wear those overalls again tomorrow. You're going to get them all wrinkled up leaning against them like that."

He didn't move. He was too tired and his legs were throbbing now that he had sat down. Besides the overalls were already wrinkled and dirty, he thought. They couldn't help but be for she'd worn them all week. He leaned farther back in the chair.

"Come on, get up," she ordered.

"Oh, what the hell," he said wearily, and got up from the chair. "I'd just as soon live in a subway. There'd be just as much place to sit down."

He saw that her sense of humor was struggling with her anger. But her sense of humor won because she giggled.

"Aw, come on and eat," she said. There was a coaxing note in her voice. "You're nothing but an old hungry nigger trying to act tough and—" she paused to giggle and then continued, "You—"

He had always found her giggling pleasant and deliberately said things that might amuse her and then waited, listening for the delicate sound to emerge from her throat. This time he didn't even hear the giggle. He didn't let her finish what she was saying. She was standing close to him and that funny tingling started in his finger tips, went fast up his arms and sent his fist shooting straight for her face.

There was the smacking sound of soft flesh being struck by a hard object and it wasn't until she screamed that he realized he had hit her in the mouth—so hard that the dark red lipstick had blurred and spread over her full lips, reaching up toward the tip of her nose, down toward her chin, out toward her cheeks.

The knowledge that he had struck her seeped through him slowly and he was appalled but he couldn't drag his hands away from her face. He kept striking her and he thought with horror that something inside him was holding him, binding him to this act, wrapping and twisting about him so that he had to continue it. He had lost all control over his hands. And he groped for a phrase, a word, something to describe what this thing was like that was happening to him and he thought it was like being enmeshed in a winding sheet—that was it—like a winding sheet. And even as the thought formed in his mind, his hands reached for her face again and yet again.

READING AND REACTING

1. This story appeared in a 1945 collection of Petry's stories. What information does this date suggest about the characters' experiences prior to the beginning of the story? Does the date help in any way to explain Johnson's character? His motivation?
2. Johnson is portrayed as exhausted, frustrated, and tense with rage. How are these character traits communicated to readers?
3. When the forelady calls Johnson a nigger, he speaks up to her quietly yet firmly, and she backs off. Given what we know about Johnson, is his action plausible? Is it consistent with his other actions?
4. How do Johnson's physical ailments help to develop his character? How do they help to explain his motivation? Do you think they in any way mitigate his final act?
5. What do readers really know about Mae besides the facts that she wears overalls to work, sings along with the radio, wears red lipstick, and chews gum? Do we really *need* to know anything else? Would the story have a different impact if Mae's character were as fully developed as Johnson's?
6. What function is served by Johnson's boss, Mrs. Scott? By the woman at the coffee urn? Are both minor characters necessary to the story? Is it essential or incidental that both are women?
7. What finally causes Johnson to snap? Why does he lose his temper at this point? Why do you think he doesn't lose it earlier?

8. Do you see the story's outcome as inevitable? How is this outcome foreshadowed?
9. **Journal Entry** Whom do you blame for Johnson's violent act? Is he alone to blame, or should someone—or something—else also be held responsible? Could you argue that Johnson is as much a victim as Mae is?

Related Works: "Barn Burning" (p. 142), "Harlem" (p. 404), *Trifles* (p. 586)

◆ Writing Suggestions: Character

1. In "A&P" and "Like a Winding Sheet," characters struggle against rules, authority figures, and inflexible social systems. Compare and contrast the struggles in which the characters are engaged.
2. Write an essay in which you contrast the character of Miss Brill with the character of Phoenix Jackson in "A Worn Path" (Chapter 9). Consider how each character interacts with those around her as well as how each seems to see her role or mission in the world.
3. Write a letter from Mae to Johnson in which you reveal information about her character that does not appear in "Like a Winding Sheet." What is her typical day like? What frustrations does *she* experience? Does she too feel a sense of rage? Conclude the letter by explaining what she plans to do now, as she recovers physically and emotionally. Will she leave Johnson or stay with him?
4. Although Sammy and Miss Brill use their active imaginations to create scenarios that help get them through the day, neither is able to sustain the illusion. As a result, each finds out how harsh reality can be. What steps could these characters take to fit more comfortably into the worlds they inhabit? *Should* they take such steps? Are they able to do so?
5. Both "A&P" and "Like a Winding Sheet" are, to some extent, about characters who are unhappy at work and frustrated with their bosses. Write an essay in which you focus on the *differences* between Sammy's and Johnson's work environments, relationships with their bosses, and reactions to conflict. How do you account for these differences?

CHAPTER 5

Setting

The **setting** of a work of fiction establishes its historical, geographical, and physical location. *Where* a work is set—on a tropical island, in a dungeon, at a crowded party, in a tent in the woods—influences our interpretation of the story's events and characters. *When* a work takes place—during the French Revolution, during the Vietnam War, today, or in the future—is equally important. Setting, however, is more than just the approximate time and place in which the work is set; setting also encompasses a wide variety of physical and cultural elements.

Clearly, setting is more important in some works than in others. In some stories, no particular time or place is specified, or even suggested, perhaps because the writer does not consider a specific setting to be important or because the writer wishes the story's events to seem timeless and universal. In Nadine Gordimer's "Once upon a Time" (p. 46), for example, the writer follows the conventions of fairy tales, which are set in unidentified, faraway places. In other stories, a writer may provide only minimal information about setting, telling readers little more than where and when the action takes place. Sometimes, however, a particular setting may be vital to the story, perhaps influencing characters' behavior, as it does in Charlotte Perkins Gilman's "The Yellow Wall-Paper" (p. 102). In such cases, of course, setting must be fully described.

Sometimes a story's central conflict is between the protagonist and the setting—for example, Alice in Wonderland; a northerner in the South; a naive, unsophisticated American tourist in an old European city; a sane person in a mental hospital; a moral person in a corrupt environment; an immigrant in a new world; or a city dweller in the country. This conflict helps to define the characters as well as drive the plot. (A conflict between events and setting—for example, the intrusion of nuclear war into a typical suburban neighborhood, the intrusion of modern social ideas into an old-fashion world, or the intrusion of a brutal, senseless murder into a peaceful English village—can also enrich a story.)

85

Historical Setting

❖ ❖ ❖

A particular historical period, and the events associated with it, can be important in a story; therefore, some familiarity with a period can be useful (or even essential) to readers who wish to understand a story fully. Historical context establishes a social, cultural, economic, and political environment. Knowing, for instance, that "The Yellow Wall-Paper" was written in the late nineteenth century, when doctors treated women as delicate and dependent creatures, helps to explain the narrator's emotional state. Likewise, it may be important to know that a story is set during a particularly volatile (or static) political era, during a time of permissive (or repressive) attitudes toward sex, during a war, or during a period of economic prosperity or recession. Any one of these factors may determine—or help to explain—characters' actions. Historical events or cultural norms may, for instance, limit or expand a character's options, and our knowledge of history may reveal to us a character's incompatibility with his or her milieu. In F. Scott Fitzgerald's "Bernice Bobs Her Hair," set in the 1920s in a midwestern town, a young girl is goaded into cutting her long hair. To understand the significance of Bernice's act— and to understand the reactions of others to that act—readers must know that during that era only racy "society vampires," not nice girls from good families, bobbed their hair.

Knowing the approximate year or historical period during which a story takes place can explain forces that act on characters, help to account for their behavior, clarify circumstances that influence the story's action, and help to justify a writer's use of plot devices that might otherwise seem improbable. For instance, stories set before the development of modern transportation and communication systems may hinge on plot devices readers would not accept in a modern story. Thus, in "Paul's Case," a 1904 story by Willa Cather, a young man who steals a large sum of money in Pittsburgh is able to spend several days enjoying it before the news of the theft reaches New York, where he has fled. In other stories we see such outdated plot devices as characters threatened by diseases that have now been eradicated (and subjected to outdated medical or psychiatric treatment). In addition, characters may be constrained by social conventions different from those that operate in our own society.

Geographical Setting

❖ ❖ ❖

In addition to knowing when a work takes place, readers need to know *where* it takes place. Knowing whether a story is set in the United States, in Europe, or in a developing nation can help to explain anything from why language and customs are unfamiliar to us to why characters act in ways we find improbable. Even in stories set in our own country, regional differences may account for differences in plot development and characters' motivation. For example, knowing that William Faulkner's "A Rose for Emily" (p. 52) is set in the post–Civil War American South helps readers understand why the townspeople are so chivalrously protective of Miss Emily. Similarly, the fact that Bret Harte's "The Outcasts of Poker Flat" is set in the American West accounts for its unusual cast of characters—including a gambler, a prostitute, and a traveling salesman.

The size of the town or city in which a story takes place may also be important. In a small town, for example, a character's problems are more likely to be subject to intense scrutiny by other characters, as they are in stories of small-town life such as "A Rose for Emily." In a large city, characters may be more likely to be isolated and anonymous.

Of course, a story may not have a recognizable geographical setting; its location may not be specified, and it may even be set in a fantasy world. Such settings may free writers from the constraints placed on them by familiar environments, allowing them to experiment with situations and characters, unaffected by readers' expectations or associations with familiar settings.

Physical Setting

The *time of day* can clearly influence a story's mood as well as its development. The gruesome murder described in Edgar Allan Poe's "The Cask of Amontillado" (p. 136) takes place in an appropriate setting: not just underground, but in the darkness of night. Conversely, the horrifying events of Shirley Jackson's "The Lottery" (p. 209) take place in broad daylight, contrasting dramatically with the darkness of the society that permits—and even participates in—such events. Many stories, of course, move through several time periods as the action unfolds, and changes in time may also be important. For instance, the approach of evening, or of dawn, can signal the end of a crisis in the plot.

Whether a story is set primarily *inside* or *out-of-doors* may also be significant. The characters may be physically constrained by a closed-in setting or liberated by an expansive landscape. Some interior settings may be psychologically limiting. For instance, the narrator in "The Yellow Wall-Paper" feels suffocated by her room, whose ugly wallpaper comes to haunt her. In many of Poe's stories, the central character is trapped, physically or psychologically, in a confined, suffocating space. In other stories, an interior setting may serve a symbolic function. For instance, in "A Rose for Emily" the house is for Miss Emily a symbol of the South's past glory as well as a refuge, a fortress, and a hiding place. Similarly, a building or house may represent society, with its rules and norms and limitations. In John Updike's "A&P" (p. 65), for instance, the supermarket establishes social as well as physical limits. This is also the case in Katherine Mansfield's "Her First Ball," where a ballroom serves as the setting for a young girl's initiation into the rules and realities of adult society.

Conversely, an outdoor setting can free a character from social norms of behavior, as it does for Ernest Hemingway's Nick Adams, a war veteran who, in "Big Two-Hearted River," finds order, comfort, and peace only when he is away from civilization. An outdoor setting can also expose characters to physical dangers, such as untamed wilderness, uncharted seas, and frighteningly empty open spaces.

Weather can be another important aspect of setting. A storm can threaten a character's life or just make the character—and readers—*think* danger is present, distracting us from other, more subtle threats. Extreme weather conditions can make characters act irrationally or uncharacteristically, as in Kate Chopin's "The Storm" (p. 89), where a storm provides the complication and determines the characters' actions. In numerous stories set in hostile landscapes, where extremes of heat and cold influence the action, weather may pose a test for characters, as in Jack London's "To Build a Fire," in which the main character struggles unsuccessfully against a brutally cold, hostile environment.

The various physical attributes of setting combine to create a story's **atmosphere** or **mood**. In "The Cask of Amontillado," for example, several factors work together to create the eerie, intense atmosphere appropriate to the story's events: it is nighttime; it is the hectic carnival season; and the catacombs are dark, damp, and filled with the bones of the narrator's ancestors. The atmosphere that is created in a story can reflect a character's mental state—for example, darkness and isolation can reflect a character's depression, whereas an idyllic, peaceful atmosphere can express a character's joy. A story's atmosphere may also *influence* the characters' reactions or state of mind, causing them to react one way in a crowded, busy, hectic atmosphere but to react very differently in a peaceful rural atmosphere. At the same time, the mood or atmosphere that is created often helps to convey a story's central theme—as the ironic contrast between the pleasant atmosphere and the horrible events that unfold communicates the theme of "The Lottery."

 CHECKLIST: WRITING ABOUT SETTING

- ✓ Is the setting specified or unidentified? Is it fully described or just sketched in?
- ✓ Is the setting just background, or is it a key force in the story?
- ✓ How does the setting influence the characters? Does it affect (or reflect) their emotional state? Does it help to explain their motivation?
- ✓ Are any characters in conflict with their environment?
- ✓ Are any situations set in sharp contrast to the setting?

> ✓ How does the setting influence the story's plot? Does it cause characters to act?
> ✓ Does the setting add irony to the story?
> ✓ In what time period does the story take place? How can you tell? What social, political, or economic characteristics of the historical period might influence the story?
> ✓ In what geographical location is the story set? Is this location important to the story?
> ✓ At what time of day is the story set? Is time important to the development of the story?
> ✓ Is the story set primarily indoors or out-of-doors? What role does this aspect of the setting play in the story?
> ✓ What role do weather conditions play in the story?
> ✓ Is the story's general atmosphere dark or bright? Clear or murky? Tumultuous or calm? Gloomy or cheerful?
> ✓ Does the atmosphere change as the story progresses? Is this change significant?

◆ **KATE CHOPIN** (1851–1904) (picture and biography on p. 43) Chopin often used the physical world—for example, the charged atmosphere of "The Storm"—to symbolize the inner truths of her characters' minds and hearts.

KATE CHOPIN

The Storm
(c. 1899)

I

The leaves were so still that even Bibi thought it was going to rain. Bobinôt, who was accustomed to converse on terms of perfect equality with his little son, called the child's attention to certain sombre clouds that were rolling with sinister intention from the west, accompanied by a sullen, threatening roar. They were at Friedheimer's store and decided to remain there till the storm had passed. They sat within the door on two empty kegs. Bibi was four years old and looked very wise.

"Mama'll be 'fraid, yes," he suggested with blinking eyes.

"She'll shut the house. Maybe she got Sylvie helpin' her this evenin'," Bobinôt responded reassuringly.

"No; she ent got Sylvie. Sylvie was helpin' her yistiday," piped Bibi.

Bobinôt arose and going across to the counter purchased a can of shrimps, of which Calixta was very fond. Then he returned to his perch on the keg and sat stolidly holding the can of shrimps while the storm burst. It shook the wooden store and seemed to be ripping great furrows in the distant field. Bibi laid his little hand on his father's knee and was not afraid.

II

Calixta, at home, felt no uneasiness for their safety. She sat at a side window sewing furiously on a sewing machine. She was greatly occupied and did not notice the approaching storm. But she felt very warm and often stopped to mop her face on which the perspiration gathered in beads. She unfastened her white sacque at the throat. It began to grow dark, and suddenly realizing the situation she got up hurriedly and went about closing windows and doors.

Out on the small front gallery she had hung Bobinôt's Sunday clothes to air and she hastened out to gather them before the rain fell. As she stepped outside, Alcée Laballière rode in at the gate. She had not seen him very often since her marriage, and never alone. She stood there with Bobinôt's coat in her hands, and the big rain drops began to fall. Alcée rode his horse under the shelter of a side projection where the chickens had huddled and there were plows and a harrow piled up in the corner.

"May I come and wait on your gallery till the storm is over, Calixta?" he asked.

"Come 'long in, M'sieur Alcée."

His voice and her own startled her as if from a trance, and she seized Bobinôt's vest. Alcée, mounting to the porch, grabbed the trousers and snatched Bibi's braided jacket that was about to be carried away by a sudden gust of wind. He expressed an intention to remain outside, but it was soon apparent that he might as well have been out in the open: the water beat in upon the boards in driving sheets, and he went inside, closing the door after him. It was even necessary to put something beneath the door to keep the water out.

"My! what a rain! It's good two years sence it rain' like that," exclaimed Calixta as she rolled up a piece of bagging and Alcée helped her to thrust it beneath the crack.

She was a little fuller of figure than five years before when she married; but she had lost nothing of her vivacity. Her blue eyes still retained their melting quality; and her yellow hair, dishevelled by the wind and rain, kinked more stubbornly than ever about her ears and temples.

The rain beat upon the low, shingled roof with a force and clatter that threatened to break an entrance and deluge them there. They were in the dining room—the sitting room—the general utility room. Adjoining was her bed room, with Bibi's couch along side her own. The door stood open, and the room with its white, monumental bed, its closed shutters, looked dim and mysterious.

Alcée flung himself into a rocker and Calixta nervously began to gather up from the floor the lengths of a cotton sheet which she had been sewing.

"If this keeps up, *Dieu sait*[1] if the levees[2] goin' to stan' it!" she exclaimed.

"What have you got to do with the levees?"

"I got enough to do! An' there's Bobinôt with Bibi out in that storm—if he only didn't left Friedheimer's!"

"Let us hope, Calixta, that Bobinôt's got sense enough to come in out of a cyclone."

She went and stood at the window with a greatly disturbed look on her face. She wiped the frame that was clouded with moisture. It was stiflingly hot. Alcée got up and joined her at the window, looking over her shoulder. The rain was coming down in sheets obscuring the view of far-off cabins and enveloping the distant wood in a gray mist. The playing of the lightning was incessant. A bolt struck a tall chinaberry tree at the edge of the field. It filled all visible space with a blinding glare and the crash seemed to invade the very boards they stood upon.

Calixta put her hands to her eyes, and with a cry, staggered backward. Alcée's arm encircled her, and for an instant he drew her close and spasmodically to him.

"*Bonté!*"[3] she cried, releasing herself from his encircling arm and retreating from the window, "the house'll go next! If I only knew w'ere Bibi was!" She would not compose herself; she would not be seated. Alcée clasped her shoulders and looked into her face. The contact of her warm, palpitating body when he had unthinkingly drawn her into his arms, had aroused all the old-time infatuation and desire for her flesh.

"Calixta," he said, "don't be frightened. Nothing can happen. The house is too low to be struck, with so many tall trees standing about. There! aren't you going to be quiet? say, aren't you?" He pushed her hair back from her face that was warm and steaming. Her lips were as red and moist as pomegranate seed. Her white neck and a glimpse of her full, firm bosom disturbed him powerfully. As she glanced up at him the fear in her liquid blue eyes had given place to a drowsy gleam that unconsciously betrayed a sensuous desire. He looked down into her eyes and there was nothing for him to do but to gather her lips in a kiss. It reminded him of Assumption.

"Do you remember—in Assumption, Calixta?" he asked in a low voice broken by passion. Oh! she remembered; for in Assumption he had kissed her and kissed and kissed her; until his senses would well nigh fail,

---

[1] God knows.
[2] A raised embankment designed to keep a river from overflowing.
[3] "Goodness!"

and to save her he would resort to a desperate flight. If she was not an immaculate dove in those days, she was still inviolate; a passionate creature whose very defenselessness had made her defense, against which his honor forbade him to prevail. Now—well, now—her lips seemed in a manner free to be tasted, as well as her round, white throat and her whiter breasts.

They did not heed the crashing torrents, and the roar of the elements made her laugh as she lay in his arms. She was a revelation in that dim, mysterious chamber; as white as the couch she lay upon. Her firm, elastic flesh that was knowing for the first time its birthright, was like a creamy lily that the sun invites to contribute its breath and perfume to the undying life of the world.

The generous abundance of her passion, without guile or trickery, was like a white flame which penetrated and found response in depths of his own sensuous nature that had never yet been reached.

When he touched her breasts they gave themselves up in quivering ecstasy, inviting his lips. Her mouth was a fountain of delight. And when he possessed her, they seemed to swoon together at the very borderland of life's mystery.

He stayed cushioned upon her, breathless, dazed, enervated, with his heart beating like a hammer upon her. With one hand she clasped his head, her lips lightly touching his forehead. The other hand stroked with a soothing rhythm his muscular shoulders.

The growl of the thunder was distant and passing away. The rain beat softly upon the shingles, inviting them to drowsiness and sleep. But they dared not yield.

The rain was over; and the sun was turning the glistening green world into a palace of gems. Calixta, on the gallery, watched Alcée ride away. He turned and smiled at her with a beaming face; and she lifted her pretty chin in the air and laughed aloud.

III

Bobinôt and Bibi, trudging home, stopped without at the cistern to make themselves presentable.

"My! Bibi, w'at will yo' mama say! You ought to be ashame'. You oughtn' put on those good pants. Look at 'em! An' that mud on yo' collar! How you got that mud on yo' collar, Bibi? I never saw such a boy!" Bibi was the picture of pathetic resignation. Bobinôt was the embodiment of serious solicitude as he strove to remove from his own person and his son's the signs of their tramp over heavy roads and through wet fields. He scraped the mud off Bibi's bare legs and feet with a stick and carefully removed all traces from his heavy brogans. Then, prepared for the worst—the meeting with an over-scrupulous housewife, they entered cautiously at the back door.

Calixta was preparing supper. She had set the table and was dripping coffee at the hearth. She sprang up as they came in.

"Oh, Bobinôt! You back! My! but I was uneasy. W'ere you been during the rain? An' Bibi? he ain't wet? he ain't hurt?" She had clasped Bibi and was kissing him effusively. Bobinôt's explanations and apologies which he had been composing all along the way, died on his lips as Calixta felt him to see if he were dry, and seemed to express nothing but satisfaction at their safe return.

"I brought you some shrimps, Calixta," offered Bobinôt, hauling the can from his ample side pocket and laying it on the table.

"Shrimps! Oh, Bobinôt! you too good fo' anything!" and she gave him a smacking kiss on the cheek that resounded. "*J'vous réponds*,[4] we'll have a feas' tonight! umph-umph!"

Bobinôt and Bibi began to relax and enjoy themselves, and when the three seated themselves at table they laughed much and so loud that anyone might have heard them as far away as Laballière's.

IV

Alcée Laballière wrote to his wife, Clarisse, that night. It was a loving letter, full of tender solicitude. He told her not to hurry back, but if she and the babies liked it at Biloxi, to stay a month longer. He was getting on nicely; and though he missed them, he was willing to bear the separation a while longer—realizing that their health and pleasure were the first things to be considered.

V

As for Clarisse, she was charmed upon receiving her husband's letter. She and the babies were doing well. The society was agreeable; many of her old friends and acquaintances were at the bay. And the first free breath since her marriage seemed to restore the pleasant liberty of her maiden days. Devoted as she was to her husband, their intimate conjugal life was something which she was more than willing to forego for a while.

So the storm passed and everyone was happy.

READING AND REACTING

1. Trace the progress of the storm through the five parts of the story. Then, trace the stages of the story's plot. How does the progress of the storm parallel the developing plot?
2. How does the weather help to create the story's atmosphere? How would you characterize this atmosphere?
3. In Part I the "sombre clouds [. . .] rolling with sinister intention" introduce the storm. In what sense does this description introduce the story's action as well?

---

[4] "I tell you."

4. In what ways does the storm *cause* the action of the story? List specific events that occur because of the storm. Is the presence of the storm essential to the story? Explain.
5. In what sense could the storm be considered a character in the story?
6. The weather is the most obvious element of the story's setting. What other aspects of setting are important to the story?
7. After Part II the storm is not mentioned again until the last line of the story. What signs of the storm remain in Parts III, IV, and V?
8. Besides denoting the weather, what else might the title suggest?
9. **JOURNAL ENTRY** The storm sets in motion the chain of events that leads to the characters' adultery. Do you think the storm excuses the characters in any way from responsibility for their actions?

Related Works: "The Faithful Wife" (p. 375), "Wild Nights—Wild Nights!" (p. 515).

◆ **TILLIE OLSEN** (1912 or 1913–) is known for her works of fiction about working-class Americans—coal miners, farm laborers, packinghouse butchers, housewives. Olsen published two poems, a short story, and part of a novel in the 1930s. After her marriage, she did not publish again for twenty-two years, spending her time raising four children and working at a variety of jobs. The collection of her short stories *Tell Me a Riddle* (1961), which includes "I Stand Here Ironing," was published when she was fifty. Her only other work of fiction is the novel *Yonnondio* (1974).

◆ ◆ ◆

TILLIE OLSEN

I Stand Here Ironing
(1961)

I stand here ironing, and what you asked me moves tormented back and forth with the iron.

"I wish you would manage the time to come and talk with me about your daughter. I'm sure you can help me understand her. She's a youngster who needs help and whom I'm deeply interested in helping."

"Who needs help." . . . Even if I came, what good would it do? You think because I am her mother I have a key, or that in some way you could use me as a key? She has lived for nineteen years. There is all that life that has happened outside of me, beyond me.

And when is there time to remember, to sift, to weigh, to estimate, to total? I will start and there will be an interruption and I will have to gather it all together again. Or I will become engulfed with all I did or did not do, with what should have been and what cannot be helped.

5   She was a beautiful baby. The first and only one of our five that was beautiful at birth. You do not guess how new and uneasy her tenancy in her now-loveliness. You did not know her all those years she was thought homely, or see her poring over her baby pictures, making me tell her over and over how beautiful she had been—and would be, I would tell her—and was now, to the seeing eye. But the seeing eyes were few or nonexistent. Including mine.

I nursed her. They feel that's important nowadays. I nursed all the children, but with her, with all the fierce rigidity of first motherhood, I did like the books then said. Though her cries battered me to trembling and my breasts ached with swollenness, I waited till the clock decreed.

Why do I put that first? I do not even know if it matters, or if it explains anything.

She was a beautiful baby. She blew shining bubbles of sound. She loved motion, loved light, loved color and music and textures. She would lie on the floor in her blue overalls patting the surface so hard in ecstasy her hands and feet would blur. She was a miracle to me, but when she was eight months old I had to leave her daytimes with the woman downstairs to whom she was no miracle at all, for I worked or looked for work and for Emily's father, who "could no longer endure" (he wrote in his good-bye note) "sharing want with us."

I was nineteen. It was the pre-relief, pre-WPA[1] world of the depression. I would start running as soon as I got off the streetcar, running up the stairs, the place smelling sour, and awake or asleep to startle awake, when she saw me she would break into a clogged weeping that could not be comforted, a weeping I can hear yet.

10   After a while I found a job hashing at night so I could be with her days, and it was better. But it came to where I had to bring her to his family and leave her.

It took a long time to raise the money for her fare back. Then she got chicken pox and I had to wait longer. When she finally came, I hardly knew her, walking quick and nervous like her father, looking like her father, thin, and dressed in a shoddy red that yellowed her skin and glared at the pockmarks. All the baby loveliness gone.

She was two. Old enough for nursery school they said, and I did not know then what I know now—the fatigue of the long day, and the

---

[1] Works Progress Administration, created in 1935 as part of President Franklin D. Roosevelt's New Deal program. The purpose of the WPA (renamed the Works Projects Administration in 1939) was to provide jobs for the unemployed during the Great Depression.

lacerations of group life in the kinds of nurseries that are only parking places for children.

Except that it would have made no difference if I had known. It was the only place there was. It was the only way we could be together, the only way I could hold a job.

And even without knowing, I knew. I knew the teacher that was evil because all these years it has curdled into my memory, the little boy hunched in the corner, her rasp, "why aren't you outside, because Alvin hits you? that's no reason, go out, scaredy." I knew Emily hated it even if she did not clutch and implore "don't go Mommy" like the other children, mornings.

15 She always had a reason why we should stay home. Momma, you look sick. Momma, I feel sick. Momma, the teachers aren't there today, they're sick. Momma, we can't go, there was a fire there last night. Momma, it's a holiday today, no school, they told me.

But never a direct protest, never rebellion. I think of our others in their three-, four-year-oldness—the explosions, the tempers, the denunciations, the demands—and I feel suddenly ill. I put the iron down. What in me demanded that goodness in her? And what was the cost, the cost to her of such goodness?

The old man living in the back once said in his gentle way: "You should smile at Emily more when you look at her." What *was* in my face when I looked at her? I loved her. There were all the acts of love.

It was only with the others I remembered what he said, and it was the face of joy, and not of care or tightness or worry I turned to them— too late for Emily. She does not smile easily, let alone almost always as her brothers and sisters do. Her face is closed and sombre, but when she wants, how fluid. You must have seen it in her pantomimes, you spoke of her rare gift for comedy on the stage that rouses laughter out of the audience so dear they applaud and applaud and do not want to let her go.

Where does it come from, that comedy? There was none of it in her when she came back to me that second time, after I had had to send her away again. She had a new daddy now to learn to love, and I think perhaps it was a better time.

20 Except when we left her alone nights, telling ourselves she was old enough.

"Can't you go some other time, Mommy, like tomorrow?" she would ask. "Will it be just a little while you'll be gone? Do you promise?"

The time we came back, the front door open, the clock on the floor in the hall. She rigid awake. "It wasn't just a little while. I didn't cry. Three times I called you, just three times, and then I ran downstairs to open the door so you could come faster. The clock talked loud. I threw it away, it scared me what it talked."

She said the clock talked loud again that night I went to the hospital to have Susan. She was delirious with the fever that comes before red measles, but she was fully conscious all the week I was gone and the week after we were home when she could not come near the new baby or me.

She did not get well. She stayed skeleton thin, not wanting to eat, and night after night she had nightmares. She would call for me, and I would rouse from exhaustion to sleepily call back: "You're all right, darling, go to sleep, it's just a dream," and if she still called, in a sterner voice, "now go to sleep, Emily, there's nothing to hurt you." Twice, only twice, when I had to get up for Susan anyhow, I went in to sit with her.

Now when it is too late (as if she would let me hold and comfort her like I do the others) I get up and go to her at once at her moan or restless stirring. "Are you awake, Emily? Can I get you something?" And the answer is always the same: "No, I'm all right, go back to sleep, Mother."

They persuaded me at the clinic to send her away to a convalescent home in the country where "she can have the kind of food and care you can't manage for her, and you'll be free to concentrate on the new baby." They still send children to that place. I see pictures on the society page of sleek young women planning affairs to raise money for it, or dancing at the affairs, or decorating Easter eggs or filling Christmas stockings for the children.

They never have a picture of the children so I do not know if the girls still wear those gigantic red bows and the ravaged looks on the every other Sunday when parents can come to visit "unless otherwise notified"—as we were notified the first six weeks.

Oh it is a handsome place, green lawns and tall trees and fluted flower beds. High up on the balconies of each cottage the children stand, the girls in their red bows and white dresses, the boys in white suits and giant red ties. The parents stand below shrieking up to be heard and the children shriek down to be heard, and between them the invisible wall: "Not to Be Contaminated by Parental Germs or Physical Affection."

There was a tiny girl who always stood hand in hand with Emily. Her parents never came. One visit she was gone. "They moved her to Rose Cottage," Emily shouted in explanation. "They don't like you to love anybody here."

She wrote once a week, the labored writing of a seven-year-old. "I am fine. How is the baby. If I write my leter nicly I will have a star. Love." There never was a star. We wrote every other day, letters she could never hold or keep but only hear read—once. "We simply do not have room for children to keep any personal possessions," they patiently explained when we pieced one Sunday's shrieking together to plead how much it would mean to Emily, who loved so to keep things, to be allowed to keep her letters and cards.

Each visit she looked frailer. "She isn't eating," they told us.

(They had runny eggs for breakfast or mush with lumps, Emily said later, I'd hold it in my mouth and not swallow. Nothing ever tasted good, just when they had chicken.)

It took us eight months to get her released home, and only the fact that she gained back so little of her seven lost pounds convinced the social worker.

I used to try to hold and love her after she came back, but her body would stay stiff, and after a while she'd push away. She ate little. Food sickened her, and I think much of life too. Oh she had physical lightness and brightness, twinkling by on skates, bouncing like a ball up and down up and down over the jump rope, skimming over the hill; but these were momentary.

35   She fretted about her appearance, thin and dark and foreign-looking at a time when every little girl was supposed to look or thought she should look a chubby blonde replica of Shirley Temple. The doorbell sometimes rang for her, but no one seemed to come and play in the house or be a best friend. Maybe because we moved so much.

There was a boy she loved painfully through two school semesters. Months later she told me how she had taken pennies from my purse to buy him candy. "Licorice was his favorite and I brought him some every day, but he still liked Jennifer better'n me. Why, Mommy?" The kind of question for which there is no answer.

School was a worry to her. She was not glib or quick in a world where glibness and quickness were easily confused with ability to learn. To her overworked and exasperated teachers she was an overconscientious "slow learner" who kept trying to catch up and was absent entirely too often.

I let her be absent, though sometimes the illness was imaginary. How different from my now-strictness about attendance with the others. I wasn't working. We had a new baby, I was home anyhow. Sometimes, after Susan grew old enough, I would keep her home from school, too, to have them all together.

Mostly Emily had asthma, and her breathing, harsh and labored, would fill the house with a curiously tranquil sound. I would bring the two old dresser mirrors and her boxes of collections to her bed. She would select beads and single earrings, bottle tops and shells, dried flowers and pebbles, old postcards and scraps, all sorts of oddments; then she and Susan would play Kingdom, setting up landscapes and furniture, peopling them with action.

40   Those were the only times of peaceful companionship between her and Susan. I have edged away from it, that poisonous feeling between them, that terrible balancing of hurts and needs I had to do between the two, and did so badly, those earlier years.

Oh there are conflicts between the others too, each one human, needing, demanding, hurting, taking—but only between Emily and Susan, no, Emily toward Susan that corroding resentment. It seems so obvious on the surface, yet it is not obvious. Susan, the second child, Susan, golden- and curly-haired and chubby, quick and articulate and assured, everything in appearance and manner Emily was not; Susan, not able to resist Emily's precious things, losing or sometimes clumsily breaking them; Susan telling jokes and riddles to company for applause while Emily sat silent (to say to me later: that was *my* riddle, Mother, I told it to Susan); Susan, who for all the five years' difference in age was just a year behind Emily in developing physically.

I am glad for that slow physical development that widened the difference between her and her contemporaries, though she suffered over it. She was too vulnerable for that terrible world of youthful competition, of preening and parading, of constant measuring of yourself against every other, of envy, "If I had that copper hair," "If I had that skin. . . ." She tormented herself enough about not looking like the others, there was enough of the unsureness, the having to be conscious of words before you speak, the constant caring—what are they thinking of me? without having it all magnified by the merciless physical drives.

Ronnie is calling. He is wet and I change him. It is rare there is such a cry now. That time of motherhood is almost behind me when the ear is not one's own but must always be racked and listening for the child cry, the child call. We sit for a while and I hold him, looking out over the city spread in charcoal with its soft aisles of light. *"Shoogily,"* he breathes and curls closer. I carry him back to bed, asleep. *Shoogily.* A funny word, a family word, inherited from Emily, invented by her to say: *comfort.*

In this and other ways she leaves her seal, I say aloud. And startle at my saying it. What do I mean? What did I start to gather together, to try and make coherent? I was at the terrible, growing years. War years. I do not remember them well. I was working, there were four smaller ones now, there was not time for her. She had to help be a mother, and housekeeper, and shopper. She had to set her seal. Mornings of crisis and near hysteria trying to get lunches packed, hair combed, coats and shoes found, everyone to school or Child Care on time, the baby ready for transportation. And always the paper scribbled on by a smaller one, the book looked at by Susan then mislaid, the homework not done. Running out to that huge school where she was one, she was lost, she was a drop; suffering over the unpreparedness, stammering and unsure in her classes.

There was so little time left at night after the kids were bedded down. She would struggle over books, always eating (it was in those years she developed her enormous appetite that is legendary in our family) and I would be ironing, or preparing food for the next day, or writing V-mail[2] to Bill, or tending the baby. Sometimes, to make me laugh, or out of her despair, she would imitate happenings or types at school.

I think I said once: "Why don't you do something like this in the school amateur show?" One morning she phoned me at work, hardly understandable through the weeping: "Mother, I did it. I won, I won; they gave me first prize; they clapped and clapped and wouldn't let me go."

---

[2] Mail sent to or from members of the armed forces during World War II. Letters were reduced onto microfilm and enlarged and printed at their destination.

Now suddenly she was Somebody, and as imprisoned in her difference as she had been in anonymity.

She began to be asked to perform at other high schools, even in colleges, then at city and statewide affairs. The first one we went to, I only recognized her that first moment when thin, shy, she almost drowned herself into the curtains. Then: Was this Emily? The control, the command, the convulsing and deadly clowning, the spell, then the roaring, stamping audience, unwilling to let this rare and precious laughter out of their lives.

Afterwards: You ought to do something about her with a gift like that—but without money or knowing how, what does one do? We have left it all to her, and the gift has as often eddied inside, clogged and clotted, as been used and growing.

She is coming. She runs up the stairs two at a time with her light graceful step, and I know she is happy tonight. Whatever it was that occasioned your call did not happen today.

"Aren't you ever going to finish the ironing, Mother? Whistler painted his mother in a rocker. I'd have to paint mine standing over an ironing board." This is one of her communicative nights and she tells me everything and nothing as she fixes herself a plate of food out of the icebox.

She is so lovely. Why did you want me to come in at all? Why were you concerned? She will find her way.

She starts up the stairs to bed. "Don't get me up with the rest in the morning." "But I thought you were having midterms." "Oh, those," she comes back in, kisses me, and says quite lightly, "in a couple of years when we'll all be atom-dead they won't matter a bit."

She has said it before. She *believes* it. But because I have been dredging the past, and all that compounds a human being is so heavy and meaningful in me, I cannot endure it tonight.

I will never total it all. I will never come in to say: She was a child seldom smiled at. Her father left me before she was a year old. I had to work her first six years when there was work, or I sent her home and to his relatives. There were years she had care she hated. She was dark and thin and foreign-looking in a world where the prestige went to blondeness and curly hair and dimples, she was slow where glibness was prized. She was a child of anxious, not proud, love. We were poor and could not afford for her the soil of easy growth. I was a young mother, I was a distracted mother. There were other children pushing up, demanding. Her younger sister seemed all that she was not. There were years she did not want me to touch her. She kept too much in herself, her life was such she had to keep too much in herself. My wisdom came too late. She has much to her and probably little will come of it. She is a child of her age, of depression, of war, of fear.

Let her be. So all that is in her will not bloom—but in how many does it? There is still enough left to live by. Only help her to know—help make it so there is cause for her to know—that she is more than this dress on the ironing board, helpless before the iron.

READING AND REACTING

1. "I Stand Here Ironing" focuses on incidents that took place in the "pre-relief, pre-WPA world" of the Depression (9). In light of social, political, and economic changes that have occurred since the 1930s, do you think the events the story presents could occur today? Explain.
2. In what sense is the image of a mother at an ironing board appropriate for this story?
3. The narrator is overwhelmed by guilt. What does she believe she has done wrong? What, if anything, do *you* think she has done wrong? Do you think she has been a good mother? Why or why not?
4. Who, or what, do you blame for the narrator's problems? For example, do you blame Emily's father? The Depression? The social institutions and "experts" to which the narrator turns?
5. Do you see the narrator as a victim limited by the times in which she lives? Do you agree with the narrator that Emily is "a child of her age, of depression, of war, of fear"? Or do you believe both women have some control over their own destinies, regardless of the story's historical setting?
6. What do you think the narrator wants for her daughter? Do you think her goals for Emily are realistic ones?
7. Paragraph 28 describes the physical setting of the convalescent home to which Emily was sent. What does this description add to the story? Why do you suppose there is no physical description of the apartment in which Emily lived as a child? How do you picture this apartment?
8. To whom do you think the mother is speaking in this story?
9. **JOURNAL ENTRY** Put yourself in Emily's position. What do you think she would like to tell her mother?

Related Works: "Everyday Use" (p. 217), "Two Kinds" (p. 285), "Those Winter Sundays" (p. 311), *The Glass Menagerie* (p. 938)

◆ **CHARLOTTE PERKINS GILMAN** (1860–1935) was a prominent feminist and social thinker at the turn of the century. Her essays, lectures, and nonfiction works are forceful statements of her opinions on women's need for economic independence and social equality.

Although "The Yellow Wall-Paper" (1892) is not typical of Gilman's fiction, it is considered her artistic masterpiece. It is particularly chilling when read with a knowledge of Gilman's personal history. In the 1880s, she married Charles Walter Stetson. After the birth of their daughter, she grew increasingly depressed and turned to a noted neurologist for help. Following the accepted practice of the time, he prescribed complete bed rest and mental inactivity—a treatment that, Gilman said later, drove her "so near the borderline of utter mental ruin that I could see over."

◆ ◆ ◆

CHARLOTTE PERKINS GILMAN

The Yellow Wall-Paper
(1892)

It is very seldom that mere ordinary people like John and myself secure ancestral halls for the summer.

A colonial mansion, a hereditary estate, I would say a haunted house, and reach the height of romantic felicity—but that would be asking too much of fate!

Still I will proudly declare that there is something queer about it.

Else, why should it be let so cheaply? And why have stood so long untenanted?

5   John laughs at me, of course, but one expects that in marriage.

John is practical in the extreme. He has no patience with faith, an intense horror of superstition, and he scoffs openly at any talk of things not to be felt and seen and put down in figures.

John is a physician, and *perhaps*—(I would not say it to a living soul, of course, but this is dead paper and a great relief to my mind—) *perhaps* that is one reason I do not get well faster.

You see he does not believe I am sick!

And what can one do?

10 If a physician of high standing, and one's own husband, assures friends and relatives that there is really nothing the matter with one but temporary nervous depression—a slight hysterical tendency—what is one to do?

My brother is also a physician, and also of high standing, and he says the same thing.

So I take phosphates or phosphites[1]—whichever it is, and tonics, and journeys, and air, and exercise, and am absolutely forbidden to "work" until I am well again.

Personally, I disagree with their ideas.

Personally, I believe that congenial work, with excitement and change, would do me good.

But what is one to do?

I did write for a while in spite of them; but it *does* exhaust me a good deal—having to be so sly about it, or else meet with heavy opposition.

I sometimes fancy that in my condition if I had less opposition and more society and stimulus—but John says the very worst thing I can do is to think about my condition, and I confess it always makes me feel bad.

So I will let it alone and talk about the house.

The most beautiful place! It is quite alone, standing well back from the road, quite three miles from the village. It makes me think of English places that you read about, for there are hedges and walls and gates that lock, and lots of separate little houses for the gardeners and people.

There is a *delicious* garden! I never saw such a garden—large and shady, full of box-bordered paths, and lined with long grape-covered arbors with seats under them.

There were greenhouses, too, but they are all broken now.

There was some legal trouble, I believe, something about the heirs and co-heirs; anyhow, the place has been empty for years.

That spoils my ghostliness, I am afraid, but I don't care—there is something strange about the house—I can feel it.

I even said so to John one moonlight evening, but he said what I felt was a *draught,* and shut the window.

I get unreasonably angry with John sometimes. I'm sure I never used to be so sensitive. I think it is due to this nervous condition.

But John says if I feel so, I shall neglect proper self-control; so I take pains to control myself—before him, at least, and that makes me very tired.

I don't like our room a bit. I wanted one downstairs that opened on the piazza and had roses all over the window, and such pretty old-fashioned chintz hangings! But John would not hear of it.

He said there was only one window and not room for two beds, and no near room for him if he took another.

---

[1] Both terms refer to salts of phosphorous acid. The narrator, however, means "phosphate," a carbonated beverage of water, flavoring, and a small amount of phosphoric acid.

He is very careful and loving, and hardly lets me stir without special direction.

I have a schedule prescription for each hour in the day; he takes all care from me, and so I feel basely ungrateful not to value it more.

He said we came here solely on my account, that I was to have perfect rest and all the air I could get. "Your exercise depends on your strength, my dear," said he, "and your food somewhat on your appetite; but air you can absorb all the time." So we took the nursery at the top of the house.

It is a big, airy room, the whole floor nearly, with windows that look all ways, and air and sunshine galore. It was nursery first and then playroom and gymnasium, I should judge; for the windows are barred for little children, and there are rings and things in the walls.

The paint and paper look as if a boys' school had used it. It is stripped off—the paper—in great patches all around the head of my bed, about as far as I can reach, and in a great place on the other side of the room low down. I never saw a worse paper in my life.

One of those sprawling flamboyant patterns committing every artistic sin.

It is dull enough to confuse the eye in following, pronounced enough to constantly irritate and provoke study, and when you follow the lame uncertain curves for a little distance they suddenly commit suicide—plunge off at outrageous angles, destroy themselves in unheard of contradictions.

The color is repellent, almost revolting; a smouldering unclean yellow, strangely faded by the slow-turning sunlight.

It is a dull yet lurid orange in some places, a sickly sulphur tint in others.

No wonder the children hated it! I should hate it myself if I had to live in this room long.

There comes John, and I must put this away,—he hates to have me write a word.

We have been here two weeks, and I haven't felt like writing before, since that first day.

I am sitting by the window now, up in this atrocious nursery, and there is nothing to hinder my writing as much as I please, save lack of strength.

John is away all day, and even some nights when his cases are serious.

I am glad my case is not serious!

But these nervous troubles are dreadfully depressing.

John does not know how much I really suffer. He knows there is no *reason* to suffer, and that satisfies him.

Of course it is only nervousness. It does weigh on me so not to do my duty in any way!

I meant to be such a help to John, such a real rest and comfort, and here I am a comparative burden already!

Nobody would believe what an effort it is to do what little I am able,—to dress and entertain, and order things.

It is fortunate Mary is so good with the baby. Such a dear baby!

And yet I *cannot* be with him, it makes me so nervous.

I suppose John never was nervous in his life. He laughs at me so about this wall-paper!

At first he meant to repaper the room, but afterwards he said that I was letting it get the better of me, and that nothing was worse for a nervous patient than to give way to such fancies.

He said that after the wall-paper was changed it would be the heavy bedstead, and then the barred windows, and then that gate at the head of the stairs, and so on.

"You know the place is doing you good," he said, "and really, dear, I don't care to renovate the house just for a three months' rental."

"Then do let us go downstairs," I said, "there are such pretty rooms there."

Then he took me in his arms and called me a blessed little goose, and said he would go down cellar, if I wished, and have it whitewashed into the bargain.

But he is right enough about the beds and windows and things.

It is an airy and comfortable room as any one need wish, and, of course, I would not be so silly as to make him uncomfortable just for a whim.

I'm really getting quite fond of the big room, all but that horrid paper.

Out of one window I can see the garden, those mysterious deep-shaded arbors, the riotous old-fashioned flowers, and bushes and gnarly trees.

Out of another I get a lovely view of the bay and a little private wharf belonging to the estate. There is a beautiful shaded lane that runs down there from the house. I always fancy I see people walking in these numerous paths and arbors, but John has cautioned me not to give way to fancy in the least. He says that with my imaginative power and habit of story-making, a nervous weakness like mine is sure to lead to all manner of excited fancies, and that I ought to use my will and good sense to check the tendency. So I try.

I think sometimes that if I were only well enough to write a little it would relieve the press of ideas and rest me.

But I find I get pretty tired when I try.

It is so discouraging not to have any advice and companionship about my work. When I get really well, John says we will ask Cousin Henry and Julia down for a long visit; but he says he would as soon put fireworks in my pillow-case as to let me have those stimulating people about now.

I wish I could get well faster.

But I must not think about that. This paper looks to me as if it *knew* what a vicious influence it had!

There is a recurrent spot where the pattern lolls like a broken neck and two bulbous eyes stare at you upside down.

I get positively angry with the impertinence of it and the everlastingness. Up and down and sideways they crawl, and those absurd, unblinking eyes are everywhere. There is one place where two breadths didn't match, and the eyes go all up and down the line, one a little higher than the other.

I never saw so much expression in an inanimate thing before, and we all know how much expression they have! I used to lie awake as a child and get more entertainment and terror out of blank walls and plain furniture than most children could find in a toy-store.

I remember what a kindly wink the knobs of our big, old bureau used to have, and there was one chair that always seemed like a strong friend.

I used to feel that if any of the other things looked too fierce I could always hop into that chair and be safe.

The furniture in this room is no worse than inharmonious, however, for we had to bring it all from downstairs. I suppose when this was used as a playroom they had to take the nursery things out, and no wonder! I never saw such ravages as the children have made here.

The wall-paper, as I said before, is torn off in spots, and it sticketh closer than a brother—they must have had perseverance as well as hatred.

Then the floor is scratched and gouged and splintered, the plaster itself is dug out here and there, and this great heavy bed which is all we found in the room, looks as if it had been through the wars.

But I don't mind it a bit—only the paper.

There comes John's sister. Such a dear girl as she is, and so careful of me! I must not let her find me writing.

She is a perfect and enthusiastic housekeeper, and hopes for no better profession. I verily believe she thinks it is the writing which made me sick!

But I can write when she is out, and see her a long way off from these windows.

There is one that commands the road, a lovely shaded winding road, and one that just looks off over the country. A lovely country, too, full of great elms and velvet meadows.

This wall-paper has a kind of sub-pattern in a different shade, a particularly irritating one, for you can only see it in certain lights, and not clearly then.

But in the places where it isn't faded and where the sun is just so—I can see a strange, provoking, formless sort of figure, that seems to skulk about behind that silly and conspicuous front design.

There's sister on the stairs!

• • •

Well, the Fourth of July is over! The people are all gone and I am tired out. John thought it might do me good to see a little company, so we just had mother and Nellie and the children down for a week.

Of course I didn't do a thing. Jennie sees to everything now.

But it tired me all the same.

John says if I don't pick up faster he shall send me to Weir Mitchell[2] in the fall.

But I don't want to go there at all. I had a friend who was in his hands once, and she says he is just like John and my brother, only more so!

Besides, it is such an undertaking to go so far.

I don't feel as if it was worth while to turn my hand over for anything, and I'm getting dreadfully fretful and querulous.

I cry at nothing, and cry most of the time.

Of course I don't when John is here, or anybody else, but when I am alone.

And I am alone a good deal just now. John is kept in town very often by serious cases, and Jennie is good and lets me alone when I want her to.

So I walk a little in the garden or down that lovely lane, sit on the porch under the roses, and lie down up here a good deal.

I'm getting really fond of the room in spite of the wall-paper. Perhaps *because* of the wall-paper.

It dwells in my mind so!

I lie here on this great immovable bed—it is nailed down, I believe—and follow that pattern about by the hour. It is as good as gymnastics, I assure you. I start, we'll say, at the bottom, down in the corner over there where it has not been touched, and I determine for the thousandth time that I *will* follow that pointless pattern to some sort of a conclusion.

I know a little of the principle of design, and I know this thing was not arranged on any laws of radiation, or alternation, or repetition, or symmetry, or anything else that I ever heard of.

It is repeated, of course, by the breadths, but not otherwise.

Looked at in one way each breadth stands alone, the bloated curves and flourishes—a kind of "debased Romanesque" with *delirium tremens*[3] go waddling up and down in isolated columns of fatuity.

But, on the other hand, they connect diagonally, and the sprawling outlines run off in great slanting waves of optic horror, like a lot of wallowing seaweeds in full chase.

The whole thing goes horizontally, too, at least it seems so, and I exhaust myself in trying to distinguish the order of its going in that direction.

---

[2] Silas Weir Mitchell (1829–1914)—a Philadelphia neurologist-psychologist who introduced the "rest cure" for nervous diseases.

[3] Mental confusion caused by alcohol poisoning and characterized by physical tremors and hallucinations.

They have used a horizontal breadth for a frieze, and that adds wonderfully to the confusion.

There is one end of the room where it is almost intact, and there, when the crosslights fade and the low sun shines directly upon it, I can almost fancy radiation after all,—the interminable grotesque seems to form around a common center and rush off in headlong plunges of equal distraction.

It makes me tired to follow it. I will take a nap I guess.

I don't know why I should write this.

I don't want to.

I don't feel able.

And I know John would think it absurd. But I *must* say what I feel and think in some way—it is such a relief!

But the effort is getting to be greater than the relief.

Half the time now I am awfully lazy, and lie down ever so much.

John says I mustn't lose my strength, and has me take cod liver oil and lots of tonics and things, to say nothing of ale and wine and rare meat.

Dear John! He loves me very dearly, and hates to have me sick. I tried to have a real earnest reasonable talk with him the other day, and tell him how I wish he would let me go and make a visit to Cousin Henry and Julia.

But he said I wasn't able to go, nor able to stand it after I got there; and I did not make out a very good case for myself, for I was crying before I had finished.

It is getting to be a great effort for me to think straight. Just this nervous weakness I suppose.

And dear John gathered me up in his arms, and just carried me upstairs and laid me on the bed, and sat by me and read to me till it tired my head.

He said I was his darling and his comfort and all he had, and that I must take care of myself for his sake, and keep well.

He says no one but myself can help me out of it, that I must use my will and self-control and not let any silly fancies run away with me.

There's one comfort, the baby is well and happy, and does not have to occupy this nursery with the horrid wall-paper.

If we had not used it, that blessed child would have! What a fortunate escape! Why, I wouldn't have a child of mine, an impressionable little thing, live in such a room for worlds.

I never thought of it before, but it is lucky that John kept me here after all, I can stand it so much easier than a baby, you see.

Of course I never mention it to them any more—I am too wise,—but I keep watch of it all the same.

There are things in that paper that nobody knows but me, or ever will.

Behind that outside pattern the dim shapes get clearer every day.

It is always the same shape, only very numerous.

And it is like a woman stooping down and creeping about behind that pattern. I don't like it a bit. I wonder—I begin to think—I wish John would take me away from here!

It is so hard to talk with John about my case, because he is so wise, and because he loves me so.

But I tried it last night.

It was moonlight. The moon shines in all around just as the sun does.

I hate to see it sometimes, it creeps so slowly, and always comes in by one window or another.

John was asleep and I hated to waken him, so I kept still and watched the moonlight on that undulating wall-paper till I felt creepy.

The faint figure behind seemed to shake the pattern, just as if she wanted to get out.

I got up softly and went to feel and see if the paper *did* move, and when I came back John was awake.

"What is it, little girl?" he said. "Don't go walking about like that—you'll get cold."

I thought it was a good time to talk, so I told him that I really was not gaining here, and that I wished he would take me away.

"Why, darling!" said he, "our lease will be up in three weeks, and I can't see how to leave before.

"The repairs are not done at home, and I cannot possibly leave town just now. Of course if you were in any danger, I could and would, but you really are better, dear, whether you can see it or not. I am a doctor, dear, and I know. You are gaining flesh and color, your appetite is better, I feel really much easier about you."

"I don't weigh a bit more," said I, "nor as much; and my appetite may be better in the evening when you are here, but it is worse in the morning when you are away!"

"Bless her little heart!" said he with a big hug, "she shall be as sick as she pleases! But now let's improve the shining hours by going to sleep, and talk about it in the morning!"

"And you won't go away?" I asked gloomily.

"Why, how can I, dear? It is only three weeks more and then we will take a nice little trip of a few days while Jennie is getting the house ready. Really dear you are better!"

"Better in body perhaps—" I began, and stopped short, for he sat up straight and looked at me with such a stern, reproachful look that I could not say another word.

"My darling," said he, "I beg of you, for my sake and for our child's sake, as well as for your own, that you will never for one instant let that idea enter your mind! There is nothing so dangerous, so fascinating, to a temperament like yours. It is a false and foolish fancy. Can you not trust me as a physician when I tell you so?"

So of course I said no more on that score, and we went to sleep before long. He thought I was asleep first, but I wasn't, and lay there for hours trying to decide whether that front pattern and the back pattern really did move together or separately.

On a pattern like this, by daylight, there is a lack of sequence, a defiance of law, that is a constant irritant to a normal mind.

The color is hideous enough, and unreliable enough, and infuriating enough, but the pattern is torturing.

You think you have mastered it, but just as you get well underway in following, it turns back-somersault and there you are. It slaps you in the face, knocks you down, and tramples upon you. It is like a bad dream.

The outside pattern is a florid arabesque, reminding one of a fungus. If you can imagine a toadstool in joints, an interminable string of toadstools, budding and sprouting in endless convolutions—why, that is something like it.

That is, sometimes!

There is one marked peculiarity about this paper, a thing nobody seems to notice but myself, and that is that it changes as the light changes.

When the sun shoots in through the east window—I always watch for that first long, straight ray—it changes so quickly that I never can quite believe it.

That is why I watch it always.

By moonlight—the moon shines in all night when there is a moon—I wouldn't know it was the same paper.

At night in any kind of light, in twilight, candlelight, lamplight, and worst of all by moonlight, it becomes bars! The outside pattern I mean, and the woman behind it is as plain as can be.

I didn't realize for a long time what the thing was that showed behind, that dim sub-pattern, but now I am quite sure it is a woman.

By daylight she is subdued, quiet. I fancy it is the pattern that keeps her so still. It is so puzzling. It keeps me quiet by the hour.

I lie down ever so much now. John says it is good for me, and to sleep all I can.

Indeed he started the habit by making me lie down for an hour after each meal.

It is a very bad habit I am convinced, for you see I don't sleep.

And that cultivates deceit, for I don't tell them I'm awake—O no!

The fact is I am getting a little afraid of John.

He seems very queer sometimes, and even Jennie has an inexplicable look.

It strikes me occasionally, just as a scientific hypothesis,—that perhaps it is the paper!

I have watched John when he did not know I was looking, and come into the room suddenly on the most innocent excuses, and I've caught him several times *looking at the paper!* And Jennie too. I caught Jennie with her hand on it once.

She didn't know I was in the room, and when I asked her in a quiet, a very quiet voice, with the most restrained manner possible, what she was doing with the paper—she turned around as if she had been caught stealing, and looked quite angry—asked me why I should frighten her so!

Then she said that the paper stained everything it touched, that she had found yellow smooches on all my clothes and John's, and she wished we would be more careful!

Did not that sound innocent? But I know she was studying that pattern, and I am determined that nobody shall find it out but myself!

Life is very much more exciting now than it used to be. You see I have something more to expect, to look forward to, to watch. I really do eat better, and am more quiet than I was.

John is so pleased to see me improve! He laughed a little the other day, and said I seemed to be flourishing in spite of my wall-paper.

I turned it off with a laugh. I had no intention of telling him it was *because* of the wall-paper—he would make fun of me. He might even want to take me away.

I don't want to leave now until I have found it out. There is a week more, and I think that will be enough.

I'm feeling ever so much better! I don't sleep much at night, for it is so interesting to watch developments; but I sleep a good deal in the daytime.

In the daytime it is tiresome and perplexing.

There are always new shoots on the fungus, and new shades of yellow all over it. I cannot keep count of them, though I have tried conscientiously.

It is the strangest yellow, that wall-paper! It makes me think of all the yellow things I ever saw—not beautiful ones like buttercups, but old foul, bad yellow things.

But there is something else about that paper—the smell! I noticed it the moment we came into the room, but with so much air and sun it was not bad. Now we have had a week of fog and rain, and whether the windows are open or not, the smell is here.

It creeps all over the house.

I find it hovering in the dining-room, skulking in the parlor, hiding in the hall, lying in wait for me on the stairs.

It gets into my hair.

Even when I go to ride, if I turn my head suddenly and surprise it—there is that smell!

Such a peculiar odor, too! I have spent hours in trying to analyze it, to find what it smelled like.

It is not bad—at first, and very gentle, but quite the subtlest, most enduring odor I ever met.

In this damp weather it is awful, I wake up in the night and find it hanging over me.

It used to disturb me at first. I thought seriously of burning the house—to reach the smell.

But now I am used to it. The only thing I can think of that it is like is the *color* of the paper! A yellow smell.

There is a very funny mark on this wall, low down, near the mopboard. A streak that runs round the room. It goes behind every piece of furniture, except the bed, a long, straight, even *smooch,* as if it had been rubbed over and over.

I wonder how it was done and who did it, and what they did it for. Round and round and round—round and round and round!—it makes me dizzy!

I really have discovered something at last.

Through watching so much at night, when it changes so, I have finally found out.

The front pattern *does* move—and no wonder! The woman behind shakes it!

Sometimes I think there are a great many women behind, and sometimes only one, and she crawls around fast, and her crawling shakes it all over.

Then in the very bright spots she keeps still, and in the very shady spots she just takes hold of the bars and shakes them hard.

And she is all the time trying to climb through. But nobody could climb through that pattern—it strangles so; I think that is why it has so many heads.

They get through, and then the pattern strangles them off and turns them upside down, and makes their eyes white!

If those heads were covered or taken off it would not be half so bad.

I think that woman gets out in the daytime!

And I'll tell you why—privately—I've seen her!

I can see her out of every one of my windows!

It is the same woman, I know, for she is always creeping, and most women do not creep by daylight.

I see her in that long shaded lane, creeping up and down. I see her in those dark grape arbors, creeping all around the garden.

I see her on that long road under the trees, creeping along, and when a carriage comes she hides under the blackberry vines.

I don't blame her a bit. It must be very humiliating to be caught creeping by daylight!

I always lock the door when I creep by daylight. I can't do it at night, for I know John would suspect something at once.

And John is so queer now, that I don't want to irritate him. I wish he would take another room! Besides, I don't want anybody to get that woman out at night but myself.

I often wonder if I could see her out of all the windows at once.

But, turn as fast as I can, I can only see out of one at one time.

And though I always see her, she *may* be able to creep faster than I can turn!

I have watched her sometimes away off in the open country, creeping as fast as a cloud shadow in a high wind.

If only that top pattern could be gotten off from the under one! I mean to try it, little by little.

I have found out another funny thing, but I shan't tell it this time! It does not do to trust people too much.

There are only two more days to get this paper off, and I believe John is beginning to notice. I don't like the look in his eyes.

And I heard him ask Jennie a lot of professional questions about me. She had a very good report to give.

She said I slept a good deal in the daytime.

John knows I don't sleep very well at night, for all I'm so quiet!

He asked me all sorts of questions, too, and pretended to be very loving and kind.

As if I couldn't see through him!

Still, I don't wonder he acts so, sleeping under this paper for three months.

It only interests me, but I feel sure John and Jennie are secretly affected by it.

Hurrah! This is the last day, but it is enough. John to stay in town over night, and won't be out until this evening.

Jennie wanted to sleep with me—the sly thing! But I told her I should undoubtedly rest better for a night all alone.

That was clever, for really I wasn't alone a bit! As soon as it was moonlight and that poor thing began to crawl and shake the pattern, I got up and ran to help her.

I pulled and she shook, I shook and she pulled, and before morning we had peeled off yards of that paper.

A strip about as high as my head and half around the room.

And then when the sun came and that awful pattern began to laugh at me, I declared I would finish it to-day!

We go away to-morrow, and they are moving all my furniture down again to leave things as they were before.

Jennie looked at the wall in amazement, but I told her merrily that I did it out of pure spite at the vicious thing.

She laughed and said she wouldn't mind doing it herself, but I must not get tired.

How she betrayed herself that time!

But I am here, and no person touches this paper but me,—not *alive!*

She tried to get me out of the room—it was too patent! But I said it was so quiet and empty and clean now that I believed I would lie down again and sleep all I could; and not to wake me even for dinner—I would call when I woke.

So now she is gone, and the servants are gone, and the things are gone, and there is nothing left but that great bedstead nailed down, with the canvas mattress we found on it.

We shall sleep downstairs to-night, and take the boat home to-morrow.

I quite enjoy the room, now it is bare again.

How those children did tear about here!

This bedstead is fairly gnawed!

But I must get to work.

I have locked the door and thrown the key down into the front path.

I don't want to go out, and I don't want to have anybody come in, till John comes.

I want to astonish him.

I've got a rope up here that even Jennie did not find. If that woman does get out, and tries to get away, I can tie her!

But I forgot I could not reach far without anything to stand on!

This bed will *not* move!

I tried to lift and push it until I was lame, and then I got so angry I bit off a little piece at one corner—but it hurt my teeth.

Then I peeled off all the paper I could reach standing on the floor. It sticks horribly and the pattern just enjoys it! All those strangled heads and bulbous eyes and waddling fungus growths just shriek with derision!

I am getting angry enough to do something desperate. To jump out of the window would be admirable exercise, but the bars are too strong even to try.

Besides I wouldn't do it. Of course not. I know well enough that a step like that is improper and might be misconstrued.

I don't like to *look* out of the windows even—there are so many of those creeping women, and they creep so fast.

I wonder if they all come out of that wall-paper as I did?

But I am securely fastened now by my well-hidden rope—you don't get *me* out in the road there!

I suppose I shall have to get back behind the pattern when it comes night, and that is hard!

It is so pleasant to be out in this great room and creep around as I please!

I don't want to go outside. I won't, even if Jennie asks me to.

For outside you have to creep on the ground, and everything is green instead of yellow.

But here I can creep smoothly on the floor, and my shoulder just fits in that long smooch around the wall, so I cannot lose my way.

Why there's John at the door!

It is no use, young man, you can't open it!

How he does call and pound!

Now he's crying for an axe.

It would be a shame to break down that beautiful door!

"John dear!" said I in the gentlest voice, "the key is down by the front steps, under a plantain leaf!"

That silenced him for a few moments.

Then he said—very quietly indeed, "Open the door, my darling!"

"I can't," said I. "The key is down by the front door under a plantain leaf!"

And then I said it again, several times, very gently and slowly, and said it so often that he had to go and see, and he got it of course, and came in. He stopped short by the door.

"What is the matter?" he cried. "For God's sake, what are you doing!"

I kept on creeping just the same, but I looked at him over my shoulder.

"I've got out at last," said I, "in spite of you and Jane. And I've pulled off most of the paper, so you can't put me back!"

Now why should that man have fainted? But he did, and right across my path by the wall, so that I had to creep over him every time!

READING AND REACTING

1. The story's narrator, who has recently given birth, is suffering from what her husband, a doctor, calls "temporary nervous depression—a slight hysterical tendency" (10). What is the relationship between this depression and the story's setting?
2. Describe the house and grounds. How do they affect the narrator's mood?
3. What aspects of the room in which the narrator lives upset her? Why?
4. Describe the wallpaper. What does the narrator actually see in it, and what does she imagine? How can you tell the difference?
5. What do the following comments reveal about the narrator's situation: "John laughs at me, of course, but one expects that in marriage" (5); "I must put this away,—he hates to have me write a word" (39); "He laughs at me so about this wall-paper" (51); "Then he took me in his arms and called me a blessed little goose" (56)?
6. What has probably caused the narrator's depression? What factors aggravate it? How much insight does the narrator seem to have into her situation?
7. How does the narrator's mood change as the story progresses? How do her descriptions of her setting change?
8. Aside from the physical setting—the room, the house, and the garden—what other aspects of the story's setting are important?
9. **JOURNAL ENTRY** Do you think a present-day physician or psychiatrist would give the narrator different advice? Do you think a present-day woman would respond differently to advice from her husband or doctor? Explain.

Related Works: "The Story of an Hour" (p. 43), "Barbie Doll" (p. 541), *A Doll House* (p. 599)

◊ Writing Suggestions: Setting

1. Both "The Storm" and "The Yellow Wall-Paper" use rich language to create a mood that dominates the story. Analyze this use of language in one of the two stories—or compare two short passages, one from each story. How does language create and enrich each story's setting?
2. In all of the three stories in this chapter, social constraints determined by the story's historical setting limit a woman's options. Explore the options each woman might reasonably exercise in order to break free of the limits that social institutions impose on her.
3. In stories in which setting is a strong presence, the danger always exists that the writer will neglect character development in favor of atmosphere. Does this problem occur in any of the stories in this chapter? Explain your answer.
4. Write an essay in which you consider how any one of the three stories in this chapter would be different if its historical, geographical, or physical setting were changed to a setting of your choice. In your essay, examine the changes (in plot development as well as in the characters' conflicts, reactions, and motivation) that might be caused by the change in setting.
5. Select a story from another chapter, and write an essay in which you consider how setting affects its plot—for example, how it creates conflict or crisis, how it forces characters to act, or how it determines how the plot is resolved.

CHAPTER 6

Point of View

All stories are told, or narrated, by someone, and one of the first choices writers make is who tells the story. This choice determines the story's **point of view**—the vantage point from which events are presented. The implications of this choice are far reaching. Consider for a moment the following scenario. Five people witness a crime and are questioned by the police. Their stories agree on certain points: a crime was committed, a body was found, and the crime occurred at noon. But in other ways their stories are different. The man who fled the scene was either tall or of average height; his hair either was dark or light; he either was carrying an object or was empty handed. The events that led up to the crime and even the description of the crime itself are markedly different depending on who tells the story. Thus, the perspective from which a story is told determines what details are included in the story and how they are arranged—in short, the plot. In addition, the perspective of the narrator affects the story's style, language, and themes.

The narrator of a work of fiction is not the same as the writer—even when a writer uses the first-person *I*. Writers create narrators, often with personalities and opinions far different from theirs, to tell their stories. (The term **persona**—which literally means "mask"—is used for this narrator.) By assuming this mask, a writer expands the creative possibilities of a work.

When deciding on a point of view for a work of fiction, a writer can choose to tell the story either in the *first person* or in the *third person*.

FIRST-PERSON NARRATOR

✦ ✦ ✦

Sometimes the narrator is a character who uses the **first person** *I* (or sometimes *we*) to tell the story. Often this narrator is a major character—Sammy in John Updike's "A&P" (p. 65) and the boy in James Joyce's "Araby" (p. 167), for example—who tells his or her own story and is the focus of that story. Sometimes, however, a first-person narrator may tell a story that is primarily about someone else. Such a narrator may be a minor character who plays a relatively small part in the story or simply an observer who reports events experienced or related by others. The narrator of William Faulkner's "A Rose for Emily" (p. 52), for example, is an unidentified witness to the story's events. By using *we* instead of *I*, this narrator speaks on behalf of all the town's residents, expressing their shared views of their neighbor, Emily Grierson:

> We did not say she was crazy then. We believed she had to do that. We remembered all the young men her father had driven away, and we knew that with nothing left, she would have to cling to that which had robbed her, as people will.

Writers gain a number of advantages when they use a first-person narrator. First, they are able to present incidents very convincingly. Readers are more willing to accept a statement like "My sister changed a lot after that day" than they are to accept the impersonal observations of a third-person narrator. The first-person narrator also simplifies a writer's task of selecting details. Only the events and details that the narrator could actually have seen or experienced can be introduced into the story.

Another major advantage of first-person narrators is that their restricted view can create **irony**—a discrepancy between what is said and what readers believe to be true. Irony may be *dramatic, situational,* or *verbal.* **Dramatic irony** occurs when a narrator or character perceives less than readers do; **situational irony** occurs when what happens is at odds with what readers are led to expect; **verbal irony** occurs when the narrator says one thing but actually means another.

Unreliable Narrators

Sometimes first-person narrators may be self-serving, mistaken, confused, unstable, or even mad. These **unreliable narrators,** whether intentionally or unintentionally, misrepresent events and misdirect readers. In Edgar Allan Poe's "The Cask of Amontillado" (p. 136), for example, the narrator, Montresor, tells his story to justify a crime he committed fifty years before. Montresor's version of what happened is not accurate, and perceptive readers know it: his obvious self-deception, his sadistic manipulation of Fortunato, his detached description of the cold-blooded murder, and his lack of remorse lead readers to question his sanity (and, therefore, to distrust his version of events). This distrust creates an ironic distance between readers and narrator.

The narrator of Charlotte Perkins Gilman's "The Yellow Wall-Paper" (p. 102) is also an unreliable narrator. Suffering from "nervous depression," she unintentionally distorts the facts when she says that the shapes in the wallpaper of her bedroom are changing and moving. Moreover, she does not realize what is wrong with her or why, or how her husband's "good intentions" are hurting her. Readers, however, see the discrepancy between the narrator's interpretation of events and their own, and this irony enriches their understanding of the story.

Some narrators are unreliable because they are naive. Because they are immature, sheltered, or innocent of evil, these narrators may not be aware of the full significance of the events they are relating. Having the benefit of experience, readers interpret events differently from the way these narrators do. When we read a passage by a child narrator—such as the following from J. D. Salinger's novel *The Catcher in the Rye*—we are aware of the narrator's innocence, and we know his interpretation of events is flawed:

> Anyway, I keep picturing all these little kids playing some game in this big field of rye and all. Thousands of little kids, and nobody's around—nobody big, I mean—except me. And I'm standing on the edge of some crazy cliff. What I have to do, I have to catch everybody if they start to go over the cliff—I mean if they're running and they don't look where they're going I have to come out from somewhere and catch them. I'd just be the catcher in the rye [. . .].

The irony in the preceding passage comes from our knowledge that the naive narrator, Holden Caulfield, cannot stop children from growing up. Ultimately, they all fall off the "crazy cliff" and mature into adults. Although he is not aware of the futility of trying to protect children from the dangers of adulthood, readers know that his efforts are doomed from the start.

A naive narrator's background can also limit his or her ability to understand a situation. The narrator in Sherwood Anderson's short story "I'm a Fool," for example, lies to impress a rich girl he meets at a race track. At the end of the story the boy laments the fact that he lied, believing that if he had told the truth, he could have seen the girl again. The reader knows, however, that the narrator is deceiving himself because the social gap that separates the narrator and the girl could never be bridged.

Keep in mind that there is a difference between an unreliable narrator and a narrator whose perspective is limited. All first-person narrators are, by definition, limited because they present a situation as only one person sees it. "In a Grove," a short story by the Japanese writer Ryūnosuke Akutagawa, illustrates this idea. In this story, seven characters act as narrators and give different accounts of a murder. Some of the characters seem to be lying or bending the facts to suit their own needs, but others simply have an incomplete or mistaken understanding of the event. No character, of course, has all the information the story's author has.

As a reader focusing on a story's point of view, you should look for discrepancies between a narrator's view of events and your own. Discovering that a story has an unreliable narrator enables you not only to question the truth of the narrative but also to recognize the irony in the narrator's version of events. By doing so, you gain insight into the story and learn something about the writer's purpose.

Third-Person Narrator

◊ ◊ ◊

Writers can also use **third-person** narrators, who are not characters in the story. These narrators fall into three categories.

Omniscient

Some third-person narrators are **omniscient** (all-knowing) narrators, moving at will from one character's mind to another. One advantage of omniscient narrators is that they are objective; they have none of the naïveté, dishonesty, gullibility, or mental instability that can characterize first-person narrators. In addition, because omniscient narrators are not characters in the story, their perception is not limited to what any one character can observe or comprehend. As a result, they can present a more inclusive overview of events and characters than first-person narrators can. Notice how the narrator of Nadine Gordimer's "Once upon a Time" (p. 46) is able to give such an overview:

> In a house, in a suburb, in a city, there were a man and his wife who loved each other very much and were living happily ever after. They had a little boy, and they loved him very much. They had a cat and a dog that the little boy loved very much. They had a car and a caravan trailer for holidays, and a swimming-pool which was fenced so that the little boy and his playmates would not fall in and drown. They had a housemaid who was absolutely trustworthy and an itinerant gardener who was highly recommended by the neighbours. For when they began to live happily ever after they were warned, by that wise old witch, the husband's mother, not to take anyone off the street.

Occasionally, omniscient narrators move not only in and out of the minds of the characters but also in and out of a persona (representing the voice of the author) that speaks directly to readers. This experimental narrative technique was popular during the eighteenth century, when the novel was a new literary form. It permitted writers to present themselves as masters of artifice, able to know and control all aspects of experience. Few contemporary writers would give themselves the license that Henry Fielding does in the following passage from *Tom Jones*:

> And true it was that [Mr. Alworthy] did many of these things; but had he done nothing more I should have left him to have

recorded his own merit on some fair freestone over the door of that hospital. Matters of a much more extraordinary kind are to be the subject of this history, or I should grossly misspend my time in writing so voluminous a work; and you my sagacious friend, might with equal profit and pleasure travel through some pages which certain droll authors have been facetiously pleased to call *The History of England.*

A contemporary example of this type of omniscient point of view occurs in Ursula K. LeGuin's "The Ones Who Walk Away from Omelas." This 1973 story presents a description of a city that in the narrator's words is "like a city in a fairy tale." As the story proceeds, however, the description of Omelas changes, and the narrator's tone changes as well: "Do you believe? Do you accept the festival, the city, the joy? No? Then let me describe one more thing." With this change of tone, the narrator suggests the impossibility of human beings ever achieving an ideal society.

LIMITED OMNISCIENT

Third-person narrators can have **limited omniscience,** focusing on only what a single character experiences. In other words, events are limited to one character's perspective, and nothing is revealed that the character does not see, hear, feel, or think. Andy in David Michael Kaplan's "Doe Season" (p. 230) is just such a limited-focus character. Limited omniscient narrators, like all third-person narrators, have certain advantages over first-person narrators. When a writer uses a first-person narrator, the narrator's personality and speech color the story, creating a personal or even idiosyncratic narrative. Also, the first-person narrator's character flaws or lack of knowledge may limit his or her awareness of the significance of events. Limited omniscient narrators are more flexible: they take readers into a particular character's mind just as a first-person narrator does, but without the first-person narrator's subjectivity, self-deception, or naiveté. In the following example from Anne Tyler's 1984 short story "Teenage Wasteland," the limited omniscient narrator presents the story from the point of view of a single character, Daisy:

> Daisy and Matt sat silent, shocked. Matt rubbed his forehead with his fingertips. Imagine, Daisy thought, how they must look to Mr. Lanham: an overweight housewife in a cotton dress and a too-tall, too-thin insurance agent in a baggy, frayed suit. Failures, both of them—the kind of people who are hurrying to catch up, missing the point of things that everyone else grasps at once. She wished she'd worn nylons instead of knee socks.

Here the narrative point of view gives readers the impression that they are standing off to the side watching Daisy and her husband Matt. At the same time we have the advantage of this objective view, however, we are also able to see into the mind of one character.

Objective

Finally, third-person narrators can tell a story from an **objective** (or *dramatic*) point of view, remaining entirely outside the characters' minds. With objective narrators, events unfold the way they would in a play or a movie: narrators tell the story only by presenting dialogue and recounting events; they do not reveal the characters' thoughts or explain their motivation. Thus, they allow readers to interpret the actions of the characters without any interference. Ernest Hemingway uses the objective point of view in his short story "A Clean, Well-Lighted Place" (p. 173):

> The waiter took the brandy bottle and another saucer from the counter inside the café and marched out to the old man's table. He put down the saucer and poured the glass full of brandy.
> "You should have killed yourself last week," he said to the deaf man. The old man motioned with his finger. "A little more," he said. The waiter poured on into the glass so that the brandy slopped over and ran down the stem into the top saucer of the pile. "Thank you," the old man said. The waiter took the bottle back inside the café. He sat down at the table with his colleague again.

The story's narrator is distant, seemingly emotionless, and this perspective is consistent with the author's purpose: for Hemingway, the attitude of the narrator reflects the stunned, almost anesthetized condition of people in the post–World War I world.

 Selecting an Appropriate Point of View: Review

First-Person Narrator (*I* or *we*)
◇ *Major character telling his or her own story* "Every morning I lay on the floor in the front parlour watching her door." (James Joyce, "Araby")
◇ *Minor character as witness or nonparticipant* "And so she died. [. . .] We did not even know she was sick; we had

long since given up trying to get information [. . .]. " (William Faulkner, "A Rose for Emily")

THIRD-PERSON NARRATOR (*HE, SHE, IT,* OR *THEY*)

- ◇ *Omniscient—able to move at will from character to character and comment about them* "In a house, in a suburb, in a city, there were a man and his wife who loved each other very much [. . .]. " (Nadine Gordimer, "Once upon a Time")
- ◇ *Limited Omniscient—restricts focus to a single character* "The wagon went on. He did not know where they were going." (William Faulkner, "Barn Burning")
- ◇ *Objective (Dramatic)—simply reports the dialogue and the actions of characters* "'You'll be drunk,' the waiter said. The old man looked at him. The waiter went away." (Ernest Hemingway, "A Clean, Well-Lighted Place")

CHECKLIST: WRITING ABOUT POINT OF VIEW

- ✓ What is the dominant point of view from which the story is told?
- ✓ Is the narrator a character in the story? If so, is he or she a participant in the story's events or just a witness?
- ✓ Does the story's point of view create irony?
- ✓ If the story has a first-person narrator, is the narrator reliable or unreliable? Are there any inconsistencies in the narrator's presentation of the story?
- ✓ If the story has a third-person narrator, is he or she omniscient? Does he or she have limited omniscience? Is the narrator objective?
- ✓ What are the advantages of the story's point of view? How does the point of view accomplish the author's purpose?
- ✓ Does the point of view remain consistent throughout the story, or does it shift?
- ✓ How might a different point of view change the story?

 ◆ **RICHARD WRIGHT** (1908–1960) was born near Natchez, Mississippi, the son of sharecroppers. He had little formal schooling but was a voracious reader. In 1935, he joined the Federal Writers' Project, an association that took him to New York City. Deeply troubled by the oppression suffered by fellow African-Americans, Wright began to reach a mainstream audience when a group of four long stories on the theme of racial oppression and violence was judged best manuscript in a contest sponsored by *Story* magazine in 1938. Two years later, Wright published his most famous work, *Native Son*.

The following story is uncharacteristic of Wright's work in a number of ways—not least of which is that it is told through the eyes of a white protagonist.

◆ ◆ ◆

RICHARD WRIGHT

Big Black Good Man
(1957)

Through the open window Olaf Jenson could smell the sea and hear the occasional foghorn of a freighter; outside, rain pelted down through an August night, drumming softly upon the pavements of Copenhagen,[1] inducing drowsiness, bringing dreamy memory, relaxing the tired muscles of his work-wracked body. He sat slumped in a swivel chair with his legs outstretched and his feet propped atop an edge of his desk. An inch of white ash tipped the end of his brown cigar and now and then he inserted the end of the stogie[2] into his mouth and drew gently upon it, letting wisps of blue smoke eddy from the corners of his wide, thin lips. The watery gray irises behind the thick lenses of his eyeglasses gave him a look of abstraction, of absentmindedness, of an almost genial idiocy. He sighed, reached for his half-empty bottle of beer, and drained it into his glass and downed it with a long slow gulp, then licked his lips. Replacing the cigar, he slapped his right palm against his thigh and said half aloud:

"Well, I'll be sixty tomorrow. I'm not rich, but I'm not poor either . . . Really, I can't complain. Got good health. Traveled all over the world and had my share of girls when I was young . . . And my Karen's a good wife. I own my home. Got no debts. And I love digging in my garden in

---

[1] The capital of Denmark.
[2] Cheap cigar.

the spring . . . Grew the biggest carrots of anybody last year. Ain't saved much money, but what the hell . . . Money ain't everything. Got a good job. Night portering ain't too bad." He shook his head and yawned. "Karen and I could of had some children, though. Would of been good company . . . 'Specially for Karen. And I could of taught 'em languages . . . English, French, German, Danish, Dutch, Swedish, Norwegian, and Spanish . . ." He took the cigar out of his mouth and eyed the white ash critically. "Hell of a lot of good language learning did me . . . Never got anything out of it. But those ten years in New York were fun . . . Maybe I could of got rich if I'd stayed in America . . . Maybe. But I'm satisfied. You can't have everything."

Behind him the office door opened and a young man, a medical student occupying room number nine, entered.

"Good evening," the student said.

"Good evening," Olaf said, turning.

The student went to the keyboard and took hold of the round, brown knob that anchored his key.

"Rain, rain, rain," the student said.

"That's Denmark for you," Olaf smiled at him.

"This dampness keeps me clogged up like a drainpipe," the student complained.

"That's Denmark for you," Olaf repeated with a smile.

"Good night," the student said.

"Good night, son," Olaf sighed, watching the door close.

Well, my tenants are my children, Olaf told himself. Almost all of his children were in their rooms now . . . Only seventy-two and forty-four were missing . . . Seventy-two might've gone to Sweden . . . And forty-four was maybe staying at his girl's place tonight, like he sometimes did . . . He studied the pear-shaped blobs of hard rubber, reddish brown like ripe fruit, that hung from the keyboard, then glanced at his watch. Only room thirty, eighty-one, and one hundred and one were empty . . . And it was almost midnight. In a few moments he could take a nap. Nobody hardly ever came looking for accommodations after midnight, unless a stray freighter came in, bringing thirsty, women-hungry sailors. Olaf chuckled softly. Why in hell was I ever a sailor? The whole time I was at sea I was thinking and dreaming about women. Then why didn't I stay on land where women could be had? Hunh? Sailors are crazy . . .

But he liked sailors. They reminded him of his youth, and there was something so direct, simple, and childlike about them. They always said straight out what they wanted, and what they wanted was almost always women and whisky . . . "Well, there's no harm in that . . . Nothing could be more natural," Olaf sighed, looking thirstily at his empty beer bottle. No; he'd not drink any more tonight; he'd had enough; he'd go to sleep . . .

He was bending forward and loosening his shoelaces when he heard the office door crack open. He lifted his eyes, then sucked in his breath.

He did not straighten; he just stared up and around at the huge black thing that filled the doorway. His reflexes refused to function; it was not fear; it was just simple astonishment. He was staring at the biggest, strangest, and blackest man he'd ever seen in all his life.

"Good evening," the black giant said in a voice that filled the small office. "Say, you got a room?"

Olaf sat up slowly, not to answer but to look at this brooding black vision; it towered darkly some six and a half feet into the air, almost touching the ceiling, and its skin was so black that it had a bluish tint. And the sheer bulk of the man! . . . His chest bulged like a barrel; his rocklike and humped shoulders hinted of mountain ridges; the stomach ballooned like a threatening stone; and the legs were like telephone poles . . . The big black cloud of a man now lumbered into the office, bending to get its buffalolike head under the door frame, then advanced slowly upon Olaf, like a stormy sky descending.

"You got a room?" the big black man asked again in a resounding voice.

Olaf now noticed that the ebony giant was well dressed, carried a wonderful new suitcase, and wore black shoes that gleamed despite the raindrops that peppered their toes.

20 "You're American?" Olaf asked him.

"Yeah, man; sure," the black giant answered.

"Sailor?"

"Yeah. American Continental Lines."

Olaf had not answered the black man's question. It was not that the hotel did not admit men of color; Olaf took in all comers—blacks, yellows, whites, and browns . . . To Olaf, men were men, and, in his day, he'd worked and eaten and slept and fought with all kinds of men. But this particular black man . . . Well, he didn't seem human. Too big, too black, too loud, too direct, and probably too violent to boot . . . Olaf's five feet seven inches scarcely reached the black giant's shoulder and his frail body weighed less, perhaps, than one of the man's gigantic legs . . . There was something about the man's intense blackness and ungainly bigness that frightened and insulted Olaf; he felt as though this man had come here expressly to remind him how puny, how tiny, and how weak and how white he was. Olaf knew, while registering his reactions, that he was being irrational and foolish; yet, for the first time in his life, he was emotionally determined to refuse a man a room solely on the basis of the man's size and color . . . Olaf's lips parted as he groped for the right words in which to couch his refusal, but the black giant bent forward and boomed:

25 "I asked you if you got a room. I got to put up somewhere tonight, man."

"Yes, we got a room," Olaf murmured.

And at once he was ashamed and confused. Sheer fear had made him yield. And he seethed against himself for his involuntary weakness.

Well, he'd look over his book and pretend that he'd made a mistake; he'd tell this hunk of blackness that there was really no free room in the hotel, and that he was so sorry . . . Then, just as he took out the hotel register to make believe that he was poring over it, a thick roll of American bank notes, crisp and green, was thrust under his nose.

"Keep this for me, will you?" the black giant commanded. "Cause I'm gonna get drunk tonight and I don't wanna lose it."

Olaf stared at the roll; it was huge, in denominations of fifties and hundreds. Olaf's eyes widened.

"How much is there?" he asked.

"Two thousand six hundred," the giant said. "Just put it into an envelope and write 'Jim' on it and lock it in your safe, hunh?"

The black mass of man had spoken in a manner that indicated that it was taking it for granted that Olaf would obey. Olaf was licked. Resentment clogged the pores of his wrinkled white skin. His hands trembled as he picked up the money. No; he couldn't refuse this man . . . The impulse to deny him was strong, but each time he was about to act upon it something thwarted him, made him shy off. He clutched about desperately for an idea. Oh yes, he could say that if he planned to stay for only one night, then he could not have the room, for it was against the policy of the hotel to rent rooms for only one night . . .

"How long are you staying? Just tonight?" Olaf asked.

"Naw. I'll be here for five or six days, I reckon," the giant answered offhandedly.

"You take room number thirty," Olaf heard himself saying. "It's forty kroner a day."

"That's all right with me," the giant said.

With slow, stiff movements, Olaf put the money in the safe and then turned and stared helplessly up into the living, breathing blackness looming above him. Suddenly he became conscious of the outstretched palm of the black giant; he was silently demanding the key to the room. His eyes downcast, Olaf surrendered the key, marveling at the black man's tremendous hands . . . He could kill me with one blow, Olaf told himself in fear.

Feeling himself beaten, Olaf reached for the suitcase, but the black hand of the giant whisked it out of his grasp.

"That's too heavy for you, big boy; I'll take it," the giant said.

Olaf let him. He thinks I'm nothing . . . He led the way down the corridor, sensing the giant's lumbering presence behind him. Olaf opened the door of number thirty and stood politely to one side, allowing the black giant to enter. At once the room seemed like a doll's house, so dwarfed and filled and tiny it was with a great living blackness . . . Flinging his suitcase upon a chair, the giant turned. The two men looked directly at each other now. Olaf saw that the giant's eyes were tiny and red, buried, it seemed, in muscle and fat. Black cheeks spread, flat and broad, topping the wide and flaring nostrils. The mouth was the biggest that Olaf had ever seen on a human face; the lips were thick, pursed, parted, showing snow-white teeth. The black neck was like a bull's . . . The giant advanced upon Olaf and stood over him.

"I want a bottle of whiskey and a woman," he said. "Can you fix me up?"

"Yes," Olaf whispered, wild with anger and insult.

But what was he angry about? He'd had requests like this every night from all sorts of men and he was used to fulfilling them; he was a night porter in a cheap, water-front Copenhagen hotel that catered to sailors and students. Yes, men needed women, but this man, Olaf felt, ought to have a special sort of woman. He felt a deep and strange reluctance to phone any of the women whom he habitually sent to men. Yet he had promised. Could he lie and say that none was available? No. That sounded too fishy. The black giant sat upon the bed, staring straight before him. Olaf moved about quickly, pulling down the window shades, taking the pink coverlet off the bed, nudging the giant with his elbow to make him move as he did so . . . That's the way to treat 'im . . . Show 'im I ain't scared of 'im . . . But he was still seeking for an excuse to refuse. And he could think of nothing. He felt hypnotized, mentally immobilized. He stood hesitantly at the door.

"You send the whiskey and the woman quick, pal?" the black giant asked, rousing himself from a brooding stare.

45 "Yes," Olaf grunted, shutting the door.

Goddamn, Olaf sighed. He sat in his office at his desk before the phone. Why did *he* have to come here? . . . I'm not prejudiced . . . No, not at all . . . But . . . He couldn't think any more. God oughtn't make men as big and black as that . . . But what the hell was he worrying about? He'd sent women of all races to men of all colors . . . So why not a woman to the black giant? Oh, only if the man were small, brown, and intelligent-looking . . . Olaf felt trapped.

With a reflex movement of his hand, he picked up the phone and dialed Lena. She was big and strong and always cut him in for fifteen per cent instead of the usual ten per cent. Lena had four small children to feed and clothe. Lena was willing; she was, she said, coming over right now. She didn't give a good goddamn about how big and black the man was . . .

"Why you ask me that?" Lena wanted to know over the phone. "You never asked that before . . ."

"But this one is *big*," Olaf found himself saying.

50 "He's just a man," Lena told him, her voice singing stridently, laughingly over the wire. "You just leave that to me. You don't have to do anything. *I'll* handle 'im."

Lena had a key to the hotel door downstairs, but tonight Olaf stayed awake. He wanted to see her. Why? He didn't know. He stretched out on the sofa in his office, but sleep was far from him. When Lena arrived, he told her again how big and black the man was.

"You told me that over the phone," Lena reminded him.

Olaf said nothing. Lena flounced off on her errand of mercy. Olaf shut the office door, then opened it and left it ajar. But why? He didn't know. He lay upon the sofa and stared at the ceiling. He glanced at his watch; it was almost two o'clock . . . She's staying in there a long time . . . Ah, God, but he could do with a drink . . . Why was he so damned worked up and nervous about a nigger and a white whore? . . . He'd never been so upset in all his life. Before he knew it, he had drifted off to sleep. Then he heard the office door swinging creakingly open on its rusty hinges. Lena stood in it, grim and businesslike, her face scrubbed free of powder and rouge. Olaf scrambled to his feet, adjusting his eyeglasses, blinking.

"How was it?" he asked her in a confidential whisper.

Lena's eyes blazed.

"What the hell's that to you?" she snapped. "There's your cut," she said, flinging him his money, tossing it upon the covers of the sofa. "You're sure nosy tonight. You wanna take over my work?"

Olaf's pasty cheeks burned red.

"You go to hell," he said, slamming the door.

"I'll meet you there!" Lena's shouting voice reached him dimly.

He was being a fool; there was no doubt about it. But, try as he might, he could not shake off a primitive hate for that black mountain of energy, of muscle, of bone; he envied the easy manner in which it moved with such a creeping and powerful motion; he winced at the booming and commanding voice that came to him when the tiny little eyes were not even looking at him; he shivered at the sight of those vast and clawlike hands that seemed always to hint of death . . .

Olaf kept his counsel. He never spoke to Karen about the sordid doings at the hotel. Such things were not for women like Karen. He knew instinctively that Karen would have been amazed had he told her that he was worried sick about a nigger and a blonde whore . . . No; he couldn't talk to anybody about it, not even the hard-bitten[3] old bitch who owned the hotel. She was concerned only about money; she didn't give a damn about how big and how black a client was as long as he paid his room rent.

Next evening, when Olaf arrived for duty, there was no sight or sound of the black giant. A little later after one o'clock in the morning he appeared, left his key, and went out wordlessly. A few moments past two the giant returned, took his key from the board, and paused.

"I want that Lena again tonight. And another bottle of whiskey," he said boomingly.

"I'll call her and see if she's in," Olaf said.

---

[3] Stubborn, tough.

"Do that," the black giant said and was gone.

He thinks he's God, Olaf fumed. He picked up the phone and ordered Lena and a bottle of whiskey, and there was a taste of ashes in his mouth. On the third night came the same request: Lena and whiskey. When the black giant appeared on the fifth night, Olaf was about to make a sarcastic remark to the effect that maybe he ought to marry Lena, but he checked it in time . . . After all, he could kill me with one hand, he told himself.

Olaf was nervous and angry with himself for being nervous. Other black sailors came and asked for girls and Olaf sent them, but with none of the fear and loathing that he sent Lena and a bottle of whiskey to the giant . . . All right, the black giant's stay was almost up. He'd said that he was staying for five or six nights; tomorrow night was the sixth night and that ought to be the end of this nameless terror.

On the sixth night Olaf sat in his swivel chair with his bottle of beer and waited, his teeth on edge, his fingers drumming the desk. But what the hell am I fretting for? . . . The hell with 'im . . . Olaf sat and dozed. Occasionally he'd awaken and listen to the foghorns of freighters sounding as ships came and went in the misty Copenhagen harbor. He was half asleep when he felt a rough hand on his shoulder. He blinked his eyes open. The giant, black and vast and powerful, all but blotted out his vision.

"What I owe you, man?" the giant demanded. "And I want my money."

"Sure," Olaf said, relieved, but filled as always with fear of this living wall of black flesh.

With fumbling hands, he made out the bill and received payment, then gave the giant his roll of money, laying it on the desk so as not to let his hands touch the flesh of the black mountain. Well, his ordeal was over. It was past two o'clock in the morning. Olaf even managed a wry smile and muttered a guttural "Thanks" for the generous tip that the giant tossed him.

Then a strange tension entered the office. The office door was shut and Olaf was alone with the black mass of power, yearning for it to leave. But the black mass of power stood still, immobile, looking down at Olaf. And Olaf could not, for the life of him, guess at what was transpiring in that mysterious black mind. The two of them simply stared at each other for a full two minutes, the giant's tiny little beady eyes blinking slowly as they seemed to measure and search Olaf's face. Olaf's vision dimmed for a second as terror seized him and he could feel a flush of heat overspread his body. Then Olaf sucked in his breath as the devil of blackness commanded:

"Stand up!"

Olaf was paralyzed. Sweat broke on his face. His worst premonitions about this black beast were coming true. This evil blackness was about to attack him, maybe kill him . . . Slowly Olaf shook his head, his terror permitting him to breathe:

75   "What're you talking about?"

"Stand up, I say!" the black giant bellowed.

As though hypnotized, Olaf tried to rise; then he felt the black paw of the beast helping him roughly to his feet.

They stood an inch apart. Olaf's pasty-white features were glued to the giant's swollen black face. The ebony ensemble of eyes and nose and mouth and cheeks looked down at Olaf, silently; then, with a slow and deliberate movement of his gorillalike arms, he lifted his mammoth hands to Olaf's throat. Olaf had long known and felt that this dreadful moment was coming; he felt trapped in a nightmare. He could not move. He wanted to scream, but could find no words. His lips refused to open; his tongue felt icy and inert. Then he knew that his end had come when the giant's black fingers slowly, softly encircled his throat while a horrible grin of delight broke out on the sooty face . . . Olaf lost control of the reflexes of his body and he felt a hot stickiness flooding his underwear . . . He stared without breathing, gazing into the grinning blackness of the face that was bent over him, feeling the black fingers caressing his throat and waiting to feel the sharp, stinging ache and pain of the bones in his neck being snapped, crushed . . . He knew all along that I hated 'im . . . Yes, and now he's going to kill me for it, Olaf told himself with despair.

The black fingers still circled Olaf's neck, not closing, but gently massaging it, as it were, moving to and fro, while the obscene face grinned into his. Olaf could feel the giant's warm breath blowing on his eyelashes and he felt like a chicken about to have its neck wrung and its body tossed to flip and flap dyingly in the dust of the barnyard . . . Then suddenly the black giant withdrew his fingers from Olaf's neck and stepped back a pace, still grinning. Olaf sighed, trembling, his body seeming to shrink; he waited. Shame sheeted him for the hot wetness that was in his trousers. Oh, God, he's teasing me . . . He's showing me how easily he can kill me . . . He swallowed, waiting, his eyes stones of gray.

80   The giant's barrel-like chest gave forth a low, rumbling chuckle of delight.

"You laugh?" Olaf asked whimperingly.

"Sure I laugh," the giant shouted.

"Please don't hurt me," Olaf managed to say.

"I wouldn't hurt you, boy," the giant said in a tone of mockery. "So long."

85   And he was gone. Olaf fell limply into the swivel chair and fought off losing consciousness. Then he wept. He was showing me how easily he could kill me . . . He made me shake with terror and then laughed and left . . . Slowly, Olaf recovered, stood, then gave vent to a string of curses:

"Goddamn 'im! My gun's right there in the desk drawer; I should of shot 'im. Jesus, I hope the ship he's on sinks . . . I hope he drowns and the sharks eat 'im . . ."

Later, he thought of going to the police, but sheer shame kept him back; and, anyway, the giant was probably on board his ship by now. And he had to get home and clean himself. Oh, Lord, what could he tell Karen? Yes, he would say that his stomach had been upset . . . He'd change clothes and return to work. He phoned the hotel owner that he was ill and wanted an hour off; the old bitch said that she was coming right over and that poor Olaf could have the evening off.

Olaf went home and lied to Karen. Then he lay awake the rest of the night dreaming of revenge. He saw that freighter on which the giant was sailing; he saw it springing a dangerous leak and saw a torrent of sea water flooding, gushing into all the compartments of the ship until it found the bunk in which the black giant slept. Ah, yes, the foamy, surging waters would surprise that sleeping black bastard of a giant and he would drown, gasping and choking like a trapped rat, his tiny eyes bulging until they glittered red, the bitter water of the sea pounding his lungs until they ached and finally burst . . . The ship would sink slowly to the bottom of the cold, black, silent depths of the sea and a shark, a *white* one, would glide aimlessly about the shut portholes until it found an open one and it would slither inside and nose about until it found that swollen, rotting, stinking carcass of the black beast and it would then begin to nibble at the decomposing mass of tarlike flesh, eating the bones clean . . . Olaf always pictured the giant's bones as being jet black and shining.

Once or twice, during these fantasies of cannibalistic revenge, Olaf felt a little guilty about all the many innocent people, women and children, all white and blonde, who would have to go down into watery graves in order that that white shark could devour the evil giant's black flesh . . . But, despite feelings of remorse, the fantasy lived persistently on, and when Olaf found himself alone, it would crowd and cloud his mind to the exclusion of all else, affording him the only revenge he knew. To make me suffer just for the pleasure of it, he fumed. Just to show me how strong he was . . . Olaf learned how to hate, and got pleasure out of it.

90   Summer fled on wings of rain. Autumn flooded Denmark with color. Winter made rain and snow fall on Copenhagen. Finally spring came, bringing violets and roses. Olaf kept to his job. For many months he feared the return of the black giant. But when a year had passed and the giant had not put in an appearance, Olaf allowed his revenge fantasy to peter out, indulging in it only when recalling the shame that the black monster had made him feel.

Then one rainy August night, a year later, Olaf sat drowsing at his desk, his bottle of beer before him, tilting back in his swivel chair, his feet resting atop a corner of his desk, his mind mulling over the more pleasant aspects of his life. The office door cracked open. Olaf glanced boredly up and around. His heart jumped and skipped a beat. The black nightmare of terror and shame that he had hoped that he had lost forever was again upon him . . . Resplendently dressed, suitcase in hand, the black looming mountain filled the doorway. Olaf's thin lips parted and a silent moan, half a curse, escaped them.

"Hi," the black giant boomed from the doorway.

Olaf could not reply. But a sudden resolve swept him: this time he would even the score. If this black beast came within so much as three feet of him, he would snatch his gun out of the drawer and shoot him dead, so help him God . . .

"No rooms tonight," Olaf heard himself announcing in a determined voice.

The black giant grinned; it was the same infernal grimace of delight and triumph that he had had when his damnable black fingers had been around his throat . . .

"Don't want no room tonight," the giant announced.

"Then what are you doing here?" Olaf asked in a loud but tremulous voice.

The giant swept toward Olaf and stood over him; and Olaf could not move, despite his oath to kill him . . .

"What do you want then?" Olaf demanded once more, ashamed that he could not lift his voice above a whisper.

The giant still grinned, then tossed what seemed the same suitcase upon Olaf's sofa and bent over it; he zippered it open with a sweep of his clawlike hand and rummaged in it, drawing forth a flat, gleaming white object done up in glowing cellophane. Olaf watched with lowered lids, wondering what trick was now being played on him. Then, before he could defend himself, the giant had whirled and again long, black, snakelike fingers were encircling Olaf's throat . . . Olaf stiffened, his right hand clawing blindly for the drawer where the gun was kept. But the giant was quick.

"Wait," he bellowed, pushing Olaf back from the desk.

The giant turned quickly to the sofa and, still holding his fingers in a wide circle that seemed a noose for Olaf's neck, he inserted the rounded fingers into the top of the flat, gleaming object. Olaf had the drawer open and his sweaty fingers were now touching the gun, but something made him freeze. The flat, gleaming object was a shirt and the black giant's circled fingers were fitting themselves into its neck . . .

"A perfect fit!" the giant shouted.

Olaf stared, trying to understand. His fingers loosened about the gun. A mixture of a laugh and a curse struggled in him. He watched the giant plunge his hands into the suitcase and pull out other flat, gleaming shirts.

"One, two, three, four, five, six," the black giant intoned, his voice crisp and businesslike. "Six nylon shirts. And they're all yours. One shirt for each time Lena came . . . See, Daddy-O?"

The black, cupped hands, filled with billowing nylon whiteness, were extended under Olaf's nose. Olaf eased his damp fingers from his gun and pushed the drawer closed, staring at the shirts and then at the black giant's grinning face.

"Don't you like 'em?" the giant asked.

Olaf began to laugh hysterically, then suddenly he was crying, his eyes so flooded with tears that the pile of dazzling nylon looked like snow in the dead of winter. Was this true? Could he believe it? Maybe this too was a trick? But, no. There were six shirts, all nylon, and the black giant had had Lena six nights.

"What's the matter with you, Daddy-O?" the giant asked. "You blowing your top? Laughing and crying . . ."

Olaf swallowed, dabbed his withered fists at his dimmed eyes; then he realized that he had his glasses on. He took them off and dried his eyes and sat up. He sighed, the tension and shame and fear and haunting dread of his fantasy went from him, and he leaned limply back in his chair . . .

"Try one on," the giant ordered.

Olaf fumbled with the buttons of his shirt, let down his suspenders, and pulled the shirt off. He donned a gleaming nylon one and the giant began buttoning it for him.

"Perfect, Daddy-O," the giant said.

His spectacled face framed in sparkling nylon, Olaf sat with trembling lips. So he'd not been trying to kill me after all.

"You want Lena, don't you?" he asked the giant in a soft whisper. "But I don't know where she is. She never came back here after you left—"

"I know where Lena is," the giant told him. "We been writing to each other. I'm going to her house. And, Daddy-O, I'm late." The giant zippered the suitcase shut and stood a moment gazing down at Olaf, his tiny little red eyes blinking slowly. Then Olaf realized that there was a compassion in that stare that he had never seen before.

"And I thought you wanted to kill me," Olaf told him. "I was scared of you . . ."

"Me? Kill you?" the giant blinked. "When?"

"That night when you put your fingers around my throat—"

"What?" the giant asked, then roared with laughter. "Daddy-O, you're a funny little man. I wouldn't hurt you. I like you. You a *good* man. You helped me."

Olaf smiled, clutching the pile of nylon shirts in his arms.

"You're a good man too," Olaf murmured. Then loudly, "You're a big black good man."

"Daddy-O, you're crazy," the giant said.

He swept his suitcase from the sofa, spun on his heel, and was at the door in one stride.

"Thanks!" Olaf cried after him.

The black giant paused, turned his vast black head, and flashed a grin.

"Daddy-O, drop dead," he said and was gone.

Reading and Reacting

1. Why do you suppose Wright has his third-person narrator see events through Olaf's eyes? How would the story be different if the sailor told it?
2. This story was published in 1957. What attitudes about race does Wright expect his American readers to have? Do these attitudes predispose readers to identify with the sailor or with Olaf? Explain.
3. Why does Olaf dislike the sailor? What does the narrator mean in paragraph 24 when he says that the sailor's "intense blackness and ungainly bigness [. . .] frightened and insulted Olaf"?
4. In what ways do the sailor's words and actions contribute to Olaf's fears? Do you think Olaf's reactions are reasonable, or do you believe he is overreacting?
5. The sailor's name is Jim, but this name is almost never used in the story. Why not? List some of the words by which Jim is identified. Why are they used? How do they affect your reaction to Jim?
6. Do you think the story's title is ironic? In what other respects is the story ironic?
7. How would "Big Black Good Man" be different if Jim were white? Would there even *be* a story?
8. Why do you think Wright set the story in Copenhagen? Could it have been set in the United States in 1957?
9. **JOURNAL ENTRY** What do you think Jim thinks of Olaf? Do you suppose he realizes the effect he has on him? How do you explain his last comment?

Related Works: "The Cask of Amontillado" (p. 136), "Girl" (p. 266), "We Wear the Mask" (p. 518), *The Brute* (p. 668)

◊ **EDGAR ALLAN POE** (1809–1849) had a profound impact on many corners of the literary world. His tales of psychological terror and the macabre, his haunting lyric poems, and his writings on poetry and the short story influenced the development of symbolism, the modern detective story, and the Gothic horror tale. In most of Poe's horror tales (as in "The Cask of Amontillado"), readers vicariously live the story through the first-person narrator.

In 1836, Poe married his frail thirteen-year-old cousin, Virginia Clemm. He produced many of his most famous stories and poems in the next few years, working feverishly to support his tubercular wife; but although his stories were widely admired, financial success never came. Less than two years after his wife's death in 1847, Poe was found barely conscious in a Baltimore street; three days later, he was dead at age forty.

◊ ◊ ◊

EDGAR ALLAN POE

The Cask of Amontillado
(1846)

The thousand injuries of Fortunato I had borne as I best could, but when he ventured upon insult I vowed revenge. You, who so well know the nature of my soul, will not suppose, however, that I gave utterance to a threat. *At length* I would be avenged; this was a point definitely settled—but the very definitiveness with which it was resolved precluded the idea of risk. I must not only punish but punish with impunity. A wrong is unredressed when retribution overtakes its redresser. It is equally unredressed when the avenger fails to make himself felt as such to him who has done the wrong.

It must be understood that neither by word nor deed had I given Fortunato cause to doubt my good will. I continued, as was my wont, to smile in his face, and he did not perceive that my smile *now* was at the thought of his immolation.

He had a weak point—this Fortunato—although in other regards he was a man to be respected and even feared. He prided himself on his connoisseurship in wine. Few Italians have the true virtuoso spirit. For the most part their enthusiasm is adopted to suit the time and opportunity, to practise imposture upon the British and Austrian *millionaires*. In painting and gemmary, Fortunato, like his countrymen, was a quack, but in the matter of old wines he was sincere. In this respect I did not differ from him materially;—I was skillful in the Italian vintages myself, and bought largely whenever I could.

It was about dusk, one evening during the supreme madness of the carnival season, that I encountered my friend. He accosted me with excessive warmth, for he had been drinking much. The man wore motley.[1] He had on a tight-fitting parti-striped dress, and his head was surmounted by the conical cap and bells. I was so pleased to see him that I thought I should never have done wringing his hand.

---
[1] The many-colored attire of a court jester.

I said to him—"My dear Fortunato, you are luckily met. How remarkably well you are looking to-day. But I have received a pipe[2] of what passes for Amontillado,[3] and I have my doubts."

"How?" said he. "Amontillado? A pipe? Impossible! And in the middle of the carnival!"

"I have my doubts," I replied; "and I was silly enough to pay the full Amontillado price without consulting you in the matter. You were not to be found, and I was fearful of losing a bargain."

"Amontillado!"

"I have my doubts."

"Amontillado!"

"And I must satisfy them."

"Amontillado!"

"As you are engaged, I am on my way to Luchresi. If any one has a critical turn it is he. He will tell me—"

"Luchresi cannot tell Amontillado from Sherry."

"And yet some fools will have it that his taste is a match for your own."

"Come, let us go."

"Whither?"

"To your vaults."

"My friend, no; I will not impose upon your good nature. I perceive you have an engagement. Luchresi—"

"I have no engagement;—come."

"My friend, no. It is not the engagement, but the severe cold with which I perceive you are afflicted. The vaults are insufferably damp. They are encrusted with nitre."[4]

"Let us go, nevertheless. The cold is merely nothing. Amontillado! You have been imposed upon. And as for Luchresi, he cannot distinguish Sherry from Amontillado."

Thus speaking, Fortunato possessed himself of my arm; and putting on a mask of black silk and drawing a *roquelaire*[5] closely about my person, I suffered him to hurry me to my palazzo.

There were no attendants at home; they had absconded to make merry in honor of the time. I had told them that I should not return until the morning, and had given them explicit orders not to stir from the house. These orders were sufficient, I well knew, to insure their immediate disappearance, one and all, as soon as my back was turned.

I took from their sconces two flambeaux, and giving one to Fortunato, bowed him through several suites of rooms to the archway that

---

[2] In the United States and England, a cask containing a volume equal to 126 gallons.

[3] A pale, dry sherry; literally, a wine "from Montilla" (Spain).

[4] Mineral deposits.

[5] A short cloak.

led into the vaults. I passed down a long and winding staircase, requesting him to be cautious as he followed. We came at length to the foot of the descent, and stood together upon the damp ground of the catacombs of the Montresors.

The gait of my friend was unsteady, and the bells upon his cap jingled as he strode.

"The pipe," he said.

"It is farther on," said I; "but observe the white web-work which gleams from these cavern walls."

He turned towards me, and looked into my eyes with two filmy orbs that distilled the rheum of intoxication.

"Nitre?" he asked at length.

"Nitre," I replied. "How long have you had that cough?"

"Ugh! ugh! ugh!—ugh! ugh! ugh!—ugh! ugh! ugh!—ugh! ugh! ugh!—ugh! ugh! ugh!"

My poor friend found it impossible to reply for many minutes.

"It is nothing," he said at last.

"Come," I said, with decision, "we will go back; your health is precious. You are rich, respected, admired, beloved; you are happy, as once I was. You are a man to be missed. For me it is no matter. We will go back; you will be ill, and I cannot be responsible. Besides, there is Luchresi—"

"Enough," he said; "the cough is a mere nothing; it will not kill me. I shall not die of a cough."

"True—true," I replied; "and, indeed, I had no intention of alarming you unnecessarily—but you should use all proper caution. A draught of this Médoc[6] will defend us from the damps."

Here I knocked off the neck of a bottle which I drew from a long row of its fellows that lay upon the mould.

"Drink," I said, presenting him the wine.

He raised it to his lips with a leer. He paused and nodded to me familiarly, while his bells jingled.

"I drink," he said, "to the buried that repose around us."

"And I to your long life."

He again took my arm, and we proceeded.

"These vaults," he said, "are extensive."

"The Montresors," I replied, "were a great and numerous family."

"I forget your arms."

"A huge human foot d'or, in a field azure; the foot crushes a serpent rampant whose fangs are imbedded in the heel."

"And the motto?"

"*Nemo me impune lacessit.*"[7]

"Good!" he said.

---

[6] A claret from the Médoc, near Bordeaux, France.
[7] "No one insults me with impunity"; this is the legend of the royal arms of Scotland.

The wine sparkled in his eyes and the bells jingled. My own fancy grew warm with the Médoc. We had passed through long walls of piled skeletons, with casks and puncheons[8] intermingling, into the inmost recesses of the catacombs. I paused again, and this time I made bold to seize Fortunato by an arm above the elbow.

"The nitre!" I said; "see, it increases. It hangs like moss upon the vaults. We are below the river's bed. The drops of moisture trickle among the bones. Come, we will go back ere it is too late. Your cough—"

"It is nothing," he said; "let us go on. But first, another draught of the Médoc."

I broke and reached him a flagon of De Grâve.[9] He emptied it at a breath. His eyes flashed with a fierce light. He laughed and threw the bottle upwards with a gesticulation I did not understand.

I looked at him in surprise. He repeated the movement—a grotesque one.

"You do not comprehend?" he said.

"Not I," I replied.

"Then you are not of the brotherhood."

"How?"

"You are not of the masons."[10]

"Yes, yes," I said; "yes, yes."

"You? Impossible! A mason?"

"A mason," I replied.

"A sign," he said, "a sign."

"It is this," I answered, producing from beneath the folds of my *roquelaire* a trowel.

"You jest," he exclaimed, recoiling a few paces. "But let us proceed to the Amontillado."

"Be it so," I said, replacing the tool beneath the cloak and again offering him my arm. He leaned upon it heavily. We continued our route in search of the Amontillado. We passed through a range of low arches, descended, passed on, and descending again, arrived at a deep crypt, in which the foulness of the air caused our flambeaux rather to glow than flame.

At the most remote end of the crypt there appeared another less spacious. Its walls had been lined with human remains, piled to the vault overhead, in the fashion of the great catacombs of Paris. Three sides of this interior crypt were still ornamented in this manner. From the fourth side the bones had been thrown down, and lay promiscuously upon the earth, forming at one point a mound of some size. Within the wall thus exposed by the displacing of the bones, we perceived a still

---

[8] Barrel.

[9] Correctly, "Gráves," a light wine from the Bordeaux area.

[10] Freemasons (members of a secret fraternity). The trowel is a symbol of their alleged origin as a guild of stonemasons.

interior crypt or recess, in depth about four feet, in width three, in height six or seven. It seemed to have been constructed for no especial use within itself, but formed merely the interval between two of the colossal supports of the roof of the catacombs, and was backed by one of their circumscribing walls of solid granite.

It was in vain that Fortunato, uplifting his dull torch, endeavored to pry into the depth of the recess. Its termination the feeble light did not enable us to see.

"Proceed," I said; "herein is the Amontillado. As for Luchresi—"

"He is an ignoramus," interrupted my friend, as he stepped unsteadily forward, while I followed immediately at his heels. In an instant he had reached the extremity of the niche, and finding his progress arrested by the rock, stood stupidly bewildered. A moment more and I had fettered him to the granite. In its surface were two iron staples, distant from each other about two feet, horizontally. From one of these depended a short chain, from the other a padlock. Throwing the links about his waist, it was but the work of a few seconds to secure it. He was too much astounded to resist. Withdrawing the key I stepped back from the recess.

"Pass your hand," I said, "over the wall; you cannot help feeling the nitre. Indeed, it is *very* damp. Once more let me *implore* you to return. No? Then I must positively leave you. But I must first render you all the little attentions in my power."

"The Amontillado!" ejaculated my friend, not yet recovered from his astonishment.

"True," I replied; "the Amontillado."

As I said these words I busied myself among the pile of bones of which I have before spoken. Throwing them aside, I soon uncovered a quantity of building stone and mortar. With these materials and with the aid of my trowel, I began vigorously to wall up the entrance of the niche.

I had scarcely laid the first tier of the masonry when I discovered that the intoxication of Fortunato had in a great measure worn off. The earliest indication I had of this was a low moaning cry from the depth of the recess. It was *not* the cry of a drunken man. There was a long and obstinate silence. I laid the second tier, and the third, and the fourth; and then I heard the furious vibrations of the chain. The noise lasted for several minutes, during which, that I might hearken to it with the more satisfaction, I ceased my labors and sat down upon the bones. When at last the clanking subsided, I resumed the trowel, and finished without interruption the fifth, the sixth, and the seventh tier. The wall was now nearly upon a level with my breast. I again paused, and holding the flambeaux over the mason-work, threw a few feeble rays upon the figure within.

A succession of loud and shrill screams, bursting suddenly from the throat of the chained form, seemed to thrust me violently back. For a brief moment I hesitated, I trembled. Unsheathing my rapier, I began to grope with it about the recess; but the thought of an instant reassured me. I placed my hand upon the solid fabric of the catacombs, and felt satisfied. I reapproached the wall; I replied to the yells of him who clamoured. I reechoed, I aided, I surpassed them in volume and in strength. I did this, and the clamourer grew still.

It was now midnight, and my task was drawing to a close. I had completed the eighth, the ninth and the tenth tier. I had finished a portion of the last and the eleventh; there remained but a single stone to be fitted and plastered in. I struggled with its weight; I placed it partially in its destined position. But now there came from out the niche a low laugh that erected the hairs upon my head. It was succeeded by a sad voice, which I had difficulty in recognizing as that of the noble Fortunato. The voice said—

"Ha! ha! ha!—he! he! he!—a very good joke, indeed—an excellent jest. We will have many a rich laugh about it at the palazzo—he! he! he!—over our wine—he! he! he!"

80 "The Amontillado!" I said.

"He! he! he!—he! he! he!—yes, the Amontillado. But is it not getting late? Will not they be awaiting us at the palazzo, the Lady Fortunato and the rest? Let us be gone."

"Yes," I said, "let us be gone."

"For the love of God, Montresor!"

"Yes," I said, "for the love of God."

85 But to these words I hearkened in vain for a reply. I grew impatient. I called aloud—

"Fortunato!"

No answer. I called again—

"Fortunato!"

No answer still. I thrust a torch through the remaining aperture and let it fall within. There came forth in return only a jingling of the bells. My heart grew sick; it was the dampness of the catacombs that made it so. I hastened to make an end of my labour. I forced the last stone into its position; I plastered it up. Against the new masonry I re-erected the old rampart of bones. For the half of a century no mortal has disturbed them. *In pace requiescat!*[11]

READING AND REACTING

1. Montresor cites a "thousand injuries" and an "insult" as his motivation for murdering Fortunato. Given what you learn about the two men during the course of the story, what do you suppose the "injuries" and "insult" might be?
2. Do you find Montresor to be a reliable narrator? If not, what makes you question his version of events?

---

[11] "May he rest in peace."

3. What is Montresor's concept of personal honor? Is it consistent or inconsistent with the values of contemporary American society? How relevant are the story's ideas about revenge and guilt to present-day society? Explain.
4. Does Fortunato ever understand why Montresor hates him? What is Fortunato's attitude toward Montresor?
5. What is the significance of Montresor's family coat of arms and motto? What is the significance of Fortunato's costume?
6. In what ways does Montresor manipulate Fortunato? What weaknesses does Montresor exploit?
7. Why does Montresor wait fifty years to tell his story? How might the story be different if he had told it the next morning?
8. Why does Montresor wait for a reply before he puts the last stone in position? What do you think he wants Fortunato to say?
9. **JOURNAL ENTRY** Do you think the use of a first-person point of view makes you more sympathetic toward Montresor than you would be if his story were told by a third-person narrator? Why or why not?

Related Works: "A Rose for Emily" (p. 52), "The Love Song of J. Alfred Prufrock" (p. 519), *Trifles* (p. 586)

◊ **WILLIAM FAULKNER** (1897–1962) (picture and biography on p. 51) "Barn Burning" marks the first appearance of the Snopes clan in Faulkner's fiction. These crafty tenant farmers and traders run roughshod over the aristocratic families of Yoknapatawpha County in three later Faulkner novels. In Southern literary circles, the name "Snopes" still serves as a shorthand term for the greedy (but frequently successful) opportunists of the "New South."

◊ ◊ ◊

WILLIAM FAULKNER

Barn Burning
(1939)

The store in which the Justice of the Peace's court was sitting smelled of cheese. The boy, crouched on his nail keg at the back of the crowded room, knew he smelled cheese, and more: from where he sat he could see the ranked shelves close-packed with the solid, squat, dynamic shapes of tin cans whose labels his stomach read, not from the lettering which meant nothing to his mind but from the scarlet devils and the silver curve of fish—this, the cheese which he knew he smelled and the hermetic meat[1] which his intestines believed he smelled coming in intermittent gusts momentary and brief between the other constant one, the smell and sense just a little of fear because mostly of despair and grief, the old fierce pull of blood. He could not see the table where the Justice sat and before which his father and his father's enemy (*our enemy* he thought in that despair; *ourn! mine and hisn both! He's my father!*) stood, but he could hear them, the two of them that is, because his father had said no word yet:

"But what proof have you, Mr. Harris?"

"I told you. The hog got into my corn. I caught it up and sent it back to him. He had no fence that would hold it. I told him so, warned him. The next time I put the hog in my pen. When he came to get it I gave him enough wire to patch up his pen. The next time I put the hog up and kept it. I rode down to his house and saw the wire I gave him still rolled on to the spool in his yard. I told him he could have the hog when he paid me a dollar pound fee. That evening a nigger came with the dollar and got the hog. He was a strange nigger. He said, 'He say to tell you wood and hay kin burn.' I said, 'What?' 'That whut he say to tell you,' the nigger said. 'Wood and hay kin burn.' That night my barn burned. I got the stock out but I lost the barn."

"Where is the nigger? Have you got him?"

5   "He was a strange nigger, I tell you. I don't know what became of him."

"But that's not proof. Don't you see that's not proof?"

"Get that boy up here. He knows." For a moment the boy thought too that the man meant his older brother until Harris said, "Not him. The little one. The boy," and, crouching, small for his age, small and wiry like his father, in patched and faded jeans even too small for him, with straight, uncombed, brown hair and eyes gray and wild as storm scud, he saw the men between himself and the table part and become a lane of grim faces, at the end of which he saw the Justice, a shabby, collarless, graying man in spectacles, beckoning him. He felt no floor under his bare feet; he seemed to walk beneath the palpable weight of the grim turning faces. His father, stiff in his black Sunday coat donned not for the trial but for the moving, did not even look at him. *He aims for me to lie,* he thought, again with that frantic grief and despair. *And I will have to do hit.*

"What's your name, boy?" the Justice said.

"Colonel Sartoris Snopes," the boy whispered.

10 "Hey?" the Justice said. "Talk louder. Colonel Sartoris? I reckon anybody named for Colonel Sartoris in this country can't help but tell the truth, can they?" The boy said nothing. *Enemy! Enemy!* he thought; for a moment he could not even see, could not see that the Justice's face was

---

[1] Canned meat.

kindly nor discern that his voice was troubled when he spoke to the man named Harris: "Do you want me to question this boy?" But he could hear, and during those subsequent long seconds while there was absolutely no sound in the crowded little room save that of quiet and intent breathing it was as if he had swung outward at the end of a grape vine, over a ravine, and at the top of the swing had been caught in a prolonged instant of mesmerized gravity, weightless in time.

"No!" Harris said violently, explosively. "Damnation! Send him out of here!" Now time, the fluid world, rushed beneath him again, the voices coming to him again through the smell of cheese and sealed meat, the fear and despair and the old grief of blood:

"This case is closed. I can't find against you, Snopes, but I can give you advice. Leave this country and don't come back to it."

His father spoke for the first time, his voice cold and harsh, level, without emphasis: "I aim to. I don't figure to stay in a country among people who . . ." he said something unprintable and vile, addressed to no one.

"That'll do," the Justice said. "Take your wagon and get out of this country before dark. Case dismissed."

15 His father turned, and he followed the stiff black coat, the wiry figure walking a little stiffly from where a Confederate provost's man's[2] musket ball had taken him in the heel on a stolen horse thirty years ago, followed the two backs now, since his older brother had appeared from somewhere in the crowd, no taller than the father but thicker, chewing tobacco steadily, between the two lines of grim-faced men and out of the store and across the worn gallery and down the sagging steps and among the dogs and half-grown boys in the mild May dust, where as he passed a voice hissed:

"Barn burner!"

Again he could not see, whirling; there was a face in a red haze, moonlike, bigger than the full moon, the owner of it half again his size, he leaping in the red haze toward the face, feeling no blow, feeling no shock when his head struck the earth, scrabbling up and leaping again, feeling no blow this time either and tasting no blood, scrabbling up to see the other boy in full flight and himself already leaping into pursuit as his father's hand jerked him back, the harsh, cold voice speaking above him: "Go get in the wagon."

It stood in a grove of locusts and mulberries across the road. His two hulking sisters in their Sunday dresses and his mother and her sister in calico and sunbonnets were already in it, sitting on and among the sorry residue of the dozen and more movings which even the boy could remember—the battered stove, the broken beds and chairs, the clock inlaid with mother-of-pearl, which would not run, stopped at some fourteen

---

[2] Military policeman.

minutes past two o'clock of a dead and forgotten day and time, which had been his mother's dowry. She was crying, though when she saw him she drew her sleeve across her face and began to descend from the wagon. "Get back," the father said.

"He's hurt. I got to get some water and wash his . . ."

"Get back in the wagon," his father said. He got in too, over the tailgate. His father mounted to the seat where the older brother already sat and struck the gaunt mules two savage blows with the peeled willow, but without heat. It was not even sadistic; it was exactly that same quality which in later years would cause his descendants to overrun the engine before putting a motor car into motion, striking and reining back in the same movement. The wagon went on, the store with its quiet crowd of grimly watching men dropped behind; a curve in the road hid it. *Forever* he thought. *Maybe he's done satisfied now, now that he has* . . . stopping himself, not to say it aloud even to himself. His mother's hand touched his shoulder.

"Does hit hurt?" she said.

"Naw," he said. "Hit don't hurt. Lemme be."

"Can't you wipe some of the blood off before hit dries?"

"I'll wash to-night," he said. "Lemme be, I tell you."

The wagon went on. He did not know where they were going. None of them ever did or ever asked, because it was always somewhere, always a house of sorts waiting for them a day or two days or even three days away. Likely his father had already arranged to make a crop on another farm before he . . . Again he had to stop himself. He (the father) always did. There was something about his wolf-like independence and even courage when the advantage was at least neutral which impressed strangers, as if they got from his latent ravening ferocity not so much a sense of dependability as a feeling that his ferocious conviction in the rightness of his own actions would be of advantage to all whose interest lay with his.

That night they camped, in a grove of oaks and beeches where a spring ran. The nights were still cool and they had a fire against it, of a rail lifted from a nearby fence and cut into lengths—a small fire, neat, niggard almost, a shrewd fire; such fires were his father's habit and custom always, even in freezing weather. Older, the boy might have remarked this and wondered why not a big one; why should not a man who had not only seen the waste and extravagance of war, but who had in his blood an inherent voracious prodigality with material not his own, have burned everything in sight? Then he might have gone a step farther and thought that that was the reason: that niggard blaze was the living fruit of nights passed during those four years in the woods hiding from all men, blue or gray, with his strings of horses (captured horses, he called them). And older still, he might have divined the true reason: that the element of fire spoke to some deep mainspring of his father's being, as the element of steel or of powder spoke to other men, as the one weapon for the preservation of integrity, else breath were not worth the breathing, and hence to be regarded with respect and used with discretion.

But he did not think this now and he had seen those same niggard blazes all his life. He merely ate his supper beside it and was already half asleep over his iron plate when his father called him, and once more he followed the stiff back, the stiff and ruthless limp, up the slope and on to the starlit road where, turning, he could see his father against the stars but without face or depth—a shape black, flat, and bloodless as though cut from tin in the iron folds of the frockcoat which had not been made for him, the voice harsh like tin and without heat like tin:

"You were fixing to tell them. You would have told him." He didn't answer. His father struck him with the flat of his hand on the side of the head, hard but without heat, exactly as he had struck the two mules at the store, exactly as he would strike either of them with any stick in order to kill a horse fly, his voice still without fear or anger: "You're getting to be a man. You got to learn. You got to learn to stick to your own blood or you ain't going to have any blood to stick to you. Do you think either of them, any man there this morning, would? Don't you know all they wanted was a chance to get at me because they knew I had them beat? Eh?" Later, twenty years later, he was to tell himself, "If I had said they wanted only truth, justice, he would have hit me again." But now he said nothing. He was not crying. He just stood there. "Answer me," his father said.

"Yes," he whispered. His father turned.

"Get on to bed. We'll be there tomorrow."

Tomorrow they were there. In the early afternoon the wagon stopped before a paintless two-room house identical almost with the dozen others it had stopped before even in the boy's ten years, and again, as on the other dozen occasions, his mother and aunt got down and began to unload the wagon, although his two sisters and his father and brother had not moved.

"Likely hit ain't fitten for hawgs," one of the sisters said.

"Nevertheless, fit it will and you'll hog it and like it," his father said. "Get out of them chairs and help your Ma unload."

The two sisters got down, big, bovine, in a flutter of cheap ribbons; one of them drew from the jumbled wagon bed a battered lantern, the other a worn broom. His father handed the reins to the older son and began to climb stiffly over the wheel. "When they get unloaded, take the team to the barn and feed them." Then he said, and at first the boy thought he was still speaking to his brother: "Come with me."

"Me?" he said.

"Yes," his father said. "You."

"Abner," his mother said. His father paused and looked back—the harsh level stare beneath the shaggy, graying, irascible brows.

"I reckon I'll have a word with the man that aims to begin tomorrow owning me body and soul for the next eight months."

They went back up the road. A week ago—or before last night, that is—he would have asked where they were going, but not now. His father had struck him before last night but never before had he paused afterward to explain why; it was as if the blow and the following calm, outrageous voice still rang, repercussed, divulging nothing to him save the terrible handicap of being young, the light weight of his few years, just heavy enough to prevent his soaring free of the world as it seemed to be ordered but not heavy enough to keep him footed solid in it, to resist it and try to change the course of its events.

40   Presently he could see the grove of oaks and cedars and the other flowering trees and shrubs, where the house would be, though not the house yet. They walked beside a fence massed with honeysuckle and Cherokee roses and came to a gate swinging open between two brick pillars, and now, beyond a sweep of drive, he saw the house for the first time and at that instant he forgot his father and the terror and despair both, and even when he remembered his father again (who had not stopped) the terror and despair did not return. Because, for all the twelve movings, they had sojourned until now in a poor country, a land of small farms and fields and houses, and he had never seen a house like this before. *Hit's big as a courthouse* he thought quietly, with a surge of peace and joy whose reason he could not have thought into words, being too young for that: *They are safe from him. People whose lives are a part of this peace and dignity are beyond his touch, he no more to them than a buzzing wasp: capable of stinging for a little moment but that's all; the spell of this peace and dignity rendering even the barns and stable and cribs which belong to it impervious to the puny flames he might contrive . . .* this, the peace and joy, ebbing for an instant as he looked again at the stiff black back, the stiff and implacable limp of the figure which was not dwarfed by the house, for the reason that it had never looked big anywhere and which now, against the serene columned backdrop, had more than ever that impervious quality of something cut ruthlessly from tin, depthless, as though, sidewise to the sun, it would cast no shadow. Watching him, the boy remarked the absolutely undeviating course which his father held and saw the stiff foot come squarely down in a pile of fresh droppings where a horse had stood in the drive and which his father could have avoided by a simple change of stride. But it ebbed only for a moment, though he could not have thought this into words either, walking on in the spell of the house, which he could even want but without envy, without sorrow, certainly never with that ravening and jealous rage which unknown to him walked in the ironlike black coat before him: *Maybe he will feel it too. Maybe it will even change him now from what maybe he couldn't help but be.*

They crossed the portico. Now he could hear his father's stiff foot as it came down on the boards with clocklike finality, a sound out of all proportion to the displacement of the body it bore and which was not dwarfed either by the white door before it, as though it had attained to a sort of vicious and ravening minimum not to be dwarfed by anything— the flat, wide, black hat, the formal coat of broadcloth which had once been black but which had now that friction-glazed greenish cast of the bodies of old house flies, the lifted sleeve which was too large, the lifted hand like a curled claw. The door opened so promptly that the boy knew the Negro must have been watching them all the time, an old man with neat grizzled hair, in a linen jacket, who stood barring the door with his body, saying, "Wipe yo foots, white man, fo you come in here. Major ain't home nohow."

"Get out of my way, nigger," his father said, without heat too, flinging the door back and the Negro also and entering, his hat still on his head. And now the boy saw the prints of the stiff foot on the doorjamb and saw them appear on the pale rug behind the machinelike deliberation of the foot which seemed to bear (or transmit) twice the weight which the body compassed. The Negro was shouting "Miss Lula! Miss Lula!" somewhere behind them, then the boy, deluged as though by a warm wave by a suave turn of carpeted stair and a pendant glitter of chandeliers and a mute gleam of gold frames, heard the swift feet and saw her too, a lady—perhaps he had never seen her like before either—in a gray, smooth gown with lace at the throat and an apron tied at the waist and the sleeves turned back, wiping cake or biscuit dough from her hands with a towel as she came up the hall, looking not at his father at all but at the tracks on the blond rug with an expression of incredulous amazement.

"I tried," the Negro cried, "I tole him to . . ."

"Will you please go away?" she said in a shaking voice. "Major de Spain is not at home. Will you please go away?"

45   His father had not spoken again. He did not speak again. He did not even look at her. He just stood stiff in the center of the rug, in his hat, the shaggy iron-gray brows twitching slightly above the pebble-colored eyes as he appeared to examine the house with brief deliberation. Then with the same deliberation he turned; the boy watched him pivot on the good leg and saw the stiff foot drag round the arc of the turning, leaving a final long and fading smear. His father never looked at it, he never once looked down at the rug. The Negro held the door. It closed behind them, upon the hysteric and indistinguishable woman-wail. His father stopped at the top of the steps and scraped his boot clean on the edge of it. At the gate he stopped again. He stood for a moment, planted stiffly on the stiff foot, looking back at the house. "Pretty and white, ain't it?" he said. "That's sweat. Nigger sweat. Maybe it ain't white enough yet to suit him. Maybe he wants to mix some white sweat with it."

Two hours later the boy was chopping wood behind the house within which his mother and aunt and the two sisters (the mother and aunt, not the two girls, he knew that; even at this distance and muffled by walls the flat loud voices of the two girls emanated an incorrigible idle inertia) were setting up the stove to prepare a meal, when he heard the hooves and saw the linen-clad man on a fine sorrel mare, whom he recognized even before he saw the rolled rug in front of the Negro youth following on a fat bay carriage horse—a suffused, angry face vanishing, still at full gallop, beyond the corner of the house where his father and brother were sitting in the two tilted chairs; and a moment later, almost before he could have put the axe down, he heard the hooves again and watched the sorrel mare go back out of the yard, already galloping again. Then his father began to shout one of the sisters' names, who presently emerged backward from the kitchen door dragging the rolled rug along the ground by one end while the other sister walked behind it.

"If you ain't going to tote, go on and set up the wash pot," the first said.

"You, Sarty!" the second shouted. "Set up the wash pot!" His father appeared at the door, framed against that shabbiness, as he had been against that other bland perfection, impervious to either, the mother's anxious face at his shoulder.

"Go on," the father said. "Pick it up." The two sisters stooped, broad, lethargic; stooping, they presented an incredible expanse of pale cloth and a flutter of tawdry ribbons.

"If I thought enough of a rug to have to git hit all the way from France I wouldn't keep hit where folks coming in would have to tromp on hit," the first said. They raised the rug.

"Abner," the mother said. "Let me do it."

"You go back and git dinner," his father said. "I'll tend to this."

From the woodpile through the rest of the afternoon the boy watched them, the rug spread flat in the dust beside the bubbling washpot, the two sisters stooping over it with that profound and lethargic reluctance, while the father stood over them in turn, implacable and grim, driving them though never raising his voice again. He could smell the harsh homemade lye[3] they were using; he saw his mother come to the door once and look toward them with an expression not anxious now but very like despair; he saw his father turn, and he fell to with the axe and saw from the corner of his eye his father raise from the ground a flattish fragment of field stone and examine it and return to the pot, and this time his mother actually spoke: "Abner. Abner. Please don't. Please, Abner."

Then he was done too. It was dusk; the whippoorwills had already begun. He could smell coffee from the room where they would presently eat the cold food remaining from the mid-afternoon meal, though when he entered the house he realized they were having coffee again probably because there was a fire on the hearth, before which the rug now lay spread over the backs of the two chairs. The tracks of his father's foot were gone. Where they had been were now long, water-cloudy scoriations resembling the sporadic course of a Lilliputian mowing machine.

It still hung there while they ate the cold food and then went to bed, scattered without order or claim up and down the two rooms, his mother in one bed, where his father would later lie, the older brother in

---

[3] A soap made from wood ashes and water, unsuitable for washing fine fabrics.

the other, himself, the aunt, and the two sisters on pallets on the floor. But his father was not in bed yet. The last thing the boy remembered was the depthless, harsh silhouette of the hat and coat bending over the rug and it seemed to him that he had not even closed his eyes when the silhouette was standing over him, the fire almost dead behind it, the stiff foot prodding him awake. "Catch up the mule," his father said.

When he returned with the mule his father was standing in the black door, the rolled rug over his shoulder. "Ain't you going to ride?" he said.

"No. Give me your foot."

He bent his knee into his father's hand, the wiry, surprising power flowed smoothly, rising, he rising with it, on to the mule's bare back (they had owned a saddle once; the boy could remember it though not when or where) and with the same effortlessness his father swung the rug up in front of him. Now in the starlight they retraced the afternoon's path, up the dusty road rife with honeysuckle, through the gate and up the black tunnel to the drive to the lightless house, where he sat on the mule and felt the rough warp of the rug drag across his thighs and vanish.

"Don't you want me to help?" he whispered. His father did not answer and now he heard again that stiff foot striking the hollow portico with that wooden and clocklike deliberation, that outrageous overstatement of the weight it carried. The rug, hunched, not flung (the boy could tell that even in the darkness) from his father's shoulder struck the angle of wall and floor with a sound unbelievably loud, thunderous, then the foot again, unhurried and enormous; a light came on in the house and the boy sat, tense, breathing steadily and quietly and just a little fast, though the foot itself did not increase its beat at all, descending the steps now; now the boy could see him.

"Don't you want to ride now?" he whispered. "We kin both ride now," the light within the house altering now, flaring up and sinking. *He's coming down the stairs now,* he thought. He had already ridden the mule up beside the horse block; presently his father was up behind him and he doubled the reins over and slashed the mule across the neck, but before the animal could begin to trot the hard, thin arm came round him, the hard, knotted hand jerking the mule back to a walk.

In the first red rays of the sun they were in the lot, putting plow gear on the mules. This time the sorrel mare was in the lot before he heard it at all, the rider collarless and even bareheaded, trembling, speaking in a shaking voice as the woman in the house had done, his father merely looking up once before stooping again to the hame[4] he was buckling, so that the man on the mare spoke to his stooping back:

"You must realize you have ruined that rug. Wasn't there anybody here, any of your women . . ." he ceased, shaking, the boy watching him,

---

[4] Harness.

the older brother leaning now in the stable door, chewing, blinking slowly and steadily at nothing apparently. "It cost a hundred dollars. But you never had a hundred dollars. You never will. So I'm going to charge you twenty bushels of corn against your crop. I'll add it in your contract and when you come to the commissary you can sign it. That won't keep Mrs. de Spain quiet but maybe it will teach you to wipe your feet off before you enter her house again."

Then he was gone. The boy looked at his father, who still had not spoken or even looked up again, who was now adjusting the loggerhead in the hame.

"Pap," he said. His father looked at him—the inscrutable face, the shaggy brows beneath which the gray eyes glinted coldly. Suddenly the boy went toward him, fast, stopping as suddenly. "You done the best you could!" he cried. "If he wanted hit done different why didn't he wait and tell you how? He won't git no twenty bushels! He won't git none! We'll gether hit and hide hit! I kin watch . . ."

"Did you put the cutter back in that straight stock like I told you?"

"No, sir," he said.

"Then go do it."

That was Wednesday. During the rest of that week he worked steadily, at what was within his scope and some which was beyond it, with an industry that did not need to be driven nor even commanded twice; he had this from his mother, with the difference that some at least of what he did he liked to do, such as splitting wood with the half-size axe which his mother and aunt had earned, or saved money somehow, to present him with at Christmas. In company with the two older women (and on one afternoon, even one of the sisters), he built pens for the shoat and the cow which were a part of his father's contract with the landlord, and one afternoon, his father being absent, gone somewhere on one of the mules, he went to the field.

They were running a middle buster now, his brother holding the plow straight while he handled the reins, and walking beside the straining mule, the rich black soil shearing cool and damp against his bare ankles, he thought *Maybe this is the end of it. Maybe even that twenty bushels that seems hard to have to pay for just a rug will be a cheap price for him to stop forever and always from being what he used to be;* thinking, dreaming now, so that his brother had to speak sharply to him to mind the mule: *Maybe he even won't collect the twenty bushels. Maybe it will all add up and balance and vanish—corn, rug, fire; the terror and grief, the being pulled two ways like between two teams of horses—gone, done with for ever and ever.*

Then it was Saturday; he looked up from beneath the mule he was harnessing and saw his father in the black coat and hat. "Not that," his father said. "The wagon gear." And then, two hours later, sitting in the wagon bed behind his father and brother on the seat, the wagon accomplished a final curve, and he saw the weathered paintless store with its tattered tobacco- and patent-medicine posters and the tethered wagons and saddle animals below the gallery. He mounted the gnawed steps behind his father and brother, and there again was the lane of quiet, watching faces for the three of them to walk through. He saw the man in spectacles sitting at the plank table and he did not need to be told this was a Justice of the Peace; he sent one glare of fierce, exultant, partisan defiance at the man in collar and cravat now, whom he had seen but twice before in his life, and that on a galloping horse, who now wore on his face an expression not of rage but of amazed unbelief which the boy could not have known was at the incredible circumstance of being sued by one of his own tenants, and came and stood against his father and cried at the Justice: "He ain't done it! He ain't burnt . . ."

"Go back to the wagon," his father said.

"Burnt?" the Justice said. "Do I understand this rug was burned too?"

"Does anybody here claim it was?" his father said. "Go back to the wagon." But he did not, he merely retreated to the rear of the room, crowded as that other had been, but not to sit down this time, instead, to stand pressing among the motionless bodies, listening to the voices:

"And you claim twenty bushels of corn is too high for the damage you did to the rug?"

"He brought the rug to me and said he wanted the tracks washed out of it. I washed the tracks out and took the rug back to him."

"But you didn't carry the rug back to him in the same condition it was in before you made the tracks on it."

His father did not answer, and now for perhaps half a minute there was no sound at all save that of breathing, the faint, steady suspiration of complete and intent listening.

"You decline to answer that, Mr. Snopes?" Again his father did not answer. "I'm going to find against you, Mr. Snopes. I'm going to find that you were responsible for the injury to Major de Spain's rug and hold you liable for it. But twenty bushels of corn seems a little high for a man in your circumstances to have to pay. Major de Spain claims it cost a hundred dollars. October corn will be worth about fifty cents. I figure that if Major de Spain can stand a ninety-five dollar loss on something he paid cash for, you can stand a five-dollar loss you haven't earned yet. I hold you in damages to Major de Spain to the amount of ten bushels of corn over and above your contract with him, to be paid to him out of your crop at gathering time. Court adjourned."

It had taken no time hardly, the morning was but half begun. He thought they would return home and perhaps back to the field, since they were late, far behind all other farmers. But instead his father passed on behind the wagon, merely indicating with his hand for the older brother to follow with it, and crossed the road toward the blacksmith shop opposite, pressing on after his father, overtaking him, speaking, whispering up at the harsh, calm face beneath the weathered hat: "He won't git no ten bushels neither. He won't git one. We'll . . ." until his father glanced for an instant down at him, the face absolutely calm, the grizzled eyebrows tangled above the cold eyes, the voice almost pleasant, almost gentle:

80 "You think so? Well, we'll wait till October anyway."

The matter of the wagon—the setting of a spoke or two and the tightening of the tires—did not take long either, the business of the tires accomplished by driving the wagon into the spring branch behind the shop and letting it stand there, the mules nuzzling into the water from time to time, and the boy on the seat with the idle reins, looking up the slope and through the sooty tunnel of the shed where the slow hammer rang and where his father sat on an upended cypress bolt, easily, either talking or listening, still sitting there when the boy brought the dripping wagon up out of the branch and halted it before the door.

"Take them on to the shade and hitch," his father said. He did so and returned. His father and the smith and a third man squatting on his heels inside the door were talking, about crops and animals; the boy, squatting too in the ammoniac dust and hoof-parings and scales of rust, heard his father tell a long and unhurried story out of the time before the birth of the older brother even when he had been a professional horsetrader. And then his father came up beside him where he stood before a tattered last year's circus poster on the other side of the store, gazing rapt and quiet at the scarlet horses, the incredible poisings and convolutions of tulle and tights and the painted leers of comedians, and said, "It's time to eat."

But not at home. Squatting beside his brother against the front wall, he watched his father emerge from the store and produce from a paper sack a segment of cheese and divide it carefully and deliberately into three with his pocket knife and produce crackers from the same sack. They all three squatted on the gallery and ate, slowly, without talking; then in the store again, they drank from a tin dipper tepid water smelling of the cedar bucket and of living beech trees. And still they did not go home. It was a horse lot this time, a tall rail fence upon and along which men stood and sat and out of which one by one horses were led, to be walked and trotted and then cantered back and forth along the road while the slow swapping and buying went on and the sun began to slant westward, they—the three of them—watching and listening, the older brother with his muddy eyes and his steady, inevitable tobacco, the father commenting now and then on certain of the animals, to no one in particular.

It was after sundown when they reached home. They ate supper by lamplight, then, sitting on the doorstep, the boy watched the night fully accomplish, listening to the whippoorwills and the frogs, when he heard his mother's voice: "Abner! No! No! Oh, God. Oh, God. Abner!" and he rose, whirled, and saw the altered light through the door where a candle stub now burned in a bottle neck on the table and his father, still in the hat and coat, at once formal and burlesque as though dressed carefully for some shabby and ceremonial violence, emptying the reservoir of the lamp back into the five-gallon kerosene can from which it had been filled, while the mother tugged at his arm until he shifted the lamp to the other hand and flung her back, not savagely or viciously, just hard, into the wall, her hands flung out against the wall for balance, her mouth open and in her face the same quality of hopeless despair as had been in her voice. Then his father saw him standing in the door.

85 "Go to the barn and get that can of oil we were oiling the wagon with," he said. The boy did not move. Then he could speak.

"What . . ." he cried. "What are you . . ."

"Go get that oil," his father said. "Go."

Then he was moving, running, outside the house, toward the stable: this the old habit, the old blood which he had not been permitted to choose for himself, which had been bequeathed him willy nilly and which had run for so long (and who knew where, battening on what of outrage and savagery and lust) before it came to him. *I could keep on,* he thought. *I could run on and on and never look back, never need to see his face again. Only I can't. I can't,* the rusted can in his hand now, the liquid sploshing in it as he ran back to the house and into it, into the sound of his mother's weeping in the next room, and handed the can to his father.

"Ain't you going to even send a nigger?" he cried. "At least you sent a nigger before!"

90 This time his father didn't strike him. The hand came even faster than the blow had, the same hand which had set the can on the table with almost excruciating care flashing from the can toward him too quick for him to follow it, gripping him by the back of his shirt and on to tiptoe before he had seen it quit the can, the face stooping at him in breathless and frozen ferocity, the cold, dead voice speaking over him to the older brother who leaned against the table, chewing with that steady, curious, sidewise motion of cows:

"Empty the can into the big one and go on. I'll catch up with you."

"Better tie him to the bedpost," the brother said.

"Do like I told you," the father said. Then the boy was moving, his bunched shirt and the hard, bony hand between his shoulderblades, his toes just touching the floor, across the room and into the other one, past the sisters sitting with spread heavy thighs in the two chairs over the cold hearth, and to where his mother and aunt sat side by side on the bed, the aunt's arms about his mother's shoulders.

"Hold him," the father said. The aunt made a startled movement. "Not you," the father said. "Lennie. Take hold of him. I want to see you do it." His mother took him by the wrist. "You'll hold him better than that. If he gets loose don't you know what he is going to do? He will go up yonder." He jerked his head toward the road. "Maybe I'd better tie him."

95 "I'll hold him," his mother whispered.

"See you do then." Then his father was gone, the stiff foot heavy and measured upon the boards, ceasing at last.

Then he began to struggle. His mother caught him in both arms, he jerking and wrenching at them. He would be stronger in the end, he knew that. But he had no time to wait for it. "Lemme go!" he cried. "I don't want to have to hit you!"

"Let him go!" the aunt said. "If he don't go, before God, I am going up there myself!"

"Don't you see I can't?" his mother cried. "Sarty! Sarty! No! No! Help me, Lizzie!"

100 Then he was free. His aunt grasped at him but it was too late. He whirled, running, his mother stumbled forward on to her knees behind him, crying to the nearest sister: "Catch him, Net! Catch him!" But that was too late too, the sister (the sisters were twins, born at the same time, yet either of them now gave the impression of being, encompassing as much living meat and volume and weight as any other two of the family) not yet having begun to rise from the chair, her head, face, alone merely turned, presenting to him in the flying instant an astonishing expanse of young female features untroubled by any surprise even, wearing only an expression of bovine interest. Then he was out of the room, out of the house, in the mild dust of the starlit road and the heavy rifeness of honeysuckle, the pale ribbon unspooling with terrific slowness under his running feet, reaching the gate at last and turning in, running, his heart and lungs drumming, on up the drive toward the lighted house, the lighted door. He did not knock, he burst in, sobbing for breath, incapable for the moment of speech; he saw the astonished face of the Negro in the linen jacket without knowing when the Negro had appeared.

"De Spain!" he cried, panted. "Where's . . ." then he saw the white man too emerging from a white door down the hall. "Barn!" he cried. "Barn!"

"What?" the white man said. "Barn?"

"Yes!" the boy cried. "Barn!"

"Catch him!" the white man shouted.

105 But it was too late this time too. The Negro grasped his shirt, but the entire sleeve, rotten with washing, carried away, and he was out that door too and in the drive again, and had actually never ceased to run even while he was screaming into the white man's face.

Behind him the white man was shouting, "My horse! Fetch my horse!" and he thought for an instant of cutting across the park and climbing the fence into the road, but he did not know the park nor how high the vine-massed fence might be and he dared not risk it. So he ran on down the drive, blood and breath roaring; presently he was in the road again though he could not see it. He could not hear either: the galloping mare was almost upon him before he heard her, and even then he held his course, as if the very urgency of his wild grief and need must in a moment more find him wings, waiting until the ultimate instant to hurl himself aside and into the weed-choked roadside ditch as the horse thundered past and on, for an instant in furious silhouette against the stars, the tranquil early summer night sky which, even before the shape of the horse and rider vanished, stained abruptly and violently upward: a long, swirling roar incredible and soundless, blotting the stars, and he springing up and into the road again, running again, knowing it was too late yet still running even after he heard the shot and, an instant later, two shots, pausing now without knowing he had ceased to run, crying "Pap! Pap!", running again before he knew he had begun to run, stumbling, tripping over something and scrabbling up again without ceasing to run, looking backward over his shoulder at the glare as he got up, running on among the invisible trees, panting, sobbing, "Father! Father!"

At midnight he was sitting on the crest of a hill. He did not know it was midnight and he did not know how far he had come. But there was no glare behind him now and he sat now, his back toward what he had called home for four days anyhow, his face toward the dark woods which he would enter when breath was strong again, small, shaking steadily in the chill darkness, hugging himself into the remainder of his thin, rotten shirt, the grief and despair now no longer terror and fear but just grief and despair. *Father. My father,* he thought. "He was brave!" he cried suddenly, aloud but not loud, no more than a whisper: "He was! He was in the war! He was in Colonel Sartoris' cav'ry!" not knowing that his father had gone to that war a private in the fine old European sense, wearing no uniform, admitting the authority of and giving fidelity to no man or army or flag, going to war as Malbrouck[5] himself did: for booty—it meant nothing and less than nothing to him if it were enemy booty or his own.

The slow constellations wheeled on. It would be dawn and then sunup after a while and he would be hungry. But that would be tomorrow and now he was only cold, and walking would cure that. His breathing was easier now and he decided to get up and go on, and then he found that he had been asleep because he knew it was almost dawn, the night almost over. He could tell that from the whippoorwills. They were everywhere now among the dark trees below him, constant and inflectioned and ceaseless, so that, as the instant for giving over to the day birds drew nearer and nearer, there was no interval at all between them. He got up. He was a little stiff, but walking would cure that too as it would the cold, and soon there would be the sun. He went on down the hill, toward the dark woods within which the liquid silver voices of the birds called unceasing—the rapid and urgent beating of the urgent and quiring heart of the late spring night. He did not look back.

---

[5] A character in a popular eighteenth-century nursery rhyme about a famous warrior.

Reading and Reacting

1. Is the third-person narrator of "Barn Burning" omniscient, or is his omniscience limited? Explain.
2. What is the point of view of the italicized passages? What do we learn from them? Do they create irony? How would the story have been different without these passages?
3. "Barn Burning" includes a great deal of dialogue. How would you characterize the **level of diction** of this dialogue? What information about various characters does it provide?
4. What conflicts are presented in "Barn Burning"? Which, if any, are resolved in the story? Are the conflicts avoidable? Explain.
5. Why does Ab Snopes burn barns? Do you think his actions are justified? Explain your reasoning.
6. What role does the Civil War play in "Barn Burning"? What does Abner Snopes's behavior during the war tell readers about his character?
7. In Books 1 and 2 of Samuel in the Old Testament, Abner was a relative of King Saul and commander in chief of his armies. Abner supported King Saul against David and was killed as a result of his own jealousy and rage. What, if any, significance is there in the fact that Faulkner names Ab Snopes, loyal to no man, fighter "for booty, and father of the Snopes clan," after this mighty biblical leader?
8. Why does Sarty Snopes insist that his father was brave? How does your knowledge of events unknown to the boy affect your reactions to this statement?
9. **JOURNAL ENTRY** How would the story be different if it were told from Ab's point of view? From Sarty's? From the point of view of Ab's wife? From the point of view of a member of a community in which the Snopeses have lived?

Related Works: "A Worn Path" (p. 256), "Child's Grave, Hale County, Alabama" (p. 480), "The Satisfaction Coal Company" (p. 516)

◆ Writing Suggestions: Point of View

1. Retell one of the stories in this chapter from a different point of view. For example, retell "The Cask of Amontillado" from Fortunato's point of view, beginning when he and Montresor were on friendly terms and ending just before the story begins. Or retell "Big Black Good Man" from Lena's point of view or "Barn Burning" from the point of view of Sarty's mother.
2. Assume that you are the sailor in "Big Black Good Man" and that you are keeping a journal of your travels. Write the journal

entries for the time you spent in Copenhagen. Include your impressions of Olaf, Lena, the hotel, and anything else that caught your attention. Make sure you present your version of the key events described in the story—especially Olaf's reaction to you.

3. Both "The Cask of Amontillado" and "Barn Burning" deal with crimes that essentially go unpunished and with the emotions that accompany these crimes. In what sense does each story's use of point of view shape its treatment of the crime in question? For instance, how does point of view determine how much readers know about the motives for the crime, the crime's basic circumstances, and the extent to which the crime is justified?

4. Both "Young Goodman Brown" (p. 198) and "The Cask of Amontillado" are about characters who encounter evil and are forever changed by the experience. Write an essay in which you compare these two characters. In what ways are their responses to evil similar, and in what ways are they different? In the end, which characte learns the most from his experience?

5. "Barn Burning" is, among other things, a story about a child's conflict with a parent's values. Write an essay in which you compare "Barn Burning" with another work that explores this theme—for example, *Death of a Salesman* (p. 782) or *The Glass Menagerie* (p. 938).

Chapter 7

Style, Tone, and Language

One of the qualities that gives a work of literature its individual personality is its **style,** the way in which a writer selects and arranges words to say what he or she wants to say. Style encompasses elements such as word choice; syntax; sentence length and structure; and the presence, frequency, and prominence of imagery and figures of speech. Closely related to style is **tone,** the attitude of the narrator or author of a work toward the subject matter, characters, or audience. Word choice and sentence structure help to create a work's tone, which may be intimate or distant, bitter or affectionate, straightforward or cautious, supportive or critical, respectful or condescending. (Tone may also be **ironic;** see Chapter 6, "Point of View," for a discussion of irony.)

Style offers almost limitless possibilities to a writer. Creative use of language (unusual word choice, word order, or sentence structure, for instance) can enrich a story and add to its overall effect. Sometimes style can help to create an atmosphere that enhances the setting or communicates the story's theme. In other cases, style can reveal a character's mental state. For instance, the breathless, disjointed style of Edgar Allan Poe's "The Tell-Tale Heart" suggests the narrator's increasing emotional instability: "Was it possible they heard not? Almighty God!—no, no! They heard!—they suspected!—they *knew!*—they were making a mockery of my horror!" In his short story "Big Two-Hearted River," Ernest Hemingway strings sentences together without transitions to create a flat, emotionless prose style that reveals his character's alienation and fragility as he struggles to maintain control: "Now things were done. There had been this to do. Now it was done. It had been a hard trip. He was very tired. That was done. He had made his camp. He was settled. Nothing could touch him." Finally, style can expand a story's possibilities through its very inventiveness. For example, James Joyce's innovative **stream-of-consciousness** style mimics thought, allowing ideas to run into one another as random associations are made, so that readers may follow and participate in the thought processes of the narrator. Here is a stream-of-consciousness passage from Joyce's experimental novel *Ulysses:*

frseeeeeeeefronnnng train somewhere whistling the strength those engines have in them like big giants and the water rolling all over and out of them all sides like the end of Loves old sweet sonnnng the poor men that have to be out all the night from their wives and families in those roasting engines stifling it was today [. . .].

The following passage from Alberto Alvaro Ríos's story "The Secret Lion" (p. 281) illustrates the power of creative language to enrich a story:

> We had read the books, after all; we knew about bridges and castles and wildtreacherousraging alligatormouth rivers. We wanted them. So we were going to go out and get them. We went back that morning into that kitchen and we said, "We're going out there, we're going into the hills, we're going away for three days, don't worry." She said, "All right."
> "You know," I said to Sergio, "if we're going to go away for three days, well, we ought to at least pack a lunch."
> But we were two young boys with no patience for what we thought at the time was mom-stuff: making sa-and-wiches. My mother didn't offer. So we got out little kid knapsacks that my mother had sewn for us, and into them we put the jar of mustard. A loaf of bread. Knivesforksplates, bottles of Coke, a can opener. This was lunch for the two of us. And we were weighed down, humped over to be strong enough to carry this stuff. But we started walking anyway, into the hills. We were going to eat berries and stuff otherwise. "Goodbye." My mom said that.

Through language, the adult narrator of the preceding paragraphs recaptures the bravado of the boys in search of "wildtreacherousraging alligatormouth rivers" even as he suggests to readers that the boys are not going far. The story's use of language is original and inventive: words are blended together ("getridofit," "knivesforksplates"), linked to form new language ("mom-stuff"), and drawn out ("sa-and-wiches") to mimic speech. These experiments with language show the narrator's willingness to move back into a child's frame of reference while maintaining the advantage of distance. The adult narrator uses sentence fragments ("A loaf of bread."), colloquialisms ("kid," "mom," "stuff"), and contractions. He also includes conversational elements such as *you know* and *well* in the dialogue, accurately re-creating the childhood scene at the same time he sees its folly and remains aware of the disillusionment that awaits him. Thus, the unique style permits the narrator to bring readers with him into the child's world even as he maintains his adult stance: "But we were two young boys with no patience for what we thought at the time was mom-stuff [. . .]."

Use of stylistic devices that place emphasis on the sounds and rhythm of words and sentences also enriches works of fiction. Consider the use of such techniques in the following sentence from James Joyce's "Araby" (p. 167):

> The light from the lamp opposite our door caught the white curve of her neck, lit up her hair that rested there and, falling, lit up the hand upon the railing.

Here the narrator is describing his first conversation with a girl who fascinates him, and the lush, lyrical, almost musical language reflects his enchantment. Note in particular the **alliteration** (<u>l</u>ight/<u>l</u>amp; <u>c</u>aught/<u>c</u>urve; <u>h</u>air/<u>h</u>and), the repetition (lit up/lit up), and the rhyme (lit up her *hair*/that rested *there*) and **near rhyme** (falling/railing); these poetic devices connect the words of the sentence into a smooth, rhythmic whole. Another example of this emphasis on sound may be found in the measured **parallelism** of this sentence from Nathaniel Hawthorne's "The Birthmark":

> He had left his laboratory to the care of an assistant, cleared his fine countenance from the furnace smoke, washed the stain of acids from his fingers, and persuaded a beautiful woman to become his wife.

The style of the preceding sentence, conveying methodical precision and order, reflects the compulsive personality of the character being described.

Although many stylistic options are available to writers, style must be consistent with the writer's purpose and with the effect he or she hopes to create. Just as writers may experiment with point of view or manipulate events to create a complex plot, so they can adjust style to suit particular narrators, characters, settings, or themes. Two elements with which writers frequently experiment are *level of diction,* and *imagery* and *figurative language.*

LEVEL OF DICTION

◊ ◊ ◊

The level of diction—how formal or informal a story's language is—can suggest a good deal about those who use the language, thus providing insights into the story's theme.

FORMAL DICTION

Formal diction is characterized by elaborate, complex sentences; a learned vocabulary; and a serious, objective, detached tone. The speaker avoids contractions, shortened word forms (like *phone*), regional expressions, and slang, and he or she may use *one* or *we* in place of *I*. At its most extreme, formal language may be stiff and stilted, far removed from everyday speech.

Formal diction, whether used by a narrator or by a character, may indicate erudition, a high educational level, a superior social or professional position, or emotional detachment. When one character's language is significantly more formal than others', he or she may seem old-fashioned or stuffy; when language is inappropriately elevated or complex, it may reveal the character to be pompous or ridiculous; when a narrator's language is noticeably more formal than that of the characters, the narrator may seem superior or even condescending. Thus, level of diction reveals a good deal about characters and about the narrator's attitude toward them.

The following passage from "The Birthmark" illustrates formal style:

> In the latter part of the last century there lived a man of science, an eminent proficient in every branch of natural philosophy, who not long before our story opens had made experience of a spiritual affinity more attractive than any chemical one. He had left his laboratory to the care of an assistant, cleared his fine countenance from the furnace smoke, washed the stain of acids from his fingers, and persuaded a beautiful woman to become his wife. In those days when the comparatively recent discovery of electricity and other kindred mysteries of Nature seemed to open paths into the region of miracle, it was not unusual for the love of science to rival the love of woman in its depth and absorbing energy. The higher intellect, the imagination, the spirit, and even the heart might all find their congenial ailment in pursuits which, as some of their ardent votaries believed, would ascend from one step of powerful intelligence to another, until the philosopher should lay his hand on the secret of creative force and perhaps make new worlds for himself.

The long, complex sentences; learned vocabulary ("countenance," "ailment," "votaries"); and absence of colloquialisms suit Hawthorne's purpose well, re-creating the formal language of the earlier era in which his story is set. The omniscient narrator, despite his use of the first person in "our story," is aloof and controlled.

INFORMAL DICTION

Informal diction, consistent with everyday speech, is characterized by slang, contractions, colloquial expressions like *you know* and *I mean*, shortened word forms, incomplete sentences, and a casual, conversational tone. A first-person narrator may use informal style, or characters may speak informally; in either case, informal style tends to narrow the distance between readers and text.

Informal language can range from the straightforward contemporary style of Arnold Friend's dialogue in "Where Are You Going, Where Have You Been?" ("I toldja shut up, Ellie, . . . you're deaf, get a hearing aid, right?") to the regionalisms and dialect employed in Flannery O'Connor's "A Good Man Is Hard to Find" ("aloose"; "you all"; "britches"). In "Where Are You Going, Where Have You Been?" (p. 268), Arnold's self-consciously slangy, conversational style tells readers a good deal about his motives and his method of operating; in "A Good Man Is Hard to Find" (p. 177), the characters' speech patterns and diction reveal the region in which they live and their social class. In other stories, a character's use of obscenities may suggest his or her crudeness or adolescent bravado, and use of racial or ethnic slurs suggests that a character is insensitive and bigoted.

The following passage from John Updike's "A&P" (p. 65) illustrates informal style:

> She had sort of oaky hair that the sun and salt had bleached, done up in a bun that was unravelling, and a kind of prim face. Walking into the A&P with your straps down, I suppose it's the only kind of face you *can* have. She held her head so high her neck, coming out of those white shoulders, looked kind of stretched, but I didn't mind. The longer her neck was, the more of her there was.

In the preceding passage, the first-person narrator uses a conversational style, including colloquialisms ("sort of," "I suppose," "kind of"), contractions ("it's," "didn't"), and the imprecise, informal *you* ("Walking into the A&P with *your* straps down [. . .]."). The narrator uses neither elaborate sentences nor learned diction.

IMAGERY AND FIGURATIVE LANGUAGE
◊ ◊ ◊

IMAGERY

Imagery—words and phrases that describe what is seen, heard, smelled, tasted, or touched—can have a significant impact in a story. A pattern of repeated imagery can help to convey a particular impression about a character or situation, or a writer may use such a pattern to communicate or reinforce a story's theme. For example, the theme of newly discovered sexuality can be conveyed through repeated use of words and phrases suggesting blooming or ripening.

In T. Coraghessan Boyle's 1985 short story "Greasy Lake," the narrator's vivid description of Greasy Lake itself uses rich visual imagery to evoke a scene:

Through the center of town, up the strip, past the housing developments and shopping malls, street lights giving way to the thin streaming illumination of the headlights, trees crowding the asphalt in a black unbroken wall: that was the way out to Greasy Lake. The Indians had called it Wakan, a reference to the clarity of its waters. Now it was fetid and murky, the mud banks glittering with broken glass and strewn with beer cans and the charred remains of bonfires. There was a single ravaged island a hundred yards from shore, so stripped of vegetation it looked as if the air force had strafed it. We went up to the lake because everyone went there, because we wanted to snuff the rich scent of possibility on the breeze, watch a girl take off her clothes and plunge into the festering murk, drink beer, smoke pot, howl at the stars, savor the incongruous full-throated roar of rock and roll against the primeval susurrus of frogs and crickets. This was nature.

By characterizing a natural setting with surprising words like "fetid," "murky," and "greasy" and unpleasant images such as the "glittering of broken glass," the "ravaged island," and the "charred remains of bonfires," Boyle creates a picture that is completely at odds with a traditional pastoral view of nature. The incongruous images are nevertheless perfectly consistent with the sordid events that take place at Greasy Lake.

Figurative Language

Figures of speech—such as *similes, metaphors,* and *personification*—can enrich a story, subtly revealing information about characters and themes. (See Chapter 14 for more information about figures of speech.)

By using **metaphors** and **similes**—figures of speech that compare two dissimilar items—writers can indicate a particular attitude toward characters and events. Thus, Flannery O'Connor's many grotesque similes in "A Good Man Is Hard to Find" help to dehumanize her characters; the children's mother, for instance, has a face "as broad and innocent as a cabbage." In Tillie Olsen's "I Stand Here Ironing" (p. 94), an extended metaphor in which a mother compares her daughter to a dress waiting to be ironed expresses the mother's attitude toward her daughter, effectively suggesting to readers the daughter's vulnerability. Similes and metaphors are used freely in Kate Chopin's "The Storm" (p. 89). In a scene of sexual awakening, Calixta's skin is "like a creamy lily," her passion is "like a white flame," and her mouth is "a fountain of delight"; these figures of speech add a lushness and sensuality to the story.

Personification—a figure of speech, closely related to metaphor, that endows inanimate objects or abstract ideas with life or with human characteristics—is used in "Araby," where houses, "conscious of decent lives within them, gazed at one another with brown imperturbable faces." This use of figurative language expands readers' vision of the story's setting and gives a dreamlike quality to the passage. (Other figures of speech, such as **hyperbole** and **understatement,** can also enrich works of fiction. See Chapter 14, "Figures of Speech," for further information.)

Allusions—references to familiar historical or literary personages or events—may also expand readers' understanding and appreciation of a work. An allusion widens a work's context by bringing it into the context of a related subject or idea. For instance, Wole Soyinka's frequent references to political figures and events in "Future Plans" (p. 489) enable readers who recognize the references to gain a deeper understanding of the speaker's position on various political and social issues. Literary and biblical allusions may be used in much the same way.

A Final Note

In analyzing the use of language in a work of fiction, you may occasionally encounter obscure allusions, foreign words and phrases, unusual comparisons, and unfamiliar regional expressions—particularly in works treating cultures and historical periods other than your own. Frequently such language will be clarified by the context, or by explanatory notes in your text; when it is not, you should consult a dictionary, encyclopedia, or other reference work.

Checklist: Writing about Style, Tone, and Language

- ✓ Is the story's tone intimate? Distant? Ironic? How does the tone advance the writer's purpose?
- ✓ Does the writer make any unusual creative use of diction, word order, or sentence structure?
- ✓ Does the style emphasize the sound and rhythm of language? For example, does the writer use alliteration and assonance? Repetition and parallelism? What do such techniques add to the story?
- ✓ Is the level of diction generally formal, informal, or somewhere in between?

- ✓ Is there a difference between the style of the narrator and the style of the characters' speech? If so, what is the effect of this difference?
- ✓ Do any of the story's characters use regionalisms, colloquial language, or nonstandard speech? If so, what effect does this language have?
- ✓ What do different characters' levels of diction reveal about them?
- ✓ What kind of imagery predominates? Where, and why, is imagery used?
- ✓ Does the story develop a pattern of imagery? How does this pattern of imagery relate to the story's themes?
- ✓ Does the story use simile and metaphor? Personification? What is the effect of these figures of speech?
- ✓ Do figures of speech reinforce the story's themes? Reveal details about characters?
- ✓ Does the story make any historical, literary, or biblical allusions? What do these allusions contribute to the story?
- ✓ What unfamiliar, obscure, or foreign words, phrases, or images are used in the story? What is the effect of these words or expressions?

◆ **JAMES JOYCE** (1884–1941) was born in Dublin. A religious and artistic rebel, he fled to Paris when he was twenty. Though he never again lived in Ireland, he wrote about Dublin throughout his career. Publication of *Dubliners* (1914), a collection of short stories that included "Araby," was delayed because the Irish publisher feared libel suits from local citizens who were thinly disguised as characters. Joyce's autobiographical *Portrait of the Artist as a Young Man* (1916) tells of a young writer's rejection of family, church, and country. In *Ulysses* (1922), Joyce begins a revolutionary journey away from traditional techniques of plot and characterization to the interior monologues and stream-of-consciousness style that mark his last great novel, *Finnegans Wake* (1939).

◊ ◊ ◊
JAMES JOYCE

Araby
(1914)

North Richmond Street, being blind,[1] was a quiet street except at the hour when the Christian Brothers' School set the boys free. An uninhabited house of two storeys stood at the blind end, detached from its neighbours in a square ground. The other houses of the street, conscious of decent lives within them, gazed at one another with brown imperturbable faces.

The former tenant of our house, a priest, had died in the back drawing-room. Air, musty from having been long enclosed, hung in all the rooms, and the waste room behind the kitchen was littered with old useless papers. Among these I found a few paper-covered books, the pages of which were curled and damp: *The Abbot*, by Walter Scott, *The Devout Communicant* and *The Memoirs of Vidocq*.[2] I liked the last best because its leaves were yellow. The wild garden behind the house contained a central apple-tree and a few straggling bushes under one of which I found the late tenant's rusty bicycle-pump. He had been a very charitable priest; in his will he had left all his money to institutions and the furniture of his house to his sister.

When the short days of winter came dusk fell before we had well eaten our dinners. When we met in the street the houses had grown sombre. The space of sky above us was the colour of ever-changing violet and towards it the lamps of the street lifted their feeble lanterns. The cold air stung us and we played till our bodies glowed. Our shouts echoed in the silent street. The career of our play brought us through the dark muddy lanes behind the houses where we ran the gauntlet of the rough tribes from the cottages, to the back doors of the dark dripping gardens where odours arose from the ashpits, to the dark odorous stables where a coachman smoothed and combed the horse or shook music from the buckled harness. When we returned to the street light from the kitchen windows had filled the areas. If my uncle was seen turning the corner we hid in the shadow until we had seen him safely housed. Or if Mangan's sister came out on the doorstep to call her brother in to his tea we watched her from our shadow peer up and down the street. We waited to see whether she would remain or go in and, if

---

[1] A dead-end street.
[2] Sir Walter Scott (1771–1832)—an English Romantic novelist; *The Devout Communicant*—a variant title for *Pious Meditations*, written by an eighteenth-century English Franciscan friar, Pacifus Baker; *The Memoirs of Vidocq*—an autobiography of François-Jules Vidocq (1775–1857), a French soldier of fortune turnedi police agent.

she remained, we left our shadow and walked up to Mangan's steps resignedly. She was waiting for us, her figure defined by the light from the half-opened door. Her brother always teased her before he obeyed and I stood by the railings looking at her. Her dress swung as she moved her body and the soft rope of her hair tossed from side to side.

Every morning I lay on the floor in the front parlour watching her door. The blind was pulled down to within an inch of the sash so that I could not be seen. When she came out on the doorstep my heart leaped. I ran to the hall, seized my books and followed her. I kept her brown figure always in my eye and, when we came near the point at which our ways diverged, I quickened my pace and passed her. This happened morning after morning. I had never spoken to her, except for a few casual words, and yet her name was like a summons to all my foolish blood.

5   Her image accompanied me even in places the most hostile to romance. On Saturday evenings when my aunt went marketing I had to go to carry some of the parcels. We walked through the flaring streets, jostled by drunken men and bargaining women, amid the curses of labourers, the shrill litanies of shop-boys who stood on guard by the barrels of pigs' cheeks, the nasal chanting of street-singers, who sang a *come-all-you* about O'Donovan Rossa,[3] or a ballad about the troubles in our native land. These noises converged in a single sensation of life for me: I imagined that I bore my chalice safely through a throng of foes. Her name sprang to my lips at moments in strange prayers and praises which I myself did not understand. My eyes were often full of tears (I could not tell why) and at times a flood from my heart seemed to pour itself out into my bosom. I thought little of the future. I did not know whether I would ever speak to her or not or, if I spoke to her, how I could tell her of my confused adoration. But my body was like a harp and her words and gestures were like fingers running upon the wires.

One evening I went into the back drawing-room in which the priest had died. It was a dark rainy evening and there was no sound in the house. Through one of the broken panes I heard the rain impinge upon the earth, the fine incessant needles of water playing in the sodden beds. Some distant lamp or lighted window gleamed below me. I was thankful that I could see so little. All my senses seemed to desire to veil themselves and, feeling that I was about to slip from them, I pressed the palms of my hands together until they trembled, murmuring: "O love! O love!" many times.

At last she spoke to me. When she addressed the first words to me I was so confused that I did not know what to answer. She asked me was I going to *Araby*. I forgot whether I answered yes or no. It would be a splendid bazaar, she said she would love to go.

---

[3] Any popular song beginning "Come all you gallant Irishmen . . ."; O'Donovan Rossa was an Irish nationalist who was banished in 1870 for advocating violent rebellion against the British.

"And why can't you?" I asked.

While she spoke she turned a silver bracelet round and round her wrist. She could not go, she said, because there would be a retreat that week in her convent.[4] Her brother and two other boys were fighting for their caps and I was alone at the railings. She held one of the spikes, bowing her head towards me. The light from the lamp opposite our door caught the white curve of her neck, lit up her hair that rested there and, falling, lit up the hand upon the railing. It fell over one side of her dress and caught the white border of a petticoat, just visible as she stood at ease.

"It's well for you," she said.

"If I go," I said, "I will bring you something."

What innumerable follies laid waste my waking and sleeping thoughts after that evening! I wished to annihilate the tedious intervening days. I chafed against the work of school. At night in my bedroom and by day in the classroom her image came between me and the page I strove to read. The syllables of the word *Araby* were called to me through the silence in which my soul luxuriated and cast an Eastern enchantment over me. I asked for leave to go to the bazaar on Saturday night. My aunt was surprised and hoped it was not some Freemason[5] affair. I answered few questions in class. I watched my master's face pass from amiability to sternness; he hoped I was not beginning to idle. I could not call my wandering thoughts together. I had hardly any patience with the serious work of life which, now that it stood between me and my desire, seemed to me child's play, ugly monotonous child's play.

On Saturday morning I reminded my uncle that I wished to go to the bazaar in the evening. He was fussing at the hallstand, looking for the hatbrush, and answered me curtly:

"Yes, boy, I know."

As he was in the hall I could not go into the front parlour and lie at the window. I left the house in bad humour and walked slowly towards the school. The air was pitilessly raw and already my heart misgave me.

When I came home to dinner my uncle had not yet been home. Still it was early. I sat staring at the clock for some time and, when its ticking began to irritate me, I left the room. I mounted the staircase and gained the upper part of the house. The high cold empty gloomy rooms liberated me and I went from room to room singing. From the front window I saw my companions playing below in the street. Their cries reached me weakened and indistinct and, leaning my forehead against the cool glass, I looked over at the dark house where she lived. I may have stood there for an hour, seeing nothing but the brown-clad figure cast by my imagination, touched discreetly by the lamplight at

---

[4] A week devoted to prayer and meditation in her convent school.
[5] At the time the story takes place, Catholics in Ireland thought the Masonic Order was a threat to the church.

the curved neck, at the hand upon the railings and at the border below the dress.

When I came downstairs again I found Mrs. Mercer sitting at the fire. She was an old garrulous woman, a pawnbroker's widow, who collected used stamps for some pious purpose. I had to endure the gossip of the tea-table. The meal was prolonged beyond an hour and still my uncle did not come. Mrs. Mercer stood up to go: she was sorry she couldn't wait any longer, but it was after eight o'clock and she did not like to be out late, as the night air was bad for her. When she had gone I began to walk up and down the room, clenching my fists. My aunt said:

"I'm afraid you may put off your bazaar for this night of Our Lord."

At nine o'clock I heard my uncle's latchkey in the halldoor. I heard him talking to himself and heard the hallstand rocking when it had received the weight of his overcoat. I could interpret these signs. When he was midway through his dinner I asked him to give me the money to go to the bazaar. He had forgotten.

"The people are in bed and after their first sleep now," he said.

I did not smile. My aunt said to him energetically:

"Can't you give him the money and let him go? You've kept him late enough as it is."

My uncle said he was very sorry he had forgotten. He said he believed in the old saying: "All work and no play makes Jack a dull boy." He asked me where I was going and, when I had told him a second time he asked me did I know *The Arab's Farewell to his Steed*.[6] When I left the kitchen he was about to recite the opening lines of the piece to my aunt.

I held a florin tightly in my hand as I strode down Buckingham Street towards the station. The sight of the streets thronged with buyers and glaring with gas recalled to me the purpose of my journey. I took my seat in a third-class carriage of a deserted train. After an intolerable delay the train moved out of the station slowly. It crept onward among ruinous houses and over the twinkling river. At Westland Row Station a crowd of people pressed to the carriage doors; but the porters moved them back, saying that it was a special train for the bazaar. I remained alone in the bare carriage. In a few minutes the train drew up beside an improvised wooden platform. I passed out on to the road and saw by the lighted dial of a clock that it was ten minutes to ten. In front of me was a large building which displayed the magical name.

I could not find any sixpenny entrance and, fearing that the bazaar would be closed, I passed in quickly through a turnstile, handing a shilling to a weary-looking man. I found myself in a big hall girdled at half its height by a gallery. Nearly all the stalls were closed and the greater part of the hall was in darkness. I recognised a silence like that which pervades a church after a service. I walked into the centre of the

---

[6] A sentimental poem by Caroline Norton (1808–1877) that tells the story of a nomad's heartbreak after selling his much-loved horse.

bazaar timidly. A few people were gathered about the stalls which were still open. Before a curtain, over which the words *Café Chantant*[7] were written in coloured lamps, two men were counting money on a salver. I listened to the fall of the coins.

Remembering with difficulty why I had come I went over to one of the stalls and examined porcelain vases and flowered tea-sets. At the door of the stall a young lady was talking and laughing with two young gentlemen. I remarked their English accents and listened vaguely to their conversation.

"O, I never said such a thing!"
"O, but you did!"
"O, but I didn't!"
"Didn't she say that?"
"Yes. I heard her."
"O, there's a . . . fib!"

Observing me the young lady came over and asked me did I wish to buy anything. The tone of her voice was not encouraging; she seemed to have spoken to me out of a sense of duty. I looked humbly at the great jars that stood like eastern guards at either side of the dark entrance to the stall and murmured:

"No, thank you."

The young lady changed the position of one of the vases and went back to the two young men. They began to talk of the same subject. Once or twice the young lady glanced at me over her shoulder.

I lingered before her stall, though I knew my stay was useless, to make my interest in her wares seem the more real. Then I turned away slowly and walked down the middle of the bazaar. I allowed the two pennies to fall against the sixpence in my pocket. I heard a voice call from one end of the gallery that the light was out. The upper part of the hall was now completely dark.

Gazing up into the darkness I saw myself as a creature driven and derided by vanity; and my eyes burned with anguish and anger.

Reading and Reacting

1. How would you characterize the story's level of diction? Is this level appropriate for a story about a young boy's experiences? Explain.
2. Identify several examples of figurative language in the story. Where is Joyce most likely to use this kind of language? Why?
3. What words and phrases express the boy's extreme idealism and romantic view of the world? In what way does such language help to communicate the story's major theme?

---

[7] A Paris café featuring musical entertainment.

4. In paragraph 4, the narrator says, "her name was like a summons to all my foolish blood." In the story's last sentence he sees himself as "a creature driven and derided by vanity." What other expressions does he use to describe his feelings? How would you characterize these feelings?
5. How does word choice illustrate the contrast between the narrator's day-to-day life and the exotic promise of the bazaar?
6. What does each of the italicized words suggest: "We walked through the *flaring* streets" (5); "I heard the rain *impinge* upon the earth" (6); "I *chafed* against the work of school" (12); "I found myself in a big hall *girdled* at half its height by a gallery" (25)? What other examples of unusual word choice can you identify in the story?
7. What is it about the events in this story that causes the narrator to remember them years later?
8. Identify words and phrases in the story that are associated with religion. What purpose do these references to religion serve?
9. **JOURNAL ENTRY** Rewrite a brief passage from this story in the voice of the young boy. Use informal style, simple figures of speech, and vocabulary appropriate for a child.

Related Works: "A&P" (p. 65), "Doe Season" (p. 230), "Shall I Compare Thee to a Summer's Day?" (p. 402)

◆ **ERNEST HEMINGWAY** (1898–1961) began his writing career as a reporter on the *Kansas City Star*. In 1922, he moved to Paris, where he talked literary shop with other expatriate writers like F. Scott Fitzgerald and James Joyce. Success came early, with publication of the short story collection *In Our Time* (1925) and his first and most acclaimed novel, *The Sun Also Rises* (1926), a portrait of a postwar "lost generation" of Americans adrift in Europe. Hemingway's novels make fiction and art out of the reality of his own life. *A Farewell to Arms* (1929) harks back to his experiences during World War I; *For Whom the Bell Tolls* (1940) emerged out of his experiences as a journalist during the Spanish Civil War. Hemingway's heroes embody the writer's belief that although life may be followed by *nada,* or nothingness, strong individuals can embrace life and live it with dignity and honor. In 1961, plagued by poor health and mental illness, Hemingway took his own life. Hemingway was awarded the 1954 Nobel Prize in literature.

ERNEST HEMINGWAY

A Clean, Well-Lighted Place
(1933)

It was late and every one had left the café except an old man who sat in the shadow the leaves of the tree made against the electric light. In the day time the street was dusty, but at night the dew settled the dust and the old man liked to sit late because he was deaf and now at night it was quiet and he felt the difference. The two waiters inside the café knew that the old man was a little drunk, and while he was a good client they knew that if he became too drunk he would leave without paying, so they kept watch on him.

"Last week he tried to commit suicide," one waiter said.

"Why?"

"He was in despair."

"What about?"

"Nothing."

"How do you know it was nothing?"

"He has plenty of money."

They sat together at a table that was close against the wall near the door of the café and looked at the terrace where the tables were all empty except where the old man sat in the shadow of the leaves of the tree that moved slightly in the wind. A girl and a soldier went by in the street. The street light shone on the brass number on his collar. The girl wore no head covering and hurried beside him.

"The guard will pick him up," one waiter said.

"What does it matter if he gets what he's after?"

"He had better get off the street now. The guard will get him. They went by five minutes ago."

The old man sitting in the shadow rapped on his saucer with his glass. The younger waiter went over to him.

"What do you want?"

The old man looked at him. "Another brandy," he said.

"You'll be drunk," the waiter said. The old man looked at him. The waiter went away.

"He'll stay all night," he said to his colleague. "I'm sleepy now. I never get into bed before three o'clock. He should have killed himself last week."

The waiter took the brandy bottle and another saucer from the counter inside the café and marched out to the old man's table. He put down the saucer and poured the glass full of brandy.

"You should have killed yourself last week," he said to the deaf man. The old man motioned with his finger. "A little more," he said. The waiter poured on into the glass so that the brandy slopped over and ran down the stem into the top saucer of the pile. "Thank you," the old man said. The waiter took the bottle back inside the café. He sat down at the table with his colleague again.

"He's drunk now," he said.
"He's drunk every night."
"What did he want to kill himself for?"
"How should I know."
"How did he do it?"
"He hung himself with a rope."
"Who cut him down?"
"His niece."
"Why did they do it?"
"Fear for his soul."
"How much money has he got?"
"He's got plenty."
"He must be eighty years old."
"Anyway I should say he was eighty."
"I wish he would go home. I never get to bed before three o'clock. What kind of hour is that to go to bed?"
"He stays up because he likes it."
"He's lonely. I'm not lonely. I have a wife waiting in bed for me."
"He had a wife once too."
"A wife would be no good to him now."
"You can't tell. He might be better with a wife."
"His niece lookes after him. You said she cut him down."
"I know."
"I wouldn't want to be that old. An old man is a nasty thing."
"Not always. This old man is clean. He drinks without spilling. Even now, drunk. Look at him."
"I don't want to look at him. I wish he would go home. He has no regard for those who must work."

The old man looked from his glass across the square, then over at the waiters.

"Another brandy," he said, pointing to his glass. The waiter who was in a hurry came over.

"Finished," he said, speaking with that omission of syntax stupid people employ when talking to drunken people or foreigners. "No more tonight. Close now."

"Another," said the old man.

"No. Finished." The waiter wiped the edge of the table with a towel and shook his head.

The old man stood up, slowly counted the saucers, took a leather coin purse from his pocket and paid for the drinks, leaving half a peseta tip.

The waiter watched him go down the street, a very old man walking unsteadily but with dignity.

"Why didn't you let him stay and drink?" the unhurried waiter asked. They were putting up the shutters. "It is not half-past two."

"I want to go home to bed."
"What is an hour?"
"More to me than to him."
"An hour is the same."
"You talk like an old man yourself. He can buy a bottle and drink at home."
"It's not the same."
"No, it is not," agreed the waiter with a wife. He did not wish to be unjust. He was only in a hurry.
"And you? You have no fear of going home before your usual hour?"
"Are you trying to insult me?"
"No, hombre, only to make a joke."
"No," the waiter who was in a hurry said, rising from pulling down the metal shutters. "I have confidence. I am all confidence."
"You have youth, confidence, and a job," the older waiter said. "You have everything."
"And what do you lack?"
"Everything but work."
"You have everything I have."
"No. I have never had confidence and I am not young."
"Come on. Stop talking nonsense and lock up."
"I am of those who like to stay late at the café," the older waiter said. "With all those who do not want to go to bed. With all those who need a light for the night."
"I want to go home and into bed."
"We are of two different kinds," the older waiter said. He was now dressed to go home. "It is not only a question of youth and confidence although those things are very beautiful. Each night I am reluctant to close up because there may be some one who needs the café."
"Hombre, there are bodegas[1] open all night long."
"You do not understand. This is a clean and pleasant café. It is well lighted. The light is very good and also, now, there are shadows of the leaves."
"Good night," said the younger waiter.
"Good night," the other said. Turning off the electric light he continued the conversation with himself. It is the light of course but it is necessary that the place be clean and pleasant. You do not want music. Certainly you do not want music. Nor can you stand before a bar with dignity although that is all that is provided for these hours. What did he fear? It was not fear or dread. It was a nothing that he knew too well. It was all a nothing and a man was nothing too. It was only that and light was all it needed and a certain cleanness and order. Some lived in it and never felt it but he knew it all was nada y pues nada y nada y pues nada.[2]

---

[1] Small grocery stores, sometimes combined with wineshops.
[2] Nothing and then nothing and nothing and then nothing.

Our nada who art in nada, nada be thy name thy kingdom nada thy will be nada in nada as it is in nada. Give us this nada our daily nada and nada us our nada as we nada our nadas and nada us not into nada but deliver us from nada; pues nada. Hail nothing full of nothing, nothing is with thee. He smiled and stood before a bar with a shining steam pressure coffee machine.

"What's yours?" asked the barman.

"Nada."

"Otro loco más,"[3] said the barman and turned away.

"A little cup," said the waiter.

The barman poured it for him.

"The light is very bright and pleasant but the bar is unpolished," the waiter said.

The barman looked at him but did not answer. It was too late at night for conversation.

"You want another copita?"[4] the barman asked.

"No, thank you," said the waiter and went out. He disliked bars and bodegas. A clean, well-lighted café was a very different thing. Now, without thinking further, he would go home to his room. He would lie in the bed and finally, with daylight, he would go to sleep. After all, he said to himself, it is probably only insomnia. Many must have it.

READING AND REACTING

1. Throughout the story certain words—*nada*, for example—are repeated. Identify as many of these repeated words as you can. What do you think such repetition achieves?
2. The story's dialogue is presented in alternating exchanges of very brief sentences. What is the effect of these clipped exchanges?
3. Characterize the tone of the story.
4. Does the story present the human condition in optimistic or pessimistic terms? In what sense are the story's style and tone well suited to this worldview?
5. The story is set in Spain, yet Hemingway uses only a few Spanish words. Why does he use these words? Would the impact of the prayer be different if it had been spoken in English? Explain.
6. The café is described as "clean" and "pleasant." Why is this description a key element of the story? In what sense, if any, is this description ironic?
7. The story's primary **point of view** is objective. At times, however, a limited omniscient point of view is used. Identify

---

[3] Another lunatic.
[4] Little cup.

such instances, and try to explain the reason for each shift in point of view.
8. Identify examples of figurative language used in the story. How does the presence (or absence) of such language help to convey the story's theme?
9. **JOURNAL ENTRY** Rewrite about half a page of the story, supplying logical transitions between sentences. How does your editing change the passage? Do your changes improve the story or take something away?

Related Works: "Dreams of Suicide" (p. 491), "Dover Beach" (p. 503), "The Love Song of J. Alfred Prufrock" (p. 519), "Not Waving but Drowning" (p. 549).

◆ **(MARY) FLANNERY O'CONNOR** (1925–1964) was born to a Catholic family in Savannah, Georgia, and spent most of her adult life on a farm near Milledgeville. She studied writing at the University of Iowa, then moved to New York to work on her first novel, *Wise Blood* (1952). On a train going south for Christmas, O'Connor fell desperately ill; she was diagnosed as having lupus, the immune system disease that would cause her death when she was only thirty-nine years old.

O'Connor delighted in local reaction to her grotesque, often grisly stories. O'Connor, said a friend, believed that an artist "should face all the truth down to the worst of it." Yet however dark, O'Connor's stories are infused with humor and a fierce belief in the possibility of spiritual redemption, even for her most tortured characters.

◆ ◆ ◆

FLANNERY O'CONNOR

A Good Man Is Hard to Find
(1955)

The grandmother didn't want to go to Florida. She wanted to visit some of her connections in east Tennessee and she was seizing at every chance to change Bailey's mind. Bailey was the son she lived with, her only boy. He was sitting on the edge of his chair at the table, bent over the orange sports section of the *Journal*. "Now look here, Bailey," she said, "see here, read this," and she stood with one hand on her thin hip and the other rattling the newspaper at his bald head. "Here this fellow that calls himself The Misfit is aloose from the Federal Pen and headed toward Florida and you read here what it says he did to these people. Just you read it. I wouldn't take my children in any direction with a criminal like that aloose in it. I couldn't answer to my conscience if I did."

Bailey didn't look up from his reading so she wheeled around then and faced the children's mother, a young woman in slacks, whose face was as broad and innocent as a cabbage and was tied around with a green headkerchief that had two points on the top like a rabbit's ears. She was sitting on the sofa, feeding the baby his apricots out of a jar. "The children have been to Florida before," the old lady said. "You all ought to take them somewhere else for a change so they would see different parts of the world and be broad. They never have been to east Tennessee."

The children's mother didn't seem to hear her but the eight-year-old boy, John Wesley, a stocky child with glasses, said, "If you don't want to go to Florida, why dontcha stay at home?" He and the little girl, June Star, were reading the funny papers on the floor.

"She wouldn't stay at home to be queen for a day," June Star said without raising her yellow head.

5   "Yes and what would you do if this fellow, The Misfit, caught you?" the grandmother asked.

"I'd smack his face," John Wesley said.

"She wouldn't stay at home for a million bucks," June Star said. "Afraid she'd miss something. She has to go everywhere we go."

"All right, Miss," the grandmother said. "Just remember that the next time you want me to curl your hair."

June Star said her hair was naturally curly.

10   The next morning the grandmother was the first one in the car, ready to go. She had her big black valise that looked like the head of a hippopotamus in one corner, and underneath it she was hiding a basket with Pitty Sing, the cat, in it. She didn't intend for the cat to be left alone in the house for three days because he would miss her too much and she was afraid he might brush against one of the gas burners and accidentally asphyxiate himself. Her son, Bailey, didn't like to arrive at a motel with a cat.

She sat in the middle of the back seat with John Wesley and June Star on either side of her. Bailey and the children's mother and the baby sat in front and they left Atlanta at eight forty-five with the mileage on the car at 55890. The grandmother wrote this down because she thought it would be interesting to say how many miles they had been when they got back. It took them twenty minutes to reach the outskirts of the city.

The old lady settled herself comfortably, removing her white cotton gloves and putting them up with her purse on the shelf in front of the back window. The children's mother still had on slacks and still had her head tied up in a green kerchief, but the grandmother had on a navy blue straw sailor hat with a bunch of white violets on the brim and a navy blue dress with a small white dot in the print. Her collars and cuffs were white organdy trimmed with lace and at her neckline she had pinned a purple spray of cloth violets containing a sachet. In case of an accident, anyone seeing her dead on the highway would know at once that she was a lady.

She said she thought it was going to be a good day for driving, neither too hot nor too cold, and she cautioned Bailey that the speed limit was fifty-five miles an hour and that the patrolmen hid themselves behind billboards and small clumps of trees and sped out after you before you had a chance to slow down. She pointed out interesting details of the scenery: Stone Mountain; the blue granite that in some places came up to both sides of the highway; the brilliant red clay banks slightly streaked with purple; and the various crops that made rows of green lace-work on the ground. The trees were full of silver-white sunlight and the meanest of them sparkled. The children were reading comic magazines and their mother had gone back to sleep.

"Let's go through Georgia fast so we won't have to look at it much," John Wesley said.

"If I were a little boy," said the grandmother, "I wouldn't talk about my native state that way. Tennessee has the mountains and Georgia has the hills."

"Tennessee is just a hillbilly dumping ground," John Wesley said, "and Georgia is a lousy state too."

"You said it," June Star said.

"In my time," said the grandmother, folding her thin veined fingers, "children were more respectful of their native states and their parents and everything else. People did right then. Oh look at the cute little pickaninny!" she said and pointed to a Negro child standing in the door of a shack. "Wouldn't that make a picture, now?" she asked and they all turned and looked at the little Negro out of the back window. He waved.

"He didn't have any britches on," June Star said.

"He probably didn't have any," the grandmother explained. "Little niggers in the country don't have things like we do. If I could paint, I'd paint that picture," she said.

The children exchanged comic books.

The grandmother offered to hold the baby and the children's mother passed him over the front seat to her. She set him on her knee and bounced him and told him about the things they were passing. She rolled her eyes and screwed up her mouth and stuck her leathery thin face into his smooth bland one. Occasionally he gave her a faraway smile. They passed a large cotton field with five or six graves fenced in the middle of it, like a small island. "Look at the graveyard!" the grandmother said, pointing it out. "That was the old family burying ground. That belonged to the plantation."

"Where's the plantation?" John Wesley asked.

"Gone With the Wind," said the grandmother. "Ha. Ha."

When the children finished all the comic books they had brought, they opened the lunch and ate it. The grandmother ate a peanut butter sandwich and an olive and would not let the children throw the box and the paper napkins out the window. When there was nothing else to do they played a game by choosing a cloud and making the other two guess what shape it suggested. John Wesley took one the shape of a cow and June Star guessed a cow and John Wesley said, no, an automobile, and June Star said he didn't play fair, and they began to slap each other over the grandmother.

The grandmother said she would tell them a story if they would keep quiet. When she told a story, she rolled her eyes and waved her head and was very dramatic. She said once when she was a maiden lady she had been courted by a Mr. Edgar Atkins Teagarden from Jasper, Georgia. She said he was a very good-looking man and a gentleman and that he brought her a watermelon every Saturday afternoon with his initials cut in it, E. A. T. Well, one Saturday, she said, Mr. Teagarden brought the watermelon and there was nobody at home and he left it on the front porch and returned in his buggy to Jasper, but she never got the watermelon, she said, because a nigger boy ate it when he saw the initials, E. A. T.! This story tickled John Wesley's funny bone and he giggled and giggled but June Star didn't think it was any good. She said she wouldn't marry a man that just brought her a watermelon on Saturday. The grandmother said she would have done well to marry Mr. Teagarden because he was a gentleman and had bought Coca-Cola stock when it first came out and that he died only a few years ago, a very wealthy man.

They stopped at The Tower for barbecued sandwiches. The Tower was a part stucco and part wood filling station and dance hall set in a clearing outside of Timothy. A fat man named Red Sammy Butts ran it and there were signs stuck here and there on the building and for miles up and down the highway saying, TRY RED SAMMY'S FAMOUS BARBECUE. NONE LIKE FAMOUS RED SAMMY'S! RED SAM! THE FAT BOY WITH THE HAPPY LAUGH. A VETERAN! RED SAMMY'S YOUR MAN!

Red Sammy was lying on the bare ground outside The Tower with his head under a truck while a gray monkey about a foot high, chained to a small chinaberry tree, chattered nearby. The monkey sprang back into the tree and got on the highest limb as soon as he saw the children jump out of the car and run toward him.

Inside, The Tower was a long dark room with a counter at one end and tables at the other and dancing space in the middle. They all sat down at a board table next to the nickelodeon and Red Sam's wife, a tall burnt-brown woman with hair and eyes lighter than her skin, came and took their order. The children's mother put a dime in the machine and played "The Tennessee Waltz," and the grandmother said that tune always made her want to dance. She asked Bailey if he would like to dance but he only glared at her. He didn't have a naturally sweet disposition like she did and trips made him nervous. The grandmother's brown eyes were very bright. She swayed her head from side to side and pretended she was dancing in her chair. June Star said play something she could tap to so the children's mother put in another dime and played a fast number and June Star stepped out onto the dance floor and did her tap routine.

"Ain't she cute?" Red Sam's wife said, leaning over the counter. "Would you like to come be my little girl?"

"No I certainly wouldn't," June Star said. "I wouldn't live in a broken-down place like this for a million bucks!" and she ran back to the table.

"Ain't she cute?" the woman repeated, stretching her mouth politely.

"Aren't you ashamed?" hissed the grandmother.

Red Sam came in and told his wife to quit lounging on the counter and hurry up with these people's order. His khaki trousers reached just to his hip bones and his stomach hung over them like a sack of meal swaying under his shirt. He came over and sat down at a table nearby and let out a combination sigh and yodel. "You can't win," he said. "You can't win," and he wiped his sweating red face off with a gray handkerchief. "These days you don't know who to trust," he said. "Ain't that the truth?"

"People are certainly not nice like they used to be," said the grandmother.

"Two fellers come in here last week," Red Sammy said, "driving a Chrysler. It was a old beat-up car but it was a good one and these boys looked all right to me. Said they worked at the mill and you know I let them fellers charge the gas they bought? Now why did I do that?"

"Because you're a good man!" the grandmother said at once.

"Yes'm, I suppose so," Red Sam said as if he were struck with this answer.

His wife brought the orders, carrying the five plates all at once without a tray, two in each hand and one balanced on her arm. "It isn't a soul in this green world of God's that you can trust," she said. "And I don't count nobody out of that, not nobody," she repeated, looking at Red Sammy.

"Did you read about that criminal, The Misfit, that's escaped?" asked the grandmother.

"I wouldn't be a bit surprised if he didn't attact this place right here," said the woman. "If he hears about it being here, I wouldn't be none surprised to see him. If he hears it's two cent in the cash register, I wouldn't be at all surprised if he . . ."

"That'll do," Red Sam said. "Go bring these people their Co'-Colas," and the woman went off to get the rest of the order.

"A good man is hard to find," Red Sammy said. "Everything is getting terrible. I remember the day you could go off and leave your screen door unlatched. Not no more."

He and the grandmother discussed better times. The old lady said that in her opinion Europe was entirely to blame for the way things were now. She said the way Europe acted you would think we were made of money and Red Sam said it was no use talking about it, she was exactly right. The children ran outside into the white sunlight and looked at the monkey in the lacy chinaberry tree. He was busy catching fleas on himself and biting each one carefully between his teeth as if it were a delicacy.

45   They drove off again into the hot afternoon. The grandmother took cat naps and woke up every few minutes with her own snoring. Outside of Toombsboro she woke up and recalled an old plantation that she had visited in this neighborhood once when she was a young lady. She said the house had six white columns across the front and that there was an avenue of oaks leading up to it and two little wooden trellis arbors on either side in front where you sat down with your suitor after a stroll in the garden. She recalled exactly which road to turn off to get to it. She knew that Bailey would not be willing to lose any time looking at an old house, but the more she talked about it, the more she wanted to see it once again and find out if the little twin arbors were still standing. "There was a secret panel in this house," she said craftily, not telling the truth but wishing that she were, "and the story went that all the family silver was hidden in it when Sherman came through but it was never found . . ."

"Hey!" John Wesley said. "Let's go see it! We'll find it! We'll poke all the woodwork and find it! Who lives there? Where do you turn off at? Hey Pop, can't we turn off there?"

"We never have seen a house with a secret panel!" June Star shrieked. "Let's go to the house with the secret panel! Hey Pop, can't we go see the house with the secret panel!"

"It's not far from here, I know," the grandmother said. "It wouldn't take over twenty minutes."

Bailey was looking straight ahead. His jaw was as rigid as a horseshoe. "No," he said.

50   The children began to yell and scream that they wanted to see the house with the secret panel. John Wesley kicked the back of the front seat and June Star hung over her mother's shoulder and whined desperately into her ear that they never had any fun even on their vacation, that they could never do what THEY wanted to do. The baby began to scream and John Wesley kicked the back of the seat so hard that his father could feel the blows in his kidney.

"All right!" he shouted and drew the car to a stop at the side of the road. "Will you all shut up? Will you all just shut up for one second? If you don't shut up, we won't go anywhere."

"It would be very educational for them," the grandmother murmured.

"All right," Bailey said, "but get this: this is the only time we're going to stop for anything like this. This is the one and only time."

"The dirt road that you have to turn down is about a mile back," the grandmother directed. "I marked it when we passed."

55   "A dirt road," Bailey groaned.

After they had turned around and were headed toward the dirt road, the grandmother recalled other points about the house, the beautiful glass over the front doorway and the candle-lamp in the hall. John Wesley said that the secret panel was probably in the fireplace.

"You can't go inside this house," Bailey said. "You don't know who lives there."

"While you all talk to the people in front, I'll run around behind and get in a window," John Wesley suggested.

"We'll all stay in the car," his mother said.

They turned onto the dirt road and the car raced roughly along in a swirl of pink dust. The grandmother recalled the times when there were no paved roads and thirty miles was a day's journey. The dirt road was hilly and there were sudden washes in it and sharp curves on dangerous embankments. All at once they would be on a hill, looking down over the blue tops of trees for miles around, then the next minute, they would be in a red depression with the dust-coated trees looking down on them.

"This place had better turn up in a minute," Bailey said, "or I'm going to turn around."

The road looked as if no one had traveled on it in months.

"It's not much farther," the grandmother said and just as she said it, a horrible thought came to her. The thought was so embarrassing that she turned red in the face and her eyes dilated and her feet jumped up, upsetting her valise in the corner. The instant the valise moved, the newspaper top she had over the basket under it rose with a snarl and Pitty Sing, the cat, sprang onto Bailey's shoulder.

The children were thrown to the floor and their mother, clutching the baby, was thrown out the door onto the ground; the old lady was thrown into the front seat. The car turned over once and landed right-side-up in a gulch off the side of the road. Bailey remained in the driver's seat with the cat—gray-striped with a broad white face and an orange nose—clinging to his neck like a caterpillar.

As soon as the children saw they could move their arms and legs, they scrambled out of the car, shouting, "We've had an ACCIDENT!" The grandmother was curled up under the dashboard, hoping she was injured so that Bailey's wrath would not come down on her all at once. The horrible thought she had had before the accident was that the house she had remembered so vividly was not in Georgia but in Tennessee.

Bailey removed the cat from his neck with both hands and flung it out the window against the side of a pine tree. Then he got out of the car and started looking for the children's mother. She was sitting against the side of the red gutted ditch, holding the screaming baby, but she only had a cut down her face and a broken shoulder. "We've had an ACCIDENT!" the children screamed in a frenzy of delight.

"But nobody's killed," June Star said with disappointment as the grandmother limped out of the car, her hat still pinned to her head but the broken front brim standing up at a jaunty angle and the violet spray hanging off the side. They all sat down in the ditch, except the children, to recover from the shock. They were all shaking.

"Maybe a car will come along," said the children's mother hoarsely.

"I believe I have injured an organ," said the grandmother, pressing her side, but no one answered her. Bailey's teeth were clattering. He had on a yellow sport shirt with bright blue parrots designed in it and his face was as yellow as the shirt. The grandmother decided that she would not mention that the house was in Tennessee.

The road was about ten feet above and they could see only the tops of the trees on the other side of it. Behind the ditch they were sitting in there were more woods, tall and dark and deep. In a few minutes they saw a car some distance away on top of a hill, coming slowly as if the occupants were watching them. The grandmother stood up and waved both arms dramatically to attract their attention. The car continued to come on slowly, disappeared around a bend and appeared again, moving even slower, on top of the hill they had gone over. It was a big black battered hearse-like automobile. There were three men in it.

It came to a stop just over them and for some minutes, the driver looked down with a steady expressionless gaze to where they were sitting, and didn't speak. Then he turned his head and muttered something to the other two and they got out. One was a fat boy in black trousers and a red sweat shirt with a silver stallion embossed on the front of it. He moved around on the right side of them and stood staring, his mouth partly open in a kind of loose grin. The other had on khaki pants and a blue striped coat and a gray hat pulled down very low, hiding most of his face. He came around slowly on the left side. Neither spoke.

The driver got out of the car and stood by the side of it, looking down at them. He was an older man than the other two. His hair was just beginning to gray and he wore silver-rimmed spectacles that gave him a scholarly look. He had a long creased face and didn't have on any shirt or undershirt. He had on blue jeans that were too tight for him and was holding a black hat and a gun. The two boys also had guns.

"We've had an ACCIDENT!" the children screamed.

The grandmother had the peculiar feeling that the bespectacled man was someone she knew. His face was as familiar to her as if she had known him all her life but she could not recall who he was. He moved away from the car and began to come down the embankment, placing his feet carefully so that he wouldn't slip. He had on tan and white shoes and no socks, and his ankles were red and thin. "Good afternoon," he said. "I see you all had you a little spill."

"We turned over twice!" said the grandmother.

"Oncet," he corrected. "We seen it happen. Try their car and see will it run, Hiram," he said quietly to the boy with the gray hat.

"What you got that gun for?" John Wesley asked. "Watcha gonna do with that gun?"

"Lady," the man said to the children's mother, "would you mind calling them children to sit down by you? Children make me nervous. I want all you all to sit down right together there where you're at."

"What are you telling US what to do for?" June Star asked.

Behind them the line of woods gaped like a dark open mouth. "Come here," said their mother.

"Look here now," Bailey began suddenly, "we're in a predicament! We're in . . ."

The grandmother shrieked. She scrambled to her feet and stood staring. "You're The Misfit!" she said. "I recognized you at once!"

"Yes'm," the man said, smiling slightly as if he were pleased in spite of himself to be known, "but it would have been better for all of you, lady, if you hadn't of reckernized me."

Bailey turned his head sharply and said something to his mother that shocked even the children. The old lady began to cry and The Misfit reddened.

"Lady," he said, "don't you get upset. Sometimes a man says things he don't mean. I don't reckon he meant to talk to you thataway."

"You wouldn't shoot a lady, would you?" the grandmother said and removed a clean handkerchief from her cuff and began to slap at her eyes with it.

The Misfit pointed the toe of his shoe into the ground and made a little hole and then covered it up again. "I would hate to have to," he said.

"Listen," the grandmother almost screamed, "I know you're a good man. You don't look a bit like you have common blood. I know you must come from nice people!"

"Yes mam," he said, "finest people in the world." When he smiled he showed a row of strong white teeth. "God never made a finer woman than my mother and my daddy's heart was pure gold," he said. The boy with the red sweat shirt had come around behind them and was standing with his gun at his hip. The Misfit squatted down on the ground. "Watch them children, Bobby Lee," he said. "You know they make me nervous." He looked at the six of them huddled together in front of him and he seemed to be embarrassed as if he couldn't think of anything to say. "Ain't a cloud in the sky," he remarked, looking up at it. "Don't see no sun but don't see no cloud neither."

"Yes, it's a beautiful day," said the grandmother. "Listen," she said, "you shouldn't call yourself The Misfit because I know you're a good man at heart. I can just look at you and tell."

"Hush!" Bailey yelled. "Hush! Everybody shut up and let me handle this!" He was squatting in the position of a runner about to sprint forward but he didn't move.

"I pre-chate that, lady," The Misfit said and drew a little circle in the ground with the butt of his gun.

"It'll take a half a hour to fix this here car," Hiram called, looking over the raised hood of it.

"Well, first you and Bobby Lee get him and that little boy to step over yonder with you," The Misfit said, pointing to Bailey and John Wesley.

"The boys want to ast you something," he said to Bailey. "Would you mind stepping back in them woods there with them?"

"Listen," Bailey began, "we're in a terrible predicament! Nobody realizes what this is," and his voice cracked. His eyes were as blue and intense as the parrots in his shirt and he remained perfectly still.

The grandmother reached up to adjust her hat brim as if she were going to the woods with him but it came off in her hand. She stood staring at it and after a second she let it fall on the ground. Hiram pulled Bailey up by the arm as if he were assisting an old man. John Wesley caught hold of his father's hand and Bobby Lee followed. They went off toward the woods and just as they reached the dark edge, Bailey turned and supporting himself against a gray naked pine trunk, he shouted, "I'll be back in a minute, Mamma, wait on me!"

"Come back this instant!" his mother shrilled but they all disappeared into the woods.

"Bailey Boy!" the grandmother called in a tragic voice but she found she was looking at The Misfit squatting on the ground in front of her. "I just know you're a good man," she said desperately. "You're not a bit common!"

"Nome, I ain't a good man," The Misfit said after a second as if he had considered her statement carefully, "but I ain't the worst in the world neither. My daddy said I was a different breed of dog from my brothers and sisters. 'You know,' Daddy said, 'it's some that can live their whole life out without asking about it and it's others has to know why it is, and this boy is one of the latters. He's going to be into everything!'" He put on his black hat and looked up suddenly and then away deep into the woods as if he were embarrassed again. "I'm sorry I don't have on a shirt before you ladies," he said, hunching his shoulders slightly. "We buried our clothes that we had on when we escaped and we're just making do until we can get better. We borrowed these from some folks we met," he explained.

"That's perfectly all right," the grandmother said. "Maybe Bailey has an extra shirt in his suitcase."

"I'll look and see terrectly," The Misfit said.

"Where are they taking him?" the children's mother screamed.

"Daddy was a card himself," The Misfit said. "You couldn't put anything over on him. He never got in trouble with the Authorities though. Just had the knack of handling them."

"You could be honest too if you'd only try," said the grandmother. "Think how wonderful it would be to settle down and live a comfortable life and not have to think about somebody chasing you all the time."

The Misfit kept scratching in the ground with the butt of his gun as if he were thinking about it. "Yes'm, somebody is always after you," he murmured.

The grandmother noticed how thin his shoulder blades were just behind his hat because she was standing up looking down on him. "Do you ever pray?" she asked.

He shook his head. All she saw was the black hat wiggle between his shoulder blades. "Nome," he said.

There was a pistol shot from the woods, followed closely by another. Then silence. The old lady's head jerked around. She could hear the wind move through the tree tops like a long satisfied insuck of breath. "Bailey Boy!" she called.

"I was a gospel singer for a while," The Misfit said. "I been most everything. Been in the arm service, both land and sea, at home and abroad, been twict married, been an undertaker, been with the railroads, plowed Mother Earth, been in a tornado, seen a man burnt alive oncet," and he looked up at the children's mother and the little girl who were sitting close together, their faces white and their eyes glassy; "I even seen a woman flogged," he said.

"Pray, pray," the grandmother began, "pray, pray . . ."

"I never was a bad boy that I remember of," The Misfit said in an almost dreamy voice, "but somewheres along the line I done something wrong and got sent to the penitentiary. I was buried alive," and he looked up and held her attention to him by a steady stare.

"That's when you should have started to pray," she said. "What did you do to get sent to the penitentiary that first time?"

"Turn to the right, it was a wall," The Misfit said, looking up again at the cloudless sky. "Turn to the left, it was a wall. Look up it was a ceiling, look down it was a floor. I forget what I done, lady. I set there and set there, trying to remember what it was I done and I ain't recalled it to this day. Oncet in a while, I would think it was coming to me, but it never come."

"Maybe they put you in by mistake," the old lady said vaguely.

"Nome," he said. "It wasn't no mistake. They had the papers on me."

"You must have stolen something," she said.

The Misfit sneered slightly. "Nobody had nothing I wanted," he said. "It was a head-doctor at the penitentiary said what I had done was kill my daddy but I known that for a lie. My daddy died in nineteen ought nineteen of the epidemic flu and I never had a thing to do with it. He was buried in the Mount Hopewell Baptist churchyard and you can go there and see for yourself."

"If you would pray," the old lady said, "Jesus would help you."

"That's right," The Misfit said.

"Well then, why don't you pray?" she asked trembling with delight suddenly.

"I don't want no hep," he said. "I'm doing all right by myself."

Bobby Lee and Hiram came ambling back from the woods. Bobby Lee was dragging a yellow shirt with bright blue parrots in it.

"Thow me that shirt, Bobby Lee," The Misfit said. The shirt came flying at him and landed on his shoulder and he put it on. The grandmother couldn't name what the shirt reminded her of. "No, lady," The Misfit said while he was buttoning it up, "I found out the crime don't matter. You can do one thing or you can do another, kill a man or take a tire off his car, because sooner or later you're going to forget what it was you done and just be punished for it."

The children's mother had begun to make heaving noises as if she couldn't get her breath. "Lady," he asked, "would you and that little girl like to step off yonder with Bobby Lee and Hiram and join your husband?"

125 "Yes, thank you," the mother said faintly. Her left arm dangled helplessly and she was holding the baby, who had gone to sleep, in the other. "Hep that lady up, Hiram," The Misfit said as she struggled to climb out of the ditch, "and Bobby Lee, you hold onto that little girl's hand."

"I don't want to hold hands with him," June Star said. "He reminds me of a pig."

The fat boy blushed and laughed and caught her by the arm and pulled her off into the woods after Hiram and her mother.

Alone with The Misfit, the grandmother found that she had lost her voice. There was not a cloud in the sky nor any sun. There was nothing around her but woods. She wanted to tell him that he must pray. She opened and closed her mouth several times before anything came out. Finally she found herself saying, "Jesus, Jesus," meaning, Jesus will help you, but the way she was saying it, it sounded as if she might be cursing.

"Yes'm," The Misfit said as if he agreed. "Jesus thown everything off balance. It was the same case with Him as with me except He hadn't committed any crime and they could prove I had committed one because they had the papers on me. Of course," he said, "they never shown me my papers. That's why I sign myself now. I said long ago, you get you a signature and sign everything you do and keep a copy of it. Then you'll know what you done and you can hold up the crime to the punishment and see do they match and in the end you'll have something to prove you ain't been treated right. I call myself The Misfit," he said, "because I can't make what all I done wrong fit what all I gone through in punishment."

130 There was a piercing scream from the woods, followed closely by a pistol report. "Does it seem right to you, lady, that one is punished a heap and another ain't punished at all?"

"Jesus!" the old lady cried. "You've got good blood! I know you wouldn't shoot a lady! I know you come from nice people! Pray! Jesus, you ought not to shoot a lady. I'll give you all the money I've got!"

"Lady," The Misfit said, looking beyond her far into the woods, "there never was a body that give the undertaker a tip."

There were two more pistol reports and the grandmother raised her head like a parched old turkey hen crying for water and called, "Bailey Boy, Bailey Boy!" as if her heart would break.

"Jesus was the only One that ever raised the dead," The Misfit continued, "and He shouldn't have done it. He thown everything off balance. If He did what He said, then it's nothing for you to do but thow away everything and follow Him, and if He didn't, then it's nothing for you to do but enjoy the few minutes you got left the best way you can—by killing somebody or burning down his house or doing some other meanness to him. No pleasure but meanness," he said and his voice became almost a snarl.

135 "Maybe He didn't raise the dead," the old lady mumbled, not knowing what she was saying and feeling so dizzy that she sank down in the ditch with her legs twisted under her.

"I wasn't there so I can't say He didn't," The Misfit said. "I wisht I had of been there," he said, hitting the ground with his fist. "It ain't right I wasn't there because if I had of been there I would of known. Listen, lady," he said in a high voice, "if I had of been there I would of known and I wouldn't be like I am now." His voice seemed about to crack and the grandmother's head cleared for an instant. She saw the man's face twisted close to her own as if he were going to cry and she murmured, "Why you're one of my babies. You're one of my own children!" She reached out and touched him on the shoulder. The Misfit sprang back as if a snake had bitten him and shot her three times through the chest. Then he put his gun down on the ground and took off his glasses and began to clean them.

Hiram and Bobby Lee returned from the woods and stood over the ditch, looking down at the grandmother who half sat and half lay in a puddle of blood with her legs crossed under her like a child's and her face smiling up at the cloudless sky.

Without his glasses, The Misfit's eyes were red-rimmed and pale and defenseless-looking. "Take her off and thow her where you thown the others," he said, picking up the cat that was rubbing itself against his leg.

"She was a talker, wasn't she?" Bobby Lee said, sliding down the ditch with a yodel.

140 "She would of been a good woman," The Misfit said, "if it had been somebody there to shoot her every minute of her life."

"Some fun!" Bobby Lee said.

"Shut up, Bobby Lee," The Misfit said. "It's no real pleasure in life."

READING AND REACTING

1. How are the style and tone of the narrator's voice different from those of the characters? What, if anything, is the significance of this difference?
2. Figurative language in this story sometimes creates unflattering, even grotesque, pictures of the characters. Find several examples of such negative figures of speech. Why do you think the author uses them?
3. What does the grandmother's use of the words *pickaninny* and *nigger* reveal about her? How are readers expected to reconcile this language with her very proper appearance and her

preoccupation with manners? How does her use of these words affect your reaction to her?
4. Explain the **irony** in this statement: "In case of an accident, anyone seeing her dead on the highway would know at once that she was a lady" (12).
5. How does The Misfit's dialect characterize him?
6. What does the allusion to *Gone with the Wind* (24) contribute to the story?
7. How do the style and tone of the two-paragraph description of the three men in the car (71–72) help to prepare readers for the events that follow?
8. When The Misfit tells the grandmother about his life, his language takes on a measured, rhythmic quality: "Been in the arm service, both land and sea, at home and abroad, been twict married, been an undertaker, been with the railroads, plowed Mother Earth, been in a tornado, seen a man burnt alive oncet, [. . .]" (109). Find other examples of parallelism and rhythmic repetition in this character's speech. How does this style help to develop The Misfit's character?
9. **JOURNAL ENTRY** Why do you think the grandmother tells The Misfit she recognizes him? Why does she fail to realize the danger of her remark?

Related Works: "The Lottery" (p. 209), "Where Are You Going, Where Have You Been?" (p. 268)

◆ WRITING SUGGESTIONS: STYLE, TONE, AND LANGUAGE

1. "A Clean, Well-Lighted Place" does not have a conventional plot in which characters grow and change and conflicts are resolved. For this reason, it might be argued that in this story language takes on more of a central role than it plays in other stories. Write an essay in which you examine this idea as it applies to "A Clean, Well-Lighted Place" and to any other story in this text.
2. All of the stories in this chapter present characters who are outsiders or misfits in their social milieus. Choose two or three characters, and explain why each is estranged from others and what efforts, if any, each makes to reconcile himself with society. Be sure to show how language helps to convey each character's alienation.
3. In each of the chapter's three stories, the title communicates a good deal of information in very few words. Write an essay in which you explain what each title communicates about the story's theme. In your thesis, try to draw a conclusion about the function of a title in a fictional work.

4. In "A Clean, Well-Lighted Place," two waiters discuss an old man, but readers do not really learn what the old man is thinking or feeling. Write a letter (or a suicide note) from the old man to a friend or family member in which you reveal his thoughts about his life and try to account for his despair. Be sure the tone of your letter is consistent with his feelings of sadness.
5. Imagine The Misfit in a prison cell, relating the violent incident at the end of "A Good Man Is Hard to Find" to another prisoner—or to a member of the clergy. Would his tone be boastful? Regretful? Apologetic? Defiant? Would he use the elaborate poetic style he sometimes uses in the story or more straightforward language? Tell his version of the incident in his own words.

Chapter 8

Symbol and Allegory

A **symbol** is a person, object, action, place, or event that, in addition to its literal meaning, suggests a more complex meaning or range of meanings. **Universal** or **archetypal symbols,** such as the Old Man, the Mother, or the Grim Reaper, are so much a part of human experience that they suggest much the same thing to most people. **Conventional symbols** are also likely to suggest the same thing to most people, provided the people have common cultural and social assumptions (a rose suggests love, a skull and crossbones denotes poison). Such symbols are often used as a kind of shorthand in films, popular literature, and advertising, where they encourage automatic responses.

Conventional symbols such as the stars and stripes of the American flag can evoke powerful feelings of pride and patriotism in a group of people who share the same orientation toward it, just as the maple leaf and the Union Jack can. Symbols used in works of literature can function in much the same way, enabling writers to convey particular emotions or messages with a high degree of predictability. Thus, spring can be expected to suggest rebirth and promise; autumn, declining years and powers; summer, youth and beauty. Because a writer expects a dark forest to evoke fear, or a rainbow to communicate hope, he or she can be quite confident in using such an image to convey a particular idea or mood (provided the audience shares the writer's frame of reference).

Many symbols, however, suggest different things to different people. (For one thing, different cultures may react differently to the same symbols. In the United States, for example, an owl suggests wisdom; in India it suggests just the opposite.) Thus, symbols enrich meaning, expanding the possibilities for interpretation and for reader interaction with the text. Because they are so potentially rich, symbols have the power to open up a work of literature.

Literary Symbols

◊ ◊ ◊

Both universal and conventional symbols can function as **literary symbols** that take on additional meanings in particular works. For instance, a watch or clock denotes time; as a conventional symbol, it suggests the passing of time; as a literary symbol in a particular work, it might also convey anything from a character's inability to recapture the past to the idea of time running out—or, it might suggest more than one of these ideas.

Considering an object's possible symbolic significance can suggest a variety of ways to interpret a text. For instance, William Faulkner focuses attention on an unseen watch in a pivotal scene in "A Rose for Emily" (p. 52). The narrator first describes Emily Grierson as "a small, fat woman in black, with a thin gold chain descending to her waist and vanishing into her belt." Several sentences later, the narrator returns to the watch, noting that Emily's visitors "could hear the invisible watch ticking at the end of the gold chain." Like these visitors, readers are drawn to the unseen watch as it ticks away. Because Emily is portrayed as a woman living in the past, readers can assume that the watch is intended to reinforce the impression that she cannot see that time (the watch) has moved on. The vivid picture of the pale, plump woman in the musty room with the watch invisibly ticking does indeed suggest both that she has been left back in time and that she remains unaware of the progress around her. Thus, the symbol enriches both the depiction of character and the story's theme.

In "Barn Burning" (p. 142), another Faulkner story, the clock is a more complex symbol. The itinerant Snopes family is without financial security and apparently without a future. The clock the mother carries from shack to shack—"The clock inlaid with mother-of-pearl, which would not run, stopped at some fourteen minutes past two o'clock of a dead and forgotten day and time, which had been [Sarty's] mother's dowry"—is their only possession of value. The fact that the clock no longer works seems at first to suggest that time has run out for the family. On another level, the clock stands in pathetic contrast to Major de Spain's grand home, with its gold and glitter and Oriental rugs. Knowing that the clock was part of the mother's dowry, and that a dowry suggests a promise, readers may decide that the broken clock symbolizes lost hope; the fact that the mother still clings to the clock, however, could suggest just the opposite—her refusal to give up.

As you read, you should not try to find the one exact equivalent for each symbol; in fact, this kind of search is very limiting and not very productive. Instead, consider the different meanings a symbol might suggest. Then, consider how these various interpretations enrich other elements of the story and the work as a whole.

Recognizing Symbols

When is a clock just a clock, and when is it also a symbol with a meaning or meanings beyond its literal significance? If a character waiting for a friend glances once at his or her watch to verify the time, there is probably nothing symbolic about the watch or about the act of looking at it. If, however, the watch keeps appearing again and again in the story, at key moments; if the narrator devotes a good deal of time to describing it; if it is placed in a conspicuous physical location; if characters keep noticing it and commenting on its presence; if it is lost (or found) at a critical moment; if its function in some way parallels the development of plot or character (for instance, if it stops as a relationship ends or as a character dies); if the story's opening or closing paragraph focuses on the timepiece; or if the story is called "The Watch"—the watch most likely has symbolic significance. In other words, considering how an image is used, how often it is used, and when it appears will help you to determine whether or not it functions as a symbol.

The Purpose of Symbols

Symbols expand the possible meanings of a story, thereby heightening interest and actively involving readers in the text. In "The Lottery" (p. 209), for example, the mysterious black box has symbolic significance. It is mentioned prominently and repeatedly, and it plays a pivotal role in the story's action. Of course, the black box is important on a purely literal level: it functions as a key component of the lottery. But the box has other associations as well, and it is these associations that suggest what its symbolic significance might be.

The black wooden box is very old, a relic of many past lotteries; the narrator observes that it represents tradition. It is also closed and closely guarded, suggesting mystery and uncertainty. It is shabby, "splintered badly along one side [. . .] and in places faded or stained," and this state of disrepair could suggest that the ritual it is part of has also deteriorated or that tradition itself has deteriorated. The box is also simple in construction and design, suggesting the primitive (and therefore perhaps outdated) nature of the ritual. Thus, this symbol encourages readers to probe the story for values and ideas, to consider and weigh the suitability of a variety of interpretations. It serves as a "hot spot" that invites questions, and the answers to these questions reinforce and enrich the story's theme.

Allegory

◊ ◊ ◊

An **allegory** communicates a doctrine, message, or moral principle by making it into a narrative in which the characters personify ideas, concepts, qualities, or other abstractions. Thus, an allegory is a story with two parallel and consistent levels of meaning—one literal and one figurative. The figurative level, which offers some moral or political lesson, is the story's main concern. The allegorical figures are significant only because they represent something beyond their literal meaning in a fixed system.

Whereas a symbol has multiple symbolic associations as well as a literal meaning, an **allegorical figure**—a character, object, place, or event in the allegory—has just one meaning within an **allegorical framework,** the set of ideas that conveys the allegory's message. (At the simplest level, for instance, one character can stand for good and another can stand for evil.) For this reason, allegorical figures do not open up a text to various interpretations the way symbols do. Because the purpose of allegory is to communicate a particular lesson, readers are not encouraged to speculate about the allegory's possible meanings; each element has only one equivalent, which readers must discover if they are to make sense of the story.

Naturally, the better a reader understands the political, religious, and literary assumptions of a writer, the easier it will be to recognize the allegorical significance of his or her work. John Bunyan's *The Pilgrim's Progress,* for example, is a famous seventeenth-century allegory based on the Christian doctrine of salvation. In order to appreciate the complexity of Bunyan's work, you would have to familiarize yourself with this doctrine—possibly by consulting an encyclopedia or a reference work such as *The Oxford Companion to English Literature.*

One type of allegory, called a **beast fable,** is a short tale, usually including a moral, in which animals assume human characteristics. Aesop's fables are the best-known examples of beast fables. More recently, contemporary writers have used beast fables to satirize the political and social conditions of our time. In one such tale, "The Gentlemen of the Jungle" by the Kenyan writer Jomo Kenyatta, an elephant is allowed to put his trunk inside a man's hut during a rainstorm. Not content with keeping his trunk dry, the elephant pushes his entire body inside the hut, displacing the man. When the man protests, the elephant takes the matter to the lion, who appoints a Commission of Enquiry to settle the matter. Eventually the man is forced not only to abandon his hut to the elephant, but also to build new huts for all the animals in the Commission. Even so, the jealous animals occupy the man's new hut and begin fighting for space; while they are arguing, the man burns down the hut, animals and all. Like the tales told by Aesop, "The Gentlemen of the Jungle" has a moral: "Peace is costly," says the man as he walks away happily, "but it's worth the expense." The following passage from "The Gentlemen of the Jungle" reveals how the allegorical figures work within the framework of the allegory:

> The elephant, obeying the command of his master (the lion), got busy with the other ministers to appoint a Commission of Enquiry. The following elders of the jungle were appointed to

sit in the Commission: (1) Mr. Rhinoceros; (2) Mr. Buffalo; (3) Mr. Alligator; (4) The Rt. Hon. Mr. Fox to act as chairman; and (5) Mr. Leopard to act as Secretary of the Commission. On seeing the personnel, the man protested and asked if it was not necessary to include in this Commission a member from his side. But he was told that it was impossible, since no one from his side was well enough educated to understand the intricacy of jungle law.

From this excerpt we can see that each character represents a particular idea. For example, the members of the Commission stand for bureaucratic smugness and inequity, and the man stands for the citizens who are victimized by the government. In order to fully understand the allegorical significance of each figure in this story, of course, readers would have to know something about government bureaucracies, colonialism in Africa, and possibly a specific historical event in Kenya.

Some works contain both symbolic elements *and* allegorical elements, as Nathaniel Hawthorne's "Young Goodman Brown" (p. 198) does. The names of the story's two main characters, "Goodman" and "Faith," suggest that they fit within an allegorical system of some sort: Young Goodman Brown represents a good person who, despite his best efforts, strays from the path of righteousness; his wife, Faith, represents the quality he must hold on to in order to avoid temptation. As characters, they have no significance outside of their allegorical functions. Other elements of the story, however, are not so clear-cut. The older man whom Young Goodman Brown meets in the woods carries a staff that has carved on it "the likeness of a great black snake, so curiously wrought, that it might almost be seen to twist and wriggle itself like a living serpent." This staff, carried by a Satanic figure who represents evil and temptation, suggests the snake in the Garden of Eden, an association that neatly fits into the allegorical context of the story. Alternately, however, the staff could suggest the "slippery," ever-changing nature of sin, the difficulty people have in perceiving sin, or sexuality (which may explain Young Goodman Brown's susceptibility to temptation). This range of possible meanings suggests that the staff functions as a symbol that enriches Hawthorne's allegory.

Other stories work entirely on a symbolic level and contain no allegorical figures. "The Lottery," despite its moral overtones, is not an allegory because its characters, events, and objects are not arranged to serve one rigid, didactic purpose. In fact, many different interpretations have been suggested for this story. When it was first published in June 1948 in *The New Yorker,* some readers believed it to be a story about an actual custom or ritual. As Shirley Jackson reports in her essay "Biography of a Story," even those who recognized it as fiction speculated about its meaning, seeing it as (among other things) an attack on prejudice, a criticism of society's need for a scapegoat, or a treatise on witchcraft, Christian martyrdom, or village gossip. Various critics have argued that

"The Lottery" is a story about the evils of violence, mob psychology, or Nazi Germany. The fact is that no single allegorical interpretation will account for every major character, object, and event in the story.

★ CHECKLIST: WRITING ABOUT SYMBOL AND ALLEGORY

- ✓ Are any universal symbols used in the work? Any conventional symbols? What is their function?
- ✓ Is any character, place, action, event, or object given unusual prominence or emphasis in the story? If so, does this element seem to have symbolic as well as literal value?
- ✓ What possible meanings does each symbol suggest?
- ✓ How do symbols help to depict the story's characters?
- ✓ How do symbols help to characterize the story's setting?
- ✓ How do symbols help to advance the story's plot?
- ✓ Are any of the symbols related? Taken together, do they seem to support a common theme?
- ✓ Does the story have a moral or didactic purpose? What is the message, idea, or moral principle the story seeks to convey?
- ✓ What equivalent may be assigned to each allegorical figure in the story?
- ✓ Does the story combine allegorical figures and symbols? How do they work together in the story?

◆ **NATHANIEL HAWTHORNE** (1804–1864) was born in Salem, Massachusetts, the great-great-grandson of a judge who presided over the infamous Salem witch trials. He published four novels, including *The Scarlet Letter* (1850), and more than one hundred short stories and sketches.

His stories frequently paint a picture of a world that is virtuous on the surface but (as young Goodman Brown comes to believe) "one stain of guilt, one mighty blood spot" beneath. Hawthorne's stories often emphasize the ambiguity of human experience. Here, for example, the reader is left to wonder whether Goodman Brown actually saw a witch's coven or dreamed a dream. For Hawthorne, what is important is Brown's recognition that evil may be found everywhere.

NATHANIEL HAWTHORNE

Young Goodman[1] Brown
(1835)

Young Goodman Brown came forth at sunset, into the street of Salem village, but put his head back, after crossing the threshold, to exchange a parting kiss with his young wife. And Faith, as the wife was aptly named, thrust her own pretty head into the street, letting the wind play with the pink ribbons of her cap, while she called to Goodman Brown.

"Dearest heart," whispered she, softly and rather sadly, when her lips were close to his ear, "prithee, put off your journey until sunrise, and sleep in your own bed to-night. A lone woman is troubled with such dreams and such thoughts, that she's afeard of herself, sometimes. Pray, tarry with me this night, dear husband, of all nights in the year!"

"My love and my Faith," replied young Goodman Brown, "of all nights in the year, this one night must I tarry away from thee. My journey, as thou callest it, forth and back again, must needs be done 'twixt now and sunrise. What, my sweet, pretty wife, dost thou doubt me already, and we but three months married!"

"Then God bless you!" said Faith with the pink ribbons, "and may you find all well, when you come back."

"Amen!" cried Goodman Brown. "Say thy prayers, dear Faith, and go to bed at dusk, and no harm will come to thee."

So they parted; and the young man pursued his way, until, being about to turn the corner by the meeting-house, he looked back and saw the head of Faith still peeping after him, with a melancholy air, in spite of her pink ribbons.

"Poor little Faith!" thought he, for his heart smote him. "What a wretch am I, to leave her on such an errand! She talks of dreams, too. Methought, as she spoke, there was trouble in her face, as if a dream had warned her what work is to be done to-night. But no, no! 't would kill her to think it. Well; she's a blessed angel on earth; and after this one night, I'll cling to her skirts and follow her to Heaven."

With this excellent resolve for the future, Goodman Brown felt himself justified in making more haste on his present evil purpose. He had taken a dreary road, darkened by all the gloomiest trees of the forest, which barely stood aside to let the narrow path creep through, and closed immediately behind. It was as lonely as could be; and there is this peculiarity in such a solitude, that the traveller knows not who may be concealed by the innumerable trunks and the thick boughs overhead; so that, with lonely footsteps, he may yet be passing through an unseen multitude.

---

[1] A form of address indicating a married man of ordinary station.

"There may be a devilish Indian behind every tree," said Goodman Brown to himself; and he glanced fearfully behind him, as he added, "What if the devil himself should be at my very elbow!"

His head being turned back, he passed a crook of the road, and looking forward again, beheld the figure of a man, in grave and decent attire, seated at the foot of an old tree. He arose at Goodman Brown's approach, and walked onward, side by side with him.

"You are late, Goodman Brown," said he. "The clock of the Old South[2] was striking, as I came through Boston; and that is full fifteen minutes agone."

"Faith kept me back awhile," replied the young man, with a tremor in his voice, caused by the sudden appearance of his companion, though not wholly unexpected.

It was now deep dusk in the forest, and deepest in that part of it where these two were journeying. As nearly as could be discerned, the second traveller was about fifty years old, apparently in the same rank of life as Goodman Brown, and bearing a considerable resemblance to him, though perhaps more in expression than features. Still, they might have been taken for father and son. And yet, though the elder person was as simply clad as the younger, and as simple in manner too, he had an indescribable air of one who knew the world, and would not have felt abashed at the governor's dinner-table, or in King William's court,[3] were it possible that his affairs should call him thither. But the only thing about him that could be fixed upon as remarkable, was his staff, which bore the likeness of a great black snake, so curiously wrought, that it might almost be seen to twist and wriggle itself like a living serpent. This, of course, must have been an ocular deception, assisted by the uncertain light.

"Come, Goodman Brown!" cried his fellow-traveller, "this is a dull pace for the beginning of a journey. Take my staff, if you are so soon weary."

"Friend," said the other, exchanging his slow pace for a full stop, "having kept covenant by meeting thee here, it is my purpose now to return whence I came. I have scruples, touching the matter thou wot'st of."

"Sayest thou so?" replied he of the serpent, smiling apart. "Let us walk on, nevertheless, reasoning as we go, and if I convince thee not, thou shalt turn back. We are but a little way in the forest, yet."

"Too far, too far!" exclaimed the goodman, unconsciously resuming his walk. "My father never went into the woods on such an errand, nor his father before him. We have been a race of honest men and good Christians, since the days of the martyrs. And shall I be the first of the name of Brown that ever took this path and kept—"

---

[2] Old South Church, Boston, renowned meeting place for American patriots during the Revolution.
[3] William III, king of England from 1689 to 1702.

"Such company, thou wouldst say," observed the elder person, interrupting his pause. "Well said, Goodman Brown! I have been as well acquainted with your family as with ever a one among the Puritans; and that's no trifle to say. I helped your grandfather, the constable, when he lashed the Quaker woman so smartly through the streets of Salem. And it was I that brought your father a pitch-pine knot, kindled at my own hearth, to set fire to an Indian village, in King Philip's war.[4] They were my good friends, both; and many a pleasant walk have we had along this path, and returned merrily after midnight. I would fain be friends with you, for their sake."

"If it be as thou sayest," replied Goodman Brown, "I marvel they never spoke of these matters. Or, verily, I marvel not, seeing that the least rumor of the sort would have driven them from New England. We are a people of prayer, and good works to boot, and abide no such wickedness."

"Wickedness or not," said the traveller with the twisted staff, "I have a very general acquaintance here in New England. The deacons of many a church have drunk the communion wine with me; the selectmen, of divers towns, make me their chairman; and a majority of the Great and General Court are firm supporters of my interest. The governor and I, too—but these are state secrets."

"Can this be so!" cried Goodman Brown, with a stare of amazement at his undisturbed companion. "Howbeit, I have nothing to do with the governor and council; they have their own ways, and are no rule for a simple husbandman like me. But, were I to go on with thee, how should I meet the eye of that good old man, our minister, at Salem village? Oh, his voice would make me tremble, both Sabbath-day and lecture-day!"[5]

Thus far, the elder traveller had listened with due gravity, but now burst into a fit of irrepressible mirth, shaking himself so violently, that his snakelike staff actually seemed to wriggle in sympathy.

"Ha, ha, ha!" shouted he, again and again; then composing himself, "Well, go on, Goodman Brown, go on; but, prithee, don't kill me with laughing!"

"Well, then, to end the matter at once," said Goodman Brown, considerably nettled, "there is my wife, Faith. It would break her dear little heart; and I'd rather break my own!"

"Nay, if that be the case," answered the other, "e'en go thy ways, Goodman Brown. I would not, for twenty old women like the one hobbling before us, that Faith should come to any harm."

As he spoke, he pointed his staff at a female figure on the path, in whom Goodman Brown recognized a very pious and exemplary dame,

---

[4] A war of Indian resistance, led by King Philip, or Metacomet, of the Wampanoags. The war, intended to halt expansion of English settlers in Massachusetts, collapsed after King Philip's death in August 1676.

[5] The day of the midweek sermon, usually Thursday.

who had taught him his catechism in youth, and was still his moral and spiritual adviser, jointly with the minister and Deacon Gookin.

"A marvel, truly, that Goody[6] Cloyse should be so far in the wilderness, at nightfall!" said he. "But, with your leave, friend, I shall take a cut through the woods, until we have left this Christian woman behind. Being a stranger to you, she might ask whom I was consorting with, and whither I was going."

"Be it so," said his fellow-traveller. "Betake you to the woods, and let me keep the path."

Accordingly, the young man turned aside, but took care to watch his companion, who advanced softly along the road, until he had come within a staff's length of the old dame. She, meanwhile, was making the best of her way, with singular speed for so aged a woman, and mumbling some indistinct words, a prayer, doubtless, as she went. The traveller put forth his staff, and touched her withered neck with what seemed the serpent's tail.

30 "The devil!" screamed the pious old lady.

"Then Goody Cloyse knows her old friend?" observed the traveller, confronting her, and leaning on his writhing stick.

"Ah, forsooth, and is it your worship, indeed?" cried the good dame. "Yea, truly is it, and in the very image of my old gossip, Goodman Brown, the grandfather of the silly fellow that now is. But, would your worship believe it? my broomstick hath strangely disappeared, stolen, as I suspect, by that unhanged witch, Goody Cory, and that, too, when I was all anointed with the juice of smallage and cinque-foil and wolf's bane—"[7]

"Mingled with fine wheat and the fat of a new-born babe," said the shape of old Goodman Brown.

"Ah, your worship knows the recipe," cried the old lady, cackling aloud. "So, as I was saying, being all ready for the meeting, and no horse to ride on, I made up my mind to foot it; for they tell me there is a nice young man to be taken into communion to-night. But now your good worship will lend me your arm, and we shall be there in a twinkling."

35 "That can hardly be," answered her friend. "I may not spare you my arm, Goody Cloyse, but here is my staff, if you will."

So saying, he threw it down at her feet, where, perhaps, it assumed life, being one of the rods which its owner had formerly lent to the Egyptian Magi. Of this fact, however, Goodman Brown could not take cognizance. He had cast his eyes in astonishment, and looking down again, beheld neither Goody Cloyse nor the serpentine staff, but his fellow-traveller alone, who waited for him as calmly as if nothing had happened.

---

[6] A contraction of "Goodwife," a term of politeness used in addressing a married woman of ordinary station. Goody Cloyse, like Goody Cory and Martha Carrier, who appear later in the story, was one of the Salem "witches" sentenced in 1692.

[7] All plants believed to have magical powers. "Smallage" is wild celery.

"That old woman taught me my catechism!" said the young man; and there was a world of meaning in this simple comment.

They continued to walk onward, while the elder traveller exhorted his companion to make good speed and persevere in the path, discoursing so aptly, that his arguments seemed rather to spring up in the bosom of his auditor, than to be suggested by himself. As they went he plucked a branch of maple, to serve for a walking-stick, and began to strip it of the twigs and little boughs, which were wet with evening dew. The moment his fingers touched them, they became strangely withered and dried up, as with a week's sunshine. Thus the pair proceeded, at a good free pace, until suddenly, in a gloomy hollow of the road, Goodman Brown sat himself down on the stump of a tree, and refused to go any farther.

"Friend," said he, stubbornly, "my mind is made up. Not another step will I budge on this errand. What if a wretched old woman do choose to go to the devil, when I thought she was going to Heaven! Is that any reason why I should quit my dear Faith, and go after her?"

"You will think better of this by and by," said his acquaintance, composedly. "Sit here and rest yourself awhile; and when you feel like moving again, there is my staff to help you along."

Without more words, he threw his companion the maple stick, and was as speedily out of sight as if he had vanished into the deepening gloom. The young man sat a few moments by the roadside, applauding himself greatly, and thinking with how clear a conscience he should meet the minister, in his morning walk, nor shrink from the eye of good old Deacon Gookin. And what calm sleep would be his, that very night, which was to have been spent so wickedly, but purely and sweetly now, in the arms of Faith! Amidst these pleasant and praiseworthy meditations, Goodman Brown heard the tramp of horses along the road, and deemed it advisable to conceal himself within the verge of the forest, conscious of the guilty purpose that had brought him thither, though now so happily turned from it.

On came the hoof-tramps and the voices of the riders, two grave old voices, conversing soberly as they drew near. These mingled sounds appeared to pass along the road, within a few yards of the young man's hiding-place; but owing, doubtless, to the depth of the gloom, at that particular spot, neither the travellers nor their steeds were visible. Though their figures brushed the small boughs by the wayside, it could not be seen that they intercepted, even for a moment, the faint gleam from the strip of bright sky, athwart which they must have passed. Goodman Brown alternately crouched and stood on tiptoe, pulling aside the branches, and thrusting forth his head as far as he durst, without discerning so much as a shadow. It vexed him the more, because he could have sworn, were such a thing possible, that he recognized the voices of the minister and Deacon Gookin, jogging along quietly, as they were wont to do, when bound to some ordination or ecclesiastical council. While yet within hearing, one of the riders stopped to pluck a switch.

"Of the two, reverend Sir," said the voice like the deacon's, "I had rather miss an ordination dinner than to-night's meeting. They tell me that some of our community are to be here from Falmouth and beyond, and others from Connecticut and Rhode Island; besides several of the Indian powwows, who, after their fashion, know almost as much deviltry as the best of us. Moreover, there is a goodly young woman to be taken into communion."

"Mighty well, Deacon Gookin!" replied the solemn old tones of the minister. "Spur up, or we shall be late. Nothing can be done, you know, until I get on the ground."

The hoofs clattered again, and the voices, talking so strangely in the empty air, passed on through the forest, where no church had ever been gathered, nor solitary Christian prayed. Whither, then, could these holy men be journeying, so deep into the heathen wilderness? Young Goodman Brown caught hold of a tree, for support, being ready to sink down on the ground, faint and over-burthened with the heavy sickness of his heart. He looked up to the sky, doubting whether there really was a Heaven above him. Yet, there was the blue arch, and the stars brightening in it.

"With Heaven above, and Faith below, I will yet stand firm against the devil!" cried Goodman Brown.

While he still gazed upward, into the deep arch of the firmament, and had lifted his hands to pray, a cloud, though no wind was stirring, hurried across the zenith, and hid the brightening stars. The blue sky was still visible, except directly overhead, where this black mass of cloud was sweeping swiftly northward. Aloft in the air, as if from the depths of the cloud, came a confused and doubtful sound of voices. Once, the listener fancied that he could distinguish the accents of townspeople of his own, men and women, both pious and ungodly, many of whom he had met at the communion-table, and had seen others rioting at the tavern. The next moment, so indistinct were the sounds, he doubted whether he had heard aught but the murmur of the old forest, whispering without a wind. Then came a stronger swell of those familiar tones, heard daily in the sunshine, at Salem village, but never, until now, from a cloud at night. There was one voice, of a young woman, uttering lamentations, yet with an uncertain sorrow, and entreating for some favor, which, perhaps, it would grieve her to obtain. And all the unseen multitude, both saints and sinners, seemed to encourage her onward.

"Faith!" shouted Goodman Brown, in a voice of agony and desperation; and the echoes of the forest mocked him, crying—"Faith! Faith!" as if bewildered wretches were seeking her, all through the wilderness.

The cry of grief, rage, and terror was yet piercing the night, when the unhappy husband held his breath for a response. There was a scream, drowned immediately in a louder murmur of voices fading into far-off laughter, as the dark cloud swept away, leaving the clear and silent sky above Goodman Brown. But something fluttered lightly down through the air, and caught on the branch of a tree. The young man seized it and beheld a pink ribbon.

"My Faith is gone!" cried he, after one stupefied moment. "There is no good on earth, and sin is but a name. Come, devil! for to thee is this world given."

And maddened with despair, so that he laughed loud and long, did Goodman Brown grasp his staff and set forth again, at such a rate, that he seemed to fly along the forest path, rather than to walk or run. The road grew wilder and drearier, and more faintly traced, and vanished at length, leaving him in the heart of the dark wilderness, still rushing onward, with the instinct that guides mortal man to evil. The whole forest was peopled with frightful sounds: the creaking of the trees, the howling of wild beasts, and the yell of Indians; while, sometimes, the wind tolled like a distant church bell, and sometimes gave a broad roar around the traveller, as if all Nature was laughing him to scorn. But he was himself the chief horror of the scene, and shrank not from its other horrors.

"Ha! ha! ha!" roared Goodman Brown, when the wind laughed at him. "Let us hear which will laugh loudest! Think not to frighten me with your deviltry! Come witch, come wizard, come Indian powwow, come devil himself! and here comes Goodman Brown. You may as well fear him as he fear you!"

In truth, all through the haunted forest, there could be nothing more frightful than the figure of Goodman Brown. On he flew, among the black pines, brandishing his staff with frenzied gestures, now giving vent to an inspiration of horrid blasphemy, and now shouting forth such laughter, as set all the echoes of the forest laughing like demons around him. The fiend in his own shape is less hideous, than when he rages in the breast of man. Thus sped the demoniac on his course, until, quivering among the trees, he saw a red light before him, as when the felled trunks and branches of a clearing have been set on fire, and throw up their lurid blaze against the sky, at the hour of midnight. He paused, in a lull of the tempest that had driven him onward, and heard the swell of what seemed a hymn, rolling solemnly from a distance, with the weight of many voices. He knew the tune. It was a familiar one in the choir of the village meeting-house. The verse died heavily away, and was lengthened by a chorus, not of human voices, but of all the sounds of the benighted wilderness, pealing in awful harmony together. Goodman Brown cried out; and his cry was lost to his own ear, by its unison with the cry of the desert.

In the interval of silence, he stole forward, until the light glared full upon his eyes. At one extremity of an open space, hemmed in by the dark wall of the forest, arose a rock, bearing some rude, natural resemblance either to an altar or a pulpit, and surrounded by four blazing pines, their tops aflame, their stems untouched, like candles at an evening meeting. The mass of foliage, that had overgrown the summit of the rock, was all on fire, blazing high into the night, and fitfully illuminating the whole field. Each pendent twig and leafy festoon was in a blaze. As the red light arose and fell, a numerous congregation alternately shone forth, then disappeared in shadow, and again grew, as it were, out of the darkness, peopling the heart of the solitary woods at once.

"A grave and dark-clad company!" quoth Goodman Brown.

In truth, they were such. Among them, quivering to-and-fro, between gloom and splendor, appeared faces that would be seen, next day, at the council-board of the province, and others which, Sabbath after Sabbath, looked devoutly heavenward, and benignantly over the crowded pews, from the holiest pulpits in the land. Some affirm, that the lady of the governor was there. At least, there were high dames well known to her, and wives of honored husbands, and widows a great multitude, and ancient maidens, all of excellent repute, and fair young girls, who trembled lest their mothers should espy them. Either the sudden gleams of light, flashing over the obscure field, bedazzled Goodman Brown, or he recognized a score of the church members of Salem village, famous for their especial sanctity. Good old Deacon Gookin had arrived, and waited at the skirts of that venerable saint, his reverend pastor. But, irreverently consorting with these grave, reputable, and pious people, these elders of the church, these chaste dames and dewy virgins, there were men of dissolute lives and women of spotted fame, wretches given over to all mean and filthy vice, and suspected even of horrid crimes. It was strange to see, that the good shrank not from the wicked, nor were the sinners abashed by the saints. Scattered, also, among their pale-faced enemies, were the Indian priests, or powwows, who had often scared their native forest with more hideous incantations than any known to English witchcraft.

"But, where is Faith?" thought Goodman Brown; and, as hope came into his heart, he trembled.

Another verse of the hymn arose, a slow and mournful strain, such as the pious love, but joined to words which expressed all that our nature can conceive of sin, and darkly hinted at far more. Unfathomable to mere mortals is the lore of fiends. Verse after verse was sung, and still the chorus of the desert swelled between, like the deepest tone of a mighty organ. And, with the final peal of that dreadful anthem, there came a sound, as if the roaring wind, the rushing streams, the howling beasts, and every other voice of the unconverted wilderness were mingling and according with the voice of guilty man, in homage to the prince of all. The four blazing pines threw up a loftier flame, and obscurely discovered shapes and visages of horror on the smoke-wreaths, above the impious assembly. At the same moment, the fire on the rock shot redly forth, and formed a glowing arch above its base, where now appeared a figure. With reverence be it spoken, the apparition bore no slight similitude, both in garb and manner, to some grave divine of the New England churches.

"Bring forth the converts!" cried a voice, that echoed through the field and rolled into the forest.

60   At the word, Goodman Brown stepped forth from the shadow of the trees, and approached the congregation, with whom he felt a loathful brotherhood, by the sympathy of all that was wicked in his heart. He could have well-nigh sworn, that the shape of his own dead father beckoned him to advance, looking downward from a smoke-wreath, while a woman, with dim features of despair, threw out her hand to warn him back. Was it his mother? But he had no power to retreat one step, nor to resist, even in thought, when the minister and good old Deacon Gookin seized his arms, and led him to the blazing rock. Thither came also the slender form of a veiled female, led between Goody Cloyse, that pious teacher of the catechism, and Martha Carrier, who had received the devil's promise to be queen of hell. A rampant hag was she! And there stood the proselytes, beneath the canopy of fire.

"Welcome, my children," said the dark figure, "to the communion of your race! Ye have found, thus young, your nature and your destiny. My children, look behind you!"

They turned; and flashing forth, as it were, in a sheet of flame, the fiend-worshippers were seen; the smile of welcome gleamed darkly on every visage.

"There," resumed the sable form, "are all whom ye have reverenced from youth. Ye deemed them holier than yourselves, and shrank from your own sin, contrasting it with their lives of righteousness and prayerful aspirations heavenward. Yet, here are they all, in my worshipping assembly! This night it shall be granted you to know their secret deeds; how hoary-bearded elders of the church have whispered wanton words to the young maids of their households; how many a woman, eager for widow's weeds, has given her husband a drink at bedtime, and let him sleep his last sleep in her bosom; how beardless youths have made haste to inherit their father's wealth; and how fair damsels—blush not, sweet ones!—have dug little graves in the garden, and bidden me, the sole guest, to an infant's funeral. By the sympathy of your human hearts for sin, ye shall scent out all the places—whether in church, bedchamber, street, field, or forest—where crime has been committed, and shall exult to behold the whole earth one stain of guilt, one mighty blood-spot. Far more than this! It shall be yours to penetrate, in every bosom, the deep mystery of sin, the fountain of all wicked arts, and which inexhaustibly supplies more evil impulses than human power—than my power, at its utmost!—can make manifest in deeds. And now, my children, look upon each other."

They did so; and, by the blaze of the hell-kindled torches, the wretched man beheld his Faith, and the wife her husband, trembling before that unhallowed altar.

65   "Lo! there ye stand, my children," said the figure, in a deep and solemn tone, almost sad, with its despairing awfulness, as if his once angelic nature could yet mourn for our miserable race. "Depending upon one another's hearts, ye had still hoped that virtue were not all a dream! Now are ye undeceived!—Evil is the nature of mankind. Evil

must be your only happiness. Welcome, again, my children, to the communion of your race!"

"Welcome!" repeated the fiend-worshippers, in one cry of despair and triumph.

And there they stood, the only pair, as it seemed, who were yet hesitating on the verge of wickedness, in this dark world. A basin was hollowed, naturally, in the rock. Did it contain water, reddened by the lurid light? or was it blood? or, perchance, a liquid flame? Herein did the Shape of Evil dip his hand, and prepare to lay the mark of baptism upon their foreheads, that they might be partakers of the mystery of sin, more conscious of the secret guilt of others, both in deed and thought, than they could now be of their own. The husband cast one look at his pale wife, and Faith at him. What polluted wretches would the next glance show them to each other, shuddering alike at what they disclosed and what they saw!

"Faith! Faith!" cried the husband. "Look up to Heaven, and resist the Wicked One!"

Whether Faith obeyed, he knew not. Hardly had he spoken, when he found himself amid calm night and solitude, listening to a roar of the wind, which died heavily away through the forest. He staggered against the rock, and felt it chill and damp, while a hanging twig, that had been all on fire, besprinkled his cheek with the coldest dew.

70　　The next morning, young Goodman Brown came slowly into the street of Salem village staring around him like a bewildered man. The good old minister was taking a walk along the grave-yard, to get an appetite for breakfast and meditate his sermon, and bestowed a blessing, as he passed, on Goodman Brown. He shrank from the venerable saint, as if to avoid an anathema. Old Deacon Gookin was at domestic worship, and the holy words of his prayer were heard through the open window. "What God doth the wizard pray to?" quoth Goodman Brown. Goody Cloyse, that excellent old Christian, stood in the early sunshine, at her own lattice, catechising a little girl, who had brought her a pint of morning's milk. Goodman Brown snatched away the child, as from the grasp of the fiend himself. Turning the corner by the meeting-house, he spied the head of Faith, with the pink ribbons, gazing anxiously forth, and bursting into such joy at sight of him that she skipt along the street, and almost kissed her husband before the whole village. But Goodman Brown looked sternly and sadly into her face, and passed on without a greeting.

Had Goodman Brown fallen asleep in the forest, and only dreamed a wild dream of a witch-meeting?

Be it so, if you will. But, alas! it was a dream of evil omen for young Goodman Brown. A stern, a sad, a darkly meditative, a distrustful, if not a desperate man did he become, from the night of that fearful dream. On the Sabbath day, when the congregation were singing a holy psalm, he could not listen, because an anthem of sin rushed loudly upon his ear, and drowned all the blessed strain. When the minister spoke from the pulpit, with power and fervid eloquence, and with his hand on the open Bible, of the sacred truths of our religion, and of saint-like lives and triumphant deaths, and of future bliss or misery unutterable, then did Goodman Brown turn pale, dreading lest the roof should thunder down upon the gray blasphemer and his hearers. Often, awaking suddenly at midnight, he shrank from the bosom of Faith, and at morning or eventide, when the family knelt down at prayer, he scowled, and muttered to himself, and gazed sternly at his wife, and turned away. And when he had lived long, and was borne to his grave, a hoary corpse, followed by Faith, an aged woman, and children and grand-children, a goodly procession, besides neighbors not a few, they carved no hopeful verse upon his tombstone; for his dying hour was gloom.

READING AND REACTING

1. Who is the narrator of "Young Goodman Brown"? What advantages does the narrative point of view give the author?
2. What does young Goodman Brown mean when he says "of all nights in the year, this one must I tarry away from thee" (3)? What is important about *this* night, and why does Goodman Brown believe he must journey "'twixt now and sunrise"?
3. Is Goodman Brown surprised to encounter the second traveler on the road, or does he seem to expect him? What is the significance of their encounter? What do you make of the fact that the stranger bears a strong resemblance to young Goodman Brown?
4. What sins are the various characters Goodman Brown meets in the woods guilty of committing?
5. "Young Goodman Brown" has two distinct settings: Salem and the woods. What are the differences between these settings? What significance does each have in the story?
6. Which figures in the story are allegorical, and which are symbols? On what evidence do you base your conclusions?
7. Why do the people gather in the woods? Why do they attend the ceremony?
8. Explain the change that takes place in young Goodman Brown at the end of the story. Why can he not listen to the singing of holy psalms or to the minister's sermons? What causes him to turn away from Faith and die in gloom?
9. **JOURNAL ENTRY** At the end of the story the narrator suggests that Goodman Brown might have fallen asleep and imagined his encounter with the witches. Do you think the events are all a dream?

Related Works: Once upon a Time (p. 46), "Where Are You Going, Where Have You Been?" (p. 268), "We Wear the Mask" (p. 518), "La Belle Dame sans Merci: A Ballad" (p. 531)

◊ **SHIRLEY JACKSON** (1916–1965) is best known for her restrained tales of horror and the supernatural, most notably her novel *The Haunting of Hill House* (1959) and the short story "The Lottery" (1948). Jackson was an intense, contradictory personality: a cookie-baking "Mom" who wrote chilling tales between loads of laundry. With her husband, she settled in the small town of Bennington, Vermont, but was never accepted by the townspeople.

"The Lottery" is set in much the same kind of small, provincial town. The story's publication in *The New Yorker* magazine provoked a torrent of letters from enraged and horrified readers. Written scarcely three years after the liberation of Auschwitz, it told Americans something they did not want to hear—that the face of human evil could look just like their next-door neighbor.

◊ ◊ ◊

SHIRLEY JACKSON

The Lottery
(1948)

The morning of June 27th was clear and sunny, with the fresh warmth of a full-summer day; the flowers were blossoming profusely and the grass was richly green. The people of the village began to gather in the square, between the post office and the bank, around ten o'clock; in some towns there were so many people that the lottery took two days and had to be started on June 26th, but in this village, where there were only about three hundred people, the whole lottery took less than two hours, so it could begin at ten o'clock in the morning and still be through in time to allow the villagers to get home for noon dinner.

The children assembled first, of course. School was recently over for the summer, and the feeling of liberty sat uneasily on most of them; they tended to gather together quietly for a while before they broke into boisterous play, and their talk was still of the classroom and the teacher, of books and reprimands. Bobby Martin had already stuffed his pockets full of stones, and the other boys soon followed his example, selecting the smoothest and roundest stones; Bobby and Harry Jones and Dickie Delacroix—the villagers pronounced this name "Dellacroy"—eventually made a great pile of stones in one corner of the square and guarded it against the raids of the other boys. The girls stood aside, talking among themselves, looking over their shoulders at the boys, and the very small children rolled in the dust or clung to the hands of their older brothers or sisters.

Soon the men began to gather, surveying their own children, speaking of planting and rain, tractors and taxes. They stood together, away from the pile of stones in the corner, and their jokes were quiet and they smiled rather than laughed. The women, wearing faded house dresses and sweaters, came shortly after their menfolk. They greeted one another and exchanged bits of gossip as they went to join their husbands. Soon the women, standing by their husbands, began to call to their children, and the children came reluctantly, having to be called four or five times. Bobby Martin ducked under his mother's grasping hand and ran, laughing, back to the pile of stones. His father spoke up sharply, and Bobby came quickly and took his place between his father and his oldest brother.

The lottery was conducted—as were the square dances, the teen-age club, the Halloween program—by Mr. Summers, who had time and energy to devote to civic activities. He was a round-faced, jovial man and he ran the coal business, and people were sorry for him, because he had no children and his wife was a scold. When he arrived in the square, carrying the black wooden box, there was a murmur of conversation among the villagers, and he waved and called, "Little late today, folks." The postmaster, Mr. Graves, followed him, carrying a three-legged stool, and the stool was put in the center of the square and Mr. Summers set the black box down on it. The villagers kept their distance, leaving a space between themselves and the stool, and when Mr. Summers said, "Some of you fellows want to give me a hand?" there was a hesitation before two men, Mr. Martin and his oldest son, Baxter, came forward to hold the box steady on the stool while Mr. Summers stirred up the papers inside it.

5 The original paraphernalia for the lottery had been lost long ago, and the black box now resting on the stool had been put into use even before Old Man Warner, the oldest man in town, was born. Mr. Summers spoke frequently to the villagers about making a new box, but no one liked to upset even as much tradition as was represented by the black box. There was a story that the present box had been made with some pieces of the box that had preceded it, the one that had been constructed when the first people settled down to make a village here. Every year, after the lottery, Mr. Summers began talking again about a new box, but every year the subject was allowed to fade off without anything's being done. The black box grew shabbier each year; by now it was no longer completely black but splintered badly along one side to show the original wood color, and in some places faded or stained.

Mr. Martin and his oldest son, Baxter, held the black box securely on the stool until Mr. Summers had stirred the papers thoroughly with his hand. Because so much of the ritual had been forgotten or discarded, Mr. Summers had been successful in having slips of paper substituted for the chips of wood that had been used for generations. Chips of wood, Mr. Summers had argued, had been all very well when the village was tiny, but now that the population was more than three hundred and likely to keep on growing, it was necessary to use something that would fit more easily into the black box. The night before the lottery, Mr. Summers and Mr. Graves made up the slips of paper and put them in the box, and it was then taken to the safe of Mr. Summers's coal company and locked up until Mr. Summers was ready to take it to the square next morning. The rest of the year, the box was put away, sometimes one place, sometimes another; it had spent one year in Mr. Graves's barn and another year underfoot in the post office, and sometimes it was set on a shelf in the Martin grocery and left there.

There was a great deal of fussing to be done before Mr. Summers declared the lottery open. There were the lists to make up—of heads of families, heads of households in each family, members of each household in each family. There was the proper swearing-in of Mr. Summers by the postmaster, as the official of the lottery; at one time, some people remembered, there had been a recital of some sort, performed by the official of the lottery, a perfunctory, tuneless chant that had been rattled off duly each year; some people believed that the official of the lottery used to stand just so when he said or sang it, others believed that he was supposed to walk among the people, but years and years ago this part of the ritual had been allowed to lapse. There had been, also, a ritual salute, which the official of the lottery had had to use in addressing each person who came up to draw from the box, but this also had changed with time, until now it was felt necessary only for the official to speak to each person approaching. Mr. Summers was very good at all this; in his clean white shirt and blue jeans, with one hand resting carelessly on the black box, he seemed very proper and important as he talked interminably to Mr. Graves and the Martins.

Just as Mr. Summers finally left off talking and turned to the assembled villagers, Mrs. Hutchinson came hurriedly along the path to the square, her sweater thrown over her shoulders, and slid into place in the back of the crowd. "Clean forgot what day it was," she said to Mrs. Delacroix, who stood next to her, and they both laughed softly. "Thought my old man was out back stacking wood," Mrs. Hutchinson went on, "and then I looked out the window and the kids was gone, and then I remembered it was the twenty-seventh and came a-running." She dried her hands on her apron, and Mrs. Delacroix said, "You're in time, though. They're still talking away up there."

Mrs. Hutchinson craned her neck to see through the crowd and found her husband and children standing near the front. She tapped Mrs. Delacroix on the arm as a farewell and began to make her way through the crowd. The people separated good-humoredly to let her through; two or three people said, in voices just loud enough to be heard across the crowd, "Here comes your Missus, Hutchinson," and "Bill, she made it after all." Mrs. Hutchinson reached her husband, and Mr. Summers, who had been waiting, said cheerfully, "Thought we were going to have to get on without you, Tessie." Mrs. Hutchinson said, grinning, "Wouldn't have me leave m'dishes in the sink, now, would you, Joe?," and soft laughter ran through the crowd as the people stirred back into position after Mrs. Hutchinson's arrival.

10 "Well, now," Mr. Summers said soberly, "guess we better get started, get this over with, so's we can go back to work. Anybody ain't here?"

"Dunbar," several people said. "Dunbar, Dunbar."

Mr. Summers consulted his list. "Clyde Dunbar," he said. "That's right. He's broke his leg, hasn't he? Who's drawing for him?"

"Me, I guess," a woman said, and Mr. Summers turned to look at her. "Wife draws for her husband," Mr. Summers said. "Don't you have a grown boy to do it for you, Janey?" Although Mr. Summers and everyone else in the village knew the answer perfectly well, it was the business of the official of the lottery to ask such questions formally. Mr. Summers waited with an expression of polite interest while Mrs. Dunbar answered.

"Horace's not but sixteen yet," Mrs. Dunbar said regretfully. "Guess I gotta fill in for the old man this year."

"Right," Mr. Summers said. He made a note on the list he was holding. Then he asked, "Watson boy drawing this year?"

A tall boy in the crowd raised his hand. "Here," he said. "I'm drawing for m'mother and me." He blinked his eyes nervously and ducked his head as several voices in the crowd said things like "Good fellow, Jack," and "Glad to see your mother's got a man to do it."

"Well," Mr. Summers said, "guess that's everyone. Old Man Warner make it?"

"Here," a voice said, and Mr. Summers nodded.

A sudden hush fell on the crowd as Mr. Summers cleared his throat and looked at the list. "All ready?" he called. "Now, I'll read the names—heads of families first—and the men come up and take a paper out of the box. Keep the paper folded in your hand without looking at it until everyone has had a turn. Everything clear?"

The people had done it so many times that they only half listened to the directions; most of them were quiet, wetting their lips, not looking around. Then Mr. Summers raised one hand high and said, "Adams." A man disengaged himself from the crowd and came forward. "Hi, Steve," Mr. Summers said, and Mr. Adams said, "Hi, Joe." They grinned at one another humorlessly and nervously. Then Mr. Adams reached into the black box and took out a folded paper. He held it firmly by one corner as he turned and went hastily back to his place in the crowd, where he stood a little apart from his family, not looking down at his hand.

"Allen," Mr. Summers said. "Anderson. . . . Bentham."

"Seems like there's no time at all between lotteries any more," Mrs. Delacroix said to Mrs. Graves in the back row. "Seems like we got through with the last one only last week."

"Time sure goes fast," Mrs. Graves said.

"Clark. . . . Delacroix."

"There goes my old man," Mrs. Delacroix said. She held her breath while her husband went forward.

"Dunbar," Mr. Summers said, and Mrs. Dunbar went steadily to the box while one of the women said, "Go on, Janey," and another said, "There she goes."

"We're next," Mrs. Graves said. She watched while Mr. Graves came around from the side of the box, greeted Mr. Summers gravely, and selected a slip of paper from the box. By now, all through the crowd there were men holding the small folded papers in their large hands, turning them over and over nervously. Mrs. Dunbar and her two sons stood together, Mrs. Dunbar holding the slip of paper.

"Harburt. . . . Hutchinson."

"Get up there, Bill," Mrs. Hutchinson said, and the people near her laughed.

"Jones."

"They do say," Mr. Adams said to Old Man Warner, who stood next to him, "that over in the north village they're talking of giving up the lottery."

Old Man Warner snorted. "Pack of crazy fools," he said. "Listening to the young folks, nothing's good enough for *them*. Next thing you know, they'll be wanting to go back to living in caves, nobody work any more, live *that* way for a while. Used to be a saying about 'Lottery in June, corn be heavy soon.' First thing you know, we'd all be eating stewed chickweed and acorns. There's *always* been a lottery," he added petulantly. "Bad enough to see young Joe Summers up there joking with everybody."

"Some places have already quit lotteries," Mrs. Adams said.

"Nothing but trouble in *that*," Old Man Warner said stoutly. "Pack of young fools."

"Martin." And Bobby Martin watched his father go forward. "Overdyke. . . . Percy."

"I wish they'd hurry," Mrs. Dunbar said to her older son. "I wish they'd hurry."

"They're almost through," her son said.

"You get ready to run tell Dad," Mrs. Dunbar said.

Mr. Summers called his own name and then stepped forward precisely and selected a slip from the box. Then he called, "Warner."

"Seventy-seventh year I been in the lottery," Old Man Warner said as he went through the crowd. "Seventy-seventh time."

"Watson." The tall boy came awkwardly through the crowd. Someone said, "Don't be nervous, Jack," and Mr. Summers said, "Take your time, son."

"Zanini."

After that, there was a long pause, a breathless pause, until Mr. Summers, holding his slip of paper in the air, said, "All right, fellows." For a minute, no one moved, and then all the slips of paper were opened. Suddenly, all the women began to speak at once, saying, "Who is it?," "Who's got it?," "Is it the Dunbars?," "Is it the Watsons?" Then the voices began to say, "It's Hutchinson. It's Bill," "Bill Hutchinson's got it."

"Go tell your father," Mrs. Dunbar said to her older son.

People began to look around to see the Hutchinsons. Bill Hutchinson was standing quiet, staring down at the paper in his hand. Suddenly, Tessie Hutchinson shouted to Mr. Summers, "You didn't give him time enough to take any paper he wanted. I saw you. It wasn't fair!"

"Be a good sport, Tessie," Mrs. Delacroix called, and Mrs. Graves said, "All of us took the same chance."

"Shut up, Tessie," Bill Hutchinson said.

"Well, everyone," Mr. Summers said, "that was done pretty fast, and now we've got to be hurrying a little more to get done in time." He consulted his next list. "Bill," he said, "you draw for the Hutchinson family. You got any other households in the Hutchinsons?"

"There's Don and Eva," Mrs. Hutchinson yelled, "Make *them* take their chance!"

"Daughters draw with their husbands' families, Tessie," Mr. Summers said gently. "You know that as well as anyone else."

"It wasn't *fair*," Tessie said.

"I guess not, Joe," Bill Hutchinson said regretfully. "My daughter draws with her husband's family, that's only fair. And I've got no other family except the kids."

"Then, as far as drawing for families is concerned, it's you," Mr. Summers said in explanation, "and as far as drawing for households is concerned, that's you, too. Right?"

"Right," Bill Hutchinson said.

"How many kids, Bill?" Mr. Summers asked formally.

"Three," Bill Hutchinson said. "There's Bill, Jr., and Nancy, and little Dave. And Tessie and me."

"All right, then," Mr. Summers said. "Harry, you got their tickets back?"

Mr. Graves nodded and held up the slips of paper. "Put them in the box, then," Mr. Summers directed. "Take Bill's and put it in."

"I think we ought to start over," Mrs. Hutchinson said, as quietly as she could. "I tell you it wasn't *fair*. You didn't give him time enough to choose. *Every*body saw that."

Mr. Graves had selected the five slips and put them in the box, and he dropped all the papers but those onto the ground, where the breeze caught them and lifted them off.

"Listen, everybody," Mrs. Hutchinson was saying to the people around her.

"Ready, Bill?" Mr. Summers asked, and Bill Hutchinson, with one quick glance around at his wife and children, nodded.

"Remember," Mr. Summers said, "take the slips and keep them folded until each person has taken one. Harry, you help little Dave." Mr. Graves took the hand of the little boy, who came willingly with him up to the box. "Take a paper out of the box, Davy," Mr. Summers said. Davy put his hand into the box and laughed. "Take just *one* paper," Mr. Summers said. "Harry, you hold it for him." Mr. Graves took the child's hand and removed the folded paper from the tight fist and held it while little Dave stood next to him and looked at him wonderingly.

"Nancy next," Mr. Summers said. Nancy was twelve, and her school friends breathed heavily as she went forward, switching her skirt, and took a slip daintily from the box. "Bill, Jr.," Mr. Summers said, and Billy, his face red and his feet overlarge, nearly knocked the box over as he got a paper out. "Tessie," Mr. Summers said. She hesitated for a minute, looking around defiantly, and then set her lips and went up to the box. She snatched a paper out and held it behind her.

"Bill," Mr. Summers said, and Bill Hutchinson reached into the box and felt around, bringing his hand out at last with the slip of paper in it.

The crowd was quiet. A girl whispered, "I hope it's not Nancy," and the sound of the whisper reached the edges of the crowd.

"It's not the way it used to be," Old Man Warner said clearly. "People ain't the way they used to be."

"All right," Mr. Summers said. "Open the papers. Harry, you open little Dave's."

Mr. Graves opened the slip of paper and there was a general sigh through the crowd as he held it up and everyone could see that it was blank. Nancy and Bill, Jr., opened theirs at the same time, and both beamed and laughed, turning around to the crowd and holding their slips of paper above their heads.

"Tessie," Mr. Summers said. There was a pause, and then Mr. Summers looked at Bill Hutchinson, and Bill unfolded his paper and showed it. It was blank.

"It's Tessie," Mr. Summers said, and his voice was hushed. "Show us her paper, Bill."

Bill Hutchinson went over to his wife and forced the slip of paper out of her hand. It had a black spot on it, the black spot Mr. Summers had made the night before with the heavy pencil in the coal-company office. Bill Hutchinson held it up, and there was a stir in the crowd.

"All right, folks," Mr. Summers said. "Let's finish quickly."

Although the villagers had forgotten the ritual and lost the original black box, they still remembered to use stones. The pile of stones the boys had made earlier was ready; there were stones on the ground with the blowing scraps of paper that had come out of the box. Mrs. Delacroix selected a stone so large she had to pick it up with both hands and turned to Mrs. Dunbar. "Come on," she said. "Hurry up."

Mrs. Dunbar had small stones in both hands, and she said, gasping for breath, "I can't run at all. You'll have to go ahead and I'll catch up with you."

The children had stones already, and someone gave little Davy Hutchinson a few pebbles.

Tessie Hutchinson was in the center of a cleared space by now, and she held her hands out desperately as the villagers moved in on her. "It isn't fair," she said. A stone hit her on the side of the head.

Old Man Warner was saying, "Come on, come on, everyone." Steve Adams was in the front of the crowd of villagers, with Mrs. Graves beside him.

"It isn't fair, it isn't right," Mrs. Hutchinson screamed, and then they were upon her.

READING AND REACTING

1. What possible significance, beyond their literal meaning, might each of these items have: the village square, Mrs. Hutchinson's apron, Old Man Warner, the slips of paper, the black spot?

2. "The Lottery" takes place in summer, a conventional symbol that has a positive connotation. What does this setting contribute to the story's plot? To its atmosphere?
3. What, if anything, might the names *Graves, Adams, Summers,* and *Delacroix* signify in the context of this story? Do you think these names are intended to have any special significance? Why or why not?
4. What role do the children play in the ritual? How can you explain their presence in the story? Do they have any symbolic role?
5. What symbolic significance might be found in the way the characters are dressed? In their conversation?
6. In what sense is the story's title ironic?
7. Throughout the story there is a general atmosphere of excitement. What indication is there of nervousness or apprehension?
8. Early in the story, the boys stuff their pockets with stones, foreshadowing the attack in the story's conclusion. What other examples of foreshadowing can you identify?
9. **Journal Entry** How can a ritual like the lottery continue to be held year after year? Why does no one move to end it? Can you think of a modern-day counterpart to this lottery—a situation in which people continue to act in ways they know to be wrong rather than challenge the status quo? How can you account for such behavior?

Related Works: "Like a Winding Sheet" (p. 76), "Where Are You Going, Where Have You Been?" (p. 268), "Patterns" (p. 342), "The Colonel" (p. 472)

◆ **Alice Walker** (1944–) is an accomplished writer of poetry, fiction, and criticism. Her characters are mainly rural African-Americans, often living in her native Georgia, who struggle to survive in hostile environments. (Walker was born to sharecroppers who raised cotton.) Her writing displays a particular sensitivity to the emotions of people who suffer physical or psychological harm in their efforts to assert their own identities. "Everyday Use" was included in *Best American Short Stories 1973,* and her third novel, *The Color Purple* (1982), won the American Book Award and a Pulitzer Prize.

In the third year of her marriage, Walker took back her maiden name to honor her great-great-great-grandmother who walked, carrying her two children, from Virginia to Georgia. Walker's renaming is consistent with one of her goals in writing: to further the process of reconnecting people to their ancestors. She has said that "it is fatal to see yourself as separate" and that if people can reaffirm the past, they can "make a different future."

◊ ◊ ◊
ALICE WALKER

Everyday Use
(1973)
for your grandma

I will wait for her in the yard that Maggie and I made so clean and wavy yesterday afternoon. A yard like this is more comfortable than most people know. It is not just a yard. It is like an extended living room. When the hard clay is swept clean as a floor and the fine sand around the edges lined with tiny, irregular grooves, anyone can come and sit and look up into the elm tree and wait for the breezes that never come inside the house.

Maggie will be nervous until after her sister goes: she will stand hopelessly in corners, homely and ashamed of the burn scars down her arms and legs, eying her sister with a mixture of envy and awe. She thinks her sister has held life always in the palm of one hand, that "no" is a word the world never learned to say to her.

You've no doubt seen those TV shows where the child who has "made it" is confronted, as a surprise, by her own mother and father, tottering in weakly from backstage. (A pleasant surprise, of course: What would they do if parent and child came on the show only to curse out and insult each other?) On TV mother and child embrace and smile into each other's faces. Sometimes the mother and father weep, the child wraps them in her arms and leans across the table to tell how she would not have made it without their help. I have seen these programs.

Sometimes I dream a dream in which Dee and I are suddenly brought together on a TV program of this sort. Out of a dark and soft-seated limousine I am ushered into a bright room filled with many people. There I meet a smiling, gray, sporty man like Johnny Carson who shakes my hand and tells me what a fine girl I have. Then we are on the stage and Dee is embracing me with tears in her eyes. She pins on my dress a large orchid, even though she has told me once that she thinks orchids are tacky flowers.

5   In real life I am a large, big-boned woman with rough, man-working hands. In the winter I wear flannel nightgowns to bed and overalls during the day. I can kill and clean a hog as mercilessly as a man. My fat keeps me hot in zero weather. I can work outside all day, breaking ice to get water for washing; I can eat pork liver cooked over the open fire minutes after it comes steaming from the hog. One winter I knocked a bull

calf straight in the brain between the eyes with a sledge hammer and had the meat hung up to chill before nightfall. But of course all this does not show on television. I am the way my daughter would want me to be: a hundred pounds lighter, my skin like an uncooked barley pancake. My hair glistens in the hot bright lights. Johnny Carson has much to do to keep up with my quick and witty tongue.

But that is a mistake. I know even before I wake up. Who ever knew a Johnson with a quick tongue? Who can even imagine me looking a strange white man in the eye? It seems to me I have talked to them always with one foot raised in flight, with my head turned in whichever way is farthest from them. Dee, though. She would always look anyone in the eye. Hesitation was no part of her nature.

"How do I look, Mama?" Maggie says, showing just enough of her thin body enveloped in pink skirt and red blouse for me to know she's there, almost hidden by the door.

"Come out into the yard," I say.

Have you ever seen a lame animal, perhaps a dog run over by some careless person rich enough to own a car, sidle up to someone who is ignorant enough to be kind to him? That is the way my Maggie walks. She has been like this, chin on chest, eyes on ground, feet in shuffle, ever since the fire that burned the other house to the ground.

10   Dee is lighter than Maggie, with nicer hair and a fuller figure. She's a woman now, though sometimes I forget. How long ago was it that the other house burned? Ten, twelve years? Sometimes I can still hear the flames and feel Maggie's arms sticking to me, her hair smoking and her dress falling off her in little black papery flakes. Her eyes seemed stretched open, blazed open by the flames reflected in them. And Dee. I see her standing off under the sweet gum tree she used to dig gum out of; a look of concentration on her face as she watched the last dingy gray board of the house fall in toward the red-hot brick chimney. Why don't you do a dance around the ashes? I'd wanted to ask her. She had hated the house that much.

I used to think she hated Maggie, too. But that was before we raised the money, the church and me, to send her to Augusta to school. She used to read to us without pity; forcing words, lies, other folks' habits, whole lives upon us two, sitting trapped and ignorant underneath her voice. She washed us in a river of make-believe, burned us with a lot of knowledge we didn't necessarily need to know. Pressed us to her with the serious way she read, to shove us away at just the moment, like dimwits, we seemed about to understand.

Dee wanted nice things. A yellow organdy dress to wear to her graduation from high school; black pumps to match a green suit she'd made from an old suit somebody gave me. She was determined to stare down any disaster in her efforts. Her eyelids would not flicker for minutes at a time. Often I fought off the temptation to shake her. At sixteen she had a style of her own, and knew what style was.

• • •

I never had an education myself. After second grade the school was closed down. Don't ask me why: in 1927 colored asked fewer questions than they do now. Sometimes Maggie reads to me. She stumbles along good-naturedly but can't see well. She knows she is not bright. Like good looks and money, quickness passed her by. She will marry John Thomas (who has mossy teeth in an earnest face) and then I'll be free to sit here and I guess just sing church songs to myself. Although I never was a good singer. Never could carry a tune. I was always better at a man's job. I used to love to milk till I was hooked in the side in '49. Cows are soothing and slow and don't bother you, unless you try to milk them the wrong way.

I have deliberately turned my back on the house. It is three rooms, just like the one that burned, except the roof is tin; they don't make shingle roofs any more. There are no real windows, just some holes cut in the sides, like the portholes in a ship, but not round and not square, with rawhide holding the shutters up on the outside. This house is in a pasture, too, like the other one. No doubt when Dee sees it she will want to tear it down. She wrote me once that no matter where we "choose" to live, she will manage to come see us. But she will never bring her friends. Maggie and I thought about this and Maggie asked me, "Mama, when did Dee ever *have* any friends?"

15   She had a few. Furtive boys in pink shirts hanging about on wash-day after school. Nervous girls who never laughed. Impressed with her they worshiped the well-turned phrase, the cute shape, the scalding humor that erupted like bubbles in lye. She read to them.

When she was courting Jimmy T she didn't have much time to pay to us, but turned all her faultfinding power on him. He *flew* to marry a cheap city girl from a family of ignorant flashy people. She hardly had time to recompose herself.

When she comes I will meet—but there they are!

Maggie attempts to make a dash for the house, in her shuffling way, but I stay her with my hand. "Come back here," I say. And she stops and tries to dig a well in the sand with her toe.

It is hard to see them clearly through the strong sun. But even the first glimpse of leg out of the car tells me it is Dee. Her feet were always neat-looking, as if God himself had shaped them with a certain style. From the other side of the car comes a short, stocky man. Hair is all over his head a foot long and hanging from his chin like a kinky mule tail. I hear Maggie suck in her breath. "Uhnnnh," is what it sounds like. Like when you see the wriggling end of a snake just in front of your foot on the road. "Uhnnnh."

20   Dee next. A dress down to the ground, in this hot weather. A dress so loud it hurts my eyes. There are yellows and oranges enough to throw back the light of the sun. I feel my whole face warming from the heat waves it throws out. Earrings gold, too, and hanging down to her shoulders. Bracelets dangling and making noises when she moves her arm up

to shake the folds of the dress out of her armpits. The dress is loose and flows, and as she walks closer, I like it. I hear Maggie go "Uhnnnh" again. It is her sister's hair. It stands straight up like the wool on a sheep. It is black as night and around the edges are two long pigtails that rope about like small lizards disappearing behind her ears.

"Wa-su-zo-Tean-o!"[1] she says, coming on in that gliding way the dress makes her move. The short stocky fellow with the hair to his navel is all grinning and he follows up with "Asalamalakim,[2] my mother and sister!" He moves to hug Maggie but she falls back, right up against the back of my chair. I feel her trembling there and when I look up I see the perspiration falling off her chin.

"Don't get up," says Dee. Since I am stout it takes something of a push. You can see me trying to move a second or two before I make it. She turns, showing white heels through her sandals, and goes back to the car. Out she peeks next with a Polaroid. She stoops down quickly and lines up picture after picture of me sitting there in front of the house with Maggie cowering behind me. She never takes a shot without making sure the house is included. When a cow comes nibbling around the edge of the yard she snaps it and me and Maggie *and* the house. Then she puts the Polaroid in the back seat of the car, and comes up and kisses me on the forehead.

Meanwhile Asalamalakim is going through motions with Maggie's hand. Maggie's hand is as limp as a fish, and probably as cold, despite the sweat, and she keeps trying to pull it back. It looks like Asalamalakim wants to shake hands but wants to do it fancy. Or maybe he don't know how people shake hands. Anyhow, he soon gives up on Maggie.

"Well," I say. "Dee."

"No, Mama," she says. "Not 'Dee,' Wangero Leewanika Kemanjo!"

"What happened to 'Dee'?" I wanted to know.

"She's dead," Wangero said. "I couldn't bear it any longer, being named after the people who oppress me."

"You know as well as me you was named after your aunt Dicie," I said. Dicie is my sister. She named Dee. We called her "Big Dee" after Dee was born.

"But who was *she* named after?" asked Wangero.

"I guess after Grandma Dee," I said.

"And who was she named after?" asked Wangero.

"Her mother," I said, and saw Wangero was getting tired. "That's about as far back as I can trace it," I said. Though, in fact, I probably could have carried it back beyond the Civil War through the branches.

"Well," said Asalamalakim, "there you are."

"Uhnnnh," I heard Maggie say.

"There I was not," I said, "before 'Dicie' cropped up in our family, so why should I try to trace it that far back?"

---

[1] Greeting in Swahili; Dee sounds it out one syllable at a time.
[2] Greeting in Arabic: "Peace be upon you."

He just stood there grinning, looking down on me like somebody inspecting a Model A car. Every once in a while he and Wangero sent eye signals over my head.

"How do you pronounce this name?" I asked.

"You don't have to call me by it if you don't want to," said Wangero.

"Why shouldn't I?" I asked. "If that's what you want us to call you, we'll call you."

"I know it might sound awkward at first," said Wangero.

"I'll get used to it," I said. "Ream it out again."

Well, soon we got the name out of the way. Asalamalakim had a name twice as long and three times as hard. After I tripped over it two or three times he told me to just call him Hakim-a-barber. I wanted to ask him was he a barber, but I didn't really think he was, so I didn't ask.

"You must belong to those beef-cattle peoples down the road," I said. They said "Asalamalakim" when they met you, too, but they didn't shake hands. Always too busy: feeding the cattle, fixing the fences, putting up salt-lick shelters, throwing down hay. When the white folks poisoned some of the herd the men stayed up all night with rifles in their hands. I walked a mile and a half just to see the sight.

Hakim-a-barber said, "I accept some of their doctrines, but farming and raising cattle is not my style." (They didn't tell me, and I didn't ask, whether Wangero [Dee] had really gone and married him.)

We sat down to eat and right away he said he didn't eat collards and pork was unclean. Wangero, though, went on through the chitlins and corn bread, the greens and everything else. She talked a blue streak over the sweet potatoes. Everything delighted her. Even the fact that we still used the benches her daddy made for the table when we couldn't afford to buy chairs.

"Oh, Mama!" she cried. Then turned to Hakim-a-barber. "I never knew how lovely these benches are. You can feel the rump prints," she said, running her hands underneath her and along the bench. Then she gave a sigh and her hand closed over Grandma Dee's butter dish. "That's it!" she said. "I knew there was something I wanted to ask you if I could have." She jumped up from the table and went over in the corner where the churn stood, the milk in it clabber by now. She looked at the churn and looked at it.

"This churn top is what I need," she said. "Didn't Uncle Buddy whittle it out of a tree you all used to have?"

"Yes," I said.

"Uh huh," she said happily. "And I want the dasher, too."

"Uncle Buddy whittle that, too?" asked the barber.

Dee (Wangero) looked up at me.

"Aunt Dee's first husband whittled the dash," said Maggie so low you almost couldn't hear her. "His name was Henry, but they called him Stash."

"Maggie's brain is like an elephant's," Wangero said, laughing. "I can use the churn top as a centerpiece for the alcove table," she said, sliding a plate over the churn, "and I'll think of something artistic to do with the dasher."

When she finished wrapping the dasher the handle stuck out. I took it for a moment in my hands. You didn't even have to look close to see where hands pushing the dasher up and down to make butter had left a kind of sink in the wood. In fact, there were a lot of small sinks; you could see where thumb and fingers had sunk into the wood. It was beautiful light yellow wood, from a tree that grew in the yard where Big Dee and Stash had lived.

After dinner Dee (Wangero) went to the trunk at the foot of my bed and started rifling through it. Maggie hung back in the kitchen over the dishpan. Out came Wangero with two quilts. They had been pieced by Grandma Dee and then Big Dee and me had hung them on the quilt frames on the front porch and quilted them. One was in the Lone Star pattern. The other was Walk Around the Mountain. In both of them were scraps of dresses Grandma Dee had worn fifty and more years ago. Bits and pieces of Grandpa Jarrell's Paisley shirts. And one teeny faded blue piece, about the size of a penny matchbox, that was from Great Grandpa Ezra's uniform that he wore in the Civil War.

"Mama," Wangero said sweet as a bird. "Can I have these old quilts?"

I heard something fall in the kitchen, and a minute later the kitchen door slammed.

"Why don't you take one or two of the others?" I asked. "These old things was just done by me and Big Dee from some tops your grandma pieced before she died."

"No," said Wangero. "I don't want those. They are stitched around the borders by machine."

"That'll make them last better," I said.

"That's not the point," said Wangero. "These are all pieces of dresses Grandma used to wear. She did all this stitching by hand. Imagine!" She held the quilts securely in her arms, stroking them.

"Some of the pieces, like those lavender ones, come from old clothes her mother handed down to her," I said, moving up to touch the quilts. Dee (Wangero) moved back just enough so that I couldn't reach the quilts. They already belonged to her.

"Imagine!" she breathed again, clutching them closely to her bosom.

"The truth is," I said, "I promised to give them quilts to Maggie, for when she marries John Thomas."

She gasped like a bee had stung her. "Maggie can't appreciate these quilts!" she said. "She'd probably be backward enough to put them to everyday use."

"I reckon she would," I said. "God knows I been saving 'em for long enough with nobody using 'em. I hope she will!" I didn't want to bring up how I had offered Dee (Wangero) a quilt when she went away to college. Then she had told me they were old-fashioned, out of style.

"But, they're *priceless!*" she was saying now, furiously; for she has a temper. "Maggie would put them on the bed and in five years they'd be in rags. Less than that!"

"She can always make some more," I said. "Maggie knows how to quilt."

Dee (Wangero) looked at me with hatred. "You just will not understand. The point is these quilts, *these* quilts!"

70 "Well," I said, stumped. "What would *you* do with them?"

"Hang them," she said. As if that was the only thing you *could* do with quilts.

Maggie by now was standing in the door. I could almost hear the sound her feet made as they scraped over each other.

"She can have them, Mama," she said, like somebody used to never winning anything, or having anything reserved for her. "I can 'member Grandma Dee without the quilts."

I looked at her hard. She had filled her bottom lip with checkerberry snuff and it gave her face a kind of dopey, hangdog look. It was Grandma Dee and Big Dee who taught her how to quilt herself. She stood there with her scarred hands hidden in the folds of her skirt. She looked at her sister with something like fear but she wasn't mad at her. This was Maggie's portion. This was the way she knew God to work.

75 When I looked at her like that something hit me in the top of my head and ran down to the soles of my feet. Just like when I'm in church and the spirit of God touches me and I get happy and shout. I did something I never had done before: hugged Maggie to me, then dragged her on into the room, snatched the quilts out of Miss Wangero's hands and dumped them into Maggie's lap. Maggie just sat there on my bed with her mouth open.

"Take one or two of the others," I said to Dee.

But she turned without a word and went out to Hakim-a-barber.

"You just don't understand," she said, as Maggie and I came out to the car.

"What don't I understand?" I wanted to know.

80 "Your heritage," she said. And then she turned to Maggie, kissed her, and said, "You ought to try to make something of yourself, too, Maggie. It's really a new day for us. But from the way you and Mama still live you'd never know it."

She put on some sunglasses that hid everything above the tip of her nose and her chin.

Maggie smiled; maybe at the sunglasses. But a real smile, not scared. After we watched the car dust settle I asked Maggie to bring me a dip of snuff. And then the two of us sat there just enjoying, until it was time to go in the house and go to bed.

READING AND REACTING

1. In American culture, what does a patchwork quilt symbolize?
2. What is the *literal* meaning of the two quilts to Maggie and her mother? To Dee? Beyond this literal meaning, what symbolic meaning, if any, do they have to Maggie and her mother? Do the quilts have any symbolic meaning to Dee?

3. How does the contrast between the two sisters' appearances, personalities, lifestyles, and feelings about the quilts help to convey the story's theme?
4. What does the name *Wangero* signify to Dee? To her mother and sister? Could the name be considered a symbol? Why or why not?
5. Why do you think Maggie relinquishes the quilts to her sister?
6. What is Dee's opinion of her mother and sister? Do you agree with her assessment?
7. What does the story's title suggest to you? Is it ironic? What other titles would be effective?
8. What possible meanings, aside from their literal meanings, might each of the following suggest: the family's yard, Maggie's burn scars, the trunk in which the quilts are kept, Dee's Polaroid camera? What symbolic functions, if any, do these items serve in the story?
9. **JOURNAL ENTRY** What objects have the kind of symbolic value to you that the quilts have to Maggie? What gives these objects this value?

Related Works: "Two Kinds" (p. 285), "Digging" (p. 312), "Aunt Jennifer's Tigers" (p. 436), *Trifles* (p. 586)

◆ WRITING SUGGESTIONS: SYMBOL AND ALLEGORY

1. Select a story from anywhere in this text, and discuss its use of symbols.
2. Strangers figure prominently in "Young Goodman Brown" and "Where Are You Going, Where Have You Been?" (p. 224). Write an essay in which you discuss the possible symbolic significance of strangers in each story.
3. Write an essay in which you discuss the conflicts present in "Young Goodman Brown," showing how the allegorical elements in the story reflect and reinforce these conflicts.
4. If Shirley Jackson had wished to write "The Lottery" as an allegory whose purpose was to expose the evils of Nazi Germany, what revisions would she have had to make to convey the dangers of blind obedience to authority? Consider the story's symbols, the characters (and their names), and the setting.
5. In a number of works in this anthology, prized possessions function as symbols—for example, the quilt in "Everyday Use," the grinding ball in "The Secret Lion," the clock and de Spain's rug in "Barn Burning," and the glass animals in *The Glass Menagerie*. Write an essay in which you discuss the symbolic significance of a prized possession in any two works in this text.

CHAPTER 9

Theme

The **theme** of a work of literature is its central or dominant idea. *Theme* is not the same as *plot* or *subject,* two terms with which it is sometimes confused. A simple *plot summary* of Tadeusz Borowski's "Silence," a story about survivors of the Holocaust, could be "Prisoners are liberated from a concentration camp and, despite the warnings of the American officer, they kill a captured German guard." The statement "'Silence' is about freed prisoners and a guard" could define the *subject* of the story. A statement of the *theme* of "Silence," however, would have to do more than summarize its plot or identify its subject; it would have to convey the values and ideas expressed by the story. Many effective stories are complex, expressing more than one theme, and "Silence" is no exception. You could say, for example, that "Silence" suggests that human beings have a need for vengeance. You could also say the story demonstrates that silence is sometimes the only response possible when one is confronting unspeakable horrors. Although both these themes—and others—are expressed in the story, one theme seems to dominate—the idea that under extreme conditions the oppressed can become as morally bankrupt as their oppressors.

When you write about theme, you need to do more than tell what happens in the story. The theme you identify should be a general idea that extends beyond the story and applies to the world outside fiction. Compare these two statements about Edgar Allan Poe's "The Cask of Amontillado" (p. 136):

> Poe's "The Cask of Amontillado" is about a man who loses his humanity because of his obsessive desire to avenge himself on Fortunato.
>
> Poe's "The Cask of Amontillado" suggests that when the desire for revenge becomes obsessive, it can deprive individuals of all that makes them human.

225

The first statement merely tells what the story is about; the second statement identifies the story's theme, a general observation about humanity.

Granted, some short works (fairy tales or fables, for example) have themes that can be summed up as *clichés*—overused phrases or expressions—or as *morals*—lessons dramatized by the work. The fairy tale "Cinderella," for example, expresses the clichéd theme that a virtuous girl who endures misfortune will eventually achieve her just reward; the fable "The Tortoise and the Hare" illustrates the moral "Slow and steady wins the race." Like "The Cask of Amontillado," however, the stories in this anthology have themes that are more complex than clichés or morals.

Understanding Theme

◊ ◊ ◊

Contemporary critical theory holds that the theme of a work of fiction is as much the creation of readers as of the writer. The readers' backgrounds, knowledge, values, and beliefs all play a part in determining the theme or themes they will identify in a work. Most readers, for example, will realize that David Michael Kaplan's story "Doe Season" (p. 230)—in which the main character goes hunting, kills her first deer, and is forced to confront suffering and death—expresses a conventional **initiation theme,** revealing growing up to be a disillusioning and painful process. Still, different readers bring different perspectives to the story and, in some cases, see different themes.

During a classroom discussion of "Doe Season," a student familiar with hunting saw more than his classmates did in the story's conventional initiation theme. He knew that in many states there really is a doe season, which lasts approximately three days. Shorter than the ten-day buck season, its purpose is to enable hunters to control the size of the deer herd by killing females. This knowledge enabled the student to conclude that by the end of the story the female child's innocence must inevitably be destroyed, just as the doe must be.

Another student pointed out that the participation of Andy—a female who uses a male name—in hunting, a traditional male rite of passage, leads to her killing the deer and to her subsequent disillusionment. It also leads to her decision to abandon her nickname. By contrasting "Andrea" with "Andy," the story reveals the inner conflict between her "female" nature (illustrated by her compassion) and her desire to emulate the men to whom killing is a sport. This interpretation led the student to conclude that the theme of "Doe Season" is that males and females have very different outlooks on life.

Other students did not accept the negative characterization of the story's male characters that the above interpretation implies. They pointed out that the father is a sympathetic figure who is extremely supportive; he encourages and defends his daughter. He takes her hunting because he loves her, not because he wants to initiate her into life or to hurt her. One student mentioned that Andy's reaction (called *buck fever*) when she sees the doe is common in children who kill their first deer. In light of this information, several students thought that far from being about irreconcilable male and female perspectives, "Doe Season" makes a statement about a young girl who is hunting for her own identity and who in the process discovers her own mortality. Her father is therefore the agent who enables her to confront the inevitability of death, a fact she must accept if she is going to take her place in the adult world. In this sense, the theme of the story is the idea that in order to mature, a child must come to terms with the reality of death.

Different readers may see different themes in a story, but any understanding of a theme must make sense in light of what is actually in the story. Evidence from the work, not just your own feelings or assumptions, must support your conclusion, and a single symbol or one statement by a character is not enough in itself to reveal a story's theme. Therefore, you must identify a cross section of examples from the text to support your understanding of the story's theme. If you say that the theme of James Joyce's "Araby" (p. 167) is that an innocent idealist is inevitably doomed to disillusionment, you have to find examples from the text to support your statement. You could begin with the title, concluding that the word *Araby* suggests dreams of exotic beauty that the boy tries to find when he goes to the bazaar. You could reinforce your idea about the elusiveness of beauty by pointing out that Mangan's unattainable sister is a symbol of this beauty that the boy wants so desperately to find. Finally, you could show how idealism is ultimately crushed by society: at the end of the story, the boy stands alone in the darkness and realizes that his dreams of beauty are childish fantasies. Although other readers may have different responses to "Araby," they should find your explanation reasonable if you support it with enough examples.

IDENTIFYING THEMES

◊ ◊ ◊

Every element of a story can shed light on its themes. As you analyze a short story, look for features that reveal and reinforce what you perceive to be the story's most important ideas.

The *title* of a story can often provide insight into the theme or themes of a story. The title of an F. Scott Fitzgerald story, "Babylon Revisited," emphasizes a major idea in the story—that Paris of the 1920s is like Babylon, the ancient city the Bible singles out as the epitome of evil and corruption. The story's protagonist, Charlie Wales, comes to realize that no matter how much money he lost after the stock market crash, he lost more—his wife and his daughter—during the boom, when he was in Paris. Charlie's search through his past—his return to "Babylon"—provides new meaning to his life and offers at least a small bit of hope for the future.

Sometimes a *narrator's or character's statement* can reveal a theme. For example, at the beginning of Alberto Alvaro Ríos's "The Secret Lion" (p. 281) the first-person narrator says, "I was twelve and in junior high school and something happened that we didn't have a name for, but it was there nonetheless like a lion, and roaring, roaring that way the biggest things do. Everything changed." Although the narrator does not directly announce the story's theme, he does suggest that the story will convey the idea that the price children pay for growing up is realizing that everything changes, that nothing stays the way it is.

The *arrangement of events* in a story can suggest a story's theme, as it does in an Ernest Hemingway story, "The Short Happy Life of Francis Macomber." At the beginning of the story, the title character is a coward who is stuck in an unhappy marriage. As the story progresses, he gradually learns the nature of courage and, finally, finds it in himself. At the moment of triumph, however, Francis is killed; his "happy life" is short indeed. The way the events of the story are presented, through foreshadowing and flashbacks, reveals the connection between Macomber's marriage and his behavior as a hunter, and this connection in turn helps to reveal a possible theme: that sometimes courage can be more important than life itself.

A story's *conflict* can offer clues to its theme. In "Araby" the young boy believes that his society neglects art and beauty and glorifies the mundane. This conflict between the boy's idealism and his world can help readers understand why the boy isolates himself in his room reading books and why he retreats into dreams of idealized love. A major theme of the story—that growing up leads to the loss of youthful idealism—is revealed by this central conflict.

Similarly, the main character in "The Yellow Wall-Paper" (p. 102), a woman who has recently had a baby, is in conflict with the larger nineteenth-century society in which she lives. She is suffering from "temporary nervous depression," what doctors today recognize as postpartum depression. Following the practice of the time, her physician has ordered complete bed rest and has instructed her husband to deprive her of all mental and physical stimulation. This harsh treatment leads the narrator to lose her grasp on reality; eventually, she begins to hallucinate. The central conflict of the story is clearly between the woman and her society, controlled by men. This conflict communicates the theme: that in nineteenth-century America, women are controlled not just by their husbands and the male medical establishment, but also by society as a whole.

The *point of view* of a story can also help shed light on theme. For instance, a writer's use of an unreliable first-person narrator can help to communicate the theme of a story. Thus, Montresor's self-serving first-person account of his crime in "The Cask of Amontillado"—and his convincing attempts to justify these actions—enable readers to understand the dangers of irrational anger and misplaced ideas about honor. The voice of a third-person narrator can also help to convey a story's theme.

For example, the detachment of the narrator in Stephen Crane's Civil War novel *The Red Badge of Courage* reinforces the theme of the novel: that bravery, cowardice, battle, and even life itself are insignificant when set beside the indifference of the universe.

Quite often a story will give names, places, and objects symbolic significance. These *symbols* can not only enrich the story, but also help to convey a central theme. For example, the rocking horse in D. H. Lawrence's "The Rocking-Horse Winner" (p. 243) can be seen as a symbol of the boy's desperate desire to remain a child. Interpreted in this way, it reinforces the theme that innocence cannot survive when it confronts greed and selfishness. Similarly, Hawthorne's "Young Goodman Brown" (p. 198) uses symbols such as the walking stick, the woods, sunset and night, and the vague shadows to develop one of its central themes: that once a person strays from the path of faith, evil is everywhere.

Finally, *changes in a character* can shed light on the theme or themes of the story. The main character in Kate Chopin's "The Story of an Hour" (p. 43), for example, comes to realize that her husband's death may be a cause for happiness rather than sadness, and her changing attitude helps to communicate the story's central theme about the nature of marriage at the time.

Checklist: Writing about Theme

- ✓ What is the central theme of the story?
- ✓ What other themes can you identify?
- ✓ Does the title of the story suggest a theme?
- ✓ Does the narrator, or any character, make statements that express or imply a theme?
- ✓ In what way does the arrangement of events in the story suggest a theme?
- ✓ In what way does the central conflict of the story suggest a theme?
- ✓ How does the point of view shed light on the story's central theme?
- ✓ Do any symbols suggest a theme?
- ✓ Do any characters in the story change in any significant way? Do their changes convey a particular theme?
- ✓ Have you clearly identified the story's central theme, rather than just summarized the plot or stated the subject?
- ✓ Does your statement of the story's central theme make a general observation that has an application beyond the story itself?

◊ **DAVID MICHAEL KAPLAN** (1946–   ) is one of a group of writers who are called "magic realists." Magic realists work outside of traditional fantasy writing, seamlessly interweaving magical elements with detailed, realistically drawn "everyday" settings.

In "Doe Season," Andy's surreal encounter with the doe may be a dream, but the beauty and horror of their meeting will affect the rest of her life.

◊ ◊ ◊

DAVID MICHAEL KAPLAN

Doe Season
(1985)

They were always the same woods, she thought sleepily as they drove through the early morning darkness—deep and immense, covered with yesterday's snowfall, which had frozen overnight. They were the same woods that lay behind her house, *and they stretch all the way to here,* she thought, *for miles and miles, longer than I could walk in a day, or a week even, but they are still the same woods.* The thought made her feel good: it was like thinking of God; it was like thinking of the space between here and the moon; it was like thinking of all the foreign countries from her geography book where even now, Andy knew, people were going to bed, while they—she and her father and Charlie Spoon and Mac, Charlie's eleven-year-old son—were driving deeper into the Pennsylvania countryside, to go hunting.

They had risen long before dawn. Her mother, yawning and not trying to hide her sleepiness, cooked them eggs and French toast. Her father smoked a cigarette and flicked ashes into his saucer while Andy listened, wondering *Why doesn't he come?* and *Won't he ever come?* until at last a car pulled into the graveled drive and honked. "That will be Charlie Spoon," her father said; he always said "Charlie Spoon," even though his real name was Spreun, because Charlie was, in a sense, shaped like a spoon, with a large head and a narrow waist and chest.

Andy's mother kissed her and her father and said, "Well, have a good time," and "Be careful." Soon they were outside in the bitter dark, loading gear by the back-porch light, their breath steaming. The woods behind the house were then only a black streak against the wash of night.

Andy dozed in the car and woke to find that it was half light. Mac—also sleeping—had slid against her. She pushed him away and looked out the window. Her breath clouded the glass, and she was cold; the car's heater didn't work right. They were riding over gentle hills, the woods on both sides now—the same woods, she knew, because she had been watching the whole way, even while she slept. They had been in her dreams, and she had never lost sight of them.

Charlie Spoon was driving. "I don't understand why she's coming," he said to her father. "How old is she anyway—eight?"

"Nine," her father replied. "She's small for her age."

"So—nine. What's the difference? She'll just add to the noise and get tired besides."

"No, she won't," her father said. "She can walk me to death. And she'll bring good luck, you'll see. Animals—I don't know how she does it, but they come right up to her. We go walking in the woods, and we'll spot more raccoons and possums and such than I ever see when I'm alone."

Charlie grunted.

"Besides, she's not a bad little shot, even if she doesn't hunt yet. She shoots the .22 real good."

"Popgun," Charlie said, and snorted. "And target shooting ain't deer hunting."

"Well, she's not gonna be shooting anyway, Charlie," her father said. "Don't worry. She'll be no bother."

"I still don't know why she's coming," Charlie said.

"Because she wants to, and I want her to. Just like you and Mac. No difference."

Charlie turned onto a side road and after a mile or so slowed down. "That's it!" he cried. He stopped, backed up, and entered a narrow dirt road almost hidden by trees. Five hundred yards down, the road ran parallel to a fenced-in field. Charlie parked in a cleared area deeply rutted by frozen tractor tracks. The gate was locked. *In the spring,* Andy thought, *there will be cows here, and a dog that chases them,* but now the field was unmarked and bare.

"This is it," Charlie Spoon declared. "Me and Mac was up here just two weeks ago, scouting it out, and there's deer. Mac saw the tracks."

"That's right," Mac said.

"Well, we'll just see about that," her father said, putting on his gloves. He turned to Andy. "How you doing, honeybun?"

"Just fine," she said.

Andy shivered and stamped as they unloaded: first the rifles, which they unsheathed and checked, sliding the bolts, sighting through scopes, adjusting the slings; then the gear, their food and tents and sleeping bags and stove stored in four backpacks—three big ones for Charlie Spoon and her father and Mac, and a day pack for her.

"That's about your size," Mac said, to tease her.

She reddened and said, "Mac, I can carry a pack big as yours any day." He laughed and pressed his knee against the back of hers, so that her leg buckled. "Cut it out," she said. She wanted to make an iceball and throw it at him, but she knew that her father and Charlie were anxious to get going, and she didn't want to displease them.

Mac slid under the gate, and they handed the packs over to him. Then they slid under and began walking across the field toward the same woods that ran all the way back to her home, where even now her mother was probably rising again to wash their breakfast dishes and make herself a fresh pot of coffee. *She is there, and we are here:* the thought satisfied Andy. There was no place else she would rather be.

Mac came up beside her. "Over there's Canada," he said, nodding toward the woods.

25 "Huh!" she said. "Not likely."

"I don't mean *right* over there. I mean farther up north. You think I'm dumb?"

Dumb as your father, she thought.

"Look at that," Mac said, pointing to a piece of cow dung lying on a spot scraped bare of snow. "A frozen meadow muffin." He picked it up and sailed it at her. "Catch!"

"Mac!" she yelled. His laugh was as gawky as he was. She walked faster. He seemed different today somehow, bundled in his yellow-and-black-checkered coat, a rifle in hand, his silly floppy hat not quite covering his ears. They all seemed different as she watched them trudge through the snow—Mac and her father and Charlie Spoon—bigger, maybe, as if the cold landscape enlarged rather than diminished them, so that they, the only figures in that landscape, took on size and meaning just by being there. If they weren't there, everything would be quieter, and the woods would be the same as before. *But they are here,* Andy thought, looking behind her at the boot prints in the snow, *and I am too, and so it's all different.*

30 "We'll go down to the cut where we found those deer tracks," Charlie said as they entered the woods. "Maybe we'll get lucky and get a late one coming through."

The woods descended into a gully. The snow was softer and deeper here, so that often Andy sank to her knees. Charlie and Mac worked the top of the gully while she and her father walked along the base some thirty yards behind them. "If they miss the first shot, we'll get the second," her father said, and she nodded as if she had known this all the time. She listened to the crunch of their boots, their breathing, and the drumming of a distant woodpecker. And the crackling. In winter the woods crackled as if everything were straining, ready to snap like dried chicken bones.

We are hunting, Andy thought. The cold air burned her nostrils.

They stopped to make lunch by a rock outcropping that protected them from the wind. Her father heated the bean soup her mother had made for them, and they ate it with bread already stiff from the cold. He and Charlie took a few pulls from a flask of Jim Beam while she scoured the plates with snow and repacked them. Then they all had coffee with sugar and powdered milk, and her father poured her a cup too. "We won't tell your momma," he said, and Mac laughed. Andy held the cup the way her father did, not by the handle but around the rim. The coffee tasted smoky. She felt a little queasy, but she drank it all.

Charlie Spoon picked his teeth with a fingernail. "Now, you might've noticed one thing," he said.

35   "What's that?" her father asked.
"You might've noticed you don't hear no rifles. That's because there ain't no other hunters here. We've got the whole damn woods to ourselves. Now, I ask you—do I know how to find 'em?"
"We haven't seen deer yet, neither."
"Oh, we will," Charlie said, "but not for a while now." He leaned back against the rock. "Deer're sleeping, resting up for the evening feed."
"I seen a deer behind our house once, and it was afternoon," Andy said.
40   "Yeah, honey, but that was *before* deer season," Charlie said, grinning. "They know something now. They're smart that way."
"That's right," Mac said.
Andy looked at her father—had she said something stupid?
"Well, Charlie," he said, "if they know so much, how come so many get themselves shot?"
"Them's the ones that don't *believe* what they know," Charlie replied. The men laughed. Andy hesitated, and then laughed with them.
45   They moved on, as much to keep warm as to find a deer. The wind became even stronger. Blowing through the treetops, it sounded like the ocean, and once Andy thought she could smell salt air. But that was impossible; the ocean was *hundreds* of miles away, farther than Canada even. She and her parents had gone last summer to stay for a week at a motel on the New Jersey shore. That was the first time she'd seen the ocean, and it frightened her. It was huge and empty, yet always moving. Everything lay hidden. If you walked in it, you couldn't see how deep it was or what might be below; if you swam, something could pull you under and you'd never be seen again. Its musky, rank smell made her think of things dying. Her mother had floated beyond the breakers, calling to her to come in, but Andy wouldn't go farther than a few feet into the surf. Her mother swam and splashed with animal-like delight while her father, smiling shyly, held his white arms above the waist-deep water as if afraid to get them wet. Once a comber rolled over and sent them both tossing, and when her mother tried to stand up, the surf receding behind, Andy saw that her mother's swimsuit top had come off, so that her breasts swayed free, her nipples like two dark eyes. Embarrassed, Andy looked around: except for two women under a yellow umbrella farther up, the beach was empty. Her mother stood up unsteadily, regained her footing. Taking what seemed the longest time, she calmly refixed her top. Andy lay on the beach towel and closed her eyes. The sound of the surf made her head ache.
And now it was winter; the sky was already dimming, not just with the absence of light but with a mist that clung to the hunters' faces like cobwebs. They made camp early. Andy was chilled. When she stood still, she kept wiggling her toes to make sure they were there. Her father rubbed her arms and held her to him briefly, and that felt better. She unpacked the food while the others put up the tents.
"How about rounding us up some firewood, Mac?" Charlie asked.

"I'll do it," Andy said. Charlie looked at her thoughtfully and then handed her the canvas carrier.

There wasn't much wood on the ground, so it took her a while to get a good load. She was about a hundred yards from camp, near a cluster of high, lichen-covered boulders, when she saw through a crack in the rock a buck and two does walking gingerly, almost daintily, through the alder trees. She tried to hush her breathing as they passed not more than twenty yards away. There was nothing she could do. If she yelled, they'd be gone; by the time she got back to camp, they'd be gone. The buck stopped, nostrils quivering, tail up and alert. He looked directly at her. Still she didn't move, not one muscle. He was a beautiful buck, the color of late-turned maple leaves. Unafraid, he lowered his tail, and he and his does silently merged into the trees. Andy walked back to camp and dropped the firewood.

"I saw three deer," she said. "A buck and two does."

"Where?" Charlie Spoon cried, looking behind her as if they might have followed her into camp.

"In the woods yonder. They're gone now."

"Well, hell!" Charlie banged his coffee cup against his knee.

"Didn't I say she could find animals?" her father said, grinning.

"Too late to go after them," Charlie muttered. "It'll be dark in a quarter hour. Damn!"

"Damn," Mac echoed.

"They just walk right up to her," her father said.

"Well, leastwise this proves there's deer here." Charlie began snapping long branches into shorter ones. "You know, I think I'll stick with you," he told Andy, "since you're so good at finding deer and all. How'd that be?"

"Okay, I guess," Andy murmured. She hoped he was kidding; no way did she want to hunt with Charlie Spoon. Still, she was pleased he had said it.

Her father and Charlie took one tent, she and Mac the other. When they were in their sleeping bags, Mac said in the darkness, "I bet you really didn't see no deer, did you?"

She sighed. "I did, Mac. Why would I lie?"

"How big was the buck?"

"Four point. I counted."

Mac snorted.

"You just believe what you want, Mac," she said testily.

"Too bad it ain't buck season," he said. "Well, I got to go pee."

"So pee."

She heard him turn in his bag. "You ever see it?" he asked.

"It? What's 'it'?"

"It. A pecker."

"Sure," she lied.

"Whose? Your father's?"

She was uncomfortable. "No," she said.

"Well, whose then?"

"Oh I don't know! Leave me be, why don't you?"

"Didn't see a deer, didn't see a pecker," Mac said teasingly.

She didn't answer right away. Then she said, "My cousin Lewis. I saw his."

"Well, how old's he?"

"One and a half."

"Ha! A baby! A baby's is like a little worm. It ain't a real one at all."

If he says he'll show me his, she thought, *I'll kick him. I'll just get out of my bag and kick him.*

"I went hunting with my daddy and Versh and Danny Simmons last year in buck season," Mac said, "and we got ourselves one. And we hog-dressed the thing. You know what that is, don't you?"

"No," she said. She was confused. What was he talking about now?

"That's when you cut him open and take out all his guts, so the meat don't spoil. Makes him lighter to pack out, too."

She tried to imagine what the deer's guts might look like, pulled from the gaping hole. "What do you do with them?" she said. "The guts?"

"Oh, just leave 'em for the bears."

She ran her finger like a knife blade along her belly.

"When we left them on the ground," Mac said, "they smoked. Like they were cooking."

"Huh," she said.

"They cut off the deer's pecker, too, you know."

Andy imagined Lewis's pecker and shuddered. "Mac, you're disgusting."

He laughed. "Well, I gotta go pee." She heard him rustle out of his bag. "Broo!" he cried, flapping his arms. "It's cold!"

He makes so much noise, she thought, *just noise and more noise.*

Her father woke them before first light. He warned them to talk softly and said that they were going to the place where Andy had seen the deer, to try to cut them off on their way back from their night feeding. Andy couldn't shake off her sleep. Stuffing her sleeping bag into its sack seemed to take an hour, and tying her boots was the strangest thing she'd ever done. Charlie Spoon made hot chocolate and oatmeal with raisins. Andy closed her eyes and, between beats of her heart, listened to the breathing of the forest. *When I open my eyes, it will be lighter,* she decided. But when she did, it was still just as dark, except for the swaths of their flashlights and the hissing blue flame of the stove. *There has to be just one moment when it all changes from dark to light,* Andy thought. She had missed it yesterday, in the car; today she would watch more closely.

But when she remembered again, it was already first light and they had moved to the rocks by the deer trail and had set up shooting positions—Mac and Charlie Spoon on the up-trail side, she and her father behind them, some six feet up on a ledge. The day became brighter, the sun piercing the tall pines, raking the hunters, yet providing little warmth. Andy now smelled alder and pine and the slightly rotten odor of rock lichen. She rubbed her hand over the stone and considered that it must be very old, had probably been here before the giant pines, *before anyone was in these woods at all.* A chipmunk sniffed on a nearby branch. She aimed an imaginary rifle and pressed the trigger. The chipmunk froze, then scurried away. Her legs were cramping on the narrow ledge. Her father seemed to doze, one hand in his parka, the other cupped lightly around the rifle. She could smell his scent of old wool and leather. His cheeks were speckled with gray-black whiskers, and he worked his jaws slightly, as if chewing a small piece of gum.

Please let us get a deer, she prayed.

A branch snapped on the other side of the rock face. Her father's hand stiffened on the rifle, startling her—*He hasn't been sleeping at all,* she marveled—and then his jaw relaxed, as did the lines around his eyes, and she heard Charlie Spoon call, "Yo, don't shoot, it's us." He and Mac appeared from around the rock. They stopped beneath the ledge. Charlie solemnly crossed his arms.

"I don't believe we're gonna get any deer here," he said drily.

Andy's father lowered his rifle to Charlie and jumped down from the ledge. Then he reached up for Andy. She dropped into his arms and he set her gently on the ground.

Mac sidled up to her. "I knew you didn't see no deer," he said.

"Just because they don't come when you want 'em to don't mean she didn't see them," her father said.

Still, she felt bad. Her telling about the deer had caused them to spend the morning there, cold and expectant, with nothing to show for it.

They tramped through the woods for another two hours, not caring much about noise. Mac found some deer tracks, and they argued about how old they were. They split up for a while and then rejoined at an old logging road that deer might use, and followed it. The road crossed a stream, which had mostly frozen over but in a few spots still caught leaves and twigs in an icy swirl. They forded it by jumping from rock to rock. The road narrowed after that, and the woods thickened.

They stopped for lunch, heating up Charlie's wife's corn chowder. Andy's father cut squares of applesauce cake with his hunting knife and handed them to her and Mac, who ate his almost daintily. Andy could faintly taste knife oil on the cake. She was tired. She stretched her leg; the muscle that had cramped on the rock still ached.

"Might as well relax," her father said, as if reading her thoughts. "We won't find deer till suppertime."

Charlie Spoon leaned back against his pack and folded his hands across his stomach. "Well, even if we don't get a deer," he said expansively, "it's still great to be out here, breathe some fresh air, clomp around a bit. Get away from the house and the old lady." He winked at Mac, who looked away.

"That's what the woods are all about, anyway," Charlie said. "It's where the women don't want to go." He bowed his head toward Andy.

"With your exception, of course, little lady." He helped himself to another piece of applesauce cake.

"She ain't a woman," Mac said.

"Well, she damn well's gonna be," Charlie said. He grinned at her. "Or will you? You're half a boy anyway. You go by a boy's name. What's your real name? Andrea, ain't it?"

110 "That's right," she said. She hoped that if she didn't look at him, Charlie would stop.

"Well, which do you like? Andy or Andrea?"

"Don't matter," she mumbled. "Either."

"She's always been Andy to me," her father said.

Charlie Spoon was still grinning. "So what are you gonna be, Andrea? A boy or a girl?"

115 "I'm a girl," she said.

"But you want to go hunting and fishing and everything, huh?"

"She can do whatever she likes," her father said.

"Hell, you might as well have just had a boy and be done with it!" Charlie exclaimed.

"That's funny," her father said, and chuckled. "That's just what her momma tells me."

120 They were looking at her, and she wanted to get away from them all, even from her father, who chose to joke with them.

"I'm going to walk a bit," she said.

She heard them laughing as she walked down the logging trail. She flapped her arms; she whistled. *I don't care how much noise I make,* she thought. Two grouse flew from the underbrush, startling her. A little farther down, the trail ended in a clearing that enlarged into a frozen meadow; beyond it the woods began again. A few moldering posts were all that was left of a fence that had once enclosed the field. The low afternoon sunlight reflected brightly off the snow, so that Andy's eyes hurt. She squinted hard. A gust of wind blew across the field, stinging her face. And then, as if it had been waiting for her, the doe emerged from the trees opposite and stepped cautiously into the field. Andy watched: it stopped and stood quietly for what seemed a long time and then ambled across. It stopped again about seventy yards away and began to browse in a patch of sugar grass uncovered by the wind. Carefully, slowly, never taking her eyes from the doe, Andy walked backward, trying to step into the boot prints she'd already made. When she was far enough back into the woods, she turned and walked faster, her heart racing. *Please let it stay,* she prayed.

"There's doe in the field yonder," she told them.

They got their rifles and hurried down the trail.

125 "No use," her father said. "We're making too much noise any way you look at it."

"At least we got us the wind in our favor," Charlie Spoon said, breathing heavily.

But the doe was still there, grazing.

"Good Lord," Charlie whispered. He looked at her father. "Well, whose shot?"

"Andy spotted it," her father said in a low voice. "Let her shoot it."

"What!" Charlie's eyes widened.

Andy couldn't believe what her father had just said. She'd only shot tin cans and targets; she'd never even fired her father's .30-.30, and she'd never killed anything.

"I can't," she whispered.

"That's right, she can't," Charlie Spoon insisted. "She's not old enough and she don't have a license even if she was!"

"Well, who's to tell?" her father said in a low voice. "Nobody's going to know but us." He looked at her. "Do you want to shoot it, punkin?"

Why doesn't it hear us? she wondered. *Why doesn't it run away?* "I don't know," she said.

"Well, I'm sure as hell gonna shoot it," Charlie said. Her father grasped Charlie's rifle barrel and held it. His voice was steady.

"Andy's a good shot. It's her deer. She found it, not you. You'd still be sitting on your ass back in camp." He turned to her again. "Now—do you want to shoot it, Andy? Yes or no."

He was looking at her; they were all looking at her. Suddenly she was angry at the deer, who refused to hear them, who wouldn't run away even when it could. "I'll shoot it," she said. Charlie turned away in disgust.

She lay on the ground and pressed the rifle stock against her shoulder bone. The snow was cold through her parka; she smelled oil and wax and damp earth. She pulled off one glove with her teeth. "It sights just like the .22," her father said gently. "Cartridge's already chambered." As she had done so many times before, she sighted down the scope; now the doe was in the reticle. She moved the barrel until the cross hairs lined up. Her father was breathing beside her.

"Aim where the chest and legs meet, or a little above, punkin," he was saying calmly. "That's the killing shot."

But now, seeing it in the scope, Andy was hesitant. Her finger weakened on the trigger. Still, she nodded at what her father said and sighted again, the cross hairs lining up in exactly the same spot—the doe had hardly moved, its brownish-gray body outlined starkly against the blue-backed snow. *It doesn't know,* Andy thought. *It just doesn't know.* And as she looked, deer and snow and faraway trees flattened within the circular frame to become like a picture on a calendar, not real, and she felt calm, as if she had been dreaming everything—the day, the deer, the hunt itself. And she, finger on trigger, was only a part of that dream.

"Shoot!" Charlie hissed.

Through the scope she saw the deer look up, ears high and straining.

Charlie groaned, and just as he did, and just at the moment when Andy knew—*knew*—the doe would bound away, as if she could feel its haunches tensing and gathering power, she pulled the trigger. Later she would think, *I felt the recoil, I smelled the smoke, but I don't remember pulling the trigger.* Through the scope the deer seemed to shrink into itself, and then slowly knelt, hind legs first, head raised as if to cry out. It trembled, still straining to keep its head high, as if that alone would save it; failing, it collapsed, shuddered, and lay still.

145 "Whoee!" Mac cried.

"One shot! One shot!" her father yelled, clapping her on the back. Charlie Spoon was shaking his head and smiling dumbly.

"I told you she was a great little shot!" her father said. "I told you!" Mac danced and clapped his hands. She was dazed, not quite understanding what had happened. And then they were crossing the field toward the fallen doe, she walking dreamlike, the men laughing and joking, released now from the tension of silence and anticipation. Suddenly Mac pointed and cried out, "Look at that!"

The doe was rising, legs unsteady. They stared at it, unable to comprehend, and in that moment the doe regained its feet and looked at them, as if it too were trying to understand. Her father whistled softly. Charlie Spoon unslung his rifle and raised it to his shoulder, but the doe was already bounding away. His hurried shot missed, and the deer disappeared into the woods.

"Damn, damn, damn," he moaned.

150 "I don't believe it," her father said. "That deer was dead."

"Dead, hell!" Charlie yelled. "It was gutshot, that's all. Stunned and gutshot. Clean shot, my ass!"

What have I done? Andy thought.

Her father slung his rifle over his shoulder. "Well, let's go. It can't get too far."

"Hell, I've seen deer run ten miles gutshot," Charlie said. He waved his arms. "We may never find her!"

155 As they crossed the field, Mac came up to her and said in a low voice, "Gutshoot a deer, you'll go to hell."

"Shut up, Mac," she said, her voice cracking. It was a terrible thing she had done, she knew. She couldn't bear to think of the doe in pain and frightened. *Please let it die,* she prayed.

But though they searched all the last hour of daylight, so that they had to recross the field and go up the logging trail in a twilight made even deeper by thick, smoky clouds, they didn't find the doe. They lost its trail almost immediately in the dense stands of alderberry and larch.

"I am cold, and I am tired," Charlie Spoon declared. "And if you ask me, that deer's in another county already."

"No one's asking you, Charlie," her father said.

160 They had a supper of hard salami and ham, bread, and the rest of the applesauce cake. It seemed a bother to heat the coffee, so they had cold chocolate instead. Everyone turned in early.

"We'll find it in the morning, honeybun," her father said, as she went to her tent.

"I don't like to think of it suffering." She was almost in tears.

"It's dead already, punkin. Don't even think about it." He kissed her, his breath sour and his beard rough against her cheek.

Andy was sure she wouldn't get to sleep; the image of the doe falling, falling, then rising again, repeated itself whenever she closed her eyes. Then she heard an owl hoot and realized that it had awakened her, so she must have been asleep after all. She hoped the owl would hush, but instead it hooted louder. She wished her father or Charlie Spoon would wake up and do something about it, but no one moved in the other tent, and suddenly she was afraid that they had all decamped, wanting nothing more to do with her. She whispered, "Mac, Mac," to the sleeping bag where he should be, but no one answered. She tried to find the flashlight she always kept by her side, but couldn't, and she cried in panic, "Mac, are you there?" He mumbled something, and immediately she felt foolish and hoped he wouldn't reply.

When she awoke again, everything had changed. The owl was gone, the woods were still, and she sensed light, blue and pale, light where before there had been none. *The moon must have come out,* she thought. And it was warm, too, warmer than it should have been. She got out of her sleeping bag and took off her parka—it was that warm. Mac was asleep, wheezing like an old man. She unzipped the tent and stepped outside.

The woods were more beautiful than she had ever seen them. The moon made everything ice-rimmed glimmer with a crystallized, immanent light, while underneath that ice the branches of trees were as stark as skeletons. She heard a crunching in the snow, the one sound in all that silence, and there, walking down the logging trail into their camp, was the doe. Its body, like everything around her, was silvered with frost and moonlight. It walked past the tent where her father and Charlie Spoon were sleeping and stopped no more than six feet from her. Andy saw that she had shot it, yes, had shot it cleanly, just where she thought she had, the wound a jagged, bloody hole in the doe's chest.

A heart shot, she thought.

The doe stepped closer, so that Andy, if she wished, could have reached out and touched it. It looked at her as if expecting her to do this, and so she did, running her hand, slowly at first, along the rough, matted fur, then down to the edge of the wound, where she stopped. The doe stood still. Hesitantly, Andy felt the edge of the wound. The torn flesh was sticky and warm. The wound parted under her touch. And then, almost without her knowing it, her fingers were within, probing, yet still the doe didn't move. Andy pressed deeper, through flesh and muscle and sinew, until her whole hand and more was inside the wound and she had found the doe's heart, warm and beating. She cupped it gently in her hand. *Alive,* she marveled. *Alive.*

The heart quickened under her touch, becoming warmer and warmer until it was hot enough to burn. In pain, Andy tried to remove her hand, but the wound closed about it and held her fast. Her hand was burning. She cried out in agony, sure they would all hear and come help, but they didn't. And then her hand pulled free, followed by a steaming rush of blood, more blood than she ever could have imagined—it covered her hand and arm, and she saw to her horror that her hand was steaming. She moaned and fell to her knees and plunged her hand into the snow. The doe looked at her gently and then turned and walked back up the trail.

170 In the morning, when she woke, Andy could still smell the blood, but she felt no pain. She looked at her hand. Even though it appeared unscathed, it felt weak and withered. She couldn't move it freely and was afraid the others would notice. *I will hide it in my jacket pocket,* she decided, *so nobody can see.* She ate the oatmeal that her father cooked and stayed apart from them all. No one spoke to her, and that suited her. A light snow began to fall. It was the last day of their hunting trip. She wanted to be home.

Her father dumped the dregs of his coffee. "Well, let's go look for her," he said.

Again they crossed the field. Andy lagged behind. She averted her eyes from the spot where the doe had fallen, already filling up with snow. Mac and Charlie entered the woods first, followed by her father. Andy remained in the field and considered the smear of gray sky, the nearby flock of crows pecking at unyielding stubble. *I will stay here,* she thought, *and not move for a long while.* But now someone—Mac—was yelling. Her father appeared at the woods' edge and waved for her to come. She ran and pushed through a brake of alderberry and larch. The thick underbrush scratched her face. For a moment she felt lost and looked wildly about. Then, where the brush thinned, she saw them standing quietly in the falling snow. They were staring down at the dead doe. A film covered its upturned eye, and its body was lightly dusted with snow.

"I told you she wouldn't get too far," Andy's father said triumphantly. "We must've just missed her yesterday. Too blind to see."

"We're just damn lucky no animal got to her last night," Charlie muttered.

175 Her father lifted the doe's foreleg. The wound was blood-clotted, brown, and caked like frozen mud. "Clean shot," he said to Charlie. He grinned. "My little girl."

Then he pulled out his knife, the blade gray as the morning. Mac whispered to Andy, "Now watch this," while Charlie Spoon lifted the doe from behind by its forelegs so that its head rested between his knees, its underside exposed. Her father's knife sliced thickly from chest to belly to crotch, and Andy was running from them, back to the field and across, scattering the crows who cawed and circled angrily. And now they were all calling to her—Charlie Spoon and Mac and her father— crying *Andy, Andy* (but that wasn't her name, she would no longer be called that); yet louder than any of them was the wind blowing through the treetops, like the ocean where her mother floated in green water, also calling *Come in, come in,* while all around her roared the mocking of the terrible, now inevitable, sea.

Reading and Reacting

1. The initiation of a child into adulthood is a very common literary theme. In this story, hunting is presented as an initiation rite. In what way is hunting an appropriate coming-of-age ritual?
2. Which characters are in conflict in this story? What ideas are in conflict? How do these conflicts help to communicate the story's initiation theme?
3. In the story's opening paragraph and elsewhere, Andy finds comfort and reassurance in the idea that the woods are "always the same"; later in the story, she remembers the ocean, "huge and empty, yet always moving. Everything lay hidden . . ." (45). How does the contrast between the woods and the ocean suggest the transition she must make from childhood to adulthood?
4. How are the references to blood consistent with the story's initiation theme? Do they suggest another theme as well?
5. Throughout the story, references are made to Andy's ability to inspire the trust of animals. As her father says, "I don't know how she does it, but they come right up to her" (8). How does his comment foreshadow later events?
6. Why do you think Andy prays that she and the others will get a deer? What makes her change her mind? How does the change in Andy's character help to convey the story's theme?
7. Andy's mother is not an active participant in the story's events. Still, her presence is important to the story. *Why* is it important? How does paragraph 45 reveal the importance of the mother's role?
8. What has Andy learned as a result of her experience? What else do you think she has to learn?
9. **JOURNAL ENTRY** How would the story be different if Andy were a boy? What would be the same?

Related Works: "A&P" (p. 65), "Traveling through the Dark" (p. 550), *The Cuban Swimmer* (p. 865)

◊ **DAVID HERBERT LAWRENCE** (1885–1930) was born in Nottinghamshire, England, the son of a coal miner and a schoolteacher. After graduating from high school, he soon began writing fiction and established himself in London literary circles. Lawrence is recognized for his impassioned portrayal of our unconscious and instinctive natures.

Lawrence's fascination with the struggle between the unconscious and the intellect is revealed in his short story "The Rocking-Horse Winner"

(1920). Lawrence sets his story in a house full of secrets and weaves symbolism with elements of the fairy tale and the gothic to produce a tale that is at once realistic and mysterious.

◊ ◊ ◊

D. H. LAWRENCE

The Rocking-Horse Winner
(1920)

There was a woman who was beautiful, who started with all the advantages, yet she had no luck. She married for love, and the love turned to dust. She had bonny children, yet she felt they had been thrust upon her, and she could not love them. They looked at her coldly, as if they were finding fault with her. And hurriedly she felt she must cover up some fault in herself. Yet what it was that she must cover up she never knew. Nevertheless, when her children were present, she always felt the centre of her heart go hard. This troubled her, and in her manner she was all the more gentle and anxious for her children, as if she loved them very much. Only she herself knew that at the centre of her heart was a hard little place that could not feel love, no, not for anybody. Everybody else said of her: "She is such a good mother. She adores her children." Only she herself, and her children themselves, knew it was not so. They read it in each other's eyes.

There were a boy and two little girls. They lived in a pleasant house, with a garden, and they had discreet servants, and felt themselves superior to anyone in the neighbourhood.

Although they lived in style, they felt always an anxiety in the house. There was never enough money. The mother had a small income, and the father had a small income, but not nearly enough for the social position which they had to keep up. The father went into town to some office. But though he had good prospects, these prospects never materialised. There was always the grinding sense of the shortage of money, though the style was always kept up.

At last the mother said: "I will see if *I* can't make something." But she did not know where to begin. She racked her brains, and tried this thing and the other, but could not find anything successful. The failure made deep lines come into her face. Her children were growing up, they would have to go to school. There must be more money, there must be more money. The father, who was always very handsome and expensive in his tastes, seemed as if he never *would* be able to do anything worth doing. And the mother, who had a great belief in herself, did not succeed any better, and her tastes were just as expensive.

5   And so the house came to be haunted by the unspoken phrase: *There must be more money! There must be more money!* The children could hear it all the time, though nobody said it aloud. They heard it at Christmas,

when the expensive and splendid toys filled the nursery. Behind the shining modern rocking-horse, behind the smart doll's house, a voice would start whispering: "There *must* be more money! There *must* be more money!" And the children would stop playing, to listen for a moment. They would look into each other's eyes, to see if they had all heard. And each one saw in the eyes of the other two that they too had heard. "There *must* be more money! There *must* be more money!"

It came whispering from the springs of the still-swaying rocking-horse, and even the horse, bending his wooden, champing head, heard it. The big doll, sitting so pink and smirking in her new pram, could hear it quite plainly, and seemed to be smirking all the more self-consciously because of it. The foolish puppy, too, that took the place of the teddybear, he was looking so extraordinarily foolish for no other reason but that he heard the secret whisper all over the house: "There *must* be more money!"

Yet nobody ever said it aloud. The whisper was everywhere, and therefore no one spoke it. Just as no one ever says: "We are breathing!" in spite of the fact that breath is coming and going all the time.

"Mother," said the boy Paul one day, "why don't we keep a car of our own? Why do we always use uncle's, or else a taxi?"

"Because we're the poor members of the family," said the mother.

"But why *are* we, mother?"

"Well—I suppose," she said slowly and bitterly, "it's because your father has no luck."

The boy was silent for some time.

"Is luck money, mother?" he asked, rather timidly.

"No, Paul. Not quite. It's what causes you to have money."

"Oh!" said Paul vaguely. "I thought when Uncle Oscar said *filthy lucker,* it meant money."

"*Filthy lucre* does mean money," said the mother. "But it's lucre, not luck."

"Oh!" said the boy. "Then what *is* luck, mother?"

"It's what causes you to have money. If you're lucky you have money. That's why it's better to be born lucky than rich. If you're rich, you may lose your money. But if you're lucky, you will always get more money."

"Oh! Will you? And is father not lucky?"

"Very unlucky, I should say," she said bitterly.

The boy watched her with unsure eyes.

"Why?" he asked.

"I don't know. Nobody ever knows why one person is lucky and another unlucky."

"Don't they? Nobody at all? Does *nobody* know?"

"Perhaps God. But He never tells."

"He ought to, then. And aren't you lucky either, mother?"

"I can't be, if I married an unlucky husband."

"But by yourself, aren't you?"

"I used to think I was, before I married. Now I think I am very unlucky indeed."

"Why?"

"Well—never mind! Perhaps I'm not really," she said.

The child looked at her to see if she meant it. But he saw, by the lines of her mouth, that she was only trying to hide something from him.

"Well, anyhow," he said stoutly, "I'm a lucky person."

"Why?" said his mother, with a sudden laugh.

He stared at her. He didn't even know why he had said it.

"God told me," he asserted, brazening it out.

"I hope He did, dear!" she said, again with a laugh, but rather bitter.

"He did, mother!"

"Excellent!" said the mother, using one of her husband's exclamations.

The boy saw she did not believe him; or rather, that she paid no attention to his assertion. This angered him somewhat, and made him want to compel her attention.

He went off by himself, vaguely, in a childish way, seeking for the clue to "luck." Absorbed, taking no heed of other people, he went about with a sort of stealth, seeking inwardly for luck. He wanted luck, he wanted it, he wanted it. When the two girls were playing dolls in the nursery, he would sit on his big rocking-horse, charging madly into space, with a frenzy that made the little girls peer at him uneasily. Wildly the horse careered, the waving dark hair of the boy tossed, his eyes had a strange glare in them. The little girls dared not speak to him.

When he had ridden to the end of his mad little journey, he climbed down and stood in front of his rocking-horse, staring fixedly into its lowered face. Its red mouth was slightly open, its big eye was wide and glassy-bright.

"Now!" he would silently command the snorting steed. "Now, take me to where there is luck! Now take me!"

And he would slash the horse on the neck with the little whip he had asked Uncle Oscar for. He *knew* the horse could take him to where there was luck, if only he forced it. So he would mount again and start on his furious ride, hoping at last to get there. He knew he could get there.

"You'll break your horse, Paul!" said the nurse.

"He's always riding like that! I wish he'd leave off!" said his elder sister Joan.

But he only glared down on them in silence. Nurse gave him up. She could make nothing of him. Anyhow, he was growing beyond her.

One day his mother and his Uncle Oscar came in when he was on one of his furious rides. He did not speak to them.

"Hallo, you young jockey! Riding a winner?" said his uncle.

"Aren't you growing too big for a rocking-horse? You're not a very little boy any longer, you know," said his mother.

But Paul only gave a blue glare from his big, rather close-set eyes. He would speak to nobody when he was in full tilt. His mother watched him with an anxious expression on her face.

At last he suddenly stopped forcing his horse into the mechanical gallop and slid down.

"Well, I got there!" he announced fiercely, his blue eyes still flaring, and his sturdy long legs straddling apart.

"Where did you get to?" asked his mother.

"Where I wanted to go," he flared back at her.

"That's right, son!" said Uncle Oscar. "Don't you stop till you get there. What's the horse's name?"

"He doesn't have a name," said the boy.

"Gets on without all right?" asked the uncle.

"Well, he has different names. He was called Sansovino last week."

"Sansovino, eh? Won the Ascot.[1] How did you know this name?"

"He always talks about horse-races with Bassett," said Joan.

The uncle was delighted to find that his small nephew was posted with all the racing news. Bassett, the young gardener, who had been wounded in the left foot in the war and had got his present job through Oscar Cresswell, whose batman[2] he had been, was a perfect blade of the "turf." He lived in the racing events, and the small boy lived with him.

Oscar Cresswell got it all from Bassett.

"Master Paul comes and asks me, so I can't do more than tell him, sir," said Bassett, his face terribly serious, as if he were speaking of religious matters.

"And does he ever put anything on a horse he fancies?"

"Well—I don't want to give him away—he's a young sport, a fine sport, sir. Would you mind asking him himself? He sort of takes a pleasure in it, and perhaps he'd feel I was giving him away, sir, if you don't mind."

Bassett was serious as a church.

The uncle went back to his nephew and took him off for a ride in the car.

"Say, Paul, old man, do you ever put anything on a horse?" the uncle asked.

The boy watched the handsome man closely.

"Why, do you think I oughtn't to?" he parried.

"Not a bit of it! I thought perhaps you might give me a tip for the Lincoln."[3]

The car sped on into the country, going down to Uncle Oscar's place in Hampshire.

"Honour bright?" said the nephew.

---

[1] The annual horse race at Ascot Heath in England.
[2] A British military officer's personal assistant.
[3] The Lincolnshire Handicap.

"Honour bright, son!" said the uncle.

"Well, then, Daffodil."

"Daffodil! I doubt it, sonny. What about Mirza?"

"I only know the winner," said the boy. "That's Daffodil."

"Daffodil, eh?"

There was a pause. Daffodil was an obscure horse comparatively.

"Uncle!"

"Yes, son?"

"You won't let it go any further, will you? I promised Bassett."

"Bassett be damned, old man! What's he got to do with it?"

"We're partners. We've been partners from the first. Uncle, he lent me my first five shillings, which I lost. I promised him, honour bright, it was only between me and him; only you gave me that ten-shilling note I started winning with, so I thought you were lucky. You won't let it go any further, will you?"

The boy gazed at his uncle from those big, hot, blue eyes, set rather close together. The uncle stirred and laughed uneasily.

"Right you are, son! I'll keep your tip private. Daffodil, eh? How much are you putting on him?"

"All except twenty pounds," said the boy. "I keep that in reserve."

The uncle thought it a good joke.

"You keep twenty pounds in reserve, do you, you young romancer? What are you betting, then?"

"I'm betting three hundred," said the boy gravely. "But it's between you and me, Uncle Oscar! Honour bright?"

The uncle burst into a roar of laughter.

"It's between you and me all right, you young Nat Gould,"[4] he said, laughing. "But where's your three hundred?"

"Bassett keeps it for me. We're partners."

"You are, are you! And what is Bassett putting on Daffodil?"

"He won't go quite as high as I do, I expect. Perhaps he'll go a hundred and fifty."

"What, pennies?" laughed the uncle.

"Pounds," said the child, with a surprised look at his uncle. "Bassett keeps a bigger reserve than I do."

Between wonder and amusement Uncle Oscar was silent. He pursued the matter no further, but he determined to take his nephew with him to the Lincoln races.

"Now, son," he said, "I'm putting twenty on Mirza, and I'll put five on for you on any horse you fancy. What's your pick?"

"Daffodil, uncle."

"No, not the fiver on Daffodil!"

"I should if it was my own fiver," said the child.

---

[4] Nathaniel Gould (1857–1919), British journalist and writer known for his stories about horse racing.

"Good! Good! Right you are! A fiver for me and a fiver for you on Daffodil."

The child had never been to a race-meeting before, and his eyes were blue fire. He pursed his mouth tight and watched. A Frenchman just in front had put his money on Lancelot. Wild with excitement, he flayed his arms up and down, yelling *"Lancelot! Lancelot!"* in his French accent.

Daffodil came in first, Lancelot second, Mirza third. The child, flushed and with eyes blazing, was curiously serene. His uncle brought him four five-pound notes, four to one.

"What am I to do with these?" he cried, waving them before the boy's eyes.

"I suppose we'll talk to Bassett," said the boy. "I expect I have fifteen hundred now; and twenty in reserve; and this twenty."

His uncle studied him for some moments.

"Look here, son!" he said. "You're not serious about Bassett and that fifteen hundred, are you?"

"Yes, I am. But it's between you and me, uncle. Honour bright?"

"Honour bright all right, son! But I must talk to Bassett."

"If you'd like to be a partner, uncle, with Bassett and me, we could all be partners. Only, you'd have to promise, honour bright, uncle, not to let it go beyond us three. Bassett and I are lucky, and you must be lucky, because it was your ten shillings I started winning with. . . ."

Uncle Oscar took both Bassett and Paul into Richmond Park for an afternoon, and there they talked.

"It's like this, you see, sir," Bassett said. "Master Paul would get me talking about racing events, spinning yarns, you know, sir. And he was always keen on knowing if I'd made or if I'd lost. It's about a year since, now, that I put five shillings on Blush of Dawn for him: and we lost. Then the luck turned, with that ten shillings he had from you: that we put on Singhalese. And since that time, it's been pretty steady, all things considering. What do you say, Master Paul?"

"We're all right when we're sure," said Paul. "It's when we're not quite sure that we go down."

"Oh, but we're careful then," said Bassett.

"But when are you *sure*?" smiled Uncle Oscar.

"It's Master Paul, sir," said Bassett in a secret, religious voice. "It's as if he had it from heaven. Like Daffodil, now, for the Lincoln. That was as sure as eggs."

"Did you put anything on Daffodil?" asked Oscar Cresswell.

"Yes, sir. I made my bit."

"And my nephew?"

Bassett was obstinately silent, looking at Paul.

"I made twelve hundred, didn't I, Bassett? I told uncle I was putting three hundred on Daffodil."

"That's right," said Bassett, nodding.

"But where's the money?" asked the uncle.

"I keep it safe locked up, sir. Master Paul can have it any minute he likes to ask for it."

"What, fifteen hundred pounds?"

"And twenty! And *forty*, that is, with the twenty he made on the course."

"It's amazing!" said the uncle.

"If Master Paul offers you to be partners, sir, I would, if I were you: if you'll excuse me," said Bassett.

Oscar Cresswell thought about it.

"I'll see the money," he said.

They drove home again, and, sure enough, Bassett came round to the garden-house with fifteen hundred pounds in notes. The twenty pounds reserve was left with Joe Glee, in the Turf Commission deposit.

"You see, it's all right, uncle, when I'm *sure*! Then we go strong, for all we're worth. Don't we, Bassett?"

"We do that, Master Paul."

"And when are you sure?" said the uncle, laughing.

"Oh, well, sometimes I'm *absolutely* sure, like about Daffodil," said the boy; "and sometimes I have an idea; and sometimes I haven't even an idea, have I, Bassett? Then we're careful, because we mostly go down."

"You do, do you! And when you're sure, like about Daffodil, what makes you sure, sonny?"

"Oh, well, I don't know," said the boy uneasily. "I'm sure, you know, uncle; that's all."

"It's as if he had it from heaven, sir," Bassett reiterated.

"I should say so!" said the uncle.

But he became a partner. And when the Leger[5] was coming on Paul was "sure" about Lively Spark, which was a quite inconsiderable horse. The boy insisted on putting a thousand on the horse, Bassett went for five hundred, and Oscar Cresswell two hundred. Lively Spark came in first, and the betting had been ten to one against him. Paul had made ten thousand.

"You see," he said, "I was absolutely sure of him."

Even Oscar Cresswell had cleared two thousand.

"Look here, son," he said, "this sort of thing makes me nervous."

"It needn't, uncle! Perhaps I shan't be sure again for a long time."

"But what are you going to do with your money?" asked the uncle.

"Of course," said the boy, "I started it for mother. She said she had no luck, because father is unlucky, so I thought if *I* was lucky, it might stop whispering."

"What might stop whispering?"

---

[5] The St. Leger Stakes.

"Our house. I *hate* our house for whispering."
"What does it whisper?"
"Why—why"—the boy fidgeted—"why, I don't know. But it's always short of money, you know, uncle."
"I know it, son, I know it."
"You know people send mother writs,[6] don't you, uncle?"
"I'm afraid I do," said the uncle.
"And then the house whispers, like people laughing at you behind your back. It's awful, that is! I thought if I was lucky . . ."
"You might stop it," added the uncle.
The boy watched him with big blue eyes, that had an uncanny cold fire in them, and he said never a word.
"Well, then!" said the uncle. "What are we doing?"
"I shouldn't like mother to know I was lucky," said the boy.
"Why not, son?"
"She'd stop me."
"I don't think she would."
"Oh!"—and the boy writhed in an odd way—"I *don't* want her to know, uncle."
"All right, son! We'll manage it without her knowing."

They managed it very easily. Paul, at the other's suggestion, handed over five thousand pounds to his uncle, who deposited it with the family lawyer, who was then to inform Paul's mother that a relative had put five thousand pounds into his hands, which sum was to be paid out a thousand pounds at a time, on the mother's birthday, for the next five years.

"So she'll have a birthday present of a thousand pounds for five successive years," said Uncle Oscar. "I hope it won't make it all the harder for her later."

Paul's mother had her birthday in November. The house had been "whispering" worse than ever lately, and, even in spite of his luck, Paul could not bear up against it. He was very anxious to see the effect of the birthday letter, telling his mother about the thousand pounds.

When there were no visitors, Paul now took his meals with his parents, as he was beyond the nursery control. His mother went into town nearly every day. She had discovered that she had an odd knack of sketching furs and dress materials, so she worked secretly in the studio of a friend who was the chief "artist" for the leading drapers. She drew the figures of ladies in furs and ladies in silk and sequins for the newspaper advertisements. This young woman artist earned several thousand pounds a year, but Paul's mother only made several hundreds, and she was again dissatisfied. She so wanted to be first in something, and she did not succeed, even in making sketches for drapery advertisements.

---

[6] Letters from creditors requesting payment.

She was down to breakfast on the morning of her birthday. Paul watched her face as she read her letters. He knew the lawyer's letter. As his mother read it, her face hardened and became more expressionless. Then a cold, determined look came on her mouth. She hid the letter under the pile of others, and said not a word about it.

"Didn't you have anything nice in the post for your birthday, mother?" said Paul.

"Quite moderately nice," she said, her voice cold and absent.

She went away to town without saying more.

But in the afternoon Uncle Oscar appeared. He said Paul's mother had had a long interview with the lawyer, asking if the whole five thousand could not be advanced at once, as she was in debt.

"What do you think, uncle?" asked the boy.

"I leave it to you, son."

"Oh, let her have it, then! We can get some more with the other," said the boy.

"A bird in the hand is worth two in the bush, laddie!" said Uncle Oscar.

"But I'm sure to *know* for the Grand National; or the Lincolnshire; or else the Derby.[7] I'm sure to know for *one* of them," said Paul.

So Uncle Oscar signed the agreement, and Paul's mother touched the whole five thousand. Then something very curious happened. The voices in the house suddenly went mad, like a chorus of frogs on a spring evening. There was certain new furnishings, and Paul had a tutor. He was *really* going to Eton, his father's school, in the following autumn. There were flowers in the winter, and a blossoming of the luxury Paul's mother had been used to. And yet the voices in the house, behind the sprays of mimosa and almond-blossom, and from under the piles of iridescent cushions, simply trilled and screamed in a sort of ecstasy: "There *must* be more money! Oh-h-h; there *must* be more money. Oh, now, now-w! Now-w-w-w—there *must* be more money!—more than ever! More than ever!"

It frightened Paul terribly. He studied away at his Latin and Greek with his tutor. But his intense hours were spent with Bassett. The Grand National had gone by: he had not "known," and had lost a hundred pounds. Summer was at hand. He was in agony for the Lincoln. But even for the Lincoln he didn't "know," and he lost fifty pounds. He became wild-eyed and strange, as if something were going to explode in him.

"Let it alone, son! Don't you bother about it!" urged Uncle Oscar. But it was as if the boy couldn't really hear what his uncle was saying.

"I've got to know for the Derby! I've got to know for the Derby!" the child reiterated, his big blue eyes blazing with a sort of madness.

---

[7] Famous British horse races. The Grand National is run at Aintree, the Derby at Epsom Downs.

185 His mother noticed how overwrought he was.

"You'd better go to the seaside. Wouldn't you like to go now to the seaside, instead of waiting? I think you'd better," she said, looking down at him anxiously, her heart curiously heavy because of him.

But the child lifted his uncanny blue eyes.

"I couldn't possibly go before the Derby, mother!" he said. "I couldn't possibly!"

"Why not?" she said, her voice becoming heavy when she was opposed. "Why not? You can still go from the seaside to see the Derby with your Uncle Oscar, if that's what you wish. No need for you to wait here. Besides, I think you care too much about these races. It's a bad sign. My family has been a gambling family, and you won't know till you grow up how much damage it has done. But it has done damage. I shall have to send Bassett away, and ask Uncle Oscar not to talk racing to you, unless you promise to be reasonable about it: go away to the seaside and forget it. You're all nerves!"

190 "I'll do what you like, mother, so long as you don't send me away till after the Derby," the boy said.

"Send you away from where? Just from this house?"

"Yes," he said, gazing at her.

"Why, you curious child, what makes you care about this house so much, suddenly? I never knew you loved it."

He gazed at her without speaking. He had a secret within a secret, something he had not divulged, even to Bassett or to his Uncle Oscar.

195 But his mother, after standing undecided and a little bit sullen for some moments, said:

"Very well, then! Don't go to the seaside till after the Derby, if you don't wish it. But promise me you won't let your nerves go to pieces. Promise you won't think so much about horse-racing and *events,* as you call them!"

"Oh no," said the boy casually. "I won't think much about them, mother. You needn't worry. I wouldn't worry, mother, if I were you."

"If you were me and I were you," said his mother, "I wonder what we *should* do!"

"But you know you needn't worry, mother, don't you?" the boy repeated.

200 "I should be awfully glad to know it," she said wearily.

"Oh, well, you *can,* you know. I mean, you *ought* to know you needn't worry," he insisted.

"Ought I? Then I'll see about it," she said.

Paul's secret of secrets was his wooden horse, that which had no name. Since he was emancipated from a nurse and a nursery-governess, he had had his rocking-horse removed to his own bedroom at the top of the house.

"Surely you're too big for a rocking-horse!" his mother had remonstrated.

"Well, you see, mother, till I can have a *real* horse, I like to have *some* sort of animal about," had been his quaint answer.

"Do you feel he keeps you company?" she laughed.

"Oh yes! He's very good, he always keeps me company, when I'm there," said Paul.

So the horse, rather shabby, stood in an arrested prance in the boy's bedroom.

The Derby was drawing near, and the boy grew more and more tense. He hardly heard what was spoken to him, he was very frail, and his eyes were really uncanny. His mother had sudden strange seizures of uneasiness about him. Sometimes, for half an hour, she would feel a sudden anxiety about him that was almost anguish. She wanted to rush to him at once, and know he was safe.

Two nights before the Derby, she was at a big party in town, when one of her rushes of anxiety about her boy, her firstborn, gripped her heart till she could hardly speak. She fought with the feeling, might and main, for she believed in common sense. But it was too strong. She had to leave the dance and go downstairs to telephone to the country. The children's nursery-governess was terribly surprised and startled at being rung up in the night.

"Are the children all right, Miss Wilmot?"

"Oh yes, they are quite all right."

"Master Paul? Is he all right?"

"He went to bed as right as a trivet. Shall I run up and look at him?"

"No," said Paul's mother reluctantly. "No! Don't trouble. It's all right. Don't sit up. We shall be home fairly soon." She did not want her son's privacy intruded upon.

"Very good," said the governess.

It was about one o'clock when Paul's mother and father drove up to their house. All was still. Paul's mother went to her room and slipped off her white fur cloak. She had told her maid not to wait up for her. She heard her husband downstairs, mixing a whisky and soda.

And then, because of the strange anxiety at her heart, she stole upstairs to her son's room. Noiselessly she went along the upper corridor. Was there a faint noise? What was it?

She stood, with arrested muscles, outside his door, listening. There was a strange, heavy, and yet not loud noise. Her heart stood still. It was a soundless noise, yet rushing and powerful. Something huge, in violent, hushed motion. What was it? What in God's name was it? She ought to know. She felt that she knew the noise. She knew what it was.

Yet she could not place it. She couldn't say what it was. And on and on it went, like a madness.

Softly, frozen with anxiety and fear, she turned the door-handle.

The room was dark. Yet in the space near the window, she heard and saw something plunging to and fro. She gazed in fear and amazement.

Then suddenly she switched on the light, and saw her son, in his green pyjamas, madly surging on the rocking-horse. The blaze of light suddenly lit him up, as he urged the wooden horse, and lit her up, as she stood, blonde, in her dress of pale green and crystal, in the doorway.

"Paul!" she cried. "Whatever are you doing?"

"It's Malabar!" he screamed in a powerful, strange voice. "It's Malabar!"

His eyes blazed at her for one strange and senseless second, as he ceased urging his wooden horse. Then he fell with a crash to the ground, and she, all her tormented motherhood flooding upon her, rushed to gather him up.

But he was unconscious, and unconscious he remained, with some brain-fever. He talked and tossed, and his mother sat stonily by his side.

"Malabar! It's Malabar! Bassett, Bassett, I *know!* It's Malabar!"

So the child cried, trying to get up and urge the rocking-horse that gave him his inspiration.

"What does he mean by Malabar?" asked the heart-frozen mother.

"I don't know," said the father stonily.

"What does he mean by Malabar?" she asked her brother Oscar.

"It's one of the horses running for the Derby," was the answer.

And, in spite of himself, Oscar Cresswell spoke to Bassett, and himself put a thousand on Malabar: at fourteen to one.

The third day of the illness was critical: they were waiting for a change. The boy, with his rather long, curly hair, was tossing ceaselessly on the pillow. He neither slept nor regained consciousness, and his eyes were like blue stones. His mother sat, feeling her heart had gone, turned actually into a stone.

In the evening, Oscar Cresswell did not come, but Bassett sent a message, saying could he come up for one moment, just one moment? Paul's mother was very angry at the intrusion, but on second thought she agreed. The boy was the same. Perhaps Bassett might bring him to consciousness.

The gardener, a shortish fellow with a little brown moustache and sharp little brown eyes, tiptoed into the room, touched his imaginary cap to Paul's mother, and stole to the bedside, staring with glittering, smallish eyes at the tossing, dying child.

"Master Paul!" he whispered. "Master Paul! Malabar came in first all right, a clean win. I did as you told me. You've made over seventy thousand pounds, you have; you've got over eighty thousand. Malabar came in all right, Master Paul."

"Malabar! Malabar! Did I say Malabar, mother? Did I say Malabar? Do you think I'm lucky, mother? I knew Malabar, didn't I? Over eighty thousand pounds! I call that lucky, don't you, mother? Over eighty thousand pounds! I knew, didn't I know I knew? Malabar came in all right. If I ride my horse till I'm sure, then I tell you, Bassett, you can go as high as you like. Did you go for all you were worth, Bassett?"

"I went a thousand on it, Master Paul."

"I never told you, mother, that if I can ride my horse, and *get there*, then I'm absolutely sure—oh, absolutely! Mother, did I ever tell you? I *am* lucky!"

"No, you never did," said his mother.

But the boy died in the night.

And even as he lay dead, his mother heard her brother's voice saying to her: "My God, Hester, you're eighty-odd thousand to the good, and a poor devil of a son to the bad. But, poor devil, poor devil, he's best gone out of a life where he rides his rocking-horse to find a winner."

READING AND REACTING

1. From what point of view is "The Rocking-Horse Winner" told? How does this point of view help to communicate the story's theme?
2. In what respects is "The Rocking-Horse Winner" like a fairy tale? How is it different?
3. Many fairy tales involve a hero who goes on a journey to search for something of great value. What journey does Paul go on? What does he search for? Is he successful?
4. In paragraph 5, the narrator says that the house is "haunted by the unspoken phrase 'There must be more money.'" In what way does the phrase "haunt" the house?
5. How would you characterize Paul's parents? His uncle? Bassett? Are they weak? Evil? What motivates them?
6. Beginning with paragraph 10, Paul's mother attempts to define the word *luck*. According to her definition, does she consider Paul lucky? Do you agree?
7. In what ways does Paul behave like other children? In what ways is he different? How do you account for these differences? How old do you think Paul is? Why is his age significant?
8. The rocking horse is an important literary symbol in the story. What possible meanings might the rocking horse suggest? In what ways does this symbol reinforce the story's theme?
9. What secrets do the various characters keep from one another? Why do they keep them? How do these secrets relate to the story's theme?
10. How does Paul know who the winners will be? Does the rocking horse really tell him? Does he get his information "from heaven" as Bassett suggests? Or, does he just guess?
11. **JOURNAL ENTRY** In your opinion, who or what is responsible for Paul's death?

Related Works: "Gretel in Darkness" (p. 330), "Suicide Note" (p. 338), "The Chimney Sweeper" (p. 504), *A Doll House* (p. 599)

◆ **EUDORA WELTY** (1909–) was born and raised in Jackson, Mississippi, where she still lives in her family's home. In 1936, she wrote the first of her many short stories, and she has also written several novels.

One of the country's most accomplished writers, Welty has focused much of her fiction on life in Southern towns peopled with dreamers, eccentrics, and close-knit families. Her sharply observed characters are sometimes presented with great humor, sometimes with poignant lyricism, but always with clarity and sympathy. In "A Worn Path," Welty creates a particularly memorable character in the tenacious Phoenix Jackson, and she explores a theme that transcends race and region.

◆ ◆ ◆

EUDORA WELTY

A Worn Path
(1940)

It was December—a bright frozen day in the early morning. Far out in the country there was an old Negro woman with her head tied in a red rag, coming along a path through the pinewoods. Her name was Phoenix Jackson. She was very old and small and she walked slowly in the dark pine shadows, moving a little from side to side in her steps, with the balanced heaviness and lightness of a pendulum in a grandfather clock. She carried a thin, small cane made from an umbrella, and with this she kept tapping the frozen earth in front of her. This made a grave and persistent noise in the still air, that seemed meditative like the chirping of a solitary little bird.

She wore a dark striped dress reaching down to her shoe tops, and an equally long apron of bleached sugar sacks, with a full pocket: all neat and tidy, but every time she took a step she might have fallen over her shoelaces, which dragged from her unlaced shoes. She looked straight ahead. Her eyes were blue with age. Her skin had a pattern all its own of numberless branching wrinkles and as though a whole little tree stood in the middle of her forehead, but a golden color ran underneath, and the two knobs of her cheeks were illuminated by a yellow burning under the dark. Under the red rag her hair came down on her neck in the frailest of ringlets, still black, and with an odor like copper.

Now and then there was a quivering in the thicket. Old Phoenix said, "Out of my way, all you foxes, owls, beetles, jack rabbits, coons and wild animals! . . . Keep out from under these feet, little bob-whites. . . . Keep the big wild hogs out of my path. Don't let none of those come running my direction. I got a long way." Under her small black-freckled hand her cane, limber as a buggy whip, would switch at the brush as if to rouse up any hiding things.

On she went. The woods were deep and still. The sun made the pine needles almost too bright to look at, up where the wind rocked. The cones dropped as light as feathers. Down in the hollow was the mourning dove—it was not too late for him.

5 The path ran up a hill. "Seem like there is chains about my feet, time I get this far," she said, in the voice of argument old people keep to use with themselves. "Something always take a hold of me on this hill—pleads I should stay."

After she got to the top she turned and gave a full, severe look behind her where she had come. "Up through pines," she said at length. "Now down through oaks."

Her eyes opened their widest, and she started down gently. But before she got to the bottom of the hill a bush caught her dress.

Her fingers were busy and intent, but her skirts were full and long, so that before she could pull them free in one place they were caught in another. It was not possible to allow the dress to tear. "I in the thorny bush," she said. "Thorns, you doing your appointed work. Never want to let folks pass, no sir. Old eyes thought you was a pretty little *green* bush."

Finally, trembling all over, she stood free, and after a moment dared to stoop for her cane.

10 "Sun so high!" she cried, leaning back and looking, while the thick tears went over her eyes. "The time getting all gone here."

At the foot of this hill was a place where a log was laid across the creek.

"Now comes the trial," said Phoenix.

Putting her right foot out, she mounted the log and shut her eyes. Lifting her skirt, leveling her cane fiercely before her, like a festival figure in some parade, she began to march across. Then she opened her eyes and she was safe on the other side.

"I wasn't as old as I thought," she said.

15 But she sat down to rest. She spread her skirts on the bank around her and folded her hands over her knees. Up above her was a tree in a pearly cloud of mistletoe. She did not dare to close her eyes, and when a little boy brought her a plate with a slice of marble-cake on it she spoke to him. "That would be acceptable," she said. But when she went to take it there was just her own hand in the air.

So she left that tree, and had to go through a barbed-wire fence. There she had to creep and crawl, spreading her knees and stretching her fingers like a baby trying to climb the steps. But she talked loudly to herself: she could not let her dress be torn now, so late in the day, and she could not pay for having her arm or her leg sawed off if she got caught fast where she was.

At last she was safe through the fence and risen up out in the clearing. Big dead trees, like black men with one arm, were standing in the purple stalks of the withered cotton field. There sat a buzzard.

"Who you watching?"

In the furrow she made her way along.

"Glad this not the season for bulls," she said, looking sideways, "and the good Lord made his snakes to curl up and sleep in the winter. A pleasure I don't see no two-headed snake coming around that tree, where it come once. It took a while to get by him, back in the summer."

She passed through the old cotton and went into a field of dead corn. It whispered and shook and was taller than her head. "Through the maze now," she said, for there was no path.

Then there was something tall, black, and skinny there, moving before her.

At first she took it for a man. It could have been a man dancing in the field. But she stood still and listened, and it did not make a sound. It was as silent as a ghost.

"Ghost," she said sharply, "who be you the ghost of? For I have heard of nary death close by."

But there was no answer—only the ragged dancing in the wind.

She shut her eyes, reached out her hand, and touched a sleeve. She found a coat and inside that an emptiness, cold as ice.

"You scarecrow," she said. Her face lighted. "I ought to be shut up for good," she said with laughter. "My senses is gone. I too old. I the oldest people I ever know. Dance, old scarecrow," she said, "while I dancing with you."

She kicked her foot over the furrow, and with mouth drawn down, shook her head once or twice in a little strutting way. Some husks blew down and whirled in streamers about her skirts.

Then she went on, parting her way from side to side with the cane, through the whispering field. At last she came to the end, to a wagon track where the silver grass blew between the red ruts. The quail were walking around like pullets, seeming all dainty and unseen.

"Walk pretty," she said. "This is the easy place. This the easy going."

She followed the track, swaying through the quiet bare fields, through the little strings of trees silver in their dead leaves, past cabins silver from weather, with the doors and windows boarded shut, all like old women under a spell sitting there. "I walking in their sleep," she said, nodding her head vigorously.

In a ravine she went where a spring was silently flowing through a hollow log. Old Phoenix bent and drank. "Sweet-gum makes the water sweet," she said, and drank more. "Nobody know who made this well, for it was here when I was born."

The track crossed a swampy part where the moss hung as white as lace from every limb. "Sleep on, alligators, and blow your bubbles." Then the track went into the road.

Deep, deep the road went down between the high green-colored banks. Overhead the live-oaks met, and it was as dark as a cave.

A black dog with a lolling tongue came up out of the weeds by the ditch. She was meditating, and not ready, and when he came at her she only hit him a little with her cane. Over she went in the ditch, like a little puff of milkweed.

Down there, her senses drifted away. A dream visited her, and she reached her hand up, but nothing reached down and gave her a pull. So she lay there and presently went to talking. "Old woman," she said to herself, "that black dog come up out of the weeds to stall you off, and now there he sitting on his fine tail, smiling at you."

A white man finally came along and found her—a hunter, a young man, with his dog on a chain.

"Well, Granny!" he laughed. "What are you doing there?"

"Lying on my back like a June-bug waiting to be turned over, mister," she said, reaching up her hand.

40 He lifted her up, gave her a swing in the air, and set her down. "Anything broken, Granny?"

"No sir, them old dead weeds is springy enough," said Phoenix, when she had got her breath. "I thank you for your trouble."

"Where do you live, Granny?" he asked, while the two dogs were growling at each other.

"Away back yonder, sir, behind the ridge. You can't even see it from here."

"On your way home?"

45 "No sir, I going to town."

"Why, that's too far! That's as far as I walk when I come out myself, and I get something for my trouble." He patted the stuffed bag he carried, and there hung down a little closed claw. It was one of the bobwhites, with its beak hooked bitterly to show it was dead. "Now you go on home, Granny!"

"I bound to go to town, mister," said Phoenix. "The time come around."

He gave another laugh, filling the whole landscape. "I know you old colored people! Wouldn't miss going to town to see Santa Claus!"

But something held old Phoenix very still. The deep lines in her face went into a fierce and different radiation. Without warning, she had seen with her own eyes a flashing nickel fall out of the man's pocket onto the ground.

50 "How old are you, Granny?" he was saying.

"There is no telling, mister," she said, "no telling."

Then she gave a little cry and clapped her hands and said, "Git on away from here, dog! Look! Look at that dog!" She laughed as if in admiration. "He ain't scared of nobody. He a big black dog." She whispered, "Sic him!"

"Watch me get rid of that cur," said the man. "Sic him, Pete! Sic him!"

Phoenix heard the dogs fighting, and heard the man running and throwing sticks. She even heard a gunshot. But she was slowly bending forward by that time, further and further forward, the lid stretched down over her eyes, as if she were doing this in her sleep. Her chin was lowered almost to her knees. The yellow palm of her hand came out from the fold of her apron. Her fingers slid down and along the ground under the piece of money with the grace and care they would have in lifting an egg from under a setting hen. Then she slowly straightened up, she stood erect, and the nickel was in her apron pocket. A bird flew by. Her lips moved. "God watching me the whole time. I come to stealing."

The man came back, and his own dog panted about them. "Well, I scared him off that time," he said, and then he laughed and lifted his gun and pointed it at Phoenix.

She stood straight and faced him.

"Doesn't the gun scare you?" he said, still pointing it.

"No, sir, I seen plenty go off closer by, in my day, and for less than what I done," she said, holding utterly still.

He smiled, and shouldered the gun. "Well, Granny," he said, "you must be a hundred years old, and scared of nothing. I'd give you a dime if I had any money with me. But you take my advice and stay home, and nothing will happen to you."

"I bound to go on my way, mister," said Phoenix. She inclined her head in the red rag. Then they went in different directions, but she could hear the gun shooting again and again over the hill.

She walked on. The shadows hung from the oak trees to the road like curtains. Then she smelled wood-smoke, and smelled the river, and she saw a steeple and the cabins on their steep steps. Dozens of little black children whirled around her. There ahead was Natchez shining. Bells were ringing. She walked on.

In the paved city it was Christmas time. There were red and green electric lights strung and crisscrossed everywhere, and all turned on in the daytime. Old Phoenix would have been lost if she had not distrusted her eyesight and depended on her feet to know where to take her.

She paused quietly on the sidewalk where people were passing by. A lady came along in the crowd, carrying an armful of red-, green- and silver-wrapped presents; she gave off perfume like the red roses in hot summer, and Phoenix stopped her.

"Please, missy, will you lace up my shoe?" She held up her foot.

"What do you want, Grandma?"

"See my shoe," said Phoenix. "Do all right for out in the country, but wouldn't look right to go in a big building."

"Stand still then, Grandma," said the lady. She put her packages down on the sidewalk beside her and laced and tied both shoes tightly.

"Can't lace 'em with a cane," said Phoenix. "Thank you, missy. I doesn't mind asking a nice lady to tie up my shoe, when I gets out on the street."

Moving slowly and from side to side, she went into the big building, and into a tower of steps, where she walked up and around and around until her feet knew to stop.

She entered a door, and there she saw nailed up on the wall the document that had been stamped with the gold seal and framed in the gold frame, which matched the dream that was hung up in her head.

"Here I be," she said. There was a fixed and ceremonial stiffness over her body.

"A charity case, I suppose," said an attendant who sat at the desk before her.

But Phoenix only looked above her head. There was sweat on her face, the wrinkles in her face shone like a bright net.

"Speak up, Grandma," the woman said. "What's your name? We must have your history, you know. Have you been here before? What seems to be the trouble with you?"

Old Phoenix only gave a twitch to her face as if a fly were bothering her.

"Are you deaf?" cried the attendant.

But then the nurse came in.

"Oh, that's just old Aunt Phoenix," she said. "She doesn't come for herself—she has a little grandson. She makes these trips just as regular as clockwork. She lives away back off the Old Natchez Trace." She bent down. "Well, Aunt Phoenix, why don't you just take a seat? We won't keep you standing after your long trip." She pointed.

The old woman sat down, bolt upright in the chair.

"Now, how is the boy?" asked the nurse.

Old Phoenix did not speak.

"I said, how is the boy?"

But Phoenix only waited and stared straight ahead, her face very solemn and withdrawn into rigidity.

"Is his throat any better?" asked the nurse. "Aunt Phoenix, don't you hear me? Is your grandson's throat any better since the last time you came for the medicine?"

With her hands on her knees, the old woman waited, silent, erect and motionless, just as if she were in armor.

"You mustn't take up our time this way, Aunt Phoenix," the nurse said. "Tell us quickly about your grandson, and get it over. He isn't dead, is he?"

At last there came a flicker and then a flame of comprehension across her face, and she spoke.

"My grandson. It was my memory had left me. There I sat and forgot why I made my long trip."

"Forgot?" The nurse frowned. "After you came so far?"

Then Phoenix was like an old woman begging a dignified forgiveness for waking up frightened in the night. "I never did go to school, I was too old at the Surrender,"[1] she said in a soft voice. "I'm an old woman without an education. It was my memory fail me. My little grandson, he is just the same, and I forgot it in the coming."

"Throat never heals, does it?" said the nurse, speaking in a loud, sure voice to old Phoenix. By now she had a card with something written on

---

[1] Of General Robert E. Lee to General Ulysses S. Grant at the end of the Civil War, April 9, 1865.

it, a little list. "Yes. Swallowed lye. When was it?—January—two-three years ago—"

Phoenix spoke unasked now. "No, missy, he not dead, he just the same. Every little while his throat begin to close up again, and he not able to swallow. He not get his breath. He not able to help himself. So the time come around, and I go on another trip for the soothing medicine."

"All right. The doctor said as long as you came to get it, you could have it," said the nurse. "But it's an obstinate case."

"My little grandson, he sit up there in the house all wrapped up, waiting by himself," Phoenix went on. "We is the only two left in the world. He suffer and it don't seem to put him back at all. He got a sweet look. He going to last. He wear a little patch quilt and peep out holding his mouth open like a little bird. I remembers so plain now. I not going to forget him again, no, the whole enduring time. I could tell him from all the others in creation."

95 "All right." The nurse was trying to hush her now. She brought her a bottle of medicine. "Charity," she said, making a check mark in a book.

Old Phoenix held the bottle close to her eyes, and then carefully put it into her pocket.

"I thank you," she said.

"It's Christmas time, Grandma," said the attendant. "Could I give you a few pennies out of my purse?"

"Five pennies is a nickel," said Phoenix stiffly.

100 "Here's a nickel," said the attendant.

Phoenix rose carefully and held out her hand. She received the nickel and then fished the other nickel out of her pocket and laid it beside the new one. She stared at her palm closely, with her head on one side.

Then she gave a tap with her cane on the floor.

"This is what come to me to do," she said. "I going to the store and buy my child a little windmill they sells, made out of paper. He going to find it hard to believe there such a thing in the world. I'll march myself back where he waiting, holding it straight up in this hand."

She lifted her free hand, gave a little nod, turned around, and walked out of the doctor's office. Then her slow step began on the stairs, going down.

READING AND REACTING

1. How does the first paragraph set the scene for the story? How does it foreshadow the events that will take place later on?
2. Traditionally, a quest is a journey in which a knight overcomes a series of obstacles in order to perform a prescribed feat. In what way is Phoenix's journey like a quest? What obstacles does she face? What feat must she perform?
3. Because Phoenix is so old, she has trouble seeing. What things does she have difficulty seeing? How do her mistakes shed light

on her character? How do they contribute to the impact of the story?
4. What is the major theme of this story? What other themes are expressed?
5. A phoenix is a mythical bird that would live for five hundred years, be consumed by fire, and then rise from its own ashes. In what way is this name appropriate for the main character of this story?
6. Phoenix is not intimidated by the man with the gun and has no difficulty asking a white woman to tie her shoe. In spite of this nobility of character, however, Phoenix has no qualms about stealing a nickel or taking charity from the doctor. How do you account for this apparent contradiction?
7. How do the various people Phoenix encounters react to her? Do they treat her with respect? With disdain? Why do you think they react the way they do?
8. In paragraph 90, Phoenix says that she is an old woman without an education. Does she nevertheless seem to have any knowledge that the other characters lack?
9. **JOURNAL ENTRY** Could "A Worn Path" be an **allegory?** If so, what might each of the characters represent?

Related Works: "Miss Brill" (p. 71), "Araby" (p. 167), "Reapers" (p. 398), *The Cuban Swimmer* (p. 865)

◆ WRITING SUGGESTIONS: THEME

1. In both "Doe Season" and "A&P" (p. 65), a young person learns a hard lesson. Write an essay in which you compare the lessons that Andy and Sammy learn and discuss the effects the knowledge they gain has on them.
2. Two of this chapter's stories deal with the importance of patience and persistence. Write an essay in which you examine the value of enduring despite difficulties, citing the main characters in "Doe Season" and "A Worn Path." Which character is more successful? How do you explain their relative degrees of success?
3. Eudora Welty has said that the question she is asked most frequently is whether Phoenix Jackson's grandson is actually dead. How would you answer this quesion? In what way would the answer to this question affect your view of Phoenix Jackson? For example, if the boy were dead, would her journey be in vain, or would it not make any difference?
4. Both "The Rocking-Horse Winner" and "A Worn Path" deal with characters who make journeys. What is the significance of each journey? How do the protagonists of these two stories overcome

the obstacles they encounter? In what sense are these journeys symbolic as well as actual?

5. Like "Doe Season," the following poem focuses on a child's experience with hunting. Write an essay in which you contrast its central theme with the central theme of "Doe Season."

◊ ◊ ◊

ROBERT HUFF
(1924–1993)

Rainbow[1]

After the shot the driven feathers rock
In the air and are by sunlight trapped.
Their moment of descent is eloquent.
It is the rainbow echo of a bird
5 Whose thunder, stopped, puts in my daughter's eyes
A question mark. She does not see the rainbow,
And the folding bird-fall was for her too quick.
It is about the stillness of the bird
Her eyes are asking. She is three years old;
10 Has cut her fingers; found blood tastes of salt;
But she has never witnessed quiet blood,
Nor ever seen before the peace of death.
I say: "The feathers—Look!" but she is torn
And wretched and draws back. And I am glad
15 That I have wounded her, have winged her heart,
And that she goes beyond my fathering.

---

[1] Publication date is not available.

FICTION

FOR FURTHER READING

◊ ◊ ◊

RAYMOND CARVER
(1938–1988)

Popular Mechanics
(1981)

Early that day the weather turned and the snow was melting into dirty water. Streaks of it ran down from the little shoulder-high window that faced the backyard. Cars slushed by on the street outside, where it was getting dark. But it was getting dark on the inside too.

He was in the bedroom pushing clothes into a suitcase when she came to the door.

I'm glad you're leaving! I'm glad you're leaving! she said. Do you hear?

He kept on putting his things into the suitcase.

Son of a bitch! I'm so glad you're leaving! She began to cry. You can't even look me in the face, can you?

Then she noticed the baby's picture on the bed and picked it up.

He looked at her and she wiped her eyes and stared at him before turning and going back to the living room.

Bring that back, he said.

Just get your things and get out, she said.

He did not answer. He fastened the suitcase, put on his coat, looked around the bedroom before turning off the light. Then he went out to the living room.

She stood in the doorway of the little kitchen, holding the baby.

I want the baby, he said.

Are you crazy?

No, but I want the baby. I'll get someone to come by for his things.

You're not touching this baby, she said.

The baby had begun to cry and she uncovered the blanket from around his head.

Oh, oh, she said, looking at the baby.

He moved toward her.

For God's sake! she said. She took a step back into the kitchen.

I want the baby.

Get out of here!

She turned and tried to hold the baby over in a corner behind the stove.

But he came up. He reached across the stove and tightened his hands on the baby.

Let go of him, he said.

Get away, get away! she cried.

The baby was red-faced and screaming. In the scuffle they knocked down a flowerpot that hung behind the stove.

He crowded her into the wall then, trying to break her grip. He held on to the baby and pushed with all his weight.

Let go of him, he said.

Don't, she said. You're hurting the baby, she said.

I'm not hurting the baby, he said.

The kitchen window gave no light. In the near-dark he worked on her fisted fingers with one hand and with the other hand he gripped the screaming baby up under an arm near the shoulder.

She felt her fingers being forced open. She felt the baby going from her.

No! she screamed just as her hands came loose.

She would have it, this baby. She grabbed for the baby's other arm. She caught the baby around the wrist and leaned back.

But he would not let go. He felt the baby slipping out of his hands and he pulled back very hard.

In this manner, the issue was decided.

◊ ◊ ◊

JAMAICA KINCAID
(1949–   )

Girl
(1984)

Wash the white clothes on Monday and put them on the stone heap; wash the color clothes on Tuesday and put them on the clothesline to dry; don't walk barehead in the hot sun; cook pumpkin fritters in very hot sweet oil; soak your little clothes right after you take them off; when buying cotton to make yourself a nice blouse, be sure that it doesn't have gum on it, because that way it won't hold up well after a wash; soak salt fish overnight before you cook it; is it true that you sing benna[1] in Sunday School?; always eat your food in such a way that it won't turn someone else's stomach; on Sundays try to walk like a lady and not like the slut you are so bent on becoming; don't sing benna in Sunday School; you mustn't speak to wharf-rat boys, not even to give directions; don't eat fruits on the street—flies will follow you; *but I don't sing benna on Sundays at all and never in Sunday school;* this is how to sew on a button; this is how to make a buttonhole for the button you have just sewed on; this is how to hem a dress when you see the hem coming down and so to prevent yourself from looking like the slut I know you are so bent on becoming; this is how you iron your father's khaki shirt so that it doesn't have a crease; this is how you iron your father's khaki pants so that they don't have a crease; this is how you grow okra—far from the house, because okra tree harbors red ants; when you are growing dasheen, make sure it gets plenty of water or else it makes your throat itch when you are eating it; this is how you sweep a corner; this is how you sweep a whole house; this is how you sweep a yard; this is how you smile to someone you don't like too much; this is how you smile to someone you don't like at all; this is how you smile to someone you like completely; this is how you set a table for tea; this is how you set a table for dinner; this is how you set a table for dinner with an important guest; this is how you set a table for lunch; this is how you set a table for breakfast; this is how to behave in the presence of men who don't know you very well, and this way they won't recognize immediately the slut I have warned you against becoming; be sure to wash every day, even if it is with your own spit; don't squat down to play marbles—you are not a boy, you know; don't pick people's flowers—you might catch something; don't throw stones at blackbirds, because it might not be a blackbird at all; this is how to make a bread pudding; this is how to make doukona;[2] this is how to make pepper pot; this is how to make a good medicine for a cold; this is how to make a good medicine to throw away a child before it even becomes a child; this is how to catch a fish; this is how to throw back a fish you don't like, and that way something bad won't fall on you; this is how to bully a man; this is how a man bullies you; this is how to love a man, and if this doesn't work there are other ways, and if they don't work don't feel too bad about giving up; this is how to spit up in the air if you feel like it, and this is how to move quick so that it doesn't fall on you; this is how to make ends meet; always squeeze bread to make sure it's fresh; *but what if the baker won't let me feel the bread?;* you mean to say that after all you are really going to be the kind of woman who the baker won't let near the bread?

---

[1] Calypso music.
[2] Spicy plantain pudding.

◊ ◊ ◊
JOYCE CAROL OATES
(1938–   )

Where Are You Going, Where Have You Been?
(1966)

For Bob Dylan

Her name was Connie. She was fifteen and she had a quick nervous giggling habit of craning her neck to glance into mirrors, or checking other people's faces to make sure her own was all right. Her mother, who noticed everything and knew everything and who hadn't much reason any longer to look at her own face, always scolded Connie about it. "Stop gawking at yourself, who are you? You think you're so pretty?" she would say. Connie would raise her eye-brows at these familiar complaints and look right through her mother, into a shadowy vision of herself as she was right at that moment: she knew she was pretty and that was everything. Her mother had been pretty once too, if you could believe those old snapshots in the album, but now her looks were gone and that was why she was always after Connie.

"Why don't you keep your room clean like your sister? How've you got your hair fixed—what the hell stinks? Hair spray? You don't see your sister using that junk."

Her sister June was twenty-four and still lived at home. She was a secretary in the high school Connie attended, and if that wasn't bad enough—with her in the same building—she was so plain and chunky and steady that Connie had to hear her praised all the time by her mother and her mother's sisters. June did this, June did that, she saved money and helped clean the house and cooked and Connie couldn't do a thing, her mind was all filled with trashy daydreams. Their father was away at work most of the time and when he came home he wanted supper and he read the newspaper at supper and after supper he went to bed. He didn't bother talking much to them, but around his bent head Connie's mother kept picking at her until Connie wished her mother was dead and she herself was dead and it was all over. "She makes me want to throw up sometimes," she complained to her friends. She had a high, breathless, amused voice which made everything she said sound a little forced, whether it was sincere or not.

There was one good thing: June went places with girl friends of hers, girls who were just as plain and steady as she, and so when Connie wanted to do that her mother had no objections. The father of Connie's best girl friend drove the girls the three miles to town and left them off at a shopping plaza, so that they could walk through the stores or go to a movie, and when he came to pick them up again at eleven he never bothered to ask what they had done.

5   They must have been familiar sights, walking around that shopping plaza in their shorts and flat ballerina slippers that always scuffed the sidewalk, with charm bracelets jingling on their thin wrists; they would lean together to whisper and laugh secretly if someone passed by who amused or interested them. Connie had long dark blond hair that drew anyone's eye to it, and she wore part of it pulled up on her head and puffed out and the rest of it she let fall down her back. She wore a pullover jersey blouse that looked one way when she was at home and another way when she was away from home. Everything about her had two sides to it, one for home and one for anywhere that was not home: her walk that could be childlike and bobbing, or languid enough to make anyone think she was hearing music in her head, her mouth which was pale and smirking most of the time, but bright and pink on these evenings out, her laugh which was cynical and drawling at home—"Ha, ha, very funny"—but high-pitched and nervous anywhere else, like the jingling of the charms on her bracelet.

Sometimes they did go shopping or to a movie, but sometimes they went across the highway, ducking fast across the busy road, to a drive-in restaurant where older kids hung out. The restaurant was shaped like a big bottle, though squatter than a real bottle, and on its cap was a revolving figure of a grinning boy who held a hamburger aloft. One night in mid-summer they ran across, breathless with daring, and right away someone leaned out a car window and invited them over, but it was just a boy from high school they didn't like. It made them feel good to be able to ignore him. They went up through the maze of parked and cruising cars to the bright-lit, fly-infested restaurant, their faces pleased and expectant as if they were entering a sacred building that loomed out of the night to give them what haven and what blessing they yearned for. They sat at the counter and crossed their legs at the ankles, their thin shoulders rigid with excitement, and listened to the music that made everything so good: the music was always in the background like music at a church service, it was something to depend upon.

A boy named Eddie came in to talk with them. He sat backwards on his stool, turning himself jerkily around in semi-circles and then stopping and turning again, and after a while he asked Connie if she would like something to eat. She said she did and so she tapped her friend's arm on her way out—her friend pulled her face up into a brave droll look—and Connie said she would meet her at eleven, across the way. "I just hate to leave her like that," Connie said earnestly, but the boy said that she wouldn't be alone for long. So they went out to his car and on the way Connie couldn't help but let her eyes wander over the windshields and faces all around her, her face gleaming with a joy that had nothing to do with Eddie or even this place; it might have been the music. She drew her shoulders up and sucked in her breath with the pure pleasure of being alive, and just at that moment she happened to glance at a face just a few feet from hers. It was a boy with shaggy black hair, in a convertible jalopy painted gold. He stared at her and then his lips widened into a grin. Connie slit her eyes at him and turned away, but she couldn't help glancing back and there he was still watching her. He wagged a finger and laughed and said, "Gonna get you, baby," and Connie turned away again without Eddie noticing anything.

She spent three hours with him, at the restaurant where they ate hamburgers and drank Cokes in wax cups that were always sweating, and then down an alley a mile or so away, and when he left her off at five to eleven only the movie house was still open at the plaza. Her girl friend was there, talking with a boy. When Connie came up the two girls smiled at each other and Connie said, "How was the movie?" and the girl said, "*You* should know." They rode off with the girl's father, sleepy and pleased, and Connie couldn't help but look at the darkened shopping plaza with its big empty parking lot and its signs that were faded and ghostly now, and over at the drive-in restaurant where cars were still circling tirelessly. She couldn't hear the music at this distance.

Next morning June asked her how the movie was and Connie said, "So-so."

10   She and that girl and occasionally another girl went out several times a week that way, and the rest of the time Connie spent around the house—it was summer vacation—getting in her mother's way and thinking, dreaming, about the boys she met. But all the boys fell back and dissolved into a single face that was not even a face, but an idea, a feeling, mixed up with the urgent insistent pounding of the music and the humid night air of July. Connie's mother kept dragging her back to the daylight by finding things for her to do or saying, suddenly, "What's this about the Pettinger girl?"

And Connie would say nervously, "Oh, her. That dope." She always drew thick clear lines between herself and such girls, and her mother was simple and kindly enough to believe her. Her mother was so simple, Connie thought, that it was maybe cruel to fool her so much. Her mother went scuffling around the house in old bedroom slippers and complained over the telephone to one sister about the other, then the other called up and the two of them complained about the third one. If June's name was mentioned her mother's tone was approving, and if Connie's name was mentioned it was disapproving. This did not really mean she disliked Connie and actually Connie thought that her mother preferred her to June because she was prettier, but the two of them kept up a pretense of exasperation, a sense that they were tugging and struggling over something of little value to either of them. Sometimes, over coffee, they were almost friends, but something would come up—some vexation that was like a fly buzzing suddenly around their heads—and their faces went hard with contempt.

One Sunday Connie got up at eleven—none of them bothered with church—and washed her hair so that it could dry all day long, in the sun. Her parents and sister were going to a barbecue at an aunt's house and Connie said no, she wasn't interested, rolling her eyes to let her mother know just what she thought of it. "Stay home alone then," her mother said sharply. Connie sat out back in a lawn chair and watched them drive away, her father quiet and bald, hunched around so that he could back the car out, her mother with a look that was still angry and not at all softened through the windshield, and in the back seat poor old June all dressed up as if she didn't know what a barbecue was, with all the running yelling kids and the flies. Connie sat with her eyes closed in the sun, dreaming and dazed with the warmth about her as if this were a kind of love, the caresses of love, and her mind slipped over onto thoughts of the boy she had been with the night before and how nice he had been, how sweet it always was, not the way someone like June would suppose but sweet, gentle, the way it was in movies and promised in songs; and when she opened her eyes she hardly knew where she was, the back yard ran off into weeds and a fence-line of trees and behind it the sky was perfectly blue and still. The asbestos "ranch house" that was now three years old startled her—it looked small. She shook her head as if to get awake.

It was too hot. She went inside the house and turned on the radio to drown out the quiet. She sat on the edge of her bed, barefoot, and listened for an hour and a half to a program called *XYZ* Sunday Jamboree, record after record of hard, fast, shrieking songs she sang along with, interspersed by exclamations from "Bobby King": "An' look here you girls at Napoleon's—Son and Charley want you to pay real close attention to this song coming up!"

And Connie paid close attention herself, bathed in a glow of slow-pulsed joy that seemed to rise mysteriously out of the music itself and lay languidly about the airless little room, breathed in and breathed out with each gentle rise and fall of her chest.

15 After a while she heard a car coming up the drive. She sat up at once, startled, because it couldn't be her father so soon. The gravel kept crunching all the way in from the road—the driveway was long—and Connie ran to the window. It was a car she didn't know. It was an open jalopy, painted a bright gold that caught the sunlight opaquely. Her heart began to pound and her fingers snatched at her hair, checking it, and she whispered "Christ. Christ," wondering how bad she looked. The car came to a stop at the side door and the horn sounded four short taps as if this were a signal Connie knew.

She went into the kitchen and approached the door slowly, then hung out the screen door, her bare toes curling down off the step. There were two boys in the car and now she recognized the driver: he had shaggy, shabby black hair that looked crazy as a wig and he was grinning at her.

"I ain't late, am I?" he said.
"Who the hell do you think you are?" Connie said.
"Toldja I'd be out, didn't I?"

"I don't even know who you are."

She spoke sullenly, careful to show no interest or pleasure, and he spoke in a fast bright monotone. Connie looked past him to the other boy, taking her time. He had fair brown hair, with a lock that fell onto his forehead. His sideburns gave him a fierce, embarrassed look, but so far he hadn't even bothered to glance at her. Both boys wore sunglasses. The driver's glasses were metallic and mirrored everything in miniature.

"You wanta come for a ride?" he said.

Connie smirked and let her hair fall loose over one shoulder.

"Don'tcha like my car? New paint job," he said. "Hey."

"What?"

"You're cute."

She pretended to fidget, chasing flies away from the door.

"Don'tcha believe me, or what?" he said.

"Look, I don't even know who you are," Connie said in disgust.

"Hey, Ellie's got a radio, see. Mine's broke down." He lifted his friend's arm and showed her the little transistor the boy was holding, and now Connie began to hear the music. It was the same program that was playing inside the house.

"Bobby King?" she said.

"I listen to him all the time. I think he's great."

"He's kind of great," Connie said reluctantly.

"Listen, that guy's *great*. He knows where the action is."

Connie blushed a little, because the glasses made it impossible for her to see just what this boy was looking at. She couldn't decide if she liked him or if he was just a jerk, and so she dawdled in the doorway and wouldn't come down or go back inside. She said, "What's all that stuff painted on your car?"

"Can'tcha read it?" He opened the door very carefully, as if he was afraid it might fall off. He slid out just as carefully, planting his feet firmly on the ground, the tiny metallic world in his glasses slowing down like gelatine hardening and in the midst of it Connie's bright green blouse. "This here is my name, to begin with," he said. ARNOLD FRIEND was written in tarlike black letters on the side, with a drawing of a round grinning face that reminded Connie of a pumpkin, except it wore sunglasses. "I wanta introduce myself, I'm Arnold Friend and that's my real name and I'm gonna be your friend, honey, and inside the car's Ellie Oscar, he's kinda shy." Ellie brought his transistor radio up to his shoulder and balanced it there. "Now these numbers are a secret code, honey," Arnold Friend explained. He read off the numbers 33, 19, 17 and raised his eyebrows at her to see what she thought of that, but she didn't think much of it. The left rear fender had been smashed and around it was written, on the gleaming gold background: DONE BY CRAZY WOMAN DRIVER. Connie had to laugh at that. Arnold Friend was pleased at her laughter and looked up at her. "Around the other side's a lot more—you wanta come and see them?"

"No."

"Why not?"
"Why should I?"
"Don'tcha wanta see what's on the car? Don'tcha wanta go for a ride?"
"I don't know."
"Why not?"
"I got things to do."
"Like what?"
"Things."

He laughed as if she had said something funny. He slapped his thighs. He was standing in a strange way, leaning back against the car as if he were balancing himself. He wasn't tall, only an inch or so taller than she would be if she came down to him. Connie liked the way he was dressed, which was the way all of them dressed: tight faded jeans stuffed into black, scuffed boots, a belt that pulled his waist in and showed how lean he was, and a white pull-over shirt that was a little soiled and showed the hard small muscles of his arms and shoulders. He looked as if he probably did hard work, lifting and carrying things. Even his neck looked muscular. And his face was a familiar face, somehow: the jaw and chin and cheeks slightly darkened, because he hadn't shaved for a day or two, and the nose long and hawk-like, sniffing as if she were a treat he was going to gobble up and it was all a joke.

"Connie, you ain't telling the truth. This is your day set aside for a ride with me and you know it," he said, still laughing. The way he straightened and recovered from his fit of laughing showed that it had been all fake.

"How do you know what my name is?" she said suspiciously.
"It's Connie."
"Maybe and maybe not."
"I know my Connie," he said, wagging his finger. Now she remembered him even better, back at the restaurant, and her cheeks warmed at the thought of how she sucked in her breath just at the moment she passed him—how she must have looked to him. And he had remembered her. "Ellie and I come out here especially for you," he said. "Ellie can sit in back. How about it?"
"Where?"
"Where what?"
"Where're we going?"

He looked at her. He took off the sunglasses and she saw how pale the skin around his eyes was, like holes that were not in shadow but instead in light. His eyes were chips of broken glass that catch the light in an amiable way. He smiled. It was as if the idea of going for a ride somewhere, to some place, was a new idea to him.

"Just for a ride, Connie sweetheart."
"I never said my name was Connie," she said.
"But I know what it is. I know your name and all about you, lots of things," Arnold Friend said. He had not moved yet but stood still leaning

back against the side of his jalopy. "I took a special interest in you, such a pretty girl, and found out all about you like I know your parents and sister are gone somewheres and I know where and how long they're going to be gone, and I know who you were with last night, and your best girl friend's name is Betty. Right?"

He spoke in a simple lilting voice, exactly as if he were reciting the words to a song. His smile assured her that everything was fine. In the car Ellie turned up the volume on his radio and did not bother to look around at them.

"Ellie can sit in the back seat," Arnold Friend said. He indicated his friend with a casual jerk of his chin, as if Ellie did not count and she should not bother with him.

"How'd you find out all that stuff?" Connie said.

"Listen: Betty Schultz and Tony Fitch and Jimmy Pettinger and Nancy Pettinger," he said, in a chant. "Raymond Stanley and Bob Hutter—"

"Do you know all those kids?"

"I know everybody."

"Look, you're kidding. You're not from around here."

"Sure."

"But—how come we never saw you before?"

"Sure you saw me before," he said. He looked down at his boots, as if he were a little offended. "You just don't remember."

"I guess I'd remember you," Connie said.

"Yeah?" He looked up at this, beaming. He was pleased. He began to mark time with the music from Ellie's radio, tapping his fists lightly together. Connie looked away from his smile to the car, which was painted so bright it almost hurt her eyes to look at it. She looked at that name, ARNOLD FRIEND. And up at the front fender was an expression that was familiar—MAN THE FLYING SAUCERS. It was an expression kids had used the year before, but didn't use this year. She looked at it for a while as if the words meant something to her that she did not yet know.

"What're you thinking about? Huh?" Arnold Friend demanded. "Not worried about your hair blowing around in the car, are you?"

"No."

"Think I maybe can't drive good?"

"How do I know?"

"You're a hard girl to handle. How come?" he said. "Don't you know I'm your friend? Didn't you see me put my sign in the air when you walked by?"

"What sign?"

"My sign." And he drew an X in the air, leaning out toward her. They were maybe ten feet apart. After his hand fell back to his side the X was still in the air, almost visible. Connie let the screen door close and stood perfectly still inside it, listening to the music from her radio and the boy's radio blend together. She stared at Arnold Friend. He stood there so stiffly relaxed, pretending to be relaxed, with one hand idly on the door handle as if he were keeping himself up that way and had no intention of ever moving again. She recognized most things about him, the tight jeans that showed his thighs and buttocks and the greasy leather boots and the tight shirt, and even that slippery friendly smile of his, that sleepy dreamy smile that all the boys used to get across ideas they didn't want to put into words. She recognized all this and also the singsong way he talked, slightly mocking, kidding, but serious and a little melancholy, and she recognized the way he tapped one fist against the other in homage to the perpetual music behind him. But all these things did not come together.

She said suddenly, "Hey, how old are you?"

His smile faded. She could see then that he wasn't a kid, he was much older—thirty, maybe more. At this knowledge her heart began to pound faster.

"That's a crazy thing to ask. Can'tcha see I'm your own age?"

"Like hell you are."

"Or maybe a coupla years older, I'm eighteen."

"Eighteen?" she said doubtfully.

He grinned to reassure her and lines appeared at the corners of his mouth. His teeth were big and white. He grinned so broadly his eyes became slits and she saw how thick the lashes were, thick and black as if painted with a black tarlike material. Then he seemed to become embarrassed, abruptly, and looked over his shoulder at Ellie. "*Him*, he's crazy," he said. "Ain't he a riot, he's a nut, a real character." Ellie was still listening to the music. His sunglasses told nothing about what he was thinking. He wore a bright orange shirt unbuttoned halfway to show his chest, which was a pale, bluish chest and not muscular like Arnold Friend's. His shirt collar was turned up all around and the very tips of the collar pointed out past his chin as if they were protecting him. He was pressing the transistor radio up against his ear and sat there in a kind of daze, right in the sun.

"He's kinda strange," Connie said.

"Hey, she says you're kinda strange! Kinda strange!" Arnold Friend cried. He pounded on the car to get Ellie's attention. Ellie turned for the first time and Connie saw with shock that he wasn't a kid either—he had a fair, hairless face, cheeks reddened slightly as if the veins grew too close to the surface of his skin, the face of a forty-year-old baby. Connie felt a wave of dizziness rise in her at this sight and she stared at him as if waiting for something to change the shock of the moment, make it all right again. Ellie's lips kept shaping words, mumbling along with the words blasting in his ear.

"Maybe you two better go away," Connie said faintly.

"What? How come?" Arnold Friend cried. "We come out here to take you for a ride. It's Sunday." He had the voice of the man on the radio now. It was the same voice, Connie thought. "Don'tcha know it's Sunday all day and honey, no matter who you were with last night today you're with Arnold Friend and don't you forget it!—Maybe you better step out here," he said, and this last was in a different voice. It was a little flatter, as if the heat was finally getting to him.

"No. I got things to do."

"Hey."
"You two better leave."
"We ain't leaving until you come with us."
"Like hell I am—"
"Connie, don't fool around with me. I mean, I mean, don't fool around," he said, shaking his head. He laughed incredulously. He placed his sunglasses on top of his head, carefully, as if he were indeed wearing a wig, and brought the stems down behind his ears. Connie stared at him, another wave of dizziness and fear rising in her so that for a moment he wasn't even in focus but was just a blur, standing there against his gold car, and she had the idea that he had driven up the driveway all right but had come from nowhere before that and belonged nowhere and that everything about him and even about the music that was so familiar to her was only half real.
"If my father comes and sees you—"
"He ain't coming. He's at a barbecue."
"How do you know that?"
"Aunt Tillie's. Right now they're—uh—they're drinking. Sitting around," he said vaguely, squinting as if he were staring all the way to town and over to Aunt Tillie's backyard. Then the vision seemed to get clear and he nodded energetically. "Yeah. Sitting around. There's your sister in a blue dress, huh? And high heels, the poor sad bitch—nothing like you sweetheart! And your mother's helping some fat woman with the corn, they're cleaning the corn—husking the corn—"
"What fat woman?" Connie cried.
"How do I know what fat woman. I don't know every goddam fat woman in the world!" Arnold Friend laughed.
"Oh, that's Mrs. Hornby. . . . Who invited her?" Connie said. She felt a little light-headed. Her breath was coming quickly.
"She's too fat. I don't like them fat. I like them the way you are, honey," he said, smiling sleepily at her. They stared at each other for a while, through the screen door. He said softly, "Now what you're going to do is this: you're going to come out that door. You're going to sit up front with me and Ellie's going to sit in the back, the hell with Ellie, right? This isn't Ellie's date. You're my date. I'm your lover, honey."
"What? You're crazy—"
"Yes, I'm your lover. You don't know what that is but you will," he said. "I know that too. I know all about you. But look: it's real nice and you couldn't ask for nobody better than me, or more polite. I always keep my word. I'll tell you how it is, I'm always nice at first, the first time. I'll hold you so tight you won't think you have to try to get away or pretend anything because you'll know you can't. And I'll come inside you where it's all secret and you'll give in to me and you'll love me—"
"Shut up! You're crazy!" Connie said. She backed away from the door. She put her hands against her ears as if she'd heard something terrible, something not meant for her. "People don't talk like that, you're crazy," she muttered. Her heart was almost too big now for her chest and

its pumping made sweat break out all over her. She looked out to see Arnold Friend pause and then take a step toward the porch lurching. He almost fell. But, like a clever drunken man, he managed to catch his balance. He wobbled in his high boots and grabbed hold of one of the porch posts.

"Honey?" he said. "You still listening?"

"Get the hell out of here!"

"Be nice, honey. Listen."

"I'm going to call the police—"

He wobbled again and out of the side of his mouth came a fast spat curse, an aside not meant for her to hear. But even this "Christ!" sounded forced. Then he began to smile again. She watched this smile come, awkward as if he were smiling from inside a mask. His whole face was a mask, she thought wildly, tanned down onto his throat but then running out as if he had plastered make-up on his face but had forgotten about his throat.

"Honey—? Listen, here's how it is. I always tell the truth and I promise you this: I ain't coming in that house after you."

"You better not! I'm going to call the police if you—if you don't—"

"Honey," he said, talking right through her voice, "honey, I'm not coming in there but you are coming out here. You know why?"

She was panting. The kitchen looked like a place she had never seen before, some room she had run inside but which wasn't good enough, wasn't going to help her. The kitchen window had never had a curtain, after three years, and there were dishes in the sink for her to do—probably—and if you ran your hand across the table you'd probably feel something sticky there.

"You listening, honey? Hey?"

"—going to call the police—"

"Soon as you touch the phone I don't need to keep my promise and can come inside. You won't want that."

She rushed forward and tried to lock the door. Her fingers were shaking. "But why lock it," Arnold Friend said gently, talking right into her face. "It's just a screen door. It's just nothing." One of his boots was at a strange angle, as if his foot wasn't in it. It pointed out to the left, bent at the ankle. "I mean, anybody can break through a screen door and glass and wood and iron or anything else if he needs to, anybody at all and specially Arnold Friend. If the place got lit up with a fire honey you'd come running out into my arms, right into my arms and safe at home—like you knew I was your lover and'd stopped fooling around. I don't mind a nice shy girl but I don't like no fooling around." Part of those words were spoken with a slight rhythmic lilt, and Connie somehow recognized them—the echo of a song from last year, about a girl rushing into her boy friend's arms and coming home again—

Connie stood barefoot on the linoleum floor, staring at him. "What do you want?" she whispered.

"I want you," he said.

"What?"

"Seen you that night and thought, that's the one, yes sir. I never needed to look any more."

"But my father's coming back. He's coming to get me. I had to wash my hair first—" She spoke in a dry, rapid voice, hardly raising it for him to hear.

"No, your daddy is not coming and yes, you had to wash your hair and you washed it for me. It's nice and shining and all for me, I thank you, sweetheart," he said, with a mock bow, but again he almost lost his balance. He had to bend and adjust his boots. Evidently his feet did not go all the way down; the boots must have been stuffed with something so that he would seem taller. Connie stared out at him and behind him Ellie in the car, who seemed to be looking off toward Connie's right, into nothing. This Ellie said, pulling the words out of the air one after another as if he were just discovering them, "You want me to pull out the phone?"

"Shut your mouth and keep it shut," Arnold Friend said, his face red from bending over or maybe from embarrassment because Connie had seen his boots. "This ain't none of your business."

"What—what are you doing? What do you want?" Connie said. "If I call the police they'll get you, they'll arrest you—"

"Promise was not to come in unless you touch that phone, and I'll keep that promise," he said. He resumed his erect position and tried to force his shoulders back. He sounded like a hero in a movie, declaring something important. He spoke too loudly and it was as if he were speaking to someone behind Connie. "I ain't made plans for coming in that house where I don't belong but just for you to come out to me, the way you should. Don't you know who I am?"

"You're crazy," she whispered. She backed away from the door but did not want to go into another part of the house, as if this would give him permission to come through the door. "What do you.... You're crazy, you..."

"Huh? What're you saying, honey?"

Her eyes darted everywhere in the kitchen. She could not remember what it was, this room.

"This is how it is, honey: you come out and we'll drive away, have a nice ride. But if you don't come out we're gonna wait till your people come home and then they're all going to get it."

"You want that telephone pulled out?" Ellie said. He held the radio away from his ear and grimaced, as if without the radio the air was too much for him.

"I toldja shut up, Ellie," Arnold Friend said, "you're deaf, get a hearing aid, right? Fix yourself up. This little girl's no trouble and's gonna be nice to me, so Ellie keep to yourself, this ain't your date—right? Don't hem in on me. Don't hog. Don't crush. Don't bird dog. Don't trail me," he said in a rapid meaningless voice, as if he were running through all the expressions he'd learned but was no longer sure which one of them was in style, then rushing on to new ones, making them up with his eyes closed, "Don't crawl under my fence, don't squeeze in my chipmunk hole, don't sniff my glue, suck my popsicle, keep your own greasy fingers on yourself!" He shaded his eyes and peered in at Connie, who was backed against the kitchen table. "Don't mind him honey he's just a creep. He's a dope. Right? I'm the boy for you and like I said you come out here nice like a lady and give me your hand, and nobody else gets hurt, I mean, your nice old bald-headed daddy and your mummy and your sister in her high heels. Because listen: why bring them in this?"

"Leave me alone," Connie whispered.

"Hey, you know that old woman down the road, the one with the chickens and stuff—you know her?"

"She's dead!"

"Dead? What? You know her?" Arnold Friend said.

"She's dead—"

"Don't you like her?"

"She's dead—she's—she isn't here any more—"

"But don't you like her, I mean, you got something against her? Some grudge or something?" Then his voice dipped as if he were conscious of a rudeness. He touched the sunglasses perched on top of his head as if to make sure they were still there. "Now you be a good girl."

"What are you going to do?"

"Just two things, or maybe three," Arnold Friend said. "But I promise it won't last long and you'll like me that way you get to like people you're close to. You will. It's all over for you here, so come on out. You don't want your people in any trouble, do you?"

She turned and bumped against a chair or something, hurting her leg, but she ran into the back room and picked up the telephone. Something roared in her ear, a tiny roaring, and she was so sick with fear that she could do nothing but listen to it—the telephone was clammy and very heavy and her fingers groped down to the dial but were too weak to touch it. She began to scream into the phone, into the roaring. She cried out, she cried for her mother, she felt her breath start jerking back and forth in her lungs as if it were something Arnold Friend were stabbing her with again and again with no tenderness. A noisy sorrowful wailing rose all about her and she was locked inside it the way she was locked inside the house.

After a while she could hear again. She was sitting on the floor with her wet back against the wall.

Arnold Friend was saying from the door, "That's a good girl. Put the phone back."

She kicked the phone away from her.

"No, honey. Pick it up. Put it back right."

She picked it up and put it back. The dial tone stopped.

"That's a good girl. Now you come outside."

She was hollow with what had been fear, but what was now just an emptiness. All that screaming had blasted it out of her. She sat, one leg cramped under her, and deep inside her brain was something like a pinpoint of light that kept going and would not let her relax. She thought, I'm not going to see my mother again. She thought, I'm not going to sleep in my bed again. Her bright green blouse was all wet.

Arnold Friend said, in a gentle-loud voice that was like a stage voice, "The place where you came from ain't there any more, and where you had in mind to go is cancelled out. This place you are now—inside your daddy's house—is nothing but a cardboard box I can knock down any time. You know that and always did know it. You hear me?"

She thought, I have got to think. I have to know what to do.

"We'll go out to a nice field, out in the country here where it smells so nice and it's sunny," Arnold Friend said. "I'll have my arms around you so you won't need to try to get away and I'll show you what love is like, what it does. The hell with this house! It looks solid all right," he said. He ran a fingernail down the screen and the noise did not make Connie shiver, as it would have the day before. "Now put your hand on your heart, honey. Feel that? That feels solid too but we know better, be nice to me, be sweet like you can because what else is there for a girl like you but to be sweet and pretty and give in?—and get away before her people come back?"

155   She felt her pounding heart. Her hand seemed to enclose it. She thought for the first time in her life that it was nothing that was hers, that belonged to her, but just a pounding, living thing inside this body that wasn't really hers either.

"You don't want them to get hurt," Arnold Friend went on. "Now get up, honey. Get up all by yourself."

She stood.

"Now turn this way. That's right. Come over here to me—Ellie, put that away, didn't I tell you? You dope. You miserable creepy dope," Arnold Friend said. His words were not angry but only part of an incantation. The incantation was kindly. "Now come out through the kitchen to me honey and let's see a smile, try it, you're a brave sweet little girl and now they're eating corn and hotdogs cooked to bursting over an outdoor fire, and they don't know one thing about you and never did and honey you're better than them because not a one of them would have done this for you."

Connie felt the linoleum under her feet; it was cool. She brushed her hair back out of her eyes. Arnold Friend let go of the post tentatively and opened his arms for her, his elbows pointing in toward each other and his wrists limp, to show that this was an embarrassed embrace and a little mocking, he didn't want to make her self-conscious.

160   She put out her hand against the screen. She watched herself push the door slowly open as if she were safe back somewhere in the other doorway, watching this body and this head of long hair moving out into the sunlight where Arnold Friend waited.

"My sweet little blue-eyed girl," he said, in a half-sung sigh that had nothing to do with her brown eyes but was taken up just the same by the vast sunlit reaches of the land behind him and on all sides of him, so much land that Connie had never seen before and did not recognize except to know that she was going to it.

◊ ◊ ◊

ALBERTO ALVARO RÍOS
(1952–   )

The Secret Lion
(1984)

I was twelve and in junior high school and something happened that we didn't have a name for, but it was there nonetheless like a lion, and roaring, roaring that way the biggest things do. Everything changed. Just that. Like the rug, the one that gets pulled—or better, like the tablecloth those magicians pull where the stuff on the table stays the same but the gasp! from the audience makes the staying-the-same part not matter. Like that.

What happened was there were teachers now, not just one teacher, teach-erz, and we felt personally abandoned somehow. When a person had all these teachers now, he didn't get taken care of the same way, even though six was more than one. Arithmetic went out the door when we walked in. And we saw girls now, but they weren't the same girls we used to know because we couldn't talk to them anymore, not the same way we used to, certainly not to Sandy, even though she was my neighbor, too. Not even to her. She just played the piano all the time. And there were words, oh there were words in junior high school, and we wanted to know what they were, and how a person did them—that's what school was supposed to be for. Only, in junior high school, school wasn't school, everything was backward-like. If you went up to a teacher and said the word to try and find out what it meant you got in trouble for saying it. So we didn't. And we figured it must have been that way about other stuff, too, so we never said anything about anything—we weren't stupid.

But my friend Sergio and I, we solved junior high school. We would come home from school on the bus, put our books away, change shoes, and go across the highway to the arroyo. It was the one place we were not supposed to go. So we did. This was, after all, what junior high had at least shown us. It was our river, though, our personal Mississippi, our friend from long back, and it was full of stories and all the branch forts we had built in it when we were still the Vikings of America, with our own symbol, which we had carved everywhere, even in the sand, which let the water take it. That was good, we had decided; whoever was at the end of this river would know about us.

At the very very top of our growing lungs, what we would do down there was shout every dirty word we could think of, in every combination we could come up with, and we would yell about girls, and all the things we wanted to do with them, as loud as we could—we didn't know what we wanted to do with them, just things—and we would yell about teachers, and how we loved some of them, like Miss Crevelone, and how we wanted to dissect some of them, making signs of the cross, like priests, and we would yell this stuff over and over because it felt good, we couldn't explain why, it just felt good and for the first time in our lives there was nobody to tell us we couldn't. So we did.

5 One Thursday we were walking along shouting this way, and the railroad, the Southern Pacific, which ran above and along the far side of the arroyo, had dropped a grinding ball down there, which was, we found out later, a cannonball thing used in mining. A bunch of them were put in a big vat which turned around and crushed the ore. One had been dropped, or thrown—what do caboose men do when they get bored—but it got down there regardless and as we were walking along yelling about one girl or another, a particular Claudia, we found it, one of these things, looked at it, picked it up, and got very very excited, and held it and passed it back and forth, and we were saying "Guythisis, this is, geeGuythis . . .": we had this perception about nature then, that nature is imperfect and that round things are perfect: we said "GuyGodthis is perfect, thisisthis is perfect, it's round, round and heavy, it'sit's the best thing we'veeverseen. Whatisit?" We didn't know. We just knew it was great. We just, whatever, we played with it, held it some more.

And then we had to decide what to do with it. We knew, because of a lot of things, that if we were going to take this and show it to anybody, this discovery, this best thing, was going to be taken away from us. That's the way it works with little kids, like all the polished quartz, the tons of it we had collected piece by piece over the years. Junior high kids too. If we took it home, my mother, we knew, was going to look at it and say "throw that dirty thing in the, get rid of it." Simple like, like that. "But ma it's the best thing I" "Getridofit." Simple.

So we didn't. Take it home. Instead, we came up with the answer. We dug a hole and buried it. And we marked it secretly. Lots of secret signs. And came back the next week to dig it up and, we didn't know, pass it around some more or something, but we didn't find it. We dug up that whole bank, and we never found it again. We tried.

Sergio and I talked about that ball or whatever it was when we couldn't find it. All we used were small words, neat, good. Kid words. What we were really saying, but didn't know the words, was how much that ball was like that place, that whole arroyo: couldn't tell anybody about it, didn't understand what it was, didn't have a name for it. It just felt good. It was just perfect in the way it was that place, that whole going to that place, that whole junior high school lion. It was just iron-heavy, it had no name, it felt good or not, we couldn't take it home to show our mothers, and once we buried it, it was gone forever.

The ball was gone, like the first reasons we had come to that arroyo years earlier, like the first time we had seen the arroyo, it was gone like everything else that had been taken away. This was not our first lesson.

We stopped going to the arroyo after not finding the thing, the same way we had stopped going there years earlier and headed for the mountains. Nature seemed to keep pushing us around one way or another, teaching us the same thing every place we ended up. Nature's gang was tough that way, teaching us stuff.

When we were young we moved away from town, me and my family. Sergio's was already out there. Out in the wilds. Or at least the new place seemed like the wilds since everything looks bigger the smaller a man is. I was five, I guess, and we had moved three miles north of Nogales where we had lived, three miles north of the Mexican border. We looked across the highway in one direction and there was the arroyo; hills stood up in the other direction. Mountains, for a small man.

When the first summer came the very first place we went to was of course the one place we weren't supposed to go, the arroyo. We went down in there and found water running, summer rain water mostly, and we went swimming. But every third or fourth or fifth day, the sewage treatment plant that was, we found out, upstream, would release whatever it was that it released, and we would never know exactly what day that was, and a person really couldn't tell right off by looking at the water, not every time, not so a person could get out in time. So, we went swimming that summer and some days we had a lot of fun. Some days we didn't. We found a thousand ways to explain what happened on those other days, constructing elaborate stories about the neighborhood dogs, and hadn't she, my mother, miscalculated her step before, too? But she knew something was up because we'd come running into the house those days, wanting to take a shower, even—if this can be imagined—in the middle of the day.

That was the first time we stopped going to the arroyo. It taught us to look the other way. We decided, as the second side of summer came, we wanted to go into the mountains. They were still mountains then. We went running in one summer Thursday morning, my friend Sergio and I, into my mother's kitchen, and said, well, what'zin, what'zin those hills over there—we used her word so she'd understand us—and she said nothingdon'tworryaboutit. So we went out, and we weren't dumb, we thought with our eyes to each other, ohhoshe'stryingtokeepsomethingfromus. We knew adults.

We had read the books, after all; we knew about bridges and castles and wildtreacherousraging alligatormouth rivers. We wanted them. So we were going to go out and get them. We went back that morning into that kitchen and we said, "We're going out there, we're going into the hills, we're going away for three days, don't worry." She said, "All right."

"You know," I said to Sergio, "if we're going to go away for three days, well, we ought to at least pack a lunch."

But we were two young boys with no patience for what we thought at the time was mom-stuff: making sa-and-wiches. My mother didn't offer. So we got out little kid knapsacks that my mother had sewn for us, and into them we put the jar of mustard. A loaf of bread. Knivesforksplates, bottles of Coke, a can opener. This was lunch for the two of us. And we were weighed down, humped over to be strong enough to carry this stuff. But we started walking anyway, into the hills. We were going to eat berries and stuff otherwise. "Goodbye." My mom said that.

After the first hill we were dead. But we walked. My mother could still see us. And we kept walking. We walked until we got to where the sun is straight overhead, noon. That place. Where that is doesn't matter; it's time to eat. The truth is we weren't anywhere close to that place. We just agreed that the sun was overhead and that it was time to eat, and by tilting our heads a little we could make that the truth.

"We really ought to start looking for a place to eat."

"Yeah. Let's look for a good place to eat." We went back and forth saying that for fifteen minutes, making it lunchtime because that's what we always said back and forth before lunchtimes at home. "Yeah, I'm hungry all right." I nodded my head. "Yeah, I'm hungry all right too. I'm hungry." He nodded his head. I nodded my head back. After a good deal more nodding, we were ready, just as we came over a little hill. We hadn't found the mountains yet. This was a little hill.

And on the other side of this hill we found heaven.

It was just what we thought it would be.

Perfect. Heaven was green, like nothing else in Arizona. And it wasn't a cemetery or like that because we had seen cemeteries and they had gravestones and stuff and this didn't. This was perfect, had trees, lots of trees, had birds, like we had never seen before. It was like "The Wizard of Oz," like when they got to Oz and everything was so green, so emerald, they had to wear those glasses, and we ran just like them, laughing, laughing that way we did that moment, and we went running down to this clearing in it all, hitting each other that good way we did.

We got down there, we kept laughing, we kept hitting each other, we unpacked our stuff, and we started acting "rich." We knew all about how to do that, like blowing on our nails, then rubbing them on our chests for the shine. We made our sandwiches, opened our Cokes, got out the rest of the stuff, the salt and pepper shakers. I found this particular hole and I put my Coke right into it, a perfect fit, and I called it my Coke-holder. I got down next to it on my back, because everyone knows that rich people eat lying down, and I got my sandwich in one hand and put my other arm around the Coke in its holder. When I wanted a drink, I lifted my neck a little, put out my lips, and tipped my Coke a little with the crook of my elbow. Ah.

We were there, lying down, eating our sandwiches, laughing, throwing bread at each other and out for the birds. This was heaven. We were laughing and we couldn't believe it. My mother was keeping something from us, ah ha, but we had found her out. We even found water over at the side of the clearing to wash our plates with—we had brought plates. Sergio started washing his plates when he was done, and I was being rich with my Coke, and this day in summer was right.

When suddenly these two men came, from around a corner of trees and the tallest grass we had ever seen. They had bags on their backs, leather bags, bags and sticks.

We didn't know what clubs were, but I learned later, like I learned about the grinding balls. The two men yelled at us. Most specifically, one wanted me to take my Coke out of my Coke-holder so he could sink his golf ball into it.

Something got taken away from us that moment. Heaven. We grew up a little bit, and couldn't go backward. We learned. No one had ever told us about golf. They had told us about heaven. And it went away. We got golf in exchange.

We went back to the arroyo for the rest of that summer, and tried to have fun the best we could. We learned to be ready for finding the grinding ball. We loved it, and when we buried it we knew what would happen. The truth is, we didn't look so hard for it. We were two boys and twelve summers then, and not stupid. Things get taken away.

We buried it because it was perfect. We didn't tell my mother, but together it was all we talked about, till we forgot. It was the lion.

◊ ◊ ◊

AMY TAN
(1952–   )

Two Kinds
(1989)

My mother believed you could be anything you wanted to be in America. You could open a restaurant. You could work for the government and get good retirement. You could buy a house with almost no money down. You could become rich. You could become instantly famous.

"Of course you can be prodigy, too," my mother told me when I was nine. "You can be best anything. What does Auntie Lindo know? Her daughter, she is only best tricky."

America was where all my mother's hopes lay. She had come here in 1949 after losing everything in China: her mother and father, her family home, her first husband, and two daughters, twin baby girls. But she never looked back with regret. There were so many ways for things to get better.

We didn't immediately pick the right kind of prodigy. At first my mother thought I could be a Chinese Shirley Temple. We'd watch Shirley's old movies on TV as though they were training films. My mother would poke my arm and say, *"Ni kan"*—You watch. And I would see Shirley tapping her feet, or singing a sailor song, or pursing her lips into a very round O while saying, "Oh my goodness."

"*Ni kan,*" said my mother as Shirley's eyes flooded with tears. "You already know how. Don't need talent for crying!"

Soon after my mother got this idea about Shirley Temple, she took me to a beauty training school in the Mission district and put me in the hands of a student who could barely hold the scissors without shaking. Instead of getting big fat curls, I emerged with an uneven mass of crinkly black fuzz. My mother dragged me off to the bathroom and tried to wet down my hair.

"You look like Negro Chinese," she lamented, as if I had done this on purpose.

The instructor of the beauty training school had to lop off these soggy clumps to make my hair even again. "Peter Pan is very popular these days," the instructor assured my mother. I now had hair the length of a boy's, with straight-across bangs that hung at a slant two inches above my eyebrows. I liked the haircut and it made me actually look forward to my future fame.

In fact, in the beginning, I was just as excited as my mother, maybe even more so. I pictured this prodigy part of me as many different images, trying each one on for size. I was a dainty ballerina girl standing by the curtains, waiting to hear the right music that would send me floating on my tiptoes. I was like the Christ child lifted out of the straw manger, crying with holy indignity. I was Cinderella stepping from her pumpkin carriage with sparkly cartoon music filling the air.

In all of my imaginings, I was filled with a sense that I would soon become *perfect*. My mother and father would adore me. I would be beyond reproach. I would never feel the need to sulk for anything.

But sometimes the prodigy in me became impatient. "If you don't hurry up and get me out of here, I'm disappearing for good," it warned. "And then you'll always be nothing."

Every night after dinner, my mother and I would sit at the Formica kitchen table. She would present new tests, taking her examples from stories of amazing children she had read in *Ripley's Believe It or Not,* or *Good Housekeeping, Reader's Digest,* and a dozen other magazines she kept in a pile in our bathroom. My mother got these magazines from people whose houses she cleaned. And since she cleaned many houses each week, we had a great assortment. She would look through them all, searching for stories about remarkable children.

The first night she brought out a story about a three-year-old boy who knew the capitals of all the states and even most of the European countries. A teacher was quoted as saying the little boy could also pronounce the names of the foreign cities correctly.

"What's the capital of Finland?" my mother asked me, looking at the magazine story.

All I knew was the capital of California, because Sacramento was the name of the street we lived on in Chinatown. "Nairobi!" I guessed, saying the most foreign word I could think of. She checked to see if that was possibly one way to pronounce "Helsinki" before showing me the answer.

The tests got harder—multiplying numbers in my head, finding the queen of hearts in a deck of cards, trying to stand on my head without using my hands, predicting the daily temperatures in Los Angeles, New York, and London.

One night I had to look at a page from the Bible for three minutes and then report everything I could remember. "Now Jehoshaphat had riches and honor in abundance and . . . that's all I remember, Ma," I said.

And after seeing my mother's disappointed face once again, something inside of me began to die. I hated the tests, the raised hopes and failed expectations. Before going to bed that night, I looked in the mirror above the bathroom sink and when I saw only my face staring back—and that it would always be this ordinary face—I began to cry. Such a sad, ugly girl! I made high-pitched noises like a crazed animal, trying to scratch out the face in the mirror.

And then I saw what seemed to be the prodigy side of me—because I had never seen that face before. I looked at my reflection, blinking so I could see more clearly. The girl staring back at me was angry, powerful. This girl and I were the same. I had new thoughts, willful thoughts, or rather thoughts filled with lots of won'ts. I won't let her change me, I promised myself. I won't be what I'm not.

20   So now on nights when my mother presented her tests, I performed listlessly, my head propped on one arm. I pretended to be bored. And I was. I got so bored I started counting the bellows of the foghorns out on the bay while my mother drilled me in other areas. The sound was comforting and reminded me of the cow jumping over the moon. And the next day, I played a game with myself, seeing if my mother would give up on me before eight bellows. After a while I usually counted only one, maybe two bellows at most. At last she was beginning to give up hope.

Two or three months had gone by without any mention of my being a prodigy again. And then one day my mother was watching *The Ed Sullivan Show* on TV. The TV was old and the sound kept shorting out. Every time my mother got halfway up from the sofa to adjust the set, the sound would go back on and Ed would be talking. As soon as she sat down, Ed would go silent again. She got up, the TV broke into loud piano music. She sat down. Silence. Up and down, back and forth, quiet and loud. It was like a stiff embraceless dance between her and the TV set. Finally she stood by the set with her hand on the sound dial.

She seemed entranced by the music, a little frenzied piano piece with this mesmerizing quality, sort of quick passages and then teasing lilting ones before it returned to the quick playful parts.

"*Ni kan,*" my mother said, calling me over with hurried hand gestures, "Look here."

I could see why my mother was fascinated by the music. It was being pounded out by a little Chinese girl, about nine years old, with a Peter Pan haircut. The girl had the sauciness of a Shirley Temple. She was proudly modest like a proper Chinese child. And she also did this fancy sweep of a curtsy, so that the fluffy skirt of her white dress cascaded slowly to the floor like the petals of a large carnation.

25   In spite of these warning signs, I wasn't worried. Our family had no piano and we couldn't afford to buy one, let alone reams of sheet music and piano lessons. So I could be generous in my comments when my mother bad-mouthed the little girl on TV.

"Play note right, but doesn't sound good! No singing sound," complained my mother.

"What are you picking on her for?" I said carelessly. "She's pretty good. Maybe she's not the best, but she's trying hard." I knew almost immediately I would be sorry I said that.

"Just like you," she said. "Not the best. Because you not trying." She gave a little huff as she let go of the sound dial and sat down on the sofa.

The little Chinese girl sat down also to play an encore of "Anitra's Dance" by Grieg. I remember the song, because later on I had to learn how to play it.

30   Three days after watching *The Ed Sullivan Show,* my mother told me what my schedule would be for piano lessons and piano practice. She had talked to Mr. Chong, who lived on the first floor of our apartment building. Mr. Chong was a retired piano teacher and my mother had traded housecleaning services for weekly lessons and a piano for me to practice on every day, two hours a day, from four until six.

When my mother told me this, I felt as though I had been sent to hell. I whined and then kicked my foot a little when I couldn't stand it anymore.

"Why don't you like me the way I am? I'm *not* a genius! I can't play the piano. And even if I could, I wouldn't go on TV if you paid me a million dollars!" I cried.

My mother slapped me. "Who ask you be genius?" she shouted. "Only ask you be your best. For you sake. You think I want you be genius? Hnnh! What for! Who ask you!"

"So ungrateful," I heard her mutter in Chinese. "If she had as much talent as she has temper, she would be famous now."

35   Mr. Chong, whom I secretly nicknamed Old Chong, was very strange, always tapping his fingers to the silent music of an invisible orchestra. He looked ancient in my eyes. He had lost most of the hair on top of his head and he wore thick glasses and had eyes that always looked tired and sleepy. But he must have been younger than I thought, since he lived with his mother and was not yet married.

I met Old Lady Chong once and that was enough. She had this peculiar smell like a baby that had done something in its pants. And her fingers felt like a dead person's, like an old peach I once found in the back of the refrigerator; the skin just slid off the meat when I picked it up.

I soon found out why Old Chong had retired from teaching piano. He was deaf. "Like Beethoven!" he shouted to me. "We're both listening only in our head!" And he would start to conduct his frantic silent sonatas.

Our lessons went like this. He would open the book and point to different things, explaining their purpose: "Key! Treble! Bass! No sharps or flats! So this is C major! Listen now and play after me!"

And then he would play the C scale a few times, a simple chord, and then, as if inspired by an old, unreachable itch, he gradually added more notes and running trills and a pounding bass until the music was really something quite grand.

40   I would play after him, the simple scale, the simple chord, and then I just played some nonsense that sounded like a cat running up and down on top of garbage cans. Old Chong smiled and applauded and then said, "Very good! But now you must learn to keep time!"

So that's how I discovered that Old Chong's eyes were too slow to keep up with the wrong notes I was playing. He went through the motions in half-time. To help me keep rhythm, he stood behind me, pushing down on my right shoulder for every beat. He balanced pennies on top of my wrists so I would keep them still as I slowly played scales and arpeggios. He had me curve my hand around an apple and keep that shape when playing chords. He marched stiffly to show me how to make each finger dance up and down, staccato like an obedient little soldier.

He taught me all these things, and that was how I also learned I could be lazy and get away with mistakes, lots of mistakes. If I hit the wrong notes because I hadn't practiced enough, I never corrected myself. I just kept playing in rhythm. And Old Chong kept conducting his own private reverie.

So maybe I never really gave myself a fair chance. I did pick up the basics pretty quickly, and I might have become a good pianist at that young age. But I was so determined not to try, not to be anybody different that I learned to play only the most ear-splitting preludes, the most discordant hymns.

Over the next year, I practiced like this, dutifully in my own way. And then one day I heard my mother and her friend Lindo Jong both talking in a loud bragging tone of voice so others could hear. It was after church, and I was leaning against the brick wall wearing a dress with stiff white petticoats. Auntie Lindo's daughter, Waverly, who was about my age, was standing farther down the wall about five feet away. We had grown up together and shared all the closeness of two sisters squabbling over crayons and dolls. In other words, for the most part, we hated each other. I thought she was snotty. Waverly Jong had gained a certain amount of fame as "Chinatown's Littlest Chinese Chess Champion."

"She bring home too many trophy," lamented Auntie Lindo that Sunday. "All day she play chess. All day I have no time do nothing but dust off her winnings." She threw a scolding look at Waverly, who pretended not to see her.

"You lucky you don't have this problem," said Auntie Lindo with a sigh to my mother.

And my mother squared her shoulders and bragged: "Our problem worser than yours. If we ask Jing-mei wash dish, she hear nothing but music. It's like you can't stop this natural talent."

And right then, I was determined to put a stop to her foolish pride.

A few weeks later, Old Chong and my mother conspired to have me play in a talent show which would be held in the church hall. By then, my parents had saved up enough to buy me a secondhand piano, a black Wurlitzer spinet with a scarred bench. It was the showpiece of our living room.

For the talent show, I was to play a piece called "Pleading Child" from Schumann's *Scenes from Childhood*. It was a simple, moody piece that sounded more difficult than it was. I was supposed to memorize the whole thing, playing the repeat parts twice to make the piece sound longer. But I dawdled over it, playing a few bars and then cheating, looking up to see what notes followed. I never really listened to what I was playing. I daydreamed about being somewhere else, about being someone else.

The part I liked to practice best was the fancy curtsy: right foot out, touch the rose on the carpet with a pointed foot, sweep to the side, left leg bends, look up and smile.

My parents invited all the couples from the Joy Luck Club[1] to witness my debut. Auntie Lindo and Uncle Tin were there. Waverly and her two older brothers had also come. The first two rows were filled with children both younger and older than I was. The littlest ones got to go first. They recited simple nursery rhymes, squawked out tunes on miniature violins, twirled Hula Hoops, pranced in pink ballet tutus, and when they bowed or curtsied, the audience would sigh in unison, "Awww," and then clap enthusiastically.

When my turn came, I was very confident. I remember my childish excitement. It was as if I knew, without a doubt, that the prodigy side of me really did exist. I had no fear whatsoever, no nervousness. I remember thinking to myself, This is it! This is it! I looked out over the audience, at my mother's blank face, my father's yawn, Auntie Lindo's stiff-lipped smile, Waverly's sulky expression. I had on a white dress layered with sheets of lace, and a pink bow in my Peter Pan haircut. As I sat

---

[1] A name denoting the mother's circle of friends, all of whom were Chinese immigrants to the United States.

down I envisioned people jumping to their feet and Ed Sullivan rushing up to introduce me to everyone on TV.

And I started to play. It was so beautiful. I was so caught up in how lovely I looked that at first I didn't worry how I would sound. So it was a surprise to me when I hit the first wrong note and I realized something didn't sound quite right. And then I hit another and another followed that. A chill started at the top of my head and began to trickle down. Yet I couldn't stop playing, as though my hands were bewitched. I kept thinking my fingers would adjust themselves back, like a train switching to the right track. I played this strange jumble through two repeats, the sour notes staying with me all the way to the end.

55   When I stood up, I discovered my legs were shaking. Maybe I had just been nervous and the audience, like Old Chong, had seen me go through the right motions and had not heard anything wrong at all. I swept my right foot out, went down on my knee, looked up and smiled. The room was quiet, except for Old Chong, who was beaming and shouting, "Bravo! Bravo! Well done!" But then I saw my mother's face, her stricken face. The audience clapped weakly, and as I walked back to my chair, with my whole face quivering as I tried not to cry, I heard a little boy whisper loudly to his mother, "That was awful," and the mother whispered back, "Well, she certainly tried."

And now I realized how many people were in the audience, the whole world it seemed. I was aware of eyes burning into my back. I felt the shame of my mother and father as they sat stiffly throughout the rest of the show.

We could have escaped during intermission. Pride and some strange sense of honor must have anchored my parents to their chairs. And so we watched it all: the eighteen-year-old boy with a fake mustache who did a magic show and juggled flaming hoops while riding a unicycle. The breasted girl with white makeup who sang from *Madama Butterfly* and got honorable mention. And the eleven-year-old boy who won first prize playing a tricky violin song that sounded like a busy bee.

After the show, the Hsus, the Jongs, and the St. Clairs from the Joy Luck Club came up to my mother and father.

"Lots of talented kids," Auntie Lindo said vaguely, smiling broadly.

60   "That was somethin' else," said my father, and I wondered if he was referring to me in a humorous way, or whether he even remembered what I had done.

Waverly looked at me and shrugged her shoulders. "You aren't a genius like me," she said matter-of-factly. And if I hadn't felt so bad, I would have pulled her braids and punched her stomach.

But my mother's expression was what devastated me: a quiet, blank look that said she had lost everything. I felt the same way, and it seemed as if everybody were now coming up, like gawkers at the scene of an accident, to see what parts were actually missing. When we got on the bus to go home, my father was humming the busy-bee tune and my mother was silent. I kept thinking she wanted to wait until we got home before shouting at me. But when my father unlocked the door to our apartment, my mother walked in and then went to the back, into the bedroom. No accusations. No blame. And in a way, I felt disappointed. I had been waiting for her to start shouting, so I could shout back and cry and blame her for all my misery.

I assumed my talent-show fiasco meant I never had to play the piano again. But two days later, after school, my mother came out of the kitchen and saw me watching TV.

"Four clock," she reminded me as if it were any other day. I was stunned, as though she were asking me to go through the talent-show torture again. I wedged myself more tightly in front of the TV.

"Turn off TV," she called from the kitchen five minutes later.

I didn't budge. And then I decided. I didn't have to do what my mother said anymore. I wasn't her slave. This wasn't China. I had listened to her before and look what happened. She was the stupid one.

She came out from the kitchen and stood in the arched entryway of the living room. "Four clock," she said once again, louder.

"I'm not going to play anymore," I said nonchalantly. "Why should I? I'm not a genius."

She walked over and stood in front of the TV. I saw her chest was heaving up and down in an angry way.

"No!" I said, and I now felt stronger, as if my true self had finally emerged. So this was what had been inside me all along.

"No! I won't!" I screamed.

She yanked me by the arm, pulled me off the floor, snapped off the TV. She was frighteningly strong, half pulling, half carrying me toward the piano as I kicked the throw rugs under my feet. She lifted me up and onto the hard bench. I was sobbing by now, looking at her bitterly. Her chest was heaving even more and her mouth was open, smiling crazily as if she were pleased I was crying.

"You want me to be someone that I'm not!" I sobbed. "I'll never be the kind of daughter you want me to be!"

"Only two kinds of daughters," she shouted in Chinese. "Those who are obedient and those who follow their own mind! Only one kind of daughter can live in this house. Obedient daughter!"

"Then I wish I wasn't your daughter. I wish you weren't my mother," I shouted. As I said these things I got scared. It felt like worms and toads and slimy things crawling out of my chest, but it also felt good, as if this awful side of me had surfaced, at last.

"Too late change this," said my mother shrilly.

And I could sense her anger rising to its breaking point. I wanted to see it spill over. And that's when I remembered the babies she had lost in China, the ones we never talked about. "Then I wish I'd never been born!" I shouted. "I wish I were dead! Like them."

It was as if I had said the magic words. Alakazam!—and her face went blank, her mouth closed, her arms went slack, and she backed out of the room, stunned, as if she were blowing away like a small brown leaf, thin, brittle, lifeless.

It was not the only disappointment my mother felt in me. In the years that followed, I failed her so many times, each time asserting my own will, my right to fall short of expectations. I didn't get straight As. I didn't become class president. I didn't get into Stanford. I dropped out of college.

For unlike my mother, I did not believe I could be anything I wanted to be. I could only be me.

And for all those years, we never talked about the disaster at the recital or my terrible accusations afterward at the piano bench. All that remained unchecked, like a betrayal that was now unspeakable. So I never found a way to ask her why she had hoped for something so large that failure was inevitable.

And even worse, I never asked her what frightened me the most: Why had she given up hope?

For after our struggle at the piano, she never mentioned my playing again. The lessons stopped. The lid to the piano was closed, shutting out the dust, my misery, and her dreams.

So she surprised me. A few years ago, she offered to give me the piano, for my thirtieth birthday. I had not played in all those years. I saw the offer as a sign of forgiveness, a tremendous burden removed.

"Are you sure?" I asked shyly. "I mean, won't you and Dad miss it?"

"No, this your piano," she said firmly. "Always your piano. You only one can play."

"Well, I probably can't play anymore," I said. "It's been years."

"You pick up fast," said my mother, as if she knew this was certain. "You have natural talent. You could been genius if you want to."

"No I couldn't."

"You just not trying," said my mother. And she was neither angry nor sad. She said it as if to announce a fact that could never be disproved. "Take it," she said.

But I didn't at first. It was enough that she had offered it to me. And after that, every time I saw it in my parents' living room, standing in front of the bay windows, it made me feel proud, as if it were a shiny trophy I had won back.

Last week I sent a tuner over to my parents' apartment and had the piano reconditioned, for purely sentimental reasons. My mother had died a few months before and I had been getting things in order for my father, a little bit at a time. I put the jewelry in special silk pouches. The sweaters she had knitted in yellow, pink, bright orange—all the colors I hated—I put those in moth-proof boxes. I found some old Chinese silk dresses, the kind with little slits up the sides. I rubbed the old silk against my skin, then wrapped them in tissue and decided to take them home with me.

After I had the piano tuned, I opened the lid and touched the keys. It sounded even richer than I remembered. Really, it was a very good piano. Inside the bench were the same exercise notes with handwritten scales, the same secondhand music books with their covers held together with yellow tape.

I opened up the Schumann book to the dark little piece I had played at the recital. It was on the left-hand side of the page, "Pleading Child." It looked more difficult than I remembered. I played a few bars, surprised at how easily the notes came back to me.

And for the first time, or so it seemed, I noticed the piece on the right-hand side. It was called "Perfectly Contented." I tried to play this one as well. It had a lighter melody but the same flowing rhythm and turned out to be quite easy. "Pleading Child" was shorter but slower; "Perfectly Contented" was longer, but faster. And after I played them both a few times, I realized they were two halves of the same song.

Poetry

Chapter 10

Understanding Poetry

NIKKI GIOVANNI
(1943–)

Poetry
(1975)

    poetry is motion graceful
    as a fawn
    gentle as a teardrop
    strong like the eye
5   finding peace in a crowded room
    we poets tend to think
    our words are golden
    though emotion speaks too
    loudly to be defined
10 by silence

    sometimes after midnight or just before
    the dawn
    we sit typewriter in hand
    pulling loneliness around us
15 forgetting our lovers or children
    who are sleeping
    ignoring the weary wariness
    of our own logic
    to compose a poem

20   no one understands it
    it never says "love me" for poets are
    beyond love
    it never says "accept me" for poems seek not
    acceptance but controversy

25 it only says "i am" and therefore
i concede that you are too
a poem is pure energy
horizontally contained
between the mind
30 of the poet and the ear of the reader
if it does not sing discard the ear
for poetry is song
if it does not delight discard
the heart for poetry is joy
35 if it does not inform then close
off the brain for it is dead
if it cannot heed the insistent message
that life is precious

which is all we poets
40 wrapped in our loneliness
are trying to say

◊ ◊ ◊

ARCHIBALD MACLEISH
(1892–1982)

Ars Poetica[1]
(1926)

A poem should be palpable and mute
As a globed fruit,

Dumb
As old medallions to the thumb,

5 Silent as the sleeve-worn stone
Of casement ledges where the moss has grown—

A poem should be wordless
As the flight of birds.
     *

A poem should be motionless in time
10 As the moon climbs,

Leaving, as the moon releases
Twig by twig the night-entangled trees,

Leaving, as the moon behind the winter leaves,
Memory by memory the mind—

---

[1] Art of Poetry.

15 A poem should be motionless in time
    As the moon climbs.

                    *

    A poem should be equal to:
    Not true.

    For all the history of grief
20 An empty doorway and a maple leaf.

    For love
    The leaning grasses and two lights above the sea—

    A poem should not mean
    But be.

◊ ◊ ◊

MARIANNE MOORE
(1887–1972)

Poetry
(1921)

I, too, dislike it: there are things that are important beyond all this
      fiddle.
   Reading it, however, with a perfect contempt for it, one
   discovers in it after all, a place for the genuine.
      Hands that can grasp, eyes
5   that can dilate, hair that can rise
            if it must, these things are important not because a

high-sounding interpretation can be put upon them but because they
   are useful. When they become so derivative as to become
   unintelligible, the same thing may be said for all of us, that we
10   do not admire what
         we cannot understand: the bat
            holding on upside down or in quest of something to

eat, elephants pushing, a wild horse taking a roll, a tireless wolf
      under
   a tree, the immovable critic twitching his skin like a horse that
   feels a flea, the base-
15   ball fan, the statistician—
         nor is it valid
            to discriminate against "business documents and

school-books";[1] all these phenomena are important. One must make
    a distinction
20   however: when dragged into prominence by half poets, the result
    is not poetry,
    nor till the poets among us can be
        "literalists of
25   the imagination"[2]—above
            insolence and triviality and can present
for inspection, "imaginary gardens with real toads in them," shall
    we have
    it. In the meantime, if you demand on the one hand,
    the raw material of poetry in
30   all its rawness and
        that which is on the other hand
            genuine, you are interested in poetry.

DEFINING POETRY

◊ ◊ ◊

Throughout history and across various national and cultural boundaries, poetry has held an important place. In ancient China and Japan, for example, poetry was prized above all else. One story tells of a samurai warrior who, when defeated, asked for a pen and paper. Thinking that he wanted to write a will before being executed, his captor granted his wish. Instead of writing a will, however, the warrior wrote a farewell poem that so moved his captor that he immediately released him.

To the ancient Greeks and Romans, poetry was the medium of spiritual and philosophical expression. Epics such as the *Iliad* and the *Aeneid* are written in verse, and so are dramas such as *Oedipus the King* (p. 879). Passages of the Bible, the Koran, and the Hindu holy books are also written in poetry. Today, throughout the world, poetry continues to delight and to inspire. For many people, in many places, poetry is the language of the emotions, the medium of expression they use when they speak from the heart.

---

[1] Moore quotes the *Diaries of Tolstoy* (New York, 1917): "Where the boundary between prose and poetry lies, I shall never be able to understand. [. . .] Poetry is verse; prose is not verse. Or else poetry is everything with the exception of business documents and school books."

[2] A reference (given by Moore) to W. B. Yeats's "William Blake and His Illustrations" (in *Ideas of Good and Evil*, 1903): "The limitation of his view was from the very intensity of his vision; he was a too literal realist of the imagination as others are of nature; and because he believed that the figures seen by the mind's eye, when exalted by inspiration, were 'external existences,' symbols of divine essences, he hated every grace of style that might obscure their lineaments."

Despite the longstanding place of poetry in our lives, however, many people—including poets themselves—have difficulty deciding just what poetry is. Is a poem "pure energy / horizontally contained / between the mind / of the poet and the ear of the reader," as Nikki Giovanni describes it? Or is a poem, as Archibald MacLeish says, "Dumb," "Silent," "wordless," and "motionless in time"? Or is it simply what Marianne Moore calls "all this fiddle"?

One way of defining poetry is to say that it uses language to condense experience into an intensely concentrated package, with each sound, each word, each image, and each line carrying great weight. But beyond this, it is difficult to pin down what makes a particular arrangement of words or lines a poem. Part of the problem is that poetry has many guises: a poem may be short or long, accessible or obscure; it may express a mood or tell a story; it may conform to a familiar poetic form—a sonnet, a couplet, a haiku—or follow no conventional pattern; it may or may not have a regular, identifiable meter or a rhyme scheme; it may depend heavily on elaborate imagery, figures of speech, irony, complex allusions or symbols, or repeated sounds—or it may include none of these features conventionally associated with poetry.

To further complicate the issue, different readers, different poets, different generations of readers and poets, and different cultures may have different expectations about poetry. As a result, they have different assumptions about poetry, and these different assumptions raise questions. Must poetry be written to delight or inspire, or can a poem have a political or social message? And must this message be conveyed subtly, embellished with imaginatively chosen sounds and words, or can it be explicit and straightforward? These questions, which have been debated by literary critics as well as by poets for many years, have no easy answers—and perhaps no answers at all. A haiku—short, rich in imagery, following a rigid formal structure—is certainly poetry, although to some Western readers, a haiku might seem too plain and understated to be considered "poetic." Still, most of these readers would agree that the following lines qualify as poetry.

◊ ◊ ◊

WILLIAM SHAKESPEARE
(1564–1616)

That Time of Year Thou Mayst in Me Behold
(1609)

That time of year thou mayst in me behold
When yellow leaves, or none, or few, do hang
Upon those boughs which shake against the cold,

Bare ruined choirs, where late the sweet birds sang.
5 In me thou see'st the twilight of such day
As after sunset fadeth in the west,
Which by and by black night doth take away,
Death's second self that seals up all in rest.
In me thou see'st the glowing of such fire,
10 That on the ashes of his youth doth lie,
As the deathbed whereon it must expire,
Consumed with that which it was nourished by
This thou perceiv'st, which makes thy love more strong,
To love that well which thou must leave ere long.

This poem possesses many of the characteristics that Western readers associate with poetry. For instance, its lines have a regular pattern of rhyme and meter that identifies it as a **sonnet**. The poem also includes a complex network of related imagery and figurative language that compares the lost youth of the aging speaker to the sunset and to autumn. Finally, the pair of rhyming lines at the end of the poem states a familiar poetic theme: the lovers' knowledge that they must eventually die makes their love stronger.

Even though the next poem is quite different from the preceding sonnet, most readers would probably agree that it too is a poem.

◊ ◊ ◊

LOUIS ZUKOFSKY
(1904–1978)

I Walk in the Old Street
(1944)

I walk in the old street
to hear the beloved songs
afresh
this spring night.
5 Like the leaves—my loves wake—
not to be the same
or look tireless to the stars
and a ripped doorbell.

Unlike Shakespeare's sonnet, Zukofsky's poem does not have a regular metrical pattern or rhyme scheme. Its diction is more conversational than poetic, and one of its images—a "ripped doorbell"—stands in stark contrast to the other, more conventionally "poetic" images. Nevertheless, the subject—love—is a traditional one; in fact, Zukofsky's poem echoes some of the sentiments of the Shakespeare sonnet. Finally, the poem's division into two four-line stanzas and its use of figurative language ("Like the leaves—my loves wake—") are unmistakably poetic.

Although the two preceding works can easily be classified as poems, readers might have trouble with the following lines.

◊ ◊ ◊

E. E. CUMMINGS
(1894–1962)

l(a
(1923)

```
    l(a

    le
    af
    fa
5   ll
    s)
    one
    l

    iness
```

Unlike the preceding two poems, "l(a" does not seem to have any of the characteristics normally associated with poetry. It has no meter, rhyme, or imagery. It has no repeated sounds, no figures of speech, no symbols. It cannot even be read aloud because its "lines" are fragments of words. In spite of its odd appearance, however, "l(a" does present an idea that is poetic. Reconstructed, the words Cummings broke apart—"l (a leaf falls) one l iness"—express a conventional poetic theme: the loneliness and isolation of the individual, as reflected in nature. Like Shakespeare and Zukofsy in the two previous poems, Cummings uses the image of a leaf to express his ideas about life and human experience. At the same time, by breaking words into bits and pieces, Cummings suggests the flexibility of language and conveys the need to break out of customary ways of using words to define experience.

As the preceding discussion illustrates, defining what a poem is (and is not) is almost impossible. It is true that most poems, particularly those divided into stanzas, look like poems, and it is also true that poems tend to use compressed language. Beyond this, however, what makes a poem a poem is more a matter of degree than a question of whether or not it conforms to a strict set of rules. A poem is likely to use *more* imagery, figurative language, rhyme, and so on than a prose piece—but, then again, it may not.

Reading Poetry

Some readers say they do not like poetry because they find it obscure or intimidating. One reason some people have difficulty reading poetry is that it tends to present information in subtle (and therefore potentially confusing) ways; it does not immediately "get to the point" as journalistic articles or business letters do. One could certainly argue that by concentrating experience, poetry actually "gets to the point" in ways—and to degrees—that other kinds of writing do not. Even so, some readers see poetry as an alien form. They have the misconception that poetry is always filled with obscure allusions, complex metrical schemes, and flowery diction. Others, feeling excluded from what they see as its secret language and mysterious structure, approach poetry as something that must be deciphered. Certainly, reading poetry often requires hard work and concentration. Because it is compressed, poetry often omits exposition and explanation; consequently, readers must be willing to take the time to read closely—to interpret ideas and supply missing connections. Many readers are simply not motivated to dig deeply for what they perceive to be uncertain rewards. But not all poems are difficult, and even those that are difficult are often well worth the effort.

The following guidelines, which focus on issues discussed elsewhere in this section of the text, may help direct your reading.

- ◇ Rephrase the poem in your own words. What does your paraphrase reveal about the poem's subject and central concerns? What is lost or gained in your paraphrase of the poem?
- ◇ Consider the poem's **voice.** Who is the poem's persona or speaker? How would you characterize the poem's tone? Is the poem ironic? (See Chapter 11.)
- ◇ Study the poem's **diction** and look up unfamiliar words in a dictionary. How does word choice affect your reaction to the poem? What do the connotations of words reveal about the poem? What level of diction is used? Is dialect used? Is word order unusual or unexpected? How does the arrangement of words contribute to your understanding of the poem? (See Chapter 12.)
- ◇ Examine the poem's **imagery.** What kind of imagery predominates? What specific images are used? Is a pattern of imagery present? How does imagery enrich the poem? (See Chapter 13.)
- ◇ Identify the poem's **figures of speech.** Does the poet use metaphor? Simile? Personification? Hyperbole? Understatement? Metonymy or synecdoche? Apostrophe? How do figures of speech affect your reading of the poem? (See Chapter 14.)

- Listen to the **sound** of the poem. Are rhythm and meter regular or irregular? How do rhythm and meter reinforce the poem's central concerns? Does the poem use alliteration? Assonance? Rhyme? How do these elements enhance the poem? (See Chapter 15.)
- Look at the poem's **form**. Is the poem written in closed or open form? Is the poem constructed as a sonnet? A sestina? A villanelle? An epigram? A haiku? Is the poem an example of concrete poetry? How does the poem's form reinforce its ideas? (See Chapter 16.)
- Consider the poem's use of **symbol, allegory, allusion,** or **myth**. Does the poem make use of symbols? Allusions? How do symbols or allusions support its theme? Is the poem an allegory? Does the poem retell or interpret a myth? (See Chapter 17.)
- Identify the poem's **theme**. What central theme or themes does the poem explore? How are the themes expressed? (See pp. 305–309.)

Recognizing Kinds of Poetry

◊ ◊ ◊

Most poems are either *narrative* poems, which recount a story, or *lyric* poems, which communicate a speaker's mood, feelings, or state of mind.

Narrative Poetry

Although any brief poem that tells a story, such as Edwin Arlington Robinson's "Richard Cory" (p. 544), may be considered a narrative poem, the two most familiar forms of narrative poetry are the *epic* and the *ballad*.

Epic poems recount the accomplishments of heroic figures, typically including expansive settings, superhuman feats, and gods and supernatural beings. The language of epic poems tends to be formal, even elevated, and often quite elaborate. Epics span many cultures—from the *Odyssey* (Greek) to *Beowulf* (Anglo-Saxon) to *The Epic of Gilgamesh* (Babylonian). In ancient times, epics were handed down orally; more recently, poets have written literary epics, such as John Milton's 1667 *Paradise Lost* and Nobel Prize–winning poet Derek Walcott's 1990 *Omeros*, which follow many of the same conventions.

The **ballad** is another type of narrative poetry with roots in an oral tradition. Originally intended to be sung, a ballad uses repeated words and phrases, including a refrain, to advance its story. Some—but not all—ballads use the **ballad stanza**. Dudley Randall's "Ballad of Birmingham" (p. 358) is an example of a contemporary ballad.

Lyric Poetry

Like narrative poems, lyric poems take various forms.

An **elegy** is a poem in which a poet mourns the death of a specific person, as in A. E. Housman's "To an Athlete Dying Young" (p. 382).

An **ode** is a long lyric poem, formal and serious in style, tone, and subject matter. An ode typically has a fairly complex stanzaic pattern, such as the **terza rima** used by Percy Bysshe Shelley in "Ode to the West Wind" (p. 546). Another ode in this text is "Ode on a Grecian Urn" (p. 533).

An **aubade** is a poem about morning, usually celebrating the coming of dawn. An example is Philip Larkin's "Aubade."

An **occasional poem** is written to celebrate a particular event or occasion. An example is Miller Williams's poem for President Clinton's second inaugural in 1997.

A **meditation** is a lyric poem that focuses on a physical object, using this object as a vehicle for considering larger issues. Edmund Waller's "Go, Lovely Rose" (p. 554) is a meditation.

A **pastoral**—for example, Christopher Marlowe's "The Passionate Shepherd to His Love" (p. 313)—is a lyric poem that celebrates the simple, idyllic pleasures of country life.

Finally, a **dramatic monologue** is a poem whose speaker addresses one or more silent listeners, often revealing much more than he or she intends. Robert Browning's "My Last Duchess" (p. 334) and "Porphyria's Lover" (p. 349) and Alfred, Lord Tennyson's "Ulysses" (p. 552) are three dramatic monologues that appear in this text.

Discovering Themes in Poetry

◊ ◊ ◊

A poem can be about anything, from the mysteries of the universe to poetry itself. Although no subject is really inappropriate for poetic treatment, certain conventional subjects recur frequently. For example, poets often write about love, war, nature, death, family, the folly of human desires, and the inevitability of growing old.

A poem's **theme,** however, is more than its general subject matter. It denotes the ideas the poet explores, the concerns the poem examines. More specifically, a poem's theme is its main point or idea. Poems "about nature," for instance, may praise the beauty of nature, assert the superiority of its simplest creatures over humans, consider its evanescence, or mourn its destruction. Similarly, poems "about death" may examine the difficulty of facing one's own mortality, eulogize a friend, assert the need for the acceptance of life's cycles, cry out against death's inevitability, or explore the **carpe diem** theme ("life is brief, so let us seize the day").

In order to discover the theme of a poem, readers consider its form, its voice, its language, its images, its allusions, its sound—all of its individual elements. Together, these elements convey the ideas that are important in the poem. (Of course, a poem may not communicate the same meaning to every reader. Different readers bring different backgrounds, attitudes, and experiences to a poem and therefore see different things and give weight to different ideas.)

The following poem is rich enough in language and content to suggest a variety of different interpretations.

ADRIENNE RICH
(1929–)

A Woman Mourned by Daughters
(1984)

Now, not a tear begun,
we sit here in your kitchen,
spent, you see, already.
You are swollen till you strain
5 this house and the whole sky.
You, whom we so often
succeeded in ignoring!
You are puffed up in death
like a corpse pulled from the sea;
10 we groan beneath your weight.
And yet you were a leaf,
a straw blown on the bed,
you had long since become
crisp as a dead insect.
15 What is it, if not you,
that settles on us now
like satins you pulled down
over our bridal heads?
What rises in our throats
20 like food you prodded in?
Nothing could be enough.
You breathe upon us now
through solid assertions
of yourself: teaspoons, goblets,
25 seas of carpet, a forest
of old plants to be watered,

an old man in an adjoining
room to be touched and fed.
And all this universe
30   dares us to lay a finger
anywhere, save exactly
as you would wish it done.

In general terms, "A Woman Mourned by Daughters" is, of course, about the speaker's mother. More specifically, this poem explores a number of different ideas: the passing of time; the relationships between mother and daughters, father and daughters, husband and wife; the power of memory. Its central theme, however, may be expressed as a **paradox:** "In death, a person may be a stronger presence than she was when she was alive."

Many different elements in the poem suggest this interpretation. The poem's speaker directly addresses her mother. Her voice is searching, questioning, and the poem's unpoetic diction ("You, whom we so often / succeeded in ignoring") and metrical irregularities give it a halting, uncertain quality. The words, images, and figurative language work together to establish the central idea: alive, the mother was light as a leaf or a straw or a dead insect; dead, she seems "swollen" and "puffed up," and the daughters feel crushed by her weight. The concrete details of her life—"teaspoons, goblets, / seas of carpet [. . .]"—weigh on her survivors and keep them under her spell. In her kitchen, her memory is alive; in death, she has tremendous power over her daughters.

Like most complex poems, this one supports several alternate readings. Some readers will focus on the negative language used to describe the mother; others might emphasize the images of domesticity; still others might concentrate on the role of the sisters and the almost-absent father. Any of these focuses can lead to a redefinition of the poem's theme.

The following poem is also about a parent who inspires ambivalent feelings in a child.

❖ ❖ ❖

RAYMOND CARVER
(1938–1988)

Photograph of My Father in His Twenty-Second Year
(1983)

October. Here in this dank, unfamiliar kitchen
I study my father's embarrassed young man's face.
Sheepish grin, he holds in one hand a string

of spiny yellow perch, in the other
5 a bottle of Carlsbad beer.

In jeans and denim shirt, he leans
against the front fender of a 1934 Ford.
He would like to pose bluff and hearty for his posterity,
wear his old hat cocked over his ear.
10 All his life my father wanted to be bold.

But the eyes give him away, and the hands
that limply offer the string of dead perch
and the bottle of beer. Father, I love you,
yet how can I say thank you, I who can't hold my liquor either,
15 and don't even know the places to fish?

Like Rich's speaker, Carver's is in a kitchen. Studying a photograph, this speaker sees through his father's façade. Instead of seeing the "bold," "bluff and hearty" young man his father wanted to be, he sees him as he was: "embarrassed" and "sheepish," with limp hands. In the last three lines of the poem, the speaker addresses his father directly, comparing his father's shortcomings and his own. This frank acknowledgment of his own vulnerability and the explicit link between father and son suggest that the poem has more to do with the speaker than with his father. Still, it is clear that the poem has something universal to say about parents and children—specifically, about the ambivalent feelings that children have for parents whose faults and failings they may have inherited.

The following poem also looks back on a parent, but here the adult speaker assumes a child's point of view.

◊ ◊ ◊

JUDITH ORTIZ COFER
(1952–   )

My Father in the Navy:
A Childhood Memory
(1982)

Stiff and immaculate
in the white cloth of his uniform
and a round cap on his head like a halo,
he was an apparition on leave from a shadow-world
5 and only flesh and blood when he rose from below
the waterline where he kept watch over the engines
and dials making sure the ship parted the waters
on a straight course.

Mother, brother and I kept vigil
10 on the nights and dawns of his arrivals,
watching the corner beyond the neon sign of a quasar
for the flash of white our father like an angel
heralding a new day.
His homecomings were the verses
15 we composed over the years making up
the siren's song that kept him coming back
from the bellies of iron whales
and into our nights
like the evening prayer.

Even as an adult, the speaker seems still not to know her father, whom she remembers as "stiff and immaculate," dressed in white, "an apparition on leave from a shadow-world." She remembers him as being "like an angel," wearing his cap "like a halo." In lines 14–16, the speaker associates her father with the long-missing, long-awaited wanderer Odysseus, hero of Homer's *Odyssey*. The reference to the "siren's song" in line 16, also an allusion to the *Odyssey*, suggests the adult speaker's realization that the father is drawn back—perhaps against his will—to the family. Together, the poem's tone and imagery convey the child's view of the father as elusive and unreal—an impression the adult speaker neither confirms nor corrects. The poem seems to suggest that the speaker is still struggling to understand her father's complex role in her life; perhaps too it suggests the universal difficulty of a child's trying to understand a parent.

❖ Poems for Further Reading: Poems about Parents

❖ ❖ ❖

THEODORE ROETHKE
(1908–1963)

My Papa's Waltz
(1948)

The whiskey on your breath
Could make a small boy dizzy;
But I hung on like death:
Such waltzing was not easy.

5 We romped until the pans
Slid from the kitchen shelf;

My mother's countenance
Could not unfrown itself.

The hand that held my wrist
10 Was battered on one knuckle;
At every step you missed
My right ear scraped a buckle.

You beat time on my head
With a palm caked hard by dirt,
15 Then waltzed me off to bed
Still clinging to your shirt.

◊ ◊ ◊

DYLAN THOMAS
(1914–1953)

Do Not Go Gentle into That Good Night[1]
(1952)

Do not go gentle into that good night,
Old age should burn and rave at close of day;
Rage, rage against the dying of the light.

Though wise men at their end know dark is right,
5 Because their words had forked no lightning they
Do not go gentle into that good night.

Good men, the last wave by, crying how bright
Their frail deeds might have danced in a green bay,
Rage, rage against the dying of the light.

10 Wild men who caught and sang the sun in flight,
And learn, too late, they grieved it on its way,
Do not go gentle into that good night.

Grave men, near death, who see with blinding sight
Blind eyes could blaze like meteors and be gay,
15 Rage, rage against the dying of the light.

---

[1] This poem was written during the last illness of the poet's father, D. J. Thomas.

And you, my father, there on the sad height,
Curse, bless, me now with your fierce tears, I pray,
Do not go gentle into that good night.
Rage, rage against the dying of the light.

◊ ◊ ◊

LUCILLE CLIFTON
(1936–   )

My Mama Moved among the Days
(1969)

My Mama moved among the days
like a dreamwalker in a field;
seemed like what she touched was hers
seemed like what touched her couldn't hold,
5 she got us almost through the high grass
then seemed like she turned around and ran
right back in
right back on in

◊ ◊ ◊

ROBERT HAYDEN
(1913–1980)

Those Winter Sundays
(1962)

Sundays too my father got up early
and put his clothes on in the blueblack cold,
then with cracked hands that ached
from labor in the weekday weather made
5 banked fires blaze. No one ever thanked him.

I'd wake and hear the cold splintering, breaking.
When the rooms were warm, he'd call,
and slowly I would rise and dress,
fearing the chronic angers of that house,

10 Speaking indifferently to him,
who had driven out the cold
and polished my good shoes as well.
What did I know, what did I know
of love's austere and lonely offices?

SEAMUS HEANEY[1]
(1939–   )

Digging
(1966)

Between my finger and my thumb
The squat pen rests; snug as a gun.

Under my window, a clean rasping sound
When the spade sinks into gravelly ground:
5   My father, digging. I look down

Till his straining rump among the flowerbeds
Bends low, comes up twenty years away
Stooping in rhythm through potato drills
Where he was digging.

10 The coarse boot nestled on the lug, the shaft
Against the inside knee was levered firmly.
He rooted out tall tops, buried the bright edge deep
To scatter new potatoes that we picked
Loving their cool hardness in our hands.
15 By God, the old man could handle a spade.
Just like his old man.

My grandfather cut more turf in a day
Than any other man on Toner's bog.
Once I carried him milk in a bottle
20 Corked sloppily with paper. He straightened up
To drink it, then fell to right away

Nicking and slicing neatly, heaving sods
Over his shoulder, going down and down
For the good turf. Digging.

25 The cold smell of potato mould, the squelch and slap
Of soggy peat, the curt cuts of an edge
Through living roots awaken in my head.
But I've no spade to follow men like them.

Between my finger and my thumb
30 The squat pen rests.
I'll dig with it.

---

[1] Winner of the 1995 Nobel Prize in Literature.

Reading and Reacting: Poems about Parents

1. What is each speaker's attitude toward his or her parent?
2. Which words and images suggest positive associations? Which help to create a negative impression?
3. How would you characterize each poem's tone? For example, is the poem sentimental, humorous, angry, resentful, or regretful?
4. What ideas about parent-child relationships are explored in each poem? What is the poem's central theme?
5. What does each poem say about the parent? What does it reveal about the speaker?

Related Works: "Two Kinds" (p. 285), "Daddy" (p. 413)

Poems for Further Reading: Poems about Love

CHRISTOPHER MARLOWE
(1564–1593)

The Passionate Shepherd to His Love
(1600)

Come live with me and be my love,
And we will all the pleasures prove
That valleys, groves, hills, and fields,
Woods, or steepy mountain yields.

5 And we will sit upon the rocks,
Seeing the shepherds feed their flocks
By shallow rivers, to whose falls
Melodious birds sing madrigals.

And I will make thee beds of roses
10 And a thousand fragrant posies,
A cap of flowers and a kirtle[1]
Embroidered all with leaves of myrtle;

A gown made of the finest wool
Which from our pretty lambs we pull;
15 Fair-linèd slippers for the cold,
With buckles of the purest gold;

---

[1] Skirt.

A belt of straw and ivy buds,
With coral clasps and amber studs.
And if these pleasures may thee move,
20 Come live with me and be my love.

The shepherds' swains shall dance and sing
For thy delight each May morning.
If these delights thy mind may move,
Then live with me and be my love.

◊ ◊ ◊

SIR WALTER RALEIGH
(1552?–1618)

The Nymph's Reply to the Shepherd
(1600)

If all the world and love were young,
And truth in every shepherd's tongue,
These pretty pleasures might me move
To live with thee and be thy love.

5 Time drives the flocks from field to fold,
When rivers rage and rocks grow cold;
And Philomel[1] becometh dumb;
The rest complains of cares to come.

The flowers do fade, and wanton fields
10 To wayward winter reckoning yields:
A honey tongue, a heart of gall,
Is fancy's spring, but sorrow's fall.

Thy gowns, thy shoes, thy beds of roses,
Thy cap, thy kirtle, and thy posies
15 Soon break, soon wither, soon forgotten,
In folly ripe, in reason rotten.

Thy belt of straw and ivy buds,
Thy coral clasps and amber studs.
All these in me no means can move
20 To come to thee and be thy love.

But could youth last, and love still breed,
Had joys no date, nor age no need,
Then these delights my mind might move
To live with thee and be thy love.

---

[1] The nightingale.

THOMAS CAMPION
(1567–1620)

There Is a Garden in Her Face
(1617)

    There is a garden in her face
    Where roses and white lilies grow;
      A heav'nly paradise is that place
    Wherein all pleasant fruits do flow.
5   There cherries grow which none may buy
      Till "Cherry-ripe" themselves do cry.

    Those cherries fairly do enclose
    Of orient pearl a double row,
      Which when her lovely laughter shows,
10 They look like rose-buds filled with snow;
      Yet them nor peer nor prince can buy,
      Till "Cherry-ripe" themselves do cry.

    Her eyes like angels watch them still;
    Her brows like bended bows do stand,
15   Threat'ning with piercing frowns to kill
    All that attempt, with eye or hand
      Those sacred cherries to come nigh
      Till "Cherry-ripe" themselves do cry.

WILLIAM SHAKESPEARE
(1564–1616)

My Mistress' Eyes Are Nothing like the Sun
(1609)

    My mistress' eyes are nothing like the sun;
    Coral is far more red than her lips' red;
    If snow be white, why then her breasts are dun;
    If hairs be wires, black wires grow on her head.
5   I have seen roses damasked red and white,
    But no such roses see I in her cheeks;
    And in some perfumes is there more delight
    Than in the breath that from my mistress reeks. .
    I love to hear her speak, yet well I know
10 That music hath a far more pleasing sound;

I grant I never saw a goddess go:
My mistress, when she walks, treads on the ground.
   And yet, by heaven, I think my love as rare
   As any she, belied with false compare.

❖ ❖ ❖

ROBERT BROWNING
(1812–1889)

Meeting at Night
(1845)

The gray sea and the long black land;
And the yellow half-moon large and low;
And the startled little waves that leap
In fiery ringlets from their sleep,
5 As I gain the cove with pushing prow,
And quench its speed i' the slushy sand.

Then a mile of warm sea-scented beach;
Three fields to cross till a farm appears;
A tap at the pane, the quick sharp scratch
10 And blue spurt of a lighted match,
And a voice less loud, through its joys and fears,
Than the two hearts beating each to each!

Parting at Morning
(1845)

Round the cape of a sudden came the sea,
And the sun looked over the mountain's rim:
And straight was a path of gold for him,
And the need of a world of men for me.

ELIZABETH BARRETT BROWNING
(1806–1861)

How Do I Love Thee?[1]
(1850)

How do I love thee? Let me count the ways.
I love thee to the depth and breadth and height
My soul can reach, when feeling out of sight
For the ends of being and ideal grace.
5 I love thee to the level of every day's
Most quiet need, by sun and candle-light.
I love thee freely, as men strive for right.
I love thee purely, as they turn from praise.
I love thee with the passion put to use
10 In my old griefs, and with my childhood's faith.
I love thee with a love I seemed to lose
With my lost saints. I love thee with the breath,
Smiles, tears, of all my life; and, if God choose,
I shall but love thee better after death.

DOROTHY PARKER
(1893–1967)

General Review of the Sex Situation
(1933)

Woman wants monogamy;
Man delights in novelty.
Love is woman's moon and sun;
Man has other forms of fun.
5 Woman lives but in her lord;
Count to ten, and man is bored.
With this the gist and sum of it,
What earthly good can come of it?

---

[1] Elizabeth Barrett Browning's "Sonnets from the Portuguese" was originally published in 1850 in a two volume publication titled *Poems*. "How Do I Love Thee?" is sonnet number XLIII from that work.

SYLVIA PLATH
(1932–1963)

Wreath for a Bridal
(1956)

What though green leaves only witness
Such pact as is made once only; what matter
That owl voice sole 'yes', while cows utter
Low moos of approve; let sun surpliced in brightness
5 Stand stock still to laud these mated ones
Whose stark act all coming double luck joins.

Couched daylong in cloisters of stinging nettle
They lie, cut-grass assaulting each separate sense
With savor; coupled so, pure paragons of constance,
10 This pair seek single state from that dual battle.
Now speak some sacrament to parry scruple
For wedlock wrought within love's proper chapel.

Call here with flying colors all watchful birds
To people the twigged aisles; lead babel tongues
15 Of animals to choir: 'Look what thresh of wings
Wields guard of honor over these!' Starred with words
Let night bless that luck-rotted mead of clover
Where, bedded like angels, two burn one in fever.

From this holy day on, all pollen blown
20 Shall strew broadcast so rare a seed on wind
That every breath, thus teeming, set the land
Sprouting fruit, flowers, children most fair in legion
To slay spawn of dragon's teeth: speaking this promise,
Let flesh be knit, and each step hence go famous.

TED HUGHES
(1930–1998)

A Pink Wool Knitted Dress
(1996)

In your pink wool knitted dress
Before anything had smudged anything
You stood at the altar. Bloomsday.

Rain—so that a just-bought umbrella
5 Was the only furnishing about me
Newer than three years inured.
My tie—sole, drab, veteran RAF black—
Was the used-up symbol of a tie.
My cord jacket—thrice-dyed black, exhausted,
10 Just hanging on to itself.

I was a post-war, utility son-in-law!
Not quite the Frog-Prince. Maybe the Swineherd
Stealing this daughter's pedigree dreams
From under her watchtowered searchlit future.

15 No ceremony could conscript me
Out of my uniform. I wore my whole wardrobe—
Except for the odd, spare, identical item.
My wedding, like Nature, wanted to hide.
However—if we were going to be married
20 It had better be Westminster Abbey. Why not?
The Dean told us why not. That is how
I learned that I had a Parish Church.
St George of the Chimney Sweeps.
So we squeezed into marriage finally.

25 Your mother, brave even in this
US Foreign Affairs gamble,
Acted all bridesmaids and all guests,
Even—magnanimity—represented
My family
30 Who had heard nothing about it.
I had invited only their ancestors.
I had not even confided my theft of you
To a closest friend. For Best Man—my squire
To hold the meanwhile rings—
35 We requisitioned the sexton. Twist of the outrage:
He was packing children into a bus,
Taking them to the Zoo—in that downpour!
All the prison animals had to be patient
While we married.
40   You were transfigured.
So slender and new and naked,
A nodding spray of wet lilac.
You shook, you sobbed with joy, you were ocean depth
Brimming with God.
45 You said you saw the heavens open
And how riches, ready to drop upon us.
Levitated beside you, I stood subjected
To a strange tense: the spellbound future.

In that echo-gaunt, weekday chancel
50 I see you
Wrestling to contain your flames
In your pink wool knitted dress
And in your eye-pupils—great cut jewels
Jostling their tear-flames, truly like big jewels
55 Shaken in a dice-cup and held up to me.

READING AND REACTING: POEMS ABOUT LOVE

1. What conventional images does each speaker use to express love?
2. Does the speaker use any images that are unexpected or shocking?
3. What ideas about love are expressed by each poem?
4. What is the tone of each poem? Is it happy? Sad? Celebratory? Regretful?
5. What does each poem reveal about the speaker? About the person to whom the poem is addressed?

Related Works: "Story of an Hour" (p. 43), "Popular Mechanics" (p. 265), "I Knew a Woman" (p. 370), "The Faithful Wife" (p. 375), "A Valediction: Forbidding Mourning" (p. 411), "To My Dear and Loving Husband" (p. 418), "You Fit into Me" (p. 423), *The Brute* (p. 668)

❖ POEMS FOR FURTHER READING: POEMS ABOUT WAR

❖ ❖ ❖

RUPERT BROOKE
(1887–1915)

The Soldier[1]
(1915)

If I should die, think only this of me;
   That there's some corner of a foreign field
That is for ever England. There shall be
   In that rich earth a richer dust concealed;
5 A dust whom England bore, shaped, made aware,
   Gave, once, her flowers to love, her ways to roam,
A body of England's breathing English air,
   Washed by the rivers, blest by suns of home.

---

[1] Brooke's poem "The Soldier" appeared in 1915 in a posthumously published collection of his work titled *1914 and Other Poems.*

And think, this heart, all evil shed away,
10   A pulse in the eternal mind, no less
            Gives somewhere back the thoughts by England
                given;
Her sights and sounds; dreams happy as her day;
    And laughter, learnt of friends; and gentleness,
        In hearts at peace, under an English heaven.

◆ ◆ ◆

WILFRED OWEN
(1893–1918)

Anthem for Doomed Youth
(1917?)

What passing-bells for these who die as cattle?
    Only the monstrous anger of the guns.
    Only the stuttering rifles' rapid rattle
Can patter out their hasty orisons.[1]
5   No mockeries now for them; no prayers nor bells,
        Nor any voice of mourning save the choirs,—
    The shrill, demented choirs of wailing shells;
        And bugles calling for them from sad shires.

What candles may be held to speed them all?
10   Not in the hands of boys, but in their eyes
        Shall shine the holy glimmers of good-byes.
    The pallor of girls' brows shall be their pall;
    Their flowers the tenderness of patient minds,
    And each slow dusk a drawing-down of blinds.

---
[1] Prayers.

WILLIAM BUTLER YEATS
(1865–1939)

An Irish Airman Foresees His Death
(1919)

    I know that I shall meet my fate
    Somewhere among the clouds above;
    Those that I fight I do not hate,
    Those that I guard I do not love;
5 My country is Kiltartan Cross
    My countrymen Kiltartan's poor,
    No likely end could bring them loss
    Or leave them happier than before.
    Nor law, nor duty bade me fight,
10 Nor public men, nor cheering crowds,
    A lonely impulse of delight
    Drove to this tumult in the clouds;
    I balanced all, brought all to mind,
    The years to come seemed waste of breath,
15 A waste of breath the years behind
    In balance with this life, this death.

ROBERT LOWELL
(1917–1977)

For the Union Dead
(1959)

"Relinquunt omnia servare rem publicam."[1]

The old South Boston Aquarium stands
in a Sahara of snow now. Its broken windows are boarded.
The bronze weathervane cod has lost half its scales.
The airy tanks are dry.

---

[1] "They gave up everything to preserve the Republic." A monument in Boston Common bears a similar form of this quotation. Designed by Augustus Saint-Gaudens, the monument is dedicated to Colonel Robert Gould Shaw and the African-American troops he commanded during a Civil War battle at Fort Wagner, South Carolina, on July 18, 1863.

5 Once my nose crawled like a snail on the glass;
my hand tingled
to burst the bubbles
drifting from the noses of the cowed, compliant fish.

My hand draws back. I often sigh still
10 for the dark downward and vegetating kingdom
of the fish and reptile. One morning last March,
I pressed against the new barbed and galvanized

fence on the Boston Common. Behind their cage,
yellow dinosaur steamshovels were grunting
15 as they cropped up tons of mush and grass
to gouge their underworld garage.

Parking spaces luxuriate like civic
sandpiles in the heart of Boston.
A girdle of orange, Puritan-pumpkin colored girders
20 braces the tingling Statehouse,

shaking over the excavations, as it faces Colonel Shaw
and his bell-cheeked Negro infantry
on St. Gauden's shaking Civil War relief,
propped by a plant splint against the garage's earthquake.

25 Two months after marching through Boston,
half the regiment was dead;
at the dedication,
William James[2] could almost hear the bronze Negroes breathe.

Their monument sticks like a fishbone
30 in the city's throat.
Its Colonel is as lean
as a compass-needle.

He has an angry wrenlike vigilance,
a greyhound's gentle tautness;
35 he seems to wince at pleasure,
and suffocate for privacy.

He is out of bounds now. He rejoices in man's lovely,
peculiar power to choose life and death—
when he leads his black soldiers to death,
40 he cannot bend his back.

On a thousand small town New England greens,
the old white churches hold their air
of sparse, sincere rebellion; frayed flags
quilt the graveyards of the Grand Army of the Republic.

---

[2] Harvard psychologist and philosopher (1842–1910).

45 The stone statues of the abstract Union Soldier
    grow slimmer and younger each year—
    wasp-waisted, they doze over muskets
    and muse through their sideburns . . .

    Shaw's father wanted no monument
50 except the ditch,
    where his son's body was thrown
    and lost with his "niggers."

    The ditch is nearer.
    There are no statues for the last war here;
55 on Boylston Street, a commercial photograph
    shows Hiroshima boiling

    over a Mosler Safe,[3] the "Rock of Ages"
    that survived the blast. Space is nearer.
    When I crouch to my television set,
60 the drained faces of Negro school-children rise like balloons.

    Colonel Shaw
    is riding on his bubble,
    he waits
    for the blessed break.

65 The Aquarium is gone. Everywhere,
    giant finned cars nose forward like fish;
    a savage servility
    slides by on grease.

◊ ◊ ◊

DENISE LEVERTOV
(1923–1997)

What Were They Like?
(1966)

    1) Did the people of Viet Nam
       use lanterns of stone?
    2) Did they hold ceremonies
       to reverence the opening of buds?
5 3) Were they inclined to rippling laughter?
    4) Did they use bone and ivory,
       jade and silver, for ornament?
    5) Had they an epic poem?
    6) Did they distinguish between speech and singing?

---

[3] A brand of safe known for being especially strong.

10 1) Sir, their light hearts turned to stone.
It is not remembered whether in gardens
stone lanterns illumined pleasant ways.
    2) Perhaps they gathered once to delight in blossom,
but after the children were killed
15   there were no more buds.
    3) Sir, laughter is bitter to the burned mouth.
    4) A dream ago, perhaps. Ornament is for joy.
All the bones were charred.
    5) It is not remembered. Remember,
20   most were peasants; their life
was in rice and bamboo.
When peaceful clouds were reflected in the paddies
and the water buffalo stepped surely along terraces,
maybe fathers told their sons old tales.
25   When bombs smashed the mirrors
there was time only to scream.
    6) There is an echo yet, it is said,
of their speech which was like a song.
It is reported their singing resembled
30   the flight of moths in moonlight.
Who can say? It is silent now.

BORIS SLUTSKY[1]

How Did They Kill My Grandmother?

Translated by Elaine Feinstein

How did they kill my grandmother?
I'll tell you how they killed her.
One morning a tank rolled up to
a building where
5 the hundred and fifty Jews of our town who,
weightless
        from a year's starvation,
and white
        with the knowledge of death,
10 were gathered holding their bundles.
And the German polizei[2] were
herding the old people briskly;

---

[1] Birth date of author and publication date of poem are not available.
[2] Police.

and their tin mugs clanked as
the young men led them away
₁₅   far away.

But my small grandmother
my seventy-year-old grandmother
began to curse and
scream at the Germans;
₂₀ shouting that I was a soldier.
She yelled at them: My grandson
is off at the front fighting!
Don't you dare
touch me!
₂₅ Listen, you
           can hear our guns!

Even as she went off, my grandmother
cried abuse,
           starting all over again
₃₀ with her curses.
From every window then
Ivanovnas and Andreyevnas
Sidorovnas and Petrovnas
sobbed: You tell them, Polina
₃₅ Matveyevna, keep it up!
They all yelled together:
           "What can we do against
this enemy, the Hun?"
Which was why the Germans chose
₄₀ to kill her inside the town.

A bullet struck her hair
and kicked her grey plait down.
My grandmother fell to the ground.
That is how she died there.

✧ ✧ ✧

YUSEF KOMUNYAKAA
(1947–   )

Facing It
(1988)

My black face fades,
hiding inside the black granite.
I said I wouldn't,
dammit: No tears.

5 I'm stone. I'm flesh.
     My clouded reflection eyes me
     like a bird of prey, the profile of night
     slanted against morning. I turn
     this way—the stone lets me go.
  10 I turn that way—I'm inside
     the Vietnam Veterans Memorial
     again, depending on the light
     to make a difference.
     I go down the 58,022 names,
  15 half-expecting to find
     my own in letters like smoke.
     I touch the name Andrew Johnson;
     I see the booby trap's white flash.
     Names shimmer on a woman's blouse
  20 but when she walks away
     the names stay on the wall.
     Brushstrokes flash, a red bird's
     wings cutting across my stare.
     The sky. A plane in the sky.
  25 A white vet's images floats
     closer to me, then his pale eyes
     look through mine. I'm a window.
     He's lost his right arm
     inside the stone. In the black mirror
  30 a woman's trying to erase names:
     No, she's brushing a boy's hair.

READING AND REACTING: POEMS ABOUT WAR

1. What is each speaker's attitude toward war?
2. What conventional images does each poem use to express its ideas about war?
3. Do any of the poems use unusual, unexpected, or shocking images?
4. How would you describe each poem's tone? Angry? Cynical? Sad? Disillusioned? Resigned?
5. What does each poem reveal about the speaker?
6. What is the central theme of each poem?

Related Works: "The Man He Killed" (p. 341), "Patterns" (p. 342), "The Death of the Ball Turret Gunner" (p. 410)

Chapter 11

Voice

❖ ❖ ❖

EMILY DICKINSON
(1830–1886)

I'm Nobody! Who Are You?
(1891)

> I'm Nobody! Who are you?
> Are you—Nobody—Too?
> Then there's a pair of us?
> Don't tell! they'd advertise—you know!
>
> 5 How dreary—to be—Somebody!
> How public—like a Frog—
> To tell one's name—the livelong June—
> To an admiring Bog!

THE SPEAKER IN THE POEM

❖ ❖ ❖

In fiction, the author's careful choice and arrangement of words enable readers to form an impression of the narrator and to decide whether he or she is sophisticated or unsophisticated, trustworthy or untrustworthy, innocent or experienced. Like fiction, poetry depends on a **speaker** who describes events, feelings, and ideas to readers. Finding out as much as possible about this speaker can help readers to interpret the poem. For example, the speaker in Emily Dickinson's "I'm Nobody! Who Are You?" seems at once shy and playful. The first stanza of the poem suggests that the speaker is a private person, perhaps with little self-esteem. As the poem continues, however, the voice becomes almost defiant. In a sense, the speaker's two voices represent two ways of relating to the world. The first voice expresses the private self—internal, isolated, and revealed through poetry; the second expresses the public self—external, self-centered, and inevitably superficial. Far from being defeated by shyness, the speaker claims to have chosen her status as "nobody."

One question readers might ask about "I'm Nobody! Who Are You?" is how close the speaker's voice is to the poet's. Readers who conclude that the poem is about the conflict between a poet's public and private responsibilities may be tempted to see the speaker and the poet as one. But this is not necessarily the case. Like the narrator of a short story, the speaker of a poem is a **persona,** or mask, that the poet assumes. Granted, in some poems little distance exists between the poet and the speaker. Without hard evidence to support a link between speaker and poet, however, readers should not assume they are one and the same.

In most cases, the speaker is quite different from the poet. And even when the speaker's voice conveys the attitude of the poet, it may do so only indirectly. In "The Chimney Sweeper" (p. 504), for example, William Blake assumes the voice of a child to criticize the system of child labor that existed in eighteenth-century England. Even though the child speaker does not understand the conditions that cause his misery, readers sense the poet's anger as the trusting speaker describes the conditions under which he works. The poet's indignation is especially apparent in the biting irony of the last line, in which the victimized speaker innocently assures readers that if all people do their duty, "they need not fear harm."

Sometimes the poem's speaker is anonymous. In this case—as in William Carlos Williams's "Red Wheelbarrow" (p. 390), for instance—the first-person voice is absent and the speaker remains outside the poem. At other times, the speaker has a set identity—a king, a beggar, a highwayman, a sheriff, a husband, a wife, a rich man, a chimney sweep, a child, a mythical figure, an explorer, a teacher, a faithless lover, a saint, or even a flower, an animal, or a clod of earth. Whatever the case, the speaker is not the poet, but rather a creation that the poet uses to convey his or her ideas. (For this reason, poems by a single poet may have very different voices. See Sylvia Plath's "Daddy" [p. 413] and "Morning Song" [p. 346], for example.)

In the following poem, the poet assumes the mask of a fictional character, Gretel from the fairy tale "Hansel and Gretel."

LOUISE GLÜCK
(1943–   )

Gretel in Darkness
(1971)

This is the world we wanted. All who would have seen us dead
Are dead. I hear the witch's cry
Break in the moonlight through a sheet of sugar: God rewards.
Her tongue shrivels into gas. . . .

5   Now, far from women's arms
And memory of women, in our father's hut
We sleep, are never hungry.
Why do I not forget?
My father bars the door, bars harm
10 From this house, and it is years.

No one remembers. Even you, my brother.
Summer afternoons you look at me as though you meant
To leave, as though it never happened. But I killed for you.
I see armed firs, the spires of that gleaming kiln come back,
    come back—

15 Nights I turn to you to hold me but you are not there.
Am I alone? Spies
Hiss in the stillness, Hansel we are there still, and it is real, real,
That black forest, and the fire in earnest.

The speaker in this poem comments on her life after her encounter with the witch in the forest. Speaking to her brother, Gretel observes that they now live in the world they wanted: they live with their father in his hut, and the witch and the wicked stepmother are dead. Even so, the memory of the events in the forest haunt Gretel and make it impossible for her to live "happily ever after." The "armed firs," the "gleaming kiln," and "the black forest" break through the "sheet of sugar" that her life has become.

By assuming the persona of Gretel, Glück is able to convey some interesting and complex ideas. On one level, Gretel represents any person who has lived through a traumatic experience. Memories of the event keep breaking through into the present, frustrating her attempts to reestablish her belief in the goodness of the world. The voice we hear is sad, alone, and frightened: "Nights I turn to you to hold me," she says, "but you are not there." Although the murder Gretel committed for her brother was justified, it seems to haunt her. "No one remembers," laments Gretel, not even her brother. At some level, she realizes that by killing the witch she has killed a part of herself, perhaps the part of women that men fear and consequently transform into witches and wicked stepmothers. The world that is left after the killing is the father's and the brother's, not hers, and she is now alone in a dark world haunted by the memories of the black forest. In this sense, Gretel—"Now, far from women's arms / And memory of women"—may be the voice of all victimized women who, because of men, act against their own best interests—and regret it.

As "Gretel in Darkness" illustrates, a title can identify a poem's speaker, but the speaker's own words can provide much more information. This is the case in the following poem, where Spanish words help to establish the poem's frame of reference and to characterize the speaker.

◊ ◊ ◊

LEONARD ADAMÉ
(1947–   )

My Grandmother Would Rock Quietly and Hum
(1973)

in her house
she would rock quietly and hum
until her swelled hands
calmed

5 in summer
she wore thick stockings
sweaters
and grey braids

(when "el cheque"[1] came
10 we went to Payless
and I laughed greedily
when given a quarter)

mornings,
sunlight barely lit
15 the kitchen
and where
there were shadows
it was not cold

---

[1] The check.

        she quietly rolled
20   flour tortillas—
     the "papas"[2]
     cracking in hot lard
     would wake me

     she had lost her teeth
25   and when we ate
     she had bread
     soaked in "café"[3]

     always her eyes
     were clear
30   and she could see
     as I cannot yet see—
     through her eyes
     she gave me herself

     she would sit
35   and talk
     of her girlhood—
     of things strange to me:
           México
           epidemics
40   relatives shot
           her father's hopes
           of this country—
     how they sank
     with cement dust
45   to his insides

     now
     when I go
     to the old house
     the worn spots
50   by the stove
     echo of her shuffling
     and
     México
     still hangs in her
55   fading
     calendar pictures

---

[2] Potatoes.
[3] Coffee.

In this poem, the speaker is an adult recalling childhood memories of his grandmother. Spanish words—*el cheque, tortillas, papas,* and *café*—identify the speaker as Latino. His easy use of English, his comment that talk of Mexico is strange to him, and his observation that he cannot yet see through his grandmother's eyes suggest, however, that he is not in touch with his ethnic identity. At one level, the grandmother evokes nostalgic memories of the speaker's youth. At another level, she is a living symbol of his ties with Mexico, connecting him to the ethnic culture he is trying to recover. The poem ends on an ambivalent note: even though the speaker is able to return to "the old house," the pictures of Mexico are fading, perhaps suggesting the speaker's assimilation into mainstream American culture.

Direct statements by the speaker can also help to characterize him. In the poem that follows, the first line of each stanza establishes the identity of the speaker—and defines his perspective.

◊ ◊ ◊

LANGSTON HUGHES
(1902–1967)

Negro
(1926)

I am a Negro:
   Black as the night is black,
   Black like the depths of my Africa.

I've been a slave:
5   Caesar told me to keep his door-steps clean.
   I brushed the boots of Washington.

I've been a worker:
   Under my hand the pyramids arose.
   I made mortar for the Woolworth Building.

10 I've been a singer:
   All the way from Africa to Georgia
   I carried my sorrow songs.
   I made ragtime.

I've been a victim:
15   The Belgians cut off my hands in the Congo.
   They lynch me still in Mississippi.

I am a Negro:
   Black as the night is black,
   Black like the depths of my Africa.

Here the speaker, identifying himself as "a Negro," assumes each of the roles African-Americans have historically played in Western society—slave, worker, singer, and victim. By so doing, he gives voice to his ancestors who, by being forced to serve others, were deprived of their identities. By presenting not just their suffering, but also their accomplishments, the speaker asserts his pride in being black. The speaker also implies that the suffering of black people has been caused by economic exploitation: Romans, Egyptians, Belgians, and Americans all used black labor to help build their societies. In this context, the speaker's implied warning is clear: except for the United States, all the societies that have exploited blacks have declined, and long after these empires have fallen, black people still endure.

In each of the preceding poems, the speaker is alone. The following poem, a **dramatic monologue,** presents a more complex situation in which the poet creates a complete dramatic scene. The speaker is developed as a character whose distinctive personality is revealed through his words as he addresses a silent listener.

◊ ◊ ◊

ROBERT BROWNING
(1812–1889)

My Last Duchess
(1842)

Ferrara

That's my last Duchess painted on the wall,
Looking as if she were alive. I call
That piece a wonder, now: Frà Pandolf's[1] hands
Worked busily a day, and there she stands.
5 Will't please you sit and look at her? I said
"Frà Pandolf" by design, for never read
Strangers like you that pictured countenance,
The depth and passion of its earnest glance,
But to myself they turned (since none puts by
10 The curtain I have drawn for you, but I)
And seemed as they would ask me, if they durst,
How such a glance came there; so, not the first
Are you to turn and ask thus. Sir, 'twas not
Her husband's presence only, called that spot
15 Of joy into the Duchess' cheek: perhaps
Frà Pandolf chanced to say "Her mantle laps

---

[1] "Brother" Pandolf, a fictive painter.

Over my lady's wrist too much," or "Paint
Must never hope to reproduce the faint
Half-flush that dies along her throat": such stuff
20   Was courtesy, she thought, and cause enough
For calling up that spot of joy. She had
A heart—how shall I say?—too soon made glad,
Too easily impressed; she liked whate'er
She looked on, and her looks went everywhere.
25   Sir, 'twas all one! My favor at her breast,
The dropping of the daylight in the West,
The bough of cherries some officious fool
Broke in the orchard for her, the white mule
She rode with round the terrace—all and each
30   Would draw from her alike the approving speech,
Or blush, at least. She thanked men—good! but thanked
Somehow—I know not how—as if she ranked
My gift of a nine-hundred-years-old name
With anybody's gift. Who'd stoop to blame
35   This sort of trifling? Even had you skill
In speech—(which I have not)—to make your will
Quite clear to such an one, and say, "Just this
Or that in you disgusts me; here you miss,
Or there exceed the mark"—and if she let
40   Herself be lessoned so, nor plainly set
Her wits to yours, forsooth, and made excuse
—E'en then would be some stooping; and I choose
Never to stoop. Oh sir, she smiled, no doubt,
Whene'er I passed her; but who passed without
45   Much the same smile? This grew; I gave commands;
Then all smiles stopped together. There she stands
As if alive. Will't please you rise? We'll meet
The company below, then. I repeat,
The Count your master's known munificence
50   Is ample warrant that no just pretense
Of mine for dowry will be disallowed;
Though his fair daughter's self, as I avowed
At starting, is my object. Nay, we'll go
Together down, sir. Notice Neptune,[2] though,
55   Taming a sea horse, thought a rarity,
Which Claus of Innsbruck[3] cast in bronze for me!

---

[2] God of the sea.

[3] An imaginary—or unidentified—sculptor. The count of Tyrol's capital was at Innsbrück, Austria.

The speaker is probably Alfonso II, duke of Ferrara, Italy, whose young wife, Lucrezia, died in 1561 after only three years of marriage. Shortly after her death, the duke began negotiations to marry again. When the poem opens, the duke is showing a portrait of his late wife to an emissary of an unnamed count who is there to arrange a marriage between the duke and the count's daughter. The duke remarks that the artist, Frà Pandolf, has caught a certain look upon the duchess's face. This look aroused the jealousy of the duke, who thought that it should have been for him alone. According to the duke, the duchess's crime was to have a heart "too soon made glad," "Too easily impressed." Eventually the duke could stand the situation no longer; he "gave commands," and "all smiles stopped together."

Much of what readers learn about the duke's state of mind comes from what is implied by his words. As he discusses the painting, the duke unintentionally reveals himself to be obsessively possessive and jealous, referring to "*my* last Duchess," "*my* favor at her breast," and "*my* gift of a nine-hundred-years-old name." He keeps the portrait of his late wife well hidden behind a curtain that no one draws except him. His interest in the picture has little to do with the memory of his wife, however. In death, the duchess has become just what the duke always wanted her to be: a personal possession that reflects his good taste.

The listener plays a subtle but important role in the poem: his presence establishes the dramatic situation that allows the character of the duke to be revealed. The purpose of the story is to communicate to the emissary exactly what the duke expects from his prospective bride and from her father. As he speaks, the duke conveys only the information that he wants the emissary to take back to his master, the count. Although he appears vain and superficial, the duke is actually extraordinarily shrewd. Throughout the poem, he turns the conversation to his own ends and gains the advantage through flattery and false modesty. Notice, for example, that he claims he has little skill in speaking when actually he is cleverly manipulating the conversation. The success of the poem lies in the poet's ability to develop the voice of this complex character, who embodies both superficial elegance and shocking cruelty.

Poems for Further Reading: The Speaker in the Poem

LESLIE MARMON SILKO
(1948–)

Where Mountain Lion Lay Down with Deer
(1973)

I climb the black rock mountain
    stepping from day to day
            silently.
I smell the wind for my ancestors
5   pale blue leaves
    crushed wild mountain smell.
Returning
    up the gray stone cliff
    where I descended
10   a thousand years ago.
Returning to faded black stone.
    where mountain lion lay down with deer.
It is better to stay up here
         watching wind's reflection
15   in tall yellow flowers.
The old ones who remember me are gone
    the old songs are all forgotten
and the story of my birth.
How I danced in snow-frost moonlight
20   distant stars to the end of the Earth,
How I swam away
       in freezing mountain water
        narrow mossy canyon tumbling down
          out of the mountain
25   out of the deep canyon stone
      down
         the memory
          spilling out
           into the world.

Reading and Reacting

1. Who is speaking in line 4? In line 9? Can you explain this shift?

2. From where is the speaker returning? What is she trying to recover?
3. **JOURNAL ENTRY** Is it important for you to know that the poet is of Native American descent? How does this information affect your interpretation of the poem?

Related Works: "Two Kinds" (p. 285), "Windigo" (p. 495)

◊ ◊ ◊

JANICE MIRIKITANI
(1942–   )

Suicide Note
(1987)

... *An Asian-American college student was reported to have jumped to her death from her dormitory window. Her body was found two days later under a deep cover of snow. Her suicide note contained an apology to her parents for having received less than a perfect four point grade average. ...*

        How many notes written ...
        ink smeared like birdprints in snow.

    not good enough   not pretty enough   not smart enough
dear mother and father.
5 I apologize
for disappointing you.
I've worked very hard,
        not good enough
harder, perhaps to please you.
10 If only I were a son, shoulders broad
as the sunset threading through pine,
I would see the light in my mother's
eyes, or the golden pride reflected
in my father's dream
15 of my wide, male hands worthy of work
and comfort.
I would swagger through life
muscled and bold and assured,
drawing praises to me
20 like currents in the bed of wind, virile
with confidence.
    not good enough   not strong enough   not good enough

I apologize.
Tasks do not come easily.
25 Each failure, a glacier.
Each disapproval, a bootprint.
Each disappointment,
ice above my river.
So I have worked hard.
30   not good enough
My sacrifice I will drop
bone by bone, perched
on the ledge of my womanhood,
fragile as wings.
35   not strong enough
It is snowing steadily
surely not good weather
for flying—this sparrow
sillied and dizzied by the wind
40 on the edge.
                    not smart enough
I make this ledge my altar
to offer penance.
This air will not hold me,
45 the snow burdens my crippled wings,
my tears drop like bitter cloth
softly into the gutter below.
        not good enough   not strong enough   not smart enough
                Choices thin as shaved
50   ice. Notes shredded
                drift like snow
on my broken body,
cover me like whispers
of sorries
55 sorries.
Perhaps when they find me
they will bury
my bird bones beneath
a sturdy pine
60 and scatter my feathers like
unspoken song
over this white and cold and silent
breast of earth.

READING AND REACTING

1. This poem is a suicide note that contains an apology. Why does the speaker feel she must apologize?

2. What attitude does the speaker convey toward her parents?
3. **Journal Entry** Is the college student who speaks in this poem a stranger to you? Or is her voice in any way like that of students you know?

Related Works: "The Rocking-Horse Winner" (p. 243), *The Cuban Swimmer* (p. 865)

The Tone of the Poem

The **tone** of a poem conveys the speaker's attitude toward his or her subject or audience. In speech, this attitude can be conveyed easily: stressing a word in a sentence can modify or color a statement, drastically affecting the meaning of a sentence. For example, the statement "Of course, you would want to go to that restaurant" is quite straightforward, but changing the emphasis to "Of course *you* would want to go to *that* restaurant" transforms a neutral statement into a sarcastic one. For poets, however, conveying a particular tone to readers represents a challenge because readers rarely hear their spoken voices. Instead, poets indicate tone by using techniques such as rhyme, meter, word choice, sentence structure, figures of speech, and imagery.

The range of possible tones is wide. For example, a poem's speaker may be joyful, sad, playful, serious, comic, intimate, formal, relaxed, condescending, or ironic. The detached tone of the following poem conveys the speaker's attitude toward his subject.

ROBERT FROST
(1874–1963)

Fire and Ice
(1923)

Some say the world will end in fire,
Some say in ice.
From what I've tasted of desire
I hold with those who favor fire.
5 But if it had to perish twice,
I think I know enough of hate
To say that for destruction ice
Is also great
And would suffice.

Here the speaker uses word choice, rhyme, and understatement to comment on the human condition. The conciseness and the simple, regular meter and rhyme suggest an **epigram**—a short poem that makes a pointed comment in an unusually clear, and often witty, manner. This pointedness is consistent with the speaker's glib, unemotional tone, as is the last line's wry understatement that ice "would suffice." The contrast between the poem's serious message—that active hatred and indifference are equally destructive—and its informal style and offhand tone is consistent with the speaker's detached, almost smug, posture.

Sometimes shifts in tone reveal changes in the speaker's attitude. In the following poem, changes in tone reveal a shift in the speaker's attitude toward war.

◊ ◊ ◊

THOMAS HARDY
(1840–1928)

The Man He Killed
(1902)

"Had he and I but met
By some old ancient inn,
We should have sat us down to wet
Right many a nipperkin!¹

5   "But ranged as infantry,
And staring face to face,
I shot at him as he at me,
And killed him in his place.

"I shot him dead because—
10   Because he was my foe,
Just so: my foe of course he was;
That's clear enough; although

"He thought he'd 'list,² perhaps,
Off-hand-like—just as I—
15 Was out of work—had sold his traps—
No other reason why.

"Yes; quaint and curious war is!
You shoot a fellow down
You'd treat if met where any bar is,
20   Or help to half-a-crown."

The speaker in this poem is a soldier relating his wartime experiences. Quotation marks indicate that he is engaged in conversation—perhaps in

---

¹ A small container of liquor.
² Enlist.

a pub—and his dialect indicates that he is probably of the English working class. For him, at least at first, the object of war is simple: kill or be killed. To Hardy, this speaker represents all men who are thrust into a war without understanding its underlying social, economic, or ideological causes. In this sense, the speaker and his enemy are both victims of forces beyond their comprehension or control.

The tone of "The Man He Killed" changes as the speaker tells his story. As the poem unfolds, its sentence structure deteriorates, and this in turn helps to convey the speaker's changing attitude toward the war in which he has fought. In the first two stanzas of the poem, sentences are smooth and unbroken, establishing the speaker's matter-of-fact tone and reflecting his confidence that he has done what he had to do. In the third and fourth stanzas, however, broken syntax reflects the narrator's increasingly disturbed state of mind as he tells about the man he killed. The poem's singsong meter and regular rhyme scheme *(met/wet, inn/nipperkin)* suggest that the speaker is trying hard to maintain his composure; the smooth sentence structure of the last stanza and the use of a cliché ("Yes; quaint and curious war is!") show the speaker's efforts to trivialize the incident.

Sometimes a poem's tone can establish an ironic contrast between the speaker and his or her subject. In the next poem, the speaker's abrupt change of tone at the end of the poem establishes just such a contrast.

◊ ◊ ◊

AMY LOWELL
(1874–1925)

Patterns
(1915)

    I walk down the garden-paths,
    And all the daffodils
    Are blowing, and the bright blue squills.
    I walk down the patterned garden-paths
5 In my stiff, brocaded gown.
    With my powdered hair and jewelled fan,
    I too am a rare
    Pattern. As I wander down
    The garden-paths.

10 My dress is richly figured,
    And the train
    Makes a pink and silver stain
    On the gravel, and the thrift
    Of the borders.
15 Just a plate of current fashion

Tripping by in high-heeled, ribboned shoes.
Not a softness anywhere about me,
Only whalebone[1] and brocade.
And I sink on a seat in the shade
20 Of a lime tree. For my passion
Wars against the stiff brocade.
The daffodils and squills
Flutter in the breeze
As they please.
25 And I weep;
For the lime-tree is in blossom
And one small flower has dropped upon my bosom.
And the plashing of waterdrops
In the marble fountain
30 Comes down the garden-paths.
The dripping never stops.
Underneath my stiffened gown
Is the softness of a woman bathing in a marble basin,
A basin in the midst of hedges grown
35 So thick, she cannot see her lover hiding,
But she guesses he is near,
And the sliding of the water
Seems the stroking of a dear
Hand upon her.
40 What is Summer in a fine brocaded gown!
I should like to see it lying in a heap upon the ground.
All the pink and silver crumpled up on the ground.

I would be the pink and silver as I ran along the paths,
And he would stumble after,
45 Bewildered by my laughter.
I should see the sun flashing from his sword-hilt and buckles
    on his shoes.
I would choose
To lead him in a maze along the patterned paths,
A bright and laughing maze for my heavy-booted lover.
50 Till he caught me in the shade,
And the buttons of his waistcoat bruised my body as he clasped me,
Aching, melting, unafraid.
With the shadows of the leaves and the sundrops,
And the plopping of the waterdrops,
55 All about us in the open afternoon—
I am very like to swoon
    With the weight of this brocade,
    For the sun sifts through the shade.

---

[1] Used in making corsets.

Underneath the fallen blossom
In my bosom,
Is a letter I have hid.
It was brought to me this morning by a rider from the Duke.
Madam, we regret to inform you that Lord Hartwell
Died in action Thursday se'nnight.[2]
As I read it in the white, morning sunlight,
The letters squirmed like snakes.
"Any answer, Madam," said my footman.
"No," I told him.
"See that the messenger takes some refreshment.
No, no answer."
And I walked into the garden,
Up and down the patterned paths,
In my stiff, correct brocade.
The blue and yellow flowers stood up proudly in the sun,
Each one.
I stood upright too,
Held rigid to the pattern
By the stiffness of my gown.
Up and down I walked.
Up and down.

In a month he would have been my husband.
In a month, here, underneath this lime,
We would have broken the pattern;
He for me, and I for him,
He as Colonel, I as Lady,
On this shady seat.
He had a whim
That sunlight carried blessing.
And I answered, "It shall be as you have said."
Now he is dead.

In Summer and in Winter I shall walk
Up and down
The patterned garden-paths
In my stiff, brocaded gown.
The squills and daffodils
Will give place to pillared roses, and to asters, and to snow.
I shall go
Up and down,
In my gown.
Gorgeously arrayed,
Boned and stayed.

---

[2] "Seven night," or a week ago Thursday.

And the softness of my body will be guarded from embrace
By each button, hook, and lace.
For the man who should loose me is dead,
105 Fighting with the Duke in Flanders,[3]
In a pattern called a war.
Christ! What are patterns for?

The speaker begins by describing herself walking down garden paths. She wears a stiff brocaded gown, has powdered hair, and carries a jewelled fan. By her own admission she is "a plate of current fashion." Although her tone is controlled, she is preoccupied by sensual thoughts. Beneath her "stiffened gown" is the "softness of a woman bathing in a marble basin," and the "sliding of the water" in a fountain reminds the speaker of the stroking of her lover's hand. She imagines herself shedding her brocaded gown and running with her lover along the maze of "patterned paths." The sensuality of the speaker's thoughts stands in ironic contrast to the images of stiffness and control that dominate the poem; her passion "wars against the stiff brocade." She is also full of repressed rage. After all, she knows that her lover has been killed, and she realizes the meaninglessness of the patterns of her life, patterns to which she has conformed, just as her lover has conformed by going to war and doing what he was supposed to do. Throughout the poem, the speaker's tone reflects her barely contained anger and frustration. In the last line of the poem, when she finally lets out her rage, the poem's point about the senselessness of war becomes apparent.

❖ POEMS FOR FURTHER READING: THE TONE OF THE POEM

WILLIAM WORDSWORTH
(1770–1850)

The World Is Too Much with Us
(1807)

The world is too much with us; late and soon,
Getting and spending, we lay waste our powers;
Little we see in Nature that is ours;
We have given our hearts away, a sordid boon!
5 This Sea that bares her bosom to the moon;
The winds that will be howling at all hours,

---

[3] Region in northwestern Europe, including part of northern France and western Belgium. Flanders was the site of a historic World War I battle.

And are up-gathered now like sleeping flowers;
For this, for everything, we are out of tune;
It moves us not. Great God! I'd rather be
10 A Pagan suckled in a creed outworn;
So might I, standing on this pleasant lea,
Have glimpses that would make me less forlorn;
Have sight of Proteus[1] rising from the sea;
Or hear old Triton[2] blow his wreathèd horn.

READING AND REACTING

1. What is the speaker's attitude toward the contemporary world? How is this attitude revealed through the poem's tone?
2. This poem is a **sonnet,** a highly structured traditional form. How do the rhyme scheme and the regular meter establish the poem's tone?
3. **JOURNAL ENTRY** Imagine you are a modern-day environmentalist, labor organizer, or corporate executive. Write a response to the sentiments expressed in this poem.

Related Works: "The Rocking-Horse Winner" (p. 243), "Dover Beach" (p. 503), "She Dwelt among the Untrodden Ways" (p. 558), "The Lake Isle of Innisfree" (p. 559)

◆ ◆ ◆

SYLVIA PLATH
(1932–1963)

Morning Song
(1962)

Love set you going like a fat gold watch.
The midwife slapped your footsoles, and your bald cry
Took its place among the elements.

Our voices echo, magnifying your arrival. New statue.
5 In a drafty museum, your nakedness
Shadows our safety. We stand round blankly as walls.

I'm no more your mother
Than the cloud that distills a mirror to reflect its own slow
Effacement at the wind's hand.

---

[1] Sometimes said to be Poseidon's son, this Greek sea god had the ability to change shapes at will and to tell the future.
[2] The trumpeter of the sea, this sea god is usually pictured blowing on a conch shell. Triton was the son of Poseidon, ruler of the sea.

10 All night your moth-breath
    Flickers among the flat pink roses. I wake to listen:
    A far sea moves in my ear.

    One cry, and I stumble from bed, cow-heavy and floral
    In my Victorian nightgown.
15 Your mouth opens clean as a cat's. The window square

    Whitens and swallows its dull stars. And now you try
    Your handful of notes;
    The clear vowels rise like balloons.

READING AND REACTING

1. Who is the speaker? To whom is she speaking? What does the poem reveal about her?
2. What is the poem's subject? What attitudes about her subject do you suppose the poet expects her readers to have?
3. How is the tone of the first stanza different from that of the third? How does the tone reflect the content of each stanza?
4. **JOURNAL ENTRY** In what sense does this poem reinforce traditional ideas about motherhood? How does it undercut them?

Related Works: "The Yellow Wall-Paper" (p. 102), "Those Winter Sundays" (p. 311), "My Son, My Executioner" (p. 422)

◊ ◊ ◊

ROBERT HERRICK
(1591–1674)

To the Virgins, to Make Much of Time
(1646)

Gather ye rosebuds while ye may,
  Old Time is still a-flying;
And this same flower that smiles today,
  Tomorrow will be dying.

5 The glorious lamp of heaven, the sun,
  The higher he's a-getting,
The sooner will his race be run,
  And nearer he's to setting.

That age is best which is the first,
10 When youth and blood are warmer;
But being spent, the worse, and worst
Times still succeed the former.

Then be not coy, but use your time,
And while ye may, go marry;
15 For having lost but once your prime,
You may forever tarry.

READING AND REACTING

1. How would you characterize the speaker? Do you think he expects his listeners to share his views? How might his expectations affect his tone?
2. This poem is developed like an argument. What is the speaker's main point? How does he support it?
3. What effect does the poem's use of rhyme have on its tone?
4. **JOURNAL ENTRY** Whose side are you on—the speaker's or those he addresses?

Related Works: "Where Are You Going, Where Have You Been?" (p. 268), "The Passionate Shepherd to His Love" (p. 313), "Cinderella" (p. 355), *The Brute* (p. 668)

IRONY

◊ ◊ ◊

Just as in fiction and drama, **irony** in poetry occurs when a discrepancy exists between two levels of meaning or experience. Consider the tone of the following lines by Stephen Crane:

Do not weep, maiden, for war is kind.
Because your lover threw wild hands toward the sky
And the afrightened steed ran on alone,
Do not weep.
War is kind.

How can war be "kind"? Isn't war exactly the opposite of "kind"? Surely the speaker does not intend his words to be taken literally. By making this ironic statement, the speaker actually conveys the opposite idea: war is a cruel, mindless exercise of violence.

Skillfully used, irony enables a poet to make a pointed comment about a situation or to manipulate a reader's emotions. Implicit in irony is the writer's assumption that readers will not be misled by the literal meaning of a statement. In order for irony to work, readers must recognize the disparity between what is said and what is meant, or between what a character or speaker thinks is occurring and what readers know to be occurring.

One kind of irony that appears in poetry is **dramatic irony,** which occurs when a speaker believes one thing and readers realize something else. In the following poem, the poet uses a deranged speaker to tell a story that is filled with irony.

◊ ◊ ◊

ROBERT BROWNING
(1812–1889)

Porphyria's Lover
(1836)

      The rain set early in to-night,
         The sullen wind was soon awake,
      It tore the elm-tops down for spite,
         And did its worst to vex the lake:
5   I listened with heart fit to break.
      When glided in Porphyria; straight
         She shut the cold out and the storm,
      And kneeled and made the cheerless grate
         Blaze up, and all the cottage warm;
10   Which done, she rose, and from her form
      Withdrew the dripping cloak and shawl,
         And laid her soiled gloves by, untied
      Her hat and let the damp hair fall,
         And, last, she sat down by my side
15   And called me. When no voice replied,
      She put my arm about her waist,
         And made her smooth white shoulder bare,
      And all her yellow hair displaced,
         And, stooping, made my cheek lie there,
20   And spread, o'er all, her yellow hair,
      Murmuring how she loved me—she
         Too weak, for all her heart's endeavour,
      To set its struggling passion free
         From pride, and vainer ties dissever,
25   And give herself to me for ever.
      But passion sometimes would prevail,
         Nor could to-night's gay feast restrain
      A sudden thought of one so pale
         For love of her, and all in vain:
30   So, she was come through wind and rain.
      Be sure I looked up at her eyes
         Happy and proud; at last I knew

Porphyria worshipped me; surprise
    Made my heart swell, and still it grew
35   While I debated what to do.
That moment she was mine, mine, fair,
    Perfectly pure and good: I found
A thing to do, and all her hair
    In one long yellow string I wound
40   Three times her little throat around,
And strangled her. No pain felt she;
    I am quite sure she felt no pain.
As a shut bud that holds a bee,
    I warily oped her lids: again
45   Laughed the blue eyes without a stain.
And I untightened next the tress
    About her neck; her cheek once more
Blushed bright beneath my burning kiss:
    I propped her head up as before,
50   Only, this time my shoulder bore
Her head, which droops upon it still:
    The smiling rosy little head,
So glad it has its utmost will,
    That all it scorned at once is fled,
55   And I, its love, am gained instead!
Porphyria's love: she guessed not how
    Her darling one wish would be heard.
And thus we sit together now,
    And all night long we have not stirred,
60   And yet God has not said a word!

Like Browning's "My Last Duchess" (p. 334) this poem is a **dramatic monologue.** The speaker recounts his story in a straightforward manner, seemingly unaware of the horror of his tale. In fact, much of the effect of this poem comes from the speaker's telling his tale of murder in a flat, unemotional tone—and from readers' gradual realization that the speaker is mad.

The irony of the poem, and of its title, becomes apparent as the monologue progresses. At first, the speaker fears that Porphyria is too weak to free herself from pride and vanity to love him. As he looks into her eyes, however, he comes to believe that she worships him. To preserve the perfection of Porphyria's love, the speaker strangles her with her own hair. He assures his silent listener, "I am quite sure she felt no pain." Like many of Browning's narrators, the speaker in this poem exhibits a selfish and perverse need to possess another person totally. The moment the speaker realizes that Porphyria loves him, he feels compelled to kill her and keep her his forever. According to him, she is at this point "mine, mine, fair, / Perfectly pure and good," and he believes that by murdering her, he actually fulfills "Her darling one wish"—to stay with him forever. As he attempts to justify his actions, the speaker reveals himself to be a deluded psychopathic killer.

Another kind of irony is **situational irony,** which occurs when the situation itself contradicts readers' expectations. For example, in "Porphyria's Lover" the meeting of two lovers results not in joy and passion but in murder. In the next poem the situation also creates irony.

◊ ◊ ◊

PERCY BYSSHE SHELLEY
(1792–1822)

Ozymandias
(1818)

I met a traveler from an antique land
Who said: Two vast and trunkless legs of stone
Stand in the desert. Near them, on the sand,
Half sunk, a shattered visage lies, whose frown,
5 And wrinkled lip, and sneer of cold command,
Tell that its sculptor well those passions read
Which yet survive, stamped on these lifeless things,
The hand that mocked them, and the heart that fed;
And on the pedestal these words appear:
10 "My name is Ozymandias,[1] king of kings:
Look on my works, ye Mighty, and despair!"
Nothing beside remains. Round the decay
Of that colossal wreck, boundless and bare
The lone and level sands stretch far away.

The speaker tells a tale about a colossal statue that lies shattered in the desert. Its head lies separated from the trunk, and the face has a wrinkled lip and a "sneer of cold command." On the pedestal of the monument are words exhorting all those who pass: "Look on my works, ye Mighty, and despair!" The situational irony of the poem has its source in the contrast between the "colossal wreck" and the boastful inscription on its base. To the speaker, Ozymandias stands for the vanity of those who mistakenly think they can withstand the ravages of time.

Perhaps the most common kind of irony found in poetry is **verbal irony,** which is created when words say one thing but mean another, often exactly the opposite. When verbal irony is particularly biting, it is called **sarcasm**—for example, Stephen Crane's use of the word *kind* in his antiwar poem "War Is Kind." In speech, verbal irony is easy to detect through the speaker's change in tone or emphasis. In writing, when

---

[1] The Greek name for Ramses II, ruler of Egypt in the thirteenth century B.C.

these signals are absent, verbal irony becomes more difficult to convey. Poets must depend on the context of a remark or on the contrast between a word and other images in the poem to create irony.

Consider how verbal irony is established in the following poem.

ARIEL DORFMAN
(1942–)

Hope
(1988)

Translated by Edith Grossman with the author

My son has been
missing
since May 8
of last year.
5   They took him
just for a few hours
they said
just for some routine
questioning.
10 After the car left,
the car with no license plate,
we couldn't

find out

anything else
15 about him.
But now things have changed.
We heard from a compañero
who just got out
that five months later
20 they were torturing him
in Villa Grimaldi,
at the end of September
they were questioning him
in the red house
25 that belonged to the Grimaldis.

They say they recognized
his voice his screams
they say.

        Somebody tell me frankly
30 what times are these
        what kind of world
        what country?
        What I'm asking is
        how can it be
35 that a father's
        joy
        a mother's
        joy
        is knowing
40 that they
        that they are still
        torturing
        their son?
        Which means
45 that he was alive
        five months later
        and our greatest
        hope
        will be to find out
50 next year
        that they're still torturing him
        eight months later

        and he may   might   could
        still be alive.

Although it is not necessary to know the background of the poet to appreciate this poem, it does help to know that Ariel Dorfman is a native of Chile. After the assassination of Salvador Allende, Chile's elected socialist president, in September 1973, the civilian government was replaced by a military dictatorship. Civil rights were suspended, and activists, students, and members of opposition parties were arrested and often detained indefinitely; sometimes they simply disappeared. The irony of this poem originates in the discrepancy between the way the word *hope* is used in the poem and the way it is usually used. For most people, hope has positive connotations, but in this poem it takes on a different meaning. This irony is not lost on the speaker.

Poems for Further Reading: Irony

W. H. AUDEN
(1907–1973)

The Unknown Citizen
(1939)

(To JS/07/M/378
This Marble Monument Is Erected by the State)

He was found by the Bureau of Statistics to be
One against whom there was no official complaint,
And all the reports on his conduct agree
That, in the modern sense of an old-fashioned word, he was a saint,
5 For in everything he did he served the Greater Community.
Except for the War till the day he retired
He worked in a factory and never got fired,
But satisfied his employers, Fudge Motors Inc.
Yet he wasn't a scab or odd in his views,
10 For his Union reports that he paid his dues,
(Our report on his Union shows it was sound)
And our Social Psychology workers found
That he was popular with his mates and liked a drink.
The Press are convinced that he bought a paper every day
15 And that his reactions to advertisements were normal in every way.
Policies taken out in his name prove that he was fully insured,
And his Health-card shows he was once in hospital but left it cured.
Both Producers Research and High-Grade Living declare
He was fully sensible to the advantages of the Installment Plan
20 And had everything necessary to the Modern Man,
A phonograph, a radio, a car and a frigidaire.
Our researchers into Public Opinion are content
That he held the proper opinions for the time of year;
When there was peace, he was for peace; when there was war, he went.
25 He was married and added five children to the population,
Which our Eugenist[1] says was the right number for a parent of his generation,
And our teachers report that he never interfered with their education.

---

[1] One who studies the science of human improvement, especially through genetic control.

Was he free? Was he happy? The question is absurd:
Had anything been wrong, we should certainly have heard.

READING AND REACTING

1. The "unknown citizen" represents modern citizens, who, according to the poem, are programmed like machines. How does the title help to establish the tone of the poem? How does the inscription on the monument also help to establish the tone?
2. Who is the speaker? What is his attitude toward the unknown citizen? How can you tell?
3. What kinds of irony are present in the poem? Identify several examples.
4. **JOURNAL ENTRY** This poem was written in 1939. Does its message apply to contemporary society, or does the poem seem dated?

Related Works: "A&P" (p. 65), "The Man He Killed" (p. 341), "next to of course god america i" (p. 513), *A Doll House* (p. 599)

◊ ◊ ◊

ANNE SEXTON
(1928–1974)

Cinderella
(1970)

You always read about it:
the plumber with twelve children
who wins the Irish Sweepstakes.
From toilets to riches.
5 That story.

Or the nursemaid,
some luscious sweet from Denmark
who captures the oldest son's heart.
From diapers to Dior.[1]
10 That story.

Or a milkman who serves the wealthy,
eggs, cream, butter, yogurt, milk,
the white truck like an ambulance
who goes into real estate

---

[1] Fashion designer Christian Dior.

15 and makes a pile.
From homogenized to martinis at lunch.

Or the charwoman
who is on the bus when it cracks up
and collects enough from the insurance.
20 From mops to Bonwit Teller.[2]
That story.

Once
the wife of a rich man was on her deathbed
and she said to her daughter Cinderella:
25 Be devout. Be good. Then I will smile
down from heaven in the seam of a cloud.
The man took another wife who had
two daughters, pretty enough
but with hearts like blackjacks.
30 Cinderella was their maid.
She slept on the sooty hearth each night
and walked around looking like Al Jolson.[3]
Her father brought presents home from town,
jewels and gowns for the other women
35 but the twig of a tree for Cinderella.
She planted that twig on her mother's grave
and it grew to a tree where a white dove sat.
Whenever she wished for anything the dove
would drop it like an egg upon the ground.
40 The bird is important, my dears, so heed him.

Next came the ball, as you all know.
It was a marriage market.
The prince was looking for a wife.
All but Cinderella were preparing
45 and gussying up for the big event.
Cinderella begged to go too.
Her stepmother threw a dish of lentils
into the cinders and said: Pick them
up in an hour and you shall go.
50 The white dove brought all his friends;
all the warm wings of the fatherland came,
and picked up the lentils in a jiffy.
No, Cinderella, said the stepmother,
you have no clothes and cannot dance.
55 That's the way with stepmothers.

---

[2] Exclusive department store.
[3] Al Jolson (Asa Yoelson; 1886–1950)—American singer and songwriter, famous for his "black-face" minstrel performances.

Cinderella went to the tree at the grave
and cried forth like a gospel singer:
Mama! Mama! My turtledove,
send me to the prince's ball!
60 The bird dropped down a golden dress
and delicate little gold slippers.
Rather a large package for a simple bird.
So she went. Which is no surprise.
Her stepmother and sisters didn't
65 recognize her without her cinder face
and the prince took her hand on the spot
and danced with no other the whole day.

As nightfall came she thought she'd better
get home. The prince walked her home
70 and she disappeared into the pigeon house
and although the prince took an axe and broke
it open she was gone. Back to her cinders.
These events repeated themselves for three days.
However on the third day the prince
75 covered the palace steps with cobbler's wax
and Cinderella's gold shoe stuck upon it.
Now he would find whom the shoe fit
and find his strange dancing girl for keeps.
He went to their house and the two sisters
80 were delighted because they had lovely feet.
The eldest went into a room to try the slipper on
but her big toe got in the way so she simply
sliced it off and put on the slipper.
The prince rode away with her until the white dove
85 told him to look at the blood pouring forth.
That is the way with amputations.
They don't just heal up like a wish.
The other sister cut off her heel
but the blood told as blood will.
90 The prince was getting tired.
He began to feel like a shoe salesman.
But he gave it one last try.
This time Cinderella fit into the shoe
like a love letter into its envelope.

95 At the wedding ceremony
the two sisters came to curry favor
and the white dove pecked their eyes out.
Two hollow spots were left
like soup spoons.

100 Cinderella and the prince
lived, they say, happily ever after,

like two dolls in a museum case
never bothered by diapers or dust,
never arguing over the timing of an egg,
105 never telling the same story twice,
never getting a middle-aged spread,
their darling smiles pasted on for eternity
Regular Bobbsey Twins.[4]
That story.

READING AND REACTING

1. The first twenty-one lines of the poem act as a prelude. How does this prelude help to establish the speaker's ironic tone?
2. At times the speaker talks directly to readers. What effect do these statements have on you? Would the poem be stronger without them?
3. Throughout the poem, the speaker mixes contemporary colloquial expressions with the conventional diction of a fairy tale. Find examples of these two kinds of language. How does the juxtaposition of these different kinds of diction create irony?j360
4. **JOURNAL ENTRY** What details of the Cinderella fairy tale does Sexton change in her poem? Why do you think she makes these changes?

Related Works: "The Story of an Hour" (p. 43), "Once upon a Time" (p. 46), "The Faithful Wife" (p. 375).

✧ ✧ ✧

DUDLEY RANDALL
(1914–   )

Ballad of Birmingham
(1969)

(On the bombing of a church in Birmingham, Alabama, 1963)

"Mother dear, may I go downtown
Instead of out to play,
And march the streets of Birmingham
In a Freedom March today?"

---

[4] The two sets of twins—Nan and Bert, Flossie and Freddie—in a popular series of early twentieth-century children's books. They led an idealized, problem-free life.

5 "No, baby, no, you may not go,
For the dogs are fierce and wild,
And clubs and hoses, guns and jails
Aren't good for a little child."

"But, mother, I won't be alone.
10 Other children will go with me,
And march the streets of Birmingham
To make our country free."

"No, baby, no, you may not go,
For I fear those guns will fire.
15 But you may go to church instead
And sing in the children's choir."

She has combed and brushed her night-dark hair,
And bathed rose petal sweet,
And drawn white gloves on her small brown hands,
20 And white shoes on her feet.

The mother smiled to know her child
Was in the sacred place,
But that smile was the last smile
To come upon her face.

25 For when she heard the explosion,
Her eyes grew wet and wild.
She raced through the streets of Birmingham
Calling for her child.

She clawed through bits of glass and brick,
30 Then lifted out a shoe.
"O, here's the shoe my baby wore,
But, baby, where are you?"

READING AND REACTING

1. Who are the two speakers in the poem? How do their attitudes differ? How does the tone of the poem convey their attitudes?
2. What kinds of irony are present in the poem? Give examples of each kind you identify.
3. This poem is a **ballad,** a form of poetry traditionally written to be sung or recited. Ballads typically repeat words and phrases and have regular meter and rhyme. How do the regular rhyme, repeated words, and singsong meter affect the poem's tone?
4. **JOURNAL ENTRY** This poem was written in response to the 1963 bombing of the 16th Street Baptist Church in Birmingham, Alabama, a bombing that killed four African-American children. How does this historical background help you to understand the irony of the poem?

Related Works: "Once upon a Time" (p. 46), "Emmett Till" (p. 523), "If We Must Die" (p. 536)

 Checklist: Writing about Voice

The Speaker in the Poem
- ✓ What do we know about the speaker?
- ✓ Is the speaker anonymous, or does he or she have a particular identity?
- ✓ How does assuming a particular persona help the poet to convey his or her ideas?
- ✓ Does the title give information about the speaker's identity?
- ✓ In what way does word choice provide information about the speaker?
- ✓ Does the speaker make any direct statements that help you to establish his or her identity or character?
- ✓ Does the speaker address anyone? How can you tell? Does the presence of a listener seem to affect the speaker?

The Tone of the Poem
- ✓ What is the speaker's attitude toward his or her subject?
- ✓ How do word choice, rhyme, meter, sentence structure, figures of speech, and imagery help to convey the attitude of the speaker?
- ✓ Is the tone of the poem consistent? How do shifts in tone reflect the changing mood or attitude of the speaker?

Irony
- ✓ Does any dramatic irony exist in the poem?
- ✓ Does the poem include situational irony?
- ✓ Does verbal irony appear in the poem?

◆ Writing Suggestions: Voice

1. Poet Robert Frost once said that he wanted to write "poetry that talked." According to Frost, "whenever I write a line it is because that line has already been spoken clearly by a voice with my mind, an audible voice." Choose some poems in this chapter (or elsewhere in the book) that you consider "talking

poems." Then, write an essay about how successful they are in communicating "an audible voice."
2. Compare the women's voices in "Cinderella" (p. 355) and "Gretel in Darkness" (p. 330). In what way are their attitudes toward men similar? In what way are they different?
3. The theme of Herrick's poem "To the Virgins, to Make Much of Time" (p. 347) is known as **carpe diem** or "seize the day." Read Andrew Marvell's "To His Coy Mistress" (p. 419), which has the same theme, and compare its tone with that of "To the Virgins, to Make Much of Time."
4. Read the following poem, and compare the speaker's use of the word *hope* with the way the speaker uses the word in Ariel Dorfman's "Hope" (p. 352).

◆ ◆ ◆

EMILY DICKINSON
(1830–1886)

"Hope" Is the Thing with Feathers
(1861)

"Hope" is the thing with feathers—
That perches in the soul—
And sings the tune without the words—
And never stops—at all—

5 And sweetest—in the Gale—is heard—
And sore must be the storm—
That could abash the little Bird—
That kept so many warm—

I've heard it in the chillest land—
10 And on the strangest Sea—
Yet, never, in Extremity,
It asked a crumb—of Me.

5. Because the speaker and the poet are not the same, poems by the same author can have different voices. Compare the voices of several poems by Sylvia Plath, W. H. Auden, William Blake, or any poet in this anthology.

Chapter 12

Word Choice, Word Order

SIPHO SEPAMLA
(1932–)

Words, Words, Words[1]

    We don't speak of tribal wars anymore
    we say simple faction fights
    there are no tribes around here
    only nations
5 it makes sense you see
    'cause from there
    one moves to multinational
    it makes sense you get me
    'cause from there
10 one gets one's homeland
    which is a reasonable idea
    'cause from there
    one can dabble with independence
    which deserves warm applause
15 —the bloodless revolution

    we are talking of words
    words tossed around as if
    denied location by the wind
    we mean those words some spit
20 others grab
    dress them up for the occasion
    fling them on the lap of an audience
    we are talking of those words

---

[1] Publication date is not available. This title is possibly an allusion to *Hamlet* 2.2.189.

that stalk our lives like policemen
25 words no dictionary can embrace
words that change sooner than seasons
we mean words
that spell out our lives
words, words, words
30 for there's a kind of poetic licence
doing the rounds in these parts

    Words identify and name, characterize and distinguish, compare and contrast. Words describe, limit, and embellish; words locate and measure. Without words, there cannot be a poem. Even though words may be elusive and uncertain and changeable, "tossed around as if / denied location by the wind" and "can change sooner than seasons," they still can "stalk our lives like policemen." In poetry, as in love and in politics, words matter.

    Beyond the quantitative—how many words, how many letters and syllables—is one much more important consideration: the *quality* of words. Which are chosen, and why? Why are certain words placed next to others? What does a word suggest in a particular context? How are the words arranged? What exactly constitutes the right word?

Word Choice

◊ ◊ ◊

In poetry, even more than in fiction or drama, words tend to become the focus—sometimes even the true subject—of a work. For this reason, the choice of one word over another can be crucial. Because poems are brief, they must compress many ideas into a few lines; poets know how much weight each individual word carries, and so they choose with great care, trying to select words that imply more than they state.

    A poet may choose a word because of its sound. For instance, a word may echo another word's sound, and such repetition may place emphasis on both words; it may rhyme with another word and therefore be needed to preserve the poem's rhyme scheme; or, it may have a certain combination of stressed and unstressed syllables needed to maintain the poem's metrical pattern. Occasionally, a poet may even choose a word because of how it looks on the page. Most often, though, poets select words because they help to communicate their ideas.

    At the same time, poets may choose words for their degree of concreteness or abstraction, specificity or generality. A *concrete* word refers to an item that is a perceivable, tangible entity—for example, a kiss or a flag. An *abstract* word refers to an intangible idea, condition, or quality, something that cannot be perceived by the senses—love, patriotism, and so on. *Specific* words refer to particular items; *general* words refer to entire classes or groups of items. As the following example illustrates, whether a word is specific or general is relative; its degree of specificity or generality depends on its relationship to other words:

> Poem → closed form poem → sonnet → seventeenth-century sonnet → Elizabethan sonnet → sonnet by Shakespeare → "My Mistress' Eyes Are Nothing Like the Sun"

Sometimes a poet wants a precise word, one that is both specific and concrete. At other times, however, a poet might prefer general or abstract language, which may allow for more subtlety—or even for intentional ambiguity.

Finally, a word may be chosen for its **connotation**—what it suggests. Every word has one or more **denotations**—what it signifies without emotional associations, judgments, or opinions. The word *family*, for example, denotes "a group of related things or people." Connotation is a more complex matter, however, because a single word may have many different associations. In general terms, a word may have a connotation that is positive, neutral, or negative. Thus, *family* may have a positive connotation when it describes a group of loving relatives, a neutral connotation when it describes a biological category, and an ironically negative connotation when it describes an organized crime family. Beyond this distinction, *family*, like any other word, may have a variety of emotional and social associations, suggesting loyalty, warmth, home, security, or duty. In fact, many words have somewhat different meanings in different contexts. When poets choose words, then, they must consider what a particular word may suggest to readers as well as what it denotes.

In the poem that follows, the poet chooses words for their sounds, their relationships to other words, and their connotations.

◊ ◊ ◊

WALT WHITMAN
(1819–1892)

When I Heard the Learn'd Astronomer
(1865)

When I heard the learn'd astronomer,
When the proofs, the figures, were ranged in columns before me,
When I was shown the charts and diagrams, to add, divide, and
   measure them,
When I sitting heard the astronomer where he lectured with much
   applause in the lecture-room,
5 How soon unaccountable I became tired and sick,

Till rising and gliding out I wander'd off by myself,
In the mystical moist night-air, and from time to time,
Look'd up in perfect silence at the stars.

This poem might be paraphrased as follows: "When I grew restless listening to an astronomy lecture, I went outside, where I found I learned more just by looking at the stars than I had learned inside." But the paraphrase is obviously neither as rich nor as complex as the poem. Through careful use of diction, Whitman establishes a dichotomy that supports the poem's central theme about the relative merits of two ways of learning.

The poem can be divided into two groups of four lines. The first four lines, unified by the repetition of "When," introduce the astronomer and his tools: "proofs," "figures," and "charts and diagrams" to be added, divided, and measured. In this section of the poem, the speaker is passive: he sits and listens ("I heard"; "I was shown"; "I sitting heard"). The repetition of "When" reinforces the dry monotony of the lecture. In the next four lines, the choice of words signals the change in the speaker's actions and reactions. The confined lecture hall is replaced by "the mystical moist night-air," and the dry lecture and automatic applause give way to "perfect silence"; instead of sitting passively, the speaker becomes active (he rises, glides, wanders); instead of listening, he looks. The mood of the first half of the poem is restrained: the language is concrete and physical, and the speaker is studying, receiving information from a "learn'd" authority. The rest of the poem, celebrating intuitive knowledge and feelings, is more abstract, freer. Throughout the poem, the lecture hall contrasts sharply with the natural world outside its walls.

After considering the poem as a whole, readers should not find it hard to understand why the poet selected certain words. Whitman's use of "lectured" in line 4 rather than a more neutral word like "spoke" is appropriate both because it suggests formality and distance and because it echoes "lecture-room" in the same line. The word "sick" in line 5 is striking because it connotes physical as well as emotional distress, more effectively conveying the extent of the speaker's discomfort than "bored" or "restless" would. "Rising" and "gliding" (6) are used rather than "standing" and "walking out" both because of the way their stressed vowel sounds echo each other (and echo "time to time" in the next line) and because of their connotation of dreaminess, which is consistent with "wander'd" (6) and "mystical" (7). The word "moist" (7) is chosen not only because its consonant sounds echo the *m* and *st* sounds in "mystical," but also because it establishes a contrast with the dry, airless lecture hall. Finally, line 8's "perfect silence" is a better choice than a reasonable substitute like "complete silence" or "total silence," either of which would suggest the degree of the silence but not its quality.

In the next poem, the poet also pays careful attention to word choice.

WILLIAM STAFFORD
(1914–1993)

For the Grave of Daniel Boone
(1957)

The farther he went the farther home grew.
Kentucky became another room;
the mansion arched over the Mississippi;
flowers were spread all over the floor.
5   He traced ahead a deepening home,
and better, with goldenrod:

Leaving the snakeskin of place after place,
going on—after the trees
the grass, a bird flying after a song.
10 Rifle so level, sighting so well
his picture freezes down to now,
a story-picture for children.

They go over the velvet falls
into the tapestry of his time,
15 heirs to the landscape, feeling no jar:
it is like evening; they are the quail
surrounding his fire, coming in for the kill;
their little feet move sacred sand.

Children, we live in a barbwire time
20 but like to follow the old hands back—
the ring in the light, the knuckle, the palm,
all the way to Daniel Boone,
hunting our own kind of deepening home.
From the land that was his I heft this rock.
25 Here on his grave I put it down.

A number of words in "For the Grave of Daniel Boone" are noteworthy for their multiple denotations and connotations. In the first stanza, for example, "home" does not mean Boone's residence; it connotes an abstract state, a dynamic concept that grows and deepens, encompassing states and rivers while becoming paradoxically more and more elusive. In literal terms, Boone's "home" at the poem's end is a narrow, confined space: his grave. In a wider sense, his home is the United States, particularly the natural landscape he explored. Thus, the word "home" comes to have a variety of associations to readers beyond its denotative meaning, suggesting both the infinite possibilities beyond the frontier and the realities of civilization's walls and fences.

The word "snakeskin" denotes "the skin of a snake"; its most immediate connotations are smoothness and slipperiness. In this poem, however, the snakeskin signifies more, because it is Daniel Boone who is "leaving the snakeskin of place after place." Like a snake, Boone belongs to the natural world—and, like a snake, he wanders from place to place, shedding his skin as he goes. Thus, the word "snakeskin," with its connotation of rebirth and its links to nature, passing time, and the inevitability of change, is consistent with the image of Boone as both a man of nature and a restless wanderer, "a bird flying after a song."

In the poem's third stanza, the phrases "velvet falls" and "tapestry of time" seem at first to have been selected solely for their pleasing repetition of sounds ("ve_l_vet fa_ll_s"; "_t_apestry of _t_ime"). But both of these paradoxical phrases also support the poem's theme. Alive, Boone was in constant movement; he was also larger than life. Now he has been reduced; "his picture freezes down to [. . .] / a story-picture for children" (11–12), and he is as static and inorganic as velvet or tapestry—no longer dynamic, like "falls" and "time."

The word "barbwire" (in line 19's phrase "barbwire time") is another word whose multiple meanings enrich the poem's theme. In the simplest terms, "barbwire" denotes a metal fencing material. In light of the poem's concern with space and distance, however, "barbwire" (with its connotations of sharpness, danger, and confinement) is also the antithesis of Boone's free or peaceful wilderness, evoking images of prisons and concentration camps and reinforcing the poem's central dichotomy between past freedom and present restriction.

The phrase "old hands" (20) might also have multiple meanings in the context of the poem. On one level, the hands could belong to an elderly person holding a storybook; on another level, "old hands" could refer to those with considerable life experience—like Boone, who was an "old hand" at scouting. On still another level, given the poem's concern with time, "old hands" could suggest the hands of a clock.

Through what it says literally and through what its words suggest, "For the Grave of Daniel Boone" communicates a good deal about the speaker's identification with Daniel Boone and with the nation he called home. Boone's horizons, his concept of "home," expanded as he wandered. Now, when he is frozen in time and space, a character in a child's picture book, a body in a grave, we are still "hunting our own kind of deepening home," but our horizons, like Boone's, have narrowed in this "barbwire time."

Poems for Further Reading: Word Choice

JAMES WRIGHT
(1927–1980)

Autumn Begins in Martins Ferry, Ohio
(1963)

In the Shreve High football stadium,
I think of Polacks nursing long beers in Tiltonsville,
And gray faces of Negroes in the blast furnace at Benwood,
And the ruptured night watchman of Wheeling Steel,
5 Dreaming of heroes.

All the proud fathers are ashamed to go home.
Their women cluck like starved pullets,
Dying for love.

Therefore,
10 Their sons grow suicidally beautiful
At the beginning of October,
And gallop terribly against each other's bodies.

READING AND REACTING

1. Evaluate Wright's decision to use each of the following words: "Polacks" (2), "ruptured" (4), "pullets" (7), "suicidally" (10), "gallop" (12). Do any of these words seem unexpected, even unsettling, in the context in which he uses them? Can you explain why each is used instead of a more conventional word?
2. What thematic relationship, if any, do you see between line 5 ("Dreaming of heroes") and line 8 ("Dying for love")? What do these lines reveal about the people who live in Martins Ferry?
3. **JOURNAL ENTRY** What comment does this poem seem to be making about small towns? About high school football?

Related Works: "To an Athlete Dying Young" (p. 382), "Ex-Basketball Player" (p. 408)

E. E. CUMMINGS
(1894–1962)

in Just-[1]
(1923)

in Just-
spring   when the world is mud-
luscious the little
lame balloonman

5   whistles   far   and wee

and eddieandbill come
running from marbles and
piracies and it's
spring

10 when the world is puddle-wonderful
the queer
old balloonman whistles
far   and   wee
and bettyandisbel come dancing

15 from hop-scotch and jump-rope and
it's
spring
and
          the
20   goat-footed

balloonMan   whistles
far
and
wee

READING AND REACTING

1. In this poem, Cummings coins a number of words that he uses to modify other words. Identify these coinages. What other, more conventional, words could be used in their place? What does Cummings accomplish by using the coined words instead?
2. What do you think Cummings means by "far and wee" in lines 5, 13, and 22–24? Why do you think he arranges the three words in a different way each time he uses them?

---

[1] Also known as "Chansons Innocentes I."

3. **Journal Entry** Evaluate this poem. Do you like it? Is it memorable or moving—or just clever?

Related Works: "The Secret Lion" (p. 281), "anyone lived in a pretty how town" (p. 381), "Constantly Risking Absurdity" (p. 405), "Jabberwocky" (p. 449), "the sky was can dy" (p. 467)

◊ ◊ ◊

THEODORE ROETHKE
(1908–1963)

I Knew a Woman
(1958)

I knew a woman, lovely in her bones,
When small birds sighed, she would sigh back at them;
Ah, when she moved, she moved more ways than one:
The shapes a bright container can contain!
5 Of her choice virtues only gods should speak,
Or English poets who grew up on Greek
(I'd have them sing in chorus, cheek to cheek).

How well her wishes went! She stroked my chin,
She taught me Turn, and Counter-turn, and Stand;
10 She taught me Touch, that undulant white skin;
I nibbled meekly from her proffered hand;
She was the sickle; I, poor I, the rake,
Coming behind her for her pretty sake
(But what prodigious mowing we did make).

15 Love likes a gander, and adores a goose:
Her full lips pursed, the errant note to seize;
She played it quick, she played it light and loose;
My eyes, they dazzled at her flowing knees;
Her several parts could keep a pure repose,
20 Or one hip quiver with a mobile nose
(She moved in circles, and those circles moved).

Let seed be grass, and grass turn into hay:
I'm martyr to a motion not my own;
What's freedom for? To know eternity.
25 I swear she cast a shadow white as stone.
But who would count eternity in days?
These old bones live to learn her wanton ways:
(I measure time by how a body sways).

Reading and Reacting

1. Many of the words in Roethke's poem have double meanings—for example, "gander" and "goose" in line 15. Identify other words that have more than one meaning, and consider the function these multiple meanings serve.
2. The poem's language contains many surprises; often, the word we expect is not the one we get. For example, "container" in line 4 is not a conventional means of describing a woman. What other words are used in unusual ways? What does Roethke achieve by choosing such words?
3. Is there a difference between the denotation or connotation of the word "bones" in the phrases "lovely in her bones" (1) and "These old bones" (27)? Explain.
4. **Journal Entry** How does this poem differ from your idea of what a love poem should be?

Related Works: "My Mistress' Eyes Are Nothing like the Sun" (p. 315), "Oh, My Love Is like a Red, Red Rose" (p. 407), "She Walks in Beauty" (p. 510)

Levels of Diction
◊ ◊ ◊

Like other writers, poets use various levels of diction to convey their ideas. The diction of a poem may be formal or informal or fall anywhere in between, depending on the identity of the speaker and on the speaker's attitude toward the reader and toward his or her subject. At one extreme, very formal poems can be far removed in style and vocabulary from everyday speech. At the other extreme, highly informal poems can be full of jargon, regionalisms, and slang. Many poems, of course, use language that falls somewhere between formal and informal diction.

Formal Diction

Formal diction is characterized by a learned vocabulary and grammatically correct forms. In general, formal diction does not include colloquialisms, such as contractions and shortened word forms (*phone* for *telephone*). As the following poem illustrates, a speaker who uses formal diction can sound aloof and impersonal.

MARGARET ATWOOD
(1939–   )

The City Planners
(1966)

Cruising these residential Sunday
streets in dry August sunlight:
what offends us is
the sanities:
5 the houses in pedantic rows, the planted
sanitary trees, assert
levelness of surface like a rebuke
to the dent in our car door.
No shouting here, or
10 shatter of glass; nothing more abrupt
than the rational whine of a power mower
cutting a straight swath in the discouraged grass.

But though the driveways neatly
sidestep hysteria
15 by being even, the roofs all display
the same slant of avoidance to the hot sky,
certain things:
the smell of spilled oil a faint

sickness lingering in the garages,
20 a splash of paint on brick surprising as a bruise,
a plastic hose poised in a vicious
coil; even the too-fixed stare of the wide windows

give momentary access to
the landscape behind or under
25 the future cracks in the plaster

when the houses, capsized, will slide
obliquely into the clay seas, gradual as glaciers
that right now nobody notices.

That is where the City Planners
30 with the insane faces of political conspirators
are scattered over unsurveyed
territories, concealed from each other,
each in his own private blizzard;

guessing directions, they sketch
35 transitory lines rigid as wooden borders
on a wall in the white vanishing air

tracing the panic of suburb
order in a bland madness of snows.

Atwood's speaker is clearly concerned about the poem's central issue, but rather than use *I*, the poem uses the first-person plural (*us*) to maintain distance and to convey emotional detachment. Although phrases such as "sickness lingering in the garages" and "insane faces of political conspirators" communicate the speaker's disapproval, formal words—"pedantic," "rebuke," "display," "poised," "obliquely," "conspirators," "transitory"—help her to maintain her distance. Both the speaker herself and her attack on the misguided city planners gain credibility through her balanced, measured tone and through the use of language that is as formal and "professional" as theirs, with no slang, nonstandard diction, or colloquialisms.

Informal Diction

Informal diction is the language closest to everyday conversation. It includes colloquialisms—contractions, shortened word forms, and the like—and may also include slang, regional expressions, and even nonstandard words.

In the poem that follows, the speaker uses informal diction to highlight the contrast between James Baca, a law student speaking to the graduating class of his old high school, and the graduating seniors.

◊ ◊ ◊

JIM SAGEL
(1947-)

Baca Grande[1]
(1982)

Una vaca se topó con un ratón y le dice:
"Tú—¿tan chiquito y con bigote?" Y le responde el ratón:
"Y tú tan grandota—¿y sin brassiere?"[2]

It was nearly a miracle
James Baca remembered anyone at all
from the old hometown gang

---

[1] *Baca* is both a phonetic spelling of the Spanish word "vaca" (cow) and the last name of one of the poem's characters. *Grande* means "large."

[2] A cow ran into a rat and said: "You—so small and with a moustache?" The rat responded: "And you—so big and without a bra?"

```
         having been two years at Yale
    5      no less
         and halfway through law school
         at the University of California at Irvine
         They hardly recognized him either
         in his three-piece grey business suit
   10    and surfer-swirl haircut
         with just the menacing hint
         of a tightly trimmed Zapata moustache
             for cultural balance
         and relevance

   15    He had come to deliver the keynote address
         to the graduating class of 80
         at his old alma mater
         and show off his well-trained lips
         which laboriously parted
   20        each Kennedyish "R"
         and drilled the first person pronoun
         through the microphone
         like an oil bit
         with the slick, elegantly honed phrases
   25    that slid so smoothly
         off his meticulously bleached
             tongue
         He talked Big Bucks
         with astronautish fervor and if he
   30        the former bootstrapless James A. Baca
         could dazzle the ass
         off the universe
         then even you
             yes you

   35    Joey Martinez toying with your yellow
             tassle
         and staring dumbly into space
         could emulate Mr. Baca someday
             possibly
   40    well
         there was of course
         such a thing
         as being an outrageously successful
         gas station attendant too
   45        let us never forget
         it doesn't really matter what you do
         so long as you excel
             James said
         never believing a word
```

50 of it
       for he had already risen
              as high as they go

    Wasn't nobody else
    from this deprived environment
55 who'd ever jumped
              straight out of college
    into the Governor's office
    and maybe one day
    he'd sit in that big chair
60   himself
    and when he did
    he'd forget this damned town
    and all the petty little people
    in it
65 once and for all

    That much he promised himself

"Baca Grande" uses numerous colloquialisms, including contractions; conversational placeholders, such as "no less" and "well"; shortened word forms, such as "gas"; slang terms, such as "Big Bucks"; whimsical coinages ("Kennedyish," "astronautish," "bootstrapless"); nonstandard grammatical constructions, such as "Wasn't nobody else"; and even profanity. The level of language is perfectly appropriate for the students Baca addresses—suspicious, streetwise, and unimpressed by Baca's "three-piece grey business suit" and "surfer-swirl haircut." In fact, the informal diction is a key element in the poem, expressing the gap between the slick James Baca, with "his well-trained lips / which laboriously parted / each Kennedyish 'R'" and members of his audience, with their unpretentious, forthright speech. In this sense "Baca Grande" is as much a linguistic commentary as a social one.

◈ Poems for Further Reading: Levels of Diction

◈ ◈ ◈

BARBARA L. GREENBERG
(1932–   )

The Faithful Wife
(1978)

But if I *were* to have a lover, it would be someone
who could take nothing from you. I would, in conscience,
not dishonor you. He and I would eat at Howard Johnson's

which you and I do not enjoy. With him I would go
fishing because it is not your sport. He would wear blue
which is your worst color; he would have none of your virtues.

Not strong, not proud, not just, not provident, my lover
would blame me for his heart's distress, which you would never
think to do. He and I would drink too much and weep together
and I would bruise his face as I would not bruise your face
even in my dreams. Yes I would dance with him, but to a music
you and I would never choose to hear, and in a place
where you and I would never wish to be. He and I would speak
Spanish, which is not your tongue, and we would take
long walks in fields of burdock, to which you are allergic.

We would make love only in the morning. It would be
altogether different. I would know him with my other body,
the one that you have never asked to see.

Reading and Reacting

1. In what respect does this poem sound like everyday speech? What colloquial elements usually present in conversation are absent here?
2. The speaker seems to be addressing her husband. What words or phrases in the poem sound out of place given the identities of the participants in the conversation?
3. **Journal Entry** How do you interpret the poem's title? In what sense is it ironic? In what sense is it not?

Related Works: "The Storm" (p. 89), "The Nymph's Reply to the Shepherd" (p. 314), "You Fit into Me" (p. 423), *A Doll House* (p. 599)

◊ ◊ ◊

RICHARD WILBUR
(1921–   )

For the Student Strikers
(1970)

Go talk with those who are rumored to be unlike you,
And whom, it is said, you are so unlike.
Stand on the stoops of their houses and tell them why
You are out on strike.

It is not yet time for the rock, the bullet, the blunt
Slogan that fuddles the mind toward force.

Let the new sound in our streets be the patient sound
Of your discourse.

Doors will be shut in your faces, I do not doubt.
10 Yet here or there, it may be, there will start,
Much as the lights blink on in a block at evening,
Changes of heart.

They are your houses; the people are not unlike you;
Talk with them, then, and let it be done
15 Even for the grey wife of your nightmare sheriff
And the guardsman's son.

READING AND REACTING

1. Is this poem's diction primarily formal or informal? List the words that support your conclusion.
2. Besides its vocabulary, what elements in the poem might lead you to characterize it as formal or informal?
3. **JOURNAL ENTRY** This poem is an *exhortation,* a form of discourse intended to incite or encourage listeners to take action. Given the speaker's audience and subject matter, is its level of diction appropriate? Explain.

Related Works: "First Fight. Then Fiddle" (p. 460), "The *Chicago Defender* Sends a Man to Little Rock" (p. 507)

◊ ◊ ◊

CHARLES BUKOWSKI
(1920–1994)

Dog Fight
(1984)

he draws up against my rear bumper in the fast lane,
I can see his head in the rear view mirror, his eyes
are blue and he sucks upon a dead cigar.
I pull over. he passes, then slows. I don't like
5 this.
I pull back into the fast lane, engage myself upon
his rear bumper. we are as a team passing through
Compton.
I turn the radio on and light a cigarette.
10 he ups it 5 mph, I do likewise. we are as a team
entering Inglewood.
he pulls out of the fast lane and I drive past.
then I slow. when I check the rear view he is

upon my bumper again.
15 he has almost made me miss my turnoff at Century.
I hit the blinker and fire across 3 lanes of
traffic, just make the off-ramp . . .
blazing past the front of an inflammable tanker.
blue eyes comes down from behind the tanker and
20 we veer down the ramp in separate lanes to the signal
and we sit there side by side, not looking at each
other.
I am caught behind an empty school bus as he idles
behind a Mercedes.
25 the signal switches and he is gone. I cut to the
inner lane behind him, then I see that the parking
lane is open and I flash by inside of him and the
Mercedes, turn up the radio, make the green as the
Mercedes and blue eyes run the yellow into the red.
30 they make it as I power it and switch back ahead of
them in their lane in order to miss a parked vegetable
truck.
now we are running 1-2-3, not a cop in sight, we are
moving through a 1980 California July
35 we are driving with skillful nonchalance
we are moving in perfect anger
we are as a team
approaching LAX:[1]
1-2-3
40 2-3-1
3-2-1.

Reading and Reacting

1. "Dog Fight" describes a car race from the emotionally charged perspective of a driver. Given this persona, comment on the appropriateness of the level of diction of the following words: "likewise" (10), "upon" (14), "nonchalance" (35), "perfect" (36).
2. Many of the words in the poem are **jargon**—specialized language associated with a particular trade or profession. In this case, Bukowski uses automotive terms and the action words and phrases that typically describe driving maneuvers. Would you characterize these words as formal, informal, or neither? Explain.
3. What colloquialisms are present in the poem? Could noncolloquial expressions be substituted for any of them? How would such substitutions change the poem?

---

[1] Los Angeles International Airport.

4. **Journal Entry** Look up the phrase *dog fight* in a dictionary. What meanings are listed? Which one do you think Bukowski had in mind? Why?

Related Works: "Popular Mechanics" (p. 265), "Chicago" (p. 464), *The Cuban Swimmer* (p. 865)

Word Order
◊ ◊ ◊

The order in which words are arranged in a poem is just as important as the choice of words. Because English sentences nearly always have a subject-verb-object sequence, with adjectives preceding the nouns they modify, a departure from this order calls attention to itself. Thus, poets can use readers' expectations about word order to their advantage. Poets often manipulate word order in order to place emphasis on a word. Sometimes they achieve this emphasis by using a very unconventional sequence; sometimes they simply place the word first or last in a line or place it in a stressed position in the line. Poets may also choose a particular word order to make two related—or startlingly unrelated—words fall in adjacent or parallel position, calling attention to the similarity (or the difference) between them. In other cases, poets may manipulate syntax to preserve a poem's rhyme or meter or highlight sound correspondences that might otherwise not be noticeable. Finally, irregular syntax may be used throughout a poem to reveal a speaker's mood—for example, to give a playful quality to a poem or to suggest a speaker's disoriented state.

In the poem that follows, the placement of many words departs from conventional English syntax.

◊ ◊ ◊

EDMUND SPENSER
(1552–1599)

One Day I Wrote Her Name upon the Strand
(1595)

> One day I wrote her name upon the strand,[1]
> But came the waves and washed it away:
> Again I wrote it with a second hand,
> But came the tide and made my pains his prey.
> 5 "Vain man," said she, "that doest in vain assay,

---
[1] Beach.

A mortal thing so to immortalize,
For I myself shall like to this decay,
And eek[2] my name be wiped out likewise."
"Not so," quod[3] I, "let baser things devise,
10 To die in dust, but you shall live by fame:
My verse your virtues rare shall eternize,
And in the heavens write your glorious name.
Where whenas death shall all the world subdue,
Our love shall live, and later life renew."

"One Day I Wrote Her Name upon the Strand," a sonnet, has a fixed metrical pattern and rhyme scheme. To accommodate the sonnet's rhyme and meter, Spenser makes a number of adjustments in syntax. For example, to make sure certain rhyming words fall at the ends of lines, the poet sometimes moves words out of their conventional order, as the following three comparisons illustrate.

Conventional Word Order	Inverted Sequence
"'Vain man,' she said, 'that doest *assay in vain*.'"	"'Vain man,' said she, 'that doest *in vain assay*.'" ("Assay" appears at end of line 5, to rhyme with line 7's "decay.")
"My verse shall *eternize your rare virtues*."	"My verse *your virtues rare shall eternize*." ("Eternize" appears at end of line 11 to rhyme with line 9's "devise.")
"Where whenas death shall *subdue all the world*, / Our love shall live, and *later renew life*."	"Where whenas death shall *all the world subdue*, / Our love shall live, and *later life renew*." (Rhyming words "subdue" and "renew" are placed at ends of lines.)

To make sure the metrical pattern stresses certain words, the poet occasionally moves a word out of order so it will fall on a stressed syllable. The following comparison illustrates this technique.

Conventional Word Order	Inverted Sequence
"But *the waves came* and washed it away."	"But *came the waves* and washed it away." (Stress in line 2 falls on "waves" rather than on "the.")

---

[2] Also, indeed.
[3] Said.

As the comparisons show, Spenser's adjustments in syntax are motivated at least in part by a desire to preserve the sonnet's rhyme and meter.

The following poem does more than simply invert words; it presents an intentionally disordered syntax.

◊ ◊ ◊

E. E. CUMMINGS
(1894–1962)

anyone lived in a pretty how town
(1940)

anyone lived in a pretty how town
(with up so floating many bells down)
spring summer autumn winter
he sang his didn't he danced his did.

5 Women and men (both little and small)
cared for anyone not at all
they sowed their isn't they reaped their same
sun moon stars rain

children guessed (but only a few
10 and down they forgot as up they grew
autumn winter spring summer)
that noone loved him more by more

when by now and tree by leaf
she laughed his joy she cried his grief
15 bird by snow and stir by still
anyone's any was all to her

someones married their everyones
laughed their cryings and did their dance
(sleep wake hope and then) they
20 said their nevers they slept their dream

stars rain sun moon
(and only the snow can begin to explain
how children are apt to forget to remember
with up so floating many bells down)

25 one day anyone died i guess
(and noone stooped to kiss his face)
busy folk buried them side by side
little by little and was by was

       all by all and deep by deep
   30 and more by more they dream their sleep
       noone and anyone earth by april
       wish by spirit and if by yes.

       Women and men (both dong and ding)
       summer autumn winter spring
   35 reaped their sowing and went their came
       sun moon stars rain

At times Cummings, like Spenser, manipulates syntax in response to the demands of rhyme and meter—for example, in line 10. But Cummings goes much further, using unconventional syntax as part of a scheme that encompasses other unusual elements of the poem, such as its unexpected departures from the musical metrical pattern (for example, in lines 3 and 8) and from the rhyme scheme (for example, in lines 3 and 4), and its use of parts of speech in unfamiliar contexts. Together, these techniques give the poem a playful quality. The refreshing disorder of the syntax (for instance, in lines 1–2, line 10, and line 24) adds to the poem's whimsical effect.

❖ **Poems for Further Reading: Word Order**

❖ ❖ ❖

A. E. HOUSMAN
(1859–1936)

To an Athlete Dying Young
(1896)

       The time you won your town the race
       We chaired you through the market-place;
       Man and boy stood cheering by,
       And home we brought you shoulder-high.

   5   Today, the road all runners come,
       Shoulder-high we bring you home,
       And set you at your threshold down,
       Townsman of a stiller town.

       Smart lad, to slip betimes away
   10 From fields where glory does not stay,
       And early though the laurel grows
       It withers quicker than the rose.

       Eyes the shady night has shut
       Cannot see the record cut,

15 And silence sounds no worse than cheers
   After earth has stopped the ears.

   Now you will not swell the rout
   Of lads that wore their honors out,
   Runners whom renown outran
20 And the name died before the man.

   So set, before its echoes fade,
   The fleet foot on the sill of shade,
   And hold to the low lintel up
   The still-defended challenge-cup.

25 And round that early-laureled head
   Will flock to gaze the strengthless dead,
   And find unwithered on its curls
   The garland briefer than a girl's.

Reading and Reacting

1. Where does the poem's meter or rhyme scheme require the poet to depart from conventional syntax?
2. Reword the poem using conventional word order. Do your changes improve the poem?
3. **Journal Entry** Who do you think the speaker is? What is his relationship to the athlete?

Related Works: "Anthem for Doomed Youth" (p. 321), "Nothing Gold Can Stay" (p. 397), "Ex-Basketball Player" (p. 408)

◊ ◊ ◊

EMILY DICKINSON
(1830–1886)

My Life Had Stood— A Loaded Gun
(c. 1863)

   My Life had stood—a Loaded Gun—
   In Corners—till a Day
   The Owner passed—identified—
   And carried Me away—

5 And now We roam in Sovereign Woods—
   And now We hunt the Doe—
   And every time I speak for Him—
   The Mountains straight reply—

And do I smile, such cordial light
10 Upon the Valley glow—
It is as a Vesuvian[1] face
Had let its pleasure through—

And when at Night—Our good Day done—
I guard My Master's Head—
15 'Tis better than the Eider-Duck's[2]
Deep Pillow—to have shared—

To foe of His—I'm deadly foe—
None stir the second time—
On whom I lay a Yellow Eye—
20 Or an emphatic Thumb—

Though I than He—may longer live
He longer must—than I—
For I have but the power to kill,
Without—the power to die—

Reading and Reacting

1. Identify lines in which word order departs from conventional English syntax. Can you explain in each case why the word order has been manipulated?
2. Do any words gain added emphasis by virtue of their unexpected position? Which ones? How are these words important to the poem's meaning?
3. **Journal Entry** Why do you think the speaker might be comparing her life to a loaded gun?

Related Works: "Because I Could Not Stop for Death" (p. 514), "I Heard a Fly Buzz—When I Died" (p. 514)

---

[1] Refers to Mount Vesuvius, a volcano that erupted in 79 A.D., destroying the city of Pompeii.
[2] Refers to the duck that produces eiderdown, used for stuffing pillows.

Checklist: Writing about Word Choice and Word Order

Word Choice

- ✓ Which words are of key importance in the poem?
- ✓ What is the denotative meaning of each of these key words?
- ✓ Why is each word chosen instead of a synonym? (For example, is the word chosen for its sound? Its connotation? Its relationship to other words in the poem? Its contribution to the poem's metrical pattern?)
- ✓ What other words could be effectively used in place of words now in the poem?
- ✓ How would substitutions change the poem's meaning?
- ✓ Which key words have neutral connotations? Which have negative connotations? Which have positive connotations? Beyond its literal meaning, what does each word suggest?
- ✓ Are any words repeated? Why?

Levels of Diction

- ✓ How would you characterize the poem's level of diction? Why is this level of diction used? Is it effective?
- ✓ Does the poem mix different levels of diction? To what end?
- ✓ Does the poem use dialect? For what purpose?

Word Order

- ✓ Is the poem's syntax conventional, or are words arranged in unexpected order?
- ✓ Which phrases represent departures from conventional syntax?
- ✓ What is the purpose of the unusual syntax? (For example, does it preserve the poem's meter or rhyme scheme? Does it highlight particular sound correspondences? Does it place emphasis on a particular word or phrase? Does it reflect the speaker's mood?)
- ✓ How would the poem's impact change if conventional syntax were used?

◊ Writing Suggestions: Word Choice, Word Order

1. Reread the two poems by E. E. Cummings—"in Just-" (p. 369) and "anyone lived in a pretty how town" (p. 381)—in this chapter. If you like, you may also read one or two additional poems in this text by Cummings. Do you believe Cummings chose words primarily for their sound? For their appearance on the page? What other factors might have influenced his choices?
2. The tone of "We Real Cool" (p. 509) is flat and unemotional; the problem on which it focuses, however, is a serious one. Expand this concise poem into an essay or story that uses more detailed, more emotional language to communicate the speaker's hopeless situation.
3. Reread "The Faithful Wife" (p. 375), and choose another poem in the text whose speaker is a woman. Compare the two speakers' levels of diction and choice of words. What does their speech reveal about their lives?
4. Reread "For the Grave of Daniel Boone" (p. 366) alongside Delmore Schwartz's "The True-Blue American" (p. 492). What does each poem's choice of words reveal about the speaker's attitude toward his subject?
5. Analyze the choice of words and the level of diction in Margaret Atwood's "The City Planners" (p. 372), William Blake's "London" (p. 506), and Denise Levertov's "What Were They Like?" (p. 324). Pay particular attention to each poem's use of language to express social or political criticism.

Chapter 13

Imagery

❖ ❖ ❖

JANE FLANDERS
(1940–   )

Cloud Painter
(1984)

Suggested by the life and art of John Constable[1]

At first, as you know, the sky is incidental—
a drape, a backdrop for trees and steeples.
Here an oak clutches a rock (already he works outdoors),
a wall buckles but does not break,
5 water pearls through a lock, a haywain[2] trembles.

The pleasures of landscape are endless. What we see
around us should be enough.
Horizons are typically high and far away.

Still, clouds let us drift and remember. He is, after all,
10 a miller's son, used to trying
to read the future in the sky, seeing instead
ships, horses, instruments of flight.
Is that his mother's wash flapping on the line?
His schoolbook, smudged, illegible?

15 In this period the sky becomes significant.
Cloud forms are technically correct—mares' tails,
sheep-in-the-meadow, thunderheads.
You can almost tell which scenes have been interrupted
by summer showers.

---

[1] John Constable (1776–1837)—British painter noted for his landscapes.
[2] An open horse-drawn wagon for carrying hay.

20 Now his young wife dies.
His landscapes achieve belated success.
He is invited to join the Academy. I forget
whether he accepts or not.

In any case, the literal forms give way
25 to something spectral, nameless. His palette shrinks
to gray, blue, white—the colors of charity.
Horizons sink and fade,
trees draw back till they are little more than frames,
then they too disappear.

30 Finally the canvas itself begins to vibrate
with waning light,
as if the wind could paint.
And we too, at last, stare into a space
which tell us nothing,
35 except that the world can vanish along with our need for it.

Because the purpose of poetry—and, for that matter, of all literature—is to expand the perception of readers, poets appeal to the senses.

◆ John Constable. *Landscape, Noon, The Haywain.* 1821. Oil on canvas, 130½ × 185½ cm. London, National Gallery.

In "Cloud Painter," for example, Jane Flanders uses details, such as the mother's wash on the line and the smudged schoolbook, to enable readers to visualize particular scenes in John Constable's early work. Clouds are described so readers can picture them—"mares' tails, / sheep-in-the-meadow, thunderheads." Thus, "Cloud Painter" is not just about the work of John Constable; it is also about the ability of an artist—poet or painter—to call up images in the minds of an audience. To achieve this end, a poet uses **imagery,** language that evokes a physical sensation produced by one of the five senses—sight, hearing, taste, touch, or smell.

Although the effect can be quite complex, the way images work is simple: when you read the word *red,* your memory of the various red things that you have seen determines how you picture the image. In addition, the word *red* may have emotional associations, or **connotations,** that define your response. A red sunset, for example, can have a positive connotation or a negative one depending on whether it is associated with the end of a perfect day or with air pollution. By choosing an image carefully, then, poets not only create pictures in a reader's mind, but also suggest a great number of imaginative associations. These associations help poets to establish the **atmosphere** or **mood** of the poem. The image of softly falling snow in "Stopping by Woods on a Snowy Evening" (p. 527), for example, creates a quiet, almost mystical mood.

Readers come to a poem with their own unique experiences, so an image in a poem does not always suggest the same thing to all readers. In "Cloud Painter," for example, the poet presents the image of an oak tree clutching a rock. Although most readers will probably see a picture that is consistent with the one the poet sees, no two images will be identical. Every reader will have his or her own distinct mental image of a tree clinging to a rock; some images will be remembered experiences, whereas others will be imaginative creations. Some readers may even be familiar enough with the work of the painter John Constable to visualize a particular tree clinging to a particular rock in one of his paintings.

By conveying what the poet sees and imagines, images open readers' minds and enrich their reading with perceptions and associations different from—and possibly more original and complex than—their own.

One advantage of imagery is its extreme economy. Just a few words enable poets to evoke a range of emotions and reactions. In the following poem, just a few visual images are enough to create a picture.

WILLIAM CARLOS WILLIAMS
(1883–1963)

Red Wheelbarrow
(1923)

so much depends
upon

a red wheel
barrow

₅ glazed with rain
water

beside the white
chickens

"Red Wheelbarrow" asks readers to pause to consider the uniqueness and mystery of everyday objects. What is immediately apparent is the poem's verbal economy. The poet does not tell readers what the barnyard smells like or what sounds the animals make. In fact, he does not even paint a detailed picture of the scene. How large is the wheelbarrow? In what condition is it? How many chickens are in the barnyard? In this poem, the answers to these questions are not important. Even without answering these questions, the poet is able to use simple imagery to create a scene upon which, he says, "so much depends."

The wheelbarrow establishes a momentary connection between the poet and his world. Like a still-life painting, the red wheelbarrow beside the white chickens gives order to a world that is full of seemingly unrelated objects. By asserting the importance of the objects in the poem, the poet suggests that our ability to perceive the objects of this world gives our lives meaning and that our ability to convey our perceptions to others is central to our lives as well as to art.

Images enable poets to present ideas that would be difficult to convey in any other way. Just one look at a dictionary will illustrate that concepts such as *beauty* and *mystery* are so abstract that they are difficult to define, let alone to discuss in specific terms. By choosing an image or series of images to embody these ideas, however, poets can effectively make their feelings known, as Ezra Pound does in the brief poem that follows.

EZRA POUND
(1885–1972)

In a Station of the Metro
(1916)

The apparition of these faces in the crowd;
Petals on a wet, black bough.

This poem is almost impossible to paraphrase because the information it communicates is less important than the feelings associated with this information. The poem's title indicates that the first line is meant to suggest a group of people gathered in a station of the Paris subway. The scene, however, is presented not as a clear picture but as an "apparition," suggesting that it is unexpected or even dreamlike. In contrast with the image of the subway platform is the image of the people's faces as flower petals on the dark branch of a tree. Thus, the subway platform—dark, cold, wet, subterranean (associated with baseness, death, and hell)—is juxtaposed with white flowers—delicate, pale, radiant, lovely (associated with the ideal, life, and heaven). These contrasting images, presented without comment, bear the entire weight of the poem.

Although images can be strikingly visual, they can also appeal to the senses of hearing, smell, taste, and touch. The following poem uses images of sound and taste as well as visual images.

GARY SNYDER
(1930–   )

Some Good Things to Be Said for the Iron Age
(1970)

      A ringing tire iron
          dropped on the pavement
      Whang of a saw
      brusht on limbs
5 the taste
      of rust

Here Snyder presents two commonplace aural images: the ringing of a tire iron and the sound of a saw. These somewhat ordinary images gain power, however, through their visual isolation in the poem. Together they produce a harsh and jarring chord that in turn creates a sense of uneasiness in the reader. This poem does more than present sensory images, though. It also conveys the speaker's interpretations of these images. The last two lines of the poem imply not only that the time in which we live (the Iron Age) is base and mundane, but also that it is declining, decaying into an age of rust. This idea is reinforced by the repeated consonant sounds in *taste* and *rust*, which encourage readers to hold the final image of the poem on their tongues. The title of the poem makes an ironic comment, suggesting that compared to the time that is approaching, the age of iron may be "good." Thus, in the mind of the poet, ordinary events gain added significance, and images that spring from everyday experience become sources of enlightenment and insight.

In shorter poems, such as most of those discussed earlier, one or two images may serve as focal points. A longer poem may introduce a cluster of related images, creating a more complex tapestry of sensory impressions—as in the following poem, where several related images are woven together.

◊ ◊ ◊

SUZANNE E. BERGER
(1944–   )

The Meal
(1984)

They have washed their faces until they are pale,
their homework is beautifully complete.
They wait for the adults to lean towards each other.
The hands of the children are oval
5 and smooth as pine-nuts.

The girls have braided and rebraided their hair,
and tied ribbons without a single mistake.
The boy has put away his coin collection.
They are waiting for the mother to straighten her lipstick,
10 and for the father to speak.

They gather around the table, carefully
as constellations waiting to be named.
Their minds shift and ready, like dunes.
It is so quiet, all waiting stars and dunes.

15 Their forks move across their plates without scraping,
they wait for the milk and the gravy
at the table with its forgotten spices.
They are waiting for a happiness to lift their eyes,
like sudden light flaring in the trees outside.

20 The white miles of the meal continue,
    the figures still travel across a screen:
    the father carving the Sunday roast,
    her mouth uneven as a torn hibiscus,
    their braids still gleaming in the silence.

"The Meal" presents related images that together evoke silence, order, and emptiness. It begins with the image of faces washed "until they are pale" and goes on to describe the children's oval hands as "smooth as pine-nuts." Forks move across plates "without scraping," and the table hints at the memory of "forgotten spices." Despite the poem's title, these children are emotionally starved. The attentive, well-scrubbed children sit at a table where, neither eating nor speaking, they wait for "the milk and the gravy" and for happiness that never comes. The "white miles of the meal" seem to go on forever, reinforcing the sterility and emptiness of the Sunday ritual. Suggesting an absence of sensation or feeling, a kind of paralysis, the poem's images challenge conventional assumptions about the family and its rituals.

Much visual imagery is **static,** freezing the moment and thereby giving it the timeless quality of painting or sculpture. ("The Meal" presents just such a tableau, and so do "Red Wheelbarrow" and "In a Station of the Metro.") Some imagery, however, is **kinetic,** conveying a sense of motion or change.

◊ ◊ ◊

WILLIAM CARLOS WILLIAMS
(1883–1963)

The Great Figure
(1938)

Among the rain
and lights
I saw the figure 5
in gold
5 on a red
firetruck
moving
tense
unheeded
10 to gong clangs
siren howls
and wheels rumbling
through the dark city.

394 CHAPTER 13 ◊ IMAGERY

◊ Charles Demuth (1883–1935). *I Saw the Figure 5 in Gold*. Oil on composition board, 36 × 29¾ in. The Metropolitan Museum of Art, the Alfred Steiglitz Collection, 1949. (49.59.1) All rights reserved, the Metropolitan Museum of Art.

Commenting on "The Great Figure" in his autobiography, Williams explains that while walking in New York, he heard the sound of a fire engine. As he turned the corner, he saw a golden figure 5 on a red background speed by. The impression was so forceful that he immediately jotted down a poem about it. In the poem, Williams attempts to re-create the sensation the figure 5 made as it moved into his consciousness, presenting the image as if it were a picture taken by a camera with a high-speed shutter. The poet presents images in the order in which he perceived them: first the 5 and then the red fire truck howling and clanging into the darkness. Thus, "The Great Figure" uses images of sight, sound, and movement to re-create for readers the poet's experience. The American painter Charles Demuth was fascinated by the kinetic quality of the poem. Working closely with his friend Williams, he attempted to capture the stop-action feature of the poem in the painting reproduced on page 394.

A special use of imagery, called **synesthesia,** occurs when one sense is described in a way that is more appropriate for another—for instance, when a sound is described with color. When people say they are feeling *blue* or describe music as *hot,* they are using synesthesia. The poet John Keats uses this technique in the following lines from "Ode to a Nightingale":

> O, for a draught of vintage! that hath been
>   Cool'd a long age in the deep-delvéd earth,
>   Tasting of Flora and the country green,
>   Dance and Provençal song, and sunburnt mirth!

In these lines, the speaker describes the taste of wine in terms of images that appeal to a variety of senses: flowers, a grassy field, dance, song, and sun.

❖ Poems for Further Reading: Imagery

❖ ❖ ❖

MATSUO BASHO
(1644?–1694)

Four Haiku[1]

Translated by Geoffrey Bownas and Anthony Thwaite

> Spring:
> A hill without a name
> Veiled in morning mist.
>
> The beginning of autumn:
> 5 Sea and emerald paddy
> Both the same green.

---

[1] Publication date is not available.

> The winds of autumn
> Blow: yet still green
> The chestnut husks.
>
> 10 A flash of lightning:
> Into the gloom
> Goes the heron's cry.

Reading and Reacting

1. A **haiku** is a three-line Japanese poem that traditionally has seventeen syllables. Haiku are admired for their extreme economy and their striking images. What are the central images in each of Basho's haiku? To what senses do these images appeal?
2. In another poem, Basho says that art begins with "The depths of the country / and a rice-planting song." What do you think he means? In what way do the preceding poems exemplify this idea?
3. Do you think the conciseness of these poems increases or decreases the impact of their images?
4. **Journal Entry** "In a Station of the Metro" (p. 391) is Ezra Pound's version of a haiku. How successful do you think Pound was? Do you think a longer poem could have conveyed the images more effectively?

Related Works: "Hokku Poems" (p. 462), "the sky was can dy" (p. 467), "Birches" (p. 524)

◊ ◊ ◊

CAROLYN KIZER
(1925–   )

After Basho
(1984)

> Tentatively, you
> slip onstage this evening,
> pallid, famous moon.

Reading and Reacting

1. What possible meanings might the word "After" have in the title? What does the title tell readers about the writer's purpose?
2. What visual picture does the poem suggest? What mood does the poem's central image create?

3. What is the impact of "tentatively" in the first line and "famous" in the last line? How do the connotations of these words affect the image of the moon?

Related Works: "Photograph of My Father in His Twenty-Second Year" (p. 307), "Widow's Lament" (p. 461)

✧ ✧ ✧

RICHARD WILBUR
(1921–   )

Sleepless at Crown Point
(1973)

All night, this headland
Lunges into the rumpling
Capework of the wind.

READING AND REACTING

1. What scene is the speaker describing?
2. What is the significance of the title?
3. What are the poem's central images? How do the words "lunges" and "capework" help to establish these images?

Related Works: "The Storm" (p. 89), "Fog" (p. 545)

✧ ✧ ✧

ROBERT FROST
(1874–1963)

Nothing Gold Can Stay
(1923)

Nature's first green is gold,
Her hardest hue to hold.
Her early leaf's a flower;
But only so an hour.
5   Then leaf subsides to leaf.
So Eden sank to grief.
So dawn goes down to day.
Nothing gold can stay.

Reading and Reacting

1. What central idea does this poem express?
2. What do you think the first line of the poem means? In what sense is this line ironic?
3. What is the significance of the colors green and gold in this poem? What do these colors have to do with "Eden" and "dawn"?
4. **Journal Entry** How do the various images in the poem prepare readers for the last line?

Related Works: "The Secret Lion" (p. 281), "Shall I Compare Thee to a Summer's Day?" (p. 402)

◊ ◊ ◊

JEAN TOOMER
(1894–1967)

Reapers
(1923)

Black reapers with the sound of steel on stones
Are sharpening scythes. I see them place the hones[1]
In their hip-pockets as a thing that's done,
And start their silent swinging, one by one.
5 Black horses drive a mower through the weeds,
And there, a field rat, startled, squealing bleeds,
His belly close to ground. I see the blade,
Blood-stained, continue cutting weeds and shade.

Reading and Reacting

1. What determines the order in which the speaker arranges the images in this poem? At what point does he comment on these images?
2. The first four lines of the poem seem to suggest that the workers are content. What image contradicts this impression? How does it do so?
3. What ideas are traditionally associated with the image of the reaper? The scythe? The harvest? (You may want to consult a reference work, such as *A Dictionary of Symbols* by J. E. Cirlot.) In what way does the speaker rely on these conventional

---

[1] Stones used to sharpen cutting instruments.

associations to help him convey his ideas? Can you appreciate the poem without understanding these associations?

Related Works: "A Worn Path" (p. 256), "Lineage" (p. 554)

WILFRED OWEN
(1893–1918)

Dulce et Decorum Est[1]
(1920)

Bent double, like old beggars under sacks,
Knock-kneed, coughing like hags, we cursed through sludge,
Till on the haunting flares we turned our backs
And towards our distant rest began to trudge.
5 Men marched asleep. Many had lost their boots
But limped on, blood-shod. All went lame; all blind;
Drunk with fatigue; deaf even to the hoots
Of tired, outstripped Five-Nines[2] that dropped behind.

Gas! Gas! Quick, boys!—An ecstasy of fumbling,
10 Fitting the clumsy helmets just in time;
But someone still was yelling out and stumbling
And flound'ring like a man in fire or lime . . .
Dim, through the misty panes and thick green light,
As under a green sea, I saw him drowning.
15 In all my dreams, before my helpless sight,
He plunges at me, guttering, choking, drowning.

If in some smothering dreams you too could pace
Behind the wagon that we flung him in,
And watch the white eyes writhing in his face,
20 His hanging face, like a devil's sick of sin;
If you could hear, at every jolt, the blood
Come gargling from the froth-corrupted lungs,
Obscene as cancer, bitter as the cud
Of vile, incurable sores on innocent tongues,—
25 My friend, you would not tell with such high zest
To children ardent for some desperate glory,
The old Lie: Dulce et decorum est
Pro patria mori.

---

[1] The title and last lines are from Horace, *Odes* 3.2: "Sweet and fitting it is to die for one's country."
[2] Shells that explode on impact and release poison gas.

Reading and Reacting

1. Who is the speaker in this poem? What is his attitude toward his subject?
2. What images are traditionally associated with soldiers? How do the images in this poem depart from these associations? Why do you think Owen selected such images?
3. To what senses (other than sight) does the poem appeal to? Is any of the imagery kinetic?
4. **Journal Entry** Does the knowledge that Owen died in World War I change your reaction to the poem, or are the poem's images compelling enough to eliminate the need for biographical background?

Related Works: "The Soldier" (p. 320), "Anthem for Doomed Youth" (p. 321), "An Irish Airman Foresees His Death" (p. 322).

Checklist: Writing about Imagery

- ✓ Do the images in the poem appeal to the sense of sight, touch, hearing, smell, or taste?
- ✓ Does the poem depend on a single image or on a variety of different images?
- ✓ Does the poem depend on a cluster of related images?
- ✓ What details make the images memorable?
- ✓ What mood do the images create?
- ✓ Are the images static or kinetic? Are there any examples of synesthesia?
- ✓ How do the poem's images help to convey its theme?
- ✓ How effective are the images? In what way do the images enhance your enjoyment of the poem?

◆ Writing Suggestions: Imagery

1. How are short poems such as "Some Good Things to Be Said for the Iron Age" (p. 391) and "In a Station of the Metro" (p. 391) like and unlike haiku?
2. Reread "Cloud Painter" (p. 387) and "The Great Figure" (p. 393), and read "Musée des Beaux Arts" (p. 499). Study the paintings accompanying the poems in the text. Then, write a

paper in which you draw some conclusions about the differences between artistic and poetic images.
3. Reread "The Meal" (p. 392) and the discussion that accompanies it. Then, analyze the role of imagery in the depiction of the parent/child relationships in "My Papa's Waltz" (p. 309) and "Those Winter Sundays" (p. 311). How does each poem's imagery convey the nature of the relationship it describes?
4. Write an essay in which you discuss the color imagery in "Nothing Gold Can Stay" (p. 397), "Reapers" (p. 398), and "The Yellow Wall-Paper" (p. 102). In what way does color reinforce the themes of these works?
5. Sometimes imagery can be used to make a comment about the society in which a scene takes place. Choose two poems in which imagery functions in this way—"For the Union Dead" (p. 322), "The Colonel" (p. 472), or "The *Chicago Defender* Sends a Man to Little Rock" (p. 507), for example—and discuss how the images chosen reinforce the social statement each poem makes

Chapter 14

Figures of Speech

◊ ◊ ◊

WILLIAM SHAKESPEARE
(1564–1616)

Shall I Compare Thee to a Summer's Day?
(1609)

Shall I compare thee to a summer's day?
Thou art more lovely and more temperate.
Rough winds do shake the darling buds of May,
And summer's lease hath all too short a date.
5 Sometime too hot the eye of heaven shines,
And often is his gold complexion dimmed;
And every fair from fair sometimes declines,
By chance, or nature's changing course, untrimmed.
But thy eternal summer shall not fade,
10 Nor lose possession of that fair thou ow'st;[1]
Nor shall death brag thou wand'rest in his shade,
When in eternal lines to time thou grow'st.
    So long as men can breathe or eyes can see,
    So long lives this, and this gives life to thee.

    Although figurative language is used in all kinds of writing, poets in particular recognize the power of a figure of speech to take readers beyond the literal meaning of a word. For this reason, **figures of speech**—expressions that use words to achieve effects beyond the power

---

[1] Beauty you possess.

of ordinary language—are more prominent in poetry than in other kinds of writing. For example, the preceding sonnet by Shakespeare compares a loved one to a summer's day in order to make the point that, unlike the fleeting summer, the loved one will—within the poem—remain forever young. But this sonnet goes beyond the obvious equation (loved one = summer's day); the speaker's assertion that his loved one will live forever in his poem actually says more about his confidence in his own talent and reputation (and about the power of figurative language) than about the loved one's beauty.

SIMILE, METAPHOR, AND PERSONIFICATION

When William Wordsworth opens a poem with "I wandered lonely as a cloud," he conveys a good deal more than he would if he simply said "I wandered, lonely." By comparing himself in his loneliness to a cloud, he suggests that like the cloud he is a part of nature and that he too is drifting, passive, blown by winds, and lacking will or substance. Thus, by using a figure of speech, the poet can suggest a wide variety of feelings and associations in very few words. The phrase "I wandered lonely as a cloud" is a **simile,** a comparison between two unlike items that includes *like* or *as*. When an imaginative comparison between two unlike items does not include *like* or *as*—that is, when it says "a is b" rather than "a is like b"—it is a **metaphor.**

Accordingly, when the speaker in Adrienne Rich's "Living in Sin" speaks of "daylight coming / like a relentless milkman up the stairs," she is using a strikingly original simile to suggest that daylight brings not the conventional associations of promise and awakening, but rather a stale, never-ending routine that is greeted without enthusiasm. This idea is consistent with the rest of the poem, an account of an unhappy relationship. However, when the speaker in Audre Lorde's poem says "Rooming houses are old women" (p. 406), she uses a metaphor, equating two elements to stress their common associations with emptiness, transience, and hopelessness. In addition, by identifying rooming houses as old women, Lorde is using **personification,** a special kind of comparison, closely related to metaphor, that gives life or human characteristics to inanimate objects or abstract ideas.

Sometimes, as in Wordsworth's "I wandered lonely as a cloud," a single brief simile or metaphor can be appreciated for what it communicates on its own. At other times, however, a simile or metaphor may be one of several related figures of speech that work together to communicate a poem's meaning. The following poem, for example, presents a series of related similes. Together, they suggest the depth of the problem the poem explores in a manner that each individual simile could not do alone.

❖ ❖ ❖

LANGSTON HUGHES
(1902–1967)

Harlem
(1951)

What happens to a dream deferred?

    Does it dry up
    like a raisin in the sun?
    Or fester like a sore—
5   And then run?
    Does it stink like rotten meat?
    Or crust and sugar over—
    like a syrupy sweet?

    Maybe it just sags
10   like a heavy load.

    Or does it explode?

The dream to which Hughes alludes in his 1951 poem is the dream of racial equality. It is also the American Dream—or, by extension, any important unrealized dream. His speaker offers six tentative answers to the question asked in the poem's first line, and five of the six are presented as similes. As the poem unfolds, the speaker considers different alternatives: The dream can shrivel up and die, fester, decay, crust over—or just sag under the weight of the burden those who hold the dream must carry. In each case, the speaker transforms an abstract entity—a dream—into a concrete item—a raisin in the sun, a sore, rotten meat, syrupy candy, a heavy load. The final line of the poem, italicized for emphasis, gains power less from what it says than from what it leaves unsaid. Unlike the other alternatives explored in the poem, *"Or does it explode?"* is not presented as a simile. Nevertheless, because of the pattern of figurative language the poem has established, readers supply the other, unspoken half of the comparison: ". . . like a bomb."

    Sometimes a single *extended simile* or *extended metaphor* is developed throughout a poem. The poem that follows, for example, develops an extended simile, comparing a poet to an acrobat.

LAWRENCE FERLINGHETTI
(1919–   )

Constantly Risking Absurdity
(1958)

    Constantly risking absurdity
                  and death
        whenever he performs
                above the heads
5   of his audience
    the poet like an acrobat
                climbs on rime
                    to a high wire of his own making
    and balancing on eyebeams
10   above a sea of faces
        paces his way
                to the other side of day
    performing entrechats
                and sleight-of-foot tricks
15 and other high theatrics
                and all without mistaking
        any thing
                for what it may not be
        For he's the super realist
20   who must perforce perceive
        taut truth
                before the taking of each stance or step
    in his supposed advance
                toward that still higher perch
25 where Beauty stands and waits
                with gravity
                    to start her death-defying leap
    And he
        a little charleychaplin man
30   who may or may not catch
    her fair eternal form
                spreadeagled in the empty air
        of existence

In his extended comparison between a poet and an acrobat, Ferlinghetti characterizes the poet as a kind of all-purpose circus performer, at once swinging recklessly on a trapeze and balancing carefully on a tightrope.

What the poem suggests is that the poet, like an acrobat, works hard at his craft but manages to make it all look easy. Something of an exhibitionist, the poet is innovative and creative, taking impossible chances yet also building on traditional skills in his quest for truth and beauty. Moreover, like an acrobat, the poet is balanced "on eyebeams / above a sea of faces," for he too depends on audience reaction to help him keep his performance focused. The poet may be "the super realist," but he also has plenty of playful tricks up his sleeve: "entrechats / and sleight-of-foot tricks / and other high theatrics," including puns ("above the heads / of his audience"), unexpected rhyme ("climbs on rime"), alliteration ("taut truth"), coinages ("a little charleychaplin man"), and all the other linguistic acrobatics available to poets. (Even the arrangement of the poem's lines on the page suggests the acrobatics it describes.) Like these tricks, the poem's central simile is a whimsical one, perhaps suggesting that Ferlinghetti is poking fun at poets who take their craft too seriously. In any case, the simile helps him to illustrate the acrobatic possibilities of language in a fresh and original manner.

The following poem develops an extended metaphor, personifying rooming houses as old women.

◊ ◊ ◊

AUDRE LORDE
(1934–1992)

Rooming Houses Are Old Women
(1968)

Rooming houses are old women
rocking dark windows into their whens
waiting incomplete circles
rocking
5   rent office to stoop to
community bathrooms to gas rings and
under-bed boxes of once useful garbage
city issued with a twice monthly check
and the young men next door
10 with their loud midnight parties
and fishy rings left in the bathtub
no longer arouse them
from midnight to mealtime no stops inbetween
light breaking to pass through jumbled up windows
15 and who was it who married the widow that Buzzie's son messed with?

To Welfare and insult form the slow shuffle
from dayswork to shopping bags
heavy with leftovers

Rooming houses
20 are old women waiting
　　searching
　　through darkening windows
　　the end or beginning of agony
　　old women seen through half-ajar doors
25 hoping
　　they are not waiting
　　but being
　　the entrance to somewhere
　　unknown and desired
30 but not new.

So closely does Lorde equate rooming houses and women in this poem that at times it is difficult to tell which of the two is actually the poem's subject. Despite the poem's assertion, rooming houses are *not* old women; however, they are *comparable to* the old women who live there, because their walls enclose a lifetime of disappointments as well as the physical detritus of life. Like the old women, rooming houses are in decline, rocking away their remaining years. Like the houses they inhabit, these women's boundaries are fixed—"rent office to stoop to / community bathrooms to gas rings"—and their hopes and expectations are few. They are surrounded by other people's loud parties, but their own lives have been reduced to a "slow shuffle" to nowhere, a hopeless, frightened—and perhaps pointless—"waiting / searching." Over time, the women and the places in which they live have become one. By using an unexpected comparison between two seemingly unrelated entities, the poem illuminates both the essence of the rooming houses and the essence of their elderly occupants.

◈ Poems for Further Reading: Simile, Metaphor, and Personification

ROBERT BURNS
(1759–1796)

Oh, My Love Is like a Red, Red Rose
(1796)

　　Oh, my love is like a red, red rose
　　　That's newly sprung in June;
　　My love is like the melody
　　　That's sweetly played in tune.

> 5 So fair art thou, my bonny lass,
>   So deep in love am I;
>   And I will love thee still, my dear,
>   Till a' the seas gang[1] dry.
>
>   Till a' the seas gang dry, my dear,
> 10 And the rocks melt wi' the sun;
>   And I will love thee still, my dear,
>   While the sands o' life shall run.
>
>   And fare thee weel, my only love!
>   And fare thee weel awhile!
> 15 And I will come again, my love
>   Though it were ten thousand mile.

READING AND REACTING

1. Why does the speaker compare his love to a rose? What other simile is used in the poem? For what purpose is it used?
2. Why do you suppose Burns begins his poem with similes? Would moving them to the end change the poem's impact?
3. Where does the speaker seem to exaggerate the extent of his love? Why does he exaggerate? Do you think this exaggeration weakens the effectiveness of the poem? Explain.

Related Works: "Araby" (p. 167), "My Mistress' Eyes Are Nothing Like the Sun" (p. 315), "To His Coy Mistress" (p. 419)

◊ ◊ ◊

JOHN UPDIKE
(1932–   )

Ex-Basketball Player
(1958)

> Pearl Avenue runs past the high-school lot,
> Bends with the trolley tracks, and stops, cut off
> Before it has a chance to go two blocks,
> At Colonel McComsky Plaza. Berth's Garage
> 5 Is on the corner facing west, and there,
> Most days, you'll find Flick Webb, who helps Berth out.

---

[1] Go.

Flick stands tall among the idiot pumps—
Five on a side, the old bubble-head style,
Their rubber elbows hanging loose and low.
10 One's nostrils are two S's, and his eyes
An E and O. And one is squat, without
A head at all—more of a football type.

Once Flick played for the high-school team, the Wizards.
He was good: in fact, the best. In '46
15 He bucketed three hundred ninety points,
A county record still. The ball loved Flick.
I saw him rack up thirty-eight or forty
In one home game. His hands were like wild birds.

He never learned a trade, he just sells gas,
20 Checks oil, and changes flats. Once in a while,
As a gag, he dribbles an inner tube,
But most of us remember anyway.
His hands are fine and nervous on the lug wrench.
It makes no difference to the lug wrench, though.

25 Off work, he hangs around Mae's luncheonette.
Grease-gray and kind of coiled, he plays pinball,
Smokes those thin cigars, nurses lemon phosphates.
Flick seldom says a word to Mae, just nods
Beyond her face toward bright applauding tiers
30 Of Necco Wafers, Nibs, and Juju Beads.

READING AND REACTING

1. Explain the use of personification in the second stanza and in the poem's last two lines. What two elements make up each figure of speech? How are the two elements in each pair alike?
2. What kind of figure of speech is each of the following: "His hands were like wild birds" (18); "Grease-gray and kind of coiled" (26)? What other figures of speech can you identify in the poem?
3. **JOURNAL ENTRY** Who do you think this poem's speaker might be? What is his attitude toward Flick Webb? Do you think Flick himself shares this assessment? Explain.

Related Works: "Miss Brill" (p. 71), "Sadie and Maud" (p. 428), *Death of a Salesman* (p. 782)

RANDALL JARRELL
(1914–1965)

The Death of the Ball Turret Gunner
(1945)

From my mother's sleep I fell into the State
And I hunched in its belly till my wet fur froze.
Six miles from earth, loosed from its dream of life,
I woke to black flak and the nightmare fighters.
5 When I died they washed me out of the turret with a hose.

Reading and Reacting

1. Who is the speaker? To what does he compare himself in the poem's first two lines? What words establish this comparison?
2. Contrast the speaker's actual identity with the one he creates for himself in lines 1–2. What elements of his actual situation do you think lead him to characterize himself as he does in these lines?
3. **Journal Entry** Both this poem and "Dulce et Decorum Est" (p. 399) use figurative language to describe the horrors of war. Which poem has a greater impact on you? How does the poem's figurative language contribute to this impact?

Related Works: "An Irish Airman Foresees His Death" (p. 322), "Dulce et Decorum Est" (p. 399)

MARGE PIERCY
(1934–   )

The Secretary Chant
(1973)

My hips are a desk.
From my ears hang
chains of paper clips.
Rubber bands form my hair.
5 My breasts are wells of mimeograph ink.
My feet bear casters.
Buzz. Click.
My head is a badly organized file.
My head is a switchboard

10 where crossed lines crackle.
  Press my fingers
  and in my eyes appear
  credit and debit.
  Zing. Tinkle.
15 My navel is a reject button.
  From my mouth issue canceled reams.
  Swollen, heavy, rectangular
  I am about to be delivered
  of a baby
20 Xerox machine.
  File me under W
  because I wonce
  was
  a woman.

Reading and Reacting

1. Examine each of the poem's figures of speech. Do they all make reasonable comparisons, or are some far-fetched or hard to visualize? Explain the relationship between the secretary and each item with which she is compared.
2. **Journal Entry** Using as many metaphors and similes as you can, write a "chant" about a job you have held.

Related Works: "Like a Winding Sheet" (p. 76), "Girl" (p. 266), "Women" (p. 474), "Metaphors" (p. 541)

◊ ◊ ◊

JOHN DONNE
(1572–1631)

A Valediction: Forbidding Mourning
(1611)

  As virtuous men pass mildly away,
   And whisper to their souls to go,
  Whilst some of their sad friends do say
   The breath goes now, and some say no:

5 So let us melt, and make no noise,
   No tear-floods, nor sigh-tempests move;
  'Twere profanation of our joys
   To tell the laity[1] our love.

---

[1] Here, "common people."

Moving of th' earth brings harms and fears;
10   Men reckon what it did and meant;
But trepidation of the spheres,
   Though greater far, is innocent.

Dull sublunary lovers' love
   (Whose soul is sense) cannot admit
15 Absence, because it doth remove
   Those things which elemented it.

But we, by a love so much refined
   That ourselves know not what it is,
Inter-assurèd of the mind,
20   Care less, eyes, lips, and hands to miss.

Our two souls, therefore, which are one,
   Though I must go, endure not yet
A breach, but an expansion,
   Like gold to airy thinness beat.

25 If they be two, they are two so
   As stiff twin compasses[2] are two:
Thy soul, the fixed foot, makes no show
   To move, but doth, if th' other do.

And though it in the center sit,
30   Yet when the other far doth roam,
It leans and harkens after it,
   And grows erect as that comes home.

Such wilt thou be to me, who must,
   Like th' other foot, obliquely run;
35 Thy firmness makes my circle just,[3]
   And makes me end where I begun.

Reading and Reacting

1. Beginning with line 25, the poem develops an extended metaphor, called a **conceit,** which compares the speaker and his loved one to "twin compasses" (26), attached and yet separate. Why is the compass an especially apt metaphor? What qualities of the compass does the poet emphasize?
2. The poem uses other figures of speech to characterize both the lovers' union and their separation. To what other events does the speaker compare his separation from his loved one? To what

---

[2] The reference here is to the V-shaped instrument used to draw circles, not to the device used to determine direction.
[3] Perfect.

other elements does he compare their attachment? Do you think these comparisons are effective?
3. **JOURNAL ENTRY** To what other object could Donne have compared his loved one and himself? Explain the logic of the extended metaphor you suggest.

Related Works: "How Do I Love Thee?" (p. 317), "To My Dear and Loving Husband" (p. 418), *A Doll House* (p. 599)

HYPERBOLE AND UNDERSTATEMENT

◊ ◊ ◊

Two additional kinds of figurative language, *hyperbole* and *understatement,* also give poets opportunities to suggest meaning beyond the literal level of language.

Hyperbole is intentional exaggeration—saying more than is actually meant. In the poem "Oh, My Love Is like a Red, Red Rose" (p. 407), when the speaker says that he will love his lady until all the seas go dry, he is using hyperbole. **Understatement** is just the opposite—saying less than is meant. When the speaker in the poem "Fire and Ice" (p. 340), weighing two equally grim alternatives for the end of the world, says that "for destruction ice / Is also great / And would suffice," he is using understatement. In both cases, poets rely on their readers to understand that their words are not to be taken literally.

By using hyperbole and understatement, poets attract readers' attention. For example, poets can use hyperbole to convey exaggerated anger or graphic images of horror—and to ridicule and satirize as well as to inflame and shock. With understatement, poets can convey the same kind of powerful emotions subtly, without artifice or embellishment, thereby leading readers to look more closely than they would otherwise do.

The emotionally charged poem that follows uses hyperbole to attract attention, conveying anger and bitterness that seem almost beyond the power of words.

◊ ◊ ◊
SYLVIA PLATH
(1932–1963)

Daddy
(1965)

You do not do, you do not do
Any more, black shoe
In which I have lived like a foot
For thirty years, poor and white,
5 Barely daring to breathe or Achoo.

Daddy, I have had to kill you.
You died before I had time—
Marble-heavy, a bag full of God,
Ghastly statue with one grey toe
10 Big as a Frisco seal

And a head in the freakish Atlantic
Where it pours bean green over blue
In the waters off beautiful Nauset.
I used to pray to recover you.
15 Ach, du.[1]

In the German tongue, in the Polish town[2]
Scraped flat by the roller
Of wars, wars, wars.
But the name of the town is common.
20 My Polack friend

Says there are a dozen or two.
So I never could tell where you
Put your foot, your root,
I never could talk to you.
25 The tongue stuck in my jaw.

It stuck in a barb wire snare.
Ich, ich, ich, ich,[3]
I could hardly speak.
I thought every German was you.
30 And the language obscene

An engine, an engine
Chuffing me off like a Jew.
A Jew to Dachau, Auschwitz, Belsen.[4]
I began to talk like a Jew.
35 I think I may well be a Jew.

The snows of the Tyrol, the clear beer of Vienna
Are not very pure or true.
With my gypsy ancestress and my weird luck
And my Taroc pack and my Taroc pack
40 I may be a bit of a Jew.

---

[1] Ah, you. (German)
[2] Grabôw, where Plath's father was born.
[3] I. (German)
[4] Nazi concentration camps.

I have always been scared of *you*,
With your Luftwaffe,[5] your gobbledygoo.
And your neat moustache
And your Aryan eye, bright blue.
45 Panzer[6]-man, panzer-man, O You—

Not God but a swastika
So black no sky could squeak through.
Every woman adores a Fascist,
The boot in the face, the brute
50 Brute heart of a brute like you.

You stand at the blackboard, daddy,
In the picture I have of you,
A cleft in your chin instead of your foot
But no less a devil for that, no not
55 Any less the black man who

Bit my pretty red heart in two.
I was ten when they buried you.
At twenty I tried to die
And get back, back, back to you.
60 I thought even the bones would do.

But they pulled me out of the sack,
And they stuck me together with glue.
And then I knew what to do.
I made a model of you,
65 A man in black with a Meinkampf[7] look

And a love of the rack and the screw.
And I said I do, I do.
So daddy, I'm finally through.
The black telephone's off at the root,
70 The voices just can't worm through.

If I've killed one man, I've killed two—
The vampire who said he was you
And drank my blood for a year,
Seven years, if you want to know.
75 Daddy, you can lie back now.

---

[5] The German air force.
[6] Protected by armor. The Panzer division was the German armored division.
[7] *Mein Kampf* (My Struggle) is Adolf Hitler's autobiography.

> There's a stake in your fat black heart
> And the villagers never liked you.
> They are dancing and stamping on you.
> They always *knew* it was you.
> 80 Daddy, daddy, you bastard, I'm through.

In her anger and frustration, the speaker sees herself as a helpless victim—a foot entrapped in a shoe, a Jew in a concentration camp—of her father's (and, later, her husband's) absolute tyranny. Thus, her hated father is characterized as a "black shoe," "a bag full of God," a "ghastly statue," and, eventually, a Nazi, a torturer, the devil, a vampire. The poem "Daddy" is widely accepted by scholars as autobiographical, and the fact that Plath's own father was actually neither a Nazi nor a sadist (nor, obviously, the devil or a vampire) makes it clear that the figurative comparisons in the poem are wildly exaggerated. Even so, they may convey the poet's true feelings toward her father—and, perhaps, toward the patriarchal society in which she lived.

Plath uses hyperbole as the medium through which to communicate these emotions to readers who she knows cannot possibly feel the way she does. Her purpose, therefore, is not just to shock but also to enlighten, to persuade, and perhaps even to empower her readers. Throughout the poem, the inflammatory language is set in ironic opposition to the childish, affectionate term "Daddy"—most strikingly in the last line's choked out "Daddy, daddy, you bastard, I'm through." The result of the exaggerated rhetoric is a poem that is vivid and shocking. And, although some might believe that Plath's almost wild exaggeration undermines the poem's impact, others would argue that the powerful figurative language is necessary to convey the extent of the speaker's rage.

Like "Daddy," the next poem presents a situation whose emotional impact is devastating. In this case, however, the poet does not use emotional language; instead, he uses understatement, presenting the events without embellishment.

◊ ◊ ◊

DAVID HUDDLE
(1942–)

Holes Commence Falling
(1979)

> The lead & zinc company
> owned the mineral rights
> to the whole town anyway,
> and after drilling holes
> 5 for 3 or 4 years,

       they finally found the right
       place and sunk a mine shaft.
       We were proud
       of all that digging,
10   even though nobody from
       town got hired. They
       were going to dig right
       under New River and hook up
       with the mine at Austinville.
15   Then people's wells
       started drying up just like
       somebody'd shut off a faucet,
       and holes commenced falling,
       big chunks of people's yards
20   would drop 5 or 6 feet,
       houses would shift and crack.
       Now and then the company'd
       pay out a little money
       in damages; they got a truck
25   to haul water and sell it
       to the people whose wells
       had dried up, but most
       everybody agreed the
       situation wasn't
30   serious.

    Although "Holes Commence Falling" relates a tragic sequence of events, the tone of the poem is matter-of-fact and the language is understated. Certainly the speaker could have overdramatized the events, using inflated rhetoric to denounce big business and to predict disastrous events for the future. At the very least, he could have colored the events with realistic emotions, assigning blame to the lead and zinc company with justifiable anger. Instead, the speaker is so restrained, so nonchalant, so passive that readers must supply the missing emotions themselves—realizing, for example, that when the speaker concludes "everybody agreed the / situation wasn't / serious," he means just the opposite.
    Throughout the poem, unpleasant events are presented without comment or emotion. As it proceeds, the poem traces the high and low points in the town's fortunes, but for every hope ("We were proud / of all that digging") there is a disappointment ("even though nobody from / town got hired"). The lead and zinc company offers some compensation for the damage it does, but never enough. The present tense verb of the poem's title indicates that the problems the town faces—wells drying up, yards dropping, houses shifting and cracking—are regular occurrences. Eventually, readers come to see that what is not expressed, what lurks just below the surface—anger, powerlessness, resentment, hopelessness—is the poem's real subject. The speaker's

laconic speech and flat tone seem to suggest an attitude of resignation, but the obvious contrast between the understated tone and the seriousness of the problem creates a sense of irony that makes the speaker's real attitude toward the lead and zinc company clear.

Poems for Further Reading: Hyperbole and Understatement

ANNE BRADSTREET
(1612?–1672)

To My Dear and Loving Husband
(1678)

If ever two were one, then surely we.
If ever man were lov'd by wife, then thee;
If ever wife was happy in a man,
Compare with me ye women if you can.
5 I prize thy love more than whole Mines of gold,
Or all the riches that the East doth hold.
My love is such that Rivers cannot quench,
Nor ought but love from thee, give recompense.
Thy love is such I can no way repay,
10 The heavens reward thee manifold I pray.
Then while we live, in love let's so persever,
That when we live no more, we may live ever.

Reading and Reacting

1. Review the claims the poem's speaker makes about her husband in lines 5–8. Are such exaggerated declarations of love necessary, or would the rest of the poem be sufficient to convey the extent of her devotion to her husband?
2. **Journal Entry** Compare this poem's declarations of love to those of John Donne's speaker in "A Valediction: Forbidding Mourning" (p. 411). Which speaker do you believe is more convincing? Why?

Related Works: "A Rose for Emily" (p. 52), "Bright Star! Would I Were Steadfast as Thou Art" (p. 533).

ANDREW MARVELL
(1621–1678)

To His Coy Mistress
(1681)

    Had we but world enough and time,
    This coyness, lady, were no crime.
    We would sit down and think which way
    To walk, and pass our long love's day.
5 Thou by the Indian Ganges' side
    Should'st rubies find; I by the tide
    Of Humber[1] would complain. I would
    Love you ten years before the Flood,
    And you should, if you please, refuse
10 Till the conversion of the Jews.
    My vegetable love should grow
    Vaster than empires, and more slow.
    An hundred years should go to praise
    Thine eyes, and on thy forehead gaze,
15 Two hundred to adore each breast,
    But thirty thousand to the rest.
    An age at least to every part,
    And the last age should show your heart.
    For, lady, you deserve this state,
20 Nor would I love at lower rate.
       But at my back I always hear
    Time's wingèd chariot hurrying near,
    And yonder all before us lie
    Deserts of vast eternity.
25 Thy beauty shall no more be found,
    Nor in thy marble vault shall sound
    My echoing song; then worms shall try
    That long preserved virginity,
    And your quaint honor turn to dust,
30 And into ashes all my lust.
    The grave's a fine and private place,
    But none, I think, do there embrace.
       Now therefore, while the youthful hue
    Sits on thy skin like morning glew[2]
35 And while thy willing soul transpires

---

[1] An estuary in the east coast of England.
[2] Dew.

At every pore with instant fires,
Now let us sport us while we may;
And now, like amorous birds of prey,
Rather at once our time devour
40 Than languish in his slow-chapped[3] power.
Let us roll all our strength and all
Our sweetness up into one ball
And tear our pleasures with rough strife
Thorough the iron gates of life.
45 Thus, though we cannot make our sun
Stand still, yet we will make him run.

READING AND REACTING

1. In this poem, Marvell's speaker sets out to convince a reluctant woman to become his lover. In order to make his case more convincing, he uses hyperbole, exaggerating time periods, sizes, spaces, and the possible fate of the woman, should she refuse him. Identify as many examples of hyperbole as you can.
2. The tone of "To His Coy Mistress" is more whimsical than serious. Given this tone, what do you see as the purpose of Marvell's use of hyperbole?
3. **JOURNAL ENTRY** Using contemporary prose, paraphrase the first four lines of the poem. Then, beginning with the word *But*, write a few additional sentences, continuing the argument Marvell's speaker makes.

Related Works: "Where Are You Going, Where Have You Been?" (p. 268), "The Passionate Shepherd to His Love" (p. 313), "To the Virgins, to Make Much of Time" (p. 347), *The Brute* (p. 668)

✧ ✧ ✧

ROBERT FROST
(1874–1963)

"Out, Out—"
(1916)

The buzz saw snarled and rattled in the yard
And made dust and dropped stove-length sticks of wood,
Sweet-scented stuff when the breeze drew across it.
And from there those that lifted eyes could count

---
[3] Slowly crushing.

  5 Five mountain ranges one behind the other
      Under the sunset far into Vermont.
      And the saw snarled and rattled, snarled and rattled,
      As it ran light, or had to bear a load.
      And nothing happened: day was all but done.
10 Call it a day, I wish they might have said
      To please the boy by giving him the half hour
      That a boy counts so much when saved from work.
      His sister stood beside them in her apron
      To tell them "Supper." At the word, the saw,
15 As if to prove saws knew what supper meant,
      Leaped out at the boy's hand, or seemed to leap—
      He must have given the hand. However it was,
      Neither refused the meeting. But the hand!
      The boy's first outcry was a rueful laugh,
20 As he swung toward them holding up the hand
      Half in appeal, but half as if to keep
      The life from spilling. Then the boy saw all—
      Since he was old enough to know, big boy
      Doing a man's work, though a child at heart—
25 He saw all spoiled. "Don't let him cut my hand off—
      The doctor, when he comes. Don't let him, sister!"
      So. But the hand was gone already.
      The doctor put him in the dark of ether.
      He lay and puffed his lips out with his breath.
30 And then—the watcher at his pulse took fright.
      No one believed. They listened at his heart.
      Little—less—nothing!—and that ended it.
      No more to build on there. And they, since they
      Were not the one dead, turned to their affairs.

READING AND REACTING

1. The poem's title is an **allusion** to a passage in Shakespeare's *Macbeth* (5.5.23–28) that attacks the brevity and meaninglessness of life in very emotional terms:

   > "Out, out brief candle!
   > Life's but a walking shadow, a poor player,
   > That struts and frets his hour upon the stage
   > And then is heard no more. It is a tale
   > Told by an idiot, full of sound and fury,
   > Signifying nothing."

   What idea do you think Frost wants to convey through the title "Out, Out—"?

2. Explain why each of the following qualifies as understatement:
   "Neither refused the meeting." (18)
   "He saw all spoiled." (25)
   ". . . that ended it." (32)
   "No more to build on there." (33)

   Can you identify any other examples of understatement in the poem?
3. **JOURNAL ENTRY** Do you think the poem's impact is strengthened or weakened by its understated tone? Why?

Related Works: "The Lottery" (p. 209), "What Were They Like?" (p. 324), "Hope" (p. 352), "The Death of the Ball Turret Gunner" (p. 410)

✧ ✧ ✧

DONALD HALL
(1928–)

My Son, My Executioner
(1955)

My son, my executioner,
   I take you in my arms,
Quiet and small and just astir,
   And whom my body warms.

5 Sweet death, small son, our instrument
   Of immortality,
Your cries and hungers document
   Our bodily decay.

We twenty-five and twenty-two,
10   Who seemed to live forever,
Observe enduring life in you
   And start to die together.

READING AND REACTING

1. Because the speaker is a young man holding his newborn son in his arms, the equation in line 1 comes as a shock. What is Hall's purpose in opening with such a startling statement?
2. In what sense is the comparison between baby and executioner a valid one? Could you argue that, given the underlying similarities between the two, Hall is *not* using hyperbole? Explain.

Related Works: "Doe Season" (p. 230), "That Time of Year Thou Mayst in Me Behold" (p. 300), "Morning Song" (p. 346), "Sailing to Byzantium" (p. 559)

MARGARET ATWOOD
(1939–)

You Fit into Me
(1971)

you fit into me
like a hook into an eye

a fish hook
an open eye

READING AND REACTING

1. What connotations does Atwood expect readers to associate with the phrase "you fit into me"? What does the speaker seem at first to mean by "like a hook into an eye" in line 2?
2. The speaker's shift to the brutal suggestions of lines 3 and 4 is calculated to shock readers. Does the use of hyperbole here have another purpose in the context of the poem? Explain.

Related Works: "Popular Mechanics" (p. 265), "Daddy" (p. 413), *A Doll House* (p. 599)

METONYMY AND SYNECDOCHE

Metonymy and synecdoche are two related figures of speech. **Metonymy** is the substitution of the name of one thing for the name of another thing that most readers associate with the first—for example, using *hired gun* to mean "paid assassin" or *suits* to mean "business executives." A specific kind of metonymy, called **synecdoche,** is the substitution of a part for the whole (for example, using *bread*—as in "Give us this day our daily bread"—to mean "food") or the whole for a part (for example, saying "You can take the boy out of Brooklyn, but you can't take Brooklyn [meaning its distinctive traits] out of the boy"). With metonymy and synecdoche, instead of describing something by saying it is like something else (as in simile) or by equating it with something else (as in metaphor), writers can characterize an object or concept by using a term that evokes it. The following poem illustrates the use of synecdoche.

RICHARD LOVELACE
(1618–1658)

To Lucasta Going to the Wars
(1649)

Tell me not, Sweet, I am unkind
   That from the nunnery
Of thy chaste breast and quiet mind,
   To war and arms I fly.

5 True, a new mistress now I chase,
   The first foe in the field;
And with a stronger faith embrace
   A sword, a horse, a shield.

Yet this inconstancy is such
10   As you too shall adore;
I could not love thee, Dear, so much,
   Loved I not Honor more.

Here, Lovelace's use of synecdoche allows him to condense a number of complex ideas into a very few words. In line 3, when the speaker says that he is flying from his loved one's "chaste breast and quiet mind," he is using "breast" and "mind" to stand for all his loved one's physical and intellectual attributes. In line 8, when he says that he is embracing "A sword, a horse, a shield," he is using these three items to represent all the trappings of war—and, thus, to represent war itself.

APOSTROPHE

With **apostrophe,** a poem's speaker addresses an absent person or thing—for example, a historical or literary figure or even an inanimate object or an abstract concept.

In the following poem, the speaker addresses Vincent van Gogh.

SONIA SANCHEZ
(1934–   )

On Passing thru Morgantown, Pa.
(1984)

i saw you
vincent van
gogh perched
on those pennsylvania
5   cornfields communing
amid secret black
bird societies. yes.
i'm sure that was
you exploding your
10 fantastic delirium
while in the
distance
red indian
hills beckoned.

Expecting her readers to be aware that van Gogh is a Dutch postimpressionist painter known for his mental instability as well as for his art, Sanchez is able to give added meaning to a phrase such as "fantastic delirium" as well as to the poem's visual images. The speaker sees van Gogh perched like a black bird on a fence, and at the same time she also sees what he sees. Like van Gogh, then, the speaker sees the Pennsylvania cornfields as both a natural landscape and an "exploding" work of art.

Checklist: Writing about Figures of Speech

- ✓ Are any figures of speech present in the poem? Identify each example of simile, metaphor, personification, hyperbole, understatement, metonymy, synecdoche, and apostrophe.
- ✓ What two elements are being compared in each use of simile, metaphor, and personification? Is the comparison logical? What characteristics are shared by the two items being compared?
- ✓ How do figures of speech contribute to the impact of the poem as a whole?

- ✓ Does the poet use hyperbole? Why? For example, is it used to move or to shock readers, or is its use intended to produce a humorous or satirical effect?
- ✓ Does the poet use understatement? For what purpose? Would more straightforward language be more effective?
- ✓ In metonymy and synecdoche, what item is being substituted for another? What purpose does the substitution serve?
- ✓ If the poem includes apostrophe, whom or what does the speaker address? What is accomplished through the use of apostrophe?

◆ Writing Suggestions: Figures of Speech

1. Various figures of speech are often used to portray characters in a poem. Choose two or three poems that focus on a single character—for example, "Ex-Basketball Player" (p. 408) or "Richard Cory" (p. 544)—and explain how figures of speech are used to characterize each poem's central figure. If you like, you may write about poems that focus on real (rather than fictional) people—for example, "Emmett Till" (p. 523) or "Medgar Evers" (p. 509).
2. Write an essay in which you discuss the different ways poets use figures of speech to examine the nature of poetry itself. What kinds of figures of speech do poets use to describe their craft? (You might begin by reading the three poems about poetry that open Chapter 10.)
3. Write a letter replying to the speaker in a poem by Marvell, Bradstreet, Donne, or Burns that appears in this chapter. Use figurative language to express the depth of your love and the extent of your devotion.
4. Choose two or three poems that have a common subject—for example, love, nature, war, art, or mortality—and write a paper in which you draw some general conclusions about the relative effectiveness of the poems' use of figurative language to examine that subject. (If you like, you may focus on the poems clustered under the heads "Poems about Love," "Poems about War," and "Poems about Parents" in Chapter 10.)
5. Select a poem and a short story that treat the same subject matter, and write a paper in which you compare their use of figures of speech.

Chapter 15

Sound

WALT WHITMAN
(1819–1892)

Had I the Choice[1]

Had I the choice to tally greatest bards,
To limn[2] their portraits, stately, beautiful, and emulate at will,
Homer with all his wars and warriors—Hector, Achilles, Ajax,
Or Shakespeare's woe-entangled Hamlet, Lear, Othello—Tennyson's fair ladies,
5 Meter or wit the best, or choice conceit to wield in perfect rhyme, delight of singers;
These, these, O sea, all these I'd gladly barter,
Would you the undulation of one wave, its trick to me transfer,
Or breathe one breath of yours upon my verse,
And leave its odor there.

Rhythm

Rhythm—the regular recurrence of sounds—is at the heart of all natural phenomena: the beating of a heart, the lapping of waves against the shore, the croaking of frogs on a summer's night, the whispering of wheat swaying in the wind. In fact, even mechanical phenomena, such as the movement of rush-hour traffic through a city's streets, have a kind of rhythm. Poetry, which explores these phenomena, often tries to reflect the same rhythms. Walt Whitman makes this point in "Had I the

---

[1] Publication date is not available.
[2] To describe, depict.

427

Choice" when he says that he would gladly trade the "perfect rhyme" of Shakespeare for the ability to reproduce "the undulation of one wave" in his verse.

Effective public speakers frequently repeat key words and phrases to create rhythm. In his speech "I Have a Dream," for example, Martin Luther King, Jr., repeats the phrase "I have a dream" to create a cadence that ties the central section of the speech together:

> I say to you today, my friends, even though we face the difficulties of today and tomorrow, *I still have a dream*. It is a dream deeply rooted in the American dream. *I have a dream* that one day this nation will rise up and live out the true meaning of its creed: "We hold these truths to be self-evident, that all men are created equal." *I have a dream* that one day, on the red hills of Georgia, sons of former slaves and the sons of former slave owners will be able to sit down together at the table of brotherhood. *I have a dream* that one day even the state of Mississippi, a state sweltering with the heat of injustice, sweltering with the heat of oppression, will be transformed into an oasis of freedom and justice. *I have a dream* that my four little children will one day live in a nation where they will not be judged by the color of their skin, but by the content of their character.

Poets too create rhythm by using repeated words and phrases, as Gwendolyn Brooks does in the poem that follows.

GWENDOLYN BROOKS
(1917–   )

Sadie and Maud
(1945)

Maud went to college.
Sadie stayed at home.
Sadie scraped life
With a fine-tooth comb.

5 She didn't leave a tangle in.
Her comb found every strand.
Sadie was one of the livingest chits
In all the land.

Sadie bore two babies
10 Under her maiden name.
Maud and Ma and Papa
Nearly died of shame.

When Sadie said her last so-long
Her girls struck out from home.
15 (Sadie had left as heritage
Her fine-tooth comb.)

Maud, who went to college,
Is a thin brown mouse.
She is living all alone
20 In this old house.

Much of the force of this poem comes from its balanced structure and regular rhyme and meter, underscored by the repeated words "Sadie" and "Maud," which shift the focus from one subject to the other and back again ("Maud went to college / Sadie stayed home"). The poem's singsong rhythm recalls the rhymes children recite when jumping rope. This evocation of carefree childhood ironically contrasts with the adult realities that both Sadie and Maud face as they grow up: Sadie stays at home and has two children out of wedlock; Maud goes to college and ends up "a thin brown mouse." The speaker implies that the alternatives Sadie and Maud represent are both undesirable. Although Sadie "scraped life / with a fine-tooth comb," she dies young and leaves nothing to her girls but her desire to experience life. Maud, who graduated from college, shuts out life and cuts herself off from her roots.

Just as the repetition of words and phrases can create rhythm, so can the distribution of words among the lines of a poem—and even the appearance of words on a printed page. How a poem looks is especially important in **open form** poetry (see p. 463), which dispenses with traditional patterns of versification. In the following excerpt from a poem by E. E. Cummings, for example, an unusual arrangement of words forces readers to slow down and then to speed up, creating a rhythm that emphasizes a key phrase—"The / lily":

the moon is hiding
in her hair.
The
lily
of heaven
full of all dreams,
draws down.

Poetic rhythm—the repetition of stresses and pauses—is an essential element in poetry. Rhythm helps to establish a poem's mood, and, in combination with other poetic elements, it conveys the poet's emphasis and helps communicate the poem's meaning. Although rhythm can be affected by the regular repetition of words and phrases or by the arrangement of words into lines, poetic rhythm is largely created by **meter,** the recurrence of regular units of stressed and unstressed syllables.

METER

◆ ◆ ◆

A **stress** (or accent) occurs when one syllable is emphasized more than another, unstressed, syllable: *fór • ceps, bá • sic, il • lú • sion, ma • lár • i • a*. In a poem, even one-syllable words can be stressed to create a particular effect. For example, in Elizabeth Barrett Browning's line "How do I love thee? Let me count the ways," the metrical pattern that places stress on "love" creates one meaning; stressing "I" would create another.

Scansion is the process of analyzing patterns of stressed and unstressed syllables within a line. The most common method of poetic notation involves indicating stressed syllables with a ´ and unstressed syllables with a ˘. Although scanning lines gives readers the "beat" of the poem, scansion only approximates the sound of spoken language, which contains an infinite variety of stresses. By providing a graphic representation of the stressed and unstressed syllables of a poem, scansion aids understanding, but it is no substitute for reading the poem aloud and experimenting with various patterns of emphasis.

The basic unit of meter is a **foot**—a group of syllables with a fixed pattern of stressed and unstressed syllables. The following chart illustrates the most common types of metrical feet in English and American verse.

Foot	Stress Pattern	Example
Iamb	˘ ´	They pace | in sleek | chi val|ric cer|tain ty (Adrienne Rich)
Trochee	´ ˘	Thou, when | thou re|turn'st, wilt | tell me. (John Donne)
Anapest	˘ ˘ ´	With a hey, | and a ho, | and a hey | nonino (William Shakespeare)
Dactyl	´ ˘ ˘	Constantly | risking ab|surdity (Lawrence Ferlinghetti)

Iambic and *anapestic* meters are called *rising meters* because they progress from unstressed to stressed syllables. *Trochaic* and *dactylic* meters are called *falling meters* because they progress from stressed to unstressed syllables.

The following types of metrical feet, less common than those listed above, are used to emphasize or to provide variety rather than to create the dominant meter of a poem.

Spondee | | Pomp, pride | and circumstance of glorious war! (William Shakespeare)

Pyrrhic   ⌣⌣   A horse! a horse! My king|dom for | a horse! (William Shakespeare)

A metric line of poetry is measured by the number of feet it contains.

monometer one foot   **pentameter** five feet
dimeter two feet   **hexameter** six feet
trimeter three feet   **heptameter** seven feet
tetrameter four feet   **octameter** eight feet

The name for a metrical pattern of a line of verse identifies the name of the foot used and the number of feet the line contains. For example, the most common foot in English poetry is the **iamb,** most often occurring in lines of three or five feet.

Eight hun|dred of | the brave   Iambic trimeter

(William Cowper)

O, how | much more | doth beau|ty beau|teous seem   Iambic pentameter

(William Shakespeare)

Because **iambic pentameter** is so well suited to the rhythms of English speech, writers frequently use it in plays and poems. Shakespeare's plays, for example, are written in unrhymed lines of iambic pentameter called **blank verse** (see p. 454).

Many other material combinations are also possible; a few are illustrated here:

    / ˘   / ˘   / ˘
Like a | high-born | maiden   Trochaic trimeter
(Percy Bysshe Shelley)

    ˘ ˘ /   ˘ ˘ /
The As|syrian came down | Anapestic tetrameter
˘ ˘ /   ˘ ˘ /
like the wolf | on the fold
(Lord Byron)

    / ˘ ˘   / ˘ ˘
Maid en most | beau ti ful | Dactylic hexameter
/ ˘ ˘   / ˘ ˘   /
mother most | boun ti ful, | la
˘ ˘ /   /
dy of | lands, (A. C. Swinburne)

    ˘ / ˘ / ˘ / ˘
The yel|low fog | that rubs | its   Iambic heptameter
/ ˘ / ˘ /
back | upon | the win |
˘ /
dow-panes (T. S. Eliot)

Scansion can be an extremely technical process, and when readers become bogged down with anapests and dactyls, they can easily forget that poetic meter is not an end in itself. Meter should be appropriate for the ideas expressed by the poem, and it should help to create a suitable tone. A light, skipping rhythm, for example, would be inappropriate for an **elegy**, and a slow, heavy rhythm would surely be out of place in an **epigram** or a limerick. The following lines from the poem "Metrical Feet," by Samuel Taylor Coleridge, illustrate the different meters discussed above:

    / ˘ / ˘   / ˘ / ˘
Trochee trips from long to short;
From long to long in solemn sort
    /   /   /   /   /
Slow Spondee stalks; strong foot! yet ill able
/ ˘ ˘   / ˘ ˘   / ˘ ˘ /
Ever to come up with Dactyl trisyllable.
    ˘ / ˘ / ˘ / ˘ /
Iambics march from short to long—

With a leap and a bound the swift Anapests throng;
One syllable long, with one short at each side,
Amphibrachys hastes with a stately stride—
First and last being long, middle short, Amphimacer
Strikes his thundering hoofs like a proud high-bred Racer.

A poet may use one kind of meter—iambic meter, for example—throughout a poem. Even so, the poet may vary line length to relieve monotony or to accommodate the demands of meaning or emphasis. In the following poem, the poet uses iambic lines of different lengths.

◊ ◊ ◊

EMILY DICKINSON
(1830–1886)

I Like to See It Lap the Miles
(1891)

I like to see it lap the Miles—
And lick the Valleys up—
And stop to feed itself at Tanks—
And then—prodigious step

5 Around a Pile of Mountains—
And supercilious peer
In Shanties—by the sides of Roads—
And then a Quarry pare

To fit its Ribs
10 And crawl between
Complaining all the while
In horrid—hooting stanza—
Then chase itself down Hill—

And neigh like Boanerges[1]—
15 Then—punctual as a Star
Stop—docile and omnipotent
At its own stable door—

---

[1] A vociferous preacher and orator. Also, the name, meaning "son of thunder," Jesus gave to apostles John and James because of their fiery zeal.

This poem is a single sentence that, except for some short pauses, stretches unbroken from beginning to end. Iambic lines of varying lengths actually suggest the movements of the train that the poet describes. Lines of iambic tetrameter, such as the first, give readers a sense of the train's steady, rhythmic movement across a flat landscape, and shorter lines ("To fit its Ribs / And crawl between") suggest the train's slowing motion. Beginning with two iambic dimeter lines and progressing to iambic trimeter lines, the third stanza increases in speed just like the train that is racing downhill "In horrid—hooting stanza—."

A poet can also use more than one type of metrical foot. Any variation in a metrical pattern—the substitution of a trochee for an iamb, for instance—immediately calls attention to itself. Poets are aware of this fact and use it to their advantage. For example, in line 16 of "I Like to See It Lap the Miles," the poet departs from iambic meter by placing unexpected stress on the first word, *stop*. By emphasizing this word, the poet brings the flow of the poem to an abrupt halt, suggesting the jolt riders experience when a train comes to a stop. In the following segment from "The Rime of the Ancient Mariner," Samuel Taylor Coleridge also departs from his poem's dominant meter:

The ship | was cheered, | the har|bor cleared,

Merri|ly did | we drop

Below | the kirk, | below | the hill,

Below | the light|house top.

Although these lines are arranged in iambic tetrameter, the poet uses a trochee in the second line, breaking the meter in order to accommodate the natural pronunciation of "merrily" as well as to place stress on the word.

Another way of varying the meter is to introduce a pause in the rhythm known as a **caesura**—a Latin word meaning "a cutting"—within a line. When scanning a poem, you indicate a caesura with two parallel lines: ‖. Unless a line of poetry is extremely short, it probably will contain a caesura.

A caesura occurs after a punctuation mark or at a natural break in phrasing:

How do I love thee? ‖ Let me count the ways.
Elizabeth Barrett Browning

Two loves I have ‖ of comfort and despair.
William Shakespeare

High on a throne of royal state, ‖ which far
Outshone the wealth of Ormus ‖ and of Ind
John Milton

Sometimes, more than one caesura occurs in a single line:

> 'Tis good. ‖ Go to the gate. ‖ Somebody knocks.
> WILLIAM SHAKESPEARE

Although the end of a line may mark the end of a metrical unit, it does not always coincide with the end of a sentence. Poets may choose to indicate a pause at this point, or they may continue, without a break, to the next line. Lines that have distinct pauses at the end—usually signaled by punctuation—are called **end-stopped lines.** Lines that do not end with strong pauses are called **run-on lines.** (Sometimes the term **enjambment** is used to describe this type of line.) End-stopped lines can seem formal, or even forced, because their length is rigidly dictated by the poem's meter, rhythm, and rhyme scheme. In the following excerpt from John Keats's "La Belle Dame sans Merci: A Ballad" (p. 531), for example, rhythm, meter, and rhyme dictate the pauses that occur at the ends of the lines:

> O, what can ail thee, knight-at-arms,
>   Alone and palely loitering?
> The sedge has withered from the lake,
>   And no birds sing.

In contrast to end-stopped lines, run-on lines seem more natural. Because their ending points are determined by the rhythms of speech and by the meaning and emphasis the poet wishes to convey rather than by meter and rhyme, run-on lines are suited to the open form of much modern poetry. In the following lines from the 1967 poem "We Have Come Home," by the poet Lenrie Peters, run-on lines give readers the sense of spoken language:

> We have come home
> From the bloodless war
> With sunken hearts
> Our boots full of pride—
> From the true massacre of the soul
> When we have asked
> 'What does it cost
> To be loved and left alone?'

Rather than relying exclusively on end-stopped or run-on lines, poets often use a combination of the two to produce the effects they want. In the following lines from "Pot Roast" by Mark Strand, for example, the juxtaposition of end-stopped and run-on lines controls the rhythm:

>   I gaze upon the roast,
>   that is sliced and laid out

on my plate
and over it
I spoon the juices
of carrot and onion.
And for once I do not regret
the passage of time.

❖ Poems for Further Reading: Rhythm and Meter

ADRIENNE RICH
(1929–)

Aunt Jennifer's Tigers
(1951)

Aunt Jennifer's tigers prance across a screen,
Bright topaz denizens of a world of green.
They do not fear the men beneath the tree;
They pace in sleek chivalric certainty.

5 Aunt Jennifer's fingers fluttering through her wool
Find even the ivory needle hard to pull.
The massive weight of Uncle's wedding band
Sits heavily upon Aunt Jennifer's hand.

When Aunt is dead, her terrified hands will lie
10 Still ringed with ordeals she was mastered by.
The tigers in the panel that she made
Will go on prancing, proud and unafraid.

Reading and Reacting

1. What is the dominant metrical pattern of the poem? In what way does the meter enhance the contrast the poem develops?
2. The lines in the first stanza are end-stopped, and those in the second and third stanzas combine end-stopped and run-on lines. What does the poet achieve by varying the rhythm?
3. What ideas do the caesuras in the first and fourth lines of the last stanza emphasize?
4. **Journal Entry** What is the speaker's opinion of Aunt Jennifer's marriage? Do you think she is commenting on this particular marriage or on marriage in general?

Related Works: "Miss Brill" (p. 71), "Everday Use" (p. 217), "Rooming Houses Are Old Women" (p. 406), "Ethics" (p. 540)

ETHERIDGE KNIGHT
(1931–1991)

For Malcolm,[1] a Year After
(1986)

Compose for Red[2] a proper verse;
Adhere to foot and strict iamb;
Control the burst of angry words
Or they might boil and break the dam.
5 Or they might boil and overflow
And drench me, drown me, drive me mad.
So swear no oath, so shed no tear,
And sing no song blue Baptist sad.
Evoke no image, stir no flame,
10 And spin no yarn across the air.
Make empty anglo tea lace words—
Make them dead white and dry bone bare.

Compose a verse for Malcolm man,
And make it rime and make it prim.
15 The verse will die—as all men do—
But not the memory of him!
Death might come singing sweet like C,
Or knocking like the old folk say,
The moon and stars may pass away,
20 But not the anger of that day.

READING AND REACTING

1. Why do you think Knight chooses to write a "proper verse" in "strict iamb"? Do you think this meter is an appropriate choice for his subject?
2. What sounds and words are repeated in this poem? How does this repetition enhance the poem's rhythm?
3. Where in the poem does Knight use caesuras? Why does he use this device in each instance?
4. **JOURNAL ENTRY** How would you describe the mood of the speaker? Is the poem's meter consistent with his mood or in conflict with it? Explain.

Related Works: "To an Athlete Dying Young" (p.382), "Medgar Evers" (p. 509), "If We Must Die" (p. 536)

---

[1] Malcolm X.
[2] Malcolm X's nickname when he was a young man.

Alliteration and Assonance

♦ ♦ ♦

Just as poetry depends on rhythm, it also depends on the sounds of individual words. An effect pleasing to the ear, such as "Did he who made the Lamb make thee?" from William Blake's "The Tyger" (p. 506), is called **euphony**. A jarring or discordant effect, such as "The vorpal blade went snicker-snack!" from Lewis Carroll's "Jabberwocky" (p. 449), is called **cacophony**.

One of the earliest, and perhaps the most primitive, methods of enhancing sound is **onomatopoeia**, which occurs when the sound of a word echoes its meaning, as it does in common words such as *bang*, *crash*, and *hiss*. Poets make broad application of this technique by using combinations of words that suggest a correspondence between sound and meaning, as Edgar Allan Poe does in the following lines from his poem "The Bells":

> Yet the ear, it fully knows,
>   By the twanging
>   And the clanging,
> How the danger ebbs and flows;
> Yet the ear distinctly tells,
>   In the jangling
>   And the wrangling
> How the danger sinks and swells
> By the sinking or the swelling in the anger of the bells—
>   Of the bells,—
>   Of the bells, bells, bells, bells [. . .].

Poe's primary objective in this poem is to re-create the sound of ringing bells. Although he succeeds, the poem (113 lines long in its entirety) is extremely tedious. A more subtle use of onomatopoetic words appears in the following passage from *An Essay on Criticism* by Alexander Pope:

> Soft is the strain when Zephyr gently blows,
> And the smooth stream in smoother numbers flows;
> But when the loud surges lash the sounding shore,
> The hoarse, rough verse should like the torrent roar:
> When Ajax strives some rock's vast weight to throw,
> The line too Labors, and the words move slow.

After earlier admonishing readers that sound must echo sense, Pope uses onomatopoetic words such as *lash* and *roar* to convey the fury of the sea, and he uses repeated consonants to echo the sounds these words suggest. Notice, for example, how the *s* and *m* sounds suggest the gently blowing Zephyr and the flowing of the smooth stream and how the series of *r* sounds echoes the torrent's roar.

Alliteration—the repetition of consonant sounds in consecutive or neighboring words, usually at the beginning of words—is another device used to enhance sound in a poem. Both Poe ("sinks and swells") and Pope ("smooth stream") make use of alliteration in the preceding excerpts, and so does Alfred, Lord Tennyson in the following poem.

◊ ◊ ◊

ALFRED, LORD TENNYSON
(1809–1892)

The Eagle
(1851)

He clasps the crag with crooked hands;
Close to the sun in lonely lands,
Ringed with the azure world, he stands.

The wrinkled sea beneath him crawls:
5   He watches from his mountain walls,
And like a thunderbolt he falls.

Throughout the poem, *c*, *l*, and *w* sounds occur repeatedly. The poem is drawn together by the recurrence of these sounds and, as a result, it flows smoothly from beginning to end.

The following poem also uses alliteration to create special aural effects.

◊ ◊ ◊

N. SCOTT MOMADAY
(1934–)

Comparatives
(1976)

Sunlit sea,
the drift of fronds,
and banners
of bobbing boats—
5   the seaside
upon the planks,
the coil and
crescent of flesh
extending
10 just into death.

       Even so,
       in the distant,
       inland sea,
       a shadow runs,
 15   radiant,
       rude in the rock:
       fossil fish,
       fissure of bone
       forever.
 20   It is perhaps
       the same thing,
       an agony
       twice perceived.

       It is most like
 25   wind on waves—
       mere commotion,
       mute and mean,
       perceptible—
       that is all.

Throughout the poem, Momaday uses alliteration to create a pleasing effect and to link certain words and ideas. Each stanza of the poem has its own alliterative pattern: the first stanza contains repeated *s* and *b* sounds, the second stanza contains repeated *r* and *f* sounds, and the third stanza contains repeated *w* and *m* sounds. Not only does this use of alliteration create a pleasing effect, but also it reinforces the development of the poem's theme from stanza to stanza.

Assonance—the repetition of the same or similar vowel sounds, especially in stressed syllables—can also enrich a poem. When used solely to produce aural effects, assonance can be distracting. Consider, for example, the clumsiness of the repeated vowel sounds in Tennyson's "Many a morning on the moorland did we hear the copses ring [. . .]." When used more subtly, however, assonance can enhance a poem's effectiveness.

Assonance can also unify an entire poem. In the following poem, assonance emphasizes the thematic connections among words and thus unifies the poem's ideas.

ROBERT HERRICK
(1591–1674)

Delight in Disorder
(1648)

  A sweet disorder in the dress
  Kindles in clothes a wantonness.
  A lawn[1] about the shoulders thrown
  Into a fine distractión;
5 An erring lace, which here and there
  Enthralls the crimson stomacher;[2]
  A cuff neglectful, and thereby
  Ribbons to flow confusedly;
  A winning wave, deserving note,
10 In the tempestuous petticoat;
  A careless shoestring, in whose tie
  I see a wild civility;
  Do more bewitch me than when art
  Is too precise in every part.

Repeated vowel sounds extend throughout this poem—for instance, "shoulders" and "thrown" in line 3; and "tie," "wild," and "precise" in lines 11, 12, and 14. Using alliteration as well as assonance, Herrick subtly links certain words—"tempestuous petticoat," for example. By connecting these words, he calls attention to the pattern of imagery that helps to convey the poem's theme.

Rhyme

In addition to alliteration and assonance, poets create sound patterns with **rhyme**—the use of matching sounds in two or more words: "tight" and "might"; "born" and "horn"; "sleep" and "deep." For a rhyme to be **perfect,** final vowel and consonant sounds must be the same, as they are in each of the preceding examples. **Imperfect rhyme** (also called *near rhyme, slant rhyme, approximate rhyme,* or *consonance*) occurs when the final consonant sounds in two words are the same but vowel sounds are different—"learn/barn" or "pads/lids," for example. William Stafford uses imperfect rhyme in "Traveling through the Dark" (p. 550) when he

---

[1] A shawl made of fine fabric.
[2] A heavily embroidered garment worn by females over the chest and stomach.

rhymes "road" with "dead." Finally, **eye rhyme** occurs when two words look as if they should rhyme but do not—for example, "watch" and "catch."

Rhyme can also be classified according to the position of the rhyming syllables in a line of verse. The most common type of rhyme is **end rhyme,** which occurs at the end of a line:

> Tyger! Tyger! burning <u>bright</u>
> In the forests of the <u>night</u>
> **WILLIAM BLAKE,** "The Tyger"

Internal rhyme occurs within a line:

> The Sun came up upon the left,
> Out of the <u>sea</u> came <u>he</u>!
> And he shone <u>bright</u> and on the <u>right</u>
> Went down into the sea.
> **SAMUEL TAYLOR COLERIDGE,**
> "The Rime of the Ancient Mariner"

Beginning rhyme occurs at the beginning of a line:

> Red River, red river,
> <u>Slow</u> flow heat is silence
> <u>No</u> will is still as a river
> Still. Will heat move
> **T. S. ELIOT,** "Virginia"

Rhyme can also be classified according to the number of corresponding syllables. **Masculine rhyme** (also called **rising rhyme**) occurs when single syllables correspond ("can"/"ran"; "descend"/"contend"). **Feminine rhyme** (also called **double rhyme** or **falling rhyme**) occurs when two syllables, a stressed one followed by an unstressed one, correspond ("ocean"/"motion"; "leaping"/"sleeping"). Finally, **triple rhyme** occurs when three syllables correspond. Less common than the other two, triple rhyme is often used for humorous or satiric purposes, as in the following lines from the long poem *Don Juan* by Lord Byron:

> Sagest of women, even of widows, she
>   Resolved that Juan should be quite a <u>paragon</u>,
> And worthy of the noblest pedigree:
>   (His sire of Castile, his dam from <u>Aragon</u>).

In some cases—for example, when it is overused or used in unexpected places—rhyme can create unusual and even comic effects. In the following poem, humor is created by the incongruous connections established by rhymes such as "priest"/"beast" and "pajama"/"lllama."

OGDEN NASH
(1902–1971)

The Lama
(1931)

The one-l lama
He's a priest.
The two-l llama,
He's a beast.
5 And I will bet
A silk pajama
There isn't any
Three-l lllama.

    The conventional way to describe a poem's rhyme scheme is to chart rhyming sounds that appear at the ends of lines. The sound that ends the first line is designated *a*, and all subsequent lines that end in that sound are also labeled *a*. The next sound to appear at the end of a line is designated *b*, and all other lines whose last sounds rhyme with it are also designated *b*—and so on through the alphabet. The lines of the poem that follow have been labeled in this manner.

RICHARD WILBUR
(1921–   )

A Sketch
(1975)

    Into the lower right   *a*
    Square of the window frame   *b*
    There came   *b*
        with scalloped flight   *a*
5 A goldfinch, lit upon   *c*
    The dead branch of a pine,   *d*
    Shining,   *d*
        and then was gone,   *c*
    Tossed in a double arc   *e*
10 Upward into the thatched   *f*
    And cross-hatched   *f*
        pine-needle dark.   *e*

	Briefly, as fresh drafts stirred	g
	The tree, he dulled and gleamed	h
15	And seemed h	
	more coal than bird,	g
	Then, dodging down, returned	i
	In a new light, his perch j	
	A birch— j	
20	twig, where he burned	i
	In the sun's broadside ray, k	
	Some seed pinched in his bill.	l
	Yet still l	
	he did not stay, k	
25	But into a leaf-choken pane,	m
	Changeful as even in heaven,	n
	Even n	
	in Saturn's reign, m	
	Tunneled away and hid.	o
30	And then? But I cannot well	p
	Tell p	
	you all that he did.	o
	It was like glancing at rough	q
	Sketches tacked on a wall,	r
35	And all r	
	so less than enough	q
	Of gold on beaten wing,	s
	I could not choose that one	t
	Be done t	
40	as the finished thing.	s

    Although the rhyme scheme of this poem (*abba, cddc,* and so on) is regular, it is hardly noticeable until it is charted. Despite its subtlety, however, the rhyme scheme is not unimportant. In fact, it reinforces the poem's meaning and binds lines into structural units, connecting the first and fourth as well as the second and third lines of each stanza. In stanza 1, "right" and "flight" draw lines 1 and 4 of the stanza together, enclosing "fame" and "came" in lines 2 and 3. The pattern begins again with the next stanza and continues through the rest of the poem. Like the elusive goldfinch the poet describes, the rhymes are difficult to follow with the eye. In this sense, the rhyme reflects the central theme of the poem: the difficulty of capturing in words a reality which, like the goldfinch, is forever shifting.

    Naturally, rhyme does not have to be subtle to enrich a poem. An obvious rhyme scheme can communicate meaning by connecting ideas that are not normally linked. Notice how Alexander Pope uses this technique in the following excerpt from *An Essay on Man:*

> Honour and shame from no condition rise;
> Act well your part, there all the honour lies.
> Fortune in men has some small diff'rence made,
> One flaunts in rags, one flutters in brocade;
> The cobbler aproned, and the parson gowned,
> The friar hooded, and the monarch crowned.
> "What differ more (you cry) than crown and cowl?"
> I'll tell you, friend; a wise man and a fool.
>
> You'll find, if once the monarch acts the monk,
> Or, cobbler-like, the parson will be drunk,
> Worth makes the man, and want of it, the fellow;
> The rest is all but leather or prunella.[1]
> Stuck o'er with titles and hung round with strings,
> That thou mayest be by kings, or whores of kings.
> Boast the pure blood of an illustrious race,
> In quiet flow from Lucrece[2] to Lucrece;
> But by your fathers' worth if yours you rate,
> Count me those only who were good and great.

This poem is written in **heroic couplets,** paired iambic pentameter lines with a rhyme scheme of *aa, bb, cc, dd,* and so on. In heroic couplets, greater stress falls on the second line of each pair, usually on the last word of the line. Coming at the end of the line, this word receives double emphasis: it is strengthened both because of its position in the line and because it is rhymed with the last word of the couplet's first line. In some cases, rhyme joins opposing ideas, thereby reinforcing a theme that runs through the passage: the contrast between the high and the low, the virtuous and the immoral. For example, "gowned" and "crowned" in lines 5 and 6 convey the opposite conditions of the parson and the monarch and exemplify the idea expressed in lines 3 and 4 that fortune, not virtue, determines one's station.

---

[1] Heavy cloth the color of prunes.
[2] In Roman legend, she stabbed herself after being defiled by Sextus Tarquinius.

Poems for Further Reading: Alliteration, Assonance, and Rhyme

GERARD MANLEY HOPKINS
(1844–1889)

Pied Beauty
(1918)

Glory be to God for dappled things—
    For skies of couple-color as a brinded[1] cow;
      For rose-moles all in stipple upon trout that swim;
Fresh-firecoal chestnut-falls; finches' wings;
5   Landscape plotted and pieced—fold, fallow, and plow;
      And áll trádes, their gear and tackle and trim.[2]

All things counter, original, spare, strange;
    Whatever is fickle, freckled (who knows how?)
      With swift, slow; sweet, sour; adazzle, dim;
10 He fathers-forth whose beauty is past change:
          Praise him.

Reading and Reacting

1. Identify examples of onomatopoeia, alliteration, assonance, imperfect rhyme, and perfect rhyme. Do you think all these techniques are essential to the poem? Are any of them annoying or distracting?
2. What is the central idea of this poem? In what way do the sounds of the poem help to communicate this idea?
3. Identify examples of masculine and feminine rhyme.
4. **Journal Entry** Hopkins uses both pleasing and discordant sounds in his poem. Identify uses of euphony and cacophony, and explain how these techniques affect your reactions to the poem.

Related Works: from "Song of Myself" (p. 556), "Composed upon Westminster Bridge, September 3, 1802" (p. 557)

---

[1] Brindled (streaked).
[2] Equipment.

W. H. AUDEN
(1907–1973)

As I Walked Out One Evening
(1940)

  As I walked out one evening,
    Walking down Bristol Street,
  The crowds upon the pavement
    Were fields of harvest wheat.

5 And down by the brimming river
    I heard a lover sing
  Under an arch of the railway:
    "Love has no ending.

  "I'll love you, dear, I'll love you
10   Till China and Africa meet,
  And the river jumps over the mountain
    And the salmon sing in the street,

  "I'll love you till the ocean
    Is folded and hung up to dry,
15 And the seven stars go squawking
    Like geese about the sky.

  "The years shall run like rabbits,
    For in my arms I hold
  The Flower of the Ages,
20   And the first love of the world."

  But all the clocks in the city
    Began to whirr and chime:
  "O let not Time deceive you,
    You cannot conquer Time.

25 "In the burrows of the Nightmare
    Where Justice naked is,
  Time watches from the shadow
    And coughs when you would kiss.

  "In headaches and in worry
30   Vaguely life leaks away,
  And Time will have his fancy
    Tomorrow or today.

  "Into many a green valley
    Drifts the appalling snow;
35 Time breaks the threaded dances
    And the diver's brilliant bow.

"O plunge your hands in water,
    Plunge them in up to the wrist;
Stare, stare in the basin
40   And wonder what you've missed.

"The glacier knocks in the cupboard,
    The desert sighs in the bed,
And the crack in the teacup opens
    A lane to the land of the dead.

45 "Where the beggars raffle the banknotes
    And the Giant is enchanting to Jack,
And the Lily-white Boy is a Roarer,
    And Jill goes down on her back.

"O look, look in the mirror,
50   O look in your distress;
Life remains a blessing
    Although you cannot bless.

"O stand, stand at the window
    As the tears scald and start;
55 You shall love your crooked neighbor
    With your crooked heart."

It was late, late in the evening,
    The lovers they were gone;
The clocks had ceased their chiming,
60   And the deep river ran on.

READING AND REACTING

1. In lines 2 and 4 of almost every stanza, Auden uses perfect end rhyme. In stanzas 5 and 7, however, he uses imperfect rhyme. Should he have been more consistent in his use of rhyme? Would the poetic effect have been better had he consistently used perfect rhyme?
2. Chart the poem's rhyme scheme. Does Auden use internal rhyme? Where does he use alliteration and assonance? In what other ways does he use sound?
3. Does Auden's use of sound reinforce the poem's content or undercut it? Explain.
4. **JOURNAL ENTRY** Could this poem be considered a love poem? How are its sentiments about love different from those conventionally expressed in poems about love?

Related Works: "Araby" (p. 167), "Oh, My Love Is like a Red, Red Rose" (p. 407), "To His Coy Mistress" (p. 419), "Not Marble, nor the Gilded Monuments" (p. 546)

LEWIS CARROLL
(1832–1898)

Jabberwocky
(1871)

'Twas brillig, and the slithy toves
  Did gyre and gimble in the wabe:
All mimsy were the borogoves,
  And the mome raths outgrabe.

5 "Beware the Jabberwock, my son!
  The jaws that bite, the claws that catch!
Beware the Jubjub bird, and shun
  The frumious Bandersnatch!"

He took his vorpal sword in hand;
10   Long time the manxome foe he sought—
So rested he by the Tumtum tree
  And stood awhile in thought.

And, as in uffish thought he stood,
  The Jabberwock, with eyes of flame,
15 Came whiffling through the tulgey wood,
  And burbled as it came!

One, two! One, two! And through and through
  The vorpal blade went snicker-snack!
He left it dead, and with its head
20   He went galumphing back.

"And hast thou slain the Jabberwock?
  Come to my arms, my beamish boy!
O frabjous day! Callooh, Callay!"
  He chortled in his joy.

25 'Twas brillig, and the slithy toves
  Did gyre and gimble in the wabe:
All mimsy were the borogoves,
  And the mome raths outgrabe.

READING AND REACTING

1. Many words in this poem may be unfamiliar to you. Are they actual words? Use a dictionary to check before you dismiss any. Do some words seem to have meaning in the context of the poem regardless of whether or not they appear in the dictionary? Explain.

2. This poem contains many examples of onomatopoeia. What ideas do the various words' sounds suggest?
3. **JOURNAL ENTRY** Summarize the story the poem tells. In what sense is this poem a story of a young man's initiation into adulthood?

Related Works: "A&P" (p. 65), "Rite of Passage" (p. 538), *The Cuban Swimmer* (p. 865)

 ## CHECKLIST: WRITING ABOUT SOUND

RHYTHM AND METER
✓ Does the poem contain repeated words and phrases? If so, how do they help to create rhythm?
✓ Does the poem have one kind of meter, or does the meter vary from line to line?
✓ How does the meter contribute to the overall effect of the poem?
✓ Which lines of the poem contain caesuras? What effect do they have?
✓ Are the lines of the poem end-stopped, run-on, or a combination of the two? What effects are produced by the presence or absence of pauses at the ends of lines?

ALLITERATION, ASSONANCE, AND RHYME
✓ Does the poem contain any examples of onomatopoeia?
✓ Are there any examples of alliteration or assonance?
✓ Does the poem have a regular rhyme scheme?
✓ Does the poem use internal rhyme? Beginning rhyme?
✓ Does the poem include examples of masculine, feminine, or triple rhyme?
✓ In what ways does rhyme unify the poem?
✓ How does rhyme reinforce the poem's ideas?

◆ WRITING SUGGESTIONS: SOUND

1. William Blake's "The Tyger" (p. 506) appeared in a collection entitled *Songs of Experience*. Compare this poem to "The Lamb" (p. 505), which appeared in a collection called *Songs of Innocence*. In what way are the speakers in these two poems

relatively "innocent" or "experienced"? How does sound help to convey the voice of the speakers in these two poems?
2. "Sadie and Maud" (p. 428), like "The Faithful Wife" (p. 375), "My Papa's Waltz" (p. 309), and "Daddy" (p. 413), communicates attitudes toward home and family. How does the presence or absence of rhyme in these poems help to reinforce their themes?
3. Robert Frost once said that writing poems that have no fixed metrical pattern is like playing tennis without a net. What do you think he meant? Do you agree? After reading "'Out, Out—'" (p. 420), "Stopping by Woods on a Snowy Evening" (p. 527), and "The Road Not Taken" (p. 526), write an essay in which you discuss Frost's use of meter.
4. Select two or three contemporary poems that have no end rhyme. Write an essay in which you discuss what these poets gain and lose by not using rhyme.
5. Prose writers as well as poets use techniques such as assonance and alliteration. Choose a passage of prose—from "Araby" (p. 167), "A Clean, Well-Lighted Place" (p. 173), or "Barn Burning" (p. 142), for example—and discuss its use of assonance and alliteration. Where do assonance and alliteration occur? How do these techniques help the writer make his or her point?

Chapter 16

Form

JOHN KEATS
(1795–1821)

On the Sonnet
(1819)

If by dull rhymes our English must be chained,
And like Andromeda,[1] the sonnet sweet
Fettered, in spite of painéd loveliness,
Let us find, if we must be constrained,
5 Sandals more interwoven and complete
To fit the naked foot of Poesy:
Let us inspect the lyre, and weigh the stress
Of every chord, and see what may be gained
By ear industrious, and attention meet;
10 Misers of sound and syllable, no less
Than Midas[2] of his coinage, let us be
Jealous of dead leaves in the bay-wreath crown;
So, if we may not let the Muse be free,
She will be bound with garlands of her own.

The **form** of a literary work is its structure or shape, the way its parts fit together to form a whole; **poetic form** is the design of a poem described in terms of rhyme, meter, and stanzaic pattern.

Until the twentieth century, most poetry was written in **closed form** (sometimes called **fixed form**), characterized by regular patterns

---

[1] In Greek mythology, Andromeda was chained to a rock to appease a sea monster.
[2] King Midas was granted his wish that all he touched would turn to gold.

of meter, rhyme, line length, and stanzaic divisions. Early poems that were passed down orally—epics and ballads, for example—relied on regular form to facilitate memorization. Even after poems began to be written down, poets tended to favor regular patterns. In fact, until relatively recently, regular form was what distinguished poetry from prose. Of course, strict adherence to regular patterns sometimes produced poems that were, in John Keats's words, "chained" by "dull rhymes" and "fettered" by the rules governing a particular form. But rather than feeling "constrained" by form, many poets experimented with imagery, figures of speech, allusion, and other techniques—stretching closed form to its limits.

As they sought new ways in which to express themselves, poets also used forms from other cultures, adapting them to the demands of their own languages. English and American poets, for example, adopted (and still use) early French forms, such as the villanelle and the sestina, and early Italian forms, such as the Petrarchan sonnet and terza rima. More recently, the nineteenth-century American poet Henry Wadsworth Longfellow studied Icelandic epics; the twentieth-century poet Ezra Pound studied the works of French troubadours; and Pound and other twentieth-century American poets, such as Richard Wright and Carolyn Kizer, were inspired by Japanese haiku. Other American poets, such as Vachel Lindsay, Langston Hughes, and Maya Angelou, looked closer to home—to the rhythms of blues, jazz, and spirituals—for inspiration.

As time went on, more and more poets moved away from closed form to experiment with **open form** poetry (sometimes called **free verse** or *vers libre*), varying line length within a poem, dispensing with stanzaic divisions, breaking lines in unexpected places, and even abandoning any semblance of formal structure. In English, nineteenth-century poets—such as William Blake and Matthew Arnold—experimented with lines of irregular meter and length, and Walt Whitman wrote **prose poems,** open form poems whose long lines made them look like prose. (Well before this time, Asian poetry and some biblical passages had used a type of free verse.) In nineteenth-century France, Symbolist poets such as Baudelaire, Rimbaud, Verlaine, and Mallarmé also used free verse. Later, in the early twentieth century, a group of American poets including Ezra Pound, William Carlos Williams, and Amy Lowell, who were associated with a movement known as **imagism,** wrote poetry that dispensed with traditional principles of English versification, creating new rhythms and meters.

Although much contemporary English and American poetry is composed in open form, many poets also write in closed form—even in very traditional, highly structured patterns. Still, new forms, and new variations of old forms, are being created all the time. And, because contemporary poets do not necessarily feel bound by rules or restrictions about what constitutes "acceptable" poetic form, they experiment freely, trying to discover the form that best suits the poem's purpose, subject, language, and theme.

Closed Form

❖ ❖ ❖

A **closed form** (or *fixed form*) poem looks symmetrical; it has an identifiable, repeated pattern, with lines of similar length arranged in groups of two, three, four, or more. Such poems also tend to rely on regular metrical patterns and rhyme schemes.

Despite what its name suggests, closed form poetry does not have to be confining or conservative. In fact, sometimes contemporary poets experiment by using characteristics of open form poetry (such as lines of varying length) within a closed form, or by moving back and forth within a single poem from open to closed to open form. Sometimes they (like their eighteenth-century counterparts) experiment with closed form by combining different stanzaic forms (stanzas of two and three lines, for example) within a single poem.

Even when poets work within a traditional closed form, such as a *sonnet, sestina,* or *villanelle,* they can break new ground. For example, they can create a sonnet with an unexpected meter or rhyme scheme, add an extra line or even extra stanzas to a traditional sonnet form, combine two different traditional sonnet forms in a single poem, or write an abbreviated version of a sestina or villanelle. (See the sections on traditional closed forms in this chapter for examples of such experiments.) In other words, poets can use traditional forms as building blocks, combining them in innovative ways to create new patterns and new forms.

Sometimes a pattern (such as *blank verse*) simply determines the meter of a poem's individual lines. At other times, the pattern extends to the level of the *stanza,* with lines arranged into groups (*couplets, quatrains,* and so on). At still other times, as in the case of traditional closed forms like sonnets, a poetic pattern gives shape to an entire poem.

Blank Verse

Blank verse is unrhymed poetry with each line written in a set pattern of five stressed and five unstressed syllables called **iambic pentameter** (see p. 432). Many passages from Shakespeare's plays, such as the following lines from *Hamlet* are written in blank verse:

> To sleep, perchance to dream, ay there's the rub,
> For in that sleep of death what dreams may come
> When we have shuffled off this mortal coil
> Must give us pause—there's the respect
> That makes calamity of so long life:

For a contemporary use of blank verse, see John Updike's "Ex-Basketball Player" (p. 408).

Stanza

A **stanza** is a group of two or more lines with the same metrical pattern—and often with a regular rhyme scheme as well—separated by blank space from other such groups of lines. The stanza in poetry is like the paragraph in prose: it groups related thoughts into units.

A two-line stanza with rhyming lines of similar length and meter is called a **couplet**. The **heroic couplet**, first used by Chaucer and especially popular throughout the eighteenth century, consists of two rhymed lines of iambic pentameter, with a weak pause after the first line and a strong pause after the second. The following example, from Alexander Pope's *An Essay on Criticism*, is a heroic couplet:

> True ease in writing comes from art, not chance,
> As those move easiest who have learned to dance.

A three-line stanza with lines of similar length and a set rhyme scheme is called a **tercet**. Percy Bysshe Shelley's "Ode to the West Wind" (p. 546) is built largely of tercets:

> O wild West Wind, thou breath of Autumn's being,
> Thou, from whose unseen presence the leaves dead
> Are driven, like ghosts from an enchanter fleeing,
>
> Yellow, and black, and pale, and hectic red,
> Pestilence-stricken multitudes: O Thou,
> Who chariotest to their dark wintry bed

Although in many tercets all three lines rhyme, "Ode to the West Wind" uses a special rhyme scheme, also used by Dante, called **terza rima**. This rhyme scheme (*aba, bcb, cdc, ded,* and so on) creates an interlocking series of stanzas. Line 2's *dead* looks ahead to the rhyming words *red* and *bed*, which close lines 4 and 6, and the pattern continues throughout the poem.

A four-line stanza with lines of similar length and a set rhyme scheme is called a **quatrain**. The quatrain, the most widely used and versatile unit in English and American poetry, is used by William Wordsworth in the following excerpt from "She Dwelt among the Untrodden Ways" (p. 558):

> A violet by a mossy stone
>   Half hidden from the eye!
> Fair as a star, when only one
>   Is shining in the sky.

Quatrains are frequently used by contemporary poets as well—for instance, in Theodore Roethke's "My Papa's Waltz" (p. 309), Adrienne

Rich's "Aunt Jennifer's Tigers" (p. 436), and William Stafford's "Traveling through the Dark" (p. 550).

One special kind of quatrain, called the **ballad stanza,** alternates lines of eight and six syllables; typically, only the second and fourth lines rhyme. The following lines from the traditional Scottish ballad "Sir Patrick Spence" illustrate the ballad stanza:

> The king sits in Dumferling toune,
>   Drinking the blude-reid wine:
> "O whar will I get guid sailor
>   To sail this schip of mine?"

Common measure, a four-line stanzaic pattern closely related to the ballad stanza, is used in hymns as well as in poetry. It differs from the ballad stanza in that its rhyme scheme is *abab* rather than *abcb*. This pattern appears in Donald Hall's 1955 poem "My Son, My Executioner" (p. 422).

Other stanzaic forms include **rhyme royal,** a seven-line stanza *(ababbcc)* set in iambic pentameter, used in Sir Thomas Wyatt's sixteenth-century poem "They Flee from Me That Sometimes Did Me Seke" as well as in Theodore Roethke's twentieth-century "I Knew a Woman" (p. 370); **ottava rima,** an eight-line stanza *(abababcc)* set in iambic pentameter; and the Spenserian stanza, a nine-line form *(ababbcbcc)* whose first eight lines are set in iambic pentameter and whose last line is in iambic hexameter. The Romantic poets John Keats and Percy Bysshe Shelley were among those who used this form. (See Chapter 15 for definitions and examples of various metrical patterns.)

The Sonnet

Perhaps the most familiar kind of traditional closed form poem written in English is the **sonnet,** a fourteen-line poem with a distinctive rhyme scheme and metrical pattern. The English or **Shakespearean sonnet,** which consists of fourteen lines divided into three quatrains and a concluding couplet, is written in iambic pentameter and follows the rhyme scheme *abab cdcd efef gg.* The **Petrarchan sonnet,** popularized in the fourteenth century by the Italian poet Francesco Petrarch, also consists of fourteen lines of iambic pentameter, but these lines are divided into an eight-line unit called an **octave** and a six-line unit (composed of two tercets) called a **sestet.** The rhyme scheme of the octave is *abba abba;* the rhyme scheme of the sestet is *cde cde.*

The conventional structures of these sonnet forms reflect the arrangement of ideas within a poem. In the Shakespearean sonnet, the poet typically presents three "paragraphs" of related thoughts, introducing an idea in the first quatrain, developing it in the two remaining quatrains, and summing up in a succinct closing couplet. In the Petrarchan sonnet, the octave introduces a problem that is resolved in the sestet.

(Many Shakespearean sonnets also have a problem-solution structure.) Some poets vary the traditional patterns somewhat to suit the poem's language or ideas. For example, they may depart from the pattern to sidestep a forced rhyme or unnatural stress on a syllable, or they may not place the problem-solution break between octave and sestet.

The following poem follows the form of a traditional English sonnet.

◊ ◊ ◊

WILLIAM SHAKESPEARE
(1564–1616)

When, in Disgrace with Fortune and Men's Eyes
(1609)

When, in disgrace with Fortune and men's eyes,
I all alone beweep my outcast state,
And trouble deaf heaven with my bootless[1] cries,
And look upon myself and curse my fate,
5 Wishing me like to one more rich in hope,
Featured like him, like him with friends possessed,
Desiring this man's art, and that man's scope,
With what I most enjoy contented least,
Yet in these thoughts myself almost despising,
10 Haply[2] I think on thee, and then my state,
Like to the lark at break of day arising
From sullen earth, sings hymns at heaven's gate;
    For thy sweet love rememb'red such wealth brings
    That then I scorn to change my state with kings.

This sonnet is written in iambic pentameter and has a conventional rhyme scheme: *abab* (eyes-state-cries-fate), *cdcd* (hope-possessed-scope-least), *efef* (despising-state-arising-gate), *gg* (brings-kings). In this poem, in which the speaker explains how thoughts of his loved one can rescue him from despair, each quatrain is unified by rhyme as well as by subject. In the first quatrain, the speaker presents his problem: he is down on his luck and out of favor with his peers, isolated in self-pity and cursing his fate. In the second quatrain, he develops this idea further: he is envious of others and dissatisfied with things that usually please him. In the third quatrain, the focus shifts. Although the first two quatrains develop a dependent clause ("When [...]") that introduces a problem, line

---

[1] Futile.
[2] Luckily.

9 begins to present the resolution. In the third quatrain, the speaker explains how, in the midst of his despair and self-hatred, he thinks of his loved one, and his spirits soar. The closing couplet sums up the mood transformation the poem describes and explains its significance: when the speaker realizes the emotional riches his loved one gives him, he is no longer envious of others.

❖ Poems for Further Reading: The Sonnet

CLAUDE MCKAY
(1890–1948)

The White City
(1922)

> I will not toy with it nor bend an inch.
> Deep in the secret chambers of my heart
> I muse my life-long hate, and without flinch
> I bear it nobly as I live my part.
> 5 My being would be a skeleton, a shell,
> If this dark Passion that fills my every mood,
> And makes my heaven in the white world's hell,
> Did not forever feed me vital blood.
> I see the mighty city through a mist—
> 10 The strident trains that speed the goaded mass,
> The poles and spires and towers vapor-kissed,
> The fortressed port through which the great ships pass,
> The tides, the wharves, the dens I contemplate,
> Are sweet like wanton loves because I hate.

Reading and Reacting

1. In what sense is the speaker's mood similar to that of the speaker in "When, in Disgrace with Fortune and Men's Eyes" (p. 457)? How is it different?
2. How is the speaker's description of the city in the third quatrain consistent with the emotions he expresses in lines 1–8?
3. The closing couplet of a Shakespearean sonnet traditionally sums up the sonnet's concerns. Is this true here? Explain.
4. **Journal Entry** What possible meanings does the phrase "the white world's hell" (7) have? How does it express the poem's main idea?

Related Works: "Like a Winding Sheet" (p. 76), "The Man He Killed" (p. 341), "For Malcolm, a Year After" (p. 437), "We Wear the Mask" (p. 518), "If We Must Die" (p. 536).

JOHN KEATS
(1795–1821)

On First Looking into Chapman's Homer[1]
(1816)

Much have I traveled in the realms of gold,
    And many goodly states and kingdoms seen;
    Round many western islands have I been
Which bards in fealty to Apollo[2] hold.
5 Oft of one wide expanse had I been told
    That deep-browed Homer ruled as his demesne,[3]
    Yet did I never breathe its pure serene[4]
Till I heard Chapman speak out loud and bold.
Then felt I like some watcher of the skies
10   When a new planet swims into his ken;
    Or like stout Cortez[5] when with eagle eyes
    He stared at the Pacific—and all his men
Looked at each other with a wild surmise—
    Silent, upon a peak in Darien.[6]

READING AND REACTING

1. Is this a Petrarchan or a Shakespearean sonnet? Explain your conclusion.
2. **JOURNAL ENTRY** The sestet's change of focus is introduced with the word "Then" in line 9. How does the mood of the sestet differ from the mood of the octave? How does the language differ?

Related Works: "Araby" (p. 167), "When I Heard the Learn'd Astronomer" (p. 364)

---

[1] The translation of Homer by Elizabethan poet George Chapman.
[2] Greek god of light, truth, reason, male beauty; associated with music and poetry.
[3] Realm, domain.
[4] Air, atmosphere.
[5] It was Vasco de Balboa (not Hernando Cortez as Keats suggests) who first saw the Pacific Ocean, from "a peak in Darien."
[6] Former name of the Isthmus of Panama.

GWENDOLYN BROOKS
(1917–   )

First Fight. Then Fiddle
(1949)

First fight. Then fiddle. Ply the slipping string
With feathery sorcery; muzzle the note
With hurting love; the music that they wrote
Bewitch, bewilder. Qualify to sing
5 Threadwise. Devise no salt, no hempen thing
For the dear instrument to bear. Devote
The bow to silks and honey. Be remote
A while from malice and from murdering.
But first to arms, to armor. Carry hate
10 In front of you and harmony behind.
Be deaf to music and to beauty blind.
Win war. Rise bloody, maybe not too late
For having first to civilize a space
Wherein to play your violin with grace.

READING AND REACTING

1. What is the subject of Brooks's poem? What do you think she means by "fight" and "fiddle"?
2. What is the poem's rhyme scheme? Is it an essential element of the poem? Would the poem be equally effective if it did not include end rhyme? Explain your position.
3. Study the poem's use of capitalization and punctuation carefully. Why do you think Brooks chooses to end many of her sentences in midline? How do her choices determine how you read the poem?

Related Works: "The Soldier" (p. 320), "The White City" (p. 458), "The *Chicago Defender* Sends a Man to Little Rock" (p. 507)

HAIKU

Like an epigram, a haiku compresses words into a very small package. Unlike an epigram, however, a haiku focuses on an image, not an idea. A traditional Japanese form, the **haiku** is a brief unrhymed poem that presents the essence of some aspect of nature, concentrating a vivid image in just three lines. Although in the strictest sense a haiku consists of seventeen syllables divided into lines of five, seven, and five syllables, respectively, not all poets conform to this rigid form.

The following poem is a translation of a classic Japanese haiku by Matsuo Basho:

> Silent and still: then
> Even sinking into the rocks,
> The cicada's screech.

Notice that this poem conforms to the haiku's three-line structure and traditional subject matter, vividly depicting a natural scene without comment or analysis.

As the next poem illustrates, haiku in English is not always consistent with the traditional haiku in form or subject matter.

◊ ◊ ◊

RICHARD BRAUTIGAN
(1935–1984)

Widow's Lament[1]

> It's not quite cold enough
> to go borrow some firewood
> from the neighbors.

Brautigan's haiku adheres to the traditional pattern's number of lines and syllables, and its central idea is expressed in very concentrated terms. The poem's focus, however, is not the natural world but human psychology. Moreover, without the title, the poem would be so ambiguous as to be meaningless. In this sense, the poet "cheats" the form, depending on the title's four syllables as well as on the seventeen of the poem itself to convey his ideas.

---

[1] Publication date is not available.

Poems for Further Reading: Haiku

RICHARD WRIGHT
(1908–1960)

Hokku Poems
(1960)

I am nobody
A red sinking autumn sun
Took my name away

*

Make up your mind snail!
You are half inside your house
And halfway out!

*

In the falling snow
A laughing boy holds out his palms
Until they are white

*

Keep straight down this block
Then turn right where you will find
A peach tree blooming

*

With a twitching nose
A dog reads a telegram
On a wet tree trunk

*

The spring lingers on
In the scent of a damp log
Rotting in the sun

*

Whose town did you leave
O wild and drowning spring rain
And where do you go?

*

The crow flew so fast
That he left his lonely caw
Behind in the fields

READING AND REACTING

1. The poems in this group of modern English haiku differ in several respects from the traditional Japanese form. Consider the form and subject matter of each haiku carefully, and explain how they are like and unlike classic haiku.
2. **JOURNAL ENTRY** Referring to the additional haiku poems in Chapter 13 as well as to those in this chapter, write a broad definition of *haiku* that applies to all of them.

Related Works: "In a Station of the Metro" (p. 391), "You Fit into Me" (p. 423), "Fog" (p. 545), "Anecdote of the Jar" (p. 551)

OPEN FORM

◊ ◊ ◊

An **open form** poem (sometimes called **free verse** or *vers libre*) makes occasional use of rhyme and meter, but it has no easily identifiable pattern or design—that is, it has no conventional stanzaic divisions, no consistent metrical pattern, and no repeated rhyme scheme. Still, although open form poetry has no distinguishable pattern of meter, rhyme, or line length, it is not necessarily shapeless, untidy, or randomly ordered. All poems have form, and the form of a poem may be determined by factors such as the appearance of words on the printed page or pauses in natural speech as well as by conventional metrical patterns or rhyme schemes.

Open form poetry invites readers to participate in the creative process, to discover the relationship between form and meaning. Some modern poets believe that only open form offers them freedom to express their ideas or that the subject matter or mood of their poetry demands a relaxed, experimental approach to form. For example, when Lawrence Ferlinghetti portrays the poet as an acrobat who "climbs on rime" (p. 405), he constructs his poem in a way that is consistent with the poet/acrobat's willingness to take risks. Thus, the poem's idiosyncratic form supports its ideas about the possibilities of poetry and the poet as experimenter.

Without a predetermined pattern, however, poets must create forms that suit their needs, and they must continue to shape and reshape the look of the poem on the page as they revise its words. Thus, open form represents a challenge, a way to experiment with fresh arrangements of words and new juxtapositions of ideas.

For some poets, such as Carl Sandburg, open form provides an opportunity to create **prose poems.**

CARL SANDBURG
(1878–1967)

Chicago
(1914)

Hog Butcher for the World,
Tool Maker, Stacker of Wheat,
Player with Railroads and the Nation's Freight Handler;
Stormy, husky, brawling,
City of the Big Shoulders:

They tell me you are wicked and I believe them, for I have seen
your painted women under the gas lamps luring the farm boys.
And they tell me you are crooked and I answer: Yes, it is true I
have seen the gunman kill and go free to kill again.
And they tell me you are brutal and my reply is: On the faces of
women and children I have seen the marks of wanton hunger.
And having answered so I turn once more to those who sneer at this
my city, and I give them back the sneer and say to them:
Come and show me another city with lifted head singing so proud
to be alive and coarse and strong and cunning.
Flinging magnetic curses amid the toil of piling job on job, here is a
tall bold slugger set vivid against the little soft cities;
Fierce as a dog with tongue lapping for action, cunning as a savage
pitted against the wilderness,
    Bareheaded,
    Shoveling,
    Wrecking,
    Planning,
    Building, breaking, rebuilding,
Under the smoke, dust all over his mouth, laughing with white
teeth,
Under the terrible burden of destiny laughing as a young man
laughs,
Laughing even as an ignorant fighter laughs who has never lost a
battle,
Bragging and laughing that under his wrist is the pulse, and under
his ribs the heart of the people,
    Laughing!
Laughing the stormy, husky, brawling laughter of Youth, half-naked,
sweating, proud to be Hog Butcher, Tool Maker, Stacker of
Wheat, Player with railroads and Freight Handler to the Nation.

"Chicago" uses capitalization and punctuation conventionally, and it
generally (although not always) divides words into lines consistent with

the natural divisions of phrases and sentences. However, the poem is not divided into stanzas, and its lines vary widely in length—from a single word isolated on a line to a line crowded with words—and follow no particular metrical pattern. Instead, its form is created through its pattern of alternating sections of long and short lines; through its repeated words and phrases ("They tell me" in lines 6–8, "under" in lines 18–19, and "laughing" in lines 18–23, for example); through alliteration (for instance, "slugger set vivid against the little soft cities" in line 11); and, most of all, through the piling up of words into catalogs in lines 1–5, 13–17, and 23.

In order to understand Sandburg's reasons for choosing such a form, we must consider the poem's subject matter and theme. "Chicago" celebrates the scope and power of a "stormy, husky, brawling" city, one that is exuberant and outgoing, not sedate and civilized. Chicago the city does not follow anyone else's rules; it is, after all, "Bareheaded, / Shoveling, / Wrecking, / Planning, / Building, breaking," constantly active, in flux, on the move, "proud to be alive." "Fierce as a dog [. . .] cunning as a savage," the city is characterized as, among other things, a worker, a fighter, and a harborer of "painted women" and killers and hungry women and children. Just as Chicago itself does not conform to the rules, the poem clearly demands a departure from the orderly confines of stanzaic form and measured rhyme and meter, a kind of form better suited to "the little soft cities" than to the "tall / bold slugger" that is Chicago.

Of course, open form poetry does not have to look like Sandburg's prose poem. The following poem experiments with a different kind of open form.

◊ ◊ ◊

LOUISE GLÜCK
(1943–)

Life Is a Nice Place
(1966)

Life is a nice place (They change
the decorations
every season; and the music,
my dear, is just too
5   marvellous, they play you
anything from birds to Bach. And
every day the Host
arranges for some clever sort
of contest and they give
10   the most
fantastic prizes; I go absolutely
green. Of course, celebrities abound;

>   I've even seen Love waltzing around
>   in amusing disguises.) to
> 15   visit. But
>   I wouldn't want to live there.

Glück's poem includes several end rhymes ("too"/"you"; "Host"/ "most"; "abound"/"around"). It also forms a recognizable pattern on the page, broadening and narrowing with some regularity. Moreover, it has a clear syntactical structure, with one main sentence interrupted by parenthetical comments, and it follows the conventions of capitalization and punctuation. The poem clearly has a form, but its idiosyncratic, stanzaic divisions and uneven patterns of rhyme and meter mark it as fresh and original.

The poem's unusual form suits both its subject and its sarcastic tone. It is divided into five sentences, but only the final sentence ends at the end of a line. Moreover, the first sentence ("Life is a nice place [. . .] to visit") begins in line 1 but does not conclude until the end of the poem. The long parenthetical intrusion, unusual in itself, keeps readers from seeing at first that the poem is a grim new twist on an old cliché: "Life is a nice place [. . .] / to visit. But / I wouldn't want to live there."

The poem's first line is ironic, because the life the speaker presents is shallow, false, and ultimately meaningless. It is a cross between a stage set and a cocktail party, where love is elusive ("waltzing around / in amusing disguises") and nature is artificially re-created by piped-in music and painted backdrops. Although a traditional structure and regular rhyme and meter could, through their contrast with the subject matter, create ironic tension, Glück chooses an unconventional form that visually reinforces the empty cycles of the life the poem describes. Breaks in lines are determined not by conventional phrasing or punctuation but largely by the poem's shape; the result is unusual word groups such as "every season; and the music, [. . .] is just too" and "fantastic prizes; I go absolutely." These odd juxtapositions suggest the random quality of the speaker's encounters and, perhaps, the unpredictability of her life.

The poem that follows, an extreme example of open form, looks almost as if it has spilled out of a box of words.

◊ ◊ ◊
E. E. CUMMINGS
(1894–1962)

the sky was can dy
(1925)

```
     the
       sky
          was
       can   dy  lu
 5   minous
           edible
     spry
        pinks shy
     lemons
10   greens    coo   l choc
     olate
     s.
           un   der,
             a   lo
15   co
     mo
           tive    s pout
                       ing
                          vi
20                     o
                        lets
```

Like many of Cummings's poems, this one seems ready to skip off the page. Its irregular line length and its unconventional capitalization, punctuation, and word divisions immediately draw readers' attention to its form. Despite these oddities, and despite the absence of orderly rhyme and meter, the poem does have its conventional elements. A closer examination reveals that the poem's theme—the beauty of the sky—is quite conventional; that the poem is divided, although somewhat crudely, into two sections; and that the poet does use some rhyme—"spry" and "shy," for example. However, Cummings's sky is described not in traditional terms, but rather as something "edible," not only in terms of color but of flavor as well. The breaks within words ("can dy lu / minous"; "coo l choc / olate / s") seem to expand each word's possibilities, visually stretching them to the limit, extending their taste and visual image over several lines and, in the case of the last two words, visually reinforcing the picture the words describe. In addition, the isolation of syllables exposes hidden rhyme, as in "lo / co /

mo" and "lu" / "coo." By using open form, Cummings makes a clear statement about the capacity of a poem to move beyond the traditional boundaries set by words and lines.

❖ Poems for Further Reading: Open Form

◊ ◊ ◊

WALT WHITMAN
(1819–1892)

from "Out of the Cradle Endlessly Rocking"
(1881)

Out of the cradle endlessly rocking,
Out of the mocking-bird's throat, the musical shuttle,
Out of the Ninth-month[1] midnight,
Over the sterile sands and the fields beyond, where the child leaving his bed wander'd alone, bareheaded, barefoot,
5 Down from the shower'd halo,
Up from the mystic play of shadows twining and twisting as if they were alive,
Out from the patches of briers and blackberries,
From the memories of the bird that chanted to me,
From your memories sad brother, from the fitful risings and fallings I heard,
10 From under that yellow half-moon late-risen and swollen as if with tears,
From those beginning notes of yearning and love there in the mist,
From the thousand responses of my heart never to cease,
From the myriad thence-arous'd words,
From the word stronger and more delicious than any,
15 From such as now they start the scene revisiting,
As a flock, twittering, rising, or overhead passing,
Borne hither, ere all eludes me, hurriedly,
A man, yet by these tears a little boy again,
Throwing myself on the sand, confronting the waves,
20 I, chanter of pains and joys, uniter of here and hereafter,
Taking all hints to use them, but swiftly leaping beyond them,
A reminiscence sing.

---

[1] The Quaker designation for September. In context, an allusion to the human birth cycle.

Reading and Reacting

1. This excerpt, the first twenty-two lines of a poem nearly two hundred lines long, has no regular metrical pattern or rhyme scheme. What gives it form?
2. How might you explain why the poem's lines vary in length?
3. **Journal Entry** Compare this excerpt with the excerpt from Whitman's "Song of Myself" (p. 556). In what respects are the forms of the two poems similar?

Related Works: "Chicago" (p. 464), from "Song of Myself" (p. 556)

◊ ◊ ◊

DIANE WAKOSKI
(1937–   )

Sleep
(1966)

The mole
lifting snouts—
full of strained black dirt
      —his perfect tunnel
5   sculptured
      to fit
      the fat
      body. Sleep
fits tight
10 —must keep bringing out.
the fine grit
to keep size
for even one day.

Reading and Reacting

1. This poem's form seems to be in direct conflict with the logical divisions its syntax and punctuation suggest. For instance, the words in lines 4–9 are set between dashes, indicating a parenthetical comment, yet only lines 4–8 are visually aligned. Also, line 10 ends with a period, but lines 11–13 are clearly part of the same sentence as line 10. How can you account for such discrepancies?
2. How might the poem's discussion of the mole's constant search for the perfect-size tunnel have suggested the form of the poem?
3. **Journal Entry** Why do you believe the poet placed the words "Sleep / fits tight" (8–9) where she did? Could—or

should—these words be relocated? If so, where could they be placed, and what changes in form or punctuation would then have to be made?

Related Works: "Red Wheelbarrow" (p. 390), "Reapers" (p. 398)

◆ ◆ ◆

ROBERT HAYDEN
(1913–)

Monet's "Waterlilies"[1]
(1966)

(for Bill and Sonja)

Today as the news from Selma[2] and Saigon[3]
poisons the air like fallout,
    I come again to see
the serene great picture that I love.

5 Here space and time exist in light
the eye like the eye of faith believes.
    The seen, the known
dissolve in irridescence, become
illusive flesh of light

10   that was not, was, forever is.

O light beheld as through refracting tears.
Here is the aura of that world
    each of us has lost.
Here is the shadow of its joy.

READING AND REACTING

1. The speaker stands before Monet's *Waterlilies,* where he takes temporary refuge from the turbulent world. Why do you

---

[1] Claude Monet (1840–1926), French impressionist painter. The poet's description of the painter's use of light in this particular painting is equally applicable to most of Monet's work.

[2] Selma, a city in central Alabama. In 1965, peaceful demonstrations in support of voting rights for blacks were brutally broken up by the Selma police. Two civil rights supporters were killed: one, minister James Reeb, was beaten to death on a town street; the other, homemaker Viola Liuzzo, was shot by Ku Klux Klansmen as she was driving along a highway.

[3] Saigon, the capital of the former South Vietnam, now known as Ho Chi Minh City. All news of the Vietnam War was cleared through Saigon by U.S. authorities.

suppose Hayden chose not to use the soothing rhythms and comforting shape of closed form to convey the serenity of the moment? Do you think he made the right choice?
2. Hayden indents lines 3, 7, 10, and 13. What purpose, if any, do these indentations serve?
3. Why do you think the last four lines are separated from the rest of the poem?

Related Works: "Facing It" (p. 326), "The World Is Too Much with Us" (p. 345), "Cloud Painter" (p. 387), "Dover Beach" (p. 503), "Ethics" (p. 540)

◊ ◊ ◊

WILLIAM CARLOS WILLIAMS
(1883–1963)

Spring and All
(1923)

By the road to the contagious hospital
under the surge of the blue
mottled clouds driven from the
northeast—a cold wind. Beyond, the
5 waste of broad, muddy fields
brown with dried weeds, standing and fallen

patches of standing water
the scattering of tall trees

All along the road the reddish
10 purplish, forked, upstanding, twiggy
stuff of bushes and small trees
with dead, brown leaves under them
leafless vines—

Lifeless in appearance, sluggish
15 dazed spring approaches—

They enter the new world naked,
cold, uncertain of all
save that they enter. All about them
the cold, familiar wind—

20 Now the grass, tomorrow
the stiff curl of wildcarrot leaf
One by one objects are defined—
It quickens: clarity, outline of leaf

> But now the stark dignity of
> 25 entrance—Still, the profound change
> has come upon them: rooted, they
> grip down and begin to awaken

Reading and Reacting

1. What elements of traditional closed form poems are present in "Spring and All"? What elements are absent?
2. What does Williams accomplish by isolating two sets of two lines each (7–8; 14–15)?
3. "Spring and All" uses assonance, alliteration, and repetition. Give several examples of each technique, and explain what each adds to the poem.
4. **Journal Entry** "Spring and All" includes only two periods. Elsewhere, where readers might expect to find end punctuation, the poet uses colons, dashes, or no punctuation at all. Why do you think the poet made these decisions about the use of punctuation?

Related Works: "Comparatives" (p. 439), "Pied Beauty" (p. 446)

❖ ❖ ❖

CAROLYN FORCHÉ
(1950–)

The Colonel
(1978)

What you have heard is true. I was in his house. His wife carried a tray of coffee and sugar. His daughter filed her nails, his son went out for the night. There were daily papers, pet dogs, a pistol on the cushion beside him. The moon swung bare on its black cord over
5 the house. On the television was a cop show. It was in English. Broken bottles were embedded in the walls around the house to scoop the kneecaps from a man's legs or cut his hands to lace. On the windows there were gratings like those in liquor stores. We had dinner, rack of lamb, good wine, a gold bell was on the table for
10 calling the maid. The maid brought green mangoes, salt, a type of bread. I was asked how I enjoyed the country. There was a brief commercial in Spanish. His wife took everything away. There was some talk then of how difficult it had become to govern. The parrot said hello on the terrace. The colonel told it to shut up, and pushed
15 himself from the table. My friend said to me with his eyes: say nothing. The colonel returned with a sack used to bring groceries home. He spilled many human ears on the table. They were like

dried peach halves. There is no other way to say this. He took one
of them in his hands, shook it in our faces, dropped it into a water
20 glass. It came alive there. I am tired of fooling around he said. As
for the rights of anyone, tell your people they can go fuck themselves. He swept the ears to the floor with his arm and held the last
of his wine in the air. Something for your poetry, no? he said. Some
of the ears on the floor caught this scrap of his voice. Some of the
25 ears on the floor were pressed to the ground.

READING AND REACTING

1. Treating Forché's prose poem as prose rather than poetry, try dividing it into paragraphs. What determines where you make your divisions?
2. If you were to reshape "The Colonel" into a more conventional-looking poem, what options might you have? Rewrite the poem so it "looks like poetry," and compare your revision to the original. Which version do you find more effective? Why?
3. What is the main point of "The Colonel"? How does the form help Forché to communicate this point?
4. **JOURNAL ENTRY** Do you think "The Colonel" is poetry or prose? Consider its subject matter and language as well as its form.

Related Works: "Once upon a Time" (p. 46), "Hope" (p. 352)

CONCRETE POETRY

◆ ◆ ◆

With roots in the ancient Greek *pattern poems* and the sixteenth- and seventeenth-century *emblem poems,* contemporary **concrete poetry** uses words—and, sometimes, different fonts and type sizes—to shape a picture on the page. The form of a concrete poem is not something that emerges from the poem's words and images, but rather something predetermined by the visual image the poet has decided to create. Although some concrete poems are little more than novelties, others—like the poem that follows—can be original and enlightening.

MAY SWENSON
(1913–1989)

Women
(1970)

```
              Women                   Or they
         should be                 should be
           pedestals              little horses
              moving             those wooden
5              pedestals            sweet
                 moving          oldfashioned
                   to the         painted
                 motions         rocking
                   of men        horses

10                   the gladdest things in the toyroom

                  The          feelingly
                pegs         and then
              of their         unfeelingly
            ears                 To be
15        so familiar          joyfully
           and dear            ridden
            to the trusting    rockingly
         fists                 ridden until
         To be chafed          the restored

20   egos dismount and the legs stride away

         Immobile              willing
           sweetlipped         to be set
             sturdy            into motion
               and smiling      Women
25              women           should be
             should always     pedestals
               be waiting       to men
```

The curved shape of the poem immediately reinforces its title, and the arrangement of words on the page suggests a variety of visual directions readers might follow. The two columns seem at first to suggest two alternatives: "Women should be [. . .]" / "Or they should be [. . .]." A closer look, however, reveals that the poem's central figures of speech, such as woman as rocking horse and woman as pedestal, move back and forth between the two columns of images. This exchange of positions might suggest that the two possibilities are really just two ways of looking at one limited role. Thus, the experimental form of the poem visually challenges the apparent complacency of its words, suggesting that women, like words, need not fall into traditional roles or satisfy conventional expectations.

❖ Poem for Further Reading: Concrete Poetry

❖ ❖ ❖

GEORGE HERBERT
(1593–1633)

Easter Wings
(1633)

```
Lord, who createdst man in wealth and store,
      Though foolishly he lost the same,
            Decaying more and more
                  Till he became
                        Most poor,
                        With thee
                  Oh, let me rise
            As larks, harmoniously,
      And sing this day thy victories;
Then shall the fall further the flight in me.

My tender age in sorrow did begin;
      And still with sicknesses and shame
            Thou didst so punish sin,
                  That I became
                        Most thin.
                        With thee
                  Let me combine,
            And feel this day thy victory;
      For if I imp my wing on thine,
Affliction shall advance the flight in me.
```

Reading and Reacting

1. In this example of an **emblem poem,** lines are arranged so that shape and language reinforce each other. Explain how this is accomplished. (For example, how does line length support the poem's images and ideas?)
2. This poem has a definite rhyme scheme. How would you describe it? What relationship do you see between the rhyme scheme and the poem's visual divisions?

Related Works: "l(a" (p. 302), "A Valediction: Forbidding Mourning" (p. 411), "Because I Could Not Stop for Death" (p. 514)

CHECKLIST: WRITING ABOUT FORM

- ✓ Is the poem written in open or closed form? On what characteristics do you base your conclusion?
- ✓ Why did the poet choose open or closed form? For example, is the poem's form consistent with its subject matter, tone, or theme? Is it determined by the conventions of the historical period in which it was written?
- ✓ If the poem is arranged in closed form, does the pattern apply to single lines, to groups of lines, or to the entire poem? What factors determine the breaks between groups of lines?
- ✓ Is the poem a sonnet? A sestina? A villanelle? An epigram? A haiku? How do the traditional form's conventions suit the poet's language and theme? Is the poem consistent with the requirements of the form at all times, or does it break any new ground?
- ✓ If the poem is arranged in open form, what determines the breaks at the ends of lines?
- ✓ Are certain words or phrases isolated on lines? Why?
- ✓ How do elements such as assonance, alliteration, rhyme, and repetition of words give the poem form?
- ✓ What use does the poet make of punctuation and capitalization? Of white space on the page?
- ✓ Is the poem a prose poem? How does this form support the poem's subject matter?
- ✓ Is the poem a concrete poem? How does the poet use the visual shape of the poem to convey meaning?

◆ Writing Suggestions: Form

1. Reread the definitions of *closed form* and *open form* in this chapter. Do you consider concrete poetry "open" or "closed"? Explain your position in a short essay, supporting your conclusion with specific references to the three concrete poems in this chapter.
2. Some poets—for example, Emily Dickinson and Robert Frost—write both open and closed form poems. Choose one open and one closed form poem by a single poet, and explain the poet's possible reasons for choosing each type of form. In your analysis of the two poems, defend the poet's choices if you can.

3. The following open form poem is an alternate version of May Swenson's "Women" (p. 474). Read the two versions carefully, and write an essay in which you compare them. What differences do you notice? Which do you think was written first? Why? Do the two poems make the same point? Which makes the point with less ambiguity? Which is more effective? Why?

◊ ◊ ◊

Women Should Be Pedestals

Women should be pedestals
moving pedestals
moving to the motions of men
Or they should be little horses
5 those wooden sweet oldfashioned painted rocking horses
the gladdest things in the toyroom
The pegs of their ears so familiar and dear
to the trusting fists
To be chafed feelingly
10 and then unfeelingly
To be joyfully ridden
until the restored egos dismount and the legs stride away
Immobile sweetlipped sturdy and smiling
women should always be waiting
15 willing to be set into motion
Women should be pedestals to men

4. Look through the "Poetry for Further Reading" section that follows Chapter 17 of this text (starting on p. 503), and identify one or two prose poems. Write an essay in which you consider why the form seems suitable for the poem or poems you have chosen. Is there a particular kind of subject matter that seems especially appropriate for a prose poem?

Chapter 17

Symbol, Allegory, Allusion, Myth

WILLIAM BLAKE
(1757–1827)

The Sick Rose
(1794)

O Rose thou art sick.
The invisible worm
That flies in the night,
In the howling storm:

5 Has found out thy bed
Of crimson joy:
And his dark secret love
Does thy life destroy.

SYMBOL

As in fiction and drama, symbols in poetry function as a kind of shorthand, as a subtle way of introducing a significant idea or attitude. A **symbol** is an idea or image that suggests something else—but not in the simple way that a dollar sign stands for money or a flag represents a country. A symbol is an image that transcends its literal, or denotative, meaning in a complex way. For instance, if someone gives a rose to a loved one, it could simply be a sign of love. But in the poem "The Sick Rose," the rose has a range of contradictory and complementary meanings. For what does the rose stand? Beauty? Perfection? Passion? Something else? As this poem illustrates, the distinctive trait of a symbol is that its meaning cannot easily be pinned down or defined.

Such ambiguity can be frustrating, but it is precisely this characteristic of a symbol that enables it to enrich a work and give it additional layers of meaning. As Robert Frost has said, a symbol is a little thing that touches a larger thing. In the poem of his that follows, the central symbol does just this.

◊ ◊ ◊

ROBERT FROST
(1874–1963)

For Once, Then, Something
(1923)

Others taunt me with having knelt at well-curbs
Always wrong to the light, so never seeing
Deeper down in the well than where the water
Gives me back in a shining surface picture
5 Me myself in the summer heaven, godlike,
Looking out of a wreath of fern and cloud puffs.
Once, when trying with chin against a well-curb,
I discerned, as I thought, beyond the picture,
Through the picture, a something white, uncertain,
10 Something more of the depths—and then I lost it.
Water came to rebuke the too clear water.
One drop fell from a fern, and lo, a ripple
Shook whatever it was lay there at bottom,
Blurred it, blotted it out. What was that whiteness?
15 Truth? A pebble of quartz? For once, then, something.

The central symbol in this poem is the "something" that the speaker thinks he discerns at the bottom of a well. Traditionally, the act of looking down a well suggests a search for truth. In this poem, the speaker remarks that he always seems to look down the well at the wrong angle, so that all he can see is his own reflection—the surface, not the depths. Once, the speaker tells us, he thought he saw something "beyond the picture," something "white, uncertain," but the image remained indistinct, disappearing when a drop of water from a fern caused the water to ripple. The poem ends with the speaker questioning the significance of what he saw. Like a reader encountering a symbol, the speaker is left trying to come to terms with images that cannot be clearly perceived and suggestions that cannot be readily understood. In light of the elusive nature of truth, all the speaker can do is ask questions that have no definite answers.

Symbols that appear in works of poetry can be *conventional* or *universal*. **Conventional symbols** are those recognized by people who share certain cultural and social assumptions. National flags, for example, evoke a general and agreed-upon response in most people of a particular country and, for better or for worse, American children have for years perceived the golden arches of McDonald's as a symbol of food and fun. **Universal symbols** are those likely to be recognized by people regardless of their culture. In 1890, the noted Scottish anthropologist Sir James George Frazer wrote the first version of his work *The Golden Bough*, in which he showed parallels between the rites and beliefs of early cultures and those of Christianity. Fascinated by Frazer's work, the psychologist Carl Jung sought to explain these parallels by formulating a theory of **archetypes,** which held that certain images or ideas reside in the subconscious of all people. According to Jung, archetypal, or universal, symbols include water, symbolizing rebirth; spring, symbolizing growth; and winter, symbolizing death.

Sometimes symbols that appear in poems can be obscure or highly idiosyncratic. The works of William Blake and W. B. Yeats, for example, combine symbols from different cultural, theological, and philosophical sources to form complex networks of symbolic associations. To Blake, for example, the scientist Isaac Newton represents the tendency of scientists to quantify experience while ignoring the beauty and mystery of nature. Readers cannot begin to understand Blake's use of Newton as a symbol until they have read a number of his more difficult poems.

Most often, however, symbols in poems are not this challenging. In the following poem, for instance, the poet introduces a cross—a symbol that has specific associations to those familiar with Christianity—and makes his own use of it.

◊ ◊ ◊

JIM SIMMERMAN[1]

Child's Grave, Hale County, Alabama
(1983)

    Someone drove a two-by-four
    through the heart of this hard land
    that even in a good year
    will notch a plow blade worthless,
5 snap the head off a shovel,
    or bow a stubborn back.

---

[1] Birth date is not available.

He'd have had to steal
the wood from a local mill
or steal, by starlight, across
his landlord's farm, to worry   10
a fencepost out of its well
and lug it the three miles home.
He'd have had to leave his wife
asleep on a corn shuck mat,
leave his broken brogans[2]   15
by the stove, to slip outside,
quiet as sin, with the child
bundled in a burlap sack.
What a thing to have to do
on a cold night in December,   20
1936, alone
but for a raspy wind
and the red, rock-ridden dirt
things come down to in the end.
Whoever it was pounded   25
this shabby half-cross
into the ground must have toiled
all night to root it so:
five feet buried with the child
for the foot of it that shows.   30
And as there are no words
carved here, it's likely that
the man was illiterate,
or addled with fatigue,
or wrenched simple-minded   35
by the one simple fact.
Or else the unscored lumber
driven deep into the land
and the hump of busted rock
spoke too plainly of his grief: 40
forty years layed by and still
there are no words for this.

Even in non-Christian cultures, the cross on a grave is a readily identifiable symbol of death and rebirth. In this poem, however, the cross is not simply presented as a conventional Christian symbol; it is also associated with the tenant farmer's hard work and difficult life. In this sense, the cross also suggests the poverty that helped bring about the death of the child and the social conditions that existed during the Depression. These associations take readers through many layers of meaning, so

---

[2] Sturdy, heavy work shoes, frequently ankle high.

that the cross may ultimately stand for the tenant farmer's whole life (the cross *he* has to bear), not just for the death of the child. This interpretation by no means exhausts the possible symbolic significance of the cross in the poem. For example, the "shabby half-cross" might also suggest the rage and grief of the individual who made it, or it might call to mind the poor who live and die in anonymity. Certainly the poet could have assigned a fixed meaning to the cross that marks the child's grave, but he chose instead, by suggesting various ideas through a single powerful symbol, to let readers arrive at their own conclusions.

How do you know when an idea or image in a poem is a symbol? At what point do you decide that a particular object or idea goes beyond the literal level and takes on symbolic significance? When, that is, is a rose more than a rose or a cross more than a cross? Frequently you can recognize a symbol by its prominence or repetition. In "Child's Grave, Hale County, Alabama," for example, the cross is introduced in the first line of the poem, and it is the focal point of the poem; in "The Sick Rose," the importance of the rose is emphasized by the title.

It is not enough, however, to identify an image or idea that seems to suggest something else. Your decision that a particular item has some symbolic significance must be supported by the details of the poem and make sense within the context of the ideas developed in the poem. Moreover, the symbol must support the poem's ideas. In the following poem, the image of the volcano helps readers to understand the poem's central theme.

◊ ◊ ◊

EMILY DICKINSON
(1830–1886)

Volcanoes Be in Sicily
(1914)

Volcanoes be in Sicily
And South America
I judge from my Geography—
Volcanoes nearer here
5 A Lava step at any time
Am I inclined to climb—
A Crater I may contemplate
Vesuvius at Home.

This poem opens with a statement of fact: volcanoes are located in Sicily and South America. In lines 3 and 4, however, the speaker makes the improbable observation that volcanoes are located near where she is at the moment. Readers familiar with Dickinson know that her poems are highly autobiographical and that she lived in Amherst, Massachusetts, a town with no volcanoes. This information leads readers to suspect that they should not take the speaker's observation literally and that in the context of the poem volcanoes may have symbolic significance. But what do volcanoes suggest here? On the one hand, volcanoes represent the awesome creative power of nature; on the other hand, they suggest its destructiveness. The speaker's contemplation of the crater of Vesuvius—the volcano that buried the ancient Roman city of Pompeii in A.D. 79—is therefore filled with contradictory associations. Because Dickinson was a recluse, volcanoes—active, destructive, unpredictable, and dangerous—may be seen as symbolic of everything she fears in the outside world and, perhaps, within herself. Or, volcanoes may even suggest her own creative power, which, like a volcano, is something to be feared as well as contemplated. She has a voyeur's attraction to danger and power, but she is also afraid of them. For this reason she (and her speaker) may feel safer contemplating Vesuvius at home—not experiencing exotic lands, but simply reading a geography book.

◆ POEMS FOR FURTHER READING: SYMBOL

LANGSTON HUGHES
(1902–1967)

Island
(1951)

Wave of sorrow,
Do not drown me now:

I see the island
Still ahead somehow.

5 I see the island
And its sands are fair:

Wave of sorrow,
Take me there.

READING AND REACTING

1. What makes you suspect that the island has symbolic significance in this poem?
2. Is the "wave of sorrow" also a symbol?
3. **JOURNAL ENTRY** Beyond its literal meaning, what might the island in this poem suggest? Consider several possibilities.

Related Works: "A Worn Path" (p. 256), "Sea Grapes" (p. 498)

THEODORE ROETHKE
(1908–1963)

Night Crow
(1944)

> When I saw that clumsy crow
> Flap from a wasted tree,
> Over the gulfs of dream
> Flew a tremendous bird
> 5 Further and further away
> Into a moonless black,
> Deep in the brain, far back.

READING AND REACTING

1. What does the title suggest? How does it help you to interpret the symbolic significance of the crow?
2. How is the "clumsy crow" different from the crow "Deep in the brain"? What visual image does each suggest?
3. **JOURNAL ENTRY** It has been suggested that "Night Crow" is a commentary on the difference between reality and imagination. Does the poem's use of symbol support such an interpretation? Explain.

Related Works: "The Cask of Amontillado" (p. 136), "The Tyger" (p. 506), "The Windhover" (p. 529)

ALLEGORY

Allegory is a form of narrative that conveys a message or doctrine by using people, places, or things to stand for abstract ideas. **Allegorical figures,** each with a strict equivalent, form an **allegorical framework,** a set of ideas that conveys the allegory's message or lesson. Thus, the allegory takes place on two levels: a literal level that tells a story and a figurative level where the allegorical figures in the story stand for ideas, concepts, and other qualities. Like symbols, allegory uses things to suggest other things. But unlike symbols, which have a range of possible meanings, allegorical figures can always be assigned specific meanings. (Because writers use allegory to instruct, they gain nothing by hiding its significance.) Thus, symbols open up possibilities for interpretation, whereas allegories tend to restrict possibilities.

Quite often an allegory involves a journey or an adventure, as in the case of Dante's *Divine Comedy,* which traces a journey through Hell, Purgatory, and Heaven. Within an allegory, everything can have meaning: the road upon which the characters walk, the people they encounter, or a phrase that one of them repeats throughout the journey. Once you understand the allegorical framework, your main task is to see how the various elements fit within this system. Some allegorical poems can be relatively straightforward, but others can be so complicated that it takes a great deal of time and effort to unlock their meaning. In the following poem, a journey is central to the allegory.

◊ ◊ ◊

CHRISTINA ROSSETTI
(1830–1894)

Uphill
(1861)

Does the road wind uphill all the way?
    Yes, to the very end.
Will the day's journey take the whole long day?
    From morn to night, my friend.

5 But is there for the night a resting-place?
    A roof for when the slow dark hours begin.
May not the darkness hide it from my face?
    You cannot miss that inn.

Shall I meet other wayfarers at night?
10   Those who have gone before.
Then must I knock, or call when just in sight?
    They will not keep you standing at that door.

Shall I find comfort, travel-sore and weak?
    Of labor you shall find the sum.
15 Will there be beds for me and all who seek?
    Yea, beds for all who come.

"Uphill" uses a question-and-answer structure to describe a journey along an uphill road. Like the one described in John Bunyan's seventeenth-century allegory *The Pilgrim's Progress,* this is a spiritual journey, one that suggests the challenges a person faces throughout life. The day-and-night duration of the journey stands for life and death, and the inn at the end of the road stands for the grave, the final resting place.

Poem for Further Reading: Allegory

ADRIENNE RICH
(1929–   )

Diving into the Wreck
(1973)

First having read the book of myths,
and loaded the camera,
and checked the edge of the knife-blade,
I put on
5 the body-armor of black rubber
the absurd flippers
the grave and awkward mask.
I am having to do this
not like Cousteau with his
10 assiduous team
aboard the sun-flooded schooner
but here alone.

There is a ladder.
The ladder is always there
15 hanging innocently
close to the side of the schooner.
We know what it is for,
we who have used it.
Otherwise
20 it's a piece of maritime floss
some sundry equipment.

I go down.
Rung after rung and still
the oxygen immerses me
25 the blue light
the clear atoms
of our human air.
I go down.
My flippers cripple me,
30 I crawl like an insect down the ladder
and there is no one
to tell me when the ocean
will begin.

First the air is blue and then
35 it is bluer and then green and then
black I am blacking out and yet
my mask is powerful
it pumps my blood with power
the sea is another story
40 the sea is not a question of power
I have to learn alone
to turn my body without force
in the deep element.

And now: it is easy to forget
45 what I came for
among so many who have always
lived here
swaying their crenellated fans
between the reefs
50 and besides
you breathe differently down here.

I came to explore the wreck.
The words are purposes.
The words are maps.
55 I came to see the damage that was done
and the treasures that prevail.
I stroke the beam of my lamp
slowly along the flank
of something more permanent
60 than fish or weed

the thing I came for:
the wreck and not the story of the wreck
the thing itself and not the myth
the drowned face always staring
65 toward the sun
the evidence of damage
worn by salt and sway into this threadbare beauty
the ribs of the disaster
curving their assertion
70 among the tentative haunters.

This is the place.
And I am here, the mermaid whose dark hair
streams black, the merman in his armored body
We circle silently
75 about the wreck
we dive into the hold.
I am she: I am he

whose drowned face sleeps with open eyes
whose breasts still bear the stress
80 whose silver, copper, vermeil cargo lies
obscurely inside barrels
half-wedged and left to rot
we are the half-destroyed instruments
that once held to a course
85 the water-eaten log
the fouled compass

We are, I am, you are
by cowardice or courage
the one who finds our way
90 back to this scene
carrying a knife, a camera
a book of myths
in which
our names do not appear.

Reading and Reacting

1. On one level, this poem is about a deep-sea diver's exploration of a wrecked ship. What details suggest that the poet wants you to see something more?
2. Explain the allegorical figures presented in the poem. What, for example, might the diver and the wreck represent?
3. Does the poem contain any symbols? How can you tell they are symbols and not allegorical figures?
4. **Journal Entry** In lines 62–63, the speaker says that she came for "the wreck and not the story of the wreck / the thing itself and not the myth." What do you think the speaker is really looking for?

Related Works: "Once upon a Time" (p. 46), "Young Goodman Brown" (p. 198), "The Love Song of J. Alfred Prufrock" (p. 519)

Allusion

◊ ◊ ◊

An **allusion** is a brief reference to a person, place, or event (fictional or actual) that readers are expected to recognize. Like symbols and allegories, allusions enrich a work by introducing associations and attitudes from another context.

When poets use allusions, they assume that they and their readers have a common body of knowledge. If, when reading a poem, you come across a reference with which you are not familiar, take the time to look it up in a dictionary or an encyclopedia. As you have probably realized by now, your understanding of a poem may depend on your ability to interpret an unfamiliar reference.

Although most poets expect readers to recognize their references, some use allusions to exclude certain readers from their work. In his 1922 poem "The Waste Land," for example, T. S. Eliot makes allusions to historical events, ancient languages, and obscure literary works. He even includes a set of notes to accompany his poem, but they do little more than complicate an already difficult text. (As you might expect, critical response to this poem was mixed, with some critics saying that it was a work of genius and others saying that it was pretentious.)

Allusions can come from any source: history, the arts, other works of literature, the Bible, current events, or even the personal life of the poet. In the following poem, the Nigerian poet and playwright Wole Soyinka alludes to several contemporary political figures.

◊ ◊ ◊

WOLE SOYINKA
(1934–   )

Future Plans
(1972)

    The meeting is called
    To odium: Forgers, framers
    Fabricators Inter-
    national. Chairman,
5 A dark horse, a circus nag turned blinkered sprinter
    Mach Three
    We rate him—one for the Knife
    Two for 'iavelli, Three—
    Breaking speed
10 Of the truth barrier by a swooping detention decree
    Projects in view:
    Mao Tse Tung in league
    With Chiang Kai. Nkrumah
    Makes a secret
15 Pact with Verwood, sworn by Hastings Banda.
    Proven: Arafat
    In flagrante cum
    Golda Meir. Castro drunk
    With Richard Nixon
20 Contraceptives stacked beneath the papal bunk . . .
                    . . . *and more to come*

This poem is structured like an agenda for a meeting. From the moment it announces that a meeting has been called "To odium" (a pun on "to *order*"), it is clear that the poem will be a bitter political satire. Those in attendance are "Forgers, framers / Fabricators." The second stanza contains three allusions that shed light on the character of the chairman. The first is to Mack the Knife, a petty criminal in Bertolt Brecht and Kurt Weill's 1933 *Threepenny Opera*. The second is to Niccolò Machiavelli, whose 1532 book *The Prince* advocates the use of unscrupulous means to strengthen the State. The last is to the term *mach*, which denotes the speed of an airplane in relation to the speed of sound—mach one, two, three, and so on. By means of these allusions, the poem implies that the meeting's chairman has been chosen for his ability to engage in violence, to be ruthless, and to break the "truth barrier"—that is, to lie.

The rest of the poem alludes to individuals involved in global politics—specifically, the politics of developing nations. According to the speaker, instead of fighting for the rights of the oppressed, these people consolidate their own political power by collaborating with those who oppose their positions. Thus, Mao Tse-tung, the former communist leader of China, is "in league with" Chiang Kai-shek, his old Nationalist Chinese enemy; Yassir Arafat, the leader of the Palestine Liberation Organization, is linked with Golda Meir, the former prime minister of Israel; Kwame Nkrumah, the first president of Ghana, conspires with Hendrick Verwoerd, the former prime minister of South Africa, assassinated in 1966; and former President Richard Nixon gets drunk with Cuba's communist leader, Fidel Castro. These allusions suggest the self-serving nature of political alliances and the extreme disorder of world politics. The ideological juxtapositions show the interchangeability of various political philosophies, none of which has the answer to the world's problems. Whether the poem is satirizing the United Nations and its idealistic agenda, criticizing the tendency of politics to make strange bedfellows, or showing how corrupt all politicians are, its allusions enable the poet to broaden his frame of reference and thus make the poem more meaningful to readers.

The following poem uses allusions to writers, as well as to a myth, to develop its theme.

WILLIAM MEREDITH
(1919–   )

Dreams of Suicide
(1980)

*(in sorrowful memory of Ernest Hemingway,
Sylvia Plath, and John Berryman)*

I

I reach for the awkward shotgun not to disarm
you, but to feel the metal horn,
furred with the downy membrane of dream.
More surely than the unicorn,
5   you are the mythical beast.

II

Or I am sniffing an oven. On all fours
I am imitating a totemic animal
but she is not my totem or the totem
of my people, this is not my magic oven.

III

10   If I hold you tight by the ankles,
still you fly upward from the iron railing.
Your father made these wings,
after he made his own, and now from beyond
he tells you *fly down,* in the voice
15   my own father might say *walk, boy.*

This poem is dedicated to the memory of three writers who committed suicide. In each stanza, the speaker envisions in a dream the death of one of the writers. In the first stanza, he dreams of Ernest Hemingway, who killed himself with a shotgun. The speaker grasps the "metal horn" of Hemingway's shotgun and transforms him into a mythical beast who, like a unicorn, represents the rare, unique talent of the artist. In the second stanza, the speaker dreams of Sylvia Plath, who asphyxiated herself in a gas oven. He sees himself, like Plath, on his knees imitating an animal sniffing an oven. Finally, in the third stanza, the speaker dreams of John Berryman, who leaped to his death. Berryman is characterized as Icarus, a mythological figure who, along with his father Daedalus, fled Crete by building wings made of feathers and wax. Together they flew away, but, ignoring his father's warning, Icarus flew too close to the sun and, when the wax melted, fell to his death in the sea. Like Icarus, Berryman ignores the warning of his father and, like Daedalus, the speaker tries to stop Berryman. In this poem, then, the speaker uses allusions to make a point about the difficult lives of writers—and, perhaps, to convey his own empathy for those who could not survive the struggle to reconcile art and life.

❖ Poem for Further Reading: Allusion

❖ ❖ ❖

DELMORE SCHWARTZ
(1913–1966)

The True-Blue American
(1959)

Jeremiah Dickson was a true-blue American,
For he was a little boy who understood America, for he felt that he must
Think about *everything;* because that's *all* there is to think about,
Knowing immediately the intimacy of truth and comedy,
5   Knowing intuitively how a sense of humor was a necessity
For one and for all who live in America. Thus, natively, and
Naturally when on an April Sunday in an ice cream parlor Jeremiah
Was requested to choose between a chocolate sundae and a banana split
He answered unhesitatingly, having no need to think of it
10 Being a true-blue American, determined to continue as he began:
Rejecting the either-or of Kierkegaard,[1] and many another European;
Refusing to accept alternatives, refusing to believe the choice of between;
Rejecting selection; denying dilemma; electing absolute affirmation: knowing
15   in his breast
              The infinite and the gold
              Of the endless frontier, the deathless West.
"Both: I will have them both!" declared this true-blue American
In Cambridge, Massachusetts, on an April Sunday, instructed
20   By the great department stores, by the Five-and-Ten,
Taught by Christmas, by the circus, by the vulgarity and grandeur of
              Niagara Falls and the Grand Canyon,

---

[1] Søren Kierkegaard (1813–1855)—Danish philosopher who greatly influenced twentieth-century existentialism. *Either-Or* (1841) is one of his best-known works.

Tutored by the grandeur, vulgarity, and infinite appetite gratified and
    Shining in the darkness, of the light
25 On Saturdays at the double bills of the moon pictures,
The consummation of the advertisements of the imagination of the
    light
Which is as it was—the infinite belief in infinite hope—of Columbus,
    Barnum, Edison, and Jeremiah Dickson.

READING AND REACTING

1. To what does the poem's title refer? Do you think this title has meaning beyond its identification of Jeremiah Dickson?
2. Read an encyclopedia article about Kierkegaard. Why do you suppose Schwartz alludes to him in line 11?
3. What do you think the significance of the name Jeremiah Dickson might be? Is it an allusion?
4. What is the significance of the allusions to places in lines 19–22 and to individuals in lines 27 and 28?
5. **JOURNAL ENTRY** How do you define a "true-blue" American? How do you think the poem's speaker would define this term?

Related Works: "The Secret Lion" (p. 281), "Chicago" (p. 464), "next to of course god america i" (p. 513), "The United Fruit Co." (p. 537), *The Glass Menagerie* (p. 938)

MYTH
◊ ◊ ◊

A **myth** is a narrative that embodies—and in some cases helps to explain—the religious, philosophical, moral, and political values of a culture. Using gods and supernatural beings, myths try to make sense of occurrences in the natural world. (The term *myth* can also refer to a private belief system invented by an individual poet as well as to any fully realized fictitious setting in which a literary work takes place, such as the myths of William Faulkner's Yoknapatawpha County or Lawrence Durrell's Alexandria.) Contrary to popular usage, *myth* is not the same as *falsehood*. In the broadest sense, myths are stories—usually whole groups of stories—that can be true or partly true as well as false; regardless of their degree of accuracy, however, myths frequently express the deepest beliefs of a culture. According to this definition, then, the *Iliad* and the *Odyssey*, the Koran, and the Old and New Testaments can all be regarded as myths.

According to the mythologist Joseph Campbell, myths contain truths that link people together, whether they live today or lived 2,500 years ago. Myths do, after all, attempt to explain phenomena that human beings care about regardless of when and where they live. It is not surprising, then, that myths frequently contain archetypal images that cut across cultural and racial boundaries and touch us on a very deep level. Many Greek myths illustrate this power. For example, when Orpheus descends into Hades to rescue his wife, Eurydice, he acts out the human desire to transcend death; and when Telemachus sets out in search of his father, Odysseus, he reminds readers that we all are lost children searching for parents. When Icarus ignores his father and flies too near the sun and when Pandora cannot resist looking into a box that she has been told not to open, we are reminded of the human weaknesses we all share.

When poets use myths, they are actually making allusions. They expect readers to bring to the poem the cultural, emotional, and ethical context of the myths to which they are alluding. At one time, when all educated individuals studied the Greek and Latin classics as well as the Bible, poets could be reasonably sure that readers would recognize the mythological allusions they made. Many contemporary readers, however, are unable to understand the full significance of an allusion or its application within the poem. Although many of the poems in this anthology are accompanied by notes, these notes may not provide all the information you will need to understand each mythological allusion and to determine its significance within a poem. Occasionally, you may have to look for answers beyond this text, in dictionaries, encyclopedias, or collections of myths, such as the *New Larousse Encyclopedia of Mythology* or *Bulfinch's Mythology,* for example.

Sometimes a poet will allude to a myth in a title; sometimes references to various myths will appear throughout a poem; at other times, an entire poem will focus on a single myth. In each case, as in the following poem, the use of myth helps to communicate the poem's theme.

◊ ◊ ◊

COUNTEE CULLEN
(1903–1946)

Yet Do I Marvel
(1925)

    I doubt not God is good, well-meaning, kind,
    And did He stoop to quibble could tell why
    The little buried mole continues blind,
    Why flesh that mirrors Him must some day die,
5 Make plain the reason tortured Tantalus
    Is baited by the fickle fruit, declare
    If merely brute caprice dooms Sisyphus
    To struggle up a never-ending stair.
    Inscrutable His ways are, and immune
10 To catechism by a mind too strewn
    With petty cares to slightly understand

What awful brain compels His awful hand.
Yet do I marvel at this curious thing:
To make a poet black, and bid him sing!

The speaker in this poem begins by affirming his belief in the benevolence of God, but he then goes on to question why God engages in what appear to be capricious acts. As part of his catalog of questions, the speaker mentions Tantalus and Sisyphus, two figures from Greek mythology. Tantalus was a king who was admitted to the society of the gods. Because he behaved so badly, he was condemned to Hades and forced to stand up to his chin in a pool of water over which hung a branch laden with fruit. When he got thirsty and tried to drink, the level of the water would drop, and when he got hungry and reached for fruit, it would move just out of his grasp. Thus, Tantalus was doomed to be near what he most desired, but forever unable to obtain it. Like Tantalus, Sisyphus was also condemned to Hades. For his disrespect to Zeus, he was sentenced to endless toil. Every day, Sisyphus would push a gigantic boulder up a steep hill. As he neared the top, the boulder would slip down the hill, and he would have to begin again. Like Tantalus, the speaker cannot have what he wants; like Sisyphus, he is forced to toil in vain. He wonders why a well-meaning God would "make a poet black, and bid him sing" in a racist society that does not listen to his voice. Thus, the poet's two allusions to Greek mythology enrich the poem by connecting the suffering of the speaker to a universal drama that has been acted out again and again.

❖ POEMS FOR FURTHER READING: MYTH

LOUISE ERDRICH
(1954–   )

Windigo
(1984)

For Angela

The Windigo is a flesh-eating, wintry demon with a man buried deep inside of it. In some Chippewa stories, a young girl vanquishes this monster by forcing boiling lard down its throat, thereby releasing the human at the core of ice.

You knew I was coming for you, little one,
when the kettle jumped into the fire.
Towels flapped on the hooks,
and the dog crept off, groaning,
5   to the deepest part of the woods.

In the hackles of dry brush a thin laughter started up.
Mother scolded the food warm and smooth in the pot
and called you to eat.
But I spoke in the cold trees:
10 *New one, I have come for you, child hide and lie still.*

The sumac pushed sour red cones through the air.
Copper burned in the raw wood.
You saw me drag toward you.
Oh touch me, I murmured, and licked the soles of your feet.
15 You dug your hands into my pale, melting fur.

I stole you off, a huge thing in my bristling armor.
Steam rolled from my wintry arms, each leaf shivered
from the bushes we passed
until they stood, naked, spread like the cleaned spines of fish.

20 Then your warm hands hummed over and shoveled themselves full
of the ice and the snow. I would darken and spill
all night running, until at last morning broke the cold earth
and I carried you home,
a river shaking in the sun.

READING AND REACTING

1. Because Erdrich writes for a diverse audience, she cannot reasonably expect all her readers to be familiar with the Native American myth in the poem. Does her epigraph provide enough information for those who are not?
2. Who is the speaker in the poem? How would you characterize the speaker? What advantage does Erdrich gain by assuming this persona?
3. What is the major theme of this poem? How does the myth of the Windigo express this theme?
4. **JOURNAL ENTRY** How is the Windigo described in the epigraph like and unlike the one portrayed in the poem?

Related Works: "Where Are You Going, Where Have You Been?" (p. 268), "Gretel in Darkness" (p. 330), "Fire and Ice" (p. 340), "Leda and the Swan" (p. 497)

WILLIAM BUTLER YEATS
(1865–1939)

Leda and the Swan
(1924)

A sudden blow: the great wings beating still
Above the staggering girl, her thighs caressed
By the dark webs, her nape caught in his bill,
He holds her helpless breast upon his breast.

5 How can those terrified vague fingers push
The feathered glory from her loosening thighs?
And how can body, laid in that white rush,
But feel the strange heart beating where it lies?

A shudder in the loins engenders there
10 The broken wall, the burning roof and tower
And Agamemnon dead.
     Being so caught up,
So mastered by the brute blood of the air,
Did she put on his knowledge with his power
15 Before the indifferent beak could let her drop?

READING AND REACTING

1. Look up the myth of Leda in an encyclopedia. What event is described in this poem? What is the mythological significance of the event?
2. How is Leda portrayed? Why is the swan described as a "feathered glory" (6)? Why in the poem's last line is Leda dropped by his "indifferent beak"?
3. The third stanza refers to the Trojan War, which was indirectly caused by the event described in the poem. How does the allusion to the Trojan War help develop the theme of the poem?
4. **JOURNAL ENTRY** Does the poem answer the question asked in its last two lines? Explain.

Related Works: "Where Are You Going, Where Have You Been?" (p. 268), "To His Coy Mistress" (p. 419), "The Second Coming" (p. 560)

DEREK WALCOTT[1]
(1930–)

Sea Grapes[2]
(1971)

That sail which leans on light,
tired of islands,
a schooner beating up the Caribbean

for home, could be Odysseus,
5 home-bound on the Aegean;
that father and husband's

longing, under gnarled sour grapes, is
like the adulterer hearing Nausicaa's[3] name
in every gull's outcry.

10 This brings nobody peace. The ancient war
between obsession and responsibility
will never finish and has been the same

for the sea-wanderer or the one on shore
now wriggling on his sandals to walk home,
15 since Troy sighed its last flame,

and the blind giant's boulder heaved the trough
from whose ground-swell the great hexameters come
to the conclusions of exhausted surf.

The classics can console. But not enough.

READING AND REACTING

1. Read a plot summary of the *Odyssey* in an encyclopedia. In the context of the myth of Odysseus, what is the "ancient war / between obsession and responsibility" (10–11) to which the speaker refers? Does this conflict have a wider application in the context of the poem? Explain.
2. Consider the following lines from the poem: "and the blind giant's boulder heaved the trough / from whose ground-swell the great hexameters come / to the conclusions of exhausted surf" (16–18). In what sense does the blind giant's boulder

---

[1] Winner of the 1992 Nobel Prize in literature.
[2] Small trees found on tropical sandy beaches.
[3] A young woman who befriended Odysseus.

create the "great hexameters"? In what way does the trough end up as "exhausted surf"?
3. **JOURNAL ENTRY** This poem includes many references to Homer's *Odyssey*. Could you have appreciated it if you had not read a plot summary of the *Odyssey?*

Related Works: "My Father in the Navy: A Childhood Memory" (p. 308), "Dover Beach" (p. 503)

◊ ◊ ◊

W. H. AUDEN
(1907–1973)

Musée des Beaux Arts
(1940)

About suffering they were never wrong,
The Old Masters: how well they understood
Its human position; how it takes place
While someone else is eating or opening a window or just walking
    dully along
5 How, when the aged are reverently, passionately waiting
For the miraculous birth, there always must be
Children who did not specially want it to happen, skating
On a pond at the edge of the wood:
They never forgot
10 That even the dreadful martyrdom must run its course
Anyhow in a corner, some untidy spot
Where the dogs go on with their doggy life and the torturer's horse
Scratches its innocent behind on a tree.
In Brueghel's *Icarus,* for instance: how everything turns away
15 Quite leisurely from the disaster; the ploughman may
Have heard the splash, the forsaken cry,
But for him it was not an important failure; the sun shone
As it had to on the white legs disappearing into the green
Water; and the expensive delicate ship that must have seen
20 Something amazing, a boy falling out of the sky,
Had somewhere to get to and sailed calmly on.

READING AND REACTING

1. Reread the summary of the myth of Icarus on page 491. Is Auden's allusion to the myth essential to the poem?
2. What point does the poet make by referring to the "Old Masters" (2)?

◊ Brueghel. *Landscape with the Fall of Icarus*. Photograph by Giraudon. Art Resource, New York.

3. **Journal Entry** Look at the painting above. How does looking at Brueghel's *Landscape with the Fall of Icarus* help you to understand the poem? To what specific details in the painting does the poet refer?

Related Works: "The Lottery" (p. 209), "One Day I Wrote Her Name upon the Strand" (p. 379), "Shall I Compare Thee to a Summer's Day?" (p. 402), "Ethics" (p. 540), "Not Waving but Drowning" (p. 549)

 Checklist: Writing about Symbol, Allegory, Allusion, Myth

Symbol
- ✓ Are there any symbols in the poem? What leads you to believe they are symbols?
- ✓ Are these symbols conventional?
- ✓ Are they universal or archetypal?

- ✓ Are any symbols obscure or highly idiosyncratic?
- ✓ What is the literal meaning of each symbol in the context of the poem?
- ✓ Beyond its literal meaning, what else could each symbol suggest?
- ✓ How does your interpretation of each symbol enhance your understanding of the poem?

ALLEGORY

- ✓ Is the poem an allegory?
- ✓ Are there any allegorical figures within the poem? How can you tell?
- ✓ What do the allegorical figures signify on a literal level?
- ✓ What lesson does the allegory illustrate?

ALLUSION

- ✓ Are there any allusions in the poem?
- ✓ Do you recognize the names, places, historical events, or literary works to which the poet alludes?
- ✓ What does each allusion add to the poem? In what way does each deepen the poem's meaning? Does any allusion interfere with your understanding or enjoyment of the poem? If so, how?
- ✓ Would the poem be more effective without a particular allusion?

MYTH

- ✓ What myths or mythological figures are alluded to?
- ✓ How does the poem use myth to convey its meaning?
- ✓ How faithful is the poem to the myth? Does the poet add material to the myth? Are any details from the original myth omitted? Is any information distorted? Why?

◆ WRITING SUGGESTIONS: SYMBOL, ALLEGORY, ALLUSION, MYTH

1. Read "Aunt Jennifer's Tigers" (p. 436) and "Diving into the Wreck" (p. 486) by Adrienne Rich. Then, write an essay in which you discuss similarities and differences in Rich's use of symbols in the two poems.

2. Many popular songs make use of allusion. Choose one or two popular songs that you know well, and analyze their use of allusion, paying particular attention to whether the allusions expand the impact and meaning of the song or create barriers to your understanding.
3. Read the Emily Dickinson poem "Because I Could Not Stop for Death" (p. 514), and then write an interpretation of the poem, identifying the allegorical figures in the poem.
4. What applications do the lessons of myth have for twentieth-century life? Choose two or three poems from the section on myth, and consider how you can use myth to make generalizations about your own life.
5. Both Judith Ortiz Cofer's "My Father in the Navy: A Childhood Memory" (p. 308) and Derek Walcott's "Sea Grapes" (p. 498) allude to Homer's *Odyssey*. Read a summary of the *Odyssey* in an encyclopedia or other reference book, and then write an essay in which you discuss the poets' treatments of Homer's tale. What specific use does each poet make of the story?

POETRY
FOR FURTHER READING

MATTHEW ARNOLD
(1822–1888)

Dover Beach
(1867)

    The sea is calm tonight.
    The tide is full, the moon lies fair
    Upon the straits;—on the French coast the light
    Gleams and is gone; the cliffs of England stand,
5 Glimmering and vast, out in the tranquil bay.
    Come to the window, sweet is the night-air!
    Only, from the long line of spray
    Where the sea meets the moon-blanched[1] land,
    Listen! you hear the grating roar
10 Of pebbles which the waves draw back, and fling,
    At their return, up the high strand,[2]
    Begin, and cease, and then again begin,
    With tremulous cadence slow, and bring
    The eternal note of sadness in.

15 Sophocles[3] long ago
    Heard it on the Aegean,[4] and it brought
    Into his mind the turbid ebb and flow
    Of human misery; we

---

[1] Whitened by the moon.
[2] Beach.
[3] Greek playwright (496–406 B.C.), author of tragedies including *Oedipus Rex* and *Antigone*.
[4] Sea between Greece and Turkey.

Find also in the sound a thought,
20 Hearing it by this distant northern sea.

The Sea of Faith
Was once, too, at the full, and round earth's shore
Lay like the folds of a bright girdle furled.
But now I only hear
25 Its melancholy, long, withdrawing roar,
Retreating, to the breath
Of the night-wind, down the vast edges drear
And naked shingles[5] of the world.

Ah, love, let us be true
30 To one another! for the world, which seems
To lie before us like a land of dreams,
So various, so beautiful, so new,
Hath really neither joy, nor love, nor light,
Nor certitude, nor peace, nor help for pain;
35 And we are here as on a darkling[6] plain
Swept with confused alarms of struggle and flight,
Where ignorant armies clash by night.

◊ ◊ ◊

WILLIAM BLAKE
(1757–1827)

The Chimney Sweeper
(1789)

When my mother died I was very young,
And my father sold me while yet my tongue
Could scarcely cry "'weep! 'weep! 'weep! 'weep!"
So your chimneys I sweep, and in soot I sleep.

5 There's little Tom Dacre, who cried when his head,
That curled like a lamb's back, was shaved: so I said
"Hush, Tom! never mind it, for when your head's bare
You know that the soot cannot spoil your white hair."

---
[5] Gravel beaches.
[6] Darkening.

And so he was quiet, and that very night,
10 As Tom was a-sleeping, he had such a sight!
That thousands of sweepers, Dick, Joe, Ned, and Jack,
Were all of them locked up in coffins of black.

And by came an Angel who had a bright key,
And he opened the coffins and set them all free;
15 Then down a green plain leaping, laughing, they run,
And wash in a river, and shine in the sun.

Then naked and white, all their bags left behind,
They rise upon clouds and sport in the wind;
And the Angel told Tom, if he'd be a good boy,
20 He'd have God for his father, and never want joy.

And so Tom awoke; and we rose in the dark,
And got with our bags and our brushes to work.
Though the morning was cold, Tom was happy and warm;
So if all do their duty they need not fear harm.

The Lamb
(1789)

Little Lamb, who made thee?
Dost thou know who made thee?
Gave thee life & bid thee feed,
By the stream & o'er the mead;
5 Gave thee clothing of delight,
Softest clothing wooly bright;
Gave thee such a tender voice,
Making all the vales rejoice!
Little Lamb who made thee?
10 Dost thou know who made thee?

Little Lamb I'll tell thee,
Little Lamb I'll tell thee!
He is calléd by thy name,
For he calls himself a Lamb:
15 He is meek & he is mild,
He became a little child:
I a child & thou a lamb,
We are calléd by his name.
Little Lamb God bless thee.
20 Little Lamb God bless thee.

London
(1794)

I wander through each chartered street,
Near where the chartered Thames does flow,
And mark in every face I meet
Marks of weakness, marks of woe.

5 In every cry of every man,
In every infant's cry of fear,
In every voice, in every ban,
The mind-forged manacles I hear.

How the chimney-sweeper's cry
10 Every black'ning church appalls;
And the hapless soldier's sigh
Runs in blood down palace walls.

But most through midnight streets I hear
How the youthful harlot's curse
15 Blasts the new born infant's tear,
And blights with plagues the marriage hearse.

The Tyger
(1794)

Tyger! Tyger! burning bright
In the forests of the night,
What immortal hand or eye
Could frame thy fearful symmetry?

5 In what distant deeps or skies
Burnt the fire of thine eyes?
On what wings dare he aspire?
What the hand dare seize the fire?

And what shoulder, and what art,
10 Could twist the sinews of thy heart?
And when thy heart began to beat,
What dread hand? and what dread feet?

What the hammer? what the chain?
In what furnace was thy brain?
15 What the anvil? what dread grasp
Dare its deadly terrors clasp?

When the stars threw down their spears,
And watered heaven with their tears,
Did he smile his work to see?
20 Did he who made the Lamb make thee?

Tyger! Tyger! burning bright
In the forests of the night,
What immortal hand or eye
Dare frame thy fearful symmetry?

◊ ◊ ◊

GWENDOLYN BROOKS
(1917–)

The *Chicago Defender*[1] Sends a Man to Little Rock
(1960)

Fall, 1957[2]

In Little Rock the people bear
Babes, and comb and part their hair
And watch the want ads, put repair
To roof and latch. While wheat toast burns
5 A woman waters multiferns.

Time upholds or overturns
The many, tight, and small concerns.

In Little Rock the people sing
Sunday hymns like anything,
10 Through Sunday pomp and polishing.

And after testament and tunes,
Some soften Sunday afternoons
With lemon tea and Lorna Doones.

I forecast
15 And I believe
Come Christmas Little Rock will cleave
To Christmas tree and trifle, weave,
From laugh and tinsel, texture fast.

---

[1] A weekly newspaper for African-American readers.
[2] When black students first entered the high school in Little Rock, Arkansas, in 1957, the city erupted in race riots protesting desegregation.

In Little Rock is baseball; Barcarolle.³
20 That hotness in July . . . the uniformed figures raw and implacable
And not intellectual,
Batting the hotness or clawing the suffering dust.
The Open Air Concert, on the special twilight green. . . .
When Beethoven is brutal or whispers to lady-like air.
25 Blanket-sitters are solemn, as Johann troubles to lean
To tell them what to mean. . . .

There is love, too, in Little Rock. Soft women softly
Opening themselves in kindness,
Or, pitying one's blindness,
30 Awaiting one's pleasure
In azure
Glory with anguished rose at the root. . . .
To wash away old semi-discomfitures.
They re-teach purple and unsullen blue.
35 The wispy soils go. And uncertain
Half-havings have they clarified to sures.

In Little Rock they know
Not answering the telephone is a way of rejecting life,
That it is our business to be bothered, is our business
40 To cherish bores or boredom, be polite
To lies and love and many-faceted fuzziness.
I scratch my head, massage the hate-I-had.
I blink across my prim and pencilled pad.
The saga I was sent for is not down.
45 Because there is a puzzle in this town.
The biggest News I do not dare
Telegraph to the Editor's chair:
"They are like people everywhere."

The angry Editor would reply
50 In hundred harryings of Why.

And true, they are hurling spittle, rock,
Garbage and fruit in Little Rock.
And I saw coiling storm a-writhe
On bright madonnas. And a scythe
55 Of men harassing brownish girls.
(The bows and barrettes in the curls
And braids declined away from joy.)

I saw a bleeding brownish boy. . . .

The lariat lynch-wish I deplored.

60 The loveliest lynchee was our Lord.

---

³ A Venetian gondolier's song, or one suggesting the rhythm of rowing.

Medgar Evers[1]
(1964)

For Charles Evers[2]

The man whose height his fear improved he
arranged to fear no further. The raw
intoxicated time was time for better birth or a final death.

Old styles, old tempos, all the engagement of
5 the day—the sedate, the regulated fray—
the antique light, the Moral rose, old gusts,
tight whistlings from the past, the mothballs
in the Love at last our man forswore.

Medgar Evers annoyed confetti and assorted
10 brands of businessmen's eyes.

The shows came down: to maxims and surprise.
And palsy.

Roaring no rapt arise-ye to the dead, he
leaned across tomorrow. People said that
15 he was holding clean globes in his hands.

We Real Cool
(1960)

The Pool Players.
Seven at the Golden Shovel.

We real cool. We
Left School. We

Lurk late. We
Strike straight. We

5 Sing sin. We
Thin gin. We

Jazz June. We
Die soon.

---

[1] African-American civil rights leader who was killed by a sniper in 1963.
[2] Medgar Evers's brother.

GEORGE GORDON, LORD BYRON
(1788–1824)

She Walks in Beauty
(1815)

1

She walks in beauty, like the night
   Of cloudless climes and starry skies;
And all that's best of dark and bright
   Meet in her aspect and her eyes:
5 Thus mellowed to that tender light
   Which heaven to gaudy day denies.

2

One shade the more, one ray the less,
   Had half impaired the nameless grace
Which waves in every raven tress,
10   Or softly lightens o'er her face;
Where thoughts serenely sweet express
   How pure, how dear their dwelling place.

3

And on that cheek, and o'er that brow,
   So soft, so calm, yet eloquent,
15 The smiles that win, the tints that glow,
   But tell of days in goodness spent,
A mind at peace with all below,
   A heart whose love is innocent!

SAMUEL TAYLOR COLERIDGE
(1772–1834)

Kubla Khan[1]
(1797, 1798)

Or, a Vision in a Dream. A Fragment.

In Xanadu did Kubla Khan
A stately pleasure-dome decree:

---

[1] Coleridge mythologizes the actual Kublai Khan, a thirteenth-century Mongol emperor, as well as the Chinese city of Xanadu.

Where Alph,² the sacred river, ran
Through caverns measureless to man
5 Down to a sunless sea.
So twice five miles of fertile ground
With walls and towers were girdled round;
And there were gardens bright with sinuous rills,
Where blossomed many an incense-bearing tree;
10 And here were forests ancient as the hills,
Enfolding sunny spots of greenery.

But oh! that deep romantic chasm which slanted
Down the green hill athwart a cedarn cover!
A savage place! as holy and enchanted
15 As e'er beneath a waning moon was haunted
By woman wailing for her demon-lover!
And from this chasm, with ceaseless turmoil seething,
As if this earth in fast thick pants were breathing,
A mighty fountain momently was forced:
20 Amid whose swift half-intermitted burst
Huge fragments vaulted like rebounding hail,
Or chaffy grain beneath the thresher's flail:
And 'mid these dancing rocks at once and ever
It flung up momently the sacred river.
25 Five miles meandering with a mazy motion
Through wood and dale the sacred river ran,
Then reached the caverns measureless to man,
And sank in tumult to a lifeless ocean:
And 'mid this tumult Kubla heard from far
30 Ancestral voices prophesying war!

    The shadow of the dome of pleasure
    Floated midway on the waves;
    Where was heard the mingled measure
    From the fountain and the caves.
35 It was a miracle of rare device,
    A sunny pleasure-dome with caves of ice!

    A damsel with a dulcimer
    In a vision once I saw:
    It was an Abyssinian maid,
40 And on her dulcimer she played,

---

² Probably derived from the Greek river Alpheus, whose waters, according to legend, rose from the Ionian Sea in Sicily as the fountain of Arethusa.

Singing of Mount Abora.³
Could I revive within me
Her symphony and song,
To such a deep delight 'twould win me,
45 That with music loud and long,
I would build that dome in air,
That sunny dome! those caves of ice!
And all who heard should see them there,
And all should cry, Beware! Beware!
50 His flashing eyes, his floating hair!
Weave a circle round him thrice,⁴
And close your eyes with holy dread,
For he on honey-dew hath fed,
And drunk the milk of Paradise.

◊ ◊ ◊

E. E. CUMMINGS
(1894–1962)

Buffalo Bill's¹
(1923)

Buffalo Bill's
defunct
     who used to
       ride a watersmooth-silver
5   stallion
and break onetwothreefourfive pigeonsjustlikethat
                                                  Jesus
he was a handsome man
                        and what i want to know is
10 how do you like your blueeyed boy
Mister Death

---

[3] Some scholars see a reminiscence here of John Milton's *Paradise Lost 4.* 280–82: "where Abassin kings their issue guard / Mount Amara, though this by some supposed / True Paradise under the Ethiop Line."
[4] A magic ritual, to keep away intruding spirits.

---

[1] William F. "Buffalo Bill" Cody (1846–1917)—frontier scout, famed buffalo hunter, and popularizer of the wild west show hero of dime novels.

next to of course god america i
(1926)

"next to of course god america i
love you land of the pilgrims' and so forth oh
say can you see by the dawn's early my
country 'tis of centuries come and go
5 and are no more what of it we should worry
in every language even deafanddumb
thy sons acclaim your glorious name by gorry
by jingo by gee by gosh by gum
why talk of beauty what could be more beaut-
10 iful than these heroic happy dead
who rushed like lions to the roaring slaughter
they did not stop to think they died instead
then shall the voice of liberty be mute?"

He spoke. And drank rapidly a glass of water

◊ ◊ ◊

EMILY DICKINSON
(1830–1886)

After Great Pain, a Formal Feeling Comes
(c. 1862)

After great pain, a formal feeling comes—
The Nerves sit ceremonious, like Tombs—
The stiff Heart questions was it He, that bore,
And Yesterday, or Centuries before?

5 The Feet, mechanical, go round—
Of Ground, or Air, or Ought—
A Wooden way
Regardless grown,
A Quartz contentment, like a stone—

10 This is the Hour of Lead—
Remembered, if outlived,
As Freezing persons, recollect the Snow—
First—Chill—then Stupor—then the letting go—

Because I Could Not Stop for Death
(1863)

Because I could not stop for Death—
He kindly stopped for me—
The Carriage held but just Ourselves—
And Immortality.

5 We slowly drove—He knew no haste
And I had put away
My labor and my leisure too,
For His Civility—

We passed the School, where Children strove
10 At Recess—in the Ring—
We passed the Fields of Gazing Grain—
We passed the Setting Sun—

Or rather—He passed Us—
The Dews drew quivering and chill—
15 For only Gossamer, my Gown—
My Tippet[1]—only Tulle—

We paused before a House that seemed
A Swelling of the Ground—
The Roof was scarcely visible—
20 The Cornice—in the Ground—

Since then—'tis Centuries—and yet
Feels shorter than the Day
I first surmised the Horses' Heads
Were toward Eternity—

I Heard a Fly Buzz—When I Died
(c. 1862)

I heard a Fly buzz—when I died—
The Stillness in the Room
Was like the Stillness in the Air—
Between the Heaves of Storm—

---

[1] Cape.

     5 The Eyes around—had wrung them dry—
       And Breaths were gathering firm
       For that last Onset—when the King
       Be witnessed—in the Room—

       I willed my Keepsakes—Signed away
   10 What portion of me be
       Assignable—and then it was
       There interposed a Fly—

       With Blue—uncertain stumbling Buzz—
       Between the light—and me—
   15 And then the Windows failed—and then
       I could not see to see—

The Soul Selects Her Own Society
(1862)

       The Soul selects her own Society—
       Then—shuts the Door—
       To her divine Majority—
       Present no more—

     5 Unmoved—she notes the Chariots—pausing—
       At her low Gate—
       Unmoved—an Emperor be kneeling
       Upon her Mat—

       I've known her—from an ample nation—
   10 Choose One—
       Then—close the Valves of her attention—
       Like Stone—

Wild Nights—Wild Nights!
(1890, c. 1861)

       Wild Nights—Wild Nights!
       Were I with thee
       Wild Nights should be
       Our luxury!

     5 Futile—the Winds—
       To a Heart in port—
       Done with the Compass—
       Done with the Chart!

Rowing in Eden—
10 Ah, the Sea!
Might I but moor—Tonight—
In Thee!

◊ ◊ ◊

JOHN DONNE
(1572–1631)

Death Be Not Proud
(c. 1610)

Death be not proud, though some have callèd thee
Mighty and dreadful, for thou art not so;
For those whom thou think'st thou dost overthrow
Die not, poor death, nor yet canst thou kill me.
5 From rest and sleep, which but thy pictures be,
Much pleasure, then from thee much more must flow,
And soonest our best men with thee do go,
Rest of their bones, and soul's delivery.
Thou art slave to fate, chance, kings, and desperate men,
10 And dost with poison, war, and sickness dwell,
And poppy, or charms can make us sleep as well,
And better than thy stroke; why swell'st thou then?
One short sleep past, we wake eternally,
And death shall be no more; death, thou shalt die.

◊ ◊ ◊

RITA DOVE
(1952–   )

The Satisfaction Coal Company
(1986)

1

What to do with a day.
Leaf through *Jet*. Watch T.V.
Freezing on the porch
but he goes anyhow, snow too high
5 for a walk, the ice treacherous.
Inside, the gas heater takes care of itself;
he doesn't even notice being warm.

Everyone says he looks great.
Across the street a drunk stands smiling
10 at something carved in a tree.
The new neighbor with the floating hips
scoots out to get the mail
and waves once, brightly,
storm door clipping her heel on the way in.

2

15 Twice a week he had taken the bus down Glendale hill
to the corner of Market. Slipped through
the alley by the canal and let himself in.
Started to sweep
with terrible care, like a woman
20 brushing shine into her hair,
same motion, same lullaby.
No curtains—the cop on the beat
stopped outside once in the hour
to swing his billy club and glare.

25 It was better on Saturdays
when the children came along:
he mopped while they emptied
ashtrays, clang of glass on metal
then a dry scutter. Next they counted
30 nailheads studding the leather cushions.
Thirty-four! they shouted,
that was the year and
they found it mighty amusing.

But during the week he noticed more—
35 lights when they gushed or dimmed
at the Portage Hotel, the 10:32
picking up speed past the B & O switchyard,
floorboards trembling and the explosive
kachook kachook kachook kachook
40 and the oiled rails ticking underneath.

3

They were poor then but everyone had been poor.
He hadn't minded the sweeping,
just the thought of it—like now
when people ask him what he's thinking
45 and he says *I'm listening.*

Those nights walking home alone,
the bucket of coal scraps banging his knee,

he'd hear a roaring furnace
with its dry, familiar heat. Now the nights
50 take care of themselves—as for the days,
there is the canary's sweet curdled song,
the wino smiling through his dribble.
Past the hill, past the gorge
choked with wild sumac in summer,
55 the corner has been upgraded.
Still, he'd like to go down there someday
to stand for a while, and get warm.

◊ ◊ ◊

PAUL LAURENCE DUNBAR
(1872–1906)

We Wear the Mask
(1913)

We wear the mask that grins and lies,
It hides our cheeks and shades our eyes—
This debt we pay to human guile;
With torn and bleeding hearts we smile,
5 And mouth with myriad subtleties.

Why should the world be over-wise,
In counting all our tears and sighs?
Nay, let them only see us, while
    We wear the mask.

10 We smile, but, O great Christ, our cries
To thee from tortured souls arise.
We sing, but oh the clay is vile
Beneath our feet, and long the mile;
But let the world dream otherwise,
15   We wear the mask!

T. S. ELIOT
(1888–1965)

The Love Song of J. Alfred Prufrock
(1917)

S'io credessi che mia risposta fosse
A persona che mai tornasse al mondo,
Questa fiamma staria senza piu scosse.
Ma perciocche giammai di questo fondo
Non torno vivo alcun, s'i'odo il vero,
Senza tema d'infamia ti rispondo.[1]

Let us go then, you and I,
When the evening is spread out against the sky
Like a patient etherized upon a table;
Let us go, through certain half-deserted streets,
5   The muttering retreats
Of restless nights in one-night cheap hotels
And sawdust restaurants with oyster-shells:
Streets that follow like a tedious argument
Of insidious intent
10 To lead you to an overwhelming question . . .
Oh, do not ask, "What is it?"
Let us go and make our visit.

In the room the women come and go
Talking of Michelangelo.

15 The yellow fog that rubs its back upon the window-panes,
The yellow smoke that rubs its muzzle on the window-panes
Licked its tongue into the corners of the evening,
Lingered upon the pools that stand in drains,
Let fall upon its back the soot that falls from chimneys,
20 Slipped by the terrace, made a sudden leap,
And seeing that it was a soft October night,
Curled once about the house, and fell asleep.

---

[1] The epigraph is from Dante's *Inferno*, Canto 27. In response to the poet's question about his identity, Guido da Montefelto, who for his sin of fraud must spend eternity wrapped in flames, replies: "If I thought that I was speaking to someone who could go back to the world, this flame would shake me no more. But since from this place nobody ever returns alive, if what I hear is true, I answer you without fear of infamy."

And indeed there will be time
For the yellow smoke that slides along the street,
25 Rubbing its back upon the window-panes;
There will be time, there will be time
To prepare a face to meet the faces that you meet;
There will be time to murder and create,
And time for all the works and days[2] of hands
30 That lift and drop a question on your plate;
Time for you and time for me,
And time yet for a hundred indecisions,
And for a hundred visions and revisions,
Before the taking of a toast and tea.

35 In the room the women come and go
Talking of Michelangelo.

And indeed there will be time
To wonder, "Do I dare?" and, "Do I dare?"
Time to turn back and descend the stair,
40 With a bald spot in the middle of my hair—
(They will say: "How his hair is growing thin!")
My morning coat, my collar mounting firmly to the chin,
My necktie rich and modest, but asserted by a simple pin—
(They will say: "But how his arms and legs are thin!")
45 Do I dare
Disturb the universe?
In a minute there is time
For decisions and revisions which a minute will reverse.

For I have known them all already, known them all—
50 Have known the evenings, mornings, afternoons,
I have measured out my life with coffee spoons;
I know the voices dying with a dying fall[3]
Beneath the music from a farther room.
   So how should I presume?

55 And I have known the eyes already, known them all—
The eyes that fix you in a formulated phrase,
And when I am formulated, sprawling on a pin,
When I am pinned and wriggling on the wall,
Then how should I begin
60 To spit out all the butt-ends of my days and ways?
   And how should I presume?

---

[2] "Works and Days" is the title of a work by the eighth-century B.C. Greek Hesiod, whose poem celebrates farmwork.
[3] Allusion to Orsino's speech in *Twelfth Night* (1.1), "That strain again! It had a dying fall."

And I have known the arms already, known them all—
Arms that are braceleted and white and bare
(But in the lamplight, downed with light brown hair!)
65 Is it perfume from a dress
That makes me so digress?
Arms that lie along a table, or wrap about a shawl.
    And should I then presume?
    And how should I begin?

* * *

70 Shall I say, I have gone at dusk through narrow streets
And watched the smoke that rises from the pipes
Of lonely men in shirt-sleeves, leaning out of windows? . . .

I should have been a pair of ragged claws
Scuttling across the floors of silent seas.

* * *

75 And the afternoon, the evening, sleeps so peacefully!
Smoothed by long fingers,
Asleep . . . tired . . . or it malingers,
Stretched on the floor, here beside you and me.
Should I, after tea and cakes and ices,
80 Have the strength to force the moment to its crisis?
But though I have wept and fasted, wept and prayed,
Though I have seen my head (grown slightly bald) brought in upon a platter,[4]
I am no prophet—and here's no great matter;
I have seen the moment of my greatness flicker,
85 And I have seen the eternal Footman[5] hold my coat, and snicker,
And in short, I was afraid.

And would it have been worth it, after all,
After the cups, the marmalade, the tea,
Among the porcelain, among some talk of you and me,
90 Would it have been worth while,
To have bitten off the matter with a smile,
To have squeezed the universe into a ball
To roll it toward some overwhelming question,
To say: "I am Lazarus,[6] come from the dead,
95 Come back to tell you all, I shall tell you all"—
If one, settling a pillow by her head,

---

[4] Like John the Baptist, who was beheaded by King Herod (see Matthew 14:3–11).
[5] Perhaps death, or fate.
[6] Lazarus was raised from the dead by Christ (see John 11:1–44).

>   Should say: "That is not what I meant at all.
>   That is not it, at all."
>
>   And would it have been worth it, after all,
> 100   Would it have been worth while,
>   After the sunsets and the dooryards and the sprinkled streets,
>   After the novels, after the teacups, after the skirts that trail along
>   the floor—
>   And this, and so much more?—
>   It is impossible to say just what I mean!
> 105   But as if a magic lantern threw the nerves in patterns on a screen:
>   Would it have been worth while
>   If one, settling a pillow or throwing off a shawl,
>   And turning toward the window, should say:
>   "That is not it at all,
> 110   That is not what I meant, at all."
>
>   * * *
>
>   No! I am not Prince Hamlet, nor was meant to be;
>   Am an attendant lord, one that will do
>   To swell a progress,[7] start a scene or two,
>   Advise the prince; no doubt, an easy tool,
> 115   Deferential, glad to be of use,
>   Politic, cautious, and meticulous;
>   Full of high sentence,[8] but a bit obtuse;
>   At times, indeed, almost ridiculous—
>   Almost, at times, the Fool.
>
> 120   I grow old . . . I grow old . . .
>   I shall wear the bottoms of my trousers rolled.
>
>   Shall I part my hair behind? Do I dare to eat a peach?
>   I shall wear white flannel trousers, and walk upon the beach.
>   I have heard the mermaids singing, each to each.
>
> 125   I do not think that they will sing to me.
>
>   I have seen them riding seaward on the waves
>   Combing the white hair of the waves blown back
>   When the wind blows the water white and black.
>
>   We have lingered in the chambers of the sea
> 130   By sea-girls wreathed with seaweed red and brown
>   Till human voices wake us, and we drown.

---

[7] Here, in the Elizabethan sense of a royal journey.
[8] Opinions.

JAMES A. EMANUEL
(1921–   )

Emmett Till[1]
(1968)

I hear a whistling
Through the water.
Little Emmett
Won't be still.
5 He keeps floating
Round the darkness,
Edging through
The silent chill.
Tell me, please,
10 That bedtime story
Of the fairy
River Boy
Who swims forever,
Deep in treasures,
15 Necklaced in
A coral toy.

ROBERT FROST
(1874–1963)

Acquainted with the Night
(1928)

I have been one acquainted with the night.
I have walked out in rain—and back in rain.
I have outwalked the furthest city light.

I have looked down the saddest city lane.
5 I have passed by the watchman on his beat
And dropped my eyes, unwilling to explain.

---

[1] Emmett Till, a fourteen-year-old black youth from Chicago, was visiting relatives in Mississippi in 1955 when he made what he thought was an innocent remark to a white woman. Several days later his body was found in the river with a heavy cotton gin fan tied around his neck with barbed wire.

I have stood still and stopped the sound of feet
When far away an interrupted cry
Came over houses from another street,

10 But not to call me back or say good-by;
And further still at an unearthly height,
One luminary clock against the sky

Proclaimed the time was neither wrong nor right.
I have been one acquainted with the night.

Birches
(1915)

When I see birches bend to left and right
Across the lines of straighter darker trees,
I like to think some boy's been swinging them.
But swinging doesn't bend them down to stay
5 As ice-storms do. Often you must have seen them
Loaded with ice a sunny winter morning
After a rain. They click upon themselves
As the breeze rises, and turn many-colored
As the stir cracks and crazes their enamel.
10 Soon the sun's warmth makes them shed crystal shells
Shattering and avalanching on the snow-crust—
Such heaps of broken glass to sweep away
You'd think the inner dome of heaven had fallen.
They are dragged to the withered bracken by the load,
15 And they seem not to break; though once they are bowed
So low for long, they never right themselves:
You may see their trunks arching in the woods
Years afterwards, trailing their leaves on the ground
Like girls on hands and knees that throw their hair
20 Before them over their heads to dry in the sun.
But I was going to say when Truth broke in
With all her matter-of-fact about the ice-storm
I should prefer to have some boy bend them
As he went out and in to fetch the cows—
25 Some boy too far from town to learn baseball,
Whose only play was what he found himself,
Summer or winter, and could play alone.
One by one he subdued his father's trees
By riding them down over and over again
30 Until he took the stiffness out of them,
And not one but hung limp, not one was left
For him to conquer. He learned all there was

To learn about not launching out too soon
And so not carrying the tree away
35 Clear to the ground. He always kept his poise
To the top branches, climbing carefully
With the same pains you use to fill a cup
Up to the brim, and even above the brim.
Then he flung outward, feet first, with a swish,
40 Kicking his way down through the air to the ground.
So was I once myself a swinger of birches.
And so I dream of going back to be.
It's when I'm weary of considerations,
And life is too much like a pathless wood
45 Where your face burns and tickles with the cobwebs
Broken across it, and one eye is weeping
From a twig's having lashed across it open.
I'd like to get away from earth awhile
And then come back to it and begin over.
50 May no fate willfully misunderstand me
And half grant what I wish and snatch me away
Not to return. Earth's the right place for love:
I don't know where it's likely to go better.
I'd like to go by climbing a birch tree,
55 And climb black branches up a snow-white trunk
Toward Heaven, till the tree could bear no more,
But dipped its top and set me down again.
That would be good both going and coming back.
One could do worse than be a swinger of birches.

Mending Wall
(1914)

Something there is that doesn't love a wall,
That sends the frozen-ground-swell under it,
And spills the upper boulders in the sun;
And makes gaps even two can pass abreast.
5 The work of hunters is another thing:
I have come after them and made repair
Where they have left not one stone on a stone,
But they would have the rabbit out of hiding,
To please the yelping dogs. The gaps I mean,
10 No one has seen them made or heard them made,
But at spring mending-time we find them there.
I let my neighbor know beyond the hill;
And on a day we meet to walk the line
And set the wall between us once again.

15 We keep the wall between us as we go.
    To each the boulders that have fallen to each.
    And some are loaves and some so nearly balls
    We have to use a spell to make them balance:
    "Stay where you are until our backs are turned!"
20 We wear our fingers rough with handling them.
    Oh, just another kind of outdoor game,
    One on a side. It comes to little more:
    There where it is we do not need the wall:
    He is all pine and I am apple orchard.
25 My apple trees will never get across
    And eat the cones under his pines, I tell him.
    He only says, "Good fences make good neighbors."
    Spring is the mischief in me, and I wonder
    If I could put a notion in his head:
30 "*Why* do they make good neighbors? Isn't it
    Where there are cows? But here there are no cows.
    Before I built a wall I'd ask to know
    What I was walling in or walling out,
    And to whom I was like to give offense.
35 Something there is that doesn't love a wall,
    That wants it down." I could say "Elves" to him,
    But it's not elves exactly, and I'd rather
    He said it for himself. I see him there
    Bringing a stone grasped firmly by the top
40 In each hand, like an old-stone savage armed.
    He moves in darkness as it seems to me,
    Not of woods only and the shade of trees.
    He will not go behind his father's saying,
    And he likes having thought of it so well
45 He says again, "Good fences make good neighbors."

The Road Not Taken
(1915)

Two roads diverged in a yellow wood,
And sorry I could not travel both
And be one traveler, long I stood
And looked down one as far as I could
5 To where it bent in the undergrowth;

Then took the other, as just as fair,
And having perhaps the better claim,
Because it was grassy and wanted wear;
Though as for that the passing there
10 Had worn them really about the same,

And both that morning equally lay
In leaves no step had trodden black.
Oh, I kept the first for another day!
Yet knowing how way leads on to way,
15 I doubted if I should ever come back.

I shall be telling this with a sigh
Somewhere ages and ages hence:
Two roads diverged in a wood, and I—
I took the one less traveled by,
20 And that has made all the difference.

Stopping by Woods on a Snowy Evening
(1923)

Whose woods these are I think I know.
His house is in the village though;
He will not see me stopping here
To watch his woods fill up with snow.

5 My little horse must think it queer
To stop without a farmhouse near
Between the woods and frozen lake
The darkest evening of the year.

He gives his harness bells a shake
10 To ask if there is some mistake.
The only other sound's the sweep
Of easy wind and downy flake.

The woods are lovely, dark and deep,
But I have promises to keep,
15 And miles to go before I sleep,
And miles to go before I sleep.

THOMAS HARDY
(1840–1928)

The Convergence of the Twain
(1912)

(Lines on the loss of the 'Titanic')

I

    In a solitude of the sea
    Deep from human vanity,
And the Pride of Life that planned her, stilly couches she.

II

    Steel chambers, late the pyres[1]
5   Of her salamandrine fires,[2]
Cold currents thrid,[3] and turn to rhythmic tidal lyres.

III

    Over the mirrors meant
    To glass the opulent
The sea-worm crawls—grotesque, slimed, dumb, indifferent.

IV

10   Jewels in joy designed
    To ravish the sensuous mind
Lie lightless, all their sparkles bleared and black and blind.

V

    Dim moon-eyed fishes near
    Gaze at the gilded gear
15 And query: "What does this vaingloriousness down here?" . . .

VI

    Well: while was fashioning
    This creature of cleaving wing,
The Immanent[4] Will that stirs and urges everything

---

[1] Funeral pyres; piles of wood on which corpses were burned in ancient rites.
[2] Refers to the old belief that salamanders could live in fire.
[3] Thread (archaic verb form).
[4] Inherent, dwelling within.

VII

    Prepared a sinister mate
20   For her—so gaily great—
    A Shape of Ice, for the time far and dissociate.

VIII

    And as the smart ship grew
    In stature, grace, and hue,
    In shadowy silent distance grew the Iceberg too.

IX

25   Alien they seemed to be:
    No mortal eye could see
    The intimate welding of their later history,

X

    Or sign that they were bent
    By paths coincident
30   On being anon[5] twin halves of one august[6] event,

XI

    Till the Spinner of the Years
    Said "Now!" And each one hears,
    And consummation comes, and jars two hemispheres.

◊ ◊ ◊

GERARD MANLEY HOPKINS
(1844–1889)

The Windhover[1]
(1877)

To Christ Our Lord

  I caught this morning morning's minion,[2] king-
    dom of daylight's dauphin, dapple-dawn-drawn Falcon, in his
      riding

---

[5] Soon.
[6] Awe-inspiring, majestic.

---

[1] The kestrel, a European falcon, so called for its ability to hover in the air with its head to the wind.
[2] Favorite.

Of the rolling level underneath him steady air, and striding
High there, how he rung upon the rein[3] of a wimpling[4] wing
5 In his ecstasy! then off, off forth on swing,
    As a skate's heel sweeps smooth on a bow-bend: the hurl and gliding
  Rebuffed the big wind. My heart in hiding
Stirred for a bird,—the achieve of, the mastery of the thing!
Brute beauty and valor and act, oh, air, pride, plume, here
10   Buckle! and the fire that breaks from thee then, a billion
Times told lovelier, more dangerous, O my chevalier!
  No wonder of it: shéer plód, makes plow down sillion[5]
Shine, and blue-bleak embers, ah my dear,
    Fall, gall themselves, and gash gold-vermilion.

◊ ◊ ◊

LANGSTON HUGHES
(1902–1967)

The Negro Speaks of Rivers
(1926)

I've known rivers:
I've known rivers ancient as the world and older than the flow of human blood in human veins.

My soul has grown deep like the rivers.

I bathed in the Euphrates when dawns were young.
5 I built my hut near the Congo and it lulled me to sleep.
I looked upon the Nile and raised the pyramids above it.
I heard the singing of the Mississippi when Abe Lincoln went down to New Orleans, and I've seen its muddy bosom turn all golden in the sunset.

I've known rivers:
Ancient, dusky rivers.

10 My soul has grown deep like rivers.

---

[3] A horse is "rung upon the rein" when it circles at the end of a long rein held by the trainer.
[4] Rippling.
[5] The ridge between two furrows.

JOHN KEATS
(1795–1821)

La Belle Dame sans Merci: A Ballad[1]
(1819, 1820)

1

O what can ail thee, knight at arms,
    Alone and palely loitering?
The sedge has wither'd from the lake,
    And no birds sing.

2

5 O what can ail thee, knight at arms,
    So haggard and so woe-begone?
The squirrel's granary is full,
    And the harvest's done.

3

I see a lily on thy brow
10   With anguish moist and fever dew,
And on thy cheeks a fading rose
    Fast withereth too.

4

I met a lady in the meads,
    Full beautiful, a fairy's child;
15 Her hair was long, her foot was light,
    And her eyes were wild.

5

I made a garland for her head,
    And bracelets too, and fragrant zone;[2]
She look'd at me as she did love,
20   And made sweet moan.

---

[1] The title, which means "The Lovely Lady without Pity," was taken from a medieval poem by Alain Chartier.
[2] Belt.

6

I set her on my pacing steed,
    And nothing else saw all day long,
For sidelong would she bend, and sing
    A fairy's song.

7

25 She found me roots of relish sweet,
    And honey wild, and manna dew,
And sure in language strange she said—
    I love thee true.

8

She took me to her elfin grot,[3]
30   And there she wept, and sigh'd full sore,
And there I shut her wild wild eyes
    With kisses four.

9

And there she lullèd me asleep,
    And there I dream'd—Ah! woe betide!
35 The latest[4] dream I ever dream'd
    On the cold hill's side.

10

I saw pale kings, and princes too,
    Pale warriors, death pale were they all;
They cried—"La belle dame sans merci
40   Hath thee in thrall!"

11

I saw their starv'd lips in the gloam[5]
    With horrid warning gapèd wide,
And I awoke and found me here
    On the cold hill's side.

---

[3] Grotto.
[4] Last.
[5] Twilight.

12

45 And this is why I sojourn here,
    Alone and palely loitering,
Though the sedge is wither'd from the lake,
    And no birds sing.

Bright Star! Would I Were Steadfast as Thou Art
(1819)

Bright star! would I were steadfast as thou art—
    Not in lone splendor hung aloft the night,
And watching, with eternal lids apart,
    Like nature's patient, sleepless Eremite[1]
5 The moving waters at their priest-like task
    Of pure ablution[2] round earth's human shores,
Or gazing on the new soft-fallen mask
    Of snow upon the mountains and the moors—
No—yet still steadfast, still unchangeable,
10   Pillowed upon my fair love's ripening breast,
To feel for ever its soft fall and swell,
    Awake for ever in a sweet unrest,
Still, still to hear her tender-taken breath,
    And so live ever—or else swoon to death.

Ode on a Grecian Urn[1]
(1819)

1

Thou still unravish'd bride of quietness,
    Thou foster-child of silence and slow time,
Sylvan[2] historian, who canst thus express
    A flowery tale more sweetly than our rhyme:
5 What leaf-fring'd legend haunts about thy shape
    Of deities or mortals, or of both,

---

[1] Hermit, religious recluse.
[2] Washing, cleansing.

---

[1] Though many urns similar to the one Keats describes actually exist, the subject of the poem is purely imaginary.
[2] Pertaining to woods or forests.

             In Tempe³ or the dales of Arcady?⁴
         What men or gods are these? What maidens loth?
     What mad pursuit? What struggle to escape?
10   What pipes and timbrels? What wild ecstasy?

                              2

     Heard melodies are sweet, but those unheard
         Are sweeter; therefore, ye soft pipes, play on;
     Not to the sensual ear, but, more endear'd,
         Pipe to the spirit ditties of no tone:
15   Fair youth, beneath the trees, thou canst not leave
         Thy song, nor ever can those trees be bare;
             Bold lover, never, never canst thou kiss,
     Though winning near the goal—yet, do not grieve;
             She cannot fade, though thou hast not thy bliss,
20   For ever wilt thou love, and she be fair!

                              3

     Ah, happy, happy boughs! that cannot shed
         Your leaves, nor ever bid the spring adieu;
     And, happy melodist, unwearied,
         For ever piping songs for ever new;
25   More happy love! more happy, happy love!
         For ever warm and still to be enjoy'd,
             For ever panting, and for ever young;
     All breathing human passion far above,
         That leaves a heart high-sorrowful and cloy'd,
30   A burning forehead, and a parching tongue.

                              4

     Who are these coming to the sacrifice?
         To what green altar, O mysterious priest,
     Lead'st thou that heifer lowing at the skies,
         And all her silken flanks with garlands drest?
35   What little town by river or sea shore,
         Or mountain-built with peaceful citadel,
             Is emptied of this folk, this pious morn?
     And, little town, thy streets for evermore
         Will silent be; and not a soul to tell
40   Why thou art desolate, can e'er return.

---

³ A beautiful valley in Greece.
⁴ The valleys of Arcadia, a mountainous region on the Greek peninsula. Like
  Tempe, they represent a rustic pastoral ideal.

5

 O Attic[5] shape! Fair attitude! with brede[6]
  Of marble men and maidens overwrought,[7]
 With forest branches and the trodden weed;
  Thou, silent form, dost tease us out of thought
45 As doth eternity: Cold Pastoral!
  When old age shall this generation waste,
   Thou shalt remain, in midst of other woe
 Than ours, a friend to man, to whom thou say'st,
 "Beauty is truth, truth beauty,"—that is all
50   Ye know on earth, and all ye need to know.

When I Have Fears
(1818)

When I have fears that I may cease to be
 Before my pen has gleaned my teeming brain,
Before high-pilèd books, in charact'ry,[1]
 Hold like rich garners the full-ripened grain;
5 When I behold, upon the night's starred face,
 Huge cloudy symbols of a high romance,
And think that I may never live to trace
 Their shadows, with the magic hand of chance;
And when I feel, fair creature of an hour,
10 That I shall never look upon thee more,
Never have relish in the faery power
 Of unreflecting love!—then on the shore
Of the wide world I stand alone, and think
Till Love and Fame to nothingness do sink.

---

[5] Characteristic of Athens or Athenians.
[6] Braid.
[7] Elaborately ornamented.

---

[1] Print.

CLAUDE MCKAY
(1890–1948)

If We Must Die
(1922)

If we must die, let it not be like hogs
Hunted and penned in an inglorious spot,
While round us bark the mad and hungry dogs,
Making their mock at our accursed lot.
5 If we must die, O let us nobly die,
So that our precious blood may not be shed
In vain; then even the monsters we defy
Shall be constrained to honor us though dead!
O kinsmen! we must meet the common foe!
10 Though far outnumbered let us show us brave,
And for their thousand blows deal one deathblow!
What though before us lies the open grave?
Like men we'll face the murderous, cowardly pack,
Pressed to the wall, dying, but fighting back!

JOHN MILTON
(1608–1674)

When I Consider How My Light Is Spent[1]
(1655?)

When I consider how my light is spent,
   Ere half my days in this dark world and wide,
   And that one talent[2] which is death to hide
Lodged with me useless, though my soul more bent
5 To serve therewith my Maker, and present
   My true account, lest He returning chide;
   "Doth God exact day-labor, light denied?"
I fondly[3] ask. But Patience, to prevent
That murmur, soon replies, "God doth not need

---

[1] A meditation on his blindness.
[2] See Jesus' parable of the talents in Matthew 25:14–30.
[3] Foolishly.

10   Either man's work or His own gifts. Who best
      Bear His mild yoke, they serve Him best. His state
  Is kingly: thousands at His bidding speed,
    And post o'er land and ocean without rest;
    They also serve who only stand and wait."

PABLO NERUDA
(1904–1973)

The United Fruit Co.[1]
(1950)

Translated by Robert Bly

    When the trumpet sounded, it was
    all prepared on the earth,
    and Jehovah parceled out the earth
    to Coca-Cola, Inc., Anaconda,
5 Ford Motors, and other entities:
    The Fruit Company, Inc.
    reserved for itself the most succulent,
    the central coast of my own land,
    the delicate waist of America.
10 It rechristened its territories
    as the "Banana Republics"
    and over the sleeping dead,
    over the restless heroes
    who brought about the greatness,
15 the liberty and the flags,
    it established the comic opera:
    abolished the independencies,
    presented crowns of Caesar,
    unsheathed envy, attracted
20 the dictatorship of the flies,
    Trujillo flies, Tacho flies,
    Carias flies, Martinez flies,
    Ubico flies,[2] damp flies

---

[1] Incorporated in New Jersey in 1899 by Andrew Preston and Minor C. Keith, United Fruit became the major force in growing, transporting, and merchandising Latin American produce, especially bananas. The company is also notorious for its involvement in politics and is a symbol for many people of "Yankee" imperialism and oppression.

[2] Trujillo, Tacho, Carias, Martinez, and Ubico are all political dictators.

of modest blood and marmalade,
25 drunken flies who zoom
over the ordinary graves,
circus flies, wise flies
well trained in tyranny.

Among the bloodthirsty flies
30 the Fruit Company lands its ships,
taking off the coffee and the fruit;
the treasure of our submerged
territories flows as though
on plates into the ships.

35 Meanwhile Indians are falling
into the sugared chasms
of the harbors, wrapped
for burial in the mist of the dawn:
a body rolls, a thing
40 that has no name, a fallen cipher,
a cluster of dead fruit
thrown down on the dump.

◆ ◆ ◆

SHARON OLDS
(1942–   )

Rite of Passage
(1983)

As the guests arrive at my son's party
they gather in the living room—
short men, men in first grade
with smooth jaws and chins.
5 Hands in pockets, they stand around
jostling, jockeying for place, small fights
breaking out and calming. One says to another
How old are you? Six. I'm seven. So?
They eye each other, seeing themselves
10 tiny in the other's pupils. They clear their
throats a lot, a room of small bankers,
they fold their arms and frown. *I could beat you
up,* a seven says to a six,
the dark cake, round and heavy as a
15 turret, behind them on the table. My son,
freckles like specks of nutmeg on his cheeks,

chest narrow as the balsa¹ keel² of a
model boat, long hands
cool and thin as the day they guided him
20 out of me, speaks up as a host
for the sake of the group.
We could easily kill a two-year-old,
he says in his clear voice. The other
men agree, they clear their throats
25 like Generals, they relax and get down to
playing war, celebrating my son's life.

◊ ◊ ◊

MICHAEL ONDAATJE
(1943–   )

Dates¹

It becomes apparent that I miss great occasions.
My birth was heralded by nothing
but the anniversary of Winston Churchill's marriage.
No monuments bled, no instruments
5 agreed on a specific weather.
It was a seasonal insignificance.

I console myself with my mother's eighth month.
While she sweated out her pregnancy in Ceylon²
a servant ambling over the lawn
10 with a tray of iced drinks,
a few friends visiting her
to placate her shape, and I
drinking the life lines,
Wallace Stevens sat down in Connecticut
15 a glass of orange juice at his table
so hot he wore only shorts
and on the back of a letter
began to write "The Well Dressed Man with a Beard."

That night while my mother slept
20 her significant belly cooled

---

¹ A lightweight wood.
² The piece of wood that runs lengthwise along the center of a ship's bottom.

---

¹ Publication date is not available.
² Now known as Sri Lanka.

    by the bedroom fan
    Stevens put words together
    that grew to sentences
    and shaved them clean and
25 shaped them, the page suddenly
    becoming thought where nothing had been,
    his head making his hand
    move where he wanted
    and he saw his hand was saying
30 the mind is never finished, no, never
    and I in my mother's stomach was growing
    as were the flowers outside the Connecticut windows.

◊ ◊ ◊

LINDA PASTAN
(1932–   )

Ethics
(1980)

   In ethics class so many years ago
   our teacher asked this question every fall:
   if there were a fire in a museum
   which would you save, a Rembrandt painting
5 or an old woman who hadn't many
   years left anyhow? Restless on hard chairs
   caring little for pictures or old age
   we'd opt one year for life, the next for art
   and always half-heartedly. Sometimes
10 the woman borrowed my grandmother's face
   leaving her usual kitchen to wander
   some drafty, half imagined museum.
   One year, feeling clever, I replied
   why not let the woman decide herself?
15 Linda, the teacher would report, eschews
   the burdens of responsibility.
   This fall in a real museum I stand
   before a real Rembrandt, old woman,
   or nearly so, myself. The colors
20 within this frame are darker than autumn,
   darker even than winter—the browns of earth,
   though earth's most radiant elements burn
   through the canvas. I know now that woman
   and painting and season are almost one
25 and all beyond saving by children.

MARGE PIERCY
(1934–)

Barbie Doll
(1973)

This girlchild was born as usual
and presented dolls that did pee-pee
and miniature GE stoves and irons
and wee lipsticks the color of cherry candy.
5 Then in the magic of puberty, a classmate said:
You have a great big nose and fat legs.

She was healthy, tested intelligent,
possessed strong arms and back,
abundant sexual drive and manual dexterity.
10 She went to and fro apologizing.
Everyone saw a fat nose on thick legs.

She was advised to play coy,
exhorted to come on hearty,
exercise, diet, smile and wheedle.
15 Her good nature wore out
like a fan belt.
So she cut off her nose and her legs
and offered them up.
In the casket displayed on satin she lay
20 with the undertaker's cosmetics painted on,
a turned-up putty nose,
dressed in a pink and white nightie.
Doesn't she look pretty? everyone said.
Consummation at last.
25 To every woman a happy ending.

SYLVIA PLATH
(1932–1963)

Metaphors
(1960)

I'm a riddle in nine syllables,
An elephant, a ponderous house,
A melon strolling on two tendrils.
O red fruit, ivory, fine timbers!

5 This loaf's big with its yeasty rising.
Money's new-minted in this fat purse.
I'm a means, a stage, a cow in calf.
I've eaten a bag of green apples,
Boarded the train there's no getting off.

❖ ❖ ❖

EZRA POUND
(1885–1972)

The River-Merchant's Wife: A Letter[1]
(1515)

While my hair was still cut straight across my forehead
I played about the front gate, pulling flowers.
You came by on bamboo stilts, playing horse,
You walked about my seat, playing with blue plums.
5 And we went on living in the village of Chokan:[2]
Two small people, without dislike or suspicion.

At fourteen I married My Lord you.
I never laughed, being bashful.
Lowering my head, I looked at the wall.
10 Called to, a thousand times, I never looked back.

At fifteen I stopped scowling,
I desired my dust to be mingled with yours
Forever and forever and forever.
Why should I climb the lookout?

15 At sixteen you departed,
You went into far Ku-to-yen,[3] by the river of swirling eddies,
And you have been gone five months.
The monkeys make sorrowful noise overhead.

You dragged your feet when you went out.
20 By the gate now, the moss is grown, the different mosses,
Too deep to clear them away!

---

[1] This is one of the many translations Pound made of Chinese poems. The poem is a free translation of Li Po's (701–762) "Two Letters from Chang-Kan."
[2] Chang-Kan.
[3] An island in the river Ch'ū-t'ang.

The leaves fall early this autumn, in wind.
The paired butterflies are already yellow with August
Over the grass in the West garden;
25 They hurt me. I grow older.
If you are coming down through the narrows of the river Kiang,[4]
Please let me know beforehand,
And I will come out to meet you
    As far as Cho-fu-sa.[5]

◊ ◊ ◊

EDWIN ARLINGTON ROBINSON
(1869–1935)

Miniver Cheevy
(1910)

Miniver Cheevy, child of scorn,
    Grew lean while he assailed the seasons;
He wept that he was ever born,
    And he had reasons.

5 Miniver loved the days of old
    When swords were bright and steeds were prancing;
The vision of a warrior bold
    Would set him dancing.

Miniver sighed for what was not,
10   And dreamed, and rested from his labors;
He dreamed of Thebes[1] and Camelot,[2]
    And Priam's[3] neighbors.

Miniver mourned the ripe renown
    That made so many a name so fragrant;
15 He mourned Romance, now on the town,
    And Art, a vagrant.

---

[4] The Japanese name for the river Ch'ū-t'ang (see note 3). Pound's translations are based on commentaries derived from Japanese scholars; therefore, he usually uses Japanese instead of Chinese names.

[5] A beach several hundred miles upstream of Nanking.

---

[1] The setting of many Greek legends, including that of Oedipus.

[2] The legendary site of King Arthur's court.

[3] Priam was the last King of Troy; his "neighbors" included Helen, Aeneas, and Hector.

Miniver loved the Medici,[4]
    Albeit he had never seen one;
He would have sinned incessantly
20   Could he have been one.

Miniver cursed the commonplace
    And eyed a khaki suit with loathing;
He missed the medieval grace
    Of iron clothing.

25 Miniver scorned the gold he sought,
    But sore annoyed was he without it;
Miniver thought, and thought, and thought,
    And thought about it.

Miniver Cheevy, born too late,
30   Scratched his head and kept on thinking;
Miniver coughed, and called it fate,
    And kept on drinking.

Richard Cory
(1897)

Whenever Richard Cory went down town,
We people on the pavement looked at him:
He was a gentleman from sole to crown,
Clean favored, and imperially slim.

5 And he was always quietly arrayed,
And he was always human when he talked;
But still he fluttered pulses when he said,
"Good-morning," and he glittered when he walked.

And he was rich—yes, richer than a king—
10 And admirably schooled in every grace:
In fine, we thought that he was everything
To make us wish that we were in his place.

So on we worked, and waited for the light,
And went without the meat, and cursed the bread;
15 And Richard Cory, one calm summer night,
Went home and put a bullet through his head.

---

[4] Rulers of Florence, Italy, from the fifteenth through the eighteenth centuries. During the Renaissance, Lorenzo de Medici was a renowned patron of the arts.

CARL SANDBURG
(1878–1967)

Fog
(1916)

The fog comes
on little cat feet.
It sits looking
over harbor and city
5 on silent haunches
and then moves on.

WILLIAM SHAKESPEARE
(1564–1616)

Let Me Not to the Marriage of True Minds
(1609)

Let me not to the marriage of true minds
Admit impediments.[1] Love is not love
Which alters when it alteration finds,
Or bends with the remover to remove:
5 Oh, no! it is an ever-fixéd mark,
That looks on tempests and is never shaken;
It is the star to every wandering bark,
Whose worth's unknown, although his height[2] be taken.
Love's not Time's fool,[3] though rosy lips and cheeks
10 Within his bending sickle's compass come;
Love alters not with his brief hours and weeks,
But bears it out even to the edge of doom.[4]
If this be error and upon me proved,
I never writ, nor no man ever loved.

---

[1] A reference to "The Order of Solemnization of Matrimony" in the Anglican *Book of Common Prayer:* "I require that if either of you know any impediments why ye may not be lawfully joined together in Matrimony, ye do now confess it."

[2] Although the altitude of a star may be measured, its worth is unknowable.

[3] That is, mocked by Time.

[4] Doomsday.

Not Marble, nor the Gilded Monuments
(1609)

Not marble, nor the gilded monuments
Of princes, shall outlive this powerful rhyme;
But you shall shine more bright in these contents
Than unswept stone, besmeared with sluttish time.
5 When wasteful war shall statues overturn,
And broils root out the work of masonry,
Nor Mars[1] his sword nor war's quick fire shall burn
The living record of your memory.
'Gainst death and all-oblivious enmity
10 Shall you pace forth; your praise shall still find room
Even in the eyes of all posterity
That wear this world out to the ending doom.
   So, till the judgment that yourself arise,
   You live in this, and dwell in lovers' eyes.

◊ ◊ ◊

PERCY BYSSHE SHELLEY
(1792–1822)

Ode to the West Wind
(1820)

I

O wild West Wind, thou breath of Autumn's being,
Thou, from whose unseen presence the leaves dead
Are driven, like ghosts from an enchanter fleeing,

Yellow, and black, and pale, and hectic[1] red,
5 Pestilence-stricken multitudes: O Thou,
Who chariotest to their dark wintry bed

The winged seeds, where they lie cold and low,
Each like a corpse within its grave, until
Thine azure sister of the Spring[2] shall blow

---

[1] God of War.

---

[1] Reference to a tubercular fever that produces flushed cheeks.
[2] The west wind of the spring.

10 Her clarion o'er the dreaming earth, and fill
 (Driving sweet buds like flocks to feed in air)
 With living hues and odours plain and hill:

 Wild Spirit, which art moving everywhere;
 Destroyer and Preserver; hear, O hear!

II

15 Thou on whose stream, mid the steep sky's commotion,
 Loose clouds like Earth's decaying leaves are shed,
 Shook from the tangled boughs of Heaven and Ocean,

 Angels of rain and lightning: there are spread
 On the blue surface of thine aery surge,
20 Like the bright hair uplifted from the head

 Of some fierce Maenad,[3] even from the dim verge
 Of the horizon to the zenith's height,
 The locks of the approaching storm. Thou Dirge

 Of the dying year, to which this closing night
25 Will be the dome of a vast sepulchre,
 Vaulted with all thy congregated might

 Of vapours, from whose solid atmosphere
 Black rain and fire and hail will burst: O hear!

III

 Thou who didst waken from his summer dreams
30 The blue Mediterranean, where he lay,
 Lulled by the coil of his crystalline streams,

 Beside a pumice isle in Baiae's bay,[4]
 And saw in sleep old palaces and towers
 Quivering within the wave's intenser day,

35 All overgrown with azure moss and flowers
 So sweet, the sense faints picturing them! Thou
 For whose path the Atlantic's level powers

 Cleave themselves into chasms, while far below
 The sea-blooms and the oozy woods which wear
40 The sapless foliage of the ocean, know

---

[3] A female votary who danced wildly in ceremonies for Dionysus (or Bacchus), Greek god of wine and vegetation, who according to legend died in the fall and was reborn in the spring.

[4] A bay in the Mediterranean Sea, west of Naples. It was known for the opulent villas built by Roman emperors along its shores.

Thy voice, and suddenly grow grey with fear,
And tremble and despoil themselves: O hear!

IV

If I were a dead leaf thou mightest bear;
If I were a swift cloud to fly with thee;
45 A wave to pant beneath thy power, and share

The impulse of thy strength, only less free
Than thou, O Uncontrollable! If even
I were as in my boyhood, and could be

The comrade of thy wanderings over Heaven,
50 As then, when to outstrip thy skiey speed
Scarce seemed a vision; I would ne'er have striven

As thus with thee in prayer in my sore need,
Oh! lift me as a wave, a leaf, a cloud!
I fall upon the thorns of life! I bleed!

55 A heavy weight of hours has chained and bowed
One too like thee: tameless, and swift, and proud.

V

Make me thy lyre,[5] even as the forest is:
What if my leaves are falling like its own!
The tumult of thy mighty harmonies

60 Will take from both a deep, autumnal tone,
Sweet though in sadness. Be thou, Spirit fierce,
My spirit! Be thou me, impetuous one!

Drive my dead thoughts over the universe
Like withered leaves to quicken a new birth!
65 And, by the incantation of this verse,

Scatter, as from an unextinguished hearth
Ashes and sparks, my words among mankind!
Be through my lips to unawakened Earth

The trumpet of a prophecy! O Wind,
70 If Winter comes, can Spring be far behind?

---

[5] An Aeolian harp, a stringed instrument that produces musical sounds when exposed to the wind.

STEVIE SMITH
(1902–1971)

Not Waving but Drowning
(1957)

Nobody heard him, the dead man,
But still he lay moaning:
I was much further out than you thought
And not waving but drowning.

5 Poor chap, he always loved larking
And now he's dead
It must have been too cold for him his heart gave way,
They said.

Oh, no no no, it was too cold always
10 (Still the dead one lay moaning)
I was much too far out all my life
And not waving but drowning.

GARY SOTO
(1952–   )

Black Hair
(1985)

At eight I was brilliant with my body.
In July, that ring of heat
We all jumped through, I sat in the bleachers
Of Romain Playground, in the lengthening
5 Shade that rose from our dirty feet.
The game before us was more than baseball.
It was a figure—Hector Moreno
Quick and hard with turned muscles,
His crouch the one I assumed before an altar
10 Of worn baseball cards, in my room.
I came here because I was Mexican, a stick
Of brown light in love with those
Who could do it—the triple and hard slide,
The gloves eating balls into double plays.
15 What could I do with 50 pounds, my shyness,
My black torch of hair, about to go out?
Father was dead, his face no longer

Hanging over the table or our sleep,
And mother was the terror of mouths
20 Twisting hurt by butter knives.

In the bleachers I was brilliant with my body,
Waving players in and stomping my feet,
Growing sweaty in the presence of white shirts.
I chewed sunflower seeds. I drank water
25 And bit my arm through the late innings.
When Hector lined balls into deep
Center, in my mind I rounded the bases
With him, my face flared, my hair lifting
Beautifully, because we were coming home
30 To the arms of brown people.

◊ ◊ ◊

WILLIAM STAFFORD
(1914–1993)

Traveling through the Dark
(1962)

Traveling through the dark I found a deer
dead on the edge of the Wilson River road.
It is usually best to roll them into the canyon:
that road is narrow; to swerve might make more dead.

5 By glow of the tail-light I stumbled back of the car
and stood by the heap, a doe, a recent killing;
she had stiffened already, almost cold.
I dragged her off; she was large in the belly.

My fingers touching her side brought me the reason—
10 her side was warm; her fawn lay there waiting,
alive, still, never to be born.
Beside that mountain road I hesitated.

The car aimed ahead its lowered parking lights;
under the hood purred the steady engine.
15 I stood in the glare of the warm exhaust turning red;
around our group I could hear the wilderness listen.

I thought hard for us all—my only swerving—
then pushed her over the edge into the river.

WALLACE STEVENS
(1879–1955)

Anecdote of the Jar
(1923)

    I placed a jar in Tennessee,
    And round it was, upon a hill.
    It made the slovenly wilderness
    Surround that hill.

5 The wilderness rose up to it,
    And sprawled around, no longer wild.
    The jar was round upon the ground
    And tall and of a port in air.

    It took dominion everywhere.
10 The jar was gray and bare.
    It did not give of bird or bush,
    Like nothing else in Tennessee.

The Emperor of Ice-Cream
(1923)

    Call the roller of big cigars,
    The muscular one, and bid him whip
    In kitchen cups concupiscent curds.
    Let the wenches dawdle in such dress
5 As they are used to wear, and let the boys
    Bring flowers in last month's newspapers.
    Let be be finale of seem.
    The only emperor is the emperor of ice-cream.

    Take from the dresser of deal,[1]
10 Lacking the three glass knobs, that sheet
    On which she embroidered fantails[2] once
    And spread it so as to cover her face.
    If her horny feet protrude, they come
    To show how cold she is, and dumb.
15 Let the lamp affix its beam.
    The only emperor is the emperor of ice-cream.

---

[1] Fir or pine wood.
[2] According to Stevens, "the word fantails does not mean fans, but fantail pigeons."

ALFRED, LORD TENNYSON
(1809–1892)

Ulysses[1]
(1833)

It little profits that an idle king,
By this still hearth, among these barren crags,
Matched with an agèd wife, I mete and dole
Unequal laws unto a savage race
5 That hoard, and sleep, and feed, and know not me.
I cannot rest from travel; I will drink
Life to the lees. All times I have enjoyed
Greatly, have suffered greatly, both with those
That loved me, and alone; on shore, and when
10 Through scudding drifts the rainy Hyades[2]
Vexed the dim sea. I am become a name;
For always roaming with a hungry heart
Much have I seen and known—cities of men
And manners, climates, councils, governments,
15 Myself not least, but honored of them all—
And drunk delight of battle with my peers,
Far on the ringing plains of windy Troy.[3]
I am a part of all that I have met;
Yet all experience is an arch wherethrough
20 Gleams that untraveled world whose margin fades
Forever and forever when I move.
How dull it is to pause, to make an end,
To rust unburnished, not to shine in use!
As though to breathe were life! Life piled on life
25 Were all too little, and of one to me
Little remains; but every hour is saved
From that eternal silence, something more,

---

[1] A legendary Greek king of Ithaca and hero of Homer's *Odyssey,* Ulysses (or Odysseus) is noted for his daring and cunning. After his many adventures—including encounters with the Cyclops, the cannibalistic Laestrygones, and the enchantress Circe—Ulysses returned home to his faithful wife, Penelope. Tennyson portrays an older Ulysses pondering his situation.

[2] A group of stars whose rising was supposedly followed by rain, and hence stormy seas.

[3] An ancient city in Asia Minor. According to legend, Paris, King of Troy, abducted Helen, initiating the famed Trojan War, in which numerous Greek heroes, including Ulysses, fought.

A bringer of new things; and vile it were
For some three suns to store and hoard myself,
30 And this grey spirit yearning in desire
To follow knowledge like a sinking star,
Beyond the utmost bound of human thought.
    This is my son, mine own Telemachus,
To whom I leave the scepter and the isle—
35 Well-loved of me, discerning to fulfill
This labor, by slow prudence to make mild
A rugged people, and through soft degrees
Subdue them to the useful and the good.
Most blameless is he, centered in the sphere
40 Of common duties, decent not to fail
In offices of tenderness, and pay
Meet adoration to my household gods,
When I am gone. He works his work, I mine.
    There lies the port; the vessel puffs her sail;
45 There gloom the dark, broad seas. My mariners,
Souls that have toiled, and wrought, and thought with me—
That ever with a frolic welcome took
The thunder and the sunshine, and opposed
Free hearts, free foreheads—you and I are old;
50 Old age hath yet his honor and his toil.
Death closes all; but something ere the end,
Some work of noble note, may yet be done,
Not unbecoming men that strove with Gods.
The lights begin to twinkle from the rocks;
55 The long day wanes; the low moon climbs; the deep
Moans round with many voices. Come, my friends,
'Tis not too late to seek a newer world.
Push off, and sitting well in order smite
The sounding furrows; for my purpose holds
60 To sail beyond the sunset, and the baths
Of all the western stars, until I die.
It may be that the gulfs will wash us down;
It may be we shall touch the Happy Isles,[4]
And see the great Achilles,[5] whom we knew.
65 Though much is taken, much abides; and though
We are not now that strength which in old days
Moved earth and heaven, that which we are, we are—
One equal temper of heroic hearts,
Made weak by time and fate, but strong in will
70 To strive, to seek, to find, and not to yield.

---

[4] Elysium, or Paradise, believed to be in the far western ocean.
[5] Famed Greek hero of the Trojan War.

MARGARET WALKER
(1915–)

Lineage
(1942)

My grandmothers were strong.
They followed plows and bent to toil.
They moved through fields sowing seed.
They touched earth and grain grew.
5 They were full of sturdiness and singing.
My grandmothers were strong.

My grandmothers are full of memories
Smelling of soap and onions and wet clay
With veins rolling roughly over quick hands
10 They have many clean words to say.
My grandmothers were strong.
Why am I not as they?

EDMUND WALLER
(1606–1687)

Go, Lovely Rose
(1645)

    Go, lovely rose,
Tell her that wastes her time and me
    That now she knows,
When I resemble her to thee,
5 How sweet and fair she seems to be.

    Tell her that's young
And shuns to have her graces spied,
    That hadst thou sprung
In deserts where no men abide,
10 Thou must have uncommended died.

    Small is the worth
Of beauty from the light retired:
    Bid her come forth,
Suffer herself to be desired,
15 And not blush so to be admired.

Then die, that she
The common fate of all things rare
May read in thee,
How small a part of time they share
20 That are so wondrous sweet and fair.

PHILLIS WHEATLEY
(1754–1784)

On Being Brought from Africa to America
(1773)

'Twas mercy brought me from my *Pagan* land,
Taught my benighted soul to understand
That there's a God, that there's a *Saviour* too:
Once I redemption neither sought nor knew.
5 Some view our sable race with scornful eye,
"Their colour is a diabolic die."
Remember, *Christians, Negroes,* black as *Cain,*
May be refin'd, and join th' angelic train.

WALT WHITMAN
(1819–1892)

A Noiseless Patient Spider
(1881)

A noiseless patient spider,
I mark'd where on a little promontory it stood isolated,
Mark'd how to explore the vacant vast surrounding,
It launch'd forth filament, filament, filament, out of itself,
5 Ever unreeling them, ever tirelessly speeding them.

And you O my soul where you stand,
Surrounded, detached, in measureless oceans of space,
Ceaselessly musing, venturing, throwing, seeking the spheres to
  connect them,
Till the bridge you will need be form'd, till the ductile anchor hold,
10 Till the gossamer thread you fling catch somewhere, O my soul.

from "Song of Myself"
(1855)

1

I celebrate myself, and sing myself,
And what I assume you shall assume,
For every atom belonging to me as good belongs to you.

I loafe and invite my soul,
5 I lean and loafe at my ease observing a spear of summer grass.

My tongue, every atom of my blood, form'd from this soil, this air,
Born here of parents born here from parents the same, and their parents the same,
I, now thirty-seven years old in perfect health begin,
Hoping to cease not till death.

10 Creeds and schools in abeyance,
Retiring back a while sufficed at what they are, but never forgotten,
I harbor for good or bad, I permit to speak at every hazard,
Nature without check with original energy.

2

Houses and rooms are full of perfumes, the shelves are crowded with perfumes,
15 I breathe the fragrance myself and know it and like it,
The distillation would intoxicate me also, but I shall not let it.

The atmosphere is not a perfume, it has no taste of the distillation, it is odorless,
It is for my mouth forever, I am in love with it,
I will go to the bank by the wood and become undisguised and naked,
20 I am mad for it to be in contact with me.

The smoke of my own breath,
Echoes, ripples, buzz'd whispers, love-root, silk-thread, crotch and vine,
My respiration and inspiration, the beating of my heart, the passing of blood and air through my lungs,
The sniff of green leaves and dry leaves, and of the shore and dark-color'd sea-rocks, and of hay in the barn,
25 The sound of the belch'd words of my voice loos'd to the eddies of the wind,
A few light kisses, a few embraces, a reaching around of arms,
The play of shine and shade on the trees as the supple boughs wag,
The delight alone or in the rush of the streets, or along the fields and hill-sides,

The feeling of health, the full-noon trill, the song of me rising from
   bed and meeting the sun.
30 Have you reckon'd a thousand acres much? have you reckon'd the
   earth much?
Have you practis'd so long to learn to read?
Have you felt so proud to get at the meaning of poems?

Stop this day and night with me and you shall possess the origin of
   all poems,
You shall possess the good of the earth and sun, (there are millions
   of suns left,)
35 You shall no longer take things at second or third hand, nor look
   through the eyes of the dead, nor feed on the spectres in books,
You shall not look through my eyes either, nor take things from me,
You shall listen to all sides and filter them from your self.

◊ ◊ ◊

WILLIAM WORDSWORTH
(1770–1850)

Composed upon Westminster Bridge, September 3, 1802
(1807)

Earth has not anything to show more fair:
Dull would he be of soul who could pass by
A sight so touching in its majesty:
This City now doth, like a garment, wear
5 The beauty of the morning; silent, bare,
Ships, towers, domes, theatres, and temples lie
Open unto the fields, and to the sky;
All bright and glittering in the smokeless air.
Never did sun more beautifully steep
10 In his first splendor, valley, rock, or hill;
Ne'er saw I, never felt, a calm so deep!
The river glideth at his own sweet will:
Dear God! the very houses seem asleep;
And all that mighty heart is lying still!

She Dwelt among the Untrodden Ways
(1800)

She dwelt among the untrodden ways
    Beside the springs of Dove,[1]
A Maid whom there were none to praise
    And very few to love:

5 A violet by a mossy stone
    Half hidden from the eye!
—Fair as a star, when only one
    Is shining in the sky.

She lived unknown, and few could know
10   When Lucy ceased to be;
But she is in her grave, and, oh,
    The difference to me!

❖ ❖ ❖

JAMES WRIGHT
(1927–1980)

A Blessing
(1961)

Just off the highway to Rochester, Minnesota,
Twilight bounds softly forth on the grass.
And the eyes of those two Indian ponies
Darken with kindness.
5 They have come gladly out of the willows
To welcome my friend and me.
We step over the barbed wire into the pasture
Where they have been grazing all day, alone.
They ripple tensely, they can hardly contain their happiness
10 That we have come.
They bow shyly as wet swans. They love each other.
There is no loneliness like theirs.
At home once more,
They begin munching the young tufts of spring in the darkness.
15 I would like to hold the slenderer one in my arms,
For she has walked over to me
And nuzzled my left hand.

---

[1] River in the Lake District of England.

      She is black and white,
      Her mane falls wild on her forehead,
20 And the light breeze moves me to caress her long ear
      That is delicate as the skin over a girl's wrist.
      Suddenly I realize
      That if I stepped out of my body I would break
      Into blossom.

WILLIAM BUTLER YEATS
(1865–1939)

The Lake Isle of Innisfree
(1892)

    I will arise and go now, and go to Innisfree,[1]
    And a small cabin build there, of clay and wattles[2] made:
    Nine bean-rows will I have there, a hive for the honey-bee,
    And live alone in the bee-loud glade.

5 And I shall have some peace there, for peace comes dropping slow,
    Dropping from the veils of the morning to where the cricket sings;
    There midnight's all a glimmer, and noon a purple glow,
    And evening full of the linnet's wings.

    I will arise and go now, for always night and day
10 I hear lake water lapping with low sounds by the shore;
    While I stand on the roadway, or on the pavements grey,
    I hear it in the deep heart's core.

Sailing to Byzantium
(1927)

    That is no country for old men. The young
    In one another's arms, birds in the trees
    —Those dying generations—at their song,
    The salmon-falls, the mackerel-crowded seas,
5 Fish, flesh, or fowl, commend all summer long
    Whatever is begotten, born, and dies.
    Caught in that sensual music all neglect
    Monuments of unaging intellect.

---

[1] An island in Lough (Lake) Gill, County Sligo, in Ireland.
[2] Stakes interwoven with twigs or branches, used for walls and roofing.

An aged man is but a paltry thing,
10 A tattered coat upon a stick, unless
Soul clap its hands and sing, and louder sing
For every tatter in its mortal dress,
Nor is there singing school but studying
Monuments of its own magnificence;
15 And therefore I have sailed the seas and come
To the holy city of Byzantium.

O sages standing in God's holy fire
As in the gold mosaic of a wall,
Come from the holy fire, perne in a gyre,
20 And be the singing-masters of my soul.
Consume my heart away; sick with desire
And fastened to a dying animal
It knows not what it is; and gather me
Into the artifice of eternity.

25 Once out of nature I shall never take
My bodily form from any natural thing,
But such a form as Grecian goldsmiths make
Of hammered gold and gold enameling
To keep a drowsy Emperor awake;
30 Or set upon a golden bough to sing
To lords and ladies of Byzantium
Of what is past, or passing, or to come.

The Second Coming[1]
(1921)

Turning and turning in the widening gyre[2]
The falcon cannot hear the falconer;
Things fall apart; the center cannot hold;
Mere anarchy is loosed upon the world,
5 The blood-dimmed tide is loosed, and everywhere
The ceremony of innocence is drowned;
The best lack all conviction, while the worst
Are full of passionate intensity.[3]

---

[1] The Second Coming usually refers to the return of Christ. Yeats theorized cycles of history, much like the turning of a wheel. Here he offers a poetic comment on his view of the dissolution of civilization at the end of one such cycle.
[2] Spiral.
[3] Lines 4–8 refer to the Russian Revolution (1917).

Surely some revelation is at hand;
10 Surely the Second Coming is at hand;
The Second Coming! Hardly are those words out
When a vast image out of *Spiritus Mundi*[4]
Troubles my sight: somewhere in sands of the desert
A shape with lion body and the head of a man,
15 A gaze blank and pitiless as the sun,
Is moving its slow thighs, while all about it
Reel shadows of the indignant desert birds.
The darkness drops again; but now I know
That twenty centuries[5] of stony sleep
20 Were vexed to nightmare by a rocking cradle,
And what rough beast, its hour come round at last,
Slouches towards Bethlehem to be born?

---

[4] The Spirit of the World. Yeats believed all souls to be connected by a "Great Memory."

[5] The centuries since the birth of Christ.

Drama

Chapter 18

Understanding Drama

Dramatic Literature

❖ ❖ ❖

The distinctive appearance of a script, with its stage directions, character parts, and divisions into acts and scenes, identifies **drama** as a unique form of literature. A play is written to be performed in front of an audience by actors who take on the roles of the characters and who present the story through dialogue and action. (An exception is **closet drama,** which is meant to be read, not performed.) Indeed, the term *theater* comes from the Greek word *theasthai,* which means "to view" or "to see." Thus, drama is different from novels and short stories, which are meant to be read.

Dramatic works differ from other prose works in a number of other ways as well. Unlike novels and short stories, plays do not usually have narrators to tell the audience what a character is thinking or what happened in the past; the audience knows only what the characters reveal. Drama develops primarily by means of **dialogue,** the lines spoken by the characters. The plot and the action of drama unfold on the stage as the characters interact. Playwrights employ various techniques to compensate for the absence of a narrator. For example, playwrights use **monologues**—extended speeches by one character. (A monologue in which a character expresses private thoughts while alone on the stage is called a **soliloquy.**) Playwrights can also use **asides**—brief comments by an actor who addresses the audience but is not heard by the other characters—to reveal the thoughts of the speaker. Like the observations of a narrator, these dramatic techniques give the audience insight into a character's motives and attitudes. In addition, makeup, costumes, scenery, and lighting enhance a dramatic performance, as do actors' and directors' interpretations of dialogue and stage directions.

THE ORIGINS OF THE MODERN THEATER

◊ ◊ ◊

THE ANCIENT GREEK THEATER

The dramatic presentations of ancient Greece developed out of religious rites performed to honor gods or to mark the coming of spring. Playwrights such as Aeschylus (525–456 B.C.), Sophocles (496–406 B.C.), and Euripides (480?–406 B.C.) composed plays to be performed and judged at competitions held during the yearly Dionysian festivals. Works were chosen by a selection board and evaluated by a panel of judges. To compete in the contest, authors had to submit three tragedies, which could be either based on a common theme or unrelated, and one comedy. Unfortunately, relatively few of these ancient Greek plays survive today.

The open-air semicircular ancient Greek theater, built into the side of a hill, looked much like a primitive version of a modern sports stadium. Some Greek theaters, such as the Athenian theater, could seat almost seventeen thousand spectators. Sitting in tiered seats, the audience would look down on the *orchestra,* or "dancing place," occupied by the **chorus**—originally a group of men (led by an individual called the *choragos*) who danced and chanted and later a group of onlookers who

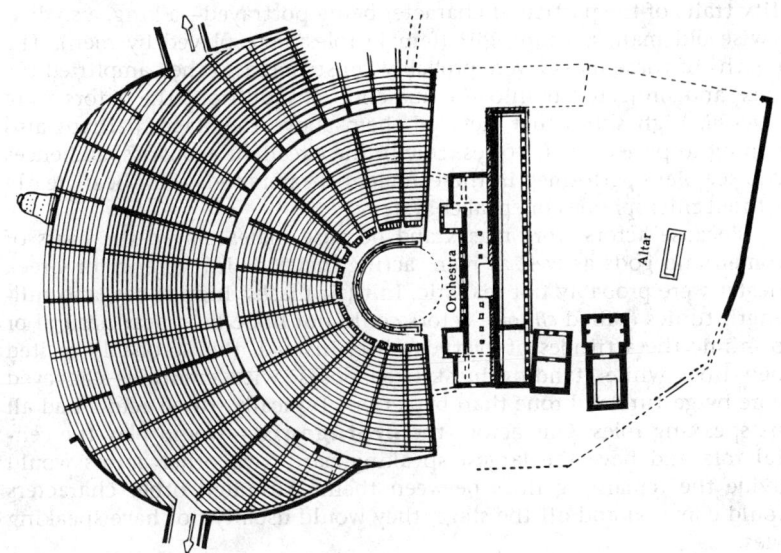

◊ **The Theater of Dionysus at Athens.** Redrawn from a drawing by R. C. Flickinger, *The Greek Theater and Its Drama* (Chicago: U of Chicago P, 1918).

commented on the drama. Raised a few steps above the orchestra was a platform on which the actors performed, behind which was a *skene*, or building, that originally served as a resting place or dressing room. (The modern term *scene* is derived from the Greek *skene*.) Behind the skene was a line of pillars called a *colonnade,* which was covered by a roof. Actors used the skene for entrances and exits; beginning with the plays of Sophocles, painted backdrops were hung there. These backdrops, however, were most likely more decorative than realistic. Historians believe that realistic props and scenery were probably absent from the ancient Greek theater. Instead, the setting was suggested by the play's dialogue, and the audience had to imagine the specific physical details of a scene.

Two mechanical devices were used. One, a rolling cart or platform, was sometimes employed to introduce action that had occurred offstage. For example, actors frozen in position could be rolled onto the roof of the skene to illustrate an event such as the killing of Oedipus's father, which occurred before the play began. Another mechanical device, a small crane, was used to show gods ascending to or descending from heaven. Such devices enabled playwrights to dramatize many of the myths that were celebrated at the Dionysian festivals.

The ancient Greek theater was designed to enhance acoustics. The flat stone wall of the skene reflected the sound from the orchestra and the stage, and the curved shape of the amphitheater captured the sound, enabling the audience to hear the lines spoken by the actors. Each actor wore a stylized mask, or **persona,** to convey to the audience the personality traits of the particular character being portrayed—a king, a soldier, a wise old man, a young girl (female roles were played by men). The mouths of these masks were probably constructed so they amplified the voice and projected it into the audience. In addition, the actors wore *kothorni*, high shoes that elevated them above the stage, perhaps also helping to project their voices. Due to the excellent acoustics, audiences who see plays performed in these ancient theaters today can hear clearly without microphones or speaker systems.

Because actors wore masks and because males played the parts of women and gods as well as men, acting methods in the ancient Greek theater were probably not realistic. In their masks, high shoes, and full-length tunics (called *chiton*), actors could not hope to appear natural or to mimic the attitudes of everyday life. Instead, they probably recited their lines while standing in stylized poses, with emotions conveyed more by gesture and tone than by action. Typically, three actors had all the speaking roles. One actor—the **protagonist**—would play the central role and have the largest speaking part. Two other actors would divide the remaining lines between them. Although other characters would come on and off the stage, they would usually not have speaking roles.

Ancient Greek tragedies were typically divided into five parts. First came the *prologos*, or prologue, in which an actor gave the background or explanations that the audience needed to follow the rest of the drama.

Then came the *párodos*, in which the chorus entered and commented on the events presented in the prologue. Following this were several *episodia*, or episodes, in which characters spoke to one another on the stage and developed the central conflict of the play. Alternating with episodes were *stasimon* (choral odes), in which the chorus commented on the exchanges that had taken place during the preceding episode. Frequently the choral odes were divided into *strophes*, or stanzas, that were recited or sung as the chorus moved across the orchestra in one direction, and *antistrophes* that were recited as it moved in the opposite direction. (Interestingly, the chorus stood between the audience and the actors, often functioning as an additional audience, expressing the political, social, and moral views of the community.) Finally came the *exodos*, the last scene of the play, during which the conflict was resolved and the actors left the stage.

Using music, dance, and verse—as well as a variety of architectural and technical innovations—the ancient Greek theater was able to convey traditional themes of tragedy. Thus, the theater powerfully expressed ideas that were central to the religious festivals in which they first appeared: the reverence for the cycles of life and death, the unavoidable dictates of the gods, and the inscrutable workings of fate.

THE ELIZABETHAN THEATER

The Elizabethan theater, influenced by the classical traditions of Roman and Greek dramatists, traces its roots back to local religious pageants performed at medieval festivals during the twelfth and thirteenth centuries. Town guilds, organizations of craftsmen who worked in the same profession, reenacted Old and New Testament stories: the fall of man, Noah and the flood, David and Goliath, and the crucifixion of Christ, for example. Church fathers encouraged these plays because they brought the Bible to a largely illiterate audience. Sometimes these spectacles, called **mystery plays,** were presented in the market square or on the church steps, and at other times actors appeared on movable stages or wagons called *pageants,* which could be wheeled to a given location. (Some of these wagons were quite elaborate, with trapdoors and pulleys and an upper tier that simulated heaven.) As mystery plays became more popular, they were performed in series over several days, presenting an entire cycle of a holiday—the death and resurrection of Christ during Easter, for example.

Related to mystery plays are **morality plays,** which developed in the fourteenth and fifteenth centuries. Unlike mystery plays, which depict scenes from the Bible, morality plays allegorize the Christian way of life. Typically, characters representing various virtues and vices struggle or debate over the soul of man. *Everyman* (1500), the best known of these plays, dramatizes the good and bad qualities of Everyman and shows his struggle to determine what is of value to him as he journeys toward death.

By the middle of the sixteenth century, mystery and morality plays had lost ground to a new secular drama. One reason for this decline was that mystery and morality plays were associated with Catholicism and consequently discouraged by the Protestant clergy. In addition, newly discovered plays of ancient Greece and Rome introduced a dramatic tradition that supplanted the traditions of religious drama. English plays that followed the classic model were sensational and bombastic, often dealing with murder, revenge, and blood retribution. Appealing to privileged classes and commoners alike, these plays were extremely popular. (One source estimates that between 20,000 and 25,000 people attended the London theaters each week.) Companies of professional actors performed works such as Christopher Marlowe's *Tamburlaine* and Thomas Kyd's *The Spanish Tragedy* in tavern courtyards and then eventually in theaters. According to scholars, the structure of the Elizabethan theater evolved from these tavern courtyards.

The Globe Theater (a corner of which was unearthed in 1989), where Shakespeare's plays were performed, consisted of a large main stage that extended out into the open-air *yard* where the *groundlings,* or common people, stood. Spectators who paid more sat on small stools in two or three levels of galleries that extended in front of and around the stage. (The theater could probably seat almost two thousand people at a performance.) Most of the play's action occurred on the stage, which had no curtain and could be seen from three sides. Beneath the stage was a space called the *hell,* which could be reached when the floorboards were removed. This space enabled actors to "disappear" or descend into a hole or grave when the play called for such action. Above the stage was a roof called the *heavens,* which protected the actors from the weather and contained ropes and pulleys used to lower props or to create special effects.

At the rear of the stage was a narrow alcove covered by a curtain that could be open or closed. This curtain, often painted, functioned as a decorative rather than a realistic backdrop. The main function of this alcove was to enable actors to hide when the script called for them to do so. Some Elizabethan theaters contained a rear stage instead of an alcove. Because the rear stage was concealed by a curtain, props could be arranged on it ahead of time. When the action on the rear stage was finished, the curtain would be drawn and the action would continue on the front stage.

On either side of the rear stage was a door through which the actors could enter and exit the front stage. Above the rear stage was an upper, curtained stage called the *chamber,* which functioned as a balcony or as any other setting located above the action taking place on the stage below. On either side of the chamber were casement windows, which actors could use when a play called for a conversation with someone leaning out a window or standing on a balcony. Above the chamber was the *music gallery,* a balcony that housed the musicians who provided musical interludes throughout the play (and that doubled as a stage if the play required it). The *huts,* windows located above the music gallery, could be

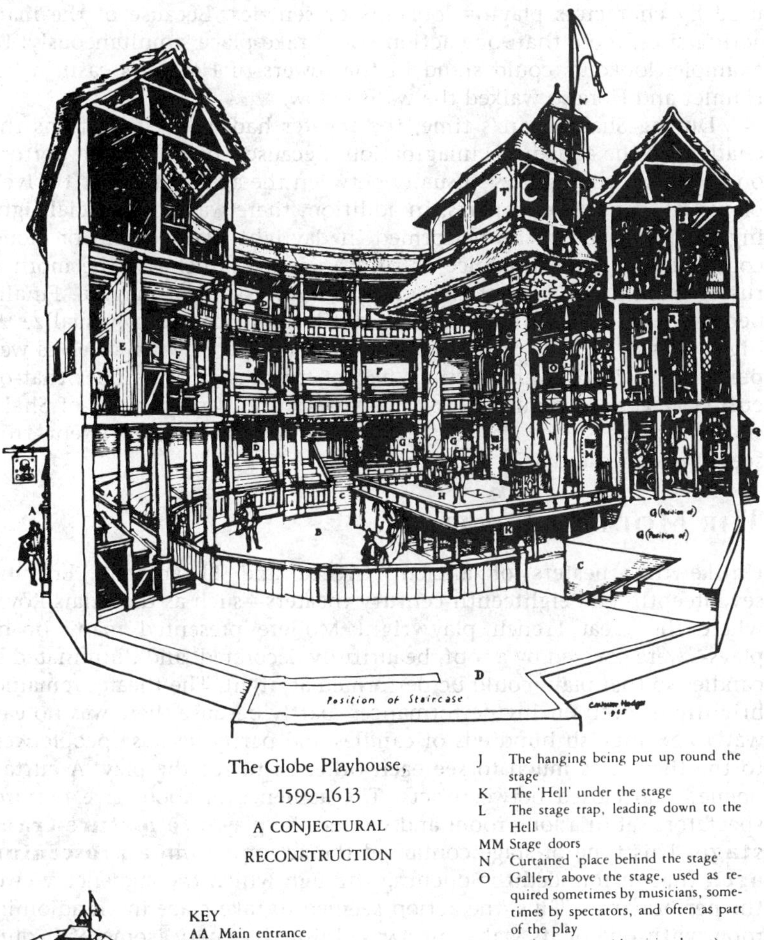

THE ORIGINS OF THE MODERN THEATER ◆ 569

The Globe Playhouse,
1599–1613

A CONJECTURAL
RECONSTRUCTION

KEY
AA Main entrance
B   The Yard
CC Entrances to lowest gallery
D   Entrances to staircase and upper galleries
E   Corridor serving the different sections of the middle gallery
F   Middle gallery ('Twopenny Rooms')
G   'Gentlemen's Rooms' or 'Lords' Rooms'
H   The stage
J   The hanging being put up round the stage
K   The 'Hell' under the stage
L   The stage trap, leading down to the Hell
MM Stage doors
N   Curtained 'place behind the stage'
O   Gallery above the stage, used as required sometimes by musicians, sometimes by spectators, and often as part of the play
P   Back-stage area (the tiring-house)
Q   Tiring-house door
R   Dressing-rooms
S   Wardrobe and storage
T   The hut housing the machine for lowering enthroned gods, etc., to the stage
U   The 'Heavens'
W   Hoisting the playhouse flag

◆ **The Globe Playhouse.** 1599–1613; a conjectural reconstruction. From C. Walter Hodges, *The Globe Restored.*

used by characters playing lookouts or sentries. Because of the many acting sites, more than one action could take place simultaneously. For example, lookouts could stand in the towers of Hamlet's castle while Hamlet and Horatio walked the walls below.

During Shakespeare's time, the theater had many limitations that challenged the audience's imagination. Because women did not perform on the stage, young boys—usually between the ages of ten and twelve—played all the women's parts. In addition, there was no artificial lighting, so plays had to be performed in daylight. Rain, wind, or clouds could disrupt a performance or ruin an image—such as "the morn in russet mantle clad"—that the audience was asked to imagine. Finally, because few sets and props were used, the audience had to visualize the high walls of a castle or the trees of a forest. The plays themselves were performed without intermission, except for musical interludes that occurred at various points. Thus, the experience of seeing one of Shakespeare's plays staged in the Elizabethan theater was different from seeing it staged today in a modern theater.

The Modern Theater

Unlike the theaters of ancient Greece and Elizabethan England, seventeenth- and eighteenth-century theaters—such as the Palais Royal, where the great French playwright Molière presented many of his plays—were covered by a roof, beautifully decorated, and illuminated by candles so that plays could be performed at night. The theater remained brightly lit even during performances, partly because there was no easy way to extinguish hundreds of candles and partly because people went to the theater as much to see each other as to see the play. A curtain opened and closed between acts. The audience of about five hundred spectators sat in a long room and viewed the play on a **picture-frame stage.** This type of stage contained the action within a **proscenium arch** that surrounded the opening through which the audience viewed the performance. Thus, the action seemed to take place in an adjoining room with one of its walls cut away. Painted scenery (some of it quite elaborate), intricately detailed costumes, and stage makeup were commonplace, and for the first time women performed female roles. Because the theaters were small, audiences were relatively close to the stage, so actors could use subtle movements and facial expressions to enhance their performances.

Many of the first innovations in the theater were quite basic. For example, the first stage lighting was produced by candles lining the front of the stage. This method of lighting was not only ineffective—actors were lit from below and had to step forward to be fully illuminated—but also dangerous. Costumes and even entire theaters could and did accidentally catch fire. Later, covered lanterns with reflectors provided more light. In the nineteenth century, a device that used an oxyhydrogen flame directed on a cylinder of lime created extremely bright illumination that could, with the aid of a lens, be concentrated into a spotlight. (It is from this method of stage lighting that we get the expression *to be in the limelight*.) Eventually, in the twentieth century, electric lights provided a dependable and safe way of lighting the stage. Electric spotlights, footlights, and ceiling light bars made the actors clearly visible and enabled playwrights to create special effects. In Arthur Miller's *Death of a Salesman* (p. 782), for example, lighting focuses attention on action in certain areas of the stage while leaving other areas in complete darkness.

Along with electric lighting came other innovations, such as electronic amplification. Microphones made it possible for actors to speak conversationally and to avoid using unnaturally loud "stage diction" to project their voices to the rear of the theater. Microphones placed at various points around the stage enabled actors and actresses to interact naturally and to deliver their lines audibly even without facing the audience. More recently, small wireless microphones eliminated the unwieldy wires and the "dead spaces" left between upright or hanging microphones, allowing characters to move freely around the stage.

The true revolutions in staging came with the advent of **realism** in the middle of the nineteenth century. Until this time, scenery was painted on canvas backdrops that trembled visibly, especially when they were intersected by doors through which actors and actresses entered. With realism came settings that were accurate down to the smallest detail. (Improved lighting, which revealed the inadequacies of painted backdrops, made such realistic stage settings necessary.) Backdrops were replaced by the **box set,** three flat panels arranged to form connected walls, with the fourth wall removed so the audience had the illusion of looking into a room. The room itself was decorated with real furniture, plants, and pictures on the walls; the door of one room might connect to another completely furnished room, or a window might open to a garden filled with realistic foliage. In addition, new methods of changing scenery were employed. Elevator stages, hydraulic lifts, and moving platforms enabled directors to make complicated changes in scenery out of the audience's view.

During the late nineteenth and early twentieth centuries, however, some playwrights reacted against what they saw as the excesses of realism. They introduced **surrealistic** stage settings, in which color and scenery mirrored the uncontrolled images of dreams, and **expressionistic** stage settings, in which costumes and scenery were exaggerated and distorted to reflect the workings of a troubled, even unbalanced mind. In addition, playwrights used lighting to create areas of light, shadow, and color that reinforced the themes of the play or reflected the emotions of the protagonist. In *The Emperor Jones,* for example, Eugene O'Neill used a series of expressionistic scenes to show the mental state of the terrified protagonist.

Sets in contemporary plays run the gamut from realistic to fantastic, from a detailed re-creation of a room in a production of Tennessee

Williams's *The Glass Menagerie* (p. 938) to a dreamlike set for Milcha Sanchez-Scott's *The Cuban Swimmer* (p. 865). Motorized devices, such as revolving turntables, and *wagons*—scenery mounted on wheels—make possible rapid changes of scenery. The Broadway musical *Les Miserables*, for example, requires scores of elaborate sets—Parisian slums, barricades, walled gardens—to be shifted as the audience watches. A gigantic barricade constructed on stage at one point in the play is later rotated to show the carnage that has taken place on both sides of a battle. Light, sound, and smoke are used to heighten the impact of the scene.

Today, as dramatists attempt to break down the barriers that separate audiences from the action they are viewing, plays are not limited to the picture-frame stage; in fact, they are performed on many different kinds of stages. Some plays, for example, take place on a **thrust stage,** which has an area that projects out into the audience. Others are performed on an **arena stage,** with the audience surrounding the actors. This kind of performance is often called **theater in the round.** In addition, experiments have been done with *environmental staging,* in which the stage surrounds the audience or several stages are situated at various locations throughout the audience. Plays may also be performed outdoors, in settings ranging from parks to city streets. Some playwrights even try to blur the line that divides the audience from the stage by

◊ **Thrust-Stage Theater.** With seats on three sides of the stage area, the thrust stage and its background can assume many forms other than the conventional living-room interior in the illustration. Entrances can be made from the aisles, from the sides, through the stage floor, and from the back.

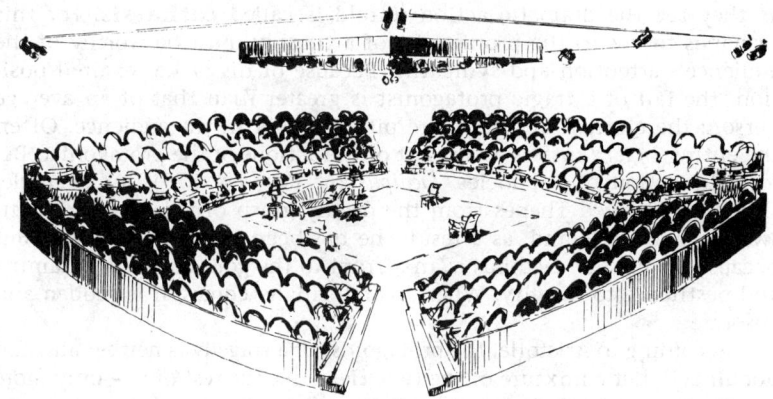

◆ **Arena Theater.** The audience surrounds the stage area, which may or may not be raised. Use of scenery is limited—perhaps to a single piece of scenery standing alone in the middle of the stage.

having actors move through or sit in the audience—or even by eliminating the stage entirely. For example, *Tony 'n Tina's Wedding,* a "participatory drama" created in 1988 by the theater group Artificial Intelligence, takes place not in a theater but at a church where a wedding is performed and then at a catering hall where the wedding reception is held. Throughout the play the members of the audience function as guests, joining in the wedding celebration and mingling with the actors, who improvise freely. More recent examples of such "interactive" drama include *Grandma Sylvia's Funeral* and *Off the Wall,* in which audiences "attend" an art auction. Today, no single architectural form defines the theater. The modern stage is a flexible space suited to the many varieties of contemporary theatrical production.

KINDS OF DRAMA

TRAGEDY

In his *Poetics,* Aristotle (384–322 B.C.) sums up ancient Greek thinking about drama when he writes that a **tragedy** is a drama treating a serious subject and involving persons of significance. According to Aristotle, when the members of an audience see a tragedy, they should feel both pity (and thus closeness to the protagonist) and fear (and thus revulsion) because they recognize in themselves the potential for similar reactions. The purging of these emotions that the audience experiences as they see the dramatic action unfold is called **catharsis.** For this catharsis to occur, the protagonist of a tragedy must be worthy of the audience's attention and sympathy. Because of his or her exalted position, the fall of a tragic protagonist is greater than that of an average person; therefore, it arouses more pity and fear in the audience. Often the entire society suffers as a result of the actions of the protagonist. Before the action of Sophocles' *Oedipus the King* (p. 879), for example, Oedipus has freed Thebes from the deadly grasp of the Sphinx by answering her riddle and, as a result, he has been welcomed as king. But because of his sins, Oedipus is an affront to the gods and brings famine and pestilence to the city. When his fall finally comes, it is sudden and absolute.

According to Aristotle, the protagonist of a tragedy is neither all good nor all evil, but a mixture of the two. He is like the rest of us—only more exalted and possessing some weakness or flaw **(hamartia).** This tragic flaw—perhaps narrowness of vision or overwhelming pride **(hubris)**—is typically the element that creates the conditions for tragedy. Shakespeare's Romeo and Juliet, for example, are so much in love they think they can ignore the blood feud that rages between their two families. However, their naive efforts to sustain their love despite the feud lead them to their tragic deaths. Similarly, Richard III's blind ambition to gain the throne causes him to murder all those who stand in his way. His unscrupulousness sets into motion the forces that eventually cause his death.

Irony is central to tragedy. **Dramatic irony** (also called **tragic irony**) emerges from a situation in which the audience knows more about the dramatic situation than a character does. As a result, the character's words and actions may be consistent with what he or she expects but at odds with what the audience knows will happen. Thus, a character may say or do something that causes the audience to infer a meaning beyond what the character intends or realizes. The dramatic irony is clear, for example, when Oedipus announces that whoever has disobeyed the dictates of the gods will be exiled. The audience knows, although Oedipus does not, that he has just condemned himself. **Cosmic irony,** also called **irony of fate,** occurs when God, fate, or some larger, uncontrollable force seems to be intentionally deceiving characters into believing they can escape their fate. Too late, they realize that trying to avoid their destiny is futile. Years before Oedipus was born, for example, the oracle of Apollo foretold that Oedipus would kill his parents. Naturally, his parents attempted to thwart the prophecy, but ironically, their actions ensured that the prophecy would be fulfilled.

At some point in a tragedy—usually after the climax—the protagonist recognizes the reasons for his or her downfall. It is this recognition (and the accompanying acceptance) that elevates tragic protagonists to grandeur and gives their suffering meaning. Without this recognition there would be no tragedy, just **pathos**—suffering that exists simply to satisfy the sentimental or morbid sensibilities of the audience. In spite of the death of the protagonist, then, tragedy enables the audience to see the nobility of the character and thus to experience a sense of elation. In Shakespeare's *King Lear*, for example, a king at the height of his powers decides to divide his kingdom among his three daughters. Too late, he realizes that without his power, he is just a bothersome old man to his ambitious children. Only after going mad does he understand the vanity of his former existence; he dies a humbled but enlightened man.

According to Aristotle, a tragedy achieves the illusion of reality only when it has *unity of action*—that is, when the play contains only those actions that lead to its tragic outcome. Later critics interpreted this to mean that including subplots or mixing tragic and comic elements would destroy this unity. To the concept of unity of action, these later critics added two other requirements: *unity of place*—the requirement that the play have a single setting—and *unity of time*—the requirement that the events depicted by the play take no longer than the actual duration of the play (or, at most, a single day).

The three unities have had a long and rather uneven history. In some of his plays—*The Tempest* and *The Comedy of Errors,* for example—Shakespeare observed the unities. Shakespeare, however, had no compunctions about writing plays with subplots and frequent changes of location. He also wrote **tragicomedies,** such as *The Merchant of Venice,* that have a serious theme appropriate for tragedy but end happily, usually because of a sudden turn of events. During the eighteenth century, with its emphasis on classic form, the unities were adhered to quite strictly, but in the late eighteenth and early nineteenth centuries, with the onset of romanticism and its emphasis on the natural, interest in the unities of place and time waned. Even though some modern dramatists occasionally observe the unities—*The Cuban Swimmer* (p. 865), for instance, has a single setting and takes place during a period of time that corresponds to the length of the play—few adhere to them strictly.

Ideas about appropriate subjects for tragedy have also changed. For Aristotle, the protagonist of a tragedy had to be exceptional—a king, for example. The protagonists of Greek tragedies were usually historical or mythical figures. Shakespeare often used kings and princes as protagonists—Richard II and Hamlet, for example—but he also used people of lesser rank, as in *Romeo and Juliet*. In our times, interest in the lives of monarchs has been overshadowed by involvement in the lives of ordinary people. Modern tragedies—*Death of a Salesman* (p. 782), for example—are more likely to focus on a traveling salesman than on a king.

With the rise of the middle class in the nineteenth century, ideas about the nature of tragedy changed. Responding to the age's desire for sentimentality, playwrights produced **melodramas,** sensational plays that appealed mainly to the emotions. Melodramas contain many of the elements of tragedy but end happily and often rely on conventional plots and stock characters. Because the protagonists in melodramas—often totally virtuous heroines suffering at the hands of impossibly wicked villains—helplessly endure their tribulations without ever gaining insight or enlightenment, they never achieve tragic status. As a result, they remain cardboard cutouts who exist only to exploit the emotions of the audience. Melodrama survives today in many films and in television soap operas.

Realism, which arose in the late nineteenth century as a response to the artificiality of melodrama, presented serious (and sometimes tragic) themes and believable characters in the context of everyday contemporary life. Writers of realistic drama used their plays to educate their audiences about the problems of the society in which they lived. For this reason, realistic drama focuses on the commonplace and eliminates the unlikely coincidences and excessive sentimentality of melodrama. Dramatists like Henrik Ibsen scrutinize the lives of ordinary people, not larger-than-life characters. After great suffering, these characters rise above the limitations of their mediocre lives and exhibit courage or emotional strength. The insight they gain often focuses attention on a social problem—the restrictive social conventions that define the behavior of women in nineteenth-century marriages, for example. Realistic drama also features settings and props similar to those used in people's daily lives and includes dialogue that reflects the way people actually speak.

Developing alongside realism was another literary movement called **naturalism.** Like realism, naturalism rejected the unrealistic plots and sentimentality of melodrama, but unlike realism, naturalism sought to explore the depths of the human condition. Influenced by Charles Darwin's ideas about evolution and natural selection and Karl Marx's ideas about economic forces that shape people's lives, naturalism is a pessimistic philosophy that presents a world which at worst is hostile and at best is indifferent to human concerns. It pictures human beings as higher-order animals who are driven by basic instincts—especially hunger, fear, and sexuality—and who are subject to economic, social, and biological forces beyond their understanding or control. It is, therefore, well suited to tragic themes.

The nineteenth-century French writer Émile Zola did much to develop the theory of naturalism, and later so did the American writers Stephen Crane, Frank Norris, and Theodore Dreiser. Naturalism also finds its way into the work of contemporary dramatists, such as Arthur Miller. Unlike other tragic protagonists, the protagonists of naturalist works are crushed not by the gods or by fate, but by poverty, animal drives, or social class. Willy Loman in *Death of a Salesman*, for example, is subject to the economic forces of a society that does not value its workers and discards those it no longer finds useful.

COMEDY

A **comedy** is a dramatic work that treats themes and characters with humor and typically has a happy ending. Whereas tragedy focuses on the hidden dimensions of the tragic hero's character, comedy focuses on the public persona, the protagonist as a social being. Tragic figures are typically seen in isolation, questioning the meaning of their lives and trying to comprehend their suffering. Hamlet—draped in sable, longing for death, and self-consciously contemplating his duty—epitomizes the isolation of the tragic hero.

Unlike tragic heroes, comic figures are seen in the public arena, where people intentionally assume the masks of pretension and self-importance. The purpose of comedy is to strip away these masks and expose human beings for what they are. Whereas tragedy reveals the nobility of the human condition, comedy reveals its inherent folly, portraying human beings as selfish, hypocritical, vain, weak, irrational, and capable of self-delusion. Thus, the basic function of comedy is critical—to tell people that things are not what they seem and that appearances are not necessarily reality. In the comic world nothing is solid or predictable, and accidents and coincidences are more important to the plot than reason. Many of Shakespeare's comedies, for example, depend on exchanged or confused identities. The wordplay and verbal nonsense of comedy add to this general confusion.

Comedies typically rely on certain familiar plot devices. Many comedies begin with a startling or unusual situation that attracts the audience's attention. In Shakespeare's *A Midsummer Night's Dream,* for example, Theseus, the duke of Athens, rules that Hermia will either marry the man her father has chosen for her or be put to death. Such an event could lead to tragedy if comedy did not intervene to save the day.

Comedy often depends on obstacles and hindrances to further its plot: the more difficult the problems the lovers face, the more satisfying their eventual triumph will be. For this reason, the plot of a comedy is usually more complex than the plot of a tragedy. Compare the rather straightforward plot of *Hamlet* (p. 681)—a prince ordered to avenge his murdered father's death is driven mad with indecision and, after finally acting decisively, is killed himself—with the mix-ups, mistaken identities, and general confusion of *A Midsummer Night's Dream.*

Finally, comedies have happy endings. Whereas tragedy ends with death, comedy ends with an affirmation of life. Eventually the confusion and misunderstandings reach a point where some resolution must be achieved: the difficulties of the lovers are overcome, the villains are banished, and the lovers marry—or at least express their intention to do so. In this way the lovers establish their connection with the rest of society, and its values are affirmed.

The first comedies, written in Greece in the fifth century B.C., heavily satirized the religious and social issues of the day. In the fourth and third centuries B.C., this **Old Comedy** gave way to **New Comedy,** a comedy of romance with stock characters—lovers and untrustworthy servants, for example—and conventional settings. Lacking the bitter satire and bawdiness of Old Comedy, New Comedy depends on outrageous plots, mistaken identities, young lovers, interfering parents, and conniving servants. Ultimately the young lovers outwit all those who stand between them and in so doing affirm the primacy of youth and love over old age and death.

Old and New Comedy represent two distinct lines of humor that extend to modern times. Old Comedy depends on **satire**—bitter humor that diminishes a person, idea, or institution by ridiculing it or holding it up to scorn. Unlike comedy, which exists simply to make people laugh, satire is social criticism, deriding hypocrisy, pretension, and vanity or condemning vice. At its best, satire appeals to the intellect, has a serious purpose, and arouses thoughtful laughter. New Comedy may also be satiric, but it frequently contains elements of **farce,** comedy in which stereotypical characters engage in boisterous horseplay and slapstick humor, all the while making jokes and sexual innuendoes—as they do in Anton Chekhov's *The Brute* (p. 668).

English comedy got its start in the sixth century A.D. in the form of farcical episodes that appeared in morality plays. During the Renaissance, comedy developed rapidly, beginning in 1533 with Nicholas Udall's *Ralph Roister Doister* and eventually evolving into Shakespeare's **romantic comedy**—such as *A Midsummer Night's Dream,* in which love is the main subject and idealized heroines and lovers endure great difficulties until the inevitable happy ending is reached.

Also during the Renaissance, particularly in the latter part of the sixteenth century, writers like Ben Jonson experimented with a different type of comedy—the **comedy of humours,** which focused on characters whose behavior was controlled by a characteristic trait, or *humour.* During the Renaissance a person's temperament was thought to be determined by the mix of fluids, or humours, in the body. When one humour dominated, a certain type of disposition resulted. Playwrights capitalized on this belief, writing comedies in which characters are motivated by stereotypical behaviors that result from the imbalance of the humours. In comedies such as Jonson's *Volpone* and *The Alchemist,* characters such as the suspicious husband and the miser can be manipulated by others because of their predictable dispositions.

Closely related to the comedy of humours is the satiric **comedy of manners,** which developed during the sixteenth century and achieved great popularity in the nineteenth century. This form focuses on the manners and customs of society and directs its satire against characters who violate social conventions and rules of behavior. These plays tend to be memorable more for their witty dialogue than for their development of characters or setting. Oliver Goldsmith's *She Stoops to Conquer,* George Bernard Shaw's *Pygmalion,* and even some television sitcoms are examples of this type of comedy.

In the eighteenth century, a reaction against the perceived immorality of the comedy of manners led to **sentimental comedy,** which eventually achieved great popularity. This kind of comedy relies on sentimental emotion rather than on wit or humor to move an audience. It also dwells on the virtues rather than on the vices of life. The heroes of sentimental comedy are unimpeachably noble, moral, and honorable; the pure, virtuous, middle-class heroines suffer trials and tribulations calculated to move the audience to tears rather than laughter. Eventually, the distress of the hero and heroine is resolved in a sometimes contrived (but always happy) ending.

In his 1877 essay *The Idea of Comedy,* novelist and critic George Meredith suggests that comedy that appeals to the intellect should be called **high comedy.** Shakespeare's *As You Like It* and Shaw's *Pygmalion* can be characterized in this way. When comedy has little or no intellectual appeal, according to Meredith, it is **low comedy.** Low comedy appears in parts of Shakespeare's *The Taming of the Shrew* and as comic relief in *Macbeth.*

The twentieth century has developed its own characteristic comic forms. Most reflect the uncertainty and pessimism of a century that has seen two world wars, the Holocaust, and nuclear destruction, as well as threats posed by environmental pollution and ethnic and racial conflict. Combining laughter and hints of tragedy, these modern tragicomedies feature **antiheroes,** characters who, instead of manifesting dignity and power, are ineffectual or petty. Their plight frequently elicits laughter, not pity and fear, from the audience. **Black** or **dark comedies,** for example, rely for their comedy on the morbid and the absurd. These works are usually so satiric and bitter that they threaten to slip over the edge into tragedy. The screenplay of Joseph Heller's novel *Catch-22,* which ends with a character dropping bombs on his own men, is a classic example of such comedy. **Theater of the absurd,** which includes comedies such as Edward Albee's *The Sandbox,* begins with the assumption that the human condition is irrational. Typically, this type of drama does not have a discernible plot; instead, it presents a series of apparently unrelated images and illogical exchanges of dialogue meant to reinforce the idea that human beings live in a remote, confusing, and often incomprehensible universe. Absurdist dramas seem to go in circles, never progressing to a climax or achieving a resolution, reinforcing the theme of the endless and meaningless repetition that characterizes modern life.

READING DRAMA

◊ ◊ ◊

When you read a play, you will notice features it shares with works of fiction—for instance, its use of language and symbols, the interaction among its characters, and its development of a theme or themes. In addition, you will notice features that distinguish it from fiction—for example, the presence of stage directions and the division into acts and scenes.

The following guidelines, designed to help you explore works of dramatic literature, focus on issues that will be examined in depth in chapters to come.

- Trace the play's **plot.** What conflicts are present? Where does the rising action reach a climax? Where does the falling action begin? What techniques move the action along? (See Chapter 19.)
- Analyze the play's **characters.** Who are the central characters? What are their most distinctive traits? How do you learn about their personalities, backgrounds, appearances, and strengths and weaknesses? (See Chapter 20.)
- Examine the play's language. How does dialogue reveal characters' emotions, conflicts, opinions, and motivation? (See Chapter 20.)
- Does the play include soliloquies or asides? What do they contribute to your knowledge of the play's characters and events? (See Chapter 20.)
- How do the characters interact with one another? Do the characters change and grow in response to the play's events, or do they remain essentially unchanged? (See Chapter 20.)
- Read the play's stage directions. What do you learn from the descriptions of the characters, including their dress, gestures, and facial expressions? (See Chapter 20.) What information do you gain from studying the playwright's descriptions of the play's setting? Do the stage directions include information about lighting, props, music, or sound effects? (See Chapter 21.)
- Consider the play's **staging.** Where and when does the action take place? What techniques are used to convey a sense of time and place to the audience? (See Chapter 21.)
- Try to interpret the play's **themes.** What main idea does the play communicate? What additional themes are explored? (See Chapter 22.)
- Identify any symbolic elements in the play. How do such symbols enhance the play's themes? (See Chapter 22.)

CHAPTER 19

Plot

Plot denotes the way events are arranged in a work of literature. Although the accepted conventions of drama require that the plot of a play be presented somewhat differently from the plot of a short story, the same components of plot are present in both. Plot in a dramatic work, like plot in a short story, presents conflicts that are revealed, intensified, and resolved during the course of the play through the characters' actions. (See Chapter 4 for a discussion of **conflict**.)

PLOT STRUCTURE

◊ ◊ ◊

In 1863, the German critic Gustav Freytag devised a pyramid to represent a prototype for the plot of a dramatic work. According to Freytag, a play typically begins with **exposition,** which presents characters and setting and introduces the basic situation in which the characters are involved. Then, during the **rising action,** complications develop, conflicts emerge, suspense builds, and crises occur. The rising action culminates in a **climax,** at which point the plot's tension peaks. Finally, during the **falling action,** the intensity subsides, eventually winding down to a **resolution,** or **denouement,** in which all loose ends are tied up.

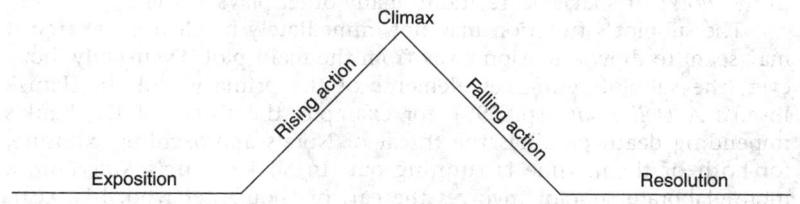

The familiar plot of a detective story follows Freytag's concept of plot: the exposition section includes the introduction of the detective and the explanation of the crime; the rising action develops as the investigation of the crime proceeds, with suspense increasing as the solution approaches; the high point of the action, the climax, comes with the revelation of the crime's solution; and the falling action presents the explanation of the solution. The story concludes with a resolution typically characterized by the capture of the criminal and the restoration of order.

The action of Susan Glaspell's one-act play *Trifles* (p. 586), which in many ways resembles a detective story, might be diagrammed as follows:

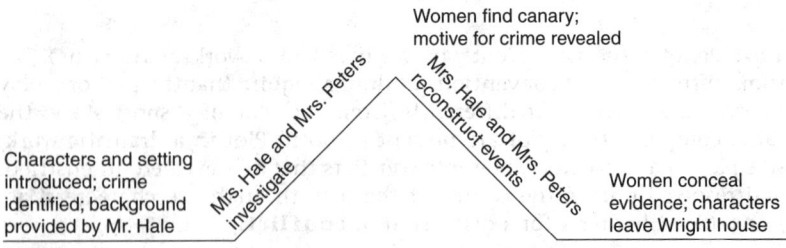

Of course, the plot of a complex dramatic work rarely conforms to the neat pattern represented by Freytag's pyramid. In fact, a play can lack exposition or resolution entirely, and the climax can occur at the beginning. Because long stretches of exposition can be dull, a playwright may arouse audience interest by moving directly into conflict. *Oedipus the King* (p. 879), for example, begins with the conflict, and so does *The Cuban Swimmer* (p. 865). Similarly, because audiences tend to lose interest after the play's climax is reached, a playwright may choose to dispense with extended falling action. Thus, after Hamlet's death, the play ends abruptly.

Plot and Subplot

While the main plot is developing, another, parallel plot, called a **subplot**, may be developing alongside it. This structural device is common in the works of Shakespeare and in many other plays as well.

The subplot's function may not immediately be clear, so at first it may seem to draw attention away from the main plot. Eventually, however, the subplot reinforces elements of the primary plot. In Henrik Ibsen's *A Doll House* (p. 599), for example, the threat of Dr. Rank's impending death parallels the threat of Nora's approaching exposure; for both of them, time is running out. In Shakespeare's *King Lear*, a more elaborate subplot involves the earl of Gloucester who, like Lear, misjudges his children, favoring a deceitful son who does not deserve his support and overlooking a more deserving one. Both families suffer greatly as a result of the fathers' misplaced loyalties. Thus, the parallel plot places additional emphasis on Lear's poor judgment and magnifies the consequences of his misguided acts: both fathers, and all but one of the five children, are dead by the play's end. A subplot can also set up a contrast—as it does in *Hamlet*, where Fortinbras acts decisively to avenge his father, an action that underscores Hamlet's hesitation and procrastination when faced with a comparable challenge.

Plot Development

◊ ◊ ◊

In a dramatic work plot unfolds through **action,** what characters say and do. Generally, a play does not include a narrator whose commentary ensures that events will move smoothly along. Instead, dialogue, stage directions, and staging techniques work together to move the play's action along.

For example, exchanges of dialogue reveal what is happening—and, sometimes, indicate what has happened in the past or suggest what will happen in the future. Characters can recount past events to other characters, announce an intention to take some action in the future, or summarize events that are occurring offstage. In such cases, dialogue takes the place of formal narrative. On the printed page, stage directions efficiently move readers from one location and time period to another by specifying entrances and exits and identifying the play's structural divisions—acts and scenes—and their accompanying changes of setting.

Staging techniques can also advance a play's action. A change in lighting, for instance, can shift the focus to another part of the stage—and thus to another place and time. Similarly, an adjustment of **scenery** or **props**—for instance, a breakfast table, complete with morning paper, replacing a bedtime setting—can indicate that the action has moved forward in time, as can a change of costumes. In Tennessee Williams's *The Glass Menagerie* (p. 938), various staging devices—such as words projected on a screen that preview words to be spoken by a character and visual images on screen that predict scenes to follow—help to keep the action moving. For example, a screen image of blue roses leads into a scene in which Laura tells her mother how Jim gave her the nickname "Blue Roses."

Music can also move a play's action along, predicting excitement or doom or a romantic interlude—or a particular character's entrance. In scene 5 of *The Glass Menagerie*, for example, stage directions announce "The Dance-Hall Music Changes to a Tango That Has a Minor and Somewhat Ominous Tone"; a "music legend" repeated throughout the play serves as a signature in scenes focusing on Laura.

Less often, a narrator advances the action. In Thornton Wilder's 1938 play *Our Town*, for example, a character known as the Stage Manager functions as a narrator, not only describing the play's setting and introducing the characters to the audience, but also soliciting questions from characters scattered around the audience, prompting characters, and interrupting dialogue. In *The Glass Menagerie* the protagonist, Tom Wingfield, also serves as a narrator, summarizing what has happened and moving readers on to the next scene: "After the fiasco at Rubicam's Business College, the idea of getting a gentleman caller for Laura began to play a more important part in Mother's calculations" (scene 3).

FLASHBACKS

Many plays—such as *The Glass Menagerie* and Arthur Miller's *Death of a Salesman* (p. 782)—include **flashbacks,** which depict events that occurred before the play's main action. In addition, dialogue can overcome the limitations set by the chronological action on stage by recounting events that occurred earlier. Thus, Mr. Hale in *Trifles* tells the other characters how he discovered John Wright's murder, and Nora in *A Doll House* confides her secret past to her friend Kristine. As characters on stage are brought up to date, the audience is also given necessary information—facts that are essential to an understanding of the characters' motivation. Naturally, characters must have plausible reasons for explaining past events. In *Trifles,* Mr. Hale is the only character who has witnessed the events he describes, and in *A Doll House,* Kristine, formerly Nora's friend and confidante, has not seen her in years. Thus, a character's need for information provides playwrights with a convenient excuse for supplying readers with necessary background. In less realistic dramas, however, no such excuse is necessary: characters can interrupt the action to deliver long monologues or soliloquies that fill in background details—or even address the audience directly, as Tom does in *The Glass Menagerie.*

FORESHADOWING

In addition to revealing past events, dialogue can **foreshadow,** or look ahead to, future action. In many cases, seemingly unimportant comments have significance that becomes clear as the play develops. For example, in act 3 of *A Doll House* Torvald Helmer says to Kristine, "An exit should always be effective, Mrs. Linde, but that's what I can't get Nora to grasp." At the end of the play, Nora's exit is not only effective, but also memorable.

Elements of staging can also suggest events to come. In *The Glass Menagerie,* for instance, the ever-present photograph of the absent father—who, Tom tells the audience, may be seen as a symbol of "the long delayed but always expected something that we live for"—foreshadows Tom's escape. Various bits of **stage business**—gestures or movements designed to attract the audience's attention—may also foreshadow future events. In *A Doll House,* for instance, Nora's sneaking forbidden macaroons seems at first to suggest her fear of her husband, but her actions actually foreshadow her eventual defiance of his authority.

CHECKLIST: WRITING ABOUT PLOT

- ✓ Summarize the play's events.
- ✓ What is the play's central conflict? How is it resolved? What other conflicts are present?
- ✓ What section of the play constitutes its rising action?
- ✓ Where does the play's climax occur?
- ✓ What crises can you identify?
- ✓ How is suspense created?
- ✓ What section of the play constitutes its falling action?
- ✓ Does the play contain a subplot? What is its purpose? How is it related to the main plot?
- ✓ Does the play have flashbacks? Does the play's dialogue contain summaries of past events or references to events in the future? How does the use of flashbacks or foreshadowing advance the play's plot?
- ✓ Does the play include a narrator?
- ✓ How does the dialogue advance the play's plot?
- ✓ How do characters' actions advance the play's plot?
- ✓ How do stage directions advance the play's plot?
- ✓ How does staging advance the play's plot?
- ✓ Does the play use any other devices to advance the plot?

◊ **SUSAN GLASPELL** (1882–1948) with her husband, George Cram Cook, founded the Provincetown Players, which became the staging ground for innovative plays by Eugene O'Neill, among others. Glaspell herself wrote plays for the Provincetown Players, beginning with *Trifles,* which she created for the 1916 season although she had never previously written a drama.

Glaspell said she wrote *Trifles* in one afternoon, sitting in the empty theater and looking at the bare stage: "After a time, the stage became a kitchen—a kitchen there all by itself." She remembered a murder trial she had covered in her early days as a reporter, and the story began to play itself out on the stage as she gazed.

SUSAN GLASPELL

Trifles
(1916)

Characters
GEORGE HENDERSON, *county attorney*
HENRY PETERS, *sheriff*
LEWIS HALE, *a neighboring farmer*
MRS. PETERS
MRS. HALE

Scene

The kitchen in the now abandoned farmhouse of John Wright, a gloomy kitchen, and left without having been put in order—unwashed pans under the sink, a loaf of bread outside the breadbox, a dish towel on the table—other signs of incompleted work. At the rear the outer door opens and the Sheriff comes in followed by the County Attorney and Hale. The Sheriff and Hale are men in middle life, the County Attorney is a young man; all are much bundled up and go at once to the stove. They are followed by two women—the Sheriff's wife first; she is a slight wiry woman, a thin nervous face. Mrs. Hale is larger and would ordinarily be called more comfortable looking, but she is disturbed now and looks fearfully about as she enters. The women have come in slowly, and stand close together near the door.

COUNTY ATTORNEY: *(rubbing his hands)* This feels good. Come up to the fire, ladies.

MRS. PETERS: *(after taking a step forward)* I'm not—cold.

SHERIFF: *(unbuttoning his overcoat and stepping away from the stove as if to mark the beginning of official business)* Now, Mr. Hale, before we move things about, you explain to Mr. Henderson just what you saw when you came here yesterday morning.

COUNTY ATTORNEY: By the way, has anything been moved? Are things just as you left them yesterday?

5 SHERIFF: *(looking about)* It's just the same. When it dropped below zero last night I thought I'd better send Frank out this morning to make a fire for us—no use getting pneumonia with a big case on, but I told him not to touch anything except the stove—and you know Frank.

COUNTY ATTORNEY: Somebody should have been left here yesterday.

SHERIFF: Oh—yesterday. When I had to send Frank to Morris Center for that man who went crazy—I want you to know I had my hands full yesterday. I knew you could get back from Omaha by today and as long as I went over everything here myself—

COUNTY ATTORNEY: Well, Mr. Hale, tell just what happened when you came here yesterday morning.

HALE: Harry and I had started to town with a load of potatoes. We came along the road from my place and as I got here I said, "I'm going to see if I can't get John Wright to go in with me on a party telephone." I spoke to Wright about it once before and he put me off, saying folks talked too much anyway, and all he asked was peace and quiet—I guess you know about how much he talked himself; but I thought maybe if I went to the house and talked about it before his wife, though I said to Harry that I didn't know as what his wife wanted made much difference to John—

10 COUNTY ATTORNEY: Let's talk about that later, Mr. Hale. I do want to talk about that, but tell now just what happened when you got to the house.

HALE: I didn't hear or see anything; I knocked at the door, and still it was all quiet inside. I knew they must be up, it was past eight o'clock. So I knocked again, and I thought I heard somebody say, "Come in." I wasn't sure, I'm not sure yet, but I opened the door—this door *(indicating the door by which the two women are still standing)* and there in that rocker—*(pointing to it)* sat Mrs. Wright.

They all look at the rocker.

COUNTY ATTORNEY: What—was she doing?
HALE: She was rockin' back and forth. She had her apron in her hand and was kind of—pleating it.
COUNTY ATTORNEY: And how did she—look?
15 HALE: Well, she looked queer.
COUNTY ATTORNEY: How do you mean—queer?
HALE: Well, as if she didn't know what she was going to do next. And kind of done up.
COUNTY ATTORNEY: How did she seem to feel about your coming?
HALE: Why, I don't think she minded—one way or other. She didn't pay much attention. I said, "How do, Mrs. Wright, it's cold, ain't it?" And she said, "Is it?"—and went on kind of pleating at her apron. Well, I was surprised; she didn't ask me to come up to the stove, or to set down, but just sat there, not even looking at me, so I said, "I want to see John." And then she—laughed. I guess you would call it a laugh. I thought of Harry and the team outside, so I said a little sharp: "Can't I see John?" "No," she says, kind o' dull like. "Ain't he home?" says I. "Yes," says she, "he's home." "Then why can't I see him?" I asked her, out of patience. "'Cause he's dead," says she. "Dead?" says I. She just nodded her head, not getting a bit excited, but rockin' back and forth. "Why—where is he?" says I, not knowing what to say. She just pointed upstairs—like that. *(Himself pointing to the room above.)* I got up, with the idea of going up there. I walked from there to here—then I says, "Why, what did he die of?" "He died of a rope round his neck," says she, and just went on pleatin' at her apron. Well, I went out and called Harry. I thought I might—need help. We went upstairs and there he was lyin'—

20 COUNTY ATTORNEY: I think I'd rather have you go into that upstairs, where you can point it all out. Just go on now with the rest of the story.

HALE: Well, my first thought was to get that rope off. It looked . . . *(stops, his face twitches)* . . . but Harry, he went up to him, and he said, "No, he's dead all right, and we'd better not touch anything." So we went back down stairs. She was still sitting that same way. "Has anybody been notified?" I asked. "No," says she, unconcerned. "Who did this, Mrs. Wright?" said Harry. He said it businesslike—and she stopped pleatin' of her apron. "I don't know," she says. "You don't *know?*" says Harry. "No," says she. "Weren't you sleepin' in the bed with him?" says Harry. "Yes," says she, "but I was on the inside." "Somebody slipped a rope round his neck and strangled him and you didn't wake up?" says Harry. "I didn't wake up," she said after him. We must 'a looked as if we didn't see how that could be, for after a minute she said, "I sleep sound." Harry was going to ask her more questions but I said maybe we ought to let her tell her story first to the coroner, or the sheriff, so Harry went fast as he could to Rivers' place, where there's a telephone.

COUNTY ATTORNEY: And what did Mrs. Wright do when she knew that you had gone for the coroner?

HALE: She moved from that chair to this one over here *(pointing to a small chair in the corner)* and just sat there with her hands held together and looking down. I got a feeling that I ought to make some conversation, so I said I had come in to see if John wanted to put in a telephone, and at that she started to laugh, and then she stopped and looked at me—scared. *(The County Attorney, who has had his notebook out, makes a note.)* I dunno, maybe it wasn't scared. I wouldn't like to say it was. Soon Harry got back, and then Dr. Lloyd came, and you, Mr. Peters, and so I guess that's all I know that you don't.

COUNTY ATTORNEY: *(looking around)* I guess we'll go upstairs first—and then out to the barn and around there. *(To the Sheriff.)* You're convinced that there was nothing important here—nothing that would point to any motive.

25 SHERIFF: Nothing here but kitchen things.

The County Attorney, after again looking around the kitchen, opens the door of a cupboard closet. He gets up on a chair and looks on a shelf. Pulls his hand away, sticky.

COUNTY ATTORNEY: Here's a nice mess.

The women draw nearer.

MRS. PETERS: *(to the other woman)* Oh, her fruit; it did freeze. *(To the County Attorney.)* She worried about that when it turned so cold. She said the fire'd go out and her jars would break.

SHERIFF: Well, can you beat the woman! Held for murder and worryin' about her preserves.
COUNTY ATTORNEY: I guess before we're through she may have something more serious than preserves to worry about.
30 HALE: Well, women are used to worrying over trifles.

The two women move a little closer together.

COUNTY ATTORNEY: *(with the gallantry of a young politician)* And yet, for all their worries, what would we do without the ladies? *(The women do not unbend. He goes to the sink, takes a dipperful of water from the pail and pouring it into a basin, washes his hands. Starts to wipe them on the roller towel, turns it for a cleaner place.)* Dirty towels! *(Kicks his foot against the pans under the sink.)* Not much of a housekeeper, would you say, ladies?
MRS. HALE: *(stiffly)* There's a great deal of work to be done on a farm.
COUNTY ATTORNEY: To be sure. And yet *(with a little bow to her)* I know there are some Dickson county farmhouses which do not have such roller towels.

He gives it a pull to expose its full length again.

MRS. HALE: Those towels get dirty awful quick. Men's hands aren't always as clean as they might be.
35 COUNTY ATTORNEY: Ah, loyal to your sex, I see. But you and Mrs. Wright were neighbors. I suppose you were friends, too.
MRS. HALE: *(shaking her head)* I've not seen much of her of late years. I've not been in this house—it's more than a year.
COUNTY ATTORNEY: And why was that? You didn't like her?
MRS. HALE: I liked her all well enough. Farmers' wives have their hands full, Mr. Henderson. And then—
COUNTY ATTORNEY: Yes—?
40 MRS. HALE: *(looking about)* It never seemed a very cheerful place.
COUNTY ATTORNEY: No—it's not cheerful. I shouldn't say she had the homemaking instinct.
MRS. HALE: Well, I don't know as Wright had, either.
COUNTY ATTORNEY: You mean that they didn't get on very well?
MRS. HALE: No, I don't mean anything. But I don't think a place'd be any cheerfuller for John Wright's being in it.
45 COUNTY ATTORNEY: I'd like to talk more of that a little later. I want to get the lay of things upstairs now.

He goes to the left, where three steps lead to a stair door.

SHERIFF: I suppose anything Mrs. Peters does'll be all right. She was to take in some clothes for her, you know, and a few little things. We left in such a hurry yesterday.
COUNTY ATTORNEY: Yes, but I would like to see what you take, Mrs. Peters, and keep an eye out for anything that might be of use to us.
MRS. PETERS: Yes, Mr. Henderson.

The women listen to the men's steps on the stairs, then look about the kitchen.

MRS. HALE: I'd hate to have men coming into my kitchen, snooping around and criticizing.

She arranges the pans under sink which the County Attorney had shoved out of place.

50 MRS. PETERS: Of course it's no more than their duty.

MRS. HALE: Duty's all right, but I guess that deputy sheriff that came out to make the fire might have got a little of this on. *(Gives the roller towel a pull.)* Wish I'd thought of that sooner. Seems mean to talk about her for not having things slicked up when she had to come away in such a hurry.

MRS. PETERS: *(who has gone to a small table in the left rear corner of the room, and lifted one end of a towel that covers a pan)* She had bread set.

Stands still.

MRS. HALE: *(eyes fixed on a loaf of bread beside the breadbox, which is on a low shelf at the other side of the room. Moves slowly toward it.)* She was going to put this in there. *(Picks up loaf, then abruptly drops it. In a manner of returning to familiar things.)* It's a shame about her fruit. I wonder if it's all gone. *(Gets up on the chair and looks.)* I think there's some here that's all right, Mrs. Peters. Yes—here; *(holding it toward the window)* this is cherries, too. *(Looking again.)* I declare I believe that's the only one. *(Gets down, bottle in her hand. Goes to the sink and wipes it off on the outside.)* She'll feel awful bad after all her hard work in the hot weather. I remember the afternoon I put up my cherries last summer.

She puts the bottle on the big kitchen table, center of the room. With a sigh, is about to sit down in the rocking-chair. Before she is seated realizes what chair it is; with a slow look at it, steps back. The chair which she has touched rocks back and forth.

MRS. PETERS: Well, I must get those things from the front room closet. *(She goes to the door at the right, but after looking into the other room, steps back.)* You coming with me, Mrs. Hale? You could help me carry them.

They go in the other room; reappear, Mrs. Peters carrying a dress and skirt, Mrs. Hale following with a pair of shoes.

55 MRS. PETERS: My, it's cold in there.

She puts the clothes on the big table, and hurries to the stove.

MRS. HALE: *(examining her skirt)* Wright was close. I think maybe that's why she kept so much to herself. She didn't even belong to the

Ladies Aid. I suppose she felt she couldn't do her part, and then you don't enjoy things when you feel shabby. She used to wear pretty clothes and be lively, when she was Minnie Foster, one of the town girls singing in the choir. But that—oh, that was thirty years ago. This all you was to take in?

Mrs. Peters: She said she wanted an apron. Funny thing to want, for there isn't much to get you dirty in jail, goodness knows. But I suppose just to make her feel more natural. She said they was in the top drawer in this cupboard. Yes, here. And then her little shawl that always hung behind the door. *(Opens stair door and looks.)* Yes, here it is.

Quickly shuts door leading upstairs.

Mrs. Hale: *(abruptly moving toward her)* Mrs. Peters?
Mrs. Peters: Yes, Mrs. Hale?
60 **Mrs. Hale:** Do you think she did it?
Mrs. Peters: *(in a frightened voice)* Oh, I don't know.
Mrs. Hale: Well, I don't think she did. Asking for an apron and her little shawl. Worrying about her fruit.
Mrs. Peters: *(starts to speak, glances up, where footsteps are heard in the room above. In a low voice.)* Mr. Peters says it looks bad for her. Mr. Henderson is awful sarcastic in a speech and he'll make fun of her sayin' she didn't wake up.
Mrs. Hale: Well, I guess John Wright didn't wake when they was slipping that rope under his neck.
65 **Mrs. Peters:** No, it's strange. It must have been done awful crafty and still. They say it was such a—funny way to kill a man, rigging it all up like that.
Mrs. Hale: That's just what Mr. Hale said. There was a gun in the house. He says that's what he can't understand.
Mrs. Peters: Mr. Henderson said coming out that what was needed for the case was a motive; something to show anger, or—sudden feeling.
Mrs. Hale: *(who is standing by the table)* Well, I don't see any signs of anger around here. *(She puts her hand on the dish towel which lies on the table, stands looking down at table, one half of which is clean, the other half messy.)* It's wiped to here. *(Makes a move as if to finish work, then turns and looks at loaf of bread outside the breadbox. Drops towel. In that voice of coming back to familiar things.)* Wonder how they are finding things upstairs. I hope she had it a little more red-up[1] up there. You know, it seems kind of *sneaking*. Locking her up in town and then coming out here and trying to get her own house to turn against her!

---

[1] Spruced up. (slang)

MRS. PETERS: But Mrs. Hale, the law is the law.

70 MRS. HALE: I s'pose 'tis. *(Unbuttoning her coat.)* Better loosen up your things, Mrs. Peters. You won't feel them when you go out.

Mrs. Peters takes off her fur tippet, goes to hang it on hook at back of room, stands looking at the under part of the small corner table.

MRS. PETERS: She was piecing a quilt.

She brings the large sewing basket and they look at the bright pieces.

MRS. HALE: It's log cabin pattern. Pretty, isn't it? I wonder if she was goin' to quilt it or just knot it?

Footsteps have been heard coming down the stairs. The Sheriff enters followed by Hale and the County Attorney.

SHERIFF: They wonder if she was going to quilt it or just knot it!

The men laugh; the women look abashed.

COUNTY ATTORNEY: *(rubbing his hands over the stove)* Frank's fire didn't do much up there, did it? Well, let's go out to the barn and get that cleared up.

The men go outside.

75 MRS. HALE: *(resentfully)* I don't know as there's anything so strange, our takin' up our time with little things while we're waiting for them to get the evidence. *(She sits down at the big table smoothing out a block with decision.)* I don't see as it's anything to laugh about.

MRS. PETERS: *(apologetically)* Of course they've got awful important things on their minds.

Pulls up a chair and joins Mrs. Hale at the table.

MRS. HALE: *(examining another block)* Mrs. Peters, look at this one. Here, this is the one she was working on, and look at the sewing! All the rest of it has been so nice and even. And look at this! It's all over the place! Why, it looks as if she didn't know what she was about!

After she has said this they look at each other, then start to glance back at the door. After an instant Mrs. Hale has pulled at a knot and ripped the sewing.

MRS. PETERS: Oh, what are you doing, Mrs. Hale?
MRS. HALE: *(mildly)* Just pulling out a stitch or two that's not sewed very good. *(Threading a needle.)* Bad sewing always made me fidgety.

80 MRS. PETERS: *(nervously)* I don't think we ought to touch things.
MRS. HALE: I'll just finish up this end. *(Suddenly stopping and leaning forward.)* Mrs. Peters?
MRS. PETERS: Yes, Mrs. Hale?
MRS. HALE: What do you suppose she was so nervous about?

MRS. PETERS: Oh—I don't know. I don't know as she was nervous. I sometimes sew awful queer when I'm just tired. *(Mrs. Hale starts to say something, looks at Mrs. Peters, then goes on sewing.)* Well, I must get these things wrapped up. They may be through sooner than we think. *(Putting apron and other things together.)* I wonder where I can find a piece of paper, and string.

MRS. HALE: In that cupboard, maybe.

MRS. PETERS: *(looking in cupboard)* Why, here's a birdcage. *(Holds it up.)* Did she have a bird, Mrs. Hale?

MRS. HALE: Why, I don't know whether she did or not—I've not been here for so long. There was a man around last year selling canaries cheap, but I don't know as she took one; maybe she did. She used to sing real pretty herself.

MRS. PETERS: *(glancing around)* Seems funny to think of a bird here. But she must have had one, or why would she have a cage? I wonder what happened to it.

MRS. HALE: I s'pose maybe the cat got it.

MRS. PETERS: No, she didn't have a cat. She's got that feeling some people have about cats—being afraid of them. My cat got in her room and she was real upset and asked me to take it out.

MRS. HALE: My sister Bessie was like that. Queer, ain't it?

MRS. PETERS: *(examining the cage)* Why, look at this door. It's broke. One hinge is pulled apart.

MRS. HALE: *(looking too)* Looks as if someone must have been rough with it.

MRS. PETERS: Why, yes.

She brings the cage forward and puts it on the table.

MRS. HALE: I wish if they're going to find any evidence they'd be about it. I don't like this place.

MRS. PETERS: But I'm awful glad you came with me, Mrs. Hale. It would be lonesome for me sitting here alone.

MRS. HALE: It would, wouldn't it? *(Dropping her sewing.)* But I tell you what I do wish, Mrs. Peters. I wish I had come over sometimes when *she* was here. I—*(looking around the room)*—wish I had.

MRS. PETERS: But of course you were awful busy, Mrs. Hale—your house and your children.

MRS. HALE: I could've come. I stayed away because it weren't cheerful—and that's why I ought to have come. I—I've never liked this place. Maybe because it's down in a hollow and you don't see the road. I dunno what it is but it's a lonesome place and always was. I wish I had come over to see Minnie Foster sometimes. I can see now—

Shakes her head.

MRS. PETERS: Well, you mustn't reproach yourself, Mrs. Hale. Somehow we just don't see how it is with other folks until—something comes up.

MRS. HALE: Not having children makes less work—but it makes a quiet house, and Wright out to work all day, and no company when he did come in. Did you know John Wright, Mrs. Peters?

MRS. PETERS: Not to know him; I've seen him in town. They say he was a good man.

MRS. HALE: Yes—good; he didn't drink, and kept his word as well as most, I guess, and paid his debts. But he was a hard man, Mrs. Peters. Just to pass the time of day with him—*(Shivers.)* Like a raw wind that gets to the bone. *(Pauses, her eye falling on the cage.)* I should think she would 'a wanted a bird. But what do you suppose went with it?

MRS. PETERS: I don't know, unless it got sick and died.

She reaches over and swings the broken door, swings it again. Both women watch it.

105 MRS. HALE: You weren't raised round here, were you? *(Mrs. Peters shakes her head.)* You didn't know—her?

MRS. PETERS: Not till they brought her yesterday.

MRS. HALE: She—come to think of it, she was kind of like a bird herself—real sweet and pretty, but kind of timid and—fluttery. How—she—did—change. *(Silence; then as if struck by a happy thought and relieved to get back to everyday things.)* Tell you what, Mrs. Peters, why don't you take the quilt in with you? It might take up her mind.

MRS. PETERS: Why, I think that's a real nice idea, Mrs. Hale. There couldn't possibly be any objection to it, could there? Now, just what would I take? I wonder if her patches are in here—and her things.

They look in the sewing basket.

MRS. HALE: Here's some red. I expect this has got sewing things in it. *(Brings out a fancy box.)* What a pretty box. Looks like something somebody would give you. Maybe her scissors are in here. *(Opens box. Suddenly puts her hand to her nose.)* Why—*(Mrs. Peters bends nearer, then turns her face away.)* There's something wrapped up in this piece of silk.

110 MRS. PETERS: Why, this isn't her scissors.

MRS. HALE: *(lifting the silk)* Oh, Mrs. Peters—it's—

Mrs. Peters bends closer.

MRS. PETERS: It's the bird.

MRS. HALE: *(jumping up)* But, Mrs. Peters—look at it! Its neck! Look at its neck! It's all—other side *to.*

MRS. PETERS: Somebody—wrung—its—neck.

Their eyes meet. A look of growing comprehension, of horror. Steps are heard outside. Mrs. Hale slips box under quilt pieces, and sinks into her chair. Enter Sheriff and County Attorney. Mrs. Peters rises.

115 COUNTY ATTORNEY: *(as one turning from serious things to little pleasantries)* Well, ladies, have you decided whether she was going to quilt it or knot it?
MRS. PETERS: We think she was going to—knot it.
COUNTY ATTORNEY: Well, that's interesting, I'm sure. *(Seeing the birdcage.)* Has the bird flown?
MRS. HALE: *(putting more quilt pieces over the box)* We think the—cat got it.
COUNTY ATTORNEY: *(preoccupied)* Is there a cat?

Mrs. Hale glances in a quick covert way at Mrs. Peters.

120 MRS. PETERS: Well, not *now*. They're superstitious, you know. They leave.
COUNTY ATTORNEY: *(to Sheriff Peters, continuing an interrupted conversation)* No sign at all of anyone having come from the outside. Their own rope. Now let's go up again and go over it piece by piece. *(They start upstairs.)* It would have to have been someone who knew just the—

Mrs. Peters sits down. The two women sit there not looking at one another, but as if peering into something and at the same time holding back. When they talk now it is in the manner of feeling their way over strange ground, as if afraid of what they are saying, but as if they can not help saying it.

MRS. HALE: She liked the bird. She was going to bury it in that pretty box.
MRS. PETERS: *(in a whisper)* When I was a girl—my kitten—there was a boy took a hatchet, and before my eyes—and before I could get there—*(Covers her face an instant.)* If they hadn't held me back I would have—*(catches herself, looks upstairs where steps are heard, falters weakly)*—hurt him.
MRS. HALE: *(with a slow look around her)* I wonder how it would seem never to have had any children around. *(Pause.)* No, Wright wouldn't like the bird—a thing that sang. She used to sing. He killed that, too.
125 MRS. PETERS: *(moving uneasily)* We don't know who killed the bird.
MRS. HALE: I knew John Wright.
MRS. PETERS: It was an awful thing was done in this house that night, Mrs. Hale. Killing a man while he slept, slipping a rope around his neck that choked the life out of him.
MRS. HALE: His neck. Choked the life out of him.

Her hand goes out and rests on the birdcage.

MRS. PETERS: *(with rising voice)* We don't know who killed him. We don't know.
130 MRS. HALE: *(her own feeling not interrupted)* If there'd been years and years of nothing, then a bird to sing to you, it would be awful—still, after the bird was still.

MRS. PETERS: *(something within her speaking)* I know what stillness is. When we homesteaded in Dakota, and my first baby died—after he was two years old, and me with no other then—
MRS. HALE: *(moving)* How soon do you suppose they'll be through, looking for the evidence?
MRS. PETERS: I know what stillness is. *(Pulling herself back.)* The law has got to punish crime, Mrs. Hale.
MRS. HALE: *(not as if answering that)* I wish you'd seen Minnie Foster when she wore a white dress with blue ribbons and stood up there in the choir and sang. *(A look around the room.)* Oh, I *wish* I'd come over here once in a while! That was a crime! That was a crime! Who's going to punish that?
135 MRS. PETERS: *(looking upstairs)* We mustn't—take on.
MRS. HALE: I might have known she needed help! I know how things can be—for women. I tell you, it's queer, Mrs. Peters. We live close together and we live far apart. We all go through the same things— it's all just a different kind of the same thing. *(Brushes her eyes; noticing the bottle of fruit, reaches out for it.)* If I was you I wouldn't tell her her fruit was gone. Tell her it *ain't*. Tell her it's all right. Take this in to prove it to her. She—she may never know whether it was broke or not.
MRS. PETERS: *(takes the bottle, looks about for something to wrap it in; takes petticoat from the clothes brought from the other room, very nervously begins winding this around the bottle. In a false voice)* My, it's a good thing the men couldn't hear us. Wouldn't they just laugh! Getting all stirred up over a little thing like a—dead canary. As if that could have anything to do with—with—wouldn't they *laugh!*

The men are heard coming down stairs.

MRS. HALE: *(under her breath)* Maybe they would—maybe they wouldn't.
COUNTY ATTORNEY: No, Peters, it's all perfectly clear except a reason for doing it. But you know juries when it comes to women. If there was some definite thing. Something to show—something to make a story about—a thing that would connect up with this strange way of doing it—

The women's eyes meet for an instant. Enter Hale from outer door.

140 HALE: Well, I've got the team around. Pretty cold out there.
COUNTY ATTORNEY: I'm going to stay here a while by myself. *(To the Sheriff.)* You can send Frank out for me, can't you? I want to go over everything. I'm not satisfied that we can't do better.
SHERIFF: Do you want to see what Mrs. Peters is going to take in?

The County Attorney goes to the table, picks up the apron, laughs.

COUNTY ATTORNEY: Oh, I guess they're not very dangerous things the ladies have picked out. *(Moves a few things about, disturbing the quilt pieces which cover the box. Steps back.)* No, Mrs. Peters doesn't need supervising. For that matter, a sheriff's wife is married to the law. Ever think of it that way, Mrs. Peters?

Mrs. Peters: Not—just that way.

145 **Sheriff:** *(chuckling)* Married to the law. *(Moves toward the other room.)* I just want you to come in here a minute, George. We ought to take a look at these windows.

County Attorney: *(scoffingly)* Oh, windows!

Sheriff: We'll be right out, Mr. Hale.

Hale goes outside. The Sheriff follows the County Attorney into the other room. Then Mrs. Hale rises, hands tight together, looking intensely at Mrs. Peters, whose eyes make a slow turn, finally meeting Mrs. Hale's. A moment Mrs. Hale holds her, then her own eyes point the way to where the box is concealed. Suddenly Mrs. Peters throws back quilt pieces and tries to put the box in the bag she is wearing. It is too big. She opens box, starts to take bird out, cannot touch it, goes to pieces, stands there helpless. Sound of a knob turning in the other room. Mrs. Hale snatches the box and puts it in the pocket of her big coat. Enter County Attorney and Sheriff.

County Attorney: *(facetiously)* Well, Henry, at least we found out that she was not going to quilt it. She was going to—what is it you call it, ladies?

Mrs. Hale: *(her hand against her pocket)* We call it—knot it, Mr. Henderson.

Reading and Reacting

1. What key events have occurred before the play begins? Why do you suppose these events are not presented in the play itself?
2. What are the "trifles" to which the title refers? How do these "trifles" advance the play's plot?
3. Glaspell's short story version of *Trifles* is called "A Jury of Her Peers." Who are Mrs. Wright's peers? What do you suppose the verdict would be if she were tried for her crime in 1916, when only men were permitted to serve on juries? If the trial were held today, do you think the jury might reach a different verdict?
4. *Trifles* is a one-act play, and all its action occurs in the Wrights' kitchen. Does this static setting slow down the flow of the plot? Are there any advantages to this setting? Explain.
5. All background information about Mrs. Wright is provided by Mrs. Hale. Do you consider her to be a reliable source of information? Why or why not?

6. Mr. Hale's summary of his conversation with Mrs. Wright is the reader's only chance to hear her version of events. How would Mrs. Wright's presence change the play?
7. *Trifles* is a relatively slow-moving, "talky" play, with very little physical action. Is this a weakness of the play, or is the slow development consistent with the effect Glaspell is trying to achieve? Explain.
8. How does each of the following events advance the play's action: the men's departure from the kitchen, the discovery of the quilt pieces, the discovery of the dead bird?
9. How do the county attorney's sarcastic comments and his patronizing attitude toward Mrs. Hale and Mrs. Peters advance the play's action?
10. How do Mrs. Peters's memories of her own life advance the action?
11. What assumptions about women do the male characters make? In what ways do the female characters conform to or depart from these assumptions?
12. In what sense is the process of making a quilt an appropriate metaphor for the plot of *Trifles*?
13. **JOURNAL ENTRY** Do you think Mrs. Hale and Mrs. Peters do the right thing by concealing evidence?

Related Works: "I Stand Here Ironing" (p. 94), "The Cask of Amontillado" (p. 136), "Everyday Use" (p. 217)

◆ **HENRIK IBSEN** (1828–1906) is Norway's foremost dramatist. In 1850, he began a life in the theater, writing plays and serving as artistic director of a theatrical company. Disillusioned by the public's lack of interest in his work, he left Norway, living in Italy and Germany between 1864 and 1891. By the time he returned to Norway, he was famous and revered.

Ibsen based *A Doll House* on a true story, which closely paralleled the main events of the play: a wife borrows money to finance a trip for an ailing husband, repayment is demanded, she forges a check and is discovered. (In the real-life story, however, the husband demanded a divorce, and the wife had a nervous breakdown and was committed to a mental institution.) The issue in *A Doll House*, he said, is that there are "two kinds of moral law, [. . .] one in man and a completely different one in woman. They do not understand each other [. . .]."

HENRIK IBSEN

A Doll House
(1879)

Translated by Rolf Fjelde

CHARACTERS

TORVALD HELMER, *a lawyer*
NORA, *his wife*
DR. RANK
MRS. LINDE
A DELIVERY BOY
NILS KROGSTAD, *a bank clerk*
THE HELMERS' THREE SMALL
   CHILDREN
ANNE-MARIE, *their nurse*
HELENE, *a maid*

The action takes place in Helmer's residence.

ACT I

A comfortable room, tastefully but not expensively furnished. A door to the right in the back wall leads to the entryway; another to the left leads to Helmer's study. Between these doors, a piano. Midway in the left-hand wall a door, and further back a window. Near the window a round table with an armchair and a small sofa. In the right-hand wall, toward the rear, a door, and nearer the foreground a porcelain stove with two armchairs and a rocking chair beside it. Between the stove and the side door, a small table. Engravings on the walls. An étagère with china figures and other small art objects; a small bookcase with richly bound books; the floor carpeted; a fire burning in the stove. It is a winter day.

A bell rings in the entryway; shortly after we hear the door being unlocked. Nora comes into the room, humming happily to herself; she is wearing street clothes and carries an armload of packages, which she puts down on the table to the right. She has left the hall door open; and through it a Delivery Boy is seen, holding a Christmas tree and a basket, which he gives to the Maid who let them in.

NORA: Hide the tree well, Helene. The children mustn't get a glimpse of it till this evening, after it's trimmed. *(To the Delivery Boy, taking out her purse.)* How much?
DELIVERY BOY: Fifty, ma'am.
NORA: There's a crown. No, keep the change. *(The Boy thanks her and leaves. Nora shuts the door. She laughs softly to herself while taking off her street things. Drawing a bag of macaroons from her pocket, she eats a couple, then steals over and listens at her husband's study door.)* Yes, he's home. *(Hums again as she moves to the table right.)*
HELMER: *(from the study)* Is that my little lark twittering out there?
5 NORA: *(busy opening some packages)* Yes, it is.

HELMER: Is that my squirrel rummaging around?
NORA: Yes!
HELMER: When did my squirrel get in?
NORA: Just now. *(Putting the macaroon bag in her pocket and wiping her mouth.)* Do come in, Torvald, and see what I've bought.
HELMER: Can't be disturbed. *(After a moment he opens the door and peers in, pen in hand.)* Bought, you say? All that there? Has the little spendthrift been out throwing money around again?
NORA: Oh, but Torvald, this year we really should let ourselves go a bit. It's the first Christmas we haven't had to economize.
HELMER: But you know we can't go squandering.
NORA: Oh yes, Torvald, we can squander a little now. Can't we? Just a tiny, wee bit. Now that you've got a big salary and are going to make piles and piles of money.
HELMER: Yes—starting New Year's. But then it's a full three months till the raise comes through.
NORA: Pooh! We can borrow that long.
HELMER: Nora! *(Goes over and playfully takes her by the ear.)* Are your scatterbrains off again? What if today I borrowed a thousand crowns, and you squandered them over Christmas week, and then on New Year's Eve a roof tile fell on my head, and I lay there—
NORA: *(putting her hand on his mouth)* Oh! Don't say such things!
HELMER: Yes, but what if it happened—then what?
NORA: If anything so awful happened, then it just wouldn't matter if I had debts or not.
HELMER: Well, but the people I'd borrowed from?
NORA: Them? Who cares about them! They're strangers.
HELMER: Nora, Nora, how like a woman! No, but seriously, Nora, you know what I think about that. No debts! Never borrow! Something of freedom's lost—and something of beauty, too—from a home that's founded on borrowing and debt. We've made a brave stand up to now, the two of us; and we'll go right on like that the little while we have to.
NORA: *(going toward the stove)* Yes, whatever you say, Torvald.
HELMER: *(following her)* Now, now, the little lark's wings mustn't droop. Come on, don't be a sulky squirrel. *(Taking out his wallet.)* Nora, guess what I have here.
NORA: *(turning quickly)* Money!
HELMER: There, see. *(Hands her some notes.)* Good grief, I know how costs go up in a house at Christmastime.
NORA: Ten—twenty—thirty—forty. Oh, thank you, Torvald; I can manage no end on this.
HELMER: You really will have to.
NORA: Oh yes, I promise I will! But come here so I can show you everything I bought. And so cheap! Look, new clothes for Ivar here—and a sword. Here a horse and a trumpet for Bob. And a doll and a doll's bed here for Emmy; they're nothing much, but she'll tear them to bits in no time anyway. And here I have dress material and

handkerchiefs for the maids. Old Anne-Marie really deserves something more.

30 HELMER: And what's in that package there?
NORA: *(with a cry)* Torvald, no! You can't see that till tonight!
HELMER: I see. But tell me now, you little prodigal, what have you thought of for yourself?
NORA: For myself? Oh, I don't want anything at all.
HELMER: Of course you do. Tell me just what—within reason—you'd most like to have.
35 NORA: I honestly don't know. Oh, listen, Torvald—
HELMER: Well?
NORA: *(fumbling at his coat buttons, without looking at him)* If you want to give me something, then maybe you could—you could—
HELMER: Come on, out with it.
NORA: *(hurriedly)* You could give me money, Torvald. No more than you think you can spare; then one of these days I'll buy something with it.
40 HELMER: But Nora—
NORA: Oh, please, Torvald darling, do that! I beg you, please. Then I could hang the bills in pretty gilt paper on the Christmas tree. Wouldn't that be fun?
HELMER: What are those little birds called that always fly through their fortunes?
NORA: Oh yes, spendthrifts; I know all that. But let's do as I say, Torvald; then I'll have time to decide what I really need most. That's very sensible, isn't it?
HELMER: *(smiling)* Yes, very—that is, if you actually hung onto the money I give you, and you actually used it to buy yourself something. But it goes for the house and for all sorts of foolish things, and then I only have to lay out some more.
45 NORA: Oh, but Torvald—
HELMER: Don't deny it, my dear little Nora. *(Putting his arm around her waist.)* Spendthrifts are sweet, but they use up a frightful amount of money. It's incredible what it costs a man to feed such birds.
NORA: Oh, how can you say that! Really, I save everything I can.
HELMER: *(laughing)* Yes, that's the truth. Everything you can. But that's nothing at all.
NORA: *(humming, with a smile of quiet satisfaction)* Hm, if you only knew what expenses we larks and squirrels have, Torvald.
50 HELMER: You're an odd little one. Exactly the way your father was. You're never at a loss for scaring up money; but the moment you have it, it runs right out through your fingers; you never know what you've done with it. Well, one takes you as you are. It's deep in your blood. Yes, these things are hereditary, Nora.
NORA: Ah, I could wish I'd inherited many of Papa's qualities.
HELMER: And I couldn't wish you anything but just what you are, my sweet little lark. But wait; it seems to me you have a very—what should I call it?—a very suspicious look today—

NORA: I do?
HELMER: You certainly do. Look me straight in the eye.
NORA: *(looking at him)* Well?
HELMER: *(shaking an admonitory finger)* Surely my sweet tooth hasn't been running riot in town today, has she?
NORA: No. Why do you imagine that?
HELMER: My sweet tooth really didn't make a little detour through the confectioner's?
NORA: No, I assure you, Torvald—
HELMER: Hasn't nibbled some pastry?
NORA: No, not at all.
HELMER: Nor even munched a macaroon or two?
NORA: No, Torvald, I assure you, really—
HELMER: There, there now. Of course I'm only joking.
NORA: *(going to the table, right)* You know I could never think of going against you.
HELMER: No, I understand that; and you *have* given me your word. *(Going over to her.)* Well, you keep your little Christmas secrets to yourself, Nora darling. I expect they'll come to light this evening, when the tree is lit.
NORA: Did you remember to ask Dr. Rank?
HELMER: No. But there's no need for that; it's assumed he'll be dining with us. All the same, I'll ask him when he stops by here this morning. I've ordered some fine wine. Nora, you can't imagine how I'm looking forward to this evening.
NORA: So am I. And what fun for the children, Torvald!
HELMER: Ah, it's so gratifying to know that one's gotten a safe, secure job, and with a comfortable salary. It's a great satisfaction, isn't it?
NORA: Oh, it's wonderful!
HELMER: Remember last Christmas? Three whole weeks before, you shut yourself in every evening till long after midnight, making flowers for the Christmas tree, and all the other decorations to surprise us. Ugh, that was the dullest time I've ever lived through.
NORA: It wasn't at all dull for me.
HELMER: *(smiling)* But the outcome *was* pretty sorry, Nora.
NORA: Oh, don't tease me with that again. How could I help it that the cat came in and tore everything to shreds.
HELMER: No, poor thing, you certainly couldn't. You wanted so much to please us all, and that's what counts. But it's just as well that the hard times are past.
NORA: Yes, it's really wonderful.
HELMER: Now I don't have to sit here alone, boring myself, and you don't have to tire your precious eyes and your fair little delicate hands—
NORA: *(clapping her hands)* No, is it really true, Torvald, I don't have to? Oh, how wonderfully lovely to hear! *(Taking his arm.)* Now I'll tell you just how I've thought we should plan things. Right after

Christmas—*(The doorbell rings.)* Oh, the bell. *(Straightening the room up a bit.)* Somebody would have to come. What a bore!
80 HELMER: I'm not at home to visitors, don't forget.
MAID: *(from the hall doorway)* Ma'am, a lady to see you—
NORA: All right, let her come in.
MAID: *(to Helmer)* And the doctor's just come too.
HELMER: Did he go right to my study?
85 MAID: Yes, he did.

Helmer goes into his room. The Maid shows in Mrs. Linde, dressed in traveling clothes, and shuts the door after her.

MRS. LINDE: *(in a dispirited and somewhat hesitant voice)* Hello, Nora.
NORA: *(uncertain)* Hello—
MRS. LINDE: You don't recognize me.
NORA: No, I don't know—but wait, I think—*(Exclaiming.)* What! Kristine! Is it really you?
90 MRS. LINDE: Yes, it's me.
NORA: *Kristine!* To think I didn't recognize you. But then, how could I? *(More quietly.)* How you've changed, Kristine!
MRS. LINDE: Yes, no doubt I have. In nine—ten long years.
NORA: Is it so long since we met! Yes, it's all of that. Oh, these last eight years have been a happy time, believe me. And so now you've come in to town, too. Made the long trip in the winter. That took courage.
MRS. LINDE: I just got here by ship this morning.
95 NORA: To enjoy yourself over Christmas, of course. Oh, how lovely! Yes, enjoy ourselves, we'll do that. But take your coat off. You're not still cold? *(Helping her.)* There now, let's get cozy here by the stove. No, the easy chair there! I'll take the rocker here. *(Seizing her hands.)* Yes, now you have your old look again; it was only in that first moment. You're a bit more pale, Kristine—and maybe a bit thinner.
MRS. LINDE: And much, much older, Nora.
NORA: Yes, perhaps a bit older; a tiny, tiny bit; not much at all. *(Stopping short; suddenly serious.)* Oh, but thoughtless me, to sit here, chattering away. Sweet, good Kristine, can you forgive me?
MRS. LINDE: What do you mean, Nora?
NORA: *(softly)* Poor Kristine, you've become a widow.
100 MRS. LINDE: Yes, three years ago.
NORA: Oh, I knew it, of course; I read it in the papers. Oh, Kristine, you must believe me; I often thought of writing you then, but I kept postponing it, and something always interfered.
MRS. LINDE: Nora dear, I understand completely.
NORA: No, it was awful of me, Kristine. You poor thing, how much you must have gone through. And he left you nothing?
MRS. LINDE: No.
105 NORA: And no children?

MRS. LINDE: No.
NORA: Nothing at all, then?
MRS. LINDE: Not even a sense of loss to feed on.
NORA: *(looking incredulously at her)* But Kristine, how could that be?
110 MRS. LINDE: *(smiling wearily and smoothing her hair)* Oh, sometimes it happens, Nora.
NORA: So completely alone. How terribly hard that must be for you. I have three lovely children. You can't see them now; they're out with the maid. But now you must tell me everything—
MRS. LINDE: No, no, no, tell me about yourself.
NORA: No, you begin. Today I don't want to be selfish. I want to think only of you today. But there *is* something I must tell you. Did you hear of the wonderful luck we had recently?
MRS. LINDE: No, what's that?
115 NORA: My husband's been made manager in the bank, just think!
MRS. LINDE: Your husband? How marvelous!
NORA: Isn't it? Being a lawyer is such an uncertain living, you know, especially if one won't touch any cases that aren't clean and decent. And of course Torvald would never do that, and I'm with him completely there. Oh, we're simply delighted, believe me! He'll join the bank right after New Year's and start getting a huge salary and lots of commissions. From now on we can live quite differently—just as we want. Oh, Kristine, I feel so light and happy! Won't it be lovely to have stacks of money and not a care in the world?
MRS. LINDE: Well, anyway, it would be lovely to have enough for necessities.
NORA: No, not just for necessities, but stacks and stacks of money!
120 MRS. LINDE: *(smiling)* Nora, Nora, aren't you sensible yet? Back in school you were such a free spender.
NORA: *(with a quiet laugh)* Yes, that's what Torvald still says. *(Shaking her finger.)* But "Nora, Nora" isn't as silly as you all think. Really, we've been in no position for me to go squandering. We've had to work, both of us.
MRS. LINDE: You too?
NORA: Yes, at odd jobs—needlework, crocheting, embroidery, and such—*(casually)* and other things too. You remember that Torvald left the department when we were married? There was no chance of promotion in his office, and of course he needed to earn more money. But that first year he drove himself terribly. He took on all kinds of extra work that kept him going morning and night. It wore him down, and then he fell deathly ill. The doctors said it was essential for him to travel south.
MRS. LINDE: Yes, didn't you spend a whole year in Italy?
125 NORA: That's right. It wasn't easy to get away, you know. Ivar had just been born. But of course we had to go. Oh, that was a beautiful

trip, and it saved Torvald's life. But it cost a frightful sum, Kristine.

MRS. LINDE: I can well imagine.

NORA: Four thousand, eight hundred crowns it cost. That's really a lot of money.

MRS. LINDE: But it's lucky you had it when you needed it.

NORA: Well, as it was, we got it from Papa.

130 MRS. LINDE: I see. It was just about the time your father died.

NORA: Yes, just about then. And, you know, I couldn't make that trip out to nurse him. I had to stay here, expecting Ivar any moment, and with my poor sick Torvald to care for. Dearest Papa, I never saw him again, Kristine. Oh, that was the worst time I've known in all my marriage.

MRS. LINDE: I know how you loved him. And then you went off to Italy?

NORA: Yes. We had the means now, and the doctors urged us. So we left a month after.

MRS. LINDE: And your husband came back completely cured?

135 NORA: Sound as a drum!

MRS. LINDE: But—the doctor?

NORA: Who?

MRS. LINDE: I thought the maid said he was a doctor, the man who came in with me.

NORA: Yes, that was Dr. Rank—but he's not making a sick call. He's our closest friend, and he stops by at least once a day. No, Torvald hasn't had a sick moment since, and the children are fit and strong, and I am, too. *(Jumping up and clapping her hands.)* Oh, dear God, Kristine, what a lovely thing to live and be happy! But how disgusting of me—I'm talking of nothing but my own affairs. *(Sits on a stool close by Kristine, arms resting across her knees.)* Oh, don't be angry with me! Tell me, is it really true that you weren't in love with your husband? Why did you marry him, then?

140 MRS. LINDE: My mother was still alive, but bedridden and helpless—and I had my two younger brothers to look after. In all conscience, I didn't think I could turn him down.

NORA: No, you were right there. But was he rich at the time?

MRS. LINDE: He was very well off, I'd say. But the business was shaky, Nora. When he died, it all fell apart, and nothing was left.

NORA: And then—?

MRS. LINDE: Yes, so I had to scrape up a living with a little shop and a little teaching and whatever else I could find. The last three years have been like one endless workday without a rest for me. Now it's over, Nora. My poor mother doesn't need me, for she's passed on. Nor the boys, either; they're working now and can take care of themselves.

145 NORA: How free you must feel—

Mrs. Linde: No—only unspeakably empty. Nothing to live for now. *(Standing up anxiously.)* That's why I couldn't take it any longer out in that desolate hole. Maybe here it'll be easier to find something to do and keep my mind occupied. If I could only be lucky enough to get a steady job, some office work—

Nora: Oh, but Kristine, that's so dreadfully tiring, and you already look so tired. It would be much better for you if you could go off to a bathing resort.

Mrs. Linde: *(going toward the window)* I have no father to give me travel money, Nora.

Nora: *(rising)* Oh, don't be angry with me.

150 **Mrs. Linde:** *(going to her)* Nora dear, don't you be angry with me. The worst of my kind of situation is all the bitterness that's stored away. No one to work for, and yet you're always having to snap up your opportunities. You have to live; and so you grow selfish. When you told me the happy change in your lot, do you know I was delighted less for your sakes than for mine?

Nora: How so? Oh, I see. You think Torvald could do something for you.

Mrs. Linde: Yes, that's what I thought.

Nora: And he will, Kristine! Just leave it to me; I'll bring it up so delicately—find something attractive to humor him with. Oh, I'm so eager to help you.

Mrs. Linde: How very kind of you, Nora, to be so concerned over me—doubly kind, considering you really know so little of life's burdens yourself.

155 **Nora:** I—? I know so little—?

Mrs. Linde: *(smiling)* Well my heavens—a little needlework and such—Nora, you're just a child.

Nora: *(tossing her head and pacing the floor)* You don't have to act so superior.

Mrs. Linde: Oh?

Nora: You're just like the others. You all think I'm incapable of anything serious—

160 **Mrs. Linde:** Come now—

Nora: That I've never had to face the raw world.

Mrs. Linde: Nora dear, you've just been telling me all your troubles.

Nora: Hm! Trivial! *(Quietly.)* I haven't told you the big thing.

Mrs. Linde: Big thing? What do you mean?

165 **Nora:** You look down on me so, Kristine, but you shouldn't. You're proud that you worked so long and hard for your mother.

Mrs. Linde: I don't look down on a soul. But it *is* true: I'm proud—and happy, too—to think it was given to me to make my mother's last days almost free of care.

Nora: And you're also proud thinking of what you've done for your brothers.

Mrs. Linde: I feel I've a right to be.

NORA: I agree. But listen to this, Kristine—I've also got something to be proud and happy for.
MRS. LINDE: I don't doubt it. But whatever do you mean?
NORA: Not so loud. What if Torvald heard! He mustn't, not for anything in the world. Nobody must know, Kristine. No one but you.
MRS. LINDE: But what is it, then?
NORA: Come here. *(Drawing her down beside her on the sofa.)* It's true—I've also got something to be proud and happy for. I'm the one who saved Torvald's life.
MRS. LINDE: Saved—? Saved how?
NORA: I told you about the trip to Italy. Torvald never would have lived if he hadn't gone south—
MRS. LINDE: Of course; your father gave you the means—
NORA: *(smiling)* That's what Torvald and all the rest think, but—
MRS. LINDE: But—?
NORA: Papa didn't give us a pin. I was the one who raised the money.
MRS. LINDE: You? That whole amount?
NORA: Four thousand, eight hundred crowns. What do you say to that?
MRS. LINDE: But Nora, how was it possible? Did you win the lottery?
NORA: *(disdainfully)* The lottery? Pooh! No art to that.
MRS. LINDE: But where did you get it from then?
NORA: *(humming, with a mysterious smile)* Hmm, tra-la-la-la.
MRS. LINDE: Because you couldn't have borrowed it.
NORA: No? Why not?
MRS. LINDE: A wife can't borrow without her husband's consent.
NORA: *(tossing her head)* Oh, but a wife with a little business sense, a wife who knows how to manage—
MRS. LINDE: Nora, I simply don't understand—
NORA: You don't have to. Whoever said I *borrowed* the money? I could have gotten it other ways. *(Throwing herself back on the sofa.)* I could have gotten it from some admirer or other. After all, a girl with my ravishing appeal—
MRS. LINDE: You lunatic.
NORA: I'll bet you're eaten up with curiosity, Kristine.
MRS. LINDE: Now listen here, Nora—you haven't done something indiscreet?
NORA: *(sitting up again)* Is it indiscreet to save your husband's life?
MRS. LINDE: I think it's indiscreet that without his knowledge you—
NORA: But that's the point: he mustn't know! My Lord, can't you understand? He mustn't ever know the close call he had. It was to *me* the doctors came to say his life was in danger—that nothing could save him but a stay in the south. Didn't I try strategy then! I began talking about how lovely it would be for me to travel abroad like other young wives; I begged and I cried; I told him please to remember my condition, to be kind and indulge me; and then I dropped a hint that he could easily take out a loan. But at that,

Kristine, he nearly exploded. He said I was frivolous, and it was his duty as man of the house not to indulge me in whims and fancies—as I think he called them. Aha, I thought, now you'll just have to be saved—and that's when I saw my chance.

MRS. LINDE: And your father never told Torvald the money wasn't from him?

NORA: No, never. Papa died right about then. I'd considered bringing him into my secret and begging him never to tell. But he was too sick at the time—and then, sadly, it didn't matter.

MRS. LINDE: And you've never confided in your husband since?

NORA: For heaven's sake, no! Are you serious? He's so strict on that subject. Besides—Torvald, with all his masculine pride—how painfully humiliating for him if he ever found out he was in debt to me. That would just ruin our relationship. Our beautiful, happy home would never be the same.

MRS. LINDE: Won't you ever tell him?

NORA: *(thoughtfully, half smiling)* Yes—maybe sometime, years from now, when I'm no longer so attractive. Don't laugh! I only mean when Torvald loves me less than now, when he stops enjoying my dancing and dressing up and reciting for him. Then it might be wise to have something in reserve—*(Breaking off.)* How ridiculous! That'll never happen—Well, Kristine, what do you think of my big secret? I'm capable of something too, hm? You can imagine, of course, how this thing hangs over me. It really hasn't been easy meeting the payments on time. In the business world there's what they call quarterly interest and what they call amortization, and these are always so terribly hard to manage. I've had to skimp a little here and there, wherever I could, you know. I could hardly spare anything from my house allowance, because Torvald has to live well. I couldn't let the children go poorly dressed; whatever I got for them, I felt I had to use up completely—the darlings!

MRS. LINDE: Poor Nora, so it had to come out of your own budget, then?

NORA: Yes, of course. But I was the one most responsible, too. Every time Torvald gave me money for new clothes and such, I never used more than half; always bought the simplest, cheapest outfits. It was a godsend that everything looks so well on me that Torvald never noticed. But it did weigh me down at times, Kristine. It *is* such a joy to wear fine things. You understand.

MRS. LINDE: Oh, of course.

NORA: And then I found other ways of making money. Last winter I was lucky enough to get a lot of copying to do. I locked myself in and sat writing every evening till late in the night. Ah, I was tired so often, dead tired. But still it was wonderful fun, sitting and working like that, earning money. It was almost like being a man.

MRS. LINDE: But how much have you paid off this way so far?

NORA: That's hard to say, exactly. These accounts, you know, aren't easy to figure. I only know that I've paid out all I could scrape together. Time and again I haven't known where to turn. *(Smiling.)* Then I'd sit here dreaming of a rich old gentleman who had fallen in love with me—

210 MRS. LINDE: What! Who is he?

NORA: Oh, really! And that he'd died, and when his will was opened, there in big letters it said, "All my fortune shall be paid over in cash, immediately, to that enchanting Mrs. Nora Helmer."

MRS. LINDE: But Nora dear—who *was* this gentleman?

NORA: Good grief, can't you understand? The old man never existed; that was only something I'd dream up time and again whenever I was at my wits' end for money. But it makes no difference now; the old fossil can go where he pleases for all I care; I don't need him or his will—because now I'm free. *(Jumping up.)* Oh, how lovely to think of that, Kristine! Carefree! To know you're carefree, utterly carefree; to be able to romp and play with the children, and to keep up a beautiful, charming home—everything just the way Torvald likes it! And think, spring is coming, with big blue skies. Maybe we can travel a little then. Maybe I'll see the ocean again. Oh yes, it *is* so marvelous to live and be happy!

The front doorbell rings.

MRS. LINDE: *(rising)* There's the bell. It's probably best that I go.

215 NORA: No, stay. No one's expected. It must be for Torvald.

MAID: *(from the hall doorway)* Excuse me, ma'am—there's a gentleman here to see Mr. Helmer, but I didn't know—since the doctor's with him—

NORA: Who is the gentleman?

KROGSTAD: *(from the doorway)* It's me, Mrs. Helmer.

Mrs. Linde starts and turns away toward the window.

NORA: *(stepping toward him, tense, her voice a whisper)* You? What is it? Why do you want to speak to my husband?

220 KROGSTAD: Bank business—after a fashion. I have a small job in the investment bank, and I hear now your husband is going to be our chief—

NORA: In other words, it's—

KROGSTAD: Just dry business, Mrs. Helmer. Nothing but that.

NORA: Yes, then please be good enough to step into the study. *(She nods indifferently as she sees him out by the hall door, then returns and begins stirring up the stove.)*

MRS. LINDE: Nora—who was that man?

225 NORA: That was a Mr. Krogstad—a lawyer.

MRS. LINDE: Then it really was him.

NORA: Do you know that person?

MRS. LINDE: I did once—many years ago. For a time he was a law clerk in our town.

NORA: Yes, he's been that.

MRS. LINDE: How he's changed.
NORA: I understand he had a very unhappy marriage.
MRS. LINDE: He's a widower now.
NORA: With a number of children. There now, it's burning. *(She closes the stove door and moves the rocker a bit to one side.)*
MRS. LINDE: They say he has a hand in all kinds of business.
NORA: Oh? That may be true: I wouldn't know. But let's not think about business. It's so dull.

Dr. Rank enters from Helmer's study.

RANK: *(still in the doorway)* No, no, really—I don't want to intrude, I'd just as soon talk a little while with your wife. *(Shuts the door, then notices Mrs. Linde.)* Oh, beg pardon. I'm intruding here too.
NORA: No, not at all. *(Introducing him.)* Dr. Rank, Mrs. Linde.
RANK: Well now, that's a name much heard in this house. I believe I passed the lady on the stairs as I came.
MRS. LINDE: Yes, I take the stairs very slowly. They're rather hard on me.
RANK: Uh-hm, some touch of internal weakness?
MRS. LINDE: More overexertion, I'd say.
RANK: Nothing else? Then you're probably here in town to rest up in a round of parties?
MRS. LINDE: I'm here to look for work.
RANK: Is that the best cure for overexertion?
MRS. LINDE: One has to live, Doctor.
RANK: Yes, there's a common prejudice to that effect.
NORA: Oh, come on, Dr. Rank—you really do want to live yourself.
RANK: Yes, I really do. Wretched as I am, I'll gladly prolong my torment indefinitely. All my patients feel like that. And it's quite the same, too, with the morally sick. Right at this moment there's one of those moral invalids in there with Helmer—
MRS. LINDE: *(softly)* Ah!
NORA: Who do you mean?
RANK: Oh, it's a lawyer, Krogstad, a type you wouldn't know. His character is rotten to the root—but even he began chattering all-importantly about how he had to *live*.
NORA: Oh? What did he want to talk to Torvald about?
RANK: I really don't know. I only heard something about the bank.
NORA: I didn't know that Krog—that this man Krogstad had anything to do with the bank.
RANK: Yes, he's gotten some kind of berth down there. *(To Mrs. Linde.)* I don't know if you also have, in your neck of the woods, a type of person who scuttles about breathlessly, sniffing out hints of moral corruption, and then maneuvers his victim into some sort of key position where he can keep an eye on him. It's the healthy these days that are out in the cold.
MRS. LINDE: All the same, it's the sick who most need to be taken in.

RANK: *(with a shrug)* Yes, there we have it. That's the concept that's turning society into a sanatorium.

Nora, lost in her thoughts, breaks out into quiet laughter and claps her hands.

RANK: Why do you laugh at that? Do you have any real idea of what society is?

NORA: What do I care about dreary old society? I was laughing at something quite different—something terribly funny. Tell me, Doctor—is everyone who works in the bank dependent now on Torvald?

260 RANK: Is that what you find so terribly funny?

NORA: *(smiling and humming)* Never mind, never mind! *(Pacing the floor.)* Yes, that's really immensely amusing: that we—that Torvald has so much power now over all those people. *(Taking the bag out of her pocket.)* Dr. Rank, a little macaroon on that?

RANK: See here, macaroons! I thought they were contraband here.

NORA: Yes, but these are some that Kristine gave me.

MRS. LINDE: What? I—?

265 NORA: Now, now, don't be afraid. You couldn't possibly know that Torvald had forbidden them. You see, he's worried they'll ruin my teeth. But hmp! Just this once! Isn't that so, Dr. Rank? Help yourself! *(Puts a macaroon in his mouth.)* And you too, Kristine. And I'll also have one, only a little one—or two, at the most. *(Walking about again.)* Now I'm really tremendously happy. Now there's just one last thing in the world that I have an enormous desire to do.

RANK: Well! And what's that?

NORA: It's something I have such a consuming desire to say so Torvald could hear.

RANK: And why can't you say it?

NORA: I don't dare. It's quite shocking.

270 MRS. LINDE: Shocking?

RANK: Well, then it isn't advisable. But in front of us you certainly can. What do you have such a desire to say so Torvald could hear?

NORA: I have such a huge desire to say—to hell and be damned!

RANK: Are you crazy?

MRS. LINDE: My goodness, Nora!

275 RANK: Go on, say it. Here he is.

NORA: *(hiding the macaroon bag)* Shh, shh, shh!

Helmer comes in from his study, hat in hand, overcoat over his arm.

NORA: *(going toward him)* Well, Torvald dear, are you through with him?

HELMER: Yes, he just left.

NORA: Let me introduce you—this is Kristine, who's arrived here in town.

280 HELMER: Kristine—? I'm sorry, but I don't know—

NORA: Mrs. Linde, Torvald dear. Mrs. Kristine Linde.

HELMER: Of course. A childhood friend of my wife's, no doubt?

MRS. LINDE: Yes, we knew each other in those days.
NORA: And just think, she made the long trip down here in order to talk with you.
285 HELMER: What's this?
MRS. LINDE: Well, not exactly—
NORA: You see, Kristine is remarkably clever in office work, and so she's terribly eager to come under a capable man's supervision and add more to what she already knows—
HELMER: Very wise, Mrs. Linde.
NORA: And then when she heard that you'd become a bank manager—the story was wired out to the papers—then she came in as fast as she could and—Really, Torvald, for my sake you can do a little something for Kristine, can't you?
290 HELMER: Yes, it's not at all impossible. Mrs. Linde, I suppose you're a widow?
MRS. LINDE: Yes.
HELMER: Any experience in office work?
MRS. LINDE: Yes, a good deal.
HELMER: Well, it's quite likely that I can make an opening for you—
295 NORA: *(clapping her hands)* You see, you see!
HELMER: You've come at a lucky moment, Mrs. Linde.
MRS. LINDE: Oh, how can I thank you?
HELMER: Not necessary. *(Putting his overcoat on.)* But today you'll have to excuse me—
RANK: Wait, I'll go with you. *(He fetches his coat from the hall and warms it at the stove.)*
300 NORA: Don't stay out long, dear.
HELMER: An hour; no more.
NORA: Are you going too, Kristine?
MRS. LINDE: *(putting on her winter garments)* Yes, I have to see about a room now.
HELMER: Then perhaps we can all walk together.
305 NORA: *(helping her)* What a shame we're so cramped here, but it's quite impossible for us to—
MRS. LINDE: Oh, don't even think of it! Good-bye, Nora dear, and thanks for everything.
NORA: Good-bye for now. Of course you'll be back this evening. And you too, Dr. Rank. What? If you're well enough? Oh, you've got to be! Wrap up tight now.

In a ripple of small talk the company moves out into the hall; children's voices are heard outside on the steps.

NORA: There they are! There they are! *(She runs to open the door. The children come in with their nurse, Anne-Marie.)* Come in, come in! *(Bends down and kisses them.)* Oh, you darlings—! Look at them, Kristine. Aren't they lovely!

RANK: No loitering in the draft here.
HELMER: Come, Mrs. Linde—this place is unbearable now for anyone but mothers.

Dr. Rank, Helmer, and Mrs. Linde go down the stairs. Anne-Marie goes into the living room with the children. Nora follows, after closing the hall door.

NORA: How fresh and strong you look. Oh, such red cheeks you have! Like apples and roses. *(The children interrupt her throughout the following.)* And it was so much fun? That's wonderful. Really? You pulled both Emmy and Bob on the sled? Imagine, all together! Yes, you're a clever boy, Ivar. Oh, let me hold her a bit, Anne-Marie. My sweet little doll baby! *(Takes the smallest from the nurse and dances with her.)* Yes, yes, Mama will dance with Bob as well. What? Did you throw snowballs? Oh, if I'd only been there! No, don't bother, Anne-Marie—I'll undress them myself. Oh yes, let me. It's such fun. Go in and rest; you look half frozen. There's hot coffee waiting for you on the stove. *(The nurse goes into the room to the left. Nora takes the children's winter things off, throwing them about, while the children talk to her all at once.)* Is that so? A big dog chased you? But it didn't bite? No, dogs never bite little, lovely doll babies. Don't peek in the packages, Ivar! What is it? Yes, wouldn't you like to know. No, no, it's an ugly something. Well? Shall we play? What shall we play? Hide-and-seek? Yes, let's play hide-and-seek. Bob must hide first. I must? Yes, let me hide first. *(Laughing and shouting, she and the children play in and out of the living room and the adjoining room to the right. At last Nora hides under the table. The children come storming in, search, but cannot find her, then hear her muffled laughter, dash over to the table, lift the cloth up and find her. Wild shouting. She creeps forward as if to scare them. More shouts. Meanwhile, a knock at the hall door; no one has noticed it. Now the door half opens, and Krogstad appears. He waits a moment; the game goes on.)*

KROGSTAD: Beg pardon, Mrs. Helmer—
NORA: *(with a strangled cry, turning and scrambling to her knees)* Oh! What do you want?
KROGSTAD: Excuse me. The outer door was ajar; it must be someone forgot to shut it—
NORA: *(rising)* My husband isn't home, Mr. Krogstad.
KROGSTAD: I know that.
NORA: Yes—then what do you want here?
KROGSTAD: A word with you.
NORA: With—? *(To the children, quietly.)* Go in to Anne-Marie. What? No, the strange man won't hurt Mama. When he's gone, we'll play some more. *(She leads the children into the room to the left and shuts the door after them. Then, tense and nervous.)* You want to speak to me?

320 KROGSTAD: Yes, I want to.
NORA: Today? But it's not yet the first of the month—
KROGSTAD: No, it's Christmas Eve. It's going to be up to you how merry a Christmas you have.
NORA: What is it you want? Today I absolutely can't—
KROGSTAD: We won't talk about that till later. This is something else. You do have a moment to spare, I suppose?
325 NORA: Oh yes, of course—I do, except—
KROGSTAD: Good. I was sitting over at Olsen's Restaurant when I saw your husband go down the street—
NORA: Yes?
KROGSTAD: With a lady.
NORA: Yes. So?
330 KROGSTAD: If you'll pardon my asking: wasn't that lady a Mrs. Linde?
NORA: Yes.
KROGSTAD: Just now come into town?
NORA: Yes, today.
KROGSTAD: She's a good friend of yours?
335 NORA: Yes, she is. But I don't see—
KROGSTAD: I also knew her once.
NORA: I'm aware of that.
KROGSTAD: Oh? You know all about it. I thought so. Well, then let me ask you short and sweet: is Mrs. Linde getting a job in the bank?
NORA: What makes you think you can cross-examine me, Mr. Krogstad—you, one of my husband's employees? But since you ask, you might as well know—yes, Mrs. Linde's going to be taken on at the bank. And I'm the one who spoke for her, Mr. Krogstad. Now you know.
340 KROGSTAD: So I guessed right.
NORA: *(pacing up and down)* Oh, one does have a tiny bit of influence, I should hope. Just because I am a woman, don't think it means that—When one has a subordinate position, Mr. Krogstad, one really ought to be careful about pushing somebody who—hm—
KROGSTAD: Who has influence?
NORA: That's right.
KROGSTAD: *(in a different tone)* Mrs. Helmer, would you be good enough to use your influence on my behalf?
345 NORA: What? What do you mean?
KROGSTAD: Would you please make sure that I keep my subordinate position in the bank?
NORA: What does that mean? Who's thinking of taking away your position?
KROGSTAD: Oh, don't play the innocent with me. I'm quite aware that your friend would hardly relish the chance of running into me again; and I'm also aware now whom I can thank for being turned out.
NORA: But I promise you—

350 KROGSTAD: Yes, yes, yes, to the point: there's still time, and I'm advising you to use your influence to prevent it.
NORA: But Mr. Krogstad, I have absolutely no influence.
KROGSTAD: You haven't? I thought you were just saying—
NORA: You shouldn't take me so literally. I! How can you believe that I have any such influence over my husband?
KROGSTAD: Oh, I've known your husband from our student days. I don't think the great bank manager's more steadfast than any other married man.
355 NORA: You speak insolently about my husband, and I'll show you the door.
KROGSTAD: The lady has spirit.
NORA: I'm not afraid of you any longer. After New Year's, I'll soon be done with the whole business.
KROGSTAD: *(restraining himself)* Now listen to me, Mrs. Helmer. If necessary, I'll fight for my little job in the bank as if it were life itself.
NORA: Yes, so it seems.
360 KROGSTAD: It's not just a matter of income; that's the least of it. It's something else—All right, out with it! Look, this is the thing. You know, just like all the others, of course, that once, a good many years ago, I did something rather rash.
NORA: I've heard rumors to that effect.
KROGSTAD: The case never got into court; but all the same, every door was closed in my face from then on. So I took up those various activities you know about. I had to grab hold somewhere; and I dare say I haven't been among the worst. But now I want to drop all that. My boys are growing up. For their sakes, I'll have to win back as much respect as possible here in town. That job in the bank was like the first rung in my ladder. And now your husband wants to kick me right back down in the mud again.
NORA: But for heaven's sake, Mr. Krogstad, it's simply not in my power to help you.
KROGSTAD: That's because you haven't the will to—but I have the means to make you.
365 NORA: You certainly won't tell my husband that I owe you money?
KROGSTAD: Hm—what if I told him that?
NORA: That would be shameful of you. *(Nearly in tears.)* This secret—my joy and my pride—that he should learn it in such a crude and disgusting way—learn it from you. You'd expose me to the most horrible unpleasantness—
KROGSTAD: Only unpleasantness?
NORA: *(vehemently)* But go on and try. It'll turn out the worse for you, because then my husband will really see what a crook you are, and then you'll *never* be able to hold your job.
370 KROGSTAD: I asked if it was just domestic unpleasantness you were afraid of.

NORA: If my husband finds out, then of course he'll pay what I owe at once, and then we'd be through with you for good.

KROGSTAD: *(a step closer)* Listen, Mrs. Helmer—you've either got a very bad memory, or else no head at all for business. I'd better put you a little more in touch with the facts.

NORA: What do you mean?

KROGSTAD: When your husband was sick, you came to me for a loan of four thousand, eight hundred crowns.

375 NORA: Where else could I go?

KROGSTAD: I promised to get you that sum—

NORA: And you got it.

KROGSTAD: I promised to get you that sum, on certain conditions. You were so involved in your husband's illness, and so eager to finance your trip, that I guess you didn't think out all the details. It might just be a good idea to remind you. I promised you the money on the strength of a note I drew up.

NORA: Yes, and that I signed.

380 KROGSTAD: Right. But at the bottom I added some lines for your father to guarantee the loan. He was supposed to sign down there.

NORA: Supposed to? He did sign.

KROGSTAD: I left the date blank. In other words, your father would have dated his signature himself. Do you remember that?

NORA: Yes, I think—

KROGSTAD: Then I gave you the note for you to mail to your father. Isn't that so?

385 NORA: Yes.

KROGSTAD: And naturally you sent it at once—because only some five, six days later you brought me the note, properly signed. And with that, the money was yours.

NORA: Well, then; I've made my payments regularly, haven't I?

KROGSTAD: More or less. But—getting back to the point—those were hard times for you then, Mrs. Helmer.

NORA: Yes, they were.

390 KROGSTAD: Your father was very ill, I believe.

NORA: He was near the end.

KROGSTAD: He died soon after?

NORA: Yes.

KROGSTAD: Tell me, Mrs. Helmer, do you happen to recall the date of your father's death? The day of the month, I mean.

395 NORA: Papa died the twenty-ninth of September.

KROGSTAD: That's quite correct; I've already looked into that. And now we come to a curious thing—*(taking out a paper)* which I simply cannot comprehend.

NORA: Curious thing? I don't know—

KROGSTAD: This is the curious thing: that your father co-signed the note for your loan three days after his death.

NORA: How—? I don't understand.
KROGSTAD: Your father died the twenty-ninth of September. But look. Here your father dated his signature October second. Isn't that curious, Mrs. Helmer? *(Nora is silent.)* Can you explain it to me? *(Nora remains silent.)* It's also remarkable that the words "October second" and the year aren't written in your father's hand, but rather in one that I think I know. Well, it's easy to understand. Your father forgot perhaps to date his signature, and then someone or other added it, a bit sloppily, before anyone knew of his death. There's nothing wrong in that. It all comes down to the signature. And there's no question about *that*, Mrs. Helmer. It really *was* your father who signed his own name here, wasn't it?
NORA: *(after a short silence, throwing her head back and looking squarely at him)* No, it wasn't. *I* signed Papa's name.
KROGSTAD: Wait, now—are you fully aware that this is a dangerous confession?
NORA: Why? You'll soon get your money.
KROGSTAD: Let me ask you a question—why didn't you send the paper to your father?
NORA: That was impossible. Papa was so sick. If I'd asked him for his signature, I also would have had to tell him what the money was for. But I couldn't tell him, sick as he was, that my husband's life was in danger. That was just impossible.
KROGSTAD: Then it would have been better if you'd given up the trip abroad.
NORA: I couldn't possibly. The trip was to save my husband's life. I couldn't give that up.
KROGSTAD: But didn't you ever consider that this was a fraud against me?
NORA: I couldn't let myself be bothered by that. You weren't any concern of mine. I couldn't stand you, with all those cold complications you made, even though you knew how badly off my husband was.
KROGSTAD: Mrs. Helmer, obviously you haven't the vaguest idea of what you've involved yourself in. But I can tell you this: it was nothing more and nothing worse than I once did—and it wrecked my whole reputation.
NORA: You? Do you expect me to believe that you ever acted bravely to save your wife's life?
KROGSTAD: Laws don't inquire into motives.
NORA: Then they must be very poor laws.
KROGSTAD: Poor or not—if I introduce this paper in court, you'll be judged according to law.
NORA: This I refuse to believe. A daughter hasn't a right to protect her dying father from anxiety and care? A wife hasn't a right to save her husband's life? I don't know much about laws, but I'm sure

that somewhere in the books these things are allowed. And you
don't know anything about it—you who practice the law? You must
be an awful lawyer, Mr. Krogstad.

KROGSTAD: Could be. But business—the kind of business we two mixed
up in—don't you think I know about that? All right. Do what you
want now. But I'm telling you *this:* if I get shoved down a second
time, you're going to keep me company. *(He bows and goes out
through the hall.)*

NORA: *(pensive for a moment, then tossing her head)* Oh, really! Trying to
frighten me! I'm not so silly as all that. *(Begins gathering up the
children's clothes, but soon stops.)* But—? No, but that's impossible! I
did it out of love.

THE CHILDREN: *(in the doorway, left)* Mama, that strange man's gone out
the door.

NORA: Yes, yes, I know it. But don't tell anyone about the strange man.
Do you hear? Not even Papa!

420 THE CHILDREN: No, Mama. But now will you play again?

NORA: No, not now.

THE CHILDREN: Oh, but Mama, you promised.

NORA: Yes, but I can't now. Go inside; I have too much to do. Go in, go
in, my sweet darlings. *(She herds them gently back in the room and
shuts the door after them. Settling on the sofa, she takes up a piece of
embroidery and makes some stitches, but soon stops abruptly.)* No!
(Throws the work aside, rises, goes to the hall door and calls out.)
Helene! Let me have the tree in here. *(Goes to the table, left, opens
the table drawer, and stops again.)* No, but that's utterly impossible!

MAID: *(with the Christmas tree)* Where should I put it, ma'am?

425 NORA: There. The middle of the floor.

MAID: Should I bring anything else?

NORA: No, thanks. I have what I need.

The Maid, who has set the tree down, goes out.

NORA: *(absorbed in trimming the tree)* Candles here—and flowers here.
That terrible creature! Talk, talk, talk! There's nothing to it at all.
The tree's going to be lovely. I'll do anything to please you,
Torvald. I'll sing for you, dance for you—

Helmer comes in from the hall, with a sheaf of papers under his arm.

NORA: Oh! You're back so soon?

430 HELMER: Yes. Has anyone been here?

NORA: Here? No.

HELMER: That's odd. I saw Krogstad leaving the front door.

NORA: So? Oh yes, that's true. Krogstad was here a moment.

HELMER: Nora, I can see by your face that he's been here, begging you
to put in a good word for him.

435 NORA: Yes.

HELMER: And it was supposed to seem like your own idea? You were to hide it from me that he'd been here. He asked you that, too, didn't he?
NORA: Yes, Torvald, but—
HELMER: Nora, Nora, and you could fall for that? Talk with that sort of person and promise him anything? And then in the bargain, tell me an untruth.
NORA: An untruth—?
440 HELMER: Didn't you say that no one had been here? *(Wagging his finger.)* My little songbird must never do that again. A songbird needs a clean beak to warble with. No false notes. *(Putting his arm about her waist.)* That's the way it should be, isn't it? Yes, I'm sure of it. *(Releasing her.)* And so, enough of that. *(Sitting by the stove.)* Ah, how snug and cozy it is here. *(Leafing among his papers.)*
NORA: *(busy with the tree, after a short pause)* Torvald!
HELMER: Yes.
NORA: I'm so much looking forward to the Stenborgs' costume party, day after tomorrow.
HELMER: And I can't wait to see what you'll surprise me with.
445 NORA: Oh, that stupid business!
HELMER: What?
NORA: I can't find anything that's right. Everything seems so ridiculous, so inane.
HELMER: So my little Nora's come to *that* recognition?
NORA: *(going behind his chair, her arms resting on its back)* Are you very busy, Torvald?
450 HELMER: Oh—
NORA: What papers are those?
HELMER: Bank matters.
NORA: Already?
HELMER: I've gotten full authority from the retiring management to make all necessary changes in personnel and procedure. I'll need Christmas week for that. I want to have everything in order by New Year's.
455 NORA: So that was the reason this poor Krogstad—
HELMER: Hm.
NORA: *(still leaning on the chair and slowly stroking the nape of his neck)* If you weren't so very busy, I would have asked you an enormous favor, Torvald.
HELMER: Let's hear. What is it?
NORA: You know, there isn't anyone who has your good taste—and I want so much to look well at the costume party. Torvald, couldn't you take over and decide what I should be and plan my costume?
460 HELMER: Ah, is my stubborn little creature calling for a lifeguard?
NORA: Yes, Torvald, I can't get anywhere without your help.
HELMER: All right—I'll think it over. We'll hit on something.

NORA: Oh, how sweet of you. *(Goes to the tree again. Pause.)* Aren't the red flowers pretty—? But tell me, was it really such a crime that this Krogstad committed?

HELMER: Forgery. Do you have any idea what that means?

NORA: Couldn't he have done it out of need?

HELMER: Yes, or thoughtlessness, like so many others. I'm not so heartless that I'd condemn a man categorically for just one mistake.

NORA: No, of course not, Torvald!

HELMER: Plenty of men have redeemed themselves by openly confessing their crimes and taking their punishment.

NORA: Punishment—?

HELMER: But now Krogstad didn't go that way. He got himself out by sharp practices, and that's the real cause of his moral breakdown.

NORA: Do you really think that would—?

HELMER: Just imagine how a man with that sort of guilt in him has to lie and cheat and deceive on all sides, has to wear a mask even with the nearest and dearest he has, even with his own wife and children. And with the children, Nora—that's where it's most horrible.

NORA: Why?

HELMER: Because that kind of atmosphere of lies infects the whole life of a home. Every breath the children take in is filled with the germs of something degenerate.

NORA: *(coming closer behind him)* Are you sure of that?

HELMER: Oh, I've seen it often enough as a lawyer. Almost everyone who goes bad early in life has a mother who's a chronic liar.

NORA: Why just—the mother?

HELMER: It's usually the mother's influence that's dominant, but the father's works in the same way, of course. Every lawyer is quite familiar with it. And still this Krogstad's been going home year in, year out, poisoning his own children with lies and pretense; that's why I call him morally lost. *(Reaching his hands out toward her.)* So my sweet little Nora must promise me never to plead his cause. Your hand on it. Come, come, what's this? Give me your hand. There, now. All settled. I can tell you it'd be impossible for me to work alongside of him. I literally feel physically revolted when I'm anywhere near such a person.

NORA: *(withdraws her hand and goes to the other side of the Christmas tree)* How hot it is here! And I've got so much to do.

HELMER: *(getting up and gathering his papers)* Yes, and I have to think about getting some of these read through before dinner. I'll think about your costume, too. And something to hang on the tree in gilt paper, I may even see about that. *(Putting his hand on her head.)* Oh you, my darling little songbird. *(He goes into his study and closes the door after him.)*

NORA: *(softly, after a silence)* Oh, really! It isn't so. It's impossible. It must be impossible.

ANNE-MARIE: *(in the doorway, left)* The children are begging so hard to come in to Mama.

NORA: No, no, no, don't let them in to me! You stay with them, Anne-Marie.

ANNE-MARIE: Of course, ma'am. *(Closes the door.)*

485 NORA: *(pale with terror)* Hurt my children—! Poison my home? *(A moment's pause; then she tosses her head.)* That's not true. Never. Never in all the world.

ACT II

Same room. Beside the piano the Christmas tree now stands stripped of ornaments, burned-down candle stubs on its ragged branches. Nora's street clothes lie on the sofa. Nora, alone in the room, moves restlessly about; at last she stops at the sofa and picks up her coat.

NORA: *(dropping the coat again)* Someone's coming! *(Goes toward the door, listens.)* No—there's no one. Of course—nobody's coming today, Christmas Day—or tomorrow, either. But maybe—*(Opens the door and looks out.)* No, nothing in the mailbox. Quite empty. *(Coming forward.)* What nonsense! He won't do anything serious. Nothing terrible could happen. It's impossible. Why, I have three small children.

Anne-Marie, with a large carton, comes in from the room to the left.

ANNE-MARIE: Well, at last I found the box with the masquerade clothes.

NORA: Thanks. Put it on the table.

ANNE-MARIE: *(does so)* But they're all pretty much of a mess.

5 NORA: Ahh! I'd love to rip them in a million pieces!

ANNE-MARIE: Oh, mercy, they can be fixed right up. Just a little patience.

NORA: Yes, I'll go get Mrs. Linde to help me.

ANNE-MARIE: Out again now? In this nasty weather? Miss Nora will catch cold—get sick.

NORA: Oh, worse things could happen—How are the children?

10 ANNE-MARIE: The poor mites are playing with their Christmas presents, but—

NORA: Do they ask for me much?

ANNE-MARIE: They're so used to having Mama around, you know.

NORA: Yes. But Anne-Marie, I *can't* be together with them as much as I was.

ANNE-MARIE: Well, small children get used to anything.

15 NORA: You think so? Do you think they'd forget their mother if she was gone for good?

ANNE-MARIE: Oh, mercy—gone for good!

NORA: Wait, tell me, Anne-Marie—I've wondered so often—how could you ever have the heart to give your child over to strangers?

ANNE-MARIE: But I had to, you know, to become little Nora's nurse.
NORA: Yes, but how could you *do* it?
20 ANNE-MARIE: When I could get such a good place? A girl who's poor and who's gotten in trouble is glad enough for that. Because that slippery fish, he didn't do a thing for me, you know.
NORA: But your daughter's surely forgotten you.
ANNE-MARIE: Oh, she certainly has not. She's written to me, both when she was confirmed and when she was married.
NORA: *(clasping her about the neck)* You old Anne-Marie, you were a good mother for me when I was little.
ANNE-MARIE: Poor little Nora, with no other mother but me.
25 NORA: And if the babies didn't have one, then I know that you'd—What silly talk! *(Opening the carton.)* Go in to them. Now I'll have to—Tomorrow you can see how lovely I'll look.
ANNE-MARIE: Oh, there won't be anyone at the party as lovely as Miss Nora. *(She goes off into the room, left.)*
NORA: *(begins unpacking the box, but soon throws it aside)* Oh, if I dared to go out. If only nobody would come. If only nothing would happen here while I'm out. What craziness—nobody's coming. Just don't think. This muff—needs a brushing. Beautiful gloves, beautiful gloves. Let it go. Let it go! One, two, three, four, five, six—*(With a cry.)* Oh, there they are! *(Poises to move toward the door, but remains irresolutely standing. Mrs. Linde enters from the hall, where she has removed her street clothes.)*
NORA: Oh, it's you, Kristine. There's no one else out there? How good that you've come.
MRS. LINDE: I hear you were up asking for me.
30 NORA: Yes, I just stopped by. There's something you really can help me with. Let's get settled on the sofa. Look, there's going to be a costume party tomorrow evening at the Stenborgs' right above us, and now Torvald wants me to go as a Neapolitan peasant girl and dance the tarantella that I learned in Capri.
MRS. LINDE: Really, are you giving a whole performance?
NORA: Torvald says yes, I should. See, here's the dress. Torvald had it made for me down there; but now it's all so tattered that I just don't know—
MRS. LINDE: Oh, we'll fix that up in no time. It's nothing more than the trimmings—they're a bit loose here and there. Needle and thread? Good, now we have what we need.
NORA: Oh, how sweet of you!
35 MRS. LINDE: *(sewing)* So you'll be in disguise tomorrow, Nora. You know what? I'll stop by then for a moment and have a look at you all dressed up. But listen, I've absolutely forgotten to thank you for that pleasant evening yesterday.
NORA: *(getting up and walking about)* I don't think it was as pleasant as usual yesterday. You should have come to town a bit sooner,

Kristine—Yes, Torvald really knows how to give a home elegance and charm.

MRS. LINDE: And you do, too, if you ask me. You're not your father's daughter for nothing. But tell me, is Dr. Rank always so down in the mouth as yesterday?

NORA: No, that was quite an exception. But he goes around critically ill all the time—tuberculosis of the spine, poor man. You know, his father was a disgusting thing who kept mistresses and so on—and that's why the son's been sickly from birth.

MRS. LINDE: *(lets her sewing fall to her lap)* But my dearest Nora, how do you know about such things?

40 NORA: *(walking more jauntily)* Hmp! When you've had three children, then you've had a few visits from—from women who know something of medicine, and they tell you this and that.

MRS. LINDE: *(resumes sewing; a short pause)* Does Dr. Rank come here every day?

NORA: Every blessed day. He's Torvald's best friend from childhood, and *my* good friend, too. Dr. Rank almost belongs to this house.

MRS. LINDE: But tell me—is he quite sincere? I mean, doesn't he rather enjoy flattering people?

NORA: Just the opposite. Why do you think that?

45 MRS. LINDE: When you introduced us yesterday, he was proclaiming that he'd often heard my name in this house; but later I noticed that your husband hadn't the slightest idea who I really was. So how could Dr. Rank—?

NORA: But it's all true, Kristine. You see, Torvald loves me beyond words, and, as he puts it, he'd like to keep me all to himself. For a long time he'd almost be jealous if I even mentioned any of my old friends back home. So of course I dropped that. But with Dr. Rank I talk a lot about such things, because he likes hearing about them.

MRS. LINDE: Now listen, Nora; in many ways you're still like a child. I'm a good deal older than you, with a little more experience. I'll tell you something: you ought to put an end to all this with Dr. Rank.

NORA: What should I put an end to?

MRS. LINDE: Both parts of it, I think. Yesterday you said something about a rich admirer who'd provide you with money—

50 NORA: Yes, one who doesn't exist—worse luck. So?

MRS. LINDE: Is Dr. Rank well off?

NORA: Yes, he is.

MRS. LINDE: With no dependents?

NORA: No, no one. But—

55 MRS. LINDE: And he's over here every day?

NORA: Yes, I told you that.

MRS. LINDE: How can a man of such refinement be so grasping?

NORA: I don't follow you at all.

MRS. LINDE: Now don't try to hide it, Nora. You think I can't guess who loaned you the forty-eight hundred crowns?

NORA: Are you out of your mind? How could you think such a thing! A friend of ours, who comes here every single day. What an intolerable situation that would have been!

MRS. LINDE: Then it really wasn't him.

NORA: No, absolutely not. It never even crossed my mind for a moment—And he had nothing to lend in those days; his inheritance came later.

MRS. LINDE: Well, I think that was a stroke of luck for you, Nora dear.

NORA: No, it never would have occurred to me to ask Dr. Rank—Still, I'm quite sure that if I had asked him—

MRS. LINDE: Which you won't, of course.

NORA: No, of course not. I can't see that I'd ever need to. But I'm quite positive that if I talked to Dr. Rank—

MRS. LINDE: Behind your husband's back?

NORA: I've got to clear up this other thing; *that's* also behind his back. I've *got* to clear it all up.

MRS. LINDE: Yes, I was saying that yesterday, but—

NORA: *(pacing up and down)* A man handles these problems so much better than a woman—

MRS. LINDE: One's husband does, yes.

NORA: Nonsense. *(Stopping.)* When you pay everything you owe, then you get your note back, right?

MRS. LINDE: Yes, naturally.

NORA: And can rip it into a million pieces and burn it up—that filthy scrap of paper!

MRS. LINDE: *(looking hard at her, laying her sewing aside, and rising slowly)* Nora, you're hiding something from me.

NORA: You can see it in my face?

MRS. LINDE: Something's happened to you since yesterday morning. Nora, what is it?

NORA: *(hurrying toward her)* Kristine! *(Listening.)* Shh! Torvald's home. Look, go in with the children a while. Torvald can't bear all this snipping and stitching. Let Anne-Marie help you.

MRS. LINDE: *(gathering up some of the things)* All right, but I'm not leaving here until we've talked this out. *(She disappears into the room, left, as Torvald enters from the hall.)*

NORA: Oh, how I've been waiting for you, Torvald dear.

HELMER: Was that the dressmaker?

NORA: No, that was Kristine. She's helping me fix up my costume. You know, it's going to be quite attractive.

HELMER: Yes, wasn't that a bright idea I had?

NORA: Brilliant! But then wasn't I good as well to give in to you?

HELMER: Good—because you give in to your husband's judgment? All right, you little goose, I know you didn't mean it like that. But I won't disturb you. You'll want to have a fitting, I suppose.

NORA: And you'll be working?
HELMER: Yes. *(Indicating a bundle of papers.)* See. I've been down to the bank. *(Starts toward his study.)*
NORA: Torvald.
HELMER: *(stops)* Yes.
NORA: If your little squirrel begged you, with all her heart and soul, for something—?
HELMER: What's that?
NORA: Then would you do it?
HELMER: First, naturally, I'd have to know what it was.
NORA: Your squirrel would scamper about and do tricks, if you'd only be sweet and give in.
HELMER: Out with it.
NORA: Your lark would be singing high and low in every room—
HELMER: Come on, she does that anyway.
NORA: I'd be a wood nymph and dance for you in the moonlight.
HELMER: Nora—don't tell me it's that same business from this morning?
NORA: *(coming closer)* Yes, Torvald, I beg you, please!
HELMER: And you actually have the nerve to drag that up again?
NORA: Yes, yes, you've got to give in to me; you *have* to let Krogstad keep his job in the bank.
HELMER: My dear Nora, I've slated his job for Mrs. Linde.
NORA: That's awfully kind of you. But you could just fire another clerk instead of Krogstad.
HELMER: This is the most incredible stubbornness! Because you go and give an impulsive promise to speak up for him, I'm expected to—
NORA: That's not the reason, Torvald. It's for your own sake. That man does writing for the worst papers; you said it yourself. He could do you any amount of harm. I'm scared to death of him—
HELMER: Ah, I understand. It's the old memories haunting you.
NORA: What do you mean by that?
HELMER: Of course, you're thinking about your father.
NORA: Yes, all right. Just remember how those nasty gossips wrote in the papers about Papa and slandered him so cruelly. I think they'd have had him dismissed if the department hadn't sent you up to investigate, and if you hadn't been so kind and open-minded toward him.
HELMER: My dear Nora, there's a notable difference between your father and me. Your father's official career was hardly above reproach. But mine is; and I hope it'll stay that way as long as I hold my position.
NORA: Oh, who can ever tell what vicious minds can invent? We could be so snug and happy now in our quiet, carefree home—you and I and the children, Torvald! That's why I'm pleading with you so—
HELMER: And just by pleading for him you make it impossible for me to keep him on. It's already known at the bank that I'm firing

Krogstad. What if it's rumored around now that the new bank manager was vetoed by his wife—

NORA: Yes, what then—?

HELMER: Oh yes—as long as our little bundle of stubbornness gets her way—! I should go and make myself ridiculous in front of the whole office—give people the idea I can be swayed by all kinds of outside pressure. Oh, you can bet I'd feel the effects of that soon enough! Besides—there's something that rules Krogstad right out at the bank as long as I'm the manager.

NORA: What's that?

HELMER: His moral failings I could maybe overlook if I had to—

NORA: Yes, Torvald, why not?

HELMER: And I hear he's quite efficient on the job. But he was a crony of mine back in my teens—one of those rash friendships that crop up again and again to embarrass you later in life. Well, I might as well say it straight out: we're on a first-name basis. And that tactless fool makes no effort at all to hide it in front of others. Quite the contrary—he thinks that entitles him to take a familiar air around me, and so every other second he comes booming out with his "Yes, Torvald!" and "Sure thing, Torvald!" I tell you, it's been excruciating for me. He's out to make my place in the bank unbearable.

NORA: Torvald, you can't be serious about all this.

HELMER: Oh no? Why not?

NORA: Because these are such petty considerations.

HELMER: What are you saying? Petty? You think I'm petty!

NORA: No, just the opposite, Torvald dear. That's exactly why—

HELMER: Never mind. You call my motives petty; then I might as well be just that. Petty! All right! We'll put a stop to this for good. *(Goes to the hall door and calls.)* Helene!

NORA: What do you want?

HELMER: *(searching among his papers)* A decision. *(The Maid comes in.)* Look here; take this letter; go out with it at once. Get hold of a messenger and have him deliver it. Quick now. It's already addressed. Wait, here's some money.

MAID: Yes, sir. *(She leaves with the letter.)*

HELMER: *(straightening his papers)* There, now, little Miss Willful.

NORA: *(breathlessly)* Torvald, what was that letter?

HELMER: Krogstad's notice.

NORA: Call it back, Torvald! There's still time. Oh, Torvald, call it back! Do it for my sake—for your sake, for the children's sake! Do you hear, Torvald; do it! You don't know how this can harm us.

HELMER: Too late.

NORA: Yes, too late.

HELMER: Nora dear, I can forgive you this panic, even though basically you're insulting me. Yes, you are! Or isn't it an insult to think that *I* should be afraid of a courtroom hack's revenge? But I forgive you anyway, because this shows so beautifully how much you love me. *(Takes her in his arms.)* This is the way it should be, my darling Nora. Whatever comes, you'll see: when it really counts, I have strength and courage enough as a man to take on the whole weight myself.

NORA: *(terrified)* What do you mean by that?

HELMER: The whole weight, I said.

NORA: *(resolutely)* No, never in all the world.

HELMER: Good. So we'll share it, Nora, as man and wife. That's as it should be. *(Fondling her.)* Are you happy now? There, there, there— not these frightened dove's eyes. It's nothing at all but empty fantasies—Now you should run through your tarantella and practice your tambourine. I'll go to the inner office and shut both doors, so I won't hear a thing; you can make all the noise you like. *(Turning in the doorway.)* And when Rank comes, just tell him where he can find me. *(He nods to her and goes with his papers into the study, closing the door.)*

140 NORA: *(standing as though rooted, dazed with fright, in a whisper)* He really could do it. He will do it. He'll do it in spite of everything. No, not that, never, never! Anything but that! Escape! A way out—*(The doorbell rings.)* Dr. Rank! Anything but that! *Anything*, whatever it is! *(Her hands pass over her face, smoothing it; she pulls herself together, goes over and opens the hall door. Dr. Rank stands outside, hanging his fur coat up. During the following scene, it begins getting dark.)*

NORA: Hello, Dr. Rank. I recognized your ring. But you mustn't go in to Torvald yet; I believe he's working.

RANK: And you?

NORA: For you, I always have an hour to spare—you know that. *(He has entered, and she shuts the door after him.)*

RANK: Many thanks. I'll make use of these hours while I can.

145 NORA: What do you mean by that? While you can?

RANK: Does that disturb you?

NORA: Well, it's such an odd phrase. Is anything going to happen?

RANK: What's going to happen is what I've been expecting so long— but I honestly didn't think it would come so soon.

NORA: *(gripping his arm)* What is it you've found out? Dr. Rank, you have to tell me!

150 RANK: *(sitting by the stove)* It's all over with me. There's nothing to be done about it.

NORA: *(breathing easier)* Is it you—then—?

RANK: Who else? There's no point in lying to one's self. I'm the most miserable of all my patients, Mrs. Helmer. These past few days I've been auditing my internal accounts. Bankrupt! Within a month I'll probably be laid out and rotting in the churchyard.

NORA: Oh, what a horrible thing to say.

RANK: The thing itself is horrible. But the worst of it is all the other horror before it's over. There's only one final examination left;

when I'm finished with that, I'll know about when my disintegration will begin. There's something I want to say. Helmer with his sensitivity has such a sharp distaste for anything ugly. I don't want him near my sickroom.

155 NORA: Oh, but Dr. Rank—

RANK: I won't have him in there. Under no condition. I'll lock my door to him—As soon as I'm completely sure of the worst, I'll send you my calling card marked with a black cross, and you'll know then the wreck has started to come apart.

NORA: No, today you're completely unreasonable. And I wanted you so much to be in a really good humor.

RANK: With death up my sleeve? And then to suffer this way for somebody else's sins. Is there any justice in that? And in every single family, in some way or another, this inevitable retribution of nature goes on—

NORA: *(her hands pressed over her ears)* Oh, stuff! Cheer up! Please— be gay!

160 RANK: Yes, I'd just as soon laugh at it all. My poor, innocent spine, serving time for my father's gay army days.

NORA: *(by the table, left)* He was so infatuated with asparagus tips and *pâté de foie gras,* wasn't that it?

RANK: Yes—and with truffles.

NORA: Truffles, yes. And then with oysters, I suppose?

RANK: Yes, tons of oysters, naturally.

165 NORA: And then the port and champagne to go with it. It's so sad that all these delectable things have to strike at our bones.

RANK: Especially when they strike at the unhappy bones that never shared in the fun.

NORA: Ah, that's the saddest of all.

RANK: *(looks searchingly at her)* Hm.

NORA: *(after a moment)* Why did you smile?

170 RANK: No, it was you who laughed.

NORA: No, it was you who smiled, Dr. Rank!

RANK: *(getting up)* You're even a bigger tease than I'd thought.

NORA: I'm full of wild ideas today.

RANK: That's obvious.

175 NORA: *(putting both hands on his shoulders)* Dear, dear Dr. Rank, you'll never die for Torvald and me.

RANK: Oh, that loss you'll easily get over. Those who go away are soon forgotten.

NORA: *(looks fearfully at him)* You believe that?

RANK: One makes new connections, and then—

NORA: Who makes new connections?

180 RANK: Both you and Torvald will when I'm gone. I'd say you're well under way already. What was that Mrs. Linde doing here last evening?

NORA: Oh, come—you can't be jealous of poor Kristine?

RANK: Oh yes, I am. She'll be my successor here in the house. When I'm down under, that woman will probably—
NORA: Shh! Not so loud. She's right in there.
RANK: Today as well. So you see.
NORA: Only to sew on my dress. Good gracious, how unreasonable you are. *(Sitting on the sofa.)* Be nice now, Dr. Rank. Tomorrow you'll see how beautifully I'll dance; and you can imagine then that I'm dancing only for you—yes, and of course for Torvald, too—that's understood. *(Takes various items out of the carton.)* Dr. Rank, sit over here and I'll show you something.
RANK: *(sitting)* What's that?
NORA: Look here. Look.
RANK: Silk stockings.
NORA: Flesh-colored. Aren't they lovely? Now it's so dark here, but tomorrow—No, no, no, just look at the feet. Oh well, you might as well look at the rest.
RANK: Hm—
NORA: Why do you look so critical? Don't you believe they'll fit?
RANK: I've never had any chance to form an opinion on that.
NORA: *(glancing at him a moment)* Shame on you. *(Hits him lightly on the ear with the stockings.)* That's for you. *(Puts them away again.)*
RANK: And what other splendors am I going to see now?
NORA: Not the least bit more, because you've been naughty. *(She hums a little and rummages among her things.)*
RANK: *(after a short silence)* When I sit here together with you like this, completely easy and open, then I don't know—I simply can't imagine—whatever would have become of me if I'd never come into this house.
NORA: *(smiling)* Yes, I really think you feel completely at ease with us.
RANK: *(more quietly, staring straight ahead)* And then to have to go away from it all—
NORA: Nonsense, you're not going away.
RANK: *(his voice unchanged)*—and not even be able to leave some poor show of gratitude behind, scarcely a fleeting regret—no more than a vacant place that anyone can fill.
NORA: And if I asked you now for—? No—
RANK: For what?
NORA: For a great proof of your friendship—
RANK: Yes, yes?
NORA: No, I mean—for an exceptionally big favor—
RANK: Would you really, for once, make me so happy?
NORA: Oh, you haven't the vaguest idea what it is.
RANK: All right, then tell me.
NORA: No, but I can't, Dr. Rank—it's all out of reason. It's advice and help, too—and a favor—
RANK: So much the better. I can't fathom what you're hinting at. Just speak out. Don't you trust me?

NORA: Of course. More than anyone else. You're my best and truest friend, I'm sure. That's why I want to talk to you. All right, then, Dr. Rank: there's something you can help me prevent. You know how deeply, how inexpressibly dearly Torvald loves me; he'd never hesitate a second to give up his life for me.
RANK: *(leaning close to her)* Nora—do you think he's the only one—
NORA: *(with a slight start)* Who—?
RANK: Who'd gladly give up his life for you.
215 NORA: *(heavily)* I see.
RANK: I swore to myself you should know this before I'm gone. I'll never find a better chance. Yes, Nora, now you know. And also you know now that you can trust me beyond anyone else.
NORA: *(rising, natural and calm)* Let me by.
RANK: *(making room for her, but still sitting)* Nora—
NORA: *(in the hall doorway)* Helene, bring the lamp in. *(Goes over to the stove.)* Ah, dear Dr. Rank, that was really mean of you.
220 RANK: *(getting up)* That I've loved you just as deeply as somebody else? Was *that* mean?
NORA: No, but that you came out and told me. That was quite unnecessary—
RANK: What do you mean? Have you known—?

The Maid comes in with the lamp, sets it on the table, and goes out again.

RANK: Nora—Mrs. Helmer—I'm asking you: have you known about it?
NORA: Oh, how can I tell what I know or don't know? Really, I don't know what to say—Why did you have to be so clumsy, Dr. Rank! Everything was so good.
225 RANK: Well, in any case, you now have the knowledge that my body and soul are at your command. So won't you speak out?
NORA: *(looking at him)* After that?
RANK: Please, just let me know what it is.
NORA: You can't know anything now.
RANK: I have to. You mustn't punish me like this. Give me the chance to do whatever is humanly possible for you.
230 NORA: Now there's nothing you can do for me. Besides, actually, I don't need any help. You'll see—it's only my fantasies. That's what it is. Of course! *(Sits in the rocker, looks at him, and smiles.)* What a nice one you are, Dr. Rank. Aren't you a little bit ashamed, now that the lamp is here?
RANK: No, not exactly. But perhaps I'd better go—for good?
NORA: No, you certainly can't do that. You must come here just as you always have. You know Torvald can't do without you.
RANK: Yes, but *you*?
NORA: You know how much I enjoy it when you're here.
235 RANK: That's precisely what threw me off. You're a mystery to me. So many times I've felt you'd almost rather be with me than with Helmer.

NORA: Yes—you see, there are some people that one loves most and other people that one would almost prefer being with.
RANK: Yes, there's something to that.
NORA: When I was back home, of course I loved Papa most. But I always thought it was so much fun when I could sneak down to the maids' quarters, because they never tried to improve me, and it was always so amusing, the way they talked to each other.
RANK: Aha, so it's *their* place that I've filled.
240 NORA: *(jumping up and going to him)* Oh, dear, sweet Dr. Rank, that's not what I mean at all. But you can understand that with Torvald it's just the same as with Papa—

The Maid enters from the hall.

MAID: Ma'am—please! *(She whispers to Nora and hands her a calling card.)*
NORA: *(glancing at the card)* Ah! *(Slips it into her pocket.)*
RANK: Anything wrong?
NORA: No, no, not at all. It's only some—it's my new dress—
245 RANK: Really? But—there's your dress.
NORA: Oh, that. But this is another one—I ordered it—Torvald mustn't know—
RANK: Ah, now we have the big secret.
NORA: That's right. Just go in with him—he's back in the inner study. Keep him there as long as—
RANK: Don't worry. He won't get away. *(Goes into the study.)*
250 NORA: *(to the Maid)* And he's standing waiting in the kitchen?
MAID: Yes, he came up by the back stairs.
NORA: But didn't you tell him somebody was here?
MAID: Yes, but that didn't do any good.
NORA: He won't leave?
255 MAID: No, he won't go till he's talked with you, ma'am.
NORA: Let him come in, then—but quietly. Helene, don't breathe a word about this. It's a surprise for my husband.
MAID: Yes, yes, I understand—*(Goes out.)*
NORA: This horror—it's going to happen. No, no, no, it can't happen, it mustn't. *(She goes and bolts Helmer's door. The Maid opens the hall door for Krogstad and shuts it behind him. He is dressed for travel in a fur coat, boots, and a fur cap.)*
NORA: *(going toward him)* Talk softly. My husband's home.
260 KROGSTAD: Well, good for him.
NORA: What do you want?
KROGSTAD: Some information.
NORA: Hurry up, then. What is it?
KROGSTAD: You know, of course, that I got my notice.
265 NORA: I couldn't prevent it, Mr. Krogstad. I fought for you to the bitter end, but nothing worked.
KROGSTAD: Does your husband's love for you run so thin? He knows everything I can expose you to, and all the same he dares to—

NORA: How can you imagine he knows anything about this?
KROGSTAD: Ah, no—I can't imagine it either, now. It's not at all like my fine Torvald Helmer to have so much guts—
NORA: Mr. Krogstad, I demand respect for my husband!
270 KROGSTAD: Why, of course—all due respect. But since the lady's keeping it so carefully hidden, may I presume to ask if you're also a bit better informed than yesterday about what you've actually done?
NORA: More than you ever could teach me.
KROGSTAD: Yes, I *am* such an awful lawyer.
NORA: What is it you want from me?
KROGSTAD: Just a glimpse of how you are, Mrs. Helmer. I've been thinking about you all day long. A cashier, a night-court scribbler, a—well, a type like me also has a little of what they call a heart, you know.
275 NORA: Then show it. Think of my children.
KROGSTAD: Did you or your husband ever think of mine? But never mind. I simply wanted to tell you that you don't need to take this thing too seriously. For the present, I'm not proceeding with any action.
NORA: Oh no, really! Well—I knew that.
KROGSTAD: Everything can be settled in a friendly spirit. It doesn't have to get around town at all; it can stay just among us three.
NORA: My husband must never know anything of this.
280 KROGSTAD: How can you manage that? Perhaps you can pay me the balance?
NORA: No, not right now.
KROGSTAD: Or you know some way of raising the money in a day or two?
NORA: No way that I'm willing to use.
KROGSTAD: Well, it wouldn't have done you any good, anyway. If you stood in front of me with a fistful of bills, you still couldn't buy your signature back.
285 NORA: Then tell me what you're going to do with it.
KROGSTAD: I'll just hold onto it—keep it on file. There's no outsider who'll even get wind of it. So if you've been thinking of taking some desperate step—
NORA: I have.
KROGSTAD: Been thinking of running away from home—
NORA: I have!
290 KROGSTAD: Or even of something worse—
NORA: How could you guess that?
KROGSTAD: You can drop those thoughts.
NORA: How could you guess I was thinking of *that*?
KROGSTAD: Most of us think about *that* at first. I thought about it too, but I discovered I hadn't the courage—
295 NORA: *(lifelessly)* I don't either.

KROGSTAD: *(relieved)* That's true, you haven't the courage? You too?
NORA: I don't have it—I don't have it.
KROGSTAD: It would be terribly stupid, anyway. After that first storm at home blows out, why, then—I have here in my pocket a letter for your husband—
NORA: Telling everything?
300 KROGSTAD: As charitably as possible.
NORA: *(quickly)* He mustn't ever get that letter. Tear it up. I'll find some way to get money.
KROGSTAD: Beg pardon, Mrs. Helmer, but I think I just told you—
NORA: Oh, I don't mean the money I owe you. Let me know how much you want from my husband, and I'll manage it.
KROGSTAD: I don't want any money from your husband.
305 NORA: What do you want, then?
KROGSTAD: I'll tell you what. I want to recoup, Mrs. Helmer; I want to get on in the world—and there's where your husband can help me. For a year and a half I've kept myself clean of anything disreputable—all that time struggling with the worst conditions; but I was satisfied, working my way up step by step. Now I've been written right off, and I'm just not in the mood to come crawling back. I tell you, I want to move on. I want to get back in the bank—in a better position. Your husband can set up a job for me—
NORA: He'll never do that!
KROGSTAD: He'll do it. I know him. He won't dare breathe a word of protest. And once I'm in there together with him, you just wait and see! Inside of a year, I'll be the manager's right-hand man. It'll be Nils Krogstad, not Torvald Helmer, who runs the bank.
NORA: You'll never see the day!
310 KROGSTAD: Maybe you think you can—
NORA: I have the courage now—for *that*.
KROGSTAD: Oh, you don't scare me. A smart, spoiled lady like you—
NORA: You'll see; you'll see!
KROGSTAD: Under the ice, maybe? Down in the freezing, coal-black water? There, till you float up in the spring, ugly, unrecognizable, with your hair falling out—
315 NORA: You don't frighten me.
KROGSTAD: Nor do you frighten me. One doesn't do these things, Mrs. Helmer. Besides, what good would it be? I'd still have him safe in my pocket.
NORA: Afterwards? When I'm no longer—?
KROGSTAD: Are you forgetting that *I'll* be in control then over your final reputation? *(Nora stands speechless, staring at him.)* Good; now I've warned you. Don't do anything stupid. When Helmer's read my letter, I'll be waiting for his reply. And bear in mind that it's your husband himself who's forced me back to my old ways. I'll never forgive him for that. Good-bye, Mrs. Helmer. *(He goes out through the hall.)*

NORA: *(goes to the hall door, opens it a crack, and listens)* He's gone. Didn't leave the letter. Oh no, no, that's impossible too! *(Opening the door more and more.)* What's that? He's standing outside—not going downstairs. He's thinking it over? Maybe he'll—? *(A letter falls in the mailbox; then Krogstad's footsteps are heard, dying away down a flight of stairs. Nora gives a muffled cry and runs over toward the sofa table. A short pause.)* In the mailbox. *(Slips warily over to the hall door.)* It's lying there. Torvald, Torvald—now we're lost!

MRS. LINDE: *(entering with the costume from the room, left)* There now, I can't see anything else to mend. Perhaps you'd like to try—
NORA: *(in a hoarse whisper)* Kristine, come here.
MRS. LINDE: *(tossing the dress on the sofa)* What's wrong? You look upset.
NORA: Come here. See that letter? *There!* Look—through the glass in the mailbox.
MRS. LINDE: Yes, yes, I see it.
NORA: That letter's from Krogstad—
MRS. LINDE: Nora—it's Krogstad who loaned you the money!
NORA: Yes, and now Torvald will find out everything.
MRS. LINDE: Believe me, Nora, it's best for both of you.
NORA: There's more you don't know. I forged a name.
MRS. LINDE: But for heaven's sake—?
NORA: I only want to tell you that, Kristine, so that you can be my witness.
MRS. LINDE: Witness? Why should I—?
NORA: If I should go out of my mind—it could easily happen—
MRS. LINDE: Nora!
NORA: Or anything else occurred—so I couldn't be present here—
MRS. LINDE: Nora, Nora, you aren't yourself at all!
NORA: And someone should try to take on the whole weight, all of the guilt, you follow me—
MRS. LINDE: Yes, of course, but why do you think—?
NORA: Then you're the witness that it isn't true, Kristine. I'm very much myself; my mind right now is perfectly clear; and I'm telling you: nobody else has known about this; I alone did everything. Remember that.
MRS. LINDE: I will. But I don't understand all this.
NORA: Oh, how could you ever understand it? It's the miracle now that's going to take place.
MRS. LINDE: The miracle?
NORA: Yes, the miracle. But it's so awful, Kristine. It mustn't take place, not for anything in the world.
MRS. LINDE: I'm going right over and talk with Krogstad.
NORA: Don't go near him; he'll do you some terrible harm!
MRS. LINDE: There was a time once when he'd gladly have done anything for me.
NORA: He?
MRS. LINDE: Where does he live?

NORA: Oh, how do I know? Yes. *(Searches in her pocket.)* Here's his card. But the letter, the letter—!
350 HELMER: *(from the study, knocking on the door)* Nora!
NORA: *(with a cry of fear)* Oh! What is it? What do you want?
HELMER: Now, now, don't be so frightened. We're not coming in. You locked the door—are you trying on the dress?
NORA: Yes, I'm trying it. I'll look just beautiful, Torvald.
MRS. LINDE: *(who has read the card)* He's living right around the corner.
355 NORA: Yes, but what's the use? We're lost. The letter's in the box.
MRS. LINDE: And your husband has the key?
NORA: Yes, always.
MRS. LINDE: Krogstad can ask for his letter back unread; he can find some excuse—
NORA: But it's just this time that Torvald usually—
360 MRS. LINDE: Stall him. Keep him in there. I'll be back as quick as I can. *(She hurries out through the hall entrance.)*
NORA: *(goes to Helmer's door, opens it, and peers in)* Torvald!
HELMER: *(from the inner study)* Well—does one dare set foot in one's own living room at last? Come on, Rank, now we'll get a look—*(In the doorway.)* But what's this?
NORA: What, Torvald dear?
HELMER: Rank had me expecting some grand masquerade.
365 RANK: *(in the doorway)* That was my impression, but I must have been wrong.
NORA: No one can admire me in my splendor—not till tomorrow.
HELMER: But Nora dear, you look so exhausted. Have you practiced too hard?
NORA: No, I haven't practiced at all yet.
HELMER: You know, it's necessary—
370 NORA: Oh, it's absolutely necessary, Torvald. But I can't get anywhere without your help. I've forgotten the whole thing completely.
HELMER: Ah, we'll soon take care of that.
NORA: Yes, take care of me, Torvald, please! Promise me that? Oh, I'm so nervous. That big party—You must give up everything this evening for me. No business—don't even touch your pen. Yes? Dear Torvald, promise?
HELMER: It's a promise. Tonight I'm totally at your service—you little helpless thing. Hm—but first there's one thing I want to—*(Goes toward the hall door.)*
NORA: What are you looking for?
375 HELMER: Just to see if there's any mail.
NORA: No, no, don't do that, Torvald!
HELMER: Now what?
NORA: Torvald, please. There isn't any.
HELMER: Let me look, though. *(Starts out. Nora, at the piano, strikes the first notes of the tarantella. Helmer, at the door, stops.)* Aha!
380 NORA: I can't dance tomorrow if I don't practice with you.

HELMER: *(going over to her)* Nora dear, are you really so frightened?
NORA: Yes, so terribly frightened. Let me practice right now; there's still time before dinner. Oh, sit down and play for me, Torvald. Direct me. Teach me, the way you always have.
HELMER: Gladly, if it's what you want. *(Sits at the piano.)*
NORA: *(snatches the tambourine up from the box, then a long, varicolored shawl, which she throws around herself, whereupon she springs forward and cries out)* Play for me now! Now I'll dance!

Helmer plays and Nora dances. Rank stands behind Helmer at the piano and looks on.

385 HELMER: *(as he plays)* Slower. Slow down.
NORA: Can't change it.
HELMER: Not so violent, Nora!
NORA: Has to be just like this.
HELMER: *(stopping)* No, no, that won't do at all.
390 NORA: *(laughing and swinging her tambourine)* Isn't that what I told you?
RANK: Let me play for her.
HELMER: *(getting up)* Yes, go on. I can teach her more easily then.

Rank sits at the piano and plays; Nora dances more and more wildly. Helmer has stationed himself by the stove and repeatedly gives her directions; she seems not to hear them; her hair loosens and falls over her shoulders; she does not notice, but goes on dancing. Mrs. Linde enters.

MRS. LINDE: *(standing dumbfounded at the door)* Ah—!
NORA: *(still dancing)* See what fun, Kristine!
395 HELMER: But Nora darling, you dance as if your life were at stake.
NORA: And it is.
HELMER: Rank, stop! This is pure madness. Stop it, I say!

Rank breaks off playing, and Nora halts abruptly.

HELMER: *(going over to her)* I never would have believed it. You've forgotten everything I taught you.
NORA: *(throwing away the tambourine)* You see for yourself.
400 HELMER: Well, there's certainly room for instruction here.
NORA: Yes, you see how important it is. You've got to teach me to the very last minute. Promise me that, Torvald?
HELMER: You can bet on it.
NORA: You mustn't, either today or tomorrow, think about anything else but me; you mustn't open any letters—or the mailbox—
HELMER: Ah, it's still the fear of that man—
405 NORA: Oh yes, yes, that too.
HELMER: Nora, it's written all over you—there's already a letter from him out there.
NORA: I don't know. I guess so. But you mustn't read such things now; there mustn't be anything ugly between us before it's all over.
RANK: *(quietly to Helmer)* You shouldn't deny her.

HELMER: *(putting his arm around her)* The child can have her way. But tomorrow night, after you've danced—
NORA: Then you'll be free.
MAID: *(in the doorway, right)* Ma'am, dinner is served.
NORA: We'll be wanting champagne, Helene.
MAID: Very good, ma'am. *(Goes out.)*
HELMER: So—a regular banquet, hm?
NORA: Yes, a banquet—champagne till daybreak! *(Calling out.)* And some macaroons, Helene. Heaps of them—just this once.
HELMER: *(taking her hands)* Now, now, now—no hysterics. Be my own little lark again.
NORA: Oh, I will soon enough. But go on in—and you, Dr. Rank. Kristine, help me put up my hair.
RANK: *(whispering, as they go)* There's nothing wrong—really wrong, is there?
HELMER: Oh, of course not. It's nothing more than this childish anxiety I was telling you about. *(They go out, right.)*
NORA: Well?
MRS. LINDE: Left town.
NORA: I could see by your face.
MRS. LINDE: He'll be home tomorrow evening. I wrote him a note.
NORA: You shouldn't have. Don't try to stop anything now. After all, it's a wonderful joy, this waiting here for the miracle.
MRS. LINDE: What is it you're waiting for?
NORA: Oh, you can't understand that. Go in to them: I'll be along in a moment.

Mrs. Linde goes into the dining room. Nora stands a short while as if composing herself; then she looks at her watch.

NORA: Five. Seven hours to midnight. Twenty-four hours to the midnight after, and then the tarantella's done. Seven and twenty-four? Thirty-one hours to live.
HELMER: *(in the doorway, right)* What's become of the little lark?
NORA: *(going toward him with open arms)* Here's your lark!

ACT III

Same scene. The table, with chairs around it, has been moved to the center of the room. A lamp on the table is lit. The hall door stands open. Dance music drifts down from the floor above. Mrs. Linde sits at the table, absently paging through a book, trying to read, but apparently unable to focus her thoughts. Once or twice she pauses, tensely listening for a sound at the outer entrance.

MRS. LINDE: *(glancing at her watch)* Not yet—and there's hardly any time left. If only he's not—*(Listening again.)* Ah, there he is. *(She goes out in the hall and cautiously opens the outer door. Quiet footsteps are heard on the stairs. She whispers:)* Come in. Nobody's here.

KROGSTAD: *(in the doorway)* I found a note from you at home. What's back of all this?
MRS. LINDE: I just *had* to talk to you.
KROGSTAD: Oh? And it just *had* to be here in this house?
MRS. LINDE: At my place it was impossible; my room hasn't a private entrance. Come in; we're all alone. The maid's asleep, and the Helmers are at the dance upstairs.
KROGSTAD: *(entering the room)* Well, well, the Helmers are dancing tonight? Really?
MRS. LINDE: Yes, why not?
KROGSTAD: How true—why not?
MRS. LINDE: All right, Krogstad, let's talk.
KROGSTAD: Do we two have anything more to talk about?
MRS. LINDE: We have a great deal to talk about.
KROGSTAD: I wouldn't have thought so.
MRS. LINDE: No, because you've never understood me, really.
KROGSTAD: Was there anything more to understand—except what's all too common in life? A calculating woman throws over a man the moment a better catch comes by.
MRS. LINDE: You think I'm so thoroughly calculating? You think I broke it off lightly?
KROGSTAD: Didn't you?
MRS. LINDE: Nils—is that what you really thought?
KROGSTAD: If you cared, then why did you write me the way you did?
MRS. LINDE: What else could I do? If I had to break off with you, then it was my job as well to root out everything you felt for me.
KROGSTAD: *(wringing his hands)* So that was it. And this—all this, simply for money!
MRS. LINDE: Don't forget I had a helpless mother and two small brothers. We couldn't wait for you, Nils; you had such a long road ahead of you then.
KROGSTAD: That may be; but you still hadn't the right to abandon me for somebody else's sake.
MRS. LINDE: Yes—I don't know. So many, many times I've asked myself if I did have that right.
KROGSTAD: *(more softly)* When I lost you, it was as if all the solid ground dissolved from under my feet. Look at me; I'm a half-drowned man now, hanging onto a wreck.
MRS. LINDE: Help may be near.
KROGSTAD: It was near—but then you came and blocked it off.
MRS. LINDE: Without my knowing it, Nils. Today for the first time I learned that it's you I'm replacing at the bank.
KROGSTAD: All right—I believe you. But now that you know, will you step aside?
MRS. LINDE: No, because that wouldn't benefit you in the slightest.
KROGSTAD: Not "benefit" me, hm! I'd step aside anyway.

MRS. LINDE: I've learned to be realistic. Life and hard, bitter necessity have taught me that.

KROGSTAD: And life's taught me never to trust fine phrases.

MRS. LINDE: Then life's taught you a very sound thing. But you do have to trust in actions, don't you?

KROGSTAD: What does that mean?

35 MRS. LINDE: You said you were hanging on like a half-drowned man to a wreck.

KROGSTAD: I've good reason to say that.

MRS. LINDE: I'm also like a half-drowned woman on a wreck. No one to suffer with; no one to care for.

KROGSTAD: You made your choice.

MRS. LINDE: There wasn't any choice then.

40 KROGSTAD: So—what of it?

MRS. LINDE: Nils, if only we two shipwrecked people could reach across to each other.

KROGSTAD: What are you saying?

MRS. LINDE: Two on one wreck are at least better off than each on his own.

KROGSTAD: Kristine!

45 MRS. LINDE: Why do you think I came into town?

KROGSTAD: Did you really have some thought of me?

MRS. LINDE: I have to work to go on living. All my born days, as long as I can remember, I've worked, and it's been my best and my only joy. But now I'm completely alone in the world; it frightens me to be so empty and lost. To work for yourself—there's no joy in that. Nils, give me something—someone to work for.

KROGSTAD: I don't believe all this. It's just some hysterical feminine urge to go out and make a noble sacrifice.

MRS. LINDE: Have you ever found me to be hysterical?

50 KROGSTAD: Can you honestly mean this? Tell me—do you know everything about my past?

MRS. LINDE: Yes.

KROGSTAD: And you know what they think I'm worth around here.

MRS. LINDE: From what you were saying before, it would seem that with me you could have been another person.

KROGSTAD: I'm positive of that.

55 MRS. LINDE: Couldn't it happen still?

KROGSTAD: Kristine—you're saying this in all seriousness? Yes, you are! I can see it in you. And do you really have the courage, then—?

MRS. LINDE: I need to have someone to care for; and your children need a mother. We both need each other. Nils, I have faith that you're good at heart—I'll risk everything together with you.

KROGSTAD: *(gripping her hands)* Kristine, thank you, thank you—Now I know I can win back a place in their eyes. Yes—but I forgot—

MRS. LINDE: *(listening)* Shh! The tarantella. Go now! Go on!

60 KROGSTAD: Why? What is it?
MRS. LINDE: Hear the dance up there? When that's over, they'll be coming down.
KROGSTAD: Oh, then I'll go. But—it's all pointless. Of course, you don't know the move I made against the Helmers.
MRS. LINDE: Yes, Nils, I know.
KROGSTAD: And all the same, you have the courage to—?
65 MRS. LINDE: I know how far despair can drive a man like you.
KROGSTAD: Oh, if I only could take it all back.
MRS. LINDE: You easily could—your letter's still lying in the mailbox.
KROGSTAD: Are you sure of that?
MRS. LINDE: Positive. But—
70 KROGSTAD: *(looks at her searchingly)* Is that the meaning of it, then? You'll save your friend at any price. Tell me straight out. Is that it?
MRS. LINDE: Nils—anyone who's sold herself for somebody else once isn't going to do it again.
KROGSTAD: I'll demand my letter back.
MRS. LINDE: No, no.
KROGSTAD: Yes, of course. I'll stay here till Helmer comes down; I'll tell him to give me my letter again—that it only involves my dismissal—that he shouldn't read it—
75 MRS. LINDE: No, Nils, don't call the letter back.
KROGSTAD: But wasn't that exactly why you wrote me to come here?
MRS. LINDE: Yes, in that first panic. But it's been a whole day and night since then, and in that time I've seen such incredible things in this house. Helmer's got to learn everything; this dreadful secret has to be aired; those two have to come to a full understanding; all these lies and evasions can't go on.
KROGSTAD: Well, then, if you want to chance it. But at least there's one thing I can do, and do right away—
MRS. LINDE: *(listening)* Go now, go, quick! The dance is over. We're not safe another second.
80 KROGSTAD: I'll wait for you downstairs.
MRS. LINDE: Yes, please do; take me home.
KROGSTAD: I can't believe it; I've never been so happy. *(He leaves by way of the outer door; the door between the room and the hall stays open.)*
MRS. LINDE: *(straightening up a bit and getting together her street clothes)* How different now! How different! Someone to work for, to live for—a home to build. Well, it is worth the try! Oh, if they'd only come! (Listening.) Ah, there they are. Bundle up. *(She picks up her hat and coat. Nora's and Helmer's voices can be heard outside; a key turns in the lock, and Helmer brings Nora into the hall almost by force. She is wearing the Italian costume with a large black shawl about her; he has on evening dress, with a black domino open over it.)*
NORA: *(struggling in the doorway)* No, no, no, not inside! I'm going up again. I don't want to leave so soon.
85 HELMER: But Nora dear—

NORA: Oh, I beg you, please, Torvald. From the bottom of my heart, *please*—only an hour more!
HELMER: Not a single minute, Nora darling. You know our agreement. Come on, in we go; you'll catch cold out here. *(In spite of her resistance, he gently draws her into the room.)*
MRS. LINDE: Good evening.
NORA: Kristine!
HELMER: Why, Mrs. Linde—are you here so late?
MRS. LINDE: Yes, I'm sorry, but I did want to see Nora in costume.
NORA: Have you been sitting here, waiting for me?
MRS. LINDE: Yes. I didn't come early enough; you were all upstairs; and then I thought I really couldn't leave without seeing you.
HELMER: *(removing Nora's shawl)* Yes, take a good look. She's worth looking at, I can tell you that, Mrs. Linde. Isn't she lovely?
MRS. LINDE: Yes, I should say—
HELMER: A dream of loveliness, isn't she? That's what everyone thought at the party, too. But she's horribly stubborn—this sweet little thing. What's to be done with her? Can you imagine, I almost had to use force to pry her away.
NORA: Oh, Torvald, you're going to regret you didn't indulge me, even for just a half hour more.
HELMER: There, you see. She danced her tarantella and got a tumultuous hand—which was well earned, although the performance may have been a bit too naturalistic—I mean it rather overstepped the proprieties of art. But never mind—what's important is, she made a success, an overwhelming success. You think I could let her stay on after that and spoil the effect? Oh no; I took my lovely little Capri girl—my capricious little Capri girl, I should say—took her under my arm; one quick tour of the ballroom, a curtsy to every side, and then—as they say in novels—the beautiful vision disappeared. An exit should always be effective, Mrs. Linde, but that's what I can't get Nora to grasp. Phew, it's hot in here. *(Flings the domino on a chair and opens the door to his room.)* Why's it dark in here? Oh yes, of course. Excuse me. *(He goes in and lights a couple of candles.)*
NORA: *(in a sharp, breathless whisper)* So?
MRS. LINDE: *(quietly)* I talked with him.
NORA: And—?
MRS. LINDE: Nora—you must tell your husband everything.
NORA: *(dully)* I knew it.
MRS. LINDE: You've got nothing to fear from Krogstad, but you have to speak out.
NORA: I won't tell.
MRS. LINDE: Then the letter will.
NORA: Thanks, Kristine. I know now what's to be done. Shh!
HELMER: *(reentering)* Well, then, Mrs. Linde—have you admired her?
MRS. LINDE: Yes, and now I'll say good night.

110   **HELMER:** Oh, come, so soon? Is this yours, this knitting?
      MRS. LINDE: Yes, thanks. I nearly forgot it.
      HELMER: Do you knit, then?
      MRS. LINDE: Oh yes.
      HELMER: You know what? You should embroider instead.
115 **MRS. LINDE:** Really? Why?
      HELMER: Yes, because it's a lot prettier. See here, one holds the embroidery so, in the left hand, and then one guides the needle with the right—so—in an easy, sweeping curve—right?
      MRS. LINDE: Yes, I guess that's—
      HELMER: But, on the other hand, knitting—it can never be anything but ugly. Look, see here, the arms tucked in, the knitting needles going up and down—there's something Chinese about it. Ah, that was really a glorious champagne they served.
      MRS. LINDE: Yes, good night, Nora, and don't be stubborn any more.
120 **HELMER:** Well put, Mrs. Linde!
      MRS. LINDE: Good night, Mr. Helmer.
      HELMER: *(accompanying her to the door)* Good night, good night. I hope you get home all right. I'd be very happy to—but you don't have far to go. Good night, good night. *(She leaves. He shuts the door after her and returns.)* There, now, at last we got her out the door. She's a deadly bore, that creature.
      NORA: Aren't you pretty tired, Torvald?
      HELMER: No, not a bit.
125 **NORA:** You're not sleepy?
      HELMER: Not at all. On the contrary, I'm feeling quite exhilarated. But you? Yes, you really look tired and sleepy.
      NORA: Yes, I'm very tired. Soon now I'll sleep.
      HELMER: See! You see! I was right all along that we shouldn't stay longer.
      NORA: Whatever you do is always right.
130 **HELMER:** *(kissing her brow)* Now my little lark talks sense. Say, did you notice what a time Rank was having tonight?
      NORA: Oh, was he? I didn't get to speak with him.
      HELMER: I scarcely did either, but it's a long time since I've seen him in such high spirits. *(Gazes at her a moment, then comes nearer her.)* Hm—it's marvelous, though, to be back home again—to be completely alone with you. Oh, you bewitchingly lovely young woman!
      NORA: Torvald, don't look at me like that!
      HELMER: Can't I look at my richest treasure? At all that beauty that's mine, mine alone—completely and utterly.
135 **NORA:** *(moving around to the other side of the table)* You mustn't talk to me that way tonight.
      HELMER: *(following her)* The tarantella is still in your blood, I can see—and it makes you even more enticing. Listen. The guests are

beginning to go. *(Dropping his voice.)* Nora—it'll soon be quiet through this whole house.

NORA: Yes, I hope so.

HELMER: You do, don't you, my love? Do you realize—when I'm out at a party like this with you—do you know why I talk to you so little, and keep such a distance away; just send you a stolen look now and then—you know why I do it? It's because I'm imagining then that you're my secret darling, my secret young bride-to-be, and that no one suspects there's anything between us.

NORA: Yes, yes; oh, yes, I know you're always thinking of me.

140 HELMER: And then when we leave and I place the shawl over those fine young rounded shoulders—over that wonderful curving neck—then I pretend that you're my young bride, that we're just coming from the wedding, that for the first time I'm bringing you into my house—that for the first time I'm alone with you—completely alone with you, your trembling young beauty! All this evening I've longed for nothing but you. When I saw you turn and sway in the tarantella—my blood was pounding till I couldn't stand it—that's why I brought you down here so early—

NORA: Go away, Torvald! Leave me alone. I don't want all this.

HELMER: What do you mean? Nora, you're teasing me. You will, won't you? Aren't I your husband—?

A knock at the outside door.

NORA: *(startled)* What's that?

HELMER: *(going toward the hall)* Who is it?

145 RANK: *(outside)* It's me. May I come in a moment?

HELMER: *(with quiet irritation)* Oh, what does he want now? *(Aloud.)* Hold on. *(Goes and opens the door.)* Oh, how nice that you didn't just pass us by!

RANK: I thought I heard your voice, and then I wanted so badly to have a look in. *(Lightly glancing about.)* Ah, me, these old familiar haunts. You have it snug and cozy in here, you two.

HELMER: You seemed to be having it pretty cozy upstairs, too.

RANK: Absolutely. Why shouldn't I? Why not take in everything in life? As much as you can, anyway, and as long as you can. The wine was superb—

150 HELMER: The champagne especially.

RANK: You noticed that too? It's amazing how much I could guzzle down.

NORA: Torvald also drank a lot of champagne this evening.

RANK: Oh?

NORA: Yes, and that always makes him so entertaining.

155 RANK: Well, why shouldn't one have a pleasant evening after a well spent day?

HELMER: Well spent? I'm afraid I can't claim that.

RANK: *(slapping him on the back)* But I can, you see!
NORA: Dr. Rank, you must have done some scientific research today.
RANK: Quite so.
HELMER: Come now—little Nora talking about scientific research!
NORA: And can I congratulate you on the results?
RANK: Indeed you may.
NORA: Then they were good?
RANK: The best possible for both doctor and patient—certainty.
NORA: *(quickly and searchingly)* Certainty?
RANK: Complete certainty. So don't I owe myself a gay evening afterwards?
NORA: Yes, you're right, Dr. Rank.
HELMER: I'm with you—just so long as you don't have to suffer for it in the morning.
RANK: Well, one never gets something for nothing in life.
NORA: Dr. Rank—are you very fond of masquerade parties?
RANK: Yes, if there's a good array of odd disguises—
NORA: Tell me, what should we two go as at the next masquerade?
HELMER: You little featherhead—already thinking of the next!
RANK: We two? I'll tell you what: you must go as Charmed Life—
HELMER: Yes, but find a costume for *that!*
RANK: Your wife can appear just as she looks every day.
HELMER: That was nicely put. But don't you know what you're going to be?
RANK: Yes, Helmer, I've made up my mind.
HELMER: Well?
RANK: At the next masquerade I'm going to be invisible.
HELMER: That's a funny idea.
RANK: They say there's a hat—black, huge—have you never heard of the hat that makes you invisible? You put it on, and then no one on earth can see you.
HELMER: *(suppressing a smile)* Ah, of course.
RANK: But I'm quite forgetting what I came for. Helmer, give me a cigar, one of the dark Havanas.
HELMER: With the greatest of pleasure. *(Holds out his case.)*
RANK: Thanks. *(Takes one and cuts off the tip.)*
NORA: *(striking a match)* Let me give you a light.
RANK: Thank you. *(She holds the match for him; he lights the cigar.)* And now good-bye.
HELMER: Good-bye, good-bye, old friend.
NORA: Sleep well, Doctor.
RANK: Thanks for that wish.
NORA: Wish me the same.
RANK: You? All right, if you like—Sleep well. And thanks for the light. *(He nods to them both and leaves.)*
HELMER: *(his voice subdued)* He's been drinking heavily.

195 NORA: *(absently)* Could be. *(Helmer takes his keys from his pocket and goes out in the hall.)* Torvald—what are you after?
HELMER: Got to empty the mailbox; it's nearly full. There won't be room for the morning papers.
NORA: Are you working tonight?
HELMER: You know I'm not. Why—what's this? Someone's been at the lock.
NORA: At the lock—?
200 HELMER: Yes, I'm positive. What do you suppose—? I can't imagine one of the maids—? Here's a broken hairpin. Nora, it's yours—
NORA: *(quickly)* Then it must be the children—
HELMER: You'd better break them of that. Hm, hm—well, opened it after all. *(Takes the contents out and calls into the kitchen.)* Helene! Helene, would you put out the lamp in the hall. *(He returns to the room, shutting the hall door, then displays the handful of mail.)* Look how it's piled up. *(Sorting through them.)* Now what's this?
NORA: *(at the window)* The letter! Oh, Torvald, no!
HELMER: Two calling cards—from Rank.
205 NORA: From Dr. Rank?
HELMER: *(examining them)* "Dr. Rank, Consulting Physician." They were on top. He must have dropped them in as he left.
NORA: Is there anything on them?
HELMER: There's a black cross over the name. See? That's a gruesome notion. He could almost be announcing his own death.
NORA: That's just what he's doing.
210 HELMER: What! You've heard something? Something he's told you?
NORA: Yes. That when those cards came, he'd be taking his leave of us. He'll shut himself in now and die.
HELMER: Ah, my poor friend! Of course I knew he wouldn't be here much longer. But so soon—And then to hide himself away like a wounded animal.
NORA: If it has to happen, then it's best it happens in silence—don't you think so, Torvald?
HELMER: *(pacing up and down)* He'd grown right into our lives. I simply can't imagine him gone. He with his suffering and loneliness—like a dark cloud setting off our sunlit happiness. Well, maybe it's best this way. For him, at least. *(Standing still.)* And maybe for us too, Nora. Now we're thrown back on each other, completely. *(Embracing her.)* Oh you, my darling wife, how can I hold you close enough? You know what, Nora—time and again I've wished you were in some terrible danger, just so I could stake my life and soul and everything, for your sake.
215 NORA: *(tearing herself away, her voice firm and decisive)* Now you must read your mail, Torvald.
HELMER: No, no, not tonight. I want to stay with you, dearest.
NORA: With a dying friend on your mind?

HELMER: You're right. We've both had a shock. There's ugliness between us—these thoughts of death and corruption. We'll have to get free of them first. Until then—we'll stay apart.
NORA: *(clinging about his neck)* Torvald—good night! Good night!
220 HELMER: *(kissing her on the cheek)* Good night, little songbird. Sleep well, Nora. I'll be reading my mail now. *(He takes the letters into his room and shuts the door after him.)*
NORA: *(with bewildered glances, groping about, seizing Helmer's domino, throwing it around her, and speaking in short, hoarse, broken whispers)* Never see him again. Never, never. *(Putting her shawl over her head.)* Never see the children either—them, too. Never, never. Oh, the freezing black water! The depths—down—Oh, I wish it were over— He has it now; he's reading it—now. Oh no, no, not yet. Torvald, good-bye, you and the children—*(She starts for the hall; as she does, Helmer throws open his door and stands with an open letter in his hand.)*
HELMER: Nora!
NORA: *(screams)* Oh—!
HELMER: What is this? You know what's in this letter?
225 NORA: Yes, I know. Let me go! Let me out!
HELMER: *(holding her back)* Where are you going?
NORA: *(struggling to break loose)* You can't save me, Torvald!
HELMER: *(slumping back)* True! Then it's true what he writes? How horrible! No, no, it's impossible—it can't be true.
NORA: It *is* true. I've loved you more than all this world.
230 HELMER: Ah, none of your slippery tricks.
NORA: *(taking one step toward him)* Torvald—!
HELMER: What *is* this you've blundered into!
NORA: Just let me loose. You're not going to suffer for my sake. You're not going to take on my guilt.
HELMER: No more playacting. *(Locks the hall door.)* You stay right here and give me a reckoning. You understand what you've done? Answer! You understand?
235 NORA: *(looking squarely at him, her face hardening)* Yes. I'm beginning to understand everything now.
HELMER: *(striding about)* Oh, what an awful awakening! In all these eight years—she who was my pride and joy—a hypocrite, a liar— worse, worse—a criminal! How infinitely disgusting it all is! The shame! *(Nora says nothing and goes on looking straight at him. He stops in front of her.)* I should have suspected something of the kind. I should have known. All your father's flimsy values—Be still! All your father's flimsy values have come out in you. No religion, no morals, no sense of duty—Oh, how I'm punished for letting him off! I did it for your sake, and you repay me like this.
NORA: Yes, like this.
HELMER: Now you've wrecked all my happiness—ruined my whole future. Oh, it's awful to think of. I'm in a cheap little grafter's hands; he can do anything he wants with me, ask for anything,

play with me like a puppet—and I can't breathe a word. I'll be swept down miserably into the depths on account of a featherbrained woman.

NORA: When I'm gone from this world, you'll be free.

HELMER: Oh, quit posing. Your father had a mess of those speeches too. What good would that ever do me if you were gone from this world, as you say? Not the slightest. He can still make the whole thing known; and if he does, I could be falsely suspected as your accomplice. They might even think that I was behind it—that I put you up to it. And all that I can thank you for—you that I've coddled the whole of our marriage. Can you see now what you've done to me?

NORA: *(icily calm)* Yes.

HELMER: It's so incredible, I just can't grasp it. But we'll have to patch up whatever we can. Take off the shawl. I said, take if off! I've got to appease him somehow or other. The thing has to be hushed up at any cost. And as for you and me, it's got to seem like everything between us is just as it was—to the outside world, that is. You'll go right on living in this house, of course. But you can't be allowed to bring up the children; I don't dare trust you with them—Oh, to have to say this to someone I've loved so much! Well, that's done with. From now on happiness doesn't matter; all that matters is saving the bits and pieces, the appearance—*(The doorbell rings. Helmer starts.)* What's that? And so late. Maybe the worst—? You think he'd—? Hide, Nora! Say you're sick. *(Nora remains standing motionless. Helmer goes and opens the door.)*

MAID: *(half dressed, in the hall)* A letter for Mrs. Helmer.

HELMER: I'll take it. *(Snatches the letter and shuts the door.)* Yes, it's from him. You don't get it; I'm reading it myself.

NORA: Then read it.

HELMER: *(by the lamp)* I hardly dare. We may be ruined, you and I. But—I've got to know. *(Rips open the letter, skims through a few lines, glances at an enclosure, then cries out joyfully.)* Nora! *(Nora looks inquiringly at him.)* Nora! Wait—better check it again—Yes, yes, it's true. I'm saved. Nora, I'm saved!

NORA: And I?

HELMER: You too, of course. We're both saved, both of us. Look. He's sent back your note. He says he's sorry and ashamed—that a happy development in his life—oh, who cares what he says! Nora, we're saved! No one can hurt you. Oh, Nora, Nora—but first, this ugliness all has to go. Let me see—*(Takes a look at the note.)* No, I don't want to see it; I want the whole thing to fade like a dream. *(Tears the note and both letters to pieces, throws them into the stove and watches them burn.)* There—now there's nothing left—He wrote that since Christmas Eve you—Oh, they must have been three terrible days for you, Nora.

NORA: I fought a hard fight.

HELMER: And suffered pain and saw no escape but—No, we're not going to dwell on anything unpleasant. We'll just be grateful and keep on repeating: it's over now, it's over! You hear me, Nora? You don't seem to realize—it's over. What's it mean—that frozen look? Oh, poor little Nora, I understand. You can't believe I've forgiven you. But I have, Nora; I swear I have. I know that what you did, you did out of love for me.

NORA: That's true.

HELMER: You loved me the way a wife ought to love her husband. It's simply the means that you couldn't judge. But you think I love you any the less for not knowing how to handle your affairs? No, no—just lean on me; I'll guide you and teach you. I wouldn't be a man if this feminine helplessness didn't make you twice as attractive to me. You mustn't mind those sharp words I said—that was all in the first confusion of thinking my world had collapsed. I've forgiven you, Nora; I swear I've forgiven you.

NORA: My thanks for your forgiveness. *(She goes out through the door, right.)*

HELMER: No, wait—*(Peers in.)* What are you doing in there?

NORA: *(inside)* Getting out of my costume.

HELMER: *(by the open door)* Yes, do that. Try to calm yourself and collect your thoughts again, my frightened little songbird. You can rest easy now; I've got wide wings to shelter you with. *(Walking about close by the door.)* How snug and nice our home is, Nora. You're safe here; I'll keep you like a hunted dove I've rescued out of a hawk's claws. I'll bring peace to your poor, shuddering heart. Gradually it'll happen, Nora; you'll see. Tomorrow all this will look different to you; then everything will be as it was. I won't have to go on repeating I forgive you; you'll feel it for yourself. How can you imagine I'd ever conceivably want to disown you—or even blame you in any way? Ah, you don't know a man's heart, Nora. For a man there's something indescribably sweet and satisfying in knowing he's forgiven his wife—and forgiven her out of a full and open heart. It's as if she belongs to him in two ways now: in a sense he's given her fresh into the world again, and she's become his wife and his child as well. From now on that's what you'll be to me—you little, bewildered, helpless thing. Don't be afraid of anything, Nora; just open your heart to me, and I'll be conscience and will to you both—*(Nora enters in her regular clothes.)* What's this? Not in bed? You've changed your dress?

NORA: Yes, Torvald, I've changed my dress.

HELMER: But why now, so late?

NORA: Tonight I'm not sleeping.

HELMER: But Nora dear—

NORA: *(looking at her watch)* It's still not so very late. Sit down, Torvald; we have a lot to talk over. *(She sits at one side of the table.)*

HELMER: Nora—what is this? That hard expression—

NORA: Sit down. This'll take some time. I have a lot to say.
HELMER: *(sitting at the table directly opposite her)* You worry me, Nora. And I don't understand you.
265 NORA: No, that's exactly it. You don't understand me. And I've never understood you either—until tonight. No, don't interrupt. You can just listen to what I say. We're closing out accounts, Torvald.
HELMER: How do you mean that?
NORA: *(after a short pause)* Doesn't anything strike you about our sitting here like this?
HELMER: What's that?
NORA: We've been married now eight years. Doesn't it occur to you that this is the first time we two, you and I, man and wife, have ever talked seriously together?
270 HELMER: What do you mean—seriously?
NORA: In eight whole years—longer even—right from our first acquaintance, we've never exchanged a serious word on any serious thing.
HELMER: You mean I should constantly go and involve you in problems you couldn't possibly help me with?
NORA: I'm not talking of problems. I'm saying that we've never sat down seriously together and tried to get to the bottom of anything.
HELMER: But dearest, what good would that ever do you?
275 NORA: That's the point right there: you've never understood me. I've been wronged greatly, Torvald—first by Papa, and then by you.
HELMER: What! By us—the two people who've loved you more than anyone else?
NORA: *(shaking her head)* You never loved me. You've thought it fun to be in love with me, that's all.
HELMER: Nora, what a thing to say!
NORA: Yes, it's true now, Torvald. When I lived at home with Papa, he told me all his opinions, so I had the same ones too; or if they were different I hid them, since he wouldn't have cared for that. He used to call me his doll-child, and he played with me the way I played with my dolls. Then I came into your house—
280 HELMER: How can you speak of our marriage like that?
NORA: *(unperturbed)* I mean, then I went from Papa's hands into yours. You arranged everything to your own taste, and so I got the same taste as you—or I pretended to; I can't remember. I guess a little of both, first one, then the other. Now when I look back, it seems as if I'd lived here like a beggar—just from hand to mouth. I've lived by doing tricks for you, Torvald. But that's the way you wanted it. It's a great sin what you and Papa did to me. You're to blame that nothing's become of me.
HELMER: Nora, how unfair and ungrateful you are! Haven't you been happy here?
NORA: No, never. I thought so—but I never have.
HELMER: Not—not happy!

285 NORA: No, only lighthearted. And you've always been so kind to me. But our home's been nothing but a playpen. I've been your doll-wife here, just as at home I was Papa's doll-child. And in turn the children have been my dolls. I thought it was fun when you played with me, just as they thought it fun when I played with them. That's been our marriage, Torvald.
HELMER: There's some truth in what you're saying—under all the raving exaggeration. But it'll all be different after this. Playtime's over; now for the schooling.
NORA: Whose schooling—mine or the children's?
HELMER: Both yours and the children's, dearest.
NORA: Oh, Torvald, you're not the man to teach me to be a good wife to you.
290 HELMER: And you can say that?
NORA: And I—how am I equipped to bring up children?
HELMER: Nora!
NORA: Didn't you say a moment ago that that was no job to trust me with?
HELMER: In a flare of temper! Why fasten on that?
295 NORA: Yes, but you were so very right. I'm not up to the job. There's another job I have to do first. I have to try to educate myself. You can't help me with that. I've got to do it alone. And that's why I'm leaving you now.
HELMER: *(jumping up)* What's that?
NORA: I have to stand completely alone, if I'm ever going to discover myself and the world out there. So I can't go on living with you.
HELMER: Nora, Nora!
NORA: I want to leave right away. Kristine should put me up for the night—
300 HELMER: You're insane! You've no right! I forbid you!
NORA: From here on, there's no use forbidding me anything. I'll take with me whatever is mine. I don't want a thing from you, either now or later.
HELMER: What kind of madness is this!
NORA: Tomorrow I'm going home—I mean, home where I came from. It'll be easier up there to find something to do.
HELMER: Oh, you blind, incompetent child!
305 NORA: I must learn to be competent, Torvald.
HELMER: Abandon your home, your husband, your children! And you're not even thinking what people will say.
NORA: I can't be concerned about that. I only know how essential this is.
HELMER: Oh, it's outrageous. So you'll run out like this on your most sacred vows.
NORA: What do you think are my most sacred vows?
310 HELMER: And I have to tell you that! Aren't they your duties to your husband and children?

NORA: I have other duties equally sacred.
HELMER: That isn't true. What duties are they?
NORA: Duties to myself.
HELMER: Before all else, you're a wife and a mother.
315 NORA: I don't believe in that any more. I believe that, before all else, I'm a human being, no less than you—or anyway, I ought to try to become one. I know the majority thinks you're right, Torvald, and plenty of books agree with you, too. But I can't go on believing what the majority says, or what's written in books. I have to think over these things myself and try to understand them.
HELMER: Why can't you understand your place in your own home? On a point like that, isn't there one everlasting guide you can turn to? Where's your religion?
NORA: Oh, Torvald, I'm really not sure what religion is.
HELMER: What—?
NORA: I only know what the minister said when I was confirmed. He told me religion was this thing and that. When I get clear and away by myself, I'll go into that problem too. I'll see if what the minister said was right, or, in any case, if it's right for me.
320 HELMER: A young woman your age shouldn't talk like that. If religion can't move you, I can try to rouse your conscience. You do have some moral feeling? Or, tell me—has that gone too?
NORA: It's not easy to answer that, Torvald. I simply don't know. I'm all confused about these things. I just know I see them so differently from you. I find out, for one thing, that the law's not at all what I'd thought—but I can't get it through my head that the law is fair. A woman hasn't a right to protect her dying father or save her husband's life! I can't believe that.
HELMER: You talk like a child. You don't know anything of the world you live in.
NORA: No, I don't. But now I'll begin to learn for myself. I'll try to discover who's right, the world or I.
HELMER: Nora, you're sick; you've got a fever. I almost think you're out of your head.
325 NORA: I've never felt more clearheaded and sure in my life.
HELMER: And—clearheaded and sure—you're leaving your husband and children?
NORA: Yes.
HELMER: Then there's only one possible reason.
NORA: What?
330 HELMER: You no longer love me.
NORA: No. That's exactly it.
HELMER: Nora! You can't be serious!
NORA: Oh, this is so hard, Torvald—you've been so kind to me always. But I can't help it. I don't love you any more.
HELMER: *(struggling for composure)* Are you also clearheaded and sure about that?

335 **NORA:** Yes, completely. That's why I can't go on staying here.
HELMER: Can you tell me what I did to lose your love?
NORA: Yes, I can tell you. It was this evening when the miraculous thing didn't come—then I knew you weren't the man I'd imagined.
HELMER: Be more explicit; I don't follow you.
NORA: I've waited now so patiently eight long years—for, my Lord, I know miracles don't come every day. Then this crisis broke over me, and such a certainty filled me: *now* the miraculous event would occur. While Krogstad's letter was lying out there, I never for an instant dreamed that you could give in to his terms. I was so utterly sure you'd say to him: go on, tell your tale to the whole wide world. And when he'd done that—
340 **HELMER:** Yes, what then? When I'd delivered my own wife into shame and disgrace—!
NORA: When he'd done that, I was so utterly sure that you'd step forward, take the blame on yourself and say: I am the guilty one.
HELMER: Nora—!
NORA: You're thinking I'd never accept such a sacrifice from you? No, of course not. But what good would my protests be against you? That was the miracle I was waiting for, in terror and hope. And to stave that off, I would have taken my life.
HELMER: I'd gladly work for you day and night, Nora—and take on pain and deprivation. But there's no one who gives up honor for love.
345 **NORA:** Millions of women have done just that.
HELMER: Oh, you think and talk like a silly child.
NORA: Perhaps. But you neither think nor talk like the man I could join myself to. When your big fright was over—and it wasn't from any threat against me, only for what might damage you—when all the danger was past, for you it was just as if nothing had happened. I was exactly the same, your little lark, your doll, that you'd have to handle with double care now that I'd turned out so brittle and frail. *(Gets up.)* Torvald—in that instant it dawned on me that for eight years I've been living here with a stranger, and that I'd even conceived three children—oh, I can't stand the thought of it! I could tear myself to bits.
HELMER: *(heavily)* I see. There's a gulf that's opened between us—that's clear. Oh, but Nora, can't we bridge it somehow?
NORA: The way I am now, I'm no wife for you.
350 **HELMER:** I have the strength to make myself over.
NORA: Maybe—if your doll gets taken away.
HELMER: But to part! To part from you! No, Nora, no—I can't imagine it.
NORA: *(going out, right)* All the more reason why it has to be. *(She reenters with her coat and a small overnight bag, which she puts on a chair by the table.)*
HELMER: Nora, Nora, not now! Wait till tomorrow.

355 **NORA:** I can't spend the night in a strange man's room.
HELMER: But couldn't we live here like brother and sister—
NORA: You know very well how long that would last. *(Throws her shawl about her.)* Good-bye, Torvald. I won't look in on the children. I know they're in better hands than mine. The way I am now, I'm no use to them.
HELMER: But someday, Nora—someday—?
NORA: How can I tell? I haven't the least idea what'll become of me.
360 **HELMER:** But you're my wife, now and wherever you go.
NORA: Listen, Torvald—I've heard that when a wife deserts her husband's house just as I'm doing, then the law frees him from all responsibility. In any case, I'm freeing you from being responsible. Don't feel yourself bound, any more than I will. There has to be absolute freedom for us both. Here, take your ring back. Give me mine.
HELMER: That too?
NORA: That too.
HELMER: There it is.
365 **NORA:** Good. Well, now it's all over. I'm putting the keys here. The maids know all about keeping up the house—better than I do. Tomorrow, after I've left town, Kristine will stop by to pack up everything that's mine from home. I'd like those things shipped up to me.
HELMER: Over! All over! Nora, won't you ever think about me?
NORA: I'm sure I'll think of you often, and about the children and the house here.
HELMER: May I write you?
NORA: No—never. You're not to do that.
370 **HELMER:** Oh, but let me send you—
NORA: Nothing. Nothing.
HELMER: Or help you if you need it.
NORA: No. I accept nothing from strangers.
HELMER: Nora—can I never be more than a stranger to you?
375 **NORA:** *(picking up the overnight bag)* Ah, Torvald—it would take the greatest miracle of all—
HELMER: Tell me the greatest miracle!
NORA: You and I both would have to transform ourselves to the point that—Oh, Torvald, I've stopped believing in miracles.
HELMER: But I'll believe. Tell me! Transform ourselves to the point that—?
NORA: That our living together could be a true marriage. *(She goes out down the hall.)*
380 **HELMER:** *(sinks down on a chair by the door, face buried in his hands)* Nora! Nora! *(Looking about and rising.)* Empty. She's gone. *(A sudden hope leaps in him.)* The greatest miracle—?

From below, the sound of a door slamming shut.

Reading and Reacting

1. What is your attitude toward Nora at the beginning of the play? How does your attitude toward her change as the play progresses? What actions and/or lines of dialogue change your assessment of her?
2. List the key events that occur before the play begins. How do we learn of each event?
3. In act 1, how do the various references to macaroons in the stage directions reinforce plot developments?
4. Explain the role of each of the following in advancing the play's action: the Christmas tree, the locked mailbox, the telegram Dr. Rank receives, Dr. Rank's calling cards.
5. In act 2, Torvald says, "Whatever comes, you'll see: when it really counts, I have strength and courage enough as a man to take on the whole weight myself." How does this statement influence Nora's subsequent actions?
6. How do the upcoming costume party and Nora's dance influence the development of the play's plot? Where does the play's climax occur?
7. Explain how the following foreshadow events that will occur later in the play: Torvald's comments about Krogstad's children (act 1); Torvald's attitude toward Nora's father (act 2); Krogstad's suggestions about suicide (act 2).
8. In addition to the play's main plot—which concerns the blackmail of Nora by Krogstad and her attempts to keep her crime secret from Torvald—the play contains several subplots, some of which have developed before the play begins and some of which unfold alongside the main plot. Identify these subplots. How do they advance the themes of survival, debt, sacrifice, and duty that run through the play?
9. Is Kristine Linde essential to the play? How might the play be different without her?
10. Is Mrs. Linde as much of a "modern woman" as Nora? Is she actually *more* of a modern woman? Explain.
11. Do you think *A Doll House* is primarily about the struggle between the needs of the individual and the needs of society, or about the conflict between women's roles in the family and in the larger society? Explain.
12. **Journal Entry** Nora makes a drastic decision at the end of the play. Do you think she overreacts? What other options does she have? What other options might she have today?

Related Works: "The Story of an Hour" (p. 43), "The Rocking-Horse Winner" (p. 243), "Girl" (p. 266), "Barbie Doll" (p. 541)

◆ Writing Suggestions: Plot

1. Central to the plots of both *Trifles* and *A Doll House* is a woman who commits a crime. Compare and contrast the reactions of the two plays' other characters, particularly each woman's friends, to her crime.
2. Write an essay in which you compare the influence of Nora's father on the plot of *A Doll House* to the role of an absent father in another play in this text, such as *The Glass Menagerie* (p. 938) or *Hamlet* (p. 681).
3. In both *Trifles* and *A Doll House,* the plot depends to some extent on the fact that male characters misjudge—and perhaps underestimate—women. Write an essay in which you compare and contrast the attitudes the men in these plays hold toward women, the ways in which they reveal these attitudes, and the ways in which the women react.
4. Both plays in this chapter deal with troubled marriages. Suppose you were a marriage counselor and one of the couples came to you for help. What would you say to them? Write an essay in which you give the troubled couple advice for saving their marriage.
5. Write a monologue for Mrs. Wright, including everything she might like to tell the other two women about her married life?

CHAPTER 20

Character

In Tennessee Williams's 1945 play *The Glass Menagerie* (p. 938) the protagonist, Tom Wingfield, functions as the play's narrator. Stepping out of his role as a character and speaking directly to the audience, he directs the play's action, music, lighting, and other elements. In addition, he summarizes characters' actions, explains their motivation, and discusses the significance of their behavior in the context of the play—commenting on his own character's actions as well. As narrator, Tom also presents useful background information about the characters. For instance, when he introduces his coworker, Jim, he prepares readers for Jim's entrance and helps them to understand his subsequent actions:

> In high school Jim was a hero. He had tremendous Irish good nature and vitality with the scrubbed and polished look of white chinaware. He seemed to move in a continual spotlight. [. . .] But Jim apparently ran into more interference after his graduation. [. . .] His speed had definitely slowed. Six years after he left high school he was holding a job that wasn't much better than mine.

Most plays, however, do not include narrators who present background. Instead, readers learn about characters from their own words and from comments by others about them, as well as from the characters' actions and from the playwright's stage directions. At a performance, the audience has the added advantage of seeing the actors' interpretations of the characters.

Characters in plays, like characters in novels and short stories, may be **round** or **flat**, **static** or **dynamic**. Generally speaking, major characters are likely to be round, whereas minor characters are likely to be flat. Through the language and the actions of the characters, audiences learn whether the characters are multidimensional, skimpily developed, or perhaps merely **foils**, players whose main purpose is to shed light on more important characters. Audiences also learn about the emotions, attitudes, and values that help to shape the characters—their hopes and fears, their strengths and weaknesses. In addition, by comparing characters' early words and actions with later ones, audiences learn from the play whether or not characters grow and change emotionally.

Characters' Words

◊ ◊ ◊

Characters' words reveal the most about their attitudes, feelings, beliefs, and values. Sometimes information is communicated (to other characters as well as to the audience) in a **monologue**—an extended speech by one character. This device is used with great success in August Strindberg's *The Stronger*. A **soliloquy**—a monologue revealing a character's thoughts and feelings, directed at the audience and presumed not to be heard by other characters—can also convey information about a character. For example, Hamlet's well-known soliloquy that begins "To be or not to be" eloquently communicates his distraught mental state—his resentment of his mother and uncle, his confusion about what course of action to take, his suicidal thoughts. Finally, **dialogue**—an exchange of words between two characters—can reveal misunderstanding or conflict between them, or it can show their agreement, mutual support, or similar beliefs.

In Henrik Ibsen's *A Doll House* (p. 599), dialogue reveals a good deal about the characters. Nora Helmer, the spoiled young wife, has broken the law and kept her crime secret from her husband. Through her words, we learn about her motivation, her emotions, and her reactions to other characters and to her potentially dangerous situation. We learn, for instance, that she is flirtatious—"If your little squirrel begged you, with all her heart and soul [. . .]" (act 2)—and that she is childishly unrealistic about the consequences of her actions. When her husband, Torvald, asks what she would do if he was seriously injured, leaving her in debt, she says, "If anything so awful happened, then it just wouldn't matter if I had debts or not" (act 1). When Torvald presses, "Well, but the people I'd borrowed from?" she dismisses them: "Them? Who cares about them! They're strangers." As the play progresses, Nora's lack of understanding of the power of the law becomes more and more significant as she struggles with her moral and ethical dilemma.

The inability of both Nora and Torvald to confront ugly truths is also revealed through their words. When, in act 1, Nora tells Krogstad, her blackmailer, that his revealing her secret could expose her to "the most horrible unpleasantness," he responds, "Only unpleasantness?" Yet later on, in act 3, Torvald uses the same word, fastidiously dismissing the horror with, "No, we're not going to dwell on anything unpleasant."

The ease with which Torvald is able to dismiss his dying friend Dr. Rank in act 3 ("He with his suffering and loneliness—like a dark cloud setting off our sunlit happiness. Well, maybe it's best this way.") exposes his egocentrism and foreshadows the lack of support he will give

Nora immediately thereafter. Especially revealing is his use of *I* and *my* and *me*, which convey his self-centeredness:

> Now you've wrecked all my happiness—ruined my whole future. Oh, it's awful to think of. I'm in a cheap little grafter's hands; he can do anything he wants with me, ask for anything, play with me like a puppet—and I can't breathe a word. I'll be swept down miserably into the depths on account of a featherbrained woman.

Just as Torvald's words reveal that he has not been changed by the play's events, Nora's words show that she has changed significantly. Her dialogue near the end of act 3 shows that she has become a responsible, determined woman—one who understands her situation and her options and is no longer blithely oblivious to her duties. When she says, "I've never felt more clearheaded and sure in my life," she is calm and decisive; when she says, "Our home's been nothing but a playpen. I've been your doll-wife here, just as at home I was Papa's doll-child," she reveals her newly found self-awareness. When she confronts her husband, she displays complete honesty—perhaps for the first time in her relationship with Torvald.

Sometimes what other characters say to or about a character can reveal more to an audience than the character's own words. (Keep in mind, however, that you should measure the accuracy of characters' comments against what you already know about them.) For instance, in act 2 of *A Doll House*, when the dying Dr. Rank says, apparently without malice, "[Torvald] Helmer with his sensitivity has such a sharp distaste for anything ugly," readers not only think ill of the man who is too "sensitive" to visit his sick friend but also question his ability to withstand situations that may be emotionally or morally "ugly" as well.

When a character is offstage for much (or even all) of the action, the audience must rely on other characters' assessments of the absent character. In Susan Glaspell's *Trifles* (p. 586) the play's focus is on an absent character, Minnie Wright, who is described solely through other characters' remarks. The evidence suggests that Mrs. Wright has killed her husband, and only Mrs. Hale's and Mrs. Peters's comments about Mrs. Wright's dreary life can delineate her character and suggest a likely motive for the murder. Although we never meet Mrs. Wright, we learn essential information from the other women: that as a young girl she liked to sing and that more recently she was so distraught about the lack of beauty in her life that even her sewing revealed her distress. Similarly, the father in *The Glass Menagerie* never appears (and therefore never speaks), but the play's other characters describe him as "A telephone man who—fell in love with long-distance" (scene 6)—the absent husband and father who symbolizes abandonment and instability to Laura and Amanda and the possibility of freedom and escape to Tom.

Whether they are in the form of a monologue, a soliloquy, or dialogue, and whether they reveal information about the character who is speaking or about someone else, a character's words are always revealing. Explicitly or implicitly, they convey a character's nature, attitudes, and relationships with other characters. A character may, for instance, use learned words, foreign words, elaborate figurative language, irony or sarcasm, regionalisms, slang, jargon, clichés, or profanity. Words can also be used to indicate tone—for example, to express irony. Any of these uses of language may communicate vital information to the audience about a character's background, attitudes, and motivation. And, of course, a character's language may change as a play progresses, and this change too may be revealing.

FORMAL AND INFORMAL LANGUAGE

One character in a dramatic work may be very formal and aloof, using absolutely correct grammar, a learned vocabulary, and long, complex sentences; another may be informal, using conversational speech, colloquialisms, and slang. At times, two characters with different levels of language may be set in opposition for dramatic effect, as they are in Irish playwright George Bernard Shaw's 1912 play *Pygmalion*, which updates the ancient Greek myth of a sculptor who creates (and falls in love with) a statue of a woman. In Shaw's version, a linguistics professor sets out to teach "proper" speech and manners to a lowly flower seller. Throughout the play, the contrasting language of Henry Higgins, the professor, and Eliza Doolittle, the flower seller, indicates their differing social standing:

> **LIZA:** I ain't got no mother. Her that turned me out was my sixth stepmother. But I done without them. And I'm a good girl, I am.
>
> **HIGGINS:** Very well, then, what on earth is all this fuss about?

A character's accent or dialect may also be significant. In comedies of manners, for instance, rustic or provincial characters, identified by their speech, were often objects of humor. In *Pygmalion* Eliza Doolittle uses cockney dialect, the dialect spoken in the East End of London. At first, her colorful, distinctive language (complete with expressions like *Nah-ow, garn,* and *ah-ah-ah-ow-ow-ow-oo*) and her nonstandard grammatical constructions make her an object of ridicule; later, the transformation of her speech parallels the dramatic changes in her character.

PLAIN AND ELABORATE STYLE

A character's speech can be simple and straightforward or complex and convoluted; it can be plain and unadorned, or it can be embellished with elaborate **figures of speech.** The relative complexity or lack of complexity of a character's speech can have different effects on the audience. For example, a character whose language is simple and unsophisticated may seem to be unintelligent, unenlightened, gullible, or naive—especially if he or she also uses slang, dialect, or colloquial expressions. Conversely, a character's plain, down-to-earth language can convey common sense or intelligence. Plain language can also be quite emotionally powerful. Thus, Willy Loman's speech in act 2 of *Death of a Salesman* (p. 782), about an eighty-four-year-old salesman named Dave Singleman, moves the audience with its sincerity and directness:

> Do you know? When he died—and by the way he died the death of a salesman, in his green velvet slippers in the smoker of the New York, New Haven and Hartford, going into Boston—when he died, hundreds of salesmen and buyers were at his funeral. Things were sad on a lotta trains for months after that.

Like plain speech, elaborate language may have different effects in different contexts. Sometimes, use of figurative language can make a character seem to have depth and insight and analytical skills absent in other characters. In the following excerpt from a soliloquy from *Hamlet*, for example, complex language reveals the depth of Hamlet's anguished self-analysis:

> **HAMLET:** O, that this too too solid flesh would melt,
>   Thaw, and resolve itself into a dew!
>   Or that the Everlasting had not fix'd
>   His canon 'gainst self-slaughter! O God! O God!
>   How weary, stale, flat, and unprofitable
>   Seem to me all the uses of this world!
>   Fie on't, O fie, 'tis an unweeded garden,
>   That grows to seed [. . .]. (1.2.129–36)

In the preceding lines, Hamlet compares the world to a garden gone to seed. His use of imagery and figurative language vividly communicates his feelings about the world and his internal struggle against the temptation to commit suicide.

Sometimes, however, elaborate figurative language may make a character seem pompous or untrustworthy. In the following passages from Shakespeare's *King Lear*, for example, Goneril and Regan, the deceitful daughters, use elaborate language to conceal their true feelings from their father, King Lear. However, Cordelia—the loyal, loving daughter—uses simple, straightforward prose that suggests her sincerity and lack of artifice. Compare the three speeches:

> **GONERIL:** Sir, I love you more than words can wield the matter;
>   Dearer than eyesight, space, and liberty;

Beyond what can be valued, rich or rare;
No less than life, with grace, health, beauty, honour;
As much as child e'er lov'd, or father found;
A love that makes breath poor, and speech unable.
Beyond all manner of so much I love you. (1.1.56–62)

REGAN: Sir, I am made
Of the selfsame metal that my sister is,
And prize me at her worth. In my true heart
I find she names my very deed of love;
Only she comes too short, that I profess
Myself an enemy to all other joys
Which the most precious square of sense possesses,
And find I am alone felicitate
In your dear Highness' love. (1.1.70–78)

CORDELIA: Unhappy that I am, I cannot heave
My heart into my mouth. I love your Majesty
According to my bond; no more no less. (1.1.93–95)

Cordelia's unwillingness, even when she is prodded by Lear, to exaggerate her feelings or misrepresent her love through inflated language shows the audience her honesty and nobility. The contrast between her language and that of her sisters makes their very different motives clear to the audience.

TONE

Tone reveals a character's mood or attitude. Tone can be flat or hysterical, bitter or accepting, affectionate or aloof, anxious or calm. Contrasts in tone can indicate differences in outlook or emotional state between two characters; changes in tone from one point in the play to another can suggest corresponding changes within a character. At the end of *A Doll House*, for instance, Nora is resigned to what she must do, and her language is appropriately controlled. Her husband, however, is desperate to change her mind, and his language reflects this desperation. The following exchanges from act 3 of the play illustrate their contrasting emotional states:

HELMER: But to part! To part from you! No, Nora, no—I can't imagine it.

NORA: *(going out, right)* All the more reason why it has to be.

HELMER: Over! All over! Nora, won't you ever think about me?

NORA: I'm sure I'll think of you often, and about the children and the house here.

In earlier scenes between the two characters, Nora is emotional—at times, hysterical—and her husband is considerably more controlled. As the preceding dialogue indicates, both Nora and Torvald Helmer change drastically during the course of the play.

IRONY

Irony, a contradiction or discrepancy between two different levels of meaning, can reveal a great deal about character. **Verbal irony**—a contradiction between what a character says and what he or she means—is very important in drama, where the verbal interplay between characters carries the weight of the play. For example, when Nora and Dr. Rank discuss the latest news about his health in *A Doll House,* there is deep irony in his use of the phrase "complete certainty." Although the phrase usually suggests reassuring news, here it is meant to suggest death, and both Nora and Dr. Rank understand this.

Dramatic irony depends on the audience's knowing something that a character has not yet realized, or on one character's knowing something that other characters do not know. In some cases, dramatic irony is created by an audience's awareness of historical background or events of which characters are unaware. (Familiar with the story of Oedipus, for instance, the audience knows that the man who has caused all the problems in Thebes—the man Oedipus vows to find and take revenge on—is Oedipus himself.) In other cases, dramatic irony emerges when the audience learns something—something the characters do not yet know or comprehend—from a play's unfolding action. The central irony in *A Doll House,* for example, is that the family's "happy home" rests on a foundation of secrets, lies, and deception. Torvald does not know about the secrets, and Nora does not understand how they have poisoned her marriage. The audience, however, quickly becomes aware of the atmosphere of deceit—and aware of how it threatens the family's happiness.

Dramatic irony may also be conveyed through dialogue. Typically, dramatic irony is revealed when a character, in conversation, delivers lines that give the audience information that other characters, offstage at the time, do not know. In *A Doll House,* the audience knows—because Nora has explained her situation to Kristine—that Nora has spent the previous Christmas season hard at work, earning money to pay her secret debt. Torvald, however, remains unaware of her activities and believes her story that she was using the time to make holiday decorations, which the cat destroyed. This belief is consistent with his impression of her as an irresponsible child, yet the audience has quite a different impression of Nora. This discrepancy, one of many contradictions between the audience's view of Nora and Torvald's view of her, helps to create dramatic tension in the play.

Finally, **asides** can create dramatic irony by undercutting dialogue, providing ironic contrast between what the characters on stage know and what the audience knows. In Anton Chekhov's *The Brute* (p. 668), for example, the audience knows that Mr. Smirnov is succumbing to Mrs. Popov's charms because he says, in an aside, "My god, what eyes she has! They're setting me on fire." Mrs. Popov, however, is not yet aware of his infatuation. The discrepancy between the audience's awareness and the character's adds to the play's humor.

CHARACTERS' ACTIONS

◊ ◊ ◊

Through their actions, characters convey their values and attitudes to the audience. Actions also reveal aspects of a character's personality. When Laura Wingfield, a character in *The Glass Menagerie*, hides rather than face the "gentleman caller," readers see just how shy she is; when Nora in *A Doll House* plays hide-and-seek with her children, eats forbidden macaroons, and takes childish joy in Christmas, her immaturity is apparent.

Readers also learn about characters from what they do *not* do. Thus, Nora's failure to remain in touch with her friend Kristine, who has had a hard life, reveals her selfishness, and the failure of Mrs. Peters and Mrs. Hale in *Trifles* to communicate their evidence to the sheriff indicates their support for Mrs. Wright and their understanding of what motivated her to take such drastic action.

Audiences also learn a good deal about characters by observing how they interact with other characters. In William Shakespeare's *Othello*, Iago is the embodiment of evil, and as the play's action unfolds, we discover his true nature. He reveals the secret marriage of Othello and Desdemona to her father; he schemes to arouse Othello's jealousy, making him believe Desdemona has been unfaithful with his lieutenant, Cassio; he persuades Cassio to ask Desdemona to plead his case with Othello, knowing this act will further arouse Othello's suspicions; he encourages Othello to be suspicious of Desdemona's defense of Cassio; he plants Desdemona's handkerchief in Cassio's room; and, finally, he persuades Othello to kill Desdemona and then kills his own wife, Emilia, to prevent her from exposing his role in the intrigue. As the play progresses, then, Iago's dealings with others consistently reveal him to be evil and corrupt.

STAGE DIRECTIONS

◊ ◊ ◊

When we read a play, we also read the playwright's italicized **stage directions,** the notes that concern **staging**—the scenery, props, lighting, music, sound effects, costumes, and other elements that contribute to the way the play looks and sounds to an audience (Chapter 21). In addition to commenting on staging, stage directions may supply physical details about the characters, suggesting their age, appearance, movements, gestures, relative positions, and facial expressions. These details may in turn convey additional information about characters: appearance may reveal social position or economic status, expressions may reveal attitudes, and so on. Stage directions may also indicate the manner in which a line of dialogue is to be delivered—haltingly, confidently, hesitantly, or loudly, for instance. The way a line is spoken may reveal a character to be excited, upset, angry, shy, or disappointed. Finally, stage directions may indicate *changes* in characters—for instance, a character whose speech is described as timid in early scenes may deliver lines emphatically and forcefully later on in the play.

Some plays' stage directions provide a good deal of detail about character; others do little more than list characters' names. Arthur Miller is one playwright who often chooses to provide detailed information about character through stage directions. In *Death of a Salesman*, for instance, Miller's stage directions characterize Willy Loman immediately and specifically:

> *He is past sixty years of age, dressed quietly. Even as he crosses the stage to the doorway of the house, his exhaustion is apparent. He unlocks the door, comes into the kitchen, and thankfully lets his burden down, feeling the soreness of his palms. A word-sigh escapes his lips—*

Subsequent stage directions indicate how lines are to be spoken. For example, in the play's opening lines, Willy's wife Linda calls out to him *"with some trepidation"*; Linda speaks *"very carefully, delicately,"* and Willy speaks *"with casual irritation."* These instructions to readers (and actors) are meant to suggest the strained relationship between the two characters.

George Bernard Shaw is notorious for the full character description in his stage directions. In these directions—seen by readers of the play but not heard by audiences—he communicates complex information about characters' attitudes and values, strengths and weaknesses, motivation and reactions, and relationships with other characters. In doing so Shaw functions as a narrator, explicitly communicating his own attitudes toward various characters. (Unlike the voice of Tom Wingfield in *The Glass Menagerie*, however, the voice in Shaw's stage directions is not also the voice of a character in the play; it is the voice of the playwright.) Shaw's stage directions for *Pygmalion* initially describe Eliza Doolittle as follows:

> *She is not at all an attractive person. She is perhaps eighteen, perhaps twenty, hardly older. She wears a little sailor hat of black straw that has long been exposed to the dust and soot of London and has seldom if ever been brushed. Her hair needs washing rather badly; its mousy color can hardly be natural. She wears a shoddy black coat*

that reaches nearly to her knees and is shaped to her waist. She has a brown skirt with a coarse apron. Her boots are much the worse for wear. She is no doubt as clean as she can afford to be; but compared to the ladies she is very dirty. Her features are no worse than theirs; but their condition leaves something to be desired; and she needs the services of a dentist.

Rather than providing an objective summary of the character's most notable physical attributes, Shaw injects subjective comments *("seldom if ever brushed"; "color can hardly be natural"; "no doubt as clean as she can afford to be")* that reveal his attitude toward Eliza. This initially supercilious attitude, which he shares with Professor Higgins, is tempered considerably by the end of the play, helping to make Eliza's transformation more obvious to readers than it would be if measured by her words and actions alone. By act 5 the tone of the stage directions characterizing Eliza has changed to admiration: *"Eliza enters, sunny, self-possessed, and giving a staggeringly convincing exhibition of ease of manner."*

Stage directions in *Hamlet* are not nearly as comprehensive. Characters are introduced with only the barest identifying tags: "Claudius, *King of Denmark*"; "Hamlet, *Son to the former, and nephew to the present King*"; "Gertrude, *Queen of Denmark, mother to Hamlet.*" Most stage directions do little more than chronicle the various characters' entrances and exits or specify particular physical actions: *"Enter Ghost"; "Spreads his arms"; "Ghost beckons Hamlet"; "He kneels"; "Sheathes his sword"; "Leaps in the grave."* Occasionally, stage directions specify a prop *("Puts down the skull")*; a sound effect *("A noise within")*; or a costume *("Enter the ghost in his night-gown")*. Such brevity is typical of Shakespeare's plays, in which characters are delineated almost solely by their words—and, not incidentally, by the way actors have interpreted the characters over the years. In fact, because Shakespeare's stage directions only suggest characters' gestures, physical reactions, movements, and facial expressions, actors have been left quite free to experiment, reading various interpretations into Shakespeare's characters.

Actors' Interpretations

◆ ◆ ◆

When we watch a play, we gain insight into a character not merely through what the character says and does or how other characters react, but also through the way an actor interprets the role. If a playwright does not specify a character's mannerisms, gestures, or movements, or does not indicate how a line is to be delivered (and sometimes even if he or she does), an actor is free to interpret the role as he or she believes it should be played. Even when a playwright *does* specify such actions, the actor has a good deal of freedom to decide which gestures or expressions will convey a certain emotion.

In "Some Thoughts on Playwriting," American dramatist Thornton Wilder argues that "the theatre is an art which reposes upon the work of many collaborators" rather than on "one governing selecting will." Citing examples from Shakespeare and Ibsen, Wilder illustrates the great degree of "intervention" that may occur in dramatic productions. For instance, Wilder observes, Shakespeare's Shylock has been portrayed by two different actors as "noble, wronged and indignant" and as "a vengeful and hysterical buffoon"—and both performances were considered positive contributions to the theater. As noted earlier, the absence of detailed stage directions in Shakespeare's plays makes possible (and perhaps even encourages) such widely diverging interpretations. However, as Wilder notes, even when playing roles created by a dramatist such as Ibsen, whose stage directions are typically quite specific, actors and directors have a good deal of leeway. Thus, actress Janet McTeer, who played the part of Ibsen's Nora in the 1997 London production of *A Doll House,* saw Nora and Torvald, despite their many problems, as "the perfect couple," deeply in love and involved in a passionate marriage. "You have to make that marriage sexually credible," McTeer told the *New York Times,* "to imagine they have a wonderful time in bed, so there becomes something to lose. If you play them as already past it or no longer attracted to each other, then there is no play." This interpretation is not inconsistent with the play, but it does go beyond what Ibsen actually wrote. In a sense, then, the playwright's words on the page are just the beginning of the character's lives.

Irish playwright Samuel Beckett devotes a good deal of attention to indicating actors' movements and gestures and their physical reactions to one another. In his 1952 play *Waiting for Godot,* for example, Beckett seems to choreograph every gesture, every emotion, every intention, with stage directions such as the following:

- *(he looks at them ostentatiously in turn to make it clear they are both meant)*
- *Vladimir seizes Lucky's hat. Silence of Lucky. He falls. Silence. Panting of the victors.*
- *Estragon hands him the boot. Vladimir inspects it, throws it down angrily.*
- *Estragon pulls, stumbles, falls. Long silence.*
- *He goes feverishly to and fro, halts finally at extreme left, broods.*

Clearly, Beckett provides full and obviously carefully thought-out stage directions and, in so doing, attempts to retain a good deal of control over his characters. Still, in a 1988 production of *Godot,* director Mike Nichols and comic actors Robin Williams and Steve Martin felt free to improvise, adding gestures and movements not specified or even hinted at—and most critics believed that this production managed to remain true to the tragicomic spirit of Beckett's existentialist play.

Checklist: Writing about Character

- ✓ Does any character serve as a narrator? If so, what information does this narrator supply about the other characters? How reliable is the narrator?
- ✓ Are the major characters fully developed?
- ✓ Do the major characters change and grow during the course of the play, or do they remain essentially unchanged?
- ✓ What function does each of the minor characters serve in the play?
- ✓ What elements reveal changes in the characters?
- ✓ What is revealed about the characters through their words?
- ✓ Do characters use foreign words, regionalisms, slang, jargon, clichés, or profanity? What does such use of language reveal about characters? About theme?
- ✓ Is the language formal or informal?
- ✓ Do characters speak in dialect? Do they have accents?
- ✓ Is the language elaborate or plain?
- ✓ Do different characters exhibit contrasting styles or levels of language? What is the significance of these differences?
- ✓ In what way does language reveal characters' emotional states?
- ✓ Does the tone or style of any character's language change significantly as the play progresses? What does this change reveal?
- ✓ Does the play include verbal irony? Dramatic irony? How is irony conveyed? What purpose does irony achieve?
- ✓ What is revealed about the characters through what others say about them?
- ✓ Is the audience encouraged to react sympathetically to the character?
- ✓ What is revealed about the characters through their actions?
- ✓ What is revealed about the characters through the playwright's stage directions?
- ✓ How might different actors' interpretations change an audience's understanding of the characters?

◊ **Anton Chekhov** (1860–1904) is the major nineteenth-century Russian playwright and short story writer. His full-length plays include *The Seagull* (1896), *Uncle Vanya* (1898), *The Three Sisters* (1901), and *The Cherry Orchard* (1904).

The Brute, or *The Bear* (1888), is one of a number of one-act farces Chekhov wrote just before his major plays. It is based on a French farce (*Les Jurons de Cadillac* by Pierre Breton) about a man who cannot refrain from swearing. The woman he loves offers to marry him if he can avoid swearing for one hour; though he can't do it, he fails so charmingly that she agrees to marry him anyway.

◊ ◊ ◊

ANTON CHEKHOV

The Brute

A Joke in One Act
(1888)

English Version by Eric Bentley

Characters

Mrs. Popov, *widow and landowner, small, with dimpled cheeks*
Mr. Grigory S. Smirnov, *gentleman farmer, middle-aged*
Luka, *Mrs. Popov's footman, an old man*
Gardener
Coachman
Hired Men

Scene

The drawing room of a country house. Mrs. Popov, in deep mourning, is staring hard at a photograph. Luka is with her.

Luka: It's not right, ma'am, you're killing yourself. The cook has gone off with the maid to pick berries. The cat's having a high old time in the yard catching birds. Every living thing is happy. But you stay moping here in the house like it was a convent, taking no pleasure in nothing. I mean it, ma'am! It must be a full year since you set foot out of doors.
Mrs. Popov: I must never set foot out of doors again, Luka. Never! I have nothing to set foot out of doors *for.* My life is done. *He* is in

his grave. I have buried myself alive in this house. We are *both* in our graves.

LUKA: You're off again, ma'am. I just won't listen to you no more. Mr. Popov is dead, but what can we do about that? It's God's doing. God's will be done. You've cried over him, you've done your share of mourning, haven't you? There's a limit to everything. You can't go on weeping and wailing forever. My old lady died, for that matter, and I wept and wailed over her a whole month long. Well, that was it. I couldn't weep and wail all my life. She just wasn't worth it. *(He sighs.)* As for the neighbors, you've forgotten all about them, ma'am. You don't visit them and you don't let them visit you. You and I are like a pair of spiders—excuse the expression, ma'am—here we are in this house like a pair of spiders, we never see the light of day. And it isn't like there was no nice people around either. The whole county's swarming with 'em. There's a regiment quartered at Riblov, and the officers are so good-looking! The girls can't take their eyes off them—There's a ball at the camp every Friday—The military band plays most every day of the week—What do you say, ma'am? You're young, you're pretty, you could enjoy yourself! Ten years from now you may want to strut and show your feathers to the officers, and it'll be too late.

MRS. POPOV: *(firmly)* You must never bring this subject up again, Luka. Since Popov died, life has been an empty dream to me, you know that. *You* may think I am alive. Poor ignorant Luka! You are wrong. I am dead. I'm in my grave. Never more shall I see the light of day, never strip from my body this . . . raiment of death! Are you listening, Luka? Let his ghost learn how I love him! Yes, *I* know, and *you* know, he was often unfair to me, he was cruel to me, and he was unfaithful to me. What of it? *I* shall be faithful to *him,* that's all. I will show him how *I* can love. Hereafter, in a better world than this, he will welcome me back, the same loyal girl I always was—

5 LUKA: Instead of carrying on this way, ma'am, you should go out in the garden and take a bit of a walk, ma'am. Or why not harness Toby and take a drive? Call on a couple of the neighbours, ma'am?

MRS. POPOV: *(breaking down)* Oh, Luka!

LUKA: Yes, ma'am? What have I said, ma'am? Oh, dear!

MRS. POPOV: Toby! You said Toby! He adored that horse. When he drove me out to the Korchagins and the Vlasovs, it was always with Toby! He was a wonderful driver, do you remember, Luka? So graceful! So strong! I can see him now, pulling at those reins with all his might and main! Toby! Luka, tell them to give Toby an extra portion of oats today.

LUKA: Yes, ma'am.

A bell rings.

MRS. POPOV: Who is that? Tell them I'm not at home.
LUKA: Very good, ma'am. *(Exit.)*
MRS. POPOV: *(gazing again at the photograph)* You shall see, my Popov, how a wife can love and forgive. Till death do us part. Longer than that. Till death re-unite us forever! *(Suddenly a titter breaks through her tears.)* Aren't you ashamed of yourself, Popov? Here's your little wife, being good, being faithful, so faithful she's locked up here waiting for her own funeral, while you—doesn't it make you ashamed, you naughty boy? You were terrible, you know. You were unfaithful, and you made those awful scenes about it, you stormed out and left me alone for weeks—

Enter Luka.

LUKA: *(upset)* There's someone asking for you, ma'am. Says he must—
MRS. POPOV: I suppose you told him that since my husband's death I see no one?
LUKA: Yes, ma'am. I did, ma'am. But he wouldn't listen, ma'am. He says it's urgent.
MRS. POPOV: *(shrilly)* I see no one!!
LUKA: He won't take no for an answer, ma'am. He just curses and swears and comes in anyway. He's a perfect monster, ma'am. He's in the dining room right now.
MRS. POPOV: In the dining room, is he? I'll give him his come-uppance. Bring him in here this minute.

Exit Luka.

(Suddenly sad again.) Why do they do this to me? Why? Insulting my grief, intruding on my solitude? *(She sighs.)* I'm afraid I'll have to enter a convent. I will, I *must* enter a convent!

Enter Mr. Smirnov and Luka.

SMIRNOV: *(to Luka)* Dolt! Idiot! You talk too much! *(Seeing Mrs. Popov. With dignity.)* May I have the honor of introducing myself, madam? Grigory S. Smirnov, landowner and lieutenant of artillery, retired. Forgive me, madam, if I disturb your peace and quiet, but my business is both urgent and weighty.
MRS. POPOV: *(declining to offer him her hand)* What is it you wish, sir?
SMIRNOV: At the time of his death, your late husband—with whom I had the honor to be acquainted, ma'am—was in my debt to the tune of twelve hundred rubles. I have two notes to prove it. Tomorrow, ma'am, I must pay the interest on a bank loan. I have therefore no alternative, ma'am, but to ask you to pay me the money today.
MRS. POPOV: Twelve hundred rubles? But what did my husband owe it to you for?
SMIRNOV: He used to buy his oats from me, madam.

MRS. POPOV: *(to Luka, with a sigh)* Remember what I said, Luka: tell them to give Toby an extra portion of oats today!

Exit Luka.

My dear Mr.—what was the name again?

SMIRNOV: Smirnov, ma'am.

MRS. POPOV: My dear Mr. Smirnov, if Mr. Popov owed you money, you shall be paid—to the last ruble, to the last kopeck. But today—you must excuse me, Mr.—what was it?

SMIRNOV: Smirnov, ma'am.

MRS. POPOV: Today, Mr. Smirnov, I have no ready cash in the house. *(Smirnov starts to speak.)* Tomorrow, Mr. Smirnov, no, the day after tomorrow, all will be well. My steward will be back from town. I shall see that he pays what is owing. Today, no. In any case, today is exactly seven months from Mr. Popov's death. On such a day you will understand that I am in no mood to think of money.

SMIRNOV: Madam, if you don't pay up now, you can carry me out feet foremost. They'll seize my estate.

MRS. POPOV: You can have your money. *(He starts to thank her.)* Tomorrow. *(He again starts to speak.)* That is: the day after tomorrow.

SMIRNOV: I don't need the money the day after tomorrow. I need it today.

MRS. POPOV: I'm sorry, Mr.—

SMIRNOV: *(shouting)* Smirnov!

MRS. POPOV: *(sweetly)* Yes, of course. But you can't have it today.

SMIRNOV: But I can't wait for it any longer!

MRS. POPOV: Be sensible, Mr. Smirnov. How can I pay you if I don't have it?

SMIRNOV: You don't have it?

MRS. POPOV: I don't have it.

SMIRNOV: Sure?

MRS. POPOV: Positive.

SMIRNOV: Very well. I'll make a note to that effect. *(Shrugging.)* And then they want me to keep cool. I meet the tax commissioner on the street, and he says, "Why are you always in such a bad humor, Smirnov?" Bad humor! How can I help it, in God's name? I need money, I need it desperately. Take yesterday: I leave home at the crack of dawn, I call on all my debtors. Not a one of them pays up. Footsore and weary, I creep at midnight into some little dive, and try to snatch a few winks of sleep on the floor by the vodka barrel. Then today, I come here, fifty miles from home, saying to myself, "At last, at last, I can be sure of something," and you're not in the mood! You give me a mood! Christ, how can I help getting all worked up?

MRS. POPOV: I thought I'd made it clear, Mr. Smirnov, that you'll get your money the minute my steward is back from town.

SMIRNOV: What the hell do I care about your steward? Pardon the expression, ma'am. But it was you I came to see.
MRS. POPOV: What language! What a tone to take to a lady! I refuse to hear another word. *(Quickly, exit.)*
45 SMIRNOV: Not in the mood, huh? "Exactly seven months since Popov's death," huh? How about me? *(Shouting after her.)* Is there this interest to pay, or isn't there? I'm asking you a question: is there this interest to pay, or isn't there? So your husband died, and you're not in the mood, and your steward's gone off some place, and so forth and so on, but what can *I* do about all that, huh? What do *you* think I should do? Take a running jump and shove my head through the wall? Take off in a balloon? You don't know my *other* debtors. I call on Gruzdeff. Not at home. I look for Yaroshevitch. He's hiding out. I find Kooritsin. He kicks up a row, and I have to throw him through the window. I work my way right down the list. Not a kopeck. Then I come to you, and God damn it to hell, if you'll pardon the expression, you're not in the mood! *(Quietly, as he realizes he's talking to air.)* I've spoiled them all, that's what, I've let them play me for a sucker. Well, I'll show them. I'll show this one. I'll stay right here till she pays up. Ugh! *(He shudders with rage.)* I'm in a rage! I'm in a positively towering rage! Every nerve in my body is trembling at forty to the dozen! I can't breathe, I feel ill, I think I'm going to faint, hey, you there!

Enter Luka.

LUKA: Yes, sir? Is there anything you wish, sir?
SMIRNOV: Water! Water! No, make it vodka.

Exit Luka.

Consider the logic of it. A fellow creature is desperately in need of cash, so desperately in need that he has to seriously contemplate hanging himself, and this woman, this mere chit of a girl, won't pay up, and why not? Because, forsooth, she isn't in the mood! Oh, the logic of women! Come to that, I never have liked them, I could do without the whole sex. Talk to a woman? I'd rather sit on a barrel of dynamite, the very thought gives me gooseflesh. Women! Creatures of poetry and romance! Just to see one in the distance gets me mad. My legs start twitching with rage. I feel like yelling for help.

Enter Luka, handing Smirnov a glass of water.

LUKA: Mrs. Popov is indisposed, sir. She is seeing no one.
SMIRNOV: Get out.

Exit Luka.

Indisposed, is she? Seeing no one, huh? Well, she can see me or not, but I'll be here, I'll be right here till she pays up. If you're sick for a week, I'll be here for a week. If you're sick for a year, I'll be here for a year. You won't get around *me* with your widow's weeds and your schoolgirl dimples. I know all about dimples. *(Shouting through the window.)* Semyon, let the horses out of those shafts, we're not leaving, we're staying, and tell them to give the horses some oats, yes, oats, you fool, what do you think? *(Walking away from the window.)* What a mess, what an unholy mess! I didn't sleep last night, the heat is terrific today, not a damn one of 'em has paid up, and here's this—this skirt in mourning that's not in the mood! My head aches, where's that—*(He drinks from the glass.)* Water, ugh! You there!

Enter Luka.

50 LUKA: Yes, sir. You wish for something, sir?
SMIRNOV: Where's that confounded vodka I asked for?

Exit Luka.

(Smirnov sits and looks himself over.) Oof! A fine figure of a man *I* am! Unwashed, uncombed, unshaven, straw on my vest, dust all over me. The little woman must've taken me for a highwayman. *(Yawns.)* I suppose it wouldn't be considered polite to barge into a drawing room in this state, but who cares? I'm not a visitor, I'm a creditor—most unwelcome of guests, second only to Death.

Enter Luka.

LUKA: *(handing him the vodka)* If I may say so, sir, you take too many liberties, sir.
SMIRNOV: What?!
LUKA: Oh, nothing, sir, nothing.
55 SMIRNOV: Who in hell do you think you're talking to? Shut your mouth!
LUKA: *(aside)* There's an evil spirit abroad. The Devil must have sent him. Oh! *(Exit Luka.)*
SMIRNOV: What a rage I'm in! I'll grind the whole world to powder. Oh, I feel ill again. You there!

Enter Mrs. Popov.

MRS. POPOV: *(looking at the floor)* In the solitude of my rural retreat, Mr. Smirnov, I've long since grown unaccustomed to the sound of the human voice. Above all, I cannot bear shouting. I must beg you not to break the silence.
SMIRNOV: Very well. Pay me my money and I'll go.
60 MRS. POPOV: I told you before, and I tell you again, Mr. Smirnov, I have no cash, you'll have to wait till the day after tomorrow. Can I express myself more plainly?
SMIRNOV: And *I* told *you* before, and *I* tell *you* again, that I need the money today, that the day after tomorrow is too late, and that if

you don't pay, and pay now, I'll have to hang myself in the morning!
MRS. POPOV: But I have no cash. This is quite a puzzle.
SMIRNOV: You won't pay, huh?
MRS. POPOV: I *can't* pay, Mr. Smirnov.
SMIRNOV: In that case, I'm going to sit here and wait. *(Sits down.)* You'll pay up the day after tomorrow? Very good. Till the day after tomorrow, here I sit. *(Pause. He jumps up.)* Now look, do I have to pay that interest tomorrow, or don't I? Or do you think I'm joking?
MRS. POPOV: I must ask you not to raise your voice, Mr. Smirnov. This is not a stable.
SMIRNOV: Who said it was? Do I have to pay the interest tomorrow or not?
MRS. POPOV: Mr. Smirnov, do you know how to behave in the presence of a lady?
SMIRNOV: No, madam, I do not know how to behave in the presence of a lady.
MRS. POPOV: Just what I thought. I look at you, and I say: ugh! I hear you talk, and I say to myself: "That man doesn't know how to talk to a lady."
SMIRNOV: You'd like me to come simpering to you in French, I suppose. "*Enchanté, madame! Merci beaucoup* for not paying zee money, *madame! Pardonnez-moi* if I 'ave disturbed you, *madame!* How *charmante* you look in mourning, *madame!*"
MRS. POPOV: Now you're being silly, Mr. Smirnov.
SMIRNOV: *(mimicking)* "Now you're being silly, Mr. Smirnov." "You don't know how to talk to a lady, Mr. Smirnov." Look here, Mrs. Popov, I've known more women than you've known pussy cats. I've fought three duels on their account. I've jilted twelve, and been jilted by nine others. Oh, yes, Mrs. Popov, I've played the fool in my time, whispered sweet nothings, bowed and scraped and endeavored to please. Don't tell me I don't know what it is to love, to pine away with longing, to have the blues, to melt like butter, to be weak as water. I was full of tender emotion. I was carried away with passion. I squandered half my fortune on the sex. I chattered about women's emancipation. But there's an end to everything, dear madam. Burning eyes, dark eyelashes, ripe, red lips, dimpled cheeks, heaving bosoms, soft whisperings, the moon above; the lake below—I don't give a rap for that sort of nonsense any more, Mrs. Popov. I've found out about women. Present company excepted, they're liars. Their behavior is mere play acting; their conversation is sheer gossip. Yes, dear lady, women, young or old, are false, petty, vain, cruel, malicious, unreasonable. As for intelligence, any sparrow could give them points. Appearances, I admit, can be deceptive. In appearance, a woman may be all poetry and romance, goddess and angel, muslin and fluff. To look at her exterior is to be transported to heaven. But I have looked at

her interior, Mrs. Popov, and what did I find there—in her very soul? A crocodile. *(He has gripped the back of the chair so firmly that it snaps.)* And, what is more revolting, a crocodile with an illusion, a crocodile that imagines tender sentiments are its own special province, a crocodile that thinks itself queen of the realm of love! Whereas, in sober fact, dear madam, if a woman can love anything except a lapdog you can hang me by the feet on that nail. For a man, love is suffering, love is sacrifice. A woman just swishes her train around and tightens her grip on your nose. Now, you're a woman, aren't you, Mrs. Popov? You must be an expert on some of this. Tell me, quite frankly, did you ever know a woman to be—faithful, for instance? Or even sincere? Only old hags, huh? Though some women are old hags from birth. But as for the others? You're right: a faithful woman is a freak of nature—like a cat with horns.

MRS. POPOV: Who *is* faithful, then? Who *have* you cast for the faithful lover? Not man?

75 SMIRNOV: Right first time, Mrs. Popov: man.

MRS. POPOV: *(going off into a peal of bitter laughter)* Man! Man is faithful! that's a new one! *(Fiercely.)* What right do you have to say this, Mr. Smirnov? Men faithful? Let me tell you something. Of all the men I have ever known my late husband Popov was the best. I loved him, and there are women who know how to love, Mr. Smirnov. I gave him my youth, my happiness, my life, my fortune. I worshipped the ground he trod on—and what happened? The best of men was unfaithful to me, Mr. Smirnov. Not once in a while. All the time. After he died, I found his desk drawer full of love letters. While he was alive, he was always going away for the week-end. He squandered my money. He made love to other women before my very eyes. But, in spite of all, Mr. Smirnov, *I* was faithful. Unto death. And beyond. I am *still* faithful, Mr. Smirnov! Buried alive in this house, I shall wear mourning till the day I, too, am called to my eternal rest.

SMIRNOV: *(laughing scornfully)* Expect me to believe that? As if I couldn't see through all this hocus-pocus. Buried alive! Till you're called to your eternal rest! Till when? Till some little poet—or some little subaltern with his first moustache—comes riding by and asks: "Can that be the house of the mysterious Tamara who for love of her late husband has buried herself alive, vowing to see no man?" Ha!

MRS. POPOV: *(flaring up)* How dare you? How dare you insinuate—?

SMIRNOV: You may have buried yourself alive, Mrs. Popov, but you haven't forgotten to powder your nose.

80 MRS. POPOV: *(incoherent)* How dare you? How—?

SMIRNOV: Who's raising his voice now? Just because I call a spade a spade. Because I shoot straight from the shoulder. Well, don't shout at me, I'm not your steward.

MRS. POPOV: I'm not shouting, you're shouting! Oh, leave me alone!
SMIRNOV: Pay me the money, and I will.
MRS. POPOV: You'll get no money out of me!
85 SMIRNOV: Oh, so that's it!
MRS. POPOV: Not a ruble, not a kopeck. Get out! Leave me alone!
SMIRNOV: Not being your husband, I must ask you not to make scenes with me. *(He sits.)* I don't like scenes.
MRS. POPOV: *(choking with rage)* You're sitting down?
SMIRNOV: Correct, I'm sitting down.
90 MRS. POPOV: I asked you to leave!
SMIRNOV: Then give me the money. *(Aside.)* Oh, what a rage I'm in, what a rage!
MRS. POPOV: The impudence of the man! I won't talk to you a moment longer. Get out. *(Pause.)* Are you going?
SMIRNOV: No.
MRS. POPOV: No?!
95 SMIRNOV: No.
MRS. POPOV: On your head be it. Luka!

Enter Luka.

    Show the gentleman out, Luka.
LUKA: *(approaching)* I'm afraid, sir, I'll have to ask you, um, to leave, sir, now, um—
SMIRNOV: *(jumping up)* Shut your mouth, you old idiot! Who do you think you're talking to? I'll make mincemeat of you.
LUKA: *(clutching his heart)* Mercy on us! Holy saints above! *(He falls into an armchair.)* I'm taken sick! I can't breathe!!
100 MRS. POPOV: Then where's Dasha? Dasha! Dasha! Come here at once! *(She rings.)*
LUKA: They gone picking berries, ma'am, I'm alone here—Water, water, I'm taken sick!
MRS. POPOV: *(to Smirnov)* Get out, you!
SMIRNOV: Can't you even be polite with me, Mrs. Popov?
MRS. POPOV: *(clenching her fists and stamping her feet)* With you? You're a wild animal, you were never house-broken!
105 SMIRNOV: What? What did you say?
MRS. POPOV: I said you were a wild animal, you were never house-broken.
SMIRNOV: *(advancing upon her)* And what right do you have to talk to me like that?
MRS. POPOV: Like what?
SMIRNOV: You have insulted me, madam.
110 MRS. POPOV: What of it? Do you think I'm scared of you?
SMIRNOV: So you think you can get away with it because you're a woman. A creature of poetry and romance, huh? Well, it doesn't go down with me. I hereby challenge you to a duel.
LUKA: Mercy on us! Holy saints alive! Water!

SMIRNOV: I propose we shoot it out.
MRS. POPOV: Trying to scare me again? Just because you have big fists and a voice like a bull? You're a brute.
SMIRNOV: No one insults Grigory S. Smirnov with impunity! And I don't care if you *are* a female.
MRS. POPOV: *(trying to outshout him)* Brute, brute, brute!
SMIRNOV: The sexes are equal, are they? Fine: then it's just prejudice to expect men alone to pay for insults. I hereby challenge—
MRS. POPOV: *(screaming)* All right! You want to shoot it out? All right! Let's shoot it out!
SMIRNOV: And let it be here and now!
MRS. POPOV: Here and now! All right! I'll have Popov's pistols here in one minute! *(Walks away, then turns.)* Putting one of Popov's bullets through your silly head will be a pleasure! Au revoir. *(Exit.)*
SMIRNOV: I'll bring her down like a duck, a sitting duck. I'm not one of your little poets, I'm no little subaltern with his first moustache. No, sir, there's no weaker sex where I'm concerned!
LUKA: Sir! Master! *(He goes down on his knees.)* Take pity on a poor old man, and do me a favor: go away. It was bad enough before, you nearly scared me to death. But a duel—!
SMIRNOV: *(ignoring him)* A duel! That's equality of the sexes for you! That's women's emancipation! Just as a matter of principle I'll bring her down like a duck. But what a woman! "Putting one of Popov's bullets through your silly head . . ." Her cheeks were flushed, her eyes were gleaming! And, by God, she's accepted the challenge! I never knew a woman like this before!
LUKA: Sir! Master! Please go away! I'll always pray for you!
SMIRNOV: *(again ignoring him)* What a woman! Phew!! *She's* no sour puss, *she's* no cry baby. She's fire and brimstone. She's a human cannon ball. What a shame I have to kill her!
LUKA: *(weeping)* Please, kind sir, please, go away!
SMIRNOV: *(as before)* I like her, isn't that funny? With those dimples and all? I like her. I'm even prepared to consider letting her off that debt. And where's my rage? It's gone. I never knew a woman like this before.

Enter Mrs. Popov with pistols.

MRS. POPOV: *(boldly)* Pistols, Mr. Smirnov! *(Matter of fact.)* But before we start, you'd better show me how it's done. I'm not too familiar with these things. In fact I never gave a pistol a second look.
LUKA: Lord, have mercy on us, I must go hunt up the gardener and the coachman. Why has this catastrophe fallen upon us, O Lord? *(Exit.)*
SMIRNOV: *(examining the pistols)* Well, it's like this. There are several makes: one is the Mortimer, with capsules, especially constructed for dueling. What you have here are Smith and Wesson triple-action revolvers, with extractor, first-rate job, worth ninety rubles

at the very least. You hold it this way. *(Aside.)* My God, what eyes she has! They're setting me on fire.

MRS. POPOV: This way?

SMIRNOV: Yes, that's right. You cock the trigger, take aim like this, head up, arm out like this. Then you just press with this finger here, and it's all over. The main thing is, keep cool, take slow aim, and don't let your arm jump.

MRS. POPOV: I see. And if it's inconvenient to do the job here, we can go out in the garden.

SMIRNOV: Very good. Of course, I should warn you: I'll be firing in the air.

135 MRS. POPOV: What? This is the end. Why?

SMIRNOV: Oh, well—because—for private reasons.

MRS. POPOV: Scared, huh? *(She laughs heartily.)* Now don't you try to get out of it, Mr. Smirnov. My blood is up. I won't be happy till I've drilled a hole through that skull of yours. Follow me. What's the matter? Scared?

SMIRNOV: That's right. I'm scared.

MRS. POPOV: Oh, come on, what's the matter with you?

140 SMIRNOV: Well, um, Mrs. Popov, I, um, I like you.

MRS. POPOV: *(laughing bitterly)* Good God! He likes me, does he? The gall of the man. *(Showing him the door.)* You may leave, Mr. Smirnov.

SMIRNOV: *(Quietly puts the gun down, takes his hat, and walks to the door. Then he stops and the pair look at each other without a word. Then, approaching gingerly.)* Listen, Mrs. Popov. Are you still mad at me? I'm in the devil of a temper myself, of course. But then, you see—what I mean is—it's this way—the fact is—*(Roaring.)* Well, is it my fault, damn it, if I like you? *(Clutches the back of a chair. It breaks.)* Christ, what fragile furniture you have here. I like you. Know what I mean? I could fall in love with you.

MRS. POPOV: I hate you. Get out!

SMIRNOV: What a woman! I never saw anything like it. Oh, I'm lost, I'm done for, I'm a mouse in a trap.

145 MRS. POPOV: Leave this house, or I shoot!

SMIRNOV: Shoot away! What bliss to die of a shot that was fired by that little velvet hand! To die gazing into those enchanting eyes. I'm out of my mind. I know: you must decide at once. Think for one second, then decide. Because if I leave now, I'll never be back. Decide! I'm a pretty decent chap. Landed gentleman, I should say. Ten thousand a year. Good stable. Throw a kopeck up in the air, and I'll put a bullet through it. Will you marry me?

MRS. POPOV: *(indignant, brandishing the gun)* We'll shoot it out! Get going! Take your pistol!

SMIRNOV: I'm out of my mind. I don't understand anything any more. *(Shouting.)* You there! That vodka!

MRS. POPOV: No excuses! No delays! We'll shoot it out!

150 SMIRNOV: I'm out of my mind. I'm falling in love. I *have* fallen in love. *(He takes her hand vigorously; she squeals.)* I love you. *(He goes down on his knees.)* I love you as I've never loved before. I jilted twelve, and was jilted by nine others. But I didn't love a one of them as I love you. I'm full of tender emotion. I'm melting like butter. I'm weak as water. I'm on my knees like a fool, and I offer you my hand. It's a shame, it's a disgrace. I haven't been in love in five years. I took a vow against it. And now, all of a sudden, to be swept off my feet, it's a scandal. I offer you my hand, dear lady. Will you or won't you? You won't? Then don't! *(He rises and walks toward the door.)*

MRS. POPOV: I didn't say anything.

SMIRNOV: *(stopping)* What?

MRS. POPOV: Oh, nothing, you can go. Well, no, just a minute. No, you can go. Go! I detest you! But, just a moment. Oh, if you knew how furious I feel! *(Throws the gun on the table.)* My fingers have gone to sleep holding that horrid thing. *(She is tearing her handkerchief to shreds.)* And what are you standing around for? Get out of here!

SMIRNOV: Goodbye.

155 MRS. POPOV: Go, go, go! *(Shouting.)* Where are you going? Wait a minute! No, no, it's all right, just go. I'm fighting mad. Don't come near me, don't come near me!

SMIRNOV: *(who is coming near her)* I'm pretty disgusted with myself—falling in love like a kid, going down on my knees like some moongazing whippersnapper, the very thought gives me gooseflesh. *(Rudely.)* I love you. But it doesn't make sense. Tomorrow, I have to pay that interest, and we've already started mowing. *(He puts his arm about her waist.)* I shall never forgive myself for this.

MRS. POPOV: Take your hands off me, I hate you! Let's shoot it out!

A long kiss. Enter Luka with an axe, the Gardener with a rake, the coachman with a pitchfork, hired men with sticks.

LUKA: *(seeing the kiss)* Mercy on us! Holy saints above!

MRS. POPOV: *(dropping her eyes)* Luka, tell them in the stable that Toby is *not* to have any oats today.

READING AND REACTING

1. Are Mr. Smirnov and Mrs. Popov round or flat characters? Are they static or dynamic?
2. Which of the two characters do you think has the upper hand in their relationship?
3. Although Mrs. Popov's husband is dead, he is, in a sense, an important character in *The Brute*. What do we know about him? How does he influence the play's two main characters?

4. Why are Mrs. Popov and Mr. Smirnov distrustful of members of the opposite sex? How is this distrust revealed to the audience?
5. Do you think this play reinforces gender stereotypes or challenges them? Explain.
6. Because *The Brute* is a **farce,** Chekhov's characters frequently exaggerate for comic effect. For instance, Smirnov tells Mrs. Popov, "I've known more women than you've known pussy cats. I've fought three duels on their account. I've jilted twelve, and been jilted by nine others." Give some additional examples of such broadly exaggerated language, and explain its function.
7. Give some examples of physical actions used to reinforce emotions or attitudes in *The Brute*.
8. Explain and illustrate how the characters' words reveal each of the following moods: Mrs. Popov's anger at Mr. Smirnov, Mrs. Popov's ambivalence toward her late husband, Mr. Smirnov's impatience with Mrs. Popov, Mr. Smirnov's stubbornness.
9. As the play progresses, Mrs. Popov's changing language communicates her changing attitude toward her husband. Give some examples that illustrate this change in attitude.
10. What can you infer about Mrs. Popov's relationship with Luka from the language she uses when she addresses him? From the language he uses with her? What function does Luka serve in the play?
11. At what point in the play does Mr. Smirnov's speech become more elaborate? What does his use of figurative language suggest?
12. Where in the play does dramatic irony occur? Is verbal irony also present?
13. Identify all the asides in the play. What is their function?
14. **Journal Entry** If you had to take a side in the dispute between Mrs. Popov and Mr. Smirnov, whose side would you be on? Why?

Related Works: "Big Black Goodman" (p. 124), "The Cask of Amontillado (p. 136), "Popular Mechanics" (p. 265), "General Review of the Sex Situation" (p. 317), "You Fit into Me" (p. 423), "Women" (p. 474)

◆ **WILLIAM SHAKESPEARE** (1564–1616), born in Stratford-on-Avon, England, spent most of his adult life in London. He was deeply involved in all aspects of the theater as an actor; an acting company shareholder; a part owner of the Globe Theater; and, most significantly, the author of at least thirty-six plays.

It is difficult to date many of Shakespeare's plays exactly, but we do know that a play called the *Revenge of Hamlett Prince Denmarke* was presented around July 26, 1602. Some scholars believe the play was composed as early as 1598.

◆ ◆ ◆

WILLIAM SHAKESPEARE

Hamlet

PRINCE OF DENMARK*
(c. 1600)

CHARACTERS

CLAUDIUS, *King of Denmark*
HAMLET, *son to the former and nephew to the present King*
POLONIUS, *Lord Chamberlain*
HORATIO, *friend to Hamlet*
LAERTES, *son to Polonius*
VOLTIMAND ⎫
CORNELIUS ⎪
ROSENCRANTZ ⎬ *courtiers*
GUILDENSTERN ⎪
OSRIC ⎭
A GENTLEMAN
A PRIEST
FRANCISCO, *a soldier*
MARCELLUS ⎫ *officers*
BERNARDO ⎭

REYNALDO, *servant to Polonius*
PLAYERS
TWO CLOWNS, *grave-diggers*
FORTINBRAS, *Prince of Norway*
A CAPTAIN
ENGLISH AMBASSADORS
GHOST OF HAMLET'S FATHER
GERTRUDE, *Queen of Denmark and mother of Hamlet*
OPHELIA, *daughter to Polonius*
LORDS, LADIES, OFFICERS, SOLDIERS, SAILORS, MESSENGERS, AND OTHER ATTENDANTS

---

*Note that individual lines are numbered in the following play. When a line is shared by two or more characters, it is counted as one line.

Act I
Scene 1

Elsinore. A platform before the castle.

(Francisco at his post. Enter to him Bernardo.)

BERNARDO: Who's there?
FRANCISCO: Nay, answer me: stand, and unfold yourself.
BERNARDO: Long live the king!
FRANCISCO: Bernardo?
5   **BERNARDO:** He.
FRANCISCO: You come most carefully upon your hour.
BERNARDO: 'Tis now struck twelve; get thee to bed, Francisco.
FRANCISCO: For this relief much thanks: 'tis bitter cold,
       And I am sick at heart.
10 **BERNARDO:** Have you had quiet guard?
FRANCISCO: Not a mouse stirring.
BERNARDO: Well, good-night.
       If you do meet Horatio and Marcellus,
       The rivals of my watch, bid them make haste.
FRANCISCO: I think I hear them.—Stand, ho! Who is there?

(Enter Horatio and Marcellus.)

15 **HORATIO:** Friends to this ground.
MARCELLUS: And liegemen to the Dane.
FRANCISCO: Give you good-night.
MARCELLUS: O, farewell, honest soldier:
       Who hath reliev'd you?
FRANCISCO: Bernardo has my place.
       Give you good-night.

(Exit.)

MARCELLUS: Holla! Bernardo!
BERNARDO: Say.
       What, is Horatio there?
HORATIO: A piece of him.
20 **BERNARDO:** Welcome, Horatio:—welcome, good Marcellus.
MARCELLUS: What, has this thing appear'd again to-night?
BERNARDO: I have seen nothing.
MARCELLUS: Horatio says 'tis but our fantasy,
       And will not let belief take hold of him
25   Touching this dreaded sight, twice seen of us:
       Therefore I have entreated him along
       With us to watch the minutes of this night;
       That, if again this apparition come
       He may approve our eyes and speak to it.
30 **HORATIO:** Tush, tush, 'twill not appear.

BERNARDO: Sit down awhile,
    And let us once again assail your ears,
    That are so fortified against our story,
    What we two nights have seen.
HORATIO: Well, sit we down,
    And let us hear Bernardo speak of this.
35 BERNARDO: Last night of all,
    When yon same star that's westward from the pole
    Had made his course to illume that part of heaven
    Where now it burns, Marcellus and myself,
    The bell then beating one,—
40 MARCELLUS: Peace, break thee off; look where it comes again!

(Enter Ghost, armed.)

BERNARDO: In the same figure, like the king that's dead.
MARCELLUS: Thou art a scholar; speak to it, Horatio.
BERNARDO: Looks it not like the king? mark it, Horatio.
HORATIO: Most like:—it harrows me with fear and wonder.
45 BERNARDO: It would be spoke to.
MARCELLUS: Question it, Horatio.
HORATIO: What art thou, that usurp'st this time of night,
    Together with that fair and warlike form
    In which the majesty of buried Denmark
    Did sometimes march? by heaven I charge thee, speak!
50 MARCELLUS: It is offended.
BERNARDO: See, it stalks away!
HORATIO: Stay! speak, speak! I charge thee, speak!

(Exit Ghost.)

MARCELLUS: 'Tis gone, and will not answer.
BERNARDO: How now, Horatio! you tremble and look pale:
    Is not this something more than fantasy?
55   What think you on't?
HORATIO: Before my God, I might not this believe
    Without the sensible and true avouch
    Of mine own eyes.
MARCELLUS: Is it not like the king?
HORATIO: As thou art to thyself:
60   Such was the very armor he had on
    When he the ambitious Norway combated;
    So frown'd he once when, in an angry parle,[1]
    He smote the sledded Polacks on the ice.
    'Tis strange.

---

[1] *parle:* parley, or conference.

65	**MARCELLUS:** Thus twice before, and just at this dead hour,
	With martial stalk hath he gone by our watch.
	HORATIO: In what particular thought to work I know not;
	But, in the gross and scope of my opinion,
	This bodes some strange eruption to our state.
70	**MARCELLUS:** Good now, sit down, and tell me, he that knows,
	Why this same strict and most observant watch
	So nightly toils the subject of the land;
	And why such daily cast of brazen cannon,
	And foreign mart for implements of war;
75	Why such impress of shipwrights, whose sore task
	Does not divide the Sunday from the week;
	What might be toward, that this sweaty haste
	Doth make the night joint-laborer with the day:
	Who is't that can inform me?
	HORATIO: That can I;
80	At least, the whisper goes so. Our last king,
	Whose image even but now appear'd to us,
	Was, as you know, by Fortinbras of Norway,
	Thereto prick'd on by a most emulate pride,
	Dar'd to the combat; in which our valiant Hamlet,—
85	For so this side of our known world esteem'd him,—
	Did slay this Fortinbras; who, by a seal'd compact,
	Well ratified by law and heraldry,
	Did forfeit, with his life, all those his lands.
	Which he stood seiz'd of,[2] to the conqueror:
90	Against the which, a moiety competent[3]
	Was gagéd[4] by our king; which had return'd
	To the inheritance of Fortinbras,
	Had he been vanquisher; as by the same cov'nant,
	And carriage of the article design'd,
95	His fell to Hamlet. Now, sir, young Fortinbras,
	Of unimproved mettle hot and full,
	Hath in the skirts of Norway, here and there,
	Shark'd up a list of landless resolutes,
	For food and diet, to some enterprise
100	That hath a stomach in't: which is no other,—
	As it doth well appear unto our state,—
	But to recover of us by strong hand,
	And terms compulsatory, those foresaid lands
	So by his father lost: and this, I take it,
105	Is the main motive of our preparations,
	The source of this our watch, and the chief head
	Of this post-haste and romage[5] in the land.

---

[2] *seiz'd of:* possessed.   [3] *moiety competent:* a sufficient portion of his lands.
[4] *gagéd:* engaged or pledged.   [5] *post-haste and romage:* general activity.

BERNARDO: I think it be no other, but e'en so:
    Well may it sort that this portentous figure
110   Comes armed through our watch; so like the king
    That was and is the question of these wars.
HORATIO: A mote it is to trouble the mind's eye.
    In the most high and palmy state of Rome,
    A little ere the mightiest Julius fell,
115   The graves stood tenantless, and the sheeted dead
    Did squeak and gibber in the Roman streets:
    As, stars with trains of fire and dews of blood,
    Disasters in the sun; and the moist star,
    Upon whose influence Neptune's empire stands,
120   Was sick almost to doomsday with eclipse:
    And even the like precurse of fierce events,—
    As harbingers preceding still the fates,
    And prologue to the omen coming on,—
    Have heaven and earth together demonstrated
125   Unto our climature and countrymen.—
    But, soft, behold! lo, where it comes again!

(Re-enter Ghost.)

    I'll cross it, though it blast me.—Stay, illusion!
    If thou hast any sound or use of voice,
    Speak to me:
130   If there be any good thing to be done,
    That may to thee do ease, and grace to me,
    Speak to me:
    If thou art privy to thy country's fate,
    Which, happily,[6] foreknowing may avoid,
135   O, speak!
    Or if thou has uphoarded in thy life
    Extorted treasure in the womb of earth,
    For which, they say, you spirits oft walk in death,

(Cock crows.)

    Speak of it:—stay, and speak!—Stop it, Marcellus.
140 MARCELLUS: Shall I strike at it with my partisan?[7]
HORATIO: Do, if it will not stand.
BERNARDO: 'Tis here!
HORATIO: 'Tis here!
MARCELLUS: 'Tis gone!

(Exit Ghost.)

    We do it wrong, being so majestical,
    To offer it the show of violence;

---

[6] *happily:* haply, or perhaps.   [7] *partisan:* pike.

145   For it is, as the air, invulnerable,
      And our vain blows malicious mockery.
   BERNARDO: It was about to speak when the cock crew.
   HORATIO: And then it started like a guilty thing
      Upon a fearful summons. I have heard,
150   The cock, that is the trumpet to the morn,
      Doth with his lofty and shrill-sounding throat
      Awake the god of day; and at his warning,
      Whether in sea or fire, in earth or air,
      The extravagant and erring spirit hies
155   To his confine: and of the truth herein
      This present object made probation.[8]
   MARCELLUS: It faded on the crowing of the cock.
      Some say that ever 'gainst that season comes
      Wherein our Saviour's birth is celebrated,
160   The bird of dawning singeth all night long:
      And then, they say, no spirit can walk abroad;
      The nights are wholesome; then no planets strike,
      No fairy takes, nor witch hath power to charm;
      So hallow'd and so gracious is the time.
165 HORATIO: So have I heard, and do in part believe.
      But, look, the morn, in russet mantle clad,
      Walks o'er the dew of yon high eastern hill:
      Break we our watch up: and, by my advice,
      Let us impart what we have seen to-night
170   Unto young Hamlet; for, upon my life,
      This spirit, dumb to us, will speak to him:
      Do you consent we shall acquaint him with it,
      As needful in our loves, fitting our duty?
   MARCELLUS: Let's do't, I pray; and I this morning know
175   Where we shall find him most conveniently.

(Exeunt.)

SCENE 2

Elsinore. A room of state in the castle.

(Enter the King, Queen, Hamlet, Polonius, Laertes, Voltimand, Cornelius, Lords, and Attendants.)

   KING: Though yet of Hamlet our dear brother's death
      The memory be green; and that it us befitted
      To bear our hearts in grief, and our whole kingdom
      To be contracted in one brow of woe;
5   Yet so far hath discretion fought with nature
      That we with wisest sorrow think on him,

---

[8] *probation:* proof.

Together with remembrance of ourselves.
Therefore our sometime sister, now our queen,
The imperial jointress of this warlike state,
10 Have we, as 'twere with defeated joy,—
With one auspicious and one dropping eye,
With mirth and funeral, and with dirge in marriage,
In equal scale weighing delight and dole,—
Taken to wife: nor have we herein barr'd
15 Your better wisdoms, which have freely gone
With this affair along:—for all, our thanks.
Now follows that you know, young Fortinbras,
Holding a weak supposal of our worth,
Or thinking by our late dear brother's death
20 Our state to be disjoint and out of frame,
Colleagued with the dream of his advantage,
He hath not fail'd to pester us with message,
Importing the surrender of those lands
Lost by his father, with all bonds of law,
25 To our most valiant brother. So much for him.—
Now for ourself, and for this time of meeting:
Thus much the business is:—we have here writ
To Norway, uncle of young Fortinbras,—
Who, impotent and bed-rid, scarcely hears
30 Of this his nephew's purpose,—to suppress
His further gait herein; in that the levies,
The lists, and full proportions, are all made
Out of his subject:—and we here despatch
You, good Cornelius, and you, Voltimand,
35 For bearers of this greeting to old Norway;
Giving to you no further personal power
To business with the king more than the scope
Of these dilated articles allow.
Farewell; and let your haste commend your duty.
40 CORNELIUS and VOLTIMAND: In that and all things will we show our
duty.
KING: We doubt it nothing: heartily farewell.

(Exeunt Voltimand and Cornelius.)

And now, Laertes, what's the news with you?
You told us of some suit; what is't, Laertes?
You cannot speak of reason to the Dane,
45 And lose your voice: what wouldst thou beg, Laertes,
That shall not be my offer, nor thy asking?
The head is not more native to the heart,
The hand more instrumental to the mouth,
Than is the throne of Denmark to thy father.
50 What wouldst thou have, Laertes?

LAERTES: Dread my lord,
    Your leave and favor to return to France;
    From whence though willingly I came to Denmark,
    To show my duty in your coronation;
    Yet now, I must confess, that duty done,
55   My thoughts and wishes bend again toward France.
    And bow them to your gracious leave and pardon.
KING: Have you your father's leave? What says Polonius?
POLONIUS: He hath, my lord, wrung from me my slow leave
    By laborsome petition; and at last
60   Upon his will I seal'd my hard consent:
    I do beseech you, give him leave to go.
KING: Take thy fair hour, Laertes; time be thine,
    And thy best graces spend it at thy will!—
    But now, my cousin Hamlet, and my son,—
65 HAMLET: *(Aside)* A little more than kin, and less than kind.
KING: How is it that the clouds still hang on you?
HAMLET: Not so, my lord; I am too much i' the sun.
QUEEN: Good Hamlet, cast thy nighted color off,
    And let thine eye look like a friend on Denmark.
70   Do not for ever with thy vailed[1] lids
    Seek for thy noble father in the dust:
    Thou know'st 'tis common,—all that live must die,
    Passing through nature to eternity.
HAMLET: Ay, madam, it is common.
QUEEN: If it be,
75   Why seems it so particular with thee?
HAMLET: Seems, madam! nay, it is; I know not seems.
    'Tis not alone my inky cloak, good mother,
    Nor customary suits of solemn black,
    Nor windy suspiration of forc'd breath,
80   No, nor the fruitful river in the eye,
    Nor the dejected 'havior of the visage,
    Together with all forms, moods, shows of grief,
    That can denote me truly: these, indeed, seem;
    For they are actions that a man might play:
85   But I have that within which passeth show;
    These but the trappings and the suits of woe.
KING: 'Tis sweet and cómmendable in your nature, Hamlet,
    To give these mourning duties to your father:
    But, you must know, your father lost a father;
90   That father lost, lost his; and the survivor bound,
    In filial obligation, for some term
    To do obsequious sorrow: but to persever[2]

---

[1] *vailed:* downcast.   [2] *persever:* persevere.

In obstinate condolement is a course
Of impious stubbornness; 'tis unmanly grief:
95 It shows a will most incorrect to heaven;
A heart unfortified, a mind impatient;
An understanding simple and unschool'd:
For what we know must be, and is as common
As any the most vulgar thing to sense,[3]
100 Why should we, in our peevish opposition,
Take it to heart? Fie! 'tis a fault to heaven,
A fault against the dead, a fault to nature,
To reason most absurd; whose common theme
Is death of fathers, and who still[4] hath cried,
105 From the first corse till he that died to-day,
This must be so. We pray you, throw to earth
This unprevailing woe; and think of us
As of a father: for let the world take note
You are the most immediate to our throne;
110 And with no less nobility of love
Than that which dearest father bears his son
Do I impart toward you. For your intent
In going back to school in Wittenberg,
It is most retrograde to our desire:
115 And we beseech you bend you to remain
Here, in the cheer and comfort of our eye,
Our chiefest courtier, cousin, and our son.
QUEEN: Let not thy mother lose her prayers, Hamlet:
I pray thee, stay with us; go not to Wittenberg.
120 HAMLET: I shall in all my best obey you, madam.
KING: Why, 'tis a loving and a fair reply:
Be as ourself in Denmark.—Madam, come;
This gentle and unforc'd accord of Hamlet
Sits smiling to my heart: in grace whereof,
125 No jocund health that Denmark drinks to-day
But the great cannon to the clouds shall tell;
And the king's rouse[5] the heavens shall bruit[6] again,
Re-speaking earthly thunder. Come away.

(Exeunt all but Hamlet.)

HAMLET: O, that this too too solid flesh would melt,
130 Thaw, and resolve itself into a dew!
Or that the Everlasting had not fix'd
His canon 'gainst self-slaughter! O God! O God!
How weary, stale, flat, and unprofitable

---

[3] *any . . . sense:* anything that is very commonly seen or heard. [4] *still:* ever, or always. [5] *rouse:* drink. [6] *bruit:* echo.

Seem to me all the uses of this world!
135   Fie on't! O fie! 'tis an unweeded garden,
That grows to seed; things rank and gross in nature
Possess it merely. That it should come to this!
But two months dead!—nay, not so much, not two:
So excellent a king; that was, to this,
140   Hyperion[7] to a satyr: so loving to my mother,
That he might not beteem the winds of heaven
Visit her face too roughly. Heaven and earth!
Must I remember? why, she would hang on him
As if increase of appetite had grown
145   By what it fed on: and yet, within a month,—
Let me not think on't,—Frailty, thy name is woman!—
A little month; or ere those shoes were old
With which she follow'd my poor father's body
Like Niobe, all tears;—why she, even she,—
150   O God! a beast, that wants discourse of reason,
Would have mourn'd longer,—married with mine uncle,
My father's brother; but no more like my father
Than I to Hercules: within a month;
Ere yet the salt of most unrighteous tears
155   Had left the flushing in her galled eyes,
She married:—O, most wicked speed, to post
With such dexterity to incestuous sheets!
It is not, nor it cannot come to good;
But break, my heart,—for I must hold my tongue!

(Enter Horatio, Marcellus, and Bernardo.)

160 HORATIO: Hail to your lordship!
  HAMLET: I am glad to see you well:
     Horatio,—or I do forget myself.
  HORATIO: The same, my lord, and your poor servant ever.
  HAMLET: Sir, my good friend; I'll change that name with you:
     And what make you from Wittenberg, Horatio?—Marcellus?
165 MARCELLUS: My good lord,—
  HAMLET: I am very glad to see you.—Good even, sir.—
     But what, in faith, make you from Wittenberg?
  HORATIO: A truant disposition, good my lord.
  HAMLET: I would not hear your enemy say so;
170   Nor shall you do mine ear that violence,
     To make it truster of your own report
     Against yourself: I know you are no truant.
     But what is your affair in Elsinore?
     We'll teach you to drink deep ere you depart.

---

[7] *Hyperion:* the Greek sun god, the brightest and most beautiful of the gods.

175 **HORATIO:** My lord, I came to see your father's funeral.
HAMLET: I pray thee, do not mock me, fellow-student;
 I think it was to see my mother's wedding.
HORATIO: Indeed, my lord, it follow'd hard upon.
HAMLET: Thrift, thrift, Horatio! the funeral-bak'd meats
180 Did coldly furnish forth the marriage tables.
 Would I had met my dearest foe[8] in heaven
 Ere I had ever seen that day, Horatio!—
 My father,—methinks I see my father.
HORATIO: Where, my lord?
HAMLET: In my mind's eye, Horatio.
185 **HORATIO:** I saw him once; he was a goodly[9] king.
HAMLET: He was a man, take him for all in all,
 I shall not look upon his like again.
HORATIO: My lord, I think I saw him yester-night.
HAMLET: Saw who?
190 **HORATIO:** My lord, the king your father.
HAMLET: The king my father!
HORATIO: Season your admiration[10] for awhile
 With an attent ear, till I may deliver,
 Upon the witness of these gentlemen,
 This marvel to you.
HAMLET: For God's love, let me hear.
195 **HORATIO:** Two nights together had these gentlemen,
 Marcellus and Bernardo, in their watch,
 In the dead vast and middle of the night,
 Been thus encounter'd. A figure like your father,
 Arm'd at all points exactly, cap-a-pe,[11]
200 Appears before them, and with solemn march
 Goes slow and stately by them: thrice he walk'd
 By their oppress'd[12] and fear-surprised eyes,
 Within his truncheon's length; whilst they, distill'd
 Almost to jelly with the act of fear,
205 Stand dumb, and speak not to him. This to me
 In dreadful secrecy impart they did;
 And I with them the third night kept the watch:
 Where, as they had deliver'd, both in time,
 Form of the thing, each word made true and good,
210 The apparition comes: I knew your father;
 These hands are not more like.
HAMLET: But where was this?
MARCELLUS: My lord, upon the platform where we watch'd.
HAMLET: Did you not speak to it?

---

[8] *dearest foe:* worst enemy. [9] *goodly:* handsome. [10] *admiration:* astonishment. [11] *cap-a-pe:* from head to toe. [12] *oppress'd:* overwhelmed.

HORATIO: My lord, I did;
      But answer made it none: yet once methought
215   It lifted up its head, and did address
      Itself to motion, like as it would speak:
      But even then the morning cock crew loud,
      And at the sound it shrunk in haste away,
      And vanish'd from our sight.
HAMLET: 'Tis very strange.
220 HORATIO: As I do live, my honor'd lord, 'tis true;
      And we did think it writ down in our duty
      To let you know of it.
HAMLET: Indeed, indeed, sirs, but this troubles me.
      Hold you the watch to-night?
225 MARCELLUS and BERNARDO: We do, my lord.
HAMLET: Arm'd, say you?
MARCELLUS and BERNARDO: Arm'd, my lord.
HAMLET: From top to toe?
MARCELLUS and BERNARDO: My lord, from head to foot.
230 HAMLET: Then saw you not his face?
HORATIO: O yes, my lord; he wore his beaver up.
HAMLET: What, look'd he frowningly?
HORATIO: A countenance more in sorrow than in anger.
HAMLET: Pale or red?
235 HORATIO: Nay, very pale.
HAMLET: And fix'd his eyes upon you?
HORATIO: Most constantly.
HAMLET: I would I had been there.
HORATIO: It would have much amaz'd you.
HAMLET: Very like, very like. Stay'd it long?
HORATIO: While one with moderate haste might tell[13] a hundred.
240 MARCELLUS and BERNARDO: Longer, longer.
HORATIO: Not when I saw't.
HAMLET: His beard was grizzled,—no?
HORATIO: It was, as I have seen it in his life,
      A sable silver'd.
HAMLET: I will watch to-night;
      Perchance 'twill walk again.
HORATIO: I warrant it will.
245 HAMLET: If it assume my noble father's person
      I'll speak to it, though hell itself should gape
      And bid me hold my peace. I pray you all,
      If you have hitherto conceal'd this sight,
      Let it be tenable in your silence still;
250   And whatsoever else shall hap to-night,

---

[13] *tell:* count.

Give it an understanding, but no tongue:
I will requite your loves. So, fare ye well:
Upon the platform, 'twixt eleven and twelve,
I'll visit you.
ALL: Our duty to your honor.
255 **HAMLET:** Your loves, as mine to you: farewell.

(Exeunt Horatio, Marcellus, and Bernardo.)

My father's spirit in arms; all is not well;
I doubt some foul play: would the night were come!
Till then sit still, my soul: foul deeds will rise,
Though all the earth o'erwhelm them, to men's eyes.

(Exit.)

SCENE 3

A room in Polonius' house.

(Enter Laertes and Ophelia.)

LAERTES: My necessaries are embark'd: farewell:
And, sister, as the winds give benefit,
And convoy[1] is assistant, do not sleep,
But let me hear from you.
OPHELIA: Do you doubt that?
5 **LAERTES:** For Hamlet, and the trifling of his favor,
Hold it a fashion and a toy in blood:
A violet in the youth of primy nature,
Forward, not permanent, sweet, not lasting,
The perfume and suppliance of a minute;
10   No more.
OPHELIA: No more but so?
LAERTES: Think it no more:
For nature, crescent,[2] does not grow alone
In thews and bulk; but as this temple[3] waxes,
The inward service of the mind and soul
Grows wide withal. Perhaps he loves you now;
15 And now no soil nor cautel[4] doth besmirch
The virtue of his will: but you must fear,
His greatness weigh'd, his will is not his own;
For he himself is subject to his birth:
He may not, as unvalu'd persons do,
20   Carve for himself; for on his choice depends
The safety and the health of the whole state;

---

[1] *convoy:* means of conveyance.   [2] *crescent:* growing.   [3] *temple:* body.   [4] *cautel:* deceit.

And therefore must his choice be circumscrib'd
Unto the voice and yielding of that body
Whereof he is the head. Then if he says he loves you,
It fits your wisdom so far to believe it
As he in his particular act and place
May give his saying deed; which is no further
Than the main[5] voice of Denmark goes withal.
Then weigh what loss your honor may sustain
If with too credent ear you list his songs,
Or lose your heart, or your chaste treasure open
To his unmaster'd importunity.
Fear it, Ophelia, fear it, my dear sister;
And keep within the rear of your affection,
Out of the shot and danger of desire.
The chariest maid is prodigal enough
If she unmask her beauty to the moon:
Virtue itself scrapes not calumnious strokes:
The canker galls the infants of the spring
Too oft before their buttons be disclos'd;
And in the morn and liquid dew of youth
Contagious blastments are most imminent.
Be wary, then; best safety lies in fear:
Youth to itself rebels, though none else near.

OPHELIA: I shall the effect of this good lesson keep
As watchman to my heart. But, good my brother,
Do not, as some ungracious pastors do,
Show me the steep and thorny way to heaven;
Whilst like a puff'd and reckless libertine,
Himself the primrose path of dalliance treads,
And recks not his own rede.[6]

LAERTES: O, fear me not.
I stay too long:—but here my father comes.

(Enter Polonius.)

A double blessing is a double grace;
Occasion smiles upon a second leave.

POLONIUS: Yet here, Laertes! aboard, aboard, for shame!
The wind sits in the shoulder of your sail,
And you are stay'd for. There,—my blessing with you!

(Laying his hand on Laertes' head.)

And these few precepts in thy memory
See thou character.[7] Give thy thoughts no tongue,

---

[5] *main:* strong, or mighty.   [6] *rede:* counsel.   [7] *in . . . character:* engrave in your mind.

60   Nor any unproportion'd thought his act.
           Be thou familiar, but by no means vulgar.
           The friends thou hast, and their adoption tried,
           Grapple them to thy soul with hoops of steel;
           But do not dull thy palm with entertainment
65   Of each new-hatch'd, unfledg'd comrade. Beware
           Of entrance to a quarrel; but, being in,
           Bear't that the opposèd may beware of thee.
           Give every man thine ear, but few thy voice:
           Take each man's censure,[8] but reserve thy judgment.
70   Costly thy habit as thy purse can buy,
           But not express'd in fancy; rich, not gaudy:
           For the apparel oft proclaims the man;
           And they in France of the best rank and station
           Are most select and generous chief in that.
75   Neither a borrower nor a lender be:
           For a loan oft loses both itself and friend;
           And borrowing dulls the edge of husbandry.
           This above all,—to thine own self be true;
           And it must follow, as the night the day,
80   Thou canst not then be false to any man.
           Farewell: my blessing season this in thee!
      LAERTES: Most humbly do I take my leave, my lord.
      POLONIUS: The time invites you; go, your servants tend.[9]
      LAERTES: Farewell, Ophelia; and remember well
85   What I have said to you.
           OPHELIA: 'Tis in my memory lock'd,
           And you yourself shall keep the key of it.
      LAERTES: Farewell. *(Exit.)*
      POLONIUS: What is't, Ophelia, he hath said to you?
      OPHELIA: So please you, something touching the Lord Hamlet.
90 **POLONIUS:** Marry, well bethought:
           'Tis told me he hath very oft of late
           Given private time to you; and you yourself
           Have of your audience been most free and bounteous:
           If it be so,—as so 'tis put on me,
95   And that in way of caution,—I must tell you,
           You do not understand yourself so clearly
           As it behoves my daughter and your honor.
           What is between you? give me up the truth.
      OPHELIA: He hath, my lord, of late made many tenders
100   Of his affection to me.
      POLONIUS: Affection! pooh! you speak like a green girl,
           Unsifted in such perilous circumstance.
           Do you believe his tenders,[10] as you call them?

---

[8] *censure:* opinion.   [9] *tend:* wait.   [10] *tenders:* offers.

OPHELIA: I do not know, my lord, what I should think.
105 POLONIUS: Marry, I'll teach you: think yourself a baby;
That you have ta'en these tenders for true pay,
Which are not sterling. Tender yourself more dearly;
Or,—not to crack the wind of the poor phrase,
Wronging it thus,—you'll tender me a fool.
110 OPHELIA: My lord, he hath impórtun'd me with love
In honorable fashion.
POLONIUS: Ay, fashion you may call it; go to, go to.
OPHELIA: And hath given countenance to his speech, my lord,
With almost all the holy vows of heaven.
115 POLONIUS: Ay, springes to catch woodcocks. I do know,
When the blood burns, how prodigal the soul
Lends the tongue vows: these blazes, daughter,
Giving more light than heat,—extinct in both,
Even in their promise, as it is a-making,—
120 You must not take for fire. From this time
Be somewhat scanter of your maiden presence;
Set your entreatments at a higher rate
Than a command to parley. For Lord Hamlet,
Believe so much in him, that he is young;
125 And with a larger tether may he walk
Than may be given you: in few, Ophelia,
Do not believe his vows; for they are brokers,[11]—
Not of that die which their investments show,
But mere implorators of unholy suits,
130 Breathing like sanctified and pious bawds,
The better to beguile. This is for all,—
I would not, in plain terms, from this time forth,
Have you so slander any moment leisure
As to give words or talk with the Lord Hamlet.
135 Look to't, I charge you; come your ways.
OPHELIA: I shall obey, my lord.

(Exeunt.)

SCENE 4

The platform.

(Enter Hamlet, Horatio, and Marcellus.)

HAMLET: The air bites shrewdly; it is very cold.
HORATIO: It is a nipping and an eager air.
HAMLET: What hour now?
HORATIO: I think it lacks of twelve.
MARCELLUS: No, it is struck.

---

[11] *brokers:* procurers.

5 HORATIO: Indeed? I heard it not: then it draws near the season
   Wherein the spirit held his wont to walk.

(A flourish of trumpets, and ordnance shot off within.)

   What does this mean, my lord?
HAMLET: The king doth wake to-night, and takes his rouse,
   Keeps wassail, and the swaggering upspring[1] reels;
10 And, as he drains his draughts of Rhenish down,
   The kettle-drum and trumpet thus bray out
   The triumph of his pledge.[2]
HORATIO: Is it a custom?
HAMLET: Ay, marry, is't:
   But to my mind,—though I am native here,
15 And to the manner born,—it is a custom
   More honor'd in the breach than the observance.
   This heavy-headed revel east and west
   Makes us traduc'd and tax'd of other nations:
   They clepe us drunkards, and with swinish phrase
20 Soil our addition;[3] and, indeed, it takes
   From our achievements, though perform'd at height,
   The pith and marrow of our attribute.
   So oft it chances in particular men
   That, for some vicious mole of nature in them,
25 As in their birth,—wherein they are not guilty,
   Since nature cannot choose his origin,—
   By the o'ergrowth of some complexion,
   Oft breaking down the pales and forts of reason;
   Or by some habit, that too much o'erleavens
30 The form of plausive[4] manners;—that these men,—
   Carrying, I say, the stamp of one defect,
   Being nature's livery or fortune's star,—
   Their virtues else,—be they as pure as grace,
   As infinite as man may undergo,—
35 Shall in the general censure take corruption
   From that particular fault: the dram of evil
   Doth all the noble substance of a doubt
   To his own scandal.
HORATIO: Look, my lord, it comes!

(Enter Ghost.)

HAMLET: Angels and ministers of grace defend us!—
40 Be thou a spirit of health or goblin damn'd,
   Bring with thee airs from heaven or blasts from hell,

---

[1] *upspring:* a dance. [2] *triumph . . . pledge:* the glory of his toasts. [3] *addition:* reputation. [4] *plausive:* pleasing.

          Be thy intents wicked or charitable,
          Thou com'st in such a questionable shape
          That I will speak to thee: I'll call thee Hamlet,
45   King, father, royal Dane: O, answer me!
          Let me not burst in ignorance; but tell
          Why thy canóniz'd bones, hearsèd in death,
          Have burst their cerements; why the sepulchre,
          Wherein we saw thee quietly in-urn'd,
50   Hath op'd his ponderous and marble jaws
          To cast thee up again! What may this mean,
          That thou, dead corse, again in còmplete steel,
          Revisit'st thus the glimpses of the moon,
          Making night hideous and we[5] fools of nature
55   So horridly to shake our disposition
          With thoughts beyond the reaches of our souls?
          Say, why is this? wherefore? what should we do?

     (Ghost beckons Hamlet.)

     HORATIO: It beckons you to go away with it,
          As if it some impartment did desire
60   To you alone.
     MARCELLUS: Look, with what courteous action
          It waves you to a more removed ground:
          But do not go with it.
     HORATIO: No, by no means.
     HAMLET: It will not speak; then will I follow it.
     HORATIO: Do not, my lord.
     HAMLET: Why, what should be the fear?
65   I do not set my life at a pin's fee;
          And for my soul, what can it do to that,
          Being a thing immortal as itself?
          It waves me forth again;—I'll follow it.
     HORATIO: What if it tempt you toward the flood, my lord.
70   Or to the dreadful summit of the cliff
          That beetles o'er his base into the sea,
          And there assume some other horrible form,
          Which might deprive your sovereignty of reason,
          And draw you into madness? think of it:
75   The very place puts toys of desperation,
          Without more motive, into every brain
          That looks so many fathoms to the sea
          And hears it roar beneath.
     HAMLET: It waves me still.—
          Go on; I'll follow thee.

---

[5] *we:* us.

80 **MARCELLUS:** You shall not go, my lord.
    HAMLET: Hold off your hands.
    HORATIO: Be rul'd; you shall not go.
    HAMLET: My fate cries out,
       And makes each petty artery in this body
       As hardy as the Némean lion's[6] nerve.—

(Ghost beckons.)

       Still am I call'd;—unhand me, gentlemen;—*(Breaking from them)*
85   By heaven, I'll make a ghost of him that lets[7] me.
       I say, away!—Go on; I'll follow thee.

(Exeunt Ghost and Hamlet.)

    HORATIO: He waxes desperate with imagination.
    MARCELLUS: Let's follow; 'tis not fit thus to obey him.
    HORATIO: Have after.—To what issue will this come?
90 **MARCELLUS:** Something is rotten in the state of Denmark.
    HORATIO: Heaven will direct it.
    MARCELLUS: Nay, let's follow him.

(Exeunt.)

SCENE 5

A more remote part of the platform.

(Enter Ghost and Hamlet.)

    HAMLET: Where wilt thou lead me? speak, I'll go no further.
    GHOST: Mark me.
    HAMLET: I will.
    GHOST: My hour is almost come,
       When I to sulphurous and tormenting flames
       Must render up myself.
    HAMLET: Alas, poor ghost!
5 **GHOST:** Pity me not, but lend thy serious hearing
       To what I shall unfold.
    HAMLET: Speak; I am bound to hear.
    GHOST: So art thou to revenge, when thou shalt hear.
    HAMLET: What?
    GHOST: I am thy father's spirit;
10   Doom'd for a certain term to walk the night,
       And, for the day, confin'd to waste in fires
       Till the foul crimes[1] done in my days of nature
       Are burnt and purg'd away. But that I am forbid

---

[6] *Némean lion's:* the fierce lion that Hercules was called upon to slay as one of his "twelve labors."   [7] *lets:* hinders.

[1] *foul crimes:* rather, sins or faults.

                To tell the secrets of my prison-house,
15   I could a tale unfold whose lightest word
                Would harrow up thy soul; freeze thy young blood;
                Make thy two eyes, like stars, start from their spheres;
                Thy knotted and combined locks to part,
                And each particular hair to stand on end,
20   Like quills upon the fretful porcupine:
                But this eternal blazon[2] must not be
                To ears of flesh and blood.—List, list, O, list!—
                If thou didst ever thy dear father love,—
        HAMLET: O God!
25   GHOST: Revenge his foul and most unnatural murder.
        HAMLET: Murder!
        GHOST: Murder—most foul, as in the best it is;
                But this most foul, strange, and unnatural.
        HAMLET: Haste me to know't, that I, with wings as swift
30   As meditation or the thoughts of love,
                May sweep to my revenge.
        GHOST: I find thee apt;
                And duller shouldst thou be than the fat weed
                That rots itself in ease on Lethe[3] wharf,
                Wouldst thou not stir in this. Now, Hamlet,
35   'Tis given out that, sleeping in mine orchard,
                A serpent stung me; so the whole ear of Denmark
                Is by a forged process of my death
                Rankly abus'd: but know, thou noble youth,
                The serpent that did sting thy father's life
40   Now wears his crown.
        HAMLET: O my prophetic soul! mine uncle!
        GHOST: Ay, that incestuous, that adulterate beast,
                With witchcraft of his wit, with traitorous gifts,—
                O wicked wit and gifts that have the power
                So to seduce!—won to his shameful lust
45   The will of my most seeming virtuous queen:
                O Hamlet, what a falling-off was there!
                From me, whose love was of that dignity
                That it went hand in hand even with the vow
                I made to her in marriage: and to decline
50   Upon a wretch whose natural gifts were poor
                To those of mine!
                But virtue, as it never will be mov'd,
                Though lewdness court it in a shape of heaven;
                So lust, though to a radiant angel link'd,

---

[2] *eternal blazon:* disclosure of information concerning the other world.
[3] *Lethe:* the river of forgetfulness of the past, out of which the dead drink.

	Will sate itself in a celestial bed

55   Will sate itself in a celestial bed
        And prey on garbage.
        But, soft! methinks I scent the morning air;
        Brief let me be.—Sleeping within mine orchard,
        My custom always in the afternoon,
60   Upon my sécure hour thy uncle stole,
        With juice of cursed hebenon[4] in a vial,
        And in the porches of mine ears did pour
        The leperous distilment; whose effect
        Holds such an enmity with blood of man
65   That, swift as quicksilver, it courses through
        The natural gates and alleys of the body;
        And with a sudden vigor it doth posset[5]
        And curd, like eager[6] droppings into milk,
        The thin and wholesome blood: so did it mine;
70   And a most instant tetter bark'd about,
        Most lazar-like,[7] with vile and loathsome crust,
        All my smooth body.
        Thus was I, sleeping, by a brother's hand,
        Of life, of crown, of queen, at once despatch'd:
75   Cut off even in the blossoms of my sin,
        Unhousel'd, unanointed, unanel'd;
        No reckoning made, but sent to my account
        With all my imperfections on my head:
        O, horrible! O, horrible! most horrible!
80   If thou hast nature in thee, bear it not;
        Let not the royal bed of Denmark be
        A couch for luxury[8] and damned incest.
        But, howsoever thou pursu'st this act,
        Taint not thy mind, nor let thy soul contrive
85   Against thy mother aught: leave her to heaven,
        And to those thorns that in her bosom lodge,
        To prick and sting her. Fare thee well at once!
        The glowworm shows the matin to be near,
        And 'gins to pale his uneffectual fire:
90   Adieu, adieu! Hamlet, remember me. *(Exit.)*
HAMLET: O all you host of heaven! O earth! what else?
        And shall I couple hell?—O, fie!—Hold, my heart;
        And you, my sinews, grow not instant old,
        But bear me stiffly up.—Remember thee!
95   Ay, thou poor ghost, while memory holds a seat
        In this distracted globe. Remember thee!
        Yea, from the table of my memory

---

[4] *hebenon:* ebony.   [5] *posset:* coagulate.   [6] *eager:* acid.   [7] *lazar-like:* like a leper, whose skin is rough.   [8] *luxury:* lechery.

                I'll wipe away all trivial fond⁹ records,
                All saws of books, all forms, all pressures past,
100   That youth and observation copied there;
                And thy commandment all alone shall live
                Within the book and volume of my brain,
                Unmix'd with baser matter: yes, by heaven.—
                O most pernicious woman!
105   O villain, villain, smiling, damned villain!
                My tables,—meet it is I set it down,
                That one may smile, and smile, and be a villain;
                At least, I am sure, it may be so in Denmark:

        (Writing.)

                So, uncle, there you are. Now to my word;
110   It is, *Adieu, adieu! remember me:*
                I have sworn't.
        HORATIO: *(Within)* My lord, my lord,—
        MARCELLUS: *(Within)*   Lord Hamlet,—
        HORATIO: *(Within)*   Heaven secure him!
        MARCELLUS: *(Within)* So be it!
        HORATIO: *(Within)* Illo, ho, ho, my lord!
        HAMLET: Hillo, ho, ho, boy! come, bird, come.¹⁰

        (Enter Horatio and Marcellus.)

115   MARCELLUS: How is't, my noble lord?
        HORATIO: What news, my lord?
        HAMLET: O, wonderful!
        HORATIO: Good my lord, tell it.
        HAMLET: No; you'll reveal it.
        HORATIO: Not I, my lord, by heaven.
        MARCELLUS: Nor I, my lord.
        HAMLET: How say you, then; would heart of man once think it?—
120   But you'll be secret?
        HORATIO and MARCELLUS: Ay, by heaven, my lord.
        HAMLET: There's ne'er a villain dwelling in all Denmark
                But he's an arrant knave.
        HORATIO: There needs no ghost, my lord, come from the grave
125   To tell us this.
        HAMLET: Why, right; you are i' the right;
                And so, without more circumstance at all,
                I hold it fit that we shake hands and part:
                You, as your business and desire shall point you,—
130   For every man has business and desire,

---

⁹ *fond:* foolish.   ¹⁰ *bird:* Hamlet uses the word "bird" because this is a falconer's call.

Such as it is;—and for mine own poor part,
Look you, I'll go pray.
HORATIO: These are but wild and whirling words, my lord.
HAMLET: I'm sorry they offend you, heartily;
135   Yes, faith, heartily.
HORATIO: There's no offence, my lord.
HAMLET: Yes, by Saint Patrick, but there is, Horatio,
And much offence too. Touching this vision here,—
It is an honest ghost, that let me tell you:
For you desire to know what is between us,
140   O'ermaster't as you may. And now, good friends,
As you are friends, scholars, and soldiers,
Give me one poor request.
HORATIO: What is't, my lord? we will.
HAMLET: Never make known what you have seen to-night.
145 HORATIO and MARCELLUS: My lord, we will not.
HAMLET: Nay, but swear't.
HORATIO: In faith,
My lord, not I.
MARCELLUS: Nor I, my lord, in faith.
HAMLET: Upon my sword.
MARCELLUS: We have sworn, my lord, already.
HAMLET: Indeed, upon my sword, indeed.
GHOST: *(Beneath)* Swear.
150 HAMLET: Ha, ha, boy! say'st thou so? art thou there, truepenny?—
Come on,—you hear this fellow in the cellarage,—
Consent to swear.
HORATIO: Propose the oath, my lord.
HAMLET: Never to speak of this that you have seen,
Swear by my sword.
155 GHOST: *(Beneath)* Swear.
HAMLET: *Hic et ubique?*[11] then we'll shift our ground.—
Come hither, gentlemen,
And lay your hands again upon my sword:
Never to speak of this that you have heard,
160   Swear by my sword.
GHOST: *(Beneath)* Swear.
HAMLET: Well said! old mole! canst work i' the earth so fast?
A worthy pioneer![12]—Once more remove, good friends.
HORATIO: O day and night, but this is wondrous strange!
165 HAMLET: And therefore as a stranger give it welcome.
There are more things in heaven and earth, Horatio,

---

[11] *Hic et ubique:* here and everywhere?   [12] *pioneer:* a soldier who digs trenches and undermines fortresses.

        Than are dreamt of in your philosophy.
        But come;—
        Here, as before, never, so help you mercy,
170   How strange or odd soe'er I bear myself,—
        As I, perchance, hereafter shall think meet
        To put an antic disposition on,—
        That you, at such times seeing me, never shall,
        With arms encumber'd[13] thus, or this headshake,
175   Or by pronouncing of some doubtful phrase,
        As, *Well, well, we know;*—or, *We could, an if we would;*—
        Or, *If we list to speak;*—or, *There be, an if they might;*—
        Or such ambiguous giving out, to note
        That you know aught of me:—this not to do,
180   So grace and mercy at your most need help you,
        Swear.
GHOST: *(Beneath)* Swear.
HAMLET: Rest, rest, perturbed spirit!—So, gentlemen,
        With all my love I do commend to you:
185   And what so poor a man as Hamlet is
        May do, to express his love and friending to you,
        God willing, shall not lack. Let us go in together;
        And still your fingers on your lips, I pray.
        The time is out of joint:—O cursed spite,
190   That ever I was born to set it right!—
        Nay, come, let's go together.

(Exeunt.)

ACT II
SCENE 1

A room in Polonius' house.

(Enter Polonius and Reynaldo.)

POLONIUS: Give him this money and these notes, Reynaldo.
REYNALDO: I will, my lord.
POLONIUS: You shall do marvelous wisely, good Reynaldo,
        Before you visit him, to make inquiry
5   On his behavior.
REYNALDO: My lord, I did intend it.
POLONIUS: Marry, well said; very well said. Look you, sir,
        Inquire me first what Danskers[1] are in Paris;
        And how, and who, what means, and where they keep,
        What company, at what expense; and finding,

---

[13] *encumber'd:* folded.

[1] *Danskers:* Danes.

10 　　　By this encompassment and drift of question,
　　　That they do know my son, come you more nearer
　　　Than your particular demands will touch it:
　　　Take you, as 'twere, some distant knowledge of him;
　　　As thus, *I know his father and his friends,*
15 　　　*And in part him;*—do you mark this, Reynaldo?
　　REYNALDO: Ay, very well, my lord.
　　POLONIUS: *And in part him;*—but, you may say, *not well:*
　　　But if't be he I mean, he's very wild;
　　　Addicted so and so; and there put on him
20 　　　What forgeries you please; marry, none so rank
　　　As may dishonor him; take heed of that;
　　　But, sir, such wanton, wild, and usual slips
　　　As are companions noted and most known
　　　To youth and liberty.
　　REYNALDO: 　　　　　　　As gaming, my lord.
25 　　POLONIUS: Ay, or drinking, fencing, swearing, quarreling,
　　　Drabbing:[2]—you may go so far.
　　REYNALDO: My lord, that would dishonor him.
　　POLONIUS: Faith, no; as you may season it in the charge.
　　　You must not put another scandal on him,
30 　　　That he is open to incontinency;
　　　That's not my meaning: but breathe his faults so quaintly
　　　That they may seem the taints of liberty;
　　　The flash and outbreak of a fiery mind;
　　　A savageness in unreclaimed blood,
35 　　　Of general assault.
　　REYNALDO: 　　　　　But, my good lord,—
　　POLONIUS: Wherefore should you do this?
　　REYNALDO: 　　　　　　　　　Ay, my lord,
　　　I would know that.
　　POLONIUS: 　　　　Marry, sir, here's my drift;
　　　And I believe it is a fetch of warrant:[3]
　　　You laying these slight sullies on my son.
40 　　　As 'twere a thing a little soil'd i' the working,
　　　Mark you,
　　　Your party in converse, him you would sound,
　　　Having ever seen in the prenominate crimes
　　　The youth you breathe of guilty, be assur'd
45 　　　He closes with you in this consequence;
　　　Good sir, or so; or *friend,* or *gentleman,*—
　　　According to the phrase or the addition[4]
　　　Of man and country.

---

[2] *Drabbing:* going about with loose women. 　[3] *fetch of warrant:* a good device.
[4] *addition:* form of address.

REYNALDO: Very good, my lord.
POLONIUS: And then, sir, does he this,—he does,—
50   What was I about to say?—By the mass, I was
        About to say something:—where did I leave?
REYNALDO: At *closes in the consequence,*
        At *friend or so,* and *gentleman.*
POLONIUS: At—closes in the consequence,—ay, marry;
55   He closes with you thus:—*I know the gentleman;*
        I saw him yesterday, or t'other day,
        Or then, or then; with such, or such; and, as you say,
        There was he gaming; there o'ertook in's rouse;
        There falling out at tennis: or perchance,
60   *I saw him enter such a house of sale,*—
        Videlicet, a brothel,—or so forth.—
        See you now;
        Your bait of falsehood takes this carp of truth:
        And thus do we of wisdom and of reach,
65   With windlasses, and with assays of bias,
        By indirections find directions out:
        So, by my former lecture and advice,
        Shall you my son. You have me, have you not?
REYNALDO: My lord, I have.
POLONIUS: God b' wi' you; fare you well.
70 REYNALDO: Good my lord!
POLONIUS: Observe his inclination in yourself.
REYNALDO: I shall, my lord.
POLONIUS: And let him ply his music.
REYNALDO: Well, my lord.
POLONIUS: Farewell!

(Exit Reynaldo.)

(Enter Ophelia.)

75   How now, Ophelia! what's the matter?
OPHELIA: Alas, my lord, I have been so affrighted.
POLONIUS: With what, i' the name of God?
OPHELIA: My lord, as I was sewing in my chamber,
        Lord Hamlet,—with his doublet all unbrac'd;
80   No hat upon his head; his stockings foul'd,
        Ungarter'd, and down-gyved[5] to his ankle;
        Pale as his shirt; his knees knocking each other;
        And with a look so piteous in purport
        As if he had been loosed out of hell
85   To speak of horrors,—he comes before me.
POLONIUS: Mad for thy love?

---

[5] *down-gyved:* dangling like chains.

OPHELIA: My lord, I do not know;
    But truly I do fear it.
POLONIUS: What said he?
OPHELIA: He took me by the wrist, and held me hard;
    Then goes he to the length of all his arm;
90 And with his other hand thus o'er his brow,
    He falls to such perusal of my face
    As he would draw it. Long stay'd he so;
    At last,—a little shaking of mine arm,
    And thrice his head thus waving up and down,—
95 He rais'd a sigh so piteous and profound
    That it did seem to shatter all his bulk
    And end his being; that done, he lets me go:
    And, with his head over his shoulder turn'd,
    He seem'd to find his way without his eyes;
100 For out o' doors he went without their help,
    And to the last bended their light on me.
POLONIUS: Come, go with me: I will go seek the king.
    This is the very ecstasy[6] of love;
    Whose violent property fordoes itself,[7]
105 And leads the will to desperate undertakings,
    As oft as any passion under heaven
    That does afflict our nature. I am sorry,—
    What, have you given him any hard words of late?
OPHELIA: No, my good lord; but, as you did command,
110 I did repel his letters, and denied
    His access to me.
POLONIUS: That hath made him mad.
    I am sorry that with better heed and judgment
    I had not quoted him: I fear'd he did but trifle,
    And meant to wreck thee; but, beshrew my jealousy!
115 It seems it is as proper to our age
    To cast beyond ourselves in our opinions
    As it is common for the younger sort
    To lack discretion. Come, go we to the king:
    This must be known; which, being kept close, might move
120 More grief to hide than hate to utter love.

(Exeunt.)

SCENE 2

A room in the castle.

(Enter King, Queen, Rosencrantz, Guildenstern, and Attendants.)

KING: Welcome, dear Rosencrantz and Guildenstern!
    Moreover that we much did long to see you,

---

[6] *ecstasy:* madness.   [7] *fordoes itself:* destroys itself.

                The need we have to use you did provoke
                Our hasty sending. Something have you heard
5   Of Hamlet's transformation; so I call it,
                Since nor the exterior nor the inward man
                Resembles that it was. What it should be,
                More than his father's death, that thus hath put him
                So much from the understanding of himself,
10   I cannot dream of: I entreat you both,
                That being of so young days brought up with him,
                And since so neighbor'd to his youth and humor,
                That you vouchsafe your rest here in our court
                Some little time: so by your companies
15   To draw him on to pleasures, and to gather,
                So much as from occasion you may glean,
                Whether aught, to us unknown, afflicts him thus,
                That, open'd, lies within our remedy.
        QUEEN: Good gentlemen, he hath much talk'd of you;
20   And sure I am two men there are not living
                To whom he more adheres. If it will please you
                To show us so much gentry and good-will
                As to expend your time with us awhile,
                For the supply and profit of our hope,
25   Your visitation shall receive such thanks
                As fits a king's remembrance.
        ROSENCRANTZ: Both your majesties
                Might, by the sovereign power you have of us,
                Put your dread pleasures more into command
                Than to entreaty.
        GUILDENSTERN: We both obey,
30   And here give up ourselves, in the full bent,
                To lay our service freely at your feet,
                To be commanded.
        KING: Thanks, Rosencrantz and gentle Guildenstern.
        QUEEN: Thanks, Guildenstern and gentle Rosencrantz:
35   And I beseech you instantly to visit
                My too-much-changed son.—Go, some of you,
                And bring these gentlemen where Hamlet is.
        GUILDENSTERN: Heavens make our presence and our practices
                Pleasant and helpful to him!
        QUEEN: Ay, amen!

        (Exeunt Rosencrantz, Guildenstern, and some Attendants.)

        (Enter Polonius.)

40   POLONIUS: The ambassadors from Norway, my good lord,
                Are joyfully return'd.
        KING: Thou still has been the father of good news.

POLONIUS: Have I, my lord? Assure you, my good liege,
  I hold my duty, as I hold my soul,
45 Both to my God and to my gracious king:
  And I do think,—or else this brain of mine
  Hunts not the trail of policy[1] so sure
  As it hath us'd to do,—that I have found
  The very cause of Hamlet's lunacy.
50 KING: O, speak of that; that do I long to hear.
POLONIUS: Give first admittance to the ambassadors;
  My news shall be the fruit to that great feast.
KING: Thyself do grace to them, and bring them in.

(Exit Polonius.)

  He tells me, my sweet queen, that he hath found
55 The head and source of all your son's distemper.
QUEEN: I doubt it is no other but the main,—
  His father's death and our o'erhasty marriage.
KING: Well, we shall sift him.

(Re-enter Polonius, with Voltimand and Cornelius.)

            Welcome, my good friends!
  Say, Voltimand, what from our brother Norway?
60 VOLTIMAND: Most fair return of greetings and desires.
  Upon our first, he sent out to suppress
  His nephew's levies; which to him appear'd
  To be a preparation 'gainst the Polack;
  But, better look'd into, he truly found
65 It was against your highness: whereat griev'd,—
  That so his sickness, age, and impotence
  Was falsely borne in hand,—sends out arrests
  On Fortinbras; which he, in brief, obeys;
  Receives rebuke from Norway; and, in fine,
70 Makes vows before his uncle never more
  To give the assay of arms against your majesty.
  Whereon old Norway, overcome with joy,
  Gives him three thousand crowns in annual fee;
  And his commission to employ those soldiers,
75 So levied as before, against the Polack:
  With an entreaty, herein further shown, *(gives a paper)*
  That it might please you to give quiet pass
  Through your dominions for this enterprise,
  On such regards of safety and allowance
80 As therein are set down.

---

[1] *trail of policy:* statecraft.

KING: It likes us well;
And at our more consider'd time we'll read,
Answer, and think upon this business.
Meantime we thank you for your well-took labor:
Go to your rest; at night we'll feast together:
85 Most welcome home!

(Exeunt Voltimand and Cornelius.)

POLONIUS: This business is well ended.—
My liege, and madam,—to expostulate
What majesty should be, what duty is,
Why day is day, night night, and time is time,
Were nothing but to waste night, day, and time.
90 Therefore, since brevity is the soul of wit,
And tediousness the limbs and outward flourishes,
I will be brief:—your noble son is mad:
Mad call I it; for to define true madness,
What is't but to be nothing else but mad?
95 But let that go.
QUEEN: More matter with less art.
POLONIUS: Madam, I swear I use no art at all.
That he is mad, 'tis true 'tis pity;
And pity 'tis 'tis true: a foolish figure;
But farewell it, for I will use no art.
100 Mad let us grant him, then: and now remains
That we find out the cause of this effect;
Or rather say, the cause of this defect,
For this effect defective comes by cause:
Thus it remains, and the remainder thus.
105 Perpend.
I have a daughter,—have whilst she is mine,—
Who, in her duty and obedience, mark,
Hath given me this: now gather, and surmise

(Reads)

To the celestial, and my soul's idol, the most beautified Ophelia,—

110 That's an ill phrase, a vile phrase,—*beautified* is a vile phrase: but
you shall hear. Thus:

(Reads)

In her excellent white bosom, these, &c.

QUEEN: Came this from Hamlet to her?
POLONIUS: Good madam, stay a while; I will be faithful.

(Reads)

115   *Doubt thou the stars are fire;*
                    Doubt that the sun doth move;
                    Doubt truth to be a liar;
                    But never doubt I love.

    O dear Ophelia, I am ill at these numbers, I have not art to reckon
120   *my groans: but that I love thee best, O most best, believe it.*
    Adieu.
    Thine evermore, most dear lady, whilst this machine is to him, Hamlet

    This, in obedience, hath my daughter show'd me:
    And more above, hath his solicitings,
125   As they fell out by time, by means, and place,
    All given to mine ear.
King: But how hath she
    Receiv'd his love?
Polonius: What do you think of me?
King: As of a man faithful and honorable.
Polonius: I would fain prove so. But what might you think,
130   When I had seen this hot love on the wing,—
    As I perceiv'd it, I must tell you that,
    Before my daughter told me,—what might you,
    Or my dear majesty your queen here, think,
    If I had play'd the desk or table-book;[2]
135   Or given my heart a winking, mute and dumb;
    Or look'd upon this love with idle sight;—
    What might you think? No, I went round to work,
    And my young mistress thus I did bespeak:
    Lord Hamlet is a prince out of thy sphere;
140   *This must not be:* and then I precepts gave her,
    That she should lock herself from his resort,
    Admit no messengers, receive no tokens.
    Which done, she took the fruits of my advice;
    And he, repulsed,—a short tale to make,—
145   Fell into a sadness; then into a fast;
    Thence to a watch; thence into a weakness;
    Thence to a lightness; and, by this declension,
    Into the madness wherein now he raves
    And all we wail for.
King: Do you think 'tis this?
150 **Queen:** It may be, very likely.
Polonius: Hath there been such a time,—I'd fain know that,—
    That I have positively said, *'Tis so,*
    When it prov'd otherwise?

---

[2] *table-book:* memorandum pad.

KING: Not that I know.
POLONIUS: Take this from this, if this be otherwise: *(Pointing to his head and shoulder)*
155   If circumstances lead me, I will find
Where truth is hid, though it were hid indeed
Within the center.
KING: How may we try it further?
POLONIUS: You know, sometimes he walks for hours together
Here in the lobby.
QUEEN: So he does, indeed.
160 POLONIUS: At such a time I'll loose my daughter to him:
Be you and I behind an arras[3] then;
Mark the encounter: if he love her not,
And be not from his reason fall'n thereon,
Let me be no assistant for a state,
165   But keep a farm and carters.
KING: We will try it.
QUEEN: But look, where sadly the poor wretch comes reading.
POLONIUS: Away, I do beseech you, both away:
I'll board[4] him presently:—O, give me leave.

(Exeunt King, Queen, and Attendants.)

(Enter Hamlet, reading.)

    How does my good Lord Hamlet?
170 HAMLET: Well, God-a-mercy.
POLONIUS: Do you know me, my lord?
HAMLET: Excellent, excellent well; you're a fishmonger.
POLONIUS: Not I, my lord.
HAMLET: Then I would you were so honest a man.
175 POLONIUS: Honest, my lord!
HAMLET: Ay, sir; to be honest, as this world goes, is to be one man picked out of ten thousand.
POLONIUS: That's very true, my lord.
HAMLET: For if the sun breed maggots in a dead dog, being a god
180   kissing carrion,—Have you a daughter?
POLONIUS: I have, my lord.
HAMLET: Let her not walk i' the sun: conception is a blessing; but not as your daughter may conceive:—friend, look to't.
POLONIUS: How say you by that?—*(Aside)* Still harping on my
185   daughter:—yet he knew me not at first; he said I was a fishmonger: he is far gone, far gone: and truly in my youth I suffered much extremity for love; very near this. I'll speak to him again.—What do you read, my lord?

---

[3] *arras:* tapestry, hung some distance away from a wall.   [4] *board:* address.

HAMLET: Words, words, words.
190 POLONIUS: What is the matter, my lord?
HAMLET: Between who?
POLONIUS: I mean, the matter that you read, my lord.
HAMLET: Slanders, sir: for the satirical slave says here that old men
have gray beards; that their faces are wrinkled; their eyes purging
195 thick amber and plum-tree gum; and that they have a plentiful
lack of wit, together with most weak hams: all which, sir, though I
most powerfully and potently believe, yet I hold it not honesty to
have it thus set down; for you yourself, sir, should be old as I am,
if, like a crab, you could go backward.
200 POLONIUS: *(Aside)* Though this be madness, yet there is method in't.—
ill you walk out of the air, my lord?
HAMLET: Into my grave?
POLONIUS: Indeed, that is out o' the air.—*(Aside)* How pregnant[5]
sometimes his replies are! a happiness that often madness hits on,
205 which reason and sanity could not so prosperously be delivered of.
I will leave him, and suddenly contrive the means of meeting
between him and my daughter.—More honorable lord, I will most
humbly take my leave of you.
HAMLET: You cannot, sir, take from me anything that I will more
210 willingly part withal,—except my life, except my life, except my life.
POLONIUS: Fare you well, my lord.
HAMLET: These tedious old fools!

(Enter Rosencrantz and Guildenstern.)

POLONIUS: You go to seek the Lord Hamlet; there he is.
ROSENCRANTZ: *(To Polonius)* God save you, sir!

(Exit Polonius.)

215 GUILDENSTERN: Mine honored lord!
ROSENCRANTZ: My most dear lord!
HAMLET: My excellent good friends! How dost thou, Guildenstern?
Ah, Rosencrantz? Good lads, how do ye both?
ROSENCRANTZ: As the indifferent children of the earth.
220 GUILDENSTERN: Happy in that we are not overhappy; on fortune's cap
we are not the very button.
HAMLET: Nor the soles of her shoe?
ROSENCRANTZ: Neither, my lord.
HAMLET: Then you live about her waist, or in the middle of her favors?
225 GUILDENSTERN: Faith, her privates we.
HAMLET: In the secret parts of fortune? O, most true; she is a strumpet.
What's the news?
ROSENCRANTZ: None, my lord, but that the world's grown honest.

---

[5] *pregnant:* ready, and clever.

HAMLET: Then is doomsday near: but your news is not true. Let me
question more in particular: what have you, my good friends,
deserved at the hands of fortune, that she sends you to prison
hither?
GUILDENSTERN: Prison, my lord!
HAMLET: Denmark's a prison.
ROSENCRANTZ: Then is the world one.
HAMLET: A goodly one; in which there are many confines, wards, and
dungeons, Denmark being one o' the worst.
ROSENCRANTZ: We think not so, my lord.
HAMLET: Why, then, 'tis none to you; for there is nothing either good
or bad, but thinking makes it so: to me it is a prison.
ROSENCRANTZ: Why, then, your ambition makes it one; 'tis too
narrow for your mind.
HAMLET: O God, I could be bounded in a nutshell, and count myself
a king of infinite space, were it not that I have bad dreams.
GUILDENSTERN: Which dreams, indeed, are ambition; for the very
substance of the ambitious is merely the shadow of a dream.
HAMLET: A dream itself is but a shadow.
ROSENCRANTZ: Truly, and I hold ambition of so airy and light a quality
that it is but a shadow's shadow.
HAMLET: Then are our beggars bodies, and our monarchs and
outstretched heroes the beggars' shadows. Shall we to the court?
for, by my fay, I cannot reason.
ROSENCRANTZ and GUILDENSTERN: We'll wait upon you.
HAMLET: No such matter: I will not sort you with the rest of my
servants, for, to speak to you like an honest man, I am most
dreadfully attended. But, in the beaten way of friendship, what
make you at Elsinore?
ROSENCRANTZ: To visit you, my lord; no other occasion.
HAMLET: Beggar that I am, I am even poor in thanks; but I thank you:
and sure, dear friends, my thanks are too dear a halfpenny. Were
you not sent for? Is it your own inclining? Is it a free visitation?
Come, deal justly with me: come, come; nay, speak.
GUILDENSTERN: What should we say, my lord?
HAMLET: Why, anything—but to the purpose. You were sent for; and
there is a kind of confession in your looks, which your modesties
have not craft enough to color: I know the good king and queen
have sent for you.
ROSENCRANTZ: To what end, my lord?
HAMLET: That you must teach me. But let me conjure you, by the rights
of our fellowship, by the consonancy of our youth, by the
obligation of our ever-preserved love, and by what more dear a
better proposer could charge you withal, be even and direct with
me, whether you were sent for or no?
ROSENCRANTZ: What say you? *(To Guildenstern)*
HAMLET: *(Aside)* Nay, then, I have an eye of you.—If you love me,
hold not off.

GUILDENSTERN: My lord, we were sent for.
HAMLET: I will tell you why; so shall my anticipation prevent your discovery, and your secrecy to the king and queen moult no
280 feather. I have of late,—but wherefore I know not,—lost all my mirth, forgone all custom of exercises; and, indeed, it goes so heavily with my disposition that this goodly frame, the earth, seems to me a sterile promontory; this most excellent canopy, the air, look you, this brave o'erhanging firmament, this majestical
285 roof fretted[6] with golden fire,—why, it appears no other thing to me than a foul and pestilent congregation of vapors. What a piece of work is man! How noble in reason! how infinite in faculties! in form and moving, how express and admirable! in action, how like an angel! in apprehension, how like a god! the beauty of the world!
290 the paragon of animals! And yet, to me, what is this quintessence of dust? man delights not me; no, nor woman neither, though by your smiling you seem to say so.
ROSENCRANTZ: My lord, there was no such stuff in my thoughts.
HAMLET: Why did you laugh, then, when I said, *Man delights not me*?
295 ROSENCRANTZ: To think, my lord, if you delight not in man, what lenten entertainment[7] the players shall receive from you: we coted[8] them on the way; and hither are they coming, to offer you service.
HAMLET: He that plays the king shall be welcome,—his majesty shall have tribute of me; the adventurous knight shall use his foil and
300 target; the lover shall not sigh gratis; the humorous[9] man shall end his part in peace; the clown shall make those laugh whose lungs are tickled o' the sere;[10] and the lady shall say her mind freely, or the blank verse shall halt[11] for't.—What players are they?
ROSENCRANTZ: Even those you were wont to take delight in,—the
305 tragedians of the city.
HAMLET: How chances it they travel? their residence, both in reputation and profit, was better both ways.
ROSENCRANTZ: I think their inhibition[12] comes by the means of the late innovation.
310 HAMLET: Do they hold the same estimation they did when I was in the city? Are they so followed?
ROSENCRANTZ: No, indeed, they are not.
HAMLET: How comes it? do they grow rusty?
ROSENCRANTZ: Nay, their endeavor keeps in the wonted pace; but there
315 is, sir, an aery[13] of children, little eyases,[14] that cry out on the top of question, and are most tyrannically clapped for't: these are now

---

[6] *roof fretted:* a roof with fretwork. [7] *lenten entertainment:* poor reception. [8] *coted:* passed. [9] *humorous:* eccentric. [10] *whose ... sere:* whose lungs, for laughter, are easily tickled. [11] *halt:* limp. [12] *inhibition:* difficulty, preventing them from remaining in the capital. [13] *aery:* brood of birds of prey. [14] *little eyases:* young hawks; a reference to the boys' companies that became popular rivals of Shakespeare's company of players.

the fashion; and so berattle the common stages,—so they call them,—that many wearing rapiers are afraid of goose-quills, and dare scarce come thither.

HAMLET: What, are they children? who maintains 'em? how are they escoted?[15] Will they pursue the quality[16] no longer than they can sing? will they not say afterwards, if they should grow themselves to common players,—as it is most like, if their means are no better, —their writers do them wrong, to make them exclaim against their own succession?

ROSENCRANTZ: Faith, there has been much to do on both sides; and the nation holds it no sin to tarre[17] them to controversy: there was for awhile no money bid for argument, unless the poet and the player went to cuffs in the question.

HAMLET: Is't possible?

GUILDENSTERN: O, there has been much throwing about of brains.

HAMLET: Do the boys carry it away?

ROSENCRANTZ: Ay, that they do, my lord; Hercules and his load[18] too.

HAMLET: It is not strange; for mine uncle is king of Denmark, and those that would make mouths at him while my father lived, give twenty, forty, fifty, an hundred ducats a-piece for his picture in little. 'Sblood, there is something in this more than natural, if philosophy could find it out.

(Flourish of trumpets within.)

GUILDENSTERN: There are the players.

HAMLET: Gentlemen, you are welcome to Elsinore. Your hands, come: the appurtenance of welcome is fashion and ceremony: let me comply with you in this garb; lest my extent[19] to the players, which, I tell you, must show fairly outward, should more appear like entertainment[20] than yours. You are welcome: but my uncle-father and aunt-mother are deceived.

GUILDENSTERN: In what, my dear lord?

HAMLET: I am but mad north-north-west: when the wind is southerly I know a hawk from a handsaw.

(Enter Polonius.)

POLONIUS: Well be with you, gentlemen!

HAMLET: Hark you, Guildenstern;—and you too;—at each ear a hearer: that great baby you see there is not yet out of his swathing-clouts.

ROSENCRANTZ: Happily he's the second time come to them; for they say an old man is twice a child.

HAMLET: I will prophesy he comes to tell me of the players; mark it. You say right, sir: o' Monday morning; 'twas so indeed.

---

[15] *escoted:* financially supported.   [16] *quality:* profession.   [17] *tarre:* egg them on.   [18] *load:* the globe, or the world.   [19] *extent:* show of friendliness.   [20] *entertainment:* welcome.

POLONIUS: My lord, I have news to tell you.
HAMLET: My lord, I have news to tell you. When Roscius was an actor in Rome,—
POLONIUS: The actors are come hither, my lord.
HAMLET: Buzz, buzz!
POLONIUS: Upon mine honor,—
HAMLET: Then came each actor on his ass,—
POLONIUS: The best actors in the world, either for tragedy, comedy, history, pastoral, pastoral-comical, historical-pastoral, tragical-historical, tragical-comical-historical-pastoral, scene individable,[21] or poem unlimited:[22] Seneca cannot be too heavy nor Plautus too light. For the law of writ and the liberty,[23] these are the only men.
HAMLET: O Jephthah, judge of Israel, what a treasure hadst thou!
POLONIUS: What a treasure had he, my lord?
HAMLET: Why—

    One fair daughter, and no more,
    The which he loved passing well.

POLONIUS: *(Aside)* Still on my daughter.
HAMLET: Am I not i' the right, old Jephthah?
POLONIUS: If you call me Jephthah, my lord, I have a daughter that I love passing well.
HAMLET: Nay, that follows not.
POLONIUS: What follows, then, my lord?
HAMLET: Why—

    As by lot, God wot,

and then, you know,

    It came to pass, as most like it was,

the first row of the pious chanson will show you more; for look where my abridgement comes.

(Enter four or five Players.)

You are welcome, masters; welcome, all:—I am glad to see thee well:—welcome, good friends.—O, my old friend! Thy face is valanced since I saw thee last; comest thou to beard me in Denmark?—What, my young lady and mistress! By'r lady, your ladyship is nearer heaven than when I saw you last, by the altitude

---

[21] *scene individable:* a play that observes the unities of time and place.
[22] *poem unlimited:* a typical multiscened Elizabethan type of drama, not restricted by the unities; examples are *Hamlet, Macbeth, King Lear,* and virtually any other play by Shakespeare. [23] *For . . . liberty:* for the laws of the unities and for playwriting that is not so restricted.

of a chopine.[24] Pray God, your voice, like a piece of uncurrent gold, be not cracked within the ring.—Masters, you are all welcome. We'll e'en to't like French falconers, fly at anything we see: we'll have a speech straight: come, give us a taste of your quality; come, a passionate speech.

1ST PLAYER: What speech, my lord?

HAMLET: I heard thee speak me a speech once,—but it was never acted; or, if it was, not above once; for the play, I remember, pleased not the million; 'twas caviare to the general: but it was,—as I received it, and others whose judgments in such matters cried in the top of mine,—an excellent play, well digested in the scenes, set down with as much modesty as cunning. I remember, one said there were no sallets in the lines to make the matter savory, nor no matter in the phrase that might indite the author of affectation; but called it an honest method, as wholesome as sweet, and by very much more handsome than fine. One speech in it I chiefly loved: 'twas Aeneas' tale to Dido; and thereabout of it especially where he speaks of Priam's slaughter: if it live in your memory, begin at this line;—let me see, let me see:—

> The rugged Pyrrhus, like the Hyrcanian beast,[25]

—it is not so:—it begins with Pyrrhus:—

> The rugged Pyrrhus,—he whose sable arms,
> Black as his purpose, did the night resemble
> When he lay couched in the ominous horse,—
> Hath now this dread and black complexion smear'd
> With heraldry more dismal; head to foot
> Now is he total gules; horridly trick'd
> With blood of fathers, mothers, daughters, sons,
> Bak'd and impasted with the parching streets,
> That lend a tyrannous and damned light
> To their vile murders: roasted in wrath and fire,
> And thus o'er-sized with coagulate gore,
> With eyes like carbuncles, the hellish Pyrrhus
> Old grandsire Priam seeks.—

So proceed you.

POLONIUS: 'Fore God, my lord, well spoken, with good accent and good discretion.

1ST PLAYER: Anon he finds him
Striking too short at Greeks; his antique sword,

---

[24] *chopine:* a wooden stilt more than a foot high used under a woman's shoe; a Venetian fashion introduced into England. [25] *The rugged . . . :* this speech is an example of the declamatory style of drama, which Shakespeare surely must have considered outmoded.

                Rebellious to his arm, lies where it falls,
430   Repugnant to command: unequal match'd,
                Pyrrhus at Priam drives; in rage strikes wide;
                But with the whiff and wind of his fell sword
                The unnerved father falls. Then senseless Ilium,
                Seeming to feel this blow, with flaming top
435   Stoops to his base; and with a hideous crash
                Takes prisoner Pyrrhus' ear: for, lo! his sword,
                Which was declining on the milky head
                Of reverend Priam, seem'd i' the air to stick:
                So, as a painted tyrant, Pyrrhus stood;
440   And, like a neutral to his will and matter,
                Did nothing.
                But as we often see, against some storm,
                A silence in the heavens, the rack stand still,
                The blood winds speechless, and the orb below
445   As hush as death, anon the dreadful thunder
                Doth rend the region; so, after Pyrrhus' pause,
                A roused vengeance sets him new a-work;
                And never did the Cyclops' hammers fall
                On Mars his armor, forg'd for proof eterne,
450   With less remorse than Pyrrhus' bleeding sword
                Now falls on Priam.—
                Out, out, thou strumpet, Fortune! All you gods,
                In general synod, take away her power;
                Break all the spokes and fellies from her wheel,
455   And bowl the round knave down the hill of heaven,
                As low as to the fiends!
            POLONIUS: This is too long.
            HAMLET: It shall to the barber's, with your beard.—Pr'ythee, say
                on.—He's for a jig, or a tale of bawdry, or he sleeps:—say on; come
460   to Hecuba.
            1ST PLAYER: But who, O, who had seen the mobled queen,—
            HAMLET: *The mobled queen?*
            POLONIUS: That's good; *mobled queen* is good.
            1ST PLAYER: Run barefoot up and down, threatening the flames
465   With bissom rheum; a clout upon that head
                Where late the diadem stood; and, for a robe,
                About her lank and all o'er-teemed loins,
                A blanket, in the alarm of fear caught up;—
                Who this had seen, with tongue in venom steep'd,
470   'Gainst Fortune's state would treason have pronounc'd:
                But if the gods themselves did see her then,
                When she saw Pyrrhus make malicious sport
                In mincing with his sword her husband's limbs,
                The instant burst of clamor that she made,—
475   Unless things mortal move them not at all,—

Would have made milch the burning eyes of heaven,
And passion in the gods.
POLONIUS: Look, whether he has not turn'd his color, and has tears in's eyes.—Pray you, no more.
480 HAMLET: 'Tis well; I'll have thee speak out the rest soon.—Good my lord, will you see the players well bestowed? Do you hear, let them be well used; for they are the abstracts and brief chronicles of the time; after your death you were better have a bad epitaph than their ill report while you live.
485 POLONIUS: My lord, I will use them according to their desert.
HAMLET: God's bodykins,[26] man, better: use every man after his desert, and who should 'scape whipping? Use them after your own honor and dignity: the less they deserve the more merit is in your bounty. Take them in.
490 POLONIUS: Come, sirs.
HAMLET: Follow him, friends: we'll hear a play to-morrow.

(Exit Polonius with all the Players but the First.)

Dost thou hear me, old friend; can you play the Murder of Gonzago?
1ST PLAYER: Ay, my lord.
HAMLET: We'll ha't to-morrow night. You could, for a need, study a
495 speech of some dozen or sixteen lines which I would set down and insert in't? could you not?
1ST PLAYER: Ay, my lord.
HAMLET: Very well.—Follow that lord; and look you mock him not.

(Exit First Player.)

—My good friends, *(to Rosencrantz and Guildenstern)* I'll leave you
500 till night: you are welcome to Elsinore.
ROSENCRANTZ: Good my lord!

(Exeunt Rosencrantz and Guildenstern.)

HAMLET: Ay, so God b' wi' ye!—Now I am alone.
O, what a rogue[27] and peasant slave am I!
Is it not monstrous that this player here,
505 But in a fiction, in a dream of passion,
Could force his soul so to his own conceit[28]
That from her working all his visage wan'd;
Tears in his eyes, distraction in's aspect,
A broken voice, and his whole function suiting
510 With forms to his conceit? And all for nothing!
For Hecuba?
What's Hecuba to him or he to Hecuba,

---

[26] *God's bodykins:* by God's little body.   [27] *rogue:* wretched creature.   [28] *conceit:* conception.

That he should weep for her? What would he do,
Had he the motive and the cue for passion
515 That I have? He would drown the stage with tears,
And cleave the general ear with horrid speech;
Make mad the guilty, and appal the free;
Confound the ignorant, and amaze, indeed,
The very faculties of eyes and ears.
520 Yet I,
A dull and muddy-mettled rascal, peak,
Like John-a-dreams, unpregnant of my cause,
And can say nothing; no, not for a king
Upon whose property and most dear life
525 A damn'd defeat was made. Am I a coward?
Who calls me villain? breaks my pate across?
Plucks off my beard and blows it in my face?
Tweaks me by the nose? gives me the lie i' the throat,
As deep as to the lungs? who does me this, ha?
530 'Swounds, I should take it: for it cannot be
But I am pigeon-liver'd, and lack gall
To make oppression bitter; or ere this
I should have fatted all the region kites
With this slave's offal:—bloody, bawdy villain!
535 Remorseless, treacherous, lecherous, kindless villain!
O, vengeance!
Why, what an ass am I! This is most brave,
That I, the son of a dear father murder'd,
Prompted to my revenge by heaven and hell,
540 Must, like a whore, unpack my heart with words,
And fall a-cursing like a very drab,
A scullion!
Fie upon't! foh!—About, my brain! I have heard
That guilty creatures, sitting at a play,
545 Have by the very cunning of the scene
Been struck so to the soul that presently
They have proclaim'd their malefactions;
For murder, though it have no tongue, will speak
With most miraculous organ. I'll have these players
550 Play something like the murder of my father
Before mine uncle: I'll observe his looks;
I'll tent[29] him to the quick: if he but blench,
I know my course. The spirit that I have seen
May be the devil: and the devil hath power
555 To assume a pleasing shape; yea, and perhaps
Out of my weakness and my melancholy,—

---

[29] *tent:* probe.

>   As he is very potent with such spirits,—
>   Abuses me to damn me: I'll have grounds
>   More relative than this:—the play's the thing
> 560   Wherein I'll catch the conscience of the king. *(Exit.)*

ACT III
SCENE 1

A room in the castle.

(Enter King, Queen, Polonius, Ophelia, Rosencrantz, and Guildenstern.)

>   KING: And can you, by no drift of circumstance,
>   Get from him why he puts on this confusion,
>   Grating so harshly all his days of quiet
>   With turbulent and dangerous lunacy?
> 5   ROSENCRANTZ: He does confess he feels himself distracted;
>   But from what cause he will by no means speak.
>   GUILDENSTERN: Nor do we find him forward to be sounded;
>   But, with a crafty madness, keeps aloof
>   When we would bring him on to some confession
> 10   Of his true state.
>   QUEEN: Did he receive you well?
>   ROSENCRANTZ: Most like a gentleman.
>   GUILDENSTERN: But with much forcing of his disposition.
>   ROSENCRANTZ: Niggard of question; but, of our demands,
>   Most free in his reply.
>   QUEEN: Did you assay him
> 15   To any pastime?
>   ROSENCRANTZ: Madam, it so fell out that certain players
>   We o'er-raught on the way: of these we told him;
>   And there did seem in him a kind of joy
>   To hear of it: they are about the court;
> 20   And, as I think, they have already order
>   This night to play before him.
>   POLONIUS: 'Tis most true:
>   And he beseech'd me to entreat your majesties
>   To hear and see the matter.
>   KING: With all my heart; and it doth much content me
> 25   To hear him so inclin'd.
>   Good gentlemen, give him a further edge,
>   And drive his purpose on to these delights.
>   ROSENCRANTZ: We shall, my lord.

(Exeunt Rosencrantz and Guildenstern.)

>   KING: Sweet Gertrude, leave us too;
>   For we have closely sent for Hamlet hither
> 30   That he, as 'twere by accident, may here

Affront Ophelia:
Her father and myself,—lawful espials,[1]—
Will so bestow ourselves that, seeing, unseen,
We may of their encounter frankly judge;
35   And gather by him, as he is behav'd,
If't be the affliction of his love or no
That thus he suffers for.
   QUEEN: I shall obey you:—
And for your part, Ophelia, I do wish
That your good beauties be the happy cause
40   Of Hamlet's wildness: so shall I hope your virtues
Will bring him to his wonted way again,
To both your honors.
   OPHELIA: Madam, I wish it may.

(Exit Queen.)

   POLONIUS: Ophelia, walk you here.—Gracious, so please you,
We will bestow ourselves.—*(To Ophelia)* Read on this book;
45   That show of such an exercise may color
Your loneliness.—We are oft to blame in this,—
'Tis too much prov'd,—that with devotion's visage
And pious action we do sugar o'er
The devil himself.
   KING: *(Aside)*   O, 'tis too true!
50   How smart a lash that speech doth give my conscience!
The harlot's cheek, beautied with plastering art,
Is not more ugly to the thing that helps it
Than is my deed to my most painted word:
O heavy burden!
55   POLONIUS: I hear him coming: let's withdraw, my lord.

(Exeunt King and Polonius.)

(Enter Hamlet.)

   HAMLET: To be, or not to be,—that is the question:
Whether 'tis nobler in the mind to suffer
The slings and arrows of outrageous fortune,
Or to take arms against a sea of troubles,
60   And by opposing end them?—To die,—to sleep,—
No more; and by a sleep to say we end
The heart-ache and the thousand natural shocks
That flesh is heir to,—'tis a consummation
Devoutly to be wish'd. To die,—to sleep;—
65   To sleep! perchance to dream:—ay, there's the rub;

---

[1] *espials:* spies.

       For in that sleep of death what dreams may come,
       When we have shuffled off this mortal coil,
       Must give us pause: there's the respect
       That makes a calamity of so long life;
70   For who would bear the whips and scorns of time,
       The oppressor's wrong, the proud man's contumely,
       The pangs of déspis'd love, the law's delay,
       The insolence of office, and the spurns
       That patient merit of the unworthy takes,
75   When he himself might his quietus make
       With a bare bodkin?[2] who would fardels[3] bear,
       To grunt[4] and sweat under a weary life,
       But that the dread of something after death,—
       The undiscover'd country, from whose bourn[5]
80   No traveler returns,—puzzles the will,
       And makes us rather bear those ills we have
       Than to fly to others that we know not of?
       Thus conscience does make cowards of us all;
       And thus the native hue of resolution
85   Is sicklied o'er with the pale cast of thought;
       And enterprises of great pith and moment,
       With this regard, their currents turn awry,
       And lose the name of action.—Soft you now!
       The fair Ophelia.—Nymph, in thy orisons[6]
90   Be all my sins remember'd.
OPHELIA: Good my lord,
       How does your honor for this many a day?
HAMLET: I humbly thank you; well, well, well.
OPHELIA: My lord, I have remembrances of yours,
       That I have longed long to re-deliver;
95   I pray you, now receive them.
HAMLET: No, not I;
       I never gave you aught.
OPHELIA: My honor'd lord, you know right well you did;
       And with them, words of so sweet breath compos'd
       As made the things more rich: their perfume lost,
100   Take these again; for to the noble mind
       Rich gifts wax poor when givers prove unkind.
       There, my lord.
HAMLET: Ha, ha! are you honest?
OPHELIA: My lord?
105 HAMLET: Are you fair?
OPHELIA: What means your lordship?

---

[2] *bodkin:* stiletto. [3] *fardels:* burdens. [4] *grunt:* groan. [5] *bourn:* boundary.
[6] *orisons:* prayers.

HAMLET: That if you be honest and fair, your honesty should admit no
   discourse to your beauty.
OPHELIA: Could beauty, my lord, have better commerce than with
   honesty?
HAMLET: Ay, truly; for the power of beauty will sooner transform
   honesty from what it is to a bawd than the force of honesty
   can translate beauty into his likeness: this was sometime a
   paradox, but now the time gives it proof. I did love you once.
OPHELIA: Indeed, my lord, you made me believe so.
HAMLET: You should not have believed me; for virtue cannot so
   inoculate our old stock but we shall relish of it: I loved you not.
OPHELIA: I was the more deceived.
HAMLET: Get thee to a nunnery: why wouldst thou be a breeder of
   sinners? I am myself indifferent[7] honest; but yet I could accuse me
   of such things that it were better my mother had not borne me: I
   am very proud, revengeful, ambitious; with more offences at my
   beck than I have thoughts to put them in, imagination to give
   them shape, or time to act them in. What should such fellows as I
   do crawling between heaven and earth? We are arrant knaves, all;
   believe none of us. Go thy ways to a nunnery. Where's your father?
OPHELIA: At home, my lord.
HAMLET: Let the doors be shut upon him, that he may play the fool
   nowhere but in's own house. Farewell.
OPHELIA: O, help him, you sweet heavens!
HAMLET: If thou dost marry, I'll give thee this plague for thy
   dowry,—be thou as chaste as ice, as pure as snow, thou shalt not
   escape calumny. Get thee to a nunnery, go: farewell. Or, if thou
   wilt needs marry, marry a fool; for wise men know well enough
   what monsters you make of them. To a nunnery, go; and quickly
   too. Farewell.
OPHELIA: O heavenly powers, restore him!
HAMLET: I have heard of your paintings too, well enough; God has
   given you one face and you make yourselves another: you jig, you
   amble, and you lisp, and nickname God's creatures, and make your
   wantonness your ignorance. Go to, I'll no more on't; it hath made
   me mad. I say, we will have no more marriages: those that are
   married already, all but one, shall live; the rest shall keep as they
   are. To a nunnery, go. *(Exit.)*
OPHELIA: O, what a noble mind is here o'erthrown!
   The courtier's, soldier's, scholar's eye, tongue, sword:
   The expectancy and rose of the fair state,
   The glass of fashion and the mould of form,
   The observ'd of all observers,—quite, quite down!
   And I, of ladies most deject and wretched

---

[7] *indifferent:* tolerably.

>   That suck'd the honey of his music vows,
>   Now see that noble and most sovereign reason,
>   Like sweet bells jangled, out of tune and harsh;
>   That unmatch'd form and feature of blown[8] youth
> 155   Blasted with ecstasy: O, woe is me,
>   To have seen what I have seen, see what I see!
>
> *(Re-enter King and Polonius.)*
>
> KING: Love! his affections do not that way tend;
>   Nor what he spake, though it lack'd form a little,
>   Was not like madness. There's something in his soul
> 160   O'er which his melancholy sits on brood;
>   And I do doubt[9] the hatch and the disclose
>   Will be some danger: which for to prevent,
>   I have in quick determination
>   Thus set it down:—he shall with speed to England
> 165   For the demand of our neglected tribute:
>   Haply, the seas and countries different,
>   With variable objects, shall expel
>   This something-settled matter in his heart;
>   Whereon his brains still beating puts him thus
> 170   From fashion of himself. What think you on't?
> POLONIUS: It shall do well: but yet do I believe
>   The origin and commencement of his grief
>   Sprung from neglected love.—How now, Ophelia!
>   You need not tell us what Lord Hamlet said;
> 175   We heard it all.—My lord, do as you please;
>   But if you hold it fit, after the play,
>   Let his queen mother all alone entreat him
>   To show his grief: let her be round with him;
>   And I'll be plac'd, so please you, in the ear
> 180   Of all their conference. If she finds him not,[10]
>   To England send him; or confine him where
>   Your wisdom best shall think.
> KING: It shall be so:
>   Madness in great ones must not unwatch'd go.
>
> *(Exeunt.)*

SCENE 2

A hall in the castle.

(Enter Hamlet and certain Players.)

HAMLET: Speak the speech, I pray you, as I pronounced it to you, trippingly on the tongue: but if you mouth it, as many of your

---

[8] *blown:* full-blown.   [9] *doubt:* fear.   [10] *she . . . not:* does not find him out.

players do, I had as lief the town-crier spoke my lines. Nor do not saw the air too much with your hand, thus; but use all gently: for in the very torrent, tempest, and, as I may say, the whirlwind of passion, you must acquire and beget a temperance that may give it smoothness. O, it offends me to the soul, to hear a robustious periwigpated fellow tear a passion to tatters, to very rags, to split the ears of the groundlings, who, for the most part, are capable of nothing but inexplicable dumb shows and noise: I could have such a fellow whipped for o'erdoing Termagant;[1] it out-herods Herod:[2] pray you, avoid it.

1ST PLAYER: I warrant your honor.

HAMLET: Be not too tame neither, but let your own discretion be your tutor; suit the action to the word, the word to the action; with this special observance, that you o'erstep not the modesty of nature: for anything so overdone is from the purpose of playing, whose end, both at the first and now, was and is, to hold, as 'twere, the mirror up to nature; to show virtue her own feature, scorn her own image, and the very age and body of the time his form and pressure. Now, this overdone or come tardy off, though it make the unskilful laugh, cannot but make the judicious grieve; the censure of the which one must, in your allowance, o'erweigh a whole theater of others. O, there be players that I have seen play,—and heard others praise, and that highly,—not to speak it profanely, that, neither having the accent of Christians, nor the gait of Christian, pagan, nor man, have so strutted and bellowed that I have thought some of nature's journeymen had made men, and not made them well, they imitated humanity so abominably.

1ST PLAYER: I hope we have reformed that indifferently with us, sir.

HAMLET: O, reform it altogether. And let those that play your clowns speak no more than is set down for them: for there be of them that will themselves laugh, to set on some quantity of barren spectators to laugh too; though, in the meantime, some necessary question of the play be then to be considered: that's villainous, and shows a most pitiful ambition in the fool that uses it. Go, make you ready.

(Exeunt Players.)

(Enter Polonius, Rosencrantz, and Guildenstern.)

How now, my lord! will the king hear this piece of work?

POLONIUS: And the queen, too, and that presently.

HAMLET: Bid the players make haste.

(Exit Polonius.)

Will you two help to hasten them?

---

[1] *Termagant:* a violent pagan deity, supposedly Mohammedan. [2] *out-herods Herod:* out-rants the ranting Herod, who figures in medieval drama.

ROSENCRANTZ and GUILDENSTERN: We will, my lord. *(Exeunt.)*
HAMLET: What, ho, Horatio!

(Enter Horatio.)

HORATIO: Here, sweet lord, at your service.
HAMLET: Horatio, thou art e'en as just a man
    As e'er my conversation cop'd withal.
HORATIO: O, my dear lord,—
HAMLET: Nay, do not think I flatter;
    For what advancement may I hope from thee,
    That no revénue hast, but thy good spirits,
    To feed and clothe thee? Why should the poor be flatter'd?
    No, let the candied tongue lick ábsurd pomp;
    And crook the pregnant hinges of the knee
    Where thrift may follow fawning. Dost thou hear?
    Since my dear soul was mistress of her choice,
    And could of men distinguish, her election
    Hath seal'd thee for herself: for thou hast been
    As one, in suffering all, that suffers nothing;
    A man that Fortune's buffets and rewards
    Hast ta'en with equal thanks: and bless'd are those
    Whose blood and judgment are so well commingled
    That they are not a pipe for Fortune's finger
    To sound what stop she please. Give me that man
    That is not passion's slave, and I will wear him
    In my heart's core, ay, in my heart of heart,
    As I do thee.—Something too much of this.—
    There is a play to-night before the king;
    One scene of it comes near the circumstance
    Which I have told thee of my father's death:
    I pr'ythee, when thou see'st that act a-foot,
    Even with the very comment of thy soul
    Observe mine uncle: if this his occulted guilt
    Do not itself unkennel in one speech,
    It is a damned ghost that we have seen;
    And my imaginations are as foul
    As Vulcan's stithy.[3] Give him heedful note:
    For I mine eyes will rivet to his face;
    And, after, we will both our judgments join
    In censure of his seeming.
HORATIO: Well, my lord:
    If he steal aught the whilst this play is playing,
    And 'scape detecting, I will pay the theft.

---

[3] *stithy:* smithy.

80 **HAMLET:** They are coming to the play; I must be idle:[4]
   Get you a place.

   (Danish march. A flourish. Enter King, Queen, Polonius, Ophelia, Rosencrantz, Guildenstern, and others.)

   KING: How fares our cousin Hamlet?
   HAMLET: Excellent, i'faith; of the chameleon's dish:[5] I eat the air, promise-crammed: you cannot feed capons so.
85 **KING:** I have nothing with this answer, Hamlet; these words are not mine.
   HAMLET: No, nor mine now. *(To Polonius)* My lord, you played once i'the university, you say?
   POLONIUS: That did I, my lord, and was accounted a good actor.
90 **HAMLET:** And what did you enact?
   POLONIUS: I did enact Julius Caesar: I was killed i' the Capitol; Brutus killed me.
   HAMLET: It was a brute part of him to kill so capital a calf there.—Be the players ready.
95 **ROSENCRANTZ:** Ay, my lord; they stay upon your patience.
   QUEEN: Come hither, my good Hamlet, sit by me.
   HAMLET: No, good mother, here's metal more attractive.
   POLONIUS: O, ho! do you mark that? *(To the King)*
   HAMLET: Lady, shall I lie in your lap? *(Lying down at Ophelia's feet)*
100 **OPHELIA:** No, my lord.
   HAMLET: I mean, my head upon your lap?
   OPHELIA: Ay, my lord.
   HAMLET: Do you think I meant country matters?
   OPHELIA: I think nothing, my lord.
105 **HAMLET:** That's a fair thought to lie between maids' legs.
   OPHELIA: What is, my lord?
   HAMLET: Nothing.
   OPHELIA: You are merry, my lord.
   HAMLET: Who, I?
110 **OPHELIA:** Ay, my lord.
   HAMLET: O, your only jig-maker. What should a man do but be merry? for, look you, how cheerfully my mother looks, and my father died within's two hours.
   OPHELIA: Nay, 'tis twice two months, my lord.
115 **HAMLET:** So long? Nay, then, let the devil wear black, for I'll have a suit of sables. O heavens! die two months ago, and not forgotten yet? Then there's hope a great man's memory may outlive his life half a year: but, by'r lady, he must build churches, then; or else shall he suffer not thinking on, with the hobby-horse, whose epitaph is,
120 *For, O, for, O, the hobby-horse is forgot.*

---

[4] *idle:* foolish.   [5] *chameleon's dish:* Chameleons were supposed to live on air.

(Trumpets sound. The dumb show enters.)

(Enter a King and a Queen, very lovingly; the Queen embracing him and he her. She kneels, and makes show of protestation unto him. He takes her up, and declines his head upon her neck: lays him down upon a bank of flowers: she, seeing him asleep, leaves him. Anon comes in a fellow, takes off his crown, kisses it, and pours poison in the King's ears, and exit. The Queen returns; finds the King dead, and makes passionate action. The Poisoner, with some two or three Mutes, comes in again, seeming to lament with her. The dead body is carried away. The Poisoner woos the Queen with gifts: she seems loth and unwilling awhile, but in the end accepts his love.)

(Exeunt.)

OPHELIA: What means this, my lord?
HAMLET: Marry, this is miching mallecho;[6] it means mischief.
OPHELIA: Belike this show imports the argument of the play.

(Enter Prologue.)

HAMLET: We shall know by this fellow: the players cannot keep counsel;
125   they'll tell all.
OPHELIA: Will he tell us what this show meant?
HAMLET: Ay, or any show that you'll show him: be not you ashamed
    to show, he'll not shame to tell you what it means.
OPHELIA: You are naught, you are naught: I'll mark the play.
PROLOGUE:
130   *For us, and for our tragedy,*
                  Here stooping to your clemency,
                  We beg your hearing patiently.

HAMLET: Is this a prologue, or the posy[7] of a ring?
OPHELIA: 'Tis brief, my lord.
135 HAMLET: As woman's love.

(Enter a King and a Queen.)

PROLOGUE KING: Full thirty times hath Phoebus' cart gone round
    Neptune's salt wash and Tellus' orbed ground,[8]
    And thirty dozen moons with borrow'd sheen
    About the world have times twelve thirties been,
140   Since love our hearts, and Hymen did our hands
    Unite commutual in most sacred bands.
PROLOGUE QUEEN: So many journeys may the sun and moon
    Make us again count o'er ere love be done!
    But, woe is me, you are so sick of late,

---

[6] *miching mallecho:* a sneaking misdeed.   [7] *posy:* motto or inscription.   [8] *Neptune's . . . ground:* the globe.

	So far from cheer and from your former state
145	That I distrust you.⁹ Yet, though I distrust,
	Discomfort you, my lord, it nothing must:
	For women's fear and love holds quantity,¹⁰
	In neither aught, or in extremity.
150	Now, what my love is, proof hath made you know;
	And as my love is siz'd, my fear is so:
	Where love is great, the littlest doubts are fear;
	Where little fears grow great, great love grows there.

PROLOGUE KING: Faith, I must leave thee, love, and shortly too;
155 My operant powers their functions leave¹¹ to do:
And thou shalt live in this fair world behind,
Honor'd, belov'd; and haply one as kind
For husband shalt thou,—

PROLOGUE QUEEN: O, confound the rest!
Such love must needs be treason in my breast:
160 In second husband let me be accurst!
None wed the second but who kill'd the first.

HAMLET: *(Aside)* Wormwood, wormwood.

PROLOGUE QUEEN: The instances that second marriage move
Are base respects of thrift, but none of love:
165 A second time I kill my husband, dead,
When second husband kisses me in bed.

PROLOGUE KING: I do believe you think what now you speak;
But what we do determine oft we break.
Purpose is but the slave to memory;
170 Of violent birth, but poor validity:
Which now, like fruit unripe, sticks on the tree;
But fall unshaken when they mellow be.
Most necessary 'tis that we forget
To pay ourselves what to ourselves is debt:
175 What to ourselves in passion we propose,
The passion ending, doth the purpose lose.
The violence of either grief or joy
Their own enactures with themselves destroy:
Where joy most revels grief doth most lament;
180 Grief joys, joy grieves, on slender accident.
This world is not for aye; nor 'tis not strange
That even our loves should with our fortunes change;
For 'tis a question left us yet to prove
Whether love lead fortune or else fortune love.
185 The great man down, you mark his favorite flies;
The poor advanc'd makes friends of enemies.

---

⁹ *distrust you:* worry about you.   ¹⁰ *holds quantity:* correspond in degree.
¹¹ *leave:* cease.

        And hitherto doth love on fortune tend:
        For who not needs shall never lack a friend;
        And who in want a hollow friend doth try,
190   Directly seasons him his enemy.
        But, orderly to end where I begun,—
        Our wills and fates do so contrary run
        That our devices still are overthrown;
        Our thoughts are ours, their ends none of our own:
195   So think thou wilt no second husband wed;
        But die thy thoughts when thy first lord is dead.
    PROLOGUE QUEEN: Nor earth to me give food, nor heaven light!
        Sport and repose lock from me day and night!
        To desperation turn my trust and hope!
200   An anchor's[12] cheer in prison be my scope!
        Each opposite, that blanks the face of joy,
        Meet what I would have well, and it destroy!
        Both here and hence, pursue me lasting strife,
        If, once a widow, ever I be wife!
205   HAMLET: If she should break it now! *(To Ophelia)*
    PROLOGUE KING: 'Tis deeply sworn. Sweet, leave me here awhile;
        My spirits grow dull, and fain I would beguile
        The tedious day with sleep. *(Sleeps)*
    PROLOGUE QUEEN: Sleep rock thy brain,
        And never come mischance between us twain! *(Exit.)*
210   HAMLET: Madam, how like you this play?
    QUEEN: The lady doth protest too much, methinks.
    HAMLET: O, but she'll keep her word.
    KING: Have you heard the argument? Is there no offence in't?
    HAMLET: No, no, they do but jest, poison in jest; no offence i' the
215   world.
    KING: What do you call the play?
    HAMLET: The Mouse-trap. Marry, how? Tropically.[13] This play is the
        image of a murder done in Vienna: Gonzago is the duke's name:
        his wife, Baptista: you shall see anon; 'tis a knavish piece of work:
220   but what o' that? your majesty, and we that have free souls, it
        touches us not: let the galled jade wince, our withers are unwrung.

    (Enter Lucianus.)

        This is one Lucianus, nephew to the king.
    OPHELIA: You are a good chorus, my lord.
    HAMLET: I could interpret between you and your love, if I could see
225   the puppets dallying.
    OPHELIA: You are keen, my lord, you are keen.

---

[12] *anchor's:* anchorite's, or hermit's.   [13] *Tropically:* figuratively, or metaphorically; by means of a "trope."

HAMLET: It would cost you a groaning to take off my edge.
OPHELIA: Still better, and worse.
HAMLET: So you must take your husbands.—Begin, murderer; pox,
leave thy damnable faces and begin. Come:—*The croaking raven doth bellow for revenge.*
LUCIANUS: Thoughts black, hands apt, drugs fit, and time agreeing;
Confederate season, else no creature seeing;
Thou mixture rank, of midnight weeds collected,
With Hecate's ban[14] thrice blasted, thrice infected,
Thy natural magic and dire property
On wholesome life usurp immediately.

(Pours the poison into the sleeper's ears.)

HAMLET: He poisons him i' the garden for's estate. His name's Gonzago: the story is extant, and writ in choice Italian: you shall see anon how the murderer gets the love of Gonzago's wife.
OPHELIA: The king rises.
HAMLET: What, frighted with false fire!
QUEEN: How fares my lord?
POLONIUS: Give o'er the play.
KING: Give me some light:—away!
ALL: Lights, lights, lights!

(Exeunt all but Hamlet and Horatio.)

HAMLET:
> Why, let the stricken deer go weep,
> The hart ungalled play;
> For some must watch, while some must sleep:
> So runs the world away.—

Would not this, sir, and a forest of feathers, if the rest of my fortunes turn Turk with me, with two Provencal roses on my razed shoes, get me a fellowship in a cry[15] of players, sir?
HORATIO: Half a share.
HAMLET: A whole one, I.

> For thou dost know, O Damon dear,
> This realm dismantled was
> Of Jove himself; and now reigns here
> A very, very—pajock.[16]

HORATIO: You might have rhymed.
HAMLET: O good Horatio, I'll take the ghost's word for a thousand pound. Didst perceive?

---

[14] *Hecate's ban:* the spell of the goddess of witchcraft. [15] *cry:* company.
[16] *pajock:* peacock.

HORATIO: Very well, my lord.
HAMLET: Upon the talk of the poisoning,—
265 HORATIO: I did very well note him.
HAMLET: Ah, ha!—Come, some music! come, the recorders!—

> For if the king like not the comedy,
> Why, then, belike,—he likes it not, perdy.
> Come, some music!

(Re-enter Rosencrantz and Guildenstern.)

270 GUILDENSTERN: Good my lord, vouchsafe me a word with you.
HAMLET: Sir, a whole history.
GUILDENSTERN: The king, sir,—
HAMLET: Ay, sir, what of him?
GUILDENSTERN: Is, in his retirement, marvelous distempered.
275 HAMLET: With drink, sir?
GUILDENSTERN: No, my lord, rather with choler.
HAMLET: Your wisdom should show itself more richer to signify this to his doctor; for, for me to put him to his purgation would perhaps plunge him into far more choler.
280 GUILDENSTERN: Good my lord, put your discourse into some frame, and start not so wildly from my affair.
HAMLET: I am tame, sir:—pronounce.
GUILDENSTERN: The queen, your mother, in most great affliction of spirit, hath sent me to you.
285 HAMLET: You are welcome.
GUILDENSTERN: Nay, good my lord, this courtesy is not of the right breed. If it shall please you to make me a wholesome answer, I will do you mother's commandment: if not, your pardon and my return shall be the end of my business.
290 HAMLET: Sir, I cannot.
GUILDENSTERN: What, my lord?
HAMLET: Make you a wholesome answer; my wit's diseas'd: but, sir, such answer as I can make, you shall command; or, rather, as you say, my mother: therefore no more, but to the matter: my mother,
295 you say,—
ROSENCRANTZ: Then thus she says: your behavior hath struck her into amazement and admiration.
HAMLET: O wonderful son, that can so astonish a mother!—But is there no sequel at the heels of this mother's admiration?
300 ROSENCRANTZ: She desires to speak with you in her closet[17] ere you go to bed.
HAMLET: We shall obey, were she ten times our mother. Have you any further trade with us?
ROSENCRANTZ: My lord, you once did love me.

---

[17] *closet:* boudoir.

305 **HAMLET:** So I do still, by these pickers and stealers.[18]
ROSENCRANTZ: Good, my lord, what is your cause of distemper? you do, surely, bar the door upon your own liberty if you deny your griefs to your friend.
HAMLET: Sir, I lack advancement.
310 **ROSENCRANTZ:** How can that be, when you have the voice of the king himself for your succession in Denmark?
HAMLET: Ay, but *While the grass grows,*—the proverb is something musty.

(Re-enter the Players, with recorders.)

O, the recorders:—let me see one.—To withdraw with you:—why
315 do you go about to recover the wind of me, as if you would drive me into a toil?
GUILDENSTERN: O, my lord, if my duty be too bold, my love is too unmannerly.
HAMLET: I do not well understand that. Will you play upon this pipe?
320 **GUILDENSTERN:** My lord, I cannot.
HAMLET: I pray you.
GUILDENSTERN: Believe me, I cannot.
HAMLET: I do beseech you.
GUILDENSTERN: I know no touch of it, my lord.
325 **HAMLET:** 'Tis as easy as lying: govern these ventages[19] with your finger and thumb, give it breath with your mouth, and it will discourse most eloquent music. Look you, these are the stops.
GUILDENSTERN: But these cannot I command to any utterance of harmony; I have not the skill.
330 **HAMLET:** Why, look you now, how unworthy a thing you make of me! You would play upon me; you would seem to know my stops; you would pluck out the heart of my mystery; you would sound me from my lowest note to the top of my compass: and there is much music, excellent voice, in this little organ; yet cannot you make it
335 speak. 'Sblood, do you think that I am easier to be played on than a pipe? Call me what instrument you will, though you can fret me you cannot play upon me.

(Enter Polonius.)

God bless you, sir!
POLONIUS: My lord, the queen would speak with you, and
340 presently.
HAMLET: Do you see yonder cloud that's almost in shape of a camel?
POLONIUS: By the mass, and 'tis like a camel indeed.
HAMLET: Methinks it is like a weasel.
POLONIUS: It is backed like a weasel.

---

[18] *pickers and stealers:* fingers.   [19] *ventages:* holes.

345 **HAMLET:** Or like a whale?
POLONIUS: Very like a whale.
HAMLET: Then will I come to my mother by and by.—They fool me
to the top of my bent.—I will come by and by.
POLONIUS: I will say so.
350 **HAMLET:** By and by is easily said.

(Exit Polonius.)

    Leave me, friends.

(Exeunt Rosencrantz, Guildenstern, Horatio, and Players.)

    'Tis now the very witching time of night,
    When churchyards yawn, and hell itself breathes out
    Contagion to this world: now could I drink hot blood,
355   And do such bitter business as the day
    Would quake to look on. Soft! now to my mother.—
    O heart, lose not thy nature; let not ever
    The soul of Nero[20] enter this firm bosom:
    Let me be cruel, not unnatural:
360   I will speak daggers to her, but use none;
    My tongue and soul in this be hypocrites,—
    How in my words soever she be shent,
    To give them seals never, my soul, consent! *(Exit.)*

SCENE 3

A room in the castle.

(Enter King, Rosencrantz, and Guildenstern.)

KING: I like him not; nor stands it safe with us
    To let his madness range. Therefore prepare you;
    I your commission with forthwith despatch,
    And he to England shall along with you:
5   The terms of our estate may not endure
    Hazard so dangerous as doth hourly grow
    Out of his lunacies.
GUILDENSTERN: We will ourselves provide:
    Most holy and religious fear it is
    To keep those many many bodies safe
10   That live and feed upon your majesty.
ROSENCRANTZ: The single and peculiar life is bound,
    With all the strength and armor of the mind,
    To keep itself from 'noyance; but much more
    That spirit upon whose weal depend and rest

---

[20] *soul of Nero:* Nero killed his mother, a crime of which Hamlet does not want to be guilty.

15   The lives of many. The cease of majesty
      Dies not alone; but like a gulf doth draw
      What's near it with it: it is a massy wheel,
      Fix'd on the summit of the highest mount,
      To whose huge spokes ten thousand lesser things
20   Are mortis'd and adjoin'd; which, when it falls,
      Each small annexment, petty consequence,
      Attends the boisterous ruin. Never alone
      Did the king sigh, but with a general groan.
   KING: Arm you, I pray you, to this speedy voyage;
25   For we will fetters put upon this fear,
      Which now goes too free-footed.
   ROSENCRANTZ and GUILDENSTERN: We will haste us.

(Exeunt Rosencrantz and Guildenstern.)

(Enter Polonius.)

   POLONIUS: My lord, he's going to his mother's closet:
      Behind the arras I'll convey myself
      To hear the process; I'll warrant she'll tax him home:[1]
30   And, as you said, and wisely was it said,
      'Tis meet that some more audience than a mother,
      Since nature makes them partial, should o'erhear
      The speech, of vantage. Fare you well, my liege:
      I'll call upon you ere you go to bed,
35   And tell you what I know.
   KING: Thanks, dear my lord.

(Exit Polonius.)

      O, my offence is rank, it smells to heaven;
      It hath the primal eldest curse upon't,—
      A brother's murder!—Pray can I not,
      Though inclination be as sharp as will:
40   My stronger guilt defeats my strong intent;
      And, like a man to double business bound,
      I stand in pause where I shall first begin,
      And both neglect. What if this cursed hand
      Were thicker than itself with brother's blood,—
45   Is there not rain enough in the sweet heavens
      To wash it white as snow? Whereto serves mercy
      But to confront the visage of offence?
      And what's in prayer but this twofold force,—
      To be forestalled ere we come to fall,
50   Or pardon'd being down? Then I'll look up;

---

[1] *tax him home:* reprove him properly.

My fault is past. But, O, what form of prayer
Can serve my turn? Forgive me my foul murder?—
That cannot be; since I am still possess'd
Of those effects for which I did the murder,—
My crown, mine own ambition, and my queen.
May one be pardon'd and retain the offence?[2]
In the corrupted currents of this world
Offence's gilded hand may shove by justice;
And oft 'tis seen the wicked prize itself
Buys out the law: but 'tis not so above;
There is no shuffling,—there the action lies
In his true nature; and we ourselves compell'd,
Even to the teeth and forehead of our faults,
To give in evidence. What then? what rests?[3]
Try what repentance can: what can it not?
Yet what can it when one can not repent?
O wretched state! O bosom black as death!
O limed[4] soul, that, struggling to be free,
Art more engag'd! Help, angels! make assay:
Bow, stubborn knees; and, heart, with strings of steel,
Be soft as sinews of the new-born babe!
All may be well. *(Retires and kneels)*

(Enter Hamlet.)

HAMLET: Now might I do it pat, now he is praying;
And now I'll do't—and so he goes to heaven;
And so am I reveng'd:—that would be scann'd:
A villain kills my father; and for that,
I, his sole son, do this same villain send
To heaven.
O, this is hire and salary, not revenge.
He took my father grossly, full of bread;
With all his crimes broad blown, as flush as May;
And how his audit stands who knows save heaven?
But in our circumstance and course of thought
'Tis heavy with him: and am I, then, reveng'd,
To take him in the purging of his soul,
When he is fit and season'd for his passage?
No.
Up, sword; and know thou a more horrid hent:[5]
When he is drunk, asleep, or in his rage;
Or in the incestuous pleasure of his bed;
At gaming, swearing; or about some act

---

[2] *offence:* that is, the gains won by the offense.   [3] *rests:* remains.   [4] *limed:* snared.   [5] *hent:* opportunity.

That has no relish of salvation in't;—
Then trip him, that his heels may kick at heaven;
And that his soul may be as damn'd and black
95 As hell, whereto it goes. My mother stays:
This physic but prolongs thy sickly days. *(Exit.)*

(The King rises and advances.)

KING: My words fly up, my thoughts remain below:
Words without thoughts never to heaven go. *(Exit.)*

Scene 4

Another room in the castle.

(Enter Queen and Polonius.)

POLONIUS: He will come straight. Look you lay home to him:
Tell him his pranks have been too broad to bear with,
And that your grace hath screen'd and stood between
Much heat and him. I'll silence me e'en here.
5 Pray you, be round with him.
HAMLET: *(Within)* Mother, mother, mother!
QUEEN: I'll warrant you:
Fear me not:—withdraw, I hear him coming.

(Polonius goes behind the arras.)

(Enter Hamlet.)

HAMLET: Now, mother, what's the matter?
QUEEN: Hamlet, thou hast thy father much offended.
10 HAMLET: Mother, you have my father much offended.
QUEEN: Come, come, you answer with an idle tongue.
HAMLET: Go, go, you question with a wicked tongue.
QUEEN: Why, how now, Hamlet!
HAMLET: What's the matter now?
QUEEN: Have you forgot me?
HAMLET: No, by the rood, not so:
15 You are the queen, your husband's brother's wife;
And,—would it were not so!—you are my mother.
QUEEN: Nay, then, I'll set those to you that can speak.
HAMLET: Come, come, and sit you down; you shall not budge;
You go not till I set you up a glass
20 Where you may see the inmost part of you.
QUEEN: What wilt thou do? thou wilt not murder me?—
Help, help, ho!
POLONIUS: *(Behind)* What, ho! help, help, help!
HAMLET: How now! a rat? *(Draws)*
Dead, for a ducat, dead! *(Makes a pass through the arras)*

25 **POLONIUS:** *(Behind)* O, I am slain! *(Falls and dies.)*
    QUEEN: O me, what hast thou done?
    HAMLET: Nay, I know not:
        Is it the king? *(Draws forth Polonius)*
    QUEEN: O, what a rash and bloody deed is this!
    HAMLET: A bloody deed!—almost as bad, good mother,
30   As kill a king and marry with his brother.
    QUEEN: As kill a king!
    HAMLET: Ay, lady, 'twas my word.—
        Thou wretched, rash, intruding fool, farewell! *(To Polonius)*
        I took thee for thy better: take thy fortune;
        Thou find'st to be too busy is some danger.—
35   Leave wringing of your hands: peace; sit you down,
        And let me wring your heart: for so I shall,
        If it be made of penetrable stuff;
        If damned custom have not braz'd it so
        That it is proof and bulwark against sense.
40 **QUEEN:** What have I done, that thou dar'st wag thy tongue
        In noise so rude against me?
    HAMLET: Such an act
        That blurs the grace and blush of modesty;
        Calls virtue hypocrite; takes off the rose
        From the fair forehead of an innocent love,
45   And sets a blister there; makes marriage-vows
        As false as dicers' oaths: O, such a deed
        As from the body of contraction plucks
        The very soul, and sweet religion makes
        A rhapsody of words: heaven's face doth glow;
50   Yea, this solidity and compound mass,
        With tristful[1] visage, as against the doom,
        Is thought-sick at the act.
    QUEEN: Ah me, what act,
        That roars so loud, and thunders in the index?
    HAMLET: Look here upon this picture and on this,—
55   The counterfeit presentment of two brothers.
        See what grace was seated on this brow;
        Hyperion's curls; the front of Jove himself;
        An eye like Mars, to threaten and command;
        A station like the herald Mercury
60   New-lighted on a heaven-kissing hill;
        A combination and a form, indeed,
        Where every god did seem to set his seal,
        To give the world assurance of a man:
        This was your husband.—Look you now, what follows:

---

[1] *tristful:* gloomy.

	Here is your husband, like a mildew'd ear
65	Blasting his wholesome brother. Have you eyes?
	Could you on this fair mountain leave to feed,
	And batten on this moor? Ha! have you eyes?
	You cannot call it love; for at your age
70	The hey-day in the blood is tame, it's humble,
	And waits upon the judgment: and what judgment
	Would step from this to this? Sense, sure, you have,
	Else could you not have motion: but sure that sense
	Is apoplex'd: for madness would not err;
75	Nor sense to ecstasy was ne'er so thrill'd
	But it reserv'd some quantity of choice
	To serve in such a difference. What devil was't
	That thus hath cozen'd you at hoodman-blind?[2]
	Eyes without feeling, feeling without sight,
80	Ears without hand or eyes, smelling sans all,
	Or but a sickly part of one true sense
	Could not so mope.
	O shame! where is thy blush! Rebellious hell,
	If thou canst mutine in a matron's bones,
85	To flaming youth let virtue be as wax,
	And melt in her own fire: proclaim no shame
	When the compulsive ardor gives the charge,
	Since frost itself as actively doth burn,
	And reason panders[3] will.

QUEEN: O Hamlet, speak no more:
90   Thou turn'st mine eyes into my very soul;
        And there I see such black and grained spots
        As will not leave their tinct.[4]

HAMLET: Nay, but to live
        In the rank sweat of an enseamed bed,
        Stew'd in corruption, honeying and making love
95   Over the nasty sty,—

QUEEN: O, speak to me no more;
        These words like daggers enter in mine ears;
        No more, sweet Hamlet.

HAMLET: A murderer and a villain;
        A slave that is not twentieth part the tithe
        Of your precedent lord; a vice of kings;[5]
100   A cutpurse of the empire and the rule,
        That from a shelf the precious diadem stole,
        And put it in his pocket!

---

[2] *cozen'd . . . hoodman-blind:* tricked you at blindman's bluff.   [3] *panders:* becomes subservient to.   [4] *As . . . tinct:* as will not yield up their color.   [5] *a vice of kings:* a buffoon among kings; the "Vice" in morality plays.

QUEEN: No more.
HAMLET: A king of shreds and patches,—

(Enter Ghost.)

  Save me, and hover o'er me with your wings,
105 You heavenly guards!—What would your gracious figure?
QUEEN: Alas, he's mad!
HAMLET: Do you not come your tardy son to chide,
  That, laps'd in time and passion, lets go by
  The important acting of your dread command?
110 O, say!
GHOST: Do not forget: this visitation
  Is but to whet thy almost blunted purpose.
  But, look, amazement on thy mother sits:
  O, step between her and her fighting soul,—
115 Conceit in weakest bodies strongest works,—
  Speak to her, Hamlet.
HAMLET: How is it with you, lady?
QUEEN: Alas, how is't with you,
  That you do bend your eye on vacancy,
  And with the incorporal air do hold discourse?
120 Forth at your eyes your spirits wildly peep;
  And, as the sleeping soldiers in the alarm,
  Your bedded hair, like life in excrements,[6]
  Starts up and stands on end. O gentle son,
  Upon the heat and flame of thy distemper
125 Sprinkle cool patience. Whereon do you look?
HAMLET: On him, on him! Look you, how pale he glares!
  His form and cause conjoin'd, preaching to stones,
  Would make them capable.—Do not look upon me;
  Lest with this piteous action you convert
130 My stern effects: then what I have to do
  Will want true color; tears perchance for blood.
QUEEN: To whom do you speak this?
HAMLET: Do you see nothing there?
QUEEN: Nothing at all; yet all that is I see.
HAMLET: Nor did you nothing hear?
135 QUEEN: No, nothing but ourselves.
HAMLET: Why, look you there! look, how it steals away!
  My father, in his habit as he liv'd!
  Look, where he goes, even now, out at the portal!

(Exit Ghost.)

---

[6] *excrements:* in outgrowths or extremities.

QUEEN: This is the very coinage of your brain:
140   This bodiless creation ecstasy
       Is very cunning in.
       HAMLET: Ecstasy!
       My pulse, as yours, doth temperately keep time,
       And makes as healthful music: it is not madness
       That I have utter'd: bring me to the test,
145   And I the matter will re-word; which madness
       Would gambol from. Mother, for love of grace,
       Lay not that flattering unction to your soul,
       That not your trespass, but my madness speaks:
       It will but skin and film the ulcerous place,
150   Whilst rank corruption, mining all within,
       Infects unseen. Confess yourself to Heaven;
       Repent what's past; avoid what is to come;
       And do not spread the compost on the weeds,
       To make them ranker. Forgive me this my virtue;
155   For in the fatness[7] of these pursy times
       Virtue itself of vice must pardon beg,
       Yea, curb and woo for leave to do him good.
QUEEN: O Hamlet, thou hast cleft my heart in twain.
HAMLET: O, throw away the worser part of it,
160   And live the purer with the other half.
       Good-night: but go not to mine uncle's bed;
       Assume a virtue, if you have it not.
       That monster custom, who all sense doth eat,
       Of habits devil, is angel yet in this,—
165   That to the use of actions fair and good
       He likewise gives a frock or livery
       That aptly is put on. Refrain to-night;
       And that shall lend a kind of easiness
       To the next abstinence: the next more easy;
170   For use almost can change the stamp of nature,
       And either curb the devil, or throw him out
       With wondrous potency. Once more, good-night:
       And when you are desirous to be bless'd,
       I'll blessing beg of you.—For this same lord *(Pointing to Polonius)*
175   I do repent: but Heaven hath pleas'd it so,
       To punish me with this, and this with me,
       That I must be their[8] scourge and minister.
       I will bestow him, and will answer well
       The death I gave him. So, again, good-night.—
180   I must be cruel only to be kind:

---

[7] *fatness:* corruption.   [8] *their:* Heaven's, or the heavens'.

Thus bad begins and worse remains behind.—
One word more, good lady.

QUEEN: What shall I do?

HAMLET: Not this, by no means, that I bid you do:
Let the bloat king tempt you again to bed;
Pinch wanton on your cheek; call you his mouse;
And let him, for a pair of reechy kisses,
Or paddling in your neck with his damn'd fingers,
Make you to ravel all this matter out,
That I essentially am not in madness,
But mad in craft. 'Twere good you let him know;
For who that's but a queen, fair, sober, wise,
Would from a paddock,[9] from a bat, a gib,[10]
Such dear concernings hide? who would do so?
No, in despite of sense and secrecy,
Unpeg the basket on the house's top,
Let the birds fly, and, like the famous ape,
To try conclusions, in the basket creep,
And break your own neck down.

QUEEN: Be thou assur'd, if words be made of breath
And breath of life, I have not life to breathe
What thou hast said to me.

HAMLET: I must to England; you know that?

QUEEN: Alack,
I had forgot: 'tis so concluded on.

HAMLET: There's letters seal'd: and my two school-fellows,—
Whom I will trust as I will adders fang'd,
They bear the mandate; they must sweep my way,
And marshal me to knavery. Let it work;
For 'tis the sport to have the éngineer
Hoist with his own petard: and't shall go hard
But I will delve one yard below their mines,
And blow them at the moon: O, 'tis most sweet,
When in one line two crafts directly meet.—
This man shall set me packing:
I'll lug the guts into the neighbor room.—
Mother, good-night.—Indeed, this counsellor
Is now most still, most secret, and most grave,
Who was in life a foolish prating knave.
Come, sir, to draw toward an end with you:—
Good-night, mother.

(Exeunt severally; Hamlet dragging out Polonius.)

---

[9] *paddock:* toad.   [10] *gib:* tomcat.

Act IV
Scene 1

A room in the castle.

(Enter King, Queen, Rosencrantz, and Guildenstern.)

KING: There's matter in these sighs, these prófound heaves:
You must translate: 'tis fit we understand them.
Where is your son?
QUEEN: Bestow this place on us a little while. *(To Rosencrantz and Guildenstern, who go out)*
5   Ah, my good lord, what have I seen to-night!
KING: What, Gertrude? How does Hamlet?
QUEEN: Mad as the sea and wind, when both contend
Which is the mightier: in his lawless fit,
Behind the arras hearing something stir,
10   He whips his rapier out, and cries, *A rat, a rat!*
And, in this brainish apprehension,[1] kills
The unseen good old man.
KING: O heavy deed!
It had been so with us had we been there:
His liberty is full of threats to all;
15   To you yourself, to us, to every one.
Alas, how shall this bloody deed be answer'd?
It will be laid to us, whose providence
Should have kept short, restrain'd, and out of haunt
This mad young man: but so much was our love,
20   We would not understand what was most fit;
But, like the owner of a foul disease,
To keep it from divulging, let it feed
Even on the pith of life. Where is he gone?
QUEEN: To draw apart the body he hath kill'd:
25   O'er whom his very madness, like some ore
Among a mineral of metals base,
Shows itself pure; he weeps for what is done.
KING: O Gertrude, come away!
The sun no sooner shall the mountains touch
30   But we will ship him hence: and this vile deed
We must, with all our majesty and skill,
Both countenance and excuse.—Ho, Guildenstern!

(Enter Rosencrantz and Guildenstern.)

Friends both, go join you with some further aid:
Hamlet in madness hath Polonius slain,

---

[1] *brainish apprehension:* mad notion.

35   And from his mother's closet hath he dragg'd him:
        Go seek him out; speak fair, and bring the body
        Into the chapel. I pray you, haste in this.

(Exeunt Rosencrantz and Guildenstern.)

        Come, Gertrude, we'll call up our wisest friends;
        And let them know both what we mean to do
40   And what's untimely done: so haply slander,—
        Whose whisper o'er the world's diameter,
        As level as the cannon to his blank,
        Transports his poison'd shot,—may amiss our name,
        And hit the woundless air.—O, come away!
45   My soul is full of discord and dismay.

(Exeunt.)

Scene 2

Another room in the castle.

(Enter Hamlet.)

Hamlet: Safely stowed.
Rosencrantz and Guildenstern: *(Within)* Hamlet! Lord Hamlet!
Hamlet: What noise? who calls on Hamlet? O, here they come.

(Enter Rosencrantz and Guildenstern.)

Rosencrantz: What have you done, my lord, with the dead body?
5 **Hamlet:** Compounded it with dust, whereto 'tis kin.
Rosencrantz: Tell us where 'tis, that we may take it thence,
        And bear it to the chapel.
Hamlet: Do not believe it.
Rosencrantz: Believe what?
10 **Hamlet:** That I can keep your counsel, and not mine own. Besides, to be demanded of a sponge!—what replication should be made by the son of a king?
Rosencrantz: Take you me for a sponge, my lord?
Hamlet: Ay, sir; that soaks up the king's countenance, his rewards,
15   his authorities. But such officers do the king best service in the end: he keeps them, like an ape, in the corner of his jaw; first mouthed, to be last swallowed: when he needs what you have gleaned, it is but squeezing you, and, sponge, you shall be dry again.
20 **Rosencrantz:** I understand you not, my lord.
Hamlet: I am glad of it: a knavish speech sleeps in a foolish ear.
Rosencrantz: My lord, you must tell us where the body is, and go with us to the king.
Hamlet: The body is with the king, but the king is not with the
25   body. The king is a thing,—

GUILDENSTERN: A thing, my lord!
HAMLET: Of nothing: bring me to him. Hide fox, and all after.

(Exeunt.)

Scene 3

Another room in the castle.

(Enter King, attended.)

KING: I have sent to seek him, and to find the body.
    How dangerous is it that this man goes loose!
    Yet must not we put the strong law on him:
    He's lov'd of the distracted multitude,
5   Who like not in their judgment, but their eyes;
    And where 'tis so, the offender's scourge is weigh'd,
    But never the offence. To bear all smooth and even,
    This sudden sending him away must seem
    Deliberate pause: diseases desperate grown
10   By desperate appliance are reliev'd,
    Or not at all.

(Enter Rosencrantz.)

              How now! what hath befallen!
ROSENCRANTZ: Where the dead body is bestow'd, my lord,
    We cannot get from him.
KING: But where is he?
ROSENCRANTZ: Without, my lord; guarded, to know your pleasure.
15 KING: Bring him before us.
    ROSENCRANTZ: Ho, Guildenstern! bring in my lord.

(Enter Hamlet and Guildenstern.)

KING: Now, Hamlet, where's Polonius?
HAMLET: At supper.
KING: At supper! where?
HAMLET: Not where he eats, but where he is eaten: a certain
20   convocation of politic worms are e'en at him. Your worm is your
    only emperor for diet: we fat all creatures else to fat us, and we fat
    ourselves for maggots: your fat king and your lean beggar is but
    variable service,—two dishes, but to one table: that's the end.
KING: Alas, alas!
25 HAMLET: A man may fish with the worm that hath eat of a king, and
    eat of the fish that hath fed of that worm.
KING: What does thou mean by this?
HAMLET: Nothing but to show you how a king may go a progress
    through the guts of a beggar.
30 KING: Where is Polonius?
HAMLET: In heaven; send thither to see: if your messenger find him
    not there, seek him i' the other place yourself. But, indeed, if you

find him not within this month, you shall nose him as you go up
the stairs into the lobby.
35 KING: Go seek him there. *(To some Attendants)*
HAMLET: He will stay till ye come.

(Exeunt Attendants.)

KING: Hamlet, this deed, for thine especial safety,—
Which we do tender, as we dearly grieve
For that which thou hast done,—must send thee hence
40 With fiery quickness: therefore prepare thyself;
The bark is ready, and the wind at help,
The associates tend, and everything is bent
For England.
HAMLET: For England!
KING: Ay, Hamlet.
HAMLET: Good.
KING: So is it, if thou knew'st our purposes.
45 HAMLET: I see a cherub that sees them.—But, come; for England!—
Farewell, dear mother.
KING: Thy loving father, Hamlet.
HAMLET: My mother: father and mother is man and wife; man and
wife is one flesh; and so, my mother.—Come, for England! *(Exit.)*
50 KING: Follow him at foot; tempt him with speed aboard;
Delay it not; I'll have him hence to-night:
Away! for everything is seal'd and done
That else leans on the affair, pray you, make haste.

(Exeunt Rosencrantz and Guildenstern.)

And, England, if my love thou hold'st at aught,—
55 As my great power thereof may give thee sense,
Since yet thy cicatrice looks raw and red
After the Danish sword, and thy free awe
Pays homage to us,—thou mayst not coldly set
Our sovereign process; which imports at full,
60 By letters conjuring to that effect,
The present death of Hamlet. Do it, England;
For like the hectic in my blood he rages,
And thou must cure me: till I know 'tis done,
Howe'er my haps, my joys will ne'er begin. *(Exit.)*

SCENE 4

A plain in Denmark.

(Enter Fortinbras, and Forces marching.)

FORTINBRAS: Go, from me greet the Danish king:
Tell him that, by his license, Fortinbras

Craves the conveyance of a promis'd march
Over his kingdom. You know the rendezvous,
5   If that his majesty would aught with us,
We shall express our duty in his eye,
And let him know so.
CAPTAIN: I will do't, my lord.
FORTINBRAS: Go softly on.

(Exeunt Fortinbras and Forces.)

(Enter Hamlet, Rosencrantz, Guildenstern, &c.)

HAMLET: Good sir, whose powers are these?
10 CAPTAIN: They are of Norway, sir.
HAMLET: How purpos'd, sir, I pray you?
CAPTAIN: Against some part of Poland.
HAMLET: Who commands them, sir?
CAPTAIN: The nephew to old Norway, Fortinbras.
15 HAMLET: Goes it against the main of Poland, sir,
Or for some frontier?
CAPTAIN: Truly to speak, and with no addition,
We go to gain a little patch of ground
That hath in it no profit but the name.
20   To pay five ducats, five, I would not farm it;
Nor will it yield to Norway or the Pole
A ranker[1] rate should it be sold in fee.
HAMLET: Why, then the Polack never will defend it.
CAPTAIN: Yes, it is already garrison'd.
25 HAMLET: Two thousand souls and twenty thousand ducats
Will not debate the question of this straw:
This is the imposthume[2] of much wealth and peace,
That inward breaks, and shows no cause without
Why the man dies.—I humbly thank you, sir.
30 CAPTAIN: God b' wi' you, sir. *(Exit.)*
ROSENCRANTZ: Will't please you go, my lord?
HAMLET: I'll be with you straight. Go a little before.

(Exeunt all but Hamlet.)

How all occasions do inform against me,
And spur my dull revenge! What is a man,
35   If his chief good and market of his time
Be but to sleep and feed? a beast, no more.
Sure he that made us with such large discourse,[3]
Looking before and after, gave us not
That capability and godlike reason

---

[1] *ranker:* dearer.   [2] *imposthume:* ulcer.   [3] *discourse:* reasoning faculty.

40   To fust[4] in us unus'd. Now, whether it be
        Bestial oblivion or some craven scruple
        Of thinking too precisely on the event,—
        A thought which, quarter'd, hath but one part wisdom
        And ever three parts coward,—I do not know
45   Why yet I live to say, *This thing's to do;*
        Sith[5] I have cause, and will, and strength, and means
        To do't. Examples, gross as earth, exhort me:
        Witness this army, of such mass and charge,
        Led by a delicate and tender prince;
50   Whose spirit, with divine ambition puff'd,
        Makes mouths at the invisible event;
        Exposing what is mortal and unsure
        To all that fortune, death, and danger dare,
        Even for an egg-shell. Rightly to be great
55   Is not to stir without great argument,
        But greatly to find quarrel in a straw
        When honor's at the stake. How stand I, then,
        That have a father kill'd, a mother stain'd,
        Excitements of my reason and my blood,
60   And let all sleep? while, to my shame, I see
        The imminent death of twenty thousand men,
        That, for a fantasy and trick of fame,
        Go to their graves like beds; fight for a plot
        Whereon the numbers cannot try the cause,
65   Which is not tomb enough and continent[6]
        To hide the slain?—O, from this time forth,
        My thoughts be bloody, or be nothing worth! *(Exit.)*

Scene 5

Elsinore. A room in the castle.

(Enter Queen and Horatio.)

Queen: I will not speak with her.
Horatio: She is importunate; indeed, distract:
    Her mood will needs be pitied.
Queen: What would she have?
Horatio: She speaks much of her father; says she hears
5   There's tricks i' the world; and hems, and beats her heart;
       Spurns enviously at straws; speaks things in doubt,
       That carry but half sense: her speech is nothing,
       Yet the unshapéd use of it doth move
       The hearers to collection; they aim at it,

---

[4] *fust:* grow musty.   [5] *Sith:* since.   [6] *continent:* container.

> And botch the words up fit to their own thoughts;
> Which, as her winks, and nods, and gestures yield them,
> Indeed would make one think there might be thought,
> Though nothing sure, yet much unhappily.
> 'Twere good she were spoken with; for she may strew
> Dangerous conjectures in ill-breeding minds.
>
> QUEEN: Let her come in.

(Exit Horatio.)

> To my sick soul, as sin's true nature is,
> Each toy seems prologue to some great amiss:
> So full of artless jealousy is guilt,
> It spills itself in fearing to be spilt.

(Re-enter Horatio and Ophelia.)

OPHELIA: Where is the beauteous majesty of Denmark?
QUEEN: How now, Ophelia!
OPHELIA: *(Sings)*

> How should I your true love know
> From another one?
> By his cockle hat and staff,
> And his sandal shoon.

QUEEN: Alas, sweet lady, what imports this song?
OPHELIA: Say you? nay, pray you, mark.

(Sings)

> He is dead and gone, lady,
> He is dead and gone;
> At his head a grass green turf,
> At his heels a stone.

QUEEN: Nay, but, Ophelia,—
OPHELIA: Pray you, mark.

(Sings)

> White his shroud as the mountain snow,

(Enter King.)

QUEEN: Alas, look here, my lord.
OPHELIA: *(Sings)*

> Larded with sweet flowers;
> Which bewept to the grave did go
> With true-love showers.

KING: How do you, pretty lady?

OPHELIA: Well, God 'ild[1] you! They say the owl was a baker's daughter.
Lord, we know what we are, but know not what we may be.
God be at your table!
KING: Conceit upon her father.
OPHELIA: Pray you, let's have no words of this; but when they ask
you what it means, say you this:

(Sings.)

> To-morrow is Saint Valentine's day
> All in the morning betime,
> And I a maid at your window,
> To be your Valentine.
>
> Then up he rose, and donn'd his clothes,
> And dupp'd the chamber-door;
> Let in the maid, that out a maid
> Never departed more.

KING: Pretty Ophelia!
OPHELIA: Indeed, la, without an oath, I'll make an end on't;

(Sings)

> By Gis[2] and by Saint Charity,
> Alack, and fie for shame!
> Young men will do't, if they come to't;
> By cock, they are to blame.
>
> Quoth she, before you tumbled me,
> You promis'd me to wed.
> So would I ha' done, by yonder sun,
> An thou hadst not come to my bed.

KING: How long hath she been thus?
OPHELIA: I hope all will be well. We must be patient: but I cannot
choose but weep, to think they should lay him i' the cold ground.
My brother shall know of it: and so I thank you; for your good
counsel.—Come, my coach!—Good-night, ladies; good-night,
sweet ladies; good-night, good-night. *(Exit.)*
KING: Follow her close; give her good watch, I pray you.

(Exit Horatio.)

> O, this is the poison of deep grief; it springs
> All from her father's death. O Gertrude, Gertrude,
> When sorrows come, they come not single spies,
> But in battalions! First, her father slain;
> Next, your son gone; and he most violent author

---

[1] *'ild:* yield you—that is, reward you.   [2] *By Gis:* a contraction for "by Jesus."

　　　　Of his own just remove: the people muddied,
　　　　Thick and unwholesome in their thoughts and whispers
　　　　For good Polonius' death; and we have done but greenly
　　　　In hugger-mugger³ to inter him: poor Ophelia
80　　　Divided from herself and her fair judgment,
　　　　Without the which we are pictures, or mere beasts:
　　　　Last, and as much containing as all these,
　　　　Her brother is in secret come from France;
　　　　Feeds on his wonder, keeps himself in clouds,
85　　　And wants not buzzers to infect his ear
　　　　With pestilent speeches of his father's death;
　　　　Wherein necessity, of matter beggar'd,
　　　　Will nothing stick our person to arraign
　　　　In ear and ear. O my dear Gertrude, this,
90　　　Like to a murdering piece,⁴ in many places
　　　　Gives me superfluous death.

(A noise within.)

QUEEN:　　　　　　　　　Alack, what noise is this?
KING: Where are my Switzers?⁵ let them guard the door.

(Enter a Gentleman.)

　　　　What is the matter?
GENTLEMAN:　　　　Save yourself, my lord:
　　　　The ocean, overpeering of his list,
95　　　Eats not the flats with more impetuous haste
　　　　Than young Laertes, in a riotous head,
　　　　O'erbears your officers. The rabble call him lord;
　　　　And, as the world were now but to begin,
　　　　Antiquity forgot, custom not known,
100　　　The ratifiers and props of every word,
　　　　They cry, *Choose we, Laertes shall be king!*
　　　　Caps, hands, and tongues applaud it to the clouds,
　　　　Laertes shall be king, Laertes king!
QUEEN: How cheerfully on the false trail they cry!
105　　　O, this is counter, you false Danish dogs!
KING: The doors are broke.

(Noise within.)

(Enter Laertes armed; Danes following.)

LAERTES: Where is this king?—Sirs, stand you all without.
DANES: No, let's come in.

---

³ *In hugger-mugger:* in great secrecy and haste.　⁴ *piece:* a cannon.　⁵ *Switzers:* bodyguard of Swiss mercenaries.

LAERTES: I pray you, give me leave.
DANES: We will, we will. *(They retire without the door.)*
110 LAERTES: I thank you:—keep the door.—O thou vile king,
Give me my father!
QUEEN: Calmly, good Laertes.
LAERTES: That drop of blood that's calm proclaims me bastard;
Cries cuckold to my father; brands the harlot
Even here, between the chaste unsmirched brow
115 Of my true mother.
KING: What is the cause, Laertes,
That thy rebellion looks so giant-like?—
Let him go, Gertrude; do not fear our person:
There's such divinity doth hedge a king,
That treason can but peep to what it would,
120 Acts little of his will.—Tell me, Laertes,
Why thou art thus incens'd.—Let him go, Gertrude:—
Speak, man.
LAERTES: Where is my father?
KING: Dead.
QUEEN: But not by him.
KING: Let him demand his fill.
125 LAERTES: How came he dead? I'll not be juggled with:
To hell, allegiance! vows, to the blackest devil!
Conscience and grace, to the profoundest pit!
I dare damnation:—to this point I stand,—
That both the worlds I give to negligence,
130 Let come what comes; only I'll be reveng'd
Most thoroughly for my father.
KING: Who shall stay you?
LAERTES: My will, not all the world:
And for my means, I'll husband them so well,
They shall go far with little.
KING: Good Laertes,
135 If you desire to know the certainty
Of your dear father's death, is't writ in your revenge
That, sweepstake, you will draw both friend and foe,
Winner or loser?
LAERTES: None but his enemies.
KING: Will you know them, then?
140 LAERTES: To his good friends thus wide I'll ope my arms;
And, like the kind life-rendering pelican,[6]
Repast them with my blood.

---

[6] *life-rendering pelican:* the pelican mother was believed to draw blood from itself to feed its young.

KING: Why, now you speak
    Like a good child and a true gentleman.
    That I am guiltless of your father's death,
145   And am most sensible in grief for it,
    It shall as level to your judgment pierce
    As day does to your eye.
DANES: *(Within)*   Let her come in.
LAERTES: How now! what noise is that?

(Re-enter Ophelia, fantastically dressed with straws and flowers.)

    O heat, dry up my brains! tears seven times salt
150   Burn out the sense and virtue of mine eyes!—
    By heaven, thy madness shall be paid by weight
    Till our scale turn the beam. O rose of May!
    Dear maid, kind sister, sweet Ophelia!—
    O heavens! is't possible a young maid's wits
155   Should be as mortal as an old man's life!
    Nature is fine in love; and where 'tis fine
    It sends some precious instance of itself
    After the thing it loves.
OPHELIA: *(Sings)*

        They bore him barefac'd on the bier;
160   Hey no nonny, nonny, hey nonny;
        And on his grave rain'd many a tear,—
        Fare you well, my dove!

LAERTES: Hadst thou thy wits, and didst persuade revenge,
    It could not move thus.
165 **OPHELIA:** You must sing, *Down-a-down, an you call him a-down-a.* O, how the wheel becomes it! It is the false steward, that stole his master's daughter.
LAERTES: This nothing's more than matter.
OPHELIA: There's rosemary, that's for remembrance; pray, love,
170   remember: and there is pansies that's for thoughts.
LAERTES: A document in madness,—thoughts and remembrance fitted.
OPHELIA: There's fennel for you, and columbines:—there's rue for you; and here's some for me:—we may call it herb-grace o' Sundays:—O, you must wear your rue with a difference.—There's a
175   daisy:—I would give you some violets, but they withered all when my father died:—they say, he made a good end,—
(Sings)

        For bonny sweet Robin is all my joy,—

LAERTES: Thoughts and affliction, passion, hell itself,
    She turns to favor and to prettiness.
OPHELIA: *(Sings)*

180   And will he not come again?
             And will he not come again?
               No, no, he is dead,
               Go to thy death-bed,
             He never will come again.

185   His beard was as white as snow
               All flaxen was his poll:
                 He is gone, he is gone,
                 And we cast away moan:
               God ha' mercy on his soul!

190   And of all Christian souls, I pray God.—God b' wi' ye. *(Exit.)*
LAERTES: Do you see this, O God?
KING: Laertes, I must commune with your grief,
    Or you deny me right. Go but apart,
    Make choice of whom your wisest friends you will,
195 And they shall hear and judge 'twixt you and me:
    If by direct or by collateral hand
    They find us touch'd, we will our kingdom give,
    Our crown, our life, and all that we call ours,
    To you in satisfaction; but if not,
200 Be you content to lend your patience to us,
    And we shall jointly labor with your soul
    To give it due content.
LAERTES: Let this be so;
    His means of death, his obscure burial,—
    No trophy, sword, nor hatchment[7] o'er his bones
205 No noble rite nor formal ostentation,—
    Cry to be heard, as 'twere from heaven to earth,
    That I must call't in question.
KING: So you shall;
    And where the offence is, let the great axe fall.
    I pray you, go with me.

(Exeunt.)

SCENE 6

Another room in the castle.

(Enter Horatio and a Servant.)

HORATIO: What are they that would speak with me?
SERVANT: Sailors, sir: they say they have letters for you.
HORATIO: Let them come in.—

(Exit Servant.)

---

[7] *hatchment:* a tablet with coat of arms.

I do not know from what part of the world
5   I should be greeted, if not from Lord Hamlet.

(Enter Sailors.)

1st Sailor: God bless you, sir.
Horatio: Let him bless thee too.
1st Sailor: He shall, sir, an't please him. There's a letter for you, sir;
it comes from the ambassador that was bound for England; if your
10 name be Horatio, as I am let to know it is.
Horatio: *(Reads)* Horatio, when thou shalt have overlooked this, give these
fellows some means to the king: they have letters for him. Ere we were
two days old at sea, a pirate of very warlike appointment gave us chase.
Finding ourselves too slow of sail, we put on a compelled valor; and in
15 he grapple I boarded them; on the instant they got clear of our ship; so I
alone became their prisoner. They have dealt with me like thieves of
mercy: but they knew what they did; I am to do a good turn for them.
Let the king have the letters I have sent; and repair thou to me with as
much haste as thou wouldst fly death. I have words to speak in thine ear
20 will make thee dumb; yet are they much too light for the bore of the
matter. These good fellows will bring thee where I am. Rosencrantz and
Guildenstern hold their course for England: of them I have much to tell
thee. Farewell. He that thou knowest thine.   Hamlet
Come, I will give you way for these your letters;
25 And do't the speedier, that you may direct me
To him from whom you brought them.

(Exeunt.)

Scene 7

Another room in the castle.

(Enter King and Laertes.)

King: Now must your conscience my acquittance seal,
And you must put me in your heart for friend,
Sith you have heard, and with a knowing ear,
That he which hath your noble father slain
5   Pursu'd my life.
Laertes: It well appears:—but tell me
Why you proceeded not against these feats,
So crimeful and so capital in nature,
As by your safety, wisdom, all things else,
You mainly were stirr'd up.
King: O, for two special reasons;
10 Which may to you, perhaps, seem much unsinew'd,
But yet to me they are strong. The queen his mother
Lives almost by his looks; and for myself,—

        My virtue or my plague, be it either which,—
        She's so conjunctive to my life and soul,
15   That, as the star moves not but in his sphere,
        I could not but by her. The other motive,
        Why to a public count I might not go,
        Is the great love the general gender bear him;
        Who, dipping all his faults in their affection,
20   Would, like the spring that turneth wood to stone,
        Convert his gyves to graces; so that my arrows,
        Too slightly timber'd for so loud a wind,
        Would have reverted to my bow again,
        And not where I had aim'd them.
25 LAERTES: And so have I a noble father lost;
        A sister driven into desperate terms,—
        Whose worth, if praises may go back again,
        Stood challenger on mount of all the age
        For her perfections:—but my revenge will come.
30 KING: Break not your sleeps for that: you must not think
        That we are made of stuff so flat and dull
        That we can let our beard be shook with danger,
        And think it pastime. You shortly shall hear more:
        I lov'd your father, and we love ourself;
35   And that, I hope, will teach you to imagine,—

(Enter a Messenger.)

        How now! what news?
MESSENGER: Letters, my lord, from Hamlet:
        This to your majesty; this to the queen.
KING: From Hamlet! Who brought them?
MESSENGER: Sailors, my lord, they say; I saw them not:
40   They were given me by Claudio,—he receiv'd them
        Of him that brought them.
KING: Laertes, you shall hear them.—Leave us.

(Exit Messenger.)

        (Reads) High and mighty,—You shall know I am set naked on your
        kingdom. To-morrow shall I beg leave to see your kingly eyes: when I
45   shall, first asking your pardon thereunto, recount the occasions of my
        sudden and more strange return.   Hamlet

        What should this mean? Are all the rest come back?
        Or is it some abuse,[1] and no such thing?
LAERTES: Know you the hand?

---

[1] *abuse:* ruse.

KING: 'Tis Hamlet's character:[2]—*Naked,*—
    And in a postscript here, he says, *alone.*
    Can you advise me?
    LAERTES: I am lost in it, my lord. But let him come;
    It warms the very sickness in my heart,
    That I shall live, and tell him to his teeth,
    Thus diddest thou.
    KING: If it be so, Laertes,—
    As how should it be so? how otherwise?—
    Will you be rul'd by me?
    LAERTES: Ay, my lord:
    So you will not o'errule me to a peace.
KING: To thine own peace. If he be now return'd,—
    As checking at his voyage, and that he means
    No more to undertake it,—I will work him
    To an exploit, now ripe in my device,
    Under the which he shall not choose but fall:
    And for his death no wind of blame shall breathe;
    But even his mother shall uncharge the practice
    And call it accident.
    LAERTES: My lord, I will be rul'd;
    The rather if you could devise it so
    That I might be the organ.
    KING: It falls right.
    You have been talk'd of since your travel much,
    And that in Hamlet's hearing, for a quality
    Wherein they say you shine: your sum of parts
    Did not together pluck such envy from him
    As did that one; and that, in my regard,
    Of the unworthiest siege.
    LAERTES: What part is that, my lord?
KING: A very riband in the cap of youth,
    Yet needful too; for youth no less becomes
    The light and careless livery that it wears
    Than settled age his sables and his weeds,
    Importing health and graveness.—Two months since,
    Here was a gentleman of Normandy,—
    I've seen myself, and serv'd against, the French,
    And they can well on horseback: but this gallant
    Had witchcraft in't; he grew unto his seat;
    And to such wondrous doing brought his horse,
    As he had been incorps'd and demi-natur'd[3]
    With the brave beast: so far he topp'd my thought,

---

[2] *character:* handwriting.   [3] *incorps'd and demi-natur'd:* made as one body and formed into half man, half horse—or centaur.

That I, in forgery of shapes and tricks,[4]
　　Come short of what he did.
LAERTES:　　　　　　　A Norman was't?
90　KING: A Norman.
LAERTES: Upon my life, Lamond.
KING:　　　　　　　The very same.
LAERTES: I know him well: he is the brooch, indeed,
　　And gem of all the nation.
KING: He made confession of you;
95　And gave you such a masterly report
　　For art and exercise in your defence,
　　And for your rapier most especially,
　　That he cried out, 'twould be a sight indeed
　　If one could match you: the scrimers[5] of their nation,
100　He swore, had neither motion, guard, nor eye,
　　If you oppos'd them. Sir, this report of his
　　Did Hamlet so envenom with his envy,
　　That he could nothing do but wish and beg
　　Your sudden coming o'er, to play with him.
105　Now, out of this,—
LAERTES:　　　　　　What out of this, my lord?
KING: Laertes, was your father dear to you?
　　Or are you like the painting of a sorrow,
　　A face without a heart?
LAERTES:　　　　　　Why ask you this?
KING: Not that I think you did not love your father;
110　But that I know love is begun by time;
　　And that I see, in passages of proof,[6]
　　Time qualifies the spark and fire of it.
　　There lives within the very flame of love
　　A kind of wick or snuff that will abate it;
115　And nothing is at a like goodness still;
　　For goodness, growing to a pleurisy,[7]
　　Dies in his own too much: that we would do
　　We should do when we would; for this *would* changes,
　　And hath abatements and delays as many
120　As there are tongues, or hands, or accidents;
　　And then this *should* is like a spendthrift sigh
　　That hurts by easing. But to the quick o' the ulcer:
　　Hamlet comes back: what would you undertake
　　To show yourself your father's son in deed
125　More than in words?

---

[4] *in . . . tricks:* in imagining tricks of horsemanship.　　[5] *scrimers:* fencers.
[6] *passages of proof:* the evidence of experience.　　[7] *pleurisy:* plethora, an excess of blood.

LAERTES: To cut his throat i' the church.
KING: No place, indeed, should murder sanctuarize;
Revenge should have no bounds. But, good Laertes,
Will you do this, keep close within your chamber.
Hamlet return'd shall know you are come home:
We'll put on those shall praise your excellence,
And set a double varnish on the fame
The Frenchman gave you; bring you, in fine, together,
And wager on your heads: he, being remiss,[8]
Most generous, and free from all contriving,
Will not peruse the foils; so that, with ease,
Or with a little shuffling, you may choose
A sword unbated, and, in a pass of practice,
Requite him for your father.
LAERTES: I will do't it:
And, for that purpose, I'll anoint my sword.
I bought an unction of a mountebank,
So mortal that but dip a knife in it,
Where it draws blood no cataplasm so rare,[9]
Collected from all simples that have virtue
Under the moon, can save the thing from death
That is but scratch'd withal: I'll touch my point
With this contagion, that, if I gall him slightly,
It may be death.
KING: Let's further think of this;
Weigh what convenience both of time and means
May fit us to our shape: if this should fail,
And that our drift look through our bad performance,
'Twere better not assay'd: therefore this project
Should have a back or second, that might hold
If this should blast in proof. Soft! let me see:—
We'll make a solemn wager on your cunnings,—
I ha't:
When in your motion you are hot and dry,—
As make your bouts more violent to that end,—
And that he calls for drink, I'll have prepar'd him
A chalice for the nonce;[10] whereon but sipping,
If he by chance escape your venom'd stuck
Our purpose may hold there.

(Enter Queen.)

How now, sweet queen!
QUEEN: One woe doth tread upon another's heel,
So fast they follow:—your sister's drown'd, Laertes.

---

[8] *remiss:* unguarded and free from suspicion.   [9] *Where . . . rare:* no poultice, however remarkably efficacious.   [10] *nonce:* purpose.

LAERTES: Drown'd! O, where?
165 QUEEN: There is a willow grows aslant a brook,
That shows his hoar leaves in the glassy stream;
There with fantastic garlands did she come
Of crowflowers, nettles, daisies, and long purples,
That liberal shepherds give a grosser name,
170 But our cold maids do dead men's fingers call them.
There, on the pendant boughs her coronet weeds
Clambering to hang, an envious[11] sliver broke;
When down her weedy trophies and herself
Fell in the weeping brook. Her clothes spread wide;
175 And, mermaid-like, awhile they bore her up:
Which time she chanted snatches of old tunes;
As one incapable of her own distress,
Or like a creature native and indu'd
Unto that element: but long it could not be
180 Till that her garments, heavy with their drink,
Pull'd the poor wretch from her melodious lay
To muddy death.
LAERTES: Alas, then, she is drown'd?
QUEEN: Drown'd, drown'd.
LAERTES: Too much of water hast thou, poor Ophelia,
And therefore I forbid my tears: but yet
185 It is our trick; nature her custom holds,
Let shame say what it will: when these are gone,
The woman will be out.[12]—Adieu, my lord:
I have a speech of fire, that fain would blaze,
190 But that this folly douts it.[13] *(Exit.)*
KING: Let's follow, Gertrude;
How much I had to do to calm his rage!
Now fear I this will give it start again;
Therefore let's follow.

(Exeunt.)

ACT V
SCENE 1

A churchyard.

(Enter two Clowns[1] with spades, &c.)

1ST CLOWN: Is she to be buried in Christian burial that wilfully seeks her own salvation?

---

[11] *envious:* malicious.   [12] *The . . . out:* that is, "I shall be ruthless."   [13] *douts it:* drowns it.

---

[1] *Clowns:* rustic fellows.

2ND CLOWN: I tell thee she is; and therefore make her grave straight: the crowner[2] hath sat on her, and finds it Christian burial.
1ST CLOWN: How can that be, unless she drowned herself in her own defence?
2ND CLOWN: Why, 'tis found so.
1ST CLOWN: It must be *se offendendo*,[3] it cannot be else. For here lies the point: if I drown myself wittingly, it argues an act: and an act hath three branches; it is to act, to do, and to perform: argal,[4] she drowned herself wittingly.
2ND CLOWN: Nay, but hear you, goodman delver,—
1ST CLOWN: Give me leave. Here lies the water; good: here stands the man; good: if the man go to this water and drown himself, it is, will he, nill he, he goes,—mark you that: but if the water come to him and drown him, he drowns not himself: argal, he that is not guilty of his own death shortens not his own life.
2ND CLOWN: But is this law?
1ST CLOWN: Ay, marry, is't; crowner's quest law.
2ND CLOWN: Will you ha' the truth on't? If this had not been a gentlewoman she should have been buried out of Christian burial.
1ST CLOWN: Why, there thou say'st: and the more pity that great folks should have countenance in this world to drown or hang themselves more than their even-Christian.[5]—Come, my spade. There is no ancient gentlemen but gardeners, ditchers, and grave-makers; they hold up Adam's profession.
2ND CLOWN: Was he a gentleman?
1ST CLOWN: He was the first that ever bore arms.
2ND CLOWN: Why, he had none.
1ST CLOWN: What, art a heathen? How dost thou understand the Scripture? The Scripture says, Adam digged: could he dig without arms? I'll put another question to thee: if thou answerest me not to the purpose, confess thyself,[6]—
2ND CLOWN: Go to.
1ST CLOWN: What is he that builds stronger than either the mason, the shipwright, or the carpenter?
2ND CLOWN: The gallows-maker; for that frame outlives a thousand tenants.
1ST CLOWN: I like thy wit well, in good faith: the gallows does well; but how does it well? it does well to those that do ill: now thou dost ill to say the gallows is built stronger than the church: argal, the gallows may do well to thee. To't again, come.
2ND CLOWN: Who builds stronger than a mason, a shipwright, or a carpenter?

---

[2] *crowner:* coroner.   [3] *se offendendo:* in self-offense; he means *se defendendo,* in self-defense.   [4] *argal:* he means *ergo,* therefore.   [5] *even-Christian:* fellow Christian.   [6] *confess thyself:* "Confess thyself an ass," perhaps.

45 **1st Clown:** Ay, tell me that, and unyoke.
2nd Clown: Marry, now I can tell.
1st Clown: To't.
2nd Clown: Mass, I cannot tell.

(Enter Hamlet and Horatio, at a distance.)

1st Clown: Cudgel thy brains no more about it, for your dull ass will
50   not mend his pace with beating; and when you are asked this
question next, say a grave-maker; the houses that he makes last till
doomsday. Go, get thee to Yaughan: fetch me a stoup of liquor.

(Exit Second Clown.)

(Digs and sings.)

>In youth, when I did love, did love,
>   Methought it was very sweet,
55   To contract, O, the time, for, ah, my behove,[7]
>   O, methought there was nothing meet.

Hamlet: Has this fellow no feeling of his business, that he sings at
grave-making?
Horatio: Custom hath made it in him a property of easiness.
60 **Hamlet:** 'Tis e'en so: the hand of little employment hath the daintier
sense.
1st Clown: *(Sings)*

>But age, with his stealing steps,
> Hath claw'd me in his clutch,
>And hath shipp'd me intil the land,
65   As if I had never been such.

(Throws up a skull)

Hamlet: That skull had a tongue in it, and could sing once: how the
knave joels[8] it to the ground, as if it were Cain's jawbone, that did
the first murder! This might be the pate of a politician, which this
ass now o'erreaches; one that would circumvent God, might it not?
70 **Horatio:** It might, my lord.
Hamlet: Or of a courtier; which could say, *Good-morrow, sweet lord!
How dost thou, good lord?* This might be my lord such-a-one, that
praised my lord such-a-one's horse, when he meant to beg it,—
might it not?
75 **Horatio:** Ay, my lord.
Hamlet: Why, e'en so: and now my Lady Worm's; chapless,[9] and
knocked about the mazard[10] with a sexton's spade: here's fine
revolution, an we had the trick to see't. Did these bones cost no

---

[7] *behove:* behoof, or advantage.   [8] *joels:* throws.   [9] *chapless:* without a lower jaw.   [10] *mazard:* head.

more the breeding but to play at loggats[11] with 'em? Mine ache
to think on't.

1ST CLOWN: *(Sings)*

> A pick-axe and a spade, a spade,
> For and a shrouding sheet:
> O, a pit of clay for to be made
> For such a guest is meet.

(Throws up another.)

HAMLET: There's another: why may not that be the skull of a lawyer? Where be his quiddits[12] now, his quillets,[13] his cases, his tenures, and his tricks? why does he suffer this rude knave now to knock him about the sconce with a dirty shovel, and will not tell him of his action of battery? Hum! This fellow might be in's time a great buyer of land, with his statutes, his recognizances, his fines, his double vouchers, his recoveries: is this the fine of his fines, and the recovery of his recoveries, to have his fine pate full of fine dirt? will his vouchers vouch him no more of his purchases, and double ones too, than the length and breadth of a pair of indentures? The very conveyances of his lands will hardly lie in this box; and must the inheritor himself have no more, ha?

HORATIO: Not a jot more, my lord.

HAMLET: Is not parchment made of sheep-skins?

HORATIO: Ay, my lord, and of calf-skins too.

HAMLET: They are sheep and calves which seek out assurance in that. I will speak to this fellow.—Whose grave's this, sir?

1ST CLOWN: Mine, sir.—*(Sings)*

> O, a pit of clay for to be made
> For such a guest is meet.

HAMLET: I think it be thine indeed; for thou liest in't.

1ST CLOWN: You lie out on't, sir, and therefore it is not yours: for my part, I do not lie in't, and yet it is mine.

HAMLET: Thou dost lie in't, to be in't, and say it is thine: 'tis for the dead, not for the quick; therefore thou liest.

1ST CLOWN: 'Tis a quick lie, sir: 'twill away again from me to you.

HAMLET: What man dost thou dig it for?

1ST CLOWN: For no man, sir.

HAMLET: What woman, then?

1ST CLOWN: For none, neither.

HAMLET: Who is to be buried in't?

---

[11] *loggats:* a game in which small pieces of wood are hurled at a stake.
[12] *quiddits:* "whatnesses"—that is, hair-splittings.   [13] *quillets:* quibbling distinctions.

1ST CLOWN: One that was a woman, sir; but, rest her soul, she's dead.
HAMLET: How absolute the knave is! we must speak by the card, or equivocation will undo us. By the Lord, Horatio, these three years I have taken note of it; the age is grown so picked[14] that the toe of the peasant comes so near the heel of the courtier, he galls his kibe.[15]—How long hast thou been a grave-maker?
1ST CLOWN: Of all the days i' the year, I came to't that day that our last King Hamlet o'ercame Fortinbras.
HAMLET: How long is that since?
1ST CLOWN: Cannot you tell that? every fool can tell that: it was the very day that young Hamlet was born,—he that is mad, and sent into England.
HAMLET: Ay, marry, why was he sent into England?
1ST CLOWN: Why, because he was mad: he shall recover his wits there; or, if he do not, it's no great matter there.
HAMLET: Why?
1ST CLOWN: 'Twill not be seen in him there; there the men are as mad as he.
HAMLET: How came he mad?
1ST CLOWN: Very strangely, they say.
HAMLET: How strangely?
1ST CLOWN: Faith, e'en with losing his wits.
HAMLET: Upon what ground?
1ST CLOWN: Why, here in Denmark: I have been sexton here, man and boy, thirty years.
HAMLET: How long will a man lie i' the earth ere he rot?
1ST CLOWN: Faith, if he be not rotten before he die,—as we have many pocky corses now-a-days, that will scarce hold the laying in,—he will last you some eight year or nine year: a tanner will last you nine year.
HAMLET: Why he more than another?
1ST CLOWN: Why, sir, his hide is so tanned with his trade that he will keep out water a great while; and your water is a sore decayer of your whoreson dead body. Here's a skull now; this skull has lain in the earth three-and-twenty years.
HAMLET: Whose was it?
1ST CLOWN: A whoreson mad fellow's it was: whose do you think it was?
HAMLET: Nay, I know not.
1ST CLOWN: A pestilence on him for a mad rogue! 'a poured a flagon of Rhenish on my head once. This same skull, sir, was Yorick's skull, the king's jester.
HAMLET: This?

---

[14] *picked:* refined or educated.   [15] *he . . . kibe:* rubs and irritates the chilblain sore on the courtier's heel.

1st Clown: E'en that.
160 Hamlet: Let me see. *(Takes the skull)*—Alas, poor Yorick!—I knew him, Horatio; a fellow of infinite jest, of most excellent fancy: he hath borne me on his back a thousand times; and now, how abhorred in my imagination it is! my gorge rises at it. Here hung those lips that I have kissed I know not how oft. Where be your
165 gibes now? your gambols? your songs? your flashes of merriment, that were wont to set the table on a roar? Not one now, to mock your own grinning? quite chap-fallen? Now get you to my lady's chamber, and tell her, let her paint an inch thick, to this favor[16] she must come; make her laugh at that.—Pr'ythee, Horatio, tell me
170 one thing.
Horatio: What's that, my lord?
Hamlet: Dost thou think Alexander looked o' this fashion i' the earth?
Horatio: E'en so.
Hamlet: And smelt so? pah! *(Throws down the skull)*
175 Horatio: E'en so, my lord.
Hamlet: To what base uses we may return, Horatio! Why may not imagination trace the noble dust of Alexander till he find it stopping a bung-hole?
Horatio: 'Twere to consider too curiously to consider so.
180 Hamlet: No, faith, not a jot; but to follow him thither with modesty enough, and likelihood to lead it: as thus; Alexander died, Alexander was buried, Alexander returneth into dust; the dust is earth; of earth we make loam; and why of that loam whereto he was converted might they not stop a beer-barrel?

185   Imperious Caesar, dead and turn'd to clay,
      Might stop a hole to keep the wind away:
    O, that that earth which kept the world in awe
    Should patch a wall to expel the winter's flaw!—

But soft! but soft! aside.—Here comes the king.

(Enter Priests, &c., in procession; the corpse of Ophelia, Laertes and Mourners following; King, Queen, their Trains, &c.)

190 The queen, the courtiers: who is that they follow?
And with such maimed rites? This doth betoken
The corse they follow did with desperate hand
Fordo its own life: 'twas of some estate.
Couch we awhile and mark. *(Retiring with Horatio)*
195 Laertes: What ceremony else?
Hamlet: That is Laertes,
A very noble youth: mark.
Laertes: What ceremony else?

---

[16] *favor*: face.

1st Priest: Her obsequies have been as far enlarg'd
As we have warrantise: her death was doubtful,
200 And, but that great command o'ersways the order,
She should in ground unsanctified have lodg'd
Till the last trumpet; for charitable prayers,
Shards, flints, and pebbles, should be thrown on her,
Yet here she is allowed her virgin rites,
205 Her maiden strewments, and the bringing home
Of bell and burial.
Laertes: Must there no more be done?
1st Priest: No more be done:
We should profane the service of the dead
To sing a *requiem*, and such rest to her
210 As to peace-parted souls.
Laertes: Lay her i' the earth;—
And from her fair and unpolluted flesh
May violets spring!—I tell thee, churlish priest,
A ministering angel shall my sister be
When thou liest howling.
Hamlet: What, the fair Ophelia!
215 Queen: Sweets to the sweet: farewell! *(Scattering flowers)*
I hop'd thou shouldst have been my Hamlet's wife;
I thought thy bride-bed to have deck'd, sweet maid,
And not have strew'd thy grave.
Laertes: O, treble woe
Fall ten times treble on that cursed head
220 Whose wicked deed thy most ingenious sense
Depriv'd thee of!—Hold off the earth awhile,
Till I have caught her once more in mine arms:

(Leaps into the grave.)

Now pile your dust upon the quick and dead,
Till of this flat a mountain you have made,
225 To o'er-top old Pelion[17] or the skyish head
Of blue Olympus.
Hamlet: *(Advancing)* What is he whose grief
Bears such an emphasis? whose phrase of sorrow
Conjures the wandering stars, and makes them stand
Like wonder-wounded hearers? this is I, Hamlet the
230 Dane. *(Leaps into the grave)*
Laertes: The devil take thy soul! *(Grappling with him)*
Hamlet: Thou pray'st not well.
I pr'ythee, take thy fingers from my throat;
For, though I am not splenitive[18] and rash,

---

[17] *Pelion:* a mountain in Greece.   [18] *splenitive:* hot-tempered.

235   Yet have I in me something dangerous,
        Which let thy wiseness fear: away thy hand.
KING: Pluck them asunder.
QUEEN: Hamlet! Hamlet!
ALL: Gentlemen,—
HORATIO: Good my lord, be quiet.

(The Attendants part them, and they come out of the grave.)
HAMLET: Why, I will fight with him upon this theme
240   Until my eyelids will no longer wag.
QUEEN: O my son, what theme?
HAMLET: I lov'd Ophelia; forty thousand brothers
        Could not, with all their quantity of love,
        Make up my sum.—What wilt thou do for her?
245 KING: O, he is mad, Laertes.
QUEEN: For love of God, forbear him.
HAMLET: 'Swounds, show me what thou'lt do:
        Woul't weep? woul't fight? woul't fast? woul't tear thyself?
        Woul't drink up eisel?[19] eat a crocodile?
250   I'll do't.—Dost thou come here to whine?
        To outface me with leaping in her grave?
        Be buried quick[20] with her, and so will I:
        And, if thou prate of mountains, let them throw
        Millions of acres on us, till our ground,
255   Singeing his pate against the burning zone,[21]
        Make Ossa[22] like a wart! Nay, an thou'lt mouth,
        I'll rant as well as thou.
QUEEN: This is mere madness:
        And thus awhile the fit will work on him;
        Anon, as patient as the female dove,
260   When that her golden couplets are disclos'd,[23]
        His silence will sit drooping.
HAMLET: Hear you, sir;
        What is the reason that you use me thus?
        I lov'd you ever: but it is no matter;
        Let Hercules himself do what he may,
265   The cat will mew, and dog will have his day. *(Exit.)*
KING: I pray thee, good Horatio, wait upon him.—

(Exit Horatio.)

        (To Laertes) Strengthen your patience in our last night's speech;
        We'll put the matter to the present push.—

---

[19] *eisel:* vinegar. [20] *quick:* alive. [21] *burning zone:* the fiery zone of the celestial sphere. [22] *Ossa:* a high mountain in Greece. [23] *golden . . . disclos'd:* when the golden twins are hatched.

Good Gertrude, set some watch over your son.—
This grave shall have a living monument:
An hour of quiet shortly shall we see;
Till then, in patience our proceeding be.

(Exeunt.)

Scene 2

A hall in the castle.

(Enter Hamlet and Horatio.)

HAMLET: So much for this, sir: now let me see the other;
   You do remember all the circumstance?
HORATIO: Remember it, my lord!
HAMLET: Sir, in my heart there was a kind of fighting
   That would not let me sleep: methought I lay
   Worse than the mutines in the bilboes.[1] Rashly,
   And prais'd be rashness for it,—let us know,
   Our indiscretion sometimes serves us well,
   When our deep plots do fail: and that should teach us
   There's a divinity that shapes our ends,
   Rough-hew them how we will.
HORATIO: This is most certain.
HAMLET: Up from my cabin,
   My sea-gown scarf'd about me, in the dark
   Grop'd I to find out them: had my desire;
   Finger'd their packet; and, in fine, withdrew
   To mine own room again: making so bold,
   My fears forgetting manners, to unseal
   Their grand commission; where I found, Horatio,
   O royal knavery! an exact command,—
   Larded with many several sorts of reasons,
   Importing Denmark's health and England's too,
   With, ho! such bugs[2] and goblins in my life,—
   That, on the supervise, no leisure bated,
   No, not to stay the grinding of the axe,
   My head should be struck off.
HORATIO: Is't possible?
HAMLET: Here's the commission: read it at more leisure.
   But wilt thou hear me how I did proceed?
HORATIO: I beseech you.
HAMLET: Being thus benetted round with villainies,—
   Ere I could make a prologue to my brains,
   They had begun the play,—I sat me down;

---

[1] *bilboes:* mutineers in the iron stocks on board ship.   [2] *bugs:* bugbears.

Devis'd a new commission; wrote it fair:
I once did hold it, as our statists do,
A baseness to write fair, and labor'd much
35 How to forget that learning; but, sir, now
It did me yeoman's service. Wilt thou know
The effect of what I wrote?
HORATIO: Ay, good my lord.
HAMLET: An earnest conjuration from the king,—
As England was his faithful tributary;
40 As love between them like the palm might flourish;
As peace should still her wheaten garland wear
And stand a comma[3] 'tween their amities;
And many such like as's of great charge,—
That, on the view and know of these contents,
45 Without debatement further, more or less,
He should the bearers put to sudden death,
Not shriving-time allow'd.
HORATIO: How was this seal'd?
HAMLET: Why, even in that was heaven ordinant.
I had my father's signet in my purse,
50 Which was the model of that Danish seal:
Folded the writ up in form of the other;
Subscrib'd it; gav't the impression; plac'd it safely,
The changeling never known. Now, the next day
Was our sea-fight; and what to this was sequent
55 Thou know'st already.
HORATIO: So Guildenstern and Rosencrantz go to't.
HAMLET: Why, man, they did make love to this employment;
They are not near my conscience; their defeat
Does by their own insinuation[4] grow:
60 'Tis dangerous when the baser nature[5] comes
Between the pass and fell[6] incensed points
Of mighty opposites.
HORATIO: Why, what a king is this!
HAMLET: Does it not, think'st thee, stand me now upon,[7]
He that hath kill'd my king and whor'd my mother;
65 Popp'd in between the election and my hopes;
Thrown out his angle for my proper life,
And with such cozenage,[8]—is't not perfect conscience
To quit him with this arm? and is't not to be damn'd,
To let this canker of our nature come
70 In further evil?

---

[3] *comma:* link.   [4] *Does . . . insinuation:* by their own "sticking their noses" into the business.   [5] *baser nature:* men of lower rank.   [6] *fell:* fierce.   [7] *Does . . . upon:* that is, "Don't you think it is my duty?"   [8] *cozenage:* deceit.

HORATIO: It must be shortly known to him from England
        What is the issue of the business there.
HAMLET: It will be short: the interim is mine;
        And a man's life's no more than to say One.
75   But I am very sorry, good Horatio,
        That to Laertes I forgot myself;
        For by the image of my cause I see
        The portraiture of his: I'll court his favors:
        But, sure, the bravery[9] of his grief did put me
80   Into a towering passion.
HORATIO: Peace; who comes here?

(Enter Osric.)

OSRIC: Your lordship is right welcome back to Denmark.
HAMLET: I humbly thank you, sir.—Dost know this water-fly?
HORATIO: No, my good lord.
HAMLET: Thy state is the more gracious; for 'tis a vice to know him.
85   He hath much land, and fertile: let a beast be lord of beasts, and
        his crib shall stand at the king's mess: 'tis a chough;[10] but, as I say,
        spacious in the possession of dirt.
OSRIC: Sweet lord, if your lordship were at leisure, I should impart a
        thing to you from his majesty.
90 HAMLET: I will receive it with all diligence of spirit. Put your bonnet
        to his right use; 'tis for the head.
OSRIC: I thank your lordship, 'tis very hot.
HAMLET: No, believe me, 'tis very cold; the wind is northerly.
OSRIC: It is indifferent cold, my lord, indeed.
95 HAMLET: Methinks it is very sultry and hot for my complexion.
OSRIC: Exceedingly, my lord; it is very sultry,—as't were,—I cannot
        tell how.—But, my lord, his majesty bade me signify to you that he
        has laid a great wager on your head. Sir, this is the matter,—
HAMLET: I beseech you, remember,—

(Hamlet moves him to put on his hat.)

100 OSRIC: Nay, in good faith; for mine ease, in good faith. Sir, here is
        newly come to court Laertes; believe me, an absolute gentleman,
        full of most excellent differences, of very soft society and great
        showing: indeed, to speak feelingly of him, he is the card or
        calendar of gentry, for you shall find in him the continent of what
105   part a gentleman would see.
HAMLET: Sir, his definement suffers no perdition in you;—though, I
        know, to divide him inventorially would dizzy the arithmetic of
        memory, and yet but yaw neither, in respect of his quick sail. But,

---

[9] *bravery:* ostentation. [10] *his ... chough:* He shall have his trough at the king's table: he is a chattering fool.

in the verity of extolment, I take him to be a soul of great article; and his infusion of such dearth[11] and rareness as, to make true diction of him, his semblable is his mirror; and who else would trace him, his umbrage,[12] nothing more.

OSRIC: Your lordship speaks most infallibly of him.

HAMLET: The concernancy, sir? why do we wrap the gentleman in our more rawer breath?

OSRIC: Sir?

HORATIO: Is't not possible to understand in another tongue? You will do't sir, really.

HAMLET: What imports the nomination[13] of this gentleman?

OSRIC: Of Laertes?

HORATIO: His purse is empty already; all's golden words are spent.

HAMLET: Of him, sir.

OSRIC: I know, you are not ignorant,—

HAMLET: I would you did, sir; yet, in faith, if you did, it would not much approve me.[14]—Well, sir.

OSRIC: You are not ignorant of what excellence Laertes is,—

HAMLET: I dare not confess that, lest I should compare with him in excellence; but to know a man well were to know himself.

OSRIC: I mean, sir, for his weapon; but in the imputation laid on him by them, in his meed he's unfellowed.[15]

HAMLET: What's his weapon?

OSRIC: Rapier and dagger.

HAMLET: That's two of his weapons: but, well.

OSRIC: The king, sir, hath wagered with him six Barbary horses: against the which he has imponed,[16] as I take it, six French rapiers and poniards, with their assigns, as girdle, hangers, and so: three of the carriages, in faith, are very dear to fancy, very responsive to the hilts, most delicate carriages, and of very liberal conceit.

HAMLET: What call you the carriages?

HORATIO: I knew you must be edified by the margent ere you had done.[17]

OSRIC: The carriages, sir, are the hangers.

HAMLET: The phrase would be more germane to the matter if we could carry cannon by our sides: I would it might be hangers till then. But, on: six Barbary horses against six French swords, their assigns, and three liberal conceited carriages; that's the French bet against the Danish: why is this imponed, as you call it?

---

[11] *dearth:* rareness, or excellence.   [12] *umbrage:* shadow.   [13] *nomination:* naming.
[14] *I . . . me:* If you, who are a fool, thought me not ignorant, that would not be particularly to my credit.   [15] *in . . . unfellowed:* In his worth he has no equal.   [16] *imponed:* staked.   [17] *edified . . . done:* informed by a note in the margin of your instructions.

OSRIC: The king, sir, hath laid, that in a dozen passes between you and him he shall not exceed you three hits: he hath laid on twelve for nine; and it would come to immediate trial if your lordship would vouchsafe the answer.
HAMLET: How if I answer no?
OSRIC: I mean, my lord, the opposition of your person in trial.[18]
HAMLET: Sir, I will walk here in the hall: if it please his majesty, it is the breathing time of day with me: let the foils be brought, the gentleman willing, and the king hold his purpose, I will win for him if I can; if not, I will gain nothing but my shame and the odd hits.
OSRIC: Shall I re-deliver you[19] e'en so?
HAMLET: To this effect, sir; after what flourish your nature will.
OSRIC: I commend my duty to your lordship.
HAMLET: Yours, yours.

(Exit Osric.)

He does well to commend it himself; there are no tongues else for's turn.
HORATIO: This lapwing runs away with the shell on his head.[20]
HAMLET: He did comply with his dug before he sucked it.[21] Thus has he,—and many more of the same bevy, that I know the drossy age dotes on,—only got the tune of the time, and outward habit of encounter; a kind of yesty collection,[22] which carries them through and through the most fanned and winnowed opinions; and do but blow them to their trial, the bubbles are out.

(Enter a Lord.)

LORD: My lord, his majesty commended him to you by young Osric, who brings back to him that you attend him in the hall: he sends to know if your pleasure hold to play with Laertes, or that you will take longer time.
HAMLET: I am constant to my purposes; they follow the king's pleasure: if his fitness speaks, mine is ready; now or whensoever, provided I be so able as now.
LORD: The king and queen and all are coming down.
HAMLET: In happy time.
LORD: The queen desires you to use some gentle entertainment to Laertes before you fall to play.
HAMLET: She well instructs me.

(Exit Lord.)

---

[18] *I . . . trial:* that is, the presence of your person as Laertes' opponent in the fencing contest. [19] *redeliver you:* carry back your answer. [20] *This . . . head:* This precocious fellow is like a lapwing that starts running when it is barely out of the shell. [21] *He . . . it:* He paid compliments to his mother's breast before he sucked it. [22] *yesty collection:* yeasty or frothy affair.

HORATIO: You will lose this wager, my lord.
HAMLET: I do not think so; since he went into France I have been in
185   continual practice: I shall win at the odds. But thou wouldst not
think how ill all's here about my heart: but it is no matter.
HORATIO: Nay, good my lord,—
HAMLET: It is but foolery; but it is such a kind of gain-giving[23] as
would perhaps trouble a woman.
190 HORATIO: If your mind dislike anything, obey it: I will forestall their
repair hither, and say you are not fit.
HAMLET: Not a whit, we defy augury: there's a special providence in
the fall of a sparrow. If it be now, 'tis not to come; if it be not to
come, it will be now; if it be not now, yet it will come: the readiness
195   is all. Since no man has aught of what he leaves, what is't to leave
betimes?[24]

(Enter King, Queen, Laertes, Lords, Osric, and Attendants with foils, &c.)

KING: Come, Hamlet, come, and take this hand from me.

(The King puts Laertes' hand into Hamlet's.)

HAMLET: Give me your pardon, sir: I have done you wrong:
But pardon't, as you are a gentleman.
200   This presence knows, and you must needs have heard,
How I am punish'd with sore distraction.
What I have done,
That might your nature, honor, and exception
Roughly awake, I here proclaim was madness.
205   Was't Hamlet wrong'd Laertes? Never Hamlet:
If Hamlet from himself be ta'en away,
And when he's not himself does wrong Laertes,
Then Hamlet does it not, Hamlet denies it.
Who does it, then? His madness: if't be so,
210   Hamlet is of the faction that is wrong'd;
His madness is poor Hamlet's enemy.
Sir, in this audience,
Let my disclaiming from a purpos'd evil
Free me so far in your most generous thoughts
215   That I have shot mine arrow o'er the house
And hurt my brother.
LAERTES: I am satisfied in nature,
Whose motive, in this case, should stir me most
To my revenge: but in my terms of honor
I stand aloof; and will no reconcilement
220   Till by some elder masters of known honor

---

[23] *gain-giving:* misgiving.   [24] *What . . . betimes?:* What does an early death matter?

>   I have a voice and precedent of peace
>   To keep my name ungor'd. But till that time
>   I do receive your offer'd love like love,
>   And will not wrong it.
> **HAMLET:**   I embrace it freely;
>   And will this brother's wager frankly play.[25]—
>   Give us the foils; come on.
> **LAERTES:**   Come, one for me.
> **HAMLET:** I'll be your foil, Laertes; in mine ignorance
>   Your skill shall, like a star in the darkest night,
>   Stick fiery off indeed.
> **LAERTES:**   You mock me, sir.
> **HAMLET:** No, by this hand.
> **KING:** Give them the foils, young Osric.
>   Cousin Hamlet,
>   You know the wager?
> **HAMLET:**   Very well, my lord;
>   Your grace hath laid the odds o' the weaker side.
> **KING:** I do not fear it; I have seen you both;
>   But since he's better'd, we have therefore odds.
> **LAERTES:** This is too heavy, let me see another.
> **HAMLET:** This likes me well. These foils have all a length?

(They prepare to play.)

> **OSRIC:** Ay, my good lord.
> **KING:** Set me the stoups of wine upon that table,—
>   If Hamlet give the first or second hit,
>   Or quit in answer of the third exchange,
>   Let all the battlements their ordnance fire;
>   The king shall drink to Hamlet's better breath;
>   And in the cup an union[26] shall he throw,
>   Richer than that which four successive kings
>   In Denmark's crown have worn. Give me the cups;
>   And let the kettle[27] to the trumpet speak,
>   The trumpet to the cannoneer without,
>   The cannons to the heavens, the heavens to earth,
>   Now the king drinks to Hamlet.—Come, begin;—
>   And you, the judges, bear a wary eye.
> **HAMLET:** Come on, sir.
> **LAERTES:**   Come, my lord.

(They play.)

---

[25] *And . . . play:* fence with a heart free from resentment.   [26] *an union:* a pearl.   [27] *kettle:* kettledrum.

HAMLET: One.
LAERTES: No.
HAMLET: Judgment.
OSRIC: A hit, a very palpable hit.
LAERTES: Well;—again.
255 KING: Stay, give me a drink.—Hamlet, this pearl is thine;
     Here's to thy health.—

(Trumpets sound, and cannon shot off within.)

     Give him the cup.
HAMLET: I'll play this bout first; set it by awhile.—
     Come.—Another hit; what say you?

(They play.)

260 LAERTES: A touch, a touch, I do confess.
KING: Our son shall win.
QUEEN: He's fat, and scant of breath.—
     Here, Hamlet, take my napkin, rub thy brows:
     The queen carouses to thy fortune, Hamlet.
HAMLET: Good madam!
KING: Gertrude, do not drink.
265 QUEEN: I will, my lord; I pray you, pardon me.
KING: *(Aside)* It is the poison'd cup; it is too late.
HAMLET: I dare not drink yet, madam; by and by.
QUEEN: Come, let me wipe thy face.
LAERTES: My lord, I'll hit him now.
KING: I do not think't.
270 LAERTES: *(Aside)* And yet 'tis almost 'gainst my conscience.
HAMLET: Come, for the third, Laertes: you but dally;
     I pray you, pass with your best violence:
     I am afeard you make a wanton of me.
LAERTES: Say you so? come on.

(They play.)

275 OSRIC: Nothing, neither way.
LAERTES: Have at you now!

(Laertes wounds Hamlet; then, in scuffling, they change rapiers, and Hamlet wounds Laertes.)

KING: Part them; they are incens'd.
HAMLET: Nay, come, again.

(The Queen falls.)

OSRIC: Look to the queen there, ho!
HORATIO: They bleed on both sides.—How is it, my lord?
OSRIC: How is't, Laertes?

LAERTES: Why, as a woodcock to my own springe, Osric;
    I am justly kill'd with mine own treachery.
HAMLET: How does the queen?
KING: She swoons to see them bleed.
QUEEN: No, no, the drink, the drink,—O my dear Hamlet,—
    The drink, the drink!—I am poison'd. *(Dies.)*
HAMLET: O villainy!—Ho! let the door be lock'd:
    Treachery! seek it out.

(Laertes falls.)

LAERTES: It is here, Hamlet: Hamlet, thou art slain;
    No medicine in the world can do thee good;
    In thee there is not half an hour of life;
    The treacherous instrument is in thy hand,
    Unbated and envenom'd: the foul practice
    Hath turn'd itself on me; lo, here I lie,
    Never to rise again: thy mother's poison'd:
    I can no more:—the king, the king's to blame.
HAMLET: The point envenom'd too!—
    Then venom to thy work. *(Stabs the King)*
OSRIC and LORDS: Treason! treason!
KING: O, yet defend me, friends; I am but hurt.
HAMLET: Here, thou incestuous, murderous, damned Dane,
    Drink off this potion.—Is thy union here?
    Follow my mother.

(King dies.)

LAERTES: He is justly serv'd;
    It is a poison temper'd by himself.—
    Exchange forgiveness with me, noble Hamlet:
    Mine and my father's death come not upon thee,
    Nor thine on me! *(Dies.)*
HAMLET: Heaven make thee free of it! I follow thee.—
    I am dead, Horatio.—Wretched queen, adieu!—
    You that look pale and tremble at this chance,
    That art but mutes or audience to this act,
    Had I but time,—as this fell sergeant, death,
    Is strict in his arrest,—O, I could tell you,—
    But let it be.—Horatio, I am dead;
    Thou liv'st; report me and my cause aright
    To the unsatisfied.[28]
HORATIO: Never believe it:
    I am more an antique Roman than a Dane,—
    Here's yet some liquor left.

---

[28] *unsatisfied:* the uninformed.

HAMLET: As thou'rt a man,
    Give me the cup; let go; by heaven, I'll have't.—
    O good Horatio, what a wounded name,
320 Things standing thus unknown, shall live behind me!
    If thou didst ever hold me in thy heart,
    Absent thee from felicity awhile,
    And in this harsh world draw thy breath in pain,
    To tell my story.—

(March afar off, and shot within.)

                    What warlike noise is this?
325 OSRIC: Young Fortinbras, with conquest come from Poland,
    To the ambassadors of England gives
    This warlike volley.
    HAMLET: O, I die, Horatio;
    The potent poison quite o'er-crows my spirit:
    I cannot live to hear the news from England;
330 But I do prophesy the election lights
    On Fortinbras: he has my dying voice;
    So tell him, with the occurrents, more and less,
    Which have solicited.[29]—The rest is silence. *(Dies)*
    HORATIO: Now cracks a noble heart.—Good-night, sweet prince,
335 And flights of angels sing thee to thy rest!
    Why does the drum come hither?

(March within. Enter Fortinbras, the English Ambassadors, and others.)

    FORTINBRAS: Where is this sight?
    HORATIO: What is it you would see?
    If aught of woe or wonder, cease your search.
    FORTINBRAS: This quarry cries on havoc.[30]—O proud death,
340 What feast is toward in thine eternal cell,
    That thou so many princes at a shot
    So bloodily hast struck?
    1ST AMBASSADOR: The sight is dismal;
    And our affairs from England come too late:
    The ears are senseless that should give us hearing,
345 To tell him his commandment is fulfill'd,
    That Rosencrantz and Guildenstern are dead:
    Where should we have our thanks?
    HORATIO: Not from his mouth,
    Had it the ability of life to thank you:
    He never gave commandment for their death.

---

[29] *So . . . solicited:* So tell him, together with the events, more or less, that have brought on this tragic affair.   [30] *This . . . havoc:* This collection of dead bodies cries out havoc.

	But since, so jump[31] upon this bloody question,
350	You from the Polack wars, and you from England,
	Are here arriv'd, give order that these bodies
	High on a stage be placed to the view;
	And let me speak to the yet unknowing world
355	How these things came about: so shall you hear
	Of carnal, bloody, and unnatural acts;
	Of accidental judgments, casual slaughters;
	Of deaths put on by cunning and forc'd cause;
	And, in this upshot, purposes mistook
360	Fall'n on the inventors' heads: all this can I
	Truly deliver.

FORTINBRAS: Let us haste to hear it,
And call the noblest to the audience.
For me, with sorrow I embrace my fortune:
I have some rights of memory in this kingdom,[32]
365   Which now to claim my vantage doth invite me.
HORATIO: Of that I shall have also cause to speak,
And from his mouth whose voice will draw on more:
But let this same be presently perform'd,
Even while men's minds are wild: lest more mischance
370   On plots and errors happen.
FORTINBRAS: Let four captains
Bear Hamlet like a soldier to the stage;
For he was likely, had he been put on,[33]
To have prov'd most royally: and, for his passage,
The soldier's music and the rites of war
375   Speak loudly for him.—
Take up the bodies.—Such a sight as this
Becomes the field, but here shows much amiss.
Go, bid the soldiers shoot.

(A dead march)

(Exeunt, bearing off the dead bodies: after which a peal of ordnance is shot off.)

READING AND REACTING

1. What are Hamlet's most notable character traits?
2. Review each of Hamlet's **soliloquies.** Judging from his own words, do you believe his assessments of his own problems are accurate? Are his assessments of other characters' behavior accurate? Point to examples from the soliloquies that reveal Hamlet's insight (or lack of insight).

---

[31] *jump:* opportunely.   [32] *I . . . kingdom:* I have some unforgotten rights to this kingdom.   [33] *had . . . on:* tested by succession to the throne.

3. Is Hamlet a sympathetic character? Where (if anywhere) do you find yourself growing impatient with him or disagreeing with him?
4. What is the emotional impact on the audience of having Hamlet behave so cruelly toward Ophelia after his "To be or not to be" soliloquy?
5. What do other characters' comments reveal about Hamlet's character *before* the key events in the play begin to unfold? For example, in what way has he changed since he returned to the castle and found out about his father's death?
6. Claudius is presented as the play's villain. Is he all bad, or does he have any redeeming qualities?
7. List those in the play whom you believe to be **flat characters.** Why do you characterize each individual in this way? What does each of these flat characters contribute to the play?
8. Is Fortinbras simply Hamlet's **foil,** or does he have another essential role? Explain.
9. Each of the play's major characters has one or more character flaws that influence plot development. What specific weaknesses do you see in Claudius, Gertrude, Polonius, Laertes, Ophelia, and in Hamlet himself? Through what words or actions is each weakness revealed? How does each weakness contribute to the play's action?
10. Why doesn't Hamlet kill Claudius as soon as the Ghost tells him what Claudius did? Why doesn't he kill him when he has the chance in act 3? What words or actions reveal his motivation for hesitating? What are the implications of his failure to act?
11. Why does Hamlet pretend to be insane? Why does he arrange for the "play within a play" to be performed? Why does he agree to the duel with Laertes? In each case, what words or actions reveal his motivation to the audience?
12. Is the Ghost an essential character, or could the information he reveals and the reactions he arouses come from another source? Explain. (Keep in mind that the ghost is a **stock character** in Elizabethan drama.)
13. Describe Hamlet's relationship with his mother. Do you consider this a typical mother/son relationship? Why or why not?
14. In the graveyard scene (act 5, scene 1), the gravediggers make many ironic comments. In what way do these comments shed light on the events taking place in the play?
15. **Journal Entry** Both Gertrude and Ophelia are usually seen as weak women, firmly under the influence of the men in their lives. Do you think this characterization of them as passive and dependent is accurate? Explain.

Related Works: "The Cask of Amontillado" (p. 136), "Young Goodman Brown" (p. 198), *Oedipus the King* (p. 879), *The Glass Menagerie* (p. 938)

◊ **ARTHUR MILLER** (1915–   ) was born in New York City and graduated from the University of Michigan, where he began to write plays. His major plays include *All My Sons* (1947), about a man who has knowingly manufactured faulty airplane parts, and *The Crucible* (1953), based on the Salem witch trials of 1692.

Death of a Salesman quickly became an American classic. Miller has said he is very much influenced by the structure of Greek tragedy, and in this play he shows that a tragedy can also be the story of an ordinary person told in realistic terms.

◊ ◊ ◊

ARTHUR MILLER

Death of a Salesman

CERTAIN PRIVATE CONVERSATIONS IN
TWO ACTS AND A REQUIEM
(1949)

CHARACTERS

WILLY LOMAN
LINDA, *his wife*
BIFF ⎱ *his sons*
HAPPY ⎰
UNCLE BEN
CHARLEY
BERNARD

THE WOMAN
HOWARD WAGNER
JENNY
STANLEY
MISS FORSYTHE
LETTA

The action takes place in Willy Loman's house and yard and in various places he visits in the New York and Boston of today.

Throughout the play, in the stage directions, left and right mean stage left and stage right.

ACT I

A melody is heard, played upon a flute. It is small and fine, telling of grass and trees and the horizon. The curtain rises.

Before us is the Salesman's house. We are aware of towering, angular shapes behind it, surrounding it on all sides. Only the blue light of the sky falls upon the house and forestage; the surrounding area shows an angry glow of orange. As more light appears, we see a solid vault of apartment houses around the small, fragile-seeming home. An air of the dream clings to the place, a dream rising out of reality. The kitchen at center seems actual enough, for there is a kitchen table with three chairs, and a refrigerator. But no other fixtures are seen. At the back of the kitchen there is a draped entrance, which leads to the livingroom. To the right of the kitchen, on a level raised two feet, is a bedroom furnished only with a brass bedstead and a straight chair. On a shelf over the bed a silver athletic trophy stands. A window opens onto the apartment house at the side.

Behind the kitchen, on a level raised six and a half feet, is the boys' bedroom, at present barely visible. Two beds are dimly seen, and at the back of the room a dormer window. (This bedroom is above the unseen livingroom.) At the left a stairway curves up to it from the kitchen.

The entire setting is wholly or, in some places, partially transparent. The roofline of the house is one-dimensional; under and over it we see the apartment buildings. Before the house lies an apron, curving beyond the forestage into the orchestra. This forward area serves as the back yard as well as the locale of all Willy's imaginings and of his city scenes. Whenever the action is in the present the actors observe the imaginary wall-lines, entering the house only through the door at the left. But in the scenes of the past these boundaries are broken, and characters enter or leave a room by stepping "through" a wall onto the forestage.

From the right, Willy Loman, the Salesman, enters, carrying two large sample cases. The flute plays on. He hears but is not aware of it. He is past sixty years of age, dressed quietly. Even as he crosses the stage to the doorway of the house, his exhaustion is apparent. He unlocks the door, comes into the kitchen, and thankfully lets his burden down, feeling the soreness of his palms. A word-sigh escapes his lips—it might be "Oh, boy, oh, boy." He closes the door, then carries his cases out into the livingroom, through the draped kitchen doorway.

Linda, his wife, has stirred in her bed at the right. She gets out and puts on a robe, listening. Most often jovial, she has developed an iron repression of her exceptions to Willy's behavior—she more than loves him, she admires him, as though his mercurial nature, his temper, his massive dreams and little cruelties, served her only as sharp reminders of the turbulent longings within him, longings which she shares but lacks the temperament to utter and follow to their end.

LINDA: *(hearing Willy outside the bedroom, calls with some trepidation)* Willy!

WILLY: It's all right. I came back.

LINDA: Why? What happened? *(Sight pause.)* Did something happen, Willy?

WILLY: No, nothing happened.

5 LINDA: You didn't smash the car, did you?

WILLY: *(with casual irritation)* I said nothing happened. Didn't you hear me?

LINDA: Don't you feel well?

WILLY: I am tired to the death. *(The flute has faded away. He sits on the bed beside her, a little numb.)* I couldn't make it. I just couldn't make it, Linda.

LINDA: *(very carefully, delicately)* Where were you all day? You look terrible.

WILLY: I got as far as a little above Yonkers. I stopped for a cup of coffee. Maybe it was the coffee.

LINDA: What?

WILLY: *(after a pause)* I suddenly couldn't drive any more. The car kept going onto the shoulder, y'know?

LINDA: *(helpfully)* Oh. Maybe it was the steering again. I don't think Angelo knows the Studebaker.

WILLY: No, it's me, it's me. Suddenly I realize I'm goin' sixty miles an hour and I don't remember the last five minutes. I'm—I can't seem to—keep my mind to it.

LINDA: Maybe it's your glasses. You never went for your new glasses.

WILLY: No, I see everything. I came back ten miles an hour. It took me nearly four hours from Yonkers.

LINDA: *(resigned)* Well, you'll just have to take a rest, Willy, you can't continue this way.

WILLY: I just got back from Florida.

LINDA: But you didn't rest your mind. Your mind is overactive, and the mind is what counts, dear.

WILLY: I'll start out in the morning. Maybe I'll feel better in the morning. *(She is taking off his shoes.)* These goddam arch supports are killing me.

LINDA: Take an aspirin. Should I get you an aspirin? It'll soothe you.

WILLY: *(with wonder)* I was driving along, you understand? And I was fine. I was even observing the scenery. You can imagine, me looking at scenery, on the road every week of my life. But it's so beautiful up there, Linda, the trees are so thick, and the sun is warm. I opened the windshield and just let the warm air bathe over me. And then all of a sudden I'm goin' off the road! I'm tellin' ya, I absolutely forgot I was driving. If I'd've gone the other way over the white line I might've killed somebody. So I went on again—and five minutes later I'm dreamin' again, and I nearly—*(He presses two fingers against his eyes.)* I have such thoughts, I have such strange thoughts.

LINDA: Willy, dear. Talk to them again. There's no reason why you can't work in New York.

WILLY: They don't need me in New York. I'm the New England man. I'm vital in New England.

LINDA: But you're sixty years old. They can't expect you to keep traveling every week.

WILLY: I'll have to send a wire to Portland. I'm supposed to see Brown and Morrison tomorrow morning at ten o'clock to show the line. Goddammit, I could sell them! *(He starts putting on his jacket.)*

LINDA: *(taking the jacket from him)* Why don't you go down to the place tomorrow and tell Howard you've simply got to work in New York? You're too accommodating, dear.

WILLY: If old man Wagner was alive I'd a been in charge of New York now! That man was a prince, he was a masterful man. But that boy of his, that Howard, he don't appreciate. When I went north the first time, the Wagner Company didn't know where New England was!

LINDA: Why don't you tell those things to Howard, dear?

30 **WILLY:** *(encouraged)* I will, I definitely will. Is there any cheese?

LINDA: I'll make you a sandwich.

WILLY: No, go to sleep. I'll take some milk. I'll be up right away. The boys in?

LINDA: They're sleeping. Happy took Biff on a date tonight.

WILLY: *(interested)* That so?

35 **LINDA:** It was so nice to see them shaving together, one behind the other, in the bathroom. And going out together. You notice? The whole house smells of shaving lotion.

WILLY: Figure it out. Work a lifetime to pay off a house. You finally own it, and there's nobody to live in it.

LINDA: Well, dear, life is a casting off. It's always that way.

WILLY: No, no, some people—some people accomplish something. Did Biff say anything after I went this morning?

LINDA: You shouldn't have criticized him, Willy, especially after he just got off the train. You mustn't lose your temper with him.

40 **WILLY:** When the hell did I lose my temper? I simply asked him if he was making any money. Is that a criticism?

LINDA: But, dear, how could he make any money?

WILLY: *(worried and angered)* There's such an undercurrent in him. He became a moody man. Did he apologize when I left this morning?

LINDA: He was crestfallen, Willy. You know how he admires you. I think if he finds himself, then you'll both be happier and not fight any more.

WILLY: How can he find himself on a farm? Is that a life? A farmhand? In the beginning, when he was young, I thought, well, a young man, it's good for him to tramp around, take a lot of different jobs. But it's more than ten years now and he has yet to make thirty-five dollars a week!

45 **LINDA:** He's finding himself, Willy.

WILLY: Not finding yourself at the age of thirty-four is a disgrace!

LINDA: Shh!

WILLY: The trouble is he's lazy, goddammit!

LINDA: Willy, please!

50 **WILLY:** Biff is a lazy bum!

LINDA: They're sleeping. Get something to eat. Go on down.

WILLY: Why did he come home? I would like to know what brought him home.

LINDA: I don't know. I think he's still lost, Willy. I think he's very lost.
WILLY: Biff Loman is lost. In the greatest country in the world a young man with such—personal attractiveness, gets lost. And such a hard worker. There's one thing about Biff—he's not lazy.
55 LINDA: Never.
WILLY: *(with pity and resolve)* I'll see him in the morning; I'll have a nice talk with him. I'll get him a job selling. He could be big in no time. My God! Remember how they used to follow him around in high school? When he smiled at one of them their faces lit up. When he walked down the street . . . *(He loses himself in reminiscences.)*
LINDA: *(trying to bring him out of it)* Willy, dear, I got a new kind of American-type cheese today. It's whipped.
WILLY: Why do you get American when I like Swiss?
LINDA: I just thought you'd like a change—
60 WILLY: I don't want a change! I want Swiss cheese. Why am I always being contradicted?
LINDA: *(with a covering laugh)* I thought it would be a surprise.
WILLY: Why don't you open a window in here, for God's sake?
LINDA: *(with infinite patience)* They're all open, dear.
WILLY: The way they boxed us in here. Bricks and windows, windows and bricks.
65 LINDA: We should've bought the land next door.
WILLY: The street is lined with cars. There's not a breath of fresh air in the neighborhood. The grass don't grow any more, you can't raise a carrot in the back yard. They should've had a law against apartment houses. Remember those two beautiful elm trees out there? When I and Biff hung the swing between them?
LINDA: Yeah, like being a million miles from the city.
WILLY: They should've arrested the builder for cutting those down. They massacred the neighborhood. *(Lost.)* More and more I think of those days, Linda. This time of year it was lilac and wisteria. And then the peonies would come out, and the daffodils. What fragrance in this room!
LINDA: Well, after all, people had to move somewhere.
70 WILLY: No, there's more people now.
LINDA: I don't think there's more people. I think—
WILLY: There's more people! That's what's ruining this country! Population is getting out of control. The competition is maddening! Smell the stink from that apartment house! And another on the other side . . . How can they whip cheese?

On Willy's last line, Biff and Happy raise themselves up in their beds, listening.

LINDA: Go down, try it. And be quiet.
WILLY: *(turning to Linda, guiltily)* You're not worried about me, are you, sweetheart?

75 BIFF: What's the matter?
   HAPPY: Listen!
   LINDA: You've got too much on the ball to worry about.
   WILLY: You're my foundation and my support, Linda.
   LINDA: Just try to relax, dear. You make mountains out of molehills.
80 WILLY: I won't fight with him any more. If he wants to go back to Texas, let him go.
   LINDA: He'll find his way.
   WILLY: Sure. Certain men just don't get started till later in life. Like Thomas Edison, I think. Or B. F. Goodrich. One of them was deaf. *(He starts for the bedroom doorway.)* I'll put my money on Biff.
   LINDA: And Willy—if it's warm Sunday we'll drive in the country. And we'll open the windshield, and take lunch.
   WILLY: No, the windshields don't open on the new cars.
85 LINDA: But you opened it today.
   WILLY: Me? I didn't. *(He stops.)* Now isn't that peculiar! Isn't that remarkable—*(He breaks off in amazement and fright as the flute is heard distantly.)*
   LINDA: What, darling?
   WILLY: That is the most remarkable thing.
   LINDA: What, dear?
90 WILLY: I was thinking of the Chevvy. *(Slight pause.)* Nineteen twenty-eight . . . when I had that red Chevvy—*(Breaks off.)* That funny? I coulda sworn I was driving that Chevvy today.
   LINDA: Well, that's nothing. Something must've reminded you.
   WILLY: Remarkable. Ts. Remember those days? The way Biff used to simonize that car? The dealer refused to believe there was eighty thousand miles on it. *(He shakes his head.)* Heh! *(To Linda.)* Close your eyes, I'll be right up. *(He walks out of the bedroom.)*
   HAPPY: *(to Biff)* Jesus, maybe he smashed up the car again!
   LINDA: *(calling after Willy)* Be careful on the stairs, dear! The cheese is on the middle shelf! *(She turns, goes over to the bed, takes his jacket, and goes out of the bedroom.)*

Light has risen on the boys' room. Unseen, Willy is heard talking to himself, "Eighty thousand miles," and a little laugh. Biff gets out of bed, comes downstage a bit, and stands attentively. Biff is two years older than his brother Happy, well built, but in these days bears a worn air and seems less self-assured. He has succeeded less, and his dreams are stronger and less acceptable than Happy's. Happy is tall, powerfully made. Sexuality is like a visible color on him, or a scent that many women have discovered. He, like his brother, is lost, but in a different way, for he has never allowed himself to turn his face toward defeat and is thus more confused and hard-skinned, although seemingly more content.

95 HAPPY: *(getting out of bed)* He's going to get his license taken away if he keeps that up. I'm getting nervous about him, y'know, Biff?

BIFF: His eyes are going.
HAPPY: No, I've driven with him. He sees all right. He just doesn't keep his mind on it. I drove into the city with him last week. He stops at a green light and then it turns red and he goes. *(He laughs.)*
BIFF: Maybe he's color-blind.
HAPPY: Pop? Why he's got the finest eye for color in the business. You know that.
100 BIFF: *(sitting down on his bed)* I'm going to sleep.
HAPPY: You're not still sour on Dad, are you, Biff?
BIFF: He's all right, I guess.
WILLY: *(underneath them, in the livingroom)* Yes, sir, eighty thousand miles—eighty-two thousand!
BIFF: You smoking?
105 HAPPY: *(holding out a pack of cigarettes)* Want one?
BIFF: *(taking a cigarette)* I can never sleep when I smell it.
WILLY: What a simonizing job, heh!
HAPPY: *(with deep sentiment)* Funny, Biff, y'know? Us sleeping in here again? The old beds. *(He pats his bed affectionately.)* All the talk that went across those two beds, huh? Our whole lives.
BIFF: Yeah. Lotta dreams and plans.
110 HAPPY: *(with a deep and masculine laugh)* About five hundred women would like to know what was said in this room.

They share a soft laugh.

BIFF: Remember that big Betsy something—what the hell was her name—over on Bushwick Avenue?
HAPPY: *(combing his hair)* With the collie dog!
BIFF: That's the one. I got you in there, remember?
HAPPY: Yeah, that was my first time—I think. Boy, there was a pig! *(They laugh, almost crudely.)* You taught me everything I know about women. Don't forget that.
115 BIFF: I bet you forgot how bashful you used to be. Especially with girls.
HAPPY: Oh, I still am, Biff.
BIFF: Oh, go on.
HAPPY: I just control it, that's all. I think I got less bashful and you got more so. What happened, Biff? Where's the old humor, the old confidence? *(He shakes Biff's knee. Biff gets up and moves restlessly about the room.)* What's the matter?
BIFF: Why does Dad mock me all the time?
120 HAPPY: He's not mocking you, he—
BIFF: Everything I say there's a twist of mockery on his face. I can't get near him.
HAPPY: He just wants you to make good, that's all. I wanted to talk to you about Dad for a long time, Biff. Something's—happening to him. He—talks to himself.
BIFF: I noticed that this morning. But he always mumbled.

HAPPY: But not so noticeable. It got so embarrassing I sent him to Florida. And you know something? Most of the time he's talking to you.
125 BIFF: What's he say about me?
HAPPY: I can't make it out.
BIFF: What's he say about me?
HAPPY: I think the fact that you're not settled, that you're still kind of up in the air . . .
BIFF: There's one or two other things depressing him, Happy.
130 HAPPY: What do you mean?
BIFF: Never mind. Just don't lay it all to me.
HAPPY: But I think if you just got started—I mean—is there any future for you out there?
BIFF: I tell ya, Hap, I don't know what the future is. I don't know—what I'm supposed to want.
HAPPY: What do you mean?
135 BIFF: Well, I spent six or seven years after high school trying to work myself up. Shipping clerk, salesman, business of one kind or another. And it's a measly manner of existence. To get on that subway on the hot mornings in summer. To devote your whole life to keeping stock, or making phone calls, or selling or buying. To suffer fifty weeks of the year for the sake of a two-week vacation, when all you really desire is to be outdoors, with your shirt off. And always to have to get ahead of the next fella. And still—that's how you build a future.
HAPPY: Well, you really enjoy it on a farm? Are you content out there?
BIFF: *(with rising agitation)* Hap, I've had twenty or thirty different kinds of jobs since I left home before the war, and it always turns out the same. I just realized it lately. In Nebraska when I herded cattle, and the Dakotas, and Arizona, and now in Texas. It's why I came home now, I guess, because I realized it. This farm I work on, it's spring there now, see? And they've got about fifteen new colts. There's nothing more inspiring or—beautiful than the sight of a mare and a new colt. And it's cool there now, see? Texas is cool now, and it's spring. And whenever spring comes to where I am, I suddenly get the feeling, my God, I'm not gettin' anywhere! What the hell am I doing, playing around with horses, twenty-eight dollars a week! I'm thirty-four years old, I oughta be makin' my future. That's when I come running home. And now, I get here, and I don't know what to do with myself. *(After a pause.)* I've always made a point of not wasting my life, and every time I come back here I know that all I've done is to waste my life.
HAPPY: You're a poet, you know that, Biff? You're a—you're an idealist!
BIFF: No, I'm mixed up very bad. Maybe I oughta get married. Maybe I oughta get stuck into something. Maybe that's my trouble. I'm like a boy. I'm not married, I'm not in business, I just—I'm like a boy. Are you content, Hap? You're a success, aren't you? Are you content?

140 **HAPPY:** Hell, no!
    BIFF: Why? You're making money, aren't you?
    HAPPY: *(moving about with energy, expressiveness)* All I can do now is wait for the merchandise manager to die. And suppose I get to be merchandise manager? He's a good friend of mine, and he just built a terrific estate on Long Island. And he lived there about two months and sold it, and now he's building another one. He can't enjoy it once it's finished. And I know that's just what I would do. I don't know what the hell I'm workin' for. Sometimes I sit in my apartment—all alone. And I think of the rent I'm paying. And it's crazy. But then, it's what I always wanted. My own apartment, a car, and plenty of women. And still, goddammit, I'm lonely.
    BIFF: *(with enthusiasm)* Listen, why don't you come out West with me?
    HAPPY: You and I, heh?
145 **BIFF:** Sure, maybe we could buy a ranch. Raise cattle, use our muscles. Men built like we are should be working out in the open.
    HAPPY: *(avidly)* The Loman Brothers, heh?
    BIFF: *(with vast affection)* Sure, we'd be known all over the counties!
    HAPPY: *(enthralled)* That's what I dream about, Biff. Sometimes I want to just rip my clothes off in the middle of the store and outbox that goddam merchandise manager. I mean I can outbox, outrun, and outlift anybody in that store, and I have to take orders from those common, petty sons-of-bitches till I can't stand it any more.
    BIFF: I'm telln' you, kid, if you were with me I'd be happy out there.
150 **HAPPY:** *(enthused)* See, Biff, everybody around me is so false that I'm constantly lowering my ideals . . .
    BIFF: Baby, together we'd stand up for one another, we'd have someone to trust.
    HAPPY: If I were around you—
    BIFF: Hap, the trouble is we weren't brought up to grub for money. I don't know how to do it.
    HAPPY: Neither can I!
155 **BIFF:** Then let's go!
    HAPPY: The only thing is—what can you make out there?
    BIFF: But look at your friend. Builds an estate and then hasn't the peace of mind to live in it.
    HAPPY: Yeah, but when he walks into the store the waves part in front of him. That's fifty-two thousand dollars a year coming through the revolving door, and I got more in my pinky finger than he's got in his head.
    BIFF: Yeah, but you just said—
160 **HAPPY:** I gotta show some of those pompous, self-important executives over there that Hap Loman can make the grade. I want to walk into the store the way he walks in. Then I'll go with you, Biff. We'll be together yet, I swear. But take those two we had tonight. Now weren't they gorgeous creatures?
    BIFF: Yeah, yeah, most gorgeous I've had in years.

HAPPY: I get that any time I want, Biff. Whenever I feel disgusted. The only trouble is, it gets like bowling or something. I just keep knockin' them over and it doesn't mean anything. You still run around a lot?
BIFF: Naa. I'd like to find a girl—steady, somebody with substance.
HAPPY: That's what I long for.
165 BIFF: Go on! You'd never come home.
HAPPY: I would! Somebody with character, with resistance! Like Mom, y'know? You're gonna call me a bastard when I tell you this. That girl Charlotte I was with tonight is engaged to be married in five weeks. *(He tries on his new hat.)*
BIFF: No kiddin'!
HAPPY: Sure, the guy's in line for the vice-presidency of the store. I don't know what gets into me, maybe I just have an overdeveloped sense of competition or something, but I went and ruined her, and furthermore I can't get rid of her. And he's the third executive I've done that to. Isn't that a crummy characteristic? And to top it all, I go to their weddings! *(Indignantly, but laughing.)* Like I'm not supposed to take bribes. Manufacturers offer me a hundred-dollar bill now and then to throw an order their way. You know how honest I am, but it's like this girl, see. I hate myself for it. Because I don't want the girl, and, still, I take it and—I love it!
BIFF: Let's go to sleep.
170 HAPPY: I guess we didn't settle anything, heh?
BIFF: I just got one idea that I think I'm going to try.
HAPPY: What's that?
BIFF: Remember Bill Oliver?
HAPPY: Sure, Oliver is very big now. You want to work for him again?
175 BIFF: No, but when I quit he said something to me. He put his arm on my shoulder, and he said, "Biff, if you ever need anything, come to me."
HAPPY: I remember that. That sounds good.
BIFF: I think I'll go to see him. If I could get ten thousand or even seven or eight thousand dollars I could buy a beautiful ranch.
HAPPY: I bet he'd back you. 'Cause he thought highly of you, Biff, I mean, they all do. You're well liked, Biff. That's why I say to come back here, and we both have the apartment. And I'm telln' you, Biff, any babe you want . . .
BIFF: No, with a ranch I could do the work I like and still be something. I just wonder though. I wonder if Oliver still thinks I stole that carton of basketballs.
180 HAPPY: Oh, he probably forgot that long ago. It's almost ten years. You're too sensitive. Anyway, he didn't really fire you.
BIFF: Well, I think he was going to. I think that's why I quit. I was never sure whether he knew or not. I know he thought the world of me, though. I was the only one he'd let lock up the place.
WILLY: *(below)* You gonna wash the engine, Biff?

HAPPY: Shh!

Biff looks at Happy, who is gazing down, listening. Willy is mumbling in the parlor.

HAPPY: You hear that?

They listen. Willy laughs warmly.

185 BIFF: *(growing angry)* Doesn't he know Mom can hear that?
WILLY: Don't get your sweater dirty, Biff!

A look of pain crosses Biff's face.

HAPPY: Isn't that terrible? Don't leave again, will you? You'll find a job here. You gotta stick around. I don't know what to do about him, it's getting embarrassing.
WILLY: What a simonizing job!
BIFF: Mom's hearing that!
190 WILLY: No kiddin', Biff, you got a date? Wonderful!
HAPPY: Go on to sleep. But talk to him in the morning, will you?
BIFF: *(reluctantly getting into bed)* With her in the house. Brother!
HAPPY: *(getting into bed)* I wish you'd have a good talk with him.

The light on their room begins to fade.

BIFF: *(to himself in bed)* That selfish, stupid . . .
195 HAPPY: Sh . . . Sleep, Biff.

Their light is out. Well before they have finished speaking, Willy's form is dimly seen below in the darkened kitchen. He opens the refrigerator, searches in there, and takes out a bottle of milk. The apartment houses are fading out, and the entire house and surroundings become covered with leaves. Music insinuates itself as the leaves appear.

WILLY: Just wanna be careful with those girls, Biff, that's all. Don't make any promises. No promises of any kind. Because a girl, y'know, they always believe what you tell 'em, and you're very young, Biff, you're too young to be talking seriously to girls.

Light rises on the kitchen. Willy, talking, shuts the refrigerator door and comes downstage to the kitchen table. He pours milk into a glass. He is totally immersed in himself, smiling faintly.

WILLY: Too young entirely, Biff. You want to watch your schooling first. Then when you're all set, there'll be plenty of girls for a boy like you. *(He smiles broadly at a kitchen chair.)* That so? The girls pay for you? *(He laughs.)* Boy, you must really be makin' a hit.

Willy is gradually addressing—physically—a point offstage, speaking through the wall of the kitchen, and his voice has been rising in volume to that of a normal conversation.

WILLY: I been wondering why you polish the car so careful. Ha! Don't leave the hubcaps, boys. Get the chamois to the hubcaps. Happy, use newspaper on the windows, it's the easiest thing. Show him how to do it, Biff! You see, Happy? Pad it up, use it like a pad. That's it, that's it, good work. You're doin' all right, Hap. *(He pauses, then nods in approbation for a few seconds, then looks upward.)* Biff, first thing we gotta do when we get time is clip that big branch over the house. Afraid it's gonna fall in a storm and hit the roof. Tell you what. We get a rope and sling her around, and then we climb up there with a couple of saws and take her down. Soon as you finish the car, boys, I wanna see ya. I got a surprise for you, boys.

BIFF: *(offstage)* Whatta ya got, Dad?

200 WILLY: No, you finish first. Never leave a job till you're finished—remember that. *(Looking toward the "big trees.")* Biff, up in Albany I saw a beautiful hammock. I think I'll buy it next trip, and we'll hang it right between those two elms. Wouldn't that be something? Just swingin' there under those branches. Boy, that would be . . .

Young Biff and Young Happy appear from the direction Willy was addressing. Happy carries rags and a pail of water. Biff, wearing a sweater with a block "S," carries a football.

BIFF: *(pointing in the direction of the car offstage)* How's that, Pop, professional?

WILLY: Terrific. Terrific job, boys. Good work, Biff.

HAPPY: Where's the surprise, Pop?

WILLY: In the back seat of the car.

205 HAPPY: Boy! *(He runs off.)*

BIFF: What is it, Dad? Tell me, what'd you buy?

WILLY: *(laughing, cuffs him)* Never mind, something I want you to have.

BIFF: *(turns and starts off)* What is it, Hap?

HAPPY: *(offstage)* It's a punching bag!

210 BIFF: Oh, Pop!

WILLY: It's got Gene Tunney's[1] signature on it!

Happy runs onstage with a punching bag.

BIFF: Gee, how'd you know we wanted a punching bag?

WILLY: Well, it's the finest thing for the timing.

HAPPY: *(lies down on his back and pedals with his feet)* I'm losing weight, you notice, Pop?

215 WILLY: *(to Happy)* Jumping rope is good too.

BIFF: Did you see the new football I got?

---

[1] Gene (James Joseph) Tunney (1897–1978)—U.S. boxer, heavyweight champion from his defeat of Jack Dempsey in 1926 until his retirement in 1928.

Willy: *(examining the ball)* Where'd you get a new ball?
Biff: The coach told me to practice my passing.
Willy: That so? And he gave you the ball, heh?
Biff: Well, I borrowed it from the locker room. *(He laughs confidentially.)*
Willy: *(laughing with him at the theft)* I want you to return that.
Happy: I told you he wouldn't like it!
Biff: *(angrily)* Well, I'm bringing it back!
Willy: *(stopping the incipient argument, to Happy)* Sure, he's gotta practice with a regulation ball, doesn't he? *(To Biff.)* Coach'll probably congratulate you on your initiative!
Biff: Oh, he keeps congratulating my initiative all the time, Pop.
Willy: That's because he likes you. If somebody else took that ball there'd be an uproar. So what's the report, boys, what's the report?
Biff: Where'd you go this time, Dad? Gee we were lonesome for you.
Willy: *(pleased, puts an arm around each boy and they come down to the apron)* Lonesome, heh?
Biff: Missed you every minute.
Willy: Don't say? Tell you a secret, boys. Don't breathe it to a soul. Someday I'll have my own business, and I'll never have to leave home any more.
Happy: Like Uncle Charley, heh?
Willy: Bigger than Uncle Charley! Because Charley is not—liked. He's liked, but he's not—well liked.
Biff: Where'd you go this time, Dad?
Willy: Well, I got on the road, and I went north to Providence. Met the Mayor.
Biff: The Mayor of Providence!
Willy: He was sitting in the hotel lobby.
Biff: What'd he say?
Willy: He said, "Morning!" And I said, "You've got a fine city here, Mayor." And then he had coffee with me. And then I went to Waterbury. Waterbury is a fine city. Big clock city, the famous Waterbury clock. Sold a nice bill there. And then Boston—Boston is the cradle of the Revolution. A fine city. And a couple of other towns in Mass., and on to Portland and Bangor and straight home!
Biff: Gee, I'd love to go with you sometime, Dad.
Willy: Soon as summer comes.
Happy: Promise?
Willy: You and Hap and I, and I'll show you all the towns. America is full of beautiful towns and fine, upstanding people. And they know me, boys, they know me up and down New England. The finest people. And when I bring you fellas up, there'll be open sesame for all of us, 'cause one thing, boys: I have friends. I can park my car in any street in New England, and the cops protect it like their own. This summer, heh?
Biff and Happy: *(together)* Yeah! You bet!

WILLY: We'll take our bathing suits.
HAPPY: We'll carry your bags, Pop!
WILLY: Oh, won't that be something! Me comin' into the Boston store with you boys carryin' my bags. What a sensation!

Biff is prancing around, practicing passing the ball.

WILLY: You nervous, Biff, about the game?
BIFF: Not if you're gonna be there.
WILLY: What do they say about you in school, now that they made you captain?
HAPPY: There's a crowd of girls behind him everytime the classes change.
BIFF: *(taking Willy's hand)* This Saturday, Pop, this Saturday—just for you, I'm going to break through for a touchdown.
HAPPY: You're supposed to pass.
BIFF: I'm takin' one play for Pop. You watch me, Pop, and when I take off my helmet, that means I'm breakin' out. Then you watch me crash through that line!
WILLY: *(kisses Biff)* Oh, wait'll I tell this in Boston!

Bernard enters in knickers. He is younger than Biff, earnest and loyal, a worried boy.

BERNARD: Biff, where are you? You're supposed to study with me today.
WILLY: Hey, looka Bernard. What're you lookin' so anemic about, Bernard?
BERNARD: He's gotta study, Uncle Willy. He's got Regents next week.
HAPPY: *(tauntingly, spinning Bernard around)* Let's box, Bernard!
BERNARD: Biff! *(He gets away from Happy.)* Listen, Biff, I heard Mr. Birnbaum say that if you don't start studyin' math he's gonna flunk you, and you won't graduate. I heard him!
WILLY: You better study with him, Biff. Go ahead now.
BERNARD: I heard him!
BIFF: Oh, Pop, you didn't see my sneakers! *(He holds up a foot for Willy to look at.)*
WILLY: Hey, that's a beautiful job of printing!
BERNARD: *(wiping his glasses)* Just because he printed University of Virginia on his sneakers doesn't mean they've got to graduate him, Uncle Willy!
WILLY: *(angrily)* What're you talking about? With scholarships to three universities they're gonna flunk him?
BERNARD: But I heard Mr. Birnbaum say—
WILLY: Don't be a pest, Bernard! *(To his boys.)* What an anemic!
BERNARD: Okay, I'm waiting for you in my house, Biff.

Bernard goes off. The Lomans laugh.

WILLY: Bernard is not well liked, is he?
BIFF: He's liked, but he's not well liked.

HAPPY: That's right, Pop.
WILLY: That's just what I mean. Bernard can get the best marks in school, y'understand, but when he gets out in the business world, y'understand, you are going to be five times ahead of him. That's why I thank Almighty God you're both built like Adonises. Because the man who makes an appearance in the business world, the man who creates personal interest, is the man who gets ahead. Be liked and you will never want. You take me, for instance. I never have to wait in line to see a buyer. "Willy Loman is here!" That's all they have to know, and I go right through.
BIFF: Did you knock them dead, Pop?
WILLY: Knocked 'em cold in Providence, slaughtered 'em in Boston.
275 HAPPY: *(on his back, pedaling again)* I'm losing weight, you notice, Pop?

Linda enters, as of old, a ribbon in her hair, carrying a basket of washing.

LINDA: *(with youthful energy)* Hello, dear!
WILLY: Sweetheart!
LINDA: How'd the Chevvy run?
WILLY: Chevrolet, Linda, is the greatest car ever built. *(To the boys.)* Since when do you let your mother carry wash up the stairs?
280 BIFF: Grab hold there, boy!
HAPPY: Where to, Mom?
LINDA: Hang them up on the line. And you better go down to your friends, Biff. The cellar is full of boys. They don't know what to do with themselves.
BIFF: Ah, when Pop comes home they can wait!
WILLY: *(laughs appreciatively)* You better go down and tell them what to do, Biff.
285 BIFF: I think I'll have them sweep out the furnace room.
WILLY: Good work, Biff.
BIFF: *(goes through wall-line of kitchen to doorway at back and calls down)* Fellas! Everybody sweep out the furnace room! I'll be right down!
VOICES: All right! Okay, Biff.
BIFF: George and Sam and Frank, come out back! We're hangin' up the wash! Come on, Hap, on the double! *(He and Happy carry out the basket.)*
290 LINDA: The way they obey him!
WILLY: Well, that's training, the training. I'm tellin' you, I was sellin' thousands and thousands, but I had to come home.
LINDA: Oh, the whole block'll be at that game. Did you sell anything?
WILLY: I did five hundred gross in Providence and seven hundred gross in Boston.
LINDA: No! Wait a minute, I've got a pencil. *(She pulls pencil and paper out of her apron pocket.)* That makes your commission . . . Two hundred—my God! Two hundred and twelve dollars!
295 WILLY: Well, I didn't figure it yet, but . . .
LINDA: How much did you do?

WILLY: Well, I—I did—about a hundred and eighty gross in Providence. Well, no—it came to—roughly two hundred gross on the whole trip.
LINDA: *(without hesitation)* Two hundred gross. That's . . . *(She figures.)*
WILLY: The trouble was that three of the stores were half closed for inventory in Boston. Otherwise I woulda broke records.
LINDA: Well, it makes seventy dollars and some pennies. That's very good.
WILLY: What do we owe?
LINDA: Well, on the first there's sixteen dollars on the refrigerator—
WILLY: Why sixteen?
LINDA: Well, the fan belt broke, so it was a dollar eighty.
WILLY: But it's brand new.
LINDA: Well, the man said that's the way it is. Till they work themselves in, y'know.

They move through the wall-line into the kitchen.

WILLY: I hope we didn't get stuck on that machine.
LINDA: They got the biggest ads of any of them!
WILLY: I know, it's a fine machine. What else?
LINDA: Well, there's nine-sixty for the washing machine. And for the vacuum cleaner there's three and a half due on the fifteenth. Then the roof, you got twenty-one dollars remaining.
WILLY: It don't leak, does it?
LINDA: No, they did a wonderful job. Then you owe Frank for the carburetor.
WILLY: I'm not going to pay that man! That goddam Chevrolet, they ought to prohibit the manufacture of that car!
LINDA: Well, you owe him three and a half. And odds and ends, comes to around a hundred and twenty dollars by the fifteenth.
WILLY: A hundred and twenty dollars! My God, if business don't pick up I don't know what I'm gonna do!
LINDA: Well, next week you'll do better.
WILLY: Oh, I'll knock them dead next week. I'll go to Hartford. I'm very well liked in Hartford. You know, the trouble is, Linda, people don't seem to take to me.

They move onto the forestage.

LINDA: Oh, don't be foolish.
WILLY: I know it when I walk in. They seem to laugh at me.
LINDA: Why? Why would they laugh at you? Don't talk that way, Willy.

Willy moves to the edge of the stage. Linda goes into the kitchen and starts to darn stockings.

WILLY: I don't know the reason for it, but they just pass me by. I'm not noticed.

LINDA: But you're doing wonderful, dear. You're making seventy to a hundred dollars a week.

WILLY: But I gotta be at it ten, twelve hours a day. Other men—I don't know—they do it easier. I don't know why—I can't stop myself—I talk too much. A man oughta come in with a few words. One thing about Charley. He's a man of few words, and they respect him.

LINDA: You don't talk too much, you're just lively.

325 WILLY: *(smiling)* Well, I figure, what the hell, life is short, a couple of jokes. *(To himself.)* I joke too much! *(The smile goes.)*

LINDA: Why? You're—

WILLY: I'm fat. I'm very—foolish to look at, Linda. I didn't tell you, but Christmas time I happened to be calling on F. H. Stewarts, and a salesman I know, as I was going in to see the buyer I heard him say something about—walrus. And I—I cracked him right across the face. I won't take that. I simply will not take that. But they do laugh at me. I know that.

LINDA: Darling . . .

WILLY: I gotta overcome it. I know I gotta overcome it. I'm not dressing to advantage, maybe.

330 LINDA: Willy, darling, you're the handsomest man in the world—

WILLY: Oh, no, Linda.

LINDA: To me you are. *(Slight pause.)* The handsomest.

From the darkness is heard the laughter of a woman. Willy doesn't turn to it, but it continues through Linda's lines.

LINDA: And the boys, Willy. Few men are idolized by their children the way you are.

Music is heard as behind a scrim, to the left of the house, The Woman, dimly seen, is dressing.

WILLY: *(with great feeling)* You're the best there is, Linda, you're a pal, you know that? On the road—on the road I want to grab you sometimes and just kiss the life outa you.

The laughter is loud now, and he moves into a brightening area at the left, where The Woman has come from behind the scrim and is standing, putting on her hat, looking into a "mirror" and laughing.

335 WILLY: 'Cause I get so lonely—especially when business is bad and there's nobody to talk to. I get the feeling that I'll never sell anything again, that I won't make a living for you, or a business, a business for the boys. *(He talks through The Woman's subsiding laughter; The Woman primps at the "mirror.")* There's so much I want to make for—

THE WOMAN: Me? You didn't make me, Willy. I picked you.

WILLY: *(pleased)* You picked me?

THE WOMAN: *(who is quite proper-looking, Willy's age)* I did. I've been sitting at that desk watching all the salesmen go by, day in, day out. But you've got such a sense of humor, and we do have such a good time together, don't we?

WILLY: Sure, sure. *(He takes her in his arms.)* Why do you have to go now?

THE WOMAN: It's two o'clock . . .

WILLY: No, come on in! *(He pulls her.)*

THE WOMAN: . . . my sisters'll be scandalized. When'll you be back?

WILLY: Oh, two weeks about. Will you come up again?

THE WOMAN: Sure thing. You do make me laugh. It's good for me. *(She squeezes his arm, kisses him.)* And I think you're a wonderful man.

WILLY: You picked me, heh?

THE WOMAN: Sure. Because you're so sweet. And such a kidder.

WILLY: Well, I'll see you next time I'm in Boston.

THE WOMAN: I'll put you right through to the buyers.

WILLY: *(slapping her bottom)* Right. Well, bottoms up!

THE WOMAN: *(slaps him gently and laughs)* You just kill me, Willy. *(He suddenly grabs her and kisses her roughly.)* You kill me. And thanks for the stockings. I love a lot of stockings. Well, good night.

WILLY: Good night. And keep your pores open!

THE WOMAN: Oh, Willy!

The Woman bursts out laughing, and Linda's laughter blends in. The Woman disappears into the dark. Now the area at the kitchen table brightens. Linda is sitting where she was at the kitchen table, but now is mending a pair of silk stockings.

LINDA: You are, Willy. The handsomest man. You've got no reason to feel that—

WILLY: *(coming out of The Woman's dimming area and going over to Linda)* I'll make it all up to you, Linda, I'll—

LINDA: There's nothing to make up, dear. You're doing fine, better than—

WILLY: *(noticing her mending)* What's that?

LINDA: Just mending my stockings. They're so expensive—

WILLY: *(angrily, taking them from her)* I won't have you mending stockings in this house! Now throw them out!

Linda puts the stockings in her pocket.

BERNARD: *(entering on the run)* Where is he? If he doesn't study!

WILLY: *(moving to the forestage, with great agitation)* You'll give him the answers!

BERNARD: I do, but I can't on a Regents! That's a state exam! They're liable to arrest me!

WILLY: Where is he? I'll whip him, I'll whip him!

LINDA: And he'd better give back that football, Willy, it's not nice.

WILLY: Biff! Where is he? Why is he taking everything?

LINDA: He's too tough with the girls, Willy. All the mothers are afraid of him!

WILLY: I'll whip him!

BERNARD: He's driving the car without a license!

The Woman's laugh is heard.

WILLY: Shut up!
LINDA: All the mothers—
WILLY: Shut up!
BERNARD: *(backing quietly away and out)* Mr. Birnbaum says he's stuck up.
WILLY: Get outa here!
BERNARD: If he doesn't buckle down he'll flunk math! *(He goes off.)*
LINDA: He's right, Willy, you've gotta—
WILLY: *(exploding at her)* There's nothing the matter with him! You want him to be a worm like Bernard? He's got spirit, personality . . .

As he speaks, Linda, almost in tears, exits into the livingroom. Willy is alone in the kitchen, wilting and staring. The leaves are gone. It is night again, and the apartment houses look down from behind.

WILLY: Loaded with it. Loaded! What is he stealing? He's giving it back, isn't he? Why is he stealing? What did I tell him? I never in my life told him anything but decent things.

Happy in pajamas has come down the stairs; Willy suddenly becomes aware of Happy's presence.

HAPPY: Let's go now, come on.
WILLY: *(sitting down at the kitchen table)* Huh! Why did she have to wax the floors herself? Everytime she waxes the floors she keels over. She knows that!
HAPPY: Shh! Take it easy. What brought you back tonight?
WILLY: I got an awful scare. Nearly hit a kid in Yonkers. God! Why didn't I go to Alaska with my brother Ben that time! Ben! That man was a genius, that man was success incarnate! What a mistake! He begged me to go.
HAPPY: Well, there's no use in—
WILLY: You guys! There was a man started with the clothes on his back and ended up with diamond mines!
HAPPY: Boy, someday I'd like to know how he did it.
WILLY: What's the mystery? The man knew what he wanted and went out and got it! Walked into a jungle, and comes out, the age of twenty-one, and he's rich! The world is an oyster, but you don't crack it open on a mattress!
HAPPY: Pop, I told you I'm gonna retire you for life.
WILLY: You'll retire me for life on seventy goddam dollars a week? And your women and your car and your apartment, and you'll retire me for life! Christ's sake, I couldn't get past Yonkers today! Where are you guys, where are you? The woods are burning! I can't drive a car!

Charley has appeared in the doorway. He is a large man, slow of speech, laconic, immovable. In all he says, despite what he says, there is pity, and now, trepidation. He has a robe over his pajamas, slippers on his feet. He enters the kitchen.

CHARLEY: Everything all right?
HAPPY: Yeah, Charley, everything's . . .
WILLY: What's the matter?
CHARLEY: I heard some noise. I thought something happened. Can't we do something about the walls? You sneeze in here, and in my house hats blow off.
HAPPY: Let's go to bed, Dad. Come on.

Charley signals to Happy to go.

WILLY: You go ahead, I'm not tired at the moment.
HAPPY: *(to Willy)* Take it easy, huh? *(He exits.)*
WILLY: What're you doin' up?
CHARLEY: *(sitting down at the kitchen table opposite Willy)* Couldn't sleep good. I had a heartburn.
WILLY: Well, you don't know how to eat.
CHARLEY: I eat with my mouth.
WILLY: No, you're ignorant. You gotta know about vitamins and things like that.
CHARLEY: Come on, let's shoot. Tire you out a little.
WILLY: *(hesitantly)* All right. You got cards?
CHARLEY: *(taking a deck from his pocket)* Yeah, I got them. Someplace. What is it with those vitamins?
WILLY: *(dealing)* They build up your bones. Chemistry.
CHARLEY: Yeah, but there's no bones in a heartburn.
WILLY: What are you talkin' about? Do you know the first thing about it?
CHARLEY: Don't get insulted.
WILLY: Don't talk about something you don't know anything about.

They are playing. Pause.

CHARLEY: What're you doin' home?
WILLY: A little trouble with the car.
CHARLEY: Oh. *(Pause.)* I'd like to take a trip to California.
WILLY: Don't say.
CHARLEY: You want a job?
WILLY: I got a job, I told you that. *(After a slight pause.)* What the hell are you offering me a job for?
CHARLEY: Don't get insulted.
WILLY: Don't insult me.
CHARLEY: I don't see no sense in it. You don't have to go on this way.
WILLY: I got a good job. *(Slight pause.)* What do you keep comin' in here for?
CHARLEY: You want me to go?
WILLY: *(after a pause, withering)* I can't understand it. He's going back to Texas again. What the hell is that?

CHARLEY: Let him go.
420 WILLY: I got nothin' to give him, Charley, I'm clean, I'm clean.
CHARLEY: He won't starve. None a them starve. Forget about him.
WILLY: Then what have I got to remember?
CHARLEY: You take it too hard. To hell with it. When a deposit bottle is broken you don't get your nickel back.
WILLY: That's easy enough for you to say.
425 CHARLEY: That ain't easy for me to say.
WILLY: Did you see the ceiling I put up in the livingroom?
CHARLEY: Yeah, that's a piece of work. To put up a ceiling is a mystery to me. How do you do it?
WILLY: What's the difference?
CHARLEY: Well, talk about it.
430 WILLY: You gonna put up a ceiling?
CHARLEY: How could I put up a ceiling?
WILLY: Then what the hell are you bothering me for?
CHARLEY: You're insulted again.
WILLY: A man who can't handle tools is not a man. You're disgusting.
435 CHARLEY: Don't call me disgusting, Willy.

Uncle Ben, carrying a valise and an umbrella, enters the forestage from around the right corner of the house. He is a stolid man, in his sixties, with a mustache and an authoritative air. He is utterly certain of his destiny, and there is an aura of far places about him. He enters exactly as Willy speaks.

WILLY: I'm getting awfully tired, Ben.

Ben's music is heard. Ben looks around at everything.

CHARLEY: Good, keep playing; you'll sleep better. Did you call me Ben?

Ben looks at his watch.

WILLY: That's funny. For a second there you reminded me of my brother Ben.
BEN: I have only a few minutes. *(He strolls, inspecting the place. Willy and Charley continue playing.)*
440 CHARLEY: You never heard from him again, heh? Since that time?
WILLY: Didn't Linda tell you? Couple of weeks ago we got a letter from his wife in Africa. He died.
CHARLEY: That so.
BEN: *(chuckling)* So this is Brooklyn, eh?
CHARLEY: Maybe you're in for some of his money.
445 WILLY: Naa, he had seven sons. There's just one opportunity I had with that man . . .
BEN: I must make a train, William. There are several properties I'm looking at in Alaska.
WILLY: Sure, sure! If I'd gone with him to Alaska that time, everything would've been totally different.
CHARLEY: Go on, you'd froze to death up there.

WILLY: What're you talking about?
BEN: Opportunity is tremendous in Alaska, William. Surprised you're not up there.
WILLY: Sure, tremendous.
CHARLEY: Heh?
WILLY: There was the only man I ever met who knew the answers.
CHARLEY: Who?
BEN: How are you all?
WILLY: *(taking a pot, smiling)* Fine, fine.
CHARLEY: Pretty sharp tonight.
BEN: Is Mother living with you?
WILLY: No, she died a long time ago.
CHARLEY: Who?
BEN: That's too bad. Fine specimen of a lady, Mother.
WILLY: *(to Charley)* Heh?
BEN: I'd hoped to see the old girl.
CHARLEY: Who died?
BEN: Heard anything from Father, have you?
WILLY: *(unnerved)* What do you mean, who died?
CHARLEY: *(taking a pot)* What're you talkin' about?
BEN: *(looking at his watch)* William, it's half-past eight!
WILLY: *(as though to dispel his confusion he angrily stops Charley's hand)* That's my build!
CHARLEY: I put the ace—
WILLY: If you don't know how to play the game I'm not gonna throw my money away on you!
CHARLEY: *(rising)* It was my ace, for God's sake!
WILLY: I'm through, I'm through!
BEN: When did Mother die?
WILLY: Long ago. Since the beginning you never knew how to play cards.
CHARLEY: *(picks up the cards and goes to the door)* All right! Next time I'll bring a deck with five aces.
WILLY: I don't play that kind of game!
CHARLEY: *(turning to him)* You should be ashamed of yourself!
WILLY: Yeah?
CHARLEY: Yeah! *(He goes out.)*
WILLY: *(slamming the door after him)* Ignoramus!
BEN: *(as Willy comes toward him through the wall-line of the kitchen)* So you're William.
WILLY: *(shaking Ben's hand)* Ben! I've been waiting for you so long! What's the answer? How did you do it?
BEN: Oh, there's a story in that.

Linda enters the forestage, as of old, carrying the wash basket.

LINDA: Is this Ben?
BEN: *(gallantly)* How do you do, my dear.

LINDA: Where've you been all these years? Willy's always wondered why you—
WILLY: *(pulling Ben away from her impatiently)* Where is Dad? Didn't you follow him? How did you get started?
BEN: Well, I don't know how much you remember.
WILLY: Well, I was just a baby, of course, only three or four years old—
BEN: Three years and eleven months.
WILLY: What a memory, Ben!
BEN: I have many enterprises, William, and I have never kept books.
WILLY: I remember I was sitting under the wagon in—was it Nebraska?
BEN: It was South Dakota, and I gave you a bunch of wild flowers.
WILLY: I remember you walking away down some open road.
BEN: *(laughing)* I was going to find Father in Alaska.
WILLY: Where is he?
BEN: At that age I had a very faulty view of geography, William. I discovered after a few days that I was heading due south, so instead of Alaska, I ended up in Africa.
LINDA: Africa!
WILLY: The Gold Coast!
BEN: Principally, diamond mines.
LINDA: Diamond mines!
BEN: Yes, my dear. But I've only a few minutes—
WILLY: No! Boys! Boys! *(Young Biff and Happy appear.)* Listen to this. This is your Uncle Ben, a great man! Tell my boys, Ben!
BEN: Why, boys, when I was seventeen I walked into the jungle, and when I was twenty-one I walked out. *(He laughs.)* And by God I was rich.
WILLY: *(to the boys)* You see what I been talking about? The greatest things can happen!
BEN: *(glancing at his watch)* I have an appointment in Ketchikan Tuesday week.
WILLY: No, Ben! Please tell about Dad. I want my boys to hear. I want them to know the kind of stock they spring from. All I remember is a man with a big beard, and I was in Mamma's lap, sitting around a fire, and some kind of high music.
BEN: His flute. He played the flute.
WILLY: Sure, the flute, that's right!

New music is heard, a high, rollicking tune.

BEN: Father was a very great and a very wild-hearted man. We would start in Boston, and he'd toss the whole family into the wagon, and then he'd drive the team right across the country; through Ohio, and Indiana, Michigan, Illinois, and all the Western states. And we'd stop in the towns and sell the flutes that he'd made on the way. Great inventor, Father. With one gadget he made more in a week than a man like you could make in a lifetime.
WILLY: That's just the way I'm bringing them up, Ben—rugged, well liked, all-around.

BEN: Yeah? *(To Biff.)* Hit that, boy—hard as you can. *(He pounds his stomach.)*
515 **BIFF:** Oh, no, sir!
BEN: *(taking boxing stance)* Come on, get to me! *(He laughs.)*
WILLY: Go to it, Biff! Go ahead, show him!
BIFF: Okay! *(He cocks his fist and starts in.)*
LINDA: *(to Willy)* Why must he fight, dear?
520 **BEN:** *(sparring with Biff)* Good boy! Good boy!
WILLY: How's that, Ben, heh?
HAPPY: Give him the left, Biff!
LINDA: Why are you fighting?
BEN: Good boy! *(Suddenly comes in, trips Biff, and stands over him, the point of his umbrella poised over Biff's eye.)*
525 **LINDA:** Look out, Biff!
BIFF: Gee!
BEN: *(patting Biff's knee)* Never fight fair with a stranger, boy. You'll never get out of the jungle that way. *(Taking Linda's hand and bowing.)* It was an honor and a pleasure to meet you, Linda.
LINDA: *(withdrawing her hand coldly, frightened)* Have a nice—trip.
BEN: *(to Willy)* And good luck with your—what do you do?
530 **WILLY:** Selling.
BEN: Yes. Well . . . *(He raises his hand in farewell to all.)*
WILLY: No, Ben, I don't want you to think . . . *(He takes Ben's arm to show him.)* It's Brooklyn, I know, but we hunt too.
BEN: Really, now.
WILLY: Oh, sure, there's snakes and rabbits and—that's why I moved out here. Why, Biff can fell any one of these trees in no time! Boys! Go right over to where they're building the apartment house and get some sand. We're gonna rebuild the entire front stoop right now! Watch this, Ben!
535 **BIFF:** Yes, sir! On the double, Hap!
HAPPY: *(as he and Biff run off)* I lost weight, Pop, you notice?

Charley enters in knickers, even before the boys are gone.

CHARLEY: Listen, if they steal any more from that building the watchman'll put the cops on them!
LINDA: *(to Willy)* Don't let Biff . . .

Ben laughs lustily.

WILLY: You shoulda seen the lumber they brought home last week. At least a dozen six-by-tens worth all kinds of money.
540 **CHARLEY:** Listen, if that watchman—
WILLY: I gave them hell, understand. But I got a couple of fearless characters there.
CHARLEY: Willy, the jails are full of fearless characters.
BEN: *(clapping Willy on the back, with a laugh at Charley)* And the stock exchange, friend!
WILLY: *(joining in Ben's laughter)* Where are the rest of your pants?

CHARLEY: My wife bought them.
WILLY: Now all you need is a golf club and you can go upstairs and go to sleep. *(To Ben.)* Great athlete! Between him and his son Bernard they can't hammer a nail!
BERNARD: *(rushing in)* The watchman's chasing Biff!
WILLY: *(angrily)* Shut up! He's not stealing anything!
LINDA: *(alarmed, hurrying off left)* Where is he? Biff, dear! *(She exits.)*
WILLY: *(moving toward the left, away from Ben)* There's nothing wrong. What's the matter with you?
BEN: Nervy boy. Good!
WILLY: *(laughing)* Oh, nerves of iron, that Biff!
CHARLEY: Don't know what it is. My New England man comes back and he's bleedin', they murdered him up there.
WILLY: It's contacts, Charley, I got important contacts!
CHARLEY: *(sarcastically)* Glad to hear it, Willy. Come in later, we'll shoot a little casino. I'll take some of your Portland money. *(He laughs at Willy and exits.)*
WILLY: *(turning to Ben)* Business is bad, it's murderous. But not for me, of course.
BEN: I'll stop by on my way back to Africa.
WILLY: *(longingly)* Can't you stay a few days? You're just what I need, Ben, because I—I have a fine position here, but I—well, Dad left when I was such a baby and I never had a chance to talk to him and I still feel—kind of temporary about myself.
BEN: I'll be late for my train.

They are at opposite ends of the stage.

WILLY: Ben, my boys—can't we talk? They'd go into the jaws of hell for me, see, but I—
BEN: William, you're being first-rate with your boys. Outstanding, manly chaps!
WILLY: *(hanging on to his words)* Oh, Ben, that's good to hear! Because sometimes I'm afraid that I'm not teaching them the right kind of—Ben, how should I teach them?
BEN: *(giving great weight to each word, and with a certain vicious audacity)* William, when I walked into the jungle, I was seventeen. When I walked out I was twenty-one. And, by God, I was rich! *(He goes off into darkness around the right corner of the house.)*
WILLY: ... was rich! That's just the spirit I want to imbue them with! To walk into a jungle! I was right! I was right! I was right!

Ben is gone, but Willy is still speaking to him as Linda, in nightgown and robe, enters the kitchen, glances around for Willy, then goes to the door of the house, looks out and sees him. Comes down to his left. He looks at her.

LINDA: Willy, dear? Willy?
WILLY: I was right!
LINDA: Did you have some cheese? *(He can't answer.)* It's very late, darling. Come to bed, heh?

WILLY: *(looking straight up)* Gotta break your neck to see a star in this yard.
LINDA: You coming in?
570 WILLY: What ever happened to that diamond watch fob? Remember? When Ben came from Africa that time? Didn't he give me a watch fob with a diamond in it?
LINDA: You pawned it, dear. Twelve, thirteen years ago. For Biff's radio correspondence course.
WILLY: Gee, that was a beautiful thing. I'll take a walk.
LINDA: But you're in your slippers.
WILLY: *(starting to go around the house at the left)* I was right! I was! *(Half to Linda, as he goes, shaking his head.)* What a man! There was a man worth talking to. I was right!
575 LINDA: *(calling after Willy)* But in your slippers, Willy!

Willy is almost gone when Biff, in his pajamas, comes down the stairs and enters the kitchen.

BIFF: What is he doing out there?
LINDA: Sh!
BIFF: God Almighty, Mom, how long has he been doing this?
LINDA: Don't, he'll hear you.
580 BIFF: What the hell is the matter with him?
LINDA: It'll pass by morning.
BIFF: Shouldn't we do anything?
LINDA: Oh, my dear, you should do a lot of things, but there's nothing to do, so go to sleep.

Happy comes down the stairs and sits on the steps.

HAPPY: I never heard him so loud, Mom.
585 LINDA: Well, come around more often; you'll hear him. *(She sits down at the table and mends the lining of Willy's jacket.)*
BIFF: Why didn't you ever write me about this, Mom?
LINDA: How would I write to you? For over three months you had no address.
BIFF: I was on the move. But you know I thought of you all the time. You know that, don't you, pal?
LINDA: I know, dear, I know. But he likes to have a letter. Just to know that there's still a possibility for better things.
590 BIFF: He's not like this all the time, is he?
LINDA: It's when you come home he's always the worst.
BIFF: When I come home?
LINDA: When you write you're coming, he's all smiles, and talks about the future, and—he's just wonderful. And then the closer you seem to come, the more shaky he gets, and then, by the time you get here, he's arguing, and he seems angry at you. I think it's just that maybe he can't bring himself to—to open up to you. Why are you so hateful to each other? Why is that?
BIFF: *(evasively)* I'm not hateful, Mom.

595 LINDA: But you no sooner come in the door than you're fighting!
BIFF: I don't know why. I mean to change. I'm tryin', Mom, you understand?
LINDA: Are you home to stay now?
BIFF: I don't know. I want to look around, see what's doin'.
LINDA: Biff, you can't look around all your life, can you?
600 BIFF: I just can't take hold, Mom. I can't take hold of some kind of a life.
LINDA: Biff, a man is not a bird, to come and go with the springtime.
BIFF: Your hair . . . *(He touches her hair.)* Your hair got so gray.
LINDA: Oh, it's been gray since you were in high school. I just stopped dyeing it, that's all.
BIFF: Dye it again, will ya? I don't want my pal looking old. *(He smiles.)*
605 LINDA: You're such a boy! You think you can go away for a year and . . . You've got to get it into your head now that one day you'll knock on this door and there'll be strange people here—
BIFF: What are you talking about? You're not even sixty, Mom.
LINDA: But what about your father?
BIFF: *(lamely)* Well, I meant him too.
HAPPY: He admires Pop.
610 LINDA: Biff, dear, if you don't have any feeling for him, then you can't have any feeling for me.
BIFF: Sure I can, Mom.
LINDA: No. You can't just come to see me, because I love him. *(With a threat, but only a threat, of tears.)* He's the dearest man in the world to me, and I won't have anyone making him feel unwanted and low and blue. You've got to make up your mind now, darling, there's no leeway any more. Either he's your father and you pay him that respect, or else you're not to come here. I know he's not easy to get along with—nobody knows that better than me—but . . .
WILLY: *(from the left, with a laugh)* Hey, hey, Biffo!
BIFF: *(starting to go out after Willy)* What the hell is the matter with him? *(Happy stops him.)*
615 LINDA: Don't—don't go near him!
BIFF: Stop making excuses for him! He always, always wiped the floor with you. Never had an ounce of respect for you.
HAPPY: He's always had respect for—
BIFF: What the hell do you know about it?
HAPPY: *(surlily)* Just don't call him crazy!
620 BIFF: He's got no character—Charley wouldn't do this. Not in his own house—spewing out that vomit from his mind.
HAPPY: Charley never had to cope with what he's got to.
BIFF: People are worse off than Willy Loman. Believe me, I've seen them!
LINDA: Then make Charley your father, Biff. You can't do that, can you? I don't say he's a great man. Willy Loman never made a lot of money. His name was never in the paper. He's not the finest

character that ever lived. But he's a human being, and a terrible thing is happening to him. So attention must be paid. He's not to be allowed to fall into his grave like an old dog. Attention, attention must be finally paid to such a person. You called him crazy—

BIFF: I didn't mean—

LINDA: No, a lot of people think he's lost his—balance. But you don't have to be very smart to know what his trouble is. The man is exhausted.

HAPPY: Sure!

LINDA: A small man can be just as exhausted as a great man. He works for a company thirty-six years this March, opens up unheard-of territories to their trademark, and now in his old age they take his salary away.

HAPPY: *(indignantly)* I didn't know that, Mom.

LINDA: You never asked, my dear! Now that you get your spending money someplace else you don't trouble your mind with him.

HAPPY: But I gave you money last—

LINDA: Christmas time, fifty dollars! To fix the hot water it cost ninety-seven fifty! For five weeks he's been on straight commission, like a beginner, an unknown!

BIFF: Those ungrateful bastards!

LINDA: Are they any worse than his sons? When he brought them business, when he was young, they were glad to see him. But now his old friends, the old buyers that loved him so and always found some order to hand him in a pinch—they're all dead, retired. He used to be able to make six, seven calls a day in Boston. Now he takes his valises out of the car and puts them back and takes them out again and he's exhausted. Instead of walking he talks now. He drives seven hundred miles, and when he gets there no one knows him any more, no one welcomes him. And what goes through a man's mind, driving seven hundred miles home without having earned a cent? Why shouldn't he talk to himself? Why? When he has to go to Charley and borrow fifty dollars a week and pretend to me that it's his pay? How long can that go on? How long? You see what I'm sitting here and waiting for? And you tell me he has no character? The man who never worked a day but for your benefit? When does he get the medal for that? Is this his reward—to turn around at the age of sixty-three and find his sons, who he loved better than his life, one a philandering bum—

HAPPY: Mom!

LINDA: That's all you are, my baby! *(To Biff.)* And you! What happened to the love you had for him? You were such pals! How you used to talk to him on the phone every night! How lonely he was till he could come home to you!

BIFF: All right, Mom. I'll live here in my room, and I'll get a job. I'll keep away from him, that's all.

LINDA: No, Biff. You can't stay here and fight all the time.
BIFF: He threw me out of this house, remember that.
LINDA: Why did he do that? I never knew why.
BIFF: Because I know he's a fake and he doesn't like anybody around who knows!
LINDA: Why a fake? In what way? What do you mean?
BIFF: Just don't lay it all at my feet. It's between me and him—that's all I have to say. I'll chip in from now on. He'll settle for half my pay check. He'll be all right. I'm going to bed. *(He starts for the stairs.)*
LINDA: He won't be all right.
BIFF: *(turning on the stairs, furiously)* I hate this city and I'll stay here. Now what do you want?
LINDA: He's dying, Biff.

Happy turns quickly to her, shocked.

BIFF: *(after a pause)* Why is he dying?
LINDA: He's been trying to kill himself.
BIFF: *(with great horror)* How?
LINDA: I live from day to day.
BIFF: What're you talking about?
LINDA: Remember I wrote you that he smashed up the car again? In February?
BIFF: Well?
LINDA: The insurance inspector came. He said that they have evidence. That all these accidents in the last year—weren't—weren't—accidents.
HAPPY: How can they tell that? That's a lie.
LINDA: It seems there's a woman . . . *(She takes a breath as—)*
BIFF: *(sharply but contained)* What woman?
LINDA: *(simultaneously)* . . . and this woman . . .
LINDA: What?
BIFF: Nothing. Go ahead.
LINDA: What did you say?
BIFF: Nothing. I just said what woman?
HAPPY: What about her?
LINDA: Well, it seems she was walking down the road and saw his car. She says that he wasn't driving fast at all, and that he didn't skid. She says he came to that little bridge, and then deliberately smashed into the railing, and it was only the shallowness of the water that saved him.
BIFF: Oh, no, he probably just fell asleep again.
LINDA: I don't think he fell asleep.
BIFF: Why not?
LINDA: Last month . . . *(With great difficulty.)* Oh, boys, it's so hard to say a thing like this! He's just a big stupid man to you, but I tell you there's more good in him than in many other people. *(She chokes, wipes her eyes.)* I was looking for a fuse. The lights blew out,

and I went down the cellar. And behind the fuse box—it happened
to fall out—was a length of rubber pipe—just short.
HAPPY: No kidding?
LINDA: There's a little attachment on the end of it. I knew right away.
And sure enough, on the bottom of the water heater there's a new
little nipple on the gas pipe.
670 HAPPY: *(angrily)* That—jerk.
BIFF: Did you have it taken off?
LINDA: I'm—I'm ashamed to. How can I mention it to him? Every day I
go down and take away that little rubber pipe. But, when he comes
home, I put it back where it was. How can I insult him that way? I
don't know what to do. I live from day to day, boys. I tell you, I
know every thought in his mind. It sounds so old-fashioned and
silly, but I tell you he put his whole life into you and you've turned
your backs on him. *(She is bent over in the chair, weeping, her face in
her hands.)* Biff, I swear to God! Biff, his life is in your hands!
HAPPY: *(to Biff)* How do you like that damned fool!
BIFF: *(kissing her)* All right, pal, all right. It's all settled now. I've been
remiss. I know that, Mom, but now I'll stay, and I swear to you, I'll
apply myself. *(Kneeling in front of her, in a fever of self-reproach.)* It's
just—you see, Mom, I don't fit in business. Not that I won't try. I'll
try, and I'll make good.
675 HAPPY: Sure you will. The trouble with you in business was you never
tried to please people.
BIFF: I know, I—
HAPPY: Like when you worked for Harrison's. Bob Harrison said you
were tops, and then you go and do some damn fool thing like
whistling whole songs in the elevator like a comedian.
BIFF: *(against Happy)* So what? I like to whistle sometimes.
HAPPY: You don't raise a guy to a responsible job who whistles in the
elevator!
680 LINDA: Well, don't argue about it now.
HAPPY: Like when you'd go off and swim in the middle of the day
instead of taking the line around.
BIFF: *(his resentment rising)* Well, don't you run off? You take off
sometimes, don't you? On a nice summer day?
HAPPY: Yeah, but I cover myself!
LINDA: Boys!
685 HAPPY: If I'm going to take a fade the boss can call any number where
I'm supposed to be and they'll swear to him that I just left. I'll tell
you something that I hate to say, Biff, but in the business world
some of them think you're crazy.
BIFF: *(angered)* Screw the business world!
HAPPY: All right, screw it! Great, but cover yourself!
LINDA: Hap, Hap!
BIFF: I don't care what they think! They've laughed at Dad for years,
and you know why? Because we don't belong in this nut-house of a

city! We should be mixing cement on some open plain, or—or carpenters. A carpenter is allowed to whistle!

Willy walks in from the entrance of the house, at left.

690 WILLY: Even your grandfather was better than a carpenter. *(Pause. They watch him.)* You never grew up. Bernard does not whistle in the elevator, I assure you.
BIFF: *(as though to laugh Willy out of it)* Yeah, but you do, Pop.
WILLY: I never in my life whistled in an elevator! And who in the business world thinks I'm crazy?
BIFF: I didn't mean it like that, Pop. Now don't make a whole thing out of it, will ya?
WILLY: Go back to the West! Be a carpenter, a cowboy, enjoy yourself!
695 LINDA: Willy, he was just saying—
WILLY: I heard what he said!
HAPPY: *(trying to quiet Willy)* Hey, Pop, come on now . . .
WILLY: *(continuing over Happy's line)* They laugh at me, heh? Go to Filene's, go to the Hub, go to Slattery's, Boston. Call out the name Willy Loman and see what happens! Big shot!
BIFF: All right, Pop.
700 WILLY: Big!
BIFF: All right!
WILLY: Why do you always insult me?
BIFF: I didn't say a word. *(To Linda.)* Did I say a word?
LINDA: He didn't say anything, Willy.
705 WILLY: *(going to the doorway of the livingroom)* All right, good night, good night.
LINDA: Willy, dear, he just decided . . .
WILLY: *(to Biff)* If you get tired hanging around tomorrow, paint the ceiling I put up in the livingroom.
BIFF: I'm leaving early tomorrow.
HAPPY: He's going to see Bill Oliver, Pop.
710 WILLY: *(interestedly)* Oliver? For what?
BIFF: *(with reserve, but trying, trying)* He always said he'd stake me. I'd like to go into business, so maybe I can take him up on it.
LINDA: Isn't that wonderful?
WILLY: Don't interrupt. What's wonderful about it? There's fifty men in the City of New York who'd stake him. *(To Biff.)* Sporting goods?
BIFF: I guess so. I know something about it and—
715 WILLY: He knows something about it! You know sporting goods better than Spalding, for God's sake! How much is he giving you?
BIFF: I don't know, I didn't even see him yet, but—
WILLY: Then what're you talkin' about?
BIFF: *(getting angry)* Well, all I said was I'm gonna see him, that's all!
WILLY: *(turning away)* Ah, you're counting your chickens again.
720 BIFF: *(starting left for the stairs)* Oh, Jesus, I'm going to sleep!
WILLY: *(calling after him)* Don't curse in this house!
BIFF: *(turning)* Since when did you get so clean!

HAPPY: *(trying to stop them)* Wait a . . .

WILLY: Don't use that language to me! I won't have it!

725 HAPPY: *(grabbing Biff, shouts)* Wait a minute! I got an idea. I got a feasible idea. Come here, Biff, let's talk this over now, let's talk some sense here. When I was down in Florida last time, I thought of a great idea to sell sporting goods. It just came back to me. You and I, Biff—we have a line, the Loman Line. We train a couple of weeks, and put on a couple of exhibitions, see?

WILLY: That's an idea!

HAPPY: Wait! We form two basketball teams, see? Two water-polo teams. We play each other. It's a million dollars' worth of publicity. Two brothers, see? The Loman Brothers. Displays in the Royal Palms—all the hotels. And banners over the ring and the basketball court: "Loman Brothers." Baby, we could sell sporting goods!

WILLY: That is a one-million-dollar idea.

LINDA: Marvelous!

730 BIFF: I'm in great shape as far as that's concerned.

HAPPY: And the beauty of it is, Biff, it wouldn't be like a business. We'd be out playin' ball again . . .

BIFF: *(enthused)* Yeah, that's . . .

WILLY: Million-dollar . . .

HAPPY: And you wouldn't get fed up with it, Biff. It'd be the family again. There'd be the old honor, and comradeship, and if you wanted to go off for a swim or somethin'—well, you'd do it! Without some smart cooky gettin' up ahead of you!

735 WILLY: Lick the world! You guys together could absolutely lick the civilized world.

BIFF: I'll see Oliver tomorrow. Hap, if we could work that out . . .

LINDA: Maybe things are beginning to—

WILLY: *(wildly enthused, to Linda)* Stop interrupting! *(To Biff.)* But don't wear sport jacket and slacks when you see Oliver.

BIFF: No, I'll—

740 WILLY: A business suit, and talk as little as possible, and don't crack any jokes.

BIFF: He did like me. Always liked me.

LINDA: He loved you!

WILLY: *(to Linda)* Will you stop! *(To Biff.)* Walk in very serious. You are not applying for a boy's job. Money is to pass. Be quiet, fine, and serious. Everybody likes a kidder, but nobody lends him money.

HAPPY: I'll try to get some myself, Biff. I'm sure I can.

745 WILLY: I can see great things for you, kids, I think your troubles are over. But remember, start big and you'll end big. Ask for fifteen. How much you gonna ask for?

BIFF: Gee, I don't know—

WILLY: And don't say "Gee." "Gee" is a boy's word. A man walking in for fifteen thousand dollars does not say "Gee!"

BIFF: Ten, I think, would be top though.

WILLY: Don't be so modest. You always started too low. Walk in with a big laugh. Don't look worried. Start off with a couple of your good stories to lighten things up. It's not what you say, it's how you say it—because personality always wins the day.

750 LINDA: Oliver always thought the highest of him—
WILLY: Will you let me talk?
BIFF: Don't yell at her, Pop, will ya?
WILLY: *(angrily)* I was talking, wasn't I!
BIFF: I don't like you yelling at her all the time, and I'm tellin' you, that's all.
755 WILLY: What're you, takin' over this house?
LINDA: Willy—
WILLY: *(turning on her)* Don't take his side all the time, goddammit!
BIFF: *(furiously)* Stop yelling at her!
WILLY: *(suddenly pulling on his cheek, beaten down, guilt ridden)* Give my best to Bill Oliver—he may remember me. *(He exits through the livingroom doorway.)*
760 LINDA: *(her voice subdued)* What'd you have to start that for? *(Biff turns away.)* You see how sweet he was as soon as you talked hopefully? *(She goes over to Biff.)* Come up and say good night to him. Don't let him go to bed that way.
HAPPY: Come on, Biff, let's buck him up.
LINDA: Please, dear. Just say good night. It takes so little to make him happy. Come. *(She goes through the livingroom doorway, calling upstairs from within the livingroom.)* Your pajamas are hanging in the bathroom. Willy!
HAPPY: *(looking toward where Linda went out)* What a woman! They broke the mold when they made her. You know that, Biff?
BIFF: He's off salary. My God, working on commission!
765 HAPPY: Well, let's face it: he's no hot-shot selling man. Except that sometimes, you have to admit, he's a sweet personality.
BIFF: *(deciding)* Lend me ten bucks, will ya? I want to buy some new ties.
HAPPY: I'll take you to a place I know. Beautiful stuff. Wear one of my striped shirts tomorrow.
BIFF: She got gray. Mom got awful old. Gee, I'm gonna go in to Oliver tomorrow and knock him for a—
HAPPY: Come on up. Tell that to Dad. Let's give him a whirl. Come on.
770 BIFF: *(steamed up)* You know, with ten thousand bucks, boy!
HAPPY: *(as they go into the livingroom)* That's the talk, Biff, that's the first time I've heard the old confidence out of you! *(From within the livingroom, fading off.)* You're gonna live with me, kid, and any babe you want you just say the word . . . (The last lines are hardly heard. They are mounting the stairs to their parents' bedroom.)*
LINDA: *(entering her bedroom and addressing Willy, who is in the bathroom. She is straightening the bed for him)* Can you do anything about the shower? It drips.

WILLY: *(from the bathroom)* All of a sudden everything falls to pieces! Goddam plumbing, oughta be sued, those people. I hardly finished putting it in and the thing . . . *(His words rumble off.)*
LINDA: I'm just wondering if Oliver will remember him. You think he might?
WILLY: *(coming out of the bathroom in his pajamas)* Remember him? What's the matter with you, you crazy? If he'd've stayed with Oliver he'd be on top by now! Wait'll Oliver gets a look at him. You don't know the average caliber any more. The average young man today—*(he is getting into bed)*—is got a caliber of zero. Greatest thing in the world for him was to bum around.

Biff and Happy enter the bedroom. Slight pause.

WILLY: *(stops short, looking at Biff)* Glad to hear it, boy.
HAPPY: He wanted to say good night to you, sport.
WILLY: *(to Biff)* Yeah. Knock him dead, boy. What'd you want to tell me?
BIFF: Just take it easy, Pop. Good night. *(He turns to go.)*
WILLY: *(unable to resist)* And if anything falls off the desk while you're talking to him—like a package or something—don't you pick it up. They have office boys for that.
LINDA: I'll make a big breakfast—
WILLY: Will you let me finish? *(To Biff.)* Tell him you were in the business in the West. Not farm work.
BIFF: All right, Dad.
LINDA: I think everything—
WILLY: *(going right through her speech)* And don't undersell yourself. No less than fifteen thousand dollars.
BIFF: *(unable to bear him)* Okay. Good night, Mom. *(He starts moving.)*
WILLY: Because you got a greatness in you, Biff, remember that. You got all kinds a greatness . . . *(He lies back, exhausted. Biff walks out.)*
LINDA: *(calling after Biff)* Sleep well, darling!
HAPPY: I'm gonna get married, Mom. I wanted to tell you.
LINDA: Go to sleep, dear.
HAPPY: *(going)* I just wanted to tell you.
WILLY: Keep up the good work. *(Happy exits.)* God . . . remember that Ebbets Field game? The championship of the city?
LINDA: Just rest. Should I sing to you?
WILLY: Yeah. Sing to me. *(Linda hums a soft lullaby.)* When that team came out—he was the tallest, remember?
LINDA: Oh, yes. And in gold.

Biff enters the darkened kitchen, takes a cigarette, and leaves the house. He comes downstage into a golden pool of light. He smokes, staring at the night.

WILLY: Like a young god. Hercules—something like that. And the sun, the sun all around him. Remember how he waved to me? Right up from the field, with the representatives of three colleges standing by? And the buyers I brought, and the cheers when he came out—Loman, Loman, Loman! God Almighty, he'll be great yet. A star like that, magnificent, can never really fade away!

The light on Willy is fading. The gas heater begins to glow through the kitchen wall, near the stairs, a blue flame beneath red coils.

LINDA: *(timidly)* Willy, dear, what has he got against you?
WILLY: I'm so tired. Don't talk any more.

Biff slowly returns to the kitchen. He stops, stares toward the heater.

LINDA: Will you ask Howard to let you work in New York?
WILLY: First thing in the morning. Everything'll be all right.

Biff reaches behind the heater and draws out a length of rubber tubing. He is horrified and turns his head toward Willy's room, still dimly lit, from which the strains of Linda's desperate but monotonous humming rise.

WILLY: *(staring through the window into the moonlight)* Gee, look at the moon moving between the buildings!

Biff wraps the tubing around his hand and quickly goes up the stairs. Curtain.

ACT II

Music is heard, gay and bright. The curtain rises as the music fades away. Willy, in shirt sleeves, is sitting at the kitchen table, sipping coffee, his hat in his lap. Linda is filling his cup when she can.

WILLY: Wonderful coffee. Meal in itself.
LINDA: Can I make you some eggs?
WILLY: No. Take a breath.
LINDA: You look so rested, dear.
WILLY: I slept like a dead one. First time in months. Imagine, sleeping till ten on a Tuesday morning. Boys left nice and early, heh?
LINDA: They were out of here by eight o'clock.
WILLY: Good work!
LINDA: It was so thrilling to see them leaving together. I can't get over the shaving lotion in this house.
WILLY: *(smiling)* Mmm—
LINDA: Biff was very changed this morning. His whole attitude seemed to be hopeful. He couldn't wait to get downtown to see Oliver.
WILLY: He's heading for a change. There's no question, there simply are certain men that take longer to get—solidified. How did he dress?
LINDA: His blue suit. He's so handsome in that suit. He could be a—anything in that suit!

Willy gets up from the table. Linda holds his jacket for him.

WILLY: There's no question, no question at all. Gee, on the way home tonight I'd like to buy some seeds.

LINDA: *(laughing)* That'd be wonderful. But not enough sun gets back there. Nothing'll grow any more.
15 WILLY: You wait, kid, before it's all over we're gonna get a little place out in the country, and I'll raise some vegetables, a couple of chickens . . .
LINDA: You'll do it yet, dear.

Willy walks out of his jacket. Linda follows him.

WILLY: And they'll get married, and come for a weekend. I'd build a little guest house. 'Cause I got so many fine tools, all I'd need would be a little lumber and some peace of mind.
LINDA: *(joyfully)* I sewed the lining . . .
WILLY: I could build two guest houses, so they'd both come. Did he decide how much he's going to ask Oliver for?
20 LINDA: *(getting him into the jacket)* He didn't mention it, but I imagine ten or fifteen thousand. You going to talk to Howard today?
WILLY: Yeah. I'll put it to him straight and simple. He'll just have to take me off the road.
LINDA: And Willy, don't forget to ask for a little advance, because we've got the insurance premium. It's the grace period now.
WILLY: That's a hundred . . . ?
LINDA: A hundred and eight, sixty-eight. Because we're a little short again.
25 WILLY: Why are we short?
LINDA: Well, you had the motor job on the car . . .
WILLY: That goddam Studebaker!
LINDA: And you got one more payment on the refrigerator . . .
WILLY: But it just broke again!
30 LINDA: Well, it's old, dear.
WILLY: I told you we should've bought a well-advertised machine. Charley bought a General Electric and it's twenty years old and it's still good, that son-of-a-bitch.
LINDA: But, Willy—
WILLY: Whoever heard of a Hastings refrigerator? Once in my life I would like to own something outright before it's broken! I'm always in a race with the junkyard! I just finished paying for the car and it's on its last legs. The refrigerator consumes belts like a goddam maniac. They time those things. They time them so when you finally paid for them, they're used up.
LINDA: *(buttoning up his jacket as he unbuttons it)* All told, about two hundred dollars would carry us, dear. But that includes the last payment on the mortgage. After this payment, Willy, the house belongs to us.
35 WILLY: It's twenty-five years!
LINDA: Biff was nine years old when we bought it.
WILLY: Well, that's a great thing. To weather a twenty-five year mortgage is—

LINDA: It's an accomplishment.
WILLY: All the cement, the lumber, the reconstruction I put in this house! There ain't a crack to be found in it any more.
LINDA: Well, it served its purpose.
WILLY: What purpose? Some stranger'll come along, move in, and that's that. If only Biff would take this house, and raise a family . . . *(He starts to go.)* Good-by, I'm late.
LINDA: *(suddenly remembering)* Oh, I forgot! You're supposed to meet them for dinner.
WILLY: Me?
LINDA: At Frank's Chop House on Forty-eighth near Sixth Avenue.
WILLY: Is that so! How about you?
LINDA: No, just the three of you. They're gonna blow you to a big meal!
WILLY: Don't say! Who thought of that?
LINDA: Biff came to me this morning, Willy, and he said, "Tell Dad, we want to blow him to a big meal." Be there six o'clock. You and your two boys are going to have dinner.
WILLY: Gee whiz! That's really somethin'. I'm gonna knock Howard for a loop, kid. I'll get an advance, and I'll come home with a New York job. Goddammit, now I'm gonna do it!
LINDA: Oh, that's the spirit, Willy!
WILLY: I will never get behind a wheel the rest of my life!
LINDA: It's changing, Willy, I can feel it changing!
WILLY: Beyond a question. G'by, I'm late. *(He starts to go again.)*
LINDA: *(calling after him as she runs to the kitchen table for a handkerchief)* You got your glasses?
WILLY: *(feels for them, then comes back in)* Yeah, yeah, got my glasses.
LINDA: *(giving him the handkerchief)* And a handkerchief.
WILLY: Yeah, handkerchief.
LINDA: And your saccharine?
WILLY: Yeah, my saccharine.
LINDA: Be careful on the subway stairs.

She kisses him, and a silk stocking is seen hanging from her hand. Willy notices it.

WILLY: Will you stop mending stockings? At least while I'm in the house. It gets me nervous. I can't tell you. Please.

Linda hides the stocking in her hand as she follows Willy across the forestage in front of the house.

LINDA: Remember, Frank's Chop House.
WILLY: *(passing the apron)* Maybe beets would grow out there.
LINDA: *(laughing)* But you tried so many times.
WILLY: Yeah. Well, don't work hard today. *(He disappears around the right corner of the house.)*
LINDA: Be careful!

As Willy vanishes, Linda waves to him. Suddenly the phone rings. She runs across the stage and into the kitchen and lifts it.

LINDA: Hello? Oh, Biff! I'm so glad you called, I just . . . Yes, sure, I just told him. Yes, he'll be there for dinner at six o'clock, I didn't forget. Listen, I was just dying to tell you. You know that little rubber pipe I told you about? That he connected to the gas heater? I finally decided to go down the cellar this morning and take it away and destroy it. But it's gone! Imagine? He took it away himself, it isn't there! *(She listens.)* When? Oh, then you took it. Oh—nothing, it's just that I'd hoped he'd taken it away himself. Oh, I'm not worried, darling, because this morning he left in such high spirits, it was like the old days! I'm not afraid any more. Did Mr. Oliver see you? . . . Well, you wait there then. And make a nice impression on him, darling. Just don't perspire too much before you see him. And have a nice time with Dad. He may have big news too! . . . That's right, a New York job. And be sweet to him tonight, dear. Be loving to him. Because he's only a little boat looking for a harbor. *(She is trembling with sorrow and joy.)* Oh, that's wonderful, Biff, you'll save his life. Thanks, darling. Just put your arm around him when he comes into the restaurant. Give him a smile. That's the boy . . . Good-by, dear. . . . You got your comb? . . . That's fine. Good-by, Biff dear.

In the middle of her speech, Howard Wagner, thirty-six, wheels in a small typewriter table on which is a wire-recording machine and proceeds to plug it in. This is on the left forestage. Light slowly fades on Linda as it rises on Howard. Howard is intent on threading the machine and only glances over his shoulder as Willy appears.

WILLY: Pst! Pst!
HOWARD: Hello, Willy, come in.
70 WILLY: Like to have a little talk with you, Howard.
HOWARD: Sorry to keep you waiting. I'll be with you in a minute.
WILLY: What's that, Howard?
HOWARD: Didn't you ever see one of these? Wire recorder.
WILLY: Oh. Can we talk a minute?
75 HOWARD: Records things. Just got delivery yesterday. Been driving me crazy, the most terrific machine I ever saw in my life. I was up all night with it.
WILLY: What do you do with it?
HOWARD: I bought it for dictation, but you can do anything with it. Listen to this. I had it home last night. Listen to what I picked up. The first one is my daughter. Get this. *(He flicks the switch and "Roll out the Barrel" is heard being whistled.)* Listen to that kid whistle.
WILLY: That is lifelike, isn't it?
HOWARD: Seven years old. Get that tone.

80 WILLY: Ts, ts. Like to ask a little favor if you . . .

The whistling breaks off, and the voice of Howard's Daughter is heard.

HIS DAUGHTER: "Now you, Daddy."
HOWARD: She's crazy for me! *(Again the same song is whistled.)* That's me! Ha! *(He winks.)*
WILLY: You're very good!

The whistling breaks off again. The machine runs silent for a moment.

HOWARD: Sh! Get this now, this is my son.
85 HIS SON: "The capital of Alabama is Montgomery; the capital of Arizona is Phoenix; the capital of Arkansas is Little Rock; the capital of California is Sacramento . . ." *(And on, and on.)*
HOWARD: *(holding up five fingers)* Five years old, Willy!
WILLY: He'll make an announcer some day!
HIS SON: *(continuing)* "The capital . . ."
HOWARD: Get that—alphabetical order! *(The machine breaks off suddenly.)* Wait a minute. The maid kicked the plug out.
90 WILLY: It certainly is a—
HOWARD: Sh, for God's sake!
HIS SON: "It's nine o'clock, Bulova watch time. So I have to go to sleep."
WILLY: That really is—
HOWARD: Wait a minute! The next is my wife.

They wait.

95 HOWARD'S VOICE: "Go on, say something." *(Pause.)* "Well, you gonna talk?"
HIS WIFE: "I can't think of anything."
HOWARD'S VOICE: "Well, talk—it's turning."
HIS WIFE: *(shyly, beaten)* "Hello." *(Silence.)* "Oh, Howard, I can't talk into this . . ."
HOWARD: *(snapping the machine off)* That was my wife.
100 WILLY: That is a wonderful machine. Can we—
HOWARD: I tell you, Willy, I'm gonna take my camera, and my bandsaw, and all my hobbies, and out they go. This is the most fascinating relaxation I ever found.
WILLY: I think I'll get one myself.
HOWARD: Sure, they're only a hundred and a half. You can't do without it. Supposing you wanna hear Jack Benny, see? But you can't be at home at that hour. So you tell the maid to turn the radio on when Jack Benny comes on, and this automatically goes on with the radio . . .
WILLY: And when you come home you . . .
105 HOWARD: You can come home twelve o'clock, one o'clock, any time you like, and you get yourself a Coke and sit yourself down, throw the

switch, and there's Jack Benny's program in the middle of the night!

WILLY: I'm definitely going to get one. Because lots of time I'm on the road, and I think to myself, what I must be missing on the radio!

HOWARD: Don't you have a radio in the car?

WILLY: Well, yeah, but who ever thinks of turning it on?

HOWARD: Say, aren't you supposed to be in Boston?

110 WILLY: That's what I want to talk to you about, Howard. You got a minute?

He draws a chair in from the wing.

HOWARD: What happened? What're you doing here?

WILLY: Well . . .

HOWARD: You didn't crack up again, did you?

WILLY: Oh, no. No . . .

115 HOWARD: Geez, you had me worried there for a minute. What's the trouble?

WILLY: Well, to tell you the truth, Howard, I've come to the decision that I'd rather not travel any more.

HOWARD: Not travel! Well, what'll you do?

WILLY: Remember, Christmas time, when you had the party here? You said you'd try to think of some spot for me here in town.

HOWARD: With us?

120 WILLY: Well, sure.

HOWARD: Oh, yeah, yeah. I remember. Well, I couldn't think of anything for you, Willy.

WILLY: I tell ya, Howard. The kids are all grown up, y'know. I don't need much any more. If I could take home—well, sixty-five dollars a week, I could swing it.

HOWARD: Yeah, but Willy, see I—

WILLY: I tell ya why, Howard. Speaking frankly and between the two of us, y'know—I'm just a little tired.

125 HOWARD: Oh, I could understand that, Willy. But you're a road man, Willy, and we do a road business. We've only got a half-dozen salesmen on the floor here.

WILLY: God knows, Howard, I never asked a favor of any man. But I was with the firm when your father used to carry you in here in his arms.

HOWARD: I know that, Willy, but—

WILLY: Your father came to me the day you were born and asked me what I thought of the name of Howard, may he rest in peace.

HOWARD: I appreciate that, Willy, but there just is no spot here for you. If I had a spot I'd slam you right in, but I just don't have a single, solitary spot.

He looks for his lighter. Willy has picked it up and gives it to him. Pause.

130 **WILLY:** *(with increasing anger)* Howard, all I need to set my table is fifty dollars a week.

HOWARD: But where am I going to put you, kid?

WILLY: Look, it isn't a question of whether I can sell merchandise, is it?

HOWARD: No, but it's a business, kid, and everybody's gotta pull his own weight.

WILLY: *(desperately)* Just let me tell you a story, Howard—

135 **HOWARD:** 'Cause you gotta admit, business is business.

WILLY: *(angrily)* Business is definitely business, but just listen for a minute. You don't understand this. When I was a boy—eighteen, nineteen—I was already on the road. And there was a question in my mind as to whether selling had a future for me. Because in those days I had a yearning to go to Alaska. See, there were three gold strikes in one month in Alaska, and I felt like going out. Just for the ride, you might say.

HOWARD: *(barely interested)* Don't say.

WILLY: Oh, yeah, my father lived many years in Alaska. He was an adventurous man. We've got quite a little streak of self-reliance in our family. I thought I'd go out with my older brother and try to locate him, and maybe settle in the North with the old man. And I was almost decided to go, when I met a salesman in the Parker House. His name was Dave Singleman. And he was eighty-four years old, and he'd drummed merchandise in thirty-one states. And old Dave, he'd go up to his room, y'understand, put on his green velvet slippers—I'll never forget—and pick up his phone and call the buyers, and without ever leaving his room, at the age of eighty-four, he made his living. And when I saw that, I realized that selling was the greatest career a man could want. 'Cause what could be more satisfying than to be able to go, at the age of eighty-four, into twenty or thirty different cities, and pick up a phone, and be remembered and loved and helped by so many different people? Do you know? when he died—and by the way he died the death of a salesman, in his green velvet slippers in the smoker of the New York, New Haven and Hartford, going into Boston—when he died, hundreds of salesmen and buyers were at his funeral. Things were sad on a lotta trains for months after that. *(He stands up. Howard has not looked at him.)* In those days there was personality in it, Howard. There was respect, and comradeship, and gratitude in it. Today, it's all cut and dried, and there's no chance for bringing friendship to bear—or personality. You see what I mean? They don't know me any more.

HOWARD: *(moving away, to the right)* That's just the thing, Willy.

140 **WILLY:** If I had forty dollars a week—that's all I'd need. Forty dollars, Howard.

HOWARD: Kid, I can't take blood from a stone, I—

WILLY: *(desperation is on him now)* Howard, the year Al Smith was nominated, your father came to me and—

HOWARD: *(starting to go off)* I've got to see some people, kid.
WILLY: *(stopping him)* I'm talking about your father! There were promises made across this desk! You mustn't tell me you've got people to see—I put thirty-four years into this firm, Howard, and now I can't pay my insurance! You can't eat the orange and throw the peel away—a man is not a piece of fruit! *(After a pause.)* Now pay attention. Your father—in 1928 I had a big year. I averaged a hundred and seventy dollars a week in commissions.
145 HOWARD: *(impatiently)* Now, Willy, you never averaged—
WILLY: *(banging his hand on the desk)* I averaged a hundred and seventy dollars a week in the year of 1928! And your father came to me—or rather, I was in the office here—it was right over this desk—and he put his hand on my shoulder—
HOWARD: *(getting up)* You'll have to excuse me, Willy, I gotta see some people. Pull yourself together. *(Going out.)* I'll be back in a little while.

On Howard's exit, the light on his chair grows very bright and strange.

WILLY: Pull myself together! What the hell did I say to him? My God, I was yelling at him! How could I! *(Willy breaks off, staring at the light, which occupies the chair, animating it. He approaches this chair, standing across the desk from it.)* Frank, Frank, don't you remember what you told me that time? How you put your hand on my shoulder, and Frank . . . *(He leans on the desk and as he speaks the dead man's name he accidentally switches on the recorder, and instantly—)*
HOWARD'S SON: ". . . of New York is Albany. The capital of Ohio is Cincinnati, the capital of Rhode Island is . . ." *(The recitation continues.)*
150 WILLY: *(leaping away with fright, shouting)* Ha! Howard! Howard! Howard!
HOWARD: *(rushing in)* What happened?
WILLY: *(pointing at the machine, which continues nasally, childishly, with the capital cities)* Shut it off! Shut it off!
HOWARD: *(pulling the plug out)* Look, Willy . . .
WILLY: *(pressing his hands to his eyes)* I gotta get myself some coffee. I'll get some coffee . . .

Willy starts to walk out. Howard stops him.

155 HOWARD: *(rolling up the cord)* Willy, look . . .
WILLY: I'll go to Boston.
HOWARD: Willy, you can't go to Boston for us.
WILLY: Why can't I go?
HOWARD: I don't want you to represent us. I've been meaning to tell you for a long time now.
160 WILLY: Howard, are you firing me?
HOWARD: I think you need a good long rest, Willy.

WILLY: Howard—
HOWARD: And when you feel better, come back, and we'll see if we can work something out.
WILLY: But I gotta earn money, Howard. I'm in no position—
165 HOWARD: Where are your sons? Why don't your sons give you a hand?
WILLY: They're working on a very big deal.
HOWARD: This is no time for false pride, Willy. You go to your sons and tell them that you're tired. You've got two great boys, haven't you?
WILLY: Oh, no question, no question, but in the meantime . . .
HOWARD: Then that's that, heh?
170 WILLY: All right, I'll go to Boston tomorrow.
HOWARD: No, no.
WILLY: I can't throw myself on my sons. I'm not a cripple!
HOWARD: Look, kid, I'm busy this morning.
WILLY: *(grasping Howard's arm)* Howard, you've got to let me go to Boston!
175 HOWARD: *(hard, keeping himself under control)* I've got a line of people to see this morning. Sit down, take five minutes, and pull yourself together, and then go home, will ya? I need the office, Willy. *(He starts to go, turns, remembering the recorder, starts to push off the table holding the recorder.)* Oh, yeah. Whenever you can this week, stop by and drop off the samples. You'll feel better, Willy, and then come back and we'll talk. Pull yourself together, kid, there's people outside.

Howard exits, pushing the table off left. Willy stares into space, exhausted. Now the music is heard—Ben's music—first distantly, then closer, closer. As Willy speaks, Ben enters from the right. He carries valise and umbrella.

WILLY: Oh, Ben, how did you do it? What is the answer? Did you wind up the Alaska deal already?
BEN: Doesn't take much time if you know what you're doing. Just a short business trip. Boarding ship in an hour. Wanted to say good-by.
WILLY: Ben, I've got to talk to you.
BEN: *(glancing at his watch)* Haven't the time, William.
180 WILLY: *(crossing the apron to Ben)* Ben, nothing's working out. I don't know what to do.
BEN: Now, look here, William. I've bought timberland in Alaska and I need a man to look after things for me.
WILLY: God, timberland! Me and my boys in those grand outdoors!
BEN: You've a new continent at your doorstep, William. Get out of these cities, they're full of talk and time payments and courts of law. Screw on your fists and you can fight for a fortune up there.
WILLY: Yes, yes! Linda! Linda!

Linda enters as of old, with the wash.

185 LINDA: Oh, you're back?
BEN: I haven't much time.
WILLY: No, wait! Linda, he's got a proposition for me in Alaska.

LINDA: But you've got—*(To Ben.)* He's got a beautiful job here.
WILLY: But in Alaska, kid, I could—
190 LINDA: You're doing well enough, Willy!
BEN: *(to Linda)* Enough for what, my dear?
LINDA: *(frightened of Ben and angry at him)* Don't say those things to him! Enough to be happy right here, right now. *(To Willy, while Ben laughs.)* Why must everybody conquer the world? You're well liked, and the boys love you, and someday—*(to Ben)*—why, old man Wagner told him just the other day that if he keeps it up he'll be a member of the firm, didn't he, Willy?
WILLY: Sure, sure. I am building something with this firm, Ben, and if a man is building something he must be on the right track, mustn't he?
BEN: What are you building? Lay your hand on it. Where is it?
195 WILLY: *(hesitantly)* That's true, Linda, there's nothing.
LINDA: Why? *(To Ben.)* There's a man eighty-four years old—
WILLY: That's right, Ben, that's right. When I look at that man I say, what is there to worry about?
BEN: Bah!
WILLY: It's true, Ben. All he has to do is go into any city, pick up the phone, and he's making his living and you know why?
200 BEN: *(picking up his valise)* I've got to go.
WILLY: *(holding Ben back)* Look at this boy!

Biff, in his high school sweater, enters carrying suitcase. Happy carries Biff's shoulder guards, gold helmet, and football pants.

WILLY: Without a penny to his name, three great universities are begging for him, and from there the sky's the limit, because it's not what you do, Ben. It's who you know and the smile on your face! It's contacts, Ben, contacts! The whole wealth of Alaska passes over the lunch table at the Commodore Hotel, and that's the wonder, the wonder of this country, that a man can end with diamonds here on the basis of being liked! *(He turns to Biff.)* And that's why when you get out on that field today it's important. Because thousands of people will be rooting for you and loving you. *(To Ben, who has again begun to leave.)* And Ben! when he walks into a business office his name will sound out like a bell and all the doors will open to him! I've seen it, Ben, I've seen it a thousand times! You can't feel it with your hand like timber, but it's there!
BEN: Good-by, William.
WILLY: Ben, am I right? Don't you think I'm right? I value your advice.
205 BEN: There's a new continent at your doorstep, William. You could walk out rich. Rich. *(He is gone.)*
WILLY: We'll do it here, Ben! You hear me? We're gonna do it here!

Young Bernard rushes in. The gay music of the boys is heard.

BERNARD: Oh, gee, I was afraid you left already!

WILLY: Why? What time is it?
BERNARD: It's half-past one!
210 WILLY: Well, come on, everybody! Ebbets Field[2] next stop! Where's the pennants? *(He rushes through the wall-line of the kitchen and out into the livingroom.)*
LINDA: *(to Biff)* Did you pack fresh underwear?
BIFF: *(who has been limbering up)* I want to go!
BERNARD: Biff, I'm carrying your helmet, ain't I?
HAPPY: No, I'm carrying the helmet.
215 BERNARD: Oh, Biff, you promised me.
HAPPY: I'm carrying the helmet.
BERNARD: How am I going to get in the locker room?
LINDA: Let him carry the shoulder guards. *(She puts her coat and hat on in the kitchen.)*
BERNARD: Can I, Biff? 'Cause I told everybody I'm going to be in the locker room.
220 HAPPY: In Ebbets Field it's the clubhouse.
BERNARD: I meant the clubhouse. Biff!
HAPPY: Biff!
BIFF: *(grandly, after a slight pause)* Let him carry the shoulder guards.
HAPPY: *(as he gives Bernard the shoulder guards)* Stay close to us now.

Willy rushes in with the pennants.

225 WILLY: *(handing them out)* Everybody wave when Biff comes out on the field. *(Happy and Bernard run off.)* You set now, boy?

The music has died away.

BIFF: Ready to go, Pop. Every muscle is ready.
WILLY: *(at the edge of the apron)* You realize what this means?
BIFF: That's right, Pop.
WILLY: *(feeling Biff's muscles)* You're comin' home this afternoon captain of the All-Scholastic Championship Team of the City of New York.
230 BIFF: I got it, Pop. And remember, pal, when I take off my helmet, that touchdown is for you.
WILLY: Let's go! *(He is starting out, with his arm around Biff, when Charley enters, as of old, in knickers.)* I got no room for you, Charley.
CHARLEY: Room? For what?
WILLY: In the car.
CHARLEY: You goin' for a ride? I wanted to shoot some casino.
235 WILLY: *(furiously)* Casino! *(Incredulously.)* Don't you realize what today is?
LINDA: Oh, he knows, Willy. He's just kidding you.
WILLY: That's nothing to kid about!
CHARLEY: No, Linda, what's goin' on?

---

[2] The home park of the Brooklyn Dodgers.

LINDA: He's playing in Ebbets Field.
CHARLEY: Baseball in this weather?
WILLY: Don't talk to him. Come on, come on! *(He is pushing them out.)*
CHARLEY: Wait a minute, didn't you hear the news?
WILLY: What?
CHARLEY: Don't you listen to the radio? Ebbets Field just blew up.
WILLY: You go to hell! *(Charley laughs. Pushing them out.)* Come on, come on! We're late.
CHARLEY: *(as they go)* Knock a homer, Biff, knock a homer!
WILLY: *(the last to leave, turning to Charley)* I don't think that was funny, Charley. This is the greatest day of his life.
CHARLEY: Willy, when are you going to grow up?
WILLY: Yeah, heh? When this game is over, Charley, you'll be laughing out of the other side of your face. They'll be calling him another Red Grange.[3] Twenty-five thousand a year.
CHARLEY: *(kidding)* Is that so?
WILLY: Yeah, that's so.
CHARLEY: Well, then, I'm sorry, Willy. But tell me something.
WILLY: What?
CHARLEY: Who is Red Grange?
WILLY: Put up your hands. Goddam you, put up your hands!

Charley, chuckling, shakes his head and walks away, around the left corner of the stage. Willy follows him. The music rises to a mocking frenzy.

WILLY: Who the hell do you think you are, better than everybody else? You don't know everything, you big, ignorant, stupid . . . Put up your hands!

Light rises, on the right side of the forestage, on a small table in the reception room of Charley's office. Traffic sounds are heard. Bernard, now mature, sits whistling to himself. A pair of tennis rackets and an overnight bag are on the floor beside him.

WILLY: *(offstage)* What are you walking away for? Don't walk away! If you're going to say something say it to my face! I know you laugh at me behind my back. You'll laugh out of the other side of your goddam face after this game. Touchdown! Touchdown! Eighty thousand people! Touchdown! Right between the goal posts.

Bernard is a quiet, earnest, but self-assured young man. Willy's voice is coming from right upstage now. Bernard lowers his feet off the table and listens. Jenny, his father's secretary, enters.

JENNY: *(distressed)* Say, Bernard, will you go out in the hall?

---

[3] Red (Harold Edward) Grange (1903–1991)—U.S. football player. A running back for the New York Yankees football team and the Chicago Bears, Grange was elected to the Football Hall of Fame in 1963.

BERNARD: What is that noise? Who is it?
JENNY: Mr. Loman. He just got off the elevator.
BERNARD: *(getting up)* Who's he arguing with?
JENNY: Nobody. There's nobody with him. I can't deal with him any more, and your father gets all upset everytime he comes. I've got a lot of typing to do, and your father's waiting to sign it. Will you see him?
WILLY: *(entering)* Touchdown! Touch—*(He sees Jenny.)* Jenny, Jenny, good to see you. How're ya? Workin'? Or still honest?
JENNY: Fine. How've you been feeling?
WILLY: Not much any more, Jenny. Ha, ha! *(He is surprised to see the rackets.)*
BERNARD: Hello, Uncle Willy.
WILLY: *(almost shocked)* Bernard! Well, look who's here! *(He comes quickly, guiltily, to Bernard and warmly shakes his hand.)*
BERNARD: How are you? Good to see you.
WILLY: What are you doing here?
BERNARD: Oh, just stopped by to see Pop. Get off my feet till my train leaves. I'm going to Washington in a few minutes.
WILLY: Is he in?
BERNARD: Yes, he's in his office with the accountant. Sit down.
WILLY: *(sitting down)* What're you going to do in Washington?
BERNARD: Oh, just a case I've got there, Willy.
WILLY: That so? *(indicating the rackets)* You going to play tennis there?
BERNARD: I'm staying with a friend who's got a court.
WILLY: Don't say. His own tennis court. Must be fine people, I bet.
BERNARD: They are, very nice. Dad tells me Biff's in town.
WILLY: *(with a big smile)* Yeah, Biff's in. Working on a very big deal, Bernard.
BERNARD: What's Biff doing?
WILLY: Well, he's been doing very big things in the West. But he decided to establish himself here. Very big. We're having dinner. Did I hear your wife had a boy?
BERNARD: That's right. Our second.
WILLY: Two boys! What do you know!
BERNARD: What kind of a deal has Biff got?
WILLY: Well, Bill Oliver—very big sporting-goods man—he wants Biff very badly. Called him in from the West. Long distance, carte blanche, special deliveries. Your friends have their own private tennis court?
BERNARD: You still with the old firm, Willy?
WILLY: *(after a pause)* I'm—I'm overjoyed to see how you made the grade, Bernard, overjoyed. It's an encouraging thing to see a young man really—really—Looks very good for Biff—very—*(He breaks off, then.)* Bernard—*(He is so full of emotion, he breaks off again.)*
BERNARD: What is it, Willy?
WILLY: *(small and alone)* What—what's the secret?

290 **BERNARD:** What secret?
WILLY: How—how did you? Why didn't he ever catch on?
BERNARD: I wouldn't know that, Willy.
WILLY: *(confidentially, desperately)* You were his friend, his boyhood friend. There's something I don't understand about it. His life ended after that Ebbets Field game. From the age of seventeen nothing good ever happened to him.
BERNARD: He never trained himself for anything.
295 **WILLY:** But he did, he did. After high school he took so many correspondence courses. Radio mechanics; television; God knows what, and never made the slightest mark.
BERNARD: *(taking off his glasses)* Willy, do you want to talk candidly?
WILLY: *(rising, faces Bernard)* I regard you as a very brilliant man, Bernard. I value your advice.
BERNARD: Oh, the hell with the advice, Willy. I couldn't advise you. There's just one thing I've always wanted to ask you. When he was supposed to graduate, and the math teacher flunked him—
WILLY: Oh, that son-of-a-bitch ruined his life.
300 **BERNARD:** Yeah, but, Willy, all he had to do was go to summer school and make up that subject.
WILLY: That's right, that's right.
BERNARD: Did you tell him not to go to summer school?
WILLY: Me? I begged him to go. I ordered him to go!
BERNARD: Then why wouldn't he go?
305 **WILLY:** Why? Why! Bernard, that question has been trailing me like a ghost for the last fifteen years. He flunked the subject, and laid down and died like a hammer hit him!
BERNARD: Take it easy, kid.
WILLY: Let me talk to you—I got nobody to talk to. Bernard, Bernard, was it my fault? Y'see? It keeps going around in my mind, maybe I did something to him. I got nothing to give him.
BERNARD: Don't take it so hard.
WILLY: Why did he lay down? What is the story there? You were his friend!
310 **BERNARD:** Willy, I remember, it was June, and our grades came out. And he'd flunked math.
WILLY: That son-of-a-bitch!
BERNARD: No, it wasn't right then. Biff just got very angry, I remember, and he was ready to enroll in summer school.
WILLY: *(surprised)* He was?
BERNARD: He wasn't beaten by it at all. But then, Willy, he disappeared from the block for almost a month. And I got the idea that he'd gone up to New England to see you. Did he have a talk with you then?

Willy stares in silence.

315 **BERNARD:** Willy?

WILLY: *(with a strong edge of resentment in his voice)* Yeah, he came to Boston. What about it?
BERNARD: Well, just that when he came back—I'll never forget this, it always mystifies me. Because I'd thought so well of Biff, even though he'd always taken advantage of me. I loved him, Willy, y'know? And he came back after that month and took his sneakers—remember those sneakers with "University of Virginia" printed on them? He was so proud of those, wore them every day. And he took them down in the cellar, and burned them up in the furnace. We had a fist fight. It lasted at least half an hour. Just the two of us, punching each other down the cellar, and crying right through it. I've often thought of how strange it was that I knew he'd given up his life. What happened in Boston, Willy?

Willy looks at him as at an intruder.

BERNARD: I just bring it up because you asked me.
WILLY: *(angrily)* Nothing. What do you mean, "What happened?" What's that got to do with anything?
BERNARD: Well, don't get sore.
WILLY: What are you trying to do, blame it on me? If a boy lays down is that my fault?
BERNARD: Now, Willy, don't get—
WILLY: Well, don't—don't talk to me that way! What does that mean, "What happened?"

Charley enters. He is in his vest, and he carries a bottle of bourbon.

CHARLEY: Hey, you're going to miss that train. *(He waves the bottle.)*
BERNARD: Yeah, I'm going. *(He takes the bottle.)* Thanks, Pop. *(He picks up his rackets and bag.)* Good-by, Willy, and don't worry about it. You know, "If at first you don't succeed . . ."
WILLY: Yes, I believe in that.
BERNARD: But sometimes, Willy, it's better for a man just to walk away.
WILLY: Walk away?
BERNARD: That's right.
WILLY: But if you can't walk away?
BERNARD: *(after a slight pause)* I guess that's when it's tough. *(Extending his hand.)* Good-by, Willy.
WILLY: *(shaking Bernard's hand)* Good-by, boy.
CHARLEY: *(an arm on Bernard's shoulder)* How do you like this kid? Gonna argue a case in front of the Supreme Court.
BERNARD: *(protesting)* Pop!
WILLY: *(genuinely shocked, pained, and happy)* No! The Supreme Court!
BERNARD: I gotta run, 'By, Dad!
CHARLEY: Knock 'em dead, Bernard!

Bernard goes off.

WILLY: *(as Charley takes out his wallet)* The Supreme Court! And he didn't even mention it!

CHARLEY: *(counting out money on the desk)* He don't have to—he's gonna do it.
WILLY: And you never told him what to do, did you? You never took any interest in him.
CHARLEY: My salvation is that I never took any interest in anything. There's some money—fifty dollars. I got an accountant inside.
WILLY: Charley, look . . . *(With difficulty.)* I got my insurance to pay. If you can manage it—I need a hundred and ten dollars.

Charley doesn't reply for a moment; merely stops moving.

WILLY: I'd draw it from my bank but Linda would know, and I . . .
CHARLEY: Sit down, Willy.
WILLY: *(moving toward the chair)* I'm keeping an account of everything, remember. I'll pay every penny back. *(He sits.)*
CHARLEY: Now listen to me, Willy.
WILLY: I want you to know I appreciate . . .
CHARLEY: *(sitting down on the table)* Willy, what're you doin'? What the hell is goin' on in your head?
WILLY: Why? I'm simply . . .
CHARLEY: I offered you a job. You can make fifty dollars a week. And I won't send you on the road.
WILLY: I've got a job.
CHARLEY: Without pay? What kind of a job is a job without pay? *(He rises.)* Now, look, kid, enough is enough. I'm no genius but I know when I'm being insulted.
WILLY: Insulted!
CHARLEY: Why don't you want to work for me?
WILLY: What's the matter with you? I've got a job.
CHARLEY: Then what're you walkin' in here every week for?
WILLY: *(getting up)* Well, if you don't want me to walk in here—
CHARLEY: I am offering you a job.
WILLY: I don't want your goddam job!
CHARLEY: When the hell are you going to grow up?
WILLY: *(furiously)* You big ignoramus, if you say that to me again I'll rap you one! I don't care how big you are! *(He's ready to fight.)*

Pause.

CHARLEY: *(kindly, going to him)* How much do you need, Willy?
WILLY: Charley, I'm strapped. I'm strapped. I don't know what to do. I was just fired.
CHARLEY: Howard fired you?
WILLY: That snotnose. Imagine that? I named him. I named him Howard.
CHARLEY: Willy, when're you gonna realize that them things don't mean anything? You named him Howard, but you can't sell that. The only thing you got in this world is what you can sell. And the funny thing is that you're a salesman, and you don't know that.

WILLY: I've always tried to think otherwise, I guess. I always felt that if a man was impressive, and well liked, that nothing—
CHARLEY: Why must everybody like you? Who liked J. P. Morgan?[4] Was he impressive? In a Turkish bath he'd look like a butcher. But with his pockets on he was very well liked. Now listen, Willy, I know you don't like me, and nobody can say I'm in love with you, but I'll give you a job because—just for the hell of it, put it that way. Now what do you say?
WILLY: I—I just can't work for you, Charley.
370 CHARLEY: What're you, jealous of me?
WILLY: I can't work for you, that's all, don't ask me why.
CHARLEY: *(angered, takes out more bills)* You been jealous of me all your life, you damned fool! Here, pay your insurance. *(He puts the money in Willy's hand.)*
WILLY: I'm keeping strict accounts.
CHARLEY: I've got some work to do. Take care of yourself. And pay your insurance.
375 WILLY: *(moving to the right)* Funny, y'know? After all the highways, and the trains, and the appointments, and the years, you end up worth more dead than alive.
CHARLEY: Willy, nobody's worth nothin' dead. *(After a slight pause.)* Did you hear what I said?

Willy stands still, dreaming.

CHARLEY: Willy!
WILLY: Apologize to Bernard for me when you see him. I didn't mean to argue with him. He's a fine boy. They're all fine boys, and they'll end up big—all of them. Someday they'll all play tennis together. Wish me luck, Charley. He saw Bill Oliver today.
CHARLEY: Good luck.
380 WILLY: *(on the verge of tears)* Charley, you're the only friend I got. Isn't that a remarkable thing? *(He goes out.)*
CHARLEY: Jesus!

Charley stares after him a moment and follows. All light blacks out. Suddenly raucous music is heard, and a red glow rises behind the screen at right. Stanley, a young waiter, appears, carrying a table, followed by Happy, who is carrying two chairs.

STANLEY: *(putting the table down)* That's all right, Mr. Loman, I can handle it myself. *(He turns and takes the chairs from Happy and places them at the table.)*
HAPPY: *(glancing around)* Oh, this is better.
STANLEY: Sure, in the front there you're in the middle of all kinds a noise. Whenever you got a party, Mr. Loman, you just tell me and

---

[4] John Pierpont Morgan (1837–1913)—U.S. financier.

I'll put you back here. Y'know, there's a lotta people they don't like it private, because when they go out they like to see a lotta action around them because they're sick and tired to stay in the house by theirself. But I know you, you ain't from Hackensack. You know what I mean?

385 HAPPY: *(sitting down)* So, how's it coming, Stanley?

STANLEY: Ah, it's a dog's life. I only wish during the war they'd a took me in the Army. I coulda been dead by now.

HAPPY: My brother's back, Stanley.

STANLEY: Oh, he come back, heh? From the Far West.

HAPPY: Yeah, big cattle man, my brother, so treat him right. And my father's coming too.

390 STANLEY: Oh, your father too!

HAPPY: You got a couple of nice lobsters?

STANLEY: Hundred per cent, big.

HAPPY: I want them with the claws.

STANLEY: Don't worry, I don't give you no mice. *(Happy laughs.)* How about some wine? It'll put a head on the meal.

395 HAPPY: No. You remember, Stanley, that recipe I brought you from overseas? With the champagne in it?

STANLEY: Oh, yeah, sure. I still got it tacked up yet in the kitchen. But that'll have to cost a buck apiece anyways.

HAPPY: That's all right.

STANLEY: What'd you, hit a number or somethin'?

HAPPY: No, it's a little celebration. My brother is—I think he pulled off a big deal today. I think we're going into business together.

400 STANLEY: Great! That's the best for you. Because a family business, you know what I mean?—that's the best.

HAPPY: That's what I think.

STANLEY: 'Cause what's the difference? Somebody steals? It's in the family. Know what I mean? *(Sotto voce.)* Like this bartender here. The boss is goin' crazy what kinda leak he's got in the cash register. You put it in but it don't come out.

HAPPY: *(raising his head)* Sh!

STANLEY: What?

405 HAPPY: You notice I wasn't lookin' right or left, was I?

STANLEY: No.

HAPPY: And my eyes are closed.

STANLEY: So what's the—

HAPPY: Strudel's comin'.

410 STANLEY: *(catching on, looks around)* Ah, no, there's no—

He breaks off as a furred, lavishly dressed Girl enters and sits at the next table. Both follow her with their eyes.

STANLEY: Geez, how'd ya know?

HAPPY: I got radar or something. *(Staring directly at her profile.)* Oooooooo . . . Stanley.

STANLEY: I think that's for you, Mr. Loman.
HAPPY: Look at that mouth. Oh, God. And the binoculars.
415 STANLEY: Geez, you got a life, Mr. Loman.
HAPPY: Wait on her.
STANLEY: *(going to The Girl's table)* Would you like a menu, ma'am?
GIRL: I'm expecting someone, but I'd like a—
HAPPY: Why don't you bring her—excuse me, miss, do you mind? I sell champagne, and I'd like you to try my brand. Bring her a champagne, Stanley.
420 GIRL: That's awfully nice of you.
HAPPY: Don't mention it. It's all company money. *(He laughs.)*
GIRL: That's a charming product to be selling, isn't it?
HAPPY: Oh, gets to be like everything else. Selling is selling, y'know.
GIRL: I suppose.
425 HAPPY: You don't happen to sell, do you?
GIRL: No, I don't sell.
HAPPY: Would you object to a compliment from a stranger? You ought to be on a magazine cover.
GIRL: *(looking at him a little archly)* I have been.

Stanley comes in with a glass of champagne.

HAPPY: What'd I say before, Stanley? You see? She's a cover girl.
430 STANLEY: Oh, I could see, I could see.
HAPPY: *(to The Girl)* What magazine?
GIRL: Oh, a lot of them. *(She takes the drink.)* Thank you.
HAPPY: You know what they say in France, don't you? "Champagne is the drink of the complexion"—Hya, Biff!

Biff has entered and sits with Happy.

BIFF: Hello, kid. Sorry I'm late.
435 HAPPY: I just got here. Uh, Miss—?
GIRL: Forsythe.
HAPPY: Miss Forsythe, this is my brother.
BIFF: Is Dad here?
HAPPY: His name is Biff. You might've heard of him. Great football player.
440 GIRL: Really? What team?
HAPPY: Are you familiar with football?
GIRL: No, I'm afraid I'm not.
HAPPY: Biff is quarterback with the New York Giants.
GIRL: Well, that is nice, isn't it? *(She drinks.)*
445 HAPPY: Good health.
GIRL: I'm happy to meet you.
HAPPY: That's my name. Hap. It's really Harold, but at West Point they called me Happy.
GIRL: *(now really impressed)* Oh, I see. How do you do? *(She turns her profile.)*
BIFF: Isn't Dad coming?

450 **HAPPY:** You want her?
BIFF: Oh, I could never make that.
HAPPY: I remember the time that idea would never come into your head. Where's the old confidence, Biff?
BIFF: I just saw Oliver—
HAPPY: Wait a minute. I've got to see that old confidence again. Do you want her? She's on call.
455 **BIFF:** Oh, no. *(He turns to look at The Girl.)*
HAPPY: I'm telling you. Watch this. *(Turning to The Girl.)* Honey? *(She turns to him.)* Are you busy?
GIRL: Well, I am . . . but I could make a phone call.
HAPPY: Do that, will you, honey? And see if you can get a friend. We'll be here for a while. Biff is one of the greatest football players in the country.
GIRL: *(standing up)* Well, I'm certainly happy to meet you.
460 **HAPPY:** Come back soon.
GIRL: I'll try.
HAPPY: Don't try, honey, try hard.

The Girl exits. Stanley follows, shaking his head in bewildered admiration.

HAPPY: Isn't that a shame now? A beautiful girl like that? That's why I can't get married. There's not a good woman in a thousand. New York is loaded with them, kid!
BIFF: Hap, look—
465 **HAPPY:** I told you she was on call!
BIFF: *(strangely unnerved)* Cut it out, will ya? I want to say something to you.
HAPPY: Did you see Oliver?
BIFF: I saw him all right. Now look, I want to tell Dad a couple of things and I want you to help me.
HAPPY: What? Is he going to back you?
470 **BIFF:** Are you crazy? You're out of your goddam head, you know that?
HAPPY: Why? What happened?
BIFF: *(breathlessly)* I did a terrible thing today, Hap. It's been the strangest day I ever went through. I'm all numb, I swear.
HAPPY: You mean he wouldn't see you?
BIFF: Well, I waited six hours for him, see? All day. Kept sending my name in. Even tried to date his secretary so she'd get me to him, but no soap.
475 **HAPPY:** Because you're not showin' the old confidence, Biff. He remembered you, didn't he?
BIFF: *(stopping Happy with a gesture)* Finally, about five o'clock, he comes out. Didn't remember who I was or anything. I felt like such an idiot, Hap.
HAPPY: Did you tell him my Florida idea?
BIFF: He walked away. I saw him for one minute. I got so mad I could've torn the walls down! How the hell did I ever get the idea I was a salesman there? I even believed myself that I'd been a salesman for

him! And then he gave me one look and—I realized what a ridiculous lie my whole life has been! We've been talking in a dream for fifteen years. I was a shipping clerk.

HAPPY: What'd you do?

BIFF: *(with great tension and wonder)* Well, he left, see. And the secretary went out. I was all alone in the waiting-room. I don't know what came over me, Hap. The next thing I know I'm in his office—paneled walls, everything. I can't explain it. I—Hap, I took his fountain pen.

HAPPY: Geez, did he catch you?

BIFF: I ran out. I ran down all eleven flights. I ran and ran and ran.

HAPPY: That was an awful dumb—what'd you do that for?

BIFF: *(agonized)* I don't know, I just—wanted to take something, I don't know. You gotta help me, Hap. I'm gonna tell Pop.

HAPPY: You crazy? What for?

BIFF: Hap, he's got to understand that I'm not the man somebody lends that kind of money to. He thinks I've been spiting him all these years and it's eating him up.

HAPPY: That's just it. You tell him something nice.

BIFF: I can't.

HAPPY: Say you got a lunch date with Oliver tomorrow.

BIFF: So what do I do tomorrow?

HAPPY: You leave the house tomorrow and come back at night and say Oliver is thinking it over. And he thinks it over for a couple of weeks, and gradually it fades away and nobody's the worse.

BIFF: But it'll go on forever!

HAPPY: Dad is never so happy as when he's looking forward to something!

Willy enters.

HAPPY: Hello, scout!

WILLY: Gee, I haven't been here in years!

Stanley has followed Willy in and sets a chair for him. Stanley starts off but Happy stops him.

HAPPY: Stanley!

Stanley stands by, waiting for an order.

BIFF: *(going to Willy with guilt, as to an invalid)* Sit down, Pop. You want a drink?

WILLY: Sure, I don't mind.

BIFF: Let's get a load on.

WILLY: You look worried.

BIFF: N-no. *(To Stanley.)* Scotch all around. Make it doubles.

STANLEY: Doubles, right. *(He goes.)*

WILLY: You had a couple already, didn't you?

BIFF: Just a couple, yeah.

505 **WILLY:** Well, what happened, boy? *(Nodding affirmatively, with a smile.)* Everything go all right?
BIFF: *(takes a breath, then reaches out and grasps Willy's hand)* Pal . . . *(He is smiling bravely, and Willy is smiling too.)* I had an experience today.
HAPPY: Terrific, Pop.
WILLY: That so? What happened?
BIFF: *(high, slightly alcoholic, above the earth)* I'm going to tell you everything from first to last. It's been a strange day. *(Silence. He looks around, composes himself as best he can, but his breath keeps breaking the rhythm of his voice.)* I had to wait quite a while for him, and—
510 **WILLY:** Oliver?
BIFF: Yeah, Oliver. All day, as a matter of cold fact. And a lot of—instances—facts, Pop, facts about my life came back to me. Who was it, Pop? Who ever said I was a salesman with Oliver?
WILLY: Well, you were.
BIFF: No, Dad, I was a shipping clerk.
WILLY: But you were practically—
515 **BIFF:** *(with determination)* Dad, I don't know who said it first, but I was never a salesman for Bill Oliver.
WILLY: What're you talking about?
BIFF: Let's hold on to the facts tonight, Pop. We're not going to get anywhere bullin' around. I was a shipping clerk.
WILLY: *(angrily)* All right, now listen to me—
BIFF: Why don't you let me finish?
520 **WILLY:** I'm not interested in stories about the past or any crap of that kind because the woods are burning, boys, you understand? There's a big blaze going on all around. I was fired today.
BIFF: *(shocked)* How could you be?
WILLY: I was fired, and I'm looking for a little good news to tell your mother, because the woman has waited and the woman has suffered. The gist of it is that I haven't got a story left in my head, Biff. So don't give me a lecture about facts and aspects. I am not interested. Now what've you got to say to me?

Stanley enters with three drinks. They wait until he leaves.

WILLY: Did you see Oliver?
BIFF: Jesus, Dad!
525 **WILLY:** You mean you didn't go up there?
HAPPY: Sure he went up there.
BIFF: I did. I—saw him. How could they fire you?
WILLY: *(on the edge of his chair)* What kind of a welcome did he give you?
BIFF: He won't even let you work on commission?
530 **WILLY:** I'm out! *(Driving.)* So tell me, he gave you a warm welcome?
HAPPY: Sure, Pop, sure!

Biff: *(driven)* Well, it was kind of—
Willy: I was wondering if he'd remember you. *(To Happy.)* Imagine, man doesn't see him for ten, twelve years and gives him that kind of a welcome!
Happy: Damn right!
Biff: *(trying to return to the offensive)* Pop, look—
Willy: You know why he remembered you, don't you? Because you impressed him in those days.
Biff: Let's talk quietly and get this down to the facts, huh?
Willy: *(as though Biff had been interrupting)* Well, what happened? It's great news, Biff. Did he take you into his office or'd you talk in the waiting-room?
Biff: Well, he came in, see, and—
Willy: *(with a big smile)* What'd he say? Betcha he threw his arm around you.
Biff: Well, he kinda—
Willy: He's a fine man. *(To Happy.)* Very hard man to see, y'know.
Happy: *(agreeing)* Oh, I know.
Willy: *(to Biff)* Is that where you had the drinks?
Biff: Yeah, he gave me a couple of—no, no!
Happy: *(cutting in)* He told him my Florida idea.
Willy: Don't interrupt. *(To Biff.)* How'd he react to the Florida idea?
Biff: Dad, will you give me a minute to explain?
Willy: I've been waiting for you to explain since I sat down here! What happened? He took you into his office and what?
Biff: Well—I talked. And—and he listened, see.
Willy: Famous for the way he listens, y'know. What was his answer?
Biff: His answer was—*(He breaks off, suddenly angry.)* Dad, you're not letting me tell you what I want to tell you!
Willy: *(accusing, angered)* You didn't see him, did you?
Biff: I did see him!
Willy: What'd you insult him or something? You insulted him, didn't you?
Biff: Listen, will you let me out of it, will you just let me out of it!
Happy: What the hell!
Willy: Tell me what happened!
Biff: *(to Happy)* I can't talk to him!

A single trumpet note jars the ear. The light of green leaves stains the house, which holds the air of night and a dream. Young Bernard enters and knocks on the door of the house.

Young Bernard: *(frantically)* Mrs. Loman, Mrs. Loman!
Happy: Tell him what happened!
Biff: *(to Happy)* Shut up and leave me alone!
Willy: No, no! You had to go and flunk math!
Biff: What math? What're you talking about?

565 **YOUNG BERNARD:** Mrs. Loman, Mrs. Loman!

Linda appears in the house, as of old.

WILLY: *(wildly)* Math, math, math!
BIFF: Take it easy, Pop!
YOUNG BERNARD: Mrs. Loman!
WILLY: *(furiously)* If you hadn't flunked you'd've been set by now!
570 **BIFF:** Now, look, I'm gonna tell you what happened, and you're going to listen to me.
YOUNG BERNARD: Mrs. Loman!
BIFF: I waited six hours—
HAPPY: What the hell are you saying?
BIFF: I kept sending in my name but he wouldn't see me. So finally he . . . *(He continues unheard as light fades low on the restaurant.)*
575 **YOUNG BERNARD:** Biff flunked math!
LINDA: No!
YOUNG BERNARD: Birnbaum flunked him! They won't graduate him!
LINDA: But they have to. He's gotta go to the university. Where is he? Biff! Biff!
YOUNG BERNARD: No, he left. He went to Grand Central.
580 **LINDA:** Grand—You mean he went to Boston!
YOUNG BERNARD: Is Uncle Willy in Boston?
LINDA: Oh, maybe Willy can talk to the teacher. Oh, the poor, poor boy!

Light on house area snaps out.

BIFF: *(at the table, now audible, holding up a gold fountain pen)* . . . so I'm washed up with Oliver, you understand? Are you listening to me?
WILLY: *(at a loss)* Yeah, sure. If you hadn't flunked—
585 **BIFF:** Flunked what? What're you talking about?
WILLY: Don't blame everything on me! I didn't flunk math—you did! What pen?
HAPPY: That was awful dumb, Biff, a pen like that is worth—
WILLY: *(seeing the pen for the first time)* You took Oliver's pen?
BIFF: *(weakening)* Dad, I just explained it to you.
590 **WILLY:** You stole Bill Oliver's fountain pen!
BIFF: I didn't exactly steal it! That's just what I've been explaining to you!
HAPPY: He had it in his hand and just then Oliver walked in, so he got nervous and stuck it in his pocket!
WILLY: My God, Biff!
BIFF: I never intended to do it, Dad!
595 **OPERATOR'S VOICE:** Standish Arms, good evening!
WILLY: *(shouting)* I'm not in my room!
BIFF: *(frightened)* Dad, what's the matter? *(He and Happy stand up.)*
OPERATOR: Ringing Mr. Loman for you!
WILLY: I'm not there, stop it!

600 BIFF: *(horrified, gets down on one knee before Willy)* Dad, I'll make good, I'll make good. *(Willy tries to get to his feet. Biff holds him down.)* Sit down now.
WILLY: No, you're no good, you're no good for anything.
BIFF: I am, Dad, I'll find something else, you understand? Now don't worry about anything. *(He holds up Willy's face.)* Talk to me, Dad.
OPERATOR: Mr. Loman does not answer. Shall I page him?
WILLY: *(attempting to stand, as though to rush and silence the Operator)* No, no, no!
605 HAPPY: He'll strike something, Pop.
WILLY: No, no . . .
BIFF: *(desperately, standing over Willy)* Pop, listen! Listen to me! I'm telling you something good. Oliver talked to his partner about the Florida idea. You listening? He—he talked to his partner, and he came to me . . . I'm going to be all right, you hear? Dad, listen to me, he said it was just a question of the amount!
WILLY: Then you . . . got it?
HAPPY: He's gonna be terrific, Pop!
610 WILLY: *(trying to stand)* Then you got it, haven't you? You got it! You got it!
BIFF: *(agonized, holds Willy down)* No, no. Look, Pop. I'm supposed to have lunch with them tomorrow. I'm just telling you this so you'll know that I can still make an impression, Pop. And I'll make good somewhere, but I can't go tomorrow, see?
WILLY: Why not? You simply—
BIFF: But the pen, Pop!
WILLY: You give it to him and tell him it was an oversight!
615 HAPPY: Sure, have lunch tomorrow!
BIFF: I can't say that—
WILLY: You were doing a crossword puzzle and accidentally used his pen!
BIFF: Listen, kid, I took those balls years ago, now I walk in with his fountain pen? That clinches it, don't you see? I can't face him like that! I'll try elsewhere.
PAGE'S VOICE: Paging Mr. Loman!
620 WILLY: Don't you want to be anything?
BIFF: Pop, how can I go back?
WILLY: You don't want to be anything, is that what's behind it?
BIFF: *(now angry at Willy for not crediting his sympathy)* Don't take it that way! You think it was easy walking into that office after what I'd done to him? A team of horses couldn't have dragged me back to Bill Oliver!
WILLY: Then why'd you go?
625 BIFF: Why did I go? Why did I go? Look at you! Look at what's become of you!

Off left, The Woman laughs.

WILLY: Biff, you're going to go to that lunch tomorrow, or—
BIFF: I can't go. I've got no appointment!
HAPPY: Biff, for . . . !
WILLY: Are you spiting me?
630 BIFF: Don't take it that way! Goddammit!
WILLY: *(strikes Biff and falters away from the table)* You rotten little louse! Are you spiting me?
THE WOMAN: Someone's at the door, Willy!
BIFF: I'm no good, can't you see what I am?
HAPPY: *(separating them)* Hey, you're in a restaurant! Now cut it out, both of you! *(The Girls enter.)* Hello, girls, sit down.

The Woman laughs, off left.

635 MISS FORSYTHE: I guess we might as well. This is Letta.
THE WOMAN: Willy, are you going to wake up?
BIFF: *(ignoring Willy)* How're ya, miss, sit down. What do you drink?
MISS FORSYTHE: Letta might not be able to stay long.
LETTA: I gotta get up very early tomorrow. I got jury duty. I'm so excited! Were you fellows ever on a jury?
640 BIFF: No, but I been in front of them! *(The Girls laugh.)* This is my father.
LETTA: Isn't he cute? Sit down with us, Pop.
HAPPY: Sit him down, Biff!
BIFF: *(going to him)* Come on, slugger, drink us under the table. To hell with it! Come on, sit down, pal.

On Biff's last insistence, Willy is about to sit.

THE WOMAN: *(now urgently)* Willy, are you going to answer the door!

The Woman's call pulls Willy back. He starts right, befuddled.

645 BIFF: Hey, where are you going?
WILLY: Open the door.
BIFF: The door?
WILLY: The washroom . . . the door . . . where's the door?
BIFF: *(leading Willy to the left)* Just go straight down.

Willy moves left.

650 THE WOMAN: Willy, Willy, are you going to get up, get up, get up, get up?

Willy exits left.

LETTA: I think it's sweet you bring your daddy along.
MISS FORSYTHE: Oh, he isn't really your father!
BIFF: *(at left, turning to her resentfully)* Miss Forsythe, you've just seen a prince walk by. A fine, troubled prince. A hard-working, unappreciated prince. A pal, you understand? A good companion. Always for his boys.

LETTA: That's so sweet.
655 HAPPY: Well, girls, what's the program? We're wasting time. Come on, Biff. Gather round. Where would you like to go?
BIFF: Why don't you do something for him?
HAPPY: Me!
BIFF: Don't you give a damn for him, Hap?
HAPPY: What're you talking about? I'm the one who—
660 BIFF: I sense it, you don't give a good goddam about him. *(He takes the rolled-up hose from his pocket and puts it on the table in front of Happy.)* Look what I found in the cellar, for Christ's sake. How can you bear to let it go on?
HAPPY: Me? Who goes away? Who runs off and—
BIFF: Yeah, but he doesn't mean anything to you. You could help him— I can't! Don't you understand what I'm talking about? He's going to kill himself, don't you know that?
HAPPY: Don't I know it! Me!
BIFF: Hap, help him! Jesus . . . help him . . . Help me, help me, I can't bear to look at his face! *(Ready to weep, he hurries out, up right.)*
665 HAPPY: *(starting after him)* Where are you going?
MISS FORSYTHE: What's he so mad about?
HAPPY: Come on, girls, we'll catch up with him.
MISS FORSYTHE: *(as Happy pushes her out)* Say, I don't like that temper of his!
HAPPY: He's just a little overstrung, he'll be all right!
670 WILLY: *(off left, as The Woman laughs)* Don't answer! Don't answer!
LETTA: Don't you want to tell your father—
HAPPY: No, that's not my father. He's just a guy. Come on, we'll catch Biff, and, honey, we're going to paint this town! Stanley, where's the check! Hey, Stanley!

They exit. Stanley looks toward left.

STANLEY: *(calling to Happy indignantly)* Mr. Loman! Mr. Loman!

Stanley picks up a chair and follows them off. Knocking is heard off left. The Woman enters, laughing. Willy follows her. She is in a black slip; he is buttoning his shirt. Raw, sensuous music accompanies their speech.

WILLY: Will you stop laughing? Will you stop?
675 THE WOMAN: Aren't you going to answer the door? He'll wake the whole hotel.
WILLY: I'm not expecting anybody.
THE WOMAN: Whyn't you have another drink, honey, and stop being so damn self-centered?
WILLY: I'm so lonely.
THE WOMAN: You know you ruined me, Willy? From now on, whenever you come to the office, I'll see that you go right through to the buyers. No waiting at my desk any more, Willy. You ruined me.

680 **WILLY:** That's nice of you to say that.
THE WOMAN: Gee, you are self-centered! Why so sad? You are the saddest self-centeredest soul I ever did see-saw. *(She laughs. He kisses her.)* Come on inside, drummer boy. It's silly to be dressing in the middle of the night. *(As knocking is heard.)* Aren't you going to answer the door?
WILLY: They're knocking on the wrong door.
THE WOMAN: But I felt the knocking. And he heard us talking in here. Maybe the hotel's on fire!
WILLY: *(his terror rising)* It's a mistake.
685 **THE WOMAN:** Then tell him to go away!
WILLY: There's nobody there.
THE WOMAN: It's getting on my nerves, Willy. There's somebody standing out there and it's getting on my nerves!
WILLY: *(pushing her away from him)* All right, stay in the bathroom here, and don't come out. I think there's a law in Massachusetts about it, so don't come out. It may be that new room clerk. He looked very mean. So don't come out. It's a mistake, there's no fire.

The knocking is heard again. He takes a few steps away from her, and she vanishes into the wing. The light follows him, and now he is facing Young Biff, who carries a suitcase. Biff steps toward him. The music is gone.

BIFF: Why didn't you answer?
690 **WILLY:** Biff! What are you doing in Boston?
BIFF: Why didn't you answer? I've been knocking for five minutes, I called you on the phone—
WILLY: I just heard you. I was in the bathroom and had the door shut. Did anything happen home?
BIFF: Dad—I let you down.
WILLY: What do you mean?
695 **BIFF:** Dad . . .
WILLY: Biffo, what's this about? *(Putting his arm around Biff.)* Come on, let's go downstairs and get you a malted.
BIFF: Dad, I flunked math.
WILLY: Not for the term?
BIFF: The term. I haven't got enough credits to graduate.
700 **WILLY:** You mean to say Bernard wouldn't give you the answers?
BIFF: He did, he tried, but I only got a sixty-one.
WILLY: And they wouldn't give you four points?
BIFF: Birnbaum refused absolutely. I begged him, Pop, but he won't give me those points. You gotta talk to him before they close the school. Because if he saw the kind of man you are, and you just talked to him in your way, I'm sure he'd come through for me. The class came right before practice, see, and I didn't go enough. Would you talk to him? He'd like you, Pop. You know the way you could talk.
WILLY: You're on. We'll drive right back.

705   **BIFF:** Oh, Dad, good work! I'm sure he'll change it for you!
      WILLY: Go downstairs and tell the clerk I'm checkin' out. Go right down.
      BIFF: Yes, Sir! See, the reason he hates me, Pop—one day he was late for class so I got up at the blackboard and imitated him. I crossed my eyes and talked with a lithp.
      WILLY: *(laughing)* You did? The kids like it?
      BIFF: They nearly died laughing!
710   **WILLY:** Yeah? What'd you do?
      BIFF: The thquare root of thixthy twee is . . . *(Willy bursts out laughing; Biff joins him.)* And in the middle of it he walked in!

Willy laughs and The Woman joins in offstage.

      WILLY: *(without hesitating)* Hurry downstairs and—
      BIFF: Somebody in there?
      WILLY: No, that was next door.

The Woman laughs offstage.

715   **BIFF:** Somebody got in your bathroom!
      WILLY: No, it's the next room, there's a party—
      THE WOMAN: *(enters, laughing. She lisps this)* Can I come in? There's something in the bathtub, Willy, and it's moving!

Willy looks at Biff, who is staring open-mouthed and horrified at The Woman.

      WILLY: Ah—you better go back to your room. They must be finished painting by now. They're painting her room so I let her take a shower here. Go back, go back . . . *(He pushes her.)*
      THE WOMAN: *(resisting)* But I've got to get dressed, Willy, I can't—
720   **WILLY:** Get out of here! Go back, go back . . . *(Suddenly striving for the ordinary.)* This is Miss Francis, Biff, she's a buyer. They're painting her room. Go back, Miss Francis, go back . . .
      THE WOMAN: But my clothes, I can't go out naked in the hall!
      WILLY: *(pushing her offstage)* Get outa here! Go back, go back!

Biff slowly sits down on his suitcase as the argument continues offstage.

      THE WOMAN: Where's my stockings? You promised me stockings, Willy!
      WILLY: I have no stockings here!
725   **THE WOMAN:** You had two boxes of size nine sheers for me, and I want them!
      WILLY: Here, for God's sake, will you get outa here!
      THE WOMAN: *(enters holding a box of stockings)* I just hope there's nobody in the hall. That's all I hope. *(To Biff.)* Are you football or baseball?
      BIFF: Football.
      THE WOMAN: *(angry, humiliated)* That's me too. G'night. *(She snatches her clothes from Willy, and walks out.)*

730 **WILLY:** *(after a pause)* Well, better get going. I want to get to the school first thing in the morning. Get my suits out of the closet. I'll get my valise. *(Biff doesn't move.)* What's the matter? *(Biff remains motionless, tears falling.)* She's a buyer. Buys for J. H. Simmons. She lives down the hall—they're painting. You don't imagine—*(He breaks off. After a pause.)* Now listen, pal, she's just a buyer. She sees merchandise in her room and they have to keep it looking just so . . . *(Pause. Assuming command.)* All right, get my suits. *(Biff doesn't move.)* Now stop crying and do as I say. I gave you an order. Biff, I gave you an order! Is that what you do when I give you an order? How dare you cry! *(Putting his arm around Biff.)* Now look, Biff, when you grow up you'll understand about these things. You mustn't—you mustn't overemphasize a thing like this. I'll see Birnbaum first thing in the morning.

BIFF: Never mind.

WILLY: *(getting down beside Biff)* Never mind! He's going to give you those points. I'll see to it.

BIFF: He wouldn't listen to you.

WILLY: He certainly will listen to me. You need those points for the U. of Virginia.

735 **BIFF:** I'm not going there.

WILLY: Heh? If I can't get him to change that mark you'll make it up in summer school. You've got all summer to—

BIFF: *(his weeping breaking from him)* Dad . . .

WILLY: *(infected by it)* Oh, my boy . . .

BIFF: Dad . . .

740 **WILLY:** She's nothing to me, Biff. I was lonely, I was terribly lonely.

BIFF: You—you gave her Mama's stockings! *(His tears break through and he rises to go.)*

WILLY: *(grabbing for Biff)* I gave you an order!

BIFF: Don't touch me, you—liar!

WILLY: Apologize for that!

745 **BIFF:** You fake! You phony little fake! You fake! *(Overcome, he turns quickly and weeping fully goes out with his suitcase. Willy is left on the floor on his knees.)*

WILLY: I gave you an order! Biff, come back here or I'll beat you! Come back here! I'll whip you!

Stanley comes quickly in from the right and stands in front of Willy.

WILLY: *(shouts at Stanley)* I gave you an order . . .

STANLEY: Hey, let's pick it up, pick it up, Mr. Loman. *(He helps Willy to his feet.)* Your boys left with the chippies. They said they'll see you home.

A second waiter watches some distance away.

WILLY: But we were supposed to have dinner together.

Music is heard, Willy's theme.

STANLEY: Can you make it?
WILLY: I'll—sure, I can make it. *(Suddenly concerned about his clothes.)* Do I—I look all right?
STANLEY: Sure, you look all right. *(He flicks a speck off Willy's lapel.)*
WILLY: Here—here's a dollar.
STANLEY: Oh, your son paid me. It's all right.
WILLY: *(putting it in Stanley's hand)* No, take it. You're a good boy.
STANLEY: Oh, no, you don't have to . . .
WILLY: Here—here's some more, I don't need it any more. *(After a slight pause.)* Tell me—is there a seed store in the neighborhood?
STANLEY: Seeds? You mean like to plant?

As Willy turns, Stanley slips the money back into his jacket pocket.

WILLY: Yes. Carrots, peas . . .
STANLEY: Well, there's hardware stores on Sixth Avenue, but it may be too late now.
WILLY: *(anxiously)* Oh, I'd better hurry. I've got to get some seeds. *(He starts off to the right.)* I've got to get some seeds, right away. Nothing's planted. I don't have a thing in the ground.

Willy hurries out as the light goes down. Stanley moves over to the right after him, watches him off. The other waiter has been staring at Willy.

STANLEY: *(to the waiter)* Well, whatta you looking at?

The waiter picks up the chairs and moves off right. Stanley takes the table and follows him. The light fades on this area. There is a long pause, the sound of the flute coming over. The light gradually rises on the kitchen, which is empty. Happy appears at the door of the house, followed by Biff. Happy is carrying a large bunch of long-stemmed roses. He enters the kitchen, looks around for Linda. Not seeing her, he turns to Biff, who is just outside the house door, and makes a gesture with his hands, indicating "Not here, I guess." He looks into the livingroom and freezes. Inside, Linda, unseen, is seated, Willy's coat on her lap. She rises ominously and quietly and moves toward Happy, who backs up into the kitchen, afraid.

HAPPY: Hey, what're you doing up? *(Linda says nothing but moves toward him implacably.)* Where's Pop? *(He keeps backing to the right, and now Linda is in full view in the doorway to the livingroom.)* Is he sleeping?
LINDA: Where were you?
HAPPY: *(trying to laugh it off)* We met two girls, Mom, very fine types. Here, we brought you some flowers. *(Offering them to her.)* Put them in your room, Ma.

She knocks them to the floor at Biff's feet. He has now come inside and closed the door behind him. She stares at Biff, silent.

HAPPY: Now what'd you do that for? Mom, I want you to have some flowers—

LINDA: *(cutting Happy off, violently to Biff)* Don't you care whether he lives or dies?
HAPPY: *(going to the stairs)* Come upstairs, Biff.
BIFF: *(with a flare of disgust, to Happy)* Go away from me! *(To Linda.)* What do you mean, lives or dies? Nobody's dying around here, pal.
770 LINDA: Get out of my sight! Get out of here!
BIFF: I wanna see the boss.
LINDA: You're not going near him!
BIFF: Where is he? *(He moves into the livingroom and Linda follows.)*
LINDA: *(shouting after Biff)* You invite him for dinner. He looks forward to it all day—*(Biff appears in his parents' bedroom, looks around, and exits)*—and then you desert him there. There's no stranger you'd do that to!
775 HAPPY: Why? He had a swell time with us. Listen, when I—*(Linda comes back into the kitchen)*—desert him I hope I don't outlive the day!
LINDA: Get out of here!
HAPPY: Now look, Mom . . .
LINDA: Did you have to go to women tonight? You and your lousy rotten whores!

Biff re-enters the kitchen.

HAPPY: Mom, all we did was follow Biff around trying to cheer him up! *(To Biff.)* Boy, what a night you gave me!
780 LINDA: Get out of here, both of you, and don't come back! I don't want you tormenting him any more. Go on now, get your things together! *(To Biff.)* You can sleep in his apartment. *(She starts to pick up the flowers and stops herself.)* Pick up this stuff, I'm not your maid any more. Pick it up, you bum, you!

Happy turns his back to her in refusal. Biff slowly moves over and gets down on his knees, picking up the flowers.

LINDA: You're a pair of animals! Not one, not another living soul would have had the cruelty to walk out on that man in a restaurant!
BIFF: *(not looking at her)* Is that what he said?
LINDA: He didn't have to say anything. He was so humiliated he nearly limped when he came in.
HAPPY: But, Mom he had a great time with us—
785 BIFF: *(cutting him off violently)* Shut up!

Without another word, Happy goes upstairs.

LINDA: You! You didn't even go in to see if he was all right!
BIFF: *(still on the floor in front of Linda, the flowers in his hand; with self-loathing)* No. Didn't. Didn't do a damned thing. How do you like that, heh? Left him babbling in a toilet.
LINDA: You louse. You . . .
BIFF: Now you hit it on the nose! *(He gets up, throws the flowers in the wastebasket.)* The scum of the earth, and you're looking at him!
790 LINDA: Get out of here!

BIFF: I gotta talk to the boss, Mom. Where is he?
LINDA: You're not going near him. Get out of this house!
BIFF: *(with absolute assurance, determination)* No. We're gonna have an abrupt conversation, him and me.
LINDA: You're not talking to him!

Hammering is heard from outside the house, off right. Biff turns toward the noise.

LINDA: *(suddenly pleading)* Will you please leave him alone?
BIFF: What's he doing out there?
LINDA: He's planting the garden!
BIFF: *(quietly)* Now? Oh, my God!

Biff moves outside, Linda following. The light dies down on them and comes up on the center of the apron as Willy walks into it. He is carrying a flashlight, a hoe and a handful of seed packets. He raps the top of the hoe sharply to fix it firmly, and then moves to the left, measuring off the distance with his foot. He holds the flashlight to look at the seed packets, reading off the instructions. He is in the blue of night.

WILLY: Carrots . . . quarter-inch apart. Rows . . . one-foot rows. *(He measures it off.)* One foot. *(He puts down a package and measures off.)* Beets. *(He puts down another package and measures again.)* Lettuce. *(He reads the package, puts it down.)* One foot—*(He breaks off as Ben appears at the right and moves slowly down to him.)* What a proposition, ts, ts. Terrific, terrific. 'Cause she's suffered, Ben, the woman has suffered. You understand me? A man can't go out the way he came in, Ben, a man has got to add up to something. You can't, you can't—*(Ben moves toward him as though to interrupt.)* You gotta consider, now. Don't answer so quick. Remember, it's a guaranteed twenty-thousand-dollar proposition. Now look, Ben, I want you to go through the ins and outs of this thing with me. I've got nobody to talk to, Ben, and the woman has suffered, you hear me?
BEN: *(standing still, considering)* What's the proposition?
WILLY: It's twenty thousand dollars on the barrelhead. Guaranteed, gilt-edged, you understand?
BEN: You don't want to make a fool of yourself. They might not honor the policy.
WILLY: How can they dare refuse? Didn't I work like a coolie to meet every premium on the nose? And now they don't pay off? Impossible!
BEN: It's called a cowardly thing, William.
WILLY: Why? Does it take more guts to stand here the rest of my life ringing up a zero?
BEN: *(yielding)* That's a point, William. *(He moves, thinking, turns.)* And twenty thousand—that *is* something one can feel with the hand, it is there.

WILLY: *(now assured, with rising power)* Oh, Ben, that's the whole beauty of it! I see it like a diamond, shining in the dark, hard and rough, that I can pick up and touch in my hand. Not like—like an appointment! This would not be another damned-fool appointment, Ben, and it changes all the aspects. Because he thinks I'm nothing, see, and so he spites me. But the funeral—*(Straightening up.)* Ben, that funeral will be massive! They'll come from Maine, Massachusetts, Vermont, New Hampshire! All the old-timers with the strange license plates—that boy will be thunder-struck, Ben, because he never realized—I am known! Rhode Island, New York, New Jersey—I am known, Ben, and he'll see it with his eyes once and for all. He'll see what I am, Ben! He's in for a shock, that boy!

BEN: *(coming down to the edge of the garden)* He'll call you a coward.

WILLY: *(suddenly fearful)* No, that would be terrible.

BEN: Yes. And a damned fool.

WILLY: No, no, he mustn't, I won't have that! *(He is broken and desperate.)*

BEN: He'll hate you, William.

The gay music of the boys is heard.

WILLY: Oh, Ben, how do we get back to all the great times? Used to be so full of light, and comradeship, the sleigh-riding in winter, and the ruddiness on his cheeks. And always some kind of good news coming up, always something nice coming up ahead. And never even let me carry the valises in the house, and simonizing, simonizing that little red car! Why, why can't I give him something and not have him hate me?

BEN: Let me think about it. *(He glances at his watch.)* I still have a little time. Remarkable proposition, but you've got to be sure you're not making a fool of yourself.

Ben drifts off upstage and goes out of sight. Biff comes down from the left.

WILLY: *(suddenly conscious of Biff, turns and looks up at him, then begins picking up the packages of seeds in confusion)* Where the hell is that seed? *(Indignantly.)* You can't see nothing out here! They boxed in the whole goddam neighborhood!

BIFF: There are people all around here. Don't you realize that?

WILLY: I'm busy. Don't bother me.

BIFF: *(taking the hoe from Willy)* I'm saying good-by to you, Pop. *(Willy looks at him, silent, unable to move.)* I'm not coming back any more.

WILLY: You're not going to see Oliver tomorrow?

BIFF: I've got no appointment, Dad.

WILLY: He put his arm around you, and you've got no appointment?

BIFF: Pop, get this now, will you? Everytime I've left it's been a fight that sent me out of here. Today I realized something about myself and I tried to explain it to you and I—I think I'm just not smart enough to make any sense out of it for you. To hell with whose fault it is or anything like that. *(He takes Willy's arm.)* Let's just wrap it up, heh? Come on in, we'll tell Mom. *(He gently tries to pull Willy to the left.)*

WILLY: *(frozen, immobile, with guilt in his voice)* No, I don't want to see her.

BIFF: Come on! *(He pulls again, and Willy tries to pull away.)*

825 WILLY: *(highly nervous)* No, no, I don't want to see her.

BIFF: *(tries to look into Willy's face, as if to find the answer there)* Why don't you want to see her?

WILLY: *(more harshly now)* Don't bother me, will you?

BIFF: What do you mean, you don't want to see her? You don't want them calling you yellow, do you? This isn't your fault; it's me, I'm a bum. Now come inside! *(Willy strains to get away.)* Did you hear what I said to you?

Willy pulls away and quickly goes by himself into the house. Biff follows.

LINDA: *(to Willy)* Did you plant, dear?

830 BIFF: *(at the door, to Linda)* All right, we had it out. I'm going and I'm not writing any more.

LINDA: *(going to Willy in the kitchen)* I think that's the best way, dear. 'Cause there's no use drawing it out, you'll just never get along.

Willy doesn't respond.

BIFF: People ask where I am and what I'm doing, you don't know, and you don't care. That way it'll be off your mind and you can start brightening up again. All right? That clears it, doesn't it? *(Willy is silent, and Biff goes to him.)* You gonna wish me luck, scout? *(He extends his hand.)* What do you say?

LINDA: Shake his hand, Willy.

WILLY: *(turning to her, seething with hurt)* There's no necessity to mention the pen at all, y'know.

835 BIFF: *(gently)* I've got no appointment, Dad.

WILLY: *(erupting fiercely)* He put his arm around . . . ?

BIFF: Dad, you're never going to see what I am, so what's the use of arguing? If I strike oil I'll send you a check. Meantime forget I'm alive.

WILLY: *(to Linda)* Spite, see?

BIFF: Shake hands, Dad.

840 WILLY: Not my hand.

BIFF: I was hoping not to go this way.

WILLY: Well, this is the way you're going. Good-by.

Biff looks at him a moment, then turns sharply and goes to the stairs.

WILLY: *(stops him with)* May you rot in hell if you leave this house!

BIFF: *(turning)* Exactly what is it that you want from me?

845 **WILLY:** I want you to know, on the train, in the mountains, in the valleys, wherever you go, that you cut down your life for spite!
BIFF: No, no.
WILLY: Spite, spite, is the word of your undoing! And when you're down and out, remember what did it. When you're rotting somewhere beside the railroad tracks, remember, and don't you dare blame it on me!
BIFF: I'm not blaming it on you!
WILLY: I won't take the rap for this, you hear?

Happy comes down the stairs and stands on the bottom step, watching.

850 **BIFF:** That's just what I'm telling you!
WILLY: *(sinking into a chair at the table, with full accusation)* You're trying to put a knife in me—don't think I don't know what you're doing!
BIFF: All right, phony! Then let's lay it on the line. *(He whips the rubber tube out of his pocket and puts it on the table.)*
HAPPY: You crazy—
LINDA: Biff! *(She moves to grab the hose, but Biff holds it down with his hand.)*
855 **BIFF:** Leave it there! Don't move it!
WILLY: *(not looking at it)* What is that?
BIFF: You know goddam well what that is.
WILLY: *(caged, wanting to escape)* I never saw that.
BIFF: You saw it. The mice didn't bring it into the cellar! What is this supposed to do, make a hero out of you? This supposed to make me sorry for you?
860 **WILLY:** Never heard of it.
BIFF: There'll be no pity for you, you hear it? No pity!
WILLY: *(to Linda)* You hear the spite!
BIFF: No, you're going to hear the truth—what you are and what I am!
LINDA: Stop it!
865 **WILLY:** Spite!
HAPPY: *(coming down toward Biff)* You cut it now!
BIFF: *(to Happy)* The man don't know who we are! The man is gonna know! *(To Willy.)* We never told the truth for ten minutes in this house!
HAPPY: We always told the truth!
BIFF: *(turning on him)* You big blow, are you the assistant buyer? You're one of the two assistants to the assistant, aren't you?
870 **HAPPY:** Well, I'm practically—
BIFF: You're practically full of it! We all are! And I'm through with it. *(To Willy.)* Now hear this, Willy, this is me.
WILLY: I know you!
BIFF: You know why I had no address for three months? I stole a suit in Kansas City and I was in jail. *(To Linda, who is sobbing.)* Stop crying. I'm through with it.

Linda turns away from them, her hands covering her face.

WILLY: I suppose that's my fault!

BIFF: I stole myself out of every good job since high school!

WILLY: And whose fault is that?

BIFF: And I never got anywhere because you blew me so full of hot air I could never stand taking orders from anybody! That's whose fault it is!

WILLY: I hear that!

LINDA: Don't, Biff!

BIFF: It's goddam time you heard that! I had to be boss big shot in two weeks, and I'm through with it!

WILLY: Then hang yourself! For spite, hang yourself!

BIFF: No! Nobody's hanging himself, Willy! I ran down eleven flights with a pen in my hand today. And suddenly I stopped, you hear me? And in the middle of that office building, do you hear this? I stopped in the middle of that building and I saw—the sky. I saw the things that I love in this world. The work and the food and time to sit and smoke. And I looked at the pen and said to myself, what the hell am I grabbing this for? Why am I trying to become what I don't want to be? What am I doing in an office, making a contemptuous, begging fool of myself, when all I want is out there, waiting for me the minute I say I know who I am! Why can't I say that, Willy? *(He tries to make Willy face him, but Willy pulls away and moves to the left.)*

WILLY: *(with hatred, threateningly)* The door of your life is wide open!

BIFF: Pop! I'm a dime a dozen, and so are you!

WILLY: *(turning on him now in an uncontrolled outburst)* I am not a dime a dozen! I am Willy Loman, and you are Biff Loman!

Biff starts for Willy, but is blocked by Happy. In his fury, Biff seems on the verge of attacking his father.

BIFF: I am not a leader of men, Willy, and neither are you. You were never anything but a hard-working drummer who landed in the ash can like all the rest of them! I'm one dollar an hour, Willy! I tried seven states and couldn't raise it. A buck an hour! Do you gather my meaning? I'm not bringing home any prizes any more, and you're going to stop waiting for me to bring them home!

WILLY: *(directly to Biff)* You vengeful, spiteful mutt!

Biff breaks from Happy. Willy, in fright, starts up the stairs. Biff grabs him.

BIFF: *(at the peak of his fury)* Pop, I'm nothing! I'm nothing, Pop. Can't you understand that? There's no spite in it any more. I'm just what I am, that's all.

Biff's fury has spent itself, and he breaks down, sobbing, holding on to Willy, who dumbly fumbles for Biff's face.

WILLY: *(astonished)* What're you doing? What're you doing? *(To Linda.)* Why is he crying?

890 **BIFF:** *(crying, broken)* Will you let me go, for Christ's sake? Will you take that phony dream and burn it before something happens? *(Struggling to contain himself, he pulls away and moves to the stairs.)* I'll go in the morning. Put him—put him to bed. *(Exhausted, Biff moves up the stairs to his room.)*

WILLY: *(after a long pause, astonished, elevated)* Isn't that remarkable? Biff—he likes me!

LINDA: He loves you, Willy!

HAPPY: *(deeply moved)* Always did, Pop.

WILLY: Oh, Biff! *(Staring wildly.)* He cried! Cried to me! *(He is choking with his love, and now cries out his promise.)* That boy—that boy is going to be magnificent!

Ben appears in the light just outside the kitchen.

895 **BEN:** Yes, outstanding, with twenty thousand behind him.

LINDA: *(sensing the racing of his mind, fearfully, carefully)* Now come to bed, Willy. It's all settled now.

WILLY: *(finding it difficult not to rush out of the house)* Yes, we'll sleep. Come on. Go to sleep, Hap.

BEN: And it does take a great kind of man to crack the jungle.

In accents of dread, Ben's idyllic music starts up.

HAPPY: *(his arm around Linda)* I'm getting married, Pop, don't forget it. I'm changing everything. I'm gonna run that department before the year is up. You'll see, Mom. *(He kisses her.)*

900 **BEN:** The jungle is dark but full of diamonds, Willy.

Willy turns, moves, listening to Ben.

LINDA: Be good. You're both good boys, just act that way, that's all.

HAPPY: 'Night, Pop. *(He goes upstairs.)*

LINDA: *(to Willy)* Come, dear.

BEN: *(with greater force)* One must go in to fetch a diamond out.

905 **WILLY:** *(to Linda, as he moves slowly along the edge of the kitchen, toward the door)* I just want to get settled down, Linda. Let me sit alone for a little.

LINDA: *(almost uttering her fear)* I want you upstairs.

WILLY: *(taking her in his arms)* In a few minutes, Linda. I couldn't sleep right now. Go on, you look awful tired. *(He kisses her.)*

BEN: Not like an appointment at all. A diamond is rough and hard to the touch.

WILLY: Go on now. I'll be right up.

910 **LINDA:** I think this is the only way, Willy.

WILLY: Sure, it's the best thing.

BEN: Best thing!

WILLY: The only way. Everything is gonna be—go on, kid, get to bed. You look so tired.
LINDA: Come right up.
915 WILLY: Two minutes.

Linda goes into the livingroom, then reappears in her bedroom. Willy moves just outside the kitchen door.

WILLY: Loves me. *(Wonderingly.)* Always loved me. Isn't that a remarkable thing? Ben, he'll worship me for it!
BEN: *(with promise)* It's dark there, but full of diamonds.
WILLY: Can you imagine that magnificence with twenty thousand dollars in his pocket?
LINDA: *(calling from her room)* Willy! Come up!
920 WILLY: *(calling from the kitchen)* Yes! Yes! Coming! It's very smart, you realize that, don't you, sweetheart? Even Ben sees it. I gotta go, baby. 'By! By! *(Going over to Ben, almost dancing.)* Imagine? When the mail comes he'll be ahead of Bernard again!
BEN: A perfect proposition all around.
WILLY: Did you see how he cried to me? Oh, if I could kiss him, Ben!
BEN: Time, William, time!
WILLY: Oh, Ben, I always knew one way or another we were gonna make it, Biff and I!
925 BEN: *(looking at his watch)* The boat. We'll be late. *(He moves slowly off into the darkness.)*
WILLY: *(elegiacally, turning to the house)* Now when you kick off, boy, I want a seventy-yard boot, and get right down the field under the ball, and when you hit, hit low and hit hard, because it's important, boy. *(He swings around and faces the audience.)* There's all kinds of important people in the stands, and the first thing you know . . . *(Suddenly realizing he is alone.)* Ben! Ben, where do I . . . ? *(He makes a sudden movement of search.)* Ben, how do I . . . ?
LINDA: *(calling)* Willy, you coming up?
WILLY: *(uttering a gasp of fear, whirling about as if to quiet her)* Sh! *(He turns around as if to find his way; sounds, faces, voices, seem to be swarming in upon him and he flicks at them, crying.)* Sh! Sh! *(Suddenly music, faint and high, stops him. It rises in intensity, almost to an unbearable scream. He goes up and down on his toes, and rushes off around the house.)* Shhh!
LINDA: Willy?

There is no answer. Linda waits. Biff gets up off his bed. He is still in his clothes. Happy sits up. Biff stands listening.

930 LINDA: *(with real fear)* Willy, answer me! Willy!

There is the sound of a car starting and moving away at full speed.

LINDA: No!
BIFF: *(rushing down the stairs)* Pop!

As the car speeds off, the music crashes down in a frenzy of sound, which becomes the soft pulsation of a single cello string. Biff slowly returns to his bedroom. He and Happy gravely don their jackets. Linda slowly walks out of her room. The music has developed into a dead march. The leaves of day are appearing over everything. Charley and Bernard, somberly dressed, appear and knock on the kitchen door. Biff and Happy slowly descend the stairs to the kitchen as Charley and Bernard enter. All stop a moment when Linda, in clothes of mourning, bearing a little bunch of roses, comes through the draped doorway into the kitchen. She goes to Charley and takes his arm. Now all move toward the audience, through the wall-line of the kitchen. At the limit of the apron, Linda lays down the flowers, kneels, and sits back on her heels. All stare down at the grave.

REQUIEM

CHARLEY: It's getting dark, Linda.

Linda doesn't react. She stares at the grave.

BIFF: How about it, Mom? Better get some rest, heh? They'll be closing the gate soon.

Linda makes no move. Pause.

HAPPY: *(deeply angered)* He had no right to do that! There was no necessity for it. We would've helped him.

CHARLEY: *(grunting)* Hmmm.

5 BIFF: Come along, Mom.

LINDA: Why didn't anybody come?

CHARLEY: It was a very nice funeral.

LINDA: But where are all the people he knew? Maybe they blame him.

CHARLEY: Naa. It's a rough world, Linda. They wouldn't blame him.

10 LINDA: I can't understand it. At this time especially. First time in thirty-five years we were just about free and clear. He only needed a little salary. He was even finished with the dentist.

CHARLEY: No man only needs a little salary.

LINDA: I can't understand it.

BIFF: There were a lot of nice days. When he'd come home from a trip; or on Sundays, making the stoop; finishing the cellar; putting on the new porch; when he built the extra bathroom; and put up the garage. You know something, Charley, there's more of him in that front stoop than in all the sales he ever made.

CHARLEY: Yeah. He was a happy man with a batch of cement.

15 LINDA: He was so wonderful with his hands.

BIFF: He had the wrong dreams. All, all, wrong.

HAPPY: *(almost ready to fight Biff)* Don't say that!

BIFF: He never knew who he was.

CHARLEY: *(stopping Happy's movement and reply. To Biff.)* Nobody dast blame this man. You don't understand: Willy was a salesman. And for a salesman, there is no rock bottom to the life. He don't put a bolt to a nut, he don't tell you the law or give you medicine. He's a man out there in the blue, riding on a smile and a shoeshine. And when they start not smiling back—that's an earthquake. And then you get yourself a couple of spots on your hat, and you're finished. Nobody dast blame this man. A salesman is got to dream, boy. It comes with the territory.

20 BIFF: Charley, the man didn't know who he was.
HAPPY: *(infuriated)* Don't say that!
BIFF: Why don't you come with me, Happy?
HAPPY: I'm not licked that easily. I'm staying right in this city, and I'm gonna beat this racket! *(He looks at Biff, his chin set.)* The Loman Brothers!
BIFF: I know who I am, kid.
25 HAPPY: All right, boy. I'm gonna show you and everybody else that Willy Loman did not die in vain. He had a good dream. It's the only dream you can have—to come out number-one man. He fought it out here, and this is where I'm gonna win it for him.
BIFF: *(with a hopeless glance at Happy, bends toward his mother)* Let's go, Mom.
LINDA: I'll be with you in a minute. Go on, Charley. *(He hesitates.)* I want to, just for a minute. I never had a chance to say good-by.

Charley moves away, followed by Happy. Biff remains a slight distance up and left of Linda. She sits there, summoning herself. The flute begins, not far away, playing behind her speech.

LINDA: Forgive me, dear. I can't cry. I don't know what it is, but I can't cry. I don't understand it. Why did you ever do that? Help me, Willy, I can't cry. It seems to me that you're just on another trip. I keep expecting you. Willy, dear, I can't cry. Why did you do it? I search and search and I search, and I can't understand it, Willy. I made the last payment on the house today. Today, dear. And there'll be nobody home. *(A sob rises in her throat.)* We're free and clear. *(Sobbing more fully, released.)* We're free. *(Biff comes slowly toward her.)* We're free . . . We're free . . .

Biff lifts her to her feet and moves out up right with her in his arms. Linda sobs quietly. Bernard and Charley come together and follow them, followed by Happy. Only the music of the flute is left on the darkening stage as over the house the hard towers of the apartment buildings rise into sharp focus, and—

The Curtain Falls

READING AND REACTING

1. With which character in the play do you most identify? Why?
2. Is Willy a likeable character? What words and actions—both Willy's and those of other characters—help you form your conclusion?

3. How does the existence of The Woman affect your overall impression of Willy? What does she reveal about his character?
4. What does Willy's attitude toward his sons indicate about his character? How is this attitude revealed?
5. Does this play have a hero? A villain? Explain.
6. In the absence of a narrator, what devices does Miller use to provide exposition—basic information about character and setting?
7. The conversation between Biff and Happy in act 1 reveals many of their differences. List some of the differences between these two characters.
8. In numerous remarks, Willy expresses his philosophy of business. Summarize some of his key ideas about the business world. How realistic do you think these ideas are? How do these ideas help to delineate his character?
9. In act 1 Linda tells Willy, "Few men are idolized by their children the way you are." Is she sincere, is she being ironic, or is she just trying to make Willy feel better?
10. How do the frequent flashbacks help to explain what motivates Willy? How else could this background information have been presented in the play? Are there advantages to using flashbacks instead of the alternative you suggest?
11. Is Linda simply a stereotype of the long-suffering wife, or is she an individualized, multidimensional character? Explain.
12. Willy Loman lives in Brooklyn, New York; his "territory" is New England. What is the significance to him of the "faraway places"—Africa, Alaska, California, Texas, and the like—mentioned in the play?
13. Explain the function of Bernard in the play.
14. The play concludes with a requiem. What is a requiem? What information about each of the major characters is supplied in this brief section? Is this information essential to your understanding or appreciation of the play, or would the play have been equally effective without the requiem? Explain.
15. **Journal Entry** Do you believe Willy Loman is an innocent victim of the society in which he lives, or do you believe there are flaws in his character that make him at least partially responsible for his own misfortune? Explain.

Related Works: "Do Not Go Gentle into That Good Night" (p. 310), "Those Winter Sundays" (p. 311), "The Love Song of J. Alfred Prufrock" (p. 519), *Oedipus the King* (p. 879)

◆ Writing Suggestions: Character

1. In *Death of a Salesman,* each character pursues his or her version of the American Dream. Choose two characters, define their idea of the American Dream, and explain how each tries

to make the dream a reality. In each case, consider the obstacles the character encounters, and try to account for their success or lack of success. If you like, you may consider other works in which the American Dream is central—for example, "Two Kinds" (p. 285).
2. The female characters in this chapter's plays—Mrs. Popov, Gertrude, Ophelia, and Linda—are all in one way or another in conflict with men. Focusing on the women in two different plays, define each conflict, and consider whether or not it is resolved in the play. (If you like, you may discuss a female character in one of the plays in another chapter.)
3. Minor characters are often flat characters; in many cases their sole function is to advance the plot or to highlight a particular trait in a major character. Sometimes, however, minor characters may be of more than minor importance. Choose one minor character from *Hamlet* or *Death of a Salesman* (or from a play in another chapter), and write a paper in which you discuss how the play would be different without this character.
4. Watch two or three versions of the plays in this chapter (for example, films with Lee J. Cobb, Dustin Hoffman, or Brian Dennehy as Willy Loman). Based on your understanding of the play, which actor's interpretation seems most accurate? Explain your conclusion in an essay.
5. Review the explanation of tragedy in Chapter 18, "Understanding Drama." Using the discussion of the tragic hero as your guide, write an essay in which you discuss either Willy Loman or Hamlet as a tragic hero.

Chapter 21

Staging

Staging refers to the elements of a play's production that determine how the play looks and sounds to an audience. It encompasses the **stage settings,** or **sets**—scenery and props—as well as the costumes, lighting, sound effects, and music that bring the play to life on the stage. In short, staging is everything that goes into making a written script a play.

Most contemporary staging in the West has concentrated on re-creating the outside world. This concept of staging, which has dominated Western theatrical productions for centuries, would seem alien in many non-Western theaters. Japanese kabuki dramas and No plays, for example, depend on staging conventions that make no attempt to mirror reality or everyday speech. Scenery and costumes are largely symbolic, and often actors wear highly stylized makeup or masks. Although some European and American playwrights have been strongly influenced by non-Western staging, the majority of plays being produced in the West still try to create the illusion of reality.

STAGE DIRECTIONS

◊ ◊ ◊

Usually a playwright presents instructions for the staging of a play in **stage directions**—notes that comment on the scenery, the movements of the performers, the lighting, and the placement of props. (In the absence of detailed stage directions, dialogue can provide information about staging.) Sometimes these stage directions are quite simple, leaving much to the imagination of the director. Consider how little specific information about the setting of the play is provided in these stage directions from Samuel Beckett's 1952 absurdist play *Waiting for Godot:*

ACT I

A country road. A tree. Evening.

Often, however, playwrights furnish much more detailed information about staging. Consider these notes from Anton Chekhov's *The Cherry Orchard:*

Act I

A room, which has always been called the nursery. One of the doors leads into Anya's room. Dawn, sun rises during the scene. May, the cherry trees in flower, but it is cold in the garden with the frost of the early morning. Windows closed.

Enter Dunyasha with a candle and Lopahin with a book in his hand.

These comments indicate that the first act takes place in a room with more than one door and that several windows reveal cherry trees in bloom. They also specify that the lighting should simulate the sun rising at dawn and that certain characters should enter carrying particular props. Still, Chekhov leaves it up to those staging the play to decide on the costumes for the characters and on the furniture that will be placed around the room.

Some stage directions are even more specific. George Bernard Shaw's long, complex stage directions are legendary in the theater. Note the degree of detail he provides in these stage directions from his comedy *The Doctor's Dilemma:*

The consulting-room has two windows looking on Queen Anne Street. Between the two is a marble-topped console, with haunched gilt legs ending in sphinx claws. The huge pier-glass [a long narrow mirror that fits between two windows] which surmounts it is mostly disabled from reflection by elaborate painting on its surface of palms, ferns, lilies, tulips, and sunflowers. The adjoining wall contains the fireplace, with two arm-chairs before it. As we happen to face the corner we see nothing of the other two walls. On the right of the fireplace, or rather on the right of any person facing the fireplace, is the door. On the left is the writing-table at which Redpenny [a medical student] sits. It is an untidy table with a microscope, several test tubes, and a spirit lamp [an alcohol burner] standing up through its litter of papers. There is a couch in the middle of the room, at right angles to the console, and parallel to the fireplace. A chair stands between the couch and the window. Another in the corner. Another at the other end of the windowed wall. [. . .] The wallpaper and carpets are mostly green. [. . .] The house, in fact, was so well furnished in the middle of the XIXth century that it stands unaltered to this day and is still quite presentable.

Not only does Shaw describe the furniture to be placed on stage, but he also includes a good deal of detail—specifying, for example, "gilt legs ending in sphinx claws" and "test tubes and a spirit lamp" that clutter the writing table. In addition, he defines furniture placement and specifies color.

Regardless of how detailed the stage directions are, they do not eliminate the need for creative interpretations on the part of the producer, director, set designers, and actors (See "Actors' Interpretations" in Chapter 20, p. 665). Stage directions—and, for that matter, the entire script—are the foundation on which to construct the play that the audience finally sees. Many directors, in fact, see stage directions as suggestions, not requirements, and some even consider them more confusing than helpful. Therefore, directors may choose to interpret a play's stage directions quite loosely—or even to ignore them entirely.

The Uses of Staging

◊ ◊ ◊

Staging is a key element of drama, and details that the audience sees and hears—such as costumes, props, scenery, lighting, and music and sound effects—communicate important information about characters and their motivation as well as about the play's theme.

Costumes

Costumes not only establish the historical period in which a play is set but also provide insight into the character who wears them. When he first appears, Hamlet is profoundly disillusioned and quite melancholy. This fact was immediately apparent to Shakespeare's audience because Hamlet is dressed in sable, which to the Elizabethans signified a melancholy nature. In Tennessee Williams's *The Glass Menagerie* (p. 938), Laura's dress of soft violet material and her hair ribbon reflect her delicate, childlike innocence. In contrast, her mother's "imitation velvety-looking cloth coat with imitation fur collar" and her "enormous black patent-leather pocketbook" reveal her somewhat pathetic attempt to achieve respectability. Later in the play, awaiting the "gentleman caller," Laura's mother wears a dress that is both outdated and inappropriately youthful, suggesting both her need to relive her own past and her increasingly desperate desire to marry off her daughter.

Props

Props (short for *properties*)—pictures, furnishings, objects, and the like—can also help audiences to interpret a play's characters and themes. For example, the handkerchief in Shakespeare's *Othello* gains significance as the play progresses. It begins as an innocent object and ends as the piece of evidence that convinces Othello his wife is committing adultery. Sometimes props can have symbolic significance. During the Renaissance, for example, flowers had symbolic meaning. In act 4 of *Hamlet*, Ophelia, who is mad, gives flowers to various characters. In a note to the play, the critic Thomas Parrott points out the symbolic significance of her gifts: to Claudius, the murderer of Hamlet's father, she gives fennel and columbines, which signify flattery and ingratitude; to the Queen, she gives rue and daisies, which symbolize sadness and unfaithfulness. Although modern audiences probably do not understand the full implications of the flowers, many people in Shakespeare's Elizabethan audience would have been aware of their meaning.

The furnishings in a room can also reveal a lot about a play's characters and themes. Willy Loman's house in Arthur Miller's *Death of a Salesman* (p. 782) is sparsely furnished, revealing the declining financial status of the family. The kitchen contains a table and three chairs, and the bedroom is furnished with only a brass bed and a straight chair. Over the bed on a shelf is Biff's silver athletic trophy, which is a constant reminder of his loss of status. Like Willy Loman's house, the Wingfield apartment in *The Glass Menagerie* reflects its inhabitants' modest economic circumstances. For example, the living room, which contains a sofa that unfolds into a bed, also serves as a bedroom for Laura. In addition, one piece of furniture highlights a central theme of the play: an old-fashioned cabinet in the living room displays a collection of transparent glass animals which, like Laura, are too fragile to be removed from their surroundings.

Scenery and Lighting

Playwrights often use scenery and lighting to create imaginative stage settings. In *Death of a Salesman* the house is surrounded by "towering angular shapes" of apartment houses that emphasize the "small, fragile-seeming home." Arthur Miller calls for a set that is "wholly, or in some places, transparent." Whenever the action is in the present, the actors observe the imaginary boundaries that separate rooms or mark the exterior walls of the house. But when the characters reenact past events, they walk over the boundaries and come to the front of the stage. By lighting up and darkening different parts of the stage, Miller shifts from the present to the past and back again.

The set of *The Glass Menagerie* is also innovative, combining imaginative backdrops with subtle lighting. As the curtain rises, the audience sees the dark rear wall of the Wingfield tenement, which is flanked on both sides by alleys lined with clotheslines, garbage cans, and fire escapes. After Tom delivers his opening narrative, the tenement wall becomes transparent, revealing the interior of the Wingfield apartment. To create this effect, Williams uses a **scrim,** a curtain that when illuminated from the front appears solid but when illuminated from the back becomes transparent. For Williams, such "atmospheric touches" represented a new direction in theater that contrasted with the theater of "realistic conventions."

Contemporary playwrights often use sets that combine realistic and nonrealistic elements. In his 1988 Tony Award–winning play *M. Butterfly*, for example, David Henry Hwang employs not only scrims but also a large red lacquered ramp that runs from the bottom to the top of the stage. The action takes place beneath, on, and above the ramp, creating an effect not unlike that created by Shakespeare's multiple stages. At several points in the play, a character who acts as the narrator sits beneath the ramp, addressing the audience, while at the same time a character on top of the ramp acts out the narrator's words.

Music and Sound Effects

Staging involves more than visual elements such as costumes and scenery; it also involves music and sound effects. The stage directions for *Death of a Salesman*, for example, begin, *"A melody is heard, played upon a flute."* Although not specifically identified, the music is described as "*small and fine, telling of grass and trees and the horizon.*" Interestingly, this music stands in stark contrast to the claustrophobic urban setting of the play. Music also has a major role in *The Glass Menagerie*, where a single recurring tune, like circus music, weaves in and out of the play. This musical motif gives emotional impact to certain lines and suggests the fantasy world into which Laura has retreated.

Sound effects play an important part in Henrik Ibsen's *A Doll House* (p. 599). At the end of the play, after his wife has left him, Torvald Helmer sits alone on the stage. Notice in the following stage directions how the final sound effect cuts short Helmer's attempt at self-deluding optimism:

> **HELMER:** *(sinks down on a chair by the door, face buried in his hands)* Nora! Nora! *(Looking about and rising.)* Empty. She's gone. *(A sudden hope leaps in him.)* The greatest miracle—?
>
> *From below, the sound of a door slamming shut.*

When you read a play, it may be difficult to appreciate the effect that staging can have on a performance. As you read, pay particular attention to the stage directions, and use your imagination to visualize the scenes the playwright describes. In addition, try to imagine the play's sights and sounds, and consider the options for staging that are suggested as characters speak to one another. Although even such careful reading cannot substitute for actually seeing a play performed, it can help you imagine the play as it might appear on the stage.

A Final Note

Because of a play's limited performance time, and because of space and financial limitations, not every action or event can be represented on stage. Frequently, incidents that would involve many actors or require elaborate scenery are only suggested. For example, a violent political riot may be suggested by a single scuffle, a full-scale wedding by the kiss between bride and groom, a gala evening at the opera by a well-dressed group in box seats, and a trip to an exotic locale by a departure scene. Other events are simply said to occur offstage, with the roar of a crowd suggesting an athletic event, for instance.

 ## Checklist: Writing about Staging

- ✓ What information about staging is contained in the stage directions of the play?
- ✓ What information about staging is suggested by the play's dialogue?
- ✓ What information about staging is left to the imagination?
- ✓ How might different decisions about staging change the play?
- ✓ Do the stage directions provide information about how characters are supposed to look or behave?
- ✓ What costumes are specified? In what ways do costumes give insight into the characters who wear them?
- ✓ What props play an important part in the play? Do these props have symbolic meaning?
- ✓ Is the scenery used in the play special or unusual in any way?
- ✓ What kind of lighting is specified by the stage directions? In what way does this lighting affect your reaction to the play?
- ✓ In what ways are music and sound effects used in the play? Are musical themes associated with any characters? Do music and sound effects heighten the emotional impact of certain lines?
- ✓ How does staging help to communicate the play's themes?
- ✓ What events occur offstage? Why? How are they suggested?

◆ **MILCHA SANCHEZ-SCOTT*** (1949 or 1950–   ) is a Los Angeles–based writer of plays that include *Dog Lady* (1984) and *Roosters* (1987). Born in Bali, she is the daughter of an Indonesian mother and a Colombian-Mexican father.

In 1984, the New York production of *The Cuban Swimmer* was noteworthy for an ingeniously designed set that realistically re-created on stage Pacific Ocean waves, a helicopter, and a boat. According to the *New York Times*, Jeannette Mirabel, as the Cuban swimmer, kept "her arms fluttering in the imaginary waters throughout the play."

◆ ◆ ◆

MILCHA SANCHEZ-SCOTT

The Cuban Swimmer
(1984)

CHARACTERS

MARGARITA SUÁREZ, *the swimmer*
EDUARDO SUÁREZ, *her father,*
    the coach
SIMÓN SUÁREZ, *her brother*
AÍDA SUÁREZ, *her mother*

ABUELA, *her grandmother*
VOICE OF MEL MUNSON
VOICE OF MARY BETH WHITE
VOICE OF RADIO OPERATOR

SETTING
The Pacific Ocean between San Pedro and Catalina Island.

TIME
Summer.
Live conga drums can be used to punctuate the action of the play.

SCENE 1
Pacific Ocean. Midday. On the horizon, in perspective, a small boat enters upstage left, crosses to upstage right, and exits. Pause. Lower on the horizon, the same boat, in larger perspective, enters upstage right, crosses and exits upstage left. Blackout.

SCENE 2
Pacific Ocean. Midday. The swimmer, Margarita Suárez, is swimming. On the boat following behind her are her father, Eduardo Suárez, holding a megaphone,

---

*No photograph available for this author.

and Simón, her brother, sitting on top of the cabin with his shirt off, punk
sunglasses on, binoculars hanging on his chest.

EDUARDO: *(leaning forward, shouting in time to Margarita's swimming)*
Uno, dos, uno, dos. Y uno, dos . . . keep your shoulders parallel to the
water.

SIMÓN: I'm gonna take these glasses off and look straight into the sun.

EDUARDO: *(through megaphone)* Muy bien, muy bien . . . but punch those
arms in, baby.

SIMÓN: *(looking directly at the sun through binoculars)* Come on, come on,
zap me. Show me something. *(He looks behind at the shoreline and
ahead at the sea.)* Stop! Stop, *Papi!* Stop!

Aída Suárez and Abuela, the swimmer's mother and grandmother, enter running from the back of the boat.

5 **AÍDA and ABUELA:** Qué? Qué es?
AÍDA: *Es un* shark?
EDUARDO: Eh?
ABUELA: Que es un shark *dicen?*

Eduardo blows whistle. Margarita looks up at the boat.

SIMÓN: No, *Papi*, no shark, no shark. We've reached the halfway mark.
10 **ABUELA:** *(looking into the water)* A dónde está?
AÍDA: It's not in the water.
ABUELA: Oh, no? Oh, no?
AÍDA: No! *A poco* do you think they're gonna have signs in the water to
say you are halfway to Santa Catalina? No. It's done very scientific.
A ver, hijo, explain it to your grandma.
SIMÓN: Well, you see, Abuela—*(He points behind.)* There's San Pedro. *(He
points ahead.)* And there's Santa Catalina. Looks halfway to me.

Abuela shakes her head and is looking back and forth, trying to make the decision, when suddenly the sound of a helicopter is heard.

15 **ABUELA:** *(looking up)* Virgencita de la Caridad del Cobre. *Qué es eso?*

Sound of helicopter gets closer. Margarita looks up.

MARGARITA: Papi, Papi!

*A small commotion on the boat, with Everybody pointing at the helicopter
above. Shadows of the helicopter fall on the boat. Simón looks up at it through
binoculars.*

Papi—*qué es?* What is it?
EDUARDO: *(through megaphone)* Uh . . . uh . . . uh, *un momentico* . . . *mi
hija.* . . . Your *papi's* got everything under control, understand?
Uh . . . you just keep stroking. And stay . . . uh . . . close to the
boat.

SIMÓN: Wow, *Papi!* We're on TV, man! Holy Christ, we're all over the fucking U.S.A.! It's Mel Munson and Mary Beth White!
AÍDA: *Por Dios!* Simón, don't swear. And put on your shirt.

Aída fluffs her hair, puts on her sunglasses and waves to the helicopter. Simón leans over the side of the boat and yells to Margarita.

20 SIMÓN: Yo, Margo! You're on TV, man.
EDUARDO: Leave your sister alone. Turn on the radio.
MARGARITA: *Papi! Qué está pasando?*
ABUELA: *Que es la televisión dicen? (She shakes her head.) Porque como yo no puedo ver nada sin mis espejuelos.*

Abuela rummages through the boat, looking for her glasses. Voices of Mel Munson and Mary Beth White are heard over the boat's radio.

MEL'S VOICE: As we take a closer look at the gallant crew of *La Havana* . . . and there . . . yes, there she is . . . the little Cuban swimmer from Long Beach, California, nineteen-year-old Margarita Suárez. The unknown swimmer is our Cinderella entry . . . a bundle of tenacity, battling her way through the choppy, murky waters of the cold Pacific to reach the Island of Romance . . . Santa Catalina . . . where should she be the first to arrive, two thousand dollars and a gold cup will be waiting for her.
25 AÍDA: Doesn't even cover our expenses.
ABUELA: *Qué dice?*
EDUARDO: Shhhh!
MARY BETH'S VOICE: This is really a family effort, Mel, and—
MEL'S VOICE: Indeed it is. Her trainer, her coach, her mentor, is her father, Eduardo Suárez. Not a swimmer himself, it says here, Mr. Suárez is head usher of the Holy Name Society and the owner-operator of Suárez Treasures of the Sea and Salvage Yard. I guess it's one of those places—
30 MARY BETH'S VOICE: If I might interject a fact here, Mel, assisting in this swim is Mrs. Suárez, who is a former Miss Cuba.
MEL'S VOICE: And a beautiful woman in her own right. Let's try and get a closer look.

Helicopter sound gets louder. Margarita, frightened, looks up again.

MARGARITA: *Papi!*
EDUARDO: *(through megaphone) Mi hija,* don't get nervous . . . it's the press. I'm handling it.
AÍDA: I see how you're handling it.
35 EDUARDO: *(through megaphone)* Do you hear? Everything is under control. Get back into your rhythm. Keep your elbows high and kick and kick and kick and kick . . .
ABUELA: *(finds her glasses and puts them on) Ay sí, es la televisión . . . (She points to helicopter.) Qué lindo mira . . . (She fluffs her hair, gives a big*

wave.) *Aló América! Viva mi Margarita, viva todo los Cubanos en los Estados Unidos!*
AÍDA: *Ay por Dios,* Cecilia, the man didn't come all this way in his helicopter to look at you jumping up and down, making a fool of yourself.
ABUELA: I don't care. I'm proud.
AÍDA: He can't understand you anyway.
40 ABUELA: *Viva . . . (She stops.) Simón, comó se dice viva?*
SIMÓN: Hurray.
ABUELA: Hurray for *mi* Margarita *y* for all the Cubans living *en* the United States, *y un abrazo . . . Simón, abrazo . . .*
SIMÓN: A big hug.
ABUELA: *Sí,* a big hug to all my friends in Miami, Long Beach, Union City, except for my son Carlos, who lives in New York in sin! He lives . . . *(she crosses herself)* in Brooklyn with a Puerto Rican woman in sin! *No decente . . .*
45 SIMÓN: Decent.
ABUELA: Carlos, *no decente.* This family, *decente.*
AÍDA: Cecilia, *por Dios.*
MEL'S VOICE: Look at that enthusiasm. The whole family has turned out to cheer little Margarita on to victory! I hope they won't be too disappointed.
MARY BETH'S VOICE: She seems to be making good time, Mel.
50 MEL'S VOICE: Yes, it takes all kinds to make a race. And it's a testimonial to the all-encompassing fairness . . . the greatness of this, the Wrigley Invitational Women's Swim to Catalina, where among all the professionals there is still room for the amateurs . . . like these, the simple people we see below us on the ragtag *La Havana,* taking their long-shot chance to victory. *Vaya con Dios!*

Helicopter sound fading as family, including Margarita, watch silently. Static as Simón turns radio off. Eduardo walks to bow of boat, looks out on the horizon.

EDUARDO: *(to himself)* Amateurs.
AÍDA: Eduardo, that person insulted us. Did you hear, Eduardo? That he called us a simple people in a ragtag boat? Did you hear . . . ?
ABUELA: *(clenching her fist at departing helicopter) Mal-Rayo los parta!*
SIMÓN: *(same gesture)* Asshole!

Aída follows Eduardo as he goes to side of boat and stares at Margarita.

55 AÍDA: This person comes in his helicopter to insult your wife, your family, your daughter . . .
MARGARITA: *(pops her head out of the water)* Papi?
AÍDA: Do you hear me, Eduardo? I am not simple.
ABUELA: *Sí.*
AÍDA: I am complicated.
60 ABUELA: *Sí, demasiada complicada.*
AÍDA: Me and my family are not so simple.

SIMÓN: Mom, the guy's an asshole.
ABUELA: *(shaking her fist at helicopter)* Asshole!
AÍDA: If my daughter was simple, she would not be in that water swimming.
65 MARGARITA: Simple? *Papi* . . . ?
AÍDA: *Ahora*, Eduardo, this is what I want you to do. When we get to Santa Catalina, I want you to call the TV station and demand an apology.
EDUARDO: *Cállete mujer! Aquí mando yo.* I will decide what is to be done.
MARGARITA: *Papi,* tell me what's going on.
EDUARDO: Do you understand what I am saying to you, Aída?
70 SIMÓN: *(leaning over side of boat, to Margarita)* Yo Margo! You know that Mel Munson guy on TV? He called you a simple amateur and said you didn't have a chance.
ABUELA: *(leaning directly behind Simón.) Mi hija, insultó a la familia. Desgraciado!*
AÍDA: *(leaning in behind Abuela)* He called us peasants! And your father is not doing anything about it. He just knows how to yell at me.
EDUARDO: *(through megaphone)* Shut up! All of you! Do you want to break her concentration? Is that what you are after? Eh?

Abuela, Aída, and Simón shrink back. Eduardo paces before them.

Swimming is rhythm and concentration. You win a race *aquí*. *(Pointing to his head.)* Now . . . *(to Simón)* you, take care of the boat, Aída y Mama . . . do something. Anything. Something practical.

Abuela and Aída get on knees and pray in Spanish.

Hija, give it everything, eh? . . . *por la familia. Uno . . . dos.* . . . You must win.

Simón *goes into cabin. The prayers continue as lights change to indicate bright sunlight, later in the afternoon.*

SCENE 3

Tableau for a couple of beats. Eduardo on bow with timer in one hand as he counts strokes per minute. Simón is in the cabin steering, wearing his sunglasses, baseball cap on backward. Abuela and Aída are at the side of the boat, heads down, hands folded, still muttering prayers in Spanish.

AÍDA and ABUELA: *(crossing themselves) En el nombre del Padre, del Hijo y del Espíritu Santo amén.*
EDUARDO: *(through megaphone)* You're stroking seventy-two!
SIMÓN: *(singing)* Mama's stroking, Mama's stroking seventy-two. . . .
EDUARDO: *(through megaphone)* You comfortable with it?
5 SIMÓN: *(singing)* Seventy-two, seventy-two, seventy-two for you.
AÍDA: *(looking at the heavens)* Ay, Eduardo, *ven acá*, we should be grateful that *Nuestro Señor* gave us such a beautiful day.

ABUELA: *(crosses herself)* Si, gracias a Dios.
EDUARDO: She's stroking seventy-two, with no problem. *(He throws a kiss to the sky.)* It's a beautiful day to win.
AÍDA: Qué hermoso! So clear and bright. Not a cloud in the sky. Mira! Mira! Even rainbows on the water . . . a sign from God.
SIMÓN: *(singing)* Rainbows on the water . . . you in my arms . . .
ABUELA and EDUARDO: *(Looking the wrong way.)* Dónde?
AÍDA: *(pointing toward Margarita)* There, dancing in front of Margarita, leading her on . . .
EDUARDO: Rainbows on . . . Ay coño! It's an oil slick! You . . . you . . . *(To Simón.)* Stop the boat. *(Runs to bow, yelling.)* Margarita! Margarita!

On the next stroke, Margarita comes up all covered in black oil.

MARGARITA: Papi! Papi . . . !

Everybody goes to the side and stares at Margarita, who stares back. Eduardo freezes.

AÍDA: Apúrate, Eduardo, move . . . what's wrong with you . . . *no me oíste*, get my daughter out of the water.
EDUARDO: *(softly)* We can't touch her. If we touch her, she's disqualified.
AÍDA: But I'm her mother.
EDUARDO: Not even by her own mother. Especially by her own mother. . . . You always want the rules to be different for you, you always want to be the exception. *(To Simón.)* And you . . . you didn't see it, eh? You were playing again?
SIMÓN: *Papi*, I was watching . . .
AÍDA: *(interrupting)* Pues, do something Eduardo. You are the big coach, the monitor.
SIMÓN: Mentor! Mentor!
EDUARDO: How can a person think around you? *(He walks off to bow, puts head in hands.)*
ABUELA: *(looking over side)* Mira como todos los little birds are dead. *(She crosses herself.)*
AÍDA: Their little wings are glued to their sides.
SIMÓN: Christ, this is like the La Brea tar pits.
AÍDA: They can't move their little wings.
ABUELA: Esa niña tiene que moverse.
SIMÓN: Yeah, Margo, you gotta move, man.

Abuela and Simón gesture for Margarita to move. Aída gestures for her to swim.

ABUELA: Anda niña, muévete.
AÍDA: Swim, *hija*, swim or the *aceite* will stick to your wings.
MARGARITA: Papi?
ABUELA: *(taking megaphone)* Your *papi* say "move it!"

Margarita with difficulty starts moving.

ABUELA, AÍDA and SIMÓN: *(laboriously counting)* Uno, dos . . . uno, dos . . . anda . . . uno, dos.
EDUARDO: *(running to take megaphone from Abuela)* Uno, dos . . .

Simón races into cabin and starts the engine. Abuela, Aída and Eduardo count together.

35 SIMÓN: *(looking ahead)* Papi, it's over there!
EDUARDO: Eh?
SIMÓN: *(pointing ahead and to the right)* It's getting clearer over there.
EDUARDO: *(through megaphone)* Now pay attention to me. Go to the right.

Simón, Abuela, Aída and Eduardo all lean over side. They point ahead and to the right, except Abuela, who points to the left.

FAMILY: *(shouting together)* Para yá! Para yá!

Lights go down on boat. A special light on Margarita, swimming through the oil, and on Abuela, watching her.

40 ABUELA: Sangre de mi sangre, you will be another to save us. En Bolondron, where your great-grandmother Luz Suárez was born, they say one day it rained blood. All the people, they run into their houses. They cry, they pray, *pero* your great-grandmother Luz she had *cojones* like a man. She run outside. She look straight at the sky. She shake her fist. And she say to the evil one, "Mira . . . *(beating her chest)* coño, Diablo, aquí estoy si me quieres." And she open her mouth, and she drunk the blood.

Blackout

SCENE 4

Lights up on boat. Aída and Eduardo are on deck watching Margarita swim. We hear the gentle, rhythmic lap, lap, lap of the water, then the sound of inhaling and exhaling as Margarita's breathing becomes louder. Then Margarita's heartbeat is heard, with the lapping of the water and the breathing under it. These sounds continue beneath the dialogue to the end of the scene.

AÍDA: Dios mío. Look how she moves through the water. . . .
EDUARDO: You see, it's very simple. It is a matter of concentration.
AÍDA: The first time I put her in water she came to life, she grew before my eyes. She moved, she smiled, she loved it more than me. She didn't want my breast any longer. She wanted the water.
EDUARDO: And of course, the rhythm. The rhythm takes away the pain and helps the concentration.

Pause. Aída and Eduardo watch Margarita.

5 AÍDA: Is that my child or a seal. . . .
EDUARDO: Ah, a seal, the reason for that is that she's keeping her arms very close to her body. She cups her hands, and then she reaches and digs, reaches and digs.
AÍDA: To think that a daughter of mine . . .
EDUARDO: It's the training, the hours in the water. I used to tie weights around her little wrists and ankles.
AÍDA: A spirit, an ocean spirit, must have entered my body when I was carrying her.
10 EDUARDO: *(to Margarita)* Your stroke is slowing down.

Pause. We hear Margarita's heartbeat with the breathing under, faster now.

AÍDA: Eduardo, that night, the night on the boat . . .
EDUARDO: Ah, the night on the boat again . . . the moon was . . .
AÍDA: The moon was full. We were coming to America. . . . Qué romantico.

Heartbeat and breathing continue.

EDUARDO: We were cold, afraid, with no money, and on top of everything, you were hysterical, yelling at me, tearing at me with your nails. *(Opens his shirt, points to the base of his neck.)* Look, I still bear the scars . . . telling me that I didn't know what I was doing . . . saying that we were going to die. . . .
15 AÍDA: You took me, you stole me from my home . . . you didn't give me a chance to prepare. You just said we have to go now, now! Now, you said. You didn't let me take anything. I left everything behind. . . . I left everything behind.
EDUARDO: Saying that I wasn't good enough, that your father didn't raise you so that I could drown you in the sea.
AÍDA: You didn't let me say even a good-bye. You took me, you stole me, you tore me from my home.
EDUARDO: I took you so we could be married.
AÍDA: That was in Miami. But that night on the boat, Eduardo. . . . We were not married, that night on the boat.
20 EDUARDO: *No pasó nada!* Once and for all get it out of your head, it was cold, you hated me, and we were afraid. . . .
AÍDA: *Mentiroso!*
EDUARDO: A man can't do it when he is afraid.
AÍDA: Liar! You did it very well.
EDUARDO: I did?
25 AÍDA: *Sí.* Gentle. You were so gentle and then strong . . . my passion for you so deep. Standing next to you . . . I would ache . . . looking at your hands I would forget to breathe, you were irresistible.
EDUARDO: I was?
AÍDA: You took me into your arms, you touched my face with your fingertips . . . you kissed my eyes . . . *la esquina de la boca y* . . .
EDUARDO: *Sí, sí,* and then . . .

AÍDA: I look at your face on top of mine, and I see the lights of Havana in your eyes. That's when you seduced me.
30 EDUARDO: Shhh, they're gonna hear you.

Lights go down. Special on Aída.

AÍDA: That was the night. A woman doesn't forget those things . . . and later that night was the dream . . . the dream of a big country with fields of fertile land and big, giant things growing. And there by a green, slimy pond I found a giant pea pod and when I opened it, it was full of little, tiny baby frogs.

Aída crosses herself as she watches Margarita. We hear louder breathing and heartbeat.

MARGARITA: Santa Teresa. Little Flower of God, pray for me. San Martín de Porres, pray for me. Santa Rosa de Lima, *Virgencita de la Caridad del Cobre*, pray for me. . . . Mother pray for me.

SCENE 5

Loud howling of wind is heard, as lights change to indicate unstable weather, fog and mist. Family on deck, braced and huddled against the wind. Simón is at the helm.

AÍDA: Ay Dios mío, qué viento.
EDUARDO: *(through megaphone)* Don't drift out . . . that wind is pushing you out. *(To Simón.)* You! Slow down. Can't you see your sister is drifting out?
SIMÓN: It's the wind, *Papi*.
AÍDA: Baby, don't go so far. . . .
5 ABUELA: *(to heaven)* Ay Gran Poder de Dios, quita este maldito viento.
SIMÓN: Margo! Margo! Stay close to the boat.
EDUARDO: Dig in. Dig in hard. . . . Reach down from your guts and dig in.
ABUELA: *(to heaven)* Ay Virgen de la Caridad del Cobre, por lo más tú quieres a pararla.
AÍDA: *(putting her hand out, reaching for Margarita)* Baby, don't go far.

Abuela crosses herself. Action freezes. Lights get dimmer, special on Margarita. She keeps swimming, stops, starts again, stops, then, finally exhausted, stops altogether. The boat stops moving.

10 EDUARDO: What's going on here? Why are we stopping?
SIMÓN: *Papi*, she's not moving! Yo Margo!

The family all run to the side.

EDUARDO: Hija! . . . Hijita! You're tired, eh?
AÍDA: *Por supuesto* she's tired. I like to see you get in the water, waving your arms and legs from San Pedro to Santa Catalina. A person isn't a machine, a person has to rest.

SIMÓN: Yo, Mama! Cool out, it ain't fucking brain surgery.
EDUARDO: *(to Simón)* Shut up, you. *(Louder to Margarita.)* I guess your mother's right for once, huh? . . . I guess you had to stop, eh? . . . Give your brother, the idiot . . . a chance to catch up with you.
SIMÓN: *(clowning like Mortimer Snerd)* Dum dee dum dee dum ooops, ah shucks . . .
EDUARDO: I don't think he's Cuban.
SIMÓN: *(like Ricky Ricardo)* Oye, Lucy! I'm home! Ba ba lu!
EDUARDO: *(joins in clowning, grabbing Simón in a headlock)* What am I gonna do with this idiot, eh? I don't understand this idiot. He's not like us, Margarita. *(Laughing.)* You think if we put him into your bathing suit with a cap on his head . . . *(He laughs hysterically.)* You think anyone would know . . . huh? Do you think anyone would know? *(Laughs.)*
SIMÓN: *(vamping)* Ay, mi amor. Anybody looking for tits would know.

Eduardo slaps Simón across the face, knocking him down. Aída runs to Simón's aid. Abuela holds Eduardo back.

MARGARITA: Mía culpa! Mía culpa!
ABUELA: Qué dices hija?
MARGARITA: Papi, it's my fault, it's all my fault. . . . I'm so cold, I can't move. . . . I put my face in the water . . . and I hear them whispering . . . laughing at me. . . .
AÍDA: Who is laughing at you?
MARGARITA: The fish are all biting me . . . they hate me . . . they whisper about me. She can't swim, they say. She can't glide. She has no grace. . . . Yellowtails, bonita, tuna, man-o'-war, snub-nose sharks, *los baracudas* . . . they all hate me . . . only the dolphins care . . . and sometimes I hear the whales crying . . . she is lost, she is dead. I'm so numb, I can't feel. *Papi! Papi!* Am I dead?
EDUARDO: *Vamos*, baby, punch those arms in. Come on . . . do you hear me?
MARGARITA: Papi . . . Papi . . . forgive me. . . .

All is silent on the boat. Eduardo drops his megaphone, his head bent down in dejection. Abuela, Aída, Simón, all leaning over the side of the boat. Simón slowly walks away.

AÍDA: Mi hija, qué tienes?
SIMÓN: Oh, Christ, don't make her say it. Please don't make her say it.
ABUELA: Say what? Qué cosa?
SIMÓN: She wants to quit, can't you see she's had enough?
ABUELA: Mira, para eso. Esta niña is turning blue.
AÍDA: Oyeme, mi hija. Do you want to come out of the water?
MARGARITA: Papi?
SIMÓN: *(to Eduardo)* She won't come out until *you* tell her.
AÍDA: Eduardo . . . answer your daughter.
EDUARDO: *Le dije* to concentrate . . . concentrate on your rhythm. Then the rhythm would carry her . . . ay, it's a beautiful thing, Aída. It's

like yoga, like meditation, the mind over matter . . . the mind controlling the body . . . that's how the great things in the world have been done. I wish you . . . I wish my wife could understand.

MARGARITA: *Papi?*

SIMÓN: *(to Margarita)* Forget him.

40 AÍDA: *(imploring)* Eduardo, *por favor.*

EDUARDO: *(walking in circles)* Why didn't you let her concentrate? Don't you understand, the concentration, the rhythm is everything. But no, you wouldn't listen. *(Screaming to the ocean.)* Goddamn Cubans, why, God, why do you make us go everywhere with our families? *(He goes to back of boat.)*

AÍDA: *(opening her arms) Mi hija, ven,* come to *Mami. (Rocking.)* Your *mami* knows.

Abuela has taken the training bottle, puts it in a net. She and Simón lower it to Margarita.

SIMÓN: Take this. Drink it. *(As Margarita drinks, Abuela crosses herself.)*

ABUELA: *Sangre de mi sangre.*

Music comes up softly. Margarita drinks, gives the bottle back, stretches out her arms, as if on a cross. Floats on her back. She begins a graceful back-stroke. Lights fade on boat as special lights come up on Margarita. She stops. Slowly turns over and starts to swim, gradually picking up speed. Suddenly as if in pain she stops, tries again, then stops in pain again. She becomes disoriented and falls to the bottom of the sea. Special on Margarita at the bottom of the sea.

45 MARGARITA: *Ya no puedo . . .* I can't. . . . A person isn't a machine . . . *es mi culpa . . .* Father forgive me . . . *Papi! Papi!* One, two. *Uno, dos. (Pause.) Papi! A dónde estás? (Pause.)* One, two, one, two. *Papi! Ay, Papi!* Where are you . . . ? Don't leave me. . . . Why don't you answer me? *(Pause. She starts to swim, slowly.) Uno, dos, uno, dos.* Dig in, dig in. *(Stops swimming.) Por favor, Papi! (Starts to swim again.)* One, two, one, two. Kick from your hip, kick from your hip. *(Stops swimming. Starts to cry.)* Oh God, please. . . . *(Pause.)* Hail Mary, full of grace . . . dig in, dig in . . . the Lord is with thee. . . . *(She swims to the rhythm of her Hail Mary.)* Hail Mary, full of grace . . . dig in, dig in . . . the Lord is with thee . . . dig in, dig in. . . . Blessed art thou among women. . . . *Mami,* it hurts. You let go of my hand. I'm lost. . . . And blessed is the fruit of thy womb, now and at the hour of our death. Amen. I don't want to die, I don't want to die.

Margarita is still swimming. Blackout. She is gone.

SCENE 6

Lights up on boat, we hear radio static. There is a heavy mist. On deck we see only black outline of Abuela with shawl over her head. We hear the voices of Eduardo, Aída, and Radio Operator.

EDUARDO'S VOICE: *La Havana!* Coming from San Pedro. Over.
RADIO OPERATOR'S VOICE: Right, DT6-6, you say you've lost a swimmer.
AÍDA'S VOICE: Our child, our only daughter . . . listen to me. Her name is Margarita Inez Suárez, she is wearing a black one-piece bathing suit cut high in the legs with a white racing stripe down the sides, a white bathing cap with goggles and her whole body covered with a . . . with a . . .
EDUARDO'S VOICE: With lanolin and paraffin.
5 AÍDA'S VOICE: *Sí . . . con lanolin and paraffin.*

More radio static. Special on Simón, on the edge of the boat.

SIMÓN: Margo! Yo Margo! *(Pause.)* Man don't do this. *(Pause.)* Come on. . . . Come on. . . . *(Pause.)* God, why does everything have to be so hard? *(Pause.)* Stupid. You know you're not supposed to die for this. Stupid. It's his dream and he can't even swim. *(Pause.)* Punch those arms in. Come home. Come home. I'm your little brother. Don't forget what Mama said. You're not supposed to leave me behind. *Vamos*, Margarita, take your little brother, hold his hand tight when you cross the street. He's so little. *(Pause.)* Oh, Christ, give us a sign. . . . I know! I know! Margo, I'll send you a message . . . like mental telepathy. I'll hold my breath, close my eyes, and I'll bring you home. *(He takes a deep breath; a few beats.)* This time I'll beep . . . I'll send out sonar signals like a dolphin. *(He imitates dolphin sounds.)*

The sound of real dolphins takes over from Simón, then fades into sound of Abuela saying the Hail Mary in Spanish, as full lights come up slowly.

SCENE 7

Eduardo coming out of cabin, sobbing, Aída holding him. Simón anxiously scanning the horizon. Abuela looking calmly ahead.

EDUARDO: *Es mi culpa, sí, es mi culpa.* (He hits his chest.)
AÍDA: *Ya, ya viejo* . . . it was my sin . . . I left my home.
EDUARDO: Forgive me, forgive me. I've lost our daughter, our sister, our granddaughter, *mi carne, mi sangre, mis ilusiones.* *(To heaven.)* *Dios mío,* take me . . . take me, I say . . . Goddammit, take me!
SIMÓN: I'm going in.
5 AÍDA and EDUARDO: No!
EDUARDO: *(grabbing and holding Simón, speaking to heaven)* God, take me, not my children. They are my dreams, my illusions . . . and not this one, this one is my mystery . . . he has my secret dreams. In him are the parts of me I cannot see.

Eduardo embraces Simón. Radio static becomes louder.

AÍDA: I . . . I think I see her.
SIMÓN: No, it's just a seal.

ABUELA: *(looking out with binoculars)* Mi nietacita, dónde estás? *(She feels her heart.)* I don't feel the knife in my heart . . . my little fish is not lost.

Radio crackles with static. As lights dim on boat, Voices of Mel and Mary Beth are heard over the radio.

10 MEL'S VOICE: Tragedy has marred the face of the Wrigley Invitational Women's Race to Catalina. The Cuban swimmer, little Margarita Suárez, has reportedly been lost at sea. Coast Guard and divers are looking for her as we speak. Yet in spite of this tragedy the race must go on because . . .
MARY BETH'S VOICE: *(interrupting loudly)* Mel!
MEL'S VOICE: *(startled)* What!
MARY BETH'S VOICE: Ah . . . excuse me, Mel . . . we have a winner. We've just received word from Catalina that one of the swimmers is just fifty yards from the breakers . . . it's, oh, it's . . . Margarita Suárez!

Special on family in cabin listening to radio.

MEL'S VOICE: What? I thought she died!

Special on Margarita, taking off bathing cap, trophy in hand, walking on the water.

15 MARY BETH'S VOICE: Ahh . . . unless . . . unless this is a tragic . . . No . . . there she is, Mel. Margarita Suárez! The only one in the race wearing a black bathing suit cut high in the legs with a racing stripe down the side.

Family cheering, embracing.

SIMÓN: *(screaming)* Way to go, Margo!
MEL'S VOICE: This is indeed a miracle! It's a resurrection! Margarita Suárez, with a flotilla of boats to meet her, is now walking on the waters, through the breakers . . . onto the beach, with crowds of people cheering her on. What a jubilation! This is a miracle!

Sound of crowds cheering. Lights and cheering sounds fade.

Blackout

READING AND REACTING

1. *The Cuban Swimmer* is a short play with a single setting. In what additional locations could Sanchez-Scott have set the play's action? What might she have gained or lost by using these additional settings?

2. What lighting and sound effects does the play call for? In what way do these effects advance the action of the play? In what way—if any—do they help to communicate the play's theme?
3. Although most of the play is in English, the characters frequently speak Spanish. What are the advantages of this use of Spanish? Are there any drawbacks?
4. What function do the voices of Mel and Mary Beth serve in the play?
5. What conflicts develop among the family members as the play proceeds? In what way might these conflicts represent the problems of other immigrants to the United States?
6. In what sense is Mel's final comment "This is a miracle!" ironic?
7. Do you think this play comments on the position of women in American culture? In Cuban-American culture?
8. Could this play be seen as an **allegory?** What is the value of seeing it in this way?
9. Throughout much of the play Margarita is swimming in full view of the audience. Devise three ways in which a director could achieve this effect on stage. Which one would you choose if you were directing the play?
10. As the headnote that precedes the play explains, the 1984 New York production of *The Cuban Swimmer* had an extremely realistic set. Could the play be staged unrealistically, with the characters on a raised platform in make-believe water? How do you think this kind of set would affect the audience?
11. **JOURNAL ENTRY** Are you able to empathize with Margarita's struggle? What elements of the play make it easy or difficult for you to do so?

Related Works: "Two Kinds" (p. 285), "Black Hair" (p. 549)

◆ **SOPHOCLES** (496–406 B.C.) is one of the great Greek tragic dramatists. He lived during the flowering of fifth-century Athens—the high point of Greek civilization. Though he wrote at least one hundred and twenty plays, only seven have survived, including three plays about Oedipus: *Oedipus the King, Oedipus at Colonus,* and *Antigone.*

Oedipus the King, or *Oedipus Rex,* was performed shortly after a great plague in Athens; the play opens with the account of a plague in Oedipus's kingdom. Over the years, *Oedipus the King* has attracted impressive critical attention, from Aristotle's use of it as a model for his definition of tragedy to Freud's use of its power as evidence of the validity of the so-called Oedipus complex.

SOPHOCLES

Oedipus the King*
(c. 430 B.C.)

Translated by Thomas Gould

CHARACTERS

OEDIPUS,[1] *the King of Thebes*
PRIEST OF ZEUS, *leader of the suppliants*
CREON, *Oedipus's brother-in-law*
CHORUS, *a group of Theban elders*
CHORAGOS, *spokesman of the Chorus*
TIRESIAS, *a blind seer or prophet*
JOCASTA, *the queen of Thebes*
MESSENGER, *from Corinth, once a shepherd*
HERDSMAN, *once a servant of Laius*
SECOND MESSENGER, *a servant of Oedipus*

MUTES
SUPPLIANTS, *Thebans seeking Oedipus's help*
ATTENDANTS, *for the Royal Family*
SERVANTS, *to lead Tiresias and Oedipus*
ANTIGONE, *daughter of Oedipus and Jocasta*
ISMENE, *daughter of Oedipus and Jocasta*

The action takes place during the day in front of the royal palace in Thebes. There are two altars (left and right) on the proscenium and several steps leading down to the orchestra. As the play opens, Thebans of various ages who have come to beg Oedipus for help are sitting on these steps and in part of the orchestra. These suppliants are holding branches of laurel or olive which have strips of wool[2] wrapped around them. Oedipus enters from the palace (the central door of the skene).

PROLOGUE[3]

OEDIPUS: My children, ancient Cadmus'[4] newest care,
why have you hurried to those seats, your boughs
wound with the emblems of the suppliant?

---

*Note that individual lines are numbered in the following play. When a line is shared by two or more characters, it is counted as one line.

---

[1] *Oedipus:* The name means "swollen foot." It refers to the mutilation of Oedipus's feet done by his father, Laius, before the infant was sent to Mount Cithaeron to be put to death by exposure.   [2] *wool:* Branches wrapped with wool are traditional symbols of prayer or supplication.   [3] *Prologue:* portion of the play containing the exposition, or explanation, of what has gone before and what is now happening.   [4] *Cadmus:* Oedipus's great great grandfather (although he does not know this) and the founder of Thebes.

The city is weighed down with fragrant smoke,
with hymns to the Healer[5] and the cries of mourners.
I thought it wrong, my sons, to hear your words
through emissaries, and have come out myself,
I, Oedipus, a name that all men know.

(Oedipus addresses the Priest.)

Old man—for it is fitting that you speak
for all—what is your mood as you entreat me,
fear or trust? You may be confident
that I'll do anything. How hard of heart
if an appeal like this did not rouse my pity!

PRIEST: You, Oedipus, who hold the power here,
you see our several ages, we who sit
before your altars—some not strong enough
to take long flight, some heavy in old age,
the priests, as I of Zeus,[6] and from our youths
a chosen band. The rest sit with their windings
in the markets, at the twin shrines of Pallas,[7]
and the prophetic embers of Ismēnos.[8]
Our city, as you see yourself, is tossed
too much, and can no longer lift its head
above the troughs of billows red with death.
It dies in the fruitful flowers of the soil,
it dies in its pastured herds, and in its women's
barren pangs. And the fire-bearing god[9]
has swooped upon the city, hateful plague,
and he has left the house of Cadmus empty.
Black Hades[10] is made rich with moans and weeping.
Not judging you an equal of the gods,
do I and the children sit here at your hearth,
but as the first of men, in troubled times
and in encounters with divinities.
You came to Cadmus' city and unbound
the tax we had to pay to the harsh singer,[11]

---

[5] *Healer:* Apollo, god of prophecy, light, healing, justice, purification, and destruction. [6] *Zeus:* father and king of the gods. [7] *Pallas:* Athena, goddess of wisdom, arts, crafts, and war. [8] *Ismēnos:* a reference to the temple of Apollo near the river Ismēnos in Thebes. Prophecies were made here by "reading" the ashes of the altar fires. [9] *fire-bearing god:* contagious fever viewed as a god. [10] *Black Hades:* refers to both the underworld where the spirits of the dead go and the god of the underworld. [11] *harsh singer:* the Sphinx, a monster with a woman's head, a lion's body, and wings. The "tax" that Oedipus freed Thebes from was the destruction of all the young men who failed to solve the Sphinx's riddle and were subsequently devoured. The Sphinx always asked the same riddle: "What goes on four legs in the

did it without a helpful word from us,
with no instruction; with a god's assistance
you raised up our life, so we believe.
40 Again now Oedipus, our greatest power,
we plead with you, as suppliants, all of us,
to find us strength, whether from a god's response,
or learned in some way from another man.
I know that the experienced among men
45 give counsels that will prosper best of all.
Noblest of men, lift up our land again!
Think also of yourself; since now the land
calls you its Savior for your zeal of old,
oh let us never look back at your rule
50 as men helped up only to fall again!
Do not stumble! Put our land on firm feet!
The bird of omen was auspicious then,
when you brought that luck; be that same man again!
The power is yours; if you will rule our country,
55 rule over men, not in an empty land.
A towered city or a ship is nothing
if desolate and no man lives within.
OEDIPUS: Pitiable children, oh I know, I know
the yearnings that have brought you. Yes, I know
60 that you are sick. And yet, though you are sick,
there is not one of you so sick as I.
For your affliction comes to each alone,
for him and no one else, but my soul mourns
for me and for you, too, and for the city.
65 You do not waken me as from a sleep,
for I have wept, bitterly and long,
tried many paths in the wanderings of thought,
and the single cure I found by careful search
I've acted on: I sent Menoeceus' son,
70 Creon, brother of my wife, to the Pythian
halls of Phoebus,[12] so that I might learn
what I must do or say to save this city.
Already, when I think what day this is,
I wonder anxiously what he is doing.

---

morning, two legs at noon, and three legs in the evening, and yet is weakest when supported by the largest number of feet?" Oedipus discovered the correct answer—man, who crawls in infancy, walks in his prime, and uses a stick in old age—and thus ended the Sphinx's reign of terror. The Sphinx destroyed herself when Oedipus answered the riddle. Oedipus's reward for freeing Thebes of the Sphinx was the throne and the hand of the recently widowed Jocasta.   [12] *Pythian . . . Phoebus:* the temple of Phoebus Apollo's oracle or prophet at Delphi.

⁷⁵ Too long, more than is right, he's been away.
But when he comes, then I shall be a traitor
if I do not do all that the god reveals.
PRIEST: Welcome words! But look, those men have signaled
that it is Creon who is now approaching!
⁸⁰ OEDIPUS: Lord Apollo! May he bring Savior Luck,
a Luck as brilliant as his eyes are now!
PRIEST: His news is happy, it appears. He comes,
forehead crowned with thickly berried laurel.[13]
OEDIPUS: We'll know, for he is near enough to hear us.

(Enter Creon along one of the parados.)

⁸⁵ Lord, brother in marriage, son of Menoeceus!
What is the god's pronouncement that you bring?
CREON: It's good. For even troubles, if they chance
to turn out well, I always count as lucky.
OEDIPUS: But what was the response? You seem to say
⁹⁰ I'm not to fear—but not to take heart either.
CREON: If you will hear me with these men present,
I'm ready to report—or go inside.

(Creon moves up the steps toward the palace.)

OEDIPUS: Speak out to all! The grief that burdens me
concerns these men more than it does my life.
⁹⁵ CREON: Then I shall tell you what I heard from the god.
The task Lord Phoebus sets for us is clear:
drive out pollution sheltered in our land,
and do not shelter what is incurable.
OEDIPUS: What is our trouble? How shall we cleanse ourselves?
¹⁰⁰ CREON: We must banish or murder to free ourselves
from a murder that blows storms through the city.
OEDIPUS: What man's bad luck does he accuse in this?
CREON: My Lord, a king named Laius ruled our land
before you came to steer the city straight.
¹⁰⁵ OEDIPUS: I know. So I was told—I never saw him.
CREON: Since he was murdered, you must raise your hand
against the men who killed him with their hands.
OEDIPUS: Where are they now? And how can we ever find
the track of ancient guilt now hard to read?
¹¹⁰ CREON: In our own land, he said. What we pursue,
that can be caught; but not what we neglect.

---

[13] *laurel:* Creon is wearing a garland of laurel leaves, sacred to Apollo.

OEDIPUS: Was Laius home, or in the countryside—
or was he murdered in some foreign land?
CREON: He left to see a sacred rite, he said;
He left, but never came home from his journey.
OEDIPUS: Did none of his party see it and report—
someone we might profitably question?
CREON: They were all killed but one, who fled in fear,
and he could tell us only one clear fact.
OEDIPUS: What fact? One thing could lead us on to more
if we could get a small start on our hope.
CREON: He said that bandits chanced on them and killed him—
with the force of many hands, not one alone.
OEDIPUS: How could a bandit dare so great an act—
unless this was a plot paid off from here!
CREON: We thought of that, but when Laius was killed,
we had no one to help us in our troubles.
OEDIPUS: It was your very kingship that was killed!
What kind of trouble blocked you from a search?
CREON: The subtle-singing Sphinx asked us to turn
from the obscure to what lay at our feet.
OEDIPUS: Then I shall begin again and make it plain.
It was quite worthy of Phoebus, and worthy of you,
to turn our thoughts back to the murdered man,
and right that you should see me join the battle
for justice to our land and to the god.
Not on behalf of any distant kinships,
it's for myself I will dispel this stain.
Whoever murdered him may also wish
to punish me—and with the selfsame hand.
In helping him I also serve myself.
Now quickly, children: up from the altar steps,
and raise the branches of the suppliant!
Let someone go and summon Cadmus' people:
say I'll do anything.

(Exit an Attendant along one of the parados.)

Our luck will prosper
if the god is with us, or we have already fallen.
PRIEST: Rise, my children; that for which we came,
he has himself proclaimed he will accomplish.
May Phoebus, who announced this, also come
as Savior and reliever from the plague.

(Exit Oedipus and Creon into the palace. The Priest and the Suppliants exit left and right along the parados. After a brief pause, the Chorus (including the Choragos) enters the orchestra from the parados.)

PARADOS[14]

STROPHE 1[15]

CHORUS: Voice from Zeus,[16] sweetly spoken, what are you
    that have arrived from golden
    Pytho[17] to our shining
    Thebes? I am on the rack, terror
155   shakes my soul.
    Delian Healer,[18] summoned by "iē!"
    I await in holy dread what obligation, something new
    or something back once more with the revolving years,
        you'll bring about for me.
160   Oh tell me, child of golden Hope,
        deathless Response!

ANTISTROPHE 1

    I appeal to you first, daughter of Zeus,
        deathless Athena,
    and to your sister who protects this land,
165   Artemis,[19] whose famous throne is the whole circle
        of the marketplace,
    and Phoebus, who shoots from afar: iō!
    Three-fold defenders against death, appear!
    If ever in the past, to stop blind ruin
170   sent against the city,
    you banished utterly the fires of suffering,
        come now again!

STROPHE 2

    Ah! Ah! Unnumbered are the miseries
    I bear. The plague claims all
175   our comrades. Nor has thought found yet a spear
    by which a man shall be protected. What our glorious
    earth gives birth to does not grow. Without a birth
    from cries of labor
        do the women rise.
180   One person after another
        you may see, like flying birds,

---

[14] *Parados:* a song sung by the chorus on the first entering.   [15] *Strophe, Antistrophe:* probably refer to the direction in which the Chorus danced while reciting specific stanzas. Strophe may have indicated dance steps to stage left, antistrophe to stage right.   [16] *Voice from Zeus:* a reference to Apollo's prophecy. Zeus taught Apollo how to prophesy.   [17] *Pytho:* Delphi.   [18] *Delian Healer:* Apollo.   [19] *Artemis:* goddess of virginity, childbirth, and hunting.

faster than indomitable fire, sped
to the shore of the god that is the sunset.[20]

ANTISTROPHE 2
And with their deaths unnumbered dies the city.
185   Her children lie unpitied on the ground,
spreading death, unmourned.
Meanwhile young wives, and gray-haired mothers with them,
on the shores of the altars, from this side and that,
suppliants from mournful trouble,
190   cry out their grief.
A hymn to the Healer shines,
    the flute a mourner's voice.
Against which, golden goddess, daughter of Zeus,
    send lovely Strength.

STROPHE 3
195   Causing raging Ares[21]—who,
    armed now with no shield of bronze,
burns me, coming on amid loud cries—
to turn his back and run from my land,
with a fair wind behind, to the great
200   hall of Amphitritē,[22]
or to the anchorage that welcomes no one,
Thrace's troubled sea!
If night lets something get away at last,
    it comes by day.
205   Fire-bearing god . . .
    you who dispense the might of lightning,
Zeus! Father! Destroy him with your thunderbolt!

(Enter Oedipus from the palace.)

ANTISTROPHE 3
Lycēan Lord![23] From your looped
    bowstring, twisted gold,
210   I wish indomitable missiles might be scattered
and stand forward, our protectors; also fire-bearing
radiance of Artemis, with which
    she darts across the Lycian mountains.
I call the god whose head is bound in gold,
215   with whom this country shares its name,

---

[20] *god . . . sunset:* Hades, god of the underworld.   [21] *Ares:* god of war and destruction.   [22] *Amphitritē:* the Atlantic Ocean.   [23] *Lycēan Lord:* Apollo.

>   Bacchus,[24] wine-flushed, summoned by "euoi!,"
>   Maenads' comrade,
>   to approach ablaze
>   with gleaming . . .
> 220   pine, opposed to that god-hated god.

Episode 1[25]

> OEDIPUS: I hear your prayer. Submit to what I say
>   and to the labors that the plague demands
>   and you'll get help and a relief from evils.
>   I'll make the proclamation, though a stranger
> 225 to the report and to the deed. Alone,
>   had I no key, I would soon lose the track.
>   Since it was only later that I joined you,
>   to all the sons of Cadmus I say this:
>   whoever has clear knowledge of the man
> 230 who murdered Laius, son of Labdacus,
>   I command him to reveal it all to me—
>   nor fear if, to remove the charge, he must
>   accuse himself: his fate will not be cruel—
>   he will depart unstumbling into exile.
> 235 But if you know another, or a stranger,
>   to be the one whose hand is guilty, speak:
>   I shall reward you and remember you.
>   But if you keep your peace because of fear,
>   and shield yourself or kin from my command,
> 240 hear you what I shall do in that event:
>   I charge all in this land where I have throne
>   and power, shut out that man—no matter who—
>   both from your shelter and all spoken words,
>   nor in your prayers or sacrifices make
> 245 him partner, nor allot him lustral[26] water.
>   All men shall drive him from their homes: for he
>   is the pollution that the god-sent Pythian
>   response has only now revealed to me.
>   In this way I ally myself in war
> 250 with the divinity and the deceased.[27]
>   And this curse, too, against the one who did it,
>   whether alone in secrecy, or with others:
>   may he wear out his life unblest and evil!
>   I pray this, too: if he is at my hearth

---

[24] *Bacchus:* Dionysus, god of fertility and wine.   [25] *Episode:* the portion of ancient Greek plays that appears betwen choric songs.   [26] *lustral:* purifying.   [27] *the deceased:* Laius.

255 and in my home, and I have knowledge of him,
may the curse pronounced on others come to me.
All this I lay to you to execute,
for my sake, for the god's, and for this land
now ruined, barren, abandoned by the gods.
260 Even if no god had driven you to it,
you ought not to have left this stain uncleansed,
the murdered man a nobleman, a king!
You should have looked! But now, since, as it happens,
It's I who have the power that he had once,
265 and have his bed, and a wife who shares our seed,
and common bond had we had common children
(had not his hope of offspring had bad luck—
but as it happened, luck lunged at his head);
because of this, as if for my own father,
270 I'll fight for him, I'll leave no means untried,
to catch the one who did it with his hand,
for the son of Labdacus, of Polydōrus,
of Cadmus before him, and of Agēnor.[28]
This prayer against all those who disobey:
275 the gods send out no harvest from their soil,
nor children from their wives. Oh, let them die
victims of this plague, or of something worse.
Yet for the rest of us, people of Cadmus,
we the obedient, may Justice, our ally,
280 and all the gods, be always on our side!

CHORAGOS:[29] I speak because I feel the grip of your curse:
the killer is not I. Nor can I point
to him. The one who set us to this search,
Phoebus, should also name the guilty man.
285 OEDIPUS: Quite right, but to compel unwilling gods—
no man has ever had that kind of power.
CHORAGOS: May I suggest to you a second way?
OEDIPUS: A second or a third—pass over nothing!
CHORAGOS: I know of no one who sees more of what
290   Lord Phoebus sees than Lord Tiresias.
My Lord, one might learn brilliantly from him.
OEDIPUS: Nor is this something I have been slow to do.
At Creon's word I sent an escort—twice now!
I am astonished that he has not come.
295 CHORAGOS: The old account is useless. It told us nothing.
OEDIPUS: But tell it to me. I'll scrutinize all stories.
CHORAGOS: He is said to have been killed by travelers.

---

[28] *Son . . . Agēnor:* refers to Laius by citing his genealogy.   [29] *Choragos:* leader of the Chorus and principal commentator on the play's action.

OEDIPUS: I have heard, but the one who did it no one sees.
CHORAGOS: If there is any fear in him at all,
300   he won't stay here once he has heard that curse.
OEDIPUS: He won't fear words: he had no fear when he did it.

(Enter Tiresias from the right, led by a Servant and two of Oedipus's Attendants.)

CHORAGOS: Look there! There is the man who will convict him!
          It's the god's prophet they are leading here,
          one gifted with the truth as no one else.
305 OEDIPUS: Tiresias, master of all omens—
          public and secret, in the sky and on the earth—
          your mind, if not your eyes, sees how the city
          lives with a plague, against which Thebes can find
          no Saviour or protector, Lord, but you.
310   For Phoebus, as the attendants surely told you,
          returned this answer to us: liberation
          from the disease would never come unless
          we learned without a doubt who murdered Laius—
          put them to death, or sent them into exile.
315   Do not begrudge us what you may learn from birds
          or any other prophet's path you know!
          Care for yourself, the city, care for me,
          care for the whole pollution of the dead!
          We're in your hands. To do all that he can
320   to help another is man's noblest labor.
TIRESIAS: How terrible to understand and get
          no profit from the knowledge! I knew this,
          but I forgot, or I had never come.
OEDIPUS: What's this? You've come with very little zeal.
325 TIRESIAS: Let me go home! If you will listen to me,
          You will endure your troubles better—and I mine.
OEDIPUS: A strange request, not very kind to the land
          that cared for you—to hold back this oracle!
TIRESIAS: I see your understanding comes to you
330   inopportunely. So that won't happen to me . . .
OEDIPUS: Oh, by the gods, if you understand about this,
          don't turn away! We're on our knees to you.
TIRESIAS: None of you understands! I'll never bring
          my grief to light—I will not speak of yours.
335 OEDIPUS: You know and won't declare it! Is your purpose
          to betray us and to destroy this land!
TIRESIAS: I will grieve neither of us. Stop this futile
          cross-examination. I'll tell you nothing!
OEDIPUS: Nothing? You vile traitor! You could provoke
340   a stone to anger! You still refuse to tell?
          Can nothing soften you, nothing convince you?

TIRESIAS: You blamed anger in me—you haven't seen.
   The kind that lives with you, so you blame me.
OEDIPUS: Who wouldn't fill with anger, listening
345   to words like yours which now disgrace this city?
TIRESIAS: It will come, even if my silence hides it.
OEDIPUS: If it will come, then why won't you declare it?
TIRESIAS: I'd rather say no more. Now if you wish,
   respond to that with all your fiercest anger!
350 OEDIPUS: Now I am angry enough to come right out
   with this conjecture: you, I think, helped plot
   the deed; you did it—even if your hand,
   cannot have struck the blow. If you could see,
   I should have said the deed was yours alone.
355 TIRESIAS: Is that right! Then I charge you to abide
   by the decree you have announced: from this day
   say no word to either these or me,
   for you are the vile polluter of this land!
OEDIPUS: Aren't you appalled to let a charge like that
360   come bounding forth? How will you get away?
TIRESIAS: You cannot catch me. I have the strength of truth.
OEDIPUS: Who taught you this? Not your prophetic craft!
TIRESIAS: You did. You made me say it. I didn't want to.
OEDIPUS: Say what? Repeat it so I'll understand.
365 TIRESIAS: I made no sense? Or are you trying me?
OEDIPUS: No sense I understood. Say it again!
TIRESIAS: I say you are the murderer you seek.
OEDIPUS: Again that horror! You'll wish you hadn't said that.
TIRESIAS: Shall I say more, and raise your anger higher?
370 OEDIPUS: Anything you like! Your words are powerless.
TIRESIAS: You live, unknowing, with those nearest to you
   in the greatest shame. You do not see the evil.
OEDIPUS: You won't go on like that and never pay!
TIRESIAS: I can if there is any strength in truth.
375 OEDIPUS: In truth, but not in you! You have no strength,
   blind in your ears, your reason, and your eyes.
TIRESIAS: Unhappy man! Those jeers you hurl at me
   before long all these men will hurl at you.
OEDIPUS: You are the child of endless night; it's not
380   for me or anyone who sees to hurt you.
TIRESIAS: It's not my fate to be struck down by you.
   Apollo is enough. That's his concern.
OEDIPUS: Are these inventions Creon's or your own?
TIRESIAS: No, your affliction is yourself, not Creon.
385 OEDIPUS: Oh success!—in wealth, kingship, artistry,
   in any life that wins much admiration—
   the envious ill will stored up for you!

        to get at my command, a gift I did not
        seek, which the city put into my hands,
390   my loyal Creon, colleague from the start,
        longs to sneak up in secret and dethrone me.
        So he's suborned this fortuneteller—schemer!
        deceitful beggar-priest!—who has good eyes
        for gains alone, though in his craft he's blind.
395   Where were your prophet's powers ever proved?
        Why, when the dog who chanted verse[30] was here,
        did you not speak and liberate this city?
        Her riddle wasn't for a man chancing by
        to interpret; prophetic art was needed,
400   but you had none, it seems—learned from birds
        or from a god. I came along, yes I,
        Oedipus the ignorant, and stopped her—
        by using thought, not augury from birds.
        And it is I whom you now wish to banish,
405   so you'll be close to the Creontian throne.
        You—and the plot's concocter—will drive out
        pollution to your grief: you look quite old
        or you would be the victim of that plot!
Choragos: It seems to us that this man's words were said
410   in anger, Oedipus, and yours as well.
        Insight, not angry words, is what we need,
        the best solution to the god's response.
Tiresias: You are the king, and yet I am your equal
        in my right to speak. In that I too am Lord.
415   for I belong to Loxias,[31] not you.
        I am not Creon's man. He's nothing to me.
        Hear this, since you have thrown my blindness at me:
        Your eyes can't see the evil to which you've come,
        nor where you live, nor who is in your house.
420   Do you know your parents? Not knowing, you are
        their enemy, in the underworld and here.
        A mother's and a father's double-lashing
        terrible-footed curse will soon drive you out.
        Now you can see, then you will stare into darkness.
425   What place will not be harbor to your cry,
        or what Cithaeron[32] not reverberate
        when you have heard the bride-song in your palace
        to which you sailed? Fair wind to evil harbor!
        Nor do you see how many other woes

---

[30] *dog . . . verse:* the Sphinx.   [31] *Loxias:* Apollo.   [32] *Cithaeron:* reference to the mountain on which Oedipus was to be exposed as an infant.

430   will level you to yourself and to your children.
      So, at my message, and at Creon, too,
      splatter muck! There will never be a man
      ground into wretchedness as you will be.
      OEDIPUS: Am I to listen to such things from him!
435   May you be damned! Get out of here at once!
      Go! Leave my palace! Turn around and go!

      (Tiresias begins to move away from Oedipus.)

      TIRESIAS: I wouldn't have come had you not sent for me.
      OEDIPUS: I did not know you'd talk stupidity,
         or I wouldn't have rushed to bring you to my house.
440   TIRESIAS: Stupid I seem to you, yet to your parents
         who gave you natural birth I seemed quite shrewd.
      OEDIPUS: Who? Wait! Who is the one who gave me birth?
      TIRESIAS: This day will give you birth,[33] and ruin too.
      OEDIPUS: What murky, riddling things you always say!
445   TIRESIAS: Don't you surpass us all at finding out?
      OEDIPUS: You sneer at what you'll find has brought me greatness.
      TIRESIAS: And that's the very luck that ruined you.
      OEDIPUS: I wouldn't care, just so I saved the city.
      TIRESIAS: In that case I shall go. Boy, lead the way!
450   OEDIPUS: Yes, let him lead you off. Here, underfoot,
         you irk me. Gone, you'll cause no further pain.
      TIRESIAS: I'll go when I have said what I was sent for.
         Your face won't scare me. You can't ruin me.
         I say to you, the man whom you have looked for
455   as you pronounced your curses, your decrees
         on the bloody death of Laius—he is here!
         A seeming stranger, he shall be shown to be
         a Theban born, though he'll take no delight
         in that solution. Blind, who once could see,
460   a beggar who was rich, through foreign lands
         he'll go and point before him with a stick.
         To his beloved children, he'll be shown
         a father who is also brother; to the one
         who bore him, son and husband; to his father,
465   his seed-fellow and killer. Go in
         and think this out; and if you find I've lied,
         say then I have no prophet's understanding!

      (Exit Tiresias, led by a Servant. Oedipus exits into the palace with his Attendants.)

---

[33] *give you birth:* that is, identify your parents.

Stasimon 1[34]

Strophe 1

CHORUS: Who is the man of whom the inspired
    rock of Delphi[35] said
470   he has committed the unspeakable
    with blood-stained hands?
Time for him to ply a foot
mightier than those of the horses
    of the storm in his escape;
475   upon him mounts and plunges the weaponed
son of Zeus,[36] with fire and thunderbolts,
and in his train the dreaded goddesses
of Death, who never miss.

Antistrophe 1

The message has just blazed,
480   gleaming from the snows
of Mount Parnassus: we must track
    everywhere the unseen man.
He wanders, hidden by wild
forests, up through caves
485   and rocks, like a bull,
anxious, with an anxious foot, forlorn.
He puts away from him the mantic[37] words come from earth's
navel,[38] at its center, yet these live
forever and still hover round him.

Strophe 2

490 Terribly he troubles me,
    the skilled interpreter of birds![39]
I can't assent, nor speak against him.
    Both paths are closed to me.
I hover on the wings of doubt,
495   not seeing what is here nor what's to come.
What quarrel started in the house of Labdacus[40]
or in the house of Polybus,[41]
    either ever in the past
    or now, I never

---

[34] *Stasimon:* Greek choral ode between episodes.   [35] *rock of Delphi:* Apollo's oracle at Delphi.   [36] *son of Zeus:* Apollo.   [37] *mantic:* prophetic.   [38] *earth's navel:* Delphi.   [39] *interpreter of birds:* Tiresias. The Chorus is troubled by his accusations.   [40] *house of Labdacus:* the line of Laius.   [41] *Polybus:* Oedipus's foster father.

500   heard, so that . . . with this fact for my touchstone
       I could attack the public
           fame of Oedipus, by the side of the Labdaceans
           an ally, against the dark assassination.

   ANTISTROPHE 2
       No, Zeus and Apollo
505   understand and know things
       mortal; but that another man
           can do more as a prophet than I can—
       for that there is no certain test,
           though, skill to skill,
510   one man might overtake another.
       No, never, not until
           I see the charges proved,
       when someone blames him shall I nod assent.
       For once, as we all saw, the winged maiden[42] came
515   against him: he was seen then to be skilled,
           proved, by that touchstone, dear to the people. So,
       never will my mind convict him of the evil.

   EPISODE 2

(Enter Creon from the right door of the skene and speaks to the Chorus.)

   CREON: Citizens, I hear that a fearful charge
       is made against me by King Oedipus!
520   I had to come. If, in this crisis,
       he thinks that he has suffered injury
       from anything that I have said or done,
       I have no appetite for a long life—
       bearing a blame like that! It's no slight blow
525   the punishment I'd take from what he said:
       it's the ultimate hurt to be called traitor
       by the city, by you, by my own people!
   CHORAGOS: The thing that forced that accusation out
       could have been anger, not the power of thought.
530 CREON: But who persuaded him that thoughts of mine
       had led the prophet into telling lies?
   CHORAGOS: I do not know the thought behind his words.
   CREON: But did he look straight at you? Was his mind right
       when he said that I was guilty of this charge?
535 CHORAGOS: I have no eyes to see what rulers do.
       But here he comes himself out of the house.

---

[42] *winged maiden:* the Sphinx.

(Enter Oedipus from the palace.)

OEDIPUS: What? You here? And can you really have
    the face and daring to approach my house
    when you're exposed as its master's murderer
540   and caught, too, as the robber of my kingship?
    Did you see cowardice in me, by the gods,
    or foolishness, when you began this plot?
    Did you suppose that I would not detect
    your stealthy moves, or that I'd not fight back?
545   It's your attempt that's folly, isn't it—
    tracking without followers or connections,
    kingship which is caught with wealth and numbers?
CREON: Now wait! Give me as long to answer back!
    Judge me for yourself when you have heard me!
550 OEDIPUS: You're eloquent, but I'd be slow to learn
    from you, now that I've seen your malice toward me.
CREON: That I deny. Hear what I have to say.
OEDIPUS: Don't you deny it! You are the traitor here!
CREON: If you consider mindless willfulness
555   a prized possession, you are not thinking sense.
OEDIPUS: If you think you can wrong a relative
    and get off free, you are not thinking sense.
CREON: Perfectly just, I won't say no. And yet
    what is this injury you say I did you?
560 OEDIPUS: Did you persuade me, yes or no, to send
    someone to bring that solemn prophet here?
CREON: And I still hold to the advice I gave.
OEDIPUS: How many years ago did your King Laius . . .
CREON: Laius! Do what? Now I don't understand.
565 OEDIPUS: Vanish—victim of a murderous violence?
CREON: That is a long count back into the past.
OEDIPUS: Well, was this seer then practicing his art?
CREON: Yes, skilled and honored just as he is today.
OEDIPUS: Did he, back then, ever refer to me?
570 CREON: He did not do so in my presence ever.
OEDIPUS: You did inquire into the murder then.
CREON: We had to, surely, though we discovered nothing.
OEDIPUS: But the "skilled" one did not say this then? Why not?
CREON: I never talk when I am ignorant.
575 OEDIPUS: But you're not ignorant of your own part.
CREON: What do you mean? I'll tell you if I know.
OEDIPUS: Just this: if he had not conferred with you
    he'd not have told about my murdering Laius.
CREON: If he said that, you are the one who knows.
580   But now it's fair that you should answer me.
OEDIPUS: Ask on! You won't convict me as the killer.
CREON: Well then, answer. My sister is your wife?

OEDIPUS: Now there's a statement that I can't deny.
CREON: You two have equal power in this country?
585 OEDIPUS: She gets from me whatever she desires.
CREON: And I'm a third? The three of us are equals?
OEDIPUS: That's where you're treacherous to your kinsman!
CREON: But think about this rationally, as I do.
    First look at this: do you think anyone
590   prefers the anxieties of being king
    to untroubled sleep—if he has equal power?
    I'm not the kind of man who falls in love
    with kingship. I am content with a king's power.
    And so would any man who's wise and prudent.
595   I get all things from you, with no distress;
    as king I would have onerous duties, too.
    How could the kingship bring me more delight
    than this untroubled power and influence?
    I'm not misguided yet to such a point
600   that profitable honors aren't enough.
    As it is, all wish me well and all salute;
    those begging you for something have me summoned,
    for their success depends on that alone.
    Why should I lose all this to become king?
605   A prudent mind is never traitorous.
    Treason's a thought I'm not enamored of;
    nor could I join a man who acted so.
    In proof of this, first go yourself to Pytho[43]
    and ask if I brought back the true response.
610   Then, if you find I plotted with that portent
    reader,[44] don't have me put to death by your vote
    only—I'll vote myself for my conviction.
    Don't let an unsupported thought convict me!
    It's not right mindlessly to take the bad
615   for good or to suppose the good are traitors.
    Rejecting a relation who is loyal
    is like rejecting life, our greatest love.
    In time you'll know securely without stumbling,
    for time alone can prove a just man just,
620   though you can know a bad man in a day.
CHORAGOS: Well said, to one who's anxious not to fall.
    Swift thinkers, Lord, are never safe from stumbling.
OEDIPUS: But when a swift and secret plotter moves
    against me, I must make swift counterplot.
625   If I lie quiet and await his move,
    he'll have achieved his aims and I'll have missed.
CREON: You surely cannot mean you want me exiled!

---

[43] *Pytho:* Delphi.   [44] *portent reader:* Apollo's oracle or prophet.

OEDIPUS: Not exiled, no. Your death is what I want!
CREON: If you would first define what envy is . . .
630 OEDIPUS: Are you still stubborn? Still disobedient?
CREON: I see you cannot think!
OEDIPUS: For me I can.
CREON: You should for me as well!
OEDIPUS: But you're a traitor!
CREON: What if you're wrong?
OEDIPUS: Authority must be maintained.
CREON: Not if the ruler's evil.
OEDIPUS: Hear that, Thebes!
635 CREON: It is my city too, not yours alone!
CHORAGOS: Please don't, my Lords! Ah, just in time, I see
    Jocasta there, coming from the palace.
    With her help you must settle your quarrel.

(Enter Jocasta from the palace.)

JOCASTA: Wretched men! What has provoked this ill-
640   advised dispute? Have you no sense of shame,
    with Thebes so sick, to stir up private troubles?
    Now go inside! And Creon, you go home!
    Don't make a general anguish out of nothing!
CREON: My sister, Oedipus your husband here
645   sees fit to do one of two hideous things:
    to have me banished from the land—or killed!
OEDIPUS: That's right: I caught him, Lady, plotting harm
    against my person—with a malignant science.
CREON: May my life fail, may I die cursed, if I
650   did any of the things you said I did!
JOCASTA: Believe his words, for the god's sake, Oedipus,
    in deference above all to his oath
    to the gods. Also for me, and for these men!

KOMMOS[45]

STROPHE 1

CHORUS: Consent, with will and mind,
655   my king, I beg of you!
OEDIPUS: What do you wish me to surrender?
CHORUS: Show deference to him who was not feeble in time past
    and is now great in the power of his oath!
OEDIPUS: Do you know what you're asking?
CHORUS: Yes.
OEDIPUS: Tell me then.

---

[45] *Kommos:* a dirge or lament sung by the Chorus and one or more of the chief characters.

660 **Chorus:** Never to cast into dishonored guilt, with an unproved
assumption, a kinsman who has bound himself by curse.
Oedipus: Now you must understand, when you ask this,
you ask my death or banishment from the land.

Strophe 2

Chorus: No, by the god who is the foremost of all gods,
665 the Sun! No! Godless,
friendless, whatever death is worst of all,
let that be my destruction, if this
thought ever moved me!
But my ill-fated soul
670 this dying land
wears out—the more if to these older troubles
she adds new troubles from the two of you!
Oedipus: Then let him go, though it must mean my death,
or else disgrace and exile from the land.
675 My pity is moved by your words, not by his—
he'll only have my hate, wherever he goes.
Creon: You're sullen as you yield; you'll be depressed
when you've passed through this anger. Natures like yours
are hardest on themselves. That's as it should be.
680 **Oedipus:** Then won't you go and let me be?
Creon: I'll go.
Though you're unreasonable, they know I'm righteous.

(Exit Creon.)

Antistrophe 1

Chorus: Why are you waiting, Lady?
Conduct him back into the palace!
Jocasta: I will, when I have heard what chanced.
685 **Chorus:** Conjectures—words alone, and nothing based on thought.
But even an injustice can devour a man.
Jocasta: Did the words come from both sides?
Chorus: Yes.
Jocasta: What was said?
Chorus: To me it seems enough! enough! the land already troubled,
that this should rest where it has stopped.
690 **Oedipus:** See what you've come to in your honest thought,
in seeking to relax and blunt my heart?

Antistrophe 2

Chorus: I have not said this only once, my Lord.
That I had lost my sanity,
without a path in thinking—
695 be sure this would be clear

                    if I put you away
                who, when my cherished land
                    wandered crazed
                with suffering, brought her back on course.
700   Now, too, be a lucky helmsman!
        JOCASTA: Please, for the god's sake, Lord, explain to me
                the reason why you have conceived this wrath?
        OEDIPUS: I honor you, not them,⁴⁶ and I'll explain
                to you how Creon has conspired against me.
705   JOCASTA: All right, if that will explain how the quarrel started.
        OEDIPUS: He says I am the murderer of Laius!
        JOCASTA: Did he claim knowledge or that someone told him?
        OEDIPUS: Here's what he did: he sent that vicious seer
                so he could keep his own mouth innocent.
710   JOCASTA: Ah then, absolve yourself of what he charges!
                Listen to this and you'll agree, no mortal
                is ever given skill in prophecy.
                I'll prove this quickly with one incident.
                It was foretold to Laius—I shall not say
715   by Phoebus himself, but by his ministers—
                that when his fate arrived he would be killed
                by a son who would be born to him and me.
                And yet, so it is told, foreign robbers
                murdered him, at a place where three roads meet.
720   As for the child I bore him, not three days passed
                before he yoked the ball-joints of its feet,⁴⁷
                then cast it, by others' hands, on a trackless mountain.
                That time Apollo did not make our child
                a patricide, or bring about what Laius
725   feared, that he be killed by his own son.
                That's how prophetic words determined things!
                Forget them. The things a god must track
                he will himself painlessly reveal.
        OEDIPUS: Just now, as I was listening to you, Lady,
730   what a profound distraction seized my mind!
        JOCASTA: What made you turn around so anxiously?
        OEDIPUS: I thought you said that Laius was attacked
                and butchered at a place where three roads meet.
        JOCASTA: That is the story, and it is told so still.
735   OEDIPUS: Where is the place where this was done to him?
        JOCASTA: The land's called Phocis, where a two-forked road
                comes in from Delphi and from Daulia.
        OEDIPUS: And how much time has passed since these events?

---

⁴⁶ *them:* the Chorus.   ⁴⁷ *ball-joints of its feet:* the ankles.

JOCASTA: Just prior to your presentation here
    as king this news was published to the city.
OEDIPUS: Oh, Zeus, what have you willed to do to me?
JOCASTA: Oedipus, what makes your heart so heavy?
OEDIPUS: No, tell me first of Laius' appearance,
    what peak of youthful vigor he had reached.
JOCASTA: A tall man, showing his first growth of white.
    He had a figure not unlike your own.
OEDIPUS: Alas! It seems that in my ignorance
    I laid those fearful curses on myself.
JOCASTA: What is it, Lord? I flinch to see your face.
OEDIPUS: I'm dreadfully afraid the prophet sees.
    But I'll know better with one more detail.
JOCASTA: I'm frightened too. But ask: I'll answer you.
OEDIPUS: Was his retinue small, or did he travel
    with a great troop, as would befit a prince?
JOCASTA: There were just five in all, one a herald.
    There was a carriage, too, bearing Laius.
OEDIPUS: Alas! Now I see it! But who was it,
    Lady, who told you what you know about this?
JOCASTA: A servant who alone was saved unharmed.
OEDIPUS: By chance, could he be now in the palace?
JOCASTA: No, he is not. When he returned and saw
    you had the power of the murdered Laius,
    he touched my hand and begged me formally
    to send him to the fields and to the pastures,
    so he'd be out of sight, far from the city.
    I did. Although a slave, he well deserved
    to win this favor, and indeed far more.
OEDIPUS: Let's have him called back in immediately.
JOCASTA: That can be done, but why do you desire it?
OEDIPUS: I fear, Lady, I have already said
    too much. That's why I wish to see him now.
JOCASTA: Then he shall come; but it is right somehow
    that I, too, Lord, should know what troubles you.
OEDIPUS: I've gone so deep into the things I feared
    I'll tell you everything. Who has a right
    greater than yours, while I cross through this chance?
    Polybus of Corinth was my father,
    my mother was the Dorian Meropē.
    I was first citizen, until this chance
    attacked me—striking enough, to be sure,
    but not worth all the gravity I gave it.
    This: at a feast a man who'd drunk too much
    denied, at the wine, I was my father's son.
    I was depressed and all that day I barely
    held it in. Next day I put the question

to my mother and father. They were enraged
at the man who'd let this fiction fly at me.
I was much cheered by them. And yet it kept
grinding into me. His words kept coming back.
790 Without my mother's or my father's knowledge
I went to Pytho. But Phoebus sent me away
dishonoring my demand. Instead, other
wretched horrors he flashed forth in speech.
He said that I would be my mother's lover,
795 show offspring to mankind they could not look at,
and be his murderer whose seed I am.[48]
When I heard this, and ever since, I gauged
the way to Corinth by the stars alone,
running to a place where I would never see
800 the disgrace in the oracle's words come true.
But I soon came to the exact location
where, as you tell of it, the king was killed.
Lady, here is the truth. As I went on,
when I was just approaching those three roads,
805 a herald and a man like him you spoke of
came on, riding a carriage drawn by colts.
Both the man out front and the old man himself[49]
tried violently to force me off the road.
The driver, when he tried to push me off,
810 I struck in anger. The old man saw this, watched
me approach, then leaned out and lunged down
with twin prongs[50] at the middle of my head!
He got more than he gave. Abruptly—struck
once by the staff in this my hand—he tumbled
815 out, head first, from the middle of the carriage.
And then I killed them all. But if there is
a kinship between Laius and this stranger,
who is more wretched than the man you see?
Who was there born more hated by the gods?
820 For neither citizen nor foreigner
may take me in his home or speak to me.
No, they must drive me off. And it is I
who have pronounced these curses on myself!
I stain the dead man's bed with these my hands,
825 by which he died. Is not my nature vile?
Unclean?—if I am banished and even
in exile I may not see my own parents,

---

[48] *be . . . am:* that is, murder my father. [49] *old man himself:* Laius.
[50] *lunged . . . prongs:* Laius strikes Oedipus with a two-pronged horse goad, or whip.

or set foot in my homeland, or else be yoked
in marriage to my mother, and kill my father,
830   Polybus, who raised me and gave me birth?
If someone judged a cruel divinity
did this to me, would he not speak the truth?
You pure and awful gods, may I not ever
see that day, may I be swept away
835   from men before I see so great and so
calamitous a stain fixed on my person!
CHORAGOS: These things seem fearful to us, Lord, and yet,
until you hear it from the witness, keep hope!
OEDIPUS: That is the single hope that's left to me,
840   to wait for him, that herdsman—until he comes.
JOCASTA: When he appears, what are you eager for?
OEDIPUS: Just this: if his account agrees with yours
then I shall have escaped this misery.
JOCASTA: But what was it that struck you in my story?
845   OEDIPUS: You said he spoke of robbers as the ones
who killed him. Now: if he continues still
to speak of many, then I could not have killed him.
One man and many men just do not jibe.
But if he says one belted man, the doubt
850   is gone. The balance tips toward me. I did it.
JOCASTA: No! He told it as I told you. Be certain.
He can't reject that and reverse himself.
The city heard these things, not I alone.
But even if he swerves from what he said,
855   he'll never show that Laius' murder, Lord,
occurred just as predicted. For Loxias
expressly said my son was doomed to kill him.
The boy—poor boy—he never had a chance
to cut him down, for he was cut down first.
860   Never again, just for some oracle
will I shoot frightened glances right and left.
OEDIPUS: That's full of sense. Nonetheless, send a man
to bring that farm hand here. Will you do it?
JOCASTA: I'll send one right away. But let's go in.
865   Would I do anything against your wishes?

(*Exit Oedipus and Jocasta through the central door into the palace.*)

STASIMON 2

STROPHE 1

CHORUS: May there accompany me
    the fate to keep a reverential purity in what I say,
    in all I do, for which the laws have been set forth
    and walk on high, born to traverse the brightest,

870   highest upper air; Olympus[51] only
        is their father, nor was it
        mortal nature
        that fathered them, and never will
        oblivion lull them into sleep;
875   the god in them is great and never ages.

Antistrophe 1

    The will to violate, seed of the tyrant,
    if it has drunk mindlessly of wealth and power,
    without a sense of time or true advantage,
    mounts to a peak, then
880   plunges to an abrupt . . . destiny,
    where the useful foot
    is of no use. But the kind
    of struggling that is good for the city
    I ask the god never to abolish.
885   The god is my protector: never will I give that up.

Strophe 2

    But if a man proceeds disdainfully
        in deeds of hand or word
    and has no fear of Justice
        or reverence for shrines of the divinities
890   (may a bad fate catch him
        for his luckless wantonness!),
    if he'll not gain what he gains with justice
    and deny himself what is unholy,
    or if he clings, in foolishness, to the untouchable
895   (what man, finally, in such an action, will have strength
    enough to fend off passion's arrows from his soul?),
    if, I say, this kind of
        deed is held in honor—
    why should I join the sacred dance?

Antistrophe 2

900   No longer shall I visit and revere
        Earth's navel,[52] the untouchable,
    nor visit Abae's[53] temple,
        or Olympia,[54]

---

[51] *Olympus:* Mount Olympus, home of the gods, treated as a god.   [52] *Earth's navel:* Delphi.   [53] *Abae:* a town in Phocis where there was another oracle of Apollo.   [54] *Olympia:* site of the oracle of Zeus.

if the prophecies are not matched by events
905   for all the world to point to.
No, you who hold the power, if you are rightly called
Zeus the king of all, let this matter not escape you
and your ever-deathless rule,
for the prophecies to Laius fade . . .
910 and men already disregard them;
nor is Apollo anywhere
        glorified with honors.
Religion slips away.

Episode 3

(Enter Jocasta from the palace carrying a branch wound with wool and a jar of incense. She is attended by two women.)

JOCASTA: Lords of the realm, the thought has come to me
915   to visit shrines of the divinities
with suppliant's branch in hand and fragrant smoke.
For Oedipus excites his soul too much
with alarms of all kinds. He will not judge
the present by the past, like a man of sense.
920 He's at the mercy of all terror-mongers.

(Jocasta approaches the altar on the right and kneels.)

Since I can do no good by counseling,
Apollo the Lycēan!—you are the closest—
I come a suppliant, with these my vows,
for a cleansing that will not pollute him.
925 For when we see him shaken we are all
afraid, like people looking at their helmsman.

(Enter a Messenger along one of the parados. He sees Jocasta at the altar and then addresses the Chorus.)

MESSENGER: I would be pleased if you would help me, stranger.
Where is the palace of King Oedipus?
Or tell me where he is himself, if you know.
930 CHORUS: This is his house, stranger. He is within.
This is his wife and mother of his children.
MESSENGER: May she and her family find prosperity,
if, as you say, her marriage is fulfilled.
JOCASTA: You also, stranger, for you deserve as much
935   for your gracious words. But tell me why you've come.
What do you wish? Or what have you to tell us?
MESSENGER: Good news, my Lady, both for your house and husband.
JOCASTA: What is your news? And who has sent you to us?
MESSENGER: I come from Corinth. When you have heard my news
940   you will rejoice, I'm sure—and grieve perhaps.

JOCASTA: What is it? How can it have this double power?
MESSENGER: They will establish him their king, so say
    the people of the land of Isthmia.[55]
JOCASTA: But is old Polybus not still in power?
945 MESSENGER: He's not, for death has clasped him in the tomb.
JOCASTA: What's this? Has Oedipus' father died?
MESSENGER: If I have lied then I deserve to die.
JOCASTA: Attendant! Go quickly to your master,
    and tell him this.

(Exit an Attendant into the palace.)

                Oracles of the gods!
950   Where are you now? The man whom Oedipus
    fled long ago, for fear that he should kill him—
    he's been destroyed by chance and not by him!

(Enter Oedipus from the palace.)

OEDIPUS: Darling Jocasta, my beloved wife,
    Why have you called me from the palace?
955 JOCASTA: First hear what this man has to say. Then see
    what the god's grave oracle has come to now!
OEDIPUS: Where is he from? What is this news he brings me?
JOCASTA: From Corinth. He brings news about your father:
    that Polybus is no more! that he is dead!
960 OEDIPUS: What's this, old man? I want to hear you say it.
MESSENGER: If this is what must first be clarified,
    please be assured that he is dead and gone.
OEDIPUS: By treachery or by the touch of sickness?
MESSENGER: Light pressures tip agéd frames into their sleep.
965 OEDIPUS: You mean the poor man died of some disease.
MESSENGER: And of the length of years that he had tallied.
OEDIPUS: Aha! Then why should we look to Pytho's vapors,[56]
    or to the birds that scream above our heads?[57]
    If we could really take those things for guides,
970   I would have killed my father. But he's dead!
    He is beneath the earth, and here am I,
    who never touched a spear. Unless he died
    of longing for me and I "killed" him that way!
    No, in this case, Polybus, by dying, took
975   the worthless oracle to Hades with him.
JOCASTA: And wasn't I telling you that just now?
OEDIPUS: You were indeed. I was misled by fear.

---

[55] *land of Isthmia:* Corinth, which was on an isthmus.   [56] *Pytho's vapors:* the prophecies of the oracle at Delphi.   [57] *birds . . . heads:* the prophecies derived from interpreting the flights of birds.

JOCASTA: You should not care about this anymore.
OEDIPUS: I must care. I must stay clear of my mother's bed.
980 JOCASTA: What's there for man to fear? The realm of chance
prevails. True foresight isn't possible.
His life is best who lives without a plan.
This marriage with your mother—don't fear it.
How many times have men in dreams, too, slept
985 with their own mothers! Those who believe such things
mean nothing endure their lives most easily.
OEDIPUS: A fine, bold speech, and you are right, perhaps,
except that my mother is still living,
so I must fear her, however well you argue.
990 JOCASTA: And yet your father's tomb is a great eye.
OEDIPUS: Illuminating, yes. But I still fear the living.
MESSENGER: Who is the woman who inspires this fear?
OEDIPUS: Meropē, Polybus' wife, old man.
MESSENGER: And what is there about her that alarms you?
995 OEDIPUS: An oracle, god-sent and fearful, stranger.
MESSENGER: Is it permitted that another know?
OEDIPUS: It is. Loxias once said to me
I must have intercourse with my own mother
and take my father's blood with these my hands.
1000 So I have long lived far away from Corinth.
This has indeed brought much good luck, and yet,
to see one's parents' eyes is happiest.
MESSENGER: Was it for this that you have lived in exile?
OEDIPUS: So I'd not be my father's killer, sir.
1005 MESSENGER: Had I not better free you from this fear,
my Lord? That's why I came—to do you service.
OEDIPUS: Indeed, what a reward you'd get for that!
MESSENGER: Indeed, this is the main point of my trip,
to be rewarded when you get back home.
1010 OEDIPUS: I'll never rejoin the givers of my seed![58]
MESSENGER: My son, clearly you don't know what you're doing.
OEDIPUS: But how is that, old man? For the gods' sake, tell me!
MESSENGER: If it's because of them you won't go home.
OEDIPUS: I fear that Phoebus will have told the truth.
1015 MESSENGER: Pollution from the ones who gave you seed?
OEDIPUS: That is the thing, old man, I always fear.
MESSENGER: Your fear is groundless. Understand that.
OEDIPUS: Groundless? Not if I was born their son.
MESSENGER: But Polybus is not related to you.
1020 OEDIPUS: Do you mean Polybus was not my father?

---

[58] *givers of my seed:* that is, my parents. Oedipus still thinks Meropē and Polybus are his parents.

MESSENGER: No more than I. We're both the same to you.
OEDIPUS: Same? One who begot me and one who didn't?
MESSENGER: He didn't beget you any more than I did.
OEDIPUS: But then, why did he say I was his son?
1025 MESSENGER: He got you as a gift from my own hands.
OEDIPUS: He loved me so, though from another's hands?
MESSENGER: His former childlessness persuaded him.
OEDIPUS: But had you bought me, or begotten me?
MESSENGER: Found you. In the forest hallows of Cithaeron.
1030 OEDIPUS: What were you doing traveling in that region?
MESSENGER: I was in charge of flocks which grazed those mountains.
OEDIPUS: A wanderer who worked the flocks for hire?
MESSENGER: Ah, but that day I was your savior, son.
OEDIPUS: From what? What was my trouble when you took me?
1035 MESSENGER: The ball-joints of your feet might testify.
OEDIPUS: What's that? What makes you name that ancient trouble?
MESSENGER: Your feet were pierced and I am your rescuer.
OEDIPUS: A fearful rebuke those tokens left for me!
MESSENGER: That was the chance that names you who you are.
1040 OEDIPUS: By the gods, did my mother or my father do this?
MESSENGER: That I don't know. He might who gave you to me.
OEDIPUS: From someone else? You didn't chance on me?
MESSENGER: Another shepherd handed you to me.
OEDIPUS: Who was he? Do you know? Will you explain!
1045 MESSENGER: They called him one of the men of—was it Laius?
OEDIPUS: The one who once was king here long ago?
MESSENGER: That is the one! The man was shepherd to him.
OEDIPUS: And is he still alive so I can see him?
MESSENGER: But you who live here ought to know that best.
1050 OEDIPUS: Does any one of you now present know
about the shepherd whom this man has named?
Have you seen him in town or in the fields? Speak out!
The time has come for the discovery!
CHORAGOS: The man he speaks of, I believe, is the same
1055 as the field hand you have already asked to see.
But it's Jocasta who would know this best.
OEDIPUS: Lady, do you remember the man we just
now sent for—is that the man he speaks of?
JOCASTA: What? The man he spoke of? Pay no attention!
1060 His words are not worth thinking about. It's nothing.
OEDIPUS: With clues like this within my grasp, give up?
Fail to solve the mystery of my birth?
JOCASTA: For the love of the gods, and if you love your life,
give up this search! My sickness is enough.
1065 OEDIPUS: Come! Though my mothers for three generations
were in slavery, you'd not be lowborn!
JOCASTA: No, listen to me! Please! Don't do this thing!
OEDIPUS: I will not listen; I will search out the truth.

JOCASTA: My thinking is for you—it would be best.
1070 OEDIPUS: This "best" of yours is starting to annoy me.
JOCASTA: Doomed man! Never find out who you are!
OEDIPUS: Will someone go and bring that shepherd here?
   Leave her to glory in her wealthy birth!
JOCASTA: Man of misery! No other name
1075   shall I address you by, ever again.

(Exit Jocasta into the palace after a long pause.)

CHORAGOS: Why has your lady left, Oedipus,
   hurled by a savage grief? I am afraid
   disaster will come bursting from this silence.
OEDIPUS: Let it burst forth! However low this seed
1080   of mine may be, yet I desire to see it.
   She, perhaps—she has a woman's pride—
   is mortified by my base origins.
   But I who count myself the child of Chance,
   the giver of good, shall never know dishonor.
1085 She is my mother,[59] and the months my brothers
   who first marked out my lowness, then my greatness.
   I shall not prove untrue to such a nature
   by giving up the search for my own birth.

STASIMON 3

STROPHE

CHORUS: If I have mantic power
1090   and excellence in thought,
   by Olympus,
      you shall not, Cithaeron, at tomorrow's
   full moon,
   fail to hear us celebrate you as the countryman
1095   of Oedipus, his nurse and mother,
   or fail to be the subject of our dance,
      since you have given pleasure
   to our king.
   Phoebus, whom we summon by "iē!,"
1100   may this be pleasing to you!

ANTISTROPHE

   Who was your mother, son?
   which of the long-lived nymphs
   after lying with Pan,[60]
      the mountain roaming . . . Or was it a bride
1105   of Loxias?[61]

---

[59] *She . . . mother:* Chance is my mother. [60] *Pan:* god of shepherds and woodlands, half man and half goat. [61] *Loxias:* Apollo.

> For dear to him are all the upland pastures.
> Or was it Mount Cyllēnē's lord,[62]
> or the Bacchic god,[63]
> > dweller of the mountain peaks,
> who received you as a joyous find
> from one of the nymphs of Helicon,
> the favorite sharers of his sport?

Episode 4

OEDIPUS: If someone like myself, who never met him,
> may calculate—elders, I think I see
> the very herdsman we've been waiting for.
> His many years would fit that man's age,
> and those who bring him on, if I am right,
> are my own men. And yet, in real knowledge,
> you can outstrip me, surely: you've seen him.

(Enter the old Herdsman escorted by two of Oedipus's Attendants. At first, the Herdsman will not look at Oedipus.)

CHORAGOS: I know him, yes, a man of the house of Laius,
> a trusty herdsman if he ever had one.

OEDIPUS: I ask you first, the stranger come from Corinth:
> is this the man you spoke of?

MESSENGER: That's he you see.

OEDIPUS: Then you, old man. First look at me! Now answer:
> did you belong to Laius' household once?

HERDSMAN: I did. Not a purchased slave but raised in the palace.

OEDIPUS: How have you spent your life? What is your work?

HERDSMAN: Most of my life now I have tended sheep.

OEDIPUS: Where is the usual place you stay with them?

HERDSMAN: On Mount Cithaeron. Or in that district.

OEDIPUS: Do you recall observing this man there?

HERDSMAN: Doing what? Which is the man you mean?

OEDIPUS: This man right here. Have you had dealings with him?

HERDSMAN: I can't say right away. I don't remember.

MESSENGER: No wonder, master. I'll bring clear memory
> to his ignorance. I'm absolutely sure
> he can recall it, the district was Cithaeron,
> he with a double flock, and I, with one,
> lived close to him, for three entire seasons,
> six months along, from spring right to Arcturus.[64]
> Then for the winter I'd drive mine to my fold,

---

[52] *Mount Cyllēnē's lord:* Hermes, messenger of the gods.   [63] *Bacchic god:* Dionysus.   [64] *Arcturus:* a star that is first seen in September in the Grecian sky.

and he'd drive his to Laius' pen again.
Did any of the things I say take place?
HERDSMAN: You speak the truth, though it's from long ago.
1145 MESSENGER: Do you remember giving me, back then,
a boy I was to care for as my own?
HERDSMAN: What are you saying? Why do you ask me that?
MESSENGER: There, sir, is the man who was that boy!
HERDSMAN: Damn you! Shut your mouth! Keep your silence!
1150 OEDIPUS: Stop! Don't you rebuke his words.
Your words ask for rebuke far more than his.
HERDSMAN: But what have I done wrong, most royal master?
OEDIPUS: Not telling of the boy of whom he asked.
HERDSMAN: He's ignorant and blundering toward ruin.
1155 OEDIPUS: Tell it willingly—or under torture.
HERDSMAN: Oh god! Don't—I am old—don't torture me!
OEDIPUS: Here! Someone put his hands behind his back!
HERDSMAN: But why? What else would you find out, poor man?
OEDIPUS: Did you give him the child he asks about?
1160 HERDSMAN: I did. I wish that I had died that day!
OEDIPUS: You'll come to that if you don't speak the truth.
HERDSMAN: It's if I speak that I shall be destroyed.
OEDIPUS: I think this fellow struggles for delay.
HERDSMAN: No, no! I said already that I gave him.
1165 OEDIPUS: From your own home, or got from someone else?
HERDSMAN: Not from my own. I got him from another.
OEDIPUS: Which of these citizens? What sort of house?
HERDSMAN: Don't—by the gods!—don't, master, ask me more!
OEDIPUS: It means your death if I must ask again.
1170 HERDSMAN: One of the children of the house of Laius.
OEDIPUS: A slave—or born into the family?
HERDSMAN: I have come to the dreaded thing, and I shall say it.
OEDIPUS: And I to hearing it, but hear I must.
HERDSMAN: He was reported to have been—his son.
1175 Your lady in the house could tell you best.
OEDIPUS: Because she gave him to you?
HERDSMAN: Yes, my lord.
OEDIPUS: What was her purpose?
HERDSMAN: I was to kill the boy.
OEDIPUS: The child she bore?
HERDSMAN: She dreaded prophecies.
OEDIPUS: What were they?
HERDSMAN: The word was that he'd kill his parents.
1180 OEDIPUS: Then why did you give him up to this old man?
HERDSMAN: In pity, master—so he would take him home,
to another land. But what he did was save him
for this supreme disaster. If you are the one
he speaks of—know your evil birth and fate!

1185 OEDIPUS: Ah! All of it was destined to be true!
Oh light, now may I look my last upon you,
shown monstrous in my birth, in marriage monstrous,
a murderer monstrous in those I killed.

(Exit Oedipus, running into the palace.)

STASIMON 4

STROPHE 1

CHORUS: Oh generations of mortal men,
1190 while you are living, I will
appraise your lives at zero!
What man
comes closer to seizing lasting blessedness
than merely to seize its semblance,
1195 and after living in this semblance, to plunge?
With your example before us,
with your destiny, yours,
suffering Oedipus, no mortal
can I judge fortunate.

ANTISTROPHE 1

1200 For he,[65] outranging everybody,
shot his arrow[66] and became the lord
of wide prosperity and blessedness,
oh Zeus, after destroying
the virgin with the crooked talons,[67]
1205 singer of oracles; and against death,
in my land, he arose a tower of defense.
From which time you were called my king
and granted privileges supreme—in mighty
Thebes the ruling lord.

STROPHE 2

1210 But now—whose story is more sorrowful than yours?
Who is more intimate with fierce calamities,
with labors, now that your life is altered?
Alas, my Oedipus, whom all men know:
one great harbor[68]—
1215 one alone sufficed for you,
as son and father,

---

[65] *he:* Oedipus. [66] *shot his arrow:* took his chances; made a guess at the Sphinx's riddle. [67] *virgin . . . talons:* the Sphinx. [68] *one great harbor:* metaphorical allusion to Jocasta's body.

when you tumbled,⁶⁹ plowman⁷⁰ of the woman's chamber.
How, how could your paternal
   furrows, wretched man,
1220   endure you silently so long.

ANTISTROPHE 2

Time, all-seeing, surprised you living an unwilled life
and sits from of old in judgment on the marriage, not a marriage,
where the begetter is the begot as well.
Ah, son of Laius . . . ,
1225 would that—oh, would that
I had never seen you!
I wail, my scream climbing beyond itself
from my whole power of voice. To say it straight:
   from you I got new breath—
1230 but I also lulled my eye to sleep.⁷¹

EXODOS⁷²

(Enter the Second Messenger from the palace.)

SECOND MESSENGER: You who are first among the citizens,
what deeds you are about to hear and see!
What grief you'll carry, if, true to your birth,
you still respect the house of Labdacus!
1235 Neither the Ister nor the Phasis river
could purify this house, such suffering
does it conceal, or soon must bring to light—
willed this time, not unwilled. Griefs hurt worst
which we perceive to be self-chosen ones.
1240 CHORAGOS: They were sufficient, the things we knew before,
to make us grieve. What can you add to those?
SECOND MESSENGER: The thing that's quickest said and quickest heard:
our own, our royal one, Jocasta's dead.
CHORAGOS: Unhappy queen! What was responsible?
1245 SECOND MESSENGER: Herself. The bitterest of these events
is not for you, you were not there to see,
but yet, exactly as I can recall it,
you'll hear what happened to that wretched lady.
She came in anger through the outer hall,
1250 and then she ran straight to her marriage bed,
tearing her hair with the fingers of both hands.
Then, slamming shut the doors when she was in,

---

⁶⁹ *tumbled:* were born and had sex.   ⁷⁰ *plowman:* plowing is used here as a sexual metaphor.   ⁷¹ *I . . . sleep:* I failed to see the corruption you brought.
⁷² *Exodus:* the final scene, containing the play's resolution.

	she called to Laius, dead so many years,
	remembering the ancient seed which caused
1255	his death, leaving the mother to the son
	to breed again an ill-born progeny.
	She mourned the bed where she, alas, bred double—
	husband by husband, children by her child.
	From this point on I don't know how she died,
1260	for Oedipus then burst in with a cry,
	and did not let us watch her final evil.
	Our eyes were fixed on him. Wildly he ran
	to each of us, asking for his spear
	and for his wife—no wife: where he might find
1265	the double mother-field, his and his children's.
	He raved, and some divinity then showed him—
	for none of us did so who stood close by.
	With a dreadful shout—as if some guide were leading—
	he lunged through the double doors; he bent the hollow
1270	bolts from the sockets, burst into the room,
	and there we saw her, hanging from above,
	entangled in some twisted hanging strands.
	He saw, was stricken, and with a wild roar
	ripped down the dangling noose. When she, poor woman,
1275	lay on the ground, there came a fearful sight:
	he snatched the pins of worked gold from her dress,
	with which her clothes were fastened: these he raised
	and struck into the ball-joints of his eyes.[73]
	He shouted that they would no longer see
1280	the evils he had suffered or had done,
	see in the dark those he should not have seen,
	and know no more those he once sought to know.
	While chanting this, not once but many times
	he raised his hand and struck into his eyes.
1285	Blood from his wounded eyes poured down his chin,
	not freed in moistening drops, but all at once
	a stormy rain of black blood burst like hail.
	These evils, coupling them, making them one,
	have broken loose upon both man and wife.
1290	The old prosperity that they had once
	was true prosperity, and yet today,
	mourning, ruin, death, disgrace, and every
	evil you could name—not one is absent.
	CHORAGOS: Has he allowed himself some peace from all this grief?
1295	SECOND MESSENGER: He shouts that someone slide the bolts and show
	to all the Cadmeians the patricide,

---

[73] *ball-joints of his eyes:* his eyeballs. Oedipus blinds himself in both eyes at the same time.

his mother's—I can't say it, it's unholy—
so he can cast himself out of the land,
not stay and curse his house by his own curse.
He lacks the strength, though, and he needs a guide,
for his is a sickness that's too great to bear.
Now you yourself will see: the bolts of the doors
are opening. You are about to see
a vision even one who hates must pity.

(Enter the blinded Oedipus from the palace, led in by a household Servant.)

CHORAGOS: Terrifying suffering for men to see,
more terrifying than any I've ever
come upon. Oh man of pain
what madness reached you? Which god from far off,
surpassing in range his longest spring,
    struck hard against your god-abandoned fate?
Oh man of pain,
I cannot look upon you—though there's so much
I would ask you, so much to hear,
so much that holds my eyes—
    such is the shudder you produce in me.
OEDIPUS: Ah! Ah! I am a man of misery.
Where am I carried? Pity me! Where
is my voice scattered abroad on wings?
Divinity, where has your lunge transported me?
CHORAGOS: To something horrible, not to be heard or seen.

KOMMOS

STROPHE 1

OEDIPUS: Oh, my cloud
of darkness, abominable, unspeakable as it attacks me,
not to be turned away, brought by an evil wind!
Alas!
Again alas! Both enter me at once:
the sting of the prongs,[74] the memory of evils!
CHORUS: I do not marvel that in these afflictions
you carry double griefs and double evils.

ANTISTROPHE 1

OEDIPUS: Ah, friend,
so you at least are there, resolute servant!
Still with a heart to care for me, the blind man.
Oh! Oh!

---

[74] *prongs:* refers to both the whip that Laius used and the two gold pins Oedipus used to blind himself.

>   I know that you are there. I recognize
>   even inside my darkness, that voice of yours.
> 1335 CHORUS: Doer of horror, how did you bear to quench
>   your vision? What divinity raised your hand?
>
> ## STROPHE 2
>
> OEDIPUS: It was Apollo there, Apollo, friends,
>   who brought my sorrows, vile sorrows to their perfection,
>   these evils that were done to me.
> 1340 But the one who struck them with his hand,
>   that one was none but I, in wretchedness.
>   For why was I to see
>   when nothing I could see would bring me joy?
>   CHORUS: Yes, that is how it was.
> 1345 OEDIPUS: What could I see, indeed,
>   or what enjoy—what greeting
>   is there I could hear with pleasure, friends?
>   Conduct me out of the land
>   as quickly as you can!
> 1350 Conduct me out, my friends,
>   the man utterly ruined,
>   supremely cursed,
>   the man who is by gods
>   the most detested of all men!
> 1355 CHORUS: Wretched in disaster and in knowledge:
>   oh, I could wish you'd never come to know!
>
> ## ANTISTROPHE 2
>
> OEDIPUS: May he be destroyed, whoever freed the savage shackles
>   from my feet when I'd been sent to the wild pasture,
>   whoever rescued me from murder
> 1360 and became my savior—
>   a bitter gift:
>   if I had died then,
>   I'd not have been such grief to self and kin.
>   CHORUS: I also would have had it so.
> 1365 OEDIPUS: I'd not have returned to be my father's
>   murderer; I'd not be called by men
>   my mother's bridegroom.
>   Now I'm without a god,
>   child of a polluted parent,
> 1370 fellow progenitor with him
>   who gave me birth in misery.
>   If there's an evil that
>   surpasses evils, that
>   has fallen to the lot of Oedipus.

1375 CHORAGOS: How can I say that you have counseled well?
       Better not to be than live a blind man.
    OEDIPUS: That this was not the best thing I could do—
       don't tell me that, or advise me any more!
       Should I descend to Hades and endure
1380   to see my father with these eyes? Or see
       my poor unhappy mother? For I have done,
       to both of these, things too great for hanging.
       Or is the sight of children to be yearned for,
       to see new shoots that sprouted as these did?
1385   Never, never with these eyes of mine!
       Nor city, nor tower, nor holy images
       of the divinities! For I, all-wretched,
       most nobly raised—as no one else in Thebes—
       deprived myself of these when I ordained
1390   that all expel the impious one—god-shown
       to be polluted, and the dead king's son![75]
       Once I exposed this great stain upon me,
       could I have looked on these with steady eyes?
       No! No! And if there were a way to block
1395   the source of hearing in my ears, I'd gladly
       have locked up my pitiable body,
       so I'd be blind and deaf. Evils shut out—
       that way my mind could live in sweetness.
       Alas, Cithaeron,[76] why did you receive me?
1400   Or when you had me, not killed me instantly?
       I'd not have had to show my birth to mankind.
       Polybus, Corinth, halls—ancestral,
       they told me—how beautiful was your ward,
       a scar that held back festering disease!
1405   Evil my nature, evil my origin.
       You, three roads, and you, secret ravine,
       you oak grove, narrow place of those three paths
       that drank my blood[77] from these hands, from him
       who fathered me, do you remember still
1410   the things I did to you? When I'd come here,
       what I then did once more? Oh marriages! Marriages!
       You gave us life and when you'd planted us
       you sent the same seed up, and then revealed
       fathers, brothers, sons, and kinsman's blood,
1415   and brides, and wives, and mothers, all the most
       atrocious things that happen to mankind!

---

[75] *I . . . son:* Oedipus refers to his own curse against the murderer as well as his sins of patricide and incest.   [76] *Cithaeron:* the mountain on which the infant Oedipus was supposed to be exposed.   [77] *my blood:* that is, the blood of my father, Laius.

One should not name what never should have been.
Somewhere out there, then, quickly, by the gods,
cover me up, or murder me, or throw me
to the ocean where you will never see me more!

(Oedipus moves toward the Chorus and they back away from him.)

Come! Don't shrink to touch this wretched man!
Believe me, do not be frightened! I alone
of all mankind can carry these afflictions.

(Enter Creon from the palace with Attendants.)

CHORAGOS: Tell Creon what you wish for. Just when we need him
he's here. He can act, he can advise you.
He's now the land's sole guardian in your place.
OEDIPUS: Ah! Are there words that I can speak to him?
What ground for trust can I present? It's proved
that I was false to him in everything.
CREON: I have not come to mock you, Oedipus,
nor to reproach you for your former falseness.
You men, if you have no respect for sons
of mortals, let your awe for the all-feeding
flames of lordy Hēlius[78] prevent
your showing unconcealed so great a stain,
abhorred by earth and sacred rain and light.
Escort him quickly back into the house!
If blood kin only see and hear their own
afflictions, we'll have no impious defilement.
OEDIPUS: By the gods, you've freed me from one terrible fear,
so nobly meeting my unworthiness:
grant me something—not for me; for you!
CREON: What do you want that you should beg me so?
OEDIPUS: To drive me from the land at once, to a place
where there will be no man to speak to me!
CREON: I would have done just that—had I not wished
to ask first of the god what I should do.
OEDIPUS: His answer was revealed in full—that I,
the patricide, unholy, be destroyed.
CREON: He said that, but our need is so extreme,
it's best to have sure knowledge what must be done.
OEDIPUS: You'll ask about a wretched man like me?
CREON: Is it not time you put your trust in the god?
OEDIPUS: But I bid you as well, and shall entreat you.
Give her who is within what burial
you will—you'll give your own her proper rites;

---

[78] *Hēlius:* the sun.

           but me—do not condemn my fathers' land
           to have me dwelling here while I'm alive,
           but let me live on mountains—on Cithaeron
1460   famed as mine, for my mother and my father,
           while they yet lived, made it my destined tomb,
           and I'll be killed by those who wished my ruin!
           And yet I know: no sickness will destroy me,
           nothing will: I'd never have been saved
1465   when left to die unless for some dread evil.
           Then let my fate continue where it will!
           As for my children, Creon, take no pains
           for my sons—they're men and they will never lack
           the means to live, wherever they may be—
1470   but my two wretched, pitiable girls,
           who never ate but at my table, never
           were without me—everything that I
           would touch, they'd always have a share of it—
           please care for them! Above all, let me touch
1475   them with my hands and weep aloud my woes!
           Please, my Lord!
           Please, noble heart! Touching with my hands,
           I'd think I held them as when I could see.

       (Enter Antigone and Ismene from the palace with Attendants.)

           What's this?
1480   Oh gods! Do I hear, somewhere, my two dear ones
           sobbing? Has Creon really pitied me
           and sent to me my dearest ones, my children?
           Is that it?
       CREON: Yes, I prepared this for you, for I knew
1485   you'd feel this joy, as you have always done.
       OEDIPUS: Good fortune, then, and, for your care, be guarded
           far better by divinity than I was!
           Where are you, children? Come to me! Come here
           to these my hands, hands of your brother, hands
1490   of him who gave you seed, hands that made
           these once bright eyes to see now in this fashion.

       (Oedipus embraces his daughters.)

           He, children, seeing nothing, knowing nothing,
           he fathered you where his own seed was plowed.
           I weep for you as well, though I can't see you,
1495   imagining your bitter life to come,
           the life you will be forced by men to live.
           What gatherings of townsmen will you join,
           what festivals, without returning home
           in tears instead of watching holy rites?

1500 And when you've reached the time for marrying,
      where, children, is the man who'll run the risk
      of taking on himself the infamy
      that will wound you as it did my parents?
      What evil is not here? Your father killed
1505 his father, plowed the one who gave him birth,
      and from the place where he was sown, from there
      he got you, from the place he too was born.
      These are the wounds: then who will marry you?
      No man, my children. No, it's clear that you
1510 must wither in dry barrenness, unmarried.

(Oedipus addresses Creon.)

      Son of Menoeceus! You are the only father
      left to them—we two who gave them seed
      are both destroyed: watch that they don't become
      poor, wanderers, unmarried—they are your kin.
1515 Let not my ruin be their ruin, too!
      No, pity them! You see how young they are,
      bereft of everyone, except for you.
      Consent, kind heart, and touch me with your hand!

(Creon grasps Oedipus's right hand.)

      You, children, if you had reached an age of sense,
1520 I would have counseled much. Now, pray you may live
      always where it's allowed, finding a life
      better than his was, who gave you seed.

CREON: Stop this now. Quiet your weeping. Move away, into the house.
OEDIPUS: Bitter words, but I obey them.
CREON: There's an end to all things.
1525 OEDIPUS: I have first this request.
CREON: Tell me. I shall judge when I will hear it.
OEDIPUS: Banish me from my homeland.
CREON: You must ask that of the god.
OEDIPUS: But I am the gods' most hated man!
CREON: Then you will soon get
      what you want.
OEDIPUS: Do you consent?
CREON: I never promise when, as now, I'm ignorant.
OEDIPUS: Then lead me in.
CREON: Come. But let your hold fall from your
      children.
1530 OEDIPUS: Do not take them from me, ever!
CREON: Do not wish to keep all of
      the power.
      You had power, but that power did not follow you through life.

(Oedipus's daughters are taken from him and led into the palace by Attendants. Oedipus is led into the palace by a Servant. Creon and the other Attendants follow. Only the Chorus remains.)

CHORUS: People of Thebes, my country, see: here is that Oedipus—
he who "knew" the famous riddle, and attained the highest power,
whom all citizens admired, even envying his luck!
1535   See the billows of wild troubles which he has entered now!
Here is the truth of each man's life: we must wait, and see his end,
scrutinize his dying day, and refuse to call him happy
till he has crossed the border of his life without pain.

(Exit the Chorus along each of the parados.)

READING AND REACTING

1. The ancient Greeks used no scenery in their theatrical productions. In the absence of scenery, how is the setting established at the beginning of *Oedipus the King*?
2. In order not to detract from the language of *Oedipus the King*, some contemporary productions use very simple costumes. Do you agree with this decision? If so, why? If not, what kind of costumes would you use?
3. In some recent productions of *Oedipus the King*, actors wear copies of ancient Greek masks. What are the advantages and disadvantages of using such masks in a contemporary production of the play?
4. In the ancient Greek theater, the *strophe* and *antistrophe* were sung or chanted by the chorus as it danced back and forth across the stage. If you were staging the play today, would you retain the chorus or do away with it entirely? What would be gained or lost with each alternative?
5. Why does Sophocles have Oedipus blind himself offstage? What would be the effect of having Oedipus perform this act in full view of the audience?
6. In what ways does Sophocles observe the unities of time, place, and action described on page 575? How does Sophocles manage to present information about what happened years before the action of the play while still maintaining the three unities?
7. The ancient Greek audience that viewed *Oedipus the King* was familiar with the plot of the play. Given this situation, how does Sophocles create suspense? What are the advantages and disadvantages of using a story that the audience already knows?
8. At the end of the play, what has Oedipus learned about himself? About the gods? About the quest for truth? Is he a

tragic or a pathetic figure? (See pp. 573–75 for a discussion of *tragedy* and *pathos*.)
9. Today, some directors employ *color-blind casting*—that is, they cast an actor in a role without regard to his or her race. Do you think this practice could be used in casting *Oedipus the King?* How, for example, would you react to an African-American as Oedipus or to an Asian-American as Creon?
10. **JOURNAL ENTRY** Do you think Oedipus deserves his fate? Why or why not?

Related Works: "Barn Burning" (p. 142), " 'Out, Out—' " (p. 420), "Ulysses" (p. 552), *Hamlet* (p. 681)

◆ WRITING SUGGESTIONS: STAGING

1. Discuss the problems the original staging in *Oedipus the King* poses for contemporary audiences.
2. Suppose you are the set designer for *The Cuban Swimmer*. Decide whether you want to use a realistic, surrealistic, or minimalist set for the production. Then, write a letter to the play's director in which you present and defend your proposal. Be sure to include specific references to the play.
3. Discuss and analyze the staging techniques used in a play that is not in this chapter—for example, *Trifles* (p. 586) or *The Glass Menagerie* (p. 938).
4. Choose a short story that appears in this anthology, and explain how you would stage it if it were a play. What props, costumes, lighting, and sound effects would you choose? What events would occur offstage? Possible subjects for this paper might include "A&P" (p. 65), "The Story of an Hour" (p. 43), or "The Storm" (p. 89).
5. What scenery, props, and costumes would you use to transform the setting of *Oedipus the King* to a contemporary drama?

CHAPTER 22

Theme

Like a short story or a novel, a play is open to interpretation. Readers' reactions are influenced by the language of the text, and audiences' reactions are influenced by the performance on stage. Just as in fiction, every element of a play—its title, its conflicts, its dialogue, its characters, and its staging, for instance—can shed light on its themes.

TITLES

◊ ◊ ◊

The title of a play can provide insight into themes. The ironic title of Susan Glaspell's *Trifles* (p. 586), for example, suggests that women's concern with "trifles" may get to the heart of the matter more effectively than the preoccupations of self-important men do. Likewise, Anton Chekhov's *The Brute* (p. 668) effectively calls attention to the play's ideas about male-female relationships. The title may refer to Smirnov, who says that he has never liked women—whom he characterizes as "creatures of poetry and romance." Or it may refer to Mrs. Popov's late husband, to whose memory she has dedicated her life despite the fact that he was repeatedly unfaithful. Either alternative reinforces the play's tongue-in-cheek characterization of men as "brutes."

CONFLICTS

◊ ◊ ◊

The unfolding plot of a play—especially the conflicts that develop—can also reveal the play's themes. In Henrik Ibsen's *A Doll House* (p. 599), for example, at least three major conflicts are present: one between Nora and her husband Torvald, one between Nora and Krogstad (an old acquaintance), and one between Nora and society. Each of these conflicts sheds light on the themes of the play.

Through Nora's conflict with Torvald, Ibsen examines the constraints placed on women and men by marriage in the nineteenth century. Both Nora and Torvald are imprisoned within their respective roles: Nora must be passive and childlike, and Torvald must be proper and always in control. Nora, therefore, expects her husband to be noble and generous and, in a crisis, to sacrifice himself for her. When he fails to live up to her expectations, she is profoundly disillusioned.

Nora's conflict with Krogstad underscores Ibsen's criticisms of the class system in nineteenth-century Norway. At the beginning of the play, Nora finds it "immensely amusing: that we—that Torvald has so much power over [. . .] people." Krogstad, a bank clerk who is in the employ of Torvald, visits Nora in act 1 to enlist her aid in saving his job. It is clear that she sees him as her social inferior. When Krogstad questions her about a woman with whom he has seen her, she replies, "What makes you think you can cross-examine me, Mr. Krogstad—you, one of my husband's employees?" Nora does not realize that she and Krogstad are, ironically, very much alike: both occupy subordinate positions and therefore have no power to determine their own destinies.

Finally, through Nora's conflict with society Ibsen examines an important theme of his play: the destructive nature of the forces that subjugate women. Nineteenth-century society was male-dominated. Married women could not borrow money without their husband's signatures, own real estate in their own names, or enter into contracts. In addition, all their assets—including inheritances and trust funds—automatically became the property of their husbands at the time of marriage. As a result of her sheltered life, Nora at the beginning of the play is completely innocent of the consequences of her actions. Most readers share Dr. Rank's confusion when he asks Nora, "Why do you laugh at that? Do you have any idea of what society is?" It is Nora's disillusionment at finding out that Torvald and the rest of society are not what she has been led to believe they are that ultimately causes her to rebel. By walking out the door at the end of the play, Nora rejects not only her husband and her children (to whom, incidentally, she has no legal right once she leaves), but also society and its laws.

These conflicts, then, underscore many of the themes that dominate *A Doll House.* First, the conflicts show that marriage in the nineteenth century imprisons both men and women in narrow, constricting roles. Next, the conflicts show that middle-class Norwegian society is narrow, smug, and judgmental. (Krogstad, for example, is looked down upon for a crime years after he committed it, and Nora is looked down upon because she borrows money to save her husband's life.) Finally, the conflicts show that society does not offer individuals—especially women—the freedom to lead happy and fulfilling lives. Only when the social and economic conditions that govern society change, Ibsen suggests, can women and men live together in mutual esteem.

Dialogue

❖ ❖ ❖

The dialogue of a play can also give insight into its themes. Sometimes a character will suggest—or even explicitly state—a theme. In act 3 of *A Doll House*, for example, Nora's friend, Mrs. Linde, comes as close as any character to expressing a central concern of the play when she says, "Helmer's got to learn everything; this dreadful secret has to be aired; those two have to come to a full understanding; all these lies can't go on." As the play goes on to demonstrate, the lies that exist both in marriage and in society are obstacles to love and happiness.

One of the main themes of Arthur Miller's *Death of a Salesman* (p. 782)—the questionable validity of the American Dream, given the nation's social, political, and economic realities—is suggested by the play's dialogue. As his son Biff points out, Willy Loman's stubborn belief in upward mobility and material success is based more on fantasy than on fact:

> **WILLY:** *(with hatred, threatening)* The door of your life is wide open!
>
> **BIFF:** Pop! I am a dime a dozen, and so are you!
>
> **WILLY:** *(turning on him now in an uncontrolled outburst)* I am not a dime a dozen! I am Willy Loman, and you are Biff Loman!
>
> *Biff starts for Willy, but is blocked by Happy. In his fury, Biff seems on the verge of attacking his father.*
>
> **BIFF:** I am not a leader of men, Willy, and neither are you. You were never anything but a hard-working drummer who landed in the ash can like all the rest of them! I'm one dollar an hour, Willy! I tried seven states and couldn't raise it. A buck an hour! Do you gather my meaning? I'm not bringing home any prizes any more, and you're going to stop waiting for me to bring them home!

Although not explicitly stating the theme of the play, this exchange strongly suggests that Biff rejects the materialistic values to which Willy clings.

Characters

❖ ❖ ❖

Because a dramatic work focuses on a central character, or protagonist, the development of this character can shed light on a play's themes. Willy Loman in *Death of a Salesman*, for example, is developed in great detail. At the beginning of the play he feels trapped, exhausted, and estranged from his surroundings. As Willy gradually sinks from depression into despair, the action of the play shifts from the present to the past, showing the events that shaped Willy's life. His attitudes, beliefs, dreams, and dashed hopes reveal him to be an embodiment of the major theme of the play—that an unquestioning belief in the American Dream of success and upward mobility is unrealistic and possibly destructive.

Nora, the main character in *A Doll House*, changes a great deal during the course of the play. At the beginning of the play, she is more her husband's possession than an adult capable of determining her own destiny. Nora's status becomes apparent in the first act when Torvald gently scolds his "little spendthrift" and refers to her as his "little lark" and his "squirrel." She is reduced to childish deceptions, such as hiding her macaroons from her husband when he enters the room. After Krogstad accuses her of committing forgery and threatens to expose her, she expects her husband to rise to the occasion and take the blame for her. When Torvald instead accuses her of being a hypocrite, a liar, and a criminal, Nora's neat little world comes crashing down. As a result of this experience, Nora changes; no longer is she the submissive and obedient wife. Instead, she becomes confident and assertive, ultimately telling Torvald that their marriage is a sham and that she can no longer stay with him. This abrupt shift in Nora's personality gives the audience a clear understanding of the major themes of the play.

Unlike Willy and Nora, Laura in Tennessee Williams's *The Glass Menagerie* (p. 938) is a character who changes very little during the course of the play. Laura suffers from such pathological shyness that she is unable to attend typing class, let alone talk to a potential suitor. Although the "gentleman caller" does draw Laura out of her shell for a short time, she soon withdraws again. Laura's inability to change reinforces the play's theme that contemporary society, with its emphasis on progress, has no place for people like Laura who live in private worlds "of glass animals and old, worn-out phonograph records."

STAGING

◊ ◊ ◊

Scenery and props may also convey the themes of a play. For example, the stage directions in Edward Albee's absurdist drama *The Sandbox* indicate that the stage is relatively bare. Containing only two chairs and a sandbox, this bare stage suggests the play's frightening emptiness, a quality Albee believes characterizes the lives of all human beings. In *Death of a Salesman,* Biff's trophy, which is constantly in the audience's view, ironically underscores the futility of Willy's efforts to achieve success. Similarly, the miniature animals in *The Glass Menagerie* reflect the fragility of Laura's character and the futility of her efforts to fit into the modern world.

Special lighting effects and music can also suggest a play's themes. Throughout *The Glass Menagerie,* for example, words and pictures are projected onto a section of the set between the front room and dining room walls. In scene 1 of the play, as Tom's mother, Amanda, tells him about her experiences with her "gentlemen callers," an image of her as a girl greeting callers appears on the screen. As Amanda continues, the words *"Où sont Les Neiges"*—"Where are the snows [of yesteryear]?"—appear on the screen. Later in the play, when Laura and her mother discuss a boy Laura knew, his picture is projected on the screen, showing him as a high school hero carrying a silver cup. In addition to the slides, Williams uses music—a recurring tune, dance music, and "Ave Maria"—to increase the emotional impact of certain scenes. Williams also uses shafts of light focused on selected areas or characters to create a dreamlike atmosphere for the play. Collectively, the slides, the music, and the lighting reinforce the theme that those who retreat obsessively into the past eventually become estranged from the present.

A Final Note

◇ ◇ ◇

As you read, your values and beliefs will influence your interpretation of a play's themes. For instance, your interest in feminism could lead you to focus your attention on the submissive, almost passive, role of Willy's wife, Linda, in *Death of a Salesman*. As a result, you could conclude that the play shows how, in the post–World War II United States, women like Linda often sacrificed their own happiness for their husbands. Remember, however, that the details of a play, not just your own feelings or assumptions, must support your interpretation.

 ## Checklist: Writing about Theme

✓ What is the central theme of the play?
✓ What other themes can you identify?
✓ Does the title of the play suggest a theme?
✓ What conflicts exist in the play? In what way do they shed light on the themes of the play?
✓ Do any characters' statements express or imply a theme of the play?
✓ Do any characters change during the play? How do these changes suggest the play's themes?
✓ Do certain characters resist change? How does their failure to change suggest a theme of the play?
✓ Do scenery and props help to communicate the play's themes?
✓ Does music reinforce certain ideas in the play?
✓ Does lighting underscore the themes of the play?

◈ **ALICE CHILDRESS** (1920–1994) was born in Charleston, South Carolina. She studied drama at the American Negro Theatre in the 1940s, where she wrote, directed, and starred in her first play, *Florence* (1949). She went on to become a leading African-American playwright, novelist, and actress. Other works by Childress include *Wine in the Wilderness* (1969), which won the Obie Award; *Gullah* (1984); and *Moms* (1987). She is also a novelist and a noted children's writer.

Florence, set in the 1940s, is about an African-American woman who meets a white actress in a railway station waiting room. Through her interchange with the woman, she gains respect for her own daughter's pursuit of an acting career.

◈ ◈ ◈

ALICE CHILDRESS

Florence
(1949)

CHARACTERS
MARGE
MAMA
PORTER
MRS. CARTER

PLACE
A very small town in the South.

TIME
The late 1940s.

SCENE
A railway station waiting room. The room is divided in two sections by a low railing. Upstage center is a double door which serves as an entrance to both sides of the room. Over the doorway stage right is a sign "Colored," over the doorway stage left is another sign "White." Stage right are two doors . . . one marked "Colored men" . . . the other "Colored women." Stage left two other doorways are "White ladies" and "White gentlemen." There are two benches, one on each side. The room is drab and empty looking. Through the double doors upstage center can be seen a gray lighting which gives the effect of an early evening and open platform.

At rise of curtain the stage remains empty for about twenty seconds . . . A middle aged Negro woman enters, looks offstage . . . then crosses to the "Colored" side and sits on the bench. A moment later she is followed by a young Negro woman about twenty-one years old. *She is carrying a large new cardboard suitcase and a wrapped shoebox. She is wearing a shoulder strap bag and a newspaper protrudes from the flap. She crosses to the "Colored" side and rests the suitcase at her feet as she looks at her mother with mild annoyance.*

MARGE: You didn't have to get here so early, Mama. Now you got to wait!

MAMA: If I'm goin' someplace . . . I like to get there in plenty time. You don't have to stay.

MARGE: You shouldn't wait 'round here alone.

MAMA: I ain't scared. Ain't a soul going to bother me.

5 MARGE: I got to get back to Ted. He don't like to be in the house by himself. *(She picks up the bag and places it on the bench by Mama.)*

MAMA: You'd best go back. *(Smiles.)* You know he misses Florence.

MARGE: He's just a little fellow. He needs his mother. You make her come home! She shouldn't be way up there in Harlem. She ain't got nobody there.

MAMA: You know Florence don't like the South.

MARGE: It ain't what we like in this world! You tell her that.

10 MAMA: If Mr. Jack ask about the rent, you tell him we gonna be a little late on account of the trip.

MARGE: I'll talk with him. Don't worry so about everything. *(Places suitcase on floor.)* What you carryin', Mama . . . bricks?

MAMA: If Mr. Jack won't wait . . . write to Rudley. He oughta send a little somethin'.

MARGE: Mama . . . Rudley ain't got nothin' fo himself. I hate to ask him to give us.

MAMA: That's your brother! If push come to shove, we got to ask.

15 MARGE: *(places box on bench)* Don't forget to eat your lunch . . . and try to get a seat near the window so you can lean on your elbow and get a little rest.

MAMA: Hmmmm . . . mmmph. Yes.

MARGE: Buy yourself some coffee when the man comes through. You'll need something hot and you can't go to the diner.

MAMA: I know that. You talk like I'm a northern greenhorn.

MARGE: You got handkerchiefs?

20 MAMA: I got everything, Marge.

MARGE: *(wanders upstage to the railing division line)* I know Florence is real bad off or she wouldn't call on us for money. Make her come home. She ain't gonna get rich up there and we can't afford to do for her.

MAMA: We talked all of that before.

MARGE: *(touches rail)* Well, you got to be strict on her. She got notions a Negro woman don't need.

MAMA: But she was in a real play. Didn't she send us twenty-five dollars a week?

25 **MARGE:** For two weeks.
MAMA: Well the play was over.
MARGE: *(crosses to Mama and sits beside her)* It's not money, Mama. Sarah wrote us about it. You know what she said Florence was doin'. Sweepin' the stage!
MAMA: She was *in* the play!
MARGE: Sure she was in it! Sweepin'! Them folks ain't gonna let her be no actress. You tell her to wake up.
30 **MAMA:** I . . . I . . . think.
MARGE: Listen, Mama . . . She won't wanna come. We know that . . . but she gotta!
MAMA: Maybe we shoulda told her to expect me. It's kind of mean to just walk in like this.
MARGE: I bet she's livin' terrible. What's the matter with her? Don't she know we're keepin' her son?
MAMA: Florence don't feel right 'bout down here since Jim got killed.
35 **MARGE:** Who does? I should be the one goin' to get her. You tell her she ain't gonna feel right in no place. Mama, honestly! She must think she's white!
MAMA: Florence is brownskin.
MARGE: I don't mean that. I'm talkin' about her attitude. Didn't she go to Strumley's down here and ask to be a salesgirl? *(Rises.)* Now ain't that somethin'? They don't hire no Colored folks.
MAMA: Others beside Florence been talkin' about their rights.
MARGE: I know it . . . but there's things we can't do cause they ain't gonna let us. *(She wanders over to the "White" side of the stage.)* Don't feel a damn bit different over here than it does on our side. *(Silence.)*
40 **MAMA:** Maybe we shoulda just sent her the money this time. This one time.
MARGE: *(coming back to the "Colored" side)* Mama! Don't you let her cash that check for nothin' but to bring her back home.
MAMA: I know.
MARGE: *(restless . . . fidgets with her hair . . . patting it in place)* I oughta go now.
MAMA: You best get back to Ted. He might play with the lamp.
45 **MARGE:** He better not let me catch him! If you got to go to the ladies' room take your grip.
MAMA: I'll be alright. Make Ted get up on time for school.
MARGE: *(kisses her quickly and gives her the newspaper)* Here's something to read. So long, Mama.
MAMA: G'bye, Margie baby.
MARGE: *(goes to door . . . stops and turns to her mother)* You got your smelling salts?
50 **MAMA:** In my pocketbook.
MARGE: *(wistfully)* Tell Florence I love her and miss her too.
PORTER: *(can be heard singing in the distance)*
MAMA: Sure.

MARGE: *(reluctant to leave)* Pin that check in your bosom, Mama. You might fall asleep and somebody'll rob you.
MAMA: I got it pinned to me. *(Feels for the check which is in her blouse.)*
MARGE: *(almost pathetic)* Bye, Ma.
MAMA: *(Sits for a moment looking at her surroundings. She opens the paper and begins to read.)*
PORTER: *(offstage)* Hello, Marge. What you doin' down here?
MARGE: I came to see Mama off.
PORTER: Where's she going?
MARGE: She's in there; she'll tell you. I got to get back to Ted.
PORTER: Bye now . . . Say, wait a minute, Marge.
MARGE: Yes?
PORTER: I told Ted he could have some of my peaches and he brought all them Brandford boys and they picked 'em all. I wouldn't lay a hand on him but I told him I was gonna tell you.
MARGE: I'm gonna give it to him!
PORTER: *(Enters and crosses to white side of waiting room. He carries a pail of water and a mop. He is about fifty years old. He is obviously tired but not lazy.)* Every peach off my tree!
MAMA: There wasn't but six peaches on that tree.
PORTER: *(smiles . . . glances at Mama as he crosses to the "White" side and begins to mop)* How d'ye do, Mrs. Whitney . . . you going on a trip?
MAMA: Fine, I thank you. I'm going to New York.
PORTER: Wish it was me. You gonna stay?
MAMA: No, Mr. Brown. I'm bringing Florence . . . I'm visiting Florence.
PORTER: Tell her I said hello. She's a fine girl.
MAMA: Thank you.
PORTER: My brother Bynum's in Georgia now.
MAMA: Well now, that's nice.
PORTER: Atlanta.
MAMA: He goin' to school?
PORTER: Yes'm. He saw Florence in a Colored picture. A moving picture.
MAMA: Do tell! She didn't say a word about it.
PORTER: They got Colored moving picture theaters in Atlanta.
MAMA: Yes. Your brother going to be a doctor?
PORTER: *(with pride)* No. He writes things.
MAMA: Oh.
PORTER: My son is goin' back to Howard next year.
MAMA: Takes an awful lot of goin' to school to be anything. Lot of money leastways.
PORTER: *(thoughtfully)* Yes'm, it sure do.
MAMA: That sure was a nice church sociable the other night.
PORTER: Yes'm. We raised 87 dollars.
MAMA: That's real nice.
PORTER: I won your cake at the bazaar.
MAMA: The chocolate one?

PORTER: *(as he wrings mop)* Yes'm . . . was light as a feather. That old train is gonna be late this evenin'. It's number 42.

MAMA: I don't mind waitin'.

PORTER: *(Lifts pail, tucks mop handle under his arm. He looks about in order to make certain no one is around and leans over and addresses Mama in a confidential tone.)* Did you buy your ticket from that Mr. Daly?

95 MAMA: *(in a low tone)* No. Marge bought it yesterday.

PORTER: *(leaning against railing)* That's good. That man is real mean. Especially if he thinks you're goin' north. *(He starts to leave . . . then turns back to Mama.)* If you go to the rest room, use the Colored men's . . . the other one is out of order.

MAMA: Thank you, sir.

MRS. CARTER: *(A white woman . . . well dressed, wearing furs and carrying a small, expensive overnight bag breezes in . . . breathless . . . flustered and smiling. She addresses the Porter as she almost collides with him.)* Boy! My bags are out there. There taxi driver just dropped them. Will they be safe?

PORTER: Yes, mam. I'll see after them.

100 MRS. CARTER: I thought I'd missed the train.

PORTER: It's late, mam.

MRS. CARTER: *(crosses to bench on the "White" side and rests her bag)* Fine! You come back here and get me when it comes. There'll be a tip in it for you.

PORTER: Thank you, mam. I'll be here. *(As he leaves.)* Miss Whitney, I'll take care of your bag too.

MAMA: Thank you, sir.

105 MRS. CARTER: *(wheels around . . . notices Mama)* Oh . . . Hello there . . .

MAMA: Howdy, mam. *(She opens her newspaper and begins to read.)*

MRS. CARTER: *(Paces up and down rather nervously. She takes a cigarette from her purse, lights it and takes a deep draw. She looks at her watch and then speaks to Mama across the railing.)* Have you any idea how late the train will be?

MAMA: No, mam. *(Starts to read again.)*

MRS. CARTER: I can't leave this place fast enough. Two days of it and I'm bored to tears. Do you live here?

110 MAMA: *(rests paper on her lap)* Yes, mam.

MRS. CARTER: Where are you going?

MAMA: New York City, mam.

MRS. CARTER: Good for you! You can stop "maming" me. My name is Mrs. Carter. I'm not a southerner really. *(Takes a handkerchief from her purse and covers her nose for a moment.)* My God! Disinfectant! This is a frightful place. My brother's here writing a book. Wants atmosphere. Well, he's got it. I'll never come back here ever.

MAMA: That's too bad, mam . . . Mrs. Carter.

115 MRS. CARTER: That's good. I'd die in this place. Really die. Jeff . . . Mr. Wiley . . . my brother . . . He's tied in knots, a bundle of problems . . . positively in knots.

MAMA: *(amazed)* That so, mam?
MRS. CARTER: You don't have to call me mam. It's so southern. Mrs. Carter! These people are still fighting the Civil War. I'm really a New Yorker now. Of course, I was born here . . . in the South I mean. Memphis. Listen . . . am I annoying you? I've simply got to talk to someone.
MAMA: *(places her newspaper on the bench)* No, Mrs. Carter. It's perfectly alright.
MRS. CARTER: Fine! You see Jeff has ceased writing. Stopped! Just like that! *(Snaps fingers.)*
120 MAMA: *(turns to her)* That so?
MRS. CARTER: Yes. The reviews came out on his last book. Poor fellow.
MAMA: I'm sorry, mam . . . Mrs. Carter. They didn't like his book?
MRS. CARTER: Well enough . . . but Jeff's . . . well, Mr. Wiley is a genius. He says they missed the point! Lost the whole message! Did you read . . . do you . . . have you heard of *Lost My Lonely Way?*
MAMA: No, mam. I can't say I have.
125 MRS. CARTER: Well, it doesn't matter. It's profound. Real . . . you know. *(Stands at the railing upstage.)* It's about your people.
MAMA: That's nice.
MRS. CARTER: Jeff poured his complete self into it. Really delved into the heart of the problem, pulled no punches! He hardly stopped for his meals . . . And of course I wasn't here to see that he didn't overdo. He suffers so with his characters.
MAMA: I guess he wants to do his best.
MRS. CARTER: Zelma! . . . That's his heroine . . . Zelma! A perfect character.
130 MAMA: *(interested . . . coming out of her shell eagerly)* She was colored, mam?
MRS. CARTER: Oh yes! . . . But of course you don't know what it's about do you?
MAMA: No, miss . . . Would you tell me?
MRS. CARTER: *(leaning on the railing)* Well . . . she's almost white, see? Really you can't tell except in small ways. She wants to be a lawyer . . . and . . . and . . . well, there she is full of complexes and this deep shame you know.
MAMA: *(excitedly but with curiosity)* Do tell! What shame has she got?
135 MRS. CARTER: *(takes off her fur neckpiece and places it on bench with overnight bag)* It's obvious! This lovely creature . . . intelligent, ambitious, and well . . . she's a Negro!
MAMA: *(waiting eagerly)* Yes'm, you said that . . .
MRS. CARTER: Surely you understand? She's constantly hating herself. Just before she dies she says it! . . . Right on the bridge . . .
MAMA: *(genuinely moved)* How sad. Ain't it a shame she had to die?
MRS. CARTER: It was inevitable . . . couldn't be any other way!
140 MAMA: What did she say on the bridge?
MRS. CARTER: Well . . . just before she jumped . . .
MAMA: *(slowly straightening)* You mean she killed *herself?*

MRS. CARTER: Of course. Close your eyes and picture it!
MAMA: *(turns front and closes her eyes tightly with enthusiasm)* Yes'm.
145 MRS. CARTER: *(center stage on "White" side)* Now . . . ! She's standing on the bridge in the moonlight . . . Out of her shabby purse she takes a mirror . . . and by the light of the moon she looks at her reflection in the glass.
MAMA: *(clasps her hands together gently)* I can see her just as plain.
MRS. CARTER: *(sincerely)* Tears roll down her cheeks as she says . . . almost! almost white . . . but I'm black! I'm a Negro! and then . . . *(Turns to Mama.)* she jumps and drowns herself!
MAMA: *(opens her eyes and speaks quietly)* Why?
MRS. CARTER: She can't face it! Living in a world where she almost belongs but not quite. *(Drifts upstage.)* Oh it's so . . . so . . . tragic.
150 MAMA: *(Carried away by her convictions . . . not anger . . . she feels challenged. She rises.)* That ain't so! Not one bit it ain't!
MRS. CARTER: *(surprised)* But it is!
MAMA: *(during the following she works her way around the railing until she crosses over about one foot to the "White" side and is face to face with Mrs. Carter)* I know it ain't! Don't my friend Essie Kitredge daughter look just like a German or somethin'? She didn't kill herself! She's teachin' the third grade in the colored school right here. Even the bus drivers ask her to sit in the front seats cause they think she's white! . . . an' . . . an' . . . she just says as clear as you please . . . "I'm sittin' where my people got to sit by law. I'm a Negro woman!"
MRS. CARTER: *(uncomfortable and not knowing why)* . . . But there you have it. The exception makes the rule. That's proof!
MAMA: No such thing! My cousin Hemsly's as white as you! . . . an' . . . an' he never . . .
155 MRS. CARTER: *(flushed with anger . . . yet lost . . . because she doesn't know why)* Are you losing your temper? *(Weakly.)* Are you angry with me?
MAMA: *(Stands silently trembling as she looks down and notices she is on the wrong side of the railing. She looks up at the "White Ladies room" sign and slowly works her way back to the "Colored" side. She feels completely lost.)* No, mam. Excuse me please. *(With bitterness.)* I just meant Hemsly works in the colored section of the shoe store . . . He never once wanted to kill his self! *(She sits down on the bench and fumbles for her newspaper. Silence.)*
MRS. CARTER: *(caught between anger and reason . . . she laughs nervously)* Well! Let's not be upset by this. It's entirely my fault you know. This whole thing is a completely controversial subject. *(Silence.)* If it's too much for Jeff . . . well naturally I shouldn't discuss it with you. *(Approaching railing.)* I'm sorry. Let *me* apologize.
MAMA: *(keeps her eyes on the paper)* No need for that, mam. *(Silence.)*
MRS. CARTER: *(painfully uncomfortable)* I've drifted away from . . . What started all of this?

160 **MAMA:** *(no comedy intended or allowed on this line)* Your brother, mam.
MRS. CARTER: *(trying valiantly to brush away the tension)* Yes . . . Well, I had to come down and sort of hold his hand over the reviews. He just thinks too much . . . and studies. He knows the Negro so well that sometimes our friends tease him and say he almost *seems* like . . . well you know . . .
MAMA: *(tightly)* Yes'm.
MRS. CARTER: *(slowly walks over the "Colored" side near the top of the rail)* You know I try but it's really difficult to understand you people. However . . . I keep trying.
MAMA: *(still tight)* Thank you, mam.
165 **MRS. CARTER:** *(retreats back to "White" side and begins to prove herself)* Last week . . . Why do you know what I did? I sent a thousand dollars to a Negro college for scholarships.
MAMA: That was right kind of you.
MRS. CARTER: *(almost pleading)* I know what's going on in your mind . . . and what you're thinking is wrong. I've . . . I've . . . eaten with Negroes.
MAMA: Yes, mam.
MRS. CARTER: *(trying to find a straw)* . . . And there's Malcolm! If it weren't for the guidance of Jeff he'd never written his poems. Malcolm is a Negro.
170 **MAMA:** *(freezing)* Yes, mam.
MRS. CARTER: *(Gives up, crosses to her bench, opens her overnight bag and takes out a book and begins to read. She glances at Mama from time to time. Mama is deeply absorbed in her newspaper. Mrs. Carter closes her book with a bang . . . determined to penetrate the wall Mama has built around her.)* Why are you going to New York?
MAMA: *(almost accusingly)* I got a daughter there.
MRS. CARTER: I lost my son in the war. *(Silence . . . Mama is ill at ease.)* Your daughter . . . what is she doing . . . studying?
MAMA: No'm, she's trying to get on stage.
175 **MRS. CARTER:** *(pleasantly)* Oh . . . a singer?
MAMA: No, mam. She's . . .
MRS. CARTER: *(warmly)* You people have such a gift. I love spirituals . . . "Steal Away," "Swing Low, Sweet Chariot."
MAMA: They are right nice. But Florence wants to act. Just say things in plays.
MRS. CARTER: A dramatic actress?
180 **MAMA:** Yes, that's what it is. She been in a colored moving picture, and a big show for two weeks on Broadway.
MRS. CARTER: The dear, precious child! . . . But this is funny . . . no! it's pathetic. She must be bitter . . . *really* bitter. Do you know what I do?
MAMA: I can't rightly say.
MRS. CARTER: I'm an actress! A dramatic actress . . . And I haven't really worked in six months . . . And I'm pretty well-known . . . And

everyone knows Jeff. I'd like to work. Of course, there are my committees, but you see, they don't need me. No really . . . not even Jeff.

MAMA: Now that's a shame.

MRS. CARTER: Now your daughter . . . you must make her stop before she's completely unhappy. Make her stop!

MAMA: Yes'm . . . why?

MRS. CARTER: I have the best of contacts and *I've* only done a few *broadcasts* lately. Of course, I'm not counting the things I just wouldn't do. Your daughter . . . make her stop.

MAMA: A drama teacher told her she has real talent.

MRS. CARTER: A drama teacher! My dear woman, there are loads of unscrupulous whites up there that just hand out opinions for . . .

MAMA: This was a colored gentleman down here.

MRS. CARTER: Oh well! . . . And she went up there on the strength of that? This makes me very unhappy. *(Puts book away in case, and snaps lock, silence.)*

MAMA: *(getting an idea)* Do you really, truly feel that way, mam?

MRS. CARTER: I do. Please . . . I want you to believe me.

MAMA: Could I ask you something?

MRS. CARTER: Anything.

MAMA: You won't be angry, mam?

MRS. CARTER: *(remembering)* I won't. I promise you.

MAMA: *(gathering courage)* Florence is proud . . . but she's having it hard.

MRS. CARTER: I'm sure she is.

MAMA: Could you help her out some, mam? Knowing all the folks you do . . . maybe . . .

MRS. CARTER: *(rubs the outside of the case)* Well . . . it isn't that simple . . . but . . . you're very sweet. If only I could . . .

MAMA: Anything you did, I feel grateful. I don't like to tell it, but she can't even pay her rent and things. And she's used to my cooking for her . . . I believe my girl goes hungry sometime up there . . . and yet she'd like to stay so bad.

MRS. CARTER: *(looks up, resting case on her knees)* How can I refuse? You seem like a good woman.

MAMA: Always lived as best I knew how and raised my children up right. We got a fine family, mam.

MRS. CARTER: And I've no family at all. I've got to! It's clearly my duty. Jeff's books . . . guiding Malcolm's poetry . . . It isn't enough . . . oh I know it isn't. Have you ever heard of Melba Rugby?

MAMA: No, mam. I don't know anybody much . . . except right here.

MRS. CARTER: *(brightening)* She's in California, but she's moving East again . . . hates California.

MAMA: Yes'm.

MRS. CARTER: A most versatile woman. Writes, directs, acts . . . everything!

210 MAMA: That's nice, mam.
MRS. CARTER: Well, she's uprooting herself and coming back to her first home . . . New York . . . to direct "Love Flowers" . . . it's a musical.
MAMA: Yes'm.
MRS. CARTER: She's grand . . . helped so many people . . . and I'm sure she'll help your . . . what's her name.
MAMA: Florence.
215 MRS. CARTER: *(turns back to bench, opens bag, takes out a pencil and an address book)* Yes, Florence. She'll have to *make* a place for her.
MAMA: Bless you, mam.
MRS. CARTER: *(holds handbag steady on rail as she uses it to write on)* Now let's see . . . the best thing to do would be to give you the telephone number . . . since you're going there.
MAMA: Yes'm.
MRS. CARTER: *(writing address on paper)* Your daughter will love her . . . and if she's a deserving girl . . .
220 MAMA: *(looking down as Mrs. Carter writes)* She's a good girl. Never a bit of trouble. Except about her husband, and neither one of them could help that.
MRS. CARTER: *(stops writing, raises her head questioning)* Oh?
MAMA: He got killed at voting time. He was a good man.
MRS. CARTER: *(embarrassed)* I guess that's worse than losing him in the war.
MAMA: We all got our troubles passing through here.
225 MRS. CARTER: *(gives her the address)* Tell your dear girl to call this number about a week from now.
MAMA: Yes, mam.
MRS. CARTER: Her experience won't matter with Melba. I know she'll understand. I'll call her too.
MAMA: Thank you, mam.
MRS. CARTER: I'll just tell her . . . no heavy washing or ironing . . . just light cleaning and a little cooking . . . does she cook?
230 MAMA: Mam? *(Slowly backs away from Mrs. Carter and sits down on bench.)*
MRS. CARTER: Don't worry, that won't matter to Melba. *(Silence, moves around the rail to "Colored" side, leans over Mama.)* I'd take your daughter myself, but I've got Binnie. She's been with me for years, and I just can't let her go . . . can I?
MAMA: *(looks at Mrs. Carter closely)* No, mam.
MRS. CARTER: Of course she must be steady. I couldn't ask Melba to take a fly-by-night. *(Touches Mama's arm.)* But she'll have her own room and bath, and above all . . . security.
MAMA: *(reaches out, clutches Mrs. Carter's wrist almost pulling her off balance)* Child!
235 MRS. CARTER: *(frightened)* You're hurting my wrist.
MAMA: *(looks down, realizes how tight she's clutching her, and releases her wrist)* I mustn't hurt you, must I.

MRS. CARTER: *(backing away rubbing her wrist)* It's all right.
MAMA: *(rises)* You better get over on the other side of that rail. It's against the law for you to be over here with me.
MRS. CARTER: *(frightened and uncomfortable)* If you think so.
240 MAMA: I don't want to break the law.
MRS. CARTER: *(keeps her eye on Mama as she drifts around railing to bench on her side, gathers overnight bag)* I know I must look a fright. The train should be along soon. When it comes, I won't see you until New York. These silly laws. *(Silence.)* I'm going to powder my nose. *(Exits into "White ladies" room.)*
PORTER: *(singing offstage)*
MAMA: *(Sits quietly, staring in front of her . . . then looks at the address for a moment . . . tears the paper into little bits and lets them flutter to the floor. She opens the suitcase, takes out notebook, an envelope and a pencil. She writes a few words on the paper.)*
PORTER: *(enters with broom and dust pan)* Number 42 will be coming along in nine minutes. *(When Mama doesn't answer him, he looks up and watches her. She reaches in her bosom, unpins the check, smooths it out, places it in the envelope with the letter. She closes the suitcase.)* I said the train's coming. Where's the lady?
245 MAMA: She's in the *ladies'* room. You got a stamp?
PORTER: No. But I can get one out of the machine. Three for a dime.
MAMA: *(hands him the letter)* Put one on here and mail it for me.
PORTER: *(looks at it)* Gee . . . you writing Florence when you're going to see her?
MAMA: *(pickes up the shoebox and puts it back on the bench)* You want a good lunch? It's chicken and fruit.
250 PORTER: Sure . . . thank you . . . but you won't . . .
MAMA: *(rises, paces up and down)* I ain't gonna see Florence for a long time. Might be never.
PORTER: How's that, Mrs. Whitney?
MAMA: She can be anything in the world she wants to be! That's her right. Marge can't make her turn back, Mrs. Carter can't make her turn back. *Lost My Lonely Way!* That's a book! People killing theyselves 'cause they look white but be black. They just don't know do they, Mr. Brown?
PORTER: Whatever happened don't you fret none. Life is too short.
255 MAMA: Oh, I'm gonna fret plenty! You know what I wrote Florence?
PORTER: No, mam. But you don't have to tell me.
MAMA: I said "Keep trying." . . . Oh, I'm going home.
PORTER: I'll take your bag. *(Picks up bag and starts out.)* Come on Mrs. Whitney. *(Porter exits.)*

Mama moves around to "White" side, stares at sign over door. She starts to knock on "White Ladies" door, but changes her mind. As she turns to leave, her eye catches the railing; she approaches it gently, touches it, turns, exits.

Stage is empty for about six or seven seconds. Sound of train whistle is heard in the distance. Slow curtain.

Curtain

Reading and Reacting

1. Review the stage directions for *Florence*. What insight into the play's themes do these stage directions provide?
2. *Florence* takes place in a train station. What is the significance of this setting?
3. In the waiting room, a railing separates whites from blacks; signs over the entrances and over the doors of the restrooms denote the white and black facilities. In what way do these elements reinforce the major themes of the play?
4. *Florence* is set in the South during the late 1940s. How might the play be different if it were set in the North? If it were set today?
5. In line 17, Marge tells Mama that she had better buy some food because she "can't go to the diner." Then again in line 23, Marge says that Florence has "notions a Negro woman don't need." What situation is Marge alluding to? Find other references to this "situation" in the play.
6. Does Mrs. Carter think of herself as a racist? Do you agree with her assessment of herself?
7. What causes Mama to disagree with Mrs. Carter about her brother's book? What does this disagreement tell the audience about both characters?
8. Does Mama's view of Mrs. Carter change or remain the same as the play progresses? Why does Mama ask Mrs. Carter to help Florence? What does she learn that causes her to reject the "help" that Mrs. Carter offers?
9. What is Mama's opinion of her daughter at the beginning of the play? How does this view change by the end? In what way is Mrs. Carter responsible for this change?
10. Although the play bears her name, Florence never appears on stage. In what sense is Florence nevertheless a character in the play? Why do you think Childress names the play for her?
11. **Journal Entry** Should Mama have confronted Mrs. Carter directly? What do you think would have happened had she done so?

Related Work: "Like a Winding Sheet" (p. 76), "Everyday Use" (p. 217), "Two Kinds" (p. 285), "Negro" (p. 333)

◆ **TENNESSEE WILLIAMS** (1911–1983) was born in Columbus, Mississippi, but moved to St. Louis, the setting of *The Glass Menagerie*, when he was eight. His plays include *A Streetcar Named Desire* (1947), *Cat on a Hot Tin Roof* (1955), and *Sweet Bird of Youth* (1959).

The Glass Menagerie was his first major success. Williams saw the play as somewhat autobiographical: he said his sister Rose had a collection of glass animals in her room in St. Louis, and he gives his real first name (Tom) to Laura's brother in the play.

◆ ◆ ◆

TENNESSEE WILLIAMS

The Glass Menagerie
(1945)

Nobody, not even the rain, has such small hands.
E. E. CUMMINGS

CHARACTERS

AMANDA WINGFIELD, *the mother. A little woman of great but confused vitality clinging frantically to another time and place. Her characterization must be carefully created, not copied from type. She is not paranoiac, but her life is paranoia. There is much to admire in Amanda, and as much to love and pity as there is to laugh at. Certainly she has endurance and a kind of heroism, and though her foolishness makes her unwittingly cruel at times, there is tenderness in her slight person.*

LAURA WINGFIELD, *her daughter. Amanda, having failed to establish contact with reality, continues to live vitally in her illusions, but Laura's situation is even graver. A childhood illness has left her crippled, one leg slightly shorter than the other, and held in a brace. This defect need not be more than suggested on the stage. Stemming from this, Laura's separation increases till she is like a piece of her own glass collection, too exquisitely fragile to move from the shelf.*

TOM WINGFIELD, *her son. And the narrator of the play. A poet with a job in a warehouse. His nature is not remorseless, but to escape from a trap he has to act without pity.*

JIM O'CONNOR, *the gentleman caller. A nice, ordinary, young man.*

SCENE
An alley in St. Louis.

Part I
Preparation for a Gentleman Caller.

Part II
The Gentleman Calls.

Time
Now and the Past.

Scene 1

The Wingfield apartment is in the rear of the building, one of those vast hive-like conglomerations of cellular living-units that flower as warty growths in overcrowded urban centers of lower middle-class population and are symptomatic of the impulse of this largest and fundamentally enslaved section of American society to avoid fluidity and differentiation and to exist and function as one interfused mass of automatism.

The apartment faces an alley and is entered by a fire-escape, a structure whose name is a touch of accidental poetic truth, for all of these huge buildings are always burning with the slow and implacable fires of human desperation. The fire-escape is included in the set—that is, the landing of it and steps descending from it.

The scene is memory and is therefore nonrealistic. Memory takes a lot of poetic license. It omits some details; others are exaggerated, according to the emotional value of the articles it touches, for memory is seated predominantly in the heart. The interior is therefore rather dim and poetic.

At the rise of the curtain, the audience is faced with the dark, grim rear wall of the Wingfield tenement. This building, which runs parallel to the footlights, is flanked on both sides by dark, narrow alleys which run into murky canyons of tangled clotheslines, garbage cans and the sinister latticework of neighboring fire-escapes. It is up and down these side alleys that exterior entrances and exits are made, during the play. At the end of Tom's opening commentary, the dark tenement wall slowly reveals (by means of a transparency) the interior of the ground floor Wingfield apartment.

Downstage is the living room, which also serves as a sleeping room for Laura, the sofa unfolding to make her bed. Upstage, center, and divided by a wide arch or second proscenium with transparent faded portieres (or second curtain), is the dining room. In an old-fashioned what-not in the living room are seen scores of transparent glass animals. A blown-up photograph of the father hangs on the wall of the living room, facing the audience, to the left of the archway. It is the face of a very handsome young man in a doughboy's First World War cap. He is gallantly smiling, ineluctably smiling, as if to say, "I will be smiling forever."

The audience hears and sees the opening scene in the dining room through both the transparent fourth wall of the building and the transparent gauze portieres of the dining-room arch. It is during this revealing scene that the *fourth wall slowly ascends, out of sight. This transparent exterior wall is not brought down again until the very end of the play, during Tom's final speech. The narrator is an undisguised convention of the play. He takes whatever license with dramatic convention as is convenient to his purposes.*

Tom enters dressed as a merchant sailor from the alley, stage left, and strolls across the front of the stage to the fire-escape. There he stops and lights a cigarette. He addresses the audience.

TOM: Yes, I have tricks in my pocket, I have things up my sleeve. But I am the opposite of a stage magician. He gives you illusion that has the appearance of truth. I give you truth in the pleasant disguise of illusion. To begin with, I turn back time. I reverse it to that quaint period, the thirties, when the huge middle class of America was matriculating in a school for the blind. Their eyes had failed them, or they had failed their eyes, and so they were having their fingers pressed forcibly down on the fiery Braille alphabet of a dissolving economy. In Spain there was revolution.[1] Here there was only shouting and confusion. In Spain there was Guernica.[2] Here there were disturbances of labor, sometimes pretty violent, in otherwise peaceful cities such as Chicago, Cleveland, Saint Louis. . . . This is the social background of the play.

(Music.)

The play is memory. Being a memory play, it is dimly lighted, it is sentimental, it is not realistic. In memory everything seems to happen to music. That explains the fiddle in the wings. I am the narrator of the play, and also a character in it. The other characters are my mother, Amanda, my sister, Laura, and a gentleman caller who appears in the final scenes. He is the most realistic character in the play, being an emissary from a world of reality that we were somehow set apart from. But since I have a poet's weakness for symbols, I am using this character also as a symbol; he is the long delayed but always expected something that we live for. There is a fifth character in the play who doesn't appear except in this larger-than-life photograph over the mantel. This is our father who left us a long time ago. He was a telephone man who fell in love with long distances; he gave up his job with the telephone company and skipped the light fantastic out of town . . . The last we heard of him was a picture post-card from Mazatlan, on the Pacific coast of Mexico, containing a message of two words—"Hello—Good-bye!" and an address. I think the rest of the play will explain itself. . . .

---

[1] The Spanish Civil War (1936–1939).
[2] A Basque town in northern Spain, bombed and virtually destroyed on April 27, 1937 by German planes aiding fascist General Francisco Franco's Nationalists. The destruction is depicted in one of Pablo Picasso's most famous paintings, *Guernica* (1937).

Amanda's voice becomes audible through the portieres.

(Legend On Screen: "Où Sont Les Neiges.")[3]

He divides the portieres and enters the upstage area.

    Amanda and Laura are seated at a drop-leaf table. Eating is indicated by gestures without food or utensils. Amanda faces the audience. Tom and Laura are seated in profile.

    The interior has lit up softly and through the scrim we see Amanda and Laura seated at the table in the upstage area.

AMANDA: *(calling)* Tom?
TOM: Yes, Mother.
AMANDA: We can't say grace until you come to the table!
5 TOM: Coming, Mother. *(He bows slightly and withdraws, reappearing a few moments later in his place at the table.)*
AMANDA: *(to her son)* Honey, don't *push* with your *fingers.* If you have to push with something, the thing to push with is a crust of bread. And chew—chew! Animals have sections in their stomachs which enable them to digest food without mastication, but human beings are supposed to chew their food before they swallow it down. Eat food leisurely, son, and really enjoy it. A well-cooked meal has lots of delicate flavors that have to be held in the mouth for appreciation. So chew your food and give your salivary glands a chance to function!

Tom deliberately lays his imaginary fork down and pushes his chair back from the table.

TOM: I haven't enjoyed one bite of this dinner because of your constant directions on how to eat it. It's you that makes me rush through meals with your hawk-like attention to every bite I take. Sickening—spoils my appetite—all this discussion of animals' secretion—salivary glands—mastication!
AMANDA: *(lightly)* Temperament like a Metropolitan star! *(He rises and crosses downstage.)* You're not excused from the table.
TOM: I am getting a cigarette.
10 AMANDA: You smoke too much.

Laura rises.

LAURA: I'll bring in the blanc mange.

He remains standing with his cigarette by the portieres during the following.

AMANDA: *(rising)* No, sister, no, sister—you be the lady this time and I'll be the darky.

---

[3] "Where are the snows [of yesteryear]." A famous line by French poet François Villon (1431–1463?).

LAURA: I'm already up.
AMANDA: Resume your seat, little sister—I want you to stay fresh and pretty—for gentlemen callers!
15 LAURA: I'm not expecting any gentlemen callers.
AMANDA: *(crossing out to kitchenette. Airily)* Sometimes they come when they are least expected! Why, I remember one Sunday afternoon in Blue Mountain—*(Enters kitchenette.)*
TOM: I know what's coming!
LAURA: Yes. But let her tell it.
TOM: Again?
20 LAURA: She loves to tell it.

Amanda returns with bowl of dessert.

AMANDA: One Sunday afternoon in Blue Mountain—your mother received—*seventeen!*—gentlemen callers! Why, sometimes there weren't chairs enough to accommodate them all. We had to send the nigger over to bring in folding chairs from the parish house.
TOM: *(remaining at portieres)* How did you entertain those gentlemen callers?
AMANDA: I understood the art of conversation!
TOM: I bet you could talk.
25 AMANDA: Girls in those days *knew* how to talk, I can tell you.
TOM: Yes?

(Image: Amanda As A Girl On A Porch Greeting Callers.)

AMANDA: They knew how to entertain their gentlemen callers. It wasn't enough for a girl to be possessed of a pretty face and a graceful figure—although I wasn't slighted in either respect. She also needed to have a nimble wit and a tongue to meet all occasions.
TOM: What did you talk about?
AMANDA: Things of importance going on in the world! Never anything coarse or common or vulgar. *(She addresses Tom as though he were seated in the vacant chair at the table though he remains by portieres. He plays this scene as though he held the book.)* My callers were gentlemen—all! Among my callers were some of the most prominent young planters of the Mississippi Delta—planters and sons of planters!

Tom motions for music and a spot of light on Amanda. Her eyes lift, her face glows, her voice becomes rich and elegiac.

(Screen Legend: "Où Sont Les Neiges.")

There was young Champ Laughlin who later became vice-president of the Delta Planters Bank. Hadley Stevenson who was drowned in Moon Lake and left his widow one hundred and fifty thousand in Government bonds. There were the Cutrere brothers, Wesley and

Bates. Bates was one of my bright particular beaux! He got in a quarrel with that wild Wainright boy. They shot it out on the floor of Moon Lake Casino. Bates was shot through the stomach. Died in the ambulance on his way to Memphis. His widow was also well-provided for, came into eight or ten thousand acres, that's all. She married him on the rebound—never loved her—carried my picture on him the night he died! And there was that boy that every girl in the Delta had set her cap for! That beautiful, brilliant young Fitzhugh boy from Green County!

30 TOM: What did he leave his widow?

AMANDA: He never married! Gracious, you talk as though all of my old admirers had turned up their toes to the daisies!

TOM: Isn't this the first you mentioned that still survives?

AMANDA: That Fitzhugh boy went North and made a fortune—came to be known as the Wolf of Wall Street! He had the Midas touch, whatever he touched turned to gold! And I could have been Mrs. Duncan J. Fitzhugh, mind you! But—I picked your *father!*

LAURA: *(rising)* Mother, let me clear the table.

35 AMANDA: No dear, you go in front and study your typewriter chart. Or practice your shorthand a little. Stay fresh and pretty!—It's almost time for our gentlemen callers to start arriving. *(She flounces girlishly toward the kitchenette.)* How many do you suppose we're going to entertain this afternoon?

Tom throws down the paper and jumps up with a groan.

LAURA: *(alone in the dining room)* I don't believe we're going to receive any, Mother.

AMANDA: *(reappearing, airily)* What? No one—not one? You must be joking! *(Laura nervously echoes her laugh. She slips in a fugitive manner through the half-open portieres and draws them gently behind her. A shaft of very clear light is thrown on her face against the faded tapestry of the curtains.)* (Music: "The Glass Menagerie" under faintly.) *(Lightly.)* Not one gentleman caller? It can't be true! There must be a flood, there must have been a tornado!

LAURA: It isn't a flood, it's not a tornado, Mother. I'm just not popular like you were in Blue Mountain. . . . *(Tom utters another groan. Laura glances at him with a faint, apologetic smile. Her voice catching a little.)* Mother's afraid I'm going to be an old maid.

(The Scene Dims Out With "Glass Menagerie" Music.)

SCENE 2

"Laura, Haven't You Ever Liked Some Boy?"
On the dark stage the screen is lighted with the image of blue roses. Gradually Laura's figure becomes apparent and the screen goes out. The music subsides.

Laura is seated in the delicate ivory chair at the small clawfoot table.
She wears a dress of soft violet material for a kimono—her hair tied back from her forehead with a ribbon.
She is washing and polishing her collection of glass.
Amanda appears on the fire-escape steps. At the sound of her ascent, Laura catches her breath, thrusts the bowl of ornaments away and seats herself stiffly before the diagram of the typewriter keyboard as though it held her spellbound. Something has happened to Amanda. It is written in her face as she climbs to the landing: a look that is grim and hopeless and a little absurd.

She has on one of those cheap or imitation velvety-looking cloth coats with imitation fur collar. Her hat is five or six years old, one of those dreadful cloche hats that were worn in the late twenties, and she is clasping an enormous black patent-leather pocketbook with nickel clasp and initials. This is her fulldress outfit, the one she usually wears to the D.A.R.[4]

Before entering she looks through the door.
She purses her lips, opens her eyes wide, rolls them upward and shakes her head.
Then she slowly lets herself in the door. Seeing her mother's expression Laura touches her lips with a nervous gesture.

LAURA: Hello, Mother, I was—*(She makes a nervous gesture toward the chart on the wall. Amanda leans against the shut door and stares at Laura with a martyred look.)*

AMANDA: Deception? Deception? *(She slowly removes her hat and gloves, continuing the swift suffering stare. She lets the hat and gloves fall on the floor—a bit of acting.)*

LAURA: *(shakily)* How was the D.A.R. meeting? *(Amanda slowly opens her purse and removes a dainty white handkerchief which she shakes out delicately and delicately touches to her lips and nostrils.)* Didn't you go to the D.A.R. meeting, Mother?

AMANDA: *(faintly, almost inaudibly)*—No.—No. *(Then more forcibly.)* I did not have the strength—to go the D.A.R. In fact, I did not have the courage! I wanted to find a hole in the ground and hide myself in it forever! *(She crosses slowly to the wall and removes the diagram of the typewriter keyboard. She holds it in front of her for a second, staring at it sweetly and sorrowfully—then bites her lips and tears it in two pieces.)*

5 LAURA: *(faintly)* Why did you do that, Mother? *(Amanda repeats the same procedure with the chart of the Gregg Alphabet.)* Why are you—

AMANDA: Why? Why? How old are you, Laura?

LAURA: Mother, you know my age.

---

[4] The Daughters of the American Revolution, an organization for female descendants of participants in the American Revolution, founded in 1890. That Amanda is a member says much about her concern with the past, as well as about her pride and affectations.

AMANDA: I thought that you were an adult; it seems that I was mistaken. *(She crosses slowly to the sofa and sinks down and stares at Laura.)*

LAURA: Please don't stare at me, Mother.

Amanda closes her eyes and lowers her head. Count ten.

10 AMANDA: What are we going to do, what is going to become of us, what is the future?

Count ten.

LAURA: Has something happened, Mother? *(Amanda draws a long breath and takes out the handkerchief again. Dabbing process.)* Mother, has—something happened?

AMANDA: I'll be all right in a minute. I'm just bewildered—*(count five)*—by life. . . .

LAURA: Mother, I wish that you would tell me what's happened.

AMANDA: As you know, I was supposed to be inducted into my office at the D.A.R. this afternoon. *(Image: A Swarm Of Typewriters.)* But I stopped off at Rubicam's Business College to speak to your teachers about your having a cold and ask them what progress they thought you were making down there.

15 LAURA: Oh. . . .

AMANDA: I went to the typing instructor and introduced myself as your mother. She didn't know who you were. Wingfield, she said. We don't have any such student enrolled at the school! I assured her she did, that you had been going to classes since early in January. "I wonder," she said, "if you could be talking about that terribly shy little girl who dropped out of school after only a few days' attendance?" "No," I said, "Laura, my daughter, has been going to school every day for the past six weeks!" "Excuse me," she said. She took the attendance book out and there was your name, unmistakably printed, and all the dates you were absent until they decided that you had dropped out of school. I still said, "No, there must have been some mistake! There must have been some mix-up in the records!" And she said, "No—I remember her perfectly now. Her hand shook so that she couldn't hit the right keys! The first time we gave a speed-test, she broke down completely—was sick at the stomach and almost had to be carried into the washroom! After that morning she never showed up any more. We phoned the house but never got any answer"—while I was working at Famous and Barr, I suppose, demonstrating those—Oh! I felt so weak I could barely keep on my feet. I had to sit down while they got me a glass of water! Fifty dollars' tuition, all of our plans—my hopes and ambitions for you—just gone up the spout, just gone up the spout like that. *(Laura draws a long breath and gets awkwardly to her feet. She crosses to the Victrola and winds it up.)* What are you doing?

LAURA: Oh! *(She releases the handle and returns to her seat.)*
AMANDA: Laura, where have you been going when you've gone out pretending that you were going to business college?
LAURA: I've just been going out walking.
20 AMANDA: That's not true.
LAURA: It is. I just went walking.
AMANDA: Walking? Walking? In winter? Deliberately courting pneumonia in that light coat? Where did you walk to, Laura?
LAURA: It was the lesser of two evils, Mother. *(Image: Winter Scene In Park.)* I couldn't go back up. I—threw up—on the floor!
AMANDA: From half past seven till after five every day you mean to tell me you walked around in the park, because you wanted to make me think that you were still going to Rubicam's Business College?
25 LAURA: It wasn't as bad as it sounds. I went inside places to get warmed up.
AMANDA: Inside where?
LAURA: I went in the art museum and the bird-houses at the Zoo. I visited the penguins every day! Sometimes I did without lunch and went to the movies. Lately I've been spending most of my afternoons in the Jewel-box, that big glass house where they raise the tropical flowers.
AMANDA: You did all this to deceive me, just for the deception? *(Laura looks down.)* Why?
LAURA: Mother, when you're disappointed, you get that awful suffering look on your face, like the picture of Jesus' mother in the museum!
30 AMANDA: Hush!
LAURA: I couldn't face it.

Pause. A whisper of strings.

(Legend: "The Crust Of Humility.")

AMANDA: *(hopelessly fingering the huge pocketbook)* So what are we going to do the rest of our lives? Stay home and watch the parades go by? Amuse ourselves with the glass menagerie, darling? Eternally play those worn-out phonograph records your father left as a painful reminder of him? We won't have a business career—we've given that up because it gave us nervous indigestion! *(Laughs wearily.)* What is there left but dependency all our lives? I know so well what becomes of unmarried women who aren't prepared to occupy a position. I've seen such pitiful cases in the South—barely tolerated spinsters living upon the grudging patronage of sister's husband or brother's wife!—stuck away in some little mouse-trap of a room—encouraged by one in-law to visit another—little birdlike women without any nest—eating the crust of humility all their life! Is that the future that we've mapped out for ourselves? I swear it's the only alternative I can think of! It isn't a very

pleasant alternative, is it? Of course—some girls *do marry*. *(Laura twists her hands nervously.)* Haven't you ever liked some boy?
LAURA: Yes I liked one once. *(Rises.)* I came across his picture a while ago.
AMANDA: *(with some interest)* He gave you his picture?
35 LAURA: No, it's in the year-book.
AMANDA: *(disappointed)* Oh—a high-school boy.

(Screen Image: Jim As A High-School Hero Bearing A Silver Cup.)

LAURA: Yes. His name was Jim. *(Laura lifts the heavy annual from the clawfoot table.)* Here he is in *The Pirates of Penzance*.[5]
AMANDA: *(absently)* The what?
LAURA: The operetta the senior class put on. He had a wonderful voice and we sat across the aisle from each other Mondays, Wednesdays and Fridays in the Aud. Here he is with the silver cup for debating! See his grin?
40 AMANDA: *(absently)* He must have had a jolly disposition.
LAURA: He used to call me—Blue Roses.

(Image: Blue Roses.)

AMANDA: Why did he call you such a name as that?
LAURA: When I had that attack of pleurosis—he asked me what was the matter when I came back. I said pleurosis—he thought that I said Blue Roses! So that's what he always called me after that. Whenever he saw me, he'd holler, "Hello, Blue Roses!" I didn't care for the girl that he went out with. Emily Meisenbach. Emily was the best-dressed girl at Soldan. She never struck me, though, as being sincere . . . It says in the Personal Section—they're engaged. That's—six years ago! They must be married by now.
AMANDA: Girls that aren't cut out for business careers usually wind up married to some nice man. *(Gets up with a spark of revival.)* Sister, that's what you'll do!

Laura utters a startled, doubtful laugh. She reaches quickly for a piece of glass.

45 LAURA: But, Mother—
AMANDA: Yes? *(Crossing to photograph.)*
LAURA: *(in a tone of frightened apology)* I'm—crippled!

(Image: Screen.)

AMANDA: Nonsense! Laura, I've told you never, never to use that word. Why, you're not crippled, you just have a little defect—hardly noticeable, even! When people have some slight disadvantage like that, they cultivate other things to make up for it—develop

---

[5] A musical by Gilbert and Sullivan.

charm—and vivacity—and—*charm!* That's all you have to do! *(She turns again to the photograph.)* One thing your father had *plenty* of—was *charm!*

Tom motions to the fiddle in the wings.

(The Scene Fades Out With Music.)

Scene 3

(Legend On The Screen: "After The Fiasco—")

Tom speaks from the fire-escape landing.

Tom: After the fiasco at Rubicam's Business College, the idea of getting a gentleman caller for Laura began to play a more important part in Mother's calculations. It became an obsession. Like some archetype of the universal unconscious, the image of the gentleman caller haunted our small apartment. . . . *(Image: Young Man At Door With Flowers.)* An evening at home rarely passed without some allusion to this image, this spectre, this hope. . . . Even when he wasn't mentioned, his presence hung in Mother's preoccupied look and in my sister's frightened, apologetic manner—hung like a sentence passed upon the Wingfields! Mother was a woman of action as well as words. She began to take logical steps in the planned direction. Late that winter and in the early spring—realizing that extra money would be needed to properly feather the nest and plume the bird—she conducted a vigorous campaign on the telephone, roping in subscribers to one of those magazines for matrons called *The Homemaker's Companion,* the type of journal that features the serialized sublimations of ladies of letters who think in terms of delicate cup-like breasts, slim, tapering waists, rich, creamy thighs, eyes like wood-smoke in autumn, fingers that soothe and caress like strains of music, bodies as powerful as Etruscan sculpture.

(Screen Image: A Glamour Magazine Cover.)

Amanda enters with phone on long extension cord. She is spotted in the dim stage.

Amanda: Ida Scott? This is Amanda Wingfield! We *missed* you at the D.A.R. last Monday! I said to myself: She's probably suffering with that sinus condition! How is that sinus condition? Horrors! Heaven have mercy!—You're a Christian martyr, yes, that's what you are, a Christian martyr! Well, I just now happened to notice that your subscription to the *Companion*'s about to expire! Yes, it expires with the next issue, honey!—just when that wonderful new serial by Bessie Mae Hopper is getting off to such an exciting start. Oh, honey, it's something that you can't miss! You remember how *Gone With the Wind* took everybody by storm? You simply couldn't go out if you hadn't read it. All everybody *talked* was Scarlett O'Hara. Well, this is a book that critics already compare to *Gone With the Wind*. It's the *Gone With the Wind* of the post-World War generation!—What?—Burning?—Oh, honey, don't let them burn, go take a look in the oven and I'll hold the wire! Heavens—I think she's hung up!

(Dim Out.)

(Legend On Screen: "You Think I'm In Love With Continental Shoemakers?")

Before the stage is lighted, the violent voices of Tom and Amanda are heard. They are quarreling behind the portieres. In front of them stands Laura with clenched hands and panicky expression.
A clear pool of light on her figure throughout this scene.

TOM: What in Christ's name am I—
AMANDA: *(shrilly)* Don't you use that—
5 TOM: Supposed to do!
AMANDA: Expression! Not in my—
TOM: Ohhh!
AMANDA: Presence! Have you gone out of your senses?
TOM: I have, that's true, *driven* out!
10 AMANDA: What is the matter with you, you—big—big—IDIOT!
TOM: Look—I've got *no* thing, no single thing—
AMANDA: Lower your voice!
TOM: In my life here that I can call my OWN! Everything is—
AMANDA: Stop that shouting!
15 TOM: Yesterday you confiscated my books! You had the nerve to—
AMANDA: I took that horrible novel back to the library—yes! That hideous book by that insane Mr. Lawrence. *(Tom laughs wildly.)* I cannot control the output of diseased minds or people who cater to them—*(Tom laughs still more wildly.)* BUT I WON'T ALLOW SUCH FILTH BROUGHT INTO MY HOUSE! No, no, no, no, no!
TOM: House, house! Who pays rent on it, who makes a slave of himself to—
AMANDA: *(fairly screeching)* Don't you DARE to—
TOM: No, no, I mustn't say things! *I've* got to just—
20 AMANDA: Let me tell you—
TOM: I don't want to hear any more! *(He tears the portieres open. The upstage area is lit with a turgid smoky red glow.)*

Amanda's hair is in metal curlers and she wears a very old bathrobe, much too large for her slight figure, a relic of the faithless Mr. Wingfield.
An upright typewriter and a wild disarray of manuscripts are on the dropleaf table. The quarrel was probably precipitated by Amanda's interruption of his creative labor. A chair lying overthrown on the floor.
Their gesticulating shadows are cast on the ceiling by the fiery glow.

AMANDA: You *will* hear more, you—

TOM: No, I won't hear more, I'm going out!
AMANDA: You come right back in—
25 TOM: Out, out out! Because I'm—
AMANDA: Come back here, Tom Wingfield! I'm not through talking to you!
TOM: Oh, go—
LAURA: *(desperately)* Tom!
AMANDA: You're going to listen, and no more insolence from you! I'm at the end of my patience! *(He comes back toward her.)*
30 TOM: What do you think I'm at? Aren't I supposed to have any patience to reach the end of, Mother? I know, I know. It seems unimportant to you, what I'm *doing*—what I *want* to do—having a little *difference* between them! You don't think that—
AMANDA: I think you've been doing things that you're ashamed of. That's why you act like this. I don't believe that you go every night to the movies. Nobody goes to the movies night after night. Nobody in their right mind goes to the movies as often as you pretend to. People don't go to the movies at nearly midnight, and movies don't let out at two A.M. Come in stumbling. Muttering to yourself like a maniac! You get three hours' sleep and then go to work. Oh, I can picture the way you're doing down there. Moping, doping, because you're in no condition.
TOM: *(wildly)* No, I'm in no condition!
AMANDA: What right have you got to jeopardize your job? Jeopardize the security of us all? How do you think we'd manage if you were—
TOM: Listen! You think I'm crazy *about* the *warehouse? (He bends fiercely toward her slight figure.)* You think I'm in love with the Continental Shoemakers? You think I want to spend fifty-five *years* down there in that—*celotex interior!* with—*fluorescent—tubes!* Look! I'd rather somebody picked up a crowbar and battered out my brains—than go back mornings! I *go!* Every time you come in yelling that God damn *"Rise and Shine!" "Rise and Shine!"* I say to myself *"How lucky dead* people are!" But I get up. I *go!* For sixty-five dollars a month I give up all that I dream of doing and being *ever!* And you say self—*self's* all I ever think of. Why, listen, if self is what I thought of, Mother, I'd be where he is—GONE! *(Pointing to father's picture.)* As far as the system of transportation reaches! *(He starts past her. She grabs his arm.)* Don't grab at me, Mother!
35 AMANDA: Where are you going?
TOM: I'm going to the *movies!*
AMANDA: I don't believe that lie!
TOM: *(crouching toward her, overtowering her tiny figure. She backs away, gasping)* I'm going to opium dens! Yes, opium dens, dens of vice and criminals' hang-outs, Mother. I've joined the Hogan gang, I'm a hired assassin, I carry a tommy-gun in a violin case! I run a string of cat-houses in the Valley! They call me Killer, Killer Wingfield, I'm leading a double-life, a simple, honest warehouse

worker by day, by night a dynamic *czar of the underworld,* Mother. I go to gambling casinos, I spin away fortunes on the roulette table! I wear a patch over one eye and a false mustache, sometimes I put on green whiskers. On those occasions they call me—*El Diablo!* Oh, I could tell you things to make you sleepless! My enemies plan to dynamite this place. They're going to blow us all sky-high some night! I'll be glad, very happy, and so will you! You'll go up, up on a broomstick, over Blue Mountain with seventeen gentlemen callers! You ugly—babbling old—*witch*. . . . *(He goes through a series of violent, clumsy movements, seizing his overcoat, lunging to the door, pulling it fiercely open. The women watch him, aghast. His arm catches in the sleeve of the coat as he struggles to pull it on. For a moment he is pinioned by the bulky garment. With an outraged groan he tears the coat off again, splitting the shoulders of it, and hurls it across the room. It strikes against the shelf of Laura's glass collection, there is a tinkle of shattering glass. Laura cries out as if wounded.)*

(Music Legend: "The Glass Menagerie.")

LAURA: *My glass!*—menagerie. . . . *(She covers her face and turns away.)*

But Amanda is still stunned and stupefied by the "ugly witch" so that she barely notices this occurrence. Now she recovers her speech.

40 AMANDA: *(in an awful voice)* I won't speak to you—until you apologize! *(She crosses through portieres and draws them together behind her. Tom is left with Laura. Laura clings weakly to the mantel with her face averted. Tom stares at her stupidly for a moment. Then he crosses to shelf. Drops awkwardly to his knees to collect the fallen glass, glancing at Laura as if he would speak but couldn't.)*

"The Glass Menagerie" steals in as

(The Scene Dims Out.)

SCENE 4

The interior is dark. Faint in the alley.

A deep-voiced bell in a church is tolling the hour of five as the scene commences.

Tom appears at the top of the alley. After each solemn boom of the bell in the tower, he shakes a little noise-maker or rattle as if to express the tiny spasm of man in contrast to the sustained power and dignity of the Almighty. This and the unsteadiness of his advance make it evident that he has been drinking.

As he climbs the few steps to the fire-escape landing light steals up inside. Laura appears in night-dress, observing Tom's empty bed in the front room.

Tom fishes in his pockets for the door-key, removing a motley assortment of articles in the search, including a perfect shower of movie-ticket stubs and an empty bottle. At last he finds the key, but just as he is about to insert it, it slips from his fingers. He strikes a match and crouches below the door.

TOM: *(bitterly)* One crack—and it falls through!

Laura opens the door.

LAURA: Tom! Tom, what are you doing?
TOM: Looking for a door-key.
LAURA: Where have you been all this time?
5 TOM: I have been to the movies.
LAURA: All this time at the movies?
TOM: There was a very long program. There was a Garbo picture and a Mickey Mouse and a travelogue and a newsreel and a preview of coming attractions. And there was an organ solo and a collection for the milk-fund—simultaneously—which ended up in a terrible fight between a fat lady and an usher!
LAURA: *(innocently)* Did you have to stay through everything?
TOM: Of course! And, oh, I forgot! There was a big stage show! The headliner on this stage show was Malvolio the Magician. He performed wonderful tricks, many of them, such as pouring water back and forth between pitchers. First it turned to wine and then it turned to beer and then it turned to whiskey. I know it was whiskey it finally turned into because he needed somebody to come up out of the audience to help him, and I came up—both shows! It was Kentucky Straight Bourbon. A very generous fellow, he gave souvenirs. *(He pulls from his back pocket a shimmering rainbow-colored scarf.)* He gave me this. This is his magic scarf. You can have it, Laura. You wave it over a canary cage and you get a bowl of gold-fish. You wave it over the gold-fish bowl and they fly away canaries. . . . But the wonderfullest trick of all was the coffin trick. We nailed him into a coffin and he got out of the coffin without removing one nail. *(He has come inside.)* There is a trick that would come in handy for me—get me out of this 2 by 4 situation! *(Flops onto bed and starts removing shoes.)*
10 LAURA: Tom—Shhh!
TOM: What you shushing me for?
LAURA: You'll wake up Mother.
TOM: Goody, goody! Pay 'er back for all those "Rise an' Shines." *(Lies down, groaning.)* You know it don't take much intelligence to get yourself into a nailed-up coffin, Laura. But who in hell ever got himself out of one without removing one nail?

As if in answer, the father's grinning photograph lights up.

(Scene Dims Out.)

Immediately following: The church bell is heard striking six. At the sixth stroke the alarm clock goes off in Amanda's room, and after a few moments we hear her calling: "Rise and Shine! Rise and Shine! Laura, go tell your brother to rise and shine!"

TOM: *(sitting up slowly)* I'll rise—but I won't shine.

The light increases.

15 AMANDA: Laura, tell your brother his coffee is ready.

Laura slips into front room.

LAURA: Tom! it's nearly seven. Don't make Mother nervous. *(He stares at her stupidly. Beseechingly.)* Tom, speak to Mother this morning. Make up with her, apologize, speak to her!
TOM: She won't to me. It's her that started not speaking.
LAURA: If you just say you're sorry she'll start speaking.
TOM: Her not speaking—is that such a tragedy?
20 LAURA: Please—please!
AMANDA: *(calling from kitchenette)* Laura, are you going to do what I asked you to do, or do I have to get dressed and go out myself?
LAURA: Going, going—soon as I get on my coat! *(She pulls on a shapeless felt hat with nervous, jerky movement, pleadingly glancing at Tom. Rushes awkwardly for coat. The coat is one of Amanda's inaccurately made-over, the sleeves too short for Laura.)* Butter and what else?
AMANDA: *(entering upstage)* Just butter. Tell them to charge it.
LAURA: Mother, they make such faces when I do that.
25 AMANDA: Sticks and stones may break my bones, but the expression on Mr. Garfinkel's face won't harm us! Tell your brother his coffee is getting cold.
LAURA: *(at door)* Do what I asked you, will you, will you, Tom?

He looks sullenly away.

AMANDA: Laura, go now or just don't go at all!
LAURA: *(rushing out)* Going—going! *(A second later she cries out. Tom springs up and crosses to the door. Amanda rushes anxiously in. Tom opens the door.)*
TOM: Laura?
30 LAURA: I'm all right. I slipped, but I'm all right.
AMANDA: *(peering anxiously after her)* If anyone breaks a leg on those fire-escape steps, the landlord ought to be sued for every cent he possesses! *(She shuts door. Remembers she isn't speaking and returns to other room.)*

As Tom enters listlessly for his coffee, she turns her back to him and stands rigidly facing the window on the gloomy gray vault of the areaway. Its light on her face with its aged but childish features is cruelly sharp, satirical as a Daumier print.

(Music Under: "Ave Maria.")

Tom glances sheepishly but sullenly at her averted figure and slumps at the table. The coffee is scalding hot; he sips it and gasps and spits it back in the cup. At his gasp, Amanda catches her breath and half turns. Then catches herself and turns back to window.

Tom blows on his coffee, glancing sidewise at his mother. She clears her throat. Tom clears his. He starts to rise. Sinks back down again, scratches his head, clears his throat again. Amanda coughs. Tom raises his cup in both hands to blow on it, his eyes staring over the rim of it at his mother for several moments. Then he slowly sets the cup down and awkwardly and hesitantly rises from the chair.

TOM: *(hoarsely)* Mother. I—I apologize. Mother. *(Amanda draws a quick, shuddering breath. Her face works grotesquely. She breaks into childlike tears.)* I'm sorry for what I said, for everything that I said, I didn't mean it.
AMANDA: *(sobbingly)* My devotion has made me a witch and so I make myself hateful to my children!
TOM: No, you *don't*.
35 AMANDA: I worry so much, don't sleep, it makes me nervous!
TOM: *(gently)* I understand that.
AMANDA: I've had to put up a solitary battle all these years. But you're my right-hand bower! Don't fall down, don't fail!
TOM: *(gently)* I try, Mother.
AMANDA: *(with great enthusiasm)* Try and you will SUCCEED! *(The notion makes her breathless.)* Why, you—you're just *full* of natural endowments! Both of my children—they're *unusual* children! Don't you think I know it? I'm so—*proud!* Happy and—feel I've—so much to be thankful for but—Promise me one thing, son!
40 TOM: What, Mother?
AMANDA: Promise, son, you'll—never be a drunkard!
TOM: *(turns to her grinning)* I will never be a drunkard, Mother.
AMANDA: That's what frightened me so, that you'd be drinking! Eat a bowl of Purina!
TOM: Just coffee, Mother.
45 AMANDA: Shredded wheat biscuit?
TOM: No. No, Mother, just coffee.
AMANDA: You can't put in a day's work on an empty stomach. You've got ten minutes—don't gulp! Drinking too-hot liquids makes cancer of the stomach. . . . Put cream in.
TOM: No, thank you.
AMANDA: To cool it.
50 TOM: No! No, thank you, I want it black.
AMANDA: I know, but it's not good for you. We have to do all that we can to build ourselves up. In these trying times we live in, all that we have to cling to is—each other. . . . That's why it's so important to—Tom, I—I sent out your sister so I could discuss something with you. If you hadn't spoken I would have spoken to you. *(Sits down.)*
TOM: *(gently)* What is it, Mother, that you want to discuss?
AMANDA: Laura!

Tom puts his cup down slowly.

(Legend On Screen: "Laura.")

(Music: "The Glass Menagerie.")

TOM: —Oh.—Laura . . .
AMANDA: *(touching his sleeve)* You know how Laura is. So quiet but—still water runs deep! She notices things and I think she—broods about them. *(Tom looks up.)* A few days ago I came in and she was crying.
TOM: What about?
AMANDA: You.
TOM: Me?
AMANDA: She has an idea that you're not happy here.
TOM: What gave her that idea?
AMANDA: What gives her any idea? However, you do act strangely. I—I'm not criticizing, understand *that!* I know your ambitions do not lie in the warehouse, that like everybody in the whole wide world—you've had to—make sacrifices, but—Tom—Tom—life's not easy, it calls for—Spartan endurance! There's so many things in my heart that I cannot describe to you! I've never told you but I—*loved* your father. . . .
TOM: *(gently)* I know that, Mother.
AMANDA: And you—when I see you taking after his ways! Staying out late—and—well, you *had* been drinking the night you were in that—terrifying condition! Laura says that you hate the apartment and that you go out nights to get away from it! Is that true, Tom?
TOM: No. You say there's so much in your heart that you can't describe to me. That's true of me, too. There's so much in my heart that I can't describe to *you!* So let's respect each other's—
AMANDA: But, why—*why*, Tom—are you always so *restless?* Where do you go to, nights?
TOM: I—go to the movies.
AMANDA: Why do you go to the movies so much, Tom?
TOM: I go to the movies because—I like adventure. Adventure is something I don't have much of at work, so I go to the movies.
AMANDA: But, Tom, you go to the movies *entirely* too *much!*
TOM: I like a lot of adventure.

Amanda looks baffled, then hurt. As the familiar inquisition resumes he becomes hard and impatient again. Amanda slips back into her querulous attitude toward him.

(Image On Screen: Sailing Vessel With Jolly Roger.)

AMANDA: Most young men find adventure in their careers.
TOM: Then most young men are not employed in a warehouse.
AMANDA: The world is full of young men employed in warehouses and offices and factories.
TOM: Do all of them find adventure in their careers?
AMANDA: They do or they do without it! Not everybody has a craze for adventure.
TOM: Man is by instinct a lover, a hunter, a fighter, and none of those instincts are given much play at the warehouse!

AMANDA: Man is by instinct! Don't quote instinct to me! Instinct is something that people have got away from! It belongs to animals! Christian adults don't want it!

TOM: What do Christian adults want, then, Mother?

AMANDA: Superior things! Things of the mind and the spirit! Only animals have to satisfy instincts! Surely your aims are somewhat higher than theirs! Than monkeys—pigs—

TOM: I reckon they're not.

AMANDA: You're joking. However, that isn't what I wanted to discuss.

TOM: *(rising)* I haven't much time.

AMANDA: *(pushing his shoulders)* Sit down.

TOM: You want me to punch in red at the warehouse, Mother?

AMANDA: You have five minutes. I want to talk about Laura.

(Legend: "Plans And Provisions.")

TOM: All right! What about Laura?

AMANDA: We have to be making plans and provisions for her. She's older than you, two years, and nothing has happened. She just drifts along doing nothing. It frightens me terribly how she just drifts along.

TOM: I guess she's the type that people call home-girls.

AMANDA: There's no such type, and if there is, it's a pity! That is unless the home is hers, with a husband!

TOM: What?

AMANDA: Oh, I can see the handwriting on the wall as plain as I see the nose in front of my face! It's terrifying! More and more you remind me of your father! He was out all hours without explanation—Then *left! Good-bye!* And me with the bag to hold. I saw that letter you got from the Merchant Marine. I know what you're dreaming of. I'm not standing here blindfolded. Very well, then. Then *do* it! But not till there's somebody to take your place.

TOM: What do you mean?

AMANDA: I mean that as soon as Laura has got somebody to take care of her, married, a home of her own, independent—why, then you'll be free to go wherever you please, on land, on sea, whichever way the wind blows! But until that time you've got to look out for your sister. I don't say me because I'm old and don't matter! I say for your sister because she's young and dependent. I put her in business college—a dismal failure! Frightened her so it made her sick to her stomach. I took her over to the Young People's League at the church. Another fiasco. She spoke to nobody, nobody spoke to her. Now all she does is fool with those pieces of glass and play those worn-out records. What kind of a life is that for a girl to lead!

TOM: What can I do about it?

AMANDA: Overcome selfishness! Self, self, self is all that you ever think of! *(Tom springs up and crosses to get his coat. It is ugly and bulky. He pulls on a cap with earmuffs.)* Where is your muffler? Put your wool muffler on! *(He snatches it angrily from the closet and tosses it around his neck and pulls both ends tight.)* Tom! I haven't said what I had in mind to ask you.

TOM: I'm too late to—

AMANDA: *(catching his arms—very importunately. Then shyly)* Down at the warehouse, aren't there some—nice young men?

TOM: No!

AMANDA: There *must* be—*some* . . .

100 TOM: Mother—

Gesture.

AMANDA: Find out one that's clean-living—doesn't drink and—ask him out for sister!

TOM: What?

AMANDA: For *sister!* To *meet!* Get *acquainted!*

TOM: *(stamping to door)* Oh, my *go-osh!*

105 AMANDA: Will you? *(He opens door. Imploringly.)* Will you? *(He starts down.)* Will you? *Will* you, dear?

TOM: *(calling back)* YES!

Amanda closes the door hesitantly and with a troubled but faintly hopeful expression.

(Screen Image: A Glamour Magazine Cover.)

Spot Amanda at phone.

AMANDA: Ella Cartwright? This is Amanda Wingfield! How are you, honey? How is that kidney condition? *(Count five.)* Horrors! *(Count five.)* You're a Christian martyr, yes, honey, that's what you are, a Christian martyr! Well, I just happened to notice in my little red book that your subscription to the *Companion* has just run out! I knew that you wouldn't want to miss out on the wonderful serial starting in this new issue. It's by Bessie Mae Hopper, the first thing she's written since *Honeymoon for Three*. Wasn't that a strange and interesting story? Well, this one is even lovelier, I believe. It has a sophisticated society background. It's all about the horsey set on Long Island!

(Fade Out.)

SCENE 5

(Legend On Screen: "Annunciation.") Fade with music.

It is early dusk of a spring evening. Supper has just been finished in the Wingfield apartment. Amanda and Laura in light colored dresses are removing dishes from the table, in the upstage area, which is shadowy, their movements formalized almost as a dance or ritual, their moving forms as pale and silent as moths.

Tom, in white shirt and trousers, rises from the table and crosses toward the fire-escape.

AMANDA: *(as he passes her)* Son, will you do me a favor?
TOM: What?
AMANDA: Comb your hair! You look so pretty when your hair is combed! *(Tom slouches on sofa with evening paper. Enormous caption "Franco Triumphs.")* There is only one respect in which I would like you to emulate your father.
TOM: What respect is that?
AMANDA: The care he always took of his appearance. He never allowed himself to look untidy. *(He throws down the paper and crosses to fire-escape.)* Where are you going?
TOM: I'm going out to smoke.
AMANDA: You smoke too much. A pack a day at fifteen cents a pack. How much would that amount to in a month? Thirty times fifteen is how much, Tom? Figure it out and you will be astounded at what you could save. Enough to give you a night-school course in accounting at Washington U! Just think what a wonderful thing that would be for you, son!

Tom is unmoved by the thought.

TOM: I'd rather smoke. *(He steps out on landing, letting the screen door slam.)*
AMANDA: *(sharply)* I know! That's the tragedy of it. . . . *(Alone, she turns to look at her husband's picture.)*

(Dance Music: "All The World Is Waiting For The Sunrise!")

TOM: *(to the audience)* Across the alley from us was the Paradise Dance Hall. On evenings in spring the windows and doors were open and the music came outdoors. Sometimes the lights were turned out except for a large glass sphere that hung from the ceiling. It would turn slowly about and filter the dusk with delicate rainbow colors. Then the orchestra played a waltz or a tango, something that had a slow and sensuous rhythm. Couples would come outside, to the relative privacy of the alley. You could see them kissing behind ash-pits and telephone poles. This was the compensation for lives that passed like mine, without any change or adventure. Adventure and change were imminent in this year. They were waiting around the corner for all these kids. Suspended in the mist over Berchtesgaden,[6] caught in the folds of Chamberlain's[7] umbrella—

---

[6] A resort in West Germany, in the Bavarian Alps, site of Hitler's fortified retreat, the Berghof.
[7] (Arthur) Neville Chamberlain (1869–1940)—Conservative party Prime Minister of England (1937–1940) who advocated a policy of appeasement toward Hitler.

In Spain there was Guernica! But here there was only hot swing music and liquor, dance halls, bars, and movies, and sex that hung in the gloom like a chandelier and flooded the world with brief, deceptive rainbows. . . . All the world was waiting for bombardments!

Amanda turns from the picture and comes outside.

AMANDA: *(sighing)* A fire-escape landing's a poor excuse for a porch. *(She spreads a newspaper on a step and sits down, gracefully and demurely as if she were settling into a swing on a Mississippi veranda.)* What are you looking at?
TOM: The moon.
AMANDA: Is there a moon this evening?
TOM: It's rising over Garfinkel's Delicatessen.
15 AMANDA: So it is! A little silver slipper of a moon. Have you made a wish on it yet?
TOM: Um-hum.
AMANDA: What did you wish for?
TOM: That's a secret.
AMANDA: A secret, huh? Well, I won't tell mine either. I will be just as mysterious as you.
20 TOM: I bet I can guess what yours is.
AMANDA: Is my head so transparent?
TOM: You're not a sphinx.
AMANDA: No, I don't have secrets. I'll tell you what I wished for on the moon. Success and happiness for my precious children! I wish for that whenever there's a moon, and when there isn't a moon, I wish for it, too.
TOM: I thought perhaps you wished for a gentleman caller.
25 AMANDA: Why do you say that?
TOM: Don't you remember asking me to fetch one?
AMANDA: I remember suggesting that it would be nice for your sister if you brought home some nice young man from the warehouse. I think I've made that suggestion more than once.
TOM: Yes, you have made it repeatedly.
AMANDA: Well?
30 TOM: We are going to have one.
AMANDA: What?
TOM: A gentleman caller!

(The Annunciation Is Celebrated With Music.)

Amanda rises.

(Image On Screen: Caller With Bouquet.)

AMANDA: You mean you have asked some nice young man to come over?
TOM: Yep. I've asked him to dinner.
35 AMANDA: You really did?

TOM: I did!
AMANDA: You did, and did he—*accept?*
TOM: He did!
AMANDA: Well, well—well, well! That's—lovely!
40 TOM: I thought that you would be pleased.
AMANDA: It's definite, then?
TOM: Very definite.
AMANDA: Soon?
TOM: Very soon.
45 AMANDA: For heaven's sake, stop putting on and tell me some things, will you?
TOM: What things do you want me to tell you?
AMANDA: Naturally I would like to know when he's *coming!*
TOM: He's coming tomorrow.
AMANDA: *Tomorrow?*
50 TOM: Yep. Tomorrow.
AMANDA: But, Tom!
TOM: Yes, Mother?
AMANDA: Tomorrow gives me no time!
TOM: Time for what?
55 AMANDA: Preparations! Why didn't you phone me at once, as soon as you asked him, the minute that he accepted? Then, don't you see, I could have been getting ready!
TOM: You don't have to make any fuss.
AMANDA: Oh, Tom, Tom, Tom, of course I have to make a fuss! I want things nice, not sloppy! Not thrown together. I'll certainly have to do some fast thinking, won't I?
TOM: I don't see why you have to think at all.
AMANDA: You just don't know. We can't have a gentleman caller in a pig-sty! All my wedding silver has to be polished, the monogrammed table linen ought to be laundered! The windows have to be washed and fresh curtains put up. And how about clothes? We have to *wear* something, don't we?
60 TOM: Mother, this boy is no one to make a fuss over!
AMANDA: Do you realize he's the first young man we've introduced to your sister? It's terrible, dreadful, disgraceful that poor little sister has never received a single gentleman caller! Tom, come inside! *(She opens the screen door.)*
TOM: What for?
AMANDA: I want to ask you some things.
TOM: If you're going to make such a fuss, I'll call it off, I'll tell him not to come.
65 AMANDA: You certainly won't do anything of the kind. Nothing offends people worse than broken engagements. It simply means I'll have to work like a Turk! We won't be brilliant, but we'll pass inspection. Come on inside. *(Tom follows, groaning.)* Sit down.
TOM: Any particular place you would like me to sit?

AMANDA: Thank heavens I've got that new sofa! I'm also making payments on a floor lamp I'll have sent out! And put the chintz covers on, they'll brighten things up! Of course I'd hoped to have these walls repapered. . . . What is the young man's name?
TOM: His name is O'Connor.
AMANDA: That, of course, means fish—tomorrow is Friday! I'll have that salmon loaf—with Durkee's dressing! What does he do? He works at the warehouse?
TOM: Of course! How else would I—
AMANDA: Tom, he—doesn't drink?
TOM: Why do you ask me that?
AMANDA: Your father *did!*
TOM: Don't get started on that!
AMANDA: He *does* drink, then?
TOM: Not that I know of!
AMANDA: Make sure, be certain! The last thing I want for my daughter's a boy who drinks!
TOM: Aren't you being a little premature? Mr. O'Connor has not yet appeared on the scene!
AMANDA: But will tomorrow. To meet your sister, and what do I know about his character? Nothing! Old maids are better off than wives of drunkards!
TOM: Oh, my God!
AMANDA: Be still!
TOM: *(leaning forward to whisper)* Lots of fellows meet girls whom they don't marry!
AMANDA: Oh, talk sensibly, Tom—and don't be sarcastic! *(She has gotten a hairbrush.)*
TOM: What are you doing?
AMANDA: I'm brushing that cow-lick down! What is this young man's position at the warehouse?
TOM: *(submitting grimly to the brush and the interrogation)* This young man's position is that of a shipping clerk, Mother.
AMANDA: Sounds to me like a fairly responsible job, the sort of a job *you* would be in if you just had more *get-up.* What is his salary? Have you got any idea?
TOM: I would judge it to be approximately eighty-five dollars a month.
AMANDA: Well—not princely, but—
TOM: Twenty more than I make.
AMANDA: Yes, how well I know! But for a family man, eighty-five dollars a month is not much more than you can just get by on. . . .
TOM: Yes, but Mr. O'Connor is not a family man.
AMANDA: He might be, mightn't he? Some time in the future?
TOM: I see. Plans and provisions.
AMANDA: You are the only young man that I know of who ignores the fact that the future becomes the present, the present the past, and the past turns into everlasting regret if you don't plan for it!

TOM: I will think that over and see what I can make of it.
AMANDA: Don't be supercilious with your mother! Tell me some more about this—what do you call him?
TOM: James D. O'Connor. The D. is for Delaney.
AMANDA: Irish on *both* sides! *Gracious!* And doesn't drink?
TOM: Shall I call him up and ask him right this minute?
AMANDA: The only way to find out about those things is to make discreet inquiries at the proper moment. When I was a girl in Blue Mountain and it was suspected that a young man drank, the girl whose attentions he had been receiving, if any girl *was*, would sometimes speak to the minister of his church, or rather her father would if her father was living, and sort of feel him out on the young man's character. That is the way such things are discreetly handled to keep a young woman from making a tragic mistake!
TOM: Then how did you happen to make a tragic mistake?
AMANDA: That innocent look of your father's had everyone fooled! He *smiled*—the world was *enchanted!* No girl can do worse than put herself at the mercy of a handsome appearance! I hope that Mr. O'Connor is not too good-looking.
TOM: No, he's not too good-looking. He's covered with freckles and hasn't too much of a nose.
AMANDA: He's not right-down homely, though?
TOM: Not right-down homely. Just medium homely, I'd say.
AMANDA: Character's what to look for in a man.
TOM: That's what I've always said, Mother.
AMANDA: You've never said anything of the kind and I suspect you would never give it a thought.
TOM: Don't be suspicious of me.
AMANDA: At least I hope he's the type that's up and coming.
TOM: I think he really goes in for self-improvement.
AMANDA: What reason have you to think so?
TOM: He goes to night school.
AMANDA: *(beaming)* Splendid! What does he do, I mean study?
TOM: Radio engineering and public speaking!
AMANDA: Then he has visions of being advanced in the world! Any young man who studies public speaking is aiming to have an executive job some day! And radio engineering? A thing for the future! Both of these facts are very illuminating. Those are the sort of things that a mother should know concerning any young man who comes to call on her daughter. Seriously or—not.
TOM: One little warning. He doesn't know about Laura. I didn't let on that we had dark ulterior motives. I just said, why don't you come have dinner with us? He said okay and that was the whole conversation.
AMANDA: I bet it was! You're eloquent as an oyster. However, he'll know about Laura when he gets here. When he sees how lovely and

sweet and pretty she is, he'll thank his lucky stars he was asked to dinner.
TOM: Mother, you mustn't expect too much of Laura.
AMANDA: What do you mean?
TOM: Laura seems all those things to you and me because she's ours and we love her. We don't even notice she's crippled any more.
AMANDA: Don't say crippled! You know that I never allow that word to be used!
TOM: But face facts, Mother. She is and—that's not all—
AMANDA: What do you mean "not all"?
TOM: Laura is very different from other girls.
AMANDA: I think the difference is all to her advantage.
TOM: Not quite all—in the eyes of others—strangers—she's terribly shy and lives in a world of her own and those things make her seem a little peculiar to people outside the house.
AMANDA: Don't say peculiar.
TOM: Face the facts. She is.

(*The Dance-Hall Music Changes To A Tango That Has A Minor And Somewhat Ominous Tone.*)

AMANDA: In what way is she peculiar—may I ask?
TOM: (*gently*) She lives in a world of her own—a world of—little glass ornaments, Mother. . . . (*Gets up. Amanda remains holding brush, looking at him, troubled.*) She plays old phonograph records and—that's about all—(*He glances at himself in the mirror and crosses to door.*)
AMANDA: (*sharply*) Where are you going?
TOM: I'm going to the movies. (*Out screen door.*)
AMANDA: Not to the movies, every night to the movies! (*Follows quickly to screen door.*) I don't believe you always go to the movies! (*He is gone. Amanda looks worriedly after him for a moment. Then vitality and optimism return and she turns from the door. Crossing to portieres.*) Laura! Laura! (*Laura answers from kitchenette.*)
LAURA: Yes, Mother.
AMANDA: Let those dishes go and come in front! (*Laura appears with dish towel. Gaily.*) Laura, come here and make a wish on the moon!
LAURA: (*entering*) Moon—moon?
AMANDA: A little silver slipper of a moon. Look over your left shoulder, Laura, and make a wish! (*Laura looks faintly puzzled as if called out of sleep. Amanda seizes her shoulders and turns her at an angle by the door.*) Now! Now, darling, *wish*!
LAURA: What shall I wish for, Mother?
AMANDA: (*her voice trembling and her eyes suddenly filling with tears*) Happiness! Good Fortune!

The violin rises and the stage dims out.

Scene 6

(Image: High-School Hero.)

TOM: And so the following evening I brought Jim home to dinner. I had known Jim slightly in high school. In high school Jim was a hero. He had tremendous Irish good nature and vitality with the scrubbed and polished look of white chinaware. He seemed to move in a continual spotlight. He was a star in basketball, captain of the debating club, president of the senior class and the glee club and he sang the male lead in the annual light operas. He was always running or bounding, never just walking. He seemed always at the point of defeating the law of gravity. He was shooting with such velocity through his adolescence that you would logically expect him to arrive at nothing short of the White House by the time he was thirty. But Jim apparently ran into more interference after his graduation from Soldan. His speed had definitely slowed. Six years after he left high school he was holding a job that wasn't much better than mine.

(Image: Clerk.)

He was the only one at the warehouse with whom I was on friendly terms. I was valuable to him as someone who could remember his former glory, who had seen him win basketball games and the silver cup in debating. He knew of my secret practice of retiring to a cabinet of the washroom to work on poems when business was slack in the warehouse. He called me Shakespeare. And while the other boys in the warehouse regarded me with suspicious hostility, Jim took a humorous attitude toward me. Gradually his attitude affected the others, their hostility wore off and they also began to smile at me as people smile at an oddly fashioned dog who trots across their path at some distance.

I knew that Jim and Laura had known each other at Soldan, and I had heard Laura speak admiringly of his voice. I didn't know if Jim remembered her or not. In high school Laura had been as unobtrusive as Jim had been astonishing. If he did remember Laura, it was not as my sister, for when I asked him to dinner, he grinned and said, "You know, Shakespeare, I never thought of you as having folks!" He was about to discover that I did. . . .

(Light Up Stage.)

(Legend On Screen: "The Accent Of A Coming Foot.")

Friday evening. It is about five o'clock of a late spring evening which comes "scattering poems in the sky."

A delicate lemony light is in the Wingfield apartment.

Amanda has worked like a Turk in preparation for the gentleman caller. The results are astonishing. The new floor lamp with its rose-silk shade is in place, a colored paper lantern conceals the broken light fixture in the ceiling,

new billowing white curtains are at the windows, chintz covers are on chairs and sofa, a pair of new sofa pillows make their initial appearance.
Open boxes and tissue paper are scattered on the floor.
Laura stands in the middle with lifted arms while Amanda crouches before her, adjusting the hem of the new dress, devout and ritualistic. The dress is colored and designed by memory. The arrangement of Laura's hair is changed; it is softer and more becoming. A fragile, unearthly prettiness has come out in Laura: she is like a piece of translucent glass touched by light, given a momentary radiance, not actual, not lasting.

AMANDA: *(impatiently)* Why are you trembling?
LAURA: Mother, you've made me so nervous!
AMANDA: How have I made you nervous?
5 LAURA: By all this fuss! You make it seem so important!
AMANDA: I don't understand you, Laura. You couldn't be satisfied with just sitting home, and yet whenever I try to arrange something for you, you seem to resist it. *(She gets up.)* Now take a look at yourself. No, wait! Wait just a moment—I have an idea!
LAURA: What is it now?

Amanda produces two powder puffs which she wraps in handkerchiefs and stuffs in Laura's bosom.

LAURA: Mother, what are you doing?
AMANDA: They call them "Gay Deceivers"!
10 LAURA: I won't wear them!
AMANDA: You will!
LAURA: Why should I?
AMANDA: Because, to be painfully honest, your chest is flat.
LAURA: You make it seem like we were setting a trap.
15 AMANDA: All pretty girls are a trap, a pretty trap, and men expect them to be. *(Legend: "A Pretty Trap.")* Now look at yourself, young lady. This is the prettiest you will ever be! I've got to fix myself now! You're going to be surprised by your mother's appearance! *(She crosses through portieres, humming gaily.)*

Laura moves slowly to the long mirror and stares solemnly at herself.
A wind blows the white curtains inward in a slow, graceful motion and with a faint, sorrowful sighing.

AMANDA: *(offstage)* It isn't dark enough yet. *(She turns slowly before the mirror with a troubled look.)*

(Legend On Screen: "This Is My Sister: Celebrate Her With Strings!" Music.)

AMANDA: *(laughing, off)* I'm going to show you something. I'm going to make a spectacular appearance!
LAURA: What is it, Mother?
AMANDA: Possess your soul in patience—you will see! Something I've resurrected from that old trunk! Styles haven't changed so terribly

much after all. . . . *(She parts the portieres.)* Now just look at your mother! *(She wears a girlish frock of yellowed voile with a blue silk sash. She carries a bunch of jonquils—the legend of her youth is nearly revived. Feverishly.)* This is the dress in which I led the cotillion. Won the cakewalk twice at Sunset Hill, wore one spring to the Governor's ball in Jackson! See how I sashayed around the ballroom, Laura? *(She raises her skirt and does a mincing step around the room.)* I wore it on Sundays for my gentlemen callers! I had it on the day I met your father—I had malaria fever all that spring. The change of climate from East Tennessee to the Delta—weakened resistance—I had a little temperature all the time—not enough to be serious—just enough to make me restless and giddy! Invitations poured in—parties all over the Delta!—"Stay in bed," said Mother, "you have fever!"—but I just wouldn't.—I took quinine but kept on going, going!—Evenings, dances!—Afternoons, long, long rides! Picnics—lovely!—So lovely, that country in May. All lacy with dogwood, literally flooded with jonquils!—That was the spring I had the craze for jonquils. Jonquils became an absolute obsession. Mother said, "Honey, there's no more room for jonquils." And still I kept bringing in more jonquils. Whenever, wherever I saw them, I'd say, "Stop! Stop! I see jonquils!" I made the young men help me gather the jonquils! It was a joke, Amanda and her jonquils! Finally there were no more vases to hold them, every available space was filled with jonquils. No vases to hold them? All right, I'll hold them myself! And then I—*(She stops in front of the picture.) (Music)* met your father! Malaria fever and jonquils and then—this—boy. . . . *(She switches on the rose-colored lamp.)* I hope they get here before it starts to rain. *(She crosses upstage and places the jonquils in bowl on table.)* I gave your brother a little extra change so he and Mr. O'Connor could take the service car home.

20 LAURA: *(with altered look)* What did you say his name was?
AMANDA: O'Connor.
LAURA: What is his first name?
AMANDA: I don't remember. Oh, yes, I do. It was—Jim!

Laura sways slightly and catches hold of a chair.

(Legend On Screen: "Not Jim!")

LAURA: *(faintly)* Not—Jim!
25 AMANDA: Yes, that was it, it was Jim! I've never known a Jim that wasn't nice!

(Music: Ominous.)

LAURA: Are you sure his name is Jim O'Connor?
AMANDA: Yes. Why?
LAURA: Is he the one that Tom used to know in high school?
AMANDA: He didn't say so. I think he just got to know him at the warehouse.

30   LAURA: There was a Jim O'Connor we both knew in high school—
(Then, with effort.) If that is the one that Tom is bringing to
dinner—you'll have to excuse me, I won't come to the table.
AMANDA: What sort of nonsense is this?
LAURA: You asked me once if I'd ever liked a boy. Don't you remember I
showed you this boy's picture?
AMANDA: You mean the boy you showed me in the year book?
LAURA: Yes, that boy.
35   AMANDA: Laura, Laura, were you in love with that boy?
LAURA: I don't know, Mother. All I know is I couldn't sit at the table if
it was him!
AMANDA: It won't be him! It isn't the least bit likely. But whether it is
or not, you will come to the table. You will not be excused.
LAURA: I'll have to be, Mother.
AMANDA: I don't intend to humor your silliness, Laura. I've had too
much from you and your brother, both! So just sit down and
compose yourself till they come. Tom has forgotten his key so
you'll have to let them in, when they arrive.
40   LAURA: *(panicky)* Oh, Mother—*you* answer the door!
AMANDA: *(lightly)* I'll be in the kitchen—busy!
LAURA: Oh, Mother, please answer the door, don't make me do it!
AMANDA: *(crossing into kitchenette)* I've got to fix the dressing for the
salmon. Fuss, fuss—silliness!—over a gentleman caller!

Door swings shut. Laura is left alone.

(Legend: "Terror!")

She utters a low moan and turns off the lamp—sits stiffly on the edge of the
sofa, knotting her fingers together.

(Legend On Screen: "The Opening Of A Door!")

Tom and Jim appear on the fire-escape steps and climb to landing. Hearing
their approach, Laura rises with a panicky gesture. She retreats to the portieres.
The doorbell. Laura catches her breath and touches her throat. Low drums.

AMANDA: *(calling)* Laura, sweetheart! The door!

Laura stares at it without moving.

45   JIM: I think we just beat the rain.
TOM: Uh-huh. *(He rings again, nervously. Jim whistles and fishes for a
cigarette.)*
AMANDA: *(very, very gaily)* Laura, that is your brother and Mr. O'Connor!
Will you let them in, darling?

Laura crosses toward kitchenette door.

LAURA: *(breathlessly)* Mother—you go to the door!

Amanda steps out of kitchenette and stares furiously at Laura. She points imperiously at the door.

LAURA: Please, please!
50 AMANDA: *(in a fierce whisper)* What is the matter with you, you silly thing?
LAURA: *(desperately)* Please, you answer it, *please!*
AMANDA: I told you I wasn't going to humor you, Laura. Why have you chosen this moment to lose your mind?
LAURA: Please, please, please, you go!
AMANDA: You'll have to go to the door because I can't!
55 LAURA: *(despairingly)* I can't either!
AMANDA: Why?
LAURA: I'm *sick!*
AMANDA: I'm sick, too—of your nonsense! Why can't you and your brother be normal people? Fantastic whims and behavior! *(Tom gives a long ring.)* Preposterous goings on! Can you give me one reason—*(Calls out lyrically.)* COMING! JUST ONE SECOND!—why should you be afraid to open a door? Now you answer it, Laura!
LAURA: Oh, oh, oh . . . *(She returns through the portieres. Darts to the Victrola and winds it frantically and turns it on.)*
60 AMANDA: Laura Wingfield, you march right to that door!
LAURA: Yes—yes, Mother!

A faraway, scratchy rendition of "Dardanella" softens the air and gives her strength to move through it. She slips to the door and draws it cautiously open. Tom enters with the caller, Jim O'Connor.

TOM: Laura, this is Jim. Jim, this is my sister, Laura.
JIM: *(stepping inside)* I didn't know that Shakespeare had a sister!
LAURA: *(retreating stiff and trembling from the door)* How—how do you do?
65 JIM: *(heartily extending his hand)* Okay!

Laura touches it hesitantly with hers.

JIM: Your hand's *cold,* Laura!
LAURA: Yes, well—I've been playing the Victrola. . . .
JIM: Must have been playing classical music on it! You ought to play a little hot swing music to warm you up!
LAURA: Excuse me—I haven't finished playing the Victrola. . . .

She turns awkwardly and hurries into the front room. She pauses a second by the Victrola. Then catches her breath and darts through the portieres like a frightened deer.

70 JIM: *(grinning)* What was the matter?
TOM: Oh—with Laura? Laura is—terribly shy.
JIM: Shy, huh? It's unusual to meet a shy girl nowadays. I don't believe you ever mentioned you had a sister.
TOM: Well, now you know. I have one. Here is the *Post Dispatch.* You want a piece of it?
JIM: Uh-huh.
75 TOM: What piece? The comics?

JIM: Sports! *(Glances at it.)* Ole Dizzy Dean is on his bad behavior.
TOM: *(disinterested)* Yeah? *(Lights cigarette and crosses back to fire-escape door.)*
JIM: Where are *you* going?
TOM: I'm going out on the terrace.
80 JIM: *(goes after him)* You know, Shakespeare—I'm going to sell you a bill of goods!
TOM: What goods?
JIM: A course I'm taking.
TOM: Huh?
JIM: In public speaking! You and me, we're not the warehouse type.
85 TOM: Thanks—that's good news. But what has public speaking got to do with it?
JIM: It fits you for—executive positions!
TOM: Awww.
JIM: I tell you it's done a helluva lot for me.

(Image: Executive At Desk.)

TOM: In what respect?
90 JIM: In every! Ask yourself what is the difference between you an' me and men in the office down front? Brains?—No!—Ability?—No! Then what? Just one little thing—
TOM: What is that one little thing?
JIM: Primarily it amounts to—social poise! Being able to square up to people and hold your own on any social level!
AMANDA: *(offstage)* Tom?
TOM: Yes, Mother?
95 AMANDA: Is that you and Mr. O'Connor?
TOM: Yes, Mother.
AMANDA: Well, you just make yourselves comfortable in there.
TOM: Yes, Mother.
AMANDA: Ask Mr. O'Connor if he would like to wash his hands.
100 JIM: Aw—no—thank you—I took care of that at the warehouse. Tom—
TOM: Yes?
JIM: Mr. Mendoza was speaking to me about you.
TOM: Favorably?
JIM: What do you think?
105 TOM: Well—
JIM: You're going to be out of a job if you don't wake up.
TOM: I am waking up—
JIM: You show no signs.
TOM: The signs are interior.

(Image On Screen: The Sailing Vessel With Jolly Roger Again.)

110 TOM: I'm planning to change. *(He leans over the rail speaking with quiet exhilaration. The incandescent marquees and signs of the first-run movie houses light his face from across the alley. He looks like a*

voyager.) I'm right at the point of committing myself to a future that doesn't include the warehouse and Mr. Mendoza or even a night-school course in public speaking.
JIM: What are you gassing about?
TOM: I'm tired of the movies.
JIM: Movies!
TOM: Yes, movies! Look at them—*(A wave toward the marvels of Grand Avenue.)* All of those glamorous people—having adventures—hogging it all, gobbling the whole thing up! You know what happens? People go to the *movies* instead of *moving!* Hollywood characters are supposed to have all the adventures for everybody in America, while everybody in America sits in a dark room and watches them have them! Yes, until there's a war. That's when adventure becomes available to the masses! *Everyone's* dish, not only Gable's! Then the people in the dark room come out of the dark room to have some adventures themselves—Goody, goody—It's our turn now, to go to the South Sea Island—to make a safari—to be exotic, far-off—But I'm not patient. I don't want to wait till then. I'm tired of the *movies* and I am *about* to *move!*

115 JIM: *(incredulously)* Move?
TOM: Yes.
JIM: When?
TOM: Soon!
JIM: Where? Where?

Theme three music seems to answer the question, while Tom thinks it over. He searches among his pockets.

120 TOM: I'm starting to boil inside. I know I seem dreary, but inside—well, I'm boiling! Whenever I pick up a shoe, I shudder a little thinking how short life is and what I am doing!—Whatever that means. I know it doesn't mean shoes—except as something to wear on a traveler's feet! *(Finds paper.)* Look—
JIM: What?
TOM: I'm a member.
JIM: *(reading)* The Union of Merchant Seamen.
TOM: I paid my dues this month, instead of the light bill.
125 JIM: You will regret it when they turn the lights off.
TOM: I won't be here.
JIM: How about your mother?
TOM: I'm like my father. The bastard son of a bastard! See how he grins? And he's been absent going on sixteen years!
JIM: You're just talking, you drip. How does your mother feel about it?
130 TOM: Shhh—Here comes Mother! Mother is not acquainted with my plans!
AMANDA: *(enters portieres)* Where are you all?
TOM: On the terrace, Mother.

They start inside. She advances to them. Tom is distinctly shocked at her appearance. Even Jim blinks a little. He is making his first contact with girlish Southern vivacity and in spite of the night-school course in public speaking is somewhat thrown off the beam by the unexpected outlay of social charm.

Certain responses are attempted by Jim but are swept aside by Amanda's gay laughter and chatter. Tom is embarrassed but after the first shock Jim reacts very warmly. Grins and chuckles, is altogether won over.

(Image: Amanda As A Girl.)

AMANDA: *(coyly smiling, shaking her girlish ringlets)* Well, well, well, so this is Mr. O'Connor. Introductions entirely unnecessary. I've heard so much about you from my boy. I finally said to him, Tom—good gracious!—why don't you bring this paragon to supper? I'd like to meet this nice young man at the warehouse!—Instead of just hearing him sing your praises so much! I don't know why my son is so stand-offish—that's not Southern behavior! Let's sit down and—I think we could stand a little more air in here! Tom, leave the door open. I felt a nice fresh breeze a moment ago. Where has it gone? Mmm, so warm already! And not quite summer, even. We're going to burn up when summer really gets started. However, we're having—we're having a very light supper. I think light things are better fo' this time of year. The same as light clothes are. Light clothes an' light food are what warm weather calls fo'. You know our blood gets so thick during th' winter—it takes a while fo' us to *adjust* ou'selves!—when the season changes . . . It's come so quick this year. I wasn't prepared. All of a sudden— heavens! Already summer!—I ran to the trunk an' pulled out this light dress—Terribly old! Historical almost! But feels so good—so good an' co-ol, y'know. . . .

TOM: Mother—

AMANDA: Yes, honey?

TOM: How about—supper?

AMANDA: Honey, you go ask Sister if supper is ready! You know that Sister is in full charge of supper! Tell her you hungry boys are waiting for it. *(To Jim.)* Have you met Laura?

JIM: She—

AMANDA: Let you in? Oh, good, you've met already! It's rare for a girl as sweet an' pretty as Laura to be domestic! But Laura is, thank heavens, not only pretty but also very domestic. I'm not at all. I never was a bit. I never could make a thing but angel-food cake. Well, in the South we had so many servants. Gone, gone, gone. All vestiges of gracious living! Gone completely! I wasn't prepared for what the future brought me. All of my gentlemen callers were sons of planters and so of course I assumed that I would be married to one and raise my family on a large piece of land with plenty of servants. But man proposes—and woman accepts the proposal!—To vary that old, old saying a little bit—I married no planter! I married a man who worked for the telephone company!—that gallantly smiling gentleman over there! *(Points to the picture.)* A telephone man who—fell in love with long-distance!—Now he travels and I don't even know where!—But what am I going on for about my—tribulations? Tell me yours—I hope you don't have any! Tom?

140 TOM: *(returning)* Yes, Mother?
AMANDA: Is supper nearly ready?
TOM: It looks to me like supper is on the table.
AMANDA: Let me look—*(She rises prettily and looks through portieres.)* Oh, lovely—But where is Sister?
TOM: Laura is not feeling well and says that she thinks she'd better not come to the table.
145 AMANDA: What?—Nonsense!—Laura? Oh, Laura!
LAURA: *(offstage, faintly)* Yes, Mother.
AMANDA: You really must come to the table. We won't be seated until you come to the table! Come in, Mr. O'Connor. You sit over there and I'll—Laura? Laura Wingfield! You're keeping us waiting, honey! We can't say grace until you come to the table!

The back door is pushed weakly open and Laura comes in. She is obviously quite faint, her lips trembling, her eyes wide and staring. She moves unsteadily toward the table.

(Legend: "Terror!")

Outside a summer storm is coming abruptly. The white curtains billow inward at the windows and there is a sorrowful murmur and deep blue dusk. Laura suddenly stumbles—She catches at a chair with a faint moan.

TOM: Laura!
AMANDA: Laura! *(There is a clap of thunder.) (Legend: "Ah!") (Despairingly.)* Why, Laura, you *are* sick, darling! Tom, help your sister into the living room, dear! Sit in the living room, Laura—rest on the sofa. Well! *(To the gentleman caller.)* Standing over the hot stove made her ill!—I told her that it was just too warm this evening, but—*(Tom comes back in. Laura is on the sofa.)* Is Laura all right now?
150 TOM: Yes.
AMANDA: What *is* that? Rain? A nice cool rain has come up! *(She gives the gentleman caller a frightened look.)* I think we may—have grace—now . . . *(Tom looks at her stupidly.)* Tom, honey—you say grace!
TOM: Oh . . . "For these and all thy mercies—" *(They bow their heads, Amanda stealing a nervous glance at Jim. In the living room Laura, stretched on the sofa, clenches her hand to her lips, to hold back a shuddering sob.)* God's Holy Name be praised—

(The Scene Dims Out.)

SCENE 7

(A Souvenir.)

Half an hour later. Dinner is just being finished in the upstage area which is concealed by the drawn portieres.

As the curtain rises Laura is still huddled upon the sofa, her feet drawn under her, her head resting on a pale blue pillow, her eyes wide and mysteriously watchful. The new floor lamp with its shade of rose-colored silk gives a soft, becoming light to her face, bringing out the fragile, unearthly prettiness which usually escapes attention. There is a steady murmur of rain, but it is slackening and stops soon after the scene begins; the air outside becomes pale and luminous as the moon breaks out.

A moment after the curtain rises, the lights in both rooms flicker and go out.

JIM: Hey, there, Mr. Light Bulb!

Amanda laughs nervously.

(Legend: "Suspension Of A Public Service.")

AMANDA: Where was Moses when the lights went out? Ha-ha. Do you know the answer to that one, Mr. O'Connor?
JIM: No, Ma'am, what's the answer?
AMANDA: In the dark! *(Jim laughs appreciatively.)* Everybody sit still. I'll light the candles. Isn't it lucky we have them on the table? Where's a match? Which of you gentlemen can provide a match?
5 JIM: Here.
AMANDA: Thank you, sir.
JIM: Not at all, Ma'am!
AMANDA: I guess the fuse has burnt out. Mr. O'Connor, can you tell a burnt-out fuse? I know I can't and Tom is a total loss when it comes to mechanics. *(Sound: Getting Up: Voices Recede A Little To Kitchenette.)* Oh, be careful you don't bump into something. We don't want our gentleman caller to break his neck. Now wouldn't that be a fine howdy-do?
JIM: Ha-ha! Where is the fuse-box?
10 AMANDA: Right here next to the stove. Can you see anything?
JIM: Just a minute.
AMANDA: Isn't electricity a mysterious thing? Wasn't it Benjamin Franklin who tied a key to a kite? We live in such a mysterious universe, don't we? Some people say that science clears up all the mysteries for us. In my opinion it only creates more! Have you found it yet?
JIM: No, Ma'am. All these fuses look okay to me.
AMANDA: Tom!
15 TOM: Yes, Mother?
AMANDA: That light bill I gave you several days ago. The one I told you we got the notices about?

TOM: Oh.—Yeah.

(Legend: "Ha!")

AMANDA: You didn't neglect to pay it by any chance?
TOM: Why, I—
AMANDA: Didn't! I might have known it!
JIM: Shakespeare probably wrote a poem on that light bill, Mrs. Wingfield.
AMANDA: I might have known better than to trust him with it! There's such a high price for negligence in this world!
JIM: Maybe the poem will win a ten-dollar prize.
AMANDA: We'll just have to spend the remainder of the evening in the nineteenth century, before Mr. Edison made the Mazda lamp!
JIM: Candlelight is my favorite kind of light.
AMANDA: That shows you're romantic! But that's no excuse for Tom. Well, we got through dinner. Very considerate of them to let us get through dinner before they plunged us into everlasting darkness, wasn't it, Mr. O'Connor?
JIM: Ha-ha!
AMANDA: Tom, as a penalty for your carelessness you can help me with the dishes.
JIM: Let me give you a hand.
AMANDA: Indeed you will not!
JIM: I ought to be good for something.
AMANDA: Good for something? *(Her tone is rhapsodic.)* You? Why, Mr. O'Connor, nobody, *nobody's* given me this much entertainment in years—as you have!
JIM: Aw, now, Mrs. Wingfield!
AMANDA: I'm not exaggerating, not one bit! But Sister is all by her lonesome. You go keep her company in the parlor! I'll give you this lovely old candelabrum that used to be on the altar at the church of the Heavenly Rest. It was melted a little out of shape when the church burnt down. Lightning struck it one spring. Gypsy Jones was holding a revival at the time and he intimated that the church was destroyed because the Episcopalians gave card parties.
JIM: Ha-ha.
AMANDA: And how about coaxing Sister to drink a little wine? I think it would be good for her! Can you carry both at once?
JIM: Sure. I'm Superman!
AMANDA: Now, Thomas, get into this apron!

The door of kitchenette swings closed on Amanda's gay laughter; the flickering light approaches the portieres.

Laura sits up nervously as he enters. Her speech at first is low and breathless from the almost intolerable strain of being alone with a stranger.

(The Legend: "I Don't Suppose You Remember Me At All!")

In her first speeches in this scene, before Jim's warmth overcomes her paralyzing shyness, Laura's voice is thin and breathless as though she has run up a steep flight of stairs.

Jim's attitude is gently humorous. In playing this scene it should be stressed that while the incident is apparently unimportant, it is to Laura the climax of her secret life.

JIM: Hello, there, Laura.
40 LAURA: *(faintly)* Hello. *(She clears her throat.)*
JIM: How are you feeling now? Better?
LAURA: Yes. Yes, thank you.
JIM: This is for you. A little dandelion wine. *(He extends it toward her with extravagant gallantry.)*
LAURA: Thank you.
45 JIM: Drink it—but don't get drunk! *(He laughs heartily. Laura takes the glass uncertainly; laughs shyly.)* Where shall I set the candles?
LAURA: Oh—oh, anywhere . . .
JIM: How about here on the floor? Any objections?
LAURA: No.
JIM: I'll spread a newspaper under to catch the drippings. I like to sit on the floor. Mind if I do?
50 LAURA: Oh, no.
JIM: Give me a pillow?
LAURA: What?
JIM: A pillow!
LAURA: Oh . . . *(Hands him one quickly.)*
55 JIM: How about you? Don't you like to sit on the floor?
LAURA: Oh—yes.
JIM: Why don't you, then?
LAURA: I—will.
JIM: Take a pillow! *(Laura does. Sits on the other side of the candelabrum. Jim crosses his legs and smiles engagingly at her.)* I can't hardly see you sitting way over there.
60 LAURA: I can—see you.
JIM: I know, but that's not fair, I'm in the limelight. *(Laura moves her pillow closer.)* Good! Now I can see you! Comfortable?
LAURA: Yes.
JIM: So am I. Comfortable as a cow. Will you have some gum?
LAURA: No, thank you.
65 JIM: I think that I will indulge, with your permission. *(Musingly unwraps it and holds it up.)* Think of the fortune made by the guy that invented the first piece of chewing gum. Amazing, huh? The Wrigley Building is one of the sights of Chicago.—I saw it summer before last when I went up to the Century of Progress. Did you take in the Century of Progress?
LAURA: No, I didn't.

JIM: Well, it was quite a wonderful exposition. What impressed me
most was the Hall of Science. Gives you an idea of what the future
will be in America, even more wonderful than the present time is!
(Pause. Smiling at her.) Your brother tells me you're shy. Is that
right, Laura?
LAURA: I—don't know.
JIM: I judge you to be an old-fashioned type of girl. Well, I think that's
a pretty good type to be. Hope you don't think I'm being too
personal—do you?
70 LAURA: *(hastily, out of embarrassment)* I believe I *will* take a piece of
gum, if you—don't mind. *(Clearing her throat.)* Mr. O'Connor, have
you—kept up with your singing?
JIM: Singing? Me?
LAURA: Yes. I remember what a beautiful voice you had.
JIM: When did you hear me sing?

(Voice Offstage In The Pause.)

Voice (offstage):

> O blow, ye winds, heigh-ho,
> A-roving I will go!
> I'm off to my love
> With a boxing glove—
> Ten thousand miles away!

JIM: You say you've heard me sing?
75 LAURA: Oh, yes! Yes, very often . . . I—don't suppose you remember
me—at all?
JIM: *(smiling doubtfully)* You know I have an idea I've seen you before. I
had that idea soon as you opened the door. It seemed almost like I
was about to remember your name. But the name that I started to
call you—wasn't a name! And so I stopped myself before I said it.
LAURA: Wasn't it—Blue Roses?
JIM: *(springs up, grinning)* Blue Roses! My gosh, yes—Blue Roses! That's
what I had on my tongue when you opened the door! Isn't it funny
what tricks your memory plays? I didn't connect you with the
high school somehow or other. But that's where it was; it was high
school. I didn't even know you were Shakespeare's sister! Gosh, I'm
sorry.
LAURA: I didn't expect you to. You—barely knew me!
80 JIM: But we did have a speaking acquaintance, huh?
LAURA: Yes, we—spoke to each other.
JIM: When did you recognize me?
LAURA: Oh, right away!
JIM: Soon as I came in the door?
85 LAURA: When I heard your name I thought it was probably you. I knew
that Tom used to know you a little in high school. So when you
came in the door—Well, then I was—sure.

JIM: Why didn't you *say* something, then?
LAURA: *(breathlessly)* I didn't know what to say, I was—too surprised!
JIM: For goodness' sakes! You know, this sure is funny!
LAURA: Yes! Yes, isn't it, though . . .
90 JIM: Didn't we have a class in something together?
LAURA: Yes, we did.
JIM: What class was that?
LAURA: It was—singing—Chorus!
JIM: Aw!
95 LAURA: I sat across the aisle from you in the Aud.
JIM: Aw.
LAURA: Mondays, Wednesdays and Fridays.
JIM: Now I remember—you always came in late.
LAURA: Yes, it was so hard for me, getting upstairs. I had that brace on my leg—it clumped so loud!
100 JIM: I never heard any clumping.
LAURA: *(wincing at the recollection)* To me it sounded like—thunder!
JIM: Well, well, well. I never even noticed.
LAURA: And everybody was seated before I came in. I had to walk in front of all those people. My seat was in the back row. I had to go clumping all the way up the aisle with everyone watching!
JIM: You shouldn't have been self-conscious.
105 LAURA: I know, but I was. It was always such a relief when the singing started.
JIM: Aw, yes, I've placed you now! I used to call you Blue Roses. How was it that I got started calling you that?
LAURA: I was out of school a little while with pleurosis. When I came back you asked me what was the matter. I said I had pleurosis—you thought I said Blue Roses. That's what you always called me after that!
JIM: I hope you didn't mind.
LAURA: Oh, no—I liked it. You see, I wasn't acquainted with many—people. . . .
110 JIM: As I remember you sort of stuck by yourself.
LAURA: I—I—never had much luck at—making friends.
JIM: I don't see why you wouldn't.
LAURA: Well, I—started out badly.
JIM: You mean being—
115 LAURA: Yes, it sort of—stood between me—
JIM: You shouldn't have let it!
LAURA: I know, but it did, and—
JIM: You were shy with people!
LAURA: I tried not to be but never could—
120 JIM: Overcome it?
LAURA: No, I—I never could!
JIM: I guess being shy is something you have to work out of kind of gradually.

LAURA: *(sorrowfully)* Yes—I guess it—
JIM: Takes time!
LAURA: Yes—
JIM: People are not so dreadful when you know them. That's what you have to remember! And everybody has problems, not just you, but practically everybody has got some problems. You think of yourself as having the only problems, as being the only one who is disappointed. But just look around you and you will see lots of people as disappointed as you are. For instance, I hoped when I was going to high school that I would be further along at this time, six years later, than I am now—You remember that wonderful write-up I had in *The Torch*?
LAURA: Yes! *(She rises and crosses to table.)*
JIM: It said I was bound to succeed in anything I went into! *(Laura returns with the annual.)* Holy Jeez! *The Torch!* *(He accepts it reverently. They smile across it with mutual wonder. Laura crouches beside him and they begin to turn through it. Laura's shyness is dissolving in his warmth.)*
LAURA: Here you are in *Pirates of Penzance!*
JIM: *(wistfully)* I sang the baritone lead in that operetta.
LAURA: *(rapidly)* So—beautifully!
JIM: *(protesting)* Aw—
LAURA: Yes, yes—beautifully—beautifully!
JIM: You heard me?
LAURA: All three times!
JIM: No!
LAURA: Yes!
JIM: All three performances?
LAURA: *(looking down)* Yes.
JIM: Why?
LAURA: I—wanted to ask you to—autograph my program.
JIM: Why didn't you ask me to?
LAURA: You were always surrounded by your own friends so much that I never had a chance to.
JIM: You should have just—
LAURA: Well, I—thought you might think I was—
JIM: Thought I might think you was—what?
LAURA: Oh—
JIM: *(with reflective relish)* I was beleaguered by females in those days.
LAURA: You were terribly popular!
JIM: Yeah—
LAURA: You had such a—friendly way—
JIM: I was spoiled in high school.
LAURA: Everybody—liked you!
JIM: Including you?
LAURA: I—yes, I—I did, too—*(She gently closes the book in her lap.)*

JIM: Well, well, well!—Give me that program, Laura. *(She hands it to him. He signs it with a flourish.)* There you are—better late than never!
LAURA: Oh, I—what a—surprise!
JIM: My signature isn't worth very much right now. But some day—maybe—it will increase in value! Being disappointed is one thing and being discouraged is something else. I am disappointed but I'm not discouraged. I'm twenty-three years old. How old are you?
LAURA: I'll be twenty-four in June.
160 JIM: That's not old age!
LAURA: No, but—
JIM: You finished high school?
LAURA: *(with difficulty)* I didn't go back.
JIM: You mean you dropped out?
165 LAURA: I made bad grades in my final examinations. *(She rises and replaces the book and the program. Her voice strained.)* How is—Emily Meisenbach getting along?
JIM: Oh, that kraut-head!
LAURA: Why do you call her that?
JIM: That's what she was.
LAURA: You're not still—going with her?
170 JIM: I never see her.
LAURA: It said in the Personal Section that you were—engaged!
JIM: I know, but I wasn't impressed by that—propaganda!
LAURA: It wasn't—the truth?
JIM: Only in Emily's optimistic opinion!
175 LAURA: Oh—

(Legend: "What Have You Done Since High School?")

Jim lights a cigarette and leans indolently back on his elbows smiling at Laura with a warmth and charm which light her inwardly with altar candles. She remains by the table and turns in her hands a piece of glass to cover her tumult.

JIM: *(after several reflective puffs on a cigarette)* What have you done since high school? *(She seems not to hear him.)* Huh? *(Laura looks up.)* I said what have you done since high school, Laura?
LAURA: Nothing much.
JIM: You must have been doing something these six long years.
LAURA: Yes.
180 JIM: Well, then, such as what?
LAURA: I took a business course at business college—
JIM: How did that work out?
LAURA: Well, not very—well—I had to drop out, it gave me—indigestion—

Jim laughs gently.

JIM: What are you doing now?
185 LAURA: I don't do anything—much. Oh, please don't think I sit around doing nothing! My glass collection takes up a good deal of my time. Glass is something you have to take good care of.
JIM: What did you say—about glass?
LAURA: Collection I said—I have one—*(She clears her throat and turns away again, acutely shy.)*
JIM: *(abruptly)* You know what I judge to be the trouble with you? Inferiority complex! Know what that is? That's what they call it when someone low-rates himself! I understand it because I had it, too. Although my case was not so aggravated as yours seems to be. I had it until I took up public speaking, developed my voice, and learned that I had an aptitude for science. Before that time I never thought of myself as being outstanding in any way whatsoever! Now I've never made a regular study of it, but I have a friend who says I can analyze people better than doctors that make a profession of it. I don't claim that to be necessarily true, but I can sure guess a person's psychology, Laura! *(Takes out his gum.)* Excuse me, Laura. I always take it out when the flavor is gone. I'll use this scrap of paper to wrap it in. I know how it is to get it stuck on a shoe. Yep—that's what I judge to be your principal trouble. A lack of confidence in yourself as a person. You don't have the proper amount of faith in yourself. I'm basing that fact on a number of your remarks and also on certain observations I've made. For instance that clumping you thought was so awful in high school. You say that you even dreaded to walk into class. You see what you did? You dropped out of school, you gave up an education because of a clump, which as far as I know was practically nonexistent! A little physical defect is what you have. Hardly noticeable even! Magnified thousands of times by imagination! You know what my strong advice to you is? Think of yourself as *superior* in some way!
LAURA: In what way would I think?
190 JIM: Why, man alive, Laura! Just look about you a little. What do you see? A world full of common people! All of 'em born and all of 'em going to die! Which of them has one-tenth of your good points! Or mine! Or anyone else's, as far as that goes—Gosh! Everybody excels in some one thing. Some in many! *(Unconsciously glances at himself in the mirror.)* All you've got to do is discover in *what!* Take me, for instance. *(He adjusts his tie at the mirror.)* My interest happens to lie in electro-dynamics. I'm taking a course in radio engineering at night school, Laura, on top of a fairly responsible job at the warehouse. I'm taking that course and studying public speaking.
LAURA: Ohhhh.
JIM: Because I believe in the future of television! *(Turning back to her.)* I wish to be ready to go up right along with it. Therefore I'm planning to get in on the ground floor. In fact, I've already made the right connections and all that remains is for the industry itself

to get underway! Full steam—*(His eyes are starry.)* Knowledge—
Zzzzzp! Money—Zzzzzzp!—Power! That's the cycle democracy is
built on! *(His attitude is convincingly dynamic. Laura stares at him,
even her shyness eclipsed in her absolute wonder. He suddenly grins.)* I
guess you think I think a lot of myself!

LAURA: No—o-o-o, I—

JIM: Now how about you? Isn't there something you take more interest
in than anything else?

195 LAURA: Well, I do—as I said—have my—glass collection—

A peal of girlish laughter from the kitchen.

JIM: I'm not right sure I know what you're talking about. What kind of
glass is it?

LAURA: Little articles of it, they're ornaments mostly! Most of them are
little animals made out of glass, the tiniest little animals in the
world. Mother calls them a glass menagerie! Here's an example of
one, if you'd like to see it! This one is one of the oldest. It's nearly
thirteen. *(He stretches out his hand.) (Music: "The Glass Menagerie.")*
Oh, be careful—if you breathe, it breaks!

JIM: I'd better not take it. I'm pretty clumsy with things.

LAURA: Go on, I trust you with him! *(Places it in his palm.)* There now—
you're holding him gently! Hold him over the light, he loves the
light! You see how the light shines through him?

200 JIM: It sure does shine!

LAURA: I shouldn't be partial, but he is my favorite one.

JIM: What kind of a thing is this one supposed to be?

LAURA: Haven't you noticed the single horn on his forehead?

JIM: A unicorn, huh?

205 LAURA: Mmm-hmmm!

JIM: Unicorns, aren't they extinct in the modern world?

LAURA: I know!

JIM: Poor little fellow, he must feel sort of lonesome.

LAURA: *(smiling)* Well, if he does he doesn't complain about it. He stays
on a shelf with some horses that don't have horns and all of them
seem to get along nicely together.

210 JIM: How do you know?

LAURA: *(lightly)* I haven't heard any arguments among them!

JIM: *(grinning)* No arguments, huh? Well, that's a pretty good sign!
Where shall I set him?

LAURA: Put him on the table. They all like a change of scenery once in
a while!

JIM: *(stretching)* Well, well, well, well—Look how big my shadow is when
I stretch!

215 LAURA: Oh, oh, yes—it stretches across the ceiling!

JIM: *(crossing to door)* I think it's stopped raining. *(Opens fire-escape
door.)* Where does the music come from?

LAURA: From the Paradise Dance Hall across the alley.

JIM: How about cutting the rug a little, Miss Wingfield?
LAURA: Oh, I—
220 JIM: Or is your program filled up? Let me have a look at it. *(Grasps imaginary card.)* Why, every dance is taken! I'll just have to scratch some out. *(Waltz Music: "La Golondrina.")* Ahhh, a waltz! *(He executes some sweeping turns by himself, then holds his arms toward Laura.)*
LAURA: *(breathlessly)* I—can't dance!
JIM: There you go, that inferiority stuff!
LAURA: I've never danced in my life!
JIM: Come on, try!
225 LAURA: Oh, but I'd step on you!
JIM: I'm not made out of glass.
LAURA: How—how—how do we start?
JIM: Just leave it to me. You hold your arms out a little.
LAURA: Like this?
230 JIM: A little bit higher. Right. Now don't tighten up, that's the main thing about it—relax.
LAURA: *(laughing breathlessly)* It's hard not to.
JIM: Okay.
LAURA: I'm afraid you can't budge me.
JIM: What do you bet I can't? *(He swings her into motion.)*
235 LAURA: Goodness, yes, you can!
JIM: Let yourself go, now, Laura, just let yourself go.
LAURA: I'm—
JIM: Come on!
LAURA: Trying!
240 JIM: Not so stiff—Easy does it!
LAURA: I know but I'm—
JIM: Loosen th' backbone! There now, that's a lot better.
LAURA: Am I?
JIM: Lots, lots better! *(He moves her about the room in a clumsy waltz.)*
245 LAURA: Oh, my!
JIM: Ha-ha!
LAURA: Goodness, yes you can!
JIM: Ha-ha-ha! *(They suddenly bump into the table, Jim stops.)* What did we hit on?
LAURA: Table.
250 JIM: Did something fall off it? I think—
LAURA: Yes.
JIM: I hope that it wasn't the little glass horse with the horn!
LAURA: Yes.
JIM: Aw, aw, aw. Is it broken?
255 LAURA: Now it is just like all the other horses.
JIM: It's lost its—
LAURA: Horn! It doesn't matter. Maybe it's a blessing in disguise.

JIM: You'll never forgive me. I bet that that was your favorite piece of glass.
LAURA: I don't have favorites much. It's no tragedy, Freckles. Glass breaks so easily. No matter how careful you are. The traffic jars the shelves and things fall off them.
260 JIM: Still I'm awfully sorry that I was the cause.
LAURA: *(smiling)* I'll just imagine he had an operation. The horn was removed to make him feel less—freakish! *(They both laugh.)* Now he will feel more at home with the other horses, the ones that don't have horns . . .
JIM: Ha-ha, that's very funny! *(Suddenly serious.)* I'm glad to see that you have a sense of humor. You know—you're—well—very different! Surprisingly different from anyone else I know! *(His voice becomes soft and hesitant with a genuine feeling.)* Do you mind me telling you that? *(Laura is abashed beyond speech.)* You make me feel sort of—I don't know how to put it! I'm usually pretty good at expressing things, but—This is something that I don't know how to say! *(Laura touches her throat and clears it—turns the broken unicorn in her hands.)* *(Even softer.)* Has anyone ever told you that you were pretty? *(Pause: Music.)* *(Laura looks up slowly, with wonder, and shakes her head.)* Well, you are! In a very different way from anyone else. And all the nicer because of the difference, too. *(His voice becomes low and husky. Laura turns away, nearly faint with the novelty of her emotions.)* I wish you were my sister. I'd teach you to have some confidence in yourself. The different people are not like other people, but being different is nothing to be ashamed of. Because other people are not such wonderful people. They're one hundred times one thousand. You're one times one! They walk all over the earth. You just stay here. They're common as—weeds, but—you—well, you're—*Blue Roses!*

(Image On Screen: Blue Roses.)

(Music Changes.)

LAURA: But blue is wrong for—roses . . .
JIM: It's right for you—You're—pretty!
265 LAURA: In what respect am I pretty?
JIM: In all respects—believe me! Your eyes—your hair—are pretty! Your hands are pretty! *(He catches hold of her hand.)* You think I'm making this up because I'm invited to dinner and have to be nice. Oh, I could do that! I could put on an act for you, Laura, and say lots of things without being very sincere. But this time I am. I'm talking to you sincerely. I happened to notice you had this inferiority complex that keeps you from feeling comfortable with people. Somebody needs to build your confidence up and make you proud instead of shy and turning away and—blushing—Somebody

ought to—ought to—*kiss you, Laura! (His hand slips slowly up her arm to her shoulder.) (Music Swells Tumultuously.) (He suddenly turns her about and kisses her on the lips. When he releases her Laura sinks on the sofa with a bright, dazed look. Jim backs away and fishes in his pocket for a cigarette.) (Legend On Screen: "Souvenir.")* Stumble-john! *(He lights the cigarette, avoiding her look. There is a peal of girlish laughter from Amanda in the kitchen. Laura slowly raises and opens her hand. It still contains the little broken glass animal. She looks at it with a tender, bewildered expression.)* Stumble-john! I shouldn't have done that—That was way off the beam. You don't smoke, do you? *(She looks up, smiling, not hearing the question. He sits beside her a little gingerly. She looks at him speechlessly—waiting. He coughs decorously and moves a little farther aside as he considers the situation and senses her feelings, dimly, with perturbation. Gently.)* Would you—care for a—mint? *(She doesn't seem to hear him but her look grows brighter even.)* Peppermint—Life Saver? My pocket's a regular drug store—wherever I go . . . *(He pops a mint in his mouth. Then gulps and decides to make a clean breast of it. He speaks slowly and gingerly.)* Laura, you know, if I had a sister like you, I'd do the same thing as Tom, I'd bring out fellows—introduce her to them. The right type of boys of a type to—appreciate her. Only—well—he made a mistake about me. Maybe I've got no call to be saying this. That may not have been the idea in having me over. But what if it was? There's nothing wrong about that. The only trouble is that in my case—I'm not in a situation to do the right thing. I can't take down your number and say I'll phone. I can't call up next week and—ask for a date. I thought I had better explain the situation in case you misunderstood it and—hurt your feelings. . . . *(Pause. Slowly, very slowly, Laura's look changes, her eyes returning slowly from his to the ornament in her palm.)*

Amanda utters another gay laugh in the kitchen.

LAURA: *(faintly)* You—won't—call again?

JIM: No, Laura. I can't. *(He rises from the sofa.)* As I was just explaining, I've—got strings on me, Laura, I've—been going steady! I go out all the time with a girl named Betty. She's a home-girl like you, and Catholic, and Irish, and in a great many ways we—get along fine. I met her last summer on a moonlight boat trip up the river to Alton, on the *Majestic*. Well—right away from the start it was—love! *(Legend: Love!) (Laura sways slightly forward and grips the arm of the sofa. He fails to notice, now enrapt in his own comfortable being.)* Being in love has made a new man of me! *(Leaning stiffly forward, clutching the arm of the sofa, Laura struggles visibly with her storm. But Jim is oblivious, she is a long way off.)* The power of love is really pretty tremendous! Love is something that—changes the whole world, Laura! *(The storm abates a little and Laura leans back. He notices her again.)* It happened that Betty's aunt took sick, she got a wire and had to go to Centralia. So Tom—when he asked me to dinner—I naturally just accepted the invitation, not knowing that you—that he—that I—*(He stops awkwardly.)* Huh—I'm a stumble-john! *(He flops back on the sofa. The holy candles in the altar of Laura's face have been snuffed out! There is a look of almost infinite desolation. Jim glances at her uneasily.)* I wish that you would—say something. *(She bites her lip which was trembling and then bravely smiles. She opens her hand again on the broken glass ornament. Then she gently takes his hand and raises it level with her own. She carefully places the unicorn in the palm of his hand, then pushes his fingers closed upon it.)* What are you—doing that for? You want me to have him?—Laura? *(She nods.)* What for?

LAURA: A—souvenir . . .

She rises unsteadily and crouches beside the Victrola to wind it up.

(Legend On Screen: "Things Have A Way Of Turning Out So Badly.")

(Or Image: "Gentleman Caller Waving Good-bye!—Gaily.")

At this moment Amanda rushes brightly back in the front room. She bears a pitcher of fruit punch in an old-fashioned cut-glass pitcher and a plate of macaroons. The plate has a gold border and poppies painted on it.

AMANDA: Well, well, well! Isn't the air delightful after the shower? I've made you children a little liquid refreshment. *(Turns gaily to the gentleman caller.)* Jim, do you know that song about lemonade?

"Lemonade, lemonade
Made in the shade and stirred with a spade—
Good enough for any old maid!"

JIM: *(uneasily)* Ha-ha! No—I never heard it.
AMANDA: Why, Laura! You look so serious!
JIM: We were having a serious conversation.
AMANDA: Good! Now you're better acquainted!
JIM: *(uncertainly)* Ha-ha! Yes.
AMANDA: You modern young people are much more serious-minded than my generation. I was so gay as a girl!
JIM: You haven't changed, Mrs. Wingfield.
AMANDA: Tonight I'm rejuvenated! The gaiety of the occasion, Mr. O'Connor! *(She tosses her head with a peal of laughter. Spills lemonade.)* Oooo! I'm baptizing myself!
JIM: Here—let me—
AMANDA: *(setting the pitcher down)* There now. I discovered we had some maraschino cherries. I dumped them in, juice and all!
JIM: You shouldn't have gone to that trouble. Mrs. Wingfield.
AMANDA: Trouble, trouble? Why it was loads of fun! Didn't you hear me cutting up in the kitchen? I bet your ears were burning! I told Tom

how outdone with him I was for keeping you to himself so long a time! He should have brought you over much, much sooner! Well, now that you've found your way, I want you to be a very frequent caller! Not just occasional but all the time. Oh, we're going to have a lot of gay times together! I see them coming! Mmm, just breathe that air! So fresh, and the moon's so pretty! I'll skip back out—I know where my place is when young folks are having a—serious conversation!

JIM: Oh, don't go out, Mrs. Wingfield. The fact of the matter is I've got to be going.

AMANDA: Going, now? You're joking! Why, it's only the shank of the evening, Mr. O'Connor!

285 JIM: Well, you know how it is.

AMANDA: You mean you're a young workingman and have to keep workingmen's hours. We'll let you off early tonight. But only on the condition that next time you stay later. What's the best night for you? Isn't Saturday night the best night for you workingmen?

JIM: I have a couple of time-clocks to punch, Mrs. Wingfield. One at morning, another one at night!

AMANDA: My, but you *are* ambitious! You work at night, too?

JIM: No, Ma'am, not work but—Betty! *(He crosses deliberately to pick up his hat. The band at the Paradise Dance Hall goes into a tender waltz.)*

290 AMANDA: Betty? Betty? Who's Betty! *(There is an ominous cracking sound in the sky.)*

JIM: Oh, just a girl. The girl I go steady with! *(He smiles charmingly. The sky falls.)*

(Legend: "The Sky Falls.")

AMANDA: *(a long-drawn exhalation)* Ohhhh . . . Is it a serious romance Mr. O'Connor?

JIM: We're going to be married the second Sunday in June.

AMANDA: Ohhhh—how nice! Tom didn't mention that you were engaged to be married.

295 JIM: The cat's not out of the bag at the warehouse yet. You know how they are. They call you Romeo and stuff like that. *(He stops at the oval mirror to put on his hat. He carefully shapes the brim and the crown to give a discreetly dashing effect.)* It's been a wonderful evening, Mrs. Wingfield. I guess this is what they mean by Southern hospitality.

AMANDA: It really wasn't anything at all.

JIM: I hope it don't seem like I'm rushing off. But I promised Betty I'd pick her up at the Wabash depot, an' by the time I get my jalopy down there her train'll be in. Some women are pretty upset if you keep 'em waiting.

AMANDA: Yes, I know—The tyranny of women! *(Extends her hand.)* Good-bye, Mr. O'Connor. I wish you luck—and happiness—and success! All three of them, and so does Laura!—Don't you, Laura?

LAURA: Yes!

300 JIM: *(taking her hand)* Good-bye, Laura. I'm certainly going to treasure that souvenir. And don't you forget the good advice I gave you. *(Raises his voice to a cheery shout.)* So long, Shakespeare! Thanks again, ladies—Good night!

He grins and ducks jauntily out.
Still bravely grimacing, Amanda closes the door on the gentleman caller. Then she turns back to the room with a puzzled expression. She and Laura don't dare to face each other. Laura crouches beside the Victrola to wind it.

AMANDA: *(faintly)* Things have a way of turning out so badly. I don't believe that I would play the Victrola. Well, well—well—Our gentleman caller was engaged to be married! Tom!

TOM: *(from back)* Yes, Mother?

AMANDA: Come in here a minute. I want to tell you something awfully funny.

TOM: *(enters with macaroon and a glass of the lemonade)* Has the gentleman caller gotten away already?

305 AMANDA: The gentleman caller has made an early departure. What a wonderful joke you played on us!

TOM: How do you mean?

AMANDA: You didn't mention that he was engaged to be married.

TOM: Jim? Engaged?

AMANDA: That's what he just informed us.

310 TOM: I'll be jiggered! I didn't know about that.

AMANDA: That seems very peculiar.

TOM: What's peculiar about it?

AMANDA: Didn't you call him your best friend down at the warehouse?

TOM: He is, but how did I know?

315 AMANDA: It seems extremely peculiar that you wouldn't know your best friend was going to be married!

TOM: The warehouse is where I work, not where I know things about people!

AMANDA: You don't know things anywhere! You live in a dream; you manufacture illusions! *(He crosses to door.)* Where are you going?

TOM: I'm going to the movies.

AMANDA: That's right, now that you've had us make such fools of ourselves. The effort, the preparations, all the expense! The new floor lamp, the rug, the clothes for Laura! All for what? To entertain some other girl's fiancé! Go to the movies, go! Don't think about us, a mother deserted, an unmarried sister who's crippled and has no job! Don't let anything interfere with your selfish pleasure! Just go, go, go—to the movies!

320 TOM: All right, I will! The more you shout about my selfishness to me the quicker I'll go, and I won't go to the movies!

AMANDA: Go, then! Then go to the moon—you selfish dreamer!

Tom smashes his glass on the floor. He plunges out on the fire-escape, slamming the door. Laura screams—cut by door.

Dance-hall music up. Tom goes to the rail and grips it desperately, lifting his face in the chill white moonlight penetrating the narrow abyss of the alley.

(Legend On Screen: "And So Good-bye . . . ")

Tom's closing speech is timed with the interior pantomime. The interior scene is played as though viewed through sound-proof glass. Amanda appears to be making a comforting speech to Laura who is huddled upon the sofa. Now that we cannot hear the mother's speech, her silliness is gone and she has dignity and tragic beauty. Laura's dark hair hides her face until at the end of the speech she lifts it to smile at her mother. Amanda's gestures are slow and graceful, almost dancelike, as she comforts the daughter. At the end of her speech she glances a moment at the father's picture—then withdraws through the portieres. At close of Tom's speech, Laura blows out the candles, ending the play.

TOM: I didn't go to the moon, I went much further—for time is the longest distance between two places—Not long after that I was fired for writing a poem on the lid of a shoe-box. I left Saint Louis. I descended the steps of this fire-escape for a last time and followed, from then on, in my father's footsteps, attempting to find in motion what was lost in space—I traveled around a great deal. The cities swept about me like dead leaves, leaves that were brightly colored but torn away from the branches. I would have stopped, but was pursued by something. It always came upon me unawares, taking me altogether by surprise. Perhaps it was a familiar bit of music. Perhaps it was only a piece of transparent glass. Perhaps I am walking along a street at night, in some strange city, before I have found companions. I pass the lighted window of a shop where perfume is sold. The window is filled with pieces of colored glass, tiny transparent bottles in delicate colors, like bits of a shattered rainbow. Then all at once my sister touches my shoulder. I turn around and look into her eyes . . . Oh, Laura, Laura, I tried to leave you behind me, but I am more faithful than I intended to be! I reach for a cigarette, I cross the street, I run into the movies or a bar, I buy a drink, I speak to the nearest stranger—anything that can blow your candles out! *(Laura bends over the candles.)*—for nowadays the world is lit by lightning! Blow out your candles, Laura—and so good-bye . . .

She blows the candles out.

(The Scene Dissolves.)

READING AND REACTING

1. Who is this play really about—Tom, Laura, or Amanda?
2. What is the function of the absent father in the play?

3. Besides serving as a possible suitor for Laura, what other roles does Jim play?
4. Identify references to historical events occurring at the time of the play's action. How are these events related to the play's central theme?
5. Is Tom's primary role in the play actor, character, playwright, or narrator?
6. How do the music, the lighting, and the words and pictures projected on slides—which Tennessee Williams called "extra-literary accents"—contribute to the play's action? Are they essential? (Note that at the urging of the director, Williams eliminated these "accents" when the play opened on Broadway.)
7. Tennessee Williams called *The Glass Menagerie* a "memory play." What events are presented as memories?
8. Discuss how props help to develop the play. For example, consider the picture of the father, the Victrola, the fire escape, the telephone, the alarm clock, the high school yearbook, the unicorn, the candles.
9. What events and dialogue foreshadow Tom's escape?
10. Do Amanda and Laura change as the play proceeds? What do you think will happen to them after the action of the play is over? What is the significance of Laura's blowing out the candles at the end of the play?
11. Identify several examples of religious imagery in the play—for example, the Paradise Dance Hall. What is the significance of this imagery? In what way does it relate to the major theme of the play?
12. **JOURNAL ENTRY** Do you think Tom's decision to leave his family is a sign of strength or of weakness?

Related Works: "A&P" (p. 65), "Barn Burning" (p. 142), "Cinderella" (p. 355), "The Soul Selects Her Own Society" (p. 515), "The Road Not Taken" (p. 526)

◊ Writing Suggestions: Theme

1. Write an essay in which you discuss how the conflict between the mother and daughter in *Florence* might reflect conflicts within the African-American community.
2. One of the themes of *The Glass Menagerie* is the dream a family has for its children. Compare the development of this theme in *The Glass Menagerie* and in another play in this book—for example, *The Cuban Swimmer* (p. 865) or *Death of a Salesman* (p. 782).

3. How do the two plays in this chapter reflect world events (or American life) in the 1940s? Write an essay in which you discuss how these events help develop the themes of each play?
4. Childress's plays often deal with an African-American woman whose life is ordinary until circumstances force her to demonstrate her strength. In what sense does *Florence* reflect Childress's own belief that "the black woman is the most heroic figure to emerge in America"?
5. Both *Florence* and *The Glass Menagerie* deal with children in single-parent households. In what way does the absence of the father affect the children in the two plays? Are the reactions similar or different?

Acknowledgments

LEONARD ADAMÉ, "My Grandmother Would Rock Quietly and Hum." Copyright © 1973 by Leonard Adamé. No portion of this text may be reprinted without written permission of the author.
MAYA ANGELOU, "My Arkansas" from *And Still I Rise* by Maya Angelou. Copyright © 1978 by Maya Angelou. Reprinted by permission of Random House, Inc.
MARGARET ATWOOD, "You Fit into Me" from *Power Politics* by Margaret Atwood. Copyright © 1971. Reprinted with the permission of Stoddart Publishing Company, Ltd., 34 Lesmill Rd., Don Mills, Ontario, Canada M3B 2T6. "The City Planners" from *The Circle Game* by Margaret Atwood. Copyright © 1966. Reprinted with the permission of Stoddart Publishing Company, Ltd., 34 Lesmill Rd., Don Mills, Ontario, Canada M3B 2T6.
W. H. AUDEN, "The Unknown Citizen" from *W. H. Auden: Collected Poems* by W. H. Auden. Copyright 1940 and renewed © 1968 by W. H. Auden. Reprinted by permission of Random House, Inc. "As I Walked Out One Evening" from *W. H. Auden: Collected Poems* by W. H. Auden. Copyright 1940 and renewed © 1968 by W. H. Auden. Reprinted by permission of Random House, Inc. "Musée des Beaux Arts" from *W. H. Auden: Collected Poems* by W. H. Auden. Copyright 1940 and renewed © 1968 by W. H. Auden. Reprinted by permission of Random House, Inc.
MATSUO BASHO, "Four Haiku" from *The Penguin Book of Japanese Verse*, translated by Geoffrey Bownas and Anthony Thwaite. Copyright © 1964 by Geoffrey Bownas and Anthony Thwaite. Reprinted by permission of Penguin Books, Ltd.
SUZANNE E. BERGER, "The Meal" from *Legacies* by Suzanne E. Berger. Originally published by Alice James Books, then again in *Tendrill*. Copyright © 1984 by and reprinted by permission of Suzanne E. Berger.
RICHARD BRAUTIGAN, "Widow's Lament" from *The Pill versus the Springhill Mine Disaster* by Richard Brautigan. Copyright © 1968 by Richard Brautigan. Reprinted by permission of Houghton Mifflin Company. All rights reserved.
GWENDOLYN BROOKS, "We Real Cool," "First Fight. Then Fiddle," "The *Chicago Defender* Sends a Man to Little Rock," "Medgar Evers," and "Sadie and Maud" from *Blacks* by Gwendolyn Brooks. Copyright © 1991. Published by Third World Press. No portion of this text may be reprinted without permission of Gwendolyn Brooks.
CHARLES BUKOWSKI, "Dog Fight." Copyright © 1984 by Charles Bukowski. Reprinted by permission of Black Sparrow Press.
RAYMOND CARVER, "Popular Mechanics" from *What We Talk about When We Talk about Love* by Raymond Carver. Copyright © 1981 by Raymond Carver. Reprinted by permission of Alfred A. Knopf, Inc. "Photograph of My Father in His Twenty-Second Year" from *Fires* by Raymond Carver. Copyright © 1983 by Raymond Carver. Reprinted by permission of Capra Press, Santa Barbara.
ANTON CHEKHOV, *The Brute* from *The Brute and Other Farces*, edited by Eric Bentley. Copyright © 1958, with kind permission of Applause Theatre Books.
ALICE CHILDRESS, *Florence*. Copyright 1950. Renewed © 1978 by Alice Childress. Used by permission of Flora Roberts, Inc.
LUCILLE CLIFTON, "My Mama Moved among the Days." Copyright © 1987 by Lucille Clifton. Reprinted from *Good Woman: Poems and a Memoir 1969–1980* with the permission of BOA Editions, Ltd., 260 East Avenue, Rochester, NY, 14604.

JUDITH ORTIZ COFER, "My Father in the Navy: A Childhood Memory" from *Hispanics in the U.S.: An Anthology of Creative Literature,* Vol. 2, 1982. Reprinted by permission of Bilingual Press/Editorial Bilingue (Arizona State University, Tempe, AZ).

COUNTEE CULLEN, "Yet Do I Marvel" from *Color* by Countee Cullen. Reprinted by permission of GRM Associates, Inc., Agents for the Estate of Ida M. Cullen. Copyright 1925 by Harper & Brothers and renewed 1953 by Ida M. Cullen.

E. E. CUMMINGS, "l(a," "in Just-," "anyone lived in a pretty how town," "the / sky / was," "Buffalo Bill's," "next to of course god america i" from *Complete Poems: 1904–1962* by E. E. Cummings, edited by George J. Firmage. Copyright 1923, 1925, 1926, 1931, 1935, 1938, 1939, 1940, 1944, 1945, 1946, 1947, 1948, 1949, 1950, 1951, 1952, 1953, 1954, © 1955, 1956, 1957, 1958, 1959, 1960, 1961, 1962, 1963, 1966, 1967, 1968, 1972, 1973, 1974, 1975, 1976, 1977, 1978, 1979, 1980, 1981, 1982, 1983, 1984, 1985, 1986, 1987, 1988, 1989, 1990, 1991 by the Trustees for the E. E. Cummings Trust. Copyright © 1973, 1976, 1978, 1979, 1981, 1983, 1985, 1991 by George James Firmage. Reprinted by permission of Liveright Publishing Corporation.

EMILY DICKINSON, "I'm Nobody! Who Are You?," "My Life Had Stood—A Loaded Gun," "Because I Could Not Stop for Death," "I Heard a Fly Buzz—When I Died," "The Soul Selects Her Own Society," "Wild Nights—Wild Nights!" "I Like to See it Lap the Miles," "Volcanoes Be in Sicily," "After Great Pain, a Formal Feeling Comes," "'Hope' Is the Thing with Feathers." Reprinted by permission of the publishers and the Trustees of Amherst College from *The Poems of Emily Dickinson* by Emily Dickinson, edited by Thomas H. Johnson. The Belknap Press of Harvard University Press, Cambridge, Mass. Copyright 1951, © 1955, 1979, 1983 by the President and Fellows of Harvard College.

ARIEL DORFMAN, "Hope" from *Last Waltz in Santiago* by Ariel Dorfman. Copyright © 1988 by Ariel Dorfman and Edith Grossman. Used by permission of Viking Penguin, a division of Penguin Putnam, Inc.

RITA DOVE, "The Satisfaction Coal Company" from *Thomas and Beulah* by Rita Dove. Published by Carnegie-Mellon University Press. Copyright © 1986 by Rita Dove. Reprinted by permission of the author.

T. S. ELIOT, "The Love Song of J. Alfred Prufrock" from *Collected Poems 1909–1962* by T. S. Eliot. Reprinted by permission of Faber & Faber.

JAMES A. EMANUEL, "Emmett Till." Copyright © 1968 by James A. Emamuel. Reprinted by permission of James A. Emanuel.

LOUISE ERDRICH, "Windigo" from *Jacklight* by Louise Erdrich. Copyright © 1984 by Louise Erdrich. Reprinted by permission of Henry Holt & Company, Inc.

WILLIAM FAULKNER, "A Rose for Emily" from *Collected Stories of William Faulkner* by William Faulkner. Copyright 1930 and renewed © 1958 by William Faulkner. Reprinted by permission of Random House, Inc. "Barn Burning" from *Collected Stories of William Faulkner* by William Faulkner. Copyright 1950 by Random House, Inc., renewed by Jill Faulkner Summers. Reprinted by permission of Random House, Inc.

LAWRENCE FERLINGHETTI, "Constantly Risking Absurdity" from *A Coney Island of the Mind* by Lawrence Ferlinghetti. Copyright © 1958 by Lawrence Ferlinghetti. Reprinted by permission of New Directions Publishing Corporation.

JANE FLANDERS, "Cloud Painter" from *Timepiece* by Jane Flanders. Copyright © 1988. Reprinted by permission of the University of Pittsburgh Press.

CAROLYN FORCHÉ, "The Colonel" from *The Country behind Us* by Carolyn Forché. Copyright © 1981 by Carolyn Forché. Originally appeared in *Women's International Resource Exchange*. Reprinted by permission of HarperCollins Publishers, Inc.

ROBERT FROST, "Fire and Ice," "Nothing Gold Can Stay," "'Out, Out—,'" "For Once, Then, Something," "Stopping by Woods on a Snowy Evening," and "Acquainted with the Night" from *The Poetry of Robert Frost* by Robert Frost, edited by Edward Connery Lathem. Copyright 1936, 1942, 1944, 1951, © 1956 by Robert Frost. Copyright © 1964, 1970 by Lesley Frost Ballantine. Copyright 1916, 1923, 1928, © 1969 by Henry Holt & Company, Inc. Reprinted by permission of Henry Holt & Company, Inc.

NIKKI GIOVANNI, "Poetry" from *The Women and the Men* by Nikki Giovanni. Copyright © 1970, 1974, 1975 by Nikki Giovanni. Reprinted by permission of William Morrow & Company, Inc.

SUSAN GLASPELL, *Trifles.* Copyright 1951 by Walter H. Baker Company. This edition published by arrangement with Baker's Plays, 100 Chauncy Street, Boston, MA 02111. No portion of this text may be reproduced without permission of Baker's Plays.

LOUISE GLÜCK, "Life Is a Nice Place" from *Mademoiselle,* 1966. Courtesy *Mademoiselle.* Copyright © 1966 by Conde Nast Publications, Inc. "Gretel in Darkness" from *The House on Marshland* by Louise Glück. Copyright © 1971, 1972, 1973, 1974, 1975 by Louise Glück. Reprinted by permission of the Ecco Press.

NADINE GORDIMER, "Once upon a Time" from *Jump* by Nadine Gordimer. Copyright © 1991 by Felix Licensing, B.V. Reprinted by permission of Farrar, Straus & Giroux, Inc., and Penguin Books Canada, Ltd.

BARBARA L. GREENBERG, "The Faithful Wife" from *Poetry Northwest* 19.2 (1979). Copyright © and reprinted by permission of Barbara Greenberg.

DONALD HALL, "My Son, My Executioner" from *Old and New Poems* by Donald Hall. Copyright © 1990 by Donald Hall. Reprinted by permission of Ticknor & Fields/Houghton Mifflin Company. All rights reserved.

ROBERT HAYDEN, "Those Winter Sundays." Copyright © 1966 by Robert Hayden. "Monet's 'Waterlilies'." Copyright © 1970 by Robert Hayden. From *Collected Poems of Robert Hayden* by Robert Hayden, edited by Frederick Glaysher. Reprinted by permission of Liveright Publishing Corporation.

SEAMUS HEANEY, "Digging" from *Opened Ground: Selected Poems 1966–1996* by Seamus Heaney. Copyright © 1998 by Seamus Heaney. Reprinted by permission of Farrar, Straus & Giroux, Inc., and Faber & Faber.

ERNEST HEMINGWAY, "A Clean, Well-Lighted Place" from *Winner Take Nothing* by Ernest Hemingway. Copyright 1933 by Charles Scribner's Sons and renewed © 1961 by Mary Hemingway. Reprinted with permission of Scribner, a division of Simon & Schuster, Inc.

DAVID HUDDLE, "Holes Commence Falling" from *Paper Boy* by David Huddle. Reprinted by permission of the author.

ROBERT HUFF, "Rainbow." May not be further reproduced without permission.

LANGSTON HUGHES, "Negro," "Island," "The Negro Speaks of Rivers," and "Harlem" ("Dream Deferred") from *Collected Poems* by Langston Hughes. Copyright © 1994 by the Estate of Langston Hughes. Reprinted by permission of Alfred A. Knopf, Inc.

TED HUGHES, "A Pink Wool Knitted Dress" from *Birthday Letters* by Ted Hughes. Copyright © 1998 by Ted Hughes. Reprinted by permission of Farrar, Straus & Giroux, Inc., and Faber & Faber, Ltd.

HENRIK IBSEN, *A Doll's House* from *The Complete Major Prose Plays of Henrik Ibsen* by Henrik Ibsen, translated by Rolf Fjelde. Translation copyright © 1965,

1970, 1978 by Rolf Fjelde. Used by permission of Dutton Signet, a division of Penguin Putnam, Inc.

SHIRLEY JACKSON, "The Lottery" from *The Lottery* by Shirley Jackson. Copyright 1948, 1949 by Shirley Jackson renewed © 1976, 1977 by Laurence Hyman, Barry Hyman, Mrs. Sarah Webster, and Mrs. Joanne Schnurer. Reprinted by permission of Farrar, Straus & Giroux, Inc.

RANDALL JARRELL, "The Death of the Ball Turret Gunner" from *The Complete Poems* by Randall Jarrell. Copyright © 1969 and renewed 1997 by Mary von S. Jarrell. Reprinted by permission of Farrar, Straus & Giroux, Inc.

JAMES JOYCE, "Araby" from *Dubliners* by James Joyce. Copyright 1916 by B. W. Heubsch. Definitive text: copyright © 1967 by the Estate of James Joyce. Used by permission of Viking Penguin, a division of Penguin Putnam, Inc.

DAVID MICHAEL KAPLAN, "Doe Season" from *Comfort* by David Michael Kaplan. Published by Viking Penguin, Inc. First appeared in the *Atlantic Monthly*. Also appeared in *Best American Short Stories 1986*. Copyright © 1987 by David Michael Kaplan. Reprinted by permission of Brand & Brandt Literary Agents, Inc.

JAMAICA KINCAID, "Girl" from *At the Bottom of the River* by Jamaica Kincaid. Copyright © 1983 by Jamaica Kincaid. Reprinted by permission of Farrar, Straus & Giroux, LLC.

CAROLYN KIZER, "After Basho" from *Yin: New Poems* by Carolyn Kizer. Copyright © 1984 by Carolyn Kizer. Reprinted with the permission of BOA Editions, Ltd., 260 East Avenue, Rochester, NY 14604.

ETHERIDGE KNIGHT, "For Malcolm, a Year After" from *The Essential Etheridge Knight* by Etheridge Knight. Copyright © 1986. Reprinted by permission of the University of Pittsburgh Press.

YUSEF KOMUNYAKAA, "Facing It" from *Neon Vernacular* by Yusef Komunyakaa. Copyright © 1993 by Yusef Komunyakaa. Reprinted by permission of Wesleyan University Press.

D. H. LAWRENCE, "The Rocking-Horse Winner." Copyright 1933 by the Estate of D. H. Lawrence and renewed © 1961 by Angelo Ravagli and C. M. Weekley, Executors of the Estate of Frieda Lawrence. Reprinted from *Complete Short Stories of D. H. Lawrence* by D. H. Lawrence. Used by permission of Viking Penguin, a division of Penguin Putnam, Inc.

DENISE LEVERTOV, "What Were They Like" from *Poems 1960–1967* by Denise Levertov. Copyright © 1966 by Denise Levertov. Reprinted by permission of New Directions Publishing Corporation.

AUDRE LORDE, "Rooming Houses Are Old Women." Copyright © 1973, 1970, 1968 by Audre Lorde. Reprinted from *Chosen Poems: Old and New* by Audre Lorde. Used by permission of W. W. Norton & Company, Inc.

ROBERT LOWELL, "For the Union Dead" from *For the Union Dead* by Robert Lowell. Copyright © 1959 by Robert Lowell and renewed 1987 by Harriet Lowell, Caroline Lowell, and Sheridan Lowell. Reprinted by permission of Farrar, Straus & Giroux, Inc.

ARCHIBALD MACLEISH, "Ars Poetica" from *Collected Poems 1917–1982* by Archibald MacLeish. Copyright © 1985 by the Estate of Archibald MacLeish. Reprinted by permission of Houghton Mifflin Company. All rights reserved.

KATHERINE MANSFIELD, "Miss Brill" from *The Short Stories of Katherine Mansfield* by Katherine Mansfield. Copyright 1922 by Alfred A. Knopf, Inc., and renewed 1950 by John Middleton Murry. Reprinted by permission of the publisher.

CLAUDE MCKAY, "If We Must Die" and "The White City" from *Selected Poems of Claude McKay* by Claude McKay.

WILLIAM MEREDITH, "Dreams of Suicide" from *Partial Accounts: New and Selected Poems* by William Meredith. Copyright © 1987 by William Meredith. No portion of this text may be reprinted without permission of Alfred A. Knopf, Inc.
ARTHUR MILLER, *Death of a Salesman.* Copyright 1949 and renewed © 1977 by Arthur Miller. Used by permission of Viking Penguin, a division of Penguin Putnam, Inc.
N. SCOTT MOMADAY, "Comparatives." Copyright © 1976 by N. Scott Momaday. Reprinted by permission of N. Scott Momaday.
MARIANNE MOORE, "Poetry" from *The Collected Poems of Marianne Moore* by Marianne Moore. Copyright 1935 by Marianne Moore and renewed © 1963 by Marianne Moore and T. S. Eliot. Reprinted with the permission of Simon & Schuster.
OGDEN NASH, "The Lama" from *Verses from 1929 On* by Ogden Nash. Copyright 1931 by Ogden Nash and renewed © 1985 by Frances Nash, Isabel Nash Eberstadt, and Linnell Nash Smith. First appeared in the *New Yorker.* Reprinted by permission of Little, Brown & Company.
PABLO NERUDA, "The United Fruit Co.," translated by Robert Bly. Copyright 1950 and reprinted by permission of Robert Bly.
JOYCE CAROL OATES, "Where Are You Going, Where Have You Been?" from *The Wheel of Love and Other Stories.* Copyright © 1970 by Joyce Carol Oates. Reprinted by permission of John Hawkins & Associates, Inc.
FLANNERY O'CONNOR, "A Good Man is Hard to Find" from *A Good Man Is Hard to Find and Other Stories.* Copyright 1953 by Flannery O'Connor and renewed © 1981 by Regina O'Connor. Reprinted by permission of Harcourt Brace & Company.
SHARON OLDS, "Rite of Passage" from *The Dead and the Living* by Sharon Olds. Copyright © 1983 by Sharon Olds. Reprinted by permission of Alfred A. Knopf, Inc.
TILLIE OLSEN, "I Stand Here Ironing." Copyright © 1956, 1957, 1960, 1961 by Tillie Olsen. Reprinted from *Tell Me a Riddle* by Tillie Olsen. Introduction by John Leonard. Used by permission of Delacorte Press/Seymour Lawrence, a division of Random House, Inc.
MICHAEL ONDAATJE, "Dates" from *The Cinnamon Peeler* by Michael Ondaatje. Copyright © 1989 by Michael Ondaatje. Reprinted by permission of Alfred A. Knopf, Inc.
DOROTHY PARKER, "General Review of the Sex Situation." Copyright 1926 and renewed 1954 by Dorothy Parker. Reprinted from *The Portable Dorothy Parker* by Dorothy Parker. Used by permission of Viking Penguin, a division of Penguin Putnam, Inc.
LINDA PASTAN, "Ethics" from *Waiting for My Life* by Linda Pastan. Copyright © 1981 by Linda Pastan. Reprinted by permission of W. W. Norton & Company, Inc.
ANN PETRY, "Like A Winding Sheet" from *Miss Muriel and Other Stories.* Reprinted by permission of Russell & Volkening as agents for the author. Copyright 1945 by Ann Petry and renewed © 1973 by Ann Petry. Originally appeared in *Crisis,* November 1945.
MARGE PIERCY, "The Secretary Chant" and "Barbie Doll" from *Circles on the Water* by Marge Piercy. Copyright © 1982 by Marge Piercy. Reprinted by permission of Alfred A. Knopf, Inc.
SYLVIA PLATH, "Daddy" from *Ariel* by Sylvia Plath. Copyright © 1963 by Ted Hughes. Copyright renewed. Reprinted by permission of HarperCollins Publishers, Inc., and Faber & Faber. "Morning Song" from *Ariel* by Sylvia Plath. Copyright © 1961 by Ted Hughes. Copyright renewed. Reprinted by

permission of HarperCollins Publishers, Inc., and Faber & Faber. "Metaphors" from *Crossing the Water* by Sylvia Plath. Copyright © 1960 by Ted Hughes. Copyright renewed. Reprinted by permission of HarperCollins Publishers, Inc., and Faber & Faber. "Wreath for a Bridal" from *The Collected Poems of Sylvia Plath*, edited by Ted Hughes. Copyright © 1960, 1965, 1971, 1981 by the Estate of Sylvia Plath. Editorial material: copyright © 1981 by Ted Hughes. Reprinted by permission of HarperCollins Publishers, Inc., and Faber & Faber.

EZRA POUND, "In A Station of the Metro" and "The River-Merchant's Wife: A Letter" from *Personae* by Ezra Pound. Copyright 1926 by Ezra Pound. Reprinted by permission of New Directions Publishing Corporation.

DUDLEY RANDALL, "Ballad of Birmingham." Copyright © by and reprinted by permission of Dudley Randall.

ADRIENNE RICH, "A Woman Mourned by Daughters," "Aunt Jennifer's Tigers," and "Diving into the Wreck" from *The Fact of a Doorframe: Poems Selected and New, 1950–1984* by Adrienne Rich. Copyright © 1984 by Adrienne Rich. Copyright © 1975, 1978 by W. W. Norton & Company, Inc. Copyright © 1981 by Adrienne Rich. Reprinted by permission of W. W. Norton & Company, Inc.

ALBERTO ALVARO RÍOS, "The Secret Lion" from *The Iguana Killer: Twelve Stories of the Heart* by Alberto Alvaro Ríos. Copyright © 1984 by Alberto Alvaro Ríos. Reprinted by permission of Lewis & Clark College.

THEODORE ROETHKE, "My Papa's Waltz." Copyright 1942 by Hearst Magazines, Inc. "I Knew a Woman." Copyright 1954 by Theodore Roethke. "Night Crow." Copyright 1944 by Saturday Review Association, Inc. Reprinted from *The Collected Poems of Theodore Roethke* by Theodore Roethke. Used by permission of Doubleday, a division of Random House, Inc.

JIM SAGEL, "Baca Grande" from *Hispanics in the U.S.: An Anthology of Creative Literature* 2 (1982). Reprinted by permission of Bilingual Press/Editorial Bilingue (Arizona State University, Tempe, AZ).

SONIA SANCHEZ, "On Passing thru Morgantown, PA" from *Homegirls and Handgrenades* by Sonia Sanchez. Copyright © 1984 by and reprinted by permission of Sonia Sanchez.

MILCHA SANCHEZ-SCOTT, *The Cuban Swimmer*. Copyright © 1994 by Milcha Sanchez-Scott. All rights reserved. Reprinted by permission of William Morris Agency, Inc., on behalf of the author. CAUTION: Professionals and amateurs are hereby warned that *The Cuban Swimmer* is subject to a royalty. It is fully protected under the copyright laws of the United States of America and of all countries covered under the copyright laws of the United States of America and of all countries covered by the International Copyright Union (including the Dominion of Canada and the rest of the British Commonwealth), the Berne Convention, the Pan-American Copyright Convention and the Universal Copyright Convention as well as all countries with which the United States has reciprocal copyright relations. All rights, including professional/amateur stage rights, motion picture, recitation, lecturing, public reading, radio broadcasting, television, video or sound recording, all other forms of mechanical or electronic reproduction, such as CD-ROM, CD-I, information storage and retrieval systems and photocopying, and the rights of translation into foreign languages, are strictly reserved. Particular emphasis is laid upon the matter of readings, permission for which must be secured from the author's agent in writing. Inquiries concerning rights should be addressed to: William Morris Agency, Inc., 1325 Avenue of the Americas, New York, NY 10019, Attn: George Lane. Originally produced in New York City by INTAR Hispanic American Arts Center.

ACKNOWLEDGMENTS ❖ 997

CARL SANDBURG, "Chicago" and "Fog" from *Chicago Poems* by Carl Sandburg. Copyright 1916 by Holt, Rinehart & Winston and renewed 1944 by Carl Sandburg. Reprinted by permission of Harcourt Brace & Company.

DELMORE SCHWARTZ, "The True-Blue American" from *Selected Poems: Summer Knowledge* by Delmore Schwartz. Copyright © 1959 by Delmore Schwartz. Reprinted by permission of New Directions Publishing Corporation.

SIPHO SEPAMLA, "Words, Words, Words." No portion of this text may be reprinted without permission.

ANNE SEXTON, "Cinderella" from *Transformations* by Anne Sexton. Copyright © 1971 by Anne Sexton. Reprinted by permission of Houghton Mifflin Company. All rights reserved.

LESLIE MARMON SILKO, "Where Mountain Lion Lay Down with Deer." Copyright © 1981 by Leslie Marmon Silko. First printed in *Storyteller*. No changes shall be made to the text of the above work without the express written consent of the Wylie Agency, Inc.

JIM SIMMERMAN, "Child's Grave, Hale County, Alabama." Copyright © 1983 by Jim Simmerman. Originally published by Dragon Gate, Inc. Reprinted by David K. Miller, Literary Agent, Inc., as agent for the author.

BORIS SLUTSKY, "How Did They Kill My Grandmother?" from *Post-War Russian Poetry*, translated by Elaine Feinstein. Copyright © 1974. Reprinted by permission of Elaine Feinstein.

STEVIE SMITH, "Not Waving but Drowning" from *Collected Poems of Stevie Smith* by Stevie Smith. Copyright © 1972 by Stevie Smith. Reprinted by permission of New Directions Publishing Corporation.

GARY SNYDER, "Some Good Things to Be Said for the Iron Age." Reprinted by permission of the author.

SOPHOCLES, *Oedipus the King,* translated by Thomas Gould. Copyright © 1970 by Thomas Gould. Reprinted by permission of Thomas Gould.

GARY SOTO, "Black Hair" from *New and Selected Poems* by Gary Soto. Copyright © 1995. Published by Chronicle Books, San Francisco. Reprinted by permission.

WOLE SOYINKA, "Future Plans" from *A Shuttle in the Crypt* by Wole Soyinka. Copyright © 1972 by Wole Soyinka. Reprinted by permission of Hill & Wang, a division of Farrar, Straus & Giroux, Inc.

WILLIAM STAFFORD, "For the Grave of Daniel Boone." Copyright © 1977 by William Stafford. Reprinted from *Stories That Could Be True* (Harper & Row). Used by permission of the Estate of William Stafford. "Traveling through the Dark." Copyright © 1962, 1998 by the Estate of William Stafford. Reprinted from *The Way It Is: New and Selected Poems* by William Stafford with the permission of Graywolf Press, Saint Paul, Minnesota.

WALLACE STEVENS, "Anecdote of the Jar" and "The Emperor of Ice-Cream" from *Collected Poems* by Wallace Stevens. Copyright 1923 and renewed 1951 by Wallace Stevens. Reprinted by permission of Alfred A. Knopf, Inc.

MAY SWENSON, "Women" from *Iconographs*. Copyright © 1970. Used with permission of the Literary Estate of May Swenson, c/o R. Knudson, Sea Cliffs, NY.

AMY TAN, "Two Kinds" from *The Joy Luck Club* by Amy Tan. Copyright © 1989 by Amy Tan. Used by permission of Putnam Berkley, a division of Penguin Putnam, Inc.

DYLAN THOMAS, "Do Not Go Gentle into That Good Night" from *The Poems of Dylan Thomas* by Dylan Thomas. Copyright 1952 by Dylan Thomas. Reprinted by permission of New Directions Publishing Corporation.

JEAN TOOMER, "Reapers" from *Cane* by Jean Toomer. Copyright 1923 by Boni & Liveright and renewed 1951 by Jean Toomer. Reprinted by permission of Liveright Publishing Corporation.

JOHN UPDIKE, "Ex-Basketball Player" from *The Carpented Hen and Other Tame Creatures* by John Updike. Copyright © 1957, 1982 by John Updike. Reprinted by permission of Alfred A. Knopf, Inc. "A&P" from *Pigeon Feathers and Other Stories* by John Updike. Copyright © 1962 by John Updike. Reprinted by permission of Alfred A. Knopf, Inc.
DIANE WAKOSKI, "Sleep." Copyright © 1966. No portion of this text may be reprinted without permission.
DEREK WALCOTT, "Sea Grapes" from *Collected Poems 1948-1984* by Derek Walcott. Copyright © 1986 by Derek Walcott. Reprinted by permission of Farrar, Straus & Giroux, Inc., and Random House UK Limited.
ALICE WALKER, "Everyday Use" from *In Love and Trouble: Stories of Black Women* by Alice Walker. Copyright © 1973 by Alice Walker. Reprinted by permission of Harcourt Brace & Company.
MARGARET WALKER, "Lineage" from *This Is My Sensory* by Margaret Walker. Copyright 1942 by Margaret Walker. Reprinted by permission of Margaret Walker.
EUDORA WELTY, "A Worn Path" from *A Curtain of Green and Other Stories* by Eudora Welty. Copyright 1941 and renewed © 1969 by Eudora Welty. Reprinted by permission of Harcourt Brace & Company.
RICHARD WILBUR, "For the Student Strikers" from *The Mind-Reader*. Copyright © 1971 by Richard Wilbur. Reprinted by permission of Harcourt Brace & Company. "A Sketch" from *The Mind-Reader*. Copyright © 1975 by Richard Wilbur. Reprinted by permission of Harcourt Brace & Company. "Sleepless at Crown Point" from *The Mind-Reader*. Copyright © 1973 by Richard Wilbur. Reprinted by permission of Harcourt Brace & Company.
TENNESSEE WILLIAMS, *The Glass Menagerie*. Copyright 1945 by Tennessee Williams and Edwina D. Williams and renewed © 1973 by Tennessee Williams. Reprinted by permission of Random House, Inc.
WILLIAM CARLOS WILLIAMS, "The Great Figure," "Spring and All," and "The Red Wheelbarrow" from *Collected Poems: 1909-1939*, Vol. 1, by William Carlos Williams. Copyright 1938 by New Directions Publishing Corporation. Reprinted by permission of New Directions Publishing Corporation.
JAMES WRIGHT, "Autumn Begins in Martins Ferry, Ohio" and "A Blessing" from *Above the River: The Complete Poems*. Copyright © 1990 by Anne Wright, Wesleyan University Press. Reprinted by permission of University Press of New England.
RICHARD WRIGHT, "Hokku Poems" from *Richard Wright Reader* by Richard Wright. Copyright © 1959 by Richard Wright. Published by Arcade Publishing, Inc., New York, NY. Reprinted by permission. "Big Black Good Man" from *Eight Men* by Richard Wright. Copyright 1940, © 1961 by Richard Wright and renewed 1989 by Ellen Wright. Reprinted by permission of HarperCollins Publishers, Inc.
WILLIAM BUTLER YEATS, "Leda and the Swan" and "Sailing to Byzantium" reprinted with the permission of Simon & Schuster from *The Poems of W. B. Yeats: A New Edition*, edited by Richard J. Finneran. Copyright 1928 by Macmillan Publishing Company and renewed © 1956 by Georgie Yeats. "The Lake Isle of Innisfree" and "An Irish Airman Foresees His Death" reprinted with the permission of Simon & Schuster from *The Poems of W. B. Yeats: A New Edition*, edited by Richard J. Finneran (New York: Macmillan, 1989). "The Second Coming" reprinted with the permission of Simon & Schuster from *The Poems of W. B. Yeats: A New Edition*, edited by Richard J. Finneran. Copyright 1924 by Macmillan Publishing Company and renewed 1952 by Bertha Georgie Yeats.

Photo Credits

p. 43, Courtesy of Louisiana State University Press.
p. 46, Wide World Photos, Inc.
p. 51, Wide World Photos, Inc.
p. 64, Copyright © 1988 Wilbur Funches/AP/Wide World Photos, Inc.
p. 70, UPI/Bettmann.
p. 75, AP/Wide World Photos, Inc.
p. 94, Copyright © AP/Wide World Photos, Inc.
p. 102, The Granger Collection, New York
p. 124, AP/Wide World Photos, Inc.
p. 135, AP/Wide World Photos, Inc.
p. 166, AP/Wide World Photos, Inc.
p. 172, AP/Wide World Photos, Inc.
p. 177, AP/Wide World Photos, Inc.
p. 197, The Bettmann Archive.
p. 209, AP/Wide World Photos, Inc.
p. 217, Wide World Photos, Inc.
p. 230, Courtesy of David Michael Kaplan.
p. 242, Copyright © Murray/Corbis-Bettmann.
p. 256, Wide World Photos, Inc.
p. 585, AP/Wide World Photos.
p. 598, AP/Wide World Photos, Inc.
p. 668, The Bettmann Archive.
p. 681, The Bettmann Archive.
p. 782, AP/Wide World Photos, Inc.
p. 878, The Bettmann Archive.
p. 926, Copyright © AP/Wide World Photos.
p. 938, UPI/Bettmann Newsphotos.

Index of Authors, Titles, and First Lines of Poetry

A&P, 65–70
A noiseless patient spider, 555
A poem should be palpable and mute, 297
A ringing tire iron, 391
A sudden blow: the great wings beating still, 497
A sweet disorder in the dress, 441
About suffering they were never wrong, 499
Acquainted with the Night, 523–24
ADAMÉ, LEONARD
   My Grandmother Would Rock Quietly and Hum, 331–32
After Basho, 396
After Great Pain, a Formal Feeling Comes, 513
After great pain, a formal feeling comes, 513
After the shot the driven feathers rock, 264
All night, this headland, 397
Among the rain, 393
Anecdote of the Jar, 551
ANGELOU, MAYA
   My Arkansas, 4
Anthem for Doomed Youth, 321
anyone lived in a pretty how town, 381–82
anyone lived in a pretty how town, 381
Araby, 167–71
ARNOLD, MATTHEW
   Dover Beach, 503–04
Ars Poetica, 297–98
As I Walked Out One Evening, 447–48
As I walked out one evening, 447
As the guests arrive at my son's party, 538
As virtuous men pass mildly away, 411
At eight I was brilliant with my body, 549
At first, as you know, the sky is incidental—, 387
ATWOOD, MARGARET
   City Planners, The, 372–73
   You Fit into Me, 423

AUDEN, W. H.
   As I Walked Out One Evening, 447–48
   Musée des Beaux Arts, 499
   Unknown Citizen, The, 354–55
Aunt Jennifer's Tigers, 436
Aunt Jennifer's tigers prance across a screen, 436
Autumn Begins in Martins Ferry, Ohio, 368

Baca Grande, 373–75
Ballad of Birmingham, 358–59
Barbie Doll, 541
Barn Burning, 142–56
BASHO, MATSUO
   Four Haiku, 395–96
Because I Could Not Stop for Death, 514
Because I could not stop for Death—, 514
Bent double, like old beggars under sacks, 399
BERGER, SUZANNE E.
   Meal, The, 392–93
Between my finger and my thumb, 312
Big Black Good Man, 124–35
Birches, 524–25
Black Hair, 549–50
Black reapers with the sound of steel on stones, 398
BLAKE, WILLIAM
   Chimney Sweeper, The, 504–05
   Lamb, The, 505
   London, 506
   Sick Rose, The, 478
   Tyger, The, 506–07
Blessing, A, 558–59
BRADSTREET, ANNE
   To My Dear and Loving Husband, 418
BRAUTIGAN, RICHARD
   Widow's Lament, 461
Bright Star! Would I Were Steadfast as Thou Art, 533
Bright star, would I were steadfast as thou art—, 533
BROOKE, RUPERT
   Soldier, The, 320–21

1001

BROOKS, GWENDOLYN
  Chicago Defender Sends a Man to
    Little Rock, The, 507–08
  First Fight. Then Fiddle, 460
  Medgar Evers, 509
  Sadie and Maud, 428–29
  We Real Cool, 509
BROWNING, ELIZABETH BARRETT
  How Do I Love Thee?, 317
BROWNING, ROBERT
  Meeting at Night, 316
  My Last Duchess, 334–35
  Parting at Morning, 316
  Pophyria's Lover, 349–50
Brute, The, 668–79
Buffalo Bill's, 512
Buffalo Bill's, 512
BUKOWSKI, CHARLES
  Dog Fight, 377–78
BURNS, ROBERT
  Oh, My Love Is like a Red, Red Rose,
    407–08
But if I were to have a lover, it would
    be someone, 375
By the road to the contagious
    hospital, 471
BYRON, GEORGE GORDON, LORD
  She Walks in Beauty, 510

Call the roller of big cigars, 551
CAMPION, THOMAS
  There Is a Garden in Her Face, 315
CARROLL, LEWIS
  Jabberwocky, 449
CARVER, RAYMOND
  Photograph of My Father in His
    Twenty-Second Year, 307–08
  Popular Mechanics, 265–66
Cask of Amontillado, The, 136–41
CHEKHOV, ANTON
  Brute, The, 668–79
Chicago, 464
Chicago Defender Sends a Man to
    Little Rock, The, 507–08
Child's Grave, Hale County, Alabama,
    480–81
CHILDRESS, ALICE
  Florence, 926–37
Chimney Sweeper, The, 504–05
CHOPIN, KATE
  Storm, The, 89–93
  Story of an Hour, The, 43–45
Cinderella, 355–58
City Planners, The, 372–73
Clean, Well-Lighted Place, A, 173–76

CLIFTON, LUCILLE
  My Mama Moved among the Days,
    311
Cloud Painter, 387–88
COFER, JUDITH ORTIZ
  My Father in the Navy: A Childhood
    Memory, 308–09
COLERIDGE, SAMUEL TAYLOR
  Kubla Khan, 510–512
Colonel, The, 472–73
Come live with me and be my love,
    313
Comparatives, 439–40
Compose for Red a proper verse, 437
Composed upon Westminster Bridge,
    September 3, 1802, 557
Constantly Risking Absurdity, 405
Constantly risking absurdity, 405
Convergence of the Twain, The, 528–29
Cruising these residential Sunday,
    372
Cuban Swimmer, The, 865–77
CULLEN, COUNTEE
  Yet Do I Marvel, 494–95
CUMMINGS, E. E.
  anyone lived in a pretty how town,
    381–82
  Buffalo Bill's, 512
  in Just-, 369
  l(a, 302
  next to of course god america i, 513
  sky was can dy, the, 467

Daddy, 413–16
Dates, 539–40
Death of the Ball Turret Gunner, The,
    410
Death Be Not Proud, 516
Death be not proud, though some
    have called thee, 516
Death of a Salesman, 782–856
Delight in Disorder, 441
DICKINSON, EMILY
  After Great Pain, a Formal Feeling
    Comes, 513
  Because I Could Not Stop for Death,
    514
  "Hope" Is the Thing with Feathers,
    361
  I Heard a Fly Buzz—When I Died,
    514–15
  I Like to See It Lap the Miles, 433
  I'm Nobody! Who Are You?, 328
  My Life Had Stood—A Loaded Gun,
    383–84

Soul Selects Her Own Society, The, 515
Volcanoes Be in Sicily, 482
Wild Nights—Wild Nights!, 515–16
Did the people of Viet Nam, 324
Digging, 312
Diving into the Wreck, 486–88
Do Not Go Gentle into That Good Night, 310–11
Do not go gentle into that good night, 310
Doe Season, 230–41
Does the road wind uphill all the way?, 485
Dog Fight, 377–78
Doll House, A, 599–653
DONNE, JOHN
   Death Be Not Proud, 516
   Valediction: Forbidding Mourning, A, 411–12
DORFMAN, ARIEL
   Hope, 352–53
DOVE, RITA
   Satisfaction Coal Company, The, 516–18
Dover Beach, 503–04
Dreams of Suicide, 491
Dulce et Decorum Est, 399
DUNBAR, PAUL LAWRENCE
   We Wear the Mask, 518

Eagle, The, 439
Earth has not anything to show more fair, 557
Easter Wings, 475
ELIOT, T. S.
   Love Song of J. Alfred Prufrock, The, 519–22
EMANUEL, JAMES A.
   Emmet Till, 523
Emmet Till, 523
Emperor of Ice-Cream, The, 551
ERDRICH, LOUISE
   Windigo, 495–96
Ethics, 540
Everyday Use, 217–23
Ex-Basketball Player, 408

Facing It, 326–27
Faithful Wife, The, 375–76
FAULKNER, WILLIAM
   Barn Burning, 142–56
   Rose for Emily, A, 52–59
FERLINGHETTI, LAWRENCE
   Constantly Risking Absurdity, 405

Fire and Ice, 340
First Fight. Then Fiddle, 460
First fight. Then fiddle. Ply the slipping string, 460
First having read the book of myths, 486
FLANDERS, JANE
   Cloud Painter, 387–88
Florence, 926–37
Fog, 545
FORCHÉ, CAROLYN
   Colonel, The, 472–73
For Malcolm, a Year After, 437
For Once, Then, Something, 479
For the Grave of Daniel Boone, 366
For the Student Strikers, 376–77
For the Union Dead, 322
Four Haiku, 395–96
From my mother's sleep I fell into the State, 410
FROST, ROBERT
   Acquainted with the Night, 523–24
   Birches, 524–25
   Fire and Ice, 340
   For Once, Then, Something, 479
   Mending Wall, 525–26
   Nothing Gold Can Stay, 397
   "Out, Out—," 420–21
   Road Not Taken, The, 526–27
   Stopping by Woods on a Snowy Evening, 527
Future Plans, 489

Gather ye rosebuds while ye may, 347
General Review of the Sex Situation, 317
GILMAN, CHARLOTTE PERKINS
   Yellow Wall-Paper, The, 102–15
GIOVANNI, NIKKI
   Poetry, 296–97
Girl, 266–67
GLASPELL, SUSAN
   Trifles, 586–98
Glass Menagerie, The, 938–89
Glory be to God for dappled things—, 446
GLÜCK, LOUISE
   Gretel in Darkness, 330
Life Is a Nice Place, 465–66
Go, Lovely Rose, 554–55
Go, lovely rose, 554
Go talk with those who are rumored to be unlike you, 376
Good Man Is Hard to Find, A, 177–89

GORDIMER, NADINE
   Once upon a Time, 46–50
Great Figure, The, 393
GREENBERG, BARBARA L.
   Faithful Wife, The, 375–76
Gretel in Darkness, 330

Had he and I but met, 341
Had I the Choice, 427
Had I the choice to tally greatest bards, 427
Had we but world enough and time, 419
HALL, DONALD
   My Son, My Executioner, 422
Hamlet, 681–780
HARDY, THOMAS
   Convergence of the Twain, The, 528–29
   Man He Killed, The, 341
Harlem, 404
HAWTHORNE, NATHANIEL
   Young Goodman Brown, 198–208
HAYDEN, ROBERT
   Monet's "Waterlillies," 470
   Those Winter Sundays, 311
He clasps the crag with crooked hands, 439
he draws up against my rear bumper in the fast lane, 377
He was found by the Bureau of Statistics to be, 354
HEANEY, SEAMUS
   Digging, 312
HEMINGWAY, ERNEST
   Clean Well-Lighted Place, A, 173–76
HERBERT GEORGE
   Easter Wings, 475
HERRICK, ROBERT
   Delight in Disorder, 441
   To the Virgins, to Make Much of Time, 347–48
Hog Butcher for the World, 464
Hokku Poems, 462–63
Holes Commence Falling, 416–17
Hope, 352–53
"Hope" Is the Thing with Feathers, 361
"Hope" is the thing with feathers—, 361
HOPKINS, GERARD MANLEY
   Pied Beauty, 446
   Windhover, The, 529–30
HOUSMAN, A. E.
   To an Athlete Dying Young, 382–83

How Did They Kill My Grandmother?, 325–26
How did they kill my grandmother?, 325
How Do I Love Thee?, 316
How do I love thee? Let me count the ways, 316
How many notes written, 338
HUDDLE, DAVID
   Holes Commence Falling, 416–417
HUFF, ROBERT
   Rainbow, 264
HUGHES, LANGSTON
   Harlem, 404
   Island, 483
   Negro, 333
   Negro Speaks of Rivers, The, 530
HUGHES, TED
   A Pink Wool Knitted Dress, 318–20

I am a Negro, 333
I am nobody, 462
I caught this morning morning's minion, king-, 529
I celebrate myself, and sing myself, 556
I climb the black rock mountain, 337
I doubt not God is good, well-meaning, kind, 494
I have been one acquainted with the night, 523
I hear a whistling, 514–15
I Heard a Fly Buzz—When I Died, 514–15
I heard a Fly buzz—when I died, 514
I Knew a Woman, 370
I knew a woman, lovely in her bones, 370
I know that I shall meet my fate, 322
I Like to See It Lap the Miles, 433
I like to see it lap the Miles, 433
I met a traveler from an antique land, 351
I placed a jar in Tennessee, 551
I reach for the awkward shotgun not to disarm, 491
i saw you, 425
I Stand Here Ironing, 94–101
I, too, dislike it: there are things that are important beyond all this fiddle, 298
I walk down the garden-paths, 342
I Walk in the Old Street, 301

I walk in the old street, 301
I wander through each chartered street, 506
I will arise and go now, and go to Innisfree, 559
I will not toy with it nor bend an inch, 458
IBSEN, HENRIK
  Doll House, A, 599–653
If all the world and love were young, 314
If by dull rhymes our English must be chained, 452
If ever two were one, then surely we, 418
If I should die, think only this of me, 320
If We Must Die, 536
If we must die, let it not be like hogs, 536
I'm a riddle in nine syllables, 541
I'm Nobody! Who Are You?, 328
I'm Nobody! Who are you?, 328
In a Station of the Metro, 391
In a solitude of the sea, 528
In ethics class so many years ago, 540
in Just-, 369
in Just-, 369
In Little Rock the people bear, 507
In the Shreve High football stadium, 368
In Xanadu did Kubla Khan, 511
In your pink wool knitted dress, 318,
Into the lower right, 443
Irish Airman Foresees His Death, An, 322
Island, 483
It becomes apparent that I miss great occasions, 539
It little profits that an idle king, 552
It was nearly a miracle, 373
It's not quite cold enough, 461
I've known rivers, 530

Jabberwocky, 449
JACKSON, SHIRLEY
  Lottery, The, 209–15
JARRELL, RANDALL
  Death of the Ball Turret Gunner, The, 410
Jeremiah Dickson was a true-blue American, 492
JOYCE, JAMES
  Araby, 167–71

Just off the highway to Rochester, Minnesota, 558

KAPLAN, DAVID MICHAEL
  Doe Season, 230–41
KEATS, JOHN
  Bright Star! Would I Were Steadfast as Thou Art, 533
  La Belle Dame sans Merci: A Ballad, 531–33
  Ode on a Grecian Urn, 533–35
  On First Looking into Chapman's Homer, 459
  On the Sonnet, 452
  When I Have Fears, 535
KINCAID, JAMAICA
  Girl, 266–67
KIZER, CAROLYN
  After Basho, 396
KNIGHT, ETHERIDGE
  For Malcolm, a Year After, 437
KOMUNYAKAA, YUSEF
  Facing It, 326–27
Kubla Khan, 510–12

l(a, 302
l(a, 302
La Belle Dame sans Merci: A Ballad, 531–33
Lake Isle of Innisfree, The, 559
Lama, The, 443
Lamb, The, 505
LAWRENCE, D. H.
  Rocking-Horse Winner, The, 243–55
Leda and the Swan, 497
Let Me Not to the Marriage of True Minds, 545
Let me not to the marriage of true minds, 545
Let us go then, you and I, 519
LEVERTOV, DENISE
  What Were They Like?, 324–25
Life Is a Nice Place, 465–66
Life is a nice place (They change, 466
Like a Winding Sheet, 76–83
Lineage, 554
Little Lamb, who made thee?, 505
London, 506
Lord, who createdst man in wealth and store, 475
LORDE, AUDRE
  Rooming Houses Are Old Women, 406–07
Lottery, The, 209–15

Love set you going like a fat gold
 watch, 346
Love Song of J. Alfred Prufrock, The,
 519–22
LOVELACE, RICHARD
 To Lucasta Going to the Wars, 424
LOWELL, AMY
 Patterns, 342–45
LOWELL, ROBERT
 For the Union Dead, 322–24

MACLEISH, ARCHIBALD
 Ars Poetica, 297–98
Man He Killed, The, 341
MANSFIELD, KATHERINE
 Miss Brill, 71–74
MARLOWE, CHRISTOPHER
 Passionate Shepherd to His Love, The,
 313–14
MARVELL, ANDREW
 To His Coy Mistress, 419–20
Maud went to college, 428
MCKAY, CLAUDE
 If We Must Die, 536
 White City, The, 458
Meal, The, 392–93
Medgar Evers, 509
Meeting at Night, 316
Mending Wall, 525–26
MEREDITH WILLIAM
 Dreams of Suicide, 491
Metaphors, 541–42
MILLER, ARTHUR
 Death of a Salesman, 782–856
MILTON, JOHN
 *When I Consider How My Light Is
 Spent*, 536–37
Miniver Cheevy, 543–44
Miniver Cheevy, child of scorn, 543
MIRIKITANI, JANICE
 Suicide Note, 338–39
Miss Brill, 71–74
MOMADAY, N. SCOTT,
 Comparatives, 439–40
MOORE, MARIANNE
 Poetry, 298–99
Morning Song, 346–47
Mother dear, may I go downtown,
 358
Much have I traveled in the realms
 of gold, 459
Musée des Beaux Arts, 499
My Arkansas, 4
My black face fades, 326

*My Father in the Navy: A Childhood
 Memory*, 308
*My Grandmother Would Rock Quietly
 and Hum*, 331–32
My grandmothers were strong, 554
My hips are a desk, 410
My Last Duchess, 334–35
My Life Had Stood—A Loaded Gun,
 383–84
My Life had stood—a Loaded Gun,
 383
My Mama Moved among the Days, 311
My mama moved among the days,
 311
*My Mistress' Eyes Are Nothing like the
 Sun*, 315–16
My mistress' eyes are nothing like
 the sun, 315
My Papa's Waltz, 309–10
My son has been, 352
My Son, My Executioner, 422
My son, my executioner, 422

NASH, OGDEN
 Lama, The, 443
Nature's first green is gold, 397
Negro, 333
Negro Speaks of Rivers, The, 530
NERUDA, PABLO
 United Fruit Co., The, 537–38
next to of course god america i, 513
next to of course god america i,
 513
Night Crow, 484
Nobody heard him, the dead man,
 549
Noiseless Patient Spider, A, 555
Not Marble, nor the Gilded Monuments,
 546
Not marble, nor the gilded
 monuments, 546
Not Waving but Drowning, 549
Now, not a tear begun, 306
Nymph's Reply to the Shepherd, The,
 314

O Rose thou art sick, 478
O what can ail thee, knight at arms,
 531
O wild West Wind, thou breath of
 Autumn's being, 546
OATES, JOYCE CAROL
 *Where are You Going, Where Have
 You Been?*, 268–81

O'CONNOR, FLANNERY
  Good Man Is Hard to Find, A, 177–89
October. Here in this dank, unfamiliar kitchen, 307
Ode on a Grecian Urn, 533–35
Ode to the West Wind, 546–49
Oedipus the King, 879–919
Oh, My Love Is like A Red, Red Rose, 407–08
Oh, my love is like a red, red rose, 407
OLDS, SHARON
  Rite of Passage, 538–39
OLSEN, TILLIE
  I Stand Here Ironing, 94–101
On Being Brought from Africa to America, 555
On First Looking into Chapman's Homer, 459
On Passing thru Morgantown, Pa., 425
On the Sonnet, 452
Once upon a Time, 46–50
ONDAATJE, MICHAEL
  Dates, 539–40
One Day I Wrote Her Name upon the Strand, 379–80
One day I wrote her name upon the strand, 379
Others taunt me with having knelt at well-curbs, 479
Out of the Cradle Endlessly Rocking, from, 468
Out of the cradle endlessly rocking, 468
"Out, Out—," 420–21
OWEN, WILFRED
  Anthem for Doomed Youth, 321
  Dulce et Decorum Est, 399
Ozymandias, 351

PARKER, DOROTHY
  General Review of the Sex Situation, 317
Parting at Morning, 316
Passionate Shepherd to His Love, The, 313–14
PASTAN, LINDA
  Ethics, 540
Patterns, 342–45
Pearl Avenue runs past the high-school lot, 408
PETRY, ANN
  Like a Winding Sheet, 76–83

Photograph of My Father in His Twenty-Second Year, 307–08
Pied Beauty, 446
PIERCY, MARGE
  Barbie Doll, 541
  Secretary Chant, The, 410–11
Pink Wool Knitted Dress, A, 318–20
PLATH, SYLVIA
  Daddy, 413–16
  Metaphors, 541–42
  Morning Song, 346–47
  Wreath for a Bridal, 318
POE, EDGAR ALLAN
  Cask of Amontillado, The, 136–41
Poetry (Giovanni), 296–97
Poetry (Moore), 298–99
poetry is motion graceful, 296
Popular Mechanics, 265–66
Porphyria's Lover, 349–50
POUND, EZRA
  In a Station of the Metro, 391
  River-Merchants Wife: A Letter, The, 542–43

Rainbow, 264
RALEIGH, SIR WALTER
  Nymph's Reply to the Shepherd, The, 314
RANDALL, DUDLEY
  Ballad of Birmingham, 358–59
Reapers, 398
Red Wheelbarrow, 390
RICH, ADRIENNE
  Aunt Jennifer's Tigers, 436
  Diving into the Wreck, 486–88
  Woman Mourned by Daughters, A, 306–07
Richard Cory, 544
RÍOS, ALBERTO ALVARO
  Secret Lion, The, 281–85
Rite of Passage, 538–39
River-Merchants Wife: A Letter, The, 542–43
Road Not Taken, The, 526–27
ROBINSON, EDWIN ARLINGTON
  Miniver Cheevy, 543–44
  Richard Cory, 544
Rocking-Horse Winner, The, 243–55
ROETHKE, THEODORE
  I Knew a Woman, 370
  My Papa's Waltz, 309–10
  Night Crow, 484
  Rooming Houses Are Old Women, 406–07

Rooming houses are old women, 406
Rose for Emily, A, 52–59
ROSETTI, CHRISTINA
  Uphill, 485
Round the cape of a sudden came the sea, 316

Sadie and Maud, 428–29
SAGEL, JIM
  Baca Grande, 373–75
Sailing to Byzantium, 559
SANCHEZ, SONIA
  On Passing thru Morgantown, Pa., 425
SANCHEZ-SCOTT, MILCHA
  Cuban Swimmer, The, 865–77
SANDBURG, CARL
  Chicago, 464
  Fog, 545
Satisfaction Coal Company, The, 516–18
SCHWARTZ, DELMORE
  True-Blue American, The, 492–93
Sea Grapes, 498
Second Coming, The, 560
Secret Lion, The, 281–85
Secretary Chant, The, 410–11
SEPAMLA, SIPHO
  Words, Words, Words, 362–63
SEXTON, ANNE
  Cinderella, 355–58
SHAKESPEARE, WILLIAM
  Hamlet, 681–780
  Let Me Not to the Marriage of True Minds, 545
  My Mistress' Eyes Are Nothing like the Sun, 315–16
  Not Marble, nor the Gilded Monuments, 546
  Shall I Compare Thee to a Summer's Day?, 402
  That Time of Year Thou Mayst in Me Behold, 300–301
  When, in Disgrace with Fortune and Men's Eyes, 457
Shall I Compare Thee to a Summer's Day?, 402
Shall I compare thee to a summer's day?, 402
She Dwelt among the Untrodden Ways, 558
She dwelt among the untrodden ways, 558
She Walks in Beauty, 510

She walks in beauty, like the night, 510
SHELLEY, PERCY BYSSHE
  Ode to the West Wind, 546–48
  Ozymandias, 351
Sick Rose, The, 478
SILKO, LESLIE MARMON
  Where Mountain Lion Lay Down with Deer, 337
SIMMERMAN, JIM
  Child's Grave, Hale County, Alabama, 480–81
Sketch, A, 443–44
sky was can dy, the, 467
Sleep, 469
Sleepless at Crown Point, 397
SLUTSKY, BORIS
  How Did They Kill My Grandmother?, 325–26
SMITH, STEVIE
  Not Waving but Drowning, 549
SNYDER, GARY
  Some Good Things to Be Said for the Iron Age, 391
so much depends, 390
Soldier, The, 320–21
Some Good Things to Be Said for the Iron Age, 391
Some say the world will end in fire, 340
Someone drove a two-by-four, 480
Something there is that doesn't love a wall, 525
Song of Myself, from, 556–57
SOPHOCLES
  Oedipus the King, 879–919
SOTO, GARY
  Black Hair, 549–50
Soul Selects Her Own Society, The, 514
SOYINKA, WOLE
  Future Plans, 489
SPENSER, EDMUND
  One Day I Wrote Her Name upon the Strand, 379–80
Spring, 395
Spring and All, 471–72
STAFFORD, WILLIAM
  For the Grave of Daniel Boone, 366
  Traveling through the Dark, 550
STEVENS, WALLACE
  Anecdote of the Jar, 551
  Emperor of Ice-Cream, The, 551
Stiff and immaculate, 308

Stopping by the Woods on a Snowy Evening, 527
Storm, The, 89–93
Story of an Hour, The, 43–45
Suicide Note, 338–39
Sundays too my father got up early, 311
Sunlit sea, 439
SWENSON, MAY
   Women, 474

TAN, AMY
   Two Kinds, 285–94
Tell me not, Sweet, I am unkind, 424
TENNYSON, ALFRED LORD
   Eagle, The, 439
   Ulysses, 552–53
Tentatively, you, 396
That is no country for old men. The young, 559
That sail which leans on light, 498
That Time of Year Thou Mayst in Me Behold, 300–01
That time of year thou mayst in me behold, 300
That's my last Duchess painted on the wall, 334
The apparition of these faces in the crowd, 391
The buzz saw snarled and rattled in the yard, 420
The farther he went the farther home grew, 366
The fog comes, 545
The gray sea and the long black land, 316
The lead & zinc company, 416
The man whose height his fear improved he, 509
The meeting is called, 489
The mole, 469
The old South Boston Aquarium stands, 322
The one-l lama, 443
The rain set early in to-night, 349
The sea is calm tonight, 503
the sky was, 467
The Soul selects her own Society–, 515
The time you won your town the race, 382
The whiskey on your breath, 309

The world is too much with us; late and soon, 345
There is a deep brooding, 4
There Is a Garden in Her Face, 315
There is a garden in her face, 315
They have washed their faces until they are pale, 392
This girlchild was born as usual, 541
This is the world we wanted. All who would have seen us dead, 330
THOMAS, DYLAN
   Do Not Go Gentle into That Good Night, 310–11
Those Winter Sundays, 311
Thou still unravish'd bride of quietness, 533
To an Athlete Dying Young, 382–83
To His Coy Mistress, 419–20
To Lucasta Going to the Wars, 424
To My Dear and Loving Husband, 418
To the Virgins, to Make Much of Time, 347–48
Today as the news from Selma and Saigon, 470
TOOMER, JEAN
   Reapers, 398
Traveling through the Dark, 550
Traveling through the dark I found a deer, 550
Trifles, 586–98
True-Blue American, The, 492–93
Turning and turning in the widening gyre, 560
'Twas brillig, ad the slithy toves, 449
'Twas mercy brought me from my *Pagan* land, 555
Two Kinds, 285–94
Two roads diverged in a yellow wood, 526
Tyger, The, 506–07
Tyger! Tyger! burning bright, 506

Ulysses, 552–53
United Fruit Co., The, 537–38
Unknown Citizen, The, 354–55
UPDIKE, JOHN
   A&P, 65–70
   Ex-Basketball Player, 408–09
Uphill, 485

Valediction: Forbidding Mourning, A, 411–12

Volcanoes Be in Sicily, 482
Volcanoes be in Sicily, 482

WAKOSKI, DIANE
   Sleep, 469
WALCOTT, DEREK
   Sea Grapes, 498
WALKER, ALICE
   Everyday Use, 217–23
WALKER, MARGARET
   Lineage, 554
WALLER, EDMUND
   Go, Lovely Rose, 554–55
Wave of sorrow, 483
We Real Cool, 509
We real cool. We, 509
We Wear the Mask, 518
We wear the mask that grins and lies, 518
WELTY, EUDORA
   Worn Path, A, 256–62
What happens to a dream deferred?, 404
What passing-bells for these who die as cattle?, 321
What though green leaves only witness, 318
What to do with a day, 516
What Were They Like?, 324–25
What you have heard is true. I was in his house. His wife carried, 472
WHEATLEY, PHILLIS
   On Being Brought from Africa to America, 555
When I Consider How My Light Is Spent, 536–37
When I consider how my light is spent, 536
When I Have Fears, 535
When I have fears that I may cease to be, 535
When I Heard the Learn'd Astronomer, 364–65
When I heard the learn'd astronomer, 364
When I saw that clumsy crow, 484
When I see birches bend to left and right, 524
When, in Disgrace with Fortune and Men's Eyes, 457
When, in disgrace with fortune and men's eyes, 457
When my mother died I was very young, 504

When the trumpet sounded, it was, 537
Whenever Richard Cory went down town, 544
Where Are You Going, Where Have You Been?, 268–81
Where Mountain Lion Lay Down with Deer, 337
While my hair was still cut straight across my forehead, 542
White City, The, 458
WHITMAN, WALT
   Had I the Choice, 427
   Noiseless Patient spider, A, 555
   Out of the Cradle Endlessly Rocking, from, 468
   Song of Myself, from, 556–57
   When I Heard the Learn'd Astronomer, 364–65
Whose woods these are I think I know, 527
Widow's Lament, 461
WILBUR, RICHARD
   For the Student Strikers, 376–77
   Sketch, A, 443–44
   Sleepless at Crown Point, 397
Wild Nights—Wild Nights!, 515–16
Wild Nights—Wild Nights!, 515
WILLIAMS, TENNESSEE
   Glass Menagerie, The, 938–89
WILLIAMS, WILLIAM CARLOS
   Great Figure, The, 393
   Red Wheelbarrow, 390
   Spring and All, 471–72
Windhover, The, 529–30
Windigo, 495–96
Woman Mourned by Daughters, A, 306–07
Woman wants monogamy, 317
Women, 474
Women, 474
Words, Words, Words, 362–63
WORDSWORTH, WILLIAM
   Composed upon Westminster Bridge September 3, 1802, 557
   She Dwelt among the Untrodden Ways, 558
   World Is Too Much with Us, The, 345–46
World Is Too Much with Us, The, 345–46
Worn Path, A, 256–62
Wreath for a Bridal, 318

WRIGHT, JAMES
   Autumn Begins in Martins Ferry, Ohio, 368
   Blessing, A, 558–59
WRIGHT, RICHARD
   Big Black Good Man, 124–35
   Hokku Poems, 462–63

YEATS, WILLIAM BUTLER
   Irish Airman Foresees His Death, An, 322
   Lake Isle of the Innisfree, The, 559–60
   Leda and the Swan, 497
   Sailing to Byzantium, 559–60
   Second Coming, The, 560–61
Yellow Wall-Paper, The, 102–15
Yet Do I Marvel, 494–95
You always read about it, 355
You do not do, you do not do, 413
You Fit into Me, 423
you fit into me, 423
You knew I was coming for you, little one, 495
Young Goodman Brown, 198–208

ZUKOFSKY, LOUIS
   I Walk in the Old Street, 301

INDEX OF KEY TERMS

action, 583
active reading, 1
allegorical figure, 195, 484
allegorical framework, 195, 484
allegory, 38, 194, 304, 484
alliteration, 161, 439–40, 450
allusion, 165, 304, 488–92
anapest, 431
annotating, 5–6
antagonist, 39
antihero, 579
antistrophe, 567
apostrophe, 424
archetype, 192, 480
arena stage, 572–73
aside, 564, 662
assonance, 440, 450
atmosphere, 88, 389
aubade, 305
audience, 6

ballad, 304, 359, 456
ballad stanza, 304, 456
beast fable, 195
beginning rhyme, 442
black comedy, 579
blank verse, 432, 454
box set, 571
brainstorming, 9

cacophony, 438
caesura, 434
caricature, 62
carpe diem theme, 306
catharsis, 573–74
chamber, 568
character, 35, 37, 61–64, 228–29, 580, 656–67, 923–24
characterization, 61
chorus, 565–67
cliché, 226
climax, 40, 581
closed form, 452–53, 454
closet drama, 564
colonnade, 566
comedy, 576–77
comedy of humours, 578
comedy of manners, 578
common measure, 456
conceit, 412
conclusion, 18
concrete poetry, 473–75
conflict, 39–40, 228, 921–22

connotation, 364, 389
convention, 6
conventional symbol, 192, 480
cosmic irony, 574
couplet, 455
costumes, 861
crisis, 40

dactyl, 431
dark comedy, 579
denotation, 364
denouement, 40, 581
deus ex machina, 40
dialogue, 14–15, 564, 657
diction, 303, 385
dimeter, 431
double rhyme, 442
drama, identified, 564
dramatic irony, 118, 349–51, 574, 662
dramatic monologue, 305, 334, 350
dynamic character, 62, 656

editing, 19–20
elegy, 305, 432
Elizabethan theater, 567–70
emblem poem, 475
end rhyme, 442
end-stopped line, 435
enjambment, 435
environmental staging, 572
epic, 34, 304
epigram, 341, 432
epiphany, 36
episodia, 567
euphony, 438
exodus, 567
exposition, 40, 581
expressionism, 571
eye rhyme, 442

fairy tale, 34–35
falling action, 581
falling rhyme, 442
farce, 578, 680
feminine rhyme, 442
figurative language, 164–65, 659–61
figures of speech, 164–65, 303, 402–26, 660
first-person point of view, 117–20, 122
fixed form, 452, 454
flashback, 41, 584
flat character, 61–62, 656
foil, 62, 656
folktale, 34–35

foot, 430–31, 434
foreshadowing, 41–42, 584
form, 304, 452–54
formal diction, 161–62, 371–73, 659
free verse, 453, 463–68

geographical setting, 86–87
Greek theater, ancient, 565–67
groundlings, 568

haiku, 396, 460–61
hamartia, 574
heavens, 568
hell, 568
heptameter, 431
heroic couplets, 445, 455
hexameter, 431
high comedy, 579
highlighting, 3
historical setting, 86
hubris, 574
humour, 578
huts, 568
hyperbole, 165, 413–18

iamb, 430–31
iambic pentameter, 432, 454
imagery, 163–64, 303, 387–401
imagism, 453
imperfect rhyme, 441
in medias res, 41
informal diction, 162–63, 373–75, 659
initiation theme, 226–27
interactive drama, 573
internal rhyme, 442
introduction, 17–18
ironic tone, 159
irony, 118, 348–53, 574, 662–63
irony of fate, 574

jargon, 378
journal, keeping a, 10

kinetic imagery, 393

language, 37–38, 163–65, 659
lighting, 862–63
limited omniscient point of view, 121–22
listing, 10–11
low comedy, 579
lyric poetry, 305